# International Marketing



The worldwide success of *International Marketing: Strategy and Theory* is without doubt due to the authors' thorough approach to the topic. Standard marketing texts tend to use anecdotes gleaned from newspapers and magazines. In contrast, Onkvisit and Shaw use cutting-edge scholarly works to provide a theoretical and decision-making framework to guide marketing strategies and applications.

This fifth edition has been fully revised to include new data from top journals, the International Monetary Fund, *Prices and Earnings* (published by UBS), and Transparency International. It is also the only textbook available to provide an in-depth treatment of such important topics as intellectual property, national competitiveness, marketing barriers, gray marketing, global advertising, bribery, countertrade, and currency strategies.

**Sak Onkvisit** is Professor of Marketing at San José State University, U.S.A. He has authored several books and has published in leading journals. An internationally recognized scholar, he has taught in several countries and has served as a Fulbright Senior Scholar and a Fulbright Senior Specialist.

**John J. Shaw** is Professor of Marketing and Director of the MBA Program at Providence College. His teaching and research interests include Marketing Management, International Marketing, and Consumer Behavior. He has co-authored over 80 papers in journals and at conferences, as well as three books.

# International Marketing

## Strategy and theory

Fifth edition

**Sak Onkvisit and John J. Shaw**

Routledge
Taylor & Francis Group
LONDON AND NEW YORK

First edition published by Charles Merrill in 1989
Second edition published by Macmillan in 1993
Third edition published by Prentice-Hall in 1997
Fourth edition published by Routledge in 2004

Fifth edition published 2009 by Routledge
2 Park Square, Milton Park, Abingdon, Oxon, OX14 4RN

Simultaneously published in the U.S.A. and Canada
by Routledge
711 Third Avenue, New York, NY 10017

*Routledge is an imprint of the Taylor & Francis Group, an informa business*



Typeset in Berling and Futura by
Keystroke, 28 High Street, Tettenhall, Wolverhampton
Printed and bound by CPI Group (UK) Ltd, Croydon, CR0 4YY



*British Library Cataloguing in Publication Data*
A catalogue record for this book is available from the British Library

*Library of Congress Cataloging in Publication Data*
Onkvisit, Sak.
International marketing: strategy and theory/Sak Onkvisit & John J. Shaw.
— 5th ed.
p. cm.
Includes bibliographical references and indexes.
1. Export marketing. 2. Export marketing—Management. I. Shaw, John J.
II. Title.
HF1416.O55 2008
658.8′4—dc22 2007048946

ISBN10: 0–415–77261–3 (hbk)
ISBN10: 0–415–77262–1 (pbk)
ISBN10: 0–203–93006–1 (ebk)

ISBN13: 978–0–415–77261–7 (hbk)
ISBN13: 978–0–415–77262–4 (pbk)
ISBN13: 978–0–203–93006–9 (ebk)

To the International Faculty of Management of Tomsk State University
and the memory of my grandparents and Lawrence X. Tarpey, Sr.
and
Ann and Jonathan, and the memory of Rebecca

# Contents

# Illustrations

## Marketing strategies



## Exhibits

## Figures

## Tables

## Cultural dimensions

## Legal dimensions



## Ethical dimensions

## Cases

# Preface

It is a known fact that all significant economies have either adopted a market-based approach or have largely moved in that direction. A very strong case may thus be made that citizens everywhere should have some basic understanding of how a market-oriented economy operates. In this regard, it is appropriate to view marketing as a universal discipline of study.

Due in large part to globalization, there is hardly any debate that the international dimension of marketing (or business administration) must be given appropriate attention. However, this kind of presumption needs to be scrutinized, analyzed, and debated. It is valid to question whether the international dimension is necessary and desirable. After all, the disciplines of medicine and engineering do not find it necessary to discuss the international aspect. Certainly, physicians and engineers recognize the influence of culture, and they take the international dimension into account from time to time when cultural practices can alter the application of certain theories or principles. Conceivably, medicine and engineering are fortunate to happen to be naturally universal, and it is unnecessary to develop courses such as international medicine and international engineering.

Marketing, as a discipline of study, is just as universal as medicine and engineering. It is definitely ideal if marketing could be taught as a universal discipline. If so, the need to distinguish national practices from international practices would be greatly diminished, and courses and textbooks focusing on international marketing and international business would be redundant and unnecessary. Unfortunately, marketing is not accorded the same kind of luxury with regard to how the discipline is taught, due to the fact that the influence of cultural factors is much more pervasive.

The fact of the matter is that international marketing has always been treated as a subset or special case of domestic marketing (e.g., U.S. marketing). Even with greater awareness of international activities in Europe, marketing courses generally have a national perspective, with international marketing as a specialty course. Without much, if any, debate, the national or domestic treatment of marketing is presumed to be universal. To make the matter worse, the international dimension is presumed to be somewhat of an aberration – a deviation from the national norm.

International marketing is the norm, and the various national marketing practices are its subsystems and not the other way around. Unfortunately, there is inadequate discussion about the meanings and essence of education from the universal perspective. It is inadequate to keep talking about the need to be global or international without elaborating what international education is and how it differs from national education. Marketing scientists and practitioners should strive to differentiate between business techniques that are universal and those that are unique to a particular country or region. International experiences are a necessity, not a luxury. To be whole, a person needs to understand global issues and their implications.

At present, a conventional approach employed by business schools all over the world to incorporate the international dimension into the curriculum is to offer a few international courses (e.g., international business, international marketing, international finance). This approach splits international marketing from domestic marketing and implies that the international aspect of marketing is distinct and different from the national (usually American or European) dimension of marketing activities. Unless and until business schools are willing to truly reorient their academic approaches and strategies by teaching marketing as a universal discipline, it is critical that a textbook covers international marketing in the most rigorous way, while trying to bridge the gap between national marketing and international marketing.

## The most authoritative textbook

Marketing is a dynamic, exciting, rigorous, and challenging discipline of study. Reflecting this belief, the fifth edition of *International Marketing: Strategy and Theory* has been written for the purpose of educating future executives and academicians to meet international challenges. Designed for marketing majors and MBA students, it provides solid foundations that are useful for explanation, prediction, and control of international business activities. Due to its depth and breadth, the text is suitable for any international marketing (and perhaps international business) courses at both the undergraduate and graduate levels. Due to its unparalleled breadth and depth, this textbook is one of the most, if not the most, authoritative in a number of ways – international perspective, comprehensiveness, substance, and rigor.

### *Global perspective*

Unlike some standard (i.e., national) marketing textbooks that merely insert foreign examples, this textbook aims to be internationally relevant by utilizing the global perspective. All regions of the world are covered, and their cultural and business practices are considered. Certainly, this text recognizes the economic and political significance of the triad (the U.S.A., the European Union, and Japan). On the other hand, the textbook also pays a great deal of attention to the emerging markets. There is a generous coverage of the BRIC (Brazil, Russia, India, and China) economies, in recognition of the growing importance of these countries.

In terms of international adoption, this textbook is one of the most successful ever. We sincerely appreciate the confidence of the instructors and students from all parts of the world. The textbook has been adopted in the U.S.A., the United Kingdom, Australia, India, and so on, thus confirming the international focus of the text.

### *Rigor*

One misconception often held by casual observers is that international business is not a rigorous field of study. Perhaps the most significant contributing factor to this unkind assessment is that many well-known texts provide only a "soft" coverage of international marketing by basically reporting anecdotes rather than scientific facts. To compound the problem, such textbooks become a travelogue and employ a simplistic approach that focus mainly on cultural differences rather than decision making.

This textbook treats international marketing as a solid discipline that is just as rigorous as such courses as consumer behavior, marketing research, and marketing management. The text has made a very serious attempt to utilize the theoretical and empirical evidence to offer marketing insights as related to actual applications. It should appeal to the instructor or student who wants *substance* as well as a meaningful integration of theories, applications, and managerial implications. The approach is analytical and managerial rather than merely descriptive.

Because of the textbook's rigor and sophistication, coupled with its strong application focus, the text has been used at all education levels – undergraduate, MBA, and Ph.D.

## The best conceptual framework and theoretical coverage

Most well-known texts use a descriptive approach and merely report isolated incidents based more on casual and personal observation than on rigorous investigation. Naturally, the descriptive materials can become obsolete very quickly. A competent textbook should not be basically a compilation of anecdotes (i.e., newspaper and magazine examples). Clearly, there must be a conceptual/theoretical framework to understand international marketing problems and guide marketing decisions.

The first edition of *International Marketing: Analysis and Strategy* broke new ground by providing fundamental principles and a theoretical framework to understand international activities and/or pursue a managerial career in international marketing. The approach has been very well received and widely praised because it fulfills a real need. The fifth edition continues this leading edge.

The text is highly distinctive in that it is essentially the only text that seriously utilizes scholarly sources to provide theoretical explanation and empirical evidence to support the actual practices. The leading international journals (i.e., *Journal of International Business Studies, Journal of World Business, European Journal of Marketing, International Marketing Review*, and *Journal of International Marketing*) are the major sources of information.

To have a complete understanding, we have considered other marketing sources as well. In particular, we rely on the two most influential sources: *Journal of Marketing* and *Journal of Marketing Research*. In addition, the two major advertising journals (i.e., *Journal of Advertising Research* and *Journal of Advertising*) provide information on international advertising practices.

There is no other international marketing book which comes close to the fifth edition of *International Marketing: Strategy and Theory* in terms of scholarly substance. Unlike other texts which still discuss the traditional concepts in a static manner, this text offers the latest findings which show the advancement of those concepts. Students will greatly benefit from this higher level of sophistication.

## Exceptionally strong application

In spite of its strong theoretical foundations, this text does not describe international marketing concepts only in abstract terms. Actually, the text is highly applications-oriented. A great deal of effort has been spent on meaningfully integrating the theoretical foundations, empirical evidence, and actual business practices.

The fifth edition of *International Marketing: Strategy and Theory* is superior to other texts in terms of application. We rely heavily on such leading business publications as *Business Week, The Wall Street*

*Journal*, *The Asian Wall Street Journal*, and *The Financial Times*. This coverage is very extensive and second to none.

Unlike others, we also rely on the most authoritative government and nonprofit organization publications such as those of the International Monetary Fund – *IMF Survey* and *Finance & Development*. Our readers will also benefit from the data and analysis of Transparency International, World Economic Forum, and Heritage Foundation.

The fifth edition provides solid foundations – strategically and theoretically. This text is more comprehensive than the others in treating in depth a number of relevant and significant topics. There are chapters on marketing barriers, foreign exchange, consumer behavior, branding and packaging, and physical distribution. There are two chapters for each of the 4 Ps of marketing (product, place, promotion, and price). Discussed in detail are financial strategies, analysis and management of political risks, bribery, jurisdiction, counterfeiting, gray marketing, subcultures, services, free-trade zones, representation agreements, dumping, and countertrade.

### *User-friendly features*

The fifth edition is very user-friendly. First, the "marketing strategy" section begins each chapter. These interesting vignettes illustrate the best practices (or marketing blunders in some cases).

Second, the book's unique feature is a collection of interesting "advertisements" to illustrate international marketing activities. These advertisements represent the marketing practices of multinational enterprises from the various parts of the world.

Third, the text includes "discussion assignments" and "minicases" to stimulate discussion. A high degree of teaching/learning flexibility is possible because the materials found in the text stress decision making. As such, they are thought-provoking and may be used for a variety of assignments, classroom discussions, term papers, and exams.

To further emphasize the real-world applications, the fifth edition includes another innovative feature that is not available elsewhere. There are "boxes" of marketing illustrations included in each chapter. These boxes cover three distinct dimensions: "Cultural Dimension," "Legal Dimension," and "Ethical Dimension." These real-world examples illustrate the effects of the legal, ethical, and cultural dimensions on the one hand and the good and poor strategies of business firms on the other.

### *Complete and meaningful revision*

We do not believe that the revision of any textbook should merely update the business examples or that it should only list new references for decorative reasons. Most international marketing texts contain references or footnotes that are mainly magazine and newspaper articles. When theoretical and empirical sources are used at all, they are not really part of the text discussion. This textbook, in contrast, reports the latest theoretical developments and empirical findings, and incorporates up-to-date scholarly works into the text materials so as to reflect the latest progress of academic study.

## Learning aids

The fifth edition gives the instructor a great deal of flexibility. Each chapter includes discussion assignments, minicases, and cases. As a result, the instructor and students are not restricted to only review questions. They can select from numerous assignments for active classroom discussion and class projects. The fifth edition has added many new cases and minicases. In addition, there is an abundance of chapter-opening vignettes, advertisements, exhibits, tables, and other illustrations that highlight the discussion and show how the business concepts are used in practice.

Each chapter in the book includes a number of pedagogical aids. The questions at the end of each chapter ask students to review or explain the concepts. In addition, discussion assignments and minicases require students to apply what they have learned in actual situations. In order to further stimulate ideas and debate so that students can become actively involved in applying the concepts, there are cases of varying length for each chapter. These cases were specifically written to address concepts and issues introduced in the chapter.

A unique feature of the book is the inclusion of two simulation games: one involving culture and another focusing on foreign exchange. These games are easy to follow; they do not require the use of a computer. They teach students about common international marketing problems. Although the games can begin at almost any point during the first half of the semester, they should be started early enough in order to maximize the potential benefits. Students should find them interesting and challenging.

In terms of research opportunities, the text suggests research topics and avenues. This will greatly aid the reader who wants to pursue research on a particular topic. Students and the instructor can expect up-to-date and extensive coverage of the literature which can be useful for research purposes.

## Acknowledgments

It is a pleasure to acknowledge the contributions of many individuals. First, we are grateful for the support, assistance, and encouragement of the instructors, students, and users of the textbook. Those who have given us kind encouragement and useful feedback include: Prafulla Agnihotri (Indian Institute of Management Calcutta), Venkata Ramana Vedulla (University of Hyderabad), Leonidas C. Leonidou (University of Cyprus), Byoung Hee Kim (Seowon University), Gabriele Suder (CERAM Business School), Jenny Darroch (Claremont Graduate University), Dana L. Alden (University of Hawaii), T. Andrew Poehlman (Southern Methodist University), Buarat Srinil (Thammasat University), and Durairaj Maheswaran (New York University).

Second, we want to thank our colleagues who have written cases for this book. Their cases represent an international collaboration and have enhanced the international perspective of the textbook. Next, for those reviewers who have given us their useful and insightful comments, we are thankful.

One of the authors would like to acknowledge his appreciation of the friendship and courtesy received while he visited Tomsk State University as a Fulbright Senior Specialist in 2006. In particular, he would like to thank Felix Tarassenko, Savelyi V. Volfson, and Elena Anatoljevna Sergeeva for making the visit possible and for their warm welcome. Sergey Sergeevich Maksimov was very gracious with his time and friendship. It was a great experience to meet new colleagues and friends. The Fulbright Program is invaluable in promoting international understanding and cooperation.

We would like to express our appreciation for the support of Routledge and all of those who are involved in the preparation and production of this textbook. In particular, we thank Francesca Heslop, Simon Whitmore and Simon Alexander for their encouragement, Vicky Claringbull for production support, and Russell George and Sharon Golan for their editorial assistance and patience. Their support is certainly valuable.

We are indebted to a number of companies and organizations for their permission to use their advertisements and materials. Such materials provide valuable information. In particular, we like to thank Asia Pacific Advertising Festival (and Vinit Suraphongchai of Plannova) for providing us with the AdFest video DVDs and other information and for their support of education. AdFest is the largest advertising contest in Asia.

A textbook is a major undertaking. It is an exhausting process. Our true reward is achieved when the students and adopters of the book have found that they have benefited from our sincere effort to meaningfully advance this important discipline of study.

Part 1

# Overview of world business

Chapter 1

# Nature of international marketing

## Challenges and opportunities

What can we do to educate politicians to the reality that a rising tide floats all ships? . . . We have to develop a less academic approach to explaining the benefits of globalization.

E. Neville Isdell, CEO, The Coca-Cola Company

## Chapter outline

- Marketing strategy: the sound of "glocal" entertainment
- Process of international marketing
- International dimensions of marketing
- Domestic marketing vs. international marketing
- The applicability of marketing
- Multinational corporations (MNCs)
  - Pros and cons
  - Multinationality and market performance
- Characteristics of MNCs
  - Definition by size
  - Definition by structure
  - Definition by performance
  - Definition by behavior
- The process of internationalization
- Benefits of international marketing
  - Survival and growth
  - Sales and profits
  - Diversification
  - Inflation and price moderation

- ❑ Employment
- ❑ Standards of living
- ❑ Understanding of marketing process

- ■ Conclusion
- ■ Case 1.1 Medical vacation: the globalization of health care

## Marketing strategy

**The sound of "glocal" entertainment**

The name Sony, derived from the Latin word *sonus* for sound and combined with the English word *sonny*, was adapted for Japanese tongues. It is the most recognized brand in the U.S.A., outranking McDonald's and Coke. Sony is No. 25 among the world's top brands as ranked by Interbrand and *Business Week*.

The size of Sony Corp. is impressive. Sony Corp. has some $75 billion in worldwide sales, with 80 percent from overseas and 30 percent alone from the U.S.A. (more than sales in Japan). Sony's stock is traded on 23 exchanges around the world, and foreigners own 23 percent of the stock. Out of 471 affiliates, 395 are foreign, making Sony No. 17 on the Internationalization Index of the UNCTAD.

According to the UNCTAD's *World Investment Report 2006*, in terms of foreign assets, Sony is No. 41. Out of its total assets of $87,309 million, it has $35,959 million in foreign assets. It also derives $48,285 million from foreign sales out of its total sales of $69,077 million.

Some years ago, the company made an early move into local (overseas) manufacturing, and 35 percent of the firm's manufacturing is conducted overseas. For instance, Sony makes TV sets in Wales and the U.S.A., thus enabling the company to earn revenues and pay its bills in the same currency. Sony has ceased its production of video products in Taiwan and has instead established a technology center there for product design, engineering, and procurement. The operation of video products has been moved to Malaysia and China in order to utilize cheaper labor.

Sony has some 151,400 employees worldwide, 90,092 of whom are non-Japanese. In the U.S.A., only 150 out of its 7100 employees are Japanese. Virtually alone among Japanese companies, Sony has a policy of giving the top position in its foreign operations to a local national. Sony was also the first major Japanese firm to have a foreigner as a director. Sony's late co-founder, Akio Morita, even talked about moving the company's headquarters to the U.S.A. but concluded that the effort would be too complicated.

Howard K. Stringer was in charge of Sony Corp. of America before becoming the first foreigner to lead the entire Sony Corp. He has directed the company's fractious divisions to work more closely together. Under his leadership, the company has become more "glocal" (i.e., both global and local). To account for local conditions, regional managers are able to tailor products to satisfy varying tastes across the world. American executives can decide whether to reject products that originate in Japan. A recently introduced Walkman, for example, was rejected because its screen was too small to compete against the dominant iPod in the U.S. market. There is also better cooperation among the units. As in the case of the Mylo, this handheld Web-browsing and text-messaging device was jointly designed in Japan and the United States to target teens. A successful launch in the U.S.A. led to an introduction in Japan.

*Sources*: "Remade in the U.S.A.," *Business Week*, May 7, 2007, 44–5; "Best Global Brands," *Business Week*, August 6, 2007, 59–64; *World Investment Report 2006: FDI from Developing and Transition Economies*, UNCTAD, 2006; and "PlayStation's New Chief Seeks to Lift Sony's Game," *Wall Street Journal*, June 22, 2007.

## Purpose of chapter

Sony Corp. provides a good illustration of the nature of international marketing in terms of both the challenges and opportunities. Both the international and local conditions must be taken into account. This chapter addresses the who, what, why, and how of international marketing by giving an overview of the nature of international business. The discussion begins with an examination of how marketing in general is defined and how that definition works for international marketing. The chapter examines the criteria that determine when a company has successfully transformed itself into a multinational firm. To dispel some popularly held misconceptions, there is an explicit treatment of the benefits of international trade.

## Process of international marketing

A study of international marketing should begin with an understanding of what marketing is and how it operates in an international context. **International marketing** is the multinational process of planning and executing the marketing mix (product, place or distribution, promotion, and price) to create exchanges that satisfy individual and organizational objectives. The word "multinational" implies that marketing activities are undertaken in several countries and that such activities should somehow be coordinated across nations.

This definition is not completely free of limitations. By placing individual objectives at one end of the definition and organizational objectives at the other, the definition stresses a relationship between a consumer and an organization. In effect, it fails to do justice to the significance of business-to-business (B2B) marketing, which involves a transaction between two organizations. In the world of international marketing, governments, quasi-government agencies, and profit-seeking and nonprofit entities are frequently buyers. Companies such as Boeing and Bechtel, for example, have nothing to do with consumer products. Likewise, Russia's export agency, Rosoboronexport, represents the country's 1700 defense plants and sells arms to governments all over the world.

Nonetheless, the definition does offer several advantages by carefully describing the essential characteristics of international marketing. First, what is to be exchanged is not restricted to tangible products (goods) but may include concepts and services as well. When the United Nations promotes such concepts as birth control and breast-feeding, this should be viewed as international marketing.

Second, the definition removes the implication that international marketing applies only to market or business transactions. International nonprofit marketing, which has received only scant attention, should not be overlooked. Governments are very active in marketing in order to attract foreign investment. Religion is also a big business and has been marketed internationally for centuries, though

## Cultural Dimension 1.1

**Marketing and matching**

For an exchange to take place, there must be at least two parties that offer something of value to each other. Yet even when there are two or more parties that have something of value, an exchange is not automatic. Matching an individual with a product is not an easy process. Likewise, it is a lengthy and cumbersome process to match a person with a compatible spouse. In India and China, traditionally, marriages require the services of family, friends, and professional matchmakers. The laborious process attempts to match candidates in terms of religion, caste, and horoscopes. So many potential marriages were ruined because the two candidates' horoscopes were deemed to be not compatible.

The role of marketing is to facilitate the exchange process. In the U.S.A., companies such as Table for Six, How About Lunch, and eHarmony.com offer matchmaking by arranging for single people to meet. Matching potential mates has become more efficient in India where scores of internet sites exist to broker marriages. Bharat Matrimony.com mentions in its advertisement that it is "No. 1 Indian Matrimony" and that it has arranged more than 60,000 marriages. In China, likewise, internet matchmaking is a booming and blooming business. One successful young businesswoman hired internet "love counselors" to find a suitable husband for her. She explained: "After age 25, you are not as beautiful. It is like the stock market: You want to sell at the peak."

*Sources*: "Internet Matchmaking Blooms in China," *San José Mercury News*, July 5, 2007; and "Here Come the Bride Sites," *Business Week*, November 6, 2006, 42.

most people prefer not to view it that way. Even the Vatican uses modern marketing by launching a mass-licensing program that puts images from the Vatican Library's art collection, architecture, and manuscripts on T-shirts, glassware, and candles.

Third, the definition recognizes that it is improper for a firm to create a product first and then look for a place to sell it. Rather than seeking consumers for a firm's existing product, it is often more logical to determine consumer needs before creating a product. For overseas markets, the process may call for a modified product. In some cases, following this approach may result in foreign needs being satisfied in a new way (i.e., a brand-new product is created specifically for overseas markets).

Fourth, the definition acknowledges that "place" (distribution) is only part of the marketing mix and that the distance between markets makes it neither more nor less important than the other parts of the mix. It is thus improper for any firms to regard their international function as simply to export (i.e., move) available products from one country to another.

Finally, the "multinational process" implies that the international marketing process is not a mere repetition of using identical strategies abroad. The four Ps of marketing (product, place, promotion, and price) must be integrated and coordinated across countries in order to bring about the most effective marketing mix that will facilitate an exchange. In some cases, the mix may have to be adjusted for a particular market for better impact. Coca-Cola's German and Turkish divisions, for example, have experimented with berry-flavored Fanta and a pear-flavored drink respectively. In other cases, a multinational marketer may find it more desirable to use a certain degree of standardization if the existing market differences are somewhat artificial and can be overcome. As in the case of General Electric Co.'s GE Medical Systems, it went too far in localizing its medical imaging products to compete with local competitors. Its managers designed and marketed similar products for different markets. Overcustomizing such big-ticket products is an expensive and wasteful duplication of effort.[1]

## International dimensions of marketing

One way to understand the concept of international marketing is to examine how international marketing differs from similar concepts. **Domestic marketing** is concerned with the marketing practices within a researcher's or marketer's home country. From the perspective of domestic marketing, marketing methods used outside the home market are **foreign marketing**. A study becomes **comparative marketing** when its purpose is to contrast two or more marketing systems rather than examine a particular country's marketing system for its own sake. Similarities and differences between systems are identified.

Some marketing textbooks differentiate international marketing from **global marketing** because international marketing in its literal sense signifies marketing between nations (*inter* means between).The word *international* may thus imply that a firm is not a corporate citizen of the world but rather operates from a home base. For those authors, multinational, global, or world marketing is the preferred term, since nothing is foreign or domestic about the world market and global opportunities.

One might, though, question whether the subtle difference between international marketing and multinational marketing is significant. For practical purposes, it is merely a distinction without a difference. As a matter of fact, multinational firms themselves do not make any distinction between the two terms. It is difficult to believe that International Business Machines will become more global if it changes its corporate name to Multinational Business Machines. Likewise, there is no compelling reason for American Express and British Petroleum to change their names to, say, Global Express and World Petroleum. For purposes of the discussion in this text, international, multinational, and global marketing are used interchangeably.

## Domestic marketing vs. international marketing

It would beg the question to say that life and death are similar in nature, except in degree. As pointed out by Lufthansa (see Figure 1.1), it would be just as incorrect to say that domestic and international marketing are similar in nature but not in scope, meaning that international marketing is nothing but domestic marketing on a larger scale.

Domestic marketing involves one set of uncontrollables derived from the domestic market. International marketing is much more complex because a marketer faces two or more sets of uncontrollable variables originating from various countries. The marketer must cope with different cultural, legal, political, and monetary systems. Intel Corporation's annual report makes this point very clear.[2] The company is subject to risks associated with doing business globally. The risks include security concerns, health concerns, natural disasters, inefficient and limited infrastructure and disruptions, differing employment practices and labor issues, local business and cultural factors, regulatory requirements that differ between jurisdictions, and government restrictions on the

You don't learn to fly overseas overnight.
Lufthansa
Overseas travel is considerably different than domestic travel. Longer flights and remote destinations require a different kind of service, one that can only be learned through experience.
Lufthansa flies to 85 countries around the world – more than any other airline. We've spent over 50 years getting to know the people, customs and languages that other airlines are just beginning to explore. So no matter how far you have to travel, you can be sure we know the territory.
After all, to Lufthansa, foreign destinations are anything but foreign.
People expect the world of us.
Lufthansa
Lufthansa is a participant in the mileage programs of United, Delta, USAir and Continental/Eastern. See your Travel Agent for details.

**FIGURE 1.1** Lufthansa: domestic marketing vs. international marketing

*Source*: Courtesy of Lufthansa German Airlines.

company's operations (e.g., nationalization of operations, restrictions on repatriation of earnings). In addition,

> fluctuations in exchange rates, including those caused by currency controls, could negatively impact our business operating results and financial condition by resulting in lower revenue or increased expenses. In addition, changes in tariff and import regulations and to U.S. and non-U.S. monetary policies may also negatively impact our revenue in those affected countries. Varying tax rates in different jurisdictions could negatively impact our overall tax rate.

As shown in Figure 1.2, the two or more sets of environmental factors overlap, indicating that some similarities are shared by the countries involved. A firm's marketing mix is determined by the uncontrollable factors within each country's environment as well as by the interaction between the sets (see Figure 1.3). For optimum results, a firm's marketing mix may have to be modified to conform to a different environment, though wholesale modification is not often necessary. The degree of overlap of the sets of uncontrollable variables will dictate the extent to which the four Ps of marketing must change – the more the overlap, the less the modification.

The varying environments within which the marketing plan is implemented may often rule out uniform marketing strategies across countries. McDonald's, although world renowned for its American symbols and standardization, has actually been flexible overseas. Recognizing the importance of foreign markets and local customs, the company customizes its menu by region. In fact, it has even excluded beef from its menu in India in deference to the country's Hindu tradition.

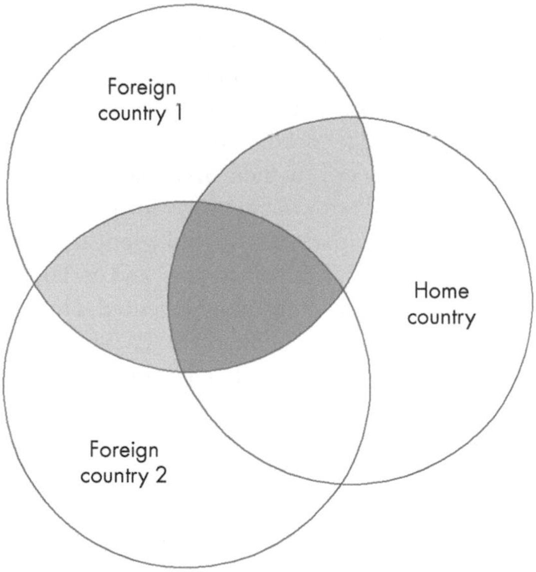
Foreign
country 1
Home
country
Foreign
country 2

**FIGURE 1.2** Environmental divergence and convergence

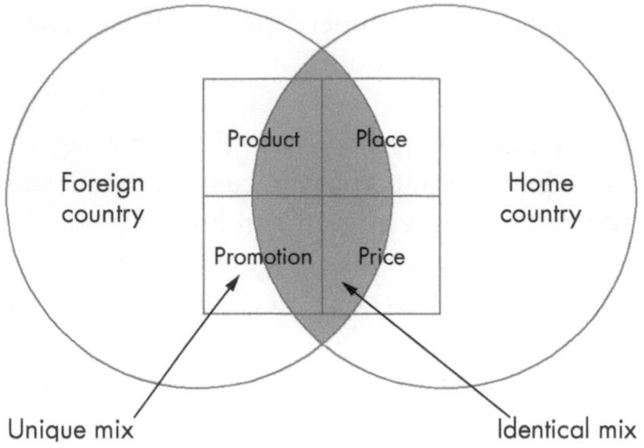
Product
Place
Foreign country
Home country
Promotion
Price
Unique mix
Identical mix

**FIGURE 1.3** Environmental effect on international marketing mix

## The applicability of marketing

Marketing is a universal activity that is widely applicable, regardless of the political, social, and economic systems of a country. It is true, however, that the practice of marketing may differ from country to country in style and scope. In Russia, where marketing is a relatively new phenomenon, marketing activities cover a narrow spectrum of the diversity of marketing practices, and these activities are not as intense in comparison with international benchmarks.[3] Likewise, in the Czech Republic, non-profit policy makers have a limited understanding of marketing practices.[4]

In spite of the universal applicability of marketing, it does not mean that consumers in all parts of the world must or should be satisfied in exactly the same way. Consumers from various countries are significantly different due to varying culture, income, level of economic development, and so on. Therefore, consumers may use the same product without having the same need or motive, and in turn may use different products to satisfy the same need. For example, different kinds of foods are used in different countries to satisfy the same hunger need. Further, Americans and Europeans may use gas or electricity to keep warm, whereas some people in India may meet the same need by burning cow dung.

Too often, marketing mix is confused with marketing principles. Sound marketing principles are universal. One basic principle states that marketers should adopt the marketing concept (i.e., using the integrated marketing approach to satisfy both customers' and corporate goals). Regardless of their nationalities, marketers everywhere should be customer-oriented. However, this universal principle in no way implies a uniform marketing mix for all markets. To be customer-oriented does not mean that the same marketing strategy should be repeated in a different environment.

## Multinational corporations (MNCs)

The United Nations Conference on Trade and Development (UNCTAD) has developed the Transnationality Index (TNI). This index is a composite of three ratios – foreign assets/total assets, foreign sales/total sales, and foreign employment/total employment. According to UNCTAD, the number of transnational corporations (TNCs) worldwide has risen to about 77,000, and these TNCs have at least 770,000 foreign affiliates. It should be noted that more than 20,000 of the TNCs originate in developing countries.[5] The world's 100 largest MNCs account for 11 percent of foreign assets, 16 percent of sales, and 12 percent of employment of all international firms. With regard to headquarters, 85 of the top 100 TNCs are located in the Triad (the U.S.A., the European Union, and Japan).[6]

## Pros and cons

Multinational corporations (MNCs) are major actors in the world of international business. The mention of MNCs usually elicits mixed reactions. On the one hand, MNCs are associated with exploitation and ruthlessness. They are often criticized for moving resources in and out of a country as they strive for profit without much regard for the country's social welfare. In addition, they erode a nation's sovereignty. One study found that globalization undermined domestic airline competition policy.[7]

### Ethical Dimension 1.1

#### National loyalty vs. global profits

Halliburton Co., an oil services firm based in Houston, Texas, is a controversial company. U.S. Vice President Dick Cheney led the company from 1995 to 2000. Cheney himself is one of the most controversial vice-presidents in U.S. history. He played a significant role in pushing the U.S.A. to invade Iraq. Halliburton's KBR unit, having booked more than $20 billion in revenues, profited handsomely from its no-bid work in the rebuilding of Iraq. KBR's pricing and quality of work have drawn a great deal of scrutiny and condemnation.

In 2006, Halliburton derived about half of its energy-services revenue from North America, a mature oil region with limited growth potential. In contrast, the Middle East accounts for almost two-thirds of the world's known reserves of oil. State-controlled oil companies in the region have been investing heavily in the fields and in other energy-related developments. In 2006, Halliburton won a multimillion-dollar contract to provide oilfield services for Saudi Aramco.

The company wants to expand its business in Africa and Russia, and its strategic goal is to lower the proportion of income generated in North America. By 2008, Halliburton's operating income from regions other than North America would jump from 40 percent to 55 percent. The company announced in 2007 that it was moving its corporate headquarters to Dubai, a booming business center in the Gulf. The CEO will run the company's entire operations from that office. The strategic location, coupled with greater presence in the region, will allow the company to be in a better position to negotiate and win large contracts in the oil-rich Middle East. It will list on a Middle East bourse after the move.

Several U.S. legislators were outraged. They felt that Halliburton had greatly benefited from its U.S. identity but that the company was willing to abandon the U.S.A. for another country for the sake of profit. As criticized by the judiciary committee chairman of the U.S. Senate, "this is an insult to the U.S. soldiers and taxpayers who paid the tab for their no-bid contracts and endured their overcharges for all these years." In defense of the company, it maintains its legal registration in the U.S.A., and the move probably shields the company from neither tax consequences nor the probes of its KBR unit.

*Sources*: "Halliburton Plays Catch Up," *Wall Street Journal*, March 14, 2007; and "Halliburton Moving to Dubai," CNNMoney.com, March 12, 2007.

Is globalization detrimental to environment? This question is based on a premise that globalization encourages the location of polluting industries in countries with low environmental regulations. Based on survey data from companies in China, globalization has positive environmental effects due to self-regulation pressures on firms in low-regulation countries. "Multinational ownership, multinational customers, and exports to developed countries increase self-regulation of environmental performance."[8] According to another study, the size of a domestic market and other factors are much more important than pollution costs. The attractiveness of China is due more to its market size than to its relatively lax pollution-control laws. From the 1970s through the early 1990s, the average amount spent by U.S. manufacturers to comply with pollution-control laws accounted for about 1 percent of their total costs, and this cost of pollution control is not high enough to justify international relocation.[9]

On a positive note, MNCs have power and prestige. Also in defense of MNCs, more and more of them have been trying to be responsible members of society. In addition, MNCs create social benefit by facilitating economic balance. Given the fact that natural resources and factors of production are unevenly distributed around the globe, MNCs can act as an effective and efficient mechanism to use these precious resources.

### *Multinationality and market performance*

At one time, it was thought that the relationship between a firm's degree of multinationality and its market performance was a linear and positive one. While studies have found a relationship, the linkage is not straightforward. Other factors complicate the relationship. One cross-sectional analysis of twelve industries over a seven-year period found that the "impact of multinationality on both financial and operational performance is moderated by a firm's R&D and marketing capabilities."[10]

## Characteristics of MNCs

MNC is not a one-dimensional concept. There is no single criterion that proves satisfactory at all times in identifying an MNC. Varying definitions are not necessarily convergent. As a result, whether or not a company is classified as an MNC depends in part on what set of criteria is used.

### *Definition by size*

The term MNC implies bigness. But bigness also has a number of dimensions. Such factors as market value, sales, profits, assets, and number of employees, when used to identify the largest multinationals, will yield varying results. While *Business Week* magazine focuses on market value, *Forbes* magazine ranks the world's largest public companies by using a composite ranking of sales, profits, assets, and market value. As measured by stock market valuation, the world's top five companies are ExxonMobil, General Electric, Microsoft, Gazprom, and Citigroup.[11] Gazprom, a Russian entity with market capitalization of $256 billion, is the world's largest natural gas company whose 49 percent of the shares were only listed for the first time in December 2005. Table 1.1 shows the global leaders based on the number of employees. Table 1.2, in contrast, shows the world's largest banks based on market value.

In the case of the *World Investment Report* of the United Nations Conference on Trade and Development (UNCTAD), it ranks transnational corporations (TNCs) by their foreign assets and spread index (see Tables 1.3 and 1.4).

Many multinational corporations are indeed large. Ownership of foreign assets is highly concentrated since half of the total is owned by just 1 percent of TNCs. Interestingly, multinationals' overseas investment has progressed to the point where sales generated by them outside their country of origin even exceed the world trade volume (total world exports).

One criterion to assess whether multinational firms are global is their penetration level of markets around the world. Very few of the 500 largest MNCs are successful globally. Out of 380 firms for which geographic sales data are available, 320 of them have an average of 80.3 percent of total sales in their home region. As such, in terms of market coverage, these companies are more regional than global.[12]

**TABLE 1.1** Global leaders: number of employees

| *Rank* | *Company* | *Number of workers* |
|---|---|---|
| 1 | Wal-Mart: | 1.8 million |
| 2 | Deutsche Post | 502,545 |
| 3 | Siemens Group | 461,000 |
| 4 | McDonald's | 447,000 |

*Source: San José Mercury News* (March 18, 2007).

**TABLE 1.2** Global leaders (banks): market value (in billions of U.S. dollars)

| *Rank* | *Company* | *Market value (in billions of US dollars)* |
|---|---|---|
| 1 | Citigroup | $273.8 |
| 2 | Bank of America | $231.7 |
| 3 | HSBC | $212.9 |
| 4 | J.P. Morgan Chase | $181.7 |
| 5 | UBS | $133.8 |
| 6 | Royal Bank of Scotland | $121.0 |
| 7 | Wells Fargo | $120.4 |
| 8 | BNP Paribas | $114.9 |
| 9 | Banco Santander Central Hispano | $114.9 |
| 10 | Mitsubishi UFJ Financial | $113.3 |

*Source:* "At Japan's Big Banks, Drive for Growth Sputters," *Wall Street Journal* (May 23, 2007).

**TABLE 1.3** Global non-financial leaders: assets (millions of dollars)

| *Rank* | *Company* | *Foreign assets* | *Total assets* |
|---|---|---|---|
| 1 | General Electric | 448,901 | 750,507 |
| 2 | Vodafone Group plc | 247,850 | 258,626 |
| 3 | Ford Motor | 179,856 | 305,341 |
| 4 | General Motors | 173,690 | 479,603 |
| 5 | British Petroleum | 154,513 | 193,213 |

*Source: World Investment Report 2006: FDI from Developing and Transition Economies* (UNCTAD, 2006).

**TABLE 1.4** Global financial leaders: UNCTAD spread index

| *Rank* | *Company* | *No. of affiliates* | *No. of host countries* |
|---|---|---|---|
| 1 | GE Capital Services | 1425 | 55 |
| 2 | Citigroup | 612 | 70 |
| 3 | UBS | 426 | 43 |
| 4 | Allianz Group | 778 | 47 |
| 5 | BNP Paribas | 622 | 53 |

*Source: World Investment Report 2006: FDI from Developing and Transition Economies* (UNCTAD, 2006).

Is corporate size an accurate indicator of international orientation? According to conventional thought, firm size should positively influence export intensity. The empirical findings have been mixed. One study shows that there is no general difference in the international marketing behavior among small and large companies.[13] Another study shows that firm size does not have a direct impact on export performance. Instead, the effect is indirect through cooperative strategy and knowledge intensity. As a result, small and medium-sized enterprises can improve their performance by employing cooperative strategies to enrich their knowledge base.[14] Furthermore, according to one study, smaller British retailers can overcome the constraints of size and they can successfully enter international markets.[15] Apparently, although smaller firms have fewer resources, they are still able to engage in international activities.

It is not unusual for corporate size to be used as a primary requirement for judging whether or not a company is multinational. However, based on this criterion, some 300,000 small and medium-sized German companies do not qualify, even though these firms (called the *Mittelstand,* or midranking) contribute mightily to Germany's export success. These medium-sized firms account for two-thirds of the country's gross national product and four-fifths of all workers.

Germany is the world's largest exporter, having surpassed the U.S.A. in 2002. Germany's exports of about $1.1 trillion account for 9.6 percent of world exports, while the shares for the U.S.A., China, and Japan are 8.9 percent, 7.4 percent, and 5.8 percent respectively. In addition, Germany, with about $206 billion, had the world's largest trade surplus. However, since 2004, Germany's trade surplus has increased by only 6.9 percent. With China's trade surplus skyrocketing nearly sixfold, China could claim the title in 2007.[16]

It should be noted that IBM did not become multinational because it was large but rather that it became large as a result of going international. Therefore, corporate size should not be used as the sole criterion for multinationalism.

### Definition by structure

According to Aharoni, an MNC has at least three significant dimensions: structural, performance, and behavioral.[17] Structural requirements for definition as an MNC include the number of countries in which the firm does business and the citizenship of corporate owners and top managers. Pfizer, stating that it is a truly global company, does business in more than 150 countries.

Schlumberger satisfies the requirement for multinationalism through the citizenship of members of its top management.[18] The company has employees from 140 nations, and its 16 highest-level executives account for 10 different nationalities. This diversity explains in part why Schlumberger has managed to get more of its revenue outside of the U.S.A. than have its competitors.

### Definition by performance

Definition by performance depends on such characteristics as foreign earnings, sales, and assets. These performance characteristics indicate the extent of the commitment of corporate resources to foreign operations and the amount of rewards from that commitment. The greater the commitment and reward, the greater the degree of internationalization. Japanese and British firms have routinely shown willingness to commit their corporate resources to overseas assets.

Kraft, North America's largest food company, has long dominated U.S. grocery store shelves with such powerful brands as Philadelphia Cream Cheese, Oreo cookies, Tang, Jell-O, Kool-Aid, Life Savers, Planters peanuts, and Lunchables prepackaged meals for kids. Remarkably, it has 61 brands with more than $100 million in sales. Virtually all U.S. grocery stores need some of Kraft's products. Internationally, it is a different matter. In Australia, Kraft Macaroni and Cheese and Oscar Mayer hot dogs are not readily available. While Kraft derives 27 percent of its total revenues from overseas, the figure pales when compared with H.J. Heinz's 44 percent, McDonald's 50+ percent, and Coca-Cola Co.'s 80+ percent. Furthermore, Kraft trails Nestlé and Unilever in foreign markets, with only 9 percent of its sales coming from developing countries.[19]

Human resources or overseas employees are customarily considered as part of the performance requirements rather than as part of the structural requirements, though the desirability of separating lower level employees from top management is questionable. A preferable analysis would be to treat the total extent of the employment of personnel in other countries as another indicator of the structure of the company. In any case, the willingness of a company to use overseas personnel satisfies a significant criterion for multinationalism. Avon, for example, employs 370,000 Japanese women to sell its products house to house across Japan. Siemens, well known worldwide for its consumer and industrial products, has some 461,000 employees in 124 countries.

## Definition by behavior

Behavior is somewhat more abstract as a measure of multinationalism than either structure or performance, though it is no less important. This requirement concerns the behavioral characteristics of top management. Thus, a company becomes more multinational as its management thinks more internationally. Such thinking, known as geocentricity, must be distinguished from two other attitudes or orientations, known as ethnocentricity and polycentricity.

### Ethnocentricity

Ethnocentricity is a strong orientation toward the home country. Markets and consumers abroad are viewed as unfamiliar and even inferior in taste, sophistication, and opportunity. The usual practice is to use the home base for the production of standardized products for export in order to gain some marginal business. Centralization of decision making is thus a necessity, regardless of whether decisions made at headquarters fit the local market.

### Polycentricity

Polycentricity, the opposite of ethnocentricity, is a strong orientation to the host country. The attitude places emphasis on differences between markets that are caused by variations within, such as in income, culture, laws, and politics. The assumption is that each market is unique and consequently difficult for outsiders to understand. Thus, managers from the host country should be employed and allowed to have a great deal of discretion in market decisions. A significant degree of decentralization is common across the overseas divisions.

A drawback of polycentricity is that it often results in duplication of effort among overseas subsidiaries. Similarities among countries might well permit the development of efficient and uniform strategies.

### Geocentricity

Geocentricity is a compromise between the two extremes of ethnocentricity and polycentricity. It could be argued that this attitude is the most important of the three. Geocentricity is an orientation that considers the whole world rather than any particular country as the target market. A geocentric company might be thought of as denationalized or supranational. As such, "international" or "foreign" departments or markets do not exist because the company does not designate anything international or foreign about a market. Corporate resources are allocated without regard to national frontiers, and there is no hesitation in making direct investment abroad when warranted. Nestlé SA mentions that Switzerland's lack of natural resources forces the company to depend on trade and adopt the geocentric perspective (see Figure 1.4).

There is a high likelihood that a geocentric company does not identify itself with a particular country. Therefore, it is often difficult to determine the firm's home country except through the location of its headquarters and its corporate registration. A multinational corporation does not have a national identity and should not mind moving its headquarters to a more hospitable environment. The chairman of Japanese retail giant Yaohan International Group, for example, moved the firm's headquarters as well as his family and personal assets to Hong Kong to take advantage of Hong Kong's low taxes and hub location in Asia. Following General Motors Corp., Hewlett-Packard Co.,

Typically Swiss...
Hard work, inventiveness, a single-minded dedication to qua-lity and a bit of luck go a long way towards explaining Swiss prosperity. With no natural resources and a beautiful, but not exactly fer-tile country, Switzerland had to put to use its one asset – its people. Nestlé, the country's biggest company, is applying its employees' knowledge, skills and experience to the cause of better nutrition and spends a lot of time and energy on research and development, trying to preserve and transform edible raw materials to satisfy the needs of expanding populations and to develop foods appropriate to the nutritional requirements and resources of consumers all over the world.
...and proud of it.
Nestlé

**FIGURE 1.4** Nestlé: MNC based on geocentricity

*Source*: Reprinted with permission of Nestlé Foods Corp.

Procter & Gamble Co., and Pfizer Inc., Kraft Foods Inc. recently moved its European headquarters to Switzerland so as to benefit from low corporate taxes.[20]

Geocentric firms take the view that, even though countries may differ, differences can be understood and managed. In coordinating and controlling the global marketing effort, the company adapts its marketing program to meet local needs within the broader framework of its total strategy. It is important to coordinate the activities of local subsidiaries and those of the headquarters. One

## Cultural Dimension 1.2

### How to be a multinational person

Ten commandments for tourists (as found in a hotel).

1 Thou shalt not expect to find things as thou hast at home, for thou hast left home to find things different.
2 Thou shalt not take anything too seriously, for a carefree mind is the start of a good holiday.
3 Thou shalt not let the other travelers get on thy nerves, for thou hast paid good money to enjoy thyself.
4 Remember to take half as many clothes as thou thinkest and twice the money.
5 Know at all times where thy passport is, for a person without a passport is a person without a country.
6 Remember that if we had been expected to stay in one place we would have been created with roots.
7 Thou shalt not worry, for he that worrieth hath no pleasure, and few things are that fatal.
8 When in a strange land, be prepared to do somewhat as its people do.
9 Thou shalt not judge the people of a country by a person who hath given thee trouble.
10 Remember thou art a guest in other lands and he that treats his host with respect shall be honored.

## Legal Dimension 1.1

### A hybrid citizen

In an ever-globalizing world, national citizenship has been giving some way to a more global kind of citizenship. The number of Latin American countries allowing some form of dual citizenship has jumped from seven in 1996 to 15 in 2003.

India, not unlike many countries, confiscates a person's citizenship of India once the person takes a new or additional citizenship. Such a practice is illogical in an ever-changing world where labor and capital are mobile. The practice alienates Indians and their children who reside abroad. About 20 million ethnic Indians live overseas, and they sent $22 billion home in 2004 – more than any national groups. Among them, 14 million are citizens of other nations.

In 2006, India reluctantly began to permit its citizens to acquire dual citizenship. As a result, among the major countries whose nationals migrate to the U.S.A., only China, South Korea, and Cuba still ban dual citizenship. India's Overseas Citizenship of India is a hybrid kind of national affiliation. Unfortunately, the new policy does not fully allow those Indians with dual citizenship full investment and voting rights.

Nationalists are not happy about the decline of patriotism. Globalists, on the other hand, look at it as a check on the power of nationalism.

*Source*: "Pledging Allegiances: Indian Passport Law Reflects Global Trend," *Wall Street Journal*, December 15, 2006.

study found important divergence between home and away in various aspects of the marketing process. This divergence may result in poor relationships, dysfunctional conflict, and ineffectiveness.[21]

The geocentric approach combines aspects of centralization and decentralization in a synthesis that allows some degree of flexibility. The firm may designate one country subsidiary as its research and development center while appointing another subsidiary in another country to specialize in manufacturing certain products. Although the corporation provides overall guidance so as to achieve maximum efficiency of its global system, the various aspects of the local operations may or may not be centralized as long as they meet local market needs. Avon Products strives for a more efficient global approach by largely centralizing manufacturing and marketing decisions that were once made by country managers.[22] Geocentric firms compete with each other on a worldwide basis rather than at a local level.

## The process of internationalization

The literature describes a number of stages of internationalization. Many companies may have begun as domestic firms concentrating on their own domestic markets before shifting or expanding the focus to also cover international markets. As they become more international, they are supposed to move from being sporadic exporters to being frequent exporters before finally doing manufacturing abroad. The process shows how firms were constrained initially by resource limitations and a lack of export commitment, and how they are able to become increasingly internationalized as more resources are allocated to international activity.

More recently, an increasingly global economy has given birth to a new theory which states that some companies are destined to go global from the outset, thus bypassing the stages of internationalization. Several Silicon Valley companies do not see the need to have a business model first for the U.S. market before going overseas. Instead, their mission is global almost from birth. As such, from the beginning, they may employ engineers in India, manufacture in Taiwan, and sell in Europe.

One definition of "**born global**" is: "a business organization that, from inception, seeks to derive significant competitive advantage from . . . the sale of outputs in multiple countries."[23] Their origins are international in the sense that management has a global focus and that resources are committed to international activities. Born-global international performance is enhanced due to managerial emphasis on foreign customer focus and marketing competence.

The born-global model has a great deal in common with the internationalization of small entrepreneurial firms.[24] Born-global companies are able to leverage a distinctive mix of orientations and strategies to succeed in diverse international markets.[25] Smaller born-global companies face a number of significant constraints: lack of economies of scale, lack of financial and knowledge resources, and aversion to risk taking. Yet they still can achieve rapid growth internationally through alliances with suppliers, distributors, and joint-venture partners.[26]

Significant differences exist between fast and gradual internationalizing firms. Firms that are in the more international active group have a proactive attitude with regard to internationalization activities, and their strategy is based on marketing differentiation advantages and strong relationships with clients and suppliers.[27] As for e-commerce companies, their speedy foreign market entry may be attributed to innovative and marketing capabilities as well as international experience of top management.[28]

At present, there is no conclusive evidence to show that domestic firms have generally indeed progressed from one stage to another as prescribed on their way to becoming more internationally oriented. Likewise, empirical evidence has so far been limited to support the competing hypothesis that some firms are "born global" in the sense that their mission is to become MNCs which engage in international business activities from the outset.

## Benefits of international marketing

International marketing affects consumers daily in many ways, though its importance is neither well understood nor appreciated. Government officials and other observers seem always to point to the negative aspects of international business. Many of their charges are more imaginary than real.

### *Survival and growth*

For companies to survive, they need to grow. Because most countries are not as fortunate as the U.S.A. in terms of market size, resources, and opportunities, they must trade with others to survive. Since most European nations are relatively small in size, they need foreign markets to achieve economies of scale so as to be competitive with American firms.

According to Friedman, the world is flattening because an explosion of digital technology has increasingly interconnected the world.[29] Even American marketers cannot ignore the vast potential of international markets. The world market is more than four times larger than the U.S. market. In the case of Amway Corp., a privately held U.S. manufacturer of cosmetics, soaps, and vitamins, Japan represents a larger market than the U.S.A..

Based on a recent report prepared by Goldman Sachs, India will grow at about 8 percent a year until 2020. India's economy will overtake those of Italy, France, and Britain by 2017. India will surpass Germany in 12 years and Japan in 18 years. The forecast is that India will overtake the U.S.A. to become the world's largest economy after China by 2042.[30]

### *Sales and profits*

Foreign markets constitute a large share of the total business of many firms that have wisely cultivated markets abroad. The case of KFC clearly emphasizes the importance of overseas markets. In 2006, KFC's third-quarter operating profit in China jumped 26 percent, while it rose less than 1 percent in the U.S.A.. KFC's sales in China increased 28 percent, while sales dropped 7 percent in the U.S.A.. Yum Brands plans to open a new KFC in China every 22 hours.[31]

Figure 1.5 shows how the state of Georgia showcases its strengths as a preferred location for companies wanting to do business with the world.

### *Diversification*

Demand for most products is affected by such cyclical factors as recession and such seasonal factors as climate. The unfortunate consequence of these variables is sales fluctuations, which can frequently be substantial enough to cause layoffs of personnel. One way to diversify a company's risk is to consider foreign markets as a solution to variable demand. Such markets even out fluctuations by providing outlets for excess production capacity. Cold weather, for instance, may depress soft drink consumption. Yet not all countries enter the winter season at the same time, and some countries are

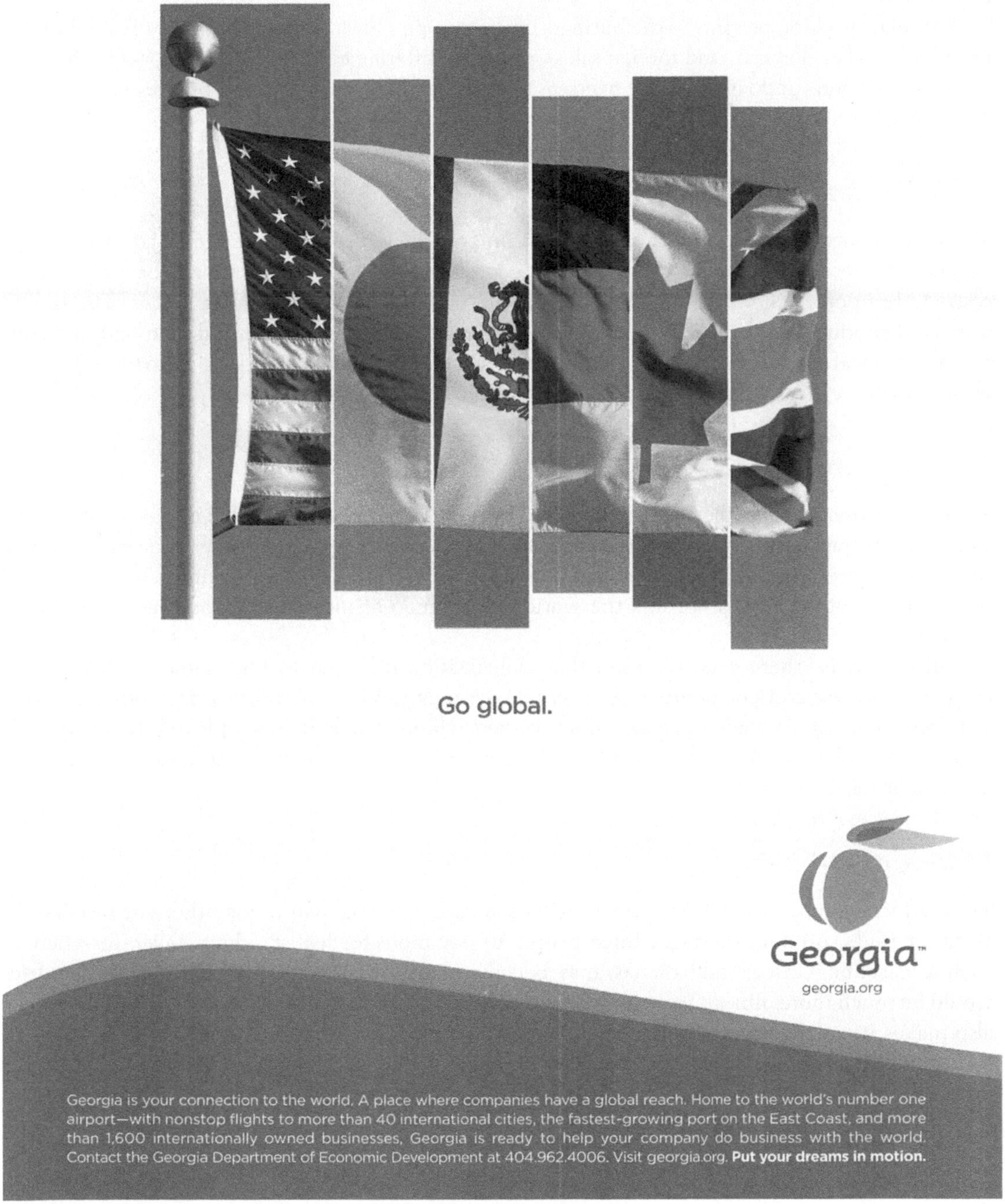
Go global.
Georgia™
georgia.org
Georgia is your connection to the world. A place where companies have a global reach. Home to the world's number one airport—with nonstop flights to more than 40 international cities, the fastest-growing port on the East Coast, and more than 1,600 internationally owned businesses, Georgia is ready to help your company do business with the world. Contact the Georgia Department of Economic Development at 404.962.4006. Visit georgia.org. **Put your dreams in motion.**

**FIGURE 1.5** Georgia: doing business with the world

*Source*: Courtesy of Georgia Department of Economic Development.

relatively warm all year round. Bird, U.S.A. Inc., a Nebraska manufacturer of go-carts and minicars for promotional purposes, has found that global selling has enabled the company to have year-round production.

A similar situation pertains to the business cycle: Europe's business cycle often lags behind that of the U.S.A.. That domestic and foreign sales operate in differing economic cycles works in the favor of General Motors and Ford because overseas operations help smooth out the business cycles of the North American market.

## Inflation and price moderation

The benefits of export are readily self-evident. Imports can also be highly beneficial to a country because they constitute reserve capacity for the local economy. Without imports (or with severely restricted imports), there is no incentive for domestic firms to moderate their prices. The lack of imported product alternatives forces consumers to pay more, resulting in inflation and excessive profits for local firms. This development usually acts as a prelude to workers' demand for higher wages, further exacerbating the problem of inflation.

## Employment

Trade restrictions, such as the high tariffs caused by the 1930 Smoot-Hawley Bill of the U.S.A., which forced the average tariff rates across the board to climb above 60 percent, contributed significantly to the Great Depression and have the potential to cause widespread unemployment again. Unrestricted trade, on the other hand, improves the world's GDP and enhances employment generally for all nations.

Unfortunately, there is no question that globalization is bound to hurt some workers whose employers are not cost-competitive. Some employers may also have to move certain jobs overseas so as to reduce costs. As a consequence, some workers will inevitably be unemployed. It is extremely difficult to explain to those who must bear the brunt of unemployment due to trade that there is a net benefit for the country.

## Standards of living

Trade affords countries and their citizens higher standards of living than would otherwise be possible. Without trade, product shortages force people to pay more for less. Products taken for granted, such as gasoline, coffee, and bananas, may become unavailable overnight. Life in most countries would be much more difficult were it not for the many strategic metals that must be imported. Trade also makes it easier for industries to specialize and gain access to raw materials, while at the same time fostering competition and efficiency. A diffusion of innovations across national boundaries is a useful by-product of international trade. A lack of such trade would inhibit the flow of innovative ideas.

The World Bank's studies have shown that increased openness to trade is associated with the reduction of poverty in most developing countries. Those developing countries which chose growth through trade grew twice as fast as those nations which chose more restrictive trade regimes. "Open trade has offered developing nations widespread gains in material well being, as well as gains in literacy, education and life expectancy."[32]

### *Understanding of marketing process*

Business schools everywhere in general and those in the U.S.A. in particular need to globalize their curricula. More than a token approach is required. It is not desirable to add "international content" as an afterthought in the form of a foreign case or article rather than as part of a fully integrated *global curriculum*.[33] Approximately 80 percent of instructional cases of Harvard Business School are out of date, and the relatively few international cases are ethnocentric in nature. Bicultural thinking is a more desirable approach.[34]

International marketing should not be considered a subset or special case of domestic marketing. When an executive is required to observe marketing in other cultures, the benefit derived is not so much the understanding of a foreign culture. Instead, the real benefit is that the executive actually develops a better understanding of marketing in one's own culture. For example, Coca-Cola Co. has applied the lessons learned in Japan to the U.S. and European markets. The study of international marketing may thus prove to be valuable in providing insights for the understanding of behavioral patterns often taken for granted at home. Ultimately, marketing as a discipline of study is more effectively understood.

## Conclusion

This chapter has provided an overview of the process and of the basic issues of international marketing. Similar to domestic marketing, international marketing is concerned with the process of creating and executing an effective marketing mix in order to satisfy the objectives of all parties seeking an exchange. International marketing is relevant regardless of whether or not the activities are for profit. It is also of little consequence whether countries have the same level of economic development or political ideology, since marketing is a universal activity that has application in a variety of circumstances.

The benefits of international marketing are considerable. Trade moderates inflation and improves both employment and the standard of living, while providing a better understanding of the marketing process at home and abroad. For many companies, survival, or the ability to diversify, depends on the growth, sales, and profits from abroad. As may be expected, the BRIC (Brazil, Russia, India, and China) economies have been getting a great deal of attention.

The more commitment a company makes to overseas markets in terms of personnel, sales, and resources, the more likely it is that it will become a multinational corporation. This is especially true when the management is geocentric rather than ethnocentric or polycentric. Since many view MNCs with envy and suspicion, the role of MNCs in society with regard to their benefits as well as their abuses will continue to be debated.

The marketing principles may be fixed, but a company's marketing mix in the international context is not. Certain marketing practices may or may not be appropriate elsewhere, and the degree of appropriateness cannot be determined without careful investigation of the market in question.

## CASE 1.1 MEDICAL VACATION: THE GLOBALIZATION OF HEALTH CARE

According to the U.S. Census Bureau, 46.6 million Americans have no medical insurance, and 120 million people have no dental insurance. Over a period of six years since 2001, health insurance premiums jumped 78 percent. In the same period, inflation went up 17 percent, while workers' wages increased 19 percent. A family pays about $11,500 a year for the coverage.

Private health care spending in Asia has reached $35 billion. Because of Asia's lower medical costs and world-class medical treatment, many people choose to combine their vacations with a medical check-up. Thailand and Malaysia are competing with Singapore to become the region's top health care center. The newcomers have joined forces with airlines and travel agents to offer medical package tours. They are able to offer comparable procedures (e.g., heart bypasses, cosmetic surgery) in comparable comfort at great savings. For heart procedures, a valve replacement may cost $160,000 in the U.S.A. but less than $10,000 in India. A heart bypass that costs $130,000 in the U.S.A. can be had for 10 percent of the amount in Thailand. Singapore at one time essentially monopolized the high-end market due to its success in attracting well-to-do patients from all over Asia. Singapore's hospital operators have fought back by conducting satellite facilities in lower cost Indonesia and Malaysia.

The CEO of Bangkok Hospital attributed the growth of medical tourists to the difficulty and unwillingness to travel to Western countries due to the global war on terrorism. Those in the Middle East, in particular, prefer to go to Thailand for medical services even though they can afford to seek treatment in the U.S.A. or Europe.

> In the past our customers were mainly Japanese; now Middle Eastern patients are dominant. Our better infrastructure and service is the main appeal for them. We also provide activities for their relatives like spas and traditional massage, tour programs, transportation and a hotel in front of our hospital.

In Southeast Asia, it is sometimes difficult to distinguish ultramodern hospitals from luxury hotels. Health care and comfort are no longer incompatible concepts. Bangkok's Bumrungrad Hospital is Thailand's top-of-the-line medical facility that has gone well beyond providing Western-trained doctors and up-to-date medical equipment. The hospital also provides guest chefs, bedside internet access, carpeted wards, and a helicopter rooftop landing pad. Patients and visitors are greeted by a white-gloved doorman, attentive bellhops, and a concierge who shows guests to their rooms (some with wet bars). An escalator connects the first two floors. If you need something to drink or eat, there are on-premise McDonald's and Starbucks outlets.

Bumrungrad Hospital first opened its doors in 1980 with a 200-bed facility. The new 554-bed facility of more than one million square feet was opened in 1997, right during the heart of the Asian economic crisis. As mentioned by Chief Executive Curtis Schroeder, Bumrungrad, unlike its competitors, decided neither to cut back services nor to lay off any staff. Instead, it took a calculated risk: going abroad. Even though it was heavily burdened by the loans taken in the rocketing U.S. dollar, it decided to use the weak baht as a vehicle to entice international patients to seek treatment in Thailand.

Bumrungrad's International Patient Center provides interpreters, an international concierge service, embassy assistance, airport transfers, and international medical and insurance coordination. Its Hospitality Residence has 74 apartments connected to the hospital, and its Hospitality Suites offer 51 fully serviced apartments with swimming pool and fitness facilities.

Bumrungrad is more than just a hospital. To reflect its growth and evolution into a global health care company focusing on clinical care, research, education, and international hospital management (international hospital management, consultancy services, and investment), the hospital has been rebranded as Bumrungrad International or BI. Its mission: "We provide efficient world class health care with caring and compassion." A giant banner proclaims: "Asia's 1st Internationally Accredited Hospital." The accreditation was granted by the U.S.-based Joint Commission on

International Accreditation. It is also the first hospital in the world to receive ISO 9001:2000 and 14001 certification. As one of Asia's first digitally electronic hospitals, Bumrungrad invests in the information system as an integral part of its operations (see Figure 1.6). Although the name Bumrungrad (meaning "serving the community") is not easy for foreigners to pronounce, the rebranding effort chose to retain the name to stress its mission as a health care company whose community has grown.

BI treats more than one million patients a year, with about one-third (or some 400,000 patients)

intel
with Intel® built in, Bumrungrad has
expansion built in
STORAGE ROOM TRANSFORMED INTO PEDIATRIC CLINIC. Bumrungrad Hospital, Southeast Asia's largest healthcare facility, created a kid-friendly pediatric clinic out of a 10,000-square-foot medical records unit. How? An ultra-scalable, 4-way Intel® Xeon® processor-based system improved data reliability and made records paperless. Read more about Bumrungrad Hospital's experience with Intel built in at intel.com/builtin.
intel inside
XEON

**FIGURE 1.6** International hospital and high technology

coming from over 150 countries. It employs more than 700 physicians and dentists as well as over 700 nurses. The company has representative offices in Bangladesh, Cambodia, Myanmar, Maldives, Nepal, the Netherlands, Vietnam, and Australia. It has won a turnkey management contract to manage Pun Hlaing International Hospital, which is Burma's first privately licensed hospital. Executives from more than 200 hospitals from all parts of the world have visited BI to observe its operations. In 2004, BI signed an equity and management agreement with a leading private hospital in the Philippines. In 2005, it entered into a joint venture with Istihmar, an investment holding company in the United Arab Emirates, to build a new hospital in Dubai. The planned hospital will be an important part of a major commercial development that includes the hospital, a hotel, and a wellness center. BI holds a 49 percent stake and will manage the hospital and its information technology system.

Asia's upscale medical facilities are not without controversy since they cater to wealthy customers. The practice thus favors the rich over the poor. The private hospital industry, on the other hand, argues that it has relieved a burden on the public system by taking care of medical tourists who can afford to pay. In addition, foreigners have been warned about not having the same kind of legal rights in the U.S.A. and Europe if something goes wrong. Yet the death rate for surgical patients in India is half of that found in most major U.S. hospitals.

*Sources*: "Asia's Middle-class Sick Find Comfort at Opulent Hospitals," *San Francisco Chronicle*, February 23, 2002; "Going Abroad for Health Care," *San José Mercury News*, October 16, 2006; "Safeguards Being Offered Overseas Clients to Cut the Risks," *San José Mercury News*, October 16, 2006; "Shopping for Surgery," *San José Mercury News*, October 16, 2006; "Seeking Health Care Abroad," *San José Mercury News*, November 5, 2006; "Medical Costs Up Again," *San José Mercury News*, September 19, 2007; "Lucrative Healing Touch," *Bangkok Post*, May 21, 2006; "Bumrungrad's Care a Standout," *Bangkok Post*, March 19, 2003; and "Bumrungrad Hospital Relaunches as Bumrungrad International," *Better Health*, No. 2, 2005, 4–5.

### *Points to consider*

Evaluate the appropriateness of the concept of "medical vacation" as well as the concept of providing health care in a luxury setting. Is medical care a culture-free product in the sense that medical treatment is universal regardless of cultures? Should culture be taken into consideration when treating and marketing to patients from the different parts of the world? What part of the hospital's marketing mix can be standardized, and what part should be adapted? Should premium health care be offered to those who can afford the high prices?

## Questions

1 Distinguish among: (a) domestic marketing, (b) foreign marketing, (c) comparative marketing, (d) international marketing, (3) multinational marketing, (f) global marketing, and (g) world marketing.
2 Are domestic marketing and international marketing different only in scope but not in nature?
3 Explain the following criteria used to identify MNCs: (a) size, (b) structure, (c) performance, and (d) behavior.
4 Distinguish among: (a) ethnocentricity, (b) polycentricity, and (c) geocentricity.
5 What are the benefits of international marketing?

# Discussion assignments and minicases

1 When Louis V. Gerstner, Jr. was a vice-chairman of American Express, he stated: "The split between international and domestic is very artificial – and at times dangerous." Do you agree with the statement? Offer your rationale.
2 Do you feel that marketing is relevant to and should be used locally as well as internationally by: (a) international agencies (e.g., the United Nations); (b) national, state, and/or city governments; (c) socialist/communist countries; (d) developing countries; and (e) priests, monks, churches, and/or evangelists?
3 Some of the best-known business schools in the U.S.A. want to emphasize discipline-based courses and eliminate international courses, based on the rationale that marketing and management principles are applicable everywhere. Is there a need to study international marketing? Discuss the pros and cons of the discipline-based approach as compared to the international approach.
4 Do MNCs provide social and economic benefits? Should they be outlawed?
5 Traditionally, American universities have served their international customers by simply admitting them to study in the U.S.A. Nowadays, no longer content to let foreign students and managers come to them, several American universities are going to their customers instead. The University of Rochester's Simon Graduate School, in conjunction with Erasmus University in Rotterdam, offers an executive MBA program. Tulane University's Freeman School of Business has a joint program with National Taiwan University. The University of Michigan has set up a program in Hong Kong for Cathay Pacific Airways managers. The University of Chicago's Graduate School of Business has transplanted its executive MBA program to Barcelona. Discuss the merits and potential problems of American and European business schools offering their graduate programs in a foreign land. Should they view themselves as international universities or merely as national universities with overseas programs?

## Notes


1 "See the World, Erase Its Border," *Business Week*, August 28, 2000, 113–14.
2 Intel Corporation, *2006 Annual Report*, 17.
3 Ralf Wagner, "Contemporary Marketing Practices in Russia," *European Journal of Marketing* 39 (Nos 1/2, 2005): 199–215.
4 Martin Bulla and David Starr-Glass, "Marketing and Non-profit Organizations in the Czech Republic," *European Journal of Marketing* 40 (Nos 1/2, 2006): 130–44.
5 *World Investment Report 2006: FDI from Developing and Transition Economies*, UNCTAD, 2006, 10.
6 *World Investment Report* 2006, 31.
7 Joseph A. Clougherty, "Globalization and the Autonomy of Domestic Competition Policy: An Empirical Test on the World Airline Industry," *Journal of International Business Studies* 32 (third quarter, 2001): 459–78.
8 Petra Christmann and Glen Taylor, "Globalization and the Environment: Determinants of Firm Self-regulation in China," *Journal of International Business Studies* 32 (third quarter, 2001): 439–58.
9 "Do Polluters Head Overseas?", *Business Week*, June 24, 2002, 26.
10 Masaaki Kotabe, Srini S. Srinivasan, and Preet S. Aulakh, "Multinationality and Firm Performance: The Moderating of R&D and Marketing Capabilities," *Journal of International Business Studies* 33 (first quarter, 2002): 79–97.
11 "Global Markets Heavyweight," *San José Mercury News*, November 26, 2006.
12 Alan M. Rugman and Alain Verbeke, "A Perspective on Regional and Global Strategies of Multinational Enterprises," *Journal of International Business Studies* 35 (January 2004): 3–18.
13 Bo Rundh, "International Marketing Behaviour Amongst Exporting Firms," *European Journal of Marketing* 41 (Nos 1/2, 2007): 181–98.
14 Antti Haahti *et al.*, "Cooperative Strategy, Knowledge Intensity and Export Performance of Small and Medium Sized Enterprises," *Journal of World Business* 40 (May 2005): 124–38.

15 Karise Hutchinson, Barry Quinn, and Nicholas Alexander, "SME Retailer Internationalisation: Case Study Evidence from British Retailers," *International Marketing Review* 23 (No. 1, 2006): 25–53.
16 "Global Export Champion," *San José Mercury News*, April 29, 2007.
17 Yair Aharoni, "On the Definition of a Multinational Corporation," *Quarterly Review of Economics and Business* (October 1971): 28–35.
18 "Star Search," *Business Week*, October 10, 2005, 69–79.
19 "Can Kraft Be a Big Cheese Abroad?", *Business Week*, June 4, 2001, 63–4.
20 "Kraft Moves Europe HQ to Switzerland," *Bangkok Post*, January 5, 2007.
21 Chi-fai Chan and Neil Bruce Holbert, "Marketing Home and Away: Perceptions of Managers in Headquarters and Subsidiaries," *Journal of World Business* 36 (No. 2, 2001): 205–21.
22 "50 Best Performers," *Business Week*, March 26, 2007, 77.
23 Gary Knight, Tage Koed Madsen, and Per Servais, "An Inquiry into Born-global Firms in Europe and the U.S.A.," *International Marketing Review* 21 (No. 6, 2004): 645–65.
24 Sylvie Chetty and Colin Campbell-Hunt, "A Strategic Approach to Internationalization: A Traditional Versus a 'Born-global' Approach," *Journal of International Marketing* 12 (No. 1, 2004): 57–81.
25 Gary A. Knight and S. Tamer Cavusgil, "Innovation, Organizational Capabilities, and the Born-global Firm," *Journal of International Business Studies* 35 (March 2004): 124–41.
26 Susan Freeman, Ron Edwards, and Bill Schroder, "How Smaller Born-global Firms Use Networks and Alliances to Overcome Constraints to Rapid Internationalization," *Journal of International Marketing* 14 (No. 3, 2006): 33–63.
27 José Pla-Barber and Alejandro Escriba-Esteve, "Accelerated Internationalisation: Evidence From a Late Investor Country," *International Marketing Review* 23 (No. 3, 2006): 255–78.
28 Yadong Luo, John Hongxin Zhao, and Jianjun Du, "The Internationalization Speed of E-commerce Companies: An Empirical Analysis," *International Marketing Review* 22 (No. 6, 2005): 693–709.
29 Thomas L. Friedman, *The World Is Flat*, Farrar, Straus & Giroux, 2006.
30 "Report Sees India as Global Economic Power," *Financial Times*, January 25, 2007.
31 "A Finger-lickin' Good Time in China," *Business Week*, October 30, 2006, 50.
32 Claudia Wolfe, "Building the Case for Global Trade," *Export America* (May 2001): 4–5.
33 Oded Shenkar, "One More Time: International Business in a Global Economy," *Journal of International Business Studies* 35 (March 2004): 161–71.
34 Gerardo R. Ungson and Daniel N. Braunstein, "The Geography of Thought," *Journal of Marketing* 68 (July 2004): 130–32.

Chapter 2

# Trade theories and economic cooperation

Capital and work – your work and your counterpart's work – can go anywhere on earth and do a job. . . . If the world operates as one big market, every employee will compete with every person anywhere in the world who is capable of doing the same job.

Andrew Grove, former CEO, Intel Corp.

## Chapter outline

- Marketing strategy: Botswana – the world's fastest growing economy
- Purpose of chapter
- Basis for international trade
    - Production possibility curve
    - Principle of absolute advantage
    - Principle of comparative/relative advantage
- Exchange ratios, trade, and gain
- Factor endowment theory
- The competitive advantage of nations
- The validity of trade theories
- Limitations of trade theories and suggested refinements
    - Land
    - Capital
    - Labor
    - Offshoring
    - Factor mobility and substitution
    - Demand
    - Marketing
    - Trade barriers

- Economic cooperation
  - Levels of economic integration
  - Economic and marketing implications
- Conclusion
- Case 2.1 The United States of America vs. the United States of Europe

## Marketing strategy

**Botswana – the world's fastest growing economy**

In 1966, Botswana had only three-and-a-half miles of paved roads to go with its three high schools in a country of 550,000 people. Water was quite scarce and precious, leading the nation to name its currency *pula*, meaning rain. At the time, Botswana's per capita income was $80 a year.

Fast forward it to the new millennium. Botswana, one of Africa's few enclaves of prosperity, is now a model for the rest of Africa or even the world. Its per capita income has rocketed to $6600. While the other African currencies are weak, the pula is strong – being backed by one of the world's highest per capita reserves ($6.2 billion).

How did Botswana do it? As a land-locked nation in southern Africa that is two-thirds desert, Botswana is a trader by necessity; but as the world's fastest growing economy, Botswana is a trader by design. Instead of being tempted by its vast diamond wealth that could easily lead to short-term solutions, the peaceful and democratic Botswana has adhered to free-market principles. Taxes are kept low. There is no nationalization of any businesses, and property rights are respected.

It is critical to note that Botswana's economic success is also due to the country's sound institutions and good governance. The country is well above the average of middle-income countries in all aspects of governance, and it even compares favorably with some high-income countries in several aspects.

For 30 years, Botswana's economic growth has averaged 9 percent per year, an extraordinary level of performance (see Figure 2.1). It has moved from being a low-income country to an upper-middle-income country. According to the World Bank's *World Development Indicators* (which reports on the world's economic and social health), the fastest growing economy over the past three decades is not in East Asia but in Africa. Since 1966, Botswana has outperformed all the others. Based on the average annual percentage growth of the GDP per capita, Botswana grew 9.2 percent. South Korea is the second fastest performer, growing at 7.3 percent. China came in third at 6.7 percent.

*Sources*: "Lessons from the Fastest-Growing Nation: Botswana?" *Business Week*, August 26, 2002, 116ff.; and "Botswana: Avoiding the Resource Curse," *IMF Survey*, August 7, 2006, 236–7.

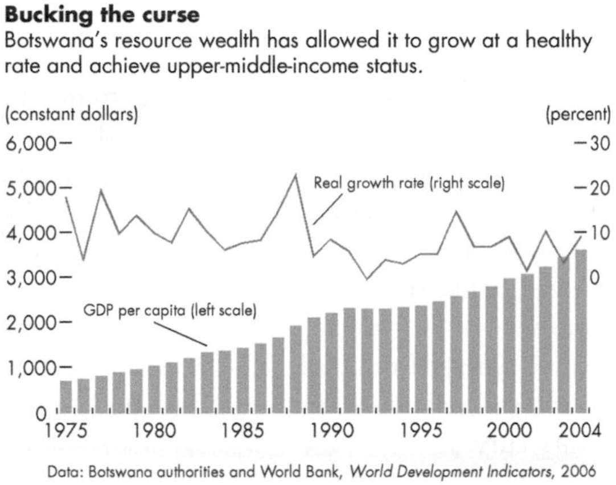
Bucking the curse
Botswana's resource wealth has allowed it to grow at a healthy rate and achieve upper-middle-income status.
(constant dollars)
(percent)
6,000
5,000
4,000
3,000
2,000
1,000
0
30
20
10
0
Real growth rate (right scale)
GDP per capita (left scale)
1975
1980
1985
1990
1995
2000
2004
Data: Botswana authorities and World Bank, World Development Indicators, 2006

**FIGURE 2.1** Avoiding the "resource curse"

*Source*: "Botswana: Avoiding the Resource Curse," *IMF Survey* (August 7, 2006, 236). © International Monetary Fund. Reprinted from *IMF Survey* (www.imf.org/imfsurvey) with the permission of the copyright holder.

## Purpose of chapter

Whenever a buyer and a seller come together, each expects to gain something from the other. The same expectation applies to nations that trade with each other. It is virtually impossible for a country to be completely self-sufficient without incurring undue costs. Therefore, trade becomes a necessary activity, though, in some cases, trade does not always work to the advantage of the nations involved. Virtually all governments feel political pressure when they experience trade deficits. Too much emphasis is often placed on the negative effects of trade, even though it is questionable whether such perceived disadvantages are real or imaginary. The benefits of trade, in contrast, are not often stressed, nor are they well communicated to workers and consumers.

The case of Botswana illustrates the necessity of trading. Botswana must import in order to survive, and it must export in order to earn funds to meet its import needs. Botswana's import and export needs are readily apparent; not so obvious is the need for other countries to do the same. There must be a logical explanation for well-endowed countries to continue to trade with other nations.

This chapter explains the rationale for international trade and examines the principles of absolute advantage and comparative advantage. These principles describe what and how nations can make gains from each other. The validity of these principles is discussed, as well as concepts that are refinements of these principles. The chapter also includes a discussion of factor endowment and competitive advantage. Finally, it concludes with a discussion of regional integration and its impact on international trade.

## Basis for international trade

Why do nations trade? A nation trades because it expects to gain something from its trading partner. One may ask whether trade is like a *zero-sum game*, in the sense that one must lose so that another will gain. The answer is no, because, though one does not mind gaining benefits at someone else's expense, no one wants to engage in a transaction that includes a high risk of loss. For trade to take place, both nations must anticipate gain from it. In other words, trade is a *positive-sum game*. Trade is about "mutual gain." However, unlike trade at the national level, competition at the company level is essentially a zero-sum game.

In order to explain how gain is derived from trade, it is necessary to examine a country's production possibility curve. How absolute and relative advantages affect trade options is based on the trading partners' production possibility curves.

### *Production possibility curve*

Without trade, a nation would have to produce all commodities by itself in order to satisfy all its needs. Figure 2.2 shows a hypothetical example of a country with a decision concerning the production of two products: computers and automobiles. This graph shows the number of units of computer or automobile the country is able to produce. The production possibility curve shows the maximum number of units manufactured when computers and automobiles are produced in various combinations, since one product may be substituted for the other within the limit of available resources. The country may elect to specialize or put all its resources into making either computers (point A) or automobiles (point B). At point C, product specialization has not been chosen, and thus a specific number of each of the two products will be produced.

Because each country has a unique set of resources, each country possesses its own unique production possibility curve. This curve, when analyzed, provides an explanation of the logic behind international trade. Regardless of whether the opportunity cost is constant or variable, a country must determine the proper mix of any two products and must decide whether it wants to specialize in one of the two. Specialization will likely occur if specialization allows the country to improve its prosperity by trading with another nation. The principles of absolute advantage and comparative advantage explain how the production possibility curve enables a country to determine what to export and what to import.

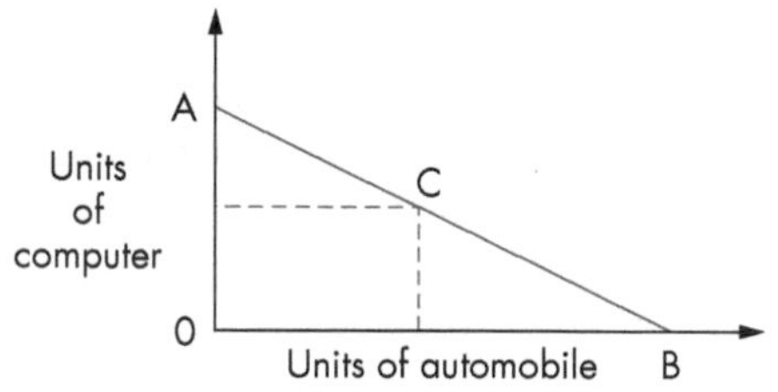
A
C
Units of computer
0
Units of automobile
B

**FIGURE 2.2** Production possibility curve: constant opportunity cost

## *Principle of absolute advantage*

Adam Smith may have been the first scholar to investigate formally the rationale behind foreign trade. In his book *The Wealth of Nations*, Smith used the principle of absolute advantage as the justification for international trade.[1] According to this principle, a country should export a commodity that can be produced at a lower cost than can other nations. Conversely, it should import a commodity that can only be produced at a higher cost than can other nations.

Consider, for example, a situation in which two nations are each producing two products. Table 2.1 provides hypothetical production figures for the U.S.A. and Japan based on two products: the computer and the automobile. Case 1 shows that, given certain resources and labor, the U.S.A. can produce 20 computers or 10 automobiles, or some combination of both. In contrast, Japan is able to produce only half as many computers (i.e., Japan produces 10 for every 20 computers the U.S.A. produces).This disparity may be the result of better skills by American workers in making this product. Therefore, the U.S.A. has an absolute advantage in computers. But the situation is reversed for automobiles: the U.S.A. makes only 10 cars for every 20 units manufactured in Japan. In this instance, Japan has an absolute advantage.

Based on Table 2.1, it should be apparent why trade should take place between the two countries. The U.S.A. has an absolute advantage for computers but an absolute disadvantage for automobiles. For Japan, the absolute advantage exists for automobiles and an absolute disadvantage for computers. If each country specializes in the product for which it has an absolute advantage, each can use its resources more effectively while improving consumer welfare at the same time. Since the U.S.A. would use fewer resources in making computers, it should produce this product for its own consumption as well as for export to Japan. Based on this same rationale, the U.S.A. should import automobiles from Japan rather than manufacture them itself. For Japan, of course, automobiles would be exported and computers imported.

An analogy may help demonstrate the value of the principle of absolute advantage. A doctor is absolutely better than a mechanic in performing surgery, whereas the mechanic is absolutely superior in repairing cars. It would be impractical for the doctor to practice medicine as well as repair the car when repairs are needed. Just as impractical would be the reverse situation, namely for the mechanic to attempt the practice of surgery. Thus, for practicality, each person should concentrate on and specialize in the craft which that person has mastered. Similarly, it would not be practical for

**TABLE 2.1** Possible physical output

| | *Product* | *U.S.A.* | *Japan* |
|---|---|---|---|
| Case 1 | Computer | 20 | 10 |
| | Automobile | 10 | 20 |
| Case 2 | Computer | 20 | 10 |
| | Automobile | 30 | 20 |
| Case 3 | Computer | 20 | 10 |
| | Automobile | 40 | 20 |

consumers to attempt to produce all the things they desire to consume. One should practice what one does well and leave the manufacture of other commodities to people who produce them well.

## *Principle of comparative/relative advantage*

One problem with the principle of absolute advantage is that it fails to explain whether trade will take place if one nation has absolute advantage for all products under consideration. Case 2 of Table 2.1 shows this situation. Note that the only difference between Case 1 and Case 2 is that the U.S.A. in Case 2 is capable of making 30 automobiles instead of the 10 in Case 1. In the second instance, the U.S.A. has absolute advantage for both products, resulting in absolute disadvantage for Japan for both. The efficiency of the U.S.A. enables it to produce more of both products at lower cost.

At first glance, it may appear that the U.S.A. has nothing to gain from trading with Japan. However, nineteenth-century British economist David Ricardo, perhaps the first economist to fully appreciate relative costs as a basis for trade, argues that absolute production costs are irrelevant.[2] More meaningful are relative production costs, which determine what trade should take place and what items to export or import. According to Ricardo's principle of relative (or comparative) advantage, one country may be better than another country in producing many products but should produce only what it produces best. Essentially, it should concentrate on either a product with the greatest comparative advantage or a product with the least comparative disadvantage. Conversely, it should import either a product for which it has the greatest comparative disadvantage or one for which it has the least comparative advantage.

Case 2 shows how the relative advantage varies from product to product. The extent of relative advantage may be found by determining the ratio of computers to automobiles. The advantage ratio for computers is 2:1 (i.e., 20:10) in favor of the U.S.A. Also in favor of the U.S.A., but to a lesser extent, is the ratio for automobiles, 1.5:1 (i.e., 30:20). These two ratios indicate that the U.S.A. possesses a 100 percent advantage over Japan for computers but only a 50 percent advantage for automobiles. Consequently, the U.S.A. has a greater relative advantage for the computer product. Therefore, the U.S.A. should specialize in producing the computer product. For Japan, having the least comparative disadvantage in automobiles indicates that it should make and export automobiles to the U.S.A.

Consider again the analogy of the doctor and the mechanic. The doctor may take up automobile repair as a hobby. It is even possible, though not probable, that the doctor may eventually be able to repair an automobile faster and better than the mechanic. In such an instance, the doctor would have an absolute advantage in both the practice of medicine and automobile repair, whereas the mechanic would have an absolute disadvantage for both activities. Yet this situation would not mean that the doctor would be better off repairing automobiles as well as performing surgery, because of the relative advantages involved. When compared to the mechanic, the doctor may be far superior in surgery but only slightly better in automobile repair. If the doctor's greatest advantage is in surgery, then the doctor should concentrate on that specialty. And when the doctor has automobile problems, the mechanic should make the repairs because the doctor has only a slight relative advantage in that skill. By leaving repairs to the mechanic, the doctor is using time more productively while maximizing income.

It should be pointed out that comparative advantage is not a static concept. John Maynard Keynes, an influential English economist, opposed India's industrialization efforts in 1911 based on his assumption of India's static comparative advantage in agriculture. However, as far back as 1791,

Alexander Hamilton had already endorsed the doctrine of **dynamic comparative advantage** as a basis of international trade.[3] This doctrine explains why Taiwan and India's Bangalore have now become high-technology centers that have attracted investments from the world's top technology companies. It also explains why or how the United Kingdom, forging more steel than the rest of the world combined in 1870, lost the lead to the U.S.A. Andrew Carnegie's mills among others were able to produce twice as much steel as Great Britain three decades later.[4]

## Exchange ratios, trade, and gain

Although an analysis of relative advantage can indicate what a country should export and import, that analysis cannot explain exactly how a country will gain from trading with a partner. In order to determine the extent of trading gain, an examination of the domestic exchange ratio is required. Based on Case 2 of Table 2.1, Japan's domestic exchange ratio between the two products in question is 1:2 (i.e., 10 computers for every 20 automobiles). In other words, Japan must give up two automobiles to make one computer. But by exporting automobiles to the U.S.A., Japan has to give up only 1.5 automobiles in order to get one computer. Thus, trading essentially enables Japan to get more computers than feasible without trading.

The U.S. domestic exchange ratio is 1:1.5 (i.e., 20 computers for every 30 automobiles). The incentive for the U.S.A. to trade with Japan occurs in the form of a gain from specializing in computer manufacturing and exchanging computers for automobiles from Japan. The extent of the gain is determined by comparing the domestic exchange ratios in the two countries. In the U.S.A., one computer brings 1.5 automobiles in exchange, but this same computer will result in two automobiles in Japan. Trading thus is the most profitable way for the U.S.A. to employ its resources.

Theoretically, trade should equalize the previously unequal domestic exchange ratios and bring about a new ratio, known as the **world market exchange ratio**, or **terms of trade**. This ratio, which will replace the two different domestic exchange ratios, will lie between the limits established by the pre-trade domestic exchange ratios.

Such benefits derived from trade do not imply that trade must always take place and that all nations will always gain from trade. We will carry the hypothetical example a step further. In Case 3 of Table 2.1, the U.S.A. now makes 40 automobiles (instead of 10 as in Case 1 and 30 as in Case 2). Not only does the U.S.A. have absolute advantage for both products, but it also has the same domestic exchange ratio as that of Japan. This situation is graphically expressed by two parallel production possibility curves (Figure 2.3).

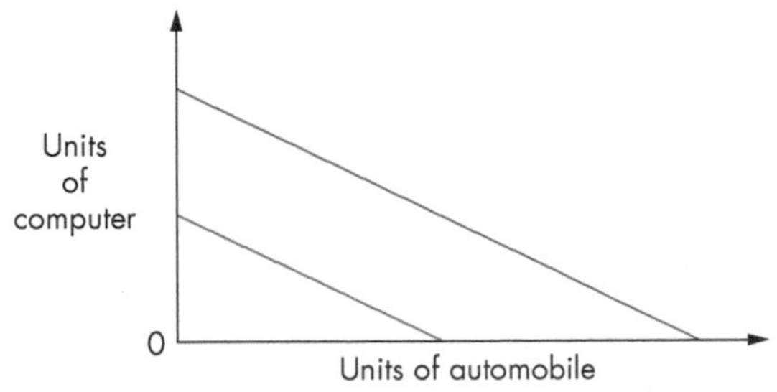
Units
of
computer
0
Units of automobile

**FIGURE 2.3** Absolute advantage without relative advantage (identical domestic exchange ratios)

Under these circumstances, trade will probably not occur for two principal reasons. First, since the U.S.A. is 100 percent better than Japan for each product, the relative advantage for the U.S.A. is identical for both products. Second, since both countries have the identical domestic exchange ratio, there is no incentive or gain from trading for either party. Whether in the U.S.A. or in Japan, one unit of computer will fetch two automobiles. When such other costs as paperwork and transportation are taken into account, it becomes too expensive to export a product from one country to another. Thus international trade is a function of the varying domestic exchange ratios, and these ratios cause variations in comparative costs or prices.

## Factor endowment theory

The principles of absolute and comparative advantage provide a primary basis for trade to occur, but the usefulness of these principles is limited by their assumptions. One basic assumption is that the advantage, whether absolute or relative, is determined solely by labor in terms of time and cost. Labor then determines comparative production costs and subsequent product prices for the same commodity.

If labor is indeed the only factor of production or even a major determinant of product content, countries with high labor cost should be in serious trouble. An interesting fact is that Japan and Germany, in spite of their very high labor costs, have remained competitive and have performed well in trade. It thus suggests that absolute labor cost is only one of several competitive inputs that determine product value. Figure 2.4 shows that the average income share of labor has been declining.

Tables 2.2 and 2.3 show incomes, working hours, and vacation days across major cities. Figure 2.5 (page 41) shows the gross and net hourly pay around the globe.

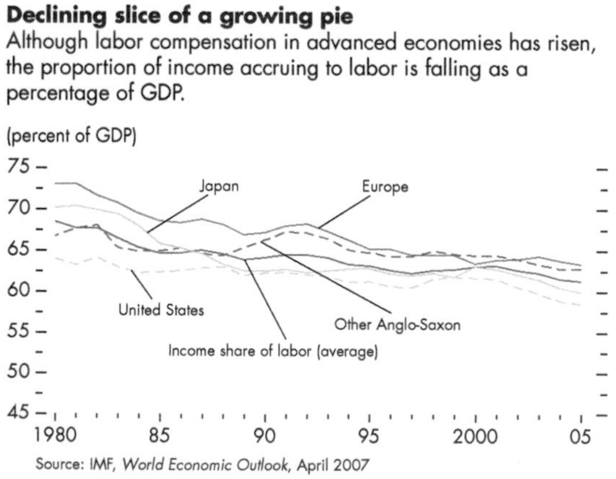
**Declining slice of a growing pie**
Although labor compensation in advanced economies has risen, the proportion of income accruing to labor is falling as a percentage of GDP.
(percent of GDP)
75
70
65
60
55
50
45
Japan
Europe
United States
Other Anglo-Saxon
Income share of labor (average)
1980
85
90
95
2000
05
Source: IMF, *World Economic Outlook*, April 2007

**FIGURE 2.4** Income share of labor

*Source*: "Labor Globalization: Bane or Boon?," *IMF Survey* (April 11, 2007, 88).

**TABLE 2.2** Wage levels around the globe

| *City*[1] | *Gross New York = 100* | *Net New York = 100* |
|---|---|---|
| Copenhagen | 118.2 | 95.7 |
| Oslo | 117.0 | 110.8 |
| Zurich | 115.1 | 124.2 |
| Geneva | 111.0 | 115.4 |
| New York | 100.0 | 100.0 |
| London | 89.2 | 96.0 |
| Chicago | 88.3 | 94.7 |
| Dublin | 88.3 | 104.6 |
| Frankfurt | 87.6 | 85.5 |
| Brussels | 86.8 | 78.2 |
| Los Angeles | 86.3 | 97.0 |
| Munich | 84.9 | 84.5 |
| Helsinki | 84.9 | 89.1 |
| Berlin | 84.3 | 82.1 |
| Luxembourg | 84.0 | 98.1 |
| Stockholm | 80.7 | 77.0 |
| Vienna | 78.7 | 81.2 |
| Tokyo | 78.0 | 87.4 |
| Amsterdam | 77.0 | 72.7 |
| Sydney | 74.6 | 79.6 |
| Toronto | 74.2 | 80.4 |
| Montreal | 74.1 | 77.3 |
| Lyon | 69.0 | 70.5 |
| Paris | 68.5 | 68.8 |
| Miami | 67.6 | 74.0 |
| Auckland | 65.7 | 73.4 |
| Barcelona | 57.6 | 66.6 |
| Milan | 56.1 | 59.9 |
| Nicosia | 55.4 | 69.5 |
| Madrid | 53.9 | 64.3 |
| Rome | 47.0 | 49.7 |
| Seoul | 44.2 | 48.2 |
| Athens | 42.8 | 48.6 |
| Dubai | 40.6 | 57.8 |
| Johannesburg | 36.5 | 37.3 |
| Taipei | 35.5 | 43.3 |
| Lisbon | 33.2 | 38.6 |
| Singapore | 32.3 | 38.9 |
| Ljubljana | 31.3 | 28.3 |

**TABLE 2.2** *continued*

| *City*[1] | *Gross* *New York = 100* | *Net* *New York = 100* |
|---|---|---|
| Hong Kong | 27.4 | 34.9 |
| Manama (Bahrain) | 26.2 | 36.6 |
| Istanbul | 25.0 | 25.9 |
| Sao Paulo | 24.7 | 29.0 |
| Prague | 24.4 | 25.8 |
| Santiago de Chile | 21.2 | 24.3 |
| Tallinn | 20.5 | 22.1 |
| Budapest | 20.0 | 20.0 |
| Moscow | 19.9 | 25.4 |
| Warsaw | 19.3 | 18.4 |
| Rio de Janeiro | 18.6 | 21.2 |
| Bratislava | 16.6 | 18.7 |
| Vilnius | 15.9 | 15.4 |
| Kuala Lumpur | 15.7 | 18.8 |
| Buenos Aires | 15.4 | 18.0 |
| Riga | 14.4 | 15.3 |
| Caracas | 14.2 | 18.7 |
| Lima | 13.7 | 15.8 |
| Bucharest | 13.1 | 13.2 |
| Shanghai | 11.5 | 13.1 |
| Mexico City | 10.9 | 14.1 |
| Bogotá | 10.3 | 13.0 |
| Kiev | 9.6 | 11.6 |
| Nairobi | 9.3 | 11.1 |
| Sofia | 9.3 | 10.2 |
| Beijing | 8.9 | 10.9 |
| Bangkok | 8.1 | 10.9 |
| Mumbai (Bombay) | 7.0 | 8.7 |
| Jakarta | 6.3 | 8.2 |
| Manila | 6.3 | 7.8 |
| Delhi | 6.1 | 7.8 |
| Tel Aviv | n.a. | n.a. |

*Note*: **Methodology** Effective hourly wages for14 professions,weighted according to distribution, net after deductions of taxes and social security contributions.

[1] Listed according to gross value of the index.

*Source*: *Prices and Earnings* (Zurich: UBS AG, 2006, 9).

**TABLE 2.3** Working hours and vacation days around the globe

| *City* | *Working hours per year* | *Vacation days[1] per year* |
|---|---|---|
| Amsterdam | 1687 | 25 |
| Athens | 1714 | 24 |
| Auckland | 1686 | 20 |
| Bangkok | 2023 | 10 |
| Barcelona | 1758 | 21 |
| Beijing | 2064 | 9 |
| Berlin | 1611 | 29 |
| Bogotá | 2065 | 15 |
| Bratislava | 1760 | 20 |
| Brussels | 1672 | 21 |
| Bucharest | 1771 | 21 |
| Budapest | 1834 | 26 |
| Buenos Aires | 2053 | 18 |
| Caracas | 1918 | 16 |
| Chicago | 1971 | 17 |
| Copenhagen | 1644 | 22 |
| Delhi | 2121 | 15 |
| Dubai | 2050 | 29 |
| Dublin | 1727 | 21 |
| Frankfurt | 1650 | 29 |
| Geneva | 1795 | 23 |
| Helsinki | 1603 | 29 |
| Hong Kong | 2231 | 9 |
| Istanbul | 2023 | 15 |
| Jakarta | 2013 | 12 |
| Johannesburg | 1902 | 21 |
| Kiev | 1712 | 23 |
| Kuala Lumpur | 2024 | 16 |
| Lima | 2052 | 25 |
| Lisbon | 1708 | 22 |
| Ljubljana | 1756 | 21 |
| London | 1782 | 20 |
| Los Angeles | 1957 | 11 |
| Luxembourg | 1725 | 25 |
| Lyon | 1572 | 25 |
| Madrid | 1724 | 22 |
| Manama (Bahrain) | 1965 | 21 |
| Manila | 2042 | 13 |
| Mexico City | 2266 | 14 |
| Miami | 1809 | 14 |

**TABLE 2.3** *continued*

| *City* | *Working hours per year* | *Vacation days[1] per year* |
|---|---|---|
| Milan | 1744 | 25 |
| Montreal | 1795 | 12 |
| Moscow | 1643 | 22 |
| Mumbai (Bombay) | 2205 | 17 |
| Munich | 1649 | 27 |
| Nairobi | 1984 | 21 |
| New York | 1869 | 13 |
| Nicosia | 1753 | 22 |
| Oslo | 1627 | 24 |
| Paris | 1481 | 27 |
| Prague | 1771 | 20 |
| Riga | 1737 | 20 |
| Rio de Janeiro | 1709 | 30 |
| Rome | 1747 | 21 |
| Santiago de Chile | 2077 | 17 |
| Sao Paulo | 1736 | 30 |
| Seoul | 2317 | 10 |

*Note:* **Methodology** Annual working hours including vacation (paid) and legal holidays: weighted average of 13 professions (excluding elementary schoolteachers).

[1] Paid working days (excluding legal holidays).

*Source: Prices and Earnings* (Zurich: UBS AG, 2006, 30).

It is misleading to analyze labor costs without also considering the quality of that labor. A country may have high labor cost on an absolute basis; yet this cost can be relatively low if productivity is high. Countries with low wages tend to have low productivity. Any subsequent productivity gains usually result in higher wages and currency appreciation.

Furthermore, the price of a product is not necessarily determined by the amount of labor it embodies, regardless of whether or not the efficiency of labor is an issue. Since product price is not determined by labor efficiency alone, other factors of production must be taken into consideration, including land and capital (i.e., equipment). Together, all of these production factors contribute significantly to the creation of value within a particular product.

One reason for the importance of identifying other factors of production is that different commodities require different factor inputs and that no country is well endowed in all production factors. The varying proportion of these factors embodied in various goods has a great deal of impact on what a country should produce. Corn, for instance, is best produced where there is an abundance of land (relative to labor and capital), even though corn can be grown in most places in the world. Oil refining, in contrast, requires relatively more capital and relatively less labor and land because of expensive equipment and specialized personnel. In clothing production, the most important input factor is that the economy is labor-intensive.

| City | USD per hour net | USD per hour gross |
|---|---|---|
| Amsterdam | 11.40 | 17.50 |
| Athens | 7.60 | 9.70 |
| Auckland | 11.50 | 14.90 |
| Bangkok | 1.70 | 1.80 |
| Barcelona | 10.50 | 13.10 |
| Beijing | 1.70 | 2.00 |
| Berlin | 12.90 | 19.20 |
| Bogotá | 2.00 | 2.30 |
| Bratislava | 2.90 | 3.80 |
| Brussels | 12.30 | 19.70 |
| Bucharest | 2.10 | 3.00 |
| Budapest | 3.20 | 4.50 |
| Buenos Aires | 2.80 | 3.50 |
| Caracus | 2.90 | 3.20 |
| Chicago | 14.90 | 20.10 |
| Copenhagen | 15.10 | 26.90 |
| Delhi | 1.20 | 1.40 |
| Dubai | 9.10 | 9.20 |
| Dublin | 16.50 | 20.10 |
| Frankfurt | 13.50 | 19.90 |
| Geneva | 18.20 | 25.20 |
| Helsinki | 14.00 | 19.30 |
| Hong Kong | 5.50 | 6.20 |
| Istanbul | 4.10 | 5.70 |
| Jakarta | 1.30 | 1.40 |
| Johannesburg | 5.90 | 8.30 |
| Kiev | 1.80 | 2.20 |
| Kuala Lumpur | 3.00 | 3.60 |
| Lima | 2.50 | 3.10 |
| Lisbon | 6.10 | 7.50 |
| Ljubljana | 4.50 | 7.10 |
| London | 15.10 | 20.30 |
| Los Angeles | 15.30 | 19.60 |
| Luxembourg | 15.40 | 19.10 |
| Lyon | 11.10 | 15.70 |
| Madrid | 10.10 | 12.30 |
| Manama | 5.80 | 6.00 |
| Manila | 1.20 | 1.40 |
| Mexico City | 2.20 | 2.50 |
| Miami | 11.60 | 15.40 |
| Milan | 9.40 | 12.70 |
| Montreal | 12.20 | 16.80 |
| Moscow | 4.00 | 4.50 |
| Mumbai | 1.40 | 1.60 |
| Munich | 13.30 | 19.30 |
| Nairobi | 1.80 | 2.10 |
| New York | 15.70 | 22.70 |
| Nicosia | 10.90 | 12.60 |
| Oslo | 17.40 | 26.60 |
| Paris | 10.80 | 15.60 |
| Prague | 4.10 | 5.50 |
| Riga | 2.40 | 3.30 |
| Rio de Janeiro | 3.30 | 4.20 |
| Rome | 7.80 | 10.70 |
| Santiago de Chile | 3.80 | 4.80 |
| São Paulo | 4.60 | 5.60 |
| Seoul | 7.60 | 10.10 |
| Shanghai | 2.10 | 2.60 |
| Singapore | 6.10 | 7.30 |
| Sofia | 1.60 | 2.10 |
| Stockholm | 12.10 | 18.30 |
| Sydney | 12.50 | 17.00 |
| Taipei | 6.80 | 8.10 |
| Tallinn | 3.50 | 4.70 |
| Tel Aviv | n.a. | n.a. |
| Tokyo | 13.70 | 17.70 |
| Toronto | 12.70 | 16.90 |
| Vienna | 12.80 | 17.90 |
| Vilnius | 2.40 | 3.60 |
| Warsaw | 2.90 | 4.40 |
| Zurich | 19.50 | 26.20 |

■ Gross income in USD per hour

■ Net income per USD per hour

**Methodology** Effective hourly wage in 14 professions, taking into account working hours, paid vacation and legal holidays. Weighting according to distribution of professions

n.a. = not available

**FIGURE 2.5** Gross and net hourly pay around the globe

*Source*: Price and Earnings (Zurich: UBS AG, 2006, 27).

The varying factor inputs and proportions for different commodities, together with the uneven distribution of such factors of production in different regions of the world, are the basis of the **Heckscher–Ohlin theory of factor endowment**.[5] This theory holds that the inequality of relative prices is a function of regional factor endowments and that comparative advantage is determined by the relative abundance of such endowments. According to Ohlin, there is a mutual interdependence among production factors, factor movements, income, prices, and trade. A change in one affects the rest. Prices of factors and subsequent product prices in each region depend on supply and demand, which in turn are affected by the desires of consumers, income levels, quantity of various factors, and physical conditions of production.

Since countries have different factor endowments, a country would have a relative advantage in a commodity that embodies in some degree that country's comparatively abundant factors. A country should thus export that commodity which is relatively plentiful (i.e., in comparison to other commodities) within the relatively abundant factor (i.e., in comparison to other countries). This exported item may then be exchanged for goods that would use large quantities of the country's scarce factors if domestically produced.

Therefore, a country that is relatively abundant in labor but relatively scarce in capital is likely to have a comparative advantage in the production of labor-intensive goods and to have deficiencies in the production of capital-intensive goods. This concept explains why China, a formidable competitor in textile products, has to depend on U.S. and European firms for oil exploration within China itself.

Interestingly or surprisingly, a nation's abundance of a particular production factor may sometimes undermine instead of enhance the country's competitive advantage. Due to the **"resource curse" hypothesis**, resource-abundant economies have a tendency to grow less rapidly than their resource-scarce counterparts. As demonstrated by Botswana, the "resource curse" phenomenon can be avoided. Resource richness, with proper government management, can generate economic growth. There are four important dimensions of good governance: voice and accountability, government effectiveness, quality of regulation, and anti-corruption policies. For developing countries, the last two dimensions are particularly important.[6]

The quality of human resources is a function of human development. The United Nations Development Program has prepared the **Human Development Index** (HDI) to measure well-being.[7] The HDI, ranging from zero (low human development) to one (high human development), is an arithmetic average of a country's achievements in three basic dimensions: longevity (measured by life expectancy at birth); educational attainment (measured by combination of adult literacy rate and enrollment ratio in primary, secondary, and tertiary education); and living standards (measured by GDP per capita in U.S. dollars at purchasing power parity). Both the HDI and per capita income are highly correlated with the other widely used measures of poverty. Table 2.4 shows a list of countries based on the HDI.

## The competitive advantage of nations

Michael Porter's book, *The Competitive Advantage of Nations*, has received a great deal of interest all over the world.[8] Based on his analysis of over a hundred case studies of industries in ten leading developed nations, Porter has identified four major determinants of international competitiveness: (1) factor conditions, (2) demand conditions, (3) related and supporting industries, and (4) firm strategy, structure, and rivalry. These four determinants interact and form the "diamond" which provides the context in which a nation's firms are born and compete.

**TABLE 2.4** Human Development Index (HDI), selected countries

| ≤ 0.50 | | 0.51–0.70 | | 0.71–0.80 | | >0.80 | |
|---|---|---|---|---|---|---|---|
| **Africa** | | **Africa** | | **Asia** | | **Europe/Industrial countries** | |
| Sudan | (0.48) | South Africa | (0.70) | Thailand | (0.74) | Canada | (0.93) |
| Mauritania | (0.45) | Botswana | (0.59) | Philippines | (0.74) | United States | (0.93) |
| Nigeria | (0.44) | Gabon | (0.59) | China | (0.71) | Australia | (0.93) |
| Congo, Dem. Rep. of the | (0.43) | Ghana | (0.56) | **Transition economies** | | Japan | (0.92) |
| Zambia | (0.42) | Zimbabwe | (0.56) | Bulgaria | (0.77) | United Kingdom | (0.92) |
| Cote d'Ivoire | (0.42) | Cameroon | (0.53) | Russia | (0.77) | France | (0.92) |
| Senegal | (0.42) | Kenya | (0.51) | Romania | (0.77) | Germany | (0.91) |
| Tanzania | (0.41) | Congo, Rep. of | (0.51) | Georgia | (0.76) | Italy | (0.90) |
| Uganda | (0.41) | **Asia** | | Ukraine | (0.74) | Spain | (0.90) |
| Angola | (0.40) | Vietnam | (0.67) | Azerbaijan | (0.72) | **Asia** | |
| Malawi | (0.38) | Indonesia | (0.67) | Albania | (0.71) | Singapore | (0.88) |
| Mozambique | (0.34) | India | (0.56) | **Middle East** | | Hong Kong SAR | (0.87) |
| Ethiopia | (0.31) | Pakistan | (0.52) | Saudi Arabia | (0.75) | Korea, Rep. of | (0.85) |
| Niger | (0.29) | **Transition economies** | | Jordan | (0.72) | **Transition economies** | |
| Sierra Leone | (0.25) | Moldova | (0.70) | Iran, Islamic Rep. of | (0.71) | Czech Republic | (0.84) |
| **Asia** | | Uzbekistan | (0.69) | **Western Hemisphere** | | Hungary | (0.82) |
| Lao, People's Dem. Rep. | (0.48) | Tajikistan | (0.66) | Mexico | (0.78) | Poland | (0.81) |
| Nepal | (0.47) | **Middle East** | | Colombia | (0.76) | **Middle East** | |
| Bangladesh | (0.46) | Syrian Arab Republic | (0.66) | Brazil | (0.75) | Israel | (0.88) |
| **Middle East** | | Egypt | (0.62) | Peru | (0.74) | Kuwait | (0.84) |
| Yemen | (0.45) | Iraq | (0.58) | | | **Western Hemisphere** | |
| **Western Hemisphere** | | **Western Hemisphere** | | | | Argentina | (0.84) |
| Haiti | (0.44) | Bolivia | (0.64) | | | Chile | (0.83) |
| | | Nicaragua | (0.63) | | | Uruguay | (0.82) |
| | | Guatemala | (0.62) | | | | |

*Source*: Paul Cashin, Paolo Mauro, and Ratna Sahay, "Macroeconomic Policies and Poverty Reduction: Some Cross-country Evidence," *Finance & Development* (June 2001, 46–9).

A nation is competitive when it has specialized assets and skills necessary for competitive advantage in an industry. Firms gain competitive advantage in industries when their home base offers better ongoing information into product and process needs. They gain competitive advantage when owners, managers, and employees support intense commitment and sustained investment. In the end, nations succeed in particular industries because their dynamic home environment stimulates firms to upgrade and widen their advantages over time. Therefore, the effect of one determinant is determined by the state of the others: the advantages in one determinant can enhance the advantages in others.

Porter's theory also includes two additional variables: chance and government. Chance events are developments outside the control of firms, and they include pure inventions, breakthroughs in basic technologies, wars, external political developments, and major shifts in market demand. Government at all levels, on the other hand, can improve or detract from a country's national advantage. Regulations and investment policies can affect domestic rivalry and home demand conditions. The government variable explains why Bermuda and the Cayman Islands, while not being well endowed in terms of factors of production, capture 31.5 percent and 12 percent respectively of the world's captive insurance operations.

As pointed out by Porter, it was falsely believed for a long time that Japan's government policy was largely responsible for the country's competitiveness. Those industries that benefited from government policies restricting competition turned out to be international failures. The successful industries are the ones that face robust internal competition. There is a positive relationship between vigorous competition, rising productivity, and economic success.[9] While the governments of South Korea and Taiwan play a fairly aggressive role in shaping economic activity, the powerful diamond-type factors have played a dominant role in their success.

The "diamond" promotes the "clustering" of a nation's competitive industries. The country's successful industries are usually linked through vertical (buyer/supplier) or horizontal (common customers, technology) relationships. This cluster of industries is mutually supporting, and the derived benefits flow forward, backward, and horizontally. As in the case of Sweden, it is successful not only in pulp and paper but also in wood-handling machinery, sulphur boilers, conveyor systems, pulp-making machinery, control instruments, paper-making machinery, and paper-drying machinery. Sweden is also internationally competitive in chemicals that are used in pulp and paper making.

Clusters influence competitiveness. The geographical concentration of firms facilitates efficient access to specialized suppliers, information and the workforce, and there are greater opportunities for innovation within clusters. Clusters also reduce barriers to entry, making it possible for new firms to gain access to an established pool of resources. Even so, any economy needs to upgrade the sophistication of its clusters towards more advanced high-value activities.[10]

While Porter's theory seems logical and is supported by empirical evidence, it has also been criticized as being "inherently case study based."[11] One may also wonder whether the broad-based generalizations are warranted. For example, it is doubtful that the theory can explain why Sweden, a relatively small country, is the third largest exporter of music. Likewise, in the case of American pastimes, one has to wonder why foreign-born Latinos are so good at playing baseball to the point that they account for 25 percent of the major league rosters, not counting thousands more from the Caribbean as well as Central and South America who play in the minors.

In fairness, Porter does offer a number of explanations or qualifications. A country's national competitive advantage in a particular industry may be eroded when conditions in the national diamond no longer support investment and innovation to match the industry's evolving structure. Some important reasons for the loss of advantage are: deterioration of factor conditions, local needs not compatible with global demand, loss of home buyers' sophistication, technological change, firms' adjustment inflexibility, and reduction in domestic rivalry. In this regard, Porter has clearly stated that his theory is dynamic. Yet by advocating clustering, the theory also looks static in the sense that it implies that newcomers (nations) will experience difficulties in gaining competitive advantage in a new area.

Table 2.5 shows Global Competitiveness Index rankings.

**TABLE 2.5** Global Competitiveness Index rankings

| *Country/Economy* | *GCI 2006 Rank* | *GCI 2006 Score* | *GCI 2005 Rank* |
|---|---|---|---|
| Switzerland | 1 | 5.81 | 4 |
| Finland | 2 | 5.76 | 2 |
| Sweden | 3 | 5.74 | 7 |
| Denmark | 4 | 5.70 | 3 |
| Singapore | 5 | 5.63 | 5 |
| United States | 6 | 5.61 | 1 |
| Japan | 7 | 5.60 | 10 |
| Germany | 8 | 5.58 | 6 |
| Netherlands | 9 | 5.56 | 11 |
| United Kingdom | 10 | 5.54 | 9 |
| Hong Kong SAR | 11 | 5.46 | 14 |
| Norway | 12 | 5.42 | 17 |
| Taiwan, China | 13 | 5.41 | 8 |
| Iceland | 14 | 5.40 | 16 |
| Israel | 15 | 5.38 | 23 |
| Canada | 16 | 5.37 | 13 |
| Austria | 17 | 5.32 | 15 |
| France | 18 | 5.31 | 12 |
| Australia | 19 | 5.29 | 18 |
| Belgium | 20 | 5.27 | 20 |
| Ireland | 21 | 5.21 | 21 |
| Luxembourg | 22 | 5.16 | 24 |
| New Zealand | 23 | 5.15 | 22 |
| Korea, Rep. | 24 | 5.13 | 19 |
| Estonia | 25 | 5.12 | 26 |
| Malaysia | 26 | 5.11 | 25 |
| Chile | 27 | 4.85 | 27 |
| Spain | 28 | 4.77 | 28 |
| Czech Republic | 29 | 4.74 | 29 |
| Tunisia | 30 | 4.71 | 37 |
| Barbados | 31 | 4.70 | – |
| United Arab Emirates | 32 | 4.66 | 32 |

**TABLE 2.5** *continued*

| *Country/Economy* | *GCI 2006 Rank* | *GCI 2006 Score* | *GCI 2005 Rank* |
|---|---|---|---|
| Slovenia | 33 | 4.64 | 30 |
| Portugal | 34 | 4.60 | 31 |
| Thailand | 35 | 4.58 | 33 |
| Latvia | 36 | 4.57 | 39 |
| Slovak Republic | 37 | 4.55 | 36 |
| Qatar | 38 | 4.55 | 46 |
| Malta | 39 | 4.54 | 44 |
| Lithuania | 40 | 4.53 | 34 |
| Hungary | 41 | 4.52 | 35 |
| Italy | 42 | 4.46 | 38 |
| India | 43 | 4.44 | 45 |
| Kuwait | 44 | 4.41 | 49 |
| South Africa | 45 | 4.36 | 40 |
| Cyprus | 46 | 4.36 | 41 |
| Greece | 47 | 4.33 | 47 |
| Poland | 48 | 4.30 | 43 |
| Bahrain | 49 | 4.28 | 50 |
| Indonesia | 50 | 4.26 | 69 |
| Croatia | 51 | 4.26 | 64 |
| Jordan | 52 | 4.25 | 42 |
| Costa Rica | 53 | 4.25 | 56 |
| China | 54 | 4.24 | 48 |
| Mauritius | 55 | 4.20 | 55 |
| Kazakhstan | 56 | 4.19 | 51 |
| Panama | 57 | 4.18 | 65 |
| Mexico | 58 | 4.18 | 59 |
| Turkey | 59 | 4.14 | 71 |
| Jamaica | 60 | 4.10 | 63 |
| El Salvador | 61 | 4.09 | 60 |
| Russian Federation | 62 | 4.08 | 53 |
| Egypt | 63 | 4.07 | 52 |
| Azerbaijan | 64 | 4.06 | 62 |
| Colombia | 65 | 4.04 | 58 |
| Brazil | 66 | 4.03 | 57 |
| Trinidad and Tobago | 67 | 4.03 | 66 |
| Romania | 68 | 4.02 | 67 |
| Argentina | 69 | 4.01 | 54 |
| Morocco | 70 | 4.01 | 76 |
| Philippines | 71 | 4.00 | 73 |
| Bulgaria | 72 | 3.96 | 61 |

**TABLE 2.5** *continued*

| *Country/Economy* | *GCI 2006 Rank* | *GCI 2006 Score* | *GCI 2005 Rank* |
|---|---|---|---|
| Uruguay | 73 | 3.96 | 70 |
| Peru | 74 | 3.94 | 77 |
| Guatemala | 75 | 3.91 | 95 |
| Algeria | 76 | 3.90 | 82 |
| Vietnam | 77 | 3.89 | 74 |
| Ukraine | 78 | 3.89 | 68 |
| Sri Lanka | 79 | 3.87 | 80 |
| Macedonia, FYR | 80 | 3.86 | 75 |
| Botswana | 81 | 3.79 | 72 |
| Armenia | 82 | 3.75 | 81 |
| Dominican Republic | 83 | 3.75 | 91 |
| Namibia | 84 | 3.74 | 79 |
| Georgia | 85 | 3.73 | 86 |
| Moldova | 86 | 3.71 | 89 |
| Serbia and Montenegro | 87 | 3.69 | 85 |
| Venezuela | 88 | 3.69 | 84 |
| Bosnia and Herzegovina | 89 | 3.67 | 88 |
| Ecuador | 90 | 3.67 | 87 |
| Pakistan | 91 | 3.66 | 94 |
| Mongolia | 92 | 3.60 | 90 |
| Honduras | 93 | 3.58 | 97 |
| Kenya | 94 | 3.57 | 93 |
| Nicaragua | 95 | 3.52 | 96 |
| Tajikistan | 96 | 3.50 | 92 |
| Bolivia | 97 | 3.46 | 101 |
| Albania | 98 | 3.46 | 100 |
| Bangladesh | 99 | 3.46 | 98 |
| Suriname | 100 | 3.45 | – |
| Nigeria | 101 | 3.45 | 83 |
| Gambia | 102 | 3.43 | 109 |
| Cambodia | 103 | 3.39 | 111 |
| Tanzania | 104 | 3.39 | 105 |
| Benin | 105 | 3.37 | 106 |
| Paraguay | 106 | 3.33 | 102 |
| Kyrgyz Republic | 107 | 3.31 | 104 |
| Cameroon | 108 | 3.30 | 99 |
| Madagascar | 109 | 3.27 | 107 |
| Nepal | 110 | 3.26 | – |
| Guyana | 111 | 3.24 | 108 |
| Lesotho | 112 | 3.22 | – |

**TABLE 2.5** *continued*

| *Country/Economy* | *GCI 2006 Rank* | *GCI 2006 Score* | *GCI 2005 Rank* |
|---|---|---|---|
| Uganda | 113 | 3.19 | 103 |
| Mauritania | 114 | 3.17 | – |
| Zambia | 115 | 3.16 | – |
| Burkina Faso | 116 | 3.07 | – |
| Malawi | 117 | 3.07 | 114 |
| Mali | 118 | 3.02 | 115 |
| Zimbabwe | 119 | 3.01 | 110 |
| Ethiopia | 120 | 2.99 | 116 |
| Mozambique | 121 | 2.94 | 112 |
| Timor-Leste | 122 | 2.90 | 113 |
| Chad | 123 | 2.61 | 117 |
| Burundi | 124 | 2.59 | – |
| Angola | 125 | 2.50 | – |

*Source*: World Economic Forum, *The Global Competitiveness Report: 2006–2007*.

## The validity of trade theories

Several studies have investigated the validity of the classical trade theories. The evidence collected by MacDougall shortly after World War II showed that comparative cost was useful in explaining trade patterns.[12] Other studies using different data and time periods have yielded results similar to MacDougall's. Thus there is support for the claim that relative labor productivities determine trade patterns.

These positive results were subsequently questioned. The studies conducted by Leontief revealed that the U.S.A. actually exports labor-intensive goods and imports capital-intensive products.[13] These paradoxical findings are now called the **Leontief Paradox**. Thus, the findings are ambiguous, indicating that, in its simplest form, the Heckscher–Ohlin theory is not supported by the evidence.

In theory, the more different two countries are, the more they stand to gain by trading with each other. There is no reason why a country should want to trade with another that is a mirror image of itself. However, a look at world trade casts some doubt on the validity of classical trade theories. Contrary to what traditional trade theory describes, there is a tendency for countries with similar endowments to trade among themselves. Developed countries trade more among themselves than with developing countries. Trade among wealthy countries accounts for a large and increasing share, and it involves countries importing and exporting similar goods (e.g., cars, machines, and cereals).[14] There is a tendency for corporations in developed countries to prefer to form direct-investment ties in the other more stable, developed countries while avoiding heavy investment in the fast-growing developing world.

The trade pattern shown is surprising theoretically, because advanced economies have similar climate and factor proportions and thus should not trade with one another since there are no comparative advantages. Apparently, other variables in addition to factor endowment play a significant role in determining trade volume and practices because considerable trade does occur among developed nations.

## Limitations of trade theories and suggested refinements

Trade theories provide logical explanations about why nations trade with one another, but such theories are limited by their underlying assumptions.

Most of the world's trade rules are based on a traditional model which assumes that (1) trade is bilateral, (2) trade involves products originating primarily in the exporting country, (3) the exporting country has a comparative advantage, and (4) competition focuses primarily on the importing country's market. However, the modern world's realities are quite different. First, trade is a multilateral process. Second, trade is often based on products assembled from components that are produced in various countries. Third, it is not easy to determine a country's comparative advantage, as evidenced by the countries that often export and import the same product. Finally, competition usually extends beyond the importing country to include the exporting country and third countries.[15]

In fairness, virtually all theories require assumptions in order to provide a focus for investigation while holding extraneous variables constant. But controlling the effect of extraneous variables acts to limit a theory's practicality and generalization.

### *Land*

One limitation of classical trade theories is that the factors of production are assumed to remain constant for each country because of the **assumed immobility** of such resources between countries. This assumption is especially true in the case of land, since physical transfer and ownership of land can only be accomplished by war or purchase (e.g., the U.S. seizure of California from Mexico and the U.S. purchase of Alaska from Russia). At present, however, such means to gain land are less and less likely. As a matter of fact, many countries have laws that prohibit foreigners from owning real estate. Thus, Japan and many other countries remain land-poor. On the other hand, outsourcing and foreign direct investment are a means to gain or use foreign land. Thus, in this regard, one can argue that land is mobile – at least indirectly.

### *Capital*

A significant difference exists in the degree of mobility between land and capital. In spite of the restrictions on the movement of capital imposed by most governments, it is possible for a country to attract foreign capital for investment or for a country to borrow money from foreign banks or international development agencies. Not surprisingly, U.S. banks, as financial institutions in a capital-rich country, provide huge loans to Latin American countries. Yet at the same time, a favorable U.S. business climate makes it possible for the U.S.A. to attract capital from abroad to help finance its enormous federal deficits. Therefore, capital is far from being immobile. As explained by Porter, "the most obvious limitation of the traditional theory is with respect to capital. You no longer need your own domestic supply of capital."[16]

Interestingly, the U.S.A., in spite of being capital rich, has attracted a great deal of foreign capital. Foreigners have spent about $5 billion in amassing U.S. bonds and equities. The U.S. equity markets vigorously protect the rights of foreign investors, while the U.S. bond markets offer unsurpassed depth and liquidity.[17] Unfortunately, as remarked by Federal Reserve Chairman Alan Greenspan, "it is difficult to imagine that we can continue indefinitely to borrow savings from abroad at a rate equivalent to 5 percent of U.S. gross domestic product." By 2006, the U.S.A. relied on foreign lending of more than $860 billion or about 6.5 percent of GDP.[18]

The extent of money laundering clearly illustrates the high degree of capital mobility (see Legal Dimension 2.1). Even in the case of legal transactions, the so-called hot capital can move instantly in search of a better return. Malaysia has imposed capital controls so as to limit capital flights. It has adopted an exit tax, and investors are taxed according to how quickly they withdraw the money. The tax gradually drops to zero for those who leave money in Malaysia for more than a year. The exchange controls continue to be enforced, and the ringgit cannot be traded outside the country. There is a limit on the amount of money one can take out of the country. In any case, an IMF study found that, once financial integration crosses a certain threshold, the positive effects of international capital flows can outweigh the negative effects.[19]

## Legal Dimension 2.1

### Capital mobility: money laundering

Like other businesspeople, criminals and terrorists need financing. As such, money laundering is their life-blood. Money laundering is a process used to transform proceeds of crime into a usable form and disguise their illegal origins. The illegal profits may be derived from drug or arms trafficking, political corruption, prostitution, and so on. To clean or launder them, criminals move the proceeds through a variety of transactions and financial vehicles before investing them in financial and related assets.

According to the IMF, poorly supervised financial institutions channel $590 billion in illicit cash a year. A recent case of money laundering was revealed when three financial institutions reported similar suspicious transactions. It turned out that drug traffickers were using go-betweens who would deliver the cash proceeds of crime to professionals in travel agencies and import/export businesses. The professionals would place the funds in their bank accounts and, for a fee, transfer them on the basis of fake invoices to bank accounts abroad. This case displays many of the common features of money laundering: cash is introduced into the banking system by people far removed from the criminal activity that gives rise to the cash being laundered; layering is achieved by splitting the funds among many small, seemingly innocuous agents (known as "smurfs"); creating a misleading paper trail; and getting funds abroad as soon as possible.

Money laundering has become increasingly sophisticated. The new tactic is "trade-based money laundering." A money launderer buys foodstuffs (e.g., sugar, vegetable oil, seeds) and ships the goods to restricted destinations (e.g., Iran). Local merchants next either sell them for cash or transfer them on. Finally, money ends up with criminals, terrorists, or governments being sanctioned.

Money laundering is global. If one country's regulations are tightened, criminals will simply shift their laundering activities to the more hospitable environment. The IMF calls for more effective information sharing among authorities. Governments are urged "to create mechanisms to enable collection and sharing, including cross-border sharing of relevant financial information with appropriate supervisory and law enforcement activities."

*Sources*: Eduardo Aninat, Daniel Hardy, and R. Barry Johnston, "Combating Money Laundering and the Financing of Terrorism," *Finance & Development* (September 2002): 44–7; "Money Laundering and Terrorist Financing," *IMF Survey*, November 26, 2001, 359; and "Trade Becomes Route for Money Tied to Terrorism," *Wall Street Journal*, July 2, 2007.

Remittance flows doubled in six years to $268 billion in 2006, and remittances sent home by migrants are the largest source of external financing in many developing countries.[20] The globalization of capital flows (flow of capital across borders) topped $6 trillion in 2005. The flows include debt, portfolio equity, and direct investment.[21] It is interesting to note that emerging market countries have become net exporters of capital and that they are an important investor class in mature markets.[22]

## Labor

Labor as a factor of production is relatively mobile because people will migrate – legally or not – in search of a better life. It is true that immigration laws in most countries severely limit the freedom of movement of labor between countries. In China, people (i.e., labor) are not even able to select residence in a city of their choice. Still, labor can and does move across borders. In the mid-nineteenth century, many Chinese peasants were brought to the U.S.A. for railroad building.

Western European nations allow their citizens to pass across borders rather freely. The U.S.A. has a farm program that allows Mexican workers to work in the U.S.A. temporarily. For Asian nations, most are so well endowed with cheap and abundant labor that the Philippines has a significant number of its citizens work as maids in Hong Kong.

For advanced economies, immigration has long been a highly controversial subject because immigrants are viewed as a threat. According to a study of the Heritage Foundation, "the average lifetime costs to the taxpayer will be $1.1 million" for each low-skilled immigrant household in the U.S.A. The *Wall Street Journal*, however, pointed out that most immigrants would have to wait many years before being eligible to receive welfare benefits.[23]

In the case of Spain, it welcomes immigrants and has accepted more than three million foreigners. Yet unemployment has dropped sharply as Spain's economic performance has become the best in Europe.[24]

## Offshoring

Due to an increasing globalization of labor, countries have access to a larger global supply of labor through immigration, offshoring, and imports of final products.[25] According to the IMF's *2007 World Economic Outlook*, the integration of China, India, and the former Eastern bloc into the world

## Ethical Dimension 2.1

### Human trafficking: the worst kind of factor mobility

Criminals make money in the worst way – even at the expense of exploiting their fellow human beings. Women and children are particularly vulnerable. In some societies, parents sell their children. In Asia and Eastern Europe, women have been abducted and forced into prostitution. At the Mexican–American border, Mexican police still have not solved the murders of many women who worked in the area or who have tried to go across the border into the U.S.A.

In the case of Thailand, it is interesting to note that laborers pay brokers to try to secure jobs in Singapore, Taiwan, and wealthy Arab nations. At the same time, labor costs in Thailand have gone up, and many employers have now turned to illegal Burmese aliens instead. While some 200,000 women and children from neighboring countries have been smuggled into Thailand for the sex trade, Thai prostitutes have been sent by gangsters to other Asian and European countries.

Forced labor became news in China in 2007 when the Chinese media reported the rescue of "slave workers." Unsuspecting people were lured with false promises of good pay. In many cases, traffickers were blatant to the point that they simply abducted people instead. Many of the abducted people were children and people with disabilities. They were forced to work in brick factories and coal-mines for 17 hours a day under harsh conditions. One factory was set up by the Communist Party chief of the village, and it was run by his son. The scandal has embarrassed Beijing.

## Ethical Dimension 2.2

### Child labor

Surgical instruments are one of the most successful exports of Pakistan. Unfortunately, the industry may be exporting child labor. Sialkot houses more than 2000 instrument makers, and it is one of the world's top producers of high-precision scalpels, forceps, and retractors. On the other hand, an outright ban on child labor may do more harm to child laborers. Many children are content to find any work at all.

There may be a happy medium. The U.S. International Labor Organization and the Surgical Instrument Manufacturers Association of Pakistan have implemented a program that makes it possible for children to attend school for two hours a day after a seven-hour work shift. The program is patterned after an initiative of the soccer ball and sports equipment industry. That similar program has won international acclaim for its attempt to reduce Sialkot child labor in manufacturing products for such companies as Nike and Adidas.

*Source*: "Pakistan Out to Curb Child Workers in Key Industry," *San José Mercury News*, December 15, 2006.

economy has quadrupled the size of the global labor force since 1980. Advanced economies have benefited from labor globalization.

While immigration laws often restrict labor movement across countries, business laws, however, tend to welcome capital movement to utilize labor in a foreign country. When wages in South Korea jumped, Goldstar Co. minimized the labor problem by importing goods from its overseas facilities back into South Korea. It may be said that, in the production of tradable goods, unskilled labor markets in the developed countries have been effectively joined with international markets. As in the case of apparel assembly and footwear, which do not lend themselves as yet to technology-intensive methods, a large share of output has already been transferred to poor countries. Even in Thailand where labor was once plentiful and cheap but where labor cost has moved up, some Thai apparel firms are transferring parts of their production operations to Cambodia and Vietnam. Likewise, Taiwanese shoe companies are establishing new operations on the mainland.

Because workers cannot easily emigrate to another country which has better wages and benefits, wages have not been equalized across countries. Conceivably, computer workstations and communications technology could lessen this problem by allowing a portion of the workforce to work for any company in any part of the world. Theoretically, if developments continue along these lines, a worldwide labor market is possible.

In the 1970s and 1980s, workers in the Western world learned a painful lesson: manufacturing could be moved virtually anywhere. History may repeat itself, since it is becoming easier for firms to shift knowledge-based labor as well. This development may be attributed to the worldwide shift to market economies, improved education, and decades of overseas training by multinationals. As a result, a global workforce is emerging, and it is capable of doing the kind of work once reserved for white-collar workers in the West. Advances in telecommunications are making these workers more accessible than ever. In electronics, Taipei, Edinburgh, Singapore, and Malaysia, although far away from the end-user and technological breakthroughs, have emerged as global product-development centers. Therefore, conventional notions of comparative advantage are rapidly changing.

DuPont has been sending out legal services to Office Tiger in the Philippines. Office Tiger manages millions of documents. These documents will be converted into digital form, coded, and indexed. A big insurance case may take 18 months to collect and process evidence. DuPont should be able to analyze evidence more quickly by relying on its global teams to reduce the time-consuming process to just three months. The company believes that 70 percent of the labor in an insurance or liability case can be outsourced. The cost saving is significant. U.S. law firms charge $150 an hour for the work of their paralegals, while offshore service providers charge about $30 an hour for document processing.[26]

A variation of offshoring is nearshoring. Instead of sending work to call centers far away, some large technology companies in the U.S.A. rely on service centers in Mexico and other countries in the Western Hemisphere. Due to language problems, Sun Microsystems' technical support jobs have moved from India to Nova Scotia. HP has shifted jobs from Western Europe to Eastern Europe as well as from the U.S.A. to Costa Rica.[27]

## *Factor mobility and substitution*

Production factors are now considered more mobile than previously assumed. However, because of government efforts to restrict the mobility of factors of production, production costs and product prices are never completely equalized across countries. Yet the amount of mobility that does exist serves to narrow the price/cost differentials. In theory, as a country exports its abundant factor, that factor becomes more scarce at home and its price rises. In contrast, as a country imports a scarce factor, it increases the abundance of that factor and its price declines. Therefore, a nation is usually interested in attracting what it lacks, and this practice will affect the distribution of production factors.

Since a country's factors of production can change owing to factor mobility, it is reasonable to expect a shift in the kinds of goods a country imports and exports. Japan, once a capital-poor country, has grown to become a major lender/supplier of money for international trade. Its trade pattern seems to reflect this change.

When considering the factors of production, another item that is very significant involves the level of quality of the production factors. It is important to understand that the quality of each factor should not be assumed to be homogeneous worldwide. Some countries have relatively better trained personnel, better equipment, better quality land, and a better climate.

Although a country should normally export products that use its abundant factors as the product's major input, a country can substitute one production factor for another to a certain extent. Cut-up chicken fryers are a good example. Japan imports chicken fryers because a scarcity of land forces it to use valuable land for products of relatively greater economic opportunity. Both the U.S.A. and Thailand sell cut-up chicken fryers to Japan. The two countries' production strategies, however, differ markedly. The U.S.A., due to its high labor costs, depends more on automation (i.e., capital) to keep production costs down. Thailand, on the other hand, has plentiful and inexpensive labor and thus produces its fryers through a labor-intensive process. Therefore, the proportion of factor inputs for a particular product is not necessarily fixed, and the identical product may be produced using alternative methods or factors.

Like Joseph Schumpeter before them, some economists argue that innovation (knowledge and its application to real business problems) counts for more than capital and labor, the traditional factors of production. Entrepreneurs, industrial research, and knowledge are what matters.

## Demand

The discussion so far has dealt with an emphasis of trade theories on the supply side, but demand is just as critical, and demand reversal (when it occurs) may serve to explain why the empirical evidence is mixed. Tastes should not be assumed to be the same among various countries. A country may have a scarcity of certain products, and yet its citizens may have no desire for those products. Frequently, less developed countries' products may not be of sufficient quality to satisfy the tastes of industrial nations' consumers. Yugo, for example, tried in vain to convince American consumers that its automobiles, despite very low prices, were not bad value or of poor quality. Even Renault, in spite of being from a developed country (France), could not win over American consumers.

In some market situations, it is possible for product quality to be too high. Companies in developed countries, for example, sometimes manufacture products with too many refinements, which make the products too costly for consumers elsewhere. German machinery, for instance, has a worldwide reputation for quality. Nonetheless, many less developed countries opt for less costly but less reliable machinery products from elsewhere. Such circumstances explain why nations with similar levels of economic development tend to trade with one another, since they share similar tastes and incomes.

### *Marketing*

Perhaps the most serious shortcoming of classical trade theories is that they ignore the marketing aspect of trade. These theories are concerned primarily with commodities rather than with manufactured goods or value-added products. It is assumed that all suppliers have identical products with similar physical attributes and quality. This habit of assuming product homogeneity is not likely to occur among those familiar with marketing.

More often than not, products are endowed with psychological attributes. Brand-name products are often promoted as having additional value based on psychological nuance. Tobacco products of Marlboro and Winston sell well worldwide because of the images of those brands. In addition, firms in two countries can produce virtually identical products in physical terms, but one product has different symbolic meaning than the other. Developing countries are just as capable as the U.S.A. or France in making good cosmetic products, but many consumers are willing to pay significantly more for the prestige of using brands such as Estée Lauder and Dior. Trade analysis, therefore, is not complete without taking into consideration the reasons for product differentiation.

### *Trade barriers*

A further shortcoming of classical trade theories is that the trade patterns as described in the theories are in reality frequently affected by trade restrictions. The direction of the flow of trade, according to some critics of free trade, is no longer determined by a country's natural comparative advantage. Rather, a country can create a comparative advantage by relying on outsourcing and other trade barriers, such as tariffs and quotas. Protectionism can thus alter the trade patterns as described by trade theories.

## Economic cooperation

Given inherent constraints in any system, conditions for the best policy rarely exist. A policy maker must then turn to the second-best policy. This practice applies to international trade as well. Worldwide free trade is ideal, but cannot be attained. The **theory of second best** suggests that the optimum policy is to have economic cooperation on a smaller scale.[28] In an attempt to reduce trade barriers and improve trade, many countries within the same geographic area often join together to establish various forms of economic cooperation. Major regional groups are shown in Exhibit 2.1. As shown in Figure 2.6, some countries are members of multiple groups.

### *Levels of economic integration*

Trade theorists have identified five levels of economic cooperation. They are: free trade area, customs union, common market, economic and monetary union, and political union. Table 2.6 shows a concise comparison of these cooperation levels.

#### *Free trade area*

In a free trade area, the countries involved eliminate duties among themselves, while maintaining separately their own tariffs against outsiders. Free trade areas include NAFTA (North American Free Trade Agreement) and EFTA (European Free Trade Association). The purpose of a free trade area is to facilitate trade among member nations. The problem with this kind of arrangement is the lack of

Exhibit 2.1

**Regional groups and their nations**

**African Financial Community**: CAEMC and WAEMU members.

**AFTA** (ASEAN Free Trade Area): ASEAN members.

**Andean Group** (the Cartagena Agreement): Bolivia, Colombia, Ecuador, Peru, and Venezuela.

**ANZCERTA** (Australia–New Zealand Closer Economic Relations Trade Agreement): Australia and New Zealand.

**APEC** (Asia Pacific Economic Cooperation): Australia, Brunei, Canada, Chile, China, Hong Kong, Indonesia, Japan, Korea, Malaysia, Mexico, New Zealand, Papua New Guinea, the Philippines, Singapore, Chinese Taipei (Taiwan), Thailand, and the U.S.A.

**Arab/Middle East Arab Common Market**: UAR, Iraq, Jordan, Sudan, Syria, and Yemen.

**ASEAN** (Association of Southeast Asian Nations): Burma, Brunei, Cambodia, Indonesia, Laos, Malaysia, the Philippines, Singapore, Thailand, and Vietnam.

**Benelux Customs Union**: Belgium, the Netherlands, and Luxembourg.

**CARICOM** (Caribbean Common Market): Antigua and Barbuda, Bahamas, Barbados, Belize, Dominica, Grenada, Guyana, Jamaica, Montserrat, Saint Christopher-Nevis, Saint Lucia, Saint Vincent and the Grenadines, and Trinidad and Tobago.

**CEMAC** (Central African Economic and Monetary Community): Cameroon, the Central African Republic, Chad, the Republic of Congo, Equatorial Guinea, and Gabon.

**Central American Community**: Costa Rica, El Salvador, Guatemala, Honduras, Nicaragua, and Panama.

**CFA Franc Zone**: the Comoros, members of the WAEMU and the CEMAC.

**CIS** (Commonwealth of Independent States): Armenia, Azerbaijan, Belarus, Georgia, Kazakhstan, Kirgizstan, Moldova, Russia, Tajikistan, Turkmenistan, Ukraine, and Uzbekistan.

**East Africa Customs Union**: Ethiopia, Kenya, Zimbabwe, Sudan, Tanzania, and Uganda.

**ECOWAS** (Economic Community of West African States): Benin, Cape Verde, Dahomey, Gambia, Ghana, Guinea, Guinea-Bissau, Ivory Coast, Liberia, Mali, Mauritania, Niger, Nigeria, Senegal, Sierra Leone, Togo, and Upper Volta.

**EEA** (European Economic Area): Iceland, Norway, and EU members.

**EFTA** (European Free Trade Association): Austria, Finland, Iceland, Liechtenstein, Norway, Sweden, and Switzerland.

**EU** (European Union): Austria, Belgium, Denmark, Finland, France, Germany, Greece, Ireland, Italy, Luxembourg, the Netherlands, Portugal, Spain, Sweden, the United Kingdom, CEE-10, Bulgaria, and Romania.

**GCC (Cooperation Council of the Arab States of the Gulf)**: Bahrain, Kuwait, Oman, Qatar, Saudi Arabia, and the United Arab Emirates.

**Group of Three**: Colombia, Mexico, and Venezuela.

**LAIA** (Latin American Integration Association): Argentina, Bolivia, Brazil, Chile, Colombia, Ecuador, Mexico, Paraguay, Peru, Uruguay, and Venezuela.

**Mahgreb Economic Community**: Algeria, Libya, Tunisia, and Morocco.

**Mercosur** (Southern Common Market): Argentina, Brazil, Paraguay, and Uruguay.

**NAFTA** (North American Free Trade Agreement): Canada, Mexico, and the United States.

**OECD** (Organization for Economic Cooperation and Development): EU members, Australia, Canada, Iceland, Japan, New Zealand, Norway, Switzerland, Turkey, and the United States.

**RCD** (Regional Cooperation for Development): Iran, Pakistan, and Turkey.

**SICA**: El Salvador, Guatemala, Honduras, and Nicaragua.

**WAEMU** (West African Economic and Monetary Union): Benin, Burkina Faso, Ivory Coast, Guinea-Bissau, Mali, Niger, Senegal, and Togo.

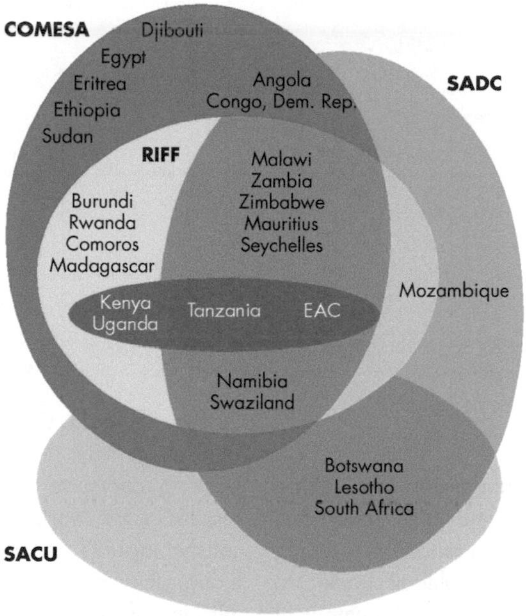
COMESA
Djibouti
Egypt
Eritrea
Ethiopia
Sudan
Angola
Congo, Dem. Rep.
SADC
RIFF
Malawi
Zambia
Zimbabwe
Mauritius
Seychelles
Burundi
Rwanda
Comoros
Madagascar
Mozambique
Kenya
Uganda
Tanzania
EAC
Namibia
Swaziland
Botswana
Lesotho
South Africa
SACU

**FIGURE 2.6** Regional trading arrangements in Eastern and Southern Africa

*Notes* COMESA: Common Market for Eastern and Southern Africa; EAC: East African Community; RIFF: Regional Integration Facilitation Forum; SADC: South African Development Community; SACU: South African Customs Union

*Source*: Robert Sharer, "An Agenda for Trade, Investment, and Regional Integration," *Finance and Development* (December 2001, 16).

coordination of tariffs against the nonmembers, enabling nonmembers to direct their exported products to enter the free trade area at the point of lowest external tariffs.

The first free trade agreement signed by the U.S.A. was with Israel in 1985, and the U.S.–Israel Free Trade Area Agreement eliminates all customs duties and most nontariff barriers between the two countries. More recently, the U.S.A. has entered into free trade agreements with Singapore, Chile, and South Korea, while Mexico has done the same with the EU. Singapore has also concluded free trade deals with Australia and Japan. It should be apparent that countries forming a free trade area do not need to share joint boundaries.

**TABLE 2.6** Levels of economic cooperation

| *Characteristics of cooperation* | *Free trade area* | *Customs union* | *Common market* | *Economic and monetary union* | *Political union* |
|---|---|---|---|---|---|
| Elimination of internal duties | Yes | Yes | Yes | Yes | Probably |
| Establishment of common barriers | No | Yes | Yes | Yes | Probably |
| Removal of restrictions on factors of production | No | No | Yes | Yes | Probably |
| Harmonization of national economic policies | No | No | No | Yes | Probably |
| Harmonization of national political policies | No | No | No | No | Yes |

## Cultural Dimension 2.1

**Exporting nurses**

Japan as a society is aging, and the welfare costs are rising. At the same time, Japan has been accused by its trading partners of being protectionist. To avoid a political backlash, Japan has agreed to accept a small number of health care workers from abroad. Up to 1,000 care workers and nurses from the Philippines in two years are allowed under the free trade agreement between Japan and the Philippines.

The Philippines' economy certainly needs remittances from the one-tenth of its population working overseas. The free trade agreement requires care workers from the Philippines to satisfy Japan's stringent requirements. Even though they may have already qualified to do this kind of work in the Philippines, they need to pass Japanese certification examinations. In addition, they must learn the Japanese language.

*Source*: "Japan FTA Takes in Filipino Nurses," *The Nation*, 5 January 2007.

### *Customs union*

A customs union is an extension of the free trade area in the sense that member countries must also agree on a common schedule of identical tariff rates. In effect, the objective of the customs union is to harmonize trade regulations and to establish common barriers against outsiders. Uniform tariffs and a common commercial policy against nonmembers are necessary to prevent them from taking advantage of the situation by shipping goods initially to a member country that has the lowest joint boundaries. The world's oldest customs union is the Benelux Customs Union. A more recent example is the one formed between Turkey and the European Union; this took effect in 1996.

### Common market

A common market is a higher and more complex level of economic integration than either a free trade area or a customs union. In a common market, countries remove all customs and other restrictions on the movement of the factors of production (such as services, raw materials, labor, and capital) among the members of the common market. As a result, business laws and labor laws are standardized to ensure undistorted competition. For an outsider, the point of entry is no longer dictated by member countries' tariff rates since those rates are uniform across countries within the common market. The point of entry is now determined by the members' nontariff barriers. The outsider's strategy should be to enter a member country that has the least non-tariff restrictions, because goods can be shipped freely once inside the common market.

In 1993, the EU and the EFTA formed the world's largest and most lucrative common market – the European Economic Area. The European Economic Area eliminates nontariff barriers between the EFTA and EU countries to create a free flow of goods, services, capital, and people in a market of more than 400 million people.

### Economic and monetary union

Cooperation among countries increases even more with an economic and monetary union (EMU). Some authorities prefer to distinguish a monetary union from an economic union. In essence, monetary union means one money (i.e., a single currency). The Delors Committee, chaired by Jacques Delors, who was then President of the European Commission, has issued a report entitled *Economic and Monetary Union in the European Community* that defines **monetary union** as having three basic characteristics: total and irreversible convertibility of currencies; complete freedom of capital movements in fully integrated financial markets; and irrevocably fixed exchange rates with no fluctuation margins between member currencies, leading ultimately to a single currency. The economic advantages of a single currency include the elimination of currency risk and lower transaction costs. One European Commission study found that European businesses were spending $12.8 billion (0.4 percent of the EU's GDP) a year on currency conversions.

The Central African and Monetary Community (CEMAC) uses the CFA franc as a common currency in Cameroon, Chad, the Central African Republic, Equatorial Guinea, Gabon, and the Republic of Congo. The CFA franc is pegged to the euro.[29]

According to the Delors Committee, the basic elements of an **economic union** include the following: a single market within which persons, goods, services, and capital could move freely; a joint competition policy to strengthen market mechanisms; common competition, structural, and regional policies; and sufficient coordination of macroeconomic policies, including binding rules on budgetary policies regarding the size and financing of national budget deficits. The EU member states have ceded substantial sovereignty to the EU. As an example, Denmark was required by the EU to comply with common packaging rules and remove its 20-year-old ban on beers and soft drinks in metal cans.

An economic union provides a number of benefits. Stronger competition policies should promote efficiency gains. In terms of inflation, the implementation of an economic union is a demonstration of a credible commitment to stable prices. Financial integration allows investors to seek higher returns and lower risks through diversification, and it enables borrowers to finance themselves less expensively and more reliably in deeper and more complete financial markets. This provides immediate benefits to consumers and businesses and, through interaction with other economic developments such as technological innovation, should allow faster productivity and economic growth.[30]

A good example of an economic and monetary union is the unification of East Germany and West Germany. The terms of the monetary union called for an average currency conversion rate of M 1.8 to DM 1 and a conversion of East German wages at parity into deutschmarks. The July 1, 1990 German Economic and Monetary Union has resulted in one Germany. In addition to sharing a common, freely convertible currency (the deutschmark), the legal environment, commercial code, and taxation requirements in the German Democratic Republic (East Germany) are now the same as those of the Federal Republic of Germany (West Germany).

Following a transition period, several European currencies were replaced by a new currency called the euro. At the beginning of 2002, twelve EU countries (not counting Denmark, Sweden, and the United Kingdom) introduced euro coins and notes. In 2003, following in the footsteps of Denmark three years earlier, the Swedes voted overwhelmingly to reject membership in the European single currency.

The euro has become a global currency and is strongly challenging the U.S. dollar for supremacy. The U.S. dollar has an edge in terms of geographic acceptance, while the euro has a more limited geographic role. However, in private use, the euro has become the most important currency of issue for international bonds and notes.[31]

The EU is unique in the sense that it is the first time that advanced economies have agreed to cooperate economically on such a grand scale. Naturally, with the fall of the Berlin wall in 1989, countries emerging from communism coveted EU memberships, while the EU leaders were stalling them. But the Yugoslav wars made the EU aware of the need to enlarge Europe's security zone. After all, if stability were not exported from the West, instability might be imported instead from the East. So the EU is expanding. Ten new members were admitted for accession in 2004, and Bulgaria and Romania followed suit in 2007. Apart from Cyprus and Malta, the other ten new members, known as the CEE-10, represent three regions: Baltics (Estonia, Latvia, and Lithuania), Central Europe (the Czech Republic, Hungary, Poland, Slovak Republic, and Slovenia), and Southeastern Europe (Bulgaria and Romania).

### *Political union*

A political union is the ultimate type of regional cooperation because it involves the integration of both economic and political policies. With France and Germany leading the way, the EU has been moving toward social, political, and economic integration. The EU's goal is to form a political union similar to the fifty states of the U.S.A. The EU's debate over political union involves issues such as having common defense and foreign policies, strengthening the role of the EU Parliament, and adopting an EU-wide social policy. In late 1991, the member countries of the EU gave the EU authority to act in defense, in foreign, and in social policies.

It is doubtful that pure forms of economic integration and political union can ever become reality. Even if they did, they would not last long because different countries eventually have different goals and inflation rates. More important is that no country would be willing to surrender its sovereignty for economic reasons. The EU, despite great strides, has been plagued by infighting among member states with conflicting national interests.

Although the Treaty of Rome calls for a free internal market and permits market forces to equalize national economic differences, Germany, France, and the Netherlands – which have expensive social welfare programs – argue that the social dimension must be taken into account in order to prevent social dumping. In other words, they seek to prevent a movement of business and jobs away from areas with high wages and strong labor organizations to areas with low wages, less organized labor forces, and weak social welfare policies. As a result, the EC Commission adopted the Social Charter in 1989 to establish workers' basic rights and to equalize EU social regulations (e.g., a minimum wage, labor participation in management decisions, and paid holidays for education purposes). Member countries accused of social dumping must subject their products to sanctions. European socialists believe that the Social Charter is necessary to prevent countries with the lowest social benefits from gaining a comparative advantage.

Countries with lower labor costs (e.g., Portugal, Spain, and Greece), however, view the Social Charter as something that forces capital-poor countries to adopt the expensive social welfare policies, in effect increasing the cost of labor and unemployment. To them, the Social Charter is nothing more than protectionism in the guise of harmonization. Such expensive policies are also a major concern to European industry. As may be expected, several initiatives are the subject of heated debate.

## *Economic and marketing implications*

Economic partnership is designed to yield economic benefits, as in the case of the CAREC program, a partnership of eight countries that occupy a land area of about 7.5 million square kilometers: Afghanistan, Azerbaijan, the People's Republic of China (focusing on Xinjiang Uygur Autonomous Region), Kazakhstan, the Kyrgyz Republic, Mongolia, Tajikistan, and Uzbekistan. Central Asia is well endowed with oil, gas, copper, gold, uranium, and water for hydropower. The participating countries have experienced strong growth performance.[32]

Marketers must pay attention to the effects of regional economic integration or cooperation because the competitive environment may change drastically over time. As in the case of the EU, although EU member countries still maintain their national identities, national borders are no longer trade barriers. Marketers must treat the EU as a single market rather than as numerous separate and fragmented markets. They need to rethink their marketing, finance, distribution, and production strategies. Foreign businesses need to make an effort to become familiar with new regulations so as to take full advantage in the changing market. For example, even though standard harmonization may exclude some U.S. firms from the EU markets, the U.S.A. should work to influence the process in order to turn the potential barrier into an advantage.

Whereas countries that are not members of the EU view the EU's ambitious goals with some concern, outsider firms can still cope successfully with the Single Internal Market program. Instead of viewing the EU's developments as obstacles, marketers should regard them as both challenges and opportunities. Not unlike coping with a single country's protectionist measures (except on a larger scale), the key to competing effectively in the EU is for an external firm to become an insider. Figure 2.7 shows how the United Kingdom can serve as a strategic location for this purpose.

General Electric Co. has formed joint ventures in major appliances and electrical equipment with Britain's largest electronics firm, has acquired France's largest medical equipment maker, and has planned to build a plastics factory in Spain. Coca-Cola has terminated some licensing agreements and has consolidated its European bottling operations to cut costs and prices. Using acquisitions to build up its European position, Sara Lee Corp. purchased a Dutch coffee and tea company and took control

Britain
THE PREFERRED LOCATION IN EUROPE FOR US INDUSTRY
Over 3,500 US companies already make Britain their base. It is by far the preferred location in Europe for US industry.
A pro-business environment; an adaptable, skilled workforce; labor practices aimed to promote flexibility and initiative; one of the lowest main corporate tax rates in Europe; excellent communications—Britain offers them all.
Our offices across the USA provide you with on the spot advice and practical assistance. Please call the Invest in Britain Bureau (212) 421-1213 or mail the coupon with your business card for further details.
My company is considering Europe as a location in which to set up or expand:
☐ a manufacturing operation
☐ a major service activity ☐ Business card attached
Mail to: Invest in Britain Bureau
British Consulate-General,
845 Third Avenue, New York, NY 10022
EC062495
Invest in Britain Bureau
FIRST LOCATE THE FACTS. THEN LOCATE IN BRITAIN.
OFFICES IN ATLANTA, BOSTON, CHICAGO, CLEVELAND, DALLAS, HOUSTON, LOS ANGELES, MIAMI, NEW YORK, SAN FRANCISCO, SEATTLE, WASHINGTON, D.C.
This material is published by Spring, O'Brien, Tolson & Co., 220 Fifth Avenue, New York, NY 10001, which is registered under the Foreign Agents Registration Act as an agency of the Trade and Investment Office, British Consulate General, New York.
This material is filed with the Department of Justice where the required registration is available for public inspection. Registration does not indicate approval of this material by the United States Government.

**FIGURE 2.7** The United Kingdom and its strategic location

of Paris-based Dim, Europe's largest maker of panty-hose. In addition, Sara Lee has experimented with the "Euro-branding" strategy by printing several languages on a single package and distributing it to several countries.

Initially, new trade policies generally tend to favor local business firms. For example, IBM encountered problems in Europe, where the EU members wanted to protect their own computer industry. Alternatively, outsider firms may be able to take advantage of the situation to overcome the barriers erected by a particular member of a regional economic community. Facing France's troublesome entry procedure, Japan could first ship its products into Germany before moving them more freely into France.

Because of the favorable economic environment in a cooperative region, additional firms desire entry and the competitive atmosphere intensifies. Firms inside the region are likely to be more competitive owing to the expansion of local markets, resulting in better economies of scale. External firms (those outside the area) are faced with overcoming trade barriers, perhaps through the establishment of local production facilities. For example, Ireland tried to attract foreign investment by mentioning in its advertisements that it is a member of the EU. Nike, a U.S. firm, was able to avoid the EU tariffs by opening a plant in Ireland.

Over time, a region will grow faster than before owing to the stimulation caused by trade creation effects, favorable policies, and more competition, but economic cooperation can create problems as well as opportunities within international markets. The expanded market offers more profit potential, but it may create an impression of collusion when subsidiaries or licensees are granted exclusive rights in certain member countries. The long-term result may be an area-wide anti-trust among new firms or nonmember countries wishing to trade within the economically integrated region.

Economic integration encourages trade liberalization internally, while it promotes trade protection externally. The tendency is for a member of an economic group to shift from the most efficient supplier in the world to the lowest cost supplier within that particular economic region. As in the case of NAFTA, the results have been generally positive.

Economic cooperation may either improve or impede international trade, depending on how the result of the cooperation is viewed. The proliferation of regional trade agreements (RTAs) runs the risk of turning the world trade system into a "noodle bowl" due to overlapping, inconsistent, and unmanageable RTAs. As of May 2007, more than 40 RTAs had been signed among Asian countries themselves or with selected partners outside the region, while an additional 70 RTAs were being negotiated. According to an IMF study, membership in an RTA promotes trade among members but does not seem to occur at the expense of trade with nonmembers. After all, most RTAs in Asia, instead of preceding, have followed trade liberalization on a multilateral basis.[33]

## Conclusion

For countries to want to trade with one another, they must be better off with trade than without it. The principles of absolute and comparative advantage explain how trade enables trading nations to increase their welfare through specialization. Trade allows a country to concentrate on the production of products with the best potential for its own consumption as well as for exports, resulting in a more efficient and effective use of its resources.

Absolute production costs are not as relevant as relative costs in determining whether trade should take place and what products to export or import. Basically, a country should specialize in manufacturing a product in which it has the greatest comparative advantage. If no comparative advantage exists, there will be no trade, since there is no difference in relative production costs between the two countries (i.e., a situation of equal relative advantage).

Comparative advantage is not determined solely by labor but rather by the required factors of production necessary to produce the product in question. This advantage is often determined by an abundance of a particular production factor in the country. Thus it is advantageous for a country to export a product that requires its abundant factor as a major production input.

Trade theories, in spite of their usefulness, simply explain what nations should do rather than describe what nations actually do. The desired trade pattern based on those theories related to comparative advantage and factor endowment often deviates significantly from the actual trade practice. It is thus necessary to modify the theories to account for the divergence caused by extraneous variables. Industrial nations' high-income levels, for instance, may foster a preference for high-quality products that less developed countries may be unable to supply. Furthermore, trade restrictions, a norm rather than an exception, heavily influence the extent and direction of trade, and any investigation is not complete without taking tariffs, quotas, and other trade barriers into consideration.

Perhaps the most serious problem with classical trade theories is their failure to incorporate marketing activities into the analysis. It is inappropriate to assume that consumers' tastes are homogeneous across national markets and that such tastes can be largely satisfied by commodities that are also homogeneous. Marketing activities such as distribution and promotion add more value to a product, and the success of the product is often determined by the planning and execution of such activities.

## CASE 2.1 THE UNITED STATES OF AMERICA VS. THE UNITED STATES OF EUROPE

### The European Union

The European Union (EU), once known as the European Common Market, is a prime example of a very high level of economic cooperation. The EU will be the first group of industrial nations to rethink national sovereignty for the sake of economic interests. Formed by the 1957 Treaty of Rome, the EU has grown from six to 27 members. The EU's institutions that function as the three traditional branches of democratic government are the European Parliament (as the legislative branch), the Court of Justice (as a judiciary), and the Council of Ministers of the European Communities (as the executive branch).The Council appoints members of the Commission of the European Communities, which initiates legislative proposals (regulations or directives) for the Council.

The passage in 1985 of the Single European Act (SEA), an amendment to the Treaties of Rome, was largely responsible for the development of the Single Internal Market. Taking effect in 1987, this legal instrument makes it possible for the Council of Ministers to adopt an Internal Market directive or regulation on the strength of a qualified majority. Council votes are assigned by a weighted average. The Council of Ministers thus no longer has to reach unanimous agreement for a directive to be passed. However, unanimity is still required for fiscal matters (e.g., taxation), decisions on the free movement of persons, and directives or regulations on the rights and interests of employed persons.

The EU member states have ceded substantial sovereignty to the EU. As an example, the EU's highest court ruled in 2001 that France was breaking an EU law by maintaining a ban on British beef, since the European Commission had already eased a worldwide embargo on British beef exports that was imposed over fears about mad cow disease (BSE).

Because an EMU envisages total fiscal and monetary integration, nations that agree to join the union must work out an economic arrangement in which trade between member countries directly benefits each of the countries' economic objectives. The features of an EMU require a common monetary policy formulated by a single institution; highly coordinated economic policies; and adequate, consistent constraints on members' public sector deficits and their financing.

It should be readily apparent that the formation of an EMU is a complex and exceedingly difficult task because this level of cooperation requires the harmonization of national economic policies – especially in the monetary and fiscal areas. A member country must give up the prospect of currency devaluation as a short-term instrument for solving economic problems. For an EMU to function effectively, member countries should have similar economic conditions. In the case of the EU, economic disparities are highly evident and will probably increase when the EU admits some Eastern European countries as new members.

Under the EU members' EMU agreements, the EU has created a central bank and adopted a single currency. According to the terms of the Maastricht Treaty, the EU nations wishing to join the monetary union must meet the following five economic criteria: annual inflation, public sector budget deficit, public sector debt, long-term interest rates, and exchange rate. In 1999, fixed conversion rates were adopted for the participating nations' currencies, and the European Central Bank (ECB) started to execute a common monetary policy. Following a transition period, the currencies were replaced by a new currency called the euro. At the beginning of 2002, twelve EU countries (not counting Denmark, Sweden, and the United Kingdom) introduced euro coins and notes. Several new member countries are eager to adopt the euro.

The EU is unique because it is the first time that advanced economies have agreed to cooperate economically on such a grand scale. To promote stability in the region, the EU has been expanding. Ten new members were admitted for accession in 2004, and they were joined by Bulgaria and Romania in 2007. Figure 2.8 shows the fast growth of the CEE-10 countries, the relatively new members of the EU.

## NAFTA

The North American Free Trade Agreement (NAFTA) is a free trade agreement. Taking effect in January 1994, NAFTA comprises Canada, Mexico, and the U.S.A.

NAFTA progressively eliminates almost all U.S.–Mexico tariffs over a 10-year period and also phases out Mexico–Canada tariffs at the same time. Such barriers to trade as import licensing requirements and customs user fees are eliminated. NAFTA establishes the principle of national treatment to ensure that NAFTA countries will treat NAFTA-origin products in

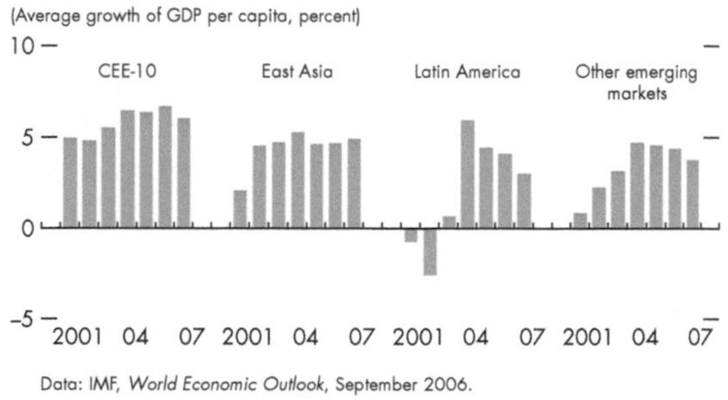
(Average growth of GDP per capita, percent)
10
5
0
-5
CEE-10
East Asia
Latin America
Other emerging markets
2001 04 07 2001 04 07 2001 04 07 2001 04 07
Data: IMF, World Economic Outlook, September 2006.

**FIGURE 2.8** The CEE-10

*Source*: "Assessing the Early Benefits of EU Membership," *IMF Survey* (November 20, 2006, 332).

the same manner as similar domestic products. Service providers of the member nations will receive equal treatment. To protect foreign investors in the free trade area, NAFTA has established five principles: (1) nondiscriminatory treatment, (2) freedom from performance requirements, (3) free transference of funds related to an investment, (4) expropriation only in conformity with international law, and (5) the right to seek international arbitration for a violation of the Agreement's protections.

Canada's locus of economic activity has always been along the U.S. border, which stretches for some 4000 miles. It is not too surprising that the natural axis of trade has always been from north to south rather than from east to west. Canada is the largest single market for U.S. exports as well as the largest manufactures market of the U.S.A.

The U.S.A. is Mexico's most important trading partner, absorbing about two-thirds of total Mexican exports worldwide. On the other hand, Mexico is the third largest U.S. trading partner, ranking after Canada and Japan. Approximately 70 percent of all of Mexico's imports come from the U.S.A., and 15 cents of every additional dollar of Mexican GDP is spent on American goods and services. To modernize its infrastructure and plant facilities, Mexico is purchasing most of the durable goods and industrial materials from the U.S.A. Not surprisingly, Mexico is the fastest growing major U.S. export market. Mexico is by far the largest U.S. trading partner in Latin America, accounting for about half of U.S. exports to and imports from the region.

Mexico has advocated a progressive move towards a North American common market that will allow free movement of labor among the three NAFTA members. Neither Canada nor the U.S.A. has shown much enthusiasm for the proposal. Instead, the U.S.A. is more interested in expanding the free trade area and thus maintaining the same level of economic cooperation.

As the EU expands, the U.S.A. itself is trying to persuade the other American countries to join the free trade area. The Free Trade Area of the Americas (FTAA), when completed, will be the world's largest free trade area stretching from the southern tip of Argentina northward to Alaska. In December 1994, at the first Summit of the Americas, the U.S.A. and 34 other democratically elected leaders in the Western Hemisphere took the first step by committing to establishing the FTAA by 2005. The idea of the FTAA is to allow import tariffs to fall to zero over a decade or more. Nontariff barriers will be gradually eliminated, and trade in services will be liberalized. Due to political and economic disputes, there is no concrete plan at present that will allow the completion of the FTAA.

## Points to consider

1. Discuss the obstacles and opportunities presented by the EU market. How should Japanese and American firms adjust their marketing strategies to meet the challenge?
2. Discuss the benefits and difficulties involved as the EU absorbs several new members.
3. Assess the likelihood that the EU will be able to establish a political union.
4. Why is it that organized labor in the United States opposes NAFTA and further expansion when it never objected to the U.S.–Canada Free Trade Agreement which preceded NAFTA?
5. Should the U.S.A. advance NAFTA to the next stage to become, say, a common market? Or instead of vertical advancement, should the U.S.A. push for horizontal advancement or enlargement by creating the FTAA?

## Questions

1 Is trade a zero-sum game or a positive-sum game?
2 Explain (a) the principle of absolute advantage and (b) the principle of comparative advantage.
3 Should there be trade if (a) a country has an absolute advantage for all products over its trading partner and (b) if the domestic exchange ratio of one country is identical to that of another country?
4 What is the theory of factor endowment.
5 Explain the Leontief Paradox.
6 Discuss the validity and limitations of trade theories.
7 Distinguish among (a) free trade area, (b) customs union, (c) common market, (d) economic and monetary union, and (e) political union.
8 Does economic cooperation improve or impede trade?

# Discussion assignments and minicases

1 Name products or industries in which the U.S.A. has a comparative advantage as well as those in which it has a comparative disadvantage.
2 Why is it beneficial for the well-endowed, resource-rich U.S.A. and European Union to trade with other nations?
3 For a country with high labor costs, how can it improve its export competitiveness?
4 Explain how the advanced economies should cope with the shift in comparative advantage.
5 There has been a proliferation of regional trading arrangements in the 1990s. The European Union and the North American Free Trade Agreement in particular have commanded a great deal of world attention. There are numerous reasons for the formation of a regional trading arrangement. Some of the reasons are economic in nature, while others are political. As a policy maker for a medium-sized and developing country, list and explain the reasons that may motivate you to consider forming or joining a regional trade group.
6 According to a UN report prepared by the International Labor Organization and released in 2007, a typical American worker puts in an average 1804 hours of work, while his French counterpart works 1564 hours. In Asia (e.g., South Korea, Hong Kong, Thailand), however, a worker surpasses 2200 hours on average.

Since the 1950s, the number of work hours has been going down in Europe. The decline has been attributed to labor regulations, strong labor unions, and an increased preference for leisure in Europe. In France, a law was passed in 1998 which requires companies to institute a 35-hour working week. The idea is to create more jobs at a time of high unemployment. Do you feel that the idea is sound? Has the law achieved its objective? What are the criteria that should be used to judge the effectiveness (or ineffectiveness) of this particular law?

## Notes

1 Adam Smith, *The Wealth of Nations* (1776; reprint, Homewood, IL: Irwin, 1963).
2 David Ricardo, *The Principles of Political Economy and Taxation* (1817; reprint, Baltimore, MD: Penguin, 1971).
3 "A Fresh Look at Keynes," *Finance & Development* (December 2001): 60–3.

4 Richard S. Tedlow, *Giants of Enterprise: Seven Business Innovators and the Empires They Built* (New York, NY: HarperBusiness, 2003).
5 Eli Heckscher, "The Effects of Foreign Trade on the Distribution of Income," in *Readings in the Theory of International Trade*, ed. Howard S. Ellis and Lloyd A. Matzler (Homewood, IL: Irwin, 1949); and Bertil Ohlin, *Interregional and International Trade* (Cambridge, MA: Harvard University Press, 1933).
6 "Botswana: Avoiding the Resource Curse," *IMF Survey*, August 7, 2006, 236–7.
7 Paul Cashin, Paolo Mauro, and Ratna Sahay,"Macroeconomic Policies and Poverty Reduction: Some Cross-country Evidence," *Finance & Development* (June 2001): 46–9.
8 Michael E. Porter, *The Competitive Advantage of Nations* (New York, NY: Free Press, 1990).
9 Brian Snowdon and George Stonehouse, "Competitiveness in a Globalised World: Michael Porter on the Microeconomic Foundations of the Competitiveness of Nations, Regions, and Firms," *Journal of International Business Studies* 37 (March 2006): 163–75.
10 Snowdon and Stonehouse, "Competitiveness."
11 Patrick Minford, "Competitiveness in a Globalised World: A Commentary," *Journal of International Business Studies* 37 (March 2006): 176–8.
12 G. D. A. MacDougall, "British and American Exports: A Study Suggested by the Theory of Comparative Costs," *Economic Journal* (December 1951); Robert Stern, "British and American Productivity and Comparative Costs in International Trade," *Oxford Economic Papers* (October 1962); and Bela Balassa, "An Empirical Demonstration of Classical Comparative Cost Theory," *Review of Economics and Statistics* (August 1963).
13 Wassily W. Leontief, "Domestic Production and Foreign Trade: The American Capital Position Re-examined," *Proceedings of the American Philosophical Society* (September 1953); and Wassily W. Leontief, "Factor Proportions and the Structure of American Trade: Further Theoretical and Empirical Analysis," *Review of Economics and Statistics* 38 (November 1956): 386–407.
14 "Economist as Crusader," *Finance & Development* (June 2006): 4–7.
15 "Trade Specialist Calls Current Rules Outdated," *IMF Survey*, July 15, 1991, 209, 216.
16 Snowdon and Stonehouse, "Competitiveness."
17 "Putting Too Many Eggs in One Basket?", *IMF Survey*, November 20, 2006, 337.
18 "How Long Can the U.S. Count on Foreign Funding?", *Business Week*, March 5, 2007, 23–4.
19 "Opening Up to Capital Flows? Be Prepared Before Plunging in," *IMF Survey*, May 19, 2003, 137.
20 "Remittance Flows Top $268 Billion," *Finance & Development* (December 2006): 3.
21 "Global Capital Flows: Defying Gravity," *Finance & Development* (March 2007): 14–15.
22 "The Changing Contours of International Financial Markets," *IMF Survey*, May 28, 2007, 135.
23 "Immigration and Welfare," *Wall Street Journal*, May 24, 2007.
24 "Immigrants Welcome," *Business Week*, May 21, 2007, 50–1.
25 "Labor Globalization: Bane or Boon?", *IMF Survey*, April 11, 2007, 88.
26 "Let's Offshore the Lawyers," *Business Week*, September 18, 2006, 42–3.
27 "Offshoring Gives Way to Nearshoring to Cut Costs, Customer Complaints," *San José Mercury News*, February 25, 2007.
28 J. E. Meade, *Trade and Welfare* (New York, NY: Oxford University Press, 1955); and R. G. Lipsey and K. Lancaster, "The General Theory of Second Best," *Review of Economic Studies* 24 (1956): 11–32.
29 "EU: From Monetary to Financial Union," *Finance & Development* (June 2006): 48.
30 "CEMAC," *Finance & Development* (December 2006): 56.
31 "The Euro: Ever More Global," *Finance & Development* (March 2007): 46–9.
32 "Encouraging Economic Cooperation in Central Asia," *IMF Survey*, June 18, 2007, 152–3.
33 "Unraveling Asia's "Noodle Bowl" of Trade Pacts," *IMF Survey*, June 18, 2007, 150–1.

Chapter 3

# Trade distortions and marketing barriers

Trade is not about warfare but about mutual gains from voluntary exchange.

Alan S. Binder, former Vice Chairman, Federal Reserve Board

## Chapter outline

- Marketing strategy: the best things in life are (not) free
- Protection of local industries
    - Keeping money at home
    - Reducing unemployment
    - Equalizing cost and price
    - Enhancing national security
    - Protecting infant industry
- Marketing barriers: tariffs
    - Direction: import and export tariffs
    - Purpose: protective and revenue tariffs
    - Length: tariff surcharge versus countervailing duty
    - Rates: specific, ad valorem, and combined
    - Distribution point: distribution and consumption taxes
- Marketing barriers: nontariff barriers
    - Government participation in trade
    - Customs and entry procedures
    - Product requirements
    - Quotas
    - Financial control
- Private barriers
- World Trade Organization (WTO)

- Generalized System of Preferences (GSP)
- Some remarks on protectionism
- Conclusion

## Marketing strategy

**The best things in life are (not) free**

South Korea is the world's sixth largest manufacturer of automobiles, and it exports some 650,000 cars annually. The country is also the world's fastest growing car market. Hyundai Motors and its subsidiary Kia have 75 percent market share.

Among auto-producing countries, South Korea is one of the most closed markets. In 1999, Volkswagen sold only two cars there. In 2006, only 3 percent of vehicles sold there were made outside. The comparable import figures for Japan and the U.S.A. were 5 percent and 37 percent respectively. Out of the 1.1 million vehicles sold in Korea in 2006, only about 40,000 vehicles were imported. U.S. companies managed to grab only 4556 cars. In contrast, the South Korean brands sold almost 800,000 vehicles in the U.S.A. in the same year.

Foreign car manufacturers have long complained about South Korea's highly protected market. Imported cars are subject to the 8 percent tariffs as well as the 15 percent acquisition tax on luxury cars. While the average tariff on industrial products in the U.S.A. is 3.7 percent, it is 11 percent in South Korea. While the U.S.A. has an average tariff on food products of 12 percent, it is 52 percent in Korea. The Korean government also restricts the number of automobile showrooms and the exhibition space which foreign-owned importers and dealers can have.

Other problems faced by foreign car manufacturers include restrictions on credit facilities and the tightly regulated advertising market. Since most advertising time on TV and radio is controlled by broadcasting authorities through contracts that may continue indefinitely, large Korean advertisers are able to lock up virtually all prime-time TV spots or sponsored programs. In addition, Korean buyers of high-priced foreign cars can expect special attention from tax officials.

To be fair, American and European cars are simply too big for most Korean consumers, especially since parking spaces are a problem. Besides, Korean consumers have strong national feelings and want to support local producers.

*Sources*: "Korea, Here We Come," *Business Week*, February 14, 2000, 8; "Foreign Automakers Set Sights on S. Korea," *San José Mercury News*, September 16, 2000; "Korea Trade Focus: Cars," *Wall Street Journal*, March 29, 2007; and "South Korea Ready to Open Up," *Wall Street Journal*, March 28, 2007.

## Purpose of chapter

Free trade makes a great deal of sense theoretically because it increases efficiency and economic welfare for all involved nations and their citizens. South Korea's trade barriers, however, do not represent an isolated case. In practice, free trade is woefully ignored by virtually all countries. Despite the advantages, nations are inclined to discourage free trade. Governments everywhere seem to be the main culprits in distorting trade and welfare arrangements in order to gain some economic and political advantage or benefit.

The *National Trade Estimate Report on Foreign Trade Barriers (NTE)*, issued by the U.S. Trade Representative, defines **trade barriers** as "government laws, regulations, policies, or practices that either protect domestic producers from foreign competition or artificially stimulate exports of particular domestic products." Restrictive business practices and government regulations designed to protect public health and national security are not considered as trade barriers. The report classifies the trade barriers into ten categories: (1) import policies (e.g., tariffs, quotas, licensing, and customs barriers); (2) standards, testing labeling, and certification; (3) government procurement; (4) export subsidies; (5) lack of intellectual property protection; (6) services barriers (e.g., restrictions on the use of foreign data processing); (7) investment barriers; (8) anti-competitive practices with trade effects tolerated by foreign governments; (9) trade restrictions affecting electronic commerce (e.g., discriminatory taxation), and (10) other barriers that encompass more than one category (e.g., bribery and corruption).[1]

This chapter catalogs the types and impact of trade and marketing barriers. It examines trade restrictions and the rationale, if any, behind them. By understanding these barriers, marketers should be in a better position to cope with them. It would be impossible to list all marketing barriers because they are simply too numerous. Furthermore, governments are forever creating new import restrictions or adjusting those currently in use.

For purposes of study, marketing barriers may be divided into two basic categories: tariff and nontariff barriers. Figure 3.1 provides details for this division. Each category and its subcategories will be described, and their marketing implications will be discussed in this chapter.

## Protection of local industries

While countries generally do not mind exporting, they simply do not like imports. Politicians as well as workers in the industries that face foreign competition tend to be against free trade. Economic cooperation among governments yields economic benefits and problems by significantly affecting internal and external trade patterns. The CAP (Common Agricultural Policy) of the European Union is a good example. The CAP, with more than twenty price systems, was adopted to satisfy France's demand to protect its farmers as a condition for joining the European Community. The practice requires the EU to impose variable-levy tariffs on many imported farm products in order to raise prices to European levels so that EU farmers will not be undersold at home regardless of world prices. Furthermore, authorities agree to buy surplus produce to maintain high target prices. The practice encourages farmers to overproduce products, which are later often sold abroad at lower prices. Based on the results of a number of studies, because of the CAP, the EU has experienced an average loss of GDP of about 1 percent as well as a large redistribution of income to farmers from consumers and taxpayers.

Many believe that the U.S.A. is the most liberal nation in promoting free trade. This notion is debatable. American farmers receive $20 billion a year in taxpayer hand-outs.[2] The U.S.A. achieves its protection goals through a variety of means. It has quotas on sugar, processed dairy products (e.g., cheese), and clothespins (see Ethical Dimension 3.1). Interestingly, in terms of combined *ad valorem* tariff equivalents (import tariffs as a percentage of the value or price of imported products), the U.S. protection is highest on products exported by the least developed countries. Japan is the same with regard to agricultural products. In contrast, the Canadian and EU protectionist measures hurt the low- and middle-income exporters the most.[3]

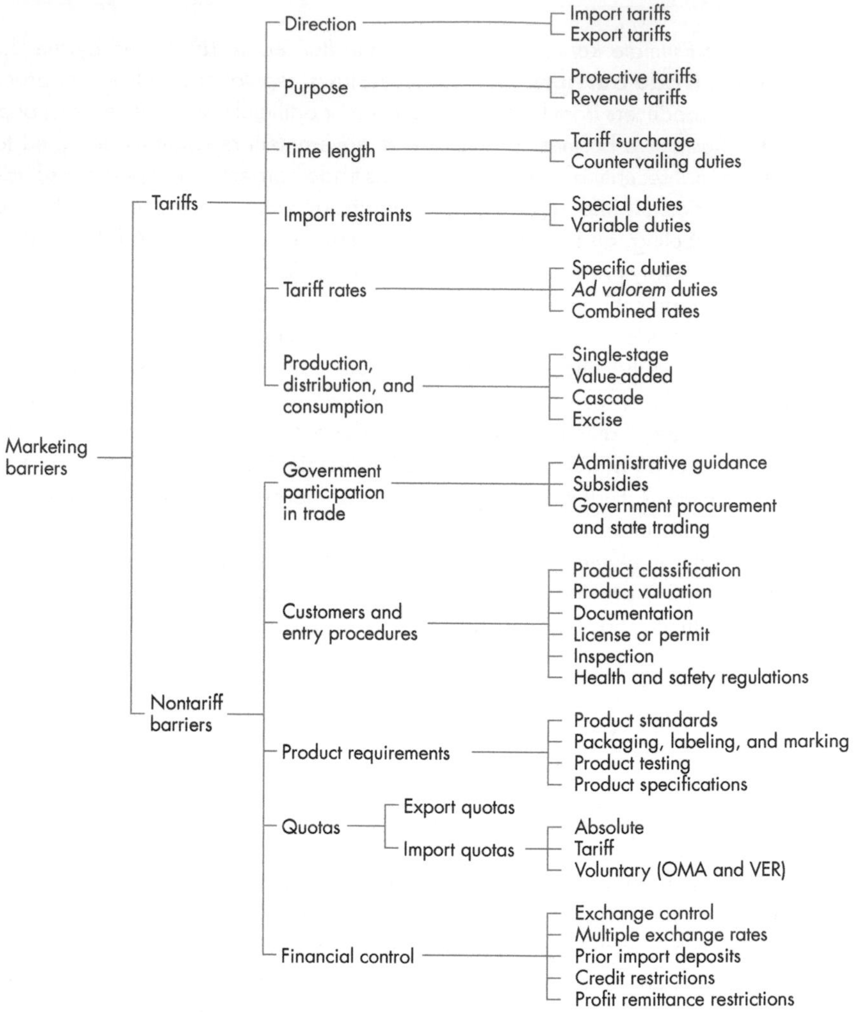
Marketing barriers
Tariffs
Direction
Import tariffs
Export tariffs
Purpose
Protective tariffs
Revenue tariffs
Time length
Tariff surcharge
Countervailing duties
Import restraints
Special duties
Variable duties
Tariff rates
Specific duties
Ad valorem duties
Combined rates
Production, distribution, and consumption
Single-stage
Value-added
Cascade
Excise
Nontariff barriers
Government participation in trade
Administrative guidance
Subsidies
Government procurement and state trading
Customers and entry procedures
Product classification
Product valuation
Documentation
License or permit
Inspection
Health and safety regulations
Product requirements
Product standards
Packaging, labeling, and marking
Product testing
Product specifications
Quotas
Export quotas
Import quotas
Absolute
Tariff
Voluntary (OMA and VER)
Financial control
Exchange control
Multiple exchange rates
Prior import deposits
Credit restrictions
Profit remittance restrictions

**FIGURE 3.1** Marketing barriers

*Source*: Adapted from Sak Onkvisit and John J. Shaw, "Marketing Barriers in International Trade," *Business Horizons* 31 (May–June 1988, 64–72).

## Ethical Dimension 3.1

### A sweet deal

The $10-billion-a-year sugar industry in the U.S.A. enjoys a sweet deal. The U.S. Department of Agriculture restricts the quantity of domestically produced sugar that may be sold in the country, while the U.S. government uses quotas and tariffs to discourage the importation of foreign sugar. Moreover, there is a federal loan program that essentially sets a minimum price for sugar. As may be expected, U.S. sugar prices are about twice as much as the world market price. Not unexpectedly, U.S. candy and soft drink manufacturers are unhappy about the high sugar prices. They are urging the government to make direct subsidy payments to sugar-cane growers instead of being in the business of restricting supply.

The sugar industry naturally sees it differently. Being second to none historically in gaining protection, it is not going to give it up without a fight. It argues that the subsidy program could further hurt its image of being dependent on corporate welfare. The subsidy will also shift the burden of $1.3 billion from consumers to taxpayers, and this move is not politically appealing. In addition, it may open the door for foreign producers to complain to the World Trade Organization that U.S. sugar growers receive an unfair advantage. Certainly, the U.S. sugar industry's lobbyists are busy making the case.

*Source*: "Lobbyists Who Want Nothing," *Business Week*, January 22, 2007, 72.

Why do nations impede free trade when the inhibition is irrational? One reason why governments interfere with free marketing is to protect local industries, often at the expense of local consumers as well as consumers worldwide. Regulations are created to keep out or hamper the entry of foreign-made products. Arguments for the protection of local industries usually take one of the following forms: (1) keeping money at home, (2) reducing unemployment, (3) equalizing cost and price, (4) enhancing national security, and (5) protecting infant industry.

## Keeping money at home

Trade unions and protectionists often argue that international trade will lead to an outflow of money, making foreigners richer and local people poorer. This argument is based on the fallacy of regarding money as the sole indicator of wealth. Other assets, even products, can also be indicators of wealth. For instance, it does not make sense to say that a man is poor just because he does not have much cash on hand when he has many valuable assets such as land and jewelry. In addition, this protectionist argument assumes that foreigners receive money without having to give something of value in return. Whether local consumers buy locally made or foreign products, they will have to spend money to pay for such products. In either case, they receive something of value for their money.

## Reducing unemployment

It is a standard practice for trade unions and politicians to attack imports and international trade in the name of job protection. Figure 3.2 presents this argument as made by the United Steelworkers of America. The argument is based on the assumption that import reduction will create more demand for local products and subsequently create more jobs. Most economists see this kind of thinking as one-sided, though not completely without merits.

Another problem with protectionism is that it may lead to inflation as local manufacturers often cannot resist the temptation of increasing their prices for quick profits. To make matters worse, other countries will often retaliate by refusing to import products.

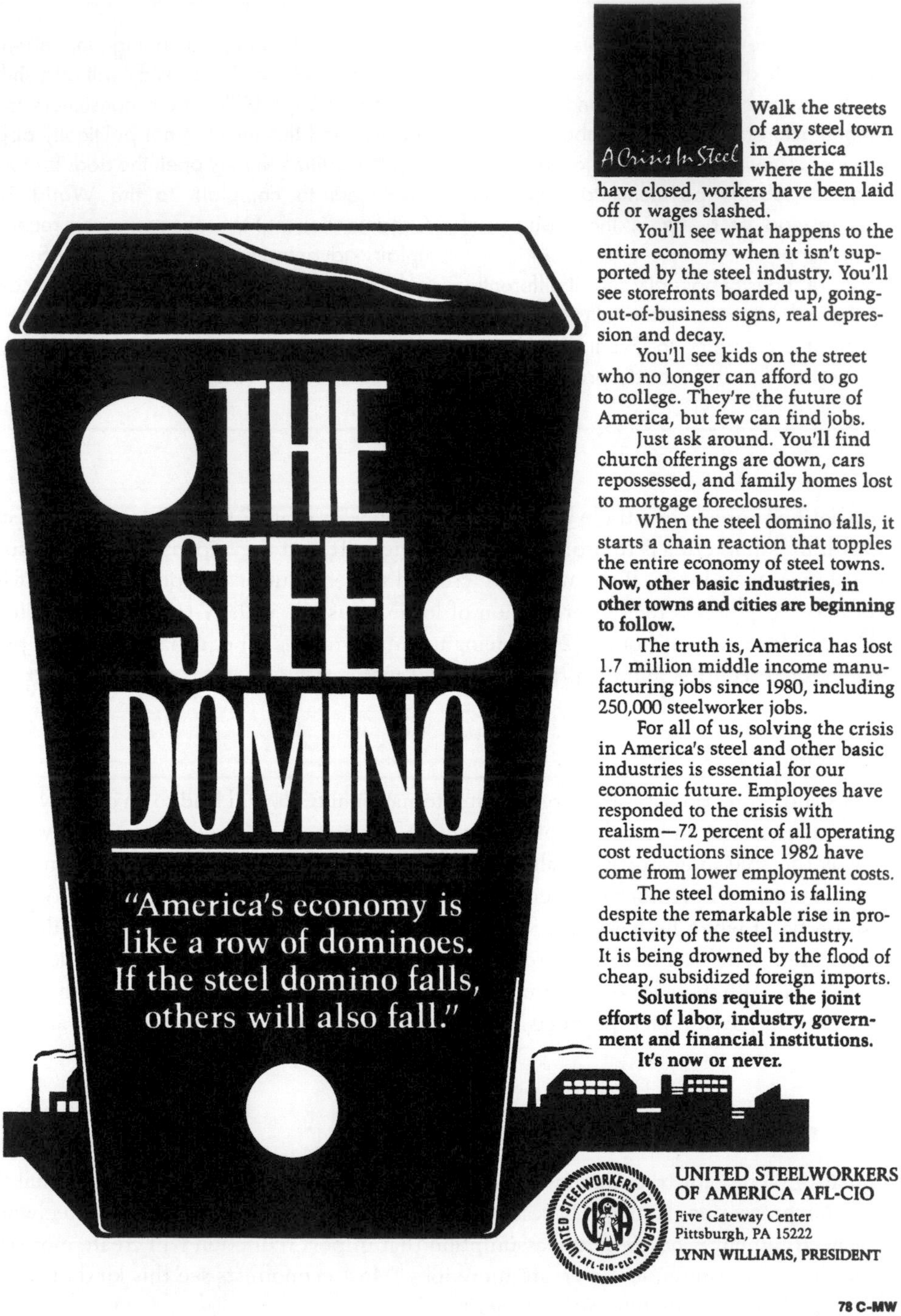
A Crisis In Steel
THE STEEL DOMINO
"America's economy is like a row of dominoes. If the steel domino falls, others will also fall."
Walk the streets of any steel town in America where the mills have closed, workers have been laid off or wages slashed.
You'll see what happens to the entire economy when it isn't supported by the steel industry. You'll see storefronts boarded up, going-out-of-business signs, real depression and decay.
You'll see kids on the street who no longer can afford to go to college. They're the future of America, but few can find jobs.
Just ask around. You'll find church offerings are down, cars repossessed, and family homes lost to mortgage foreclosures.
When the steel domino falls, it starts a chain reaction that topples the entire economy of steel towns. Now, other basic industries, in other towns and cities are beginning to follow.
The truth is, America has lost 1.7 million middle income manufacturing jobs since 1980, including 250,000 steelworker jobs.
For all of us, solving the crisis in America's steel and other basic industries is essential for our economic future. Employees have responded to the crisis with realism—72 percent of all operating cost reductions since 1982 have come from lower employment costs.
The steel domino is falling despite the remarkable rise in productivity of the steel industry.
It is being drowned by the flood of cheap, subsidized foreign imports.
Solutions require the joint efforts of labor, industry, government and financial institutions.
It's now or never.
UNITED STEELWORKERS OF AMERICA AFL-CIO
Five Gateway Center
Pittsburgh, PA 15222
LYNN WILLIAMS, PRESIDENT
78 C-MW

**FIGURE 3.2** Protectionism – labor's view

*Source*: Reprinted with permission of the United Steel Workers of America.

### Equalizing cost and price

Some protectionists attempt to justify their actions by invoking economic theory. They argue that foreign goods command lower prices because of lower production costs. Therefore, trade barriers are needed to make prices of imported products less competitive and local items more competitive. This argument is not persuasive to most analysts for several reasons. First, to determine the cause of price differential is unusually difficult. Is it caused by labor, raw materials, efficiency, or subsidy? Furthermore, costs and objectives vary greatly among countries, making it impossible to determine just what costs need to be equalized.

Second, even if the causes of price differentials can be isolated and determined, it is hard to understand why price and cost have to be artificially equalized in the first place. Trade between nations takes place due to price differentials; otherwise there is no incentive to trade at all.

Although the estimates of the cost of protection vary, they all point to the same conclusion: the costs to consumers are enormous. As an example, according to the Consuming Industries Trade Action Coalition, quotas and tariffs on steel imports cost consumers between $2 billion and $4 billion and between 36,000 and 75,000 jobs (or eight times the number of steel industry jobs saved). In any case, the WTO also ruled in 2003 that steel tariffs imposed by the U.S.A. were illegal.

If cost/price equalization is a desired end, then international trade may be the only instrument that can achieve it. For example, if wages are too high in one country, that country will attract labor from a lower wage country. That process will increase the labor supply in the high-wage country, driving the wages down. On the other hand, the labor supply in the lower wage nation will decrease, driving the wages up. Thus, equalization is achieved.

### Enhancing national security

Protectionists often use the patriotic theme. They usually claim that a nation should be self-sufficient and even willing to pay for inefficiency in order to enhance national security (see Figure 3.3). That point of view has some justification – to a certain extent.

Opponents of protectionism dismiss appeals to national security. A nation can never be completely self-sufficient because raw materials are not found in the same proportion in all areas of the world. The U.S.A. itself would be vulnerable if the supply of certain minerals were cut off. Moreover, national security is achieved at the cost of higher product prices, and money could be used for something more productive to the national interest. In addition, in the case of such scarce resources as oil, if the U.S.A. were to try to be self-sufficient, it would quickly use up its own limited resources. The country may be better off exploiting or depleting the resources of others. North Korea's brand of self-sufficiency, coupled with its defense budget, has virtually driven the nation to starvation.

### Protecting infant industry

The necessity to protect an infant industry is perhaps the most credible argument for protectionist measures. Some industries need to be protected until they become viable. South Korea serves as a good example. It has performed well by selectively protecting infant industries for export purpose.

In practice, it is not an easy task to protect industries. First, the government must identify deserving industries. Next, appropriate incentives must be created to encourage productivity. Finally, the government has to make sure that the resultant protection is only temporary. There is a question of

FOREIGN OIL
IT'S ONLY A MATTER OF TIME.
We now import more than 40 percent of all the oil we use. And that percentage is growing. Our excessive dependence on foreign oil could blow up in our faces at any moment if our supply were somehow disrupted.
But the more we use nuclear energy, instead of imported oil, to generate our electricity, the less we have to depend on uncertain foreign oil supplies.
America's 112 nuclear electric plants already have cut foreign oil dependence by 4 billion barrels since the oil embargo of 1973, saving us $115 billion in foreign oil payments.
But 112 nuclear plants will not be enough to meet our rapidly growing demand for electricity. We need more plants.
Importing so much oil is a danger we must not ignore. We need to rely more on energy sources we can count on, like nuclear energy.
For a free booklet on nuclear energy, write to the U.S. Council for Energy Awareness, P.O. Box 66080, Dept. BB01, Washington, D.C. 20035.
U.S. COUNCIL FOR ENERGY AWARENESS
Nuclear energy means more energy independence.
©1990 USCEA
As seen in February 1990 issues of U.S. News & World Report, The New York Times, The Economist, Barrons, and Congressional Quarterly; March 1990 issues of TIME, Sports Illustrated, Newsweek, Business Week, The Washington Post, Forbes, and National Journal; April 1990 issues of Reader's Digest, National Geographic, Ladies' Home Journal, Good Housekeeping, Smithsonian, The Wall Street Journal, Scientific American, Natural History, The Atlantic, American Heritage, Governing, and State Legislatures; and May 1990 issues of The Leadership Network.

**FIGURE 3.3** National security

*Source*: Courtesy of the U.S. Council for Energy Awareness.

how long an "infant" needs to grow up to be an "adult." A spoiled child often remains spoiled. A person taught to be helpless often wants to remain helpless or does not know how to stop being helpless. In a practical sense, there is no incentive for an infant industry to abandon protection and eliminate inefficiency.

## Marketing barriers: tariffs

Tariff, derived from a French word meaning rate, price, or list of charges, is a customs duty or a tax on products that move across borders. Tariffs may be classified in several ways. The classification scheme used here is based on direction, purpose, length, rate, and distribution point. These classifications are not necessarily mutually exclusive.

### *Direction: import and export tariffs*

Tariffs are often imposed on the basis of the direction of product movement; that is, on imports or exports, with the latter being the less common one. When export tariffs are levied, they usually apply to an exporting country's scarce resources or raw materials (rather than finished manufactured products).

### *Purpose: protective and revenue tariffs*

Tariffs may be classified as protective tariffs and revenue tariffs. The distinction is based on purpose. The purpose of a protective tariff is to protect home industry, agriculture, and labor against foreign competitors by trying to keep foreign goods out of the country.

The purpose of a revenue tariff, in contrast, is to generate tax revenues for the government. Compared to a protective tariff, a revenue tariff is relatively low. As in the case of the EU, it applies tariffs of up to 236 percent on meat and 180 percent on cereals, while its tariffs on raw materials and electronics rarely exceed 5 percent.[4]

### *Length: tariff surcharge versus countervailing duty*

Protective tariffs may be further classified according to length of time. A tariff surcharge is a temporary action, whereas a countervailing duty is a permanent surcharge. When Harley-Davidson claimed that it needed time to adjust to Japanese imports, President Reagan felt that it was in the national interest to provide import relief. To protect the local industry, a tariff surcharge was used. In this particular case, the tariff achieved its purpose, and the company roared back. In 2002, it shipped 263,653 units, totaled $4.1 billion in sales, earned $580 million in profit, and captured 46 percent of the North American heavyweight motorcycle market.[5] More than 100,000 people rode their Harley-Davidson motorcycles to Wisconsin in 2003 to celebrate the company's 100-year anniversary.

Countervailing duties are imposed on certain imports when products are subsidized by foreign governments. These duties are thus assessed to offset a special advantage or discount allowed by an exporter's government. Usually, a government provides an export subsidy by rebating certain taxes if goods are exported.

## Rates: specific, ad valorem, and combined

How are tax rates applied? To understand the computation, three kinds of tax rates must be distinguished: specific, *ad valorem*, and combined.

**Specific duties** are a fixed or specified amount of money per unit of weight, gauge, or other measure of quantity. Based on a standard physical unit of a product, they are specific rates of so many dollars or cents for a given unit of measure (e.g., 350 euros/ton on sugar imports into the EU). Product costs or prices are irrelevant in this case. Because the duties are constant for low- and high-priced products of the same kind, this method is discriminatory and effective for protection against cheap products because of their lower unit value. That is, there is a reverse relationship between product value and duty percentage. As product price goes up, a duty when expressed as a percentage of this price will fall. On the other hand, for a cheap product whose value is low, the duty percentage will rise accordingly.

***Ad valorem*** duties are duties "according to value." They are stated as a fixed percentage of the invoice value and are applied at a percentage to the dutiable value of the imported goods. This is the opposite of specific duties since the percentage is fixed but the total duty is not. Based on this method, there is a direct relationship between the total duties collected and the prices of products. That is, the absolute amount of total duties collected will increase or decrease with the prices of imported products. The strength of this method is that it provides a continuous and relative protection against all price levels of a particular product. Such protection becomes even more critical when inflation increases prices of imports. If specific duties were used, their effect will lessen with time because inflation reduces the proportionate effect. Another advantage is that *ad valorem* duties provide an easy comparison of rates across countries and across products.

**Combined rates** (or **compound duty**) are a combination of the specific and *ad valorem* duties on a single product. They are duties based on both the specific rate and the *ad valorem* rate that are applied to an imported product. For example, the tariff may be 10 cents per pound plus 5 percent *ad valorem*. Under this system, both rates are used together, though in some countries only the rate producing more revenue may apply.

One important fact is that the average tariff rates affect the poor the most. After all, working-class consumers spend a large share of their income on the necessities of daily life, and many of such necessities are imported. Affluent consumers, in comparison, are not bothered as much by tariffs because these necessities are only a fraction of what they earn.

## Distribution point: distribution and consumption taxes

Some taxes are collected at a particular point of distribution or when purchases and consumption occur. These indirect taxes, frequently adjusted at the border, are of four kinds: single-stage, value-added, cascade, and excise.

**Single-stage sales tax** is a tax collected only at one point in the manufacturing and distribution chain. This tax is perhaps most common in the U.S.A., where retailers and wholesalers make purchases without paying any taxes simply by showing a sales tax permit. The single-stage sales tax is not collected until products are purchased by final consumers.

A **value-added tax (VAT)** is a multistage, noncumulative tax on consumption. It is a national sales tax levied at each stage of the production and distribution system, though only on the value added at that stage. Its important feature is that it credits taxes paid by companies on their material inputs against taxes they must collect on their own sales. In other words, each time a product changes hands, even between middlemen, a tax must be paid. But the tax collected at a certain stage is based on the added value and not the total value of the product at that point. Sellers in the chain collect the VAT from a buyer, deduct the amount of VAT they have already paid on their purchase of the product, and remit the balance to the government. European Union customs officers collect the VAT upon importation of goods based on the CIF (cost, insurance, and freight) value plus the duty charged on the product.

Even though the VAT was first proposed in France in 1920, it was not until 1948 that the first recognizable VAT appeared in France. At that time, this tax was largely unknown outside the theoretical discussions. At present, more than 120 countries rely on it to raise $18 trillion or about a quarter of the world's tax revenue, affecting 4 billion people or 70 percent of the world's population.[6]

The VAT is supposed to be non-discriminatory because it applies to both products sold on the domestic market and imported goods. The importance of the value-added tax is due to the fact that GATT allows a producing country to rebate the value-added tax when products are exported. Foreign firms trying to get a refund from European governments have found the refund process to be anything but easy.

Since the tax applies to imports at the border but because it is fully rebated on exports, the VAT may improve a country's trade balance. The evidence, however, offers a mixed picture.

To strengthen the VAT collections, a country should employ a single VAT rate, thus reducing administrative complexity. Value-added taxes should have few exceptions, and any exceptions should apply only to educational, medical, and social services. In addition, only exports should be zero rated (i.e., VAT exempt).[7]

**Cascade taxes** are collected at each point in the manufacturing and distribution chain and are levied on the total value of a product, including taxes borne by the product at earlier stages (i.e., tax on tax). Of the tax systems examined, this appears to be the most severe of them all.

Table 3.1 shows how the tax varies among the three systems.

An **excise tax** is a one-time charge levied on the sales of specified products. Alcoholic beverages and cigarettes are good examples. It is also common to levy excise taxes on motor vehicles, petroleum, and consumer durables. Excise taxes account for about 19 percent of all tax revenues.[8]

**TABLE 3.1** A comparison of distribution taxes

| *Point in chain (seller)* | *Price charged* | *Payer of tax* | *Single-stage sales tax* | *Value-added tax* | *Cascade tax* |
|---|---|---|---|---|---|
| Farmer | $4 | Manufacturer | None | On $4 | On $4 |
| Manufacturer | $5 | Wholesaler | None | On $(5–4) | On $5 + previous tax |
| Wholesaler | $7 | Retailer | None | On $(7–5) | On $7 + previous taxes |
| Retailer | $10 | Consumer | On $10 | On $(10–7) | On $10 + previous taxes |

## Marketing barriers: nontariff barriers

Tariffs, though generally undesirable, are at least straightforward and obvious. Nontariff barriers, in comparison, are more elusive or nontransparent. Tariffs have declined in importance, reaching the lowest level ever of about 4 percent on average after 50 years and eight global rounds of trade negotiation (see Table 3.2).[9] In the meantime, nontariff barriers have become more prominent. Often disguised, the impact of nontariff barriers can be just as devastating, if not more, as the impact of tariffs. Figure 3.4 describes how one U.S. firm, Allen-Edmonds Shoe Corporation, intended to overcome frustrating Japanese import barriers.

There are several hundred types of nontariff barriers. According to the U.S. Trade Representative, countries use a variety of barriers that include nonscientific sanitary standards, customs procedures, and government monopolies. Japan's telecommunications, agriculture, and pharmaceuticals sectors have "structural rigidity, excessive regulation, and market access barriers." China, on the other hand, has import standards and sanitary requirements that act as import barriers. China must act to improve the protection of intellectual property rights.[10]

**TABLE 3.2** Trade rounds

| *Year* | *Place/name* | *Subjects covered* | *Number of countries* |
|---|---|---|---|
| 1947 | Geneva | Tariffs | 12 |
| 1949 | Annecy | Tariffs | 13 |
| 1951 | Torquay | Tariffs | 38 |
| 1956 | Geneva | Tariffs | 26 |
| 1960–1 | Geneva (Dillon round) | Tariffs | 26 |
| 1964–7 | Geneva (Kennedy round) | Tariffs and anti-dumping measures | 62 |
| 1973–9 | Geneva (Tokyo round) | Tariffs, nontariff measures, "framework" agreements | 102 |
| 1986–94 | Geneva (Uruguay round) | Tariffs, nontariff measures, rules, services, intellectual property, dispute settlements, textiles, agriculture, creation of WTO | 123 |
| 2002–4 | Doha | All goods and services, tariffs, non-tariff measures, anti-dumping and subsidies, regional trade agreements, intellectual property, environment, dispute settlement, Singapore issues | 144 |

*Source*: Anne McGuirk, "The Doha Development Agenda," *Finance & Development* (September 2002, 6).

WHEN THE JAPANESE
TOLD US IT WAS CUSTOMARY TO LEAVE
OUR SHOES AT THE DOOR,
THIS IS THE DOOR THEY HAD IN MIND.
ALLEN-EDMONDS
SHOE CORP.
SHIPPING
Keep your shoes to yourself. That's the clear message the Japanese government has given Allen-Edmonds and other U.S. shoe manufacturers. Tough licensing, even tougher tariffs and various other obstacles are making it nearly impossible to do business in Japan.
There is a market for our shoes there. The people have shown great interest in our classic styles and our superior quality. But the duty makes them terribly expensive. Fact is, U.S. shoes sold in Japan are taxed up to 60% higher than Japanese shoes sold in this country.
Don't misunderstand. We're not looking for help or sympathy. In fact, we're making headway with some good old-fashioned pushiness. Just recently our president literally crashed a Tokyo trade show we had been excluded from – and promptly sold over 300 pairs of shoes.
The point is this. A company – even a small one like our own – can't wait for political solutions to unfair trade barriers. Manufacturers must initiate action in a friendly but firm manner. Whether it's the Japanese market or any other, for now it's the best way we know to get a foot in the door.
ALLEN EDMONDS
The Handcrafted World of Allen-Edmonds.
Allen-Edmonds Shoe Corporation
Port Washington, WI 53074 U.S.A.
(414) 284-3461 Telex 229715
FAX (414) 284-3462

**FIGURE 3.4** Japanese import barriers

*Source*: Reprinted with permission of Allen-Edmonds Shoe Corporation.

Nontariff barriers may be grouped in five major categories. Each category contains a number of different nontariff barriers.

## Government participation in trade

The degree of government involvement in trade varies from passive to active. The types of participation include administrative guidance, state trading, and subsidies.

### Administrative guidance

Many governments routinely provide trade consultation to private companies. Japan has been doing this on a regular basis to help implement its industrial policies. This systematic cooperation between the government and business is labeled "Japan, Inc." To get private firms to conform to the Japanese government's guidance, the government uses a carrot-and-stick approach by exerting the influence through regulations, recommendations, encouragement, discouragement, or prohibition. Japan's government agencies' administrative councils are influential enough to make importers restrict their purchases to an amount not exceeding a certain percentage of local demand. The Japanese government denies that such a practice exists, claiming that it merely seeks reports on the amounts purchased by each firm.

### Government procurement and state trading

State trading is the ultimate in government participation, because the government itself is now the customer or buyer who determines what, when, where, how, and how much to buy. In this practice, the state engages in commercial operations, either directly or indirectly, through the agencies under its control. Such business activities are either in place of or in addition to private firms.

Although government involvement in business is most common with the communist countries, whose governments are responsible for the central planning of the whole economy, the practice is definitely not restricted to those nations. The U.S. government, as the largest buyer in the world, is required by the Buy American Act to give a bidding edge to U.S. suppliers in spite of their higher prices.

The Government Procurement Act requires the signatory nations to guarantee that they will provide suppliers from other signatory countries treatment equal to that which they provide their own suppliers. This guarantee of "*national treatment*" means that a foreign government must choose the goods with the lowest price that best meet the specifications regardless of the supplier's nationality. The Code requires that technical specifications not be prepared, adopted, or applied with a view to creating obstacles to international trade. The purchasing agency must adopt specifications geared towards performance rather than design and must base the specifications on international standards, national technical regulations, or recognized national standards, when appropriate.

### Subsidies

According to GATT, subsidy is a "financial contribution provided directly or indirectly by a government and which confers a benefit." Subsidies can take many forms – including cash, interest rate, value-added tax, corporate income tax, sales tax, freight, insurance, and infrastructure.

Subsidized loans for priority sectors, preferential rediscount rates, and budgetary subsidies are among the various subsidy policies of several Asian countries.

There are several other kinds of subsidies that are not so obvious. Brazil's rebates of the various taxes, coupled with other forms of assistance, may be viewed as subsidies. Tennessee, Ohio, Michigan, and Illinois, in order to attract foreign auto makers to locate their plants in those states, provided such services as highway construction, training of workers, and tax breaks, which are simply subsidies in disguise.

**Sheltered profit** is another kind of subsidy. A country may allow a corporation to shelter its profit from abroad. The U.S.A. in 1971 allowed companies to form domestic international sales corporations (DISCs) even though they cost the U.S. Treasury Department more than $1 billion a year in revenue. GATT, the multilateral treaty, eventually ruled that a DISC was an illegal export subsidy. A new U.S. law then allowed companies that met more stringent requirements to form foreign sales corporations (FSCs). As in the case of Boeing Co., it was the biggest user of this tool, enabling it to avoid $130 million in U.S. taxes in 1998, about 12 percent of its entire earnings.[11] Ultimately, FSCs were also found to be illegal.

It is a common practice for governments in developing countries to control the price of gasoline, supposedly to protect low-income consumers. Unfortunately, universal energy subsidies do not encourage efficient use of energy and actually entail a great deal of leakage of benefits to higher-income groups. According to a study of the International Monetary Fund, energy subsidies are expensive and ineffective. Such subsidies should instead be directed towards higher priorities such as education, health care, infrastructure, and tax reduction.[12]

The **Subsidies Code**, technically named the Agreement on Interpretation and Application of Article VI, XVI, and XXIII of the General Agreement on Tariffs and Trade, recognizes that government subsidies distort the competitive forces at work in international trade. The rules of the international agreement negotiated during the Tokyo Round of Multilateral Trade Negotiations differentiate between *export subsidies* and *domestic subsidies*. The Code's rules also differentiate between subsidies paid on *primary products* (e.g., manufactures) and those paid on *nonprimary products* and primary minerals. A primary product is any product of farm, forest, or fishery in its natural form or that has undergone such processing as is customarily required to prepare it for transportation and marketing in substantial volume in international trade (e.g., frozen and cured meat). The Code prohibits the use of export subsidies on nonprimary products and primary mineral products.

Agricultural export subsidies have long been a persistent source of conflict. The figures for the following countries are: Switzerland ($292 million), Norway ($128 million), and the U.S.A. ($80 million). The EU by itself incredibly spent $5,985 million. In 2003, the EU trade ministers applauded an agreement to put limits on the EU's 40-year-old practice of paying farmers subsidies based on the amount of their production. However, the EU has not reduced its $30.5 billion a year paid in production-linked subsidies, nor has it made any changes to its export subsidies – the highest in the world. Developing countries complain bitterly that these subsidies are harmful to trade by encouraging European farmers to sell their produce abroad.[13]

Interestingly, affluent countries have been heavily subsidizing their agricultural businesses. Their agricultural subsidies total almost $1 a day (about six times the level of aid to developing countries). While 75 percent of people in sub-Saharan Africa live on less than $2 a day, an average European cow receives about $2.50 a day in subsidy. On average, a Japanese cow does even better, getting about $7 a day in subsidy.[14] According to the UNCTAD Secretary-General, "six or seven of the top ten agricultural exporters are developed countries, and I don't think they could reach that status without export subsidies."[15]

## Customs and entry procedures

Customs and entry procedures may be employed as nontariff barriers. These restrictions involve classification, valuation, documentation, license, inspection, and health and safety regulations.

### Classification

How a product is classified can be arbitrary and inconsistent and is often based on a customs officer's judgment, at least at the time of entry. Product classification is important because the way in which a product is classified determines its duty status. A company can sometimes take action to affect the classification of its product. Sony argued that its PlayStation 2, equipped with a 128-bit microprocessor, a DVD player, and internet connection, was a big improvement over its PlayStation original and that it should thus qualify as a computer. However, the British customs office chose to continue to classify PlayStation 2 in the video games category, in effect imposing a duty of 2.2 percent or about $9. Had Sony prevailed in getting the "digital processing units" (computers) classification, there would be no import tax.

### Valuation

Regardless of how products are classified, each product must still be valued. The value affects the amount of tariffs levied. A customs appraiser is the one who determines the value. The process can be highly subjective, and the valuation of a product may be interpreted in different ways, depending on what value is used (e.g., foreign, export, import, or manufacturing costs) and how this value is constructed. In Japan, a commodity tax is applied to the FOB factory price of Japanese cars. Yet American cars are valued on the CIF basis, adding $1000 more to the final retail price of these cars.

### Documentation

Documentation can present another problem at entry because many documents and forms are often necessary, and the documents required can be complicated. Japan held up Givenchy's import application because the company left out an apostrophe for its I'Interdit perfume.

Without proper documentation, goods may not be cleared through customs. At the very least, such complicated and lengthy documents serve to slow down product clearance. France, requiring customs documentation to be in French, even held up trucks from other European countries for hours while looking for products' non-French instruction manuals which were banned.

### License or permit

Not all products can be freely imported; controlled imports require licenses or permits. For example, importations of distilled spirits, wines, malt beverages, arms, ammunition, and explosives into the U.S.A. require a license issued by the Bureau of Alcohol, Tobacco, and Firearms. India requires a license for all imported goods. An article is considered prohibited if not accompanied by a license. It is not always easy to obtain an import license, since many countries will issue one only if goods can be certified as necessary.

Japan simplified its licensing procedure in 1986. Previously, a separate license application had been required for any new cosmetic product, even when only a change in shade was involved. The new requirements categorize cosmetics into 78 groups and list permitted ingredients. A marketer simply notifies the government of any new product using those ingredients.

### Inspection

Inspection is an integral part of product clearance. Goods must be examined to determine quality and quantity. This step is highly related to other customs and entry procedures. First, inspection classifies and values products for tariff purposes. Second, inspection reveals whether imported items are consistent with those specified in the accompanying documents and whether such items require any licenses. Third, inspection determines whether products meet health and safety regulations in order to make certain that food products are fit for human consumption or that the products can be operated safely. Fourth, inspection prevents the importation of prohibited articles.

Marketers should be careful in stating the amount and quality of products, as well as in providing an accurate description of products. Any deviation from the statements contained in invoices necessitates further measurements and determination, more delay, and more expenses.

Inspection may be used intentionally to discourage imports. Metal baseball bats from the U.S.A., for instance, are required by Japan to carry a stamp of consumer safety, and this must be "ascertained" only after expensive on-dock inspection.

### Health and safety regulations

Many products are subject to health and safety regulations, which are necessary to protect the public health and environment (see Cultural Dimension 3.1). Health and safety regulations are not restricted to agricultural products. The regulations also apply to TV receivers, microwave ovens, X-ray devices, cosmetics, chemical substances, and clothing.

#### Cultural Dimension 3.1

**Flowers: a symbol of love?**

The Netherlands is the world's largest cut-flower producer. In second place is Colombia which is responsible for 62 percent of all flowers sold in the U.S.A. The U.S.A. requires imported flowers to be free of bugs, and the use of chemicals is inevitable. However, unlike edible fruits and vegetables, flowers are not tested for chemical residues. Several of the toxic chemicals used are listed by the World Health Organization as being extremely or highly toxic. Naturally, farm workers as well as consumers have cause to be concerned.

To address the concern, Colombia's flower exporters have launched Florverde. This flower exporters' association claims that its members have reduced the use of pesticide by 38 percent since 1998. Florverde has also certified that 86 of its 200 members have taken steps to improve worker safety and welfare.

Source: "Imported Flowers Express Love in U.S., Danger at Home," *San José Mercury News*, February 13, 2007.

Concern for safety was used by Japan against aluminum softball bats from the U.S.A. The manufacturing process leaves a small hole in the top filled with a rubber stopper. Japan thus bans the bats on the ground that the stopper may fly out and hurt someone. According to U.S. manufacturers, this fear is unfounded.

In 2007, China was greatly embarrassed due to a series of highly negative events.[16] Global concern started when contaminated wheat flour used to make pet food caused the deaths of cats and dogs in the U.S.A., resulting in a massive pet food recall. Next, counterfeited Colgate toothpaste containing harmful chemicals made its way to overseas markets. Then Mattel had to announce three big recalls of its toys that were made in China due to lead being used. The U.S.A. and EU moved to ban some Chinese products from entry. In an unrelated case, the former head of China's State Food and Drug Administration was sentenced to death due to the "huge amount of bribes involved and the great damage inflicted on the country." The drugs approved by him severely harmed a number of children.

## Product requirements

For goods to enter a country, product requirements set by that country must be met. Requirements may apply to product standards and product specifications as well as to packaging, labeling, and marking.

### Product standards

Each country determines its own product standards to protect the health and safety of its consumers. Such standards may also be erected as barriers to prevent or to slow down importation of foreign goods. Because of U.S. grade, size, quality, and maturity requirements, many Mexican agricultural commodities are barred from entering the U.S.A. Japanese product standards are even more complex, and they are based on physical characteristics instead of product performance. Such standards make it necessary to repeat the product approval process when a slight product modification occurs (such as color), even though the performance of the product in question remains the same. Furthermore, these standards are frequently changed in Japan in order to exclude imports.

### Packaging, labeling, and marking

Packaging, labeling, and marking are considered together because they are highly interrelated. Many products must be packaged in a certain way for safety and other reasons. Canada requires imported canned foods to be packed in specified can sizes, and instructions contained within packages or on them must be in English and French. The Canadian Labeling Act also requires all imported clothing to carry labels in both languages.

### Product testing

Many products must be tested to determine their safety and suitability before they can be marketed. This is another area in which the U.S.A. has some troubles in Japan. Although products may have won approval everywhere else for safety and effectiveness, such products as medical equipment and pharmaceuticals must go through elaborate standard testing that can take a few years – just long enough for Japanese companies to develop competing products. Moreover, the reviews take place behind the Health and Welfare Ministry's closed doors. In 1995, Japan's Ministry of International

Trade and Industry started requiring imported software products to be certified by agents of the Japan Accreditation Bureau. The accreditation requirement may reveal how U.S. software is designed while delaying U.S. bids on public contracts.

The EU's Global Approach to testing and certification for product safety provides manufacturers with one set of procedures for certifying product compliance with EU health, safety, and environmental requirements. The various means by which manufacturers can certify product conformance include manufacturer self-declaration of conformity, third-party testing, quality assurance audit, and/or approval by a body authorized by an EU member state and recognized by the EU Commission. The mark *CE* on the product signifies that all legal requirements concerning product standards have been met. Unfortunately, certification of product tests and registrations for information technology, medical devices, and certain products can only be carried out in Europe, and the practice is costly and uncompetitive.

### Product specifications

Product specifications, though appearing to be an innocent process, can wreak havoc on imports. Specifications can be written in such a way as to favor local bidders and to keep out foreign suppliers. For example, specifications may be extremely detailed, or they may be written to closely resemble domestic products. Thus, they may be used against foreign suppliers who cannot satisfy the specifications without expensive or lengthy modification. Japan's Nippon Telephone & Telegraph Company (NTT) was able to use product specifications as a built-in barrier when it was forced to accept bids from foreign firms. At one time, it did not even provide specifications and bidding details in any language but Japanese. Its specifications are highly restrictive and written with existing Japanese products in mind. Instead of outlining functional characteristics, NTT specifies physical features right down to the location of ventilation holes, the details of which are almost identical to those of Nippon Electric. For example, NTT requires metal cabinets for modems, whereas most U.S. makers use plastic. Parts must be made by the Japanese to qualify for bidding. In general, NTT goes well beyond specifications for performance. GATT has established procedures for setting product standards using performance standards rather than detailed physical specifications.

## Quotas

Quotas are a quantity control on imported goods. Generally, they are specific provisions limiting the amount of foreign products imported in order to protect local firms and to conserve foreign currency. Quotas may be used for export control as well. An export quota is sometimes required by national planning to preserve scarce resources. From a policy standpoint, a quota is not as desirable as a tariff since a quota generates no revenues for a country. There are three kinds of quotas: absolute, tariff, and voluntary.

### Absolute quotas

An absolute quota is the most restrictive of all. It limits in absolute terms the amount imported during a quota period. Once filled, further entries are prohibited. Some quotas are global, but others are allocated to specific foreign countries. Japan imposes strict quotas on oranges and beef. To appease the EU, it has lifted quotas on skimmed milk powder and tobacco for Europe. The most extreme of the absolute quota is an embargo, or a zero quota, as shown in the case of the U.S. trade embargoes against Libya and North Korea.

### *Tariff quotas*

A tariff quota permits the entry of a limited quantity of the quota product at a reduced rate of duty. Quantities in excess of the quota may be imported but are subject to a higher duty rate. Through the use of tariff quotas, a combination of tariffs and quotas is applied with the primary purpose of importing what is needed and discouraging excessive quantities through higher tariffs. When the U.S.A. increased tariffs on imported motorcycles in order to protect the U.S. motorcycle industry, it exempted from this tax the first 6000 big motorcycles from Japan and the first 4000 to 5000 units from Europe.

### *Voluntary quotas*

A voluntary quota differs from the other two kinds of quotas, which are unilaterally imposed. A voluntary quota is a formal agreement between nations or between a nation and an industry. This agreement usually specifies the limit of supply by product, country, and volume.

Two kinds of voluntary quotas can be legally distinguished: **VER (voluntary export restraint)** and **OMA (orderly marketing agreement)**. Whereas an OMA involves negotiation between two governments to specify export management rules, the monitoring of trade volumes, and consultation rights, a VER is a direct agreement between an importing nation's government and a foreign exporting industry (i.e., a quota with industry participation). Both enable the importing country to circumvent GATT's rules (Article XIX) that require the country to reciprocate for the quota received and to impose that market safeguard on a most-favored-nation basis. Because this is a gray area, the OMA and VER may be applied in a discriminatory manner to a certain country. In the case of a VER involving private industries, a public disclosure is not necessary.

As implied, a country may negotiate to limit voluntarily its export to a particular market. This may sound peculiar because the country appears to be acting against its own self-interest. But a country's unwillingness to accept these unfavorable terms will eventually invite trade retaliation and tougher terms in the form of forced quotas. It is thus voluntary only in the sense that the exporting country tries to avoid alternative trade barriers that are even less desirable. For example, Japan agreed to restrict and re-price some exports within Great Britain. In reality, there is nothing voluntary about a voluntary quota.

## Financial control

Financial regulations may also function to restrict international trade. These restrictive monetary policies are designed to control capital flow so that currencies can be defended or imports controlled. For example, to defend the weak Italian lira, Italy imposed a 7 percent tax on the purchase of foreign currencies. There are several forms that financial restrictions can take.

### *Exchange control*

An exchange control is a technique that limits the amount of the currency that may be taken abroad. The reason exchange controls are usually applied is that the local currency is overvalued, thus causing imports to be paid for in smaller amounts of currency. Purchasers then try to use the relatively cheap foreign exchange to obtain items that are either unavailable or more expensive in the local currency.

Exchange controls also limit the length of time and amount of money an exporter can hold for the goods sold. French exporters at one time were required to exchange the foreign currencies for francs within one month. By regulating all types of the capital outflows in foreign currencies, the government either makes it difficult to obtain imported products or makes such items available only at higher prices.

### *Multiple exchange rates*

Multiple exchange rates are another form of exchange regulation or barrier. The objectives of multiple exchange rates are twofold: to encourage exports and imports of certain goods, and to discourage exports and imports of others. This means that there is no single rate for all products or industries, but with the application of multiple exchange rates, some products and industries will benefit and some will not. Spain once used low exchange rates for goods designated for export and high rates for those it desired to retain at home. Multiple exchange rates may also apply to imports. The high rates may be used for imports of particular goods with the government's approval, whereas low rates may be used for other imports.

Because multiple exchange rates are used to bring in hard currencies (through exports) as well as to restrict imports, this system is condemned by the International Monetary Fund (IMF). According to the IMF, any unapproved multiple currency practices are a breach of obligations, and the member may become ineligible to use the Fund's resources.

### *Prior import deposits and credit restrictions*

Financial barriers may also include specific limitations on import restraints, such as prior import deposits and credit restrictions. Both of these barriers operate by imposing certain financial restrictions on importers. A government may require prior import deposits (forced deposits) that make imports difficult by tying up an importer's capital. In effect, the importer is paying interest for money borrowed without being able to use the money or get interest earnings on the money from the government. Importers in Brazil and Italy must deposit a large sum of money with their central banks if they intend to buy foreign goods. To help initiate an aircraft industry, the Brazilian government has required an importer of "flyaway" planes to deposit the full price of the imported aircraft for one year with no interest.

**Credit restrictions** apply only to imports; that is, exporters may be able to get loans from the government, usually at very favorable rates, but importers will not be able to receive any credit or financing from the government. Importers must look for loans in the private sector – very likely at significantly higher rates, if such loans are available at all.

### *Profit remittance restrictions*

Another form of exchange barrier is the profit remittance restriction. ASEAN countries share a common philosophy in allowing unrestricted repatriation of profits earned by foreign companies. Singapore, in particular, allows the unrestricted movement of capital, but many countries regulate the remittance of profits earned in local operations and sent to a parent organization located abroad. Brazil uses progressive rates in taxing all profits remitted to a parent company abroad, with such rates going up to 60 percent. Other countries practice a form of profit remittance restriction by simply having long delays in permission for profit expatriation. To overcome these practices, MNCs have looked to legal loopholes. Many employ various tactics such as countertrading, currency swaps, and other parallel schemes. For example, a multinational firm wanting to repatriate a currency may swap it with another firm which needs that currency. Or these firms may lend to each other in the currency desired by each party.

Another tactic is to negotiate for a higher value of an investment than the investment's actual worth. By charging its foreign subsidiary higher prices and fees, an MNC is able to increase the equity base from which dividend repatriations are calculated. In addition, compared to profit repatriations, the higher prices and fees are treated as costs or expenses and are thus more freely paid to the parent firm.

## Private barriers

As conventional trade barriers are lowered, governments are shifting their attention to competition policy to address environmental and labor objectives and private barriers. Private barriers are certain business practices or arrangements between or among affiliated firms.

Japan's *keiretsu* is a good example of private barriers. The *keiretsu* system deals with cooperative business groups. Such a group includes manufacturers, suppliers, retailers, and customers. Members of the group seek long-term security through interlocking directorates and through owning shares in each other's companies. Toyota Motor Corp. provided $83 million to help out Tomen Corp., a money-losing trading firm. Both belong to the same *keiretsu*, and it is a tradition for members of the *keiretsu* to subsidize each other.[17] Mitsubishi even arranges for the executives of its affiliated companies to have lunch together so as to discuss business dealings. Naturally, the companies that belong to the same *keiretsu* will grant preferential treatment to the other members. Korea's *chaebol* system also functions in a similar fashion.

Private barriers are not unique to Asia. In Germany, banks are strong and often take a leadership role. As in the case of Deutsche Bank, it owns at least 10 percent of some 70 companies, and its bank executives sit on some 400 corporate boards. As such, it is in a position to encourage its clients to do business with each other – rather than with outsiders.

While nontariff barriers are not as transparent as tariffs, private barriers are the worst in terms of transparency (or the lack of it). It is difficult for an outsider to gain business if potential buyers refuse to explain why they do not want to buy from a foreign firm. Certainly, private barriers will be the next significant challenge.

## The World Trade Organization (WTO)

Virtually all nations seek to pursue their best interests in international trade. The result is that sooner or later international trade and marketing may be disrupted. To prevent or at least alleviate any problems, there is a world organization in Geneva known as the WTO (with **General Agreement on Tariffs and Trade** or **GATT** as its predecessor).

Created in January 1948, the objective of GATT is to achieve a broad, multilateral, and free worldwide system of trading. For example, its code requires international bidding on major projects. GATT provides the forum for tariff negotiations and the elimination of trade discrimination.

The four basic principles of GATT are:

1 Member countries will *consult* each other concerning trade problems.
2 The agreement provides a framework for *negotiation* and embodies results of negotiations in a legal instrument.
3 Countries should protect domestic industries *only through tariffs*, when needed and if permitted. There should be no other restrictive devices such as quotas prohibiting imports.
4 Trade should be conducted on a *nondiscriminatory* basis.

Reductions of barriers should be mutual and reciprocal because any country's import increases caused by such reductions will be offset by export increases caused by other countries' reduction of restrictions. This concept is the basis of the principle of the **most favored nation (MFN)**, which is the cornerstone of GATT. According to this principle, countries should grant one another treatment as favorable as the treatment given to their best trading partners or any other country. For example, reductions accorded to France by the U.S.A. should be extended to other countries with which the U.S.A. exchanges the MFN principle (e.g., to Brazil). Likewise, if a country decides to temporarily protect its local industry because that industry is seriously threatened, then the newly erected barriers must apply to all countries even though the threat to its industry may only come from a single nation. The MFN principle thus moves countries away from bilateral bargaining to multilateral (or simultaneous bilateral) bargaining. Each country must be concerned with the implications that its concessions for one country would mean for other countries. The only exception is that an advanced country should not expect reciprocity from less developed countries. To better reflect actual practice, the MFN principle is now called **NTR (Normal Trade Relations)** by the U.S.A.

The U.S.A. does not accord MFN status to communist countries that restrict emigration, but this requirement can be waived by the President. After China first received MFN status from the U.S.A. in 1980, mushroom imports from China jumped from nothing to nearly 50 percent of all U.S. mushroom imports. This increase owed much to the decline of canned mushroom duties, from 45 percent to 10 percent.

Seven successive rounds of multilateral trade negotiations under GATT auspices produced a decline in average tariff on industrial products in industrial countries from more than 40 percent in 1947 to about 5 percent in 1988. The Uruguay Round of multilateral trade negotiations, launched in Punta del Este, Uruguay, in September 1986, aimed to liberalize trade further, to strengthen GATT's role, to foster cooperation, and to enhance the interrelationships between trade and other economic policies that affect growth and development. The Uruguay Round attempted to deal with new areas such as services, intellectual property rights, and trade-related investment. Developed nations offered to reduce trade protection to their agriculture and textile industries in exchange for less developed countries' greater imports of services and greater respect for intellectual property. However, the various countries' varying interests repeatedly stalled the talks. Agricultural disputes even led to violent protests by farmers in France, Japan, South Korea, and others.

Not surprisingly, Lee Kuan Yew of Singapore once called GATT the General Agreement to Talk and Talk. Fortunately, delegations from more than 100 countries were finally able to conclude negotiations at the end of 1993 after seven years of talks. The 109 nations signed the 22,000-page agreement in 1994.

Just like the Uruguay Round, the 2002 to 2004 Doha Round has generated a great deal of controversy and conflict. While the richer economies press the developing countries to open up their markets, the poorer countries have accused the advanced economies of maintaining a very high level of agricultural supports, thus damaging the poor countries' farm-dependent economies. The talks in Cancun in mid-2003 ended up with the delegates from the poorer countries walking out in protest at the advanced economies' insincere efforts to end agriculture subsidies.[18] The talks broke down again in 2006 because the U.S.A. and EU refused to lower tariffs and subsidies for their farmers. Subsequent attempts to resurrect the negotiation have gone nowhere. As a result, the future of the WTO itself could be jeopardized. Hopefully, logic and practicality should ultimately prevail.

Countries like Brazil have become wary of a multilateral negotiation because they will have to open up their markets for just about everyone, including low-cost China. In a somewhat backward move, they now seek bilateral deals with wealthy countries so that concessions can be tailored to the needs of the two sides.[19] Such deals, if continuing to proliferate, may harm global economic growth.

Because GATT was set up in 1948 as a temporary body, the Uruguay Round agreement replaced GATT with the World Trade Organization (WTO) in 1995. The WTO, being more permanent and legally secure, has more authority to settle trade disputes and serves along with the International Monetary Fund and the World Bank to monitor trade and resolve disputes. The WTO encompasses the current GATT structure as well as the Uruguay Round agreements. It provides a single, coordinated mechanism to ensure full, effective implementation of the trading system, and it also provides a permanent, comprehensive forum to address the new or evolving issues of the global market.

The WTO's strengthened dispute settlement system should be better able to limit the scope for unilateral and bilateral actions outside the multilateral system. Under GATT's dispute resolution system, the U.S.A. and other members could and indeed did veto the decisions of arbitration boards. As a result, nations could refuse to adopt negative decisions. For example, a GATT panel twice found that the European Union's oilseed subsidies impeded the tariff-free access to the EU market that was promised to the U.S.A. in a 1962 trade agreement. Yet the EU failed to adequately reform subsidies harmful to U.S. oilseed producers.

Under the WTO, a nation's veto of a panel's decision is eliminated. Other important changes under the new dispute settlement mechanism include: (1) fixed time limits for each stage of the dispute settlement process, (2) automatic adoption of dispute settlement reports, (3) automatic authority to retaliate on request if recommendations are not implemented, (4) creation of a new appellate body to review panel interpretations of WTO agreements, and (5) improved procedural transparency and access to information in the dispute settlement process. The new procedures yield a panel ruling within 16 months of requesting consultations. Unfortunately for the U.S.A., one early finding involved a challenge of Venezuela and Brazil concerning an Environmental Protection Agency (EPA) regulation governing U.S. imports of gasoline. The WTO panel ruled that the EPA's treatment of imported gasoline was inconsistent with GATT provisions.

The WTO has 150 members (see Exhibit 3.1). China, wanting the prestige of being a founding member, tried unsuccessfully to complete its negotiations in 1994 on an accelerated basis. China felt that it should not be held to the terms that apply to industrialized countries. The United States, however, wanted China to fully observe the WTO rules. After years of negotiation with the EU and the United States, China has finally gained membership. Nepal, one of the poorest countries, became the 148th member in 2003. Vietnam joined in 2007, and it is expected that it will take 12 years for Vietnam to achieve full "market economy" status. The WTO accession should facilitate Vietnam's further global integration efforts.[20]

Exhibit 3.1

**World Trade Organization: members (January 2007)**

Albania*
Angola
Antigua and Barbuda
Argentina
Armenia
Australia
Austria
Bahrain, Kingdom of
Bangladesh*
Barbados
Belgium
Belize
Benin*
Boliva
Botswana
Brazil
Brunei Darussalam
Bulgaria
Burkina Faso*
Burundi*
Cambodia*
Cameroon
Canada
Central African Republic*
Chad*
Chile
China
Colombia
Congo
Costa Rica
Cote d'Ivoire
Croatia
Cuba
Cyprus
Czech Republic
Democratic Republic of the Congo*
Denmark
Djibouti*
Dominica
Dominican Republic
Ecuador
Egypt
El Salvador
Estonia
European Communities
Fiji
Finland
Former Yugoslav Republic of Macedonia
France
Gabon
The Gambia*
Georgia
Germany
Ghana
Greece
Guatemala
Guinea*
Guinea Bissau*
Guyana
Haiti*
Honduras
Hong Kong, China
Hungary
Iceland
India
Indonesia
Ireland\Israel
Italy
Jamaica
Japan
Jordan

Kenya
Korea, Republic of
Kuwait
Kyrgyz Republic
Latvia
Lesotho*
Liechtenstein
Lithuania
Luxembourg
Macao, China
Madagascar*
Malawi*
Malaysia
Maldives*
Mali*
Malta
Mauritania*
Mauritius
Mexico
Moldova
Mongolia
Morocco
Mozambique*
Myanmar*
Namibia
Nepal*
Netherlands
New Zealand
Nicaragua
Niger*
Nigeria
Norway
Oman
Pakistan
Panama
Papua New Guinea
Paraguay
Peru
Philippines
Poland
Portugal
Qatar
Romania
Rwanda*
Saint Kitts and Nevis
Saint Lucia
Saint Vincent and the Grenadines
Saudi Arabia
Senegal*
Sierra Leone*
Singapore
Slovak Republic
Slovenia
Solomon Islands*
South Africa
Spain
Sri Lanka
Suriname
Swaziland
Sweden
Switzerland
Chinese Taipei
Tanzania*
Thailand
Togo*
Trinidad and Tobago
Tunisia
Turkey
Uganda*
United Arab Emirates
United Kingdom
U.S.A.
Uruguay
Venezuela
Vietnam
Zambia*
Zimbabwe

*Note*: *Of the 50 least developed countries on the UN list, 32 are WTO members.

These 10 least developed countries are in the process of accession to the WTO: Afghanistan, Bhutan, Cape Verde, Ethiopia, Laos, Sao Tome and Principe, Samoa, Sudan, Vanuatu, and Yemen.

Supporters of the WTO have long argued that a reduction of trade barriers will boost global trade. However, there is hardly any rigorous empirical investigation of whether the WTO has an impact on trade or trade policy. A recent study shows that any impact is very little.[21]

## Generalized System of Preferences (GSP)

Although the benefits derived from the creation of the WTO are rarely disputed, less developed countries do not necessarily embrace GATT because those countries believe that the benefits are not evenly distributed. Tariff reduction generally favors manufactured goods rather than primary goods. Less developed countries rely mainly on exports of primary products, which are then converted by advanced nations into manufactured products for export back to less developed countries. As a result, a less developed country's exports will usually be lower in value than its imports, thus exacerbating the country's poverty status.

In response to less developed countries' needs, the United Nations Conference on Trade and Development (UNCTAD) was created as a permanent organ of the UN General Assembly. Efforts by the UNCTAD led to the establishment of the New International Economic Order (NIEO) program. The program seeks to assist less developed countries through the stabilization of prices of primary products, the expansion of less developed countries' manufacturing capabilities, and the acquisition by less developed countries of advanced technology.

The goal of the UNCTAD is to encourage development in Third World countries and enhance their export positions. This goal led to the establishment of a tariff preference system for less developed countries' manufactured products. In spite of GATT's nondiscrimination principle, advanced nations agreed to grant such preferences to less developed countries' goods. The UNCTAD also played a key role in the emergence of a maritime shipping code, special international programs to help the least developed countries, and international aid targets.

Under the Generalized System of Preferences, developed countries are allowed to deviate from GATT's traditional nondiscrimination principle. Most developing countries have preferential access to the markets of industrial countries. There are about 15 such arrangements in effect. Although the lower tariffs help the exports of many low-income countries, they also divert trade from some other countries that may be just as poor. Furthermore, according to evidence, the GSP schemes may perpetuate anti-export biases by undermining incentives to engage in trade liberalization.[22]

The U.S. Congress passed the Trade Act of 1974, authorizing the initiation of the GSP. The purpose of the act is to aid development by providing duty-free entry on 4000 products from more than 30 developing countries. Products manufactured wholly or substantially (at least 35 percent for single country products) in the designated countries are permitted to enter the U.S.A. duty-free as long as a particular item does not exceed $50.9 million in sales or 50 percent of all U.S. imports of this product. Not all products qualify for such preferential treatment, however, and one should consult the Harmonized Tariff Schedule of the U.S.A. to determine whether a product may enter duty-free.

For a country to qualify, a number of economic variables are considered, such as per capita GDP and living standard. Burma and the Central African Republic had their benefits suspended under the U.S. GSP for failing to meet the labor requirements. Venezuela was challenged as a result of a claim by Occidental Petroleum that its assets were expropriated without compensation. The Four Tigers (Hong Kong, Taiwan, Singapore, and South Korea), once receiving almost 60 percent of the benefits under GSP, were permanently graduated from the program in the beginning of 1989 as a result of their high degree of economic development and export competitiveness. Therefore, Black & Decker, which makes electric irons in Singapore, lost more than $3 million a year because of the new duties. Clearly, foreign exporters and American importers can find the GSP system highly advantageous.

Among the 140 countries and territories covered by the U.S. GSP program, Thailand ranks second behind Angola for receiving the highest GSP privileges. Given the fact that GSP is product-specific and that some of Thailand's products (e.g., silver jewelry, microwave ovens, rubber gloves, and indicator panels) have reached their "competitive need" limit, certain benefits will be either reduced or withdrawn. In general, a product that has export sales of $95 million to the U.S.A. is not entitled to GSP tariff reductions. In addition, once a country's per capita GDP exceeds $3115, the country will have officially graduated from the U.S. GSP program.[23]

## Some remarks on protectionism

Protectionist policies rarely achieve their objectives. As noted by a deputy U.S. trade representative, "the price you pay for protection is inefficiency." Inward-looking strategies are based on the *positive externalities* assumption. That is, government intervention is appropriate because the development of a certain industry has a positive impact on a broader segment of the economy. Unfortunately, externalities are usually presumed rather than documented.[24]

No nation can dominate all industries. According to research, the protection of domestic economies against international competition is responsible for major economic losses for most sub-Saharan African countries. These countries need to open up their economies, and structural adjustment programs need to be implemented.

Most politicians are shortsighted; they simply desire to keep wealth within the home country. The possibility of retaliation is not fully considered. They want the best of both worlds. Artificial trade barriers reduce the world output of goods and services and subsequently world economic welfare; in the end, everyone suffers. The costs of distortions in agricultural trade are large, probably exceeding $120 billion in welfare costs. Countries, developing and industrial, must pay for protectionism. Elimination of barriers to merchandise trade will result in welfare gains of $250 billion to $620 billion.

A country has a choice of opening or closing its borders to trade. If it adopts the open system, it has a much better chance of fostering economic growth and maximizing consumer welfare. By adopting this approach, Hong Kong has been doing well economically. In response to the first oil price shock in the early 1970s, Brazil and Korea increased protection for domestic industry and achieved poor economic results. After the second oil price shock in the late 1970s, Korea adopted outward-oriented trade policies and has greatly benefited from international integration and the strong growth of world trade. Brazil's less outward-oriented policies (e.g., substantial import restrictions), in comparison, reduced competitive pressures at home, accelerated inflation, and led to stagnation.[25] The trade regimes are also more restrictive in Africa than in the rest of the world.[26]

Nations usually take a short cut and try to find a quick-fix solution for their trade problems. Preoccupation with immediate problems often makes them lose sight of the long-term objectives. Without a proper perspective, they can easily end up with more serious problems later.

Trade barriers slow down specialization, diversification, investment efficiency, and growth. Government leaders must have the political will to resist protectionist measures. Governments must make concerted and determined efforts to publicize the costs of protectionism. Trade policy should include a systematic consideration of such costs.

Openness of an economy is the degree to which foreigners and nationals can transact without government-imposed costs that are not levied on a transaction between two national citizens. One should note that trade openness and financial openness are complementary. This positive relationship applies to both industrial and developing countries.[27] Even in the case of intraregional growth, as in China, the evidence shows that the more open areas grow faster than their less open counterparts.[28]

> The breadth of evidence on openness, growth, and poverty reduction, and the strength of the association between openness and other important determinants of high per capita income, such as the quality of institutions, should give long pause to anyone contemplating the adoption of a novel (or tested and failed) development strategy that does not center on openness to trade.[29]

## Conclusion

This chapter has discussed various trade barriers that can inhibit international marketing and, in turn, the world economic welfare of all consumers. It is important to understand that these are only some of the many trade barriers – others are not discussed. For example, more and more countries have now turned to "performance requirements" in order to gain trade advantage. Foreign suppliers are required to use local materials or to conduct exporting on behalf of an importing nation before they are allowed to sell their products there.

Africa has not been an easy region to do business. Red tape is everywhere. "Nowhere is it harder to form a business, nowhere is it harder for banks to get comfortable with the credit history of prospective borrowers, and nowhere is it more cumbersome to trade."[30] In the case of labor regulation, Sierra Leone leads the world in requiring 38 remunerated vacation days a year for formally employed workers. Nevertheless, there are encouraging signs as governments throughout the continent have embraced the microeconomic reform agenda. As a matter of fact, Ghana and Tanzania were among the top reformers in 2006. Simplification of business registration is the most popular reform. Reforms in the areas of property titling and registration have gained momentum.

Africa does not have a monopoly on bureaucracy and red tape. The number of days needed to start a business on average is 57, and the number varies widely: Denmark (4), Ireland (12), Malaysia (31), New Zealand (3), Singapore (8), South Africa (38), Switzerland (20), and Great Britain (18). It takes 14 steps to enforce a contract in Denmark, but Germany requires 26 steps. As concluded by the World Bank's International Finance Corp., "heavier regulation brings bad outcomes."[31]

WTO economists have analyzed the use and the impact of government support. While some subsidies are beneficial and offset the negative externalities of economic activity, others can be damaging. As commented by Pascal Lamy, Director-General of the WTO,

> One significant part of our Doha round negotiations involves reducing subsidies which distort trade while encouraging governments to use other forms of support which can facilitate development and environmental protection. Shifting support in this way is politically difficult and requires determination and courage, but the evidence is clear that such reforms can level the playing field and provide real rewards across the board.[32]

Regardless of the inappropriateness or injustice of many of these practices, they are part of international marketing. Although nations have used the WTO to lessen many of these restrictions, many restrictions will undoubtedly remain. In fact, most countries in recent years have initiated more protective measures. Since an international marketer has no control over these wide-reaching forces, the best defense is to understand and to be knowledgable about these trade practices. These barriers may be frustrating but are not necessarily insurmountable. By understanding them, the marketer can learn what to expect and how to cope (see Legal Dimension 3.1). One must always remember that additional problems are often accompanied by additional opportunities – for additional profits.

## Legal Dimension 3.1

### Green fuels: how sweet it is

Sugar-cane is better than corn as a base for ethanol. In addition, as corn is switched to the production of ethanol, the price of corn has risen, adversely affecting livestock and poultry farmers who need corn to feed their animals. In a world free of trade barriers, the U.S.A. would be importing ethanol from Brazil. Brazil produces sugar-cane ethanol, and it is among the world's lowest cost producers. Brazil's cost of about 90 cents a gallon is about two-thirds of the cost of corn ethanol.

Unfortunately, the world is not free, and the U.S.A. imposes a tariff of 54 cents a gallon on imported ethanol, in effect until the year 2010. Fortunately, there is a way to circumvent the barrier. Caribbean Basin countries are allowed to export certain products to the U.S.A. duty free as long as such products originate or are "substantially transformed" there. Caribbean companies though are not likely to make ethanol from their own sugar-cane. It is more cost effective for them to import ethanol from Brazil and then process it before shipping it to the U.S. market. To qualify, Caribbean firms dehydrate the ethanol from its original state, and American refiners then add gasoline to make the fuel usable. The dehydrating step substantially transforms products.

Archer-Daniels-Midland Co., a grain giant, is the largest ethanol producer in the U.S.A., and it markets corn-based ethanol. ADM is considering the possibility of producing ethanol in Brazil. It may ship Brazilian ethanol to Caribbean countries first so as to take advantage of the duty-free arrangement.

*Sources*: "Ethanol Tariff Loophole Sparks a Boom in Caribbean," *Wall Street Journal*, March 9, 2007; and "ADM Plans Entry into Sugar-cane Ethanol in Brazil," *Wall Street Journal*, June 22, 2007.

## Questions

1 Explain the rationale and discuss the weaknesses of each of these arguments for the protection of local industries: (a) keeping money at home, (b) reducing unemployment, (c) equalizing cost and price, (d) enhancing national security, and (e) protecting infant industry.

2 Distinguish between these types of tariffs: (a) import and export tariffs, (b) protective and revenue tariffs, (c) surcharge and countervailing duty, and (d) specific and *ad valorem* duties.
3 Explain how these distribution/consumption taxes differ from one another: single-stage, value-added, cascade, and excise taxes.
4 Explain these various forms of government participation in trade: administrative guidance, subsidies, and state trading.
5 Other than cash, what are the various forms of subsidies?
6 Explain these customs and entry procedures and discuss how each one can be used deliberately to restrict imports: (a) product classification, (b) product valuation, (c) documentation, (d) license/permit, (e) inspection, and (f) health and safety regulations.
7 Explain these various types of product requirements and discuss how each one can be used deliberately to restrict imports: (a) product standards, (b) packaging, labeling, and marking, (c) product testing, and (d) product specifications.
8 What is the rationale for an export quota?
9 Distinguish these types of import quotas: (a) absolute, (b) tariff, (c) OMA, and (d) VER.
10 Discuss how these financial control methods adversely affect free trade: exchange control, multiple exchange rates, prior import deposits, credit restrictions, and profit remittance restrictions.
11 What is WTO? What is its purpose?
12 What is GSP?
13 On January 11, 2007, Vietnam joined the WTO as its 150th member. The entry requires Vietnam to reduce import barriers. It has agreed to bound tariff rates or legal ceilings on most products between zero and 35 percent. Even so, tariffs on cars and motorcycles will be higher, and such sensitive products as eggs, tobacco, sugar, and salt will be subject to tariff quotas. Discuss the benefits and problems of Vietnam's global integration in terms of both the internal and external markets (i.e., imports and exports).

## Discussion assignments and minicases

1 If the simple existence of government can distort trade inside and outside of its area, should governments be abolished in order to eliminate trade distortion?
2 Will tariffs play a more significant role than nontariff barriers during the 2000s in affecting world trade?
3 Discuss how you can overcome the financial control imposed by the host country.
4 Do you agree that the WTO has served a useful purpose and has achieved its goals?
5 Should the advanced economies continue the GSP system?
6 How should MNCs generally cope with trade barriers?
7 A value-added tax (VAT) is a multistage, noncumulative tax on consumption, and it is levied at each stage of the production and distribution system. At the retail level, a retailer sends VAT payments to the government only on the value it adds to a particular product (i.e., its markup).

The balance of the VAT on that product is remitted to the government by all other registered firms involved in the production of any inputs used in making or distributing that product. Each party's responsibility is in proportion to its share in the total value-added embodied in the final product. Because all the firms involved in the production and distribution will be fully reimbursed by means of successive VAT tax credits, consumers are the ones ultimately bearing the entire VAT liability.

Some U.S. government officials and elected officials have advocated the adoption of the European VAT system for revenue and balance of trade reasons. What is their reasoning? Do you agree with their position? Will VAT enhance U.S. trade competitiveness? Will it discourage tax avoidance and evasion?

8 Presumably a statement of fact, foreign subsidies are supposed to be both unfair and harmful to the U.S. economy. Any American politicians would be foolish to argue otherwise. Do you agree with the conventional wisdom that foreign subsidies are unfair? Are subsidies harmful to the U.S.A.? How should the U.S.A. deal with imported products which are subsidized?

9 As in many countries, the cigarette market in Thailand is a regulated and largely monopolistic one. A quasi-government agency was granted an exclusive right to manufacture and market cigarettes. The U.S. Cigarette Export Association complained that Thailand's discriminatory acts and policies created barriers in the sale of foreign cigarettes. As a result, American firms lost at least $166 million in exports annually. The Association filed a petition under Section 301 of the U.S. trade law, thus instigating the U.S. Trade Representative's investigation. Subsequently, American trade negotiators put a great deal of pressure on the Thai government. Eventually, Thailand was forced to reluctantly open its cigarette market to imports in 1990. Do you agree with the U.S. government's involvement in pressuring other countries to open their markets to American products in general and American tobacco products in particular?

## Notes

1 *2003 National Trade Estimate Report on Foreign Trade Barriers*, U.S. Trade Representative, 2003.
2 "Farming for Dollars," *Wall Street Journal*, July 6, 2007.
3 Hans Peter Lankes, "Market Access for Developing Countries," *Finance & Development* (September 2002): 8–13.
4 "The Truth about Industrial Country Tariffs," *Finance & Development* (September 2002): 14–15.
5 "Harley Hits 100," *San José Mercury News*, August 31, 2003.
6 Liam Ebrill *et al.*, *The Modern VAT*, IMF, 2001, and Liam Ebrill *et al.*, "The Allure of the Value-added Tax," *Finance & Development* (June 2002): 44–7.
7 "How Can Central American Countries Improve Their Tax System?", *IMF Survey*, March 17, 2003, 70–1.
8 "How Can Central American Countries."
9 "Tariff Reductions Aren't Enough," *Asian Wall Street Journal*, June 19, 2001.
10 "U.S. Attacks Use of Non-tariff Barriers," *The AFTA Monitor*, May 15, 2002.
11 "Banned by the WTO, Corporate America Is Scrambling," *Business Week*, March 20, 2000, 118.
12 "Rethinking Fuel Subsidies," *IMF Survey*, January 15, 2007, 14.
13 "WTO Trade Talks Are Deadlocked Over Concessions," *Asian Wall Street Journal*, July 15, 2003.
14 "Rich Countries Urged to Lead by Example on Trade Access," *IMF Survey*, October 21, 2002, 321–3.
15 "UNCTAD Stresses Gap Between Nations," *San José Mercury News*, February 16, 2000.
16 "China Confronts Crisis Over Food Safety," *Wall Street Journal*, May 30, 2007; and "FDA Blocks Imports of Chinese Toothpaste," *Wall Street Journal*, May 24, 2007.

17 "Stop Feeding the Losers, Toyota," *Business Week*, January 13, 2003, 48.

18 "Delegates from Poorer Nations Walk Out of World Trade Talks," *New York Times*, September 15, 2003; and "Coming U.S. Vote Figures in Walkout at Trade Talks," *New York Times*, September 16, 2003.

19 "Brazil, Others Push Outside Doha for Trade Pacts," *Wall Street Journal*, July 5, 2007.

20 "WTO Accession Will Help Vietnam Strengthen Economy," *IMF Survey*, January 29, 2007, 23.

21 "Do We Really Know That the WTO Increases Trade?", *IMF Survey*, August 18, 2003, 243–5.

22 Lankes, "Market Access."

23 "Thais Urged to Plan for Loss of Tariff Breaks," *Bangkok Post*, April 16, 2002.

24 "Structural Policies Shift in Developing Countries," *IMF Survey*, February 6, 1995, 45–6.

25 "Brazil and Korea: Good Policies Matter," *IMF Survey*, May 22, 1995, 161–3.

26 Robert Sharer, "An Agenda for Trade, Investment, and Regional Integration," *Finance & Development* (December 2001): 14–17.

27 "Trade and Finance Links Warrant Closer Attention," *IMF Survey*, September 16, 2002, 273–6.

28 Shang-Jin Wei, "Is Globalization Good for the Poor in China?", *Finance & Development* (September 2002): 26–9.

29 Andrew Berg and Anne Krueger, "Lifting All Boats," *Finance & Development* (September 2002): 16–19.

30 Michael Klein, "Taking Care of Business," *Finance & Development* (December 2006): 30–3.

31 "In Search of Fair Business Climes," *Forbes Global*, July 26, 2004, 48.

32 *World Trade Report 2006.*

Part 2

# World market environment

Chapter 4

# Political environment

In an authoritarian state, it is only the prisoner of conscience who is genuinely free.

Nobel laureate, Aung San Suu Kyi

## Chapter outline

- Marketing strategy: the Indian Bengals of information services
- Multiplicity of political environments
- Types of government: political systems
- Types of government: economic systems
- Political risks
- Privatization
- Indicators of political instability
  - Attitudes of nationals
  - Policies of the host government
- Analysis of political risk or country risk
- Management of political risk
- Measures to minimize political risk
  - Stimulation of the local economy
  - Employment of nationals
  - Sharing ownership
  - Being civic minded
  - Political neutrality
  - Behind-the-scenes lobby
  - Observation of political mood and reduction of exposure
  - Other measures

- Political insurance
  - Private insurance
  - Government insurance
  - MIGA
- Conclusion
- Case 4.1: Toyota: how to win friends and influence people

## Marketing strategy

### The Indian Bengals of information services

With more than 1.1 billion people, India is the world's second most populous nation. After decades of economic mismanagement, India is making up for lost time. The economy is hot, and incomes are rising rapidly. The country is also young. India has more than 115 million teenagers (between 15 and 21 years old), more than anywhere else on Earth.

In the late 1970s, India passed new rules that required foreign computer companies to operate through Indian-owned affiliates. IBM reacted to the regulations by quitting its Indian operations. Wipro Ltd, once a peanut oil company, took advantage of the situation by entering the computer market. However, by the early 1990s, the Indian government began liberalizing the economy and relaxed the rules (including the local-partner requirement). The world's top technology companies rushed in. Wipro, facing fierce competition, had to reinvent itself. The competitive threat was a blessing in disguise when Wipro successfully emerged as a technology services powerhouse. It now sells engineering expertise to the world's top technology firms. Part of the success of the company may be attributed to its hunger and work ethic.

Indian software service providers account for 26 percent of the market for the development and maintenance of such applications as updating the payroll software. Infosys Technologies, with 70 percent of its workforce being based in India, generates 98 percent of its revenues from abroad. While it took Infosys 23 years to reach $1 billion in annual revenue, the $2 billion mark was achieved two years later. Starting out with $250 and a few engineers, Infosys has become an outsourcing powerhouse. It does work for Airbus, Boeing, Goldman Sachs, Apple Computer, and Cisco Systems.

To capitalize on India's engineering skills, IBM and Oracle are among numerous technology firms that have gone to India and grabbed qualified engineers. In three years, IBM's workforce in India jumped from 9000 to 43,000.

In spite of India's booming economy and its expanding role in world business, India has a long way to go. The country's infrastructure is a mess due to six decades of politics and underinvestment. On the bright side, both the government and the private sector have finally plowed money into infrastructure. It is not a subject of debate that India is an important player in the $650 billion worldwide technology services industry.

*Sources*: "Young, Rich and Restless," *Business Today*, December 31, 2006, 96–100; "How This Tiger Got Its Roar," *Business Week*, October 30, 2006, 92–100; "Outsourcing Giant Infosys Believes It's the New Model for Global Business," *San José Mercury News*, December 5, 2006; and "The Trouble with India," *Business Week*, March 19, 2007, 49–58.

## Purpose of chapter

Whether political interests precede or follow economic interests is debatable, but certainly the two are closely interrelated. A country or company may play politics in order to pursue its economic interests, but economic means may also be used to achieve the political objectives.

Often, politics and economics do not mix well. For a very long time, the U.S.A. imposed economic censure against Vietnam. While the economic sanction was achieving the desired goal of adversely affecting international investment and trade with Vietnam, Asian and European companies took advantage of the absence of American firms and entered the market. Vietnam is an attractive market – not just for its market size and natural resources but also for other economic reasons. Vietnam welcomes foreign investment in all economic sectors (except defense industries), offers generous tax concessions and duty exemptions, allows 100 percent foreign ownership, imposes no minimum capital requirement, and promises the unrestricted repatriation of capital and profits. In addition, the political climate has greatly improved. The U.S. government finally permitted American companies to enter the Vietnamese market in the mid-1990s.

The economic interests of MNCs can differ widely from the economic interests of the countries in which these firms do business. A lack of convergent interests often exists between a company's home country and its various host countries. In the absence of mutual interests, political pressures can lead to political decisions, resulting in laws and proclamations that affect business. The experiences of IBM and Wipro in India provide an introduction to the political and legal dimensions of international business. Such efforts also show that political risks, thought to be largely uncontrollable, can nevertheless be reasonably managed. It is thus important to understand the role of political risk in international marketing and its impact on each of the four Ps of marketing.

This chapter examines the interrelationships among political, legal, and business decisions. The discussion will focus on how the political climate affects the investment climate. Among political topics covered are forms of government, indicators of political instability, and political risks. The chapter ends with the investigation of strategies used to manage political risks.

## Multiplicity of political environments

The political environment that MNCs face is a complex one because they must cope with the politics of more than one nation. That complexity forces MNCs to consider the three different types of political environment: foreign, domestic, and international.

Although political and economic motives are two distinct components, they are often highly intertwined. A country may use economic sanctions to make a political statement. Likewise, a political action may be taken so as to enhance the country's economic prospects. It is also hardly uncommon for governments as well as companies to ignore politics for the purpose of economic interests. Even while the economic sanctions were in place, the U.S.A. was actually importing a large amount of oil from Iraq. While Taiwan and China are supposedly enemies which do not want to do business with one another, the truth of the matter is that there are some 50,000 Taiwanese-owned factories in China. Since the early 1990s, Taiwanese companies have invested more than $100 billion there.[1]

Although the benefits of foreign investment far outweigh the costs, developing countries often view foreign firms and foreign capital investment with distrust and even resentment, owing primarily to a concern over potential foreign exploitation of local natural resources. Developed countries themselves are also concerned about foreign investment. Many Americans have expressed their concern that the increasing foreign ownership of American assets poses a threat to their country's national security, both politically and economically. In 2005, there was a political uproar when state-owned Chinese oil company Cnooc Ltd. attempted to buy California-based oil giant Unocal. A much bigger uproar ensued in 2006 when a Dubai-owned company attempted to buy operations at five American ports.

In some cases, the opposition to imported goods and foreign investment is based on moral principle. For example, the citizens of many nations pressured companies in their countries not to invest in South Africa because of that country's policy of apartheid. In the mid-1980s, the pressure became so great that the South African government ran advertisements in the United States in an attempt to minimize damage, as shown in Figure 4.1.

Regardless of whether the politics are foreign, domestic, or international, the company should keep in mind that political climate does not remain stationary. The political relationship between the U.S.A. and a long-time adversary, China, is a prime example. After decades as bitter enemies, both countries became very interested in improving their political and economic ties so as to dilute the power of the Soviet Union. However, in 2007, China and Russia conducted a joint military exercise to show the neighboring countries that China and Russia could counter the military power of the U.S.A.

Although most companies have little control in affecting changes in international politics, they must be prepared to respond to new developments. Companies can derive positive economic benefits when the relationship between two countries improves or when the host government adopts a new investment policy. As in the case of India, the country was a highly regulated, closed economy which discouraged foreign investment. It was not until 1991 that a new government began a reform program which could transform India into one of the world's most dynamic economies.

On the other hand, serious problems can develop when political conditions deteriorate. A favorable investment climate can disappear almost overnight. In one case, the U.S.A. withdrew Chile's duty-free trade status because of Chile's failure to take "steps to afford internationally recognized worker rights." Chile thus joined Romania, Nicaragua, and Paraguay in being suspended from the GSP (Generalized System of Preferences).

## Types of government: political systems

A knowledge of the form governments may take can be useful in appraising the political climate. One way to classify governments is to consider them as either parliamentary (open) or absolutist (closed). Table 4.1 shows the political features of oil-exporting nations.

**Parliamentary** governments consult with citizens from time to time for the purpose of learning about opinions and preferences. Government policies are thus intended to reflect the desire of the majority segment of the society. Most industrialized nations and all democratic nations may be classified as parliamentary.

At the other end of the spectrum are absolutist governments, which include monarchies and dictatorships. In an **absolutist** system, the ruling regime dictates government policy without

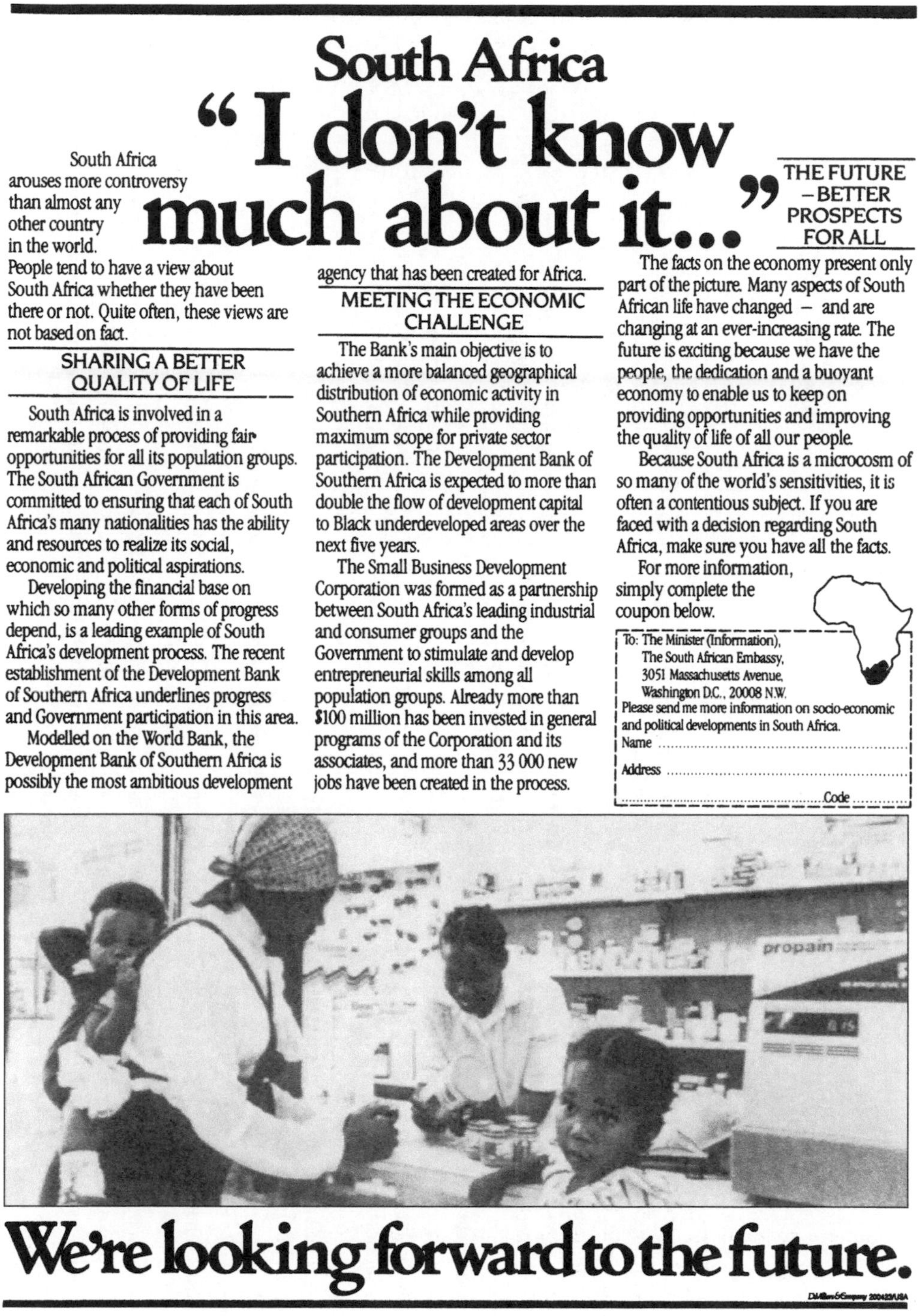
South Africa
" I don't know much about it..."
South Africa arouses more controversy than almost any other country in the world.
People tend to have a view about South Africa whether they have been there or not. Quite often, these views are not based on fact.
SHARING A BETTER QUALITY OF LIFE
South Africa is involved in a remarkable process of providing fair opportunities for all its population groups. The South African Government is committed to ensuring that each of South Africa's many nationalities has the ability and resources to realize its social, economic and political aspirations.
Developing the financial base on which so many other forms of progress depend, is a leading example of South Africa's development process. The recent establishment of the Development Bank of Southern Africa underlines progress and Government participation in this area.
Modelled on the World Bank, the Development Bank of Southern Africa is possibly the most ambitious development agency that has been created for Africa.
MEETING THE ECONOMIC CHALLENGE
The Bank's main objective is to achieve a more balanced geographical distribution of economic activity in Southern Africa while providing maximum scope for private sector participation. The Development Bank of Southern Africa is expected to more than double the flow of development capital to Black underdeveloped areas over the next five years.
The Small Business Development Corporation was formed as a partnership between South Africa's leading industrial and consumer groups and the Government to stimulate and develop entrepreneurial skills among all population groups. Already more than $100 million has been invested in general programs of the Corporation and its associates, and more than 33 000 new jobs have been created in the process.
THE FUTURE – BETTER PROSPECTS FOR ALL
The facts on the economy present only part of the picture. Many aspects of South African life have changed – and are changing at an ever-increasing rate. The future is exciting because we have the people, the dedication and a buoyant economy to enable us to keep on providing opportunities and improving the quality of life of all our people.
Because South Africa is a microcosm of so many of the world's sensitivities, it is often a contentious subject. If you are faced with a decision regarding South Africa, make sure you have all the facts.
For more information, simply complete the coupon below.
To: The Minister (Information), The South African Embassy, 3051 Massachusetts Avenue, Washington D.C., 20008 N.W.
Please send me more information on socio-economic and political developments in South Africa.
Name
Address
Code
propain
We're looking forward to the future.

**FIGURE 4.1** South Africa: dealing with political pressure

*Source*: Reprinted with permission of the South African Consulate General.

**TABLE 4.1** Oil exporters' political systems. Classifying oil exporters.[1] The type of political system affects how oil revenue is spent.

| *Political features* | *Institutional implications* | *Economic implications* |
|---|---|---|
| **Mature democracy** | | |
| Stable party system | Long policy horizon | Saving likely |
| Range of social consensus | Policy stability, transparency | Expenditure smoothing, stabilization |
| Strong, competent, insulated bureaucracy | High competitiveness, low transaction costs | Rents transferred to public through government-provided social services and insurance or direct transfers |
| Competent, professional judicial system | Strong private/traded sector, prostabilization interests vis-à-vis prospending interests | |
| Highly educated electorate | | |
| **Factional democracy** | | |
| Government and parties often unstable relative to interest groups | Short policy horizon | Saving very difficult |
| Political support gained through clientelistic ties and provision of patronage | Policy instability, nontransparency, high transaction costs | Procyclical expenditure; instability |
| Wide social disparities, lack of consensus | Strong state role in production | Rents transferred to different interests and to public through subsidies, policy distortions, public employment |
| Politicized bureaucracy and judicial system | Strong interests attached directly to state expenditures; politically weak private non-oil sector and prostabilization interests | |
| **Paternalistic autocracy** | | |
| Stable government; legitimacy originally from traditional role, maintained through rent distribution | Long horizon | Procyclical expenditure, mixed success with stabilization |
| Strong cultural elements of consensus, clientelistic, and nationalistic patterns | Policy stability, nontransparency | Risk of unsustainable long-term spending |
| Bureaucracy provides both services and public employment | Low competitiveness, high transaction costs | trajectory leading to political crisis |
| | Strong state role in production | Little economic diversification |
| | Strong interests attached directly to state expenditures | |
| | Weak private sector | |

| | | |
|---|---|---|
| **Reformist autocracy** | | |
| Stable government, legitimized by development | Long horizon | Expenditure smoothing, stabilization |
| Social range of consensus toward development | Policy stability, nontransparency | State investment complementary to competitive private sector |
| Constituency in non-oil traded sectors | Drive for competitiveness, low transaction costs | Active exchange rate management to limit Dutch disease |
| Insulated technocracy | Strong constituency for stabilization and fiscal restraint | |
| **Predatory autocracy** | | |
| Unstable government, legitimized by military force | Short horizon | No saving |
| Lack of consensus-building mechanisms | Policy instability, nontransparency | Highly procyclical expenditure |
| Bureaucracy exists as mechanism of rent capture and distribution; corrupt judicial system | Low competitiveness, high transaction costs | Very high government consumption, rent absorption by elites through petty corruption and patronage, capital flight |
| Little or no civic counterweight | Spending interests strong vis-à-vis private sector or prostabilization interests | |

*Note*

[1] These classifications are not exhaustive, and some countries have a blend of features from different categories. For example, fiscal federalism is one factor cutting across the categories. The aim is not to create a rigid classification of oil countries but to help provide insights into the policy options available to governments. For use of a similar classification, see, for example, D. Lal, 1995, "Why Growth Rates Differ. The Political Economy of Social Capability in 21 Developing Countries," in *Social Capability and Long-Term Economic Growth*, edited by Bon Ho Koo and Dwight H. Perkins (New York, NY: St. Martin's Press).

*Source*: Benn Eifert, Alan Gelb, and Nils Borje Tallroth, "Managing Oil Wealth," *Finance & Development* (March 2003, 42).

considering citizens' needs or opinions. Frequently, absolutist countries are newly formed nations or those undergoing some kind of political transition. Absolute monarchies are now relatively rare. The United Kingdom is a good example of a constitutional hereditary monarchy; despite the monarch, the government is classified as parliamentary.

Many countries' political systems do not fall neatly into one of these two categories. Some monarchies and dictatorships (e.g., Saudi Arabia and North Korea) have parliamentary elections. The former Soviet Union had elections and mandatory voting but was not classified as parliamentary because the ruling party never allowed an alternative on the ballot. Countries such as the Philippines under Marcos and Nicaragua under Somoza held elections, but the results were suspect because of government involvement in voting fraud.

Another way to classify governments is by number of political parties. This classification results in four types of governments: two-party, multi-party, single-party, and dominated one-party.

In a **two-party** system, there are typically two strong parties that take turns controlling the government, although other parties are allowed. The U.S.A. and the United Kingdom are prime examples. The two parties generally have different philosophies, resulting in a change in government policy when one party succeeds the other. In the U.S.A., the Republican Party is often viewed as representing business interests, whereas the Democratic Party is often viewed as representing labor interests, as well as the poor and disaffected.

In a **multi-party** system, there are several political parties, none of which is strong enough to gain control of the government. Even though some parties may be large, their elected representatives fall short of a majority. A government must then be formed through coalitions between the various parties, each of which wants to protect its own interests. The longevity of the coalition depends largely on the cooperation of party partners. Usually, the coalition is continuously challenged by various opposing parties. A change in a few votes may be sufficient to bring the coalition government down. If the government does not survive a vote of no confidence (i.e., does not have the support of the majority of the representatives), the government is disbanded and a new election is called. Countries operating with this system include Germany, France, and Israel. In Africa, after decades of military governments, countries have been increasingly adopting multi-party political systems.[2]

In a **single-party** system, there may be several parties, but one party is so dominant that there is little opportunity for others to elect representatives to govern the country. Egypt has operated under single-party rule for several decades. This form of government is often used by countries in the early stages of the development of a true parliamentary system. Because the ruling party holds support from the vast majority, the system is not necessarily a poor one, especially when it can provide the stability and continuity necessary for rapid growth. But when serious economic problems persist, citizens' dissatisfaction and frustration may create an explosive situation. For example, Mexico was ruled since its revolution by the institutional Revolutionary Party (PRI). Economic problems caused dissatisfaction with the PRI in the 1980s, and the National Action Party (PAN), Mexico's main opposition party, began gaining strength.

In a **dominated one-party** system, the dominant party does not allow any opposition, resulting in no alternative for the people. In contrast, a single-party system does allow some opposition parties. Cuba, Libya, North Korea, and China are good examples of dominated one-party systems. Such a system may easily transform itself into a dictatorship. The party, to maintain its power, is prepared to use force or any necessary means to eliminate the introduction and growth of other parties. Such countries as Burma and Cambodia have tried to reject outside influences, and it is no accident that they were or are among the most repressive regimes.

In addition, countries' electoral systems may be either majoritarianism or proportionality. In the case of **majoritarianism**, a country is ruled by a simple numerical majority in an organized group. **Proportionality** occurs when the number of parliamentary seats is based on vote share. Research shows that spending on social security and welfare is lower under majoritarian systems. In contrast, "certain political factors, such as an electoral system that emphasizes proportionality or a fragmented parliament or government, lead simultaneously to higher transfers, bigger government, and a revenue system that emphasizes labor taxes over consumption taxes."[3]

One should not be hasty in making generalizations about the ideal form of government in terms of political stability. It may be tempting to believe that stability is a function of economic development. Italy, a developed country, has been beset with internal and external problems. The political atmosphere is marred from time to time by a weak economy, recurring labor unrest, and internal dissension. In contrast, it may be argued that Vietnam, despite being a developing economy, is politically more stable. This stability is due in part to Vietnam's relatively closed economy.

It may be just as tempting to conclude that a democratic political system is a prerequisite for political stability. India, the world's largest democracy, possesses a solid political infrastructure and political institutions that have withstood many crises over time. The democratic system is strongly established in India, and it is almost inconceivable that the Indians would choose any other system. Yet India's political stability is hampered by regional, ethnic, language, religious, and economic problems. Unlike such other democratic nations as Australia, where such problems have largely been resolved, India's difficulties remain. These geographic, ideological, and ethnic problems inhibit the government's ability to respond to one sector's demands without alienating others.

Democracy does not guarantee peace. When religious fundamentalists won elections in Algeria, Indonesia, Nigeria, and Pakistan, violence followed. Yugoslavia's citizens appeared to endorse Slobodan Milosevic's policy of ethnic cleansing. Adolf Hitler's rise to power was the result of a free vote. On the other hand, some authoritarian rulers may be more progressive than their followers. While Suharto was in power, his authoritarian style, rightly or wrongly, brought ethnic peace and strong economic growth. Free elections have given rise to anti-American Muslim extremists, Christians being killed, and declining growth. It is debatable whether elections in Egypt, Jordan, Pakistan, and Saudi Arabia will make the countries better off if fundamentalists come to power.[4]

Dictatorial systems, monarchies, and oligarchies may be able to provide great stability for a country, especially one with a relatively closed society, which exists in many communist countries and Arab nations. If a country's ruler and military are strong, any instability that may occur can be kept under control. The problem, however, is that such systems frequently exist in a divided society where dissident groups are waiting for an opportunity to challenge the regime. When a ruler suddenly dies, the risk of widespread disruption and revolution can be quite high.

Democracy itself is not a perfect system. Japan's multi-year recession was caused in part by its divided, ineffective government. India continues to cope with chaos because of a coalition of a dozen fractured parties that runs the government. While representative democracy is generally a good thing, it can create an explosive situation when democracy is combined with capitalism to create "market-dominant minorities." The ethnic Chinese, for example, constitute 1 percent of the Philippines population but control 60 percent of the country's wealth, while two-thirds of the ethnic Filipinos struggle on less than $2 a day. The oppressed majority may violently strike back at the easily identified ethnic minority group (e.g., the ethnic Chinese in the Philippines and Indonesia, the Lebanese in West Africa, the Asian Indians in East Africa, the Jews in Russia, and the whites in Zimbabwe, the indigenous Ibo tribe in Nigeria, and the Tutsi tribe in Rwanda).[5]

Policy makers naturally want to know whether there is a direct relationship between democracy and economic progress. Latin America and Eastern Europe have moved in the democratic direction, and democracies have done relatively well in economic reform. Econometric results also point in the same direction.[6]

## Types of government: economic systems

Economic systems provide another basis for classification of governments. These systems serve to explain whether businesses are privately owned or government owned, or whether there is a combination of private and government ownership. Some people have argued that economic freedom is just as important as democracy.

Basically, three systems may be identified: communism, socialism, and capitalism. Based on the degree of government control of business activity, the various economic systems can be placed along a continuum, with communism at one end and capitalism at another. A movement towards communism is accompanied by an increase in government interference and more control of factors of production. A movement towards capitalism is accompanied by an increase in private ownership.

**Communist theory** holds that all resources should be owned and shared by all the people (i.e., not by profit-seeking enterprises) for the benefit of the society. In practice, it is the government that controls all productive assets and industries and, as a result, the government determines jobs, production, price, education, and just about anything else. The emphasis is on human welfare. Because profit making is not the government's main motive, there is a lack of incentive for workers and managers to improve productivity.

The term **centrally planned economies** is often used to refer to the former Soviet Union, Eastern European countries, China, Vietnam, and North Korea. These economies tend to have the following characteristics: a communist philosophy, an active government role in economic planning, a non-market economy, a weak economy, large foreign debt, and rigid and bureaucratic political/economic systems. A contrast between North Korea and South Korea is quite striking. While North Korea's economy has contracted, South Korea's economy has been booming. South Korea's GDP dwarfs that of North Korea. North Korea's exports are only a fraction of South Korea's exports. It should be noted that North Korea is much better endowed than its southern counterpart in terms of natural resources.

Despite communist countries' preoccupation with control of industries, it would be an error to conclude that all communist governments are exactly alike. Although the former Soviet Union and China adhered to the same basic ideology, there was a marked difference between these two largest communist nations. China has been experimenting with a new type of communism by allowing its citizens to work for themselves and to keep any profit in the process. Yet one must remember that "free markets" can exist in China only with the state's permission, and the operations of such markets are still overseen by government officials.

The degree of government control that occurs under **socialism** is somewhat less than under communism. A socialist government owns and operates the basic, major industries but leaves small businesses to private ownership. Socialism is a matter of degree, and not all socialist countries are the same. A socialist country such as Poland at one time leaned toward communism, as evidenced by its rigid control over prices, and distribution. France's socialist system, in comparison, is much closer to capitalism than it is to communism.

At the opposite end of the continuum from communism is capitalism. The philosophy of **capitalism** provides for a *free-market* system that allows business competition and freedom of choice for both consumers and companies. It is a *market-oriented* system in which individuals, motivated by private gain, are allowed to produce goods or services for public consumption under competitive conditions. Product price is determined by demand and supply. This system serves the needs of society by encouraging decentralized decision making, risk taking, and innovation. The results include product variety, product quality, efficiency, and relatively lower prices.

As with the other two economic systems, there are degrees of capitalism. Japan, when compared to the United States, is relatively less capitalistic. Although practically all Japanese businesses are privately owned, industries are very closely supervised by the state. Japan has the MITI and other government agencies that vigorously advise companies what to produce, buy, sell, and so on. Japan's aim is to allocate scarce resources in such a way as to efficiently produce those products that have the best potential for the country overall. Japan's central bank also intervenes by buying shares of the listed companies from banks so as to manipulate the stock market.

In search of the common characteristics of successful corporations, Chandler examined the 200 largest companies in the United States, Britain, and Germany from the 1880s through the 1940s and found that capitalism adopted a different form in each country.[7] "*Managerial capitalism*" took place in the U.S.A., where managers with little ownership ran companies and competed fiercely for markets and products. In Britain, "*personal capitalism*" took place as owners managed their companies. In Germany, it was "*cooperative capitalism*;" professional managers were in charge, and companies were urged to share markets and profits among themselves. This kind of Rhineland capitalism attempts to forge social consensus through behind-the-scenes deal making among big business, trade unions, and politicians. However, global competition is now threatening this type of cooperation.

Baumol, Litan, and Schramm have identified four major variations of capitalism. First, *state-guided capitalism* is based on a government's attempt to pick winners by supporting chosen industries. Second, *oligarchic capitalism* is where a small group of individuals and families control a large proportion of power and wealth. Third, in the case of *big-firm capitalism*, giant enterprises carry out the major economic activities. Finally, with regard to *entrepreneurial capitalism*, small and innovative companies play a significant role. Most countries rely on some blend of at least two of these models of capitalism, and the blend may change over time. For example, Russia has moved first from communism to oligarchy and now towards authoritarian state-guided capitalism. Of the four economic models, oligarchic capitalism is the worst in terms of performance. State-guided capitalism may perform well for a while but not in the long term. The blend of big-firm capitalism and entrepreneurial capitalism looks the best.[8]

Dunning has proposed the concept of *Responsible Global Capitalism*, an inclusive system that includes individuals, companies, nongovernment organizations, governments, and supranational agencies.[9] The Indian philosophy, called *karma capitalism* by *Business Week* magazine, has gained popularity in the West, and its theme is that companies should take a more holistic approach to business by considering the needs of shareholders, workers, customers, society, and the environment.[10] Both types of capitalism mentioned above are similar to the concept of cooperative capitalism. On the other hand, Jack Welch, the former CEO of General Electric, feels strongly that shareholders must be emphasized and that it would be a mistake for a company to start reacting to the various stakeholders.[11]

There are some other variants of capitalism. Quebec has state-assisted capitalism as the government runs the health system, all colleges and universities, liquor stores, and even a parking monopoly in downtown Montreal. While Quebecers seems to endorse the idea that the government is looking after their economic interests, they do not realize that there are hidden costs in terms of higher taxes, higher prices, and lost economic output.

In the case of China, Russia, Cambodia, and Vietnam, their economic system can be called *frontier capitalism*. These communist or socialist countries are essentially at a new frontier as they experiment with capitalism. Government agencies themselves may even be involved in production for profit. While they are moving away from communism, their capitalistic infrastructure is not quite in place yet. It is thus difficult for anyone, including the government, to tell with certainty whether the property rights of local and foreign investors will be respected. Business laws simply fail to keep up with economic changes.

At a new frontier are China's economic and legal systems. The Chinese legal system was discarded following the 1949 Communist Revolution that sent attorneys and law professors to farm collectives. At present, China's rule of law is quite rudimentary. Private business contracts are routinely enforced by bureaucrats who rely on government directives rather than on written case laws. Regulations are largely unpublished.

Similarly, Russia is representative of transition economies. It is difficult to verify and enforce contracts there. Private property rights are neither secure nor credible. Given the lack of efficient methods for resolving commercial disputes, market entry costs increase substantially. Even when one wins in court, it is difficult to collect debts due to a notoriously weak enforcement system. Not surprisingly, most businesspeople, instead of taking their cases to the overburdened courts, prefer to try to resolve any disputes among themselves. In addition, oligarchy is common in Russia. Unfortunately, a study has shown that greater oligarchic family control over large corporations correlates with bureaucracy, government intervention, price controls, and the lack of shareholder rights. Thus, society is worse off when wealthy families own the large corporate sectors.[12]

No nation operates under pure communism or pure capitalism, and most countries find it necessary to reach some compromise between the two extremes. Even Eastern Bloc countries provide incentives for their managers, and China allows farmers to sell directly to consumers in local markets. Western European countries encourage free enterprise but intervene to provide support and subsidies for steel and farm products. The U.S.A. is also not a perfect model of capitalism. It has support prices for many dairy and farm products and has imposed price controls from time to time. Furthermore, the U.S. economy is greatly affected by the Federal Reserve Board's control of the money supply and interest rates. *Laissez-faire*, the purest form of capitalism, is rare. In any case, there are no nations that allow businesses to be completely controlled by either the private or public sector.

Perhaps the only place that bears a strong resemblance to an ideal free trade market is Hong Kong. It does not even have a central bank, and the legal tender notes are issued by private commercial banks. In 2006, based on the work of the Washington-based Heritage Foundation, Hong Kong retained the highest ranking for economic freedom (see Table 4.2). Hong Kong is followed by Singapore, New Zealand, Switzerland, and the U.S.A. The Heritage Foundation's index uses ten criteria (e.g., government policies toward trade, taxation, foreign investment, and money supply) to determine how far a government interferes in economic freedom. The Washington-based Cato Institute also gave first place to Hong Kong. Cato's index, based on an economic freedom scale ranging from one to ten, relies on economic variables (e.g., inflation stability, tax rates, government spending) and social indicators (e.g., legal fairness and freedom to open a foreign bank account).

*Doing Business* was launched in 2004. This report ranks 175 economies in terms of the ease of doing business. The 2006 report, focusing on regulatory reform, examines 213 reforms in more than 100

**TABLE 4.2** Index of Economic Freedom

| *Country* | *Rank [Freedom %]* | | | | | | | |
|---|---|---|---|---|---|---|---|---|
| **Hong Kong** | **1** | [89.3] | **Bahamas** | **25** | [71.4] | **Panama** | **47** | [65.9] |
| **Singapore** | **2** | [85.7] | **Austria** | **25** | [71.3] | **Malaysia** | **48** | [65.8] |
| **Australia** | **3** | [82.7] | **Taiwan** | **26** | [71.1] | **Mexico** | **49** | [65.8] |
| **United States** | **4** | [82.0] | **Spain** | **27** | [70.9] | **Thailand** | **50** | [65.6] |
| **New Zealand** | **5** | [81.6] | **Barbados** | **28** | [70.5] | **Costa Rica** | **51** | [65.1] |
| **United Kingdom** | **6** | [81.6] | **El Salvador** | **29** | [70.3] | **South Africa** | **52** | [64.1] |
| **Ireland** | **7** | [81.3] | **Norway** | **30** | [70.1] | **Jordan** | **53** | [64.0] |
| **Luxembourg** | **8** | [79.3] | **Czech Republic** | **31** | [69.7] | **Oman** | **54** | [63.9] |
| **Switzerland** | **9** | [79.1] | **Armenia** | **32** | [69.4] | **Namibia** | **55** | [63.8] |
| **Canada** | **10** | [78.7] | **Uruguay** | **33** | [69.3] | **Belize** | **56** | [63.7] |
| **Chile** | **11** | [78.3] | **Mauritius** | **34** | [69.0] | **Kuwait** | **57** | [63.7] |
| **Estonia** | **12** | [78.1] | **Georgia** | **35** | [68.7] | **Slovenia** | **58** | [63.6] |
| **Denmark** | **13** | [77.6] | **Korea, South** | **36** | [68.6] | **Uganda** | **59** | [63.4] |
| **Netherlands** | **14** | [77.1] | **Israel** | **37** | [68.4] | **Italy** | **60** | [63.4] |
| **Iceland** | **15** | [77.1] | **Botswana** | **38** | [68.4] | **Nicaragua** | **61** | [62.7] |
| **Finland** | **16** | [76.5] | **Bahrain** | **39** | [68.4] | **Bulgaria** | **62** | [62.2] |
| **Belgium** | **17** | [74.5] | **Slovak Republic, The** | **40** | [68.4] | **Peru** | **63** | [62.1] |
| **Japan** | **18** | [73.6] | **Latvia** | **41** | [68.2] | **Swaziland** | **64** | [61.6] |
| **Germany** | **19** | [73.5] | **Malta** | **42** | [67.8] | **Madagascar** | **65** | [61.4] |
| **Cyprus** | **20** | [73.1] | **Portugal** | **43** | [66.7] | **Albania** | **66** | [61.4] |
| **Sweden** | **21** | [72.6] | **Hungary** | **44** | [66.2] | **Romania** | **67** | [61.3] |
| **Lithuania** | **22** | [72.0] | **France** | **45** | [66.1] | **Guatemala** | **68** | [61.2] |
| **Trinidad and Tobago** | **23** | [71.4] | **Jamaica** | **46** | [66.1] | **Tunisia** | **69** | [61.0] |

**TABLE 4.2** *continued*

| *Country* | *Rank [Freedom %]* | | | | |
|---|---|---|---|---|---|
| **Brazil** | **70** [60.9] | **Cambodia** | **102** [56.5] | **Suriname** | **133** [52.6] |
| **Macedonia** | **71** [60.8] | **Tanzania** | **103** [56.4] | **Algeria** | **134** [52.2] |
| **Qatar** | **72** [60.7] | **India** | **104** [55.6] | **Haiti** | **135** [52.2] |
| **Colombia** | **73** [60.5] | **Ivory Coast** | **105** [55.5] | **Rwanda** | **136** [52.1] |
| **United Arab Emirates** | **74** [60.4] | **Malawi** | **106** [55.5] | **Central African Republic** | **137** [50.3] |
| **Kazakhstan** | **75** [60.4] | **Azerbaijan** | **107** [55.4] | **Vietnam** | **138** [50.0] |
| **Honduras** | **76** [60.3] | **Ecuador** | **108** [55.3] | **Togo** | **139** [49.8] |
| **Lebanon** | **77** [60.3] | **Croatia** | **109** [55.3] | **Laos** | **140** [49.1] |
| **Mongolia** | **78** [60.1] | **Indonesia** | **110** [55.1] | **Sierra Leone** | **141** [48.4] |
| **Kyrgyz Republic, The** | **79** [59.9] | **Guinea** | **111** [55.1] | **Syria** | **142** [48.2] |
| **Fiji** | **80** [59.8] | **Bolivia** | **112** [55.0] | **Bangladesh** | **143** [47.8] |
| **Moldova** | **81** [59.5] | **Burkina Faso** | **113** [55.0] | **Venezuela** | **144** [47.7] |
| **Kenya** | **82** [59.4] | **Benin** | **114** [54.8] | **Belarus** | **145** [47.4] |
| **Turkey** | **83** [59.3] | **Bosnia and Herzegovina** | **115** [54.7] | **Burundi** | **146** [46.8] |
| **Sri Lanka** | **84** [59.3] | **Ethiopia** | **116** [54.4] | **Chad** | **147** [46.4] |
| **Saudi Arabia** | **85** [59.1] | | | | |

| | | | | | | | | |
|---|---|---|---|---|---|---|---|---|
| **Senegal** | **86** | [58.8] | **Cameroon** | **117** | [54.4] | **Guinea Bissau** | **148** | [45.7] |
| **Poland** | **87** | [58.8] | **Lesotho** | **118** | [54.1] | **Angola** | **149** | [43.5] |
| **Cape Verde** | **88** | [58.4] | **China** | **119** | [54.0] | **Iran** | **150** | [43.1] |
| **Pakistan** | **89** | [58.2] | **Russia** | **120** | [54.0] | **Congo Republic of** | **151** | [43.0] |
| **Guyana** | **90** | [58.2] | **Nepal** | **121** | [54.0] | **Turkmenistan** | **152** | [42.5] |
| **Ghana** | **91** | [58.1] | **Yemen** | **122** | [53.8] | **Burma** | **153** | [40.1] |
| **Zambia** | **92** | [57.9] | **Mali** | **123** | [53.7] | **Zimbabwe** | **154** | [35.8] |
| **Gambia, The** | **93** | [57.6] | **Niger** | **124** | [53.5] | **Libya** | **155** | [34.5] |
| **Greece** | **94** | [57.6] | **Ukraine** | **125** | [53.3] | **Cuba** | **156** | [29.7] |
| **Argentina** | **95** | [57.5] | **Mauritania** | **126** | [53.2] | **Korea, North** | **157** | [3.0] |
| **Morocco** | **96** | [57.4] | **Egypt** | **127** | [53.2] | **Sudan** | – | *Not ranked* |
| **Philippines, The** | **97** | [57.4] | **Ecuatorial Guinea** | **128** | [53.2] | **Serbia** | – | *Not ranked* |
| **Tajikistan** | **98** | [56.9] | **Gabon** | **129** | [53.0] | **Congo, Dem. Republic of** | – | *Not ranked* |
| **Paraguay** | **99** | [56.8] | **Djibouti** | **130** | [52.6] | **Iraq** | – | *Not ranked* |
| **Dominican Republic** | **100** | [56.7] | **Nigeria** | **131** | [52.6] | **Montenegro** | – | *Not ranked* |
| **Mozambique** | **101** | [56.6] | **Uzbekistan** | **132** | [52.6] | | | |

*Source*: The Heritage Foundation, *2007 Index of Economic Freedom*.

economies and highlights governments' best practices. Singapore is the top country, followed by New Zealand.[13] Cote d'Ivoire has abolished the requirement of getting ministerial approval for property transfer. Rwanda has finally repealed a law that allowed only one notary public for the whole country.

It would be presumptuous to say that capitalism, a system that encourages competition and efficiency, is the ideal system for all countries. It is true that Russia and Poland, for example, once set prices artificially low and thus had a great deal of difficulty in solving a supply dilemma. As a result, citizens were forced to stand in long lines for a small ration to meet their needs. But capitalism may be inappropriate for such countries as China because the system would allow wealth to be concentrated in the hands of a few people and subsequently leave the majority poor and hungry. Market action does not always serve the nation's best interests, particularly in areas of social need. Efficiency may be derived at the expense of jobs for the people, and the profit motive may intensify the inflation problem.

In Eastern Europe and to a lesser but significant extent in Latin America, widespread government interference and reliance on inefficient public enterprises have obstructed the normal operation of markets. After decades of state control and ownership, the worldwide movement toward market alliance and political freedom has forced both regions to replace their command systems with thriving private enterprises, which should allow producers to manufacture efficiently the goods that consumers want.

The 1990s witnessed dramatic economic transformations. The former Soviet Union and Eastern European countries abandoned central planning. There was an initial outcry as output declined sharply, but by the late 1990s recovery took place, albeit unevenly across countries. As in the case of the CIS, real output fell 50 percent and did not recover until 1999, but by 2000 Central and Southeastern Europe and the Baltics (CSB) had more than restored their original output levels.[14] Transition economies have shown a varying degree of economic performance. Those that have performed best are the ones that were most committed to the reform at the start and they have carried out those reforms rapidly and consistently.[15]

Figure 4.2 shows that a country's strength of institutions affects its efficiency.[16] It should be noted that economic freedom positively affects human development but that corruption has a negative effect on human development.[17]

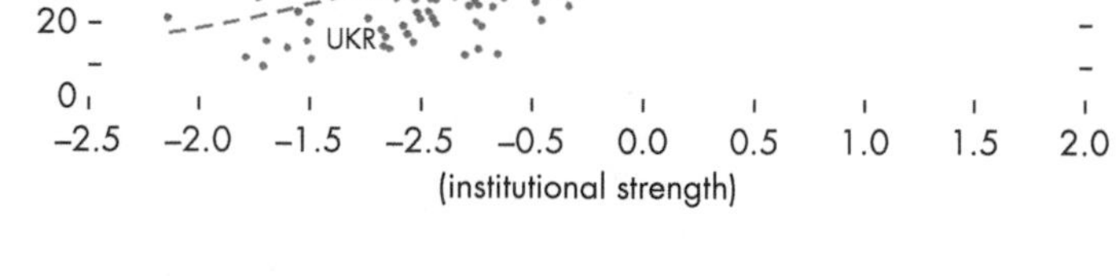
(Technical efficiency, 2000; percent)
100
80
60
40
20
0
-2.5
-2.0
-1.5
-2.5
-0.5
0.0
0.5
1.0
1.5
2.0
(institutional strength)
BEL
USA
IRL
FRA
DEU
AUS
NZL
HUN
ROM
POL
RUS
BGR
UKR

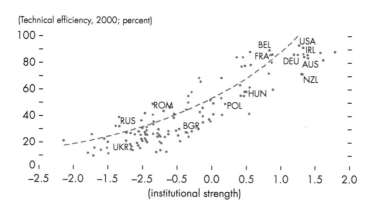

Note: Institutional strength is measured by an index ranging from –2.5 to 2.5; the smaller the number, the weaker a country's institutions. See Chart 1 for country acronyms; NZL = New Zealand. Data: World Bank and author's calculations

**FIGURE 4.2** The institutional difference

*Source*: "Institutional Improvement in Ukraine Could Lead to Growth Boom," *IMF Survey* (October 16, 2006, 301).

## Political risks

There are a number of political risks with which marketers must contend. Hazards based on a host government's actions include confiscation, expropriation, nationalization, domestication, and creeping expropriation. Such actions are more likely to be levied against foreign investments, though local firms' properties are not totally immune. Charles de Gaulle nationalized France's three largest banks in 1945, and more nationalization occurred in 1982 under the French socialists. Coca-Cola Co. managed to re-enter India in 1993, after being thrown out of the country 15 years earlier by India's socialist government.

**Confiscation** is the process of a government's taking ownership of a property without compensation. An example of confiscation is the Chinese government's seizure of American property after the Chinese communists took power in 1949. A more recent example involves Occidental Petroleum Corp. whose assets were confiscated without compensation by Venezuela. In 2006, Ecuador cancelled Occidental's contract and alleged that Occidental illegally transferred its fields to another company without permission.

**Expropriation** differs somewhat from confiscation in that there is some compensation, though not necessarily just compensation. More often than not, a company whose property is being expropriated agrees to sell its operations – not by choice but rather because of some explicit or implied coercion. In 2007, Venezuela took over the country's last remaining privately run oilfields.

After property has been confiscated or expropriated, it can be either nationalized or domesticated. **Nationalization** involves government ownership, and it is the government that operates the business being taken over. Burma's foreign trade, for example, is completely nationalized. Generally, this action affects the whole industry rather than just a single company. When Mexico attempted to control its debt problem, then-President José Lopez Portillo nationalized the country's banking system. In another case of nationalization, Libya's Colonel Gadhafi's vision of Islamic socialism led him to nationalize all private business in 1981. Unlike communists in Hungary and Poland, Czech communists nationalized 100 percent of their economy.

In the case of **domestication**, foreign companies relinquish control and ownership, either completely or partially, to the nationals. The result is that private entities are allowed to operate the confiscated or expropriated property. The French government, after finding out that the state was not sufficiently proficient to run the banking business, developed a plan to sell 36 French banks.

Domestication may sometimes be a voluntary act that takes place in the absence of confiscation or nationalization. Usually, the causes of this action are either poor economic performance or social pressures. When situations worsened in South Africa and political pressures mounted at home, Pepsi sold its South African bottling operation to local investors, and Coca-Cola signaled that it would give control to a local company. General Motors followed suit by selling its operations to local South African management in 1986. Shortly thereafter, Barclays Bank made similar moves.

Another classification system of political risks is the one used by Root.[18] Based on this classification, four sets of political risks may be identified: general instability risk, ownership/control risk, operation risk, and transfer risk.

**General instability risk** is related to uncertainty about the future viability of a host country's political system. The Iranian revolution that overthrew the Shah is an example of this kind of risk. In contrast, **ownership/control risk** is related to the possibility that a host government might take action (e.g., expropriation) to restrict an investor's ownership and control of a subsidiary in that host country.

**Operation risk** proceeds from the uncertainty that a host government might constrain the investor's business operations in all areas, including production, marketing, and finance. Finally, **transfer risk** applies to any future acts by a host government that might constrain the ability of a subsidiary to transfer payments capital, or profit out of the host country back to the parent firm.

The 1970s was the peak period for expropriation activities. The trend was reversed in the 1980s and 1990s as developing countries tried to attract foreign direct investment by promising to protect foreign investors. Unfortunately, recent actions taken by Russia and Venezuela have signaled the return of expropriation. Venezuela's state oil company, PDVSA, has seized control of at least 60 percent of each of the Orinoco operations.[19] Ecuador kicked out Occidental Petroleum Corp. in 2006, alleging that the company illegally transferred an interest in its fields to another company without government permission. For more than 20 years, Occidental was Ecuador's largest private oil producer, most profitable company, and biggest taxpayer.[20]

Governments' rationale for nationalization varies widely and includes national interests, vote getting, prevention of foreigners' exploitation, and an easy, cheap, and quick way of acquiring wealth. The risk of expropriation will likely be less in the future for several reasons. Many governments have experienced very poor records in running the businesses nationalized and have found that their optimistic projections have not materialized. Furthermore, many nations have realized that such actions have created difficulties in attracting new technology and foreign investment as well as in borrowing from foreign banks. There is also the possibility of open retaliation by other governments.

Although the threat of direct confiscation or expropriation is somewhat remote in most countries, a new kind of threat has appeared. MNCs have generally been concerned with coups, revolutions, and confiscation, but they now have to pay attention to so-called creeping expropriation. The Overseas Private Investment Corporation (OPIC) defines **creeping expropriation** as "a set of actions whose cumulative effect is to deprive investors of their fundamental rights in the investment."[21] Laws that affect corporate ownership, control, profit, and reinvestment (e.g., currency inconvertibility or cancellation of import license) can be easily enacted. Because countries can change the rules in the middle of the game, companies must adopt adequate safeguards. Various defensive and protective measures will be discussed later.

A more recent but increasingly significant risk is creeping expropriation. As in the case of Conoco, it reached a joint venture agreement in 1992 and set up Polar Lights in Russia.[22] At that point in time in the early days of post-communist Russia, potential rewards for a pioneering oil company appeared to exceed risks, but in recent years, Russian government officials have issued demands from time to time to renegotiate the terms of the agreement. The government has claimed that its officials who negotiated the original deal did so illegally. A great deal of confusion and disagreement came from Russia's evolving laws dealing with underground resources. Since Russia is a good example of frontier capitalism, such ambiguities have to be expected.

BP, likewise, invested $500 million in Sidanco.[23] BP was upset when TNK bought Chernogorneft, a prized Siberian oilfield, from Sidanco in a 1999 bankruptcy auction. Claiming that the purchase was illegal, BP threatened to leave. An understanding was reached in 2001 to return the oilfield to Sidanco. Subsequently, BP completed the biggest foreign direct investment in post-communist Russia – a $7.7 billion deal giving BP a 50 percent share in the newly formed TNK-BP. Given the fact that Russia is the world's biggest crude oil producer, the country offers a great deal of potential. However, this potential in the country with frontier capitalism is also accompanied by a significant risk.

## Privatization

Both multinational and local firms should notice a trend toward privatization and its competitive implications. Government-owned enterprises are often characterized by overstaffing, poor service, poor financial performance, politicized organizations, and lack of competition. Among the objectives of privatization are: promotion of competition and efficiency, reduction of debt and subsidies, and broadening domestic equity ownership.

Countries which are likely to pursue privatization tend to have the following characteristics: high budget deficits, high foreign debt, and high dependence on such international agencies as the World Bank and the International Monetary Fund. Governments have learned a number of lessons from privatization. Policy makers need to understand that privatization is a political process and that support from the highest political level is necessary. A successful program requires economic reform, and the privatization strategy should be tailored to a country's circumstances. In addition, the privatization process should be transparent.

Should centrally planned economies adopt the *big bang* approach or *gradualism* in reforming their economies? In the case of Eastern Europe, all transition economies adopted the big bang approach by rapidly liberalizing the goods and foreign exchange markets, resulting initially in a steep fall in output. On the other hand, China and Vietnam chose the gradualist approach and have fared better. However, both countries, unlike their Eastern European counterparts, did not begin the reform process in the wake of revolutionary political changes and a collapse of central governing systems which forced the Eastern European economies to move quickly to free prices while imposing current account convertibility. Therefore, the choice of strategy is dependent on the economy's political circumstances and economic structure.

## Indicators of political instability

To assess a potential marketing environment, a company should identify and evaluate the relevant indicators of political difficulty. Potential sources of political complications include social unrest, the attitudes of nationals, and the policies of the host government.

The breakup of the Soviet Union should not come as a surprise. Human nature involves **monostasy** (the urge to stand alone) as well as **systasy** (the urge to stand together), and the two concepts provide alternative ways of utilizing resources to meet a society's needs.[24] Monostasy encourages competition, but systasy emphasizes cooperation. As explained by Alderson, "a cooperative society tends to be a closed society. Closure is essential if the group is in some sense to act as one." Not surprisingly, China, although wanting to modernize its economy, does not fully embrace an open economy, which is likely to encourage dissension among the various groups. For the sake of its own survival, a cooperative society may have to obstruct the dissemination of new ideas and neutralize an external group that poses a threat. China has apparently learned a lesson from the Soviet Union's experience.

A liberated political climate may easily lead to a call of the long-suppressed national minority groups for cultural and territorial independence. The groups' past conflicts, unsettled but subdued during the communist period, are likely to escalate. A domestic dispute may escalate into violence that is confined within the boundaries of the country in question. The civil war that started in 1991 between Serb and Croats in Yugoslavia is a good example. An internal dispute may draw interested parties outside the country in question into the conflict.

### Attitudes of nationals

An assessment of the political climate is not complete without an investigation of the attitudes of the citizens and government of the host country. The nationals' attitude toward foreign enterprises and citizens can be quite inhospitable. Nationals are often concerned with foreigners' intentions in regard to exploitation and colonialism, and these concerns are often linked to concerns over foreign governments' actions that may be seen as improper. Such attitudes may arise out of local socialist or nationalist philosophies, which may be in conflict with the policy of the company's home-country government. Any such inherent hostility is certain to present major problems because of its relative permanence.

### Policies of the host government

Unlike citizens' inherent hostility, a government's attitude toward foreigners is often relatively short-lived. The mood can either alter with time or a change in leadership, and it can change for either better or worse. The impact of a change in mood can be quite dramatic, especially in the short run.

Government policy formulation can affect business operations either internally or externally (see Legal Dimension 4.1). The effect is internal when the policy regulates the firm's operations within the home country. The effect is external when the policy regulates the firm's activities in another country.

Although an external government policy is irrelevant to firms doing business only in one country, such a policy can create complex problems for firms doing business in countries that are in conflict

Legal Dimension 4.1

**Capitalism in North Korea**

North Korea and capitalism are two things that are anything but compatible. Yet the North Korean special economic zone of Kaesong is booming. Twenty-three South Korean companies are already operating there, and they employ about 15,000 North Korean workers. A group of 45 more South Korean companies will soon join them, and Seoul may allow 300 more companies to set up shop there.

The move makes both political and economic sense for South Korea. Economically, South Korea is caught between high-technology Japan and low-cost China. North Korean workers solve the problem since they earn only $57.50 a month, one-third of what a Chinese factory worker makes. Politically, the industrial park may serve as a first step toward the integration of the Korean peninsula.

The U.S.A. is none too pleased with the development. The Trading with the Enemy Act severely restricts North Korean exports to the U.S.A., and the restrictions apply to goods produced in Kaesong as well. Such goods must face tariffs of up to 90 percent, while most goods from South Korea are eligible to enter the U.S.A. duty free. Without these restrictions, Kaesong could serve as a production haven for South Korean firms doing business with the U.S.A.

*Source*: "A Capitalist Toehold in North Korea," *Business Week*, June 11, 2007, 45.

with each other. Disputes among countries often spill over into business activities. A company in one country may be prohibited from doing business with other countries that are viewed as hostile.

A company should pay particular attention to election time. Elections pose a special problem because of many candidates' instinctive tendency to use demagoguery to acquire votes. Candidate activities and tactics can very easily create an unwelcome atmosphere for foreign firms. When French politicians cited the fact that one French worker became unemployed for every five to ten Japanese cars imported, the government held up imported cars when the election was a few weeks away. The industry minister used every conceivable excuse to avoid signing the required certificates.

The use of unfriendly rhetoric before an election may be nothing but a smokescreen, and the "bark" will not necessarily be followed by a "bite." In such a case, a company need not take drastic action if it is able to endure through the election. Ronald Reagan, long an advocate of free trade, became something of a protectionist immediately before his re-election in 1984. After the election, a policy of free trade was reinstituted. Therefore, a company must determine whether early threats are just that and nothing more or whether such threats constitute the political candidates' real intentions and attitude for the future.

One theory focuses on the cooperation-based relations between MNCs and the host government. There are four building blocks that will allow MNCs to improve their cooperative relationships with governments: (1) resource commitment, (2) personal relations, (3) political accommodation, and (4) organizational credibility. A study of 131 MNCs in China confirms the importance of these blocks.[25]

One model proposes that organizations may employ three political strategies: information, financial incentive, and constituency building. While an MNC may have a particular global strategy when dealing with governments, its subsidiaries may still have to employ specific activities in host-country contexts. As such, a subsidiary's response must be consistent with a host country's characteristics as well as with the imperatives of the headquarters. The more integrated a subsidiary is with its affiliates in a strategic sense, the greater it is integrated with the other subsidiaries in a political sense.[26]

## Analysis of political risk or country risk

Although political scientists, economists, businesspeople, and business scholars have some ideas about what political risk is, they seem to have difficulties agreeing both on its definition and on methods to predict danger. Perhaps, because of this lack of agreement on the definition, many different methods have been employed to measure, analyze, and predict political risks.

Political risk is an uncertainty that stems from the exercise of power by governments and nongovernmental actors. Typical hazards include political instability, politicized government policy, political violence, expropriation, creeping expropriation, contract frustration, and currency inconvertibility.

Some assessment methods are country specific in the sense that a risk report is based on a particular country's unique political and economic circumstances. As such, there is a lack of a consistent framework that would allow comparison across countries. Because an MNC must decide to allocate resources based on potential opportunities and risk associated with each country, a common methodology is essential.

Even when a systematic attempt is made for cross-national comparisons, the methods used vary greatly. Some are nothing more than checklists consisting of a large number of relevant issues that are applicable to each country. Other systems rely on questionnaires sent to experts or local citizens in order to gauge the political mood. Such scoring systems, which permit numerical ratings of countries, have gained acceptance. Some institutions have turned to econometrics for this purpose. Marine Midland Bank, for example, uses econometrics to rate various countries in terms of economic risk. The method, however, is not perfect.

To many small and medium-sized firms, doing their own country-risk analyses is out of the question because of the cost, expertise, and resources required. However, there are some alternatives that can provide a useful assessment of political risk. One is to interview people who have some knowledge or experience with the countries of interest, including businesspersons, bankers, and government officials. Molex Inc., a manufacturer of high-technology electrical products, has been able to protect itself by listening to international bankers, lawyers, and accounting firms. Another method is to rely on the advice of firms specializing in this area. Controlled Risks, a Washington area firm, advises about 400 U.S. companies on the danger of doing business in 70 countries. For fees that can total $9,000 a year, the firm offers information and provides training for executives on how to protect themselves, cope with kidnapping and extortion, and guide their employees in political crises.

Many banks can help their clients to assess business risks overseas. Bank of America, for example, provides international economic analyses and forecasts to customers through World Information Services (WIS). Subscribers to WIS receive Country Outlooks, Country Data Forecasts, and Country Risk Monitor. Bank of America uses a ranking system based on a common set of economic and financial criteria to evaluate 80 countries for business risk. In addition to current rankings, a 10-year historical track of each country is shown. Country Risk Monitor allows risk comparisons of countries with benchmark risk indicators for major country groupings. Updates are regularly provided.

Another alternative is to subscribe to reports prepared for this purpose. One valuable report is the **country credit rating** prepared by *Institutional Investor* magazine. Based on a survey of approximately 100 leading international banks concerning a country's creditworthiness and the chance of payment default, rankings are assigned to 100 countries every six months. Greater weight is given to the responses of those banks that have the largest global exposures and possess the most sophisticated systems of risk analysis. Yet the loan problems encountered by the Bank of America and Citicorp make it clear that the risk-analysis systems used by some of the world's largest banks are anything but foolproof.

Another relatively simple method is based on **LIBOR (London Interbank rate)**. The LIBOR, relatively risk-free, is the interest rate charged for loans between banks. Nonbank borrowers, of course, have to pay a premium over LIBOR, with the premium (i.e., the spread between the loan rate and LIBOR) indicating the extent of risk involved. A borrower from a country with a high risk of default must expect a high premium. The premium is thus a good indicator of risk because it reflects a lender's assessment of the country in terms of debt levels and payment records. Because all loans are not comparable, adjustment must be made for volume and maturity. *Euromoney* magazine has devised a formula to allow for this adjustment, and its formula to compute a country's spread index is the following:

[(volume X spread) / *Euromoney* index] / (volume X maturity)

By simply examining the spread index of a particular country and comparing it with those of other countries, an investor can arrive at the conclusion of a degree of risk associated with the country of interest.

Although *Euromoney*'s and *Institutional Investor*'s country risk ratings are derived in different ways, the two measures are highly correlated and strongly agree on the creditworthiness of the assessed countries. Both magazines' ratings can be replicated to a significant degree with a few economic variables. "In particular, both the level of per capita income and propensity to invest affect positively the rating of a country. In addition, high-ranking countries are less indebted than low-ranking countries."[27]

One study examined 11 widely-used measures of country risk across 17 countries over 19 years. According to the results, "commercial risk measures are very poor at predicting actual realized risks." Yet managers still continue to rely on ratings agencies. One reason is that the purchasing cost of this type of information is miniscule when compared to the amount of FDI to be committed.[28]

As assessment methods of political risks have become more sophisticated, there has been a shift from the earlier conceptual and qualitative approaches to approaches that are quantitative and derivative of applied research. There is a need, however, to integrate these two major kinds of approach.

## Management of political risk

Risk and reward are related. Country risk is compensated with a higher return on assets. One study found that unexplained country risk was compensated with a higher return on assets.[29]

To manage political risk, an MNC can pursue a strategy of either avoidance or insurance. **Avoidance** means screening out politically uncertain countries. In this, measurement and analysis of political risk can be useful. **Insurance**, in contrast, is a strategy to shift the risk to other parties. This strategy will be covered in detail below.

There are other strategies that MNCs can use to safeguard their foreign investments. They may want to come to an understanding with a foreign government as to their rights and responsibilities. They may increase and maintain their bargaining power when their technical, operational, and managerial complexity requirements are not within reach of a host country's abilities.

In addition, there are several managerial strategies which are relevant. A firm may try to gain "control" of the situation through political activities, market power, exchange of threats, vertical integration, and horizontal mergers and acquisitions. Or it may try to gain "cooperation" through long-term contractual agreements, alliances, interlocking directorates, interfirm personnel flows, and so on. Furthermore, it may pursue product and/or geographic diversification to gain "flexibility." Operational flexibility can also be achieved through flexible input sourcing and multinational production.[30]

The rapid changes in Eastern Europe present both challenges and opportunities. In the former days of centralization, a trade minister in the capital could speak for the entire nation, but with decentralized decision making, an MNC has to go to the many republics for information and approval. When doing business there, companies need to be creative in terms of long-term thinking and financing.

## Measures to minimize political risk

Political risk, though impossible to eliminate, can at the very least be minimized. There are several measures that MNCs can implement in order to discourage a host country from taking control of MNC assets.

Cultural Dimension 4.1

**Better safe than sorry**

Chubb, IG, and Lloyd's of London are among a small group of insurers which have long offered policies to cover ransom demands for kidnappers. The coverage has been expanded to include legal and psychiatric fees and compensation for loss of trade secrets and product tampering. Some policies may cover costs incurred when evacuating a politically unstable country. Executives may receive training on how to avoid being kidnapped.

Premiums may run from $1000 to $100,000 a year – depending on the coverage. The premium also varies according to the countries which executives visit most often. As an example, the premium is higher if it involves Latin America and lower in the case of Europe and Japan. Individuals may buy the insurance if their employers do not provide such coverage. There is extra cost to cover accidental death and dismemberment. Because it is illegal to purchase ransom insurance in Germany and Colombia, executives visiting these countries need to buy the coverage elsewhere.

The U.S. government sent $50 billion to state and local governments for homeland security, and private contractors will benefit from it. Security companies guard against employee theft, train bodyguards in evasive driving techniques, teach executives to minimize dangers (e.g., no name and title on a limousine window), and arrange ransom payoffs. Now they offer emergency response (e.g., evacuation and repatriation of overseas personnel), business continuity (e.g., backing up the data system and anti-hacker defenses), vulnerability assessment (e.g., identifying weak points in anti-terror defense), and background checks (e.g., identifying problem workers and subcontractors).

## *Stimulation of the local economy*

One defensive investment strategy calls for a company to link its business activities with the host country's national economic interests. Brazil expelled Mellon Bank because of the bank's refusal to cooperate in renegotiating the country's massive foreign debt.

A local economy can be stimulated in a number of different ways. One strategy may involve the company's purchasing local products and raw materials for its production and operations. By assisting local firms, it can develop local allies who can provide valuable political contacts. A modification of this strategy would be to use subcontractors. For example, some military tank manufacturers tried to secure tank contracts from the Netherlands by agreeing to subcontract part of the work on the new tanks to Dutch companies.

Sometimes local sourcing is compulsory. Governments may require products to contain locally manufactured components because local content improves the economy in two ways: (1) it stimulates demand for domestic components, and (2) it saves the necessity of a foreign exchange transaction. Further investment in local production facilities by the company will please the government that much more.

Finally, the company should attempt to assist the host country by being export oriented. Both United Brands and Castle and Cooke were able to survive the Sandinista revolution in Nicaragua by implementing this strategy. Their export dollars became vital to the Nicaraguan government, thus shielding their Latin American operations from expropriation.

## *Employment of nationals*

Frequently, foreigners make the simple but costly mistake of assuming that citizens of less developed countries are poor by choice. It serves no useful purpose for a company to assume that local people are lazy, unintelligent, unmotivated, or uneducated. Such an attitude may become a self-fulfilling prophecy. Thus, the hiring of local workers should go beyond the filling of labor positions. United Brands' policy, for example, is to hire only locals as managers.

Firms should also carefully weigh the impact of automation in a cheap-labor, high-unemployment area. Automation does not go down well in India, where job creation, not job elimination, is national policy. Technology is neither always welcomed nor always socially desirable. An inability to automate production completely does not necessarily constitute a negative for MNCs. MNCs may gain more in less developed countries by using "intermediate technology" instead of the most advanced equipment. Intermediate technology, accompanied by additional labor, is less expensive, and it promotes goodwill by increasing employment.

## *Sharing ownership*

Instead of keeping complete ownership for itself, a company should try to share ownership with others, especially with local companies. One method is to convert from a private company to a public one or from a foreign company to a local one. Dragon Airline, claiming it is a real Chinese company, charged that Cathay Pacific Airways' Hong Kong landing rights should be curtailed because Cathay Pacific was more British than Chinese. The threat forced Cathay Pacific to sell a new public issue to allow Chinese investors to have minority interests in the company. The move was made to convince Hong Kong and China that the company had Chinese roots.

One of the most common techniques for shared ownership is to simply form a joint venture. Any loss of control as a result can, in most cases, be more than compensated for by the derived benefits. United Brands' policy in South America is not to initiate any business unless local joint-venture partners can be found to help spread the risk.

In some overseas business ventures, it is not always necessary to have local firms as partners. Sometimes, having co-owners from other nations can work almost as well. Having multiple nationalities for international business projects not only reduces exposure; it also makes it difficult for the host government to take over the business venture without offending a number of nations all at once. The political situation in South Africa was one of the reasons why Ford chose to merge its automobile operations there with Anglo American. The merger reduced Ford's exposure to a 40 percent minority position.

Voluntary domestication, in most cases, is not a desirable course of action because it is usually a forced decision. The company should therefore plan for domestication in advance instead of waiting until it is required, because by that time the company has lost much of its leverage and bargaining power. This strategy is also likely to be perceived as a gesture of goodwill, an accomplishment in addition to the desired reduction of exposure. A wise strategy may be for the company to retain the marketing or technical side of the business while allowing heavy local ownership in the physical assets and capital-intensive portions of the investment.

## Being civic minded

MNCs whose home country is the U.S.A. often encounter the "ugly American" label abroad, and this image should be avoided. It is not sufficient that the company simply does business in a foreign country; it should also be a good corporate citizen there. To shed the undesirable perception, multinationals should combine investment projects with civic projects.

Corporations rarely undertake civic projects out of total generosity, but such projects make economic sense in the long run. It is highly desirable to provide basic assistance because many civic entities exist in areas with slight or nonexistent municipal infrastructures that would normally provide these facilities. A good idea is to assist in building schools, hospitals, roads, and water systems because such projects benefit the host country as well as the company, especially in terms of the valuable goodwill generated in the long run. Toyota has invested in local communities. A portion of its U.S. profits is allocated each year to support community programs. Over a period of three years, it has contributed $38 million to such philanthropic organizations as United Negro College Fund, Teach for America, and Special Olympics.

There are many examples of global philanthropy. It is wise to remember that in many less developed countries, a small sum of money can go a long way.

## Political neutrality

For the best long-term interests of the company, it is not wise to become involved in political disputes among local groups or between countries. A company should state clearly but discreetly that it is not in the political business and that its primary concerns are economic in nature. Brazilian firms employ this strategy and keep a low profile in matters related to Central American revolutions and Cuban troops in foreign countries. Brazilian arms are thus attractive to the Third World because those arms are free of ideological ties. In such a case, a purchasing country does not feel obligated to become politically aligned with a seller, as when buying from the United States or China.

## Behind-the-scenes lobby

As with the variables affecting business, political risks can be reasonably managed. Companies as well as special interest groups have varying interests, and each party will want to make its own opinion known. When the U.S. mushroom industry asked for a quota against imports from China, Pizza Hut came to China's rescue by claiming that most domestic and other foreign suppliers could not meet its specifications. Pizza Hut has a great deal at stake because it is one of China's largest customers as well as a user of half of some nine million pounds of mushrooms for pizzas – not to mention the desire of PepsiCo., its parent, to open a factory in southern China. Subsequently, the petition of the U.S. mushroom industry was denied.

Where practical, firms should attempt to influence political decisions. Mobil Corporation, for example, ran newspaper advertisements emphasizing the importance of the U.S.–China relations (see Figure 4.3).

Even though a firm's operation is affected by the political environment, the direction of the influence does not have to flow in one direction only. Lobbying activities can be undertaken, and it is wise to lobby quietly behind the scenes in order not to cause unnecessary political clamor. For importers, they must let their government know why imports are crucial to them and to their consumers.

# China trade: self-interest and statesmanship

This month, the Congress will again consider the critical American interests related to China and international trade. The House of Representatives will soon vote whether to extend normal trade relations with China for another year. We urge the House to do what it and the rest of the U.S. government have done for many years: support ongoing trade with China, encourage engagement with that country and its people, and underscore America's commitment to open international trade and investment.

Last year, Congress passed and President Clinton signed legislation establishing **permanent** normal trade relations with China. However, permanent normalization was contingent upon China joining the World Trade Organization (WTO). Negotiation of the many bilateral and multilateral agreements necessary to do this has been prolonged, forcing the normal trade status to be renewed annually until China joins the WTO.

President Bush has wisely chosen to continue normal trade. Recently, U.S. Trade Representative Robert Zoellick announced that the U.S. and China have reached consensus on bilateral trade arrangements. This will help pave the way for China's WTO membership, possibly this year.

Because China and the United States have a number of disagreements in important areas unrelated to trade, some in the House would like to "send a message" to China by passing a resolution withdrawing normal trade relations. It is our view that this would be unwise.

**The importance of U.S.-China relations transcends dollars and cents**

The importance of U.S.-Chinese economic relations transcends dollars and cents. A healthy economic relationship helps establish a solid platform for cooperation and dialogue on many other matters. It presents an arena in which understanding can grow, and a vehicle through which beneficial change can take place.

Normal trade relations are important in promoting economic reform in China. The economic links are vital to Chinese citizens who depend to a great extent on overseas trade for their livelihood and their hopes for the future. And the economic relationship between American and Chinese firms has been a key element in opening China to greater reliance on market-based approaches and greater familiarity with advanced business practices.

Economic relations have been one of the most successful areas of cooperation and growth involving our two countries. China is America's second-largest trading partner, with total trade exceeding $120 billion. U.S. exports to China grew 36 percent in the first quarter of this year, helping cushion the U.S. economic slowdown. U.S. investments in China now approach $30 billion. These economic links strengthen our economy and bring benefits to virtually every American consumer through lower prices.

Accordingly, we urge the House to reject the call for a suspension of normal trade relations with China. Both statesmanship and self-interest argue for continued support of this vital intergovernmental and economic relationship.

ExxonMobil™

**FIGURE 4.3** Politics and economics

*Source*: ExxonMobil.

Companies may not only have to lobby in their own country, but they also may have to lobby in the host country. Companies may want to do the lobbying themselves, or they may allow their government to do it on their behalf. Their government can be requested to apply pressure against foreign governments.

## Observation of political mood and reduction of exposure

Marketers should be sensitive to changes in political mood. A contingency plan should be devised in readiness. When the political climate turns hostile, measures are necessary to reduce exposure. Some major banks and MNCs adopted measures to reduce their exposure in France in response to a fear that a Socialist–Communist coalition might gain control of the legislature in the elections of 1978. Their concern was understandable, as most of these companies were on the Left's nationalization list. Their defensive strategy included the outflow of capital, the transfer of patents and other assets to foreign subsidiaries, and the sale of equity holdings to foreigners and French nationals living abroad. Such activities once concluded made it difficult for the Socialist government to nationalize the companies' properties. Prudence required that these transactions be kept quiet so as to avoid reprisals.

## Other measures

There are a few other steps that MNCs can undertake to minimize political risk. One strategy could involve keeping a low profile. Because it is difficult to please all the people all the time, it may be desirable for a company to be relatively inconspicuous. For example, in the 1980s, Texas Instruments removed identifying logos and signs in El Salvador.

Another tactic could involve trying to adopt a local personality. A practice approach may require that the company blend in with the environment. There is not much to be gained by a company being ethnocentric and trying to Americanize, Europeanize, or Japanize the host country's citizens. A veteran of international business would very likely realize that it is far better to be flexible and adaptable. Such a firm would know that it should behave like a chameleon, adapting itself to fit the environment. The main reason why McDonald's uses local corporate staff is to look like a local company. This is also the goal of Hawley Group. That company is thought to be American in the United States, British in the United Kingdom, and Australian in Australia.

For S&P 500 companies alone, the direct and indirect costs of terrorism are $107 billion a year. The costs include extra spending on insurance, redundant capacity, and so on. In addition, the costs include lost revenues due to fearful consumers' decreased capacity.[31]

Multinational firms, due to their presence in a large number of countries, must be mindful of terrorist threats. According to the World Markets Research Center, the top ten countries deemed to be the most likely targets of a terrorist attack are: (1) Colombia, (2) Israel, (3) Pakistan, (4) the U.S.A., (5) the Philippines, (6) Afghanistan, (7) Indonesia, (8) Iraq, (9) India, and (10) the United Kingdom.[32]

Many or most U.S.-based MNCs do not have formal programs to deal with a terrorist attack. Rather, in addition to a focus on security equipment, they should also focus on training executives and their families. Some of the activities included in anti-terrorist training are: defensive driving, self-defense, kidnapping avoidance, behavior after/during kidnapping, negotiating skills, weapon handling, and protection of assets.

Ethical Dimension 4.1

**Good-faith concern**

Chiquita Brands International's wholly owned subsidiary Banadex was found to have paid $1.7 million to far-right paramilitary groups deemed by the U.S. government to be terrorists. These groups took over banana-growing lands in the state of Antioquia and killed human rights workers and trade unionists. At the same time, Chiquita's business was booming. The company offered the following justification for its actions: Banadex "had been forced to make payments to right- and left-wing paramilitary groups in Colombia to protect the lives of its employees. The payments made by the company were always motivated by our good-faith concern for the safety of our employees."

In the U.S. federal court, Chiquita pleaded guilty to one count of doing business with a terrorist organization. It admitted that it paid Colombian terrorists for years to protect its most profitable banana-growing operation. The plea required paying a fine of $25 million.

*Sources*: "Chiquita Pleads Guilty in Payment to Terrorists," *San José Mercury News*, 20 March 2007; and "Colombians Seek Probe of Chiquita," *San José Mercury News*, 17 March 2007.

Finally, various defensive precautions can be implemented. Automobile drivers should be trained in how to react to a kidnapping attempt, and managers themselves should be instructed in how to deal with the unexpected and taught especially to avoid driving routine routes. Very basic precautions might be undertaken. For example, in El Salvador, Texas Instruments erected protective walls for its facilities and employed extra guards. It is better to be safe than sorry.

## Political insurance

In addition to the strategies of risk avoidance and risk reduction. MNCs can employ the strategy of risk shifting. Insurance coverage may be obtained from a number of sources.

### *Private insurance*

Through ignorance, a large number of companies end up as self-insurers. A better plan would be to follow Club Med's example of shifting political risk to a third party through the purchase of political insurance.

Some insurance companies even insure sales and profits. British Aerospace, for example, has a $70 million policy that guarantees $3.7 billion in revenue from aircraft leasing until the end of 2013. Honeywell has a blanket policy to insure its foreign exchange exposure and other risks, and may expand to include interest rate hedges, weather, and commodity prices.

Currency inconvertibility is often the most common type of political risk claim. A coverage of this type does not protect against currency devaluation. On the other hand, political violence (e.g., civil disturbances and wars) has been increasing. In addition, political disruption can stem from such multilateral bodies as the United Nations, and the disruption may include sanctions and embargoes.

Once a company plans to cover commercial risk, it may as well include political risk. After all, the extra premium is not that great.[33]

Although property expropriation seems to be the most common reason for obtaining political insurance, the policy should include coverage for kidnapping, terrorism, and creeping expropriation. Information about most companies' coverage is rather scarce, because it is both imprudent and impermissible for companies to reveal that they are carrying kidnap insurance. Revelation of such coverage would only serve to encourage such activity. While AIG and other insurers have been offering corporate and individual kidnapping-and-ransom insurance policies for quite some time, Chubb now offers a free kidnapping-and-ransom upgrade for homeowners' insurance.[34]

## Government insurance

MNCs do not have to rely solely on private insurers. There are nonprofit, public agencies that can provide essentially the same kind of coverage. For U.S. firms, the two primary ones are OPIC and FCIA. Overseas Private Investment Corporation (OPIC) is a U.S. government agency that assists economic development through investment insurance and a credit financing program. To support U.S. private investments, OPIC provides several forms of assistance, with political risk insurance as its primary business. It has three types of insurance protection to cover the risks of: (1) currency inconvertibility, (2) expropriation (including creeping expropriation), and (3) loss or damage caused by war, revolution, or insurrection. A typical insurance contract runs for up to 20 years at a combined annual premium of 1.5 percent for all three types of cover. OPIC's assistance was instrumental in Motorola Inc.'s decision to enter the Nicaraguan market to install, operate, and maintain a cellular telephone service.

## MIGA

MIGA (Multilateral Investment Guarantee Agency) was established in 1988 to help its more than 100 member states to create an attractive investment climate. Its mission is to promote private investment in developing countries through insuring investment against noncommercial (i.e., political) risk. MIGA works as a co-insurer with, or a reinsurer of, other insurers. It offers four types of coverage: currency transfer, expropriation, war and civil disturbances, and breach of contract. Premiums depend on the type of project, type of coverage, and project-specific conditions. Annual premiums for each type of cover are in the range of 0.50–1.25 percent of the amount insured. MIGA's rates are slightly higher than those of other national insurers.

In sum, when it comes to political risk, companies tend to be reactive. As a result, they often have to devise an expensive strategy to deal with damage control. It is much more desirable to be proactive by developing a comprehensive and systematic view of the factors that drive risks.[35] There are three basic sets. First, there are external drivers such as political instability (e.g., coups and riots) and poor public policy (e.g., hyperinflation and currency crises). Second, interaction drives are based on relationships between a company and external actors. Finally, internal drivers include the company's quality of its political risk management processes. In general, the company is not in a position to influence external drivers (e.g., making a host country more politically or economically stable). Thus it should focus on assessing risks and managing their impacts. As an example, since kidnapping is a significant risk, one should assess the likelihood of its occurrence. In statistical terms, it is more likely for a person to become a road traffic accident victim than being a kidnap victim. On the other hand, being kidnapped and held for ransom is arguably the most traumatic experience for anyone. As such, firms should train their employees to take precautions and may want to offer them kidnapping and ransom insurance.

## Conclusion

The international marketer's political environment is complex and difficult due to the interaction among domestic, foreign, and international politics. If a product is imported or produced overseas, political groups and labor organizations accuse the marketer of taking jobs from people in the home country. On the other hand, foreign governments are not always receptive to overseas capital and investment because of suspicions about the marketer's motives and commitment. When both the host country and the home country have different political and national interests, their conflicting policies can complicate the problem further.

This chapter has covered the political dimension of international trade. Due to the diversity of political and economic systems, governments develop varying philosophies. In some circumstances, their political motives overshadow their economic logic. The result is often that political risks – such as expropriation, nationalization, and restrictions – are created against exports and/or imports and are likely inevitable.

Marketing decisions are thus affected by political considerations. When investing in a foreign country, companies must be sensitive to that country's political concerns. Due to the dynamic nature of politics in general, companies should prepare a contingency plan to cope with changes that occur in the political environment. To minimize political risk, companies should attempt to accommodate the host country's national interests by stimulating the economy, employing nationals, sharing business ownership with local firms, and being civic-oriented. On the other hand, to protect their own economic interests, companies should maintain political neutrality, quietly lobby for their goals, and shift risks to a third party through the purchase of political insurance. Finally, a company should institute a monitoring system that allows it to systematically and routinely evaluate the political situation.

Some companies view politics as an obstacle to their effort to enter foreign markets and as a barrier to the efficient use of resources. For other companies, political problems, instead of being perceived as entry barriers, are seen as challenges and opportunities. According to firms with the more optimistic view, political situations are merely environmental conditions that can be overcome and managed. Political risks, through skillful adaptation and control, can thus be reduced or neutralized.

## CASE 4.1 TOYOTA: HOW TO WIN FRIENDS AND INFLUENCE PEOPLE

In 1957, Toyota ventured into the U.S. market with two of its bestsellers in Japan. It got a cool reception: those two cars were perceived to be "overpriced, underpowered, and built like tanks" (see Figure 4.4). The two cars were taken back to Japan. Toyota persevered. By the early 1980s, Toyota had become America's leading auto import and captured 6 percent of the U.S. market. Toyota is now selling more vehicles in the U.S.A. than in Japan, and it derives 35 percent of sales and 43 percent of operating profit from North America.

In 1985, all the Toyota vehicles sold in America were imported. When President Clinton was considering a 100 percent tax on luxury car imports,

PRESIDENT LINES
Back in 1957 we brought our first two cars to America. And took them home again.
They were the best cars we'd ever made. They'd been bestsellers in Japan. But how would they do in the bigtime – in America?
We didn't know. We couldn't know, until we brought them here.
We brought them in August, 1957. And showed them with great hope. And even greater fear. What would happen if America didn't like them?
As it turned out, America *didn't* like them; our cars, the critics said, were "overpriced, underpowered, and built like tanks."
We had to start all over.
The message was painful and very clear: if we wanted to sell cars in a place like America, we had to start all over. And make a better car.
So we started over. And worked very hard for many frustrating years.
We stretched our technology farther than we had ever stretched it before.
We tried out ideas that had never been tried before.
We made every mistake that we could possibly make.
And one day we did it: we made a better car.
And the rest, as they say, is history.
And now comes the future.
Toyota is now, and has been for years, America's leading auto import.
But soon this import will be made right here.
On May 5 we broke ground for a new Toyota manufacturing plant in Kentucky.
The plant will cost $800,000,000, will employ 3,000, and will produce 200,000 cars a year.
Site of Toyota's new $800,000,000 auto plant in Kentucky.
It's a major investment in the future of the American automobile industry, and in the future of the American economy.
It's also a down payment on our debt.
We owe a lot to America. America gave us a chance when we were small and scared. It gave us the challenge that helped us become who we are.
This is something we will never forget.
TOYOTA

**FIGURE 4.4** Toyota: from Japan to the U.S.A.

*Source*: Reprinted with permission of Toyota Motor Corporation.

Toyota made an offer to build three plants in the U.S.A. The tax was never implemented. Soon after that, in 1996, West Virginia had a $400 million engine plant, and the investment has increased to $1 billion and 1,000 workers.

Since the 1980s, Toyota has positioned itself as an American car manufacturer. U.S. politicians have been reminded that Toyota employs 38,000 American workers and that it has invested $17 billion over 20 years in new plants. The company works with more than 400 U.S. suppliers to forge economic ties, and its purchases of American parts and materials have risen to more than $5 billion annually. Toyota boasts that nearly every dollar earned by its U.S. operations since U.S. manufacturing began has been reinvested in American payrolls, purchases, plants, and other facilities. The company's American factories and dealerships employ more American workers than the combined number of Coca-Cola, Microsoft, and Oracle. Its advertisements now trumpet the fact that Toyota has plants in Kentucky, California, West Virginia, and Texas. The company operates vehicle, engine, and parts factories in eight states, and the Tupelo plant in Mississippi is its eighth North American vehicle-assembly plant.

Toyota's top executives in the U.S.A. are increasingly American. Jim Press, before his surprise departure for Chrysler in 2007, was the head of Toyota Motor North America Inc. operations, and he was the first person outside of Japan to be appointed to Toyota's board.

For General Motors, Ford, and Chrysler, they can run, but they cannot hide. Having conquered the passenger car market, Toyota has mounted an assault on the truck market with its full-sized Tundra. Backed by a $300 million marketing campaign, the Tundra is billed as "the all-new, built-in-America, Toyota truck." To ward off a backlash, Toyota uses public relations and lobbying. It is active in the area of corporate philanthropy. Its literacy programs in Texas are a prime example. Its lobbying budget has been on the rise.

As Toyota unseated General Motors Corp. to become the leader in worldwide vehicle sales in 2007, it has become concerned that protectionist sentiment might resurface in the U.S.A., a market of paramount importance to Toyota. The cheap yen also makes it advantageous for Toyota to increase manufacturing capacity and export cars from Japan. According to a senior executive, "it's much, much more profitable to produce cars in Japan and ship them all to the U.S. right now, if it wasn't for the political problems that might cause."

## *Points to consider*

Toyota has made a pledge to produce in North America at least two-thirds of the vehicles that it sells in the region. Building vehicles in the U.S.A. is viewed as a form of political insurance. These manufacturing jobs across many states allow the company to build a network of friendly politicians. However, the company's top executives wonder whether Toyota may have built too many U.S. factories for the sake of political support. Evaluate Toyota's political and business activities in the U.S.A. What are the activities and strategies that have been effective for Toyota? Is there anything that Toyota needs to do or that it should have done differently?

*Sources*: "Why Toyota Is Afraid of Being Number One," *Business Week*, March 5, 2007, 42–50; "Toyota's New U.S. Plan: Stop Building Factories," *Wall Street Journal*, June 20, 2007; and "'Face of Toyota' Steps Up at a Delicate Time," *Wall Street Journal*, June 21, 2007.

## Questions

1. Explain the multiplicity of political environments.
2. Distinguish between parliamentary (open) and absolutist (closed) governments.
3. Distinguish among these types of governments: two-party, multi-party, single-party, and dominated one-party.
4. Distinguish among these economic systems: communism, socialism, and capitalism.
5. Is country stability a function of (a) economic development, (b) democracy, and (c) capitalism?
6. Explain: confiscation, expropriation, nationalization, and domestication.
7. What is creeping expropriation? What is its economic impact on foreign investors?
8. What are the potential sources and indicators of political instability?
9. How can a company conduct country-risk analysis for investment purposes?
10. Explain these methods of political-risk management: avoidance, insurance, negotiating the environment, and structuring investment.
11. What are measures that can be undertaken to minimize political risk?
12. What is OPIC and how can it assist U.S. investors abroad?
13. What is MIGA and how can it assist international marketers?

## Discussion assignments and minicases

1. According to a vice-president of Merrill Lynch, "you're better off making any car in Japan than in the U.S. But the political realities don't allow that." Discuss this comment from both economic and political perspectives and as related to the U.S.A. and Japan.
2. Why is a host country (including the U.S.A.) not always receptive to foreign firms' investment in local production facilities?
3. Once viewing each other with great distrust, the U.S.A. and China have dramatically improved their economic and political ties. What are the reasons for this development?
4. How likely is it for a country to adopt a system of either 100 percent capitalism or 100 percent communism?
5. Is capitalism the best system – economically as well as socially – for all countries?
6. Indonesia is a country of approximately 200 million citizens. This is a land where Islam, Christianity, and Hinduism coexist. This is a land where there is a huge income gap between the wealthy ethnic Chinese and the remaining 190 million Indonesians. This is also a land which was ruled for decades with an iron hand by President Suharto. His 1994 crackdown included closures of publications, beatings of demonstrators, and arrests of labor activists. Matters have changed since then. Assess Indonesia in terms of market potential and risks.

## Notes


1 "Taiwan's Acer Gains Ground on Chinese Rival Lenovo," *San José Mercury News*, April 2, 2007.
2 Robert H. Bates, "Beyond the Ballot Box," *Finance & Development* (December 2006): 26–9.
3 "Politics and Budgets," *IMF Survey*, February 17, 2003, 42–3.
4 Fareed Zakaria, *The Future of Freedom: Illiberal Democracy at Home and Abroad* (New York: Norton, 2003).
5 Amy Chua, *World on Fire: How Exporting Free Market Democracy Breeds Ethnic Hatred and Global Instability* (New York: Doubleday, 2002).
6 "Fischer Reviews His Eventful Seven-year Tenure," *IMF Survey*, September 3, 2001, 278.
7 Alfred D. Chandler, Jr., *Scale and Scope: The Dynamics of Industrial Capitalism* (Cambridge, MA: Belknap Press, 1990).
8 William J. Baumol, Robert E. Litan, and Carl J. Schramm, *Good Capitalism, Bad Capitalism, and the Economics of Growth and Prosperity* (New Haven, CT: Yale University Press, 2007).
9 John H. Dunning (ed.), *Making Globalization Good: The Moral Challenges of Global Capitalism* (Oxford: Oxford University Press, 2003).
10 "Karma Capitalism," *Business Week*, October 30, 2006, 84–91.
11 Jack Welch and Suzy Welch, "Whose Company Is It Anyway," *Business Week*, October 9, 2006, 122.
12 Kathy Fogel, "Oligarchic Family Control, Social Economic Outcomes, and the Quality of Government," *Journal of International Business Studies* 37 (September 2006): 603–22.
13 "Measuring Success," *IMF Survey*, October 30, 2006, 324.
14 Pradeep K. Mitra and Marcelo Selowsky, "Lessons from a Decade of Transition in Eastern Europe and the Former Soviet Union," *Finance & Development* (June 2002): 48–51.
15 Stanley Fischer and Ratna Sahay, "Taking Stock," *Finance & Development* (September 2000): 2–6.
16 "Institutional Improvement in Ukraine Could Lead to Growth Boom," *IMF Survey*, October 16, 2006, 300–1.
17 Syed H. Akhter, "Is Globalization What It's Cracked Up to Be? Economic Freedom, Corruption, and Human Development," *Journal of World Business* 39 (August 2004): 283–95.
18 Franklin R. Root, *Foreign Market Entry Strategies* (New York: AMACOM, 1982), 146.
19 "Venezuela Pulls Control from Big Oil," CNNMoney.com, May 1, 2007.
20 "In Ecuador, One Slippery Oil Patch," *Business Week*, October 23, 2006, 50.
21 *Overseas Private Investment Corporation* (Washington, DC: OPIC), 2.
22 "U.S. Oil Giants Are Slow to Invest in Russia," *San José Mercury News*, January 13, 2003.
23 "BP to Own Half of New Russian Energy Company," *San José Mercury News*, August 30, 2003.
24 Wroe Alderson, *Dynamic Marketing Behavior* (Homewood, IL: Richard D. Irwin, 1965); and Sak Onkvisit and John J. Shaw, "Myopic Management: The Hollow Strength of American Competitiveness," *Business Horizons* 34 (January–February 1991): 13–19.
25 Yadong Luo, "Toward a Cooperative View of MNC–Host Government Relations: Building Blocks and Performance Implications," *Journal of International Business Studies* 32 (third quarter 2001): 401–19.
26 Timothy P. Blumentritt and Douglas Nigh, "The Integration of Subsidiary Political Activities in Multinational Corporations," *Journal of International Business Studies* 33 (first quarter 2002): 57–77.
27 Jean-Claude Cossett and Jean Roy, "The Determinants of Country Risk Ratings," *Journal of International Business Studies* 22 (No. 1, 1991): 135–42.
28 Jennifer M. Oetzel, Richard A. Bettis, and Marc Zenner, "Country Risk Measures: How Risky Are They?," *Journal of World Business* 36 (No. 2, 2001): 128–45.
29 Reid W. Click, "Financial and Political Risks in U.S. Direct Foreign Investment," *Journal of International Business Studies* 36 (September 2005): 559–75.
30 Kent D. Miller, "A Framework for Integrated Risk Management in International Business," *Journal of International Business Studies* 23 (No. 2, 1992): 321.

31 "The High Cost of Fear," *Business Week*, November 6, 2006, 16.
32 "Report: U.S. Ranks 4th in World for Terror Risk," *San José Mercury News*, August 17, 2003.
33 Kit Ladwig, "Political Risk Coverage – Is It Worth It?", *Collections and Credit Risk*, February 2001, 43–5.
34 "Insurance Imitates Art," *Business Week*, January 22, 2001, 16.
35 Marvin Zonis and Sam Wilkin, "Driving Defensively Through a Minefield of Political Risk," *Mastering Risk, Financial Times*, May 30, 2000.

Chapter 5

# Legal environment

The merchant will manage commerce the better, the more they are left to manage for themselves.
Thomas Jefferson, 1800

## Chapter outline

- Marketing strategy: the long arm of the law
- Multiplicity of legal environments
- Legal systems
- Jurisdiction and extraterritoriality
- Legal form of organization
- Branch vs. subsidiary
- Litigation vs. arbitration
- Bribery
    - Legal dimension
    - Ethical dimension
- Intellectual property
    - Categories of intellectual property
    - Legal rights and requirements
- Counterfeiting
- Conclusion
- Case 5.1 Bribery: a matter of national perspective

## Marketing strategy

### The long arm of the law

Siemens is a 160-year-old German institution. This conglomerate is Europe's largest engineering company. The company has global presence, including large and profitable operations in the U.S.A. and India. Unfortunately, Siemens has been caught in a web of suspicious deals. In 2005, according to a United Nations-appointed panel, three of Siemens' subsidiaries paid $1.6 million in kickbacks tied to the oil-for-food program of the United Nations.

In late 2006, Siemens announced that it had found about half a billion dollars in suspicious transactions that spanned over seven years. According to German, Italian, and Swiss prosecutors, the company was suspected of running a network of secret bank accounts and sham consulting contracts for the purpose of bribing potential customers. Earlier in the year, Germany charged two former employees of the company's power-generation unit with offering $7.8 million in bribes to win Italian natural gas contracts. In the U.S.A., American authorities indicted the company's medical unit. This subsidiary was charged with creating a sham business with a minority company so that it could win a $49 million contract from a hospital system in the state of Illinois.

Prosecutors in Munich have been investigating allegations that Siemens executives used sham consulting contracts to funnel hundreds of millions of euros into slush funds. The funds were used to bribe potential customers overseas. The probe led to arrests of several senior company officials and a former management board member. It should be noted that, as recently as 1999, German companies could write off bribes as expenses.

Although Siemens has performed well in the marketplace, CEO Klaus Kleinfeld was forced out by the Siemens supervisory board in 2007. There was no evidence to implicate Kleinfeld, but the board simply wanted to minimize damages stemming from the corruption scandal.

The situation at Siemens is certainly not pretty. The German chapter of Transparency International, a corruption watchdog, suspended Siemens' membership in 2004 and took an unusual step in 2006 to move to expel Siemens.

Sources: "Corruption Scandal at Siemens May Derail Restructuring Drive," *Wall Street Journal*, December 18, 2006; and "Siemens Executive Arrested," *Wall Street Journal*, March 28, 2007.

## Purpose of chapter

The case of Siemens in the marketing illustration above provides an example of the complexity of the legal environment. As may be expected, regulations can sometimes be ambiguous, and they can change over time. Because regulations do not allow marketers to plead ignorance, they must themselves somehow try to take control of the situation. They must attempt to conform to the legal requirements for each of the product categories they are selling. The impact of the laws at both the national and international levels must be assessed.

The purpose of this chapter is to discuss the impact of the legal environment on business decisions and to explain how the legal and political dimensions are interdependent. The chapter examines how countries' varying laws and interpretations affect imports, exports, and the marketing mix. In addition to a look at the major legal systems, issues discussed include jurisdiction, extraterritoriality, and bribery. A section is also devoted to discussion of the various legal forms of business organizations.

## Multiciplicity of legal environments

Similar to the political environment discussed in an earlier chapter, there is a multiplicity of legal environments: domestic, foreign, and international. At their worst, laws can prohibit the marketing of a product altogether. To most businesspeople, laws act as an inconvenience. Club Med's policy of rotating its international staff every six months, for example, is hampered by the U.S. immigration law, which makes the process of rotation both time-consuming and costly.

There are many products that cannot be legally imported into most countries. Examples include counterfeit money, illicit drugs, pornographic materials, and espionage equipment. It is usually also illegal to import live animals and fresh fruit unless accompanied by the required certificates. Furthermore, many products have to be modified to conform to local laws before these products are allowed to cross the border. The modification may be quite technical from an engineering standpoint or may only be cosmetic, as in the case of certain packaging changes.

A company's production strategy may also be affected by the legal environment. The U.S.A. bans the importation of the so-called Saturday night specials – cheap, short-barreled pistols – because they are often used in violent crime. Curiously, the gun control legislation does not prohibit the sale of such inexpensive weapons; only the import of such weapons is banned. As a result, Beretta, an Italian gun maker, is able to overcome the import ban by setting up a manufacturing operation in the state of Maryland.

In general, except for certain international treaties, there is no international law per se that prescribes acceptable and legal behavior of international business enterprises. There are only national laws – often in conflict with one another, especially when national politics are involved. This complexity creates a special problem for those companies that do business in various countries, where various laws may demand contradictory actions. For example, Wal-Mart Canada, to comply with the demand of the U.S. government, removed 10,000 pairs of Cuban-made pajamas. Canada was not pleased and ordered the Canadian branch of Wal-Mart to put the pajamas back on the shelves.[1]

## Legal systems

To understand and appreciate the varying legal philosophies among countries, it is useful to distinguish between the two major legal systems: common law and statute law.

There are some twenty-five common law or British law countries. A **common law system** is a legal system that relies heavily on precedents and conventions. Judges' decisions are guided not so much by statutes as by previous court decisions and interpretations of what certain laws are or should be. As a result, these countries' laws are tradition-oriented. Countries with such a system include the U.S.A., Great Britain, Canada, India, and other British colonies.

Countries employing a **statute law system**, also known as code or civil law, include most continental European countries and Japan. Most countries – over seventy – are guided by a statute law legal system. As the name implies, the main rules of the law are embodied in legislative codes. Every circumstance is clearly spelled out to indicate what is legal and what is not. There is also a strict and literal interpretation of the law under this system.

In practice, the two systems greatly overlap, and the distinction between them is not clear-cut. Although U.S. judges rely greatly on other judges' previous rulings and interpretations, they still refer to many laws that are contained in the statutes or codes. For statute law countries, many laws are developed by courts and are never reduced to statutes. Therefore, the only major distinction between the systems is the freedom of the judge in interpreting laws. In a common law country, the judge's ability to interpret laws in a personal way gives the judge a great deal of power to apply the law as it fits the situation. In contrast, a judge in a civil law country has a lesser role in using personal judgment to create or interpret laws because the judge must strictly follow the "letter of the law."

There are four sources of European Community law: treaties, regulations, directives, and European Court of Justice case law. Member states are bound by European law, and their adopted measures must conform with it. The European Court of Justice ensures that Community law is observed in the interpretation and application of treaties. Treaties are "primary" Community law. Regulations and directives, as "secondary" Community law, expand the treaties and make them more specific. Directives are measures taken by the Community to harmonize the laws of the member states. Directives are binding. Member states' national courts and tribunals must apply Community law alongside provisions of their own national law.[2]

## Jurisdiction and extraterritoriality

National laws vary from one country to another. The EU area, for example, has high minimum wages, generous unemployment benefits, and employment protection measures. Dismissal restrictions include notice and severance pay requirements, and they can affect labor productivity. Among the advanced economies, Portugal is most restrictive in employment protection, and it has particularly stringent dismissal restrictions.[3]

In preparing a contract, a seller or buyer should stipulate the particular legal system that is to take precedence in resolving any contract dispute. The court to be used for legal remedy should also be specified. The company must keep in mind that to earn a legal victory in its home court is one thing, but to enforce a judgment against a foreign party is something else altogether. Enforcement is difficult unless that foreign party has the desire to continue to do business in the country where the judgment is obtained. Given the disparity of national laws, an international marketer will need to seek assistance from either a local lawyer or an international law firm (see Figure 5.1).

It is often necessary to file a lawsuit in the defendant's home country. To make certain that the foreign court will have jurisdiction to hear the case, the contract should contain a clause that allows the company to bring a lawsuit in either the home country or the host country. According to Article 17 of the Brussels Convention on Jurisdiction and the Enforcement of Judgments, the place where the matter in controversy is located is the exclusive forum for disputes regarding real property, status of a corporate entity, public records, trademark, copyright and patent, and enforcement of judgments.

Based on an analysis of legal cases over the 1985 to 2005 period, there are two litigation dissolution processes as related to international distribution relationships: proactive and reactive. The two processes have distinct triggers and outcomes.[4] Whenever possible and practical, companies should consider commercial arbitration in place of judicial trials. Arbitration proceedings provide such advantages as an impartial hearing, a quick result, and a decision made by experts. Both IBM and Fujitsu seemed satisfied with the ruling of their two arbitrators in settling a copyright dispute. Intel, in contrast, did not want arbitration and was frustrated by the slow pace of its copyright lawsuit against NEC.

Three important multilateral agreements on international arbitration address the enforcement of agreements to arbitrate and judicial assistance in the execution of arbitral awards. **The New York**

Today, Business is Global.
Is Your Law Firm?
To realize a vision, a company must be poised to take advantage of opportunities quickly — before they are seized by others. Combining an understanding of our clients' needs with the broad transactional and litigation experience of a 1,000 lawyer international law firm, Morrison & Foerster lawyers help clients recognize opportunities, resolve problems, and create value in today's fast-changing global marketplace.
MORRISON & FOERSTER LLP
Lawyers for the global economy℠
MoFo
on the web at www.mofo.com

**FIGURE 5.1** International law firm

**Convention** has received broad worldwide acceptance and is now in force in 82 countries. The Inter-American Convention, closely paralleling the framework of the New York Convention, states that parties which have agreed to arbitrate may be compelled to do so and that arbitral awards shall be recognized and enforced in the same manner as final judicial decisions. **The ICSID Convention (The Convention on the Settlement of Investment Disputes between States and Nationals of Other States)** has established the International Centre for the Settlement of Investment Disputes (ICSID) in Washington, D.C. to facilitate the arbitration of disputes between foreign investors and host governments.

Many Latin American countries adhere to the **Calvo Doctrine** (after the Argentine jurist Carlos Calvo), which is generally hostile to international arbitration. Under the Calvo Doctrine, disputes between foreign investors and a host government must be submitted to the domestic courts of the host government instead of to an independent third party.

One aspect of the law that does not have universal acceptance involves **extraterritorial application** of the law. A nation wishing to protect its own interests often applies its laws to activities outside its own territory. Spanish laws allow crimes such as genocide to be tried in Spain even though such crimes were not committed there. In 2003, a Spanish judge asked the government to seek the extradition of 40 Argentines, including two former leaders of the military junta. Judges in France, Sweden, and Italy also sought the extradition of several former military officers.

Not as clear-cut and much more controversial are the activities of an MNC's foreign subsidiaries and affiliates. In the case of U.S. firms' foreign subsidiaries on foreign soil, it is questionable whether these subsidiaries must comply with the U.S. government's decrees. In response to the U.S. government's prohibition of U.S. firms from doing business with Libya, American firms complied with the order but did not forbid their foreign subsidiaries from doing business as usual with Libya, as long as American personnel were not stationed there.

According to an Equal Opportunity Commission (EEOC) lawyer, "employers can't go around discriminating, discharging, and harassing people simply because they're overseas." Ali Bouresland, a Lebanese-born naturalized U.S. citizen, claimed that his supervisor at the Arabian American Oil Co. harassed him, denied him time off for Muslim holidays, and fired him because of his race, religion, and national origin. But the U.S. Supreme Court stated that a provision of the 1964 Civil Rights Act barring employment bias based on race, sex, religion, and national origin does not apply to U.S. citizens working abroad for American firms. The ruling stressed a principle of American law that limits federal legislation to U.S. territory. As a rule, American courts will not apply laws beyond their border (i.e., **extraterritorially**) unless Congress expresses a different intent. John Pfeiffer, a high-ranking executive for Wrigley Corp. in the U.S.A., was protected under U.S. law from discrimination based on his age. After his transfer to a high position in Wrigley's German office, Pfeiffer turned 65 and was immediately fired on the basis of his age. Because of the transfer, he had no recourse.

When a nation attempts to apply its laws extraterritorially, it may upset its trading or political partners. The U.S.A. has been placed in this awkward position a number of times in the past. The U.S.A. angered Canada when the U.S. government tried to prevent U.S. firms' Canadian subsidiaries from selling products to Cuba. The U.S.A. created another uproar in Europe when it prohibited European subsidiaries of American firms from participating in a Soviet pipeline project. In spite of past mistakes, the U.S.A. once again greatly upset its allies by passing the so-called Helms-Burton law in 1996. The law attempts to tighten economic sanctions against Cuba by penalizing foreign companies investing in Cuba. Mexico, Canada, and the European Union have voiced their strong objection to the extraterritorial measures of the U.S. law which interfere with the foreign policies of other countries. Reacting to their plans to enact retaliatory laws, the U.S.A. has assured these trading partners that the controversial law will not be enforced.

Jurisdiction is crucial for a number of reasons. Plaintiffs want to file lawsuits in countries which give them judicial advantages and maximum compensation. Defendants want to minimize any damage amounts that can be collected. In general, a company prefers a lawsuit in its own home country, but in some cases it is more advantageous to shift the legal action somewhere else. For example, a lawyer representing 58 Mexicans argued that the accident cases against Bridgestone/ Firestone and Ford Motor should be heard in Nashville where the headquarters of Bridgestone/ Firestone is located. Furthermore, regarding Firestone and Ford hiding the information that Ford Explorers equipped with Firestone tires were more prone to crash, these allegations took place in the U.S.A. The defendants, on the other hand, argued that the accidents occurred in Mexico and that it would be impractical to take witnesses and plaintiffs to the U.S.A., not to mention the need to employ translators to help English-speaking jurors to understand the Spanish-language testimony. The defendants did not mention, however, that plaintiffs could not seek punitive damages in Mexico.

A trend toward extraterritoriality is unclear. Belgium's law of universal jurisdiction allowed its legal system to exert criminal authority over war crimes, genocide, and crimes against humanity that took place anywhere in the world, and it does not matter whether Belgium had any connection with the matter. In other words, the law gave Belgian courts "universal jurisdiction" and allowed them to try any person accused of having committed war crimes and genocide anywhere in the world. Cases were brought against such heads of states as George W. Bush, Tony Blair, and Ariel Sharon. Because of the controversy, Belgium repealed this war crimes law in 2003.

Nations have negotiated a treaty to establish an International Criminal Court. This permanent court in The Hague is empowered to try individuals accused of genocide, war crimes, and crimes against humanity. The court should bring order to such ad hoc tribunals as the ones in Rwanda and Yugoslavia underwritten by the U.S.A. For 50 years, the U.S.A. had supported the idea, but when it was time to ratify it, the Bush administration refused. Likewise, those countries targeted for investigations refused to sign, and they include India (for Kashmir), China (for Tibet), Russia (for Chechnya), Iraq, Libya, and Israel. Since 66 nations have ratified the treaty, the court came into existence on July 1, 2002.

MNCs, by operating in a number of countries, are particularly vulnerable to countries and courts that want to exert their jurisdiction. For instance, the 1789 Alien Tort Claims Act was passed in 1789 by the fledgling U.S.A. to assure Europe that it would not harbor pirates or assassins. The law allows foreigners to sue in U.S. courts for violations of the "law of nations" (see Legal Dimension 5.1). Nobody would have thought that the law could be used in 1976 by a Paraguayan doctor who asked the U.S. court to try a former Paraguayan police official for the murder of the doctor's son. A federal appeals court ruled in 1980 that this law permitted foreigners to bring a lawsuit in a U.S. court over acts committed overseas. A precedent was set when a case involving mining company Drummon Co. was allowed to proceed to trial in 2007. It was alleged that Drummon collaborated with Colombian paramilitaries to kill three union leaders in 2001. The company denied any involvement. Such legal cases have alarmed and upset business groups, who have argued that it is not the role of U.S. courts to resolve murky disputes that took place thousands of miles away.[5]

Given the fact that cyberspace and e-commerce are inherently international, any attempts to regulate and tax their activities on the internet through the existing territorial jurisdiction will be problematic. Any successful governance regime will need to involve international public–private sector cooperation. The cooperation may combine self-regulation with government oversight and enforcement.[6]

Legal Dimension 5.1

**Pirates and human rights**

The 1789 Alien Tort Claims Act was enacted to combat seafaring pirates. Now it is Unocal's turn. Burmese citizens asserted that Unocal relied on the Burmese army to force villagers to clear jungle for this Californian energy giant's natural-gas pipeline. Those peasants who resisted were tortured or killed.

Unocal denied any knowledge of these acts. It also argued that it had no control over the Burmese military and that it did not actively participate in the alleged human rights violations (unlike the Nazis and their active collaborators at the Nuremberg trials). According to the Ninth Circuit U.S. Court of Appeals, Unocal could be liable if it "provided practical assistance or encouragement to the Burmese military" or if it simply knew that the crimes were taking place. However, the justices are divided on whether the international or U.S. Common Law should be used to assess a private corporation's liability of this type. Conceivably, MNCs can be held liable for foreign governments' human-rights abuses.

Unocal Corp. settled the claims in 2004. It was later acquired by Chevron Corp.

*Source*: "Drummon Trial Is Set to Open," *Wall Street Journal*, July 9, 2007.

## Legal form of organization

Firms doing business in Great Britain have three primary choices for the legal form of their organization: British branch, limited company, or partnership. If a limited company is the choice, more decision is needed. A limited company may be either a *public limited company (PLC)*, which can raise capital by selling securities to the public, or a *private company (Ltd)*, which is not allowed to offer shares or debentures to the public. In general, a public company must meet a number of requirements in terms of registration and capital structure, subscription for shares, and profits and assets available for distribution.

In the U.S.A., a business is able to select from among these forms: sole proprietorship, partnership, and corporation. For firms involved in international trade, the most common choice is the corporation due to the limited liability associated with the corporate form, its relatively permanent structure, and its ability to raise money by selling securities. Most large U.S. firms have a Corp. or Inc. nomenclature as part of their trade names.

The nomenclature indicating incorporation is different in other countries. For most British Commonwealth countries, corporate names include Ltd. or Ltd. co. to indicate that the liability of the company is "limited." Equivalencies in civil law countries include the following: in France, *SA* (*société anonyme* or *sociedad anónima*) for a "formal" corporation/stock company and *SARL* (*société à responsabilité limitée* or *sociedad de responsabilidad limitada*) for an "informal" corporation/limited liability company; in Germany and Switzerland, *AG* (*aktiengesellschaft*) for a stock company and *GmbH* (*Gesellschaft mit beschrankter Haftung*) for a limited liability company; in Japan, *KK* (*kabushiki kaisha*) for a stock company; in Sweden, *AB*; and in the Netherlands, *NV*. To eliminate confusion and to ensure some uniformity, European countries are now encouraging the use of *PLC* instead of other nomenclature to indicate that a company is incorporated.

## Branch vs. subsidiary

One legal decision that an MNC must make is whether to use branches or subsidiaries to carry out its plans and to manage its operations in a foreign country. A branch is the company's extension or outpost at another location. Although physically detached, it is not legally separated from its parent. A subsidiary, in contrast, is both physically and legally independent. It is considered a separate legal entity in spite of its ownership by another corporation.

A subsidiary may either be wholly owned (i.e., 100 percent owned) or partially owned. GE receives some $1 billion in revenues from its wholly owned and partially owned subsidiaries in Europe. The usual practice of Pillsbury, Coca-Cola, and IBM is to have wholly owned subsidiaries. Although a parent company has total control when its subsidiary is wholly owned, it is difficult to generalize about the superiority of one approach over the other.

As a rule, multinationals prefer subsidiaries to branches. General Electric has 1157 affiliated firms, 787 of which are foreign entities. GE Capital Services has 1425 affiliates, 1085 of which are in 55 host countries.[7] The question that must be asked is why GE, like other MNCs, would go through the trouble and expense of forming hundreds of foreign companies elsewhere. When compared to the use of branches, the use of subsidiaries adds complexity to the corporate structure. They are also expensive, requiring substantial sales volume to justify their expense.

There are several reasons why a subsidiary is the preferred structure. One reason has to do with *recruitment of management*. Titles mean a great deal in virtually all parts of the world. A top administrator of an overseas operation wants a prestigious title of president, chief executive, or managing director rather than being merely a "branch manager."

Another reason for forming a subsidiary may involve gaining *quick access* to a particular market by acquiring an existing company within the market and making it a subsidiary. The Swiss-based Ciba-Geigy Corporation acquired Airwick, a U.S. firm, with two goals in mind: gaining access to the U.S. consumer market and acquiring a well-known brand.

Furthermore, subsidiaries are preferred because of the *flexibility* created, which may allow the parent company to take advantage of legal loopholes or of the opportunity to circumvent certain government requirements. Since 1987, the U.S.A. has banned imports of Iranian crude oil. In reality, some $3.5 to $4 billion of Iranian oil found its way into the U.S.A. annually. Exxon bought 250,000 to 300,000 barrels daily from Iran for refineries in Europe and Asia. American oil companies were able to circumvent the ban by using their overseas subsidiaries to buy and sell Iranian crude.

There is an inherent conflict among corporate interests, government policy, and consumer welfare. A company must decide whether it should fully comply with the intention or spirit of the law designed to enhance foreign policy or whether it should look after the interests of consumers or its stockholders. Such a legal loophole probably does not exist if a company's operations abroad are structured as branches rather than as subsidiaries. Laws could be changed to close loopholes by requiring foreign subsidiaries and foreign-owned operations to adhere to the same rules. However, the effectiveness of such attempts is questionable, and there is the issue concerning the extraterritorial application of the law.

Another advantage in favor of maintaining subsidiaries is the *tax benefit*. When formed in a foreign country, a subsidiary is considered a local company, enabling it to receive tax benefits granted to other national companies. Moreover, a subsidiary provides the parent company with some flexibility in terms of when the parent has to pay tax on the income generated by its subsidiary. With a foreign branch, the income is immediately taxable through the parent firm, regardless of whether there is the remittance for the profit. Given this situation, there is no opportunity for the parent to defer any profit or loss.

The *limited liability* advantage may be one of the most important reasons why a subsidiary is formed. With this organizational structure, the parent firm's liability is limited to its investment in the foreign subsidiary. That is, its maximum loss can be no greater than the assets invested in its subsidiary. In addition, the formation of a separate company provides some protection against hostile acts. During World War II, for example, Philips formed North American Philips (NAP) as a separate entity by placing its U.S. operations in a trust in order to protect the company from takeover attempts by the Nazis. The problem in this case was that NAP eventually grew to be too independent and would not even buy the parent's video cassette recorders for sale in the U.S. market. Philips finally dissolved the trust in 1986, reclaiming the 58 percent interest in NAP in order to have "one face to the world, one central policy."

MNCs generally believe that they are protected against their subsidiaries' actions and liabilities because of the separate incorporation of parent firms and subsidiaries, making them separate legal entities. This precept has come under severe test in a lawsuit filed by India against Union Carbide over an industrial disaster at Bhopal, India. A gas leak at a Union Carbide plant on December 3, 1984 killed 3800 people and injured 200,000 more. In addition, the lawsuit against Union Carbide, the victims' lawyers, alleging plant design defects as contributing factor, sued Humphreys & Glasgow Consultants Pvt. Ltd., Union Carbide's prime contractor. This Bombay-based firm is affiliated with Humphreys & Glasgow Ltd., a London engineering firm, which in turn is owned by Enserch Corp., a Dallas diversified energy company.

The main legal issue in the Bhopal case is whether the parent company is also responsible for the damage caused by its subsidiary. The issue in most cases could probably be decided easily if the parent company owns 100 percent of its subsidiary's voting stock. With full control over a wholly owned subsidiary, there is little question about whether the parent and its foreign subsidiary are indeed independent and separate. In the Union Carbide case, the issue was complicated by the fact that Union Carbide India Ltd. is not a wholly owned subsidiary. Although theoretically and legally autonomous in terms of decision making and responsibility, the subsidiary does not function independently in practice, as its authority is granted by the parent. This is exactly the issue that was legally raised in India in regard to who was responsible for the disaster.

India's contention was that MNCs that are engaged in hazardous activities should not be insulated from their subsidiaries' actions. The liability issue hinged largely on the extent of Union Carbide's involvement in managing its Indian subsidiary. According to India, the two should not be considered legally separate because of their close links. Evidence included the Indian subsidiary's inability to spend large sums of money without authorization from the Connecticut headquarters. Union Carbide's defense was that, although it had the power to veto large outlays as a majority shareholder, the day-to-day operations were run locally. A settlement between India and Union Carbide was finally reached, but many legal issues as well as lawsuits are yet to be resolved.

Warren M. Anderson, the company's chairman, rushed to Bhopal to personally take moral responsibility. He was arrested as soon as he stepped off the airplane. The U.S. government intervened, and he was released on bail after six hours. Union Carbide thought that it had settled the matter in 1989 when it paid $470 million to the Indian government to settle a civil suit. Many Bhopal residents were unhappy with the settlement, and much of the money has still not reached the victims. Claimants received about $600 for injuries and about $3,000 in case of death. Subsequently, the Indian Supreme Court, probably bowing to public pressure, reinstated criminal charges of "culpable homicide" against Anderson. Victims' groups have utilized the Alien Torts Claims Act to sue American companies in the U.S.A. for actions taking place overseas. The lawsuit, charging that Union Carbide violated international law and human rights, states: "the defendants are liable for fraud and civil contempt for their total failure to comply with the lawful orders of the courts of both the United States and India."

## Litigation vs. arbitration

Litigation, no matter where it takes place, is never easy. In certain places, it can be much more complicated. India has more than 30 million civil and criminal cases pending. This should not come as a surprise, given the fact that India has 11 judges for every one million people.[8] It will take more than 300 years to go through this backlog.[9]

In the U.S.A., a lawyer may be found at virtually every corner. Actually, the U.S.A. has about 900,000 lawyers, and there is one lawyer for every 400 Americans. Americans spend many billions of dollars a year on direct litigation costs and higher insurance premiums, not to mention indirect costs which include the expense of avoiding legal liability.

In Japan, there are about 18,000 lawyers, amounting to one lawyer per 7000 Japanese. Japan's legal approach is different. To be a lawyer, one must pass the national bar exam, among the world's toughest. Only one attempt per year is allowed. For decades, only the top 500 people pass the bar exam each year. As a non-litigious, consensus-based society, Japan limits the number of attorneys passing the bar exam to only 1 or 2 percent of applicants. On average, a person makes five attempts before successfully passing the bar exam. Not surprisingly, fewer than 1000 new lawyers, judges, and prosecutors are certified annually.[10]

Also in Japan, plaintiffs must pay their lawyers an up-front fee of up to 8 percent of damages sought. The system prohibits contingency fees, class actions, and other fee-sharing devices that encourage filing a lawsuit. Judges, not juries, are the ones setting damage awards. Even when a victim is killed, awards rarely exceed $150,000. There is no "discovery," thus denying plaintiffs access before trial to an opponent's evidence. In addition, the Japanese culture discourages confrontation and does not view those who sue positively. While the American system encourages excessive and frivolous lawsuits, the Japanese system does not fully protect the rights of victims. Incidentally, when Hitachi Ltd. was sued by IBM for industrial spying in 1982, Hitachi was shocked to find that its first bill alone from its U.S. law firm exceeded its total payments for legal services in Japan since the founding of the company in 1920.

In the 1990s, U.S. law firms marched into Europe. Between 2000 and 2005, the number of lawyers working for the largest 250 American firms in England nearly tripled to more than 4200. U.S. law firms have been expanding their operations in Asia. The number of lawyers from U.S. firms has jumped to 975 in China and 470 in Japan. The rise has to do with the activities of the law firms' clients as related to mergers and acquisitions, corporate buyouts, and financial restructurings.[11]

To save time, expenses, and relationships, it may be wise to look at litigation as the last resort. To resolve a dispute in China, a company has three options: negotiation, arbitration, and litigation (see Cultural Dimension 5.1). Negotiation is usually best because it is quick and inexpensive while preserving a working relationship with one's partner. As a matter of fact, most business contracts in China require companies to employ negotiation before pursuing other dispute settlement mechanisms. Chinese government officials may be requested to negotiate a solution. A time limit for this

Cultural Dimension 5.1

**Dispute resolution**

There are several ways to deal with a trade dispute with a foreign buyer. One of them is mediation (also known as conciliation). This is a process in which parties to a dispute appoint a neutral third party to assist them in resolving their disputes. Unlike a judge or an arbitrator, the mediator does not have the power to compel the parties to accept a recommended solution. The goal of mediation is a voluntarily negotiated settlement.

One common method of dispute resolution is arbitration. Arbitration is a primary form of alternative dispute resolution. The parties agree to submit their disputes to an arbitrator or a panel of arbitrators. Arbitrators have binding authority to render awards that are enforceable in the courts of most countries. Arbitration is often less costly, less litigious, and less time-consuming, and offers more privacy to the parties than litigation.

The parties agree to arbitration in the event of a dispute in the contracting stage by including an arbitration clause in their contract. Depending on what the parties have agreed to, either the parties will choose their own arbitrators and procedures (ad hoc arbitration) or submit their dispute to an arbitral institution. There are many different arbitral institutions to which parties may turn in the event of a dispute.

*Source*: Jim Robb, "Legal Resources and Options for the Exporter," *Export America*, January 2001.

process should be specified. Arbitration is the second best method. Contracts allowing arbitration should specify a choice of arbitration body as well as a choice of law. Because of China's accession to the United Nations Convention on the Recognition and Enforcement of Foreign Arbitral Awards (the New York Convention), arbitral awards rendered in other signatory countries are recognized and enforceable in China, and vice versa.[12]

## Bribery

At first glance, bribery is both unethical and illegal. A closer look, however, reveals that bribery is not really that straightforward an issue. There are many questions about what bribery is, how it is used, and why it is used. The ethical and legal problems associated with bribery can also be quite complex.

### *Legal dimension*

According to the **Foreign Corrupt Practices Act (FCPA) of 1977**, bribery is "the use of interstate commerce to offer, pay, promise to pay, or authorize giving anything of value to influence an act or decision by a foreign government, politician, or political party to assist in obtaining, retaining, or directing business to any person." A bribe is also known as a "payoff," "grease money," "lubricant," "little envelope," *mordida* or "bite" (Mexico), and "under-the-table payment," as well as by other terms. A bribe may take the form of cash, gifts, jobs, and free trips.

Instances of firms paying bribes are numerous. The U.S. government learned in 1995 of almost ninety cases of foreign firms paying bribes to undercut American firms' efforts to win international contracts worth $45 billion. Germany's Siemens, France's Alcatel Alsthom, and Airbus Industrie are among the major practitioners. Germany found 1500 cases of public officials on the take between 1987 and 1995 in Frankfurt, adding 20 to 30 percent to the cost of a building contract. Lockheed Corp. admitted paying $38 million in bribes, kickbacks, and other questionable payments to foreign officials to facilitate aircraft sales between 1970 and 1975. The FCPA was passed as a result of the company's bribery scandal. However, in 1995, Lockheed was forced to admit that it had paid $1 million to a member of the Egyptian Parliament so that she would help the company sell three C-130 Hercules transport planes to Egypt. Subsequently, the company paid a record $24.8 million in penalties and for violating the FCPA, and a former vice-president was sentenced to 18 months in prison.

There are several reasons why a bribe is solicited, offered, and accepted. Low salaries of public officials is one reason; simple greed is another. According to EU officials, Romania's corruption stems from the fact that judges and government officials are vulnerable to bribes because their salaries are among the lowest in Europe.[13] The loyalties and commitments which public servants have to their political parties, families, and friends can cause them to ask for favors that will benefit those groups. The proliferation of bureaucratic regulations seems to be another cause. Complex regulations create the opportunity for bribery because by paying a bribe a company can cut through bureaucratic red tape quickly. Brazil's governmental system is so complicated that it even has a Debureaucratization Ministry.

Some of the reasons why some businesspersons are willing and even eager to offer a bribe are:

- To speed up the required work or processing
- To secure a contract
- To avoid the cancellation of the contract
- To prevent competitors from getting the contract.

Bribery is not always an absolute; rather it may be a matter of degree. What may seem like a bribe to one person may not be to another – especially to the one who accepts the payment. This problem of interpretation can perhaps be better understood by considering the tipping system that is so prevalent in the Western world. When considered in this light, there is a fine line between a bribe and a gratuity. The tip is given "to ensure promptness" – the same purposes for which a bribe is tendered. Those who provide services expect a tip, and this is true even when the service given may be routine and of poor quality.

The determination of whether something is a bribe or not is complicated further by particular types of payments. When a businessperson gives a public employee a few dollars for extra services so that a delay can be avoided, is this payment a tip or a bribe? The same question in a broader sphere may be asked about compensation and commissions for middlemen. Lockheed paid large sums of money for the services of Prince Bernhardt of the Netherlands and Prime Minister Tanaka of Japan. Under normal circumstances, payments to middlemen pose no problem whatsoever. In the Lockheed case, however, the two middlemen happened to be well-known personalities – a prince and a prime minister – who were in the position of being able to secure favorable treatment for the company. The U.S. Securities and Exchange Commission (SEC) takes the position that payments made to low- and middle-level officials for tasks performed routinely by such officials are not illegal but that payments to high-level government officials for special favors are unlawful.

Another kind of questionable payment involves political contributions. When Gulf Oil was forced to contribute $4 million toward the re-election of Korea's President Park, this was viewed by the

Koreans as a political contribution and by U.S. officials as extortion. It is rather ironic that U.S. senators and congressmen would be upset by Gulf's compliance with the Koreans' request when such politicians routinely solicit corporate contributions for their own re-election in the U.S.A. Many attempts to reform political donations in the U.S.A. have been slow and difficult.

There has also been debate about gifts. Traditionally, U.S. firms provide Christmas gifts for their customers, employees, and those who have assisted the firm. In foreign countries, gifts may be given for other occasions, such as a New Year holiday or birthday. These gifts are often considered by Westerners as bribes when in reality they serve the same purpose as Christmas gifts.

To answer clearly the question of whether a bribe is illegal and unethical is difficult for two reasons – legal and cultural. Legally speaking, bribery is not an either/or proposition. There are several kinds of payments that fall on the borderline of legality and illegality. To provide clarification, Sections 5001 to 5003 of the 1988 Trade Act amended the FCPA in many respects. The primary change concerns payments to third parties by a U.S. firm "knowing or having reason to know" that the third party would use the payment for prohibited purposes. Under the new law, the U.S. firm must have actual knowledge of or willful blindness to the prohibited use of the payment.

The Act also clarifies the types of payments that are permissible. For example, under the FCPA as originally enacted, although payments to low-level officials who exercise only "ministerial" or "clerical" functions were exempt, the provision provided little guidance to exporters in determining whether a given foreign official exercised discretionary authority. The fact that the Middle East and Africa employ part-time officials complicates the matter even more. The Trade Act provides guidance by specifying the types of payments that are permissible rather than which individuals can receive them. A payment for a routine governmental action (e.g., processing papers, stamping visas, and scheduling inspections) may be made without subjecting the exporter to the worry of whether this type of payment may lead to criminal liability. In spite of the clarifications, the law still contains several gray areas.

In addition, the interpretation of legality depends on the particular laws of a particular country. What is illegal in one country is not necessarily so elsewhere. In the former Soviet Union, a simple gift – such as clothing for a public official – was considered a bribe. Unlike U.S. laws, the laws of many countries do not deal specifically with foreign bribery. Canada takes the position that Canadian firms should comply with the host country's law.

Most countries do not provide for legal sanctions for the bribery of foreign officials by their companies or nationals to obtain or retain business. The U.S.A. feels that it is important to have equitable competitive conditions. As such, there should be internationally recognized standards of behavior that marketers can refer to so as to be able to refuse to engage in illicit practices. While OECD members have agreed with the U.S. government that international cooperation is needed to discourage companies and public officials from resorting to bribery, it was several years before the 26 OECD countries agreed in 1996 to prevent bribes (often listed as fees) from being tax deductible.

The U.S.A. has been pushing OECD members to take a concerted action in criminalizing the bribery of foreign officials in international business transactions. It took more than 20 years for the majority of the leading industrial countries to ratify the OECD Anti-bribery Convention. The Convention was ratified in 1998. Britain did not pass its domestic law in this regard until 2001. Even then, the OECD complained in 2005 that the United Kingdom was stalling its implementation of the Convention.[14] There is evidence that corruption reduces FDI from countries that have signed the OECD Convention on Combating Bribery of Foreign Public Officials in International Business Transactions. Unfortunately, corruption also results in higher FDI from countries with high levels of corruption, implying that investors being used to corruption at home actually seek countries with prevalent corruption.[15]

## Ethical dimension

Ethical considerations about bribery are even more ambiguous than legal definitions. Generally, ethics precedes law. What is illegal is almost always considered unethical, whereas what is unethical may not be illegal (see Ethical Dimension 5.1). Whether bribery is unethical or not depends on the standards used. Morality exists only in the context of a particular culture. As such, many foreign officials view the holier-than-thou attitude of the U.S.A. as being naive and hypocritical. To South Koreans, bribes are part of life. Korean business executives feel obligated to award each cabinet minister "rice-cake expenses" as holiday gifts.

What is unethical in one culture is not necessarily so in another. Bribery may thus be acceptable in some countries. In many less developed countries, the practice of providing bribes is so common that not to do so may be interpreted as an insult or a lack of respect. The Japanese view payments to foreign officials to secure business deals as a normal practice.

There is also another side to ethics. If a company tries to be ethical by refusing to make questionable payments, it may risk having its cargo left on the dock or in a customs warehouse where its goods can easily be damaged or stolen. Moreover, to refuse giving a bribe may result in the loss of a contract, thus hurting stockholders and employees. Generally, it is a good idea for a company to maintain its integrity. However, this task is difficult if the company's efforts are adversely affected by competitors that routinely offer bribes and thus take advantage of the company's ethical conduct.

Marketing professionals' divergence in ethical behavior and attitudes may be attributed to differences in perceptions regarding the importance of ethics and social responsibility. Such perceptions are due to country differences (cultural, economic, and legal/political environments), organizational ethical climate, and demographic variables (gender and age). On the one hand, American, Australian, and Malaysian marketers exhibited different levels of idealism and relativism. On the other hand, irrespective of country, corporate ethical values were positively related to

### Ethical Dimension 5.1

#### A legal bribe

In general, American companies and the U.S. government are at the forefront of fighting bribery. While criticizing other countries for being lax, U.S. lawmakers themselves are not exactly bashful in using questionable means and accepting questionable funds. While the ethics rules restrict personal gifts, the rules do not ban payment to a lawmaker's re-election campaigns. They routinely offer lavish outings and invite lobbyists to attend under the guise of fundraising. A birthday party in honor of a lawmaker costs $1,000 per lobbyist. Joining the legislator on a hunting or fishing trip will set the lobbyist back at least $2,500. The lobbyist pays a political fundraising committee, which then pays the lawmaker for his activities. This indirect method of payment is a result of the new ethics rules. Somehow, the indirect payment method is supposed to be more ethically sound.

marketers' idealism and negatively related to their relativism. In addition, relativism increased with age, and women were more idealistic than men.[16]

Although Thai and American managers do not differ in their perceptions about the importance of ethics, American managers have higher corporate ethical values.[17] Ethical perceptions may vary even within a country. According to a study of marketers in Egypt, Jordan, and Saudi Arabia, compared to Middle-Eastern marketers who do not perceive ethics to be important, those perceiving ethics to be important are more likely to have an ethical intention.[18]

Based on an analysis of the contents of 197 corporate codes of ethics, culture has an influence on corporate codes. The Australian and Canadian codes are similar, and they are quite different from the Swedish codes.[19] Because of religious teachings, Austrian Christians are less idealistic and relativistic than those of other religions, including other Christians from the U.S.A. and the United Kingdom.[20]

Despite the lack of agreement about what a bribe is and whether bribes are always undesirable, companies must nevertheless cope with the practice. A good rule of thumb may be to be discreet and not to pursue a bribe too aggressively. It may be prudent to wait for the other party either to bring up the issue or to provide a hint. Perhaps occasions for giving should be considered, and holidays can often provide an appropriate excuse. In fact, the absence of a gift at major holidays can be quite conspicuous. In some cultures, it is acceptable to give a gift upon being introduced or when first meeting someone. In other cultures, an occasion for gift giving is upon the consummation of a deal or when departing. If a U.S. firm decides not to comply with a request for bribe, it should cite the Foreign Corrupt Practices Act as a legitimate excuse. In any case, no matter how distasteful bribery may appear to be, marketers must realize that it is part of the international "game" that many businesspersons play.

International marketers need to develop strategies to deal with bribery problems (see Exhibits 5.1 and 5.2 and Figure 5.2). Good strategies should include having corporate codes of ethics, sensitization of ethics in managers though training and education, and conducting ethics audits. Regarding the use and contents of corporate codes of ethics, U.S. firms are more likely than their European counterparts to have adopted codes of ethics. In Europe, the adoption of such codes is a relatively new phenomenon, and many of these codes have made their way into Europe via subsidiaries of U.S. firms.

Perceptions of ethical issues vary by country. In a study of the relationship between cultural values and marketing ethics, India and the U.S.A. are culturally different.[21] One study of the human resources practices of 50 leading multinational corporations compares universal ethical norms and relativist ethical norms (related to adaptive human resources management and multi-domestic strategies). While some companies adhere to universal ethical norms, the practices are largely muti-domestic. Child labor, for example, does not have a universal meaning.[22]

Therefore, all corporate ethics policies should not look alike since a code of ethics developed in a country in which a firm's headquarters is located may not match the perceptions of ethical issues of the firm's employees in another country. However, country differences are not a sufficient reason to preclude a formulation of universal ethical principles. In spite of variations across countries, it is crucial to note that certain core values are largely universal. The five core values that shape ethics are: honesty, responsibility, respect, fairness, and compassion. This commonality defines people's notion of ethics – regardless of religions, political systems, and gender.[23]

One possible solution is for a government to scale down its role in the economy so as to reduce the opportunities for officials to engage in corruption. The combat may have to be a multiple-step process. The focus of a country's anti-corruption efforts should begin with consciousness raising, shift to making the government less susceptible, and then address the problems of a corrupt system.[24]

Exhibit 5.1

### The Coca-Cola Company: the Code of Business Conduct

#### Some highlights of the Code

- Employees must follow the law wherever they are around the world.
- Employees must avoid conflicts of interest. Be aware of appearances.
- Financial records – both for internal activities and external transactions – must be timely and accurate.
- Company assets – including computers, materials and work time – must not be used for personal benefit.
- Customers and suppliers must be dealt with fairly and at arm's length.
- Employees must never attempt to bribe or improperly influence a government official.
- Employees must safeguard the company's non-public information.
- Violations of the Code include asking other employees to violate the Code, not reporting a Code violation or failing to cooperate in a Code investigation.
- Violating the Code will result in discipline. Discipline will vary depending on the circumstances and may include, alone or in combination, a letter of reprimand, demotion, loss of merit increase, bonus or stock options, suspension or even termination.
- Under the Code, certain actions require written approval by your Principal Manager. The Principal Manager is your Division President, Group President, Corporate function head, or the General Manager of your operating unit.
- For those who are themselves Principal Managers, written approvals must come from the General Counsel and Chief Financial Officer. Written approvals for executive officers and directors must come from the Board of Directors or its designated committee.
- If you have questions about any situation, ask. Always ask.

This Code should help guide your conduct. But the Code cannot address every circumstance and isn't meant to; this is not a catalogue of workplace rules. You should be aware that the company has policies in such areas as fair competition, securities trading, workplace conduct and environmental protection. Employees should consult the policies of The Coca-Cola Company in specific areas as they apply.

#### Your responsibilities

- It is your responsibility to read and understand the Code of Business Conduct. You must comply with the Code in both letter and spirit. Ignorance of the Code will not excuse you from its requirements.
- Follow the law wherever you are and in all circumstances.
- Never engage in behavior that harms the reputation of the company. If you wouldn't want to tell your parents or your children about your action – or wouldn't want to read about it in a newspaper – don't do it.
- Some situations may seem ambiguous. Exercise caution when you hear yourself or someone else say, "Everybody does it," "Maybe just this once," 'No one will ever know" or "It won't matter in the end." These are signs to stop, think through the situation and seek guidance. Most importantly, don't ignore your instincts. Ultimately, you are responsible for your actions.
- You have several options for seeking guidance. You may discuss concerns with your manager, responsible employees in the Finance or Legal Divisions or, in the case of potential criminal issues, with Strategic Security.

Exhibit 5.2

### The Coca-Cola Company: the Code of Business Conduct – working with governments

#### Overview

Conducting business with governments is not the same as conducting business with private parties. These transactions often are covered by special legal rules. You should consult with company legal counsel to be certain that you must have approval of local legal counsel before providing anything of value to a government official.

The company prohibits the payment of bribes to government officials. "Government officials" are employees of any government anywhere in the world, even low-ranking employees or employees of government-controlled entities. The term "government officials" also includes political parties and candidates for political office. It is your obligation to understand whether someone you deal with is a government official. When in doubt, consult legal counsel.

In some countries it may be customary at times to pay government employees for performing their required duties. These facilitating payments, as they are known, are small sums paid to facilitate or expedite routine, non-discretionary government actions, such as obtaining phone service or an ordinary license. In contrast, a bribe, which is never permissible, is giving or offering to give anything of value to a government official to influence a discretionary decision.

Understanding the difference between a bribe and a facilitating payment is critically important. Consult with your division legal counsel before acting.

Our company and its subsidiaries must comply with all applicable trade restrictions and boycotts imposed by the U.S. government. (A boycott is a restriction on a company's ability to ship goods into a specific country or do business there.) Moreover, our company and its subsidiaries also must abide by U.S. anti-boycott laws that prohibit companies from participating in any international boycott not sanctioned by the U.S. government. If questions arise, contact legal counsel.

#### General principles

- The ban on bribes applies to third parties acting on behalf of the company, including all contractors and consultants. Employees must not engage a contractor or consultant if the employee has reason to believe that the contractor or consultant may attempt to bribe a government official.
- The company may hire government officials or employees to perform services that have a legitimate business purpose, with the prior approval of the Principal Manager. For example, an off-duty police officer might provide security. Government officials should never be hired to perform services that conflict with their official duties.
- All facilitating payments must be approved in advance by division legal counsel and recorded appropriately.
- Employees must comply with all U.S. boycott and anti-boycott restrictions.
- The company may operate and fund through its employees one or more political action committees.
- Political contributions by the company must be in accordance with local law. They must be approved by both your Principal Manager and the General Counsel and they must be properly recorded.
- Employees will not be reimbursed for political contributions. Your job will not be affected by your choices in personal political contributions.

**The Code in real life**

*The action*: A finance manager paid $20 to an employee of a government-owned telephone company to ensure a telephone line was installed at a company office on time. Even for that small amount, she sought approval from Division Legal Counsel and recorded the transaction as a "facilitating payment."

*The decision*: That was smart. If the payment had been large, say $600, that might be an indication that this was not a routine governmental action and might constitute a bribe. In every case, employees must seek approval for facilitating payments, and must record these actions appropriately.

*The action*: An account executive was traveling in a country experiencing civil unrest. A soldier stopped him at a bridge and demanded payment.

*The decision*: When personal safety is at risk, the employee should, of course, make the payment. Still, the fee must be reported to the Division Legal Counsel and recorded appropriately.

*The action*: A general manager entertained a government official in charge of issuing special permits to allow route trucks in a restricted area. During the meeting, the general manager gave a television and DVD player to the official as "a token of respect for the esteemed minister."

*The decision*: That was a bribe. It was a violation of both the Code and the law.

Multinational firms can play a positive role in fighting corruption. One study shows that multinational companies focusing more on ethics tend to use arm's-length bargaining to deal with a government.[25] They can also have a positive impact on the host institutions via regulatory pressure effect, demonstration effect, and professionalization effect.[26]

There is strength in numbers. A coalition of groups has been working with the World Economic Forum to sponsor a "zero-tolerance" pact against paying bribes. Altogether, 47 large multinational companies (e.g., Newmont Mining Corp., Rio Tinto, and Bechtel Group Inc.) have committed to the pact. These companies represent at least $300 billion in annual revenue.[27]

As stated by Peter Eigen, Chairman of Transparency International, "corruption takes many forms and is a universal cancer." As the world's leading anti-corruption organization, Transparency annually publishes its Corruption Perceptions Index (CPI) and Bribe Payers Index (BPI) (see Tables 5.1 and 5.2). It is encouraging that companies seem to take ethical behavior more seriously than before.

## Intellectual property

Intellectual property (IP), as defined by the World Intellectual Property Organization (WIPO), is "creations of the mind: inventions, literary and artistic works, and symbols, names, images, and designs used in commerce." Individuals and firms have the freedom to own and control the rights to intellectual property (i.e., inventions and creative works). The terms *patent*, *trademark*, *copyright*, and *trade secret* are often used interchangeably. In fact, there are four basic forms of intellectual property, and they hold different meanings. A study found a low correlation of the copyright and trademark variables with Rapp and Rozek's patent variable. This is an indication of the theoretical importance of treating intellectual property law components separately. One component cannot be used as a proxy for the other because countries do not assign equal importance and attention to them.[28]

# Corrosive corruption

All around the world, in every language, corruption has a name. Baksheesh. Soborno. Dash. Bribe. And everywhere it occurs, it is corrosive.

Corruption can take many forms, and the effects can accumulate. Where government officials seek special favors or bribes, the costs can discourage honest companies and deter needed investments. Scarce public resources are squandered on nonessential, shoddily built, or too-costly projects, while needed investments go begging. Corrupt officials may thwart the growth of more honest and democratic institutions. Public cynicism, contempt and disillusionment can become widespread.

**Companies that participate in corrupted dealings do themselves no favors**

Companies that participate in corrupted dealings also do themselves no favors. Although a business deal here or there may be obtained, the cost includes creating a culture of dishonesty within the company. If cheating or bribery or fixing the books are tolerated for certain purposes, a company can never again be sure that these dealings are not tolerated for others. The whole organization can come to believe that dishonesty is an accepted approach. That's one reason ExxonMobil maintains strong and clear policies to guard against such dishonesty.

The United States has long been in the forefront of a laudable effort to reduce corruption, and its Foreign Corrupt Practices Act has contributed positively to discouraging extortion and bribery around the world. In 1999, the OECD Convention on Combating Bribery of Foreign Public Officials went into effect. Almost all of the OECD countries have now ratified the convention and enacted enabling legislation. This convention holds great promise for reducing corruption, as long as the signatory nations live up to their enforcement obligations.

And some private-sector groups, such as the International Association of Oil & Gas Producers, are helping to meet the OECD standards.

The Organization of American States has also obtained ratification of an Inter-American Convention Against Corruption by most of its member countries. The U.S. ratified the Convention on September 29 of last year.

Also encouraging are steps by international financial institutions such as the World Bank, the International Monetary Fund and the Asian Development Bank to focus more on reducing corruption in the developing world. Innovative arrangements such as the revenue management plan for oil revenues established by the government of Chad and the World Bank are path-breaking advances.

Central to the anti-corruption drive has been the work of the nongovernmental organization Transparency International. Its advisory group of important business and government leaders has included Olusegun Obasanjo, president of Nigeria, who has been at the forefront of efforts to reduce official corruption and private-sector bribery.

There is good reason to be optimistic about the growing efforts to combat the most widespread and damaging effects of corruption. But optimism must be tempered by realism and strengthened by determination, because reducing the impact of corruption will remain a long and difficult struggle.

ExxonMobil™

**FIGURE 5.2** Corruption and business

*Source*: Mobil Corp.

**TABLE 5.1** Corruption Perceptions Index

| *Country rank* | *Country/territory* | *CPI score 2007* | *Confidence intervals** | *Surveys used*** |
|---|---|---|---|---|
| 1 | New Zealand | **9.4** | 9.2–9.6 | 6 |
| | Denmark | **9.4** | 9.2–9.6 | 6 |
| | Finland | **9.4** | 9.2–9.6 | 6 |
| 4 | Singapore | **9.3** | 9.0–9.5 | 9 |
| | Sweden | **9.3** | 9.1–9.4 | 6 |
| 6 | Iceland | **9.2** | 8.3–9.6 | 6 |
| 7 | Netherlands | **9.0** | 8.8–9.2 | 6 |
| | Switzerland | **9.0** | 8.8–9.2 | 6 |
| 9 | Norway | **8.7** | 8.0–9.2 | 6 |
| | Canada | **8.7** | 8.3–9.1 | 6 |
| 11 | Australia | **8.6** | 8.1–9.0 | 8 |
| 12 | Luxembourg | **8.4** | 7.7–8.7 | 5 |
| | United Kingdom | **8.4** | 7.9–8.9 | 6 |
| 14 | Hong Kong | **8.3** | 7.6–8.8 | 8 |
| 15 | Austria | **8.1** | 7.5–8.7 | 6 |
| 16 | Germany | **7.8** | 7.3–8.4 | 6 |
| 17 | Japan | **7.5** | 7.1–8.0 | 8 |
| | Ireland | **7.5** | 7.3–7.7 | 6 |
| 19 | France | **7.3** | 6.9–7.8 | 6 |
| 20 | USA | **7.2** | 6.5–7.6 | 8 |
| 21 | Belgium | **7.1** | 7.1–7.1 | 6 |
| 22 | Chile | **7.0** | 6.5–7.4 | 7 |
| 23 | Barbados | **6.9** | 6.6–7.1 | 4 |
| 24 | Saint Lucia | **6.8** | 6.1–7.1 | 3 |
| 25 | Uruguay | **6.7** | 6.4–7.0 | 5 |
| | Spain | **6.7** | 6.2–7.0 | 6 |
| 27 | Slovenia | **6.6** | 6.1–6.9 | 8 |
| 28 | Estonia | **6.5** | 6.0–7.0 | 8 |
| | Portugal | **6.5** | 5.8–7.2 | 6 |
| 30 | Israel | **6.1** | 5.6–6.7 | 6 |
| | Saint Vincent and the Grenadines | **6.1** | 4.0–7.1 | 3 |
| 32 | Qatar | **6.0** | 5.4–6.4 | 4 |
| 33 | Malta | **5.8** | 5.3–6.2 | 4 |
| 34 | Macao | **5.7** | 4.7–6.4 | 4 |
| | Taiwan | **5.7** | 5.4–6.1 | 9 |
| | United Arab Emirates | **5.7** | 4.8–6.5 | 5 |
| 37 | Dominica | **5.6** | 4.0–6.1 | 3 |
| 38 | Botswana | **5.4** | 4.8–6.1 | 7 |
| 39 | Hungary | **5.3** | 4.9–5.5 | 8 |

**TABLE 5.1** *continued*

| *Country rank* | *Country/territory* | *CPI score 2007* | *Confidence intervals** | *Surveys used*** |
|---|---|---|---|---|
| | Cyprus | **5.3** | 5.1–5.5 | 3 |
| 41 | Czech Republic | **5.2** | 4.9–5.8 | 8 |
| | Italy | **5.2** | 4.7–5.7 | 6 |
| 43 | Malaysia | **5.1** | 4.5–5.7 | 9 |
| | South Korea | **5.1** | 4.7–5.5 | 9 |
| | South Africa | **5.1** | 4.9–5.5 | 9 |
| 46 | Costa Rica | **5.0** | 4.7–5.3 | 5 |
| | Bhutan | **5.0** | 4.1–5.7 | 5 |
| | Bahrain | **5.0** | 4.2–5.7 | 5 |
| 49 | Slovakia | **4.9** | 4.5–5.2 | 8 |
| | Cape Verde | **4.9** | 3.4–5.5 | 3 |
| 51 | Latvia | **4.8** | 4.4–5.1 | 6 |
| | Lithuania | **4.8** | 4.4–5.3 | 7 |
| 53 | Oman | **4.7** | 3.9–5.3 | 4 |
| | Jordan | **4.7** | 3.8–5.6 | 7 |
| | Mauritius | **4.7** | 4.1–5.7 | 6 |
| 56 | Greece | **4.6** | 4.3–5.0 | 6 |
| 57 | Namibia | **4.5** | 3.9–5.2 | 7 |
| | Seychelles | **4.5** | 2.9–5.7 | 4 |
| | Samoa | **4.5** | 3.4–5.5 | 3 |
| 60 | Kuwait | **4.3** | 3.3–5.1 | 5 |
| 61 | Cuba | **4.2** | 3.5–4.7 | 4 |
| | Poland | **4.2** | 3.6–4.9 | 8 |
| | Tunisia | **4.2** | 3.4–4.8 | 6 |
| 64 | Bulgaria | **4.1** | 3.6–4.8 | 8 |
| | Croatia | **4.1** | 3.6–4.5 | 8 |
| | Turkey | **4.1** | 3.8–4.5 | 7 |
| 67 | El Salvador | **4.0** | 3.2–4.6 | 5 |
| 68 | Colombia | **3.8** | 3.4–4.3 | 7 |
| 69 | Ghana | **3.7** | 3.5–3.9 | 7 |
| | Romania | **3.7** | 3.4–4.1 | 8 |
| 71 | Senegal | **3.6** | 3.2–4.2 | 7 |
| 72 | Morocco | **3.5** | 3.0–4.2 | 7 |
| | China | **3.5** | 3.0–4.2 | 9 |
| | Suriname | **3.5** | 3.0–3.9 | 4 |
| | India | **3.5** | 3.3–3.7 | 10 |
| | Mexico | **3.5** | 3.3–3.8 | 7 |
| | Peru | **3.5** | 3.4–3.7 | 5 |
| | Brazil | **3.5** | 3.2–4.0 | 7 |

**TABLE 5.1** *continued*

| *Country rank* | *Country/territory* | *CPI score 2007* | *Confidence intervals** | *Surveys used*** |
|---|---|---|---|---|
| 79 | Serbia | **3.4** | 3.0–4.0 | 6 |
| | Georgia | **3.4** | 2.9–4.3 | 6 |
| | Grenada | **3.4** | 2.0–4.1 | 3 |
| | Trinidad and Tobago | **3.4** | 2.7–3.9 | 4 |
| | Saudi Arabia | **3.4** | 2.7–3.9 | 4 |
| 84 | Bosnia and Herzegovina | **3.3** | 2.9–3.7 | 7 |
| | Montenegro | **3.3** | 2.4–4.0 | 4 |
| | Maldives | **3.3** | 2.3–4.3 | 4 |
| | Jamaica | **3.3** | 3.1–3.4 | 5 |
| | Kiribati | **3.3** | 2.4–3.9 | 3 |
| | Gabon | **3.3** | 3.0–3.5 | 5 |
| | Swaziland | **3.3** | 2.6–4.2 | 5 |
| | Thailand | **3.3** | 2.9–3.7 | 9 |
| | Lesotho | **3.3** | 3.1–3.5 | 6 |
| | FYR Macedonia | **3.3** | 2.9–3.8 | 6 |
| 94 | Madagascar | **3.2** | 2.5–3.9 | 7 |
| | Sri Lanka | **3.2** | 2.9–3.5 | 7 |
| | Panama | **3.2** | 2.8–3.4 | 5 |
| | Tanzania | **3.2** | 2.9–3.4 | 8 |
| 98 | Vanuatu | **3.1** | 2.4–3.7 | 3 |
| 99 | Domincan Republic | **3.0** | 2.8–3.3 | 5 |
| | Armenia | **3.0** | 2.8–3.2 | 7 |
| | Lebanon | **3.0** | 2.2–3.6 | 4 |
| | Mongolia | **3.0** | 2.6–3.3 | 6 |
| | Algeria | **3.0** | 2.7–3.2 | 6 |
| | Belize | **3.0** | 2.0–3.7 | 3 |
| 105 | Argentina | **2.9** | 2.6–3.2 | 7 |
| | Djibouti | **2.9** | 2.2–3.4 | 3 |
| | Albania | **2.9** | 2.6–3.1 | 6 |
| | Burkina Faso | **2.9** | 2.6–3.4 | 7 |
| | Bolivia | **2.9** | 2.7–3.2 | 6 |
| | Egypt | **2.9** | 2.6–3.3 | 7 |
| 111 | Moldova | **2.8** | 2.5–3.3 | 7 |
| | Eritrea | **2.8** | 2.1–3.5 | 5 |
| | Guatemala | **2.8** | 2.4–3.2 | 5 |
| | Rwanda | **2.8** | 2.3–3.3 | 5 |
| | Solomon Islands | **2.8** | 2.4–3.1 | 3 |
| | Mozambique | **2.8** | 2.5–3.1 | 8 |
| | Uganda | **2.8** | 2.5–3.0 | 8 |

**TABLE 5.1** *continued*

| *Country rank* | *Country/territory* | *CPI score 2007* | *Confidence intervals** | *Surveys used*** |
|---|---|---|---|---|
| 118 | Mali | **2.7** | 2.4–3.0 | 8 |
| | Malawi | **2.7** | 2.4–3.0 | 8 |
| | Sao Tome and Principe | **2.7** | 2.4–3.0 | 3 |
| | Ukraine | **2.7** | 2.4–3.0 | 7 |
| | Benin | **2.7** | 2.3–3.2 | 7 |
| 123 | Guyana | **2.6** | 2.3–2.7 | 7 |
| | Zambia | **2.6** | 2.3–2.9 | 8 |
| | Comoros | **2.6** | 2.2–3.0 | 3 |
| | Nicaragua | **2.6** | 2.3–2.7 | 6 |
| | Viet Nam | **2.6** | 2.4–2.9 | 9 |
| | Mauritania | **2.6** | 2.0–3.3 | 6 |
| | Niger | **2.6** | 2.3–2.9 | 7 |
| | Timor-Leste | **2.6** | 2.5–2.6 | 3 |
| 131 | Nepal | **2.5** | 2.3–2.7 | 7 |
| 131 | Yemen | **2.5** | 2.1–3.0 | 5 |
| | Philippines | **2.5** | 2.3–2.7 | 9 |
| | Burundi | **2.5** | 2.0–3.0 | 7 |
| | Libya | **2.5** | 2.1–2.6 | 4 |
| | Iran | **2.5** | 2.0–3.0 | 4 |
| | Honduras | **2.5** | 2.3–2.6 | 6 |
| 138 | Pakistan | **2.4** | 2.0–2.8 | 7 |
| | Ethiopia | **2.4** | 2.1–2.7 | 8 |
| | Paraguay | **2.4** | 2.1–2.6 | 5 |
| | Cameroon | **2.4** | 2.1–2.7 | 8 |
| | Syria | **2.4** | 1.7–2.9 | 4 |
| 143 | Gambia | **2.3** | 2.0–2.6 | 6 |
| | Indonesia | **2.3** | 2.1–2.4 | 11 |
| | Togo | **2.3** | 1.9–2.8 | 5 |
| | Russia | **2.3** | 2.1–2.6 | 8 |
| 147 | Angola | **2.2** | 1.8–2.4 | 7 |
| | Nigeria | **2.2** | 2.0–2.4 | 8 |
| | Guinea-Bissau | **2.2** | 2.0–2.3 | 3 |
| 150 | Sierra Leone | **2.1** | 2.0–2.2 | 5 |
| | Kazakhstan | **2.1** | 1.7–2.5 | 6 |
| | Belarus | **2.1** | 1.7–2.6 | 5 |
| | Zimbabwe | **2.1** | 1.8–2.4 | 8 |
| | Côte d'Ivoire | **2.1** | 1.7–2.6 | 6 |
| | Tajikistan | **2.1** | 1.9–2.3 | 8 |
| | Liberia | **2.1** | 1.8–2.4 | 4 |

**TABLE 5.1** *continued*

| *Country rank* | *Country/territory* | *CPI score 2007* | *Confidence intervals** | *Surveys used*** |
|---|---|---|---|---|
| | Congo, Republic | **2.1** | 2.0–2.2 | 6 |
| | Ecuador | **2.1** | 2.0–2.3 | 5 |
| | Azerbaijan | **2.1** | 1.9–2.3 | 8 |
| | Kenya | **2.1** | 1.9–2.3 | 8 |
| | Kyrgyzstan | **2.1** | 2.0–2.2 | 7 |
| 162 | Bangladesh | **2.0** | 1.8–2.3 | 7 |
| | Papua New Guinea | **2.0** | 1.7–2.3 | 6 |
| | Turkmenistan | **2.0** | 1.8–2.3 | 5 |
| | Central African Republic | **2.0** | 1.8–2.3 | 5 |
| | Cambodia | **2.0** | 1.8–2.1 | 7 |
| | Venezuela | **2.0** | 1.9–2.1 | 7 |
| 168 | Laos | **1.9** | 1.7–2.2 | 6 |
| | Equatorial Guinea | **1.9** | 1.7–2.0 | 4 |
| | Guinea | **1.9** | 1.4–2.6 | 6 |
| | Congo, Democratic Republic | **1.9** | 1.8–2.1 | 6 |
| 172 | Afghanistan | **1.8** | 1.4–2.0 | 4 |
| | Sudan | **1.8** | 1.6–1.9 | 6 |
| | Chad | **1.8** | 1.7–1.9 | 7 |
| 175 | Uzbekistan | **1.7** | 1.6–1.9 | 7 |
| | Tonga | **1.7** | 1.5–1.8 | 3 |
| 177 | Haiti | **1.6** | 1.3–1.8 | 4 |
| 178 | Iraq | **1.5** | 1.3–1.7 | 4 |
| 179 | Somalia | **1.4** | 1.1–1.7 | 4 |
| | Myanmar | **1.4** | 1.1–1.7 | 4 |

*Notes*

* Confidence range provides a range of possible values of the CPI score. This reflects how a country's score may vary, depending on measurement precision. Nominally, with 5 percent probability the score is above this range and with another 5 percent it is below. However, particularly when only few sources are available, an unbiased estimate of the mean coverage probability is lower than the nominal value of 90 percent.

** Surveys used refers to the number of surveys that assessed a country's performance. Fourteen surveys and expert assessments were used and at least three were required for a country to be included in the CPL.

*Source*: Transparency International, reprinted (or adapted) from TI's Corruption Perceptions Index 2007, http://www.transparency.org/policy_research/surveys_indices/cpi/2007. Transparency International: the global coalition against corruption. Used with permission. For more information, visit http://www.transparency.org.

**TABLE 5.2** Bribe Payers Index

| *Rank* | *Country/territory* | *Number of respondents* | *Average score (Scale 0–10)* | *Standard Deviation* | *Margin of error (at 95% confidence)* |
|---|---|---|---|---|---|
| 1 | Switzerland | 1744 | 7.81 | 2.65 | 0.12 |
| 2 | Sweden | 1451 | 7.62 | 2.66 | 0.14 |
| 3 | Australia | 1447 | 7.59 | 2.62 | 0.14 |
| 4 | Austria | 1560 | 7.50 | 2.60 | 0.13 |
| 5 | Canada | 1870 | 7.46 | 2.70 | 0.12 |
| 6 | UK | 3442 | 7.39 | 2.67 | 0.09 |
| 7 | Germany | 3873 | 7.34 | 2.74 | 0.09 |
| 8 | Netherlands | 1821 | 7.28 | 2.69 | 0.12 |
| 9 | Belgium | 1329 | 7.22 | 2.70 | 0.15 |
| 10 | U.S. | 5401 | 7.22 | 2.77 | 0.07 |
| 11 | Japan | 3279 | 7.10 | 2.87 | 0.10 |
| 12 | Singapore | 1297 | 6.78 | 3.04 | 0.17 |
| 13 | Spain | 2111 | 6.63 | 2.73 | 0.12 |
| 14 | UAE | 1928 | 6.62 | 3.09 | 0.14 |
| 15 | France | 3085 | 6.50 | 3.00 | 0.11 |
| 16 | Portugal | 973 | 6.47 | 2.79 | 0.18 |
| 17 | Mexico | 1765 | 6.45 | 3.17 | 0.15 |
| 18 | Hong Kong | 1556 | 6.01 | 3.13 | 0.16 |
| 19 | Israel | 1482 | 6.01 | 3.14 | 0.16 |
| 20 | Italy | 2525 | 5.94 | 2.99 | 0.12 |
| 21 | South Korea | 1930 | 5.83 | 2.93 | 0.13 |
| 22 | Saudi Arabia | 1302 | 5.75 | 3.17 | 0.17 |
| 23 | Brazil | 1317 | 5.65 | 3.02 | 0.16 |
| 24 | South Africa | 1488 | 5.61 | 3.11 | 0.16 |
| 25 | Malaysia | 1319 | 5.59 | 3.07 | 0.17 |
| 26 | Taiwan | 1731 | 5.41 | 3.08 | 0.15 |
| 27 | Turkey | 1755 | 5.23 | 3.14 | 0.15 |
| 28 | Russia | 2203 | 5.16 | 3.34 | 0.14 |
| 29 | China | 3448 | 4.94 | 3.29 | 0.11 |
| 30 | India | 2145 | 4.62 | 3.28 | 0.14 |

*Note*: The margin of error at 95 percent confidence is provided to demonstrate the precision of the results. The confidence level indicates that there is a 95 percent probability that the true value of the results lies within the range given by the margin of error above and below each score.

*Source*: Transparency International, reprinted (or adapted) from TI's Bribe Payer's Index 2006, http://www.transparency.org/policy_research/surveys_indices/bpi/bpi_2006. Transparency International: the global coalition against corruption. Used with permission. For more information, visit http://www.transparency.org.

### *Categories of intellectual property*

A **trademark** is a symbol, word, or thing used to identify a product made or marketed by a particular firm. It becomes a registered trademark when the mark is accepted for registration by the Trademark Office.

A **copyright**, which is the responsibility of the Copyright Office, offers protection against unauthorized copying by others to an author or artist for his or her literary, musical, dramatic, and artistic works. A copyright protects the form of expression rather than the subject matter. A copyright has now been extended to computer software as well. According to the U.S. Supreme Court, databases such as telephone books are not covered by copyright law.

In 1790, the U.S. Congress limited copyrights to 14 years, renewable for 14 more years if the author was living. Since then, copyrights have been extended 11 times and are now good for 70 years beyond the life of an author and 95 years for copyrights owned by corporations. The latest law is the Sonny Bono Copyright Term Extension Act which was proposed by The Walt Disney Company, thus dubbed the Mickey Mouse Protection Act.[29] Ironically, Walt Disney himself greatly benefited from the value of public domain. By updating an out-of-copyright character, he created Mickey Mouse. The latest extension maintains copyright protection for the early portrayals of Mickey Mouse, George Gerschwin's *Rhapsody in Blue*, Robert Frost's poems, and such films as *Gone With the Wind, Casablanca*, and *The Wizard of Oz*.[30]

In European Union countries, copyright protection lasts for 50 years. As a result, recordings made in the early to mid-1950s by such artists as Elvis Presley, Maria Callas, and Ella Fitzgerald have entered the public domain. A European company can thus release albums that were once exclusively owned by particular labels.[31]

All EU countries (except the UK, Ireland, and Luxembourg) impose fees on copying equipment. The charges began in the 1960s at the time when copyright holders had no way to protect their work from being copied without authorization. Fees were thus imposed on photocopiers and magnetic tape-recorders. At present, depending on the country, copying equipment can include paper, blank DVDs, MP3 players, and mobile phones. Unfortunately, due to opposition from France, the European Commission postponed its plan to harmonize national charges on copying equipment.[32]

The U.S.A. has finally joined the 80-nation **Berne Convention for the Protection of Literary and Artistic Works**, allowing greater protection against foreign pirating of U.S. copyrighted works in twenty-five additional countries. In order to conform to the Berne Copyright Convention, changes in the copyright law in the U.S.A. were necessary. Under the new amendment, affixing a copyright notice is optional. For works created after January 1, 1989, mere publication and use are enough to obtain copyright protection.

Even though the copyright notice is no longer required, it is still a good idea to place a ©, the author's name, and date of publication on the original work. A clear notice entitles the author to obtain more effective remedies against infringers.

A **patent** protects an invention of a scientific or technical nature. It is a statutory grant from the government (the Patent Office) to an inventor in exchange for public disclosure giving the patent holder exclusive right to the functional and design inventions patented and excluding others from using those inventions for a certain period of time (20 years for a functional patent and 14 years for a design patent). The purpose of ownership rights is to spur inventiveness. Popular drugs that have recently lost their patent protection include Merck's Zantac (heartburn drug), and Schering-Plough's Claritin (allergy drug).

According to the WTO's Agreement on Trade-related Aspects of Intellectual Property Rights, "patents shall be available for any inventions, whether products or processes, in all fields of technology, provided that they are new, involve an inventive step and are capable of industrial application." However, members may bar a patent "to protect *ordre public* or morality, including to protect human, animal or plant life, or health, or to avoid serious prejudice to the environment."

Some have criticized the U.S. Patent Office for a proliferation of patents – an average of more than 3,000 patents a week. The definition of invention has gone beyond substantial and concrete items such as mechanical devices, manufacturing processes, and chemical processes to include genetically engineered animal and human genes and proteins – things that were considered to be mere "discoveries" at one time. Now thought and abstraction can be patented. Software and algorithms used to be unpatentable, but software is now the fastest growing patent category. The trivial things that have won patent protection include a technique for measuring a breast with a tape to determine bra size and a technique for executing a tennis stroke while wearing a kneepad.[33]

An invention that is obvious is not patentable. The definition of "obviousness" has received clarification in an important case. KSR International Corp., a Canadian company, manufactures gas pedals for General Motors. The pedal can be adjusted for a driver's height. It uses electronic signals instead of a mechanical cable to accelerate when pushing the pedal. Both features were developed independently. Teleflex Corp. sued KSR by claiming that KSR's combination of the features infringed Teleflex's patent. KSR countered that Teleflex's patent should be invalidated because the combination of the two features was obvious. In late 2006, the U.S. Supreme Court chided the U.S. Court of Appeals for the Federal Circuit for allowing patent holders to claim a patent monopoly for incremental advances. Combining a digital sensor with a mechanical pedal should have been obvious to a skilled engineer. The U.S. Supreme Court states: "granting patent protection advances that would occur in the ordinary course without real innovation retards progress."[34]

When Lucent was spun off by AT&T in 1996, it retained control of the famous Bell Labs. When Lucent merged with Alcatel in 2006, it held 15,000 Bell Labs patents. The other Bell Labs patents were allocated to Agere Systems Inc., Avaya Inc., and the current AT&T. Avaya has 3500 active patents, with 1500 dating back to Bell Labs. Agere has some 6000 patents, with a majority coming from Bell Labs.[35]

The top patent holder is IBM. For ten years in a row, IBM generated the most U.S. patents. In 2002, by receiving 3288 patents, it was the only company that was awarded more than 3000 U.S. patents in a single year. The past decade brought IBM 22,357 patents and allowed the company to beat Canon, the next closest rival, by 7000 patents. During the same period, Motorola was the only other American company that managed to land in the top ten. The top ten was dominated by mostly Japanese electronics giants – Canon, NEC, Hitachi, Toshiba, and Sony. Having the world's largest patent portfolio, IBM collects $1 billion a year in royalties.[36]

Apple's iPod, with 26 percent of the market, is the world's leader in digital music players. Creative Technology is a distant second with 6.6 percent, even though it invented the first digital music player in 1999. In 2006, Creative claimed that Apple Computer infringed its Zen patent for the interface that allows users to navigate between files on iPods, cellular phones, and other digital music players. Apple countersued. It faced a risk of receiving an adverse ruling from the U.S. International Trade Commission. If the decision went against Apple, the importation of iPods, which are made overseas, could be barred. It was a gamble Apple did not want to take. In the end, Apple grudgingly settled the case and paid Creative $100 million for the use of the technology in question.[37]

The term **trade secret** refers to know-how (e.g., manufacturing methods, formulas, plans, and so on) that is kept secret within a particular business. This know-how, generally unknown in the industry, may offer the firm a competitive advantage. KFC was alarmed to learn that a handwritten note was found in the basement of a home once owned by Colonel Harland Sanders and that the note might contain his secret KFC recipe. It immediately filed a lawsuit to keep the contents of the note secret but dropped it later after determining that the recipe found did not resemble the Colonel's original recipe of 11 herbs and spices. Colonel Sanders first came up with his famous fried chicken recipe in the late 1930s for his roadside eatery, Sanders Court and Café. Only a few people know the recipe, and they have all signed strict confidentiality agreements.

A secretary working at Coca-Cola Co. stole confidential documents and samples of products not yet launched. She and her accomplices tried to sell the trade secrets to PepsiCo. Inc. (or the "highest bidder") for at least $1.5 million. In 2007, she was sentenced to eight years in prison.[38]

**Infringement** occurs when there is commercial use (i.e., copying or imitating) without the owner's consent, with the intent of confusing or deceiving the public. For example, Texas Instruments charged that eight Japanese firms made memory chips based on its patents following the expiration of license agreements, and the U.S. company was able to force the Japanese firms to pay nearly $300 million in royalties. Texas Instruments also obtained an International Trade Commission ruling to seize Samsung's DRAM (dynamic random access memory) chips, which infringed Texas Instruments' semiconductor patents. Samsung then joined the eight Japanese companies in agreeing to pay royalties.

In a recent case, Intel filed a lawsuit against Via Technologies, a Taiwanese chip maker. Intel alleged that Via's chip set violated its patents. The legal dispute subsequently led to 11 cases in five countries involving 27 patents. In the end, the two companies settled all litigation related to microprocessors and chip sets. Under the agreement, Via got a three-year license to make Intel-compatible microprocessors and a four-year license to make Pentium 4 chip sets. In addition, both would cross-license each other on patents for ten years.

The largest patent infringement award took place in 1990 when Eastman Kodak, as a patent infringer, paid $909.5 million to Polaroid. In 2007, Microsoft paid $769 million to patent holder Lucent Technologies.

## Legal rights and requirements

Although patent, trademark, and copyright are distinctly different, they have one thing in common in that all have something to do with the protection of an owner's property. All require applications to be filed – not at the same office, however. Although this section deals with patents more specifically, the same basic ideas apply as well to the trademarks and copyrights.

When a firm develops an innovation, a patent should be obtained. The purpose of a patent is to enable the company to exploit its invention commercially while preventing others from interfering. Not all new ideas are patentable. A patent is granted only if the item under consideration is able to satisfy certain criteria. In general, the item must be new, unobvious, and useful, and must also involve an inventive step.

The problem of getting a patent granted is often difficult in many communist countries and developing countries because patent laws do not exist or are ignored. China did not enact its first patent law until 1984. Such countries may refuse to recognize certain patents granted elsewhere, or they may refuse to approve foreign firms' patent applications in their countries. Items not covered by patents in China include computer software, animals, plants, food beverages, and atomic energy-related inventions. Also not fully protected are those items relating to national defense, the economy, and public health. China does not give patents for chemicals and pharmaceuticals, reasoning that countries at similar stages of economic development have not granted such patents. However, as a new member of the WTO, China is required to observe intellectual property rights.

Patent laws vary widely, and one should not jump to the conclusion that patent problems are restricted only to communist or developing countries. Industrial nations may also exclude items from protection. Canada is the only industrialized nation requiring compulsory licensing of drugs. Smith Kline achieved success with Tagamet, a drug for treating ulcers, but Canada issued Novopharm a license for a generic version only four years after Tagamet first appeared on the U.S. market. As a result, Smith Kline sued the Canadian government for violation of patent rights. Another dispute erupted in 2007 when Thailand decided not to honor Abbott's patents in order to make drugs available to treat AIDs patients.

An inventor should understand that the patent obtained in one country does not extend protection beyond that nation's territorial limits. For further protection, it is necessary for the inventor to file application in other import markets. A few international agreements help simplify this cumbersome process. One such agreement is the **Patent Cooperation Treaty (PCT)**. The PCT is a multilateral treaty that makes it possible to file an international application simultaneously in up to 115 countries. It thus eliminates the need for separate applications.[39]

Another international agreement is provided by the **Paris Union (Paris Convention)** or the International Convention for the Protection of Industrial Property of 1883. The Paris Union claims about eighty countries as its members. The most important provision is the "**priority right**," which means that the registering of a patent in one member country gives the inventor one year from the filing date to do the same in other countries before losing the protection. In addition, the convention establishes other rules, principles, and rights. The "**national treatment**" rule prevents discrimination by requiring member countries to treat foreign applicants and their own nationals in the same manner. The principle of "**independence of patents**" provides further protection because the revocation or expiration in the country of original filing has no effect on its validity in other countries.

Centralized protection of trademarks is easier to accomplish than centralized protection of patents. One treaty for the purpose of international registration is the **Madrid Agreement for the International Registration of Marks**. Twenty-two countries, mostly in Europe, are signatories, though the U.S.A. is not one of them. The Madrid Agreement provides an automatic extension of protection to all member countries when a company pays a single fee of about $300 for the period of protection of 20 years. After a trademark owner has registered a mark in a member country, the **International Bureau of the World Intellectual Property Organization (WIPO)** in Geneva will then issue and deposit an international registration with the trademark offices in member countries for examination in accordance with their own laws.

The **Trademark Registration Treaty (TRT)** simplifies the application process further by not requiring a prior home registration, as in the case of the Madrid Agreement. If member countries designated in the application do not refuse registration under their national laws in 15 months, the mark is treated as being registered there.

There are other treaty arrangements. For example, the **European Patent Convention (EPC)** establishes a regional patent system for Western Europe. A person can thus file a single international application for a European Patent at the European Patent Office, which administers patent applications. For Latin America, there is the **Inter-American Convention on Inventions, Patents, Designs, and Industrial Models**.

The cost of preparing and registering patents can be quite high. There are costs other than the initial filing fees as well. Periodic maintenance fees (i.e., annual taxes) must be paid during the life of the patent to keep it active. Other requirements must often be met for both the initial patent and the renewal of the patent. The required evidence in support of the application usually includes the use and continuous use of the patent.

Because of the high costs associated with patent application and maintenance, the costs must be weighed against the benefits. As a rule of thumb, patent applications and registration are very important and necessary in the major markets (i.e., the U.S.A., the EU, and Japan). For other industrialized countries, the potential benefits should justify the costs. In Eastern Europe and Taiwan, it may not be economically worthwhile to file for patents because patent enforcement there is so weak as to be practically nonexistent. Gucci and Rolex fought long and largely unsuccessful battles in those markets.

In spite of the cost, the marketer must realize that, without a valid patent, it can be more costly to do business in the long run. A manufacturer that takes legal action against patent violators is often faced with the burden of proof of ownership. The failure to obtain a patent encourages active infringement and increases the subsequent legal costs and difficulty of proving a case. The legal costs incurred in a single court can easily exceed the registration costs in several countries.

In the process of filing for patent protection, it is a good idea to make a distinction between common law countries and statute law countries. A common law country determines patent ownership by **priority in use.** In comparison, the ownership in a statute law country is determined by **priority in registration**. That is, the first-to-file is granted a patent even if an innovation was actually created or used earlier by someone else. Europe, Japan, China, and most countries have the first-to-file patent system, and they make patent applications public 18 months after filing. The U.S.A., as a common law country, relies on the first-to-invent system. The U.S. system's first-to-invent standard is different because it awards patents to the original inventor even though someone else may have got to the patent office first. Based on the U.S. system, the person who thought of the idea first receives a patent, and patent applications are kept secret – sometimes for years – until a patent is granted. It is true that the European and Japanese systems, by publishing patent information early, encourage imitators, but at the same time, this practice alerts other inventors early enough to avoid redundant research.

The U.S.A. was not consistent in treating American and foreign inventors. Although the U.S.A. insisted on giving ownership to the first-to-invent, that rule did not protect overseas inventors. U.S. patent law made it clear that research efforts taking place outside the U.S.A. could not be used to prove when an invention was conceived. Thus an American inventor would still get ownership if he or she started working on a certain concept before a foreigner's application for a U.S. patent – even though the foreigner actually discovered that idea earlier overseas. After decades of favoritism, the U.S. Patent and Trademark Office, as mandated by GATT, began giving equal treatment to overseas inventors in 1996.

The Japanese patent practices appear to discriminate against foreign applicants who have to wait longer than their Japanese counterparts for a patent to be granted. In contrast, the U.S., German, and British practices may discriminate against foreign applicants with lower patent grant ratios than for domestic applicants. Countries seem to have different philosophies concerning patents. Should patents be viewed as one's property, or should they be regarded as public good?

The U.S.A. has complained about other countries' systems, while those countries have urged the U.S.A. to become more efficient and consistent with the rest of the world by adopting the system of awarding a patent to the first inventor who applies on an invention. The rationale of the U.S.A. is that it attempts to provide a balance between innovation and competition. However, the current practice can and does result in redundant research, since other inventors have no knowledge whether someone has filed a patent application on the same idea.

Companies have to put up with the U.S. system because, without U.S. patents, they may be excluded from the world's largest market. Most large companies favor the international first-to-file system due to certainty. One benefit is in terms of the reduction of the threat of "submarine patents" or those applications for major innovations which the Patent Office has kept secret for decades due to indecision about patent approval. When such patents are granted to obscure inventors who claim to have an idea first, they can torpedo other firms which do not know that a patent is pending on the same idea. As in the case of the microprocessor patent, it took the Patent Office 20 years before awarding a patent to Gilbert P. Hyatt in 1990. As a result, North American Philips Corp. and others had to scramble to obtain a license. Critics believe that some inventors have manipulated the process by continually filing revisions to the original patent applications so as to extend such applications for years or decades. Then these inventors suddenly claim patent rights to a widely used technology and demand that companies which use the technology pay them a license fee.

Because of the outcry, in 1994, the U.S.A. agreed to bring its patent system in line with those of Japan and Europe. Patent applications will be published 18 months after filing. At the same time, based on a GATT provision, the 17-year patent life after granting was changed to a 20-year term from the filing date. This change should partially solve the problems of submarine patents.

The WTO has reached unanimous agreement to alter international trade rules so as to give poor nations greater access to inexpensive life-saving medicines. Poor countries will be able to import generic versions of expensive patented medicines by buying them from countries such as India and Brazil without violating trade laws protecting patent rights. African countries and their supporters in non-profit health groups have argued that moral and political arguments outweigh commercial considerations in the face of epidemics such as AIDS, malaria, and tuberculosis. This agreement could save millions of lives.

## Counterfeiting

Counterfeiting is the practice of unauthorized and illegal copying of a product. In essence, it involves an infringement on a patent or trademark, or both. According to the U.S. Lanham Act, a counterfeit trademark is a "spurious trademark which is identical with, or substantially indistinguishable from, a registered trademark." A true counterfeit product uses the name and design of the original so as to look exactly like the original. On the other hand, some counterfeiters partially duplicate the original's design and/or trademark in order to mislead or confuse buyers. Section 42 of the U.S. Trademark Act prohibits imports of counterfeit goods into the U.S.A.

The extent of counterfeiting is great. Two out of every five recordings sold worldwide are illegal copies. In the case of pirated software as a percentage of the total market, the figures are as follows: Ukraine (89 percent), Russia (88 percent), Bulgaria (78 percent), and Romania (77 percent).[40] U.S. film studies lost $6.1 billion in 2005.[41] According to the International Chamber of Commerce, counterfeiters cost businesses about $600 billion a year, and the loss could grow to $1.2 trillion by 2009.[42]

Counterfeiting is a serious business problem. In addition to the direct monetary loss, companies face indirect losses as well. Counterfeit goods injure the reputation of companies whose brand names are placed on low-quality products. In Ecuador, it is easy to see why people will have a difficult time buying a $15 CD. Not surprisingly, in terms of sales, illegal CDs far exceed their legal counterparts.

Products affected by counterfeiting cover a wide range. At one end of the spectrum are prestigious and highly advertised consumer products, such as Hennessy brandy, Dior and Pierre Cardin fashion apparel, Samsonite luggage, Levi's jeans, and Cartier and Rolex watches. At the other end of the spectrum are industrial products, such as Pfizer animal feed supplement, medical vaccines, heart pacemakers, and helicopter parts. Counterfeits include such fashion products as Gucci and Louis Vuitton handbags, as well as such mundane products as Fram oil filters and Caterpillar tractor parts. Although fakes are more likely to be premium-priced consumer products, low-unit-value products have not escaped the attention of counterfeiters. Even Coke is not always the "real" thing," as it is very easy for counterfeiters in developing countries to put something else that looks and tastes like Coke into genuine Coke bottles.

Fakes can come from anywhere, including industrialized countries. Italy may even be a bigger counterfeit offender than some Asian countries.

Controlling the counterfeit trade is difficult in part because counterfeiting is a low-risk, high-profit venture. It is difficult and time-consuming to obtain a search warrant. Low prosecution rates and minimal penalties in terms of jail sentences and fines do not make a good deterrent. Walt Disney and Microsoft, in winning two trademark infringement cases in China, were awarded only $91 and $2600 respectively. Moreover, there are many small-time counterfeiters who could just pack up and go to a new location to escape the police.

Just as crucial, if not more so, is the attitude of law enforcement agencies and consumers. Many consumers understand neither the seriousness of the violation nor the need to respect trademark rights. Law enforcement agencies often believe that the crime does not warrant special effort. The problem is severe in Taiwan, because so many local manufacturers pay no attention to copyrights and patents. The strong export potential for bogus merchandise makes the government there look the other way. In Mexico, one counterfeiter openly operated several "Cartier" stores in American-owned hotels. After many years in Mexican courts and at least 49 legal decisions against the retailer, Cartier was still unable to gain the cooperation of the Mexican officials to close down the counterfeiter.

The U.S. Trade Representative (USTR) annually submits to Congress a national Trade Estimate Report (NTE) on significant foreign barriers to trade. After submission of the report, the USTR is required to review U.S. trade expansion priorities and identify priority foreign country practices in the **Super 301 Report**. The Super 301 Report identifies foreign practices, if eliminated, that would have the most significant potential to increase U.S. exports. The **Special 301 Report**, on the other hand, identifies annually those countries which deny adequate and effective protection of intellectual property rights (IPR) or which deny fair and equitable market access to Americans that rely on intellectual property protection.[43]

The annual Special 301 report, issued in 2007 by the U.S. Trade Representative's office, placed certain countries on a special "priority watch list" for monitoring to "encourage and maintain" effective intellectual property rights protections. According to the report, Thailand has insufficient penalties for violations, and there are indications of a further "weakening of respect" for patents such as pharmaceutical products. Thirty-one countries were put on lower levels of monitoring.[44]

The other countries on the priority watch list are Russia, Egypt, Argentina, Chile, Israel, Lebanon, Turkey, Ukraine, and Venezuela. In China, it is believed that 85 to 93 percent of all copyrighted material sold is pirated. Russian piracy sales deprived U.S. copyright holders of $2.1 billion in 2006. Chile and Venezuela remain on the top priority list due to increasing levels of piracy and failure to make progress in enforcement and cooperation.

Many trade partners of the U.S.A. have bitterly complained about the Super 301 and Special 301 reports because of their retaliatory implications. However, as far the U.S.A. is concerned, this U.S. law has brought results. Because of China's failure to protect U.S. intellectual property, the U.S.A. imposed 100 percent tariffs in 1995 on $108 billion of imports of Chinese product, representing the largest retaliation ever taken by the U.S. government. Soon after that, China signed the Intellectual Property Rights (IPR) Enforcement Agreement and took action to curb piracy. However, although pirated products are no longer sold openly over the counter, the hidden transactions are still common. In addition, while China has done something about illegal retailing, it has not done much about illegal manufacturing. As a matter of fact, production of illegal compact disks has greatly increased. The factories making counterfeit products are able to operate quite freely due to their political connections.

It is not sufficient for a company to fight counterfeiting only in its home country. The battle must be carried to the counterfeiters' own country and to other major markets. Apple has filed suits against imitators in Taiwan, Hong Kong, and New Zealand. The overall idea is to prevent bogus goods from entering the industrialized nations that make up the major markets. To make the tactic more effective, it is necessary to go after the distributors and importers in addition to the manufacturers of counterfeit goods. Cartier, for example, has filed 120 lawsuits against retailers in almost every major city. Because it is difficult and time-consuming to shut down foreign counterfeiters in their home countries, major middlemen must be targeted so that they become aware of the risks in handling fakes.

The cooperation a company receives from foreign governments in reducing the amount of counterfeiting varies greatly. Hong Kong has customarily done a credible job of enforcing court judgments against counterfeiters. Taiwan, in contrast, has been reluctant and unpredictable in going after counterfeiters. It has ignored most criticism because its economy depends significantly on the export of bogus goods. In a case such as this, the injured firm should request that its own government intervene by applying pressure on a country that harbors counterfeiters. The U.S. Tariff and Trade Act, passed in 1984, is intended to deal with this problem on an international basis. It allows the U.S.A. to deny tariff preferences and duty-free imports to developing countries that do not make a satisfactory attempt to control a counterfeit problem originating in their countries.

Finally, the company must invest in and establish its own monitoring system. Its best defense is to strike back rather than relying solely on government enforcement. One computer firm in Taiwan allows consumers to bring in fakes that it then exchanges for the purchase of genuine computers at a discount. Chanel spends more than $1 million a year on security. It goes after counterfeiters by using a computer to keep track of protected names in various countries, the names of suspected counterfeiters, and the near names, such as Channel, Chabel, or Replica No. 5. Another innovative tactic has been employed by Cartier. It opened its own store directly across the street from the store selling fakes, forcing the retailer of the bogus merchandise to stop selling forgeries in return for a sole local distributorship in Mexico.

When the cost of surveillance is high, it may be more desirable to form an association for the purpose of gathering information and evidence. Apple, Lotus, Ashton-Tate, Microsoft, Autodesk, and Word Perfect formed the Business Software Association as an investigative team. The team was successful in providing information to authorities for the arrest of pirates. This strategy reduces costs whole increasing cooperation and effectiveness.

Although counterfeiting is a serious problem, it seems strange that counterfeiting may still benefit a trademark owner or a patent holder in some way. In the case of software piracy, it provides the shadow diffusion of a software parallel to the legal diffusion in the marketplace, thus increasing the user base in the process. This shadow software diffusion may influence potential software users to adopt the software, and some of them may become new software buyers.

Business Software Alliance's recent study shows that countries reducing piracy have experienced faster economic growth.[45] Its explanation is that reduction in piracy spurs sales, leading to more jobs and tax revenues. For example, Egypt reduced its piracy rate by 30 percent and saw its software sector grow by 160 percent. Critics of the study, however, countered that it could not be determined whether a country's economic growth was a result of piracy reduction.

Technology allows owners of intellectual property to stay one step ahead of counterfeiters. Movie makers can utilize video fingerprinting to spot illegal copies, while other products can utilize nanotracers, DNA markers, and microscopic laser etchings.[46]

## Conclusion

This chapter has examined the various legal issues relating to the conduct of international business activities. Because of the variety of legal systems and the different interpretations and enforcement mechanisms, the discussion must, of necessity, be somewhat general. Based on the same rationale, it is impossible for the top management and legal staff at corporate headquarters to completely master the knowledge of foreign law on their own.

To appreciate the problem and subtlety of foreign law, it is clearly necessary to consult local attorneys to find out how a company's operation may be constrained by particular laws. To deal with problems relating to bribery, incorporation, counterfeiting, and infringement, the services of local attorneys are essential. Just as essential is the cooperation of the governments of both the host and home countries.

The legal environment is complex and dynamic, with different countries claiming jurisdiction (or a lack of jurisdiction) over business operations. The interaction among domestic, foreign, and international legal environments creates new obstacles as well as new opportunities. A host country may use an MNC's subsidiary in its country as a method of influencing the MNC and subsequently its home country's policies. Likewise, the home country may instruct the parent company to dictate its foreign subsidiary's activities. It is thus not uncommon to find a situation in which the firm is being pressured in opposing directions by two governments. However, the MNC can use its global network to counter such a threat by shifting or threatening to shift the affected operations to other countries, thus lessening the governments' influence on its behavior. It is this countervailing power that allows the company to exercise a great deal of freedom in adjusting its marketing mix strategies.

It is important to keep in mind that legal contracts and agreements can only be as good as the parties who create them and the countries that enforce them. Therefore, a contract cannot be used as a substitute for trust and understanding between parties or careful screening of business partners.

## CASE 5.1 BRIBERY: A MATTER OF NATIONAL PERSPECTIVE

At one time, the cost of bribing foreign officials was considered to be business costs that were tax deductible in the United Kingdom. For some reason, England was not and is not eager to deal with bribery of foreign officials. Any efforts to deal with bribery have been half-hearted and were taken only because of pressure from non-government agencies and the OECD.

The United Kingdom ratified the OECD's convention against bribery in 1998 but basically did nothing else. After having received considerable pressure and negative publicity, Great Britain finally moved to explicitly ban British citizens and companies from bribing foreign officials, regardless of where the act took place. The ban is part of the anti-terrorism act of 2001.

As with the Foreign Corrupt Practices Act of the U.S.A., the British law allows "facilitation payments." These supposedly "little" bribes are tolerated when it is normal in a certain country for officials to demand them. British firms will not be penalized for their subsidiaries' corrupt practices as long as the parent firms did not order or approve them. Not surprisingly, the OECD complained in 2005 about England's slow progress in implementing the convention and updating of its anti-bribery laws. The convention requires the UK to investigate bribes paid overseas. As noted by the OECD, Britain has never prosecuted anyone for paying bribes abroad.

BAE Systems PLC, Britain's largest defense contractor, secured a major deal in 1986 that generated $84 billion over two decades and that yielded more than £200 million in annual operating profit for the company. The deal involved BAE supplying and training the Saudi air force.

The BBC program *Panorama*, aired on June 11, 2007, alleged that BAE paid £1 billion to Prince Bandar bin Sultan of Saudi Arabia, in exchange for facilitating the defense contract. The payments were made with the UK Ministry of Defence's full knowledge but were concealed from Parliament and the public. The BBC and *Guardian* newspaper reported that BAE secretly paid millions of dollars to a U.S. bank account of Prince Bandar, who was Saudi ambassador to Washington for 20 years.

BAE as well as Prince Bandar, as expected, denied any wrongdoing. As part of its defense (or offense), BAE and the government of Saudi Arabia spent weeks of intense lobbying. It was reported that Saudi Arabia threatened to cancel a follow-up purchase of 72 Typhoon jet fighters. It was big news when the Serious Fraud Office announced in December 2006 that it had decided to drop its two-year investigation of BAE regarding the bribes paid to Saudi officials.

The attorney-general, the country's top law enforcement officer, explained that the decision to drop the investigation was reluctantly made after balancing the rule of law with the "wider public interest." He carefully emphasized that the investigation was halted because national security was a prime concern. In other words, Saudi Arabia threatened to stop cooperating with Britain in the fight against al-Qaeda. Incidentally, the attorney-general was a political appointee.

Tony Blair, the Prime Minister at the time, offered his rationale for intervening in the bribery investigation. His explanation was that the investigation could harm relations with Saudi Arabia. In his own words, he did not believe that the probe "would have led anywhere, except to the complete wreckage of a vital strategic relationship for our country in terms of fighting terrorism, in terms of the Middle East, in terms of British interests" in Saudi Arabia. Shortly after, Blair also mentioned that thousands of British jobs could be jeopardized due to "ill feeling between us and a key partner and ally." The British government also claimed that the acts which were investigated took place before the OECD Anti-Bribery Convention of 1999, a claim which was rejected by the OECD.

It is anything but surprising that the British government's decision has attracted a great deal of criticism and condemnation. Saudi Arabia, likewise, has been criticized for treating government accounts and the royal family's property as one and the same thing. In spite of the intense criticism, Gordon Brown did not show any inclination to revive the investigation when he became Prime Minister in 2007. Surprisingly, the Serious Fraud Office is still pursuing corruption investigations involving BAE in the Czech Republic,

Romania, and Chile. At least in private, OECD officials said that England violated the treaty by allowing political officials to intervene in judicial cases. Transparency International issued a press release stating that "UK actions on Saudi defence contract are blow to the Anti-Bribery Convention."

### Points to consider

Offer your critical evaluation of the British government's decision to drop its investigation into allegations that BAE and Saudi officials engaged in bribery. On the one hand, you should try to justify Tony Blair's decision. After having done that, you need to take the other perspective by attacking the flaws of those excuses.

As an ethics officer of a multinational corporation, what are the guidelines that you offer to your employees with regard to what they can or cannot offer customers as well as what they can or cannot receive from those who want to do business with your company?

*Sources*: "Barefaced," *The Economist*, December 23, 2006; "Bribe Britannia," *The Economist*, December 23, 2006, 85–87; "Saudi Affairs Ripple in the West," *Wall Street Journal*, June 12, 2007; and "Probe of BAE Cloud U.S. Deals," *Wall Street Journal*, June 27, 2007.

## Questions

1 Describe the multiplicity of the legal environments.
2 Distinguish between common law and statute law systems.
3 Cite examples of products that cannot be imported into the U.S.A.
4 Explain how the legal environment can have an impact on an MNC's marketing mix.
5 What is the extraterritorial application of law?
6 Why do MNCs prefer to use corporate subsidiaries in foreign markets?
7 Distinguish among patent, trademark, copyright, and infringement.
8 Distinguish between priority in use and priority in registration.

## Discussion assignments and minicases

1 Why is it so difficult for an MNC to deal with bribery?
2 According to Scott McNealy, Chairman of Sun Microsystems, business school ethics courses are a waste of time. Regarding ethics, "either you're born with it or you learn it from your parents." Thus it is too late to instill ethics by the time a person enrolls in a business school. Discuss the merits (or lack of merits) of this position.
3 What can trademark owners do to minimize counterfeiting?
4 As an owner of a software product, what form of legal protection will you try to obtain: patent, copyright, or trademark?

## Notes


1 "German Court Rules Against Wal-Mart," *San José Mercury News*, November 13, 2002.
2 Sarah L. Croft and Beatrice Harichaux de Tourdonnet, "France and England: The European Product Liability Directive in Practice," *For the Defense* (February 2000): 8–13.
3 "Offsetting the Costs of Employment Protection?", *IMF Survey*, June 30, 2003, 197–8.
4 Chun Zhang, David A. Griffith, and S. Tamer Cavusgil, "The Litigated Dissolution of International Distribution Relationships: A Process Framework and Propositions," *Journal of International Marketing* 14 (No. 2, 2006): 85–115.
5 "Drummon Trial Is Set to Open," *Wall Street Journal*, July 9, 2007; "Making a Federal Case Out of Overseas Abuses," *Business Week*, November 25, 2002, 78; and "Citing Nazis, Lawyers Say Unocal Should Be Tried," *Bangkok Post*, June 19, 2003.
6 Stephen J. Kobrin, "Territoriality and the Governance of Cyberspace," *Journal of International Business Studies* 32 (fourth quarter 2001): 687–704.
7 *World Investment Report 2006: FDI from Developing and Transition Economies* (UNCTAD, 2006).
8 "Indian Justice: Slow But Fairly Sure," *The Economist*, December 23, 2006, 48.
9 "Lawlessness and Economics," *IMF Survey*, May 19, 2003, 145–7.
10 "Non-litigious Japan Faces Critical Shortage of Lawyers," *San José Mercury News*, September 11, 2000; "More Business in Japan?", *Collections and Credit Risk* (May 2000): 10; and "Don't Kill All the Lawyers – Send Them to Japan," *Business Week*, June 14, 1999, 66.
11 "U.S. Law Firms Expand Operations Across Asia," *Wall Street Journal*, December 18, 2006.
12 "Dispute Avoidance and Dispute Resolution in China," *Export America*, June 2001, 14.
13 "Going Straight to Get in the EU," *Wall Street Journal*, February 3, 2005.
14 "Bribe Britannia," *The Economist*, December 23, 2006, 85–7.
15 Alvaro Cuervo-Cazurra, "Who Cares About Corruption?", *Journal of International Business Studies* 37 (November 2006): 807–22.
16 Anusorn Singhapakdi *et al.*, "How Important Are Ethics and Social Responsibility? – A Multinational Study of Marketing Professions," *European Journal of Marketing* 35 (No. 1, 2001): 133–53; and Kiran Karande, C.P. Rao, and Anusorn Singhapakdi, "Moral Philosophies of Marketing Managers: A Comparison of American, Australian, and Malaysian Cultures," *European Journal of Marketing* 36 (No. 7, 2002): 768–91.
17 Janet K. M. Marta and Anusorn Singhapakdi, "Comparing Thai and U.S. Businesspeople: Perceived Intensity of Unethical Marketing Practices, Corporate Ethical Values, and Perceived Importance of Ethics," *International Marketing Review* 22 (No. 5, 2005): 562–77.
18 Janet K. M. Marta *et al.*, "Some Important Factors Underlying Ethical Decisions of Middle-Eastern Marketers," *International Marketing Review* 21 (No. 1, 2004): 53–67.
19 Jang Singh *et al.*, "A Comparative Study of the Contents of Corporate Codes of Ethics in Australia, Canada, and Sweden," *Journal of World Business* 40 (February 2005): 91–109.
20 Bettina Cornwell *et al.*, "A Cross-cultural Study of the Role of Religion in Consumers' Ethical Positions," *International Marketing Review* 22 (No. 5, 2005): 531–46.
21 Pallab Paul, Abhijit Roy, and Kausiki Mukhopadhyay, "The Impact of Cultural Values on Marketing Ethical Norms: A Study in India and the United States," *Journal of International Marketing* 14 (No. 4, 2006): 28–56.
22 Ans Kolk and Rob Van Tulder, "Ethics in International Business: Multinational Approaches to Child Labor," *Journal of World Business* 39 (February 2004): 49–60.
23 "Gaining Perspective," *BGS International Exchange* (Fall 2006): 6–8.
24 Robert Klitgaard, "Subverting Corruption," *Finance & Development* (June 2000): 2–5.
25 Yadong Luo, "Political Behavior, Social Responsibility, and Perceived Corruption: A Structuration Perspective," *Journal of International Business Studies* 37 (November 2006): 747–66.

26 Chuck CY Kwok and Solomon Tadesse, "The MNC as an Agent of Change for Host-Country Institutions: FDI and Corruption," *Journal of International Business Studies* 37 (November 2006): 767–85.

27 "Multinational Companies Unite to Fight Bribery," *Wall Street Journal*, January 27, 2005.

28 Robert L. Ostergard, Jr., "The Measurement of Intellectual Property Rights Protection," *Journal of International Business Studies* 31 (second quarter 2000): 349–60.

29 "Mickey Mouse Goes to War," *San José Mercury News*, October 4, 2002.

30 "Supreme Court Extends Copyright Protections," *San José Mercury News*, January 16, 2003; and "Ruling a Ripoff of Consumers," *San José Mercury News*, January 16, 2003.

31 "Copyrights Expiring in Europe," *San José Mercury News*, January 3, 2003.

32 "EU Shelves Plans to Overhaul Collection of Copyright Fees," *Wall Street Journal*, December 14, 2006.

33 "Patently Absurd," *New York Times Magazine*, March 12, 2000, 44–49.

34 "Big Firms Face Off Over Patent Case," *San José Mercury News*, November 25, 2006; "Patent Holders' Power Is Curtailed," *Wall Street Journal*, April 30, 2007; and "Patently Obvious," *Wall Street Journal*, May 3, 2007.

35 "Bell Labs Legend Haunts Courtroom Tech Rivals," Marketwatch.com, April 9, 2007.

36 "The Business Week News You Need to Know," *Business Week*, November 6, 2006; and "Top Court Chips Away at Patents," *San José Mercury News*, May 1, 2007.

37 "A Bite Out of Apple," *San José Mercury News*, August 24, 2006.

38 "Former Coke Secretary Sentenced in Trade-secret Case," *Wall Street Journal*, May 24, 2007.

39 Dean Matlack, "Protecting Intellectual Property Rights Abroad: Resources for U.S. Exporters," *Export America*, June 2002; and "The Advantages of Using the Patent Cooperation Treaty," *Export America*, January 2002.

40 "Study Shows Costs of Software Piracy," *Asian Wall Street Journal*, June 26, 2001.

41 "Pirate-proofing Hollywood," *Business Week*, June 11, 2007, 58.

42 "Faking Out the Fakers," *Business Week*, June 4, 2007, 76–80.

43 Katherine Wiehagen, "Section 301 Reports," *Export America* (May 2000): 12.

44 "Thailand Hits Top 10 of Copyright Pirates," *Bangkok Post*, May 1, 2007.

45 "New Study Reveals Significant Decline in World Software Piracy Since 1994," Business Software Alliance, Press release, June 3, 2003.

46 "Faking Out the Fakers;" and "Pirate-proofing Hollywood."

Chapter 6

# Culture

> I do not want my house to be walled in on sides and my windows to be stuffed. I want the cultures of all the lands to be blown about my house as freely as possible. But I refuse to be blown off my feet by any.
>
> Mahatma Gandhi

## Chapter outline

- Marketing strategy: fish story
- Culture and its characteristics
- Influence of culture on consumption
- Influence of culture on thinking processes
- Influence of culture on communication processes
- Cultural universals
- Cultural similarities: an illusion
- Communication through verbal language
    - Language acquisition
    - Translation
    - The world's best language
    - Marketing and languages
- Communication through nonverbal language
    - Language of time
    - Language of space
    - Language of agreement
    - Language of friendship
    - Language of negotiation
    - Language of religion
    - Language of superstition

- ❑ Language of color
- ❑ Language of gifts

- Subculture
- Conclusion
- Case 6.1 Cultural considerations in international marketing: a classroom simulation
- Case 6.2 When in Rome do as the Romans do: useful tips for those who do business in Russia
- Case 6.3 Language of color

## Marketing strategy

**Fish story**

After achieving independence in 1991 from Russia, Estonia has strived for a post-Soviet national identity. According to an Estonian Agriculture Ministry official, "food has a political dimension." In Soviet times, recipes and their names had to be approved by Moscow. Estonian recipes were suppressed as nationalist. A 1955 Moscow-sanctioned Estonian cookbook is a 416-page book which has only 18 pages of Estonian recipes at the back of the book. Many Estonian dishes largely disappeared.

To show that Estonia is an independent nation, having symbols such as a national fish is crucial. After an emotional debate, the Baltic herring is now Estonia's national fish. The Baltic herring is a traditional staple of the Estonian diet.

Over the years, due to the influence of Germany and Russia, Estonians have become partial to pork, sauerkraut, blood sausage, and fried potato. The government has run a "fish makes good" campaign to encourage people to improve their diet. The advertisements show a woman in a bikini and a fish in her mouth emerging from the sea. The irony is that the Baltic Sea is one of the most polluted in the world, and some Baltic herring are found to have high amounts of dioxin. In addition, at the retail price of about $1.60 per pound, the fish is too expensive for many Estonians.

To the British, catching the slippery *Cyprinus carpio* is a sport. The British used to eat carp but now view them as inedible bottom feeders. To Polish fishermen in England, carp are food. Of the half million Poles in Great Britain, many like to serve carp on Christmas Eve, instead of a goose or turkey.

At private lakes, people pay $15 to $40 a day to fish for carp, take a photo, and then throw them back. Polish fishermen on the other hand think that it is illogical to catch carp and not to eat them. The culture clash has led an owner of several fisheries to ban all Eastern Europeans from his lakes.

*Sources*: "Russia, Beware: Estonia Chooses a National Fish," *Wall Street Journal*, June 13, 2007; and "In Great Britain, a Fish Culture Clash: To Eat or Release," *Wall Street Journal*, December 20, 2006.

## Purpose of chapter

A worldwide business success requires a respect for local customs. International marketers need to recognize and appreciate varying cultures. Culture plays a significant role in influencing consumer perception, which in turn influences preference and purchase. A good marketing plan can easily go awry when it clashes with tradition. A marketing mix can be effective only as long as it is relevant to a given culture. One should expect that a product may have to be modified, that a new distribution may have to be found, or that a new promotional strategy may have to be considered.

What is more surprising than the blunders that occur are the underlying causes for these mistakes. The most fundamental problem appears to be the indifferent attitude of many American firms toward international markets. The firms often enter foreign markets with a complete disregard for the customs and traditions there – something they would never do at home. In marked contrast, many Japanese firms have been highly successful in the U.S.A. and elsewhere because of their keen awareness and understanding of the local culture.

In order to develop an appreciation for the role of culture in society as well as the marketing implications of culture, this chapter will explore the following: (1) what culture is, (2) what its characteristics are, and (3) how culture affects consumer behavior. The varying methods of developing cross-cultural communication, verbally and otherwise, are discussed. To lend an understanding of how cultures vary, the chapter will compare a number of cultures. Finally, because population homogeneity within a country is an exception rather than a rule, it is necessary to examine the relevance and bases of subcultural groups.

## Culture and its characteristics

Culture, an inclusive term, may be conceptualized in many different ways. Not surprisingly, the concept is often accompanied by numerous definitions. In any case, a good basic definition of the concept is that culture is a set of traditional beliefs and values that are transmitted and shared in a given society. Culture is also the total way of life and thinking patterns that are passed from generation to generation. Culture means many things to many people because the concept encompasses norms, values, customs, art, and mores.

Culture is **prescriptive**. It prescribes the kinds of behavior considered acceptable in a society (see Ethical Dimension 6.1). As a result, culture provides guidance for decision making. For example, principles enjoining compromise are more salient in East Asian cultures than in the North American culture. As confirmed by one study, Hong Kong decision makers are more likely than their American counterparts to compromise.[1] According to another study, compared to Americans, Chinese tend to avoid conflict because it will hurt the relationship with the other party. Avoidance is further heightened when the other party is of higher status.[2]

The prescriptive characteristic of culture simplifies a consumer's decision-making process by limiting product choices to those which are socially acceptable. This same characteristic creates problems for those products not in tune with the consumer's cultural beliefs. Smoking, for instance, was once socially acceptable behavior, but recently it has become more and more undesirable – both socially and medically.

Culture is **socially shared**. Culture, out of necessity, must be based on social interaction and creation. It cannot exist by itself. It must be shared by members of a society, thus acting to reinforce culture's prescriptive nature. For example, Chinese parents at one time shared the preference of wanting their girl children to have small feet. Large feet, viewed as characteristic of peasants and low-class people, were scorned. As a result, parents from the upper class bound a daughter's feet tightly

## Ethical Dimension 6.1

**A token of appreciation or coercion**

In Asia, it is hardly uncommon for clients and patients to give their doctors and lawyers something extra above and beyond the required fees. Patients often treat their doctors like customers by trying to please them so as to get special care in return. Neither side seems to understand that this kind of extra payment may be construed as a bribe. Sometimes, a doctor may even make an overt suggestion. One surgeon at Mahatma Gandhi Hospital was convicted of corruption. For him to perform surgery, he demanded a bribe of Rs 1000 from his patient. He was given a one-year prison term.

MY Hospital, a hospital in India, had to postpone some 50 major operations on poor patients at the end of 2006. Several doctors and heads of departments were not available because they were overseas for the New Year celebrations. Their New Year package tour was arranged by a multinational drug company so that the senior doctors would prescribe its drugs and conduct clinical trials. It is not uncommon for national and multinational corporations to bribe doctors with meals, gifts, and free trips to exotic locations – supposedly for the purpose of taking "continuing medical education courses."

*Sources*: "1-Yr jail to Retd Doc for Graft," *Free Press Indore Journal*, December 31, 2006; and "Docs on Leave, Surgeries Postponed," *Free Press Indore Journal*, December 30, 2006.

so that her feet would not grow large. It did not matter to the parents that their daughter would grow up having difficulty walking about with distortedly small feet.

Culture **facilitates communication**. One useful function provided by culture is to facilitate communication. Culture usually imposes common habits of thought and feeling among people. Thus, within a given group, culture makes it easier for people to communicate with one another. But culture may also impede communication across groups due to a lack of shared common cultural values. This is one reason why a standardized advertisement may have difficulty communicating with consumers in foreign countries.

Culture is **learned**. Culture is not inherited genetically – it must be learned and acquired. **Socialization** or **enculturation** occurs when a person absorbs or learns the culture in which he or she is raised. In contrast, if a person learns the culture of a society other than the one in which he or she was raised, the process of **acculturation** occurs. The ability to learn culture makes it possible for people to absorb new cultural trends. Asian countries have complained, sometimes bitterly, about how their cultures are being contaminated by rock-and-roll music and Western sexual and social permissiveness – foreign elements they consider undesirable and harmful. South Korea has been unsuccessful in banning rock music, as was the former Soviet Union.

Culture is **subjective**. People in different cultures often have different ideas about the same object. What is acceptable in one culture may not necessarily be so in another. In this regard, culture is both unique and arbitrary (see Cultural Dimension 6.1). As a result, the same phenomenon appearing in different cultures may be interpreted in very different ways. It is customary in many cultures for a bridegroom's family to offer a dowry to a bride's family, either for the bride's future security or to compensate her family for raising her. In India, an entirely different set of cultural rules applies. A woman there is viewed as a burden to both her own family and her husband-to-be. When she marries, her family must offer a dowry to the bridegroom. Some men have been so unhappy with what they perceive as an inadequate dowry that they have set their new wives on fire. Although India outlawed dowry payments in 1961, the practice is still being observed by many Hindus who may make both pre- and post-marriage demands. Still dowries are disguised by families as gifts to newlyweds. Interestingly, according to a survey conducted four decades earlier, almost two-thirds of Indian communities reported that local custom required a groom to pay his bride's family.[3]

Culture is **enduring**. Because culture is shared and passed from generation to generation, it is relatively stable and somewhat permanent. Old habits are hard to break, and a people tends to maintain its own heritage in spite of a continuously changing world. This explains why India and China, despite severe overcrowding, have a great deal of difficulty with birth control. The Chinese view a large family as a blessing and assume that children will take care of parents when they grow old. They also have a strong desire to have sons in order to preserve their family name. The modern Chinese government's mandate of one child per family has resulted in numerous deaths of firstborn daughters. The suspicion is that parents murder their daughters in order to circumvent the quota – they want to be able to have another child, hoping for a son.

Culture is **cumulative**. Culture is based on hundreds or even thousands of years of accumulated circumstances. Each generation adds something of its own to the culture before passing the heritage on to the next generation. Therefore, culture tends to become broader-based over time, because new ideas are incorporated and become a part of that culture. Of course, during the process, some old ideas are also discarded.

Culture is **dynamic**. Culture is passed from generation to generation, but one should not assume that culture is static and immune to change. Far from being the case, culture is constantly changing – it adapts itself to new situations and new sources of knowledge. As explained by Craig and Douglas, "culture is becoming increasingly deterritorialized and penetrated by elements from other cultures. This is resulting in cultural contamination, cultural pluralism and hybridization."[4]

## Cultural Dimension 6.1

### One man's culture

Until his death in 2006, Saparmurat Niyazov ruled Turkmenistan, a former Soviet republic, with an iron fist. He called himself Turkmenbashi (Father of the Turkmens). Like all dictators, he put his image on virtually everything: bank notes, statues, vodka bottles, chocolate, tea labels, and watches. The days and months of the years were renamed in honor of himself and his family. He even renamed "bread" after his mother. According to him, because Turkmen do not read books, rural libraries were closed. Opera and ballet were banned.

Niyazov used state security services to spread fear through the population. Due to widespread abuses, there were torture, disappearances, detentions, exile, and forced labor. The U.S.A., while voicing concern over human rights, did nothing. Instead, it has chosen to maintain cooperation. After all, Niyazov offered landing rights and allowed U.S. forces to use the country's airspace for operations in Afghanistan. Apparently, dictatorship is not necessarily bad as long as the regime can provide assistance to the U.S.A.

*Source*: "U.S. and Russia Seek Control of Region's Energy," *San José Mercury News*, December 22, 2006.

The dynamic aspect of culture can make some products obsolete and usher in new buying habits. Japanese tastes, for example, have been changing from a diet of fish and rice to an accommodation of meat and dairy products. In the case of Singapore, it was illegal for concert goers to dance or stand up from their seats during performance. The government at first merely tolerated dancing in the audience if it was not violent or offensive. In 2003, the government has finally declared that bar-top dancing is legal, allowing patrons to dance on countertops. This new stance is due to Singapore's desire to transform compliant people into innovators and entrepreneurs in the name of global competitiveness. As endorsed by Prime Minister Goh Chok Tong, "if we want our people to make more decisions for themselves . . . we must allow some risk-taking and a little excitement."

## Influence of culture on consumption

Consumption patterns, lifestyles, and the priority of needs are all dictated by culture. Culture prescribes the manner in which people satisfy their desires. Hindus and some Chinese do not consume beef at all, believing that it is improper to eat cattle that work on farms, thus helping to provide foods such as rice and vegetables. In Japan, the per capita annual consumption of beef has increased to 11 pounds, still a very small amount when compared to the more than 100 pounds consumed per capita in the United States and Argentina.

The eating habits of many peoples seem exotic to Westerners. The Chinese eat such things as fish stomachs and bird's nest soup (made from bird's saliva). The Japanese eat uncooked seafood, and the Iraqis eat dried, salted locusts as snacks while drinking. Although such eating habits may seem repulsive to Westerners, consumption habits of the West are just as strange to foreigners. The French eat snails, Americans and Europeans use honey (bee expectorate or bee spit) and blue cheese or Roquefort salad dressing, which is made with a strong cheese with bluish mold. No society has a monopoly on unusual eating habits when comparisons are made among various societies.

Not only does culture influence what is to be consumed, but it also affects what should not be purchased. Jews require kosher ("pure") food. Kosher rules about food preparation prohibit pork or shellfish, and there is no mixing of milk and meat products. Coca-Cola was declared kosher in 1935.

Likewise, Muslims do not eat pork, and foods cannot be processed with alcohol and non-halal animal products (e.g., lard). Muslims do not purchase chickens unless they have been halalled, and, like Jews, no consumption of pork is allowed. They also do not smoke or drink alcoholic beverages, a habit shared by some strict Protestants. Although these restrictions exist in Islamic countries, the situation is not entirely without market possibilities. The marketing challenge is to create a product that fits the needs of a particular culture. Moussy, a nonalcoholic beer from Switzerland, is a product that was seen as being able to overcome the religious restriction of consuming alcoholic beverages. By conforming to the religious beliefs of Islam that ban alcohol, Moussy has become so successful in Saudi Arabia that half of its worldwide sales are accounted for in that country. Other international brewers have also finally reached the lucrative Middle-East market by promoting malt beverages that resemble beer – without alcohol.[5]

## Influence of culture on thinking processes

In addition to consumption habits, thinking processes are also affected by culture. Based on one study, independent consumers in individualistic cultures place an emphasis on choice, variety seeking, and personal freedom.[6]

When traveling overseas, it is virtually impossible for a person to observe foreign cultures without making reference, perhaps unconsciously, back to personal cultural values. This phenomenon is known as the **self-reference criterion (SRC)**. Because of the effect of the SRC, the individual tends to be bound by his or her own cultural assumptions. It is thus important for the traveler to recognize how perception of overseas events can be distorted by the effects of the SRC.

Animals provide a good illustration of the impact of the SRC on the thinking processes. Americans and Europeans commonly treat dogs as family members, addressing the animals affectionately and even letting dogs sleep on family members' beds. Arabs, however, view dogs as filthy animals. Some in the Far East go so far as to cook and eat dogs – a consumption habit viewed as revolting and compared to cannibalism by Americans. Hindus, in contrast, revere cows and do not understand how Westerners can eat beef.

In order to investigate a phenomenon in another country, a researcher or marketing manager must attempt to eliminate the SRC effect. The presence of the SRC, if not controlled, can invalidate the results of a research study. Lee suggests a multi-step approach to remove the undue influence of the SRC.[7] First, the problem should be defined in terms of the culture of the researcher's home country. Second, the same problem is defined again, except that it is defined in terms of the cultural norms of the host country. Third, a comparison is made of the two cultural composites. Any difference noted between the composites indicates an existence of the SRC, necessitating another look at the problem with the SRC removed.

The value of this approach is that it forces the manager/researcher to make objective evaluations about assumptions. This, in turn, compels the marketing manager to examine the applicability of initial assumptions in terms of another culture. By being aware of the influence of the SRC, a manager can isolate the SRC, making it possible to redefine a problem from a more neutral viewpoint. An awareness of this undue influence should sensitize a person to think in terms of the host country's culture. The end result should be that the manager thinks in international terms and not in terms of his or her native culture.

One study relied on self-referencing as a mechanism to explain ethnicity effects in advertising. It found that Asians exhibited greater self-referencing of Asian models than did whites. In addition, high self-referencing Asians had a more favorable attitude toward the advertisement in question.[8]

An awareness of the influence of the SRC is valuable because such awareness can help a manager to prevent a transfer of personal cultural norms on a wholesale basis to an overseas market. This awareness should make a manager more customer-oriented, and the marketing strategy developed will more likely reflect true market needs. The marketing of fire insurance may be used to explain this rationale. For American consumers, the purchase of fire insurance is a sensible and practical acquisition. However, it is difficult to encourage Brazilian consumers to purchase insurance because of superstition. In Brazil, many consumers hold the belief that, by purchasing fire insurance, they may somehow encourage a fire to occur. Therefore, they do not want to think about such an occurrence and avoid the discussion and purchase of fire insurance.

## Influence of culture on communication processes

A country may be classified as either a high-context culture or a low-context culture.[9] The context of a culture is either high or low in terms of in-depth background information. This classification provides an understanding of various cultural orientations and explains how communication is conveyed and perceived. North America and Northern Europe (e.g., Germany, Switzerland, and Scandinavian countries) are examples of **low-context cultures**. In these types of society, messages are explicit and clear in the sense that actual words are used to convey the main part of information in communication. The words and their meanings, being independent entities, can be separated from the context in which they occur. What is important, then, is what is said, not how it is said and not the environment within which it is said.

Japan, France, Spain, Italy, Asia, Africa, and the Middle Eastern Arab nations, in contrast, are **high-context cultures**. In such cultures, the communication may be indirect, and the expressive manner in which the message is delivered becomes crucial. Because the verbal part (i.e., words) does not carry most of the information, much of the information is contained in the nonverbal part of the message to be communicated. The context of communication is high because it includes a great deal of additional information, such as the message sender's values, position, background, and associations in the society. As such, the message cannot be understood without its context. One's individual environment (i.e., physical setting and social circumstances) determines what one says and how one is interpreted by others. This type of communication emphasizes one's character and words as determinants of one's integrity, making it possible for businesspersons to come to terms without detailed legal paperwork.

In his well-researched book, Nisbett explains that Westerners tend to be categorical. Americans, Europeans, and citizens of the British Commonwealth focus on particular objects in isolation from their context. They believe that, if they know the rules that govern objects, they should be able to control the behavior of these objects. By comparison, East Asians have a tendency to be broader and contextual. They feel that the underlying context must be taken into account before complex events can be properly interpreted.[10]

It is also possible that a subcontext can exist in a broader but different context of the culture. The U.S.A., for example, is a low-context culture that consists of several subcultures operating within the framework of a much higher context. Therefore, communication strategy requires a proper adjustment if it is to be effective.

One common method used by U.S. advertisers is to present an advertisement as an **illustrated lecture**. In this low-context method, a product is discussed in the absence of its natural setting. Such a message is not easily understood in high-context cultures due to the omission of essential contextual and nonverbal details.

According to Hall, cultures also vary in the manner by which information processing occurs.[11] Some cultures handle information in a direct, linear fashion and are thus **monochronic** in nature. Schedules, punctuality, and sense that time forms a purposeful straight line are indicators of such cultures. Being monochronic, however, is a matter of degree. Although the Germans, Swiss, and Americans are all monochronic cultures, the Americans are generally more monochronic than most other societies, and their fast tempo and demand for instant responses are often viewed as pushy and impatient.

Other cultures are relatively **polychronic** in the sense that people work on several fronts simultaneously instead of pursuing a single task. Both Japanese and Hispanic cultures are good examples of a polychronic culture. The Japanese are often misunderstood and are accused by Westerners of not volunteering detailed information. The truth of the matter is that the Japanese do not want to be too direct because, by saying things directly, they may be perceived as being insensitive and offensive. The Japanese are also not comfortable in getting right down to substantive business without first becoming familiar with the other business party. For them, it is premature to discuss business matters seriously without first establishing a personal relationship. Furthermore, American businesspersons consider the failure of the Japanese to make eye contact as a sign of rudeness, whereas the Japanese do not want to look each other in the eye because eye contact is an act of confrontation and aggression.

The cultural context and the manner in which the processing of information occurs can be combined to develop a more precise description of how communication takes place in a particular country. Germany, for example, is a monochronic and low-context culture. France, in comparison, is a polychronic and high-context culture. A low-context German may insult a high-context French counterpart by giving too much information about what is already known. Or a low-context German may become upset if he feels that he does not get enough details from the high-context Frenchman.

## Cultural universals

The failure to consider cultural universals results in a tendency to overemphasize cultural differences. As human beings, regardless of race or religion, we all have similar basic needs, and it is reasonable to expect that certain cultural traits transcend national boundaries. For example, people everywhere have a love for music and a need for fun. Some of the cultural universals identified by Murdock are athletic sports, bodily adornment, the calendar, cooking, courtship, dancing, dream interpretation, education, food taboos, inheritance rules, joking, kin groups, status differentiation, and superstition.[12]

Because of the universality of basic desires, some products can be marketed overseas with little modification. The need to have fun, for instance, makes it natural for people everywhere to accept video games. Likewise, culture is not a barrier to computer software dealing with engineering and scientific applications that manipulate schematic drawings and numbers rather than words.

Note that shared values do not necessarily mean shared or identical behavior. The manner of expressing culturally universal traits still varies across countries. Music is a cultural universal, but that does not mean that the same kind of music is acceptable everywhere. Because musical tastes are not internationally uniform, the type of music used must be varied to appeal to a particular country. Likewise, all peoples admire the beautiful, but cultural definitions of beauty vary greatly. As a matter of fact, beauty is not a unidimensional concept, and there are different types of beauty.

The ideal beauty can be both universal and divergent. Many Asian and Hispanic women reshape their faces to look more white. Some feel that minorities seeking cosmetic procedures, by getting rid of "ethnic markers," represents the worst kind of ethnic imperialism.[13] In Vietnam, as in other Asian countries, women associate whiteness with beauty. As a result, in the name of beauty, millions of Vietnamese women resort to using gloves, masks, and other items to cover up just about every inch of flesh to block out the damage from the sun. Vietnamese men, however, do not have this kind of obsession.[14]

In Niger and many places in Africa, fat is the beauty ideal for women. Amazingly, women take steroids to gain bulk or pills to increase their appetites. Some ingest feed or vitamins meant for animals. Fattening pills and animal feed are some of the bestsellers. Married women do not want to be thin because people may have the idea that they are not being taken care of or that they have been abandoned by their husbands. While the African concept of beauty is the reverse of that in the West, the motivation is the same: seeking men's approval.[15]

Some cultural values remain unchanged over time. For products appealing to basic generic values, certain successful products need not be changed, in spite of the changing environment. Such is the case with *Reader's Digest's* extraordinary success for more than three-quarters of a century. In the face of violent shifts in lifestyles and cultural tastes around the world, *Reader's Digest* magazine, founded in 1922, has maintained a bland, lowbrow editorial formula. It continues to tell people that laughter is the best medicine, that difficulties can be overcome, and that the world is a good, though not perfect, place. The magazine provides people with spirit-lifting stories. These cultural traits are also quite universal, as evidenced by the fact that some 100 million people read the magazine's 48 editions in 19 languages. Its success should remind the marketer that, while cultural values may be constantly shifting, there are basic or generic values that are universal and constant. For some products, that market will always be there as a viable alternative in a fast-changing world.

## Cultural similarities: an illusion

Cultural universals, when they exist, should not be interpreted as meaning that two cultures are very much alike. Too often, cultural similarities at first glance may in fact be just an illusion. A marketer must thus guard against taking any market for granted. For many Americans, Canada is merely a northward extension of the U.S.A., a notion resented by most Canadians, who resist cultural absorption by the U.S.A.

According to Zhou and Belk, global images and foreign appeals in advertising are used as evidence of the globalization of local culture. Their analysis of upscale Chinese consumers' understandings of global and local TV and print advertising indicates that it is incorrect to conclude that local culture is becoming globalized and that consumer values are changing accordingly. Chinese consumers have two reactions. On the one hand, they are driven by the desire for global cosmopolitanism and status goods. On the other hand, they are motivated by a more nationalistic desire to invoke Chinese values seen as local in origin.[16]

The perceived cultural difference, real or imagined, explains not only why some American products have been unsuccessful in Canada but also why some Canadian products have failed in the U.S. market. Repeated campaigns to sell the electric tea kettle, an indispensable part of Canadian home life, in the U.S. market have been unsuccessful. Likewise, Vegemite is the closest thing to Australia's national food, with 90 percent of Australian homes having it. Yet this black yeast spread has never been able to find its way into the American consumer's diet.

## Communication through verbal language

Language is a significant part of culture, and communication is impossible without it. A language can be spoken, written, or nonverbal. There are more than 6000 spoken languages. While Australia has 268 languages, Papua New Guinea has 832 languages. Eight countries claim more than half of all languages, and they are (in order): Papua New Guinea, Indonesia, Nigeria, India, Mexico, Cameroon,

**TABLE 6.1** The world's top languages

| *Rank* | *Language name* | *Primary country* |
|---|---|---|
| 1 | Chinese, Mandarin | China |
| 2 | Spanish | Spain |
| 3 | English | United Kingdom |
| 4 | Bengali | Bangladesh |
| 5 | Hindi | India |
| 6 | Portuguese | Portugal |
| 7 | Russian | Russia |
| 8 | Japanese | Japan |
| 9 | German | Germany |
| 10 | Chinese, Wu | China |
| 11 | Javanese | Indonesia |
| 12 | Korean | Korea |
| 13 | French | France |
| 14 | Vietnamese | Vietnam |
| 15 | Telugu | India |
| 16 | Chinese, Yue | China |
| 17 | Marathi | India |
| 18 | Tamil | India |
| 19 | Turkish | Turkey |
| 20 | Urdu | Pakistan |

*Source:* Adapted from *Ethnologue*, 13th ed., ed. Barbara Grimes, (Summer Institute of Linguistics, Inc., 1996).

Australia, and Brazil.[17] Asia accounts for 32 percent of the world's languages. Table 6.1 shows the world's most popular languages.

Some languages are just like endangered species. It is conceivable that more than half of the world's spoken languages could disappear over this century, at the rate of one language death every two weeks.[18] These losses are on top of the thousands of languages that have already disappeared. The Manx language (from the Isle of Man in the Irish Sea) was lost in 1974 when the last speaker died. In 1992, the death of a Turkish farmer was spelled end of the Ubykh language, which claimed a record of 81 consonants. It is difficult to preserve these dying languages when they are spoken by fewer than 2500 people. According to the United Nations Educational, Scientific, and Cultural Organization, a language needs at least 100,000 speakers to pass it from one generation to the next.

## *Language acquisition*

There are a number of theories that explain how people acquire languages. According to the "use it or lose it" hypothesis, people were born with an inherent ability to learn a language. However, this natural ability will diminish with age. Hence, a person must utilize this ability early. After a certain age, the ability will be lost forever, and one can no longer acquire a language in a natural and effortless way.

Language acquisition may have a biological component. A team of geneticists and linguists has discovered a gene that underlies speech and language. The discovery supports the point of view that language is acquired and generated by the brain's specific neural circuitry. This gene appears to switch on other genes in developing the brain of a fetus. Some scientists argue that the gene may not be so specific to language. Therefore, the discovery has still not settled a long-standing debate on whether the brain handles language through dedicated or general mechanisms.[19]

Several studies have confirmed a widely held belief that the U.S. population in general has very low foreign language fluency. Not surprisingly, many American managers believe that it is not necessary for them to learn another language. They prefer to believe that English is the universal language of business communication. Although this assumption is partially true, it can cause difficulty in carrying out business in parts of the world where English is not spoken.

Many U.S. firms complain that the Japanese market is closed to them, but Japanese officials and businessmen see the situation in another way. They feel that U.S. firms are at fault because U.S. managers do not try hard enough to understand the Japanese market. Japanese managers make a conscientious effort to learn the English language, but very few European and Americans reciprocate. Western managers have difficulty in communicating with Japanese suppliers, distributors, and customers. In addition, such managers cannot lobby effectively for their causes in Japan.

Not all individuals can master a foreign language. There are, however, a few indicators that can predict a person's ability to succeed in learning a language. It is quite easy for a very young person to learn a new language because the ear is still able to pick up the nuances of the spoken word. For older people, some have better linguistic aptitude and are thus better able to acquire another language. Those who are cosmopolitan also do better because of their exposure to foreigners. On the other hand, those who are rigid in their thinking usually encounter learning difficulties in languages. Being too analytical or logical is not a positive attribute. For example, it is not useful to wonder why the German language puts its verb at the end of the sentence or why some letters in certain French words are silent.

If a person wants to learn a foreign language, that person must attempt to become internationalized in the sense of thinking multilingually or thinking like a foreigner in that foreign language. In other words, one should be able to think in the foreign language without going through a translation process first. As such, the person should be flexible and spontaneous.

## *Translation*

A marketer must be careful even when the same language is used in two or more markets, such as Great Britain and the U.S.A. Although the two countries have a great deal in common, there are many differences important to a marketer. As noted by Oscar Wilde, "the English have really everything in common with the Americans except of course language."

There are significant differences between American English and British English. Different words are used to indicate the same thing, as shown in Table 6.2. For the American *apartment* and *elevator*, the British use *flat* and *lift* respectively. People use *subways* in New York, but they use the *underground* in London.

Citizens of the two countries may sometimes use the same word or phrase when they mean different things. A *billion* is a thousand million to the Americans but a million million to the Britons. When the Americans *table a motion*, the item is set aside without further discussion, but the British take this expression to mean that the item should be placed on the agenda for immediate discussion. A movie that *went like a bomb* was a success to the Briton but a failure to the American. An American vacuums the carpet, but the Briton *hoovers* or *bissels* it instead.

Even when the same word with the same meaning is used, the spelling may vary. For example, *color* and *theater* are used in the United States, whereas *colour* and *theatre* are used in Great Britain.

**TABLE 6.2** American English vs. British English

| *American* | *English* | *American* | *English* |
|---|---|---|---|
| aisle | gangway | mezzanine | dress circle |
| baby carriage | pram | molasses | black treacle |
| bacon | gammon | monkey wrench | spanner |
| baggage room | left luggage office | moving van | removal van |
| balcony | gallery | mutual fund | unit trust |
| band-aid | elastoplast | newspaper stand | news agent |
| bobby pin | kirby grip | one-way ticket | single ticket |
| bookie | turf accountant | orchestra seats | stalls |
| checkers | draughts | person-to-person call | personal call |
| chicory coffee with or without cream | endive black or white coffee | phone booth | telephone kiosk |
| | | pier | quay |
| dessert | sweet | popsicle | iced lolly |
| diaper | nappy | radio | wireless |
| druggist | chemist | raincoat | mackintosh |
| eggplant | aubergine | raisin | sultana |
| electric cord | flex | round-trip ticket | return ticket |
| elevator | lift | Scotch tape | sellotape |
| endive | chicory | second floor | first floor |
| flashlight | torch | sidewalk | pavement |
| French fried potatoes | chips | soft rolls | baps |
| grade crossing | level crossing | subway | underground |
| installment buying | hire purchase | superhighway | motorway |
| kerosene | paraffin | suspenders | garters |
| lady fingers | boudoir biscuits | thumb tack | drawing pin |
| lawyer | solicitor | tic-tac-toe | naughts and crosses |
| lease (rent) | let | toilet | WC or cloakroom |
| leash | lead | trolley car | tram |
| line | queue | truck | lorry |
| liquor store | wine merchant | two weeks | fortnight |
| long distance call | trunk call | underwear | smalls |
| lost and found | lost property | vacation | holiday |
| mail box | post box | vanilla pudding | blancmange |
| | | yellow turnips | swedes |

The pronunciation can also be different, especially with the letter Z, which is pronounced as *zee* in the U.S.A. but *zed* in the United Kingdom. An American brand name such as E-Z is puzzling in England.

Language differences often necessitate marketing strategy modification. Singer provides its salespeople with instruction books printed in more than 50 languages. Some of these books consist entirely of pictures. In many cases, more than a basic translation of the manual is needed. Computer marketers, for example, have to change software and hardware processes for use in a foreign language. Accounting and financial programs must be completely rewritten because accounting rules and financial reporting systems vary greatly from country to country.

Less obvious than the variations in accounting and financial rules are the writing and reading rules in different countries. Americans take it for granted that, when they read and write, they should begin from left to right, one row at a time before going to the next lower row. The Chinese system requires the reader to read from top to bottom, one column at a time rather than row by row. The Chinese also read from right to left (i.e., they start with the column nearest to the right of the page before moving to the next column on the left). These differences usually require a product to be adjusted to some extent. Computer makers have also found that they must change their system for Arab countries, so that the computer can produce a printout reading from right to left.

When a marketing campaign is exported, careful translation is needed. It is critical to keep in mind that the thought, not the words, must be translated. Examples of careless translation abound. Because differences in languages go beyond differences in words, it is ineffective to have a word-for-word translation. Although dictionaries may help a person understand foreign words, dictionaries cannot include subtle differences in syntax, grammar, pitch, and pronunciation. As a result, advertising copy may have to be interpreted rather than translated.

Another practice that perplexes non-Americans is the system of dating used in the U.S.A. Americans are taught to begin the date with the month, followed by the day and year. For much of the world, it is more logical to start out with the smallest unit (i.e., day). Therefore, a date written as February 3, 2011 by an American seems illogical to foreigners, who find more sense in 3 February 2011.

The confusion increases significantly when the written date consists solely of numerals. Consider 2/3/2011. Americans read that date as February 3, 2011, whereas others read that date as the second day of the third month (i.e., March) in the year 2011. One can easily imagine the difficulty that may result through a misunderstanding between an American firm and its foreign consumer about delivery and payment dates.

When communicating with customers, it cannot be emphasized strongly enough that there is no place for slang, idioms, and unfamiliar phrases in business correspondence or negotiation. There are many other words or phrases that when translated literally can be misunderstood or insulting. It is wise to avoid such American phrases as "call it a day," "big shot," "lay your cards on the table," and "bottom line."

Safe rules of thumb in international communication are:

- When in doubt, overpunctuate.
- Keep ideas separate, making only one point at a time.
- Confirm discussion in writing.
- Write down all figures using the style of the person you are talking to.
- Adjust your English to the level of your foreign counterpart.

- Use visual aids whenever possible.
- Avoid technical, sports, and business jargon.

To put it another way, "Speak to the rest of the world as if you were answering a slightly deaf, very rich auntie who just asked you how much to leave you in her will."[20]

## The world's best language

Each native speaker is going to naturally feel that one's own native language is superior. Actually, virtually all languages are not logical. Grammar, spelling, and pronunciation rules are anything but easy. There are exceptions to the rules and even exceptions to the exceptions.

Some may argue that Chinese should be the world's No. 1 language based on the sheer number of speakers. In China, Putonghua ("common speech") or Mandarin, the national language, is used throughout the country. Although the written language in China is uniform, there are actually hundreds of local dialects. Others may additionally counter by saying that Spanish is spoken in more countries. England and France are going to claim that their many former colonies use their languages.

There is no question that English is the world's language of business, diplomacy, and aviation (see Cultural Dimensions 6.2 and 6.3). At Vivendi in France, all the board and executive meetings are conducted in English, and all documents are in English. English is also the official language of Totalfina Elf, France's second-largest company. Within Western Europe, English is spoken by 77 percent of college students, 69 percent of managers, and 67 percent of those between 15 and 24 years old.[21]

There are approximately 322 million native English speakers and another billion people who can speak it reasonably well. Some have argued that the popularity of the English language is due to its merit. When compared to the French and German languages, English has a huge vocabulary and a simple grammar, and English is open to change to accommodate foreign words and grammatical

### Cultural Dimension 6.2

**Official language**

SAP AG is Germany's largest software company. The company was founded in 1972 by five German IBM engineers. It has grown to become the world's largest maker of software for back-office systems such as accounting and procurement. By the 1980s and 1990s, the company's sales force grew to the point of being global. Yet almost all of SAP's software was written in Germany.

By the early 2000s, SAP realized that it had to become less German and more global. SAP began to employ thousands of programmers in the U.S.A., India, and others. Key projects that were once handled in the home country were assigned to those new programmers. English became the official language for corporate meetings – at home and abroad. Hundreds of foreign managers were recruited. In 2000, non-Germans accounted for one-third of SAP's top ranks. By 2006, they made up half of the top managers. These new employees sought a faster pace while injecting outside influences into the company's insular culture.

*Source*: "SAP's Plan to Globalize Hits Cultural Barriers," *Wall Street Journal*, May 11, 2007.

## Cultural Dimension 6.3

**How to speak English properly**

English is the world's must studied language. It is a global language of business, finance, and technology. In countries where English is not a native language, those who can speak English invariably command higher salaries than those who cannot. However, it is important to recognize that non-native English speakers have a smaller vocabulary and that they may take certain words or phrases literally – rather than figuratively. Certainly, they will have difficulties with culture-bound expressions.

To use the English language properly and effectively when interacting with non-native speakers, the following rules should be followed.

- Avoid idioms (e.g., pushing the envelope).
- Avoid jargon (e.g., bottom line) and acronyms (e.g., OECD).
- Avoid complex sentences. Sentences are difficult to follow when they have dependent, coordinate, subordinate, and relative clauses.
- When delivering a message, speak slowly and pause. Do not run words and sentences together. Pause before beginning a new thought, sentence, or point.

*Source*: Patricia L. Kurtz, "But They Said Everyone Spoke English," Special Advertising Section, *Business Week*, December 17, 2001.

shifts, not to mention new words or slangs (e.g., get crunk, shock jock). But critics can easily point out all those irregular verbs that do not seem to follow any rhyme or reason, not to mention the fact that some irregular verbs have become regularized. To have a command of these verbs and strange pronunciations and spellings, drilling – not reasoning – is the only way to go.

Unlike the English language, which is relatively straightforward, many languages are quite subtle. The Italian language allows several different ways of addressing someone that show a speaker's position and feelings. Likewise, the Japanese language has literary and conversational styles, male and female styles, young and old styles, and various degrees of politeness. In this regard, some may argue that the English language is too black and white and that it does not have words to delineate all subtle meanings.

If there is one language that can lay claim to being truly universal, it is Esperanto. This is the UNESCO-resolutioned planned language. The strengths of Esperanto are its neutral and universal features. The grammar is extremely regular and easy to learn. The language possesses power, flexibility, and beauty, and promotes as well as protects linguistic cultural diversity. As an international language, Esperanto provides a low-cost high-quality trans-Babel communication medium, and it is possible in a short period of time to be fluent in this dialect-free international auxiliary language (see Exhibit 6.1).

### Marketing and languages

An observation made by Berlo explains in accurate terms the importance and influence of language. Because languages affect thought, "systems that employ different codes may well employ different methods of thought. A German's language is different from an American's language. It may follow that his methods of thinking are also different."[22]

Exhibit 6.1

**Quick grammar of Esperanto**

### Spelling

Every word in Esperanto is pronounced just as it is spelt, with each letter corresponding to a single sound. There are no silent letters. The stress is always on the penultimate a/e/i/o/u, for example, rapide (quickly) is spoken rah-PEA-deh.

- **c** = ts
- **^c** (circumflex over c) = ch, tsh
- **g** = (hard as in get)
- **^g** (circumlex over g) = g (soft as in ginger), dzh
- **h** = h (never silent)
- **^h** (circumflex over h) (rare) = ch in Scottish loch
- **i** = ee
- **j** = y
  - **aj** = eye
  - **ej** = ay in hay
  - **oj** = oy
  - **uj** = u + short I
- **^j** (circumflex over j) = s in pleasure, zh
- **s** = ss (never like z)
- **^s** (circumlex over s) = sh
- **u** = oo
- **ù** (breve over u) (rare) = w
  - **aù** = ow in now or how
  - **eù** (rare) = e + short u
- x = extending letter. X is not one of the 28 letters of the Esperanto alphabet, but some people do use it to indicate a circumflex or breve on the preceding letter (cx = ^c, gx = ^g, hx = ^h, jx = ^j, sx = ^s, ux - ù). This is only a temporary measure used on the Net: the true Esperanto letters will be used when Unicode WWW browsers become widespread.

### Verbs

There are no irregular verbs. All verbs (even esti = to be, havi = have, iri = to go, and fair = to do/make) take the same simple declination: add -is -as -os -us -u or -I to the root (est- hav- ir- far-). This is illustrated in the following examples.

- **-is** for past: Li vidis kaj ^si aùdis = He saw and she heard
- **-as** for present: Mi sidas, sed ili staras = I sit/am sitting, but they stand/are standing
- **-os** for future: Mi ferios julie = I will go on holiday in July
- **-us** for conditional: Se me estus rica, (tiam) mi a^cetus helikopteron = If I were rich, (then) I would buy a helicopter
- **u** for imperative: Envenu! = Come in!
- **-i** for infinitive: Mi volas na^gi en la maro = I want to swim in the sea

### Nouns

There are no word genders in Esperanto, and "the" is always "la". There is no word for "a", so Domo = A house = House. Plurals are always formed by adding -j.

- **-o** for singular nouns: Viro kun hundo = A man with a dog
- **oj** (pronounced -oy) for plural nouns: Homoj en la lando de espero = People in the land of hope

Pronouns are short words ending in I (li = he, ^se = she, ^gi = it). Objects are without exception formed by adding -n: La kato rigardas lin.^sin/^gin = the cat watches him/her/it.

**Adjectives and adverbs**

- **-a** for singular adjectives: Unu verda stelo = One green star
- **-aj** (pronounced -eye) for plural adjectives: Du feli^caj amantoj = Two happy lovers
- **-e** for adverbs: Ni kuros rapide = We will run quickly
- **-ant** => -ing: La ku^santa viro = The lying man (Ku^si = to lie, mensogi = to tell a lie)
- **-it** => -ed: La fermita pordo = The closed door (fermi = to close)

**Asking questions**

- **^Cu** = Is it true that. This word is used to make simple yes/no questions: ^Cu mi rajtas eniri? = Can (may) I enter?
- **Kial** (pronounced K E E-al) = Why. Kial vi volas transiri? = Why do you want to cross (over)?
- **Kiam** (pronounced K E E-am) = When. Kiam vi devas foriro? = When must you leave?
- **Kie** (pronounced K E E-eh) = Where. Kie oni povas eniri? = Where can you (one) enter?
- **Kio** (pronounced K E E-oh) = What. Kion vi diris? = What did you say? (-n because kio is used as the object here)
- **Kiu** (pronounced K E E-oh) = Who. Kiu donos la bluajn al mia amiko? - Who will give the blue ones to my friend? (No -n because kiu is used as the subject here)

*Source*: Courtesy of Travlang.com

Marketers should attempt to understand how consumers process linguistic information. About one quarter of the world's population read logographs. A prime example is the Chinese logographs that have also been adapted to Japanese *kanji* and Korean *hancha*, thus maintaining the same meanings but not the same pronunciation. While logographs represent meaning, most modern languages use alphabetic scripts consisting of symbols that represent sound. These sound-based scripts include Latin and Arabic. It is thus useful to determine whether the cognitive processing of words would vary based on whether such words are written in logographic and alphabetic scripts. Conceivably, processing of words written in alphabetic scripts relies more heavily on storage of the short-term memory's phonological loop. In comparison, the processing of words written in logographic scripts may rely more on the storage of visual short-term memory. According to one study, auditory contextual interference was higher for alphabetic words than for logographic words, while visual distracters produced the opposite results. Therefore, advertisements containing alphabetic words should minimize the use of distracting auditory information. However, in the case of advertisements containing logographic words, they should minimize use of distracting graphics or complex visual displays.[23]

Many managers and consumers are bilingual. Given the popularity of the English language in world business, it is reasonable to believe that English is the second language of most of these individuals. One marketing question has to do with the language to be used to communicate with bilingual consumers. One study focusing on how bilingual individuals process advertising messages examines the assumption that advertisements in the consumers' first language gave better results than those advertisements in their second language. The results indicate that second-language messages do not have to result in inferior memory. When the advertisement's picture and text are highly congruent, memory for second-language advertisements, compared to memory for first-language advertisements, is raised to a similar level. At the same time, these second-language advertisements can also maintain product evaluations at a relatively high level.[24]

Marketers may want to consider how bilingual consumers process bilingual information. Language proficiency should also be taken into account. According to one study involving evaluation of dual brand names by Chinese-English bilinguals, "proficient consumers prefer sound translation when the English name is emphasized but meaning translation when the Chinese name is emphasized." For less proficient bilinguals, they engage in semantic processing of the dual names.[25]

## Communication through nonverbal language

People do not always communicate solely through the spoken word or written word. Knowingly or not, people routinely communicate with one another in a nonverbal manner (see Figure 6.1). Body language includes movement, appearance, dress, facial expressions, gestures, posture, use of silence, use of touch, timing, distance between speakers and listeners, physical surroundings, tone, and rhythm of speech. Some body language "phrases" (e.g., a smile) are universal. But other phrases vary in meaning across cultural lines. Whereas the Japanese view prolonged eye contact as rude, Americans instead feel that avoidance of eye contact is impolite. In Latino cultures, it is also rude to sustain eye contact. In addition, nonverbal cues may vary with a person's gender and social or economic class. Sitting at a table around a corner signals cooperation and active listening. Sitting straight across from one another, on the other hand, may be perceived as being confrontational. But sitting side by side makes conversation awkward.

Beckoning someone with a wave of the hand with the palm up is fine in America, but very rude in Japan. Foreigners in Indonesia should also think about local nonverbal communication. Indonesians do not use the left hand when offering food and other objects because it is supposedly the unclean hand.

Figures 6.2 and 6.3 describe the impact of Asian cultures and how to do business in Japan and Korea.

In a popular and often-quoted article, "The Silent Language in Overseas Business," Edward T. Hall explains that there is a need to appreciate cultural differences in matters concerning the language of time, space, things, friendship patterns, and agreements. For the purpose of illustration, these languages are discussed here, modified but derived from work done by Hall and by Arning.[26]

### *Language of time*

Time has different meanings in different countries. An American and an Asian do not mean the same thing when they say, "Why don't you come over sometime?" In the U.S.A., the statement takes a formal tone, implying that advance notice should be given if the visit is to take place. For an Asian, the meaning is exactly what is said – drop in any time without any appointment, regardless of how early or late it may be in the day.

In Saudi Arabia, a Western-style calendar or daily appointment book is unsuitable as a gift because the first of January is already halfway into the Islamic year. In Jordan, an Islamic country, the official weekend is on Friday, and the new week begins on Saturday. Therefore, Fridays in Jordan and most of the Middle East are like Sundays in the West. As a result, the outside world can do business with Jordan and other Muslim countries only on Mondays, Tuesdays, Wednesdays, and half of Thursdays (when most businesses close down early).

In the U.S.A., there is a direct relationship between time and the importance of a matter. When a matter is important, it requires immediate attention and action. In some countries, a reverse

1956.
1965.
1969.
1972.
1975.
1985.
1988.
1991.
You always come back to the basics.
JIM BEAM

**FIGURE 6.1** Nonverbal communication and enduring culture

*Source*: Reprinted courtesy of Jim Beam Brands Co.

relationship exists. A matter of importance requires more time to ponder, and to declare a deadline is to exert undue pressure.

Perceptions of time are culture bound. In the case of **linear-separable time**, common in most European and North American cultures, time is linear in the sense that it has a past, present, and future. Therefore, time is valuable – time spent in the past will make some contribution to the future. In the case of **circular-traditional time**, life is supposed to follow a cycle, and the future thus cannot be altered. As a result, the future is seen as the past repeated, and there is no need to plan because time is not valuable.

Anyone who does business in Japan knows that aggression often leads to disaster.
The slightest hint of aggression can kill a business deal. Be sure to make your point but don't push it. Many Japanese find it difficult to say no—instead, they may say your request would be hard to fulfill. If you do not get a definite answer, just let the subject drop. Your wisdom should speak for itself.
Bathe in mud.
Or sand. Or sulfur. Or just plain water. You will find all kinds of hot-spring spas and baths throughout Japan. First wash yourself with a bathside basin, leaving no traces of soap, then slip gently into the bath. It's very hot at first, but once you get used to it, there's nothing more relaxing after a hard day's work.
Help!
No problem is too big or small for the Tokyo English Lifeline. They'll answer questions on everything from culture to medical emergencies. Telephone 03/264-4347.
Tipping tips.
There's no such thing as tipping in Japan. More expensive restaurants and hotels add a 10%-15% service charge to your bill, but don't tip cab drivers, waitresses, or bellhops. And do not count your change—it'll be considered a sign of distrust.
Northwest notes.
We now offer exclusive nonstop service from Los Angeles to Osaka and the only daily nonstops from Chicago to Tokyo. And, in addition to providing more service to Japan from the U.S. than any other carrier, we offer something no other airline can: the knowledge that comes from over 40 years of helping people do business in Asia. For international reservations, call your travel agent or Northwest at 1-800-447-4747. To find out more about doing business in Asia, call 1-800-553-2215, ext. 77.
NORTHWEST AIRLINES
Asia Series


**FIGURE 6.2** Doing business in Japan

*Source*: Courtesy of Northwest Airlines.

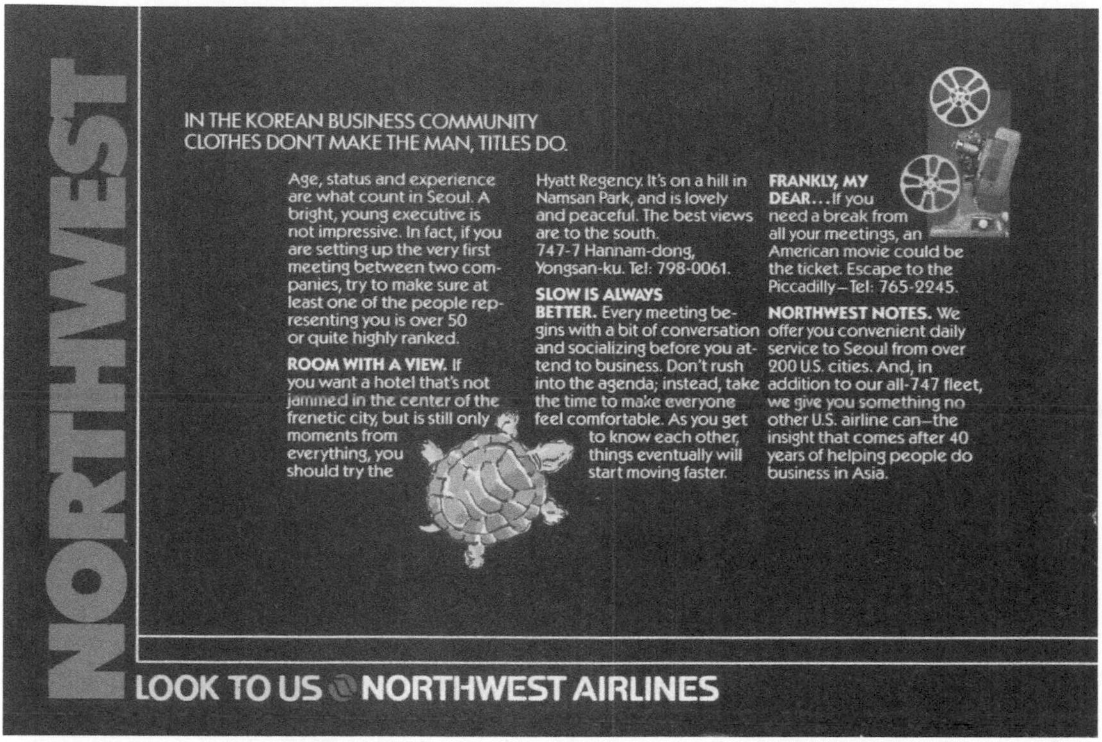
NORTHWEST
IN THE KOREAN BUSINESS COMMUNITY CLOTHES DON'T MAKE THE MAN, TITLES DO.
Age, status and experience are what count in Seoul. A bright, young executive is not impressive. In fact, if you are setting up the very first meeting between two companies, try to make sure at least one of the people representing you is over 50 or quite highly ranked.
ROOM WITH A VIEW. If you want a hotel that's not jammed in the center of the frenetic city, but is still only moments from everything, you should try the Hyatt Regency. It's on a hill in Namsan Park, and is lovely and peaceful. The best views are to the south. 747-7 Hannam-dong, Yongsan-ku. Tel: 798-0061.
SLOW IS ALWAYS BETTER. Every meeting begins with a bit of conversation and socializing before you attend to business. Don't rush into the agenda; instead, take the time to make everyone feel comfortable. As you get to know each other, things eventually will start moving faster.
FRANKLY, MY DEAR... If you need a break from all your meetings, an American movie could be the ticket. Escape to the Piccadilly—Tel: 765-2245.
NORTHWEST NOTES. We offer you convenient daily service to Seoul from over 200 U.S. cities. And, in addition to our all-747 fleet, we give you something no other U.S. airline can—the insight that comes after 40 years of helping people do business in Asia.
LOOK TO US NORTHWEST AIRLINES

**FIGURE 6.3** Doing business in Korea

*Source*: Reprinted courtesy of Northwest Airlines.

Americans tend to value time highly – both work time and leisure time – because "time is money." They often feel that things need to be settled and completed as soon as possible and that they have no time to waste or spare. American impatience is not a virtue in dealing with foreign firms. In general, American negotiators tend to skip the nontask activities and go directly to the agreement stage. Russians, in contrast, have formal classroom training in bargaining and chess. They are patient and careful before making a move, often taking extra time just to gain an advantage in the process of negotiation.

Time takes a more "leisurely walk" in many non-Western societies, where people have ample time and see no need why any situation should be urgent. Whereas Latin American people are usually late, Swedish people are very prompt. Actually, lack of punctuality may even imply importance and status in some places, but any generalization about punctuality is risky. Asians, for instance, tend not to be punctual, but the Chinese observe strict punctuality for social occasions and appointments. In general, there is a lack of punctuality in Asia and Africa, and it is not uncommon for people to be half an hour or an hour late for an appointment. Usually, no excuse is offered to those who are kept waiting. However, if an excuse is needed, it may sound something like this: "If I would have hurried through the traffic, I may have been involved in an accident that would have delayed me even more."

Societies hold various views on urgency and punctuality. Time may be important to non-Westerners in different ways. Astrologers and monks are frequently consulted in order to determine the proper time for personal and business matters. The beginning of a construction project, the ceremonial opening of a new building or business, and the right time to marry or to sign a contract are all affected by timing. In India, one should not travel in a time period determined to be unsafe or unlucky. This creates a dilemma for those who are traveling on a plane whose departure time is deemed to be inappropriate. The traveler may, however, circumvent the inappropriate departure time by being flexible. To accommodate both the modern world of travel and the traditional belief concerning the inappropriate departure time of his plane, a traveler may choose to view the departure from home, not from the airport, as the actual time of beginning the journey. If the departure time from home is also inappropriate, the traveler may leave home an hour earlier and drive around for an hour or two before going to the airport.

## Language of space

Space has its own special meaning. Its importance is most evident when people converse with one another. When the other party is nearby, such as in the same room, communication is easily facilitated. Difficulty in communicating severely increases when the distance between the receiver and sender of a message is great (e.g., when one party is across the street, on another floor, or in another room). In such cases, people have to speak loudly or shout in order to be heard, and the other party still may not hear every word, if any words at all.

Space also has implications for personal selling. Latin Americans are comfortable with just a few inches of distance and repeated embracing. Asians, on the other hand, prefer substantial conversational distance and no physical contact. For Americans, a comfortable distance is something in between those extremes. An American can give the impression of crowding to an Asian and of running away to a Latin American.

Space is also relative: what is perceived as crowded in the U.S.A. may be perceived as spacious somewhere else. A small room with low ceilings, by U.S. standards, is not small to the Japanese. In U.S. department stores, executive suites are on the top floor and the budget store is in the basement. In Japan, top executives have offices on the ground floor, and the top floor is reserved for bargain-priced merchandise.

## Language of agreement

The U.S.A. is a very legalistic society. Americans are both specific and explicit in terms of agreement, making legal contracts common and indispensable. Not surprisingly, lawyers become partners in virtually all business deals. When Japan wanted clarification concerning AT&T's products, the company reacted in a typically American fashion by sending a lawyer instead of a manager. Per capita, the U.S.A. has more lawyers than any other country in the world. American lawyers earn good money and are accorded social status not found elsewhere.

According to an old saying in Thailand, "It is better to eat a dog's feces than to engage in a lawsuit." Such thinking explains why the Chinese abhor litigation and why they prefer to withdraw from a deal rather than be involved in potential legal disputes. In many cultures, written contracts are not as binding as one's word. According to people in these societies, if a person cannot be trusted as a friend, then it is futile to expect that person to live up to obligations – written or otherwise.

Even when an agreement is reached, the agreement may not necessarily be ironclad because the agreement can be modified by changing circumstances. In South Korea, a businessperson considers a contract a loosely structured consensus statement that allows flexibility and adjustment. In some societies, agreements merely signify intention and have little relation to capacity to perform.

Culture dictates how a disagreement is expressed and resolved. North Americans generally prefer a straightforward approach. Elsewhere, one must be careful in a disagreement never to make someone else lose face. Asians, in particular, are sensitive to affronts and may become violent when "loss of face" results. Public humiliation or criticism must thus be avoided in Asia, where politeness is valued over blunt truth.

In Mexico, direct statements of criticism are considered rude, and thus Mexicans practice circumlocution, making it difficult to determine the true meaning. In Latin America, disagreements may be viewed as personal attacks against the individual. Subordinates are expected either to support their managers openly or to keep silent. Similarly, in Japan, silence is perceived as a positive concurrence, and open exchanges and debates are considered inappropriate. Only the top decision maker can comment freely. Japanese stockholders are not allowed to question management critically; companies may hire "guards" to dissuade those who ask too many questions from asking more questions.

U.S. firms prefer to base decisions on objective criteria, or at least they make that claim. The system makes allowances for those who strongly criticize decisions, but such a process would be unacceptable in countries where it is inappropriate to question an executive's personal judgment. Managers often find themselves in a dilemma, as one cannot consult with others on matters about which one is presumed to be the expert.

As might be expected, the different forms of disagreement may confuse American managers. When potential customers keep quiet, nod their heads, or state that they will think about it, American managers may think that a deal is developing. But foreign buyers may stay quiet even when the product in question is clearly unsuitable for their needs, because they do not want to offend the American by saying something critical.

## *Language of friendship*

Americans have the unique characteristic of being friendly, even at first meeting. Americans seem to have no difficulty in developing friendship in a very short time, and this trait is carried over into business relationships. American businesspersons are impatient to develop the deep personal ties that are crucial overseas. In many countries, friendship is not taken lightly – it involves real obligations such as providing financial and personal help when friends are down and out. It is thus not uncommon that an American businessperson is expected to help his foreign partner to find a school in the U.S.A. for the partner's son or daughter. Friendship is not developed as fast in these other countries, but when it is developed it tends to be deeper and longer lasting.

Quite often, it is necessary for potential business partners to become friends first before business is transacted. General Motors Corp. has learned that, in China, the Chinese dine together first before talking business, unlike the U.S. approach of talking business before having a meal together if things go well. Likewise, business is a personal matter in Turkey where friendship should be developed first before determining whether a business relationship is feasible. This is different from the practice in the U.S.A. where businesspeople want to do business first before thinking about becoming friends later.

The manner of addressing a friend can vary depending on the person being addressed, whether a colleague, a business acquaintance, or a customer. The quick friendship characteristic of the U.S.A. prompts Americans to use first names in social as well as business encounters soon after a first meeting.

This informal approach, claimed to be used to make foreigners feel comfortable, actually makes Americans themselves comfortable at the expense of foreigners.

The American practice of using first names can be very offensive in other countries, where formality and respect are strongly established traditions. Foreigners find it distasteful for American children to address their parents by their first names. The French as well as most Northern Europeans find the practice offensive. Germans are also formal, and addressing each other by first names is reserved for relatives and close friends. Germans answer the telephone by announcing their last name only. First names, often considered a secret, are revealed only to good friends. In China, it must be understood that the name mentioned first is actually the family name, and thus it would be a mistake to assume that Chinese social customs permit addressing someone by the first or given name.

Addressing someone by a first name is not common outside of the Western hemisphere, unless the first name is accompanied by the proper pronoun or adjective (e.g., Mr. or Mrs.). This formal first-name approach is customary in Asia, Latin America, and the Arab world, whereas the formal last-name approach should be used in Europe. It is thus very important for a businessperson to remember to address foreign counterparts with formal pronouns unless or until being asked to do something else.

## Language of negotiation

Negotiation styles vary greatly. One study found that negotiating styles differed between as well as within cultures.[27] Hispanic businesspeople are surprised by Anglos' resistance to bargaining. In the United States, a lack of eye contact is usually viewed as an indication that something is not quite right. But the cultural style of communication negotiation in Japan requires a great deal less eye contact between speakers. Furthermore, In Japan, periods of silence are common during interactions, and a response of silence should not come as a surprise. Americans should learn to be more comfortable with this negotiating tactic, instead of reacting by quickly offering either more concessions or new arguments.

Americans' straightforward style may prove a handicap in business negotiations. Chinese negotiations are generally tough-minded, well prepared, and under no significant time constraints. They are prepared to use various tactics to secure the best deal. While proclaiming ignorance of foreign technology and foreign business practices, these negotiators may actually be willing to play off one competitor against another. In China, foreigners should expect repetitious and time-consuming negotiations. Concessions from the Chinese may not come until Western negotiators, after many days of unproductive negotiations, are ready to give up and head to the airport. Only then will they be called back for further negotiations.

## Language of religion

In search of spiritual guidance, people turn to religion. The major religions are familiar to everyone. In some parts of the world, animism (the belief in the existence of such things as souls, spirits, demons, magic, and witchcraft) may be considered a form of religion. Regardless of the religion involved, it is safe to say, specific religious protocols are observed by the faithful (e.g., having evil spirits exorcised).

Religion affects people in many ways because it prescribes proper behavior, including work habits. The Protestant work ethic encourages Christians to glorify God by working hard and being thrifty. Thus, many Europeans and Americans believe that work is a moral virtue and disapprove of the idle.

Likewise, Islam exalts work, and idleness is seen as a sign of a person's lack of faith in the religion. As such, anyone who is able to work is not allowed to become voluntarily idle. Some religions, however, seem to guide people in the opposite direction. In Hinduism and Buddhism, the emphasis is on the elimination of desires because desires cause worrying. Not striving brings peace, and a person at peace does not suffer.

Religion influences social and consumer behavior (see Legal Dimension 6.1). As in the case of attitudes toward the advertising of controversial products and services, consumers in six countries and of four main religious groups exhibited different responses.[28] Another study showed that Austrian Christians were significantly less idealistic and relativistic than all other religions, including other Christians from the U.S.A. and Britain.[29]

Marketers must pay attention to religious activities. Buddhists observe the days associated with the birth and death of Buddha and, to a lesser extent, those days of full moon, half moon, and no moon. The entire month of Ramadan is a religious holiday for Muslims, who fast from dawn to dusk each day during that month. Therefore, workers must use part of normal sleeping time for eating. Work productivity can be greatly affected. Furthermore, Muslims pray five times a day, and they stop all work to do so.

There is no doubt that international marketing is affected by religious beliefs. Saudi Arabian publications will not accept any advertisement that has a picture of a woman in it. Sleeveless dresses are considered offensive to Islamic rules, and all advertisements that include pictures of such dresses are banned in Malaysia. In addition, religious requirements may prohibit consumption of certain items. Religious taboos include pork and alcohol for Muslims, beef for Hindus, and pork and shellfish for Jews, and once included meat on Friday for Roman Catholics.

### *Language of superstition*

In the modern world, it is easy to dismiss superstition as nonsense. Yet superstitious beliefs play a critical role in explaining personal as well as business behavior in all parts of the world. In Asia, fortune

#### Legal Dimension 6.1

**Playboy without nudity**

In 2006, Playboy entered Indonesia, the most populous Muslim country. Being mindful of the religious influence, Playboy publishes a local edition that is aimed to conform to local customs. The Indonesian edition contains no nudity, a feature that is expected of the U.S. edition as well as all other editions in dozens of countries. Yet the editor-in-chief of the Indonesian edition was charged with violation of anti-decency laws due to pictures of scantily dressed women. Some of these women were in underwear, and their breasts were partially exposed. The truth of the matter is that such photos can easily be found in many local magazines.

In 2007, an Indonesia district court ruled that the photos in question "could not be categorized as pornography." The editor-in-chief was acquitted.

*Source*: "Indonesia Playboy Editor Acquitted," *Bangkok Post*, April 5, 2007.

telling, palm reading, dream analysis and interpretation, phases of the moon, birthdate and handwriting analysis, communication with ghosts, and many other beliefs are part of everyday life. Physical appearance is often used to judge a person's character. Long ears, for example, supposedly belong to those who have good fortune.

Some Westerners may be amused to see foreigners take superstition so seriously. They may not place much credence in animal sacrifices or other ceremonial means used to get rid of evil spirits, but they should realize that their own beliefs and superstitions are just as silly when viewed by foreigners. Americans knock on wood, cross their fingers, and feel uneasy when a black cat crosses their path. They do not want to walk under ladders and may be extra careful on Friday the thirteenth.

It must be remembered that people everywhere are human beings with emotions and idiosyncrasies. They cannot be expected to always behave in a rational and objective manner. In a number of countries (e.g., Colombia), it is not uncommon for priests or monks to bless cars with holy water. While the practice may not have scientific value, it does give owners and drivers peace of mind. Instead of belittling or making fun of superstition, one is prudent to show respect for local customs and beliefs. A show of respect will go a long way in gaining friendship and cooperation from local people.

## Language of color

Flowers and colors have their own language and meaning. Preferences for particular colors are determined by culture. Because of custom and taboo, some colors are viewed negatively. A color deemed positive and acceptable in one culture may be inappropriate in another. According to FTD and Interflora Inc. which send flowers by wire to some 140 countries, the color red is used to cast spells in Mexico, and a white bouquet is necessary to lift the spell. In Spain, red roses are associated more with lust than with love. In France, a dozen as well as 13 yellow roses are inappropriate: yellow suggests infidelity, and cut flowers by the dozen or any other even number are unlucky. A bouquet of 13 blooms is also inappropriate in Latin America where yellow is associated with death rather than infidelity. In Italy, roses serve as tokens of affection when they are sent in odd numbers to women. In Japan, on the other hand, men are on the receiving end of Valentine's Day.

Other than flowers, colors by themselves have special meaning. Yellow is associated with disease in Africa. White is an appropriate color for a wedding gown in the United States, yet white is used alternately with black for mourning in India, Hong Kong, and Japan. Americans see red when they are angry, but red is a lucky color for the Chinese. It is customary for the Chinese to put money in red envelopes as gifts for employees and children on special occasions, especially on the Chinese New Year's Day.

Marketing managers should be careful in using certain colors with their products because using the wrong color can make or break a deal. A manufacturer of medical systems lost a large order for CAT (computerized axial tomography) scanners in one Middle Eastern country because of the whiteness of the equipment. Parker's white pens did not fare well in China, where white is the color of mourning. Its green pens suffered the same fate in India, where green is associated with bad luck.

## Language of gifts

Cultural attitudes concerning the presentation of gifts vary greatly across the globe. Because of varying perceptions of gifts and their appropriateness, good intentions can turn into surprises and even embarrassment when particular gifts violate cultural beliefs. Apparel is not commonly given in the

U.S.A., where it is considered too personal a gift, nor in Russia, where it is considered a bribe. In France, Russia, Germany, Taiwan, and Thailand, giving a knife as a gift is inappropriate because it may "cut" or "wound" a friendship. Although improper to be given, cutlery can be sold – for a small sum of money as token payment.

Handkerchiefs should never be given in Thailand, Italy, Venezuela, and Brazil because such a gift is akin to wishing a tragedy upon the recipient, implying that something distressing will happen in the near future which will necessitate the use of a handkerchief to wipe away the tears. Prudence requires one not to give potted plants to the sick in Japan because the illness may become more severe by taking deeper root. It is also wise to avoid giving four of anything or any item with four in the name to the Chinese and Japanese because the word sounds like *si* in these languages and means death.

Many Americans think of gift giving as a waste of time, yet they embrace Christmas gift buying and giving in spite of the excessive commercial overtones. In many parts of the world, a gift is a symbol of thoughtfulness or consideration, and one does not visit another person's home empty-handed. In Japan, the practice is extended to Japanese officials' overseas trips. This old tradition requires the prime minister to carry a gift (*miyage*) to a country being visited. The gift may take the form of trade policy concessions.

Gift giving is, to a certain extent, an art. Gifts are given in Europe only after a personal relationship has developed, but they are given in Japan when people first meet as well as when they part. In Japan, every act of generosity, no matter how small, must be paid back. In addition, form is more important than content. As a result, gift wrapping (*tsutsumi*) has been an art in Japan for over ten centuries. Special rules apply to wrapping particular items, and the occasion dictates materials and style. An American businessperson should keep in mind that often a gift is most conspicuous by its absence. Therefore, a cardinal rule in international gift giving is that, when in doubt, one should study closely the customs of a society.

It is useful to distinguish among the parties that receive gifts: good friends, just friends, hi/bye friends, and romantic other. These parties can be arranged on the gift continuum scale (from most to least intimate) of social friendships. There are three models of social exchange that explain gift giving. The first model is mainly economic, and it uses the utilitarian motives of equivalence and equality. The second model relies on the concept of generalized reciprocity and stresses the symbolic value of a gift in strengthening relationships. Such relationships do not seek equivalence and equality, and the relationships permit one-way flows of goods over an extended period of time. The third model is "pure gift." Financial or equivalence considerations are not important. Gift giving is motivated by one's deep desire to please the other person. A Hong Kong study confirms the existence of the gift continuum, which may be used to determine and guide gift exchanges.[30]

## Subculture

Because of differing cultures, worldwide consumer homogeneity does not exist. Neither does it exist in the United States. Differences in consumer groups are everywhere. There are white, black, Jewish, Catholic, farmer, truckdriver, young, old Eastern, and Western consumers, among other numerous groups. Communication problems between speakers of different languages are apparent to all, but people who presumably speak the same language may also encounter serious communication problems. Subgroups within societies utilize specialized vocabularies. Anyone listening to truckdrivers' conversations on CB radio could easily verify this point.

A subculture is a distinct and identifiable cultural group that has values in common with the overall society but also has certain characteristics that are unique to itself. Thus, subcultures are groups of people within a larger society. Although the various subcultures share some basic traits of the wider culture, they also preserve their own customs and lifestyles, making them significantly different from other groups within the larger culture of which they are a part. Indonesia, for instance, has more than 300 ethnic groups, with lifestyles and cultures that seem thousands of years apart.

There are many different ways to classify subcultures. Although race or ethnic origin is one obvious way, it is not the only one. Other demographic and social variables can be just as suitable for establishing subcultures within a nation.

The degree of intra-country homogeneity varies from one country to another. In the case of Japan, the society as a whole is remarkably homogeneous. Although some regional and racial diversities as well as differences among income classes are to be found, the differentials are not pronounced. There are several reasons why Japan is a relatively homogeneous country. It is a small country in terms of area, making its population geographically concentrated. National pride and management philosophy also help to forge a high degree of unity. As a result, people work together harmoniously to achieve the same common goals. The need to work hard together was initially fostered by the need to repair the economy following World War II, and the lessons learned from this experience have not been forgotten.

Canada, in contrast, is a large country in terms of geography. Its population, though much smaller than that of Japan, is much more geographically dispersed, and regional differences exist among the provinces, each having its own unique characteristics. Furthermore, ethnic differences are clearly visible to anyone who travels across Canada.

Canada's social environment makes it possible for ethnic groups to be active members of Canadian society while having the freedom to pursue their own native customs. The environment thus accommodates what is known as ethnic pluralism. Canadians not only tolerate but even encourage diversity in ethnic customs. Ethnically speaking, two prominent subcultures emerge: English-speaking and French-speaking. Studies have repeatedly shown that the French-speaking and English-speaking households differ from each other significantly in terms of demographics, subculture, and consumption habits. French Canadians' consumer behavior is a cross between that of North Americans and that of the continental French, being both similar to and different from those of these two groups.

In the U.S.A., the number of minority residents has surpassed 100 million, accounting for one-third of the total U.S. population. There are 40 million African Americans and 14.95 million Asian Americans. A significant demographic change is that, while most people over age 60 are non-Hispanic whites, most of those who are under age 40 are not.[31] Latinos are the largest minority group, and they are also the fastest growing minority group. The Hispanic population has reached 44.2 million, and the 13.1 million of them represent more than one-third of the population of California. Latinos of any race were the fastest growing minority group nationwide. While they account for 14.1 percent of the U.S. population and 8.9 percent of the country's purchasing power, they have captured only 2.4 percent of U.S. total advertising expenditures.[32]

Demographically, Hispanic households are larger than whites' households, with 30.6 percent of Hispanic households comprising five people or more. In addition, they have their own distinctive consumption habits. They are less likely to use credit, and soccer is an integral part of their lives. Latino holidays and cultural events are marketing opportunities. Other than holidays and holy days, religious passageways (christenings, communions, and anniversaries) are important events. Likewise,

*Quinceanera* (a girl's fifteenth birthday) requires make-up, high heels, nylons, gowns, cards, and so on. Interestingly, the Hispanic has grown to the point that Procter & Gamble even aired a Spanish-language commercial for its Crest Whitening Plus Scope toothpaste during the Grammy Awards. Titled "Goodbye Kiss," the commercial's tagline was in English – "white teeth and fresh breath . . . in any language."[33]

Given the fact that each subcultural group is a part of the larger culture while possessing its own unique cultural, demographic, and consumption characteristics, the issue of market heterogeneity must be recognized. Because individuals' values vary across subcultures, business outcomes may vary as well. As in the case of Brazil's four regional subcultures, subculture affects both motivational domains and business performance.[34] Another study investigated the decision-making patterns of blacks, Hispanics, and whites in the U.S.A. when purchasing social clothes (value-expressive product) and small electronics (utilitarian product). These groups differed in their informational influences (media and reference group) as well as their perceptions of store attribute importance, and the patterns also differed between the two product types. Advertisers should thus adjust their advertising messages according to the ethnic groups and product types.[35]

"Ethnic self-awareness" is a temporary state during which a person is more sensitive to information relating to one's ethnicity. It occurs when the person engages in a process of self-categorization and uses ethnic criteria as a basis for this categorization. This awareness can be aroused by individual difference variables, situational factors, and other contextual or stimulus primes in the environment (e.g., visual or verbal cues that draw attention to ethnicity). When aroused, this awareness can moderate consumer responses to an advertising message. A study of 109 Asian and Caucasian participants found that ethnic prime increased the participants' likelihood to spontaneously mention their ethnicity in self-descriptions. This then led to a more favorable response to the same ethnicity spokesperson and the advertisement that targeted their ethnicity. In other words, the use of ethnic actors alone is not meaningful unless consumers can be aroused first to evoke ethnic self-awareness.[36]

Subculture may provide an effective basis for market segmentation. American firms attempt to attract various subcultural groups in many different ways. Carnival Cruise Lines has an entire cruise ship (*Fiesta Marina*) just for the Hispanic market. McDonald's has created a Mac Report series of Spanish infomercials. J.C. Penney has outfitted 170 stores to carry merchandise for Hispanic and African American consumers. AT&T, MCI, and Sprint have advertised their long-distance phone services in a variety of Asian dialects.

One marketing question is which language should be used so as to effectively appeal to a particular subculture. While Sears Roebuck and Co. advertises in a generic form of Spanish, it also recognizes regional differences. It adopts a Mexican flavor in the southwest of the U.S.A. and a Caribbean theme in the east. Along the same lines, marketers need to appreciate linguistic variations. *Delincuente* means delinquent in Puerto Rico but may mean criminal in Mexico. *Cancelar*, depending on a person's origin, may mean either to cancel or to pay off an account. Beans are *frijoles* in Cuba but *habicheulas* in Puerto Rico.[37]

## Conclusion

Culture prescribes acceptable beliefs, traditions, customs, and values that are then socially shared. Culture is subjective, enduring yet dynamic, and cumulative. It affects people's behavior in diverse ways through logic, communication, and consumption. Although some cultural traits are universal, many others are unique and vary from country to country. In spite of national norms, cultural differences as a rule even exist within each country.

While there may be a tendency to misunderstand different cultures and subcultures, this temptation should be resisted. Being the force that it is, the culture of one country should not be judged as superior to the culture of another country. Each culture has its own particular (and sometimes peculiar) values and social practices, and the international marketer will be much further ahead if he or she tries to walk in the other person's shoes in order to understand more clearly that person's concerns and ideas.

Because marketing takes place within a given culture, a firm's marketing plan takes on meaning or is appropriate only when it is relevant to that culture. A U.S. company should understand that foreign consumers are not obligated to take on American values – nor may those consumers desire to do so. In addition, it is more important to know what a person thinks than what that person's language is. Because of the great differences in language and culture around the world, firms need to adjust their approach to solving marketing problems in different countries. In a foreign cultural environment, the marketing plan that has worked well at home may no longer be effective. As a result, the firm's marketing mix may have to undergo significant adaptation and adjustment. Effective marketing in this environment will thus mandate that the company be culturally responsive.

## CASE 6.1 CULTURAL CONSIDERATIONS IN INTERNATIONAL MARKETING: A CLASSROOM SIMULATION

### James B Stull, San José State University

This simulation is designed for a fifteen-week, two seventy-five minute periods per week consumer behavior course, with approximately forty students per section; adaptations for course length and size are encouraged. Before commencing with the simulation, naturally an explanation to the students is necessary to show how the simulation meets the objectives of the course.

- *Week 1* Assign students to research groups, one group for each cultural component (language, attitudes, religion, social organization, education, technology, politics and law); five students per group. Provide groups with bibliographies if available. Have the groups focus on the major considerations within each component.
- *Weeks 1–5* Pace student research groups through their research procedures, keeping them aware that they will be presenting their findings to the class during weeks six through nine. Provide sufficient in-class time for brainstorming, problem-solving and question-feedback sessions. These first five weeks may also be spent covering or highlighting portions of the textbook not highlighted by simulation.
- *Weeks 6–9* Groups present their findings; for current simulation, one cultural component is presented each class period for eight successive meetings. Students should be encouraged to participate and take notes because the information will be used during the third module of the simulation.
- *Weeks 10–15* During week 10, form new groups; assign one member from each *research* group to each new group so that each new group has eight members, one specialist from each previous group. Each new group will function as a business organization representing a separate, unique culture. Distribute handout similar to Table 6.3.

**TABLE 6.3** Cultural variables

| *Variables* | *Culture* | | | | |
|---|---|---|---|---|---|
| | *BWANA* | *FELIZ* | *LEUNG* | *KORAN* | *DHARMA* |
| Language | Swahili | Spanish | Cantonese | Arabic | Hindi |
| Religion (major) | Animistic | Catholicism | Buddhism | Muslim | Hindu |
| Education | Informal | Secondary (urban only) | Formal Tech/trade | *Koran* | Formal/ developing |
| Technology | Low/ developing | Moderate/ developing | Low– moderate/ developing | Low | Agricultural/ low/ developing |
| Politics | Republic | Republic/ unstable | Communist/ nationalist | Muslim | Socialist– British colony |
| Legal system | Indigenous | Civil | Common/ communist | Muslim | Common |
| Attitudes | (to find)[1] | | | | |
| Social organization | (to find)[2] | | | | |

*Notes*

1 Attitudes: find out general attitudes toward time, space, work, achievement, wealth and material gain, change, etc.

2 Social organization: find out general role relationships in terms of families, friendships, reference groups, social classes, unions, etc.

## Procedure

1 *Each culture should gain its own identity early.* Have each culture consult its specialists to develop a clear understanding of its own identity regarding each component. Focus on developing specific verbal and non-verbal language norms which will be observed during negotiations with other cultures. This may take a few class days.

2 Have cultures study other cultures to gain familiarity with each cultural component.

3 Instruct cultures that their overall goal is to market a product (or product line), service or idea to each other culture, and that their success depends upon how well they know their own culture and how it compares with other cultures.

4 Have cultures develop a product, service or idea which they feel is compatible with their own culture and which they feel they can market successfully to each other culture. This does not have to be an invention, merely an innovation for the new market.

5 Have cultures develop a marketing strategy for each other target culture, being sensitive to the idiosyncrasies of each.

6 Have cultures negotiate with each other, persisting until a contract has been settled or until a perceived stalemate has been reached.

7 Discuss the simulation, focusing on affective and cognitive realizations and cultural sensitivity developed.

Each step may take a few class periods, especially those involving cultural self-identity and assessment of other cultures. Depending upon the population of the course, various levels of marketing and advertising activity may be reached by participants.

## Discussion

During this simulation, students are exposed to conditions utilizing a variety of communication skills: brainstorming, encoding, decoding, role playing, decision making, problem solving, library research, cultural sensitivity and more.

Further research is currently underway to determine learning, cross-cultural sensitivity development, and student attitudes towards and perceptions of benefits of the simulation. Additional research is being conducted to apply this simulation to Latin American markets.

This simulation also strengthens interpersonal awareness on a *micro* level. If *macro* – cross-cultural – differences are stressed, it may be safe to assume that participants will recognize that any behavioral differences, even where major cultural differences do not apply, are due to the infinite variety of experiences of each member of any society.

Adaptations of this exercise are feasible to meet the needs of industrial and government training programs.

*Source*: James B. Stull, San José State University. Copyright 1980. Reprinted with permission.

## CASE 6.2 WHEN IN ROME DO AS THE ROMANS DO: USEFUL TIPS FOR THOSE WHO DO BUSINESS IN RUSSIA

### L. A. Prokopenko and E. A. Sergeeva, Tomsk State University, Russia

With the collapse of the USSR and communism in the early 1990s, large numbers of businesspeople from the U.S.A. as well as other countries are traveling to the new Russia. With the changeover from communism to the new Russian democracy, the country's population has been in a period of adjustment trying to learn the new system and way of life. Some traditions continue to exist as they always have but new ideas and ways are being implemented. The following information should help alert the traveling businessperson to some of the ways Russians view certain issues and live life.

Before going to Russia to work, expatriates should try to master the basics of the Russian language. In such a different country it is difficult to live and work with the locals and not be aware of what is going on around you. If there are serious intentions of setting up a business relationship in Russia, it would be wise to acclimatize oneself to the native culture, language, and way of life.

When in conversation with a Russian, there are certain practices and topics with which the foreign visitor should be familiar. Russians are a modest people. They do not care to listen to people who praise themselves and try to impress others in terms of their talents, achievements, and career accomplishments. They are more interested in hearing about information that an individual may share with them such as family or problems one may be having in terms of one's occupation, health, and financial circumstances. Russians are also not interested in hearing about how much money a person makes, and they are especially suspicious of anyone who appears to be making a great deal of money, as they may believe this money is being earned through illegal means. When receiving money Russians prefer cash and not checks or credit cards due to their economic system which is undergoing change, some of it unpredictable, which may make collecting money from checks or credit cards difficult. Certain subjects of conversation should be avoided in order not to cause the conversation to become socially embarrassing. To be avoided are questions about age, discussions about sex and intimate topics, the telling of rude and dirty jokes, and conversations about the weather.

Russians are also very interested in the human qualities within people they meet. They are interested in hearing about a person's hopes, aspirations, feelings, and affections. They are a very kind people and are very willing to offer help, sympathy, compassion, and empathy to someone who may be experiencing difficulties and problems. Russians are thoughtful and serious, and, once trust and sincerity are demonstrated, they will become loyal and firm friends. Once they receive and accept your trust and sincerity, they will enjoy their relationship with you. Often conversations are carried out at close physical distances (25–35 cm or 10–15 inches) and may involve careful observation of your facial expressions and touching your arm or hand as an indication of their trust and liking for you. Russians do not care for people who "put on airs" or who are constantly smiling, as they view these mannerisms as insincere and artificial. They may thus seem somber much of the time, but they do smile if the occasion truly warrants it. Russians also like giving and receiving presents and gifts. Occasions such as a visit to a Russian home, arrival or departure on a trip, or attendance at a party may involve the giving and/or receiving of a gift or present. Suitable gifts and presents would involve flowers for women, alcoholic beverages, chocolates and other sweets, books, and souvenirs symbolic of the traveler's home country.

When socializing or dining out with Russian friends, there are certain practices and activities of which the foreign businessperson should be aware. For example, when a waiter presents the bill, the customer should be very discreet if the customer wishes to review the bill. Openly adding up the bill or counting the change which the waiter returns would be viewed by Russian guests as petty and an affront to their dignity. If a Russian offers to share a drink, this invitation should not be refused. Refusal of such an invitation is interpreted as a mark of disrespect and likely seen as not being interested in developing a friendly relationship. Russians, in general, are quite experienced in consuming all sorts and combinations of alcohol. They are capable of consuming large amounts of alcohol and showing minimal effects. When having drinks with a Russian, a smaller glass (*rumka*) is a wise choice, and this will allow for keeping up with the Russian drink for drink and not become "fuzzy headed" too quickly. Russians like to drink frequent toasts that are offered with feeling and creative wording. When an especially important toast is offered, the person offering the toast may ask everyone to "drink to the bottom" of the glass. When this is done, this practice indicates solidarity and approval by everyone sharing in the toast. The foreign guest should make an effort to learn how to make a toast and, if the toast can be made in Russian, this will receive high approval and admiration from the Russian guests.

Certain topics of discussion carry a great deal of sensitivity and feeling with Russians and should be carefully discussed if the subject is brought up in conversation by a Russian. One subject of high sensitivity is the mention of war. Mention of World War II is especially sensitive because 40,000,000 Russians lost their lives in this war. Nearly every family experienced the loss of one or more family members or friends in this war. Because Russians are great patriots, they remember and honor the casualties of this war. Surviving veterans are also highly honored for their service and sacrifice to their country. Other wars are also remembered such as the conflicts in Afghanistan, Chechnya, and World War I. Most Russians are very knowledgable about these wars and have deep personal feelings about them. To become involved in a conversation about war can be a very emotional and delicate experience and give rise to strong expressions of opinion. The Russian patriot may have very diverse views about these wars if they are brought up in conversation. The wise recommendation on this subject is for the traveler not to bring up this topic in conversation. Doing so may result in the loss of a Russian friend or in feelings that may severely strain the relationship.

Another topic which holds serious feelings and thoughts for Russians would involve discussions about democracy and freedom. With the collapse of the USSR in the early 1990s, democracy came to Russia. Each Russian has had his or her experience of Russian "democracy" and "freedom," some of it good and some of it not so good. Strong feelings exist about these recently available political concepts. Some Russians continue to be hopeful and optimistic about democracy and freedom, whereas other Russians are having a difficult time accepting and adapting to this new "democracy" and "freedom." Having lived under communism for 75 years, the changes over recent years have been too slow, unfair, and confusing for many Russians. Russians are sensitive about the shortcomings that have occurred since democracy has arrived and do not like being informed about the democracy and freedoms that exist in the U.S.A. Like the war topic, the recommendation for the foreign businessperson would be not to initiate discussions about democracy and freedom. Here, as with the war topic, the situation of Russian democracy and freedom is a sensitive issue and could result in hurt feelings, strong emotions, anger, and damage to a relationship with a Russian friend or business contact.

As a final note, the traditional Russian possesses qualities that may be both favorable and curious to the foreign businessperson. When it comes to business qualities, Russian business negotiations require a great deal of patience and understanding. Often, after negotiation, Russian business expectations may appear to be very modest. However, these negotiations are usually characterized as being very open, kind, and sincere, with a spirit of strong fellowship, hospitality and emotion, creativity, and a devotion to negotiate in good faith toward the mutual completion of an agreement.

### *Points to consider*

Evaluate the social and business practices in Russia. Are those practices unique to Russia, or do they also apply to the neighboring countries that were once part of the Soviet Union? How are these practices similar to or different from those in other parts of the world?

## CASE 6.3 LANGUAGE OF COLOR

**Sergey Sergeevich Maksimov, Tomsk State University, Tomsk, Russia**

From an advertisement's point of view, the potential that color has in marketing is endless. In particular color is able to:

- provide a 38 percent increase in the chance that a commercial will be seen;
- increase the efficacy of an advertising appeal by 26 percent;
- increase the degree of informational perception by 40 percent;
- increase the value perception of a product by 22 percent.

The advertising industry has regularly researched the impact of color on consumers' perceptions. The research has generally found that the most successful colors in promotion are yellow, blue-violet, and ruby. Luxury items, the research has found, are best promoted using a combination of black and gold colors. On the other hand, common items are better promoted if red colors are used. Across the color spectrum, each color possesses its own psychophysical sphere of influence and this concept should be taken into account when designing an advertisement.

Research has shown that the following list of colors generates the following perceptions and impressions when presented to individuals.

***Red***. This color may create the impression of a scream that reaches out and touches and encourages a person to move energetically, but this feeling tends to dissipate very quickly. Emotional, amorous, and sexual people prefer red. Its use in promotion characterizes a product as something that should be purchased without hesitation. For this reason, the color red is widely used in cigarette advertisements.

***Orange***. This color suggests vigor, speeds up a person's heart rate, provides the individual with a positive mental outlook, and generates feelings of spiritual harmony and inner balance. Ancient people thought of orange as the color which gave health and creativity. It is useful for promoting products to children, as well as various medical and health care services.

***Yellow***. This is a light color which suggests a festive mood, and it helps to make a person easygoing. This color tends to generate an interest in the external world and brings about a sense of energetic activity. Yellow is highly suitable in advertisements for travel companies, advertising services, and informational technologies. Advisedly, this color is best used in combination with other colors.

***Green***. This color suggests nature, freshness, reality. The color green appeals to customers when promoting furniture such as lampshades, table lamps, and pool tables. Green has a healing and relaxing effect on individuals and is preferred by consumers who are calm and even-tempered. It is an appropriate color when promoting medicines, clinics, health care centers, and in information that preserves the environment.

***Pale blue***. This color can encourage lofty feelings. This color is associated with feelings of peace, general harmony, and spiritual relationships. Pale blue is said to relax, ease concerns, and give us comfort.

***Blue***. This is the color of self-absorption and helps in focusing our thoughts. It encourages us to sense the invisible connection between the universe and eternity. Blue color in promotion is considered to be effective because it helps a person to concentrate attention on the main point of an advertisement. It attracts attention and seldom has a negative effect on the customer.

***Violet***. This color is thought to unify body and soul, conciliate feelings, and help balance emotions. It is a thought-provoking color, assists us in achieving better spiritual insight, and stimulates brain functioning. When seeing this color, people tend to reduce their attention on secondary details. It is irreplaceable as a color when promoting and appealing to painters, designers, and musicians.

***Black***. Black personifies darkness and melancholy, and is capable of causing feelings of depression, loneliness, and isolation. Basically, black is not highly recommended for use in advertisements, but it does hold a fascination for some individuals.

***White***. White is associated with emptiness. It is also related to impressions of coldness, and the white light connected with the Beginning and the End. It embodies feelings of openness, purity, and loftiness without any disagreeable emotions. The use of white in advertising is minimal. The color, if used, will rise to its own power and causes a neutrality in information provided within commercials.

The color spectrum of an advertisement will be perceived differently in different countries. For instance, the color red and its various shades are favored by Russian women. This color symbolizes different impressions: for example, in the U.S.A. – love; in China – kindness, luck, celebration; in Russia – aggression, struggle; and in India – life.

Research shows that the following color combinations are considered in general to be the most successful:

- Black and yellow
- Yellow and black
- Green and white
- Red and white
- Black and white
- White and blue
- Blue and yellow
- Blue and white
- White and black
- Green and yellow.

In circumstances where the appropriate color spectrum is being used, the effectiveness of a message can be increased. When the right spectrum of color has been selected, and if it is used consistently, this color may become identified with a particular company as its unique mark and can contribute substantially to the success of its promotional efforts.

The most dynamic effect in color psychology is aggression and this effect is usually generated unintentionally. Red tints are highly aggressive, but a combination of red and black ("dismal aggression") can draw much more attention to an advertisement. Red with orange combinations can create a very strong effect among consumers. Remarkably, though, red in combination with white, pale blue, and green diminishes the impression of aggression.

Knowing the fundamentals of the psychological impact of colors allows marketers to create not just an image to please the eye, but also an effective and powerful advertisement, able to sell and therefore provide a company with an effective competitive advantage.

### *Points to consider*

Do certain colors have universal connotations, or are their meanings unique to a particular country or region? Pick a few primary colors and show them to people from your country and gauge their reactions. In particular, identify the colors that have negative meanings in the culture in question.

*Sources*: I. Andreeva, "Color Psychology in Advertising (the Art of Emotion Manipulation)," *Promotional Technologies* (No. 6, 2004): 26–28; E. Pesotskij, *Contemporary Advertisement: Theory and Practice* (Rostov-on-Don: Phoenix, 2001), 229; and O. Rasskazova, "Aggression in Advertising," *Promotional Technologies* (No. 9, 2002): 17.

## Questions

1 What are the characteristics of culture?
2 Explain the impact of culture on consumption.
3 What is the SRC (self-reference criterion)?
4 Distinguish between high-context and low-context cultures.
5 Distinguish between monochronic and polychronic cultures.
6 Explain how the meanings of time, space, agreement/disagreement, and friendship can vary from one culture to another. Discuss their business implications.

## Discussion assignments and minicases

1 Which of the following seems to better characterize the world: cultural commonality or cultural diversity?
2 Because English is the world language of business, is it necessary for U.S. managers to learn a foreign language?
3 Do you agree that the U.S.A. is a "melting-pot"?
4 As Hispanic consumers in the U.S.A. are also American consumers, is it necessary for marketers to adjust their marketing mix for this market segment?
5 Explain how culture affects the ways people use eating utensils (e.g., fork, spoon, knife, chopsticks).
6 Explain why people in several countries are upset when they see: (a) an advertisement showing an American crossing his legs at the reader or putting his legs on a table; and (b) Americans wearing shoes in their homes.
7 According to Edward T. Hall, a renowned anthropologist, Americans are more comfortable with Germans than with the Japanese because Germans generally make eye contact to indicate attention to a speaker. However, the Americans feel that the Germans do not smile often enough. How do the Germans and Japanese regard the Americans' frequent smiles and eye contact?
8 According to William Wells of the DDB Needham Worldwide advertising agency, American TV commercials are usually shown either as an illustrated lecture or as a drama in which a product

is a prop (or a mixture of both techniques). Why is the lecture approach (a low-context technique) inappropriate for high-context cultures? Why is the drama approach (a high-context technique) appropriate for Japan? Note that Japanese commercials go to great lengths to present cues that are not product-related before devoting only a few seconds to the product itself at the end. To American advertisers, this advertising approach is ambiguous and puzzling.

9 What are the stereotypes of the following groups: Arabs, Asians, Africans, and Latin Americans? Why is it undesirable to use stereotyping as a basis to understand foreigners? Identify the positive traits and values of the groups mentioned above.

10 What are some of the unique characteristics of the U.S. culture? What are some of the unique business characteristics of the Japanese culture?

## Notes

1 Donnel A. Briley, Michael W. Morris, and Itamar Simonson, "Reasons as Carriers of Culture: Dynamic versus Dispositional Models of Cultural Influence on Decision Making," *Journal of Consumer Research* 27 (September 2000): 157–78.

2 Ray Friedman, Shu-Cheng Chi, and Leigh Anne Liu, "An Expectancy Model of Chinese–American Differences in Conflict-avoiding," *Journal of International Business Studies* 37 (January 2006): 76–91.

3 "India Honors Bride Who Fought Dowry," *San José Mercury News*, May 17, 2003.

4 C. Samuel Craig and Susan P. Douglas, "Beyond National Culture: Implications of Cultural Dynamics for Consumer Research," *International Marketing Review* 23 (No. 3, 2006): 322–42.

5 "Malts Hot in Mideast," *San José Mercury News*, February 13, 2003.

6 Andreas Herrmann and Mark Heitmann, "Providing More or Providing Less? Accounting for Cultural Differences in Consumers' Preference for Variety," *International Marketing Review* 23 (No. 1, 2006): 7–24.

7 James A. Lee, "Cultural Analysis in Overseas Operations," *Harvard Business Review* 44 (March–April 1966): 106, 111.

8 Brett A. S. Martin, Christina Kwai-Choi Lee, and Feng Yang, "The Influence of Ad Model Ethnicity and Self-referencing on Attitudes: Evidence from New Zealand," *Journal of Advertising* 33 (winter 2004): 27–37.

9 Edward T. Hall, *Beyond Culture* (Garden City, NY: Anchor Press/Doubleday, 1976).

10 Richard Nisbett, *The Geography of Thought: How Asians and Westerners Think Differently . . . and Why* (New York: The Free Press, 2003).

11 Hall, *Beyond Culture*.

12 George P. Murdock, "The Common Denominator of Cultures," in *The Science of Man in the World Crisis*, ed. Ralph Linden (New York: Columbia University Press, 1945), 123–42.

13 "Plastic Surgery for Minorities," *San José Mercury News*, August 24, 2002.

14 "Vietnamese Women Make an Anti-sun Fashion Statement," *San José Mercury News*, November 18, 2002.

15 "Fat Is Ideal Body Shape in West Africa," *San José Mercury News*, February 17, 2001.

16 Nan Zhou and Russell W. Belk, "Chinese Consumer Readings of Global and Local Advertising Appeals," *Journal of Advertising* 33 (fall 2004): 63–76.

17 "Lost Languages," *San José Mercury News*, August 26, 2001.

18 "Lost Languages."

19 "Gene That Generates Language Found, English Scientists Say," *San José Mercury News*, October 4, 2001.

20 *The Tower of Business Babel: A Guide for the Correct Use of the English Language in International Trade* (Janesville, WI: Parker Pen Co., 1983).

21 Justin Fox, "The Triumph of English," *FORTUNE*, September 18, 2000, 209ff.

22 David R. Berlo, *The Process of Communication* (New York: Holt, Rinehart, & Winston, 1960), 164.

23 Nader T. Tavassoli and Jin K. Han, "Scripted Thought: Processing Korean Hancha and Hangul in a Multimedia Context," *Journal of Consumer Research* 28 (December 2001): 482–93.

24 David Luna and Laura A. Peracchio, "Moderators of Language Effects in Advertising to Bilinguals: A Psycholinguistic Approach," *Journal of Consumer Research* 28 (September 2001): 284–95.

25 Shi Zhang and Bernd H. Schmitt, "Activating Sound and Meaning: The Role of Language Proficiency in Bilingual Consumer Environments," *Journal of Consumer Research* 31 (June 2004): 220–8.

26 Edward T. Hall, "The Silent Language in Overseas Business," *Harvard Business Review* 38 (May–June 1960): 87–96; and H. K. Arning, "Business Customs from Malaya to Murmansk," *Management Review* 53 (October 1964): 5–14.

27 Lynn E. Metcalf *et al.*, "Cultural Tendencies in Negotiation: A Comparison of Finland, India, Mexico, Turkey, and the United States," *Journal of World Business* 41 (December 2006): 382–94.

28 Kim Shyan Fam, David S. Waller, and B. Zafer Erdogan, "The Influence of Religion on Attitudes Towards the Advertising of Controversial Products," *European Journal of Marketing* 38 (Nos 5/6, 2004): 537–55.

29 Bettina Cornwell *et al.*, "A Cross-cultural Study of the Role of Religion in Consumers' Ethical Positions," *International Marketing Review* 22 (No. 5, 2005): 531–46.

30 Annamma Joy, "Gift Giving in Hong Kong and the Continuum of Social Ties," *Journal of Consumer Research* 28 (September 2001): 239–56.

31 "Minority Population Grows to 100 Million – 1 of 3 in U.S.," SFGate.com, May 17, 2007.

32 "Sampling Smarts," *PROMO* (September 2006): 10, 64.

33 "Crest's Prime-time Ad Targets Hispanics," *San José Mercury News*, February 22, 2003.

34 Tomasz Lenartowicz and Kendall Roth, "Does Subculture within a Country Matter? A Cross-cultural Study of Motivational Domains and Business Performance in Brazil," *Journal of International Business Studies* 32 (second quarter 2001): 305–25.

35 Youn-Kyung Kim and Jikyeong Kang, "The Effects of Ethnicity and Product on Purchase Decision Making," *Journal of Advertising Research* 41 (March–April 2001): 39–48.

36 Mark R. Forehand and Rohit Deshpande, "What We See Makes Us Who We Are: Priming Ethnic Self-awareness and Advertising Response," *Journal of Marketing Research* 38 (August 2001): 336–48.

37 "In Pursuit of El Dorado," *Credit Card Management* (October 2000): 61–8.

Chapter 7

# Consumer behavior in the international context

## Psychological and social dimensions

Oh what power . . . to see ourselves as others see us!
Robert Burns

## Chapter outline

- Marketing strategy: the samurai and luxury cars
- Perspectives on consumer behavior
- Motivation
- Learning
- Personality
  - National character
  - Hofstede's national cultures
  - Clustering: commonality and diversity
- Psychographics
- Perception
  - Formation of perception
  - Country of origin and perceived product quality
- Attitude
- Social class
- Group
- Family
- Opinion leadership
- Diffusion process of innovation
- Conclusion
- Case 7.1 Tropical drink for the U.S. Market

## Marketing strategy

### The samurai and luxury cars

Introduced into the U.S.A. in 1989, Toyota's Lexus brand is the bestselling luxury brand there. However, Toyota did not launch the Lexus brand in Japan until 2005. Lexus has more than 160 showrooms that feature marble floors and lounges with leather couches. Its European competitors, having small showrooms in Tokyo, have to make house visits to sell their cars.

It has not been plain sailing. Although Toyota commands almost 45 percent of Japan's passenger-car market, it has not done as well in the luxury segment. The segment's market leaders are BMW and Mercedes Benz. Together these two European brands sell nearly four times as many cars as Lexus does. Lexus certainly does not have the same kind of brand recognition.

Toyota wants to rely on Japan's unique customs and ancient hospitality traditions to set the Lexus brand apart from its competitors. In 2003, Toyota approached a number of etiquette schools to teach the art of beautifying daily behavior and to adapt the techniques for selling cars. Although most schools turned down Toyota's request, the Ogasawara Rye Reihou institute accepted the request. The institute's teachings have been passed down since the 1300s, and its clients are well-bred families. All employees are required to attend a three-day training course.

Based on the training, Lexus sales consultants point with all five fingers to the car handle, and the left hand follows the right hand. The door is opened with both hands, just like how Japanese samurai in the fourteenth century opened a sliding screen door. While a customer is looking at a car, sales consultants lean five to ten degrees forward, just like a warrior assuming a "waiting position." When serving coffee or tea to customers, employees must have both knees on the ground, and the teacup must not make a noise when placed on the table. A sales consultant is taught to stand about two arms' lengths from a customer who is looking at a car. He will move in closer to close a deal. He should bow more deeply to a customer who has purchased a car than to a casual window shopper. While standing idly, employees need to place their left hand over their right hand, with fingers together and thumbs interlocked. This is the posture used by samurai to indicate that they were not about to draw their swords. Because the Japanese are not so good at smiling, employees are told to practice the "Lexus face," a peaceful, closed-mouth smile to put customers at ease.

One customer complained about being given a bouquet as well as a formal ceremony to hand over a car key when he went to pick up his new Lexus hybrid. Apparently, it can be too much of a good thing. Lexus acknowledges that it needs to recognize when customers want to be left alone.

*Source*: "The Samurai Sell: Lexus Dealers Bow to Move Swank Cars," *Wall Street Journal*, July 9, 2007.

## Purpose of chapter

Domestically, marketing scholars have employed a variety of techniques and concepts, including the cultural approach, to study consumer behavior. Yet consumer study on an international basis has almost exclusively employed the cultural approach without much regard for other psychological and social concepts. This is a very curious approach since it is the norm for virtually all consumer behavior textbooks to treat culture as only one of the many theoretical concepts which can affect purchase and the other behavioral dimensions.

It is a questionable practice to rely on culture as the sole determinant of behavior or as the only concept that largely, if not entirely, explains behavior. One study found that life stage is as important as, if not more so than culture in explaining the ethical perceptions of upward influence behavior.[1] Likewise, although managerial values have an impact on managerial practices when comparing two generations, young managers in India emphasize different managerial values and practices.[2]

The complex nature of consumers makes the study and understanding of consumer behavior imperative. Culture undoubtedly affects the psychological and social processes and thus affects consumer behavior. However, too much emphasis has been placed on a single concept (i.e., culture). Differences in behavioral dimensions among national groups should not be automatically or largely attributed to differences in culture. For group differences to be meaningful, there should be some explanation as to why these differences should exist. Psychological and social factors need to be taken into account.

Because the influence of culture has already been discussed in depth in Chapter 6, this chapter covers other relevant concepts. The focus is on the major approaches used to study consumer behavior. The basic purpose of the chapter is to acknowledge the role determinants other than culture play in influencing consumer behavior. The chapter thus examines the psychological and social dimensions, and these include motivation, learning, personality, psychographics, perception, attitude, social class, group, family, opinion leadership, and the diffusion process of innovations.

## Perspectives on consumer behavior

Consumer behavior may be defined as a study of human behavior within the consumer role and includes all the steps in the decision-making process. The study must go beyond the explicit act of purchase to include an examination of less observable processes, as well as a discussion of why, where, and how a particular purchase occurs.

The major behavioral sciences relevant to consumer study are psychology, sociology, and cultural anthropology. **Psychology**, with the *individual* as its central unit of analysis, is the study of individual and interpersonal behavior. Behavior is governed by a person's cognitions, such as values, attitudes, experiences, needs, and other psychological phenomena. Purchase, then, becomes a function of the psychological view of products, and the consumer buys a product not only for consumption but also because of a perception of how a product may be used to communicate with other people. Some psychological concepts relevant to the study of consumer behavior are motivation, learning, personality, perception, and attitude.

**Sociology** is a study of groups and human interactions. The unit of analysis is not the individual but rather the *group*. The group, consisting of a set of individuals who interact over time, is important because it can exert a significant influence on a person's preferences and consumption behavior. In many instances, it may be useful for a marketer to think of consumers as a group. For example, a family, not an individual, often makes a purchase decision that affects all members of the family group. Important sociological concepts are reference group and family.

**Cultural anthropology** is the study of human culture. Thus, the analytic perspective may be quite large. Culture involves an aggregate, social category level (i.e., a large group), and the social categories are significant in the sense that they influence consumers' cognitive and personality development. The concepts from this discipline usually included in the analysis of consumer behavior are culture, subculture, and social class.

## Motivation

Motivation is fundamental in initiating consumer behavior. Motivation may be thought of as a drive that is directed by a motive formed in relation to a particular goal. Once the motive–drive relationship is developed, the consumer initiates some forms of motivated behavior to satisfy a previously recognized need.

Consumer motives are largely determined by buying habits, though motives may vary, and it is important to recognize the various types of motives. Motives may be classified as rational and nonrational. Examples of **rational motives** are price, durability, and economy in operation. **Nonrational appeals**, in comparison, include prestige, comfort, and pleasure.

According to Adidas, Indian consumers are rational when making purchase decisions. While the brand name is important, they need a rational argument about the functionality and utility of the brand before making a purchase decision.[3]

The problem with the conventional classification (i.e., rational vs. emotional) is that a consumer may not recognize emotional motives and may have the tendency to rationalize personal behavior by assigning only rational and socially acceptable motives. In addition, the process of classification is not always straightforward. Convenience, for instance, can be both rational and nonrational at the same time.

In the end, the success of a product is greatly affected by whether its target customers are properly motivated. Whether a buying motive is rational or irrational is not particularly important. What is important is to identify specific motives relevant for marketing purposes. A crucial task is to select, carefully and properly, a relevant motive for the purpose of product promotion. Since its customers expect performance and excitement, Porsche advertises its Cayman as "a body built for sin" that allows "self-expression" and "performance art" (see Figures 7.1 and 7.2).

In addition, the relevance of a particular motive may vary across countries. For example, one study of youths in Hong Kong, Singapore, Canada, and Hawaii compared their beliefs in money, business ethics, *quanxi*, and Machiavellian personality. Surprisingly, Canadians believe that money can work wonders – even more so than their Hong Kong and Singapore counterparts.[4]

## Learning

Like all habits, food and drink habits are learned. Before World War II, the British were accustomed to drinking tea, not coffee. Then came the American troops, who brought the American taste for coffee – at first a relatively light, almost blond coffee. Before long, Britons had learned to drink coffee too. In another example, a large lunch with wine presents no problem to a Swiss, but the same will put an American to sleep. On the other hand, American-style cocktails may prove to be too much for Europeans, who are accustomed to milder drinks. Marketers must take these habits into consideration.

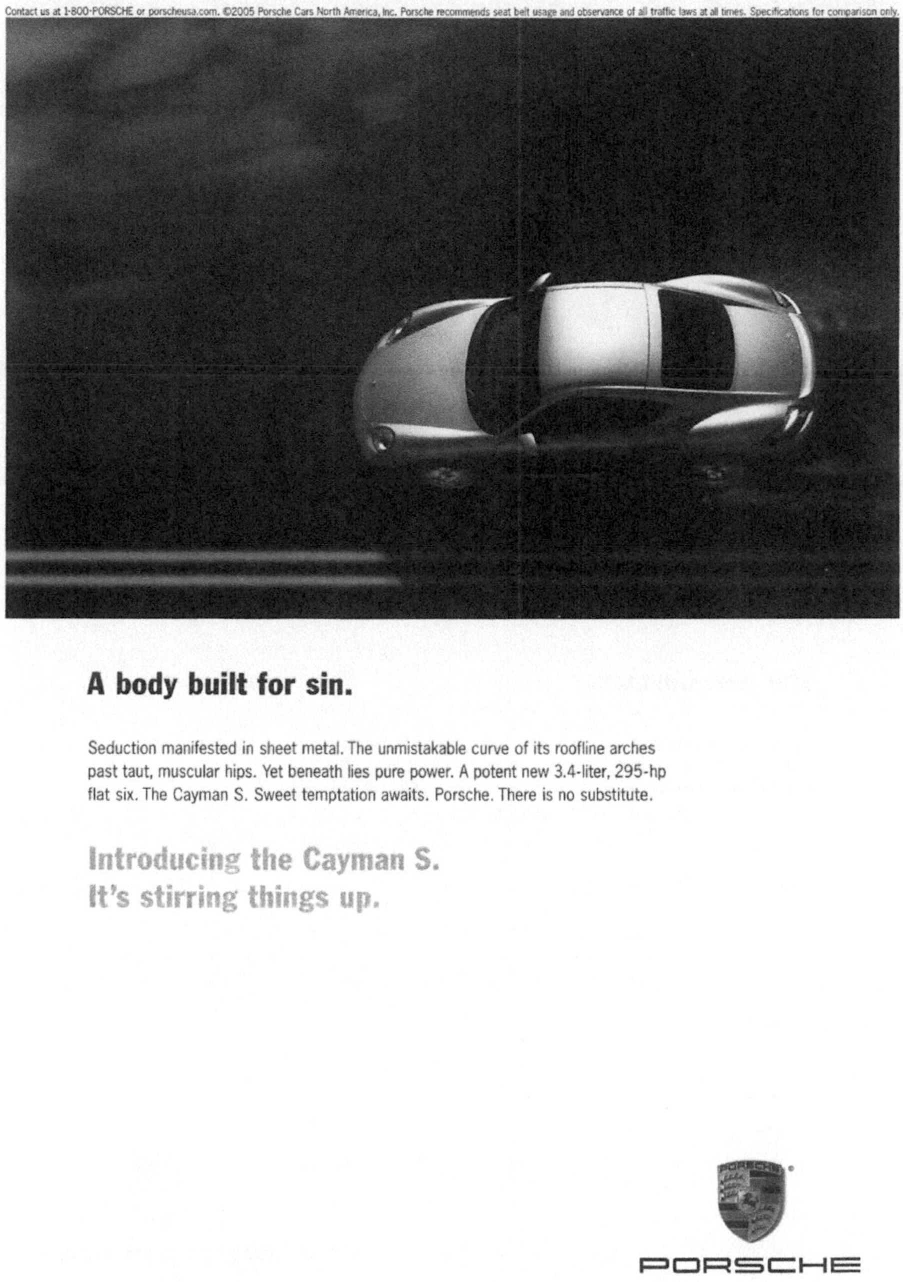
Contact us at 1-800-PORSCHE or porscheusa.com. ©2005 Porsche Cars North America, Inc. Porsche recommends seat belt usage and observance of all traffic laws at all times. Specifications for comparison only.
A body built for sin.
Seduction manifested in sheet metal. The unmistakable curve of its roofline arches past taut, muscular hips. Yet beneath lies pure power. A potent new 3.4-liter, 295-hp flat six. The Cayman S. Sweet temptation awaits. Porsche. There is no substitute.
Introducing the Cayman S.
It's stirring things up.
PORSCHE
PORSCHE

**FIGURE 7.1** Porsche: seductive and muscular

Porsche, Cayenne, and the Porsche Crest are registered trademarks, and Cayman and the distinctive shapes of the Porsche automobiles are trademarks of Dr. Ing.h.c.F. Porsche AG. Used with permission of Dr. Ing.h.c.F. Porsche AG and Porsche Cars North America, Inc. © Porsche Cars North America, Inc. Photographer: Eric Chimil.

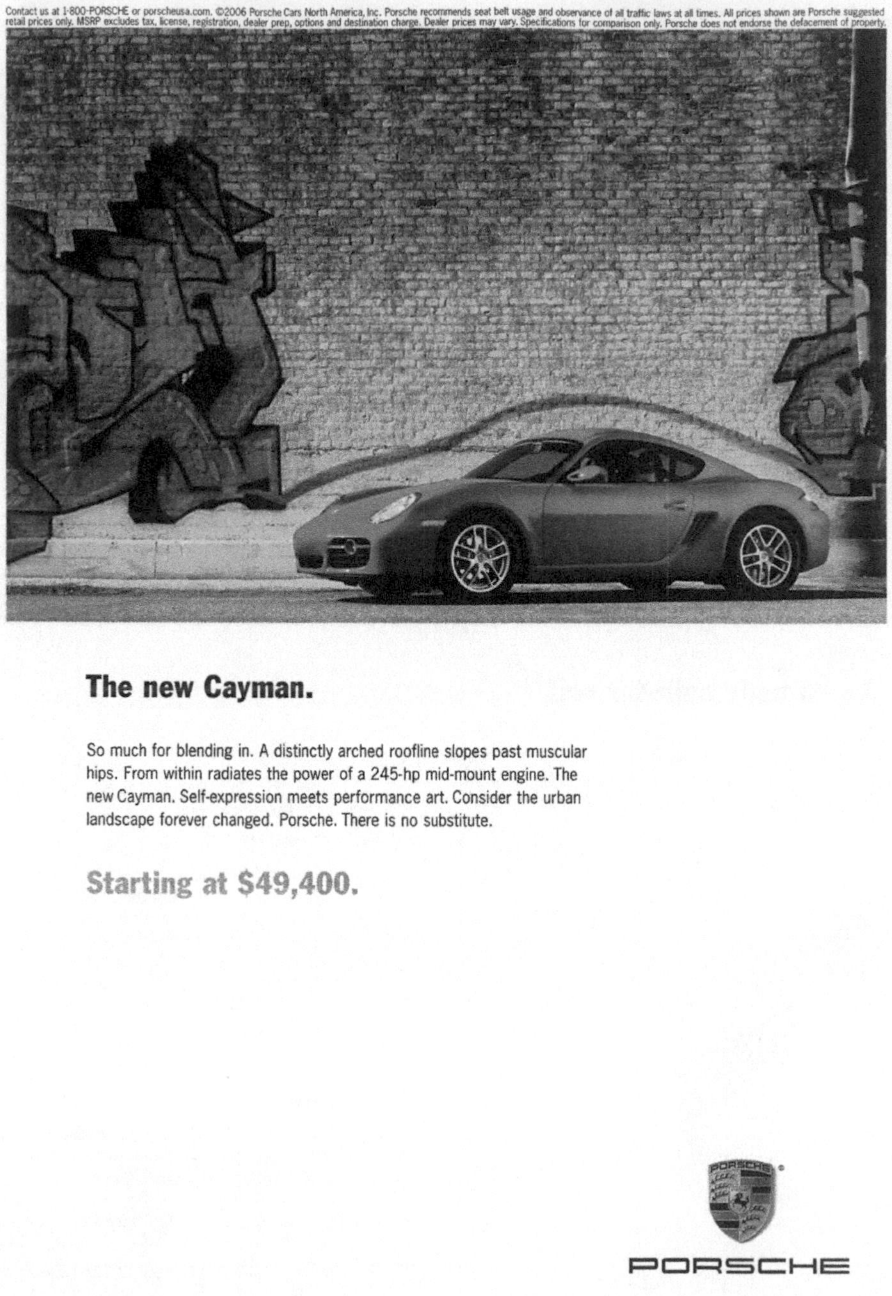
Contact us at 1-800-PORSCHE or porscheusa.com. ©2006 Porsche Cars North America, Inc. Porsche recommends seat belt usage and observance of all traffic laws at all times. All prices shown are Porsche suggested retail prices only. MSRP excludes tax, license, registration, dealer prep, options and destination charge. Dealer prices may vary. Specifications for comparison only. Porsche does not endorse the defacement of property.
The new Cayman.
So much for blending in. A distinctly arched roofline slopes past muscular hips. From within radiates the power of a 245-hp mid-mount engine. The new Cayman. Self-expression meets performance art. Consider the urban landscape forever changed. Porsche. There is no substitute.
Starting at $49,400.
PORSCHE
PORSCHE

**FIGURE 7.2** Porsche: unique and distinctive

Porsche, Cayenne, and the Porsche Crest are registered trademarks, and Cayman and the distinctive shapes of the Porsche automobiles are trademarks of Dr. Ing.h.c.F. Porsche AG. Used with permission of Dr. Ing.h.c.F. Porsche AG and Porsche Cars North America, Inc. © Porsche Cars North America, Inc. Photographer: Simon Stock.

Cultural Dimension 7.1

**Universal stress and localized remedies**

Western-style stress may be universal. Managers in China are paying more attention to performance and money rather than to family and friends. They are exhibiting the classic symptoms: eating disorders, depression, and substance abuse. In the Western world, an employee will probably seek psychological therapy. In face-saving China, this kind of treatment is unthinkable.

U.S. employee-assistance companies are offering their services to local clients. Chestnut Global Partners has signed up Minsheng Bank. It did not take long for Chestnut to learn that the techniques that worked well in the U.S.A. did not necessarily work in China. Because of the stigma attached to behavioral counseling, the company instead provides a "personal well-being service." It is "workplace harmony" instead of "conflict management." Because Chinese employees hate a one-to-one meeting and because the society emphasizes group relationships, Chestnut uses online and group sessions. Interestingly, compared to Americans, twice as many Chinese employees take advantage of Chestnut's services.

*Source*: "Go-go-going to Pieces in China," *Business Week*, April 23, 2007, 88.

Before the 1990s, instant coffee was visibly absent in Russia where people preferred tea. Things have certainly changed. On average, each Russian drinks 250 cups of instant coffee per year, exceeding consumption anywhere else in the world. Not surprisingly, Nestlé recently spent $120 million on an instant coffee factory in Russia.[5]

Motives, cultural norms, and consumption habits are all learned. Therefore, a marketer should understand the learning process. Learning is a change in behavior that occurs over time relative to a given set of external stimulus conditions. Baskin-Robbins, as the first fast food franchise in Vietnam, has to teach the Vietnamese about the concept of fast food. When the ice-cream parlor first opened, most Vietnamese customers walked in and sat down, expecting to be waited on. When they were asked to go to the counter, some felt insulted and left. In addition, the Vietnamese are accustomed to linger at café tables and are thus not used to having to pay immediately. Naturally, a number of them became angry and felt that Baskin-Robbins did not trust them by asking them to pay for the ice-cream immediately. Interestingly, one learned behavior is that the rum and raisin flavor, not that popular in the plain vanilla U.S. market, is quite popular among the Vietnamese as well as among many other Asians.

A marketer can play a significant role in facilitating the learning process by using a variety of rewards to encourage learning (see Ethical Dimension 7.1). Infant formula, as an example, is useful in many non-Western countries for well-to-do women who do not want to bother with breast-feeding. Poor women seek the reward of using this status symbol and of having fatter babies – a benefit implied by this product. Furthermore, young mothers like the prestige of using American or European products.

### Ethical Dimension 7.1

**Drink and be merry**

When it comes to alcohol, Indians strongly prefer distilled spirits. Drinkers propel India to the top rank in terms of whisky consumption. Beer is a completely different story. Annual per capita consumption of beer in India is 0.6 liters, while the figures for China, Europe, and the U.S.A. are 23, 73, and 78 liters respectively. As one drinker comments, it makes no sense to waste money on beer when whisky does the job much faster and more cheaply.

However, beer makers are tempted by India's population size, a hot climate, a hot economy, rising incomes, and an enormous youth population (with about 60 percent of the population being under 30 years old). International brewers aim to cultivate a beer culture. Anheuser-Busch Cos. has a 50:50 joint venture with Crown Beers, a local company. SABMiller spent $600 million in six years to acquire 11 local breweries, and its five brands have grabbed 37 percent of the market.

Marketing beer is no easy task, thanks to bureaucratic restrictions. First, steep tariffs add to the price. State excise taxes may reach 150 percent, pushing the price of a pint of domestic brew above $3 or three times the price of a shot of local whisky. Beer advertising is banned. The ban encourages brewers to be creative. SABMiller markets a mineral water called Royal Challenge. The name of the water is not an accident since it happens to also be the name of one of the lagers of the company. TV commercials for the water resemble traditional beer commercials and even show the same label.

*Source*: "The Great Indian Beer Rush," *Business Week*, April 23, 2007, 50.

## Personality

Personality study has long been a subject of interest to marketers due to the assumption that product purchases are an extension of a consumer's personality. Saab advertisements used to make a reference to a person's personality as a factor in choosing a car. Personality, derived from a Latin word meaning "personal" or "relating to a person," is the individual characteristics that make a person unique as well as consistent in adjustments to a changing environment. Personality is an integrated system that holds attitude, motivation, and perception together. To study a personality is to study the person as a whole – not just the separate, individual elements that make up a person.

### *National character*

Personality traits are relatively stable qualities, but they do vary in degree from person to person. Because personality study applies to a person rather than to a group, it is difficult to make generalizations about personality traits among people of a particular country. Nevertheless, it is useful to consider the concept of national character, which states that people of each nation are distinctive with regard to their pattern of behavioral or personality characteristics. The English, for example, are highly impulse-restrained and unassertive.

Despite the difficulty, particular personality traits seem dominant in certain countries. Koreans see themselves as being driven by two complementary passions that are uniquely theirs: *han* (bitterness) and *jong* (devoted love). The interplay of the two explains Korea's ability to be at once intensely productive and violent, to both drive and stall a society, and to be capable simultaneously of love and hate.[6]

While both South Korea and Japan display a mixture of ancient and modern Asian cultures, they also differ in a number of ways. In spite of South Korea's Confucian culture and the bowing, deference, traditions, and formality, the Koreans are also passionate, emotional, intense, energetic, emotional, fun-loving, and impatient. As a matter of fact, one of the phrases that is most often heard in South Korea is "*balli, balli*" (hurry, hurry). Compared to Tokyo, Seoul is more chaotic.[7]

One personality trait that has gained significant attention is consumer ethnocentrism.[8] Adapted from the general concept of ethnocentrism, consumer ethnocentrism explains that, due to patriotic and nationalistic sentiments as well as a personal level of prejudice against imports, some consumers feel that it is inappropriate or even immoral to buy imported products. Highly ethnocentric consumers thus tend to buy domestic products. Ethnocentricity appears to have a negative effect on attitudes toward an advertisement for Kazakhstan (a newly transitioning economy) but not Slovenia.[9]

The national markets also possess some other personality characteristics which may affect marketing strategies. Scotland set up Project Galore to develop a strategy to leverage the commercial power of Scottishness. Based on the reactions received in Scotland and the other parts of the world, tenacity is a true Scottish characteristic. Integrity is another core value as Scotland and the world believe that Scotland has this attribute to a greater extent than most, if not all, other countries. Spirit is another virtue that defines Scotland. However, although the Scots (as well as the English) believe that they have inventiveness, the rest of the world does not seem to subscribe to the same notion, as they do not have enough knowledge of Scotland's inventiveness.[10]

While the European Union is unifying markets, it will take time to construct a unified set of European marketing theories. There is still a wide divergence in terms of economic development levels, languages, religions, and legal systems. Generalizations are both difficult and dangerous. Marketers must still consider a country's history, national character, and cognitive styles.[11]

## Hofstede's national cultures

Hofstede has strongly indicated that ethnocentric management theories (i.e., based on a particular country's value system) are untenable. Based on his study of work-related values in fifty countries, national cultures have four largely independent dimensions: (1) individualism vs. collectivism, (2) large or small power distance, (3) strong or weak uncertainty avoidance, and (4) masculinity vs. femininity. **Power distance** describes how a society treats unequal people. "**Collectivist** countries always shows large power distances, but **individualist** countries do not always show small power distance." Regarding **uncertainty avoidance**, some countries have weak uncertainty avoidance in the sense that they accept uncertainty and that they are thus able to take risks easily. In contrast, strong uncertainty avoidance societies create institutions to offer security and avoid risk. With regard to **masculinity/femininity**, the classification is derived from whether a society has well-defined roles for men and women. A masculine society clearly expects men to be assertive and dominant and women to assume more service-oriented and caring roles. This society clearly differentiates between what men should do and what women are supposed to do.[12]

The second edition of Hofstede's book adds the fifth dimension: **temporal orientation**.[13] This dimension is sometimes called Confucian work dynamism. It has to do with short-term vs. long-term orientation.

Based on Hofstede's research, countries that are low in power distance, masculinity, and uncertainty avoidance include Australia, Canada, Denmark, the United Kingdom, the Netherlands, Norway, New Zealand, Sweden, and the United States. In comparison, those cultures that are low in individualism but high in power distance, masculinity, and uncertainty avoidance include Greece, Mexico, Pakistan, Peru, the Philippines, Taiwan, Thailand, Venezuela, and Japan.[14]

As explained by Hofstede, management is an American invention. But the practices of management in many parts of the world can deviate greatly from management as practiced in the U.S.A. American management theories emphasize market processes, managers, and individualism – characteristics that assume less significance elsewhere. In Japan, the emphasis is on workers – not managers. As a matter of fact, management as practiced in the U.S.A. does not bear much of a resemblance to how things are managed in Japan.[15]

The dimensions of national culture have marketing relevance. A study of TV commercials from Japan, Russia, Sweden, and the U.S.A. in terms of the masculine–feminine continuum found that feminine countries showed a higher degree of utilization of relationships for male and female characters. Since not all cultures share the same values, advertising standardization appears to be strategically unwise.[16] Based on another study focusing on professional service employees of an international public relations firm, employees from higher power distance, high uncertainty avoidance and high-context cultures prefer greater standardization.[17] In addition, advertisements focused on individual versus collective outcomes may affect East Asian and Western audiences differently. Marketing messages and cues that are presented in isolation rather than embedded in social backgrounds may help reduce or enhance the rate of recall, depending on which audience is targeted.[18]

According to one study, the individualism–collectivism and uncertainty avoidance dimensions (as well as their interaction) affect internet shopping rates. "For countries lower in uncertainty avoidance, individualist cultures show higher Internet shopping rates than do collectivist cultures."[19]

Hofstede's book has been cited more than any other work in social sciences. A review of 180 studies based on Hofstede's cultural values framework found these research studies to be "fragmented, redundant, and overly reliant on certain levels of analysis and direction of effects."[20] A review of the second edition of his book was critical of Hofstede's use of the same data (IBM workers), analysis, and measurement scales as in the first edition.[21] Hofstede defends the relevance of his scores by denying that a particular country's national culture could change. One thing is certain: his work has generated a huge reception.

## Clustering: commonality and diversity

The impact of Hofstede's 50-country study requires no debate. It has spawned a great deal of discussion as well as numerous studies. Another rigorous and large-scale study is just as valuable even though it is yet to attract the same kind of attention. Project GLOBE (Global Leadership and Organizational Behavior Effectiveness), based on a collaboration of scholars in all parts of the world, is a study of thousands of middle managers in food processing, finance, and telecommunications industries in 61 countries. The study focuses on nine dimensions of national cultures: performance orientation, future orientation, assertiveness, power distance, humane orientation, institutional collectivism, in-group collectivism, uncertainty avoidance, and gender egalitarianism. In the process, six global leadership attributes have been identified.[22]

The project uses discriminant analysis to confirm the ten a priori clusters: South Asia, Anglo, Arab, Germanic Europe, Latin Europe, Eastern Europe, Confucian Asia, Latin America, Sub-Saharan

Africa, and Nordic Europe. The results offer strong support for the existence of these proposed clusters.

Reflecting Latin America's paternalistic orientation, this cluster shows the practices of high power distance, and low performance orientation, uncertainty avoidance, future orientation, and institutional collectivism.[23] The hallmark of the southern Asia cluster is its high power distance and group and family collectivism practices. Charismatic, team-oriented, and humane leadership is highly valued.[24] The members of the Anglo cluster are all developed countries, and their orientation is toward individualist performance. A leader is expected to provide charismatic inspiration and a participative style.[25]

The societies found in the Arabic cluster are predominantly Muslim, and they share common literature, architecture, educational background, and religious characteristics. They are highly group-oriented, hierarchical, and masculine while being low on future orientation.[26] The cluster of Germanic Europe is a model of cooperation between labor and capital. Co-determination leads to participative leadership.[27]

The Eastern European cluster, reflecting both tradition and transition, stresses high power distance and high family and group collectivism.[28] The Latin Europe cluster scores close to mid-range on all but one dimension of societal practices. The only exception is in terms of a high average of over five on power distance. The societies in this cluster attempt to balance the need for competitiveness with their traditional preference for a paternalistic and interventionist government.[29]

One GLOBE study of 15 countries on five continents found that institutional collectivism, power distance, and CEO visionary leadership and integrity predicted social responsibility values on the part of top management team members.[30] Another 12-nation study tested the relationships among societal cultural values, individual social beliefs (cynicism, fate control, reward for application, and religiosity), perceived effectiveness of different influence strategies (persuasive, assertive, and relationship based), and four dimensions of individual beliefs. Different dimensions of individual social beliefs were found to predict the perceived effectiveness of the three types of influence strategy. Three of Project GLOBE's cultural values (in-group collectivism, uncertainty avoidance, and future orientation) moderated the strength of those relationships.[31]

## Psychographics

Because of the disappointing results in using personality to predict purchase behavior, marketers have turned to other meaningful purchase variables that may be used in conjunction with personality characteristics. This area of purchase behavior study is known as psychographics, also known as lifestyle or AIO (activities, interests, and opinions) study. Psychographics is a quantitative analysis of consumers' lifestyles and activities with the purpose of relating these variables to buying behavior. The analysis encompasses both the strength of the qualitative nature of Sigmund Freud's psychoanalytic theory and the statistical and methodological sophistication of trait and factor theories. As a result, questions are well organized, and responses are subject to numerical representation and multivariate analysis.

Questions normally included in psychographic studies are those related to demographics, personality traits, and activities such as media habits, retail patronage, and general interests. People can be classified by their lifestyles and then be contrasted in terms of their consumption habits. For example, respondents from England and Denmark do not view Denmark's furnishing interiors in the same way. The two cultures have different ideas of appropriate product syntax or how furnishing items could and should be combined.[32]

Values and lifestyles may be used to segment a market. A study of the consumer Gulf market has yielded three distinct segments: "principled purchasers," "suspicious shoppers," and "corrupt consumers." Principled purchasers tend to be less Machiavellian, less opportunistic, more trusting of others, less relativistic, and more idealistic. They also perceive questionable actions in a negative light. Suspicious shoppers are less trusting and place a high emphasis on ethical behavior. Like the suspicious shoppers, the corrupt consumers were not trusting individuals. Regarding corrupt consumers, they take advantage of opportunities and are not ethically oriented. Based on these three segments, marketers should adjust their strategies accordingly. For example, when targeting principled purchasers, there should be an emphasis on customer satisfaction and honesty in their transactions.[33]

Certain values are universal. There is a universal value structure, and the *World Values Compass* has identified six distinct consumer types: striver, fun seeker, creative, devout, intimate, and altruist. This value system is consistent across 30 countries. In spite of the universality of particular values, it must be noted that the distribution of value segments varies from country to country. In England, the fun seeker is the largest group. It is the devout group in Saudi Arabia and the intimate group in Sweden. For France, the two largest groups are fun seeker and intimate.[34]

## Perception

To learn, a person must perceive. Perception goes beyond sensation by providing meaning to sensory stimulations. It is the process of interpreting nervous impulses or stimuli received, and it requires the brain to organize and give meaning through cognitive interpretations. The Chinese, for instance, perceive Coke to look and taste like medicine.

One's culture greatly affects one's perception and behavior. Americans, for example, generally prefer steak on the "rare" side in order to maintain moisture and flavor. Asians, on the other hand, would not dream of eating steak cooked this way, believing that meat in that condition is raw and unsafe. Furthermore, Americans prefer to cook a big piece of meat, to be cut up or sliced on a serving plate at the dining table when they are ready to eat. The Chinese, however, prefer to cut the meat into small, bite-sized pieces before cooking and thus have no need for a knife at the dining table.

### *Formation of perception*

It is important to keep in mind that perceptions are formed through a highly subjective and selective process. The consumer's cognitive map of the environment is not a photograph of that physical environment. It is instead a partial and personal construction of a situation in which certain cues – selected and given emphasis – are perceived in an individual manner. More precisely, when one forms a perception, one is not a photographer but rather an artist who draws or paints an object in the way one thinks it is or should be. Therefore, no object or product is ever perceived exactly in the way it actually appears.

Because of the selectivity and subjectivity characteristics of perception, people "seeing" the same thing can have vastly different interpretations. In England, people perceive fancy, iced cakes as extra special, and such cakes are usually purchased from a bakery or made with great effort and care at home. Ready-prepared cake mixes are viewed as unacceptable and as a slight to a homemaker's role.

Whether a product will be successful or not depends significantly on how it is perceived. A marketer should provide some cues about a product in order to aid consumers in perceiving the product in the desired manner. Volvo, for example, has done quite well by emphasizing safety features.

A country, like a brand, can conjure up an image. One study used the *Anholt Nation Brands Index* to determine how 10,000 consumers in ten countries perceived America's cultural, political, commercial and human assets, investment potential, and tourist appeal. Although the U.S.A. obtained a relatively high rank in terms of U.S. exports, investment potential, immigration, tourism, and people, the global opinion of U.S. governance and culture and heritage was very low.[35] Figure 7.3 shows how Taiwan uses hospitality and culture to promote the country's image. The advertisement invites and re-invites investors and tourists by using the elegance of calligraphy to show the smiling image.

## Country of origin and perceived product quality

One of the cues often used by consumers in evaluating products is where a product is made. It is not unusual for consumers to categorize countries (e.g., rich, poor, developed, developing) and to use these categories to judge product quality. There is evidence of **country-category effect** in the sense that consumers use stereotyping in assessing product classes and brands.

At a more specific level, consumers may use **country of origin** as a guide to product quality. Not only do consumers have general images about certain countries, but they also form specific attitudes about products made in those countries. This topic has received a great deal of interest and has been researched in great depth.[36] Many empirical studies support the hypothesis that consumers have stereotyped opinions about specific products from particular countries. For example, an investigation of product-country images and ethnocentric behaviors found that Turkish consumers' perceptions of product attributes were influenced by products coming from countries of different levels of socioeconomic and technological development.[37] Country stereotypes may be spontaneously activated. The effects can occur automatically without consumers' intention to base their product judgments on country of origin.[38]

One company that has benefited from country image is Haagen-Dazs. Around 1960, Rose Mattus created a foreign-sounding name and put a map of Denmark on the ice-cream carton. She also put an umlaut over the first "a" in Häagen, when no umlaut is actually used in Danish. Häagen-Dazs was acquired by Pillsbury for $70 million in 1983, and Nestlé now owns it.[39]

When a "made in" designation is not favorably received, a marketer may want to deliberately conceal or not mention the product's origin. Many countries, however, including the U.S.A., require proper origin identification in the form of tag, label, or other identification means before foreign products can be imported.

The effects of country of origin can be moderated by consumer expertise and the type of attribute information. Motivational intensity and direction moderate the effect of information type of country of origin evaluations. When country of origin is salient and when consumers find new information relevant to their judgment, evaluations of the country of origin become more favorable.[40]

"人"means "people" or "human being"
"入"means "into" or "entrance"
Touching hospitality
Breathtaking natural splendor
Culinary delights
Imperial treasures
Herbal spas
World-class museums
Ecological adventure
Taiwan welcomes you with a smile
TODAY'S TAIWAN
REPUBLIC OF CHINA
www.gio.gov.tw

**FIGURE 7.3** Taiwan: culture and country image

*Source*: Courtesy of Government Information Office, Republic of China (Taiwan).

There is a relationship between consumer ethnocentrism and consumer attitude toward foreign products (when there is no domestic alternative). According to one study, consumers with high levels of consumer ethnocentrism have more favorable attitudes toward products from culturally similar countries when compared to products from culturally dissimilar countries.[41]

Country of origin is a multidimensional construct. As such, its effect is neither simple nor straightforward. Two particular dimensions are **country of assembly** and **country of design**. According to traditional wisdom, a manufacturer in a newly developed country or less developed country should conceal the identity of its manufacturing locations. However, if its product is *designed* in an advanced country, that fact can improve consumers' ratings of the product. One study focused on televisions and stereos in terms of the country of origin for parts, assembly, and design. Respondents have more favorable attitudes and higher purchase intention when a product assembled in the U.S.A. uses American parts rather than Mexican parts.[42]

It should be pointed out that *single-cue* studies demonstrated larger country of origin effect than did *multiple-cue studies*. The effect of country of origin is strongest when it is the only cue, but when other explicit multiple cues are included, the effect weakens.

In general, products from less developed countries are less favorably received than those from industrialized countries. However, even for high-risk products from less developed countries, consumers are still willing to buy them as long as they carry known brand names, indicating the power of a brand name to moderate the negative influence of a country's negative image. When there is congruence between brand origin and country of manufacture (e.g., a Sony TV set made in Japan), country of manufacture has impact on product beliefs and brand attitudes. Incongruence takes place when a branded product is made in a country whose image is not as favorable as that of brand origin (e.g., a Sony TV set made in Mexico). In this case, country of manufacture information adversely affects product evaluations – but only for low equity brands rather than high equity brands. Apparently, a brand can be strong enough to mitigate any negative perceptions derived from country of manufacture information.[43]

In addition, attribute claims become more credible when the products are distributed through a prestigious retailer. Distributors and/or retailers can have an impact on how a brand is perceived. Samsung Electronics Co.'s initial strategy was to use Wal-Mart Stores Inc. to distribute its low-end electronic gadgets. The company has now outgrown that strategy as it pushes toward innovative, higher margin products, such as voice-activated mobile phones that are also digital music players and personal digital assistants. For many consumers, this will be the very first time that they try such products, and it will also be the first time that they are exposed to brand names associated with these product categories. Thus Samsung has an opportunity to create brand equity and loyalty. As a result, it made a tough decision to abandon Wal-Mart in favor of specialty stores (e.g., Best Buy and Circuit City). Samsung's strong commitment to its brand strategy has propelled it to be among the world's top 50 brands. As a matter of fact, among all brands, Samsung's rise in brand value was the fastest.[44]

It may be incorrect to treat country of origin as a **halo effect**. A country's image varies across product categories. While consumers may prefer Japanese and German cars, they also prefer crystal from Ireland and leather shoes from Italy. Consumer preference is thus a function of **product–country match**. Consumer willingness to buy a country's particular product increases when the country image is also an important characteristic for that product category. One study of Bangladeshi consumers and their perceptions of products from nine foreign countries found that they overwhelmingly preferred

Western-made products. At the same time, their perceptions varied across product classes as well as across the sourcing countries.[45]

One study found that country of origin had an impact on brand equity when consumers perceived substantive differences between the countries in terms of their product category–country associations.[46] Another study found the presense of the effect of country of origin in a newly industrialized country (Singapore), even in the case of low-involvement products (bread and coffee). However, the effect was weak when brand information was included. Furthermore, a country's positive image in some product categories does not carry over to other product categories.[47] As in the case of Brazil, it conjures up the image of soccer, coffee, and samba. This image is out of date. Brazil's largest exports are airplanes and aircraft parts. The country now wants to be known for its high-technology products and services.[48]

To compete with Brazil and Mexico, the Federation of Colombian Coffee Growers needed an image (see Figure 7.4). Based on its composite Colombian coffee man, it wanted a Latin name that was both pronounceable and easy to remember for Americans. Thus, Juan was chosen as the first name because it is easy and rhymes with one (coffee beans are picked one by one). Because Rodriguez is too complicated a name for Americans, Valdez was picked as the last name. A nationwide search was made for a Colombian actor who would fit the American conception of the Latin male. The screening led to Carlos Sanchez, a relatively impoverished, university-educated silk-screen artist and sometime actor. The Federation's marketing campaign has been very effective.

The findings of the various studies have several marketing implications. Because consumers are more wary of products from developing countries, especially when there is a high degree of financial risk, developing countries naturally need to solve this marketing problem. Because consumers continuously merge product information with country image, quality control is necessary. The industry association and the government should establish quality standards and provide such incentives as tax benefits and subsidies to exporters who meet the standards, while penalizing those who do not by imposing export taxes or withholding export licenses. To help consumers generalize product information over the country's products, individual marketers can benefit from favorable country image by highlighting products of superior quality from the same country. For example, Mitsubishi may claim that its TV sets are as good as those manufactured by Sony. Alternatively, to prevent consumers from using the country's negative image in product evaluation, marketers should dissociate their products from unsuccessful products from that country.

An international marketer should pay attention to the relationship between country of origin and the perception of product quality. In general, engineering and technical products from Germany, electronics products from Japan, fashion products from France, and tobacco products from the U.S.A. are favorably received in most parts of the world. In addition, consumers in less developed countries usually prefer imported or foreign goods, believing that those goods are of higher quality and prestige.

A company must keep in mind that a product's image may change once its production facilities are moved from one country to a new location. Lowenbrau lost its image as a prestigious import beer once American drinkers became aware that the beer was licensed to be made by Miller in the U.S.A.

Because of the constancy or stability of perceptions, a negative perception associated with a particular country tends to persist. The failure of Yugoslavia's Yugo automobiles had to do with the negative perception, but the problem can be overcome if a firm or country perseveres and is determined to improve its product quality. A case in point is Japan. Its initial effort to penetrate

Some people can't wait for their next coffee break.

**FIGURE 7.4** Colombian coffee and product image

*Source*: Reprinted courtesy of the National Federation of Coffee Growers of Colombia.

the U.S. market after World War II was greeted with the perception that its products were cheap, imitative, and shoddy. Ironically, many consumers, including those in the U.S.A., have come to the conclusion that Japanese products are superior to American goods, offering better value for money. South Korea is currently striving to match Japan in this perception game. In the meantime, its Hyundai automobiles have perception hurdles to overcome. One experiment manipulated the level of warranty coverage and a warrantor's reputation. The findings indicate that warranty strategies can overcome consumers' negative perception about the quality of a company's hybrid product.[49]

Because of its poor reputation due to a decade of quality problems, Hyundai considered withdrawing from the U.S. market in 1998. It decided against this because a car maker could not be global without the U.S. market. From the marketing standpoint, the company has tried to solve the perception problem by setting aside hundreds of millions of dollars a year to cover its 100,000-mile/10-year warranty program. From the production standpoint, the company has become obsessed with quality. Hyundai has been shedding its image as a cheap car. Based on the quality scores from J.D. Power & Associates, Hyundai is the top-rated non-luxury brand, even ahead of Toyota. As a matter of fact, a quality survey of new car owners shows only Porsche and Lexus being ahead of Hyundai. Hyundai's sales in the U.S.A. have gone up, and so has the brand's global value.[50]

Finally, it should be noted that consumers are not necessarily knowledgeable of where a product originates. According to the results of one study, consumers have only modest knowledge of brand origins. Their recognition of foreign brand origins has to do with their socioeconomic status, international travel, foreign-language skills, and gender. They associate brand names with languages that suggest country of origin. Therefore, the influence of country of origin, as previously implied, may have been inflated.[51]

## Attitude

Attitude is the learned tendency to respond to an object in a consistently favorable or unfavorable way. Attitude is a complex and multidimensional concept. It consists of three components: cognition, affect, and conation (behavioral intention). Based on this definition, a few properties of attitude may be identified. First, the relationship between an individual and an object is not neutral: the reaction to the object is either favorable or unfavorable. Most people, for example, have favorable attitudes toward such automobiles as Mercedes-Benz, BMW, and Rolls-Royce, viewing them as status symbols. On the other hand, except for American consumers who have long been conditioned to prefer large automobiles, most consumers have strong reservations about large cars because they look unsightly and are difficult to maneuver on the narrow roads found in most parts of the world.

Second, attitudes are relatively enduring and patterned and not temporary or transient. As a person grows older, attitudes become more established. This becomes a challenge for international marketers who want to introduce change. A new product often involves a change in a long-held attitude. Finally, attitude is not innate – it must be learned. One's attitude about an object is formed by one's experience with the object, either directly or indirectly.

There is a relationship between consumer attitudes and their purchases and behavior (see Cultural Dimension 7.2). For instance, many Singaporeans are outshoppers who go to Malaysia to buy food, beverages, and grocery products because of competitive prices and ample parking space. Compared to their infrequent counterparts, frequent outshoppers perceive fewer secondary costs. In addition, because they engage in outshopping primarily for economic reasons, they do not feel guilty (i.e., a lack of national pride or low consumer ethnocentrism).[52]

It should be noted that consumers have similar attitudes while focusing on different product attributes, as in the case of England and Germany. Although consumers from the two countries have similar attitudes toward organic foods, the two groups seek different product attributes to achieve similar values (i.e., health, well-being, and enjoyment of life). Noticeably, the British group does not perceive any connection between organic food and the environment.[53] Another cross-cultural comparison has also found cultural differences with regard to the impact of different determinants on perceived customer benefits.[54]

Attitude is greatly influenced by culture. Attitudes toward women, for example, vary from country to country. In many countries, women are still considered as a man's property, and a woman must

## Cultural Dimension 7.2

### Celebrations and superstitions

The Chinese, Vietnamese, and Koreans celebrate Lunar New Year. Their celebrations include certain foods that resemble things considered to be lucky. The names of particular foods are homonyms for auspicious qualities.

For the Chinese, bird's nest soup signifies youthfulness, while shark fin soup offers prosperity. Lotus seeds bring about the birth of sons. Whole fish means abundance. Long noodles offer long life. While tangerines bring luck, oranges give sweetness and wealth.

For the Vietnamese, both whole chickens and whole fish mean abundance. Red melon seeds are supposed to bring joy, happiness, truth, and sincerity.

For the Koreans, rice cake soup is important. A person eating it is assured of living another year.

During Chinese New Year, the Las Vegas Strip becomes a festive red, decorated with dragons and Chinese characters. Baccarat tables welcome wealthy Chinese gamblers. Las Vegas Sands has five of its Chairman Suites designed based on the advice of a feng shui master. MGM Mirage incorporates Chinese culture into its resorts. Mandalay Bay's hotel towers avoid the unlucky numbers in the forties and fifties by going directly from the 39th floor to the 60th floor. The Mansion in MGM Grand has 31 luxury villas, with the numbers going from one to 34 so as to bypass unlucky 8, 18, and 28.

*Sources*: "Food for Luck, Joy, Fortune," *San José Mercury News*, February 8–14, 2007; and "Gung Hay Fat Choy – Vegas Style," *San José Mercury News*, February 20, 2007.

seek her husband's approval before entering into a contract or being allowed to apply for a visa or passport. In Saudi Arabia, strict Muslim restrictions make it very uncommon for women to work and impossible for them to drive a car. In Japan, working women are common but rarely have the opportunity to rise to a managerial position. Therefore, when women are portrayed in advertisements, the portrayal should be consistent with the expected role of women in that particular culture.

Attitude can affect marketing plans in other ways. Some countries have favorable attitudes toward foreigners, wealth, and change, making it relatively easy for MNCs to introduce new products. In fact, attitudes toward marketing itself should be considered. In India, marketing is viewed as unnecessary, annoying, and wasteful. Nestlé's infant formula received enormous adverse publicity because of the negative view in less developed countries about the company's marketing activities in poor countries.

One problem firms have in marketing their products overseas involves the negative attitudes toward situations associated with their products and sometimes toward the products themselves. For example, customers may have favorable attitudes toward German machinery but not toward the purchase of such machinery due to the high cost, service, or availability of parts.

It is important for a marketer to distinguish between private and public attitudes, because an expressed public attitude can differ widely from a private attitude, especially when the private attitude contradicts a society's cultural norms.

## Social class

Social class implies inequality. Even in the U.S.A., where all are supposed to be equal, some people seem to be much more equal than others. Social class exists because it provides for and ensures the smooth operation of a society. For a society to exist, many functions must be performed – some of which are not very pleasant. In this regard, members of a society are not that different from the bees in a hive – different types of bees exist for different purposes (e.g., working bees, queen bees, soldier bees, and so on). In Japan, even though the government long ago abolished the social caste system to allow for the mixing and reshuffling of people at all social levels, the selective access to higher education still impedes certain individuals from becoming career officials within the government.

Many societies see nothing wrong with the existence of a social hierarchy. As a matter of fact, many Asian and Middle-Eastern countries view status differences positively. Elders and superiors command respect. Connections with socially acceptable persons are often important in securing business.

The criteria used to assign people into social classes vary from country to country. In the U.S.A., relevant characteristics usually used in the construction of a social class index for classification purposes are occupation, source of income, house type, and dwelling area. In other countries, occupation and/or amount of income (rather than source of income) are the dominant discriminating variables. In some societies, royalty affiliation is employed as well to distinguish one social class from another.

The U.S. social system differs from those of other countries in several respects. Its greatest representation occurs approximately at the middle (i.e., the lower-middle and upper-lower categories) of the social class scale. Many developing countries have a very large lower class, and the graphic composition of all social classes is very similar to a pyramid: the upper class is a small minority group at the top and the vast number of lower-class people occupy the large base at the bottom. Furthermore, the U.S. system allows for social class mobility, while the systems elsewhere may be much more rigid.

Even when the same distinguishing variable is used in different countries for classification, it may not have the same meaning and does not necessarily yield the same result. If the classification of occupation is considered, in the U.S.A., financial considerations very likely explain why attorneys are accorded the kind of status and prestige rarely found elsewhere. Engineering positions, on the other hand, are regarded much more highly in societies outside of the U.S.A.

Social class has a great deal of relevance for marketing strategies. It influences store selection, product selection, media selection, advertising appeal selection, and sales promotion selection. Different motives may thus have to be employed for different social classes. Thresher, a British liquor store chain of 990 outlets, used the results of its marketing research to divide its shops into three designations: Drinks Stores, Wine Shops, and Wine Racks. The designations are based on the social status of a neighborhood. The downmarket Drinks Stores are located in working-class areas, and they stock mostly beer. Wine Racks, offering a larger selection of wines and champagnes, are found in wealthier locations and have a better educated staff. The middlebrow Wine Shops are somewhere in between.

## Group

A group consists of two or more persons who share a set of norms and have certain implicitly or explicitly defined relationships with one another in such a way that their behavior is interdependent. Group norms influence both general behavior and consumption behavior.

Originally formed for defense and survival, a group now serves its members more for needs of social and psychological satisfaction. An individual cannot operate well in isolation because all persons are biologically and socially interdependent. An individual needs to belong to a group to interact with those who can provide identification and help meet needs in a more efficient manner. The influence of a reference group is derived in part from its capacity to disseminate information.

The relevance and strength of influence of a reference group is not constant across product categories. Its influence is determined in part by the conspicuousness of the product in question. A product can be conspicuous in two ways: by having the qualities of visibility and by standing out. The more the product is visible and stands out, the more conspicuous it becomes. Product conspicuousness allows a reference group to operate in exerting its influence on consumer behavior. For example, Philip Morris's Galaxy brand was at one time perceived as a "diet" cigarette, and for that reason Brazilians became ashamed to be seen with it because social and personal pressures were placed on those who smoked Galaxy.

The relevance of group appeal may be dictated by cultural norms. In contrast to Americans, who are more individually oriented, the Japanese are more committed to group membership and are consensus-oriented. Group pressure is very great in Japan.

## Family

In the U.S.A., the word *family* has a narrow meaning because it encompasses only the husband, wife, and their offspring (if any). This family is known as a *nuclear* or *conjugal* family. In the other parts of the world, the word has a much broader meaning because it is based on the concept of an *extended* or *consanguineous* family. A family can be vertically extended when it includes several generations. It can also be horizontally extended when such family members as uncles, aunts, and cousins are included. Thus non-Americans count vertical and horizontal relatives of either the husband or wife or both as part of their family. It is not uncommon for a son to live in his parents' home even after getting married. When his parents become old, it will become his responsibility to take care of his parents, the home, and the business. In such a country, nursing homes are relatively rare, and the placement of elderly or ill parents in homes for the aged is disdained.

The Chinese culture emphasizes familial over private self. Attainment of family-oriented goals is a measure of self-realization and self-fulfillment. Boundaries of familial self may include romantic partners and close friends who are "like family." In family and like-family contexts, there is no need for reciprocity.[55]

As a subset and special kind of reference group, the family can be distinguished by its characteristics. First, a family allows its members ample opportunity to interact with one another on a face-to-face basis. In effect, each member operates as both a counselor and an information provider. Second, the family is a consuming unit in the sense that most members share the consumption of many products, especially those that are durables or that affect the family budget. Third, individual needs are usually subordinated to family needs. Finally, one member is often assigned the primary duty of buying products for other users, thus acting as a gatekeeper or purchasing agent.

American and non-American families raise their families in very different ways. Americans emphasize individual freedom, and children are taught to be self-sufficient and independent. In Japan and China, the family is the main focal point. Similar to the Hispanic's strong family orientation, the Japanese feel a strong sense of responsibility and obligation to their families, and these obligations predominate in family decisions.

Because of the emphasis on family orientation, nepotism is an expected and accepted practice in most parts of the world. The tradition may even be carried on to include business partners. In Japan, close bonds among all members of a manufacturer's distribution channel explain why unprofitable members are not dropped from the system. Pillsbury has to accommodate this different style of doing business in Japan, where the emphasis is on long courtship, trust, sincerity, and Asian "old friends." Joint ventures are akin to a marriage, and a divorce of this kind is strongly frowned upon. The family tradition also explains why Japanese corporate priorities are employees, suppliers, customers, community, government, bankers, and finally shareholders.

A family functions more efficiently when its members specialize in the roles they are most comfortable with or are capable of performing better than other family members. A marketer must determine the kind of decision making that is relevant to the product. Once that fact is known, the marketer can direct a promotional effort toward the party making the purchase decision. It is thus useful to consider and to assess the relative influence of each spouse in the decision-making process.

## Opinion leadership

Within each social group, there are some individuals who are able to exert a significant influence on other members in such a way as to affect their thinking and behavior in a desired direction. These individuals are known as opinion leaders. In the context of consumer behavior, their opinions about products can affect subsequent purchases made by others.

In marketing products overseas, MNCs should attempt to appeal to opinion leaders. In general, these are likely to be people who command respect from others. In Ghana, government health workers gain better cooperation and reception by asking for village witch-doctors' approval before inoculating people or spraying huts to fight malaria. In developing countries, it is a good strategy to market new ideas to teachers, monks, or priests first, because their opinions influence the acceptance of these ideas by others.

When it is doubtful who the opinion leaders are, marketers should try to identify those with influence and affluence. BMW, for example, sells its cars at a discount to diplomats, believing that its target consumers will take notice of the kinds of cars driven by those in power. In foreign countries, business periodicals and English-language newspapers are usually an effective means of reaching government and business leaders who are potential opinion leaders.

## Diffusion process of innovation

The diffusion process of innovation is an acceptance over time of a product or idea by consumers, linked to a given social structure and a given system of values or culture. Innovators possess certain characteristics that distinguish them from noninnovators. Innovators are frequently opinion leaders, and it is thus desirable to identify and contact innovators.

The diffusion process varies from culture to culture. The conservative business etiquette in South Korea is reflected in Korean firms' organizational structure as well as in their managerial approach, which emphasizes harmony and structure over innovation and experimentation. Diffusion of the internet is not similar in the U.S.A. and Japan. Japan, as a collectivist culture, values high uncertainty avoidance and has large power distance. As such, Japan has a slower adoption process.[56]

One study investigated consumer innovativeness in a cross-cultural context by examining data collected from 2283 consumers in 11 EU countries. According to the findings, innovation orientation differs both among consumers and among countries, reflecting the fact that national cultural variables can explain systematic differences in innovativeness between countries. In collectivistic countries, a marketing message should emphasize social acceptance and a product's local origin. In contrast, Australia, New Zealand, the United Kingdom, the U.S.A., and Canada have national cultures that are characterized by low uncertainty avoidance, high individualism, and high masculinity. As such, they are receptive to product innovation.[57]

Culture not only affects the diffusion process in general, but it also exerts a great deal of influence on the adoption of a product in particular. A product that is suitable in one culture may be totally inappropriate elsewhere. The Italian and Asian preference for fresh meat and vegetables has hampered the acceptance of frozen foods. In Italy and Southeast Asia, markets open and close early, and shoppers who wish to select the best items must get to market very early in the morning. By the early afternoon the market is ready to be closed, with only a few poor-quality items left for selection.

## Conclusion

Consumer behavior, as a discipline, has been studied so extensively in the U.S.A. that it has been thoroughly researched at both the macro and micro levels. Surprisingly, it has not been rigorously and diligently investigated in the international context. Much too frequently, studies that compare consumers in various countries attribute differences in consumer characteristics and behavior to cultural differences. This convenient approach (i.e., culture) by itself is inadequate and does not enhance the understanding of consumption behavior overseas.

Instead of explicitly or implicitly attempting to use culture to explain most variations in consumption, researchers should redirect their attention toward smaller units of analysis. This requires a study of psychological concepts as well as social concepts which are not solely based on cultural determinants.

At the psychological level, relevant concepts such as motivation, learning, personality, psychographics, perception, and attitude should be closely examined. Because consumer needs vary across countries, as does the degree of importance attached to a particular need, it is unrealistic to expect consumers everywhere to be motivated in the same way. The varying motives that occur are due in part to individual personality traits and lifestyles. The learning and perception of a product and the attitude toward it will also affect consumers' motivations in acquiring the product.

At the social level, it is redundant to state that consumer behavior is affected by the cultural environment. It is more important to list specifically the cultural norms in a country and to understand why those norms vary from country to country. It is thus important to appreciate how these norms are shaped by reference groups, social class, family, opinion leadership, and the diffusion process of

Legal Dimension 7.1

**Film in a digital world**

Eastman Kodak pioneered mass-market photography and prospered from its celluloid film business. However, this prosperity was threatened by the arrival of digital technology. Interestingly, that threat came from Kodak's own invention. Kodak invented the world's first digital camera in 1975. That camera was the size of a toaster and weighed eight pounds. It captured a black-and-white image on a digital cassette tape at a resolution of .01 megapixels. It has accumulated more than 1,000 digital-imaging patents. Almost all digital cameras are based on these inventions.

In 2004, Kodak took Sony Corp. to court, alleging that Sony had infringed 10 patents involving digital and video technologies such as image compression and digital storage. Sony countersued and claimed that Kodak had infringed Sony's patents that included an indicator that displays the number of pictures taken and an electronic shutter with adjustable speeds. The patent dispute, dating back to 1987, was settled in 2007. Both parties agreed to a cross-licensing deal that gave both sides access to each other's patent.

Because of the success and profit of its film business, Kodak was reluctant to move aggressively toward the new technology. It was surprised by the speed at which Chinese consumers moved from conventional cameras to digital cameras.

*Source*: "Kodak Ends Patent Row with Sony," *Bangkok Post*, January 5, 2007.

innovation. Consumer preference depends in part on how well a product fits into the cultural circumstances and on whether the product will have the approval of a consumer's reference group, social class, and family.

In conclusion, marketers and researchers should guard against using culture as a catchall term and should not use it on a wholesale basis to explain overseas behavior. It is necessary to go beyond noticing cultural differences and instead to attempt to understand the underlying causes of cultural variations. This goal requires researchers to be more specific and rigorous in their investigations by extending the application of relevant psychological and social concepts to the international scene. It is time to move a way from a vague and generic explanation of consumption behavior to a more precise and better-focused avenue of research.

## CASE 7.1 TROPICAL DRINK FOR THE U.S. MARKET

**Buarat Srinil, Thammasat University, Thailand**

One afternoon in late June 2007, T. Chai, the Managing Director of Taratip Co. Ltd., had a meeting with his business consultant. They were discussing the idea of introducing the company's tropical drink product line into the Hispanic segment of the U.S. market. The tropical drink product had been initially introduced to the U.S. Asian market seven years before and had been very successful.

Taratip Co. Ltd. was founded in 1977 in the province of Nakhon Pathom in Thailand. The province is very well known for its tropical fruit plantations and is located about 35 miles from Bangkok, the capital of Thailand. During its first years of operation, the Taratip Company marketed only one line of business and this was the processing of rice for export. At that time, only those companies that were awarded an export license were allowed to export rice. As time went on the company expanded its product line to cover additional food products such as pickled lemon, pickled ginger, and pickled hot chili as well as canned vegetables such as bamboo shoots, baby corn, and bean sprouts. The major customers for these products were Asian agents who distributed these products to Thai restaurants in the U.S.A.

Beginning in 1985, very strong competition emerged from China as it began to distribute substantially lower priced canned vegetables in the U.S. market. At about this time, the Thai government declared that rice exports would no longer require an export license, thus rendering the company's once-valuable asset worthless. Because of these added costs of doing business, the management of Taratip decided to stop exporting rice as well as canned vegetables in 1987.

Taratip subsequently developed a new line of products in the form of canned fruits such as mango, rambutan, longan, lychee, and jackfruit. New problems emerged for this line of business due to the fact that these fruis are harvested seasonally and therefore, after canning, must be warehoused, which resulted in high storage and inventory costs. The management of Taratip thus felt that it had to consider other new lines and looked into alternative possible products such as canned coconut milk, coconut cream, and Thai ready-to-eat coconut dessert. However, these considerations did not seem to be worth pursuing because a competitor, the Chao Koa Company, had entered this product line 20 years before and dominated the market.

Taratip's management continued to search for new market opportunities. Chai and his business consultant discussed the concept of product differentiation. If a new product could be successfully developed through differentiation and introduced to the market, then the chances of success could be increased. After looking into the coconut product and differentiating it, a new product was developed and called "coconut juice with pulp." The advantage this product enjoyed was that coconuts are in large supply and are grown year round, thus eliminating the need for and cost of warehousing and storage. Three years after its introduction, young coconut juice with pulp became very successful within the Asian consumer market in the U.S.A.

The management of Taratip believed that a tropical drink product line could be the right product for the U.S. market. A large amount of research funding was allocated for formulating a variety of tropical drink products as well as improving the container from a tin can to an aluminum can. Taratip's research resulted in formulating more than 15 different kinds of tropical drinks such as Thai tea drink, pineapple drink, tamarind drink, pennywort drink, mangosteen juice drink, and Jamica hibiscus drink. In 2003, Taratip began entering the Hispanic market in the U.S.A. with its tropical drink product line through its distributor export management company. The acceptance of the tropical drink product line among Hispanic consumers provided very encouraging results. In the overall sales of the tropical drink product in the U.S. market, young coconut juice accounts for 80 percent of the market. Taratip's own sales account for 30 percent of this volume while the distributor export management company's volume accounts for 70 percent of sales. The Taratip management has set a long-term objective of having its own marketing efforts account for 50 percent of the market through a multibrand strategy.

According to consumer feedback research, the Asian market in the U.S.A. was very satisfied with the taste and product form of young coconut juice, while Hispanic consumers were also very pleased with the taste of young coconut juice and Jamica hibiscus drink.

Before continuing the discussion with the business consultant, Chai had looked into some demographic statistics within the U.S. population. He determined that the number of Asian consumers approximated 10 million consumers whereas the Hispanic population consisted of around 60 million people.

## Points to consider

What steps should Chai and the Taratip management take to determine if it would be wise to establish its brand with the Hispanic market segment, and why?

## Questions

1 Distinguish among these three disciplines in terms of the unit of analysis: psychology, sociology, and anthropology.
2 Are rational motives more effective than their emotional counterparts in motivating consumers to make a purchase?
3 Are consumers' perceptions of products affected by the information concerning the products' countries of origin?
4 Explain how attitudes toward (a) marketing and (b) women may vary across countries.
5 Do social classes exist in the U.S.A., supposedly the land of equality?

# Discussion assignments and minicases

1 Do you feel that consumer differences can be adequately explained by the all-encompassing concept of culture? Is it a waste of time to employ other psychological and social concepts to understand consumer behavior?
2 Are the same buying motives effective worldwide?
3 Because personality is related to an individual person, is it possible for citizens of a country to have unique personality traits? Does a nation have its own national character?
4 Compared to Americans, are Asians and Africans: (1) more group-oriented, (b) more family-oriented, and (c) more concerned with social status? How might such orientations affect the way you market your product to Asian and African consumers?
5 Do you think it is worthwhile to appeal to opinion leaders and innovators in foreign markets?

## Notes


1 David A. Ralston *et al.*, "The Effects of Culture and Life Stage on Workplace Strategies of Upward Influence: A Comparison of Thailand and the United States," *Journal of World Business* 40 (August 2005): 321–37.
2 Kamel Mellahi and Cherif Guermat, "Does Age Matter? An Empirical Examination of the Effect of Age on Managerial Values and Practices in India," *Journal of World Business* 39 (May 2004): 199–215.
3 "60 Minutes," *Business Today*, December 31, 2006, 134–7.
4 Swee Hoon Ang, "The Power of Money: A Cross-cultural Analysis of Business-related Beliefs," *Journal of World Business*, 35 (No. 1, 2000): 43–60.

5 "Shoppers Gone Wild," *Business Week*, February 20, 2006, 46–7.

6 Michael Shapiro, *The Shadow in the Sun: A Korean Year of Love and Sorrow* (New York: Atlantic Monthly Press, 1990).

7 "Frenetic People in a Hurry," *Financial Times*, May 28, 2002.

8 Terence A. Shimp and Subhash Sharma, "Consumer Ethnocentrism: Construction and Validation of the CETSCALE," *Journal of Marketing Research* 24 (August 1987): 280–9; and Subhash Sharma, Terence A. Shimp, and Jeongshin Shin, "Consumer Ethnocentrism: A Test of Antecedents and Moderators," *Journal of the Academy of Marketing Science* 23 (winter 1995): 26–37.

9 James Reardon *et al.*, "The Effects of Ethnocentrism and Economic Development on the Formation of Brand and Ad Attitudes in Transitional Economies," *European Journal of Marketing* 39 (Nos 7/8, 2005): 737–54.

10 Kate Hamilton, "Project Galore: Qualitative Research and Leveraging Scotland's Brand Equity," *Journal of Advertising Research* 40 (January–April 2000): 107–11.

11 Frederic Jallat and Allan J. Kimmel, "Marketing in Culturally Diverse Environments: The Case of Western Europe," *Business Horizons* 45 (July–August 2002): 30–6.

12 Geert Hofstede, "The Cultural Relativity of Organizational Practices and Theories," *Journal of International Business Studies* 14 (fall 1983): 75–89.

13 Geert Hofstede, *Culture's Consequences: Comparing Values, Behaviors, Institutions and Organizations Across Nations*, 2nd edn (Thousand Oaks, CA: Sage, 2001).

14 Geert Hofstede, *Culture's Consequences: International Differences in Work-related Values* (Beverly Hills, CA: Sage, 1980).

15 Geert Hofstede, "Cultural Constraints in Management Theories," *Academy of Management Executive* 7 (No. 1, 1993): 81–94.

16 Laura M. Milner and James M. Collins, "Sex-role Portrayals and the Gender of Nations," *Journal of Advertising* 29 (spring 2000): 67–79.

17 William Newburry and Nevena Yakova, "Standardization Preferences: A Function of National Culture, Work Interdependence and Local Embeddedness," *Journal of International Business Studies* 37 (January 2006): 44–60.

18 Richard Nisbett, *The Geography of Thought: How Asians and Westerners Think Differently . . . and Why* (New York: The Free Press, 2003).

19 Kai H. Lim *et al.*, "Is eCommerce Boundary-less? Effects of Individualism-collectivism and Uncertainty Avoidance on Internet Shopping," *Journal of International Business Studies* 35 (November 2004): 545–59.

20 Bradley L. Kirkman, Kevin B. Lowe, and Cristina B. Gibson, "A Quarter Century of *Culture's Consequences*: A Review of Empirical Research Incorporating Hofstede's Cultural Values Framework," *Journal of International Business Studies* 37 (May 2006): 285–320.

21 Boonghee Yoo and Naveen Donthu, "New Books in Review," *Journal of Marketing Research* 39 (August 2002): 388–9.

22 Mansour Javidan and Robert J. House, "Leadership and Cultures around the World: Findings from GLOBE," *Journal of World Business* 37 (spring 2002): 1–2; and Robert House *et al.*, "Understanding Cultures and Implicit Leadership Theories across the Globe: An Introduction to Project GLOBE," *Journal of World Business* 37 (spring 2002): 3–10.

23 Vipin Gupta, Paul J. Hanges, and Peter Dorfman, "Cultural Clusters: Methodology and Findings," *Journal of World Business* 37 (spring 2002): 11–15.

24 Vipin Gupta *et al.*, "Southern Asia Cluster: Where the Old Meets the New?", *Journal of World Business* 37 (spring 2002): 16–27.

25 Neal M. Ashkanasy, Edwin Trevor-Roberts, and Louise Earnshaw, "The Anglo Cluster: Legacy of the British Empire," *Journal of World Business* 37 (spring 2002): 28–39.

26 Hayat Kabasakal and Muzaffer Bodur, "Arabic Cluster: A Bridge between East and West," *Journal of World Business* 37 (spring 2002): 40–54.

27 Erna Szabo *et al.*, "The Germanic Europe Cluster: Where Employees Have a Voice," *Journal of World Business* 37 (spring 2002): 55–68.
28 Gyula Bakacsi *et al.*, "Eastern European Cluster: Tradition and Transition," *Journal of World Business* 37 (spring 2002): 69–80.
29 Jorge Correia Jesuino, "Latin Europe Cluster: From South to North," *Journal of World Business* 37 (spring 2002): 81–9.
30 David A. Waldman *et al.*, "Cultural and Leadership Predictors of Corporate Social Responsibility Values of Top Management: A GLOBE Study of 15 Countries," *Journal of International Business Studies* 37 (November 2006): 823–37.
31 Ping Ping Fu *et al.*, "The Impact of Societal Cultural Values and Individual Social Beliefs on the Perceived Effectiveness of Managerial Influence Strategies: A Meso Approach," *Journal of International Business Studies* 35 (July 2004): 284–305.
32 Simon Ulrik Kragh and Malene Djursaa, "Product Syntax and Cross-cultural Marketing Strategies," *European Journal of Marketing* 35 (No. 11, 2001): 1301–20.
33 Jamal A. Al-Khatib, Angela D'Auria Stanton, and Mohammed Y. A. Rawwas, "Ethical Segmentation of Consumers in Developing Countries: A Comparative Analysis," *International Marketing Review* 22 (No. 2, 2005): 225–46.
34 Simeon Chow and Sarit Amir, "The Universality of Values: Implications for Global Advertising Strategy," *Journal of Advertising Research* 46 (September 2006): 301–14.
35 Simon Anholt, "Anholt Nation Brand Index: How Does the World See America?", *Journal of Advertising Research* 45 (September 2005): 296–304.
36 For a list of studies focusing on country of origin, see the previous editions of this textbook.
37 Erdener Kaynak and Ali Kara, "Consumer Perceptions of Foreign Products: An Analysis of Product–Country Images and Ethnocentrism," *European Journal of Marketing* 36 (No. 7, 2002): 928–49.
38 Scott S. Liu and Keith F. Johnson, "The Automatic Country-of-origin Effects on Brand Judgments," *Journal of Advertising* 34 (spring 2005): 87–97.
39 "Rose Mattus, Helped Nation Get a Taste of Häagen-Dazs," *San José Mercury News*, December 4, 2006.
40 Zeynep Gurhan-Canli and Durairaj Maheswaran, "Determinants of Country-of-Origin Evaluations," *Journal of Consumer Research* 27 (June 2000): 96–108.
41 John J. Watson and Katrina Wright, "Consumer Ethnocentrism and Attitudes toward Domestic and Foreign Products," *European Journal of Marketing* 34 (No. 9, 2000): 1149–66.
42 Paul Chao, "The Moderating Effects of Country of Assembly, Country of Parts, and Country of Design on Hybrid Product Evaluations," *Journal of Advertising* 30 (winter 2001): 67–81.
43 Michael K. Hui and Lianxi Zhou, "Country-of-manufacture Effects for Known Brands," *European Journal of Marketing* 37 (No. 1, 2003): 133–53.
44 "The Best Global Brands," *Business Week*, August 6, 2001, 50–7; and "The Best Global Brands," *Business Week*, August 5, 2002, 92–9.
45 Ravi Pappu, Pascale G. Quester, and Ray W. Cooksey, "Consumer-based Brand Equity and Country-of-origin Relationships: Some Empirical Evidence," *European Journal of Marketing* 40 (Nos 5/6, 2006): 696–717.
46 Erdener Kaynak, Orsay Kucukemiroglu, and Akmal S. Hyder, "Consumers' Country-of-origin (COO) Perceptions of Imported Products in a Homogeneous Less-developed Country," *European Journal of Marketing* 34 (No. 9, 2000): 1221–41.
47 Zafar U. Ahmed *et al.*, "Does Country of Origin Matter for Low-involvement Products?", *International Marketing Review* 21 (No. 1, 2004): 102–20.
48 "Image Problem Hurting Brazil," *Wall Street Journal*, April 23, 2005.
49 Soo J. Tan *et al.*, "Warranty and Warrantor Reputations as Signals of Hybrid Product Quality," *European Journal of Marketing* 35 (No. 1, 2001): 110–32.
50 "Best Global Brands," *Business Week*, August 7, 2006, 54–66.

51 Saeed Samiee, Terence A. Shimp, and Subhash Sharma, "Brand Origin Recognition Accuracy: Its Antecedents and Consumers' Cognitive Limitations," *Journal of International Business Studies* 36 (July 2005): 379–97.

52 Francis Piron, "International Outshopping and Ethnocentrism," *European Journal of Marketing* 36 (No. 1, 2002): 189–210.

53 Susan Baker, Keith E. Thompson, and Julia Engelken, "Mapping the Values Driving Organic Food Choice: Germany vs the UK," *European Journal of Marketing* 38 (No. 8, 2004): 995–1012.

54 Christian Homburg *et al.*, "Determinants of Customer Benefits in Business-to-business Markets: A Cross-cultural Comparison," *Journal of International Marketing* 13 (No. 3, 2005): 1–31.

55 Annamma Joy, "Gift Giving in Hong Kong and the Continuum of Social Ties," *Journal of Consumer Research* 28 (September 2001): 239–56.

56 Carrie La Ferle, Steven M. Edwards, and Yutaka Mizuno, "Internet Diffusion in Japan: Cultural Considerations," *Journal of Advertising Research* 42 (March–April 2002): 65–79.

57 Jan-Benedict E.M. Steenkamp, Frenkel ter Hofstede, and Michel Wedel, "A Cross-national Investigation into the Individual and National Cultural Antecedents of Consumer Innovativeness," *Journal of Marketing* 63 (April 1999): 55–69.

Part 3

# Planning for international marketing

Chapter 8

# Marketing research and information systems

The faster and further you move information, the more valuable it becomes.

Glen McG. Renfrew, managing director, Reuters Holdings PLC

## Chapter outline

- Marketing strategy: phones as companions
- Nature of marketing research
- Marketing information sources
- Secondary research
  - Private sources
  - Public sources
- Primary research
- Sampling
- Basic methods of data collection
  - Observation
  - Questioning
- Measurement
  - Conceptual equivalence
  - Instrument equivalence
  - Measurement scales
  - Linguistic equivalence
  - Response style
  - Measurement timing
  - External validity

- Marketing information system
  - System development
  - Desirable characteristics
  - Subsystems
- Conclusion
- Case 8.1 Mapping Japanese tourism behavior

## Marketing strategy

**Phones as companions**

Although Nokia supplies one-third of the world's mobile phones, it does not stand still. The company's scouts regularly invade the world's centers of fashion and youth culture. They observe and talk to engineers, students, architects, and users. The information obtained has resulted in a number of products. One of them is the L'Amour collection which targets fashion-conscious consumers.

Nokia watches how people interact and how they do things. Users' strange rituals have yielded insights. Watching businesspeople has led Nokia to equip its new E61 handset with a button that gives immediate access to e-mail. Because people tend to share photos by passing the handset to a family member or friend, Nokia's newest N series models have screens that fold out and can be pivoted for easier sharing and viewing.

To make low-cost phones for emerging markets, Nokia uses a combination of basic ethnographic and long-term user research in China, India, and Nepal. The research allows the company to understand how illiterate customers function in a world full of letters and numbers. Based on that knowledge, Nokia has created an "iconic" menu that lets users navigate contact lists made up of images. Because mobile phones may be the most expensive item ever bought by some poor consumers, the company has made its phones more durable. The phones are also more moisture-resistant to cope with a tropical climate. Special screens facilitate viewing in bright sunlight.

Research results have led Nokia to conclude that users want to be connected all the time. They see their handsets as entertainment centers as well as a way to share their lives with family and friends. Phones are no longer mere tools but are becoming companions.

*Sources*: "Staying Cool at Nokia," *Business Week*, July 17, 2006, 62, 65; and "The World's Most Innovative Companies," *Business Week*, April 24, 2006, 62–74.

## Purpose of chapter

Lack of knowledge and unfamiliarity with foreign markets usually heighten the risks for a company wanting to do business in a foreign land. The problem is further complicated by the fact that international marketing research is more difficult and more complex than domestic research. The case of Nokia illustrates the value of marketing information and how such information can make the difference between success and failure. The data allow the firm to make timely adjustments to its marketing mix, and the company's understanding of consumer habits makes it possible for Nokia to better satisfy its customers' needs.

Given the complexity of today's fast-changing world and the unpredictability of consumer demands, the use of marketing research is essential if a company is to reduce the serious risks associated with marketing a product. Thus, the purpose of this chapter is to examine the nature and techniques of international marketing research. The chapter investigates such topics as types of data, types of data-collection methods, sampling, and measure. The discussion emphasizes the difficulties associated with cross-cultural research and the necessity for adapting marketing research techniques to international markets.

Cultural Dimension 8.1

**Home cooking traditions**

According to Whirlpool's research, in spite of the popularity of drive-through diners, most Latino families still prefer home cooking and "making everything as far as possible from scratch." In response, Whirlpool markets Sabor in the U.S.A. (and uses the Agros label in Mexico). Sabor is a free-standing gas range with a built-in comal (griddle), which is actually interchangeable with a fifth burner. An integrated comal frees up a burner for a family that cooks frequently. It has a dual Spanish–English control panel, and it is offered in 140 U.S. markets which have significant Latino populations. For those who grew up in Mexico and Latin America, Sabor invokes a sense of home and familiarity.

Source: "Whirlpool Taps into Latino Traditions," *San José Mercury News*, February 17, 2007.

## Nature of marketing research

According to the American Marketing Association, **marketing research** involves the "systematic gathering, recording, and analyzing of data about problems relating to the marketing of goods and services." This definition provides a useful description of the nature of marketing research, but it fails to include preresearch analysis, which is an important aspect of the research process. Before data collection, careful planning is required to specify both the kind of information needed and the purpose of such information. Without preresearch activities, there is a great danger that critical information may not be obtained and that what is obtained may turn out to be irrelevant or unsuitable. The letter in Exhibit 8.1 shows a lack of problem definition, research objectives, and preresearch activities.

The gathering of information can never be a substitute for good managerial judgment. A story told by the founder of Bata (the world's largest shoe company) illustrates this point. Two shoe salesmen from two companies visited the same island and came away with vastly different interpretations of people not wearing shoes there. One gave up and returned home immediately because of a non-existent marketing opportunity. The other salesman, however, was very enthusiastic since all these

Exhibit 8.1

**Poorly formulated research**

To: International Trade Administration
U.S. Department of Commerce
Washington, DC

Dear Sir/Madam:

I am in the process of planning the importation of a foreign product into the United States for wholesale distribution.

I have not yet determined the nature of the product. I am certain, however, that it is neither a food item nor automotive products. I am also undecided about the country of origin, even though I am leaning in the direction of the European or Asian manufacturing firms. These requirements should be able to minimize the research required to locate the research materials which I would like to receive from you.

Thank you for your assistance in providing me with the requested information.

Sincerely,

Potential Importer

potential customers were still without shoes. The moral of the story is that marketing research is only one part of the equation, and proper analysis and judgmental decisions are required.

In terms of marketing research expenditures, the U.S.A. is the leader. Internationally, larger firms dominate research activities. The top 25 commercial firms account for more than half of total world expenditures for marketing, advertising, and opinion research.

## Marketing information sources

Once a researcher has identified the marketing problem and has completed a preresearch analysis, the relevant information must be collected. The two major sources of information are primary data and secondary data.

**Primary data** may be defined as information that is collected firsthand, generated by original research tailor-made to answer specific, current research questions. The major advantage of primary data is that the information is specific, relevant, and up-to-date. The desirability of primary data is, however, somewhat moderated by the high cost and amount of time associated with the collection of this type of data.

**Secondary data**, in contrast, may be defined as information that has already been collected for other purposes and is thus readily available. Note that the advantages of primary data are the disadvantages of secondary data, and that the advantages of secondary data become the disadvantages of primary data. While the cost associated with the collection of secondary data is lower, the type of information is not as specific or current.

As a rule, no research should be done without a search for secondary information first, and secondary data should be used whenever available and appropriate. To determine the suitability of the secondary data, a researcher should employ relevant criteria to evaluate the purpose, methodology, definitions of the concepts, and time period covered in the study yielding the information. Transition economies, in particular, pose a special challenge in terms of data quality. Great caution should be used when interpreting foreign trade statistics in the Baltics, Russia, and the other countries of the former Soviet Union. Economic and political conditions there have greatly changed, as has the methodology of collecting and recording data.

The evaluation process becomes much more complicated if secondary data from various countries must be compared in order to analyze the business potential of each country. A problem for marketers is that secondary data on international marketing may not be comparable for several reasons. First, countries may employ different data-collection methods. Second, there might be a problem with classification differences. Third, the unit of measurement employed could differ. Finally, definitional differences are another common problem because countries tend to use various definitions in collecting the same kind of information. For example, regarding the "urban" concept, Denmark defines it as a locality of 200 or more inhabitants, while it must be at least 20,000 for Nigeria. In the case of Bermuda and Singapore, the entire countries are an urban area.

## Secondary research

There are many different ways to collect secondary data, and there are many information sources for this purpose. Such sources may be grouped under either public or private sources.

### *Private sources*

A very basic method of finding business information is to begin with a public library or a university library. A library with a reasonable collection should contain standard reference guides, commercial and industrial directories, financial reference manuals, and other materials containing pertinent business information.

One useful source of information is the World Trade Centers Association (WTCA) which has more than 300 World Trade Centers in 89 countries. Established as a non-profit organization in 1970, the WTCA promotes international business relationships through a network of members worldwide. These centers offer referrals, contacts, and information for businesses. A local chamber of commerce in a metropolitan area pays a licensing fee to join the WTCA.

Another good source of information is a chamber of commerce. Being well informed on local business, this organization is capable of providing helpful advice. In addition to a chamber of commerce at the national level (e.g., the U.S. Chamber of Commerce), local chambers of commerce are often some of the best sources of information on trade and industry in specific localities (e.g., cities). Larger organizations may publish classified buyers' guides, manufacturers' guides, or lists of international traders in their areas. Finally, foreign chambers of commerce are in a position to provide a great deal of relevant information about their countries because they act as public relations offices.

Concerning country information, Dun's Marketing Services offers *Exporter's Encyclopaedia*, which provides comprehensive country-by-country information for over 200 markets. Several large accounting firms also publish their own country-by-country books.

## Public sources

Public sources of market information are numerous. Foreign governments, their embassies and consulates, and trade promotion agencies either have the information desired or are in a position to guide the marketer to the proper source of information (see Figure 8.1). Germany, for example, has the Society for Information and Documentation, which promotes development of information science and exchanges scientific and technical data with other countries. France's Center for Information and Documentation offers services similar to those provided by U.S. information brokers. Furthermore, regional and international organizations, such as the World Bank, the OECD, and the IMF, routinely collect information on population and a nation's financial circumstances.

The World Bank and its affiliates offer a number of publications. As in the case of its *Global Development Finance*, it allows users to: (1) generate market analysis, forecasts, and comparisons, (2) examine current trends and assess their impact on investment opportunities, (3) develop investment strategies, and (4) analyze the investment risks associated with specific emerging markets. The World Bank has launched the Country Analytic Work Website to enable multilateral agencies to share information. Both the donor agencies and their clients, through the website, can use development resources more efficiently while avoiding duplication.

One relatively new report is *Doing Business*. Prepared by the International Finance Corporation of the World Bank, the report ranks 175 economies in terms of the ease of doing business. The 2007 report examines 213 reforms in over 100 economies and highlights best practices for governments.[1]

The Organization for Economic Cooperation and Development (OECD) is the international organization of the industrialized, market economy countries of Western Europe, North America, and Asia. At OECD headquarters in Paris, it regularly gathers statistical information on the foreign trade of its member countries and makes the statistics internationally comparable by converting the information into uniform units. The OECD Secretariat compiles economic data and policy information, formulates forecasts, and provides analytical work to support the work of government representatives.

The IMF has worldwide information-gathering resources. The IMF's research activities rely on the expertise of its more than 1,100 economists who conduct a wide range of financial and monetary studies. Based on these studies, the IMF publishes the *Occasional Papers* and *Economic and Financial Surveys* series, both of which are proven references. *Occasional Papers* are studies on economic and financial subjects of importance to the world economy. *World Economic and Financial Surveys* series, in contrast, are special topic studies, and the core of the series is derived from *World Economic Outlook*. Twice a year, the IMF prepares *World Economic Outlook* which is a comprehensive assessment of each country's economic situation and prospects. In May, *World Economic Outlook* examines what is happening and what is likely to happen in various countries; in October, it provides updated projections, showing the impact of key developments. In addition, the IMF's *Staff Country Reports* cover a variety of topics on economic developments in individual member countries. Each in-depth report includes an overview, economic and financial data, analysis of trends, factors to consider in forecasting, comparative charts and graphs, and tabular presentations with interpretive comments. Because the IMF's projections affect the decisions of the IMF and its member countries, the IMF's research is based on the latest facts and figures.

The World Trade Organization (WTO) has several resources for global trade statistics. Its website provides selected statistics on trade in merchandise and services at world and regional levels, developments in major product categories, and historical developments in international trade at the aggregate level. Its trilingual (English, French, and Spanish) CD-ROM contains statistical reports.

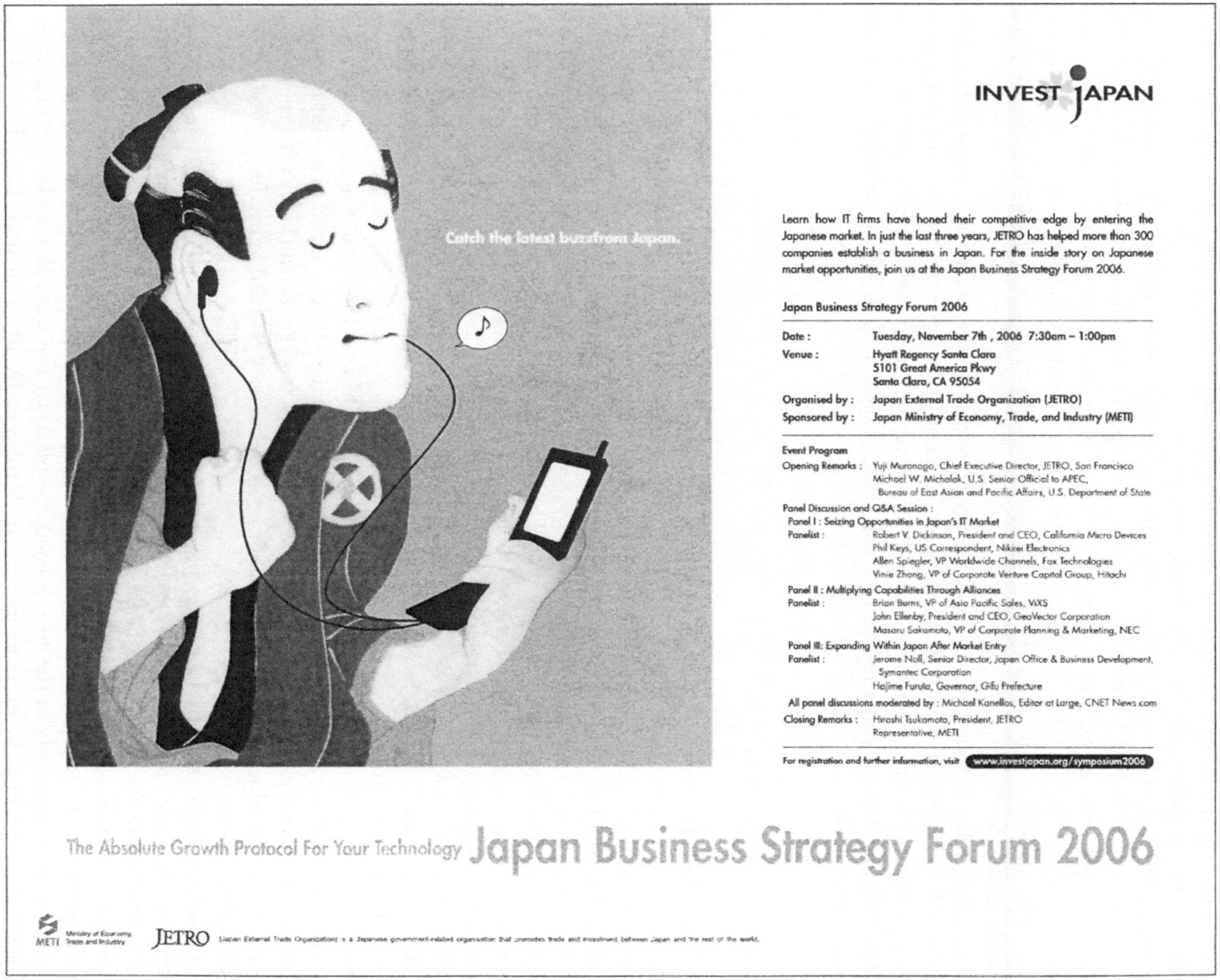
Catch the latest buzz from Japan.
INVEST JAPAN
Learn how IT firms have honed their competitive edge by entering the Japanese market. In just the last three years, JETRO has helped more than 300 companies establish a business in Japan. For the inside story on Japanese market opportunities, join us at the Japan Business Strategy Forum 2006.
Japan Business Strategy Forum 2006
Date : Tuesday, November 7th , 2006 7:30am – 1:00pm
Venue : Hyatt Regency Santa Clara
5101 Great America Pkwy
Santa Clara, CA 95054
Organised by : Japan External Trade Organization (JETRO)
Sponsored by : Japan Ministry of Economy, Trade, and Industry (METI)
Event Program
Opening Remarks : Yuji Muranago, Chief Executive Director, JETRO, San Francisco
Michael W. Michalak, U.S. Senior Official to APEC,
Bureau of East Asian and Pacific Affairs, U.S. Department of State
Panel Discussion and Q&A Session :
Panel I : Seizing Opportunities in Japan's IT Market
Panelist : Robert V. Dickinson, President and CEO, California Micro Devices
Phil Keys, US Correspondent, Nikkei Electronics
Allen Spiegler, VP Worldwide Channels, Fox Technologies
Vinie Zhang, VP of Corporate Venture Capital Group, Hitachi
Panel II : Multiplying Capabilities Through Alliances
Panelist : Brian Burns, VP of Asia Pacific Sales, VIXS
John Ellenby, President and CEO, GeoVector Corporation
Masaru Sakamoto, VP of Corporate Planning & Marketing, NEC
Panel III: Expanding Within Japan After Market Entry
Panelist : Jerome Noll, Senior Director, Japan Office & Business Development, Symantec Corporation
Hajime Furuta, Governor, Gifu Prefecture
All panel discussions moderated by : Michael Kanellos, Editor at Large, CNET News.com
Closing Remarks : Hiroshi Tsukamoto, President, JETRO
Representative, METI
For registration and further information, visit www.investjapan.org/symposium2006
The Absolute Growth Protocol For Your Technology Japan Business Strategy Forum 2006
METI Ministry of Economy, Trade and Industry
JETRO (Japan External Trade Organization) is a Japanese government-related organisation that promotes trade and investment between Japan and the rest of the world.

**FIGURE 8.1** JETRO and trade promotion

For U.S. firms, the most logical public source of information is the U.S. government and its agencies. A good starting point would be to contact the International Trade Division of the Department of Commerce. The International Trade Division maintains reference libraries in major cities where one can talk to trade experts and find statistical and trade reports for each country. At its main office in Washington, DC, there are experts assigned to cover a particular country. One U.S. company interested in selling microwave toilets to Nigeria avoided a costly mistake after being advised that what Nigeria really needed was basic sewage systems.

Getting information from the U.S. government has become easier. The federal government now offers a one-stop data site. Its firstgov.com is a one-stop site that has consolidated some 20,000 government sites and 27 million Web pages into one. One can learn about statistics, laws, and regulations. The CIA publishes the *World Factbook* that provides countries' basic statistics (e.g., demographic data) and cultural and political/legal information. The *World Factbook* may also be accessed online.

In conclusion, the U.S. government collects large amounts of relevant data that it makes available at reasonable cost. From this large database, several data products and services are produced. Many of these services differ only in terms of how the information is retrieved and packaged for sale. A marketer should thus consult the International Trade Administration before ordering too many services, some of which may turn out to be redundant.

## Primary research

When secondary data are unavailable, irrelevant, or obsolete, the marketer must then turn to primary research. One decision that must be made is whether to make or buy the information. In other words, the question to be decided is whether outside agencies such as marketing research firms should be used to collect the information needed or whether the firm should use its own personnel for this purpose.

A list of international marketing research firms may be found in the U.S. Department of Commerce's *Trade List: Market Research Organizations Worldwide*, the American Marketing Association's *International Directory of Marketing Research Houses and Services* (Green Book), and *Bradford's Directory of Marketing Research Agencies and Management Consultants in the United States and the World*. Figures 8.2 and 8.3 show that marketing research firms can help marketers obtain marketing data in Japan.

If outside personnel are to be used, the company should make a distinction among various types of information brokers who differ in terms of the extent to which value is added to the information delivered. Some merely retrieve printed materials ordered by their clients who know what they want. Other brokers add value by locating information sources and may proceed to conduct interviews on behalf of their clients.

If a marketer decides to conduct his or her own research without hiring outside consultants or researchers, there are many alternatives available to collect primary information. First, the marketer should subscribe to the newspapers in the competitor's home country. These newspapers should include the local language papers and dailies with large circulations. Even a newspaper in a small town near the potential market area is useful, because that paper is likely to cover the news concerning a major company or employer in the area. Second, the marketer can learn about a foreign market by personally visiting it or by being a member of a trade mission. By attending trade fairs, the marketer

The Japanese market isn't closed
If you have the key.
And that key is information.
Accurate, complete, up-to-date information from A&S • MRS, the leading market research company in Japan.
Try our All-Japan Retail Store Audit, for instance. If you want to tap Japan's growing market for imported food products and household goods, we'll give you the latest data on sales, inventories, and prices. Our professional staff of 1,200 auditors regularly surveys over 6,500 grocery stores and supermarkets throughout Japan.
Or if you need to know more about Japanese consumers, we'll design and run a comprehensive survey of their attitudes, shopping habits, and advertising awareness. We have over 800 well-trained interviewers ready to get the information you need.
Or if you aren't sure which way to go, we'll design a research package that's tailored precisely to your goals. Each of our research managers is an expert at assessing your requirements and providing incisive, practical anaylses.
A&S • MRS is a joint venture of Audits & Surveys, the largest privately-held research company in the United States, and Market Research Service, the oldest and most experienced market research firm in Japan. And our extensive coverage of the Japanese market is just the beginning. We can also open doors to markets in South Korea, Thailand, the Philippines, Singapore and Australia. In fact, we cover the entire Pacific basin.
So if you are feeling locked out, contact A&S • MRS,
We'll help you find the key.
For more information about what A&S • MRS can do for you, send us a letter by mail or fax.
A&S • MRS Co., Ltd.
2-2-3 Irifune, Chuo-ku, Tokyo 104, Japan
Fax 81-3-552-0743 Telephone 81-3-553-8461

SUCCESS BREEDS SUCCESS
For over 25 years we at ASI-Japan have taken pride in helping our clients to grow, because their successes have contributed to ours. We have seen their families of new products and services—many from other countries —take root in Japan and prosper.
Our team of professionals is committed to working with yours to develop the Japanese marketplace for you. Our quarter century of bilingual and bi-cultural experience in market research in Japan, as well as the hands-on business experience of many of our Japanese and non-Japanese professionals, have aided hundreds of multinational companies in succeeding in Japan.
From idea generation to rollout, from trend analysis to expansion of your existing markets—whether you are new to this market or already well-established, ASI-Japan can be your partner in growth.
For more information call George Fields, Chairman, (03) 3432-3737 or Jim Conte, Executive Vice President, (03) 3432-2288, or send for the ASI-Japan capabilities brochure.
A member of the AGB International plc group
ASI MARKET RESEARCH (JAPAN), INC.
Yoneda Building, 17-20, Shimbashi 6-chome, Minato-ku, Tokyo 105, Japan
Tel: (03) 3432-1701, Fax: (03) 3433-3394

**FIGURES 8.2 and 8.3** Marketing research in Japan

*Source*: Courtesy of A&S MRS Co., Ltd and ASI Market Research (Japan), Inc.

can observe competitors' display booths and have the opportunity to talk with potential customers and distributors.

A company should make an attempt to determine the effectiveness of the planned marketing mix. Some type of *experimental study* may be necessary to determine a cause-and-effect relationship. One type of field experimentation is test marketing. This technique may be used to test a planned national marketing program for a new product in a limited geographic area. A good test market should possess the following characteristics: (1) representativeness, (2) self-contained media, and (3) self-contained trading area.

The concern about representativeness involves demographic comparability. The test market should be demographically similar to the country of which it is part and its population should portray the country's typical characteristics. This market should be large enough to provide meaningful data and yet not be so large as to make the costs of the study prohibitive.

The market should be self-contained from a media standpoint in order to avoid media spillage out of the market. If the market is not isolated in terms of media coverage, communication costs are wasted because an audience is being contacted outside of the intended market. Media should also be available at a reasonable cost. A city such as Tokyo is unsuitable for test marketing because of the exorbitant prices charged for TV time – time not at all readily available.

Finally, the test market should be self-contained in terms of trading area. This is necessary in order to avoid transshipments into and out of the area. If the city gains population during the daytime because outside people travel into the city for work or if a distributor distributes the product in other nearby cities, it is difficult to achieve accurate readings of sales because the sales figure is actually overstated. Cities such as Tokyo and New York are definitely not self-contained.

In North America, Winnipeg, the capital of the Canadian province of Manitoba, is considered a premier test market. Its fairly cosmopolitan and conservative population displays the same characteristics as a larger target audience or general market. This city is favorably isolated because the nearest urban centers are Regina, Saskatchewan, and Minneapolis, Minnesota, both of which are approximately 300 miles away. Thus, the market is controllable because its residents are not exposed to conflicting or competing information from outside sources. In terms of media, Winnipeg has its own newspapers and TV stations; their easy access eliminates any problems related to media availability and waste. Winnipeg has been used to test several product concepts before those products were made available in the U.S. market. McDonald's first tested its chicken product in Winnipeg by combining it with french fries. Consumers, however, considered chicken to be a diet food and preferred the product without a bun or fries. Subsequently, McDonald's Chicken and Chips became Chicken McNuggets.

If certain countries are demographically and psychologically similar, a firm may use a city in one country as a test market to research market conditions in another country. As in the case of Hong Kong, it may serve as a useful test market to determine the future of the other affluent Asian markets. A product's success here may influence market development elsewhere.

While Japan in general and Tokyo in particular are significantly different from the other countries and cities, Tokyo has emerged as a significant test market. Gola, a British brand of athletic shoes and apparel, has collaborated with EuroPacific (Japan) Ltd., a retailer of fashion footwear. EuroPacific adapted Gola's designs for the Japanese market and came up with shin-high boxing boots to women. The boots were a hit with Japanese teenagers and young people. When taken to the other markets, the boots were snapped up in Europe.[2]

## Sampling

As with virtually all consumer market studies, it is neither feasible nor practical for a researcher to contact all the members of the population. What is usually done is to contact a select group of consumers considered to be representative of the entire population. This practice is known as sampling.

There are several kinds of sampling techniques, with probability and nonprobability sampling methods being the two major categories. In probability sampling, it is possible to specify in advance the chance each element in the population will have of being included in that sample, though not necessarily in equal probability for every element. In nonprobability sampling, it is not possible to determine such probability or to estimate the sampling error.

The problem of poor sampling methods is not always within the control of the researcher. An ideal sampling method, for instance, may not be practical for many reasons when used in the various markets of the world. In the U.S.A., it is possible to use virtually all types of probability and nonprobability sampling methods that closely reflect the population of a target market. The luxury of these options may not be available in other advanced countries. This problem is of a greater magnitude with sampling in developing economies.

Probability sampling methods, though theoretically superior, may be difficult to employ, and the temptation to use nonprobability methods becomes great. There are several reasons for this difficulty. A map of the country may be not available or out of date. Some cities in Saudi Arabia, for example, have no street names, and houses have no numbers. In Hong Kong, a number of people live on boats. The unavailability of block statistics thus precludes meaningful stratification. Lists of residents may be nonexistent or inaccurate. Poor people may illegally build shacks and pay their neighbors to allow illegal hookups of electricity and water – thus, even utility companies' lists may not be as accurate as they might first appear.

Poor road systems can create another problem because they preclude the use of the dispersed sample. Even when a proper location is identified, it is still difficult to identify the selected sample element. For example, if the element is a homemaker of particular housing unit, the researcher may be surprised upon arrival that that particular household has more than one homemaker. This can be a common situation in many parts of the world. The prevalence of extended families and joint tenancy makes it very easy for a housing unit to consist of several primary family units. In some countries, a husband may be a polygamist, and all of his wives may live together in the same house. In sum, while one should pay attention to sampling design, one should not be obsessed with it in light of sampling limitations in most parts of the world.

In cross-national studies, sampling procedures become even more complicated. A researcher may desire to use the same sampling method for all countries in order to maintain consistency. Theoretical desirability, however, often gives way to practicality and flexibility. Sampling procedures may need to vary across countries in order to ensure the reasonable comparability of national groups. For durable products, a random sample may work well in the U.S.A. and the European Union, but a judgmental sample based on the more upscale segment of the population may be more meaningful in a less developed country, because relatively affluent consumers there are more likely to purchase and use such products. Thus, the relevance of the sampling method depends on whether it will yield a sample that is representative of a country's population and on whether comparable samples may be obtained from the intended groups of different countries. Furthermore, a researcher may have to distinguish samples obtained from rural and urban areas because dual economies exist in many countries, resulting in rural and urban inhabitants being distinctly different.

It is quite rare for a study to simultaneously investigate some 40 or 50 countries. A researcher conducting international business research typically focuses on a few countries for comparison. Sivakumar and Nakata have proposed a methodology that aims to choose country combinations so as to strengthen hypothesis testing.[3] Using a series of algorithms, they have rank-ordered the sets of countries by their power in hypothesis testing. Their tables eliminate judgmental or ad hoc selection so that a sample can be better justified in terms of methodological rigor. Still, in the end, practical considerations must also be given to access to field sites, availability of research collaboration, and non-culture variables to be studied.

The experience of Honda demonstrates why it is critical to have an appropriate sample. Honda initially pushed to recycle a platform developed in Japan for its American sport-utility vehicle (SUV), while the American team insisted on a genuine American platform. The American subsidiary wanted an "apartment on wheels" SUV to target surfers, mountain bikers, and other youthful outdoor types who could live in a vehicle while on the road. It was critical for this SUV, Acura MDX, to have American features that included a third row of seats. On the other hand, the top Japanese product development executives felt that people who needed a third row would buy a minivan instead. To overcome the resistance, the American team insisted that a top research and development Japanese executive visit Denver. There, he visited the homes of the families that drove Ford Expeditions, and observed how mothers transported their own children and those of their neighbors to soccer games. He also saw firsthand how so many families used a vehicle's third row for their dogs. Had the research been done in Japan, the Japanese executive would have missed the dog-friendly behavior of the American middle class.[4]

## Basic methods of data collection

There are two principal methods for the collection of primary data: (1) observation, and (2) the administration of survey questions. In the case of observation, respondents are visually observed, regardless of whether they realize it or not. When the survey question method is used, respondents are asked certain questions relating to their characteristics or behavior.

### *Observation*

The principal advantage of the observation method is that, on a theoretical basis, it is supposed to be more objective than the use of survey questions. When using observation, a researcher does not have to depend on what respondents say or are willing to say. Another reason the observation method tends to yield more objective information lies in the fact that there is no influence exerted by an interviewer, regardless of whether such influence would be real or imagined by respondents. The lack of social interaction eliminates the possibility of influencing the respondent.

Individuals are usually reluctant to discuss personal habits or consumption, and observation avoids this problem. In the Middle East, Latin America, and Asia, interviewers are suspected of being tax investigators in disguise, making it difficult to obtain data about income and purchases. The degree of openness in a society may also vary. Because of the effectiveness of the observation technique, Edward T. Hall, an internationally known anthropologist, has replaced listening and asking with watching.

Toyota and its U.S. subsidiaries often disagree on the design choices for the U.S. market, and the disagreements range from major product strategy decisions to minor ones such as interior color schemes. In the late 1990s, Toyota's Japanese product planners did not endorse the idea of their American counterparts to build a V8 pickup truck. As a result, the American executives took the Japanese colleagues to a Dallas Cowboys football game. To their surprise, the Japanese saw rows of full-size pickup trucks at the Texas Stadium parking lot. They quickly realized that, to many Americans, a pickup was more than just a commercial vehicle but that it was considered to be primary transportation as well. Thus, the successful Toyota Tundra was born.[5]

Ethnography has gained popularity in the area of consumer research. By observing what people do at the place where they live and work, marketers may learn about consumers' unarticulated desires. As in the case of Motorola, it observed the popularity of Chinese character text messaging in Shanghai. Subsequently, the Motorola A732 was developed, and this mobile phone allows a user to send messages by using a finger to write directly on the keypad.[6]

There are conflicting opinions about the kinds of personnel that should be involved in direct observation. Some contend that local observers should be used due to their familiarity and understanding of the local culture. Others, on the other hand, believe that familiarity breeds carelessness. Local observers, by being familiar with local events, tend to take those occurrences for granted. Consequently, essential and rich detail may be left out of a report. For example, a local observer may fail to notice that students wear school uniforms if that is a common local practice. The failure to include this piece of information may be quite critical for an American firm wanting to sell clothing to schoolchildren. If an American observer were used in the same way, it would be unlikely that such information would be missing, since school uniforms are the exception in the U.S.A. Of course, the situation can also be reversed. An American observer may see nothing unusual about students wearing blue jeans to school, but this kind of behavior might be very conspicuous to a non-American observer.

Whereas familiarity may result in some details being left out, lack of familiarity may lead an inexperienced observer to draw a wrong conclusion. An American observer seeing two foreign males holding hands could draw a hasty conclusion that these men must be homosexual. But this conclusion could be based on an ignorance of the local culture. In many countries, there is nothing sexual or unusual about friends of the same sex holding hands. In such countries, what is unusual is for members of the opposite sex to hold hands in public.

The only safe conclusion that can be made about observers is that there is no substitute for careful training. Observers must be explicitly instructed about what they are supposed to notice. Training and practice are necessary if desired details are to be systematically noted and recorded. If bias cannot be completely eliminated through training, it may be necessary to use observers of various backgrounds to cover each other's blind spots.

Clearly, no company can learn about the competition by interviewing competitors. This is one situation where the observation technique can prove useful in gathering information. One common method used to gather data involves such traditional sources as media and business indexes. A marketer can learn about competitors by reading newspaper or magazine stories about those companies. A former competitive-intelligence executive at Visa International often scanned advertisements and news clippings about rivals, trying to search for some hidden patterns that might yield a clue as to their strategies.[7]

Problems with such media sources are that stories appearing in the print media may be too general and that standard business sources are often out of date. Furthermore, print media may not provide information on competitors' plant operations, capacity, sales force, management structure, and distribution.

The gathering of commercial intelligence needs to take into account the legal and ethical implications (see Ethical Dimension 8.1). Oracle created a controversy in 2000 because its detectives rummaged through a pro-Microsoft organization's trash. Likewise, Procter & Gamble was forced to admit that its employees hired investigators to go through Unilever's trash for shampoo secrets.

## Ethical Dimension 8.1

### I spy – for money

According to the American Society for Industrial Security (ASIS), in 1997, there were more than 1,100 documented incidents of economic espionage and 550 suspected incidents that could not be fully documented. American companies lost $25 billion in 1995 as a result of economic espionage. The loss jumped to $1 trillion in 2000. The highly prized information includes research and development strategies, manufacturing and marketing plans, and customer lists.

The CIA has reported that intelligence services of several countries (including some close U.S. allies) are active in stealing U.S. proprietary economic information, company trade secrets, and critical technologies. Japan, the United Kingdom, South Korea, Taiwan, China, and France have been known to target the U.S.A. for industrial spying.

The French, in particular, are notorious for their active industrial espionage. Their tactics include: (1) steering U.S. defense officials and business executives to bugged Air France seats as well as bugged Paris hotel rooms, (2) tapping French phone lines to obtain contract bids and new product designs faxed to France by American companies, (3) placing moles in U.S. computer firms in Paris and Silicon Valley to pass along breakthrough technology, (4) stealing garbage in Houston in search of industrial secrets, (5) posing as nondefense customers to obtain classified U.S. "stealth" technology for France's aerospace industry, and (6) recruiting French people employed by the U.S. Embassy in Paris to spy on visiting American VIPs.

There are other techniques that are probably legal but not necessarily ethical. Industrial spies can attend trade shows and talk to their clients' competitors. One technologist regularly attends scientific conferences. When technical experts present their papers, she is able to learn about a competitor's new product development.

To protect the security of the high-technology industry, the U.S. Congress passed the Economic Espionage Act of 1996. As a result, theft of trade secrets is a federal crime. Foreign economic spies, if caught, face penalties as high as 25 years in jail and $10 million in fines. It is not easy to implement the law, however, because criminal intent must be proven.

What can be done to minimize a company's vulnerability? Precautions must be taken when a person possessing valuable information is on the move. That is when proprietary information is most vulnerable. Executives must also carefully weigh the costs and benefits of employing foreign nationals. In addition, they must sensitize their employees to the possible consequences of leaking information. After all, the ultimate cost is a loss of jobs if the company loses markets.

*Sources*: French Techno-spies Bugging U.S. Industries," *San José Mercury News*, October 21, 1992; John J. Fialka, *War by Others Means*, Norton, 1999; "Attention, Business Travelers: You May Be Targeted by Spies," *San José Mercury News*, March 12, 2000; and "Foreign Spies in High Tech Hard to Catch," *San José Mercury News*, February 11, 2001.

## Questioning

Survey questions may be used more frequently than observation due to speed and cost. With questioning, data can be collected quickly and at a minimum cost because the researcher does not have to spend idle time waiting for an event to happen to be observed. The survey question method is also quite versatile, because it may be used to explore virtually all types of marketing problems. Survey questions can be employed to acquire information on the past, present, and future. They are even useful to learn about a consumer's internal workings – such as motives and attitudes – that are not observable.

Traditionally, there are three basic ways of administering questions: personal interview, telephone interview, and mail questionnaire. The Internet has recently become another viable mode of inquiry. The popularity of each questioning mode varies from country to country. In many developing countries, telephone and mail surveys are impractical for a variety of reasons. Although personal, door-to-door, in-home interviews are the dominant mode for gathering research data in Great Britain and Switzerland, central location/street interviews are the dominant technique in France. While telephone interviews are quite popular in the U.S.A., face-to-face interviews account for 77 percent of all interviews conducted in Portugal. In the Nordic countries where the education level is very high, mail interviews are common.[8]

When the **personal interview** is used, an interviewer must know and understand the local language. This imperative can present a problem in a country such as India, where there are 14 official languages. In addition, a great deal of personal and social interaction occurs in a personal interview, and the appearance of the interviewer must thus be taken into account. If an interviewer is dressed too well, farmers and villagers may be intimidated and may claim to use expensive products just to impress the interviewer.

Personal interview style and technique may need to be adjusted from country to country. A researcher will not be able to ask too many questions in Hong Kong. People there, who are constantly in a hurry, will not tolerate lengthy interviews.

**Telephone interviews** pose a special challenge for international researchers. State-run telephone monopolies are usually associated with poor service, and it is therefore difficult and at times impossible to conduct a telephone survey. It is exceedingly difficult for residents in many countries to receive their own telephone lines – something Americans have always taken for granted. Consumers in other countries may have to pay several hundred dollars for the privilege of being put on a waiting list in the hope that new telephone lines and numbers become available. Often, a person will wait several years before eventually receiving a telephone. Interestingly, when Led Zeppelin's Jimmy Page visited the U.S.A. in the late 1960s, one thing that impressed him greatly was that, unlike at home, telephones worked in the U.S.A.[9]

Assuming that private telephones are available, there remain several problems associated with a telephone interview. First, some cities do not have telephone books. Second, foreign telephone owners are much more likely than their Western counterparts to be members of the educated and higher income groups, making them untypical of the larger population. Finally, telephone conversational habits can be vastly different, and an interviewer may experience great difficulty in obtaining information over the telephone. Some people may be reluctant to give any information over the telephone to an unknown person.

Cellular phones may be significantly changing the face of interviews. The number of mobile phones has exploded all over the world. Phone ownership is now within reach of people of all social strata. In Japan, the number of mobile phones exceeds the number of fixed telephones. In Russia, mobile phone ownership has skyrocketed from 3 million in 2000 to 80 million in 2006.[10] In the context of a telephone interview, mobile phone owners are not likely to grant interviews in a public place. On the other hand, a short interview via text messaging is a possibility.

The **mail questionnaire** is a popular survey method due to its low cost and high degree of standardization. Despite these advantages, its effectiveness is contingent on the country in which it is used. Unilever, for instance, will not use the mail questionnaire in Italy.

One problem involves the scarcity of good mailing lists. No population is as mobile as the U.S. population, but people in most countries generally do not bother to report their new address, not even for the purpose of mail forwarding. As a result, a government's list based on the census report and household registration is, as a rule, woefully out of date.

Another problem is illiteracy. Without doubt, this is a significant problem in many less developed countries, but the U.S.A. is hardly immune to this problem. Lack of familiarity with the mailed survey question method should be given careful consideration, because many people are not used to responding by mail. This may be due in part to the low volume of mail received outside of the U.S.A. Finally, poor postal service, especially in rural areas, is a cause for complaint in most parts of the world.

The website of ESOMAR (European Society for Opinion and Market Research) provides tips on nuances to consider when conducting business research overseas. The site offers a guide to opinion polls. There are guidelines on tape and video recording, interviewing children, mystery shopping, and pharmaceutical marketing research.[11]

## Measurement

The best research design and the best sample are useless without proper measurements. A measuring method or instrument that works quite satisfactorily in one culture may fail to achieve the intended purpose in another country. Special care must therefore be taken if the reliability and validity of the measurement are to be ensured. Questions and scales must be assessed in order to make certain that they perform the function properly.

A measuring instrument exhibits **reliability** when it yields the same result repeatedly, assuming no change in the object being measured. As an example, if a person steps on to a weighing scale five times and gets five different results, then certainly something is wrong with the scale, because the person's weight does not change appreciably within a short span of time.

The same reliability problem applies to international marketing research. An English-language questionnaire, when used within foreign markets, increases the chance that misinterpretation, misunderstanding, and administration variation will occur. Respondents' inconsistent answers are likely to be an indicator of the possible unreliability of the instrument.

**Validity** is an indication of whether a measuring instrument is able to measure what it purports to measure (i.e., whether the measure reflects an accurate representation of the object being measured). A thermometer has been universally accepted as being a valid instrument for measuring temperature, but its validity must be seriously questioned if it is used to measure something else, such as the length of a room or the amount of rainfall.

Reliability is a prerequisite for the existence of validity. If an instrument is not reliable, there are no circumstances under which it can be valid. Reliability, although a necessary condition for validity, is not a sufficient condition. Just because an instrument is reliable, the instrument is not automatically valid.

Craig and Douglas define equivalence as "data that have, as far as possible, the same meaning or interpretation, and the same level of accuracy, precision of measurement, or reliability in all countries and cultures."[12] There are three aspects of measurement equivalence: translation equivalence, calibration equivalence (with regard to units of measurement), and metric equivalence (with regard to the specific scale or scoring procedure). Most studies appear to fail to take adequate measures to ensure data equivalence.[13]

Linguistic and conceptual nonequivalencies in questionnaire instruments that are used in cross-national surveys could conceivably operate to produce differences in the reliabilities of measurements, thus affecting the validity of conclusions drawn about market similarities or differences. The occurrence of reliability differentials in cross-national samples varies according to the type of variable. Data equivalence cannot be addressed without reference to theory.[14]

International marketing research often necessitates some measurement adaptation to overcome the problems of reliability and validity. The remainder of this section on measurement is devoted to the problems and adjustments of measurement in terms of conceptual equivalence, instrument equivalence, linguistic equivalence (translation), response style, measurement timing, and external validity.

## *Conceptual equivalence*

**Conceptual equivalence** is concerned with whether a particular concept of interest is interpreted and understood in the same manner by people in various cultures. Such concepts as hunger and family welfare are universally understood and pose few problems. Other concepts, however, are culturally specific. The concept of dating between the sexes, which is taken for granted by Americans, is incomprehensible to citizens of countries where the arranged marriage is the norm and where a man can see a member of the opposite sex only in the presence of her family or a chaperon. Culture-specific concepts such as these can have implications for marketers. For example, Pizza Hut initially found that it could not conduct marketing research in Thailand because Thai consumers at the time did not know what a pizza was.

Demographics, in spite of being apparent and easily understood, should not be readily embraced in terms of conceptual equivalence without an examination of the varying frames of reference. A demographic variable such as sex is universal, and a question of this nature may be used in a cross-cultural study. Age, on the other hand, is not always considered in the same way – the Chinese include the time during pregnancy in their age. Educational level, likewise, does not have the same meaning everywhere. The meaning of primary school, grade school, secondary school, high school, college, and university varies greatly. A primary school may range from four years to eight years, depending on the country. In some countries, a college may be nothing more than a vocational school. A college education in one country may in no way be equivalent to that in another. It is thus wise in many instances to ask about the number of years of schooling attended by the respondent.

Let us consider the measurement of poverty. The measurement process usually has three steps: (1) choosing an indicator of individual economic welfare (which tends to be household expenditure or income over a certain period, adjusted for differences in household size and cost of living), (2) setting a poverty line (that defines the level of welfare deemed necessary for an individual to escape poverty), and (3) identifying an aggregate poverty measure (one that summarizes the information from the first two steps).[15]

These three steps are anything but easy because the process contains a number of contentious issues. There are several conceptual difficulties associated with each step. In the case of the household welfare indicator, the disputes include such issues as: should the indicator be consumption or income, what should each one include, and should it consider cost-of-living differences? Regarding the poverty line, at what overall level should it be set, and should the level vary in real terms by subgroup or date? Finally, with regard to the aggregate poverty measure, how should it treat inequality among the poor? One has to wonder whether economists are well equipped to answer these questions or whether behavioral scientists (e.g., psychologists) can do a better job by focusing on individuals' perceptions of their well-being.

The measurement issues and debates mentioned above play an important role in the debate over globalization's impact on poverty and inequality. While some point out that the proportion of people living in extreme poverty in the developing world fell sharply in the 1990s, others argue that globalization has created greater poverty. Some contend that income equality has been rising in the world, whereas others argue the opposite. Such conflicting claims stem not only from differences in data and methods used but also from the important conceptual distinctions previously discussed. The opposing positions of pro-globalizers and anti-globalizers represent a question of interpretation.

One kind of conceptual equivalence a researcher should pay close attention to is **functional equivalence**. A particular object may perform varying functions or may satisfy different needs in different countries. A bicycle is a recreation device in some countries and a basic transportation device in others. Antifreeze is used to prevent freezing of engine coolant in cold countries but to prevent overheating in countries with warm climates. A hot milk-based drink is perceived as having restful, relaxing, and sleep-inducing properties in the United Kingdom; Thai consumers, in contrast, view the same drink as stimulating, energy-giving, and invigorating. Thais consume hot milk as either a substitute for or a supplement to breakfast. Therefore, a valid comparison requires the use behavior to have been developed in response to similar problems in different cultures. Use differences must be built into the measuring instrument if meaningless results are to be avoided.

**Definitional** or **classification equivalence** is another type of conceptual equivalence that requires careful treatment. This factor involves the way in which an object is defined or categorized – either perceptually by consumers or officially by law or government agencies. In addition, even demographic characteristics are subject to the problem of definitional or classification equivalence. Age is one such example. Persons in the same age group in different countries are not necessarily at the same stage of life or family life. The age at which a boy becomes a man or a legal adult depends on the definition used by a particular country. The age of legal adulthood may vary anywhere from the very early teens to 21 years. In India, a "boy" of only 13 or 14 years of age could at one time legally marry a girl who was a few years younger. As a result, chronologically identical age groups within two or more countries do not necessarily lead to comparable equivalent groups. It is thus not possible to standardize age groupings and have the same definitional or classification equivalence on an international basis.

## *Instrument equivalence*

In devising and using a measure, a researcher should distinguish between two kinds of measuring instruments: emic and etic. **Emic instruments** are tests constructed to study a phenomenon within one culture only. **Etic instruments**, on the other hand, are those that are "culture universal" or "culture independent." As such, when properly translated, etic measuring instruments may be used in other cultures.

It is important to note that about 80 percent of cross-cultural organizational studies use an etic approach.[16] Far too many studies have failed to address weaknesses of their analytical techniques. The most glaring problem has to do with researchers' inadequate assessment of the psychometric integrity of their measurement models, lack of cross-cultural equivalence in measures, and reliance on items without adequate measurement efforts.[17] Researchers and practitioners, when studying cross-cultural differences, need to be aware that distribution of scores obtained in various countries should not be interpreted at face value.[18]

Conceivably, the reliability and validity of an instrument may even vary when used with different groups of audience in the same country. One research utilized the NATID (national identity) scale in Russia to compare two age cohorts (Soviet Russians and contemporary Russians). Soviet Russians reached their "age of socialization" before the breakup of the Soviet Union. The scale consists of the following components: national heritage, cultural homogeneity, belief system, and consumer ethnocentrism. These components and overall national identity are likely to vary in strength across groups in the same country.[19]

It is a good idea to determine whether a measuring instrument provides measurement equivalence when it is used for cross-national research. Lages and Lages have developed the STEP (short-term export performance) scale. The scale captures three dimensions of managerial judgment: (1) satisfaction with short-term performance improvement, (2) short-term exporting intensity improvement, and (3) expected short-term performance improvement. Based on a cross-national survey of exporting firms, the scale appears to have reliability and validity.[20] A study of customer satisfaction in four cultures was conducted to examine the equivalence of measurement. The measurement of satisfaction in four culturally divergent contexts showed more similarities than differences across cultures. Therefore, it should be possible to construct a measuring instrument that allows comparison of consumer satisfaction across cultures and languages.[21]

A measuring instrument should be evaluated in terms of its international suitability. Let us consider the CETSCALE instrument which is used to measure consumer ethnocentrism (see Table 8.1). Consumers who are ethnocentric do not like to purchase foreign products because such purchases are unpatriotic and hurt the domestic economy and employment. The instrument was originally validated with samples of American consumers only. Subsequently, the instrument was applied to samples from France, Japan, Germany, and the U.S.A. The CETSCALE was found to be a reliable measure across the four countries. It also has some degree of validity as evidenced by the consistent pattern of correlations across each country's sample.[22]

An investigation of product country images, lifestyles, and ethnocentric behaviors of Turkish consumers detected the robustness of the CETSCALE, thus lending further support to the earlier studies which were conducted in Western countries.[23] Another study investigated whether the CETSCALE could be used as a measure of consumer ethnocentricism on an international basis. In order to assess the instrument's reliability and validity in as many countries and different conditions as possible, the study focused on Spanish consumers' ethnocentric tendencies. The findings indicated that the scale measured a unidimensional construct and that the degree of measurement error was quite acceptable.[24]

One approach to establishing equivalence is the psychometric approach to test characteristics of parameters in measurement models for invariance across countries.[25] Assessing the reliability and validity of the CETSCALE, one study found a consistent pattern of support for the CETSCALE across eight samples from six countries. The scale may thus be used in transitional economies such as China and Russia.[26]

**TABLE 8.1** CETSCALE. 17-item CETSCALE[1]

| | *Item* | *Reliability*[2] |
|---|---|---|
| 1 | American people should always buy American-made products instead of imports. | 0.65 |
| 2 | Only those products that are unavailable in the U.S.A. should be imported. | 0.63 |
| 3 | Buy American-made products. Keep America working. | 0.51 |
| 4 | American products, first, last, and foremost. | 0.65 |
| 5 | Purchasing foreign-made products is unAmerican. | 0.64 |
| 6 | It is not right to purchase foreign products, because it puts Americans out of jobs. | 0.72 |
| 7 | A real American should always buy American-made products. | 0.70 |
| 8 | We should purchase products manufactured in America instead of letting other countries get rich off us. | 0.67 |
| 9 | It is always best to purchase American products. | 0.59 |
| 10 | There should be very little trading or purchasing of goods from other countries unless out of necessity. | 0.53 |
| 11 | Americans should not buy foreign products, because this hurts American business and causes unemployment. | 0.67 |
| 12 | Curbs should be put on all imports. | 0.52 |
| 13 | It may cost me in the long-run but I prefer to support American products. | 0.55 |
| 14 | Foreigners should not be allowed to put their products on our markets. | 0.52 |
| 15 | Foreign products should be taxed heavily to reduce their entry into the U.S.A. | 0.58 |
| 16 | We should buy from foreign countries only those products that we cannot obtain within our own country. | 0.60 |
| 17 | American consumers who purchase products made in other countries are responsible for putting their fellow Americans out of work. | 0.65 |

*Notes*

1 Response format is 7-point Likert-type scale (strongly agree = 7, strongly disagree = 1). Range of scores is from 17 to 119.

2 Calculated from confirmatory factor analysis of data from four-areas study.

*Source*: Terence A. Shimp and Subhash Sharma, "Consumer Ethnocentrism: Construction and Validation of the CETSCALE," *Journal of Marketing Research* 24 (August 1987, 282).

## *Measurement scales*

In consumer research, the most popular rating scales are the Likert scale and the semantic differential scale. When a **Likert scale** is employed, a respondent is asked to respond by indicating agreement (or disagreement) and the relative intensity of such an agreement to each item or question (see Exhibit 8.2). The degree of agreement (or disagreement) usually ranges from "strongly agree" to "strongly disagree."

The **semantic differential scale** measures the meaning of an object to a respondent who is asked to rate that concept on a series of bipolar rating scales (i.e., the extremes of each scale employ adjectives of opposite meanings).

Exhibit 8.2

**Likert scale: service encounter**

Construct and scale items (9-point scale from strongly disagree to strongly agree)

**Physical good quality**

1 They have excellent products.
2 They have an excellent variety of products.
3 Their products are among the best.

**Service quality**

4 Their employees offer the personal attention I need from them.
5 The behavior of their employees instills confidence in me.
6 Their employees are courteous.
7 I receive enough individual attention from their employees.

**Servicescape**

8 They have attractive facilities.
9 The layout of their facilities makes it easy to use them.
10 Their facilities are comfortable.

**Behavioral intentions**

11 If asked, I would say good things about their organization.
12 I would recommend their organization to a friend.

*Source*: Adapted from Bruce D. Keillor, G. Tomas M. Hult, and Destan Kandemir, "A Study of the Service Encounter in Eight Countries," *Journal of International Marketing* (No. 1, 2004): 9–35.

A researcher must keep in mind that the Likert and semantic differential scales, though proven to be satisfactory in measuring behavior and opinion in the U.S.A., may not be understood or may not elicit the same manner of response in other markets. These scales may have emic (culture-bound) properties and should be treated as culture-specific instruments until proven otherwise.

The nature of the measurement scale can affect responses. Asking whether a particular object is a 10 on a scale of 1 to 10 may be meaningful to American respondents but may not be understood by respondents in most other countries, where this rating scheme is uncommon. It is imperative that scales be tailor-made and carefully tested in each culture in terms of relevance and appropriateness.

One issue that may pose a problem is whether a scale should be in balance. A balanced scale is one that has the same number of choices for the positive as well as for the negative side of the scale. Should scales have a positive or negative skew? It is possible that people in certain cultures may tend to rate positively. As such, should a researcher offer a larger number of alternatives among the positive categories to achieve discrimination?

Another issue related to rating scales is the number of choices (possible answers) provided with each question. A 7-point scale, for example, may not yield more information than a 5-point scale in the U.S.A., but the former may prove useful elsewhere. In general, a higher point scale is needed when a group is relatively homogeneous, since more information is required to distinguish among members of the group.

According to one study, the three-category scales were more equivalent than the five-category scales. This finding raises several interesting questions. "Do scales with fewer categories pose fewer equivalence problems? Is it more difficult to systematically bias scales with fewer categories because choices are constrained? If so, it would create a tradeoff between designing items to capture variance more accurately and designing items less susceptible to response bias."[27]

**Content validity** should be routinely examined. Content validity is critical when a measuring instrument developed for one population is going to be used with another population. A test has content validity when it consists of items or questions judged to be representative of the specified universe of content. A test to measure the spelling ability of fifth-grade students should consist of words which students at that level of education are supposed to have learned. If a test were to contain a relatively large number of sports terms, for example, it would not have content validity because it would be unfair to those not interested in sports. One researcher has constructed a scale to measure *Guanxi* (relationship or connection), a behavior that is pervasive in China. Naturally, the items used must reflect the typical activities in Chinese society.[28]

Standardized tests, such as IQ, SAT, and GMAT tests, are somewhat controversial because of content validity or the lack of it. In the U.S.A., such tests are criticized by the poor and various ethnic minorities for being biased because the questions purportedly reflect the experience of white, middle-class Americans. The content of the IQ test, for example, may not properly represent the universe of content of the concept of intelligence. As such, the questions are not representative of the universe of content of the concept or subject interest. The problem is greatly amplified when U.S. colleges require foreign students to take these standardized tests to determine admission eligibility.

Uniformity is usually desirable, but should not be achieved at the expense of content validity. A researcher must keep in mind that some questions are culturally specific, making them difficult for foreigners, no matter how acculturated or smart they might be, to understand. A foreign language can complicate matters even more. It would be unreasonable to say that non-English-speaking children are unintelligent just because they cannot answer questions written in English.

A researcher must remember that the content validity of an instrument depends on the purpose of the study as well as on the groups of people under investigation. The universe of content can vary from group to group and from culture to culture. Standardized tests, therefore, may not necessarily work. Identical questions do not guarantee comparable data from different countries, and some variations in questions may be necessary.

## *Linguistic equivalence*

Linguistic differences can easily invalidate the results of a study. There is no question that poor translation works against sound research methodology. Particularly disadvantageous are imprecise literal translations made without regard to the intended purpose or meaning of the study. **Linguistic equivalence** must be ensured when cross-cultural studies are conducted in different languages.

The goal of linguistic equivalence requires the researcher to pay close attention to potential translation problems. According to Sekaran, translators should pay attention to idiomatic vocabulary, grammatical and syntactical differences in languages, and the experiential differences between cultures as expressed in language.[29] Vocabulary equivalence requires a translation that is equivalent to the original language in which the instrument was developed. Idiomatic equivalence becomes a problem when idioms or colloquialisms unique to one language cannot be translated properly to another. Grammatical and syntactical equivalence poses a problem when long passages must be translated. With regard to experiential equivalence, care must be taken that accurate inferences in a given statement are drawn by respondents from various cultures. As in the case of one study exploring strategic alliances in the emerging Latin American countries, the survey instrument was developed in English and was translated into Portuguese and Spanish by native speakers who were business professors. Back translation was later performed on each local language instrument until conceptual and functional equivalence was achieved.[30]

There are several translation techniques that may be used: back translation, parallel-blind translation, committee approach, random probe, and decentering.[31] With *back translation*, the research question is translated by one translator and then translated back into the source language by another translator. Any discrepancy between the first and last research questions indicates translation problems. This direct or literal translation does not address issues of conceptual equivalence, and issues of respondents' comprehension may not be addressed either.[32]

In a *parallel-blind translation*, the question is translated by several individuals independently, and their translated statements are then compared. The *committee approach* differs from the *parallel-blind* technique in the sense that the former permits committee members to discuss the research questions with one another during the translation.

A *random probe* involves placing probes at random locations in both the source and translated question during pretesting in order to ensure that respondents understand questions in the same way. In *decentering*, both the source version and target version are viewed as open to modification. If translation problems are recognized for the source document, then it should be modified to be more easily translatable. Consequently, the source question becomes more lucid and precise. For example, the statement "I am an aerobic instructor" may be changed to "I am a dance-exercise teacher."

Regardless of the method of translation, there will always be concepts that cannot be translated into certain languages or that cannot be asked in a meaningful way in certain cultures. 7Up's "uncola" slogan is an example of such a concept. Some language purists may even contend that linguistic comparability is an unattainable goal. In any case, none of the translation methods can guarantee linguistic equivalence, but the recognition of potential translation problems should at least minimize problems.

When Gillette globally launched Venus, a triple-blade razor for women, the product hit 29 countries simultaneously.[33] Since a global campaign must pay attention to local languages and requirements, a website was designed to serve as a global template for 15 regional sites. Since a package might contain as many three languages, the company set up a translation war room in London filled with designers, translators, and lawyers. Because the promotional phrases of "soft, protective cushions" and "reveal the goddess in you" carried significance nuances, the translators were required to express back the core idea in their native language. In the case of the word "goddess," Gillette chose the lower case so as to avoid a cultural or religious controversy.

## Response style

Response styles are "tendencies to respond systematically to questionnaire items on some basis other than what items were specifically designed to measure."[34] Some common response styles are: acquiescence, extreme responding, use of the middle response category on the rating scales, and socially desirable responding (see Exhibit 8.3). Such response styles, by contaminating respondents' answers to substantive questions, threaten the validity of empirical findings of both domestic and international marketing research. One large, representative sample of consumers from 11 European Union countries showed systematic effects of response styles on the scale scores as a function of two scale characteristics (proportion of reverse-scored items and extent of deviation of scale mean from the midpoint of the response scale). The correlations between the scales could be biased upward or downward depending on correlation between response style components. Furthermore, a secondary analysis of a comprehensive collection of measurement scales found that many scales failed to control adequately for response styles.

Exhibit 8.3

**Response styles**

*Acquiescence*: The tendency to agree with items regardless of content. Also called agreement tendency, yea-saying or positivity.

*Disacquiescence*: The tendency to disagree with items regardless of content. Also called disagreement tendency, nay-saying, or negativity.

*Extreme response*: The tendency to endorse the most extreme response categories regardless of content.

*Response range*: The tendency to use a narrow or wide range of response categories around the mean response.

*Midpoint*: The tendency to use the middle scale category regardless of content.

*Noncontingent*: The tendency to respond to items carelessly, randomly, or nonpurposefully.

*Source*: Adapted from Hans Baumgartner and Jan-Benedict E.M. Steenkamp, "Response Styles in Marketing Research: A Cross-national Investigation," *Journal of Marketing Research* 38 (May 2001): 145.

People from different cultures have different response styles when dealing with the same questions. Asian people, for example, are generally very polite and may avoid making negative statements about a product. In such a case, a researcher may have to employ an even-number scale (e.g., yes/no) in order to receive an objective response. The even-number scale, however, may create another problem in the sense that it may elicit an opinion that does not truly exist. A researcher may then want to consider whether to use an odd-number scale so that respondents have an option of making a neutral response.

Another issue concerning response style variation is the willingness – or lack of it – on the part of a respondent to take an extreme position, especially when such a position is not a popular one. It may thus be appropriate to adjust for respondents' extreme positions and/or response style by using "normalized" scores rather than raw scores.

More often than not, one must be sensitive to the logic of a language. English-speaking people, for example, use the words *yes* and *no* in a manner that differs from the way non-English-speaking people do. Thus, "yes" is not always "yes," and sometimes "no" may mean "yes" instead. The English and Western languages require the answer to be "yes" when the answer is affirmative. It is "no" when the answer is negative. For other languages, however, "yes" or "no" refers to whether a person's answer affirms or negates the question asked. Consider the question, "Don't you like it?" An American who does not like the item in question would say "no." But a non-Westerner would probably say "yes," indicating agreement with the question. For the non-Westerner, the statement "Yes, I don't like it" is perfectly logical. Therefore, it is a good idea to phrase questions in simple, positive terms. Questions with negatives should be avoided.

It should be noted that an interviewer is part of the measuring instrument. As such, the characteristics of the interviewer may interact with a respondent's response style. Response quality may be affected by interaction effects of respondent and interviewer gender and ethnicity. Such factors as race and gender of an interviewer may have an impact on both the quality and quantity of responses obtained.

## *Measurement timing*

A cross-national study may be conducted simultaneously, sequentially, or independently. A researcher may initially think it advantageous for a study to be conducted simultaneously in the countries of interest. But simultaneous studies in different markets may present problems of data comparability, especially due to seasonal factors. Consider a study of soft drink consumption, which is generally highest in the summer. Winter in Canada occurs when it is summer in Argentina. Simultaneous studies in such a case would yield invalid results.

**History** is a specific external event that may affect the outcome or respondent behavior within a study. Acting as an extraneous variable, history complicates cross-national studies. For example, an important election (i.e., history) held in one country and not in another may considerably affect the results of a study. Likewise, sales in the U.S.A. during the Christmas season are much higher than sales during the rest of the year, whereas sales in China and Hong Kong tend to be higher than normal during the period of the Chinese New Year.

Another complicating factor can be a product's life-cycle stage. The same product may be in different stages of its life cycle in different countries. Because of the phenomenon of an international product's life cycle, less developed countries may lag behind more advanced nations in adopting the product. The sales of the product in two or more countries for the same period may not be comparable, casting doubts on the wisdom of conducting simultaneous studies. Because of this problem, it may be better in some cases to conduct "simultaneous" studies when the countries are in the same product life-cycle stage. In addition, it may be prudent to conduct sequential studies for a particular stage in the product's life cycle when the product is not introduced at the same time in the countries of interest.

## *External validity*

There are two major types of validity: internal and external. So far this chapter has only discussed internal validity. A study is said to have **internal validity** when it accurately measures the characteristic or behavior of interest.

However, a researcher is prudent to ask whether the findings concerning a particular sample in a particular study will hold true for subjects who did not take part in the study. **External validity** is concerned with the generalization of research results to other populations. Ordinarily, there is a limit on how far research findings may be generalized. Consequently, the findings may not be applicable to other groups or populations, other products, other cities, other countries, or other cultures.

Consider the health concerns about the use of saccharin. Many studies have provided evidence for a link between saccharin and cancer. The scientific evidence has shown that saccharin is a carcinogen (cancer-causing substance) and that it may act as a cancer catalyst in the sense that it assists the carcinogen to work. Internal validity has never been much of an issue because studies have repeatedly proven that saccharin indeed causes cancer, at least in laboratory rats. Critics of this evidence have concentrated on the issue of external validity. According to the critics, producing a disease in rats is not a valid basis for predicting the effect of saccharin on humans. The U.S. Food and Drug Administration (FDA), however, has dismissed this criticism by pointing out that the analysis is not accompanied by any proof that the mechanism causing cancer in rats would be different in humans. As far as the FDA is concerned, the studies in question are both internally and externally valid. Ironically, after several decades, new evidence seems to indicate that saccharin is safe for consumption after all.

The FDA, surprisingly, has reacted conservatively when test results submitted have used foreign subjects. Although the FDA has accepted results using rats (whether American or not) as surrogates for human beings, it had long shown great reluctance in accepting foreigners as being similar to Americans in terms of the impact of drug treatment. New FDA rules now permit a drug company to submit the results of clinical studies conducted abroad to support claims of safety and efficacy. Such studies are permitted so long as they have been conducted by competent foreign researchers, can be validated, and are applicable to the U.S. population.

External validity is generally not a problem when the matter of concern is physiological in nature. The same cannot be said about psychological matters. Thus, people may have similar demographics but diverse attitudes and behavior. The behavior of one consumer group or the general behavior of the people in one country should not automatically be extended to another group or people. It may not be reasonable to assume that a study of a marketing problem in one country or the results obtained within one culture will also be applicable to a marketing problem or people in other cultures. Because of differences between cultures, the problem of external validity is amplified when marketers engage in international marketing research.

One study evaluates the applicability of the Narver and Slater market orientation scale in the context of service firms in Central Europe's transition economies.[35] The survey measures the levels of market orientation in 205 business-to-business services companies and 141 consumer services companies in Hungary, Poland, and Slovenia. The results are consistent with the prediction found in predominantly Western marketing literature, thus establishing the scale's reliability and validity. Service firms with the higher levels of market orientation are: (1) more often found in turbulent, rapidly changing markets, (2) more likely to pursue longer term market-building goals (vs. short-term efficiency objectives), (3) more likely to pursue differentiated positioning through superior levels of service, and (4) better performers on both financial and market-based criteria.

It is important to assess the generalizability of a theory or concept that is developed in a particular country. Too often, there is an implicit assumption that a theory developed in the Western region is automatically applicable elsewhere. One study investigated whether a model based on U.S. studies could be applicable in the Eastern setting of Korea. The model focuses on importers' perceptions of an exporter with regard to trust, dependence, cooperation, satisfaction, and commitment. The findings derived from 198 Korean importers provide support for the model.[36]

It has been a tempting practice for researchers to replicate a study by automatically adopting the same conceptual model, research design, and measuring instrument as used in the original work. If the instrument happens to show a reasonable degree of internal reliability, it is proclaimed that the underlying theory and measuring instrument are relevant and satisfactory. As commented by Douglas and Craig,

> a common procedure in many marketing studies is to take a conceptual model or research design used in one country (often the U.S.) and to extend or "replicate" the study in another country without consideration of the applicability or relevance of the research design in this new context. This approach assumes that the theory and constructs are universal, or "etic." It assumes that they are relevant in any other research context and not specific to the context in which they were developed.

Not much attention has been given to the appropriateness of a conceptual model or a research instrument in another setting. "There may be factors specific to a given context that affect the hypothesized relationship. Insofar as contexts may differ at both the macro and/or the micro level, their impact on the attitudes and behavior studied needs to be considered."[37] Definitely, the extent of the universality of a theoretical model and a measuring instrument that accompanies it need to be carefully assessed.

## Marketing information system

A marketing information system (MIS) is an integrated network of information designed to provide marketing managers with relevant and useful information at the right time and place for planning, decision-making, and control. As such, the MIS helps management identify opportunities, become aware of potential problems, and develop marketing plans. The MIS is an integral part of the broader management information system. For example, Benetton's stores around the world are linked by computer. When an item is sold, its color is noted. The data collected make it possible for Benetton to determine the shade and amount of fabric to be dyed each day, enabling the firm to respond to color trends very quickly.

In spite of computer and other advanced technologies, "dark-age" methods of data collection and maintenance are still prevalent. In many parts of the world, a knowledge and application of modern management systems is nonexistent. In many offices, scores of desks are crammed together in the same room. Each employee may have his or her own unique and disorganized system for filing documents and information. New employees inherit these filing and accounting systems and modify them to suit their needs. The unindexed filing system, a long-honored custom, makes each employee practically indispensable since no one knows how to find a document that has been filed by someone else.

These problems are not only confined to less developed countries. Advanced nations such as some European countries and Japan are still struggling with the automation of their information systems.

There is often a misconception that an MIS must be automated or computerized. Although many firms' systems are computerized, it is possible for a company to set up and utilize a manual system that can later be computerized if desired. With modern technology and the availability of affordable computers, it seems worthwhile for an international firm to install a computer-based information system. Yet no one should assume that the computer is a panacea for all system problems, especially if flaws are designed into the MIS. A poorly designed system, whether computerized or not, will never perform satisfactorily.

### *System development*

For the MIS to achieve its desired purpose, the system must be carefully designed and developed. Development involves the three steps of system analysis, design, and implementation. **System analysis** involves the investigation of all users' information needs. The relevant parties must be contacted to determine the kinds of information they need, when it is needed, and the suitable format through which the information is made available. Perceived value of information is the primary reason for use of export market information, while perceived quality and cost serve as indicators of value.[38] An integrative review of 27 studies focusing on the export marketing information system reveals that export information is primarily obtained on a person-to-person basis and that the information emphasizes customers, competitors, and pricing. Furthermore, the gathered information tends to be disseminated in an informal and bottom-up basis. In any case, proper utilization of the information can enhance export management decisions.[39]

Because information is not cost-free, it may not be feasible to satisfy all kinds of information needs. The benefit of the information provided must be compared with the cost of obtaining and maintaining it. Only when the benefit is greater than the cost can a particular information need be accommodated.

**System design** should be the next major consideration. System design transforms the various information requirements into one or more plans that clearly specify the procedures and programs in obtaining, recording, and analyzing marketing data. Alternative or competing plans are developed and compared, and the most suitable one is ultimately selected.

The final step comprises **system implementation**. The chosen system is installed and checked to make certain that it functions as planned. Both those who operate the system and those who use it must be trained, and their comments should be evaluated to ensure the smooth operation of the system. Even after implementation, the system should continue to be monitored and audited. In this way, management can make certain that the system serves the needs of all users properly while preventing unqualified persons from gaining access to the system. Security Pacific Bank, for example, lost $10.3 million when a consultant was able to obtain an electronics fund transfer code and use it to deposit money into his Swiss bank account.

## *Desirable characteristics*

For the MIS to be effective and efficient, it should possess certain characteristics. In general, the system should be user-oriented, systematic, expandable, comprehensive, flexible, integrated, reliable, timely, and controllable. Marketing and environmental information should be routinely received, evaluated, and continuously updated.

As implied above, certain characteristics are universal in the sense that all information systems, whether large or small and whether domestic or global, should possess them. But unlike a domestic MIS, an international marketing information system (IMIS) needs to satisfy additional criteria in order to ensure that the system can effectively serve a company's international marketing strategy. Some of these criteria are time independence, location independence, cultural and linguistic compatibility, legal compatibility, standardization/uniformity, flexibility, and integration. An IMIS should be time independent by providing round-the-clock services. Being location independent means that the system must be capable of allowing submission and use of data at the various strategic points globally. Cultural knowledge and linguistic capability, whenever possible, should be built into the software and system. Naturally, the implementation of an IMIS must conform to local laws. To assure uniformity, certain kinds of information need to be standardized. Yet some degree of flexibility is required as well since a good information system should be user-oriented. Finally, given the number of users, countries, and locations involved, an IMIS must be designed to allow data integration.

According to the CEO of Peoplesoft, there are 12 imperatives for a real-time enterprise: (1) standardization of business processes, (2) pure Internet architecture, (3) minimizing customizations, (4) holding software vendors accountable, (5) accommodating multiple databases, (6) highly scalable applications, (7) multilingual, multicurrency, (8) interoperability between vendors, (9) embedded business analytics, (10) fewer vendors, broader product lines, (11) change management, and (12) CIO (Chief Information Officer).[40] Regardless of size, each company needs to have the capability to operate on a global basis. Therefore, it is important that, whenever possible, business processes should be standardized across subsidiaries, geographies, and divisions.

When operating in multiple countries, a company may have a number of databases (or sub-databases). Such databases should be defined by international standards so as to allow for efficient access and data comparison. While such factors as language, consumption habits, and retail trade structure may continue to maintain distinct local character, the uniform methods allow for a quick examination of market situations across the world or a particular region.

A company that has only one website for the world needs to design the site to take national or cultural differences into account. The needs of local consumers must be accommodated. To improve service, the company must design the registration and order forms to accept foreign addresses and currencies. A U.S. website thus must add a "country" field and set the postal code to accept more than five alphanumeric digits, while not making "state" a mandatory field.[41]

## Subsystems

The MIS consists of several systems: internal reporting, marketing research, and marketing intelligence. The internal reporting subsystem is vital to the system because a company handles a great deal of information on a daily basis. The marketing department has sales reports. The consumer service department receives consumers' praises and complaints. The accounting department routinely generates and collects such information as sales orders, shipments, inventory levels, promotional costs, and so on. All of these types of internally generated information should be stored and made available to all concerned and affected parties.

For externally generated information, the MIS should consist of two subsystems. One of these is the marketing research subsystem. The activities of this subsystem have already been discussed extensively. The other subsystem is the marketing intelligence or environmental scanning subsystem. The responsibility of this subsystem is to track environmental changes or trends. This subsystem collects data from salespersons, distributors, syndicated research services, government agencies, and from publications about technology, social and cultural norms, the legal and political climate, economic conditions, and competitors' activities.

The implementation of the MIS must conform to local laws (see Legal Dimension 8.1). Many countries, concerned with citizens' privacy, have laws that restrict free flow of information. In England, data users are required by the Data Protection Act to register with the Office of Data Protection Registrar; otherwise, heavy fines are levied. Computer users must state how personal information was obtained and how it will be used. Furthermore, British residents have the right to see personal data about themselves. Similarly, Quebec's privacy legislation restricts the activities of direct marketers who target the French-speaking province. The law requires marketers to notify customers that a file is being created on them and to explain why a database record has been set up. Consumers must be given a "reasonable opportunity" to remove their names from mailing lists.

The MIS should be designed to do more than data collection and maintenance. It should go beyond data collection by adding value to the data so that the information will be of most use to users. The MIS thus requires an analytical component that is responsible for conceptually and statistically analyzing the data. This component may even go a step further by offering conclusions and recommendations based on the analysis of the data. In the case of Shiseido Co., a new computer network finally links factories, sales staff, and 16,000 stores and enables managers to more accurately forecast demand for its beauty products. As a result, the company has reduced inventory by one-third.[42]

Legal Dimension 8.1

**Keep it private**

Because there is no pan-European law, each country's law must be analyzed. In France, it is illegal to collect data having to do – directly or indirectly – with membership of trade unions. In Germany, as a consequence of the Nazis' use of personal information to identify enemies, the country's data-protection laws may be the most restrictive in the European Union. Germany prohibits virtually all activities regarding collecting, storing, and processing personal data. In general, all storage, communication, and erasure of personal data are not allowed unless expressly permitted by the data-protection act. Data processing is prohibited unless a person has given his or her written consent. In England, the Direct Marketing Association Code of Practice requires list owners to warrant that "the data have been fairly and lawfully obtained and all private individuals whose data are included have been given an opportunity to object to the use of their data by persons other than the list owner and that the data of those who have objected have either been deleted from or so marked in the list."

Unlike the U.S.A. which has relied on the industry's self-regulatory approach, the European Union has adopted the government-led approach. European privacy laws, based on Europe's history and legal traditions, are comprehensive and applicable to all industries. After all, protection of information privacy is regarded as a fundamental human right in Europe.

The European Directive on Data Protection, taking effect in 1998, requires the European Commission to determine the adequacy of data protection in third countries and to prohibit personal data flows to countries without adequate privacy regimes. Any organizations wanting to receive personally identifiable information from the European Union must provide adequate privacy protection. Electronic commerce certainly needs data transfers. Multinational corporations and their affiliates routinely exchange a huge amount of information. The information ranges from personnel phone directories to more sensitive information such as personnel records and credit card bills. As a result, Microsoft and hundreds of American companies have agreed to comply with the European Union's Safe Harbor framework. Information may be collected for "specified, explicit and legitimate purposes, and [. . .] held only if it relevant, accurate and up to date."

*Sources*: James A. Reiman, "Understanding Variations in European Market Laws," *DM News*, July 25, 1994, 8–9; Jeff Rohlmeier and William Yue, "The Safe Harbor Privacy Framework," *Export America*, January 2001, 21–4; and "Europe's Tough Privacy Rules Spill Over to U.S.," *San José Mercury News*, August 30, 2002.

The Internet provides benefits in terms of data-collection speed and accuracy, cost savings, and better interaction and relationships with customers. The integration of database marketing and the Internet can greatly enhance the effectiveness of customer relationship management practices.[43]

## Conclusion

This chapter has discussed the need for information on the one hand and the difficulty of managing information on the other hand. The primary goal is to provide a basic understanding of the research process and the utilization of information. Special attention has been given to the information-collection process and the use of marketing information. This coverage is far from being exhaustive, and the reader should consult marketing research textbooks for specific details related to particular research topics.

Regardless of where the intended market is, a company must understand the market and its consumers. Japan and Western Europe are successful abroad because of their adoption of the marketing concept. Basically, the marketing concept requires companies to understand consumer needs, and marketing research is a necessary undertaking in making that determination. Although it may be true that foreign market information is frequently lacking or of poor quality, this general problem can be a blessing in disguise, because competitors do not have either adequate or reliable information. A company that does a better job in acquiring information can gain a competitive advantage.

A marketer should initiate research by searching first for any relevant secondary data. There is a great deal of information readily available, and the researcher needs to know how to identify and locate the various sources of secondary information both at home and abroad. Private sources of information are provided by general reference publications, trade journals from trade and business associations, syndicated services, and marketing research agencies. Government sources also have many kinds of information available in various forms for free or at reasonable cost.

When it is necessary to gather primary data, the marketer should not approach its collection from a perspective of the home country. A marketer should be aware of numerous extra constraints that exist overseas, since such constraints can affect virtually all steps of the research process. Because of these constraints, the process of data collection in the international context is anything but simple. One cannot simply replicate the methodology used in one country and apply it in all countries. The marketer should expect to encounter problems unique to a particular country, and some adaptation in research strategies may be necessary. In order to make certain that a study is reliable and internally and externally valid, it is important to have conceptual, instrumental, and linguistic equivalence.

A company should set up an MIS to handle the information efficiently and effectively. The system should integrate all information inputs from the various sources or departments within the company. For a multinational operation, this means the integration and coordination of all the information generated by the overseas operations as well. The system should be capable of being more than a compilation of data. It should routinely make meaningful outputs available in the desired format for its users in a timely fashion. With the advanced development of artificial intelligence, it may be possible in the near future for a computer to perform all necessary functions, including the making of recommendations for marketing strategies. Still, in the final analysis, every marketer must keep in mind that information can never replace judgment. Remember, it is useless to have "data, data everywhere, and not a thought to think."

## CASE 8.1 MAPPING JAPANESE TOURISM BEHAVIOURS

**Drew Martin, University of Hawaii at Hilo**

Understanding international tourist behavior is difficult because many variables affect the decisions and interpretations. This complexity is a daunting task for researchers and managers attempting to collect large samples using structured questionnaires, employing quantitative analysis techniques, and interpreting survey findings. An alterative method is grounded theory development, a qualitative approach. Grounded theory development is a holistic approach that captures the complexities and nuances of travel experiences. Grounded theory includes thick descriptions of behavior processes. These descriptions allow both emic (self) and etic (e.g., researcher) interpretations of the informant's lived experiences and plans. Combining both emic and etic reporting, researchers gain a deep understanding of travel decisions and tourism behavior.

The following exercise demonstrates how grounded theory enables useful mapping and description of flows of thoughts, decisions, events, and outcomes within specific contexts in leisure travel. The data from a long interview provide insights on a visitor's planning processes, motivations, and experiences while visiting Hawaii's Big Island (BI), U.S.A. From the data, streams of processing and behaviors surface showing relationships among: (1) antecedent-to-trip conditions, (2) trip-planning strategies, (3) destination activities–outcomes, and (4) outcome evaluations. The results include Gestalt understandings of conscious and unconscious thinking and behaviors. The findings provide nuances on key activities and events affecting travelers' selection of BI as a destination. In addition, the data include insights on whether or not participants perceive themselves as likely to return to BI. This exercise offers unique insights for building theory and collecting interpretative data that are useful for studying leisure behavior relevant for other destinations and for analysts and executives considering applications of ground theory.

## Japanese tourist behavior

Due to their volume and spending habits, Japanese visitors are an important market segment in Hawaii's tourism industry. In 2005, visitors from Japan represented almost 21 percent of all tourists, outnumbering Canadian visitors, the second largest source of international visitors, by almost threefold. While Oahu is the most popular destination for Japanese tourists, their visits to Hawaii's Big Island are increasing. According to the Hawaii Visitors and Convention Bureau, the Big Island is the second most popular location for Japanese tourists and the only destination in the state to show an increase in Japanese tourists between the years 2000 and 2005. In addition, Japanese tourists historically have been big spenders in Hawaii. Daily spending by Japanese tourists is the highest among all visitors with a daily average of $255 per person.

A number of studies focus on specific demographic groups of Japanese tourists. For example, single Japanese females are a unique type of tourist because they have a high level of discretionary income and exhibit characteristics of individualism not typically associated with their culture. In addition, some evidence suggests that Japan's aging population will affect travel growth in the future. While older Japanese are less constrained by schedules and likely are less price sensitive, their concerns about foreign food, language barriers, and personal health present a different set of challenges for tourism managers. Finally, there are at least eight life-cycle stages of Japanese tourists; however, four of these eight segments are identified as high growth opportunities in Australia: school excursion, language study, family, and overseas wedding. The common link in these studies is the notion that demographic variables affect tourist behavior.

The travel literature also examines socio-cultural influences on Japanese tourist perceptions and choices. The assumption is that a traveler's self-reference criterion affects behavior. Japanese tourists' cultural values influence perceptions of service and interpersonal relations with hosts. Socio-cultural foundations affect trip pre-planning and framing leisure choices too. For example, Japanese tourists tend to use friends or relatives as information sources. Visitors' activities, both planned and unplanned, can also be influenced by cultural differences. Compared to Anglo-Americans, Japanese tourists show more collective characteristics in their travel motivation by emphasizing family togetherness. To maintain social networks back at home, many Japanese buy *omiyage* gifts. The strength of this social responsibility is evident in a study which finds that 83 percent of Japanese tourists purchase *omiyage*, spending an average of $566 per person.

Japanese tourist studies provide evidence that many variables can affect emic interpretations of travel experiences. In some cases, tourists may not understand their own behavior, so etic interpretations are also useful. To address the complexity of these variables and challenges of interpreting the meaning, a holistic approach to analysis is needed. Grounded theory is useful for understanding the complexities of leisure travel decisions and tourism behaviors.

## Grounded theory propositions

In Figure 8.4, the arrows represent propositions relevant to develop grounded theory and to construct guiding questions for thick descriptions of visitors' behavior. It provides a template of topics covered during the long interview process rather than a list for variable-based analysis. The following descriptions summarize each proposition.

*Proposition 1* (P1), (box 1 to 2 in Figure 8.4) suggests that the demographics and lifestyles of visitors affect how they frame leisure choices. For example, a family with teenage children might frame their leisure trip in terms of the types of learning opportunities they may experience. Hiking across lava fields to watch volcanic magma flow into the ocean might be more attractive to the family with teenage children than one with toddlers.

*Proposition 2* (P2), (box 3 to 2) implies unexpected or unplanned events occurring that may or may not affect the framing of leisure choices. For example, a television advertisement promoting a destination triggers initial thoughts about planning a visit. The advertisement represents a catalyst for collecting information, or an affirmation that a specific destination should be a priority. Although the thoughts that the ad exposure triggers are necessary, they are not sufficient motivation to visit the destination.

*Proposition 3* (P3), (box 4 to 2) proposes that external and internal personal influences affect the framing of leisure choices. Comments by friends or family members about positive experiences while visiting a destination might be retrieved from memory and mentioned during the framing of leisure choices.

*Proposition 4* (P4), (box 2 to 5) includes features and benefits in consumers framing leisure choices relating to destination choice. For example, an opportunity to go star gazing may tip the balance for a traveler choosing between a visit to Oahu or to Hawaii's Big Island.

*Proposition 5* (P5), (box 3 to 5) states that information collected for framing and trip planning affects the process of selecting and rejecting destination alternatives. External stimuli affect both the framing of leisure choices (P2) and information retrieval for the final destination choice.

According to *Proposition* 6 (P6), (box 4 to 5), friends' opinions and thoughts retrieved from memory influence the selection or rejection of destination alternatives. This proposition is consistent with previous studies on the role of reference groups in leisure trip planning.

*Proposition* 7 (P7), (box 5 to 6) contends that key activity drivers help solidify the decision to visit the destination selected. Examples of key activity drivers include concrete plans and pre-trip actions (e.g., bookings) regarding a visit to a specific destination.

In *Proposition* 8 (P8), (box 6 to 7), key activity drivers affect what is planned and done in a destination. Box 7 notes that leisure activities can be categorized into four quadrants: planned-done; planned-undone; unplanned-done; and unplanned-undone. Planned-done activities typically are key activity drivers. Visitors' decisions to choose a destination are influenced by planned participation in these activities. Since many travelers do not engage in in-depth planning, unplanned-done activities may represent the largest share of leisure-time pursuits done by visitors. Planned-undone activities may be the result of loss of interest, an unexpected situational contingency, or the result of a tradeoff/replacement with a more desirable activity. Finally, unplanned-undone activities are when an activity is a possibility; however, the visitor does not plan or engage in the pursuit. For example, a visitor may be aware of a parasailing opportunity, but he or she does not have any interest in pursuing it.

*Proposition* 9 (P9), (box 8 to 7) proposes that visitors learn about events and activities while visiting. Exposure to the destination serves as a catalyst for affecting behavior. This behavior is consistent with the contention that visitors sometimes only think about involvement in an activity after seeing it.

Finally, *Proposition 10* (P10), (box 7 to 9) concludes that activities done (and not done) affect much of the attitude and intention consequences resulting from, and associating with, visiting a destination. In other words, visitor experiences that result in specific outcomes are the antecedents to the visitor's assessment that the destination provides a good or bad trip experience.

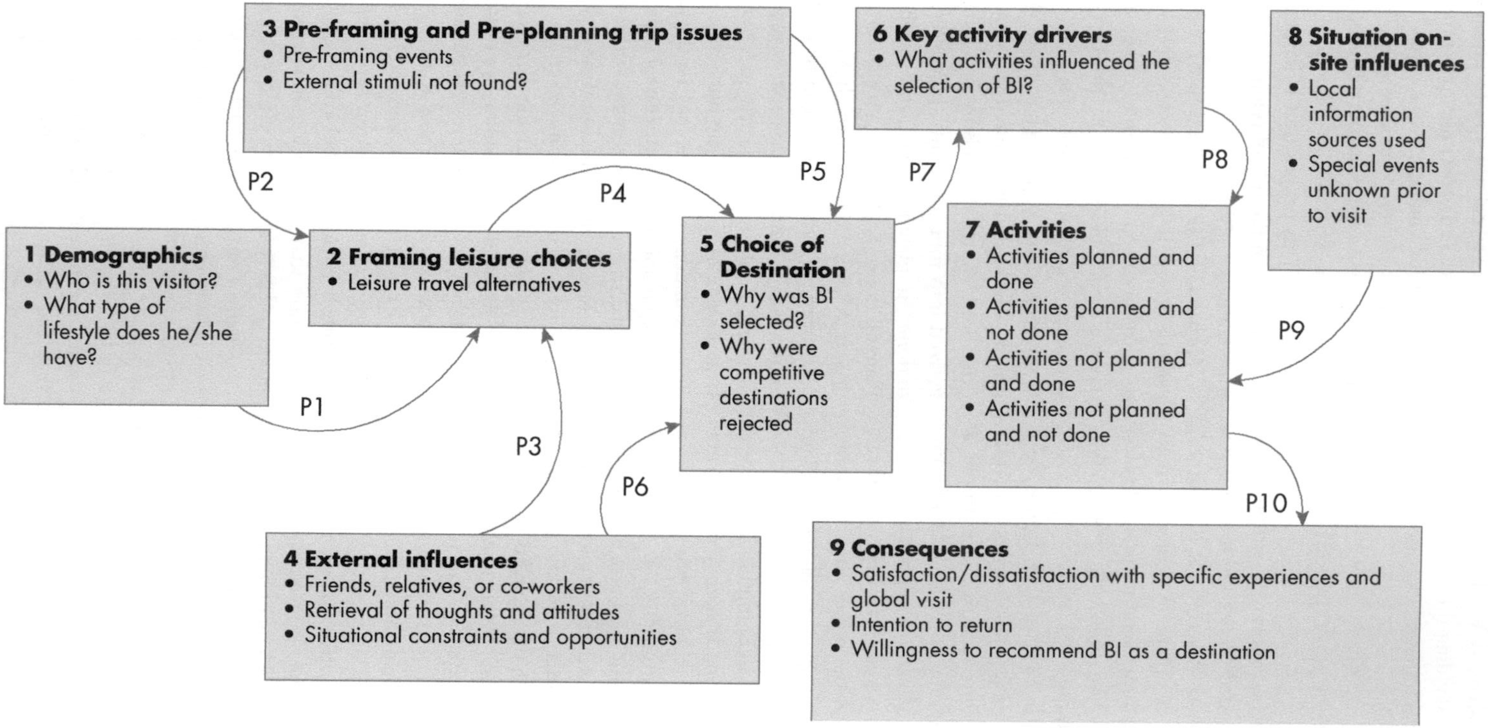
3 Pre-framing and Pre-planning trip issues
• Pre-framing events
• External stimuli not found?
6 Key activity drivers
• What activities influenced the selection of BI?
8 Situation on-site influences
• Local information sources used
• Special events unknown prior to visit
P2
P4
P5
P7
P8
1 Demographics
• Who is this visitor?
• What type of lifestyle does he/she have?
2 Framing leisure choices
• Leisure travel alternatives
5 Choice of Destination
• Why was BI selected?
• Why were competitive destinations rejected
7 Activities
• Activities planned and done
• Activities planned and not done
• Activities not planned and done
• Activities not planned and not done
P9
P1
P3
P6
P10
4 External influences
• Friends, relatives, or co-workers
• Retrieval of thoughts and attitudes
• Situational constraints and opportunities
9 Consequences
• Satisfaction/dissatisfaction with specific experiences and global visit
• Intention to return
• Willingness to recommend BI as a destination

**FIGURE 8.4** Theoretical map

Source: Adapted from Arch G. Woodside, Roberta MacDonald, and Marion Burford, "Grounded Theory of Leisure Travel," *Journal of Travel and Tourism Marketing* 17 (No.1 2004: 7–39).

## The data

To test the grounded theory propositions a questionnaire was developed to gather information about: (1) travel party's demographics, (2) pre-trip planning and sources of information, (3) activities and destinations – both planned and unplanned, (4) issues surrounding flights, accommodation, and ground transportation, (5) eating and dining experiences, and (6) overall impressions of the travel experience. The informant received U.S. $50 and a Hawaii-themed T-shirt for his co-operation. He was informed that his compensation was not dependent on answering all the questions and the interview could end at any time. The interview's duration was about 80 minutes. All questions were answered by the informant.

## Mapping Japanese behavior

The Eiji family visited Hawaii's Big Island for a one-week vacation. The Appendix shows the results of Eiji's long interview. From Eiji's responses, complete the following tasks and answer the questions.

1 Create a summary of Eiji's answers using Table 8.2's Tourism Behavior Matrix, entitling your summary, "Table 8.3 – Analysis of Eiji's Trip."
2 Applying the theoretical map (see Figure 8.4), create a map of the visitor interview. Entitle your theoretical map "Figure 8.5 – Grounded Theory Map of Eiji's Trip."
3 Based on the interview map responses in Question 2, do the results support the ten grounded theory propositions discussed? If so why, or if not, why not?

## *Appendix 2006 Hawaii visitor self-report study*

Date: *7/23/06*. Informant: *Eiji, a white male in his mid-thirties*

Location: *King's Shops; he and his family have just finished eating lunch*

## Part 1 Type of trip

1 How would you classify the trip that brings you to Hawaii? Is this a pure pleasure trip, partly, or

**TABLE 8.2** Tourism behavior matrix

| *Decision area* | *Destinations* | *Route/mode to and in the BI* | *Accommodation while in BI* | *Activities in BI* | *BI regions visited* | *Attractions visited* |
|---|---|---|---|---|---|---|
| *Consideration set and choices* | | | | | | |
| *Motives* | | | | | | |
| *Information search and use* | | | | | | |
| *Outcomes* | | | | | | |

entirely a trip related to work? If a conference, what is the name of the conference you are attending?
*We are on a one-month family vacation.*

2 Did you start this current trip that brings you to Hawaii from your home in another state, or in some other country other than the U.S.A.? Please name the city, state, and country where this current trip began.
*We live in Toyota city in Aichi prefecture (near Nagoya).*

3 Please describe the members of your immediate travel party for this trip. For example, are you traveling with family members? If yes, what are the relationships within the travel party?
*I came with my wife and two children (ages 8 and 10).*

4 Is your immediate travel party part of a larger group? For example, are you visiting Hawaii on a group tour? If yes, please name/describe the group.
*Our trip party is just the immediate family.*

5 What are some of things that happened a few years, months, or weeks ago that brought about this visit that includes you coming to Hawaii? [Use prompts: Please provide details.]
*I like Hawaii. This is my 12th trip here. I like the blue sky, ocean, and the weather. The first time, I came with a friend. I visit almost every year.*

6 Has any other member of your immediate travel party been to Hawaii before this current visit? If yes, please name the persons and describe the prior visits that have been completed.
*Yes, I have brought my wife to Hawaii 10 times. My children have accompanied me as well.*

7 Are you visiting one or more of the islands in the State of Hawaii on this current trip, or just the Big Island?
*We are going to spend one week on the Big Island, two weeks on Kauai, and 10 days on Oahu.*

8 What made the difference in this current trip to the State of Hawaii versus not making the trip, doing some other activity, or just staying home?
*I have worked 20 years for my company. As a reward, the company has allowed me to take a one-month holiday. Hawaii was the only option. I can't think about any other place. I love it here!*

9 Please describe the things that happened and thoughts you may have had during the years, months, or weeks before the trip about how many nights that were scheduled for this current visit in Hawaii and the total number of nights away from home.
*I always visit Hawaii on my vacation. We knew that the extended vacation would be spent here.*

10 Is there anything in particular on the Big Island that brings you here on this current trip? If yes, please describe.
*I really like the beach at Kona. Also, we want to visit a coffee farm. My oldest son's summer project is about coffee farming.*

11 Please describe the things that you are doing on the Big Island. What have you done and what will you be doing for the duration of your stay?
*Today, we are shopping, eating lunch, and swimming in the pool. We will be having brunch at the Mauna Kea Hotel, going to the beach, and shopping.*

## Part 2 Flights, accommodation, and ground transportation

1 What steps/events/thoughts occurred that relate to you getting flight tickets for this visit to the State of Hawaii? For example, did you use frequent flyer miles, did you reserve tickets online, or visit a travel agent? Please describe the steps.
*One ticket was obtained from the redemption of Japan Airlines frequent travel miles. The other three tickets were purchased at the travel agency that we always use.*

2 Was the airline company that you flew with something you thought about before getting tickets to visit the State of Hawaii or the Big Island? Please describe your thoughts about different airlines relating to the current visit to Hawaii.
*Yes, the frequent mileage program for Japan Airlines was the driving force in deciding which airline to use.*

3 Please describe your actual flights to the State of Hawaii and to the Big Island. What would you change, if anything?
*There was a lot of turbulence during the flight. Also, the service of the airplane was a little slow. Japan Airline's service quality is slipping.*

4 What steps/events/thoughts occurred that relate to you getting accommodation for this visit to the State of Hawaii? For example, did you reserve accommodation online, telephone for a place to stay, or visit a travel agent?
*From the Internet, we found accommodation. On the "I love Hawaii" website, a posting listed a vacancy at The Shores condominium. The owner of the unit is Japanese and he was willing to rent us the condo at a reduced rate.*

5 Was the accommodation that you are using here on the Big Island something you thought about before the visit to the State of Hawaii or the Big Island? If yes or if no, please describe the thoughts you had before this trip about different accommodation relating to the current visit to Hawaii.
*We knew about The Shores from our previous trip to Hawaii, but the high price has kept us from booking a room there. Usually, we stay at the Bay Club and purchase a package tour. To our surprise the price was very reasonable for the condo at The Shores. We looked at the web page that shows the room. It looked good, so I booked it.*

6 What steps/events/thoughts occurred that relate to you getting ground transportation (such as taking taxi-cabs) for this visit to the State of Hawaii? For example, did you reserve ground transportation online, telephone, or visit a travel agent? Please describe the steps.
*We called Alamo's Japan office to book the car. By using my JCB credit card to hold the reservation, I got a cheaper rate. At the time, JCB had a sales promotion campaign that provided discounts when the card was used.*

7 Were the ground transportations that you are using here on the Big Island something you thought about before visiting the State of Hawaii or the Big Island? If yes or if no, please describe your thoughts you had before this trip about different ground transportations relating to the current visit to Hawaii.
*We knew that a car would be needed to get around the island. We wanted to see as much of the Big Island as possible.*

## Part 3 Sources of information about Hawaii and the Big Island

1 Before this visit to Hawaii, did you talk with friends, travel agents, family members, and/or local Hawaii persons about this current trip to Hawaii?
*Yes, we talked with co-workers, friends, and family members. We asked them what they had seen, how they felt about their experience, and whether they would go back again.*

2 What information did you learn and/or was useful before visiting Hawaii? Please describe.
*A friend told me about a good beach to visit and a good restaurant, the Puka Puka Kitchen in Hilo.*

3 Did you or anyone else in your immediate travel party get a travel book in the months or weeks before this visit to Hawaii and the Big Island? If yes, what books did you get?
*We looked at several guidebooks. We found* Chikyo no Arukikata *(How to travel the globe):* Big Island *to be a very useful book.*

4 Did you talk to a travel agent or visit travel agents in person or online before starting this visit to Hawaii?
*When we reserved the air tickets, I talked to the travel agent about places to visit and things to do.*

## Part 4 Places visited and doing activities on the Big Island

Where did you visit or definitely will visit during your visit to the Big Island?

*Kailua-Kona* *Volcanoes National Park*
*Parker Ranch* *Umauma Falls*

*Waikoloa Village*
*Kapa'a Beach Park*
*Akaka Falls*
*Imiloa Astronomy Center*
*Snorkeling*
*Hapuna Beach*
*King's Shops*
*Huggo's Bubba Gump*
*Boiling Pots*
*Big Island Candy*
*Chain of Craters Road*
*Prince Kuhio Plaza*
*Mauna Loa Visitor Center*
*Waiamea*
*Coffee Farm*
*Rainbow Falls*

## Part 5 Eating out and dining experiences

Please name and describe some of your eating out and dining experiences during your visit to the Big Island.
*At King's Village, we ate at Merryman's Café – very delicious. Wanted to eat Japanese food, but the Japanese restaurant was closed. Also, at Merryman's we wanted to order pizza, but they were out.*

## Part 6 Memories of the Big Island

What do you think will be your memories of your visit to the Big Island after this trip is over?
*The lava and the stars are amazing here. Also, we liked looking at the words and pictures that were created by people that put white rock/dead coral on top of the black lava rock.*

## Part 7 Alternatives

If you had the chance to not make this trip to the Big Island and to spend your time and money on something else, what would you spend your time and money on?
*There really was no alternative in my mind. I love Hawaii. I suppose that other destinations of interest would include Australia or the mainland U.S.A.*

## Questions

1 What are the difficulties in using and comparing secondary data from a number of countries?
2 Why is it difficult to employ probability sampling techniques in developing countries?
3 Distinguish among: back translation, parallel-blind translation, committee approach, random probe, and decentering.
4 Distinguish between internal and external validity. What are the implications of external validity for international marketers?
5 What are the desirable characteristics of the MIS and IMIS?

## Discussion assignments and minicases

1 Would Tokyo be a good test market? If so why, or if not, why not?
2 Do you prefer observation or questioning in collecting overseas data?
3 Cite certain kinds of behavior so common in the U.S.A. that they are often taken for granted by Americans – but not by foreign observers.
4 Discuss the reliability and validity problems in conducting a cross-national comparison study with the use of a standardized questionnaire.
5 Dieting and jogging are concepts which Westerners can easily relate to. Are they understood by non-Westerners?

6 Do demographic variables have universal meanings? Is there a likelihood that they may be interpreted differently in different cultures?
7 After learning of no import barriers to its product, a U.S. processed food manufacturer conducted market research in Japan to determine the degree of interest in cake mixes. The results were encouraging: the Japanese enjoy eating cakes. Concluding that there was no reason why Japanese consumers would not want to buy ready-made cake mixes, the company proceeded to get Japanese supermarkets to carry its product. The sales were extremely disappointing. Did the Japanese interviewed mislead the manufacturer? Or did the manufacturer fail to ask enough or the right questions?
8 As a researcher, you have just been asked to do market research in order to make recommendations on how to market coffee in a number of Asian, European, and South American countries. What questions do you need to ask in order to understand the varying buying motives, consumption habits, and uses of this particular product?

## Notes


1 "Measuring Success," *IMF Survey*, October 30, 2006, 324.
2 "Testing What's Hot in the Cradle of Cool," *Business Week*, May 7, 2007, 46.
3 K. Sivakumar and Cheryl Nakata, "The Stampede Toward Hofstede's Framework: Avoiding the Sample Design Pit in Cross-cultural Research," *Journal of International Business Studies* 32 (third quarter 2001): 555–74.
4 "Tailoring Cars to U.S. Tastes," *Asian Wall Street Journal*, January 16, 2001.
5 "The Americanization of Toyota," *Business Week*, 15 April 2002, 54–64.
6 "The Science of Desire," *Business Week*, June 5, 2006, 98–106.
7 Leonard M. Fuld, *The Secret Language of Competitive Intelligence*, (Crown Business, 2006).
8 "U.S. Research Firms Must Put Time, Thought into European Studies," *Marketing News*, September 11, 2000.
9 "London's New Media Lessons," *Business Week*, December 4, 2006, 26.
10 "Shoppers Gone Wild," *Business Week*, February 20, 2006, 46–7.
11 See note 8.
12 C. Samuel Craig and Susan P. Douglas, *International Marketing Research* (2nd edn), New York: Wiley, 2000, p. 141.
13 Charles R. Taylor, "Moving International Advertising Research Forward: A New Research Agenda," *Journal of Advertising* 34 (spring 2005): 7–16.
14 Thomas Salzberger and Rudolf R. Sinkovics, "Reconsidering the Problem of Data Equivalence in International Marketing Research: Contrasting Approaches Based on CFA and the Rasch Model for Measurement," *International Marketing Review* 23 (No. 4, 2006): 390–417.
15 "Measuring Poverty: Pitfalls, Prescriptions, and Policy Implications," *IMF Survey*, 17 March 2003, 76–7.
16 B.S. Schaffer and C.M. Riordan, "A Review of Cross-cultural Methodologies for Organizational Research: A Best-practices Approach," *Organizational Research Methods* 6 (No. 2, 2003): 169–215.
17 S. Tamer Cavusgil, Seyda Deligonul, and Attila Yaprak, "International Marketing as a Field of Study: A Critical Assessment of Earlier Development and a Look Forward," *Journal of International Marketing* 13 (No. 4, 2005): 1–27.
18 Hester van Herk, Ype H. Poortinga, and Theo M. M. Verhallen, "Equivalence of Survey Data: Relevance for International Marketing," *European Journal of Marketing* 39 (Nos 3/4, 2005): 351–64.
19 Shawn T. Thelan and Earl D. Honeycutt Jr., "Assessing National Identity in Russia Between Generations Using the National Identity Scale," *Journal of International Marketing* 12 (No. 2, 2004): 58–81.
20 Luis Filipe Lages and Cristiana Raquel Lages, "The STEP Scale: A Measure of Short-term Export Performance Improvement," *Journal of International Marketing* 12 (No. 1, 2004): 36–56.

21 Cleopatra Veloutsou *et al.*, "Measuring Transaction-specific Satisfaction in Services: Are the Measures Transferable Across Cultures," *European Journal of Marketing* 39 (Nos 5/6, 2005): 606–28.
22 Richard G. Netemeyer, Srinivas Durvasula, and Donald R. Lichtenstein, "A Cross-national Assessment of the Reliability and Validity of the CETSCALE," *Journal of Marketing Research* 28 (August 1991): 320–7.
23 Erdener Kaynak and Ali Kara, "Consumer Perceptions of Foreign Products: An Analysis of Product-country Images and Ethnocentrism," *European Journal of Marketing* 36 (No. 7, 2002): 928–49.
24 Teodoro Luque-Martinez, José-Angel Ibanez-Zapata, and Salvador del Barrio-Garcia, "Consumer Ethonocentricism Measurement – An Assessment of the Reliability and Validity of the CETSCALE in Spain," *European Journal of Marketing* 34 (No. 11, 2000): 1353–74.
25 Jan-Benedict E.M. Steenkamp and Hans Baumgartner, "Assessing Measurement Invariance in Cross-national Consumer Research," *Journal of Consumer Research* 25 (June 1998): 78–90.
26 Jill Gabrielle Klein, Richard Ettenson, and Balaji C. Krishnan, "Extending the Construct of Consumer Ethnocentrism: When Foreign Products Are Preferred," *International Marketing Review* 23 (No. 3, 2006): 304–21.
27 Michael R. Mullen, "Diagnosing Measurement Equivalence in Cross-national Research," *Journal of International Business Studies* 26 (No. 3, 1995): 573–96.
28 Swee Hoon Ang, "The Power of Money: A Cross-cultural Analysis of Business-related Beliefs," *Journal of World Business* 35 (No. 1, 2000): 43–60.
29 Uma Sekaran, "Methodological and Theoretical Issues and Advancements in Cross-Cultural Research," *Journal of International Business Studies* 14 (Fall 1983): 61–72.
30 Masaaki Kotabe *et al.*, "Strategic Alliances in Emerging Latin America: A View from Brazilian, Chilean, and Mexican Companies," *Journal of World Business* 35 (No. 2, 2000): 114–32.
31 Charles S. Mayer, "Multinational Marketing Research: The Magnifying Glass of Methodological Problems," *European Research* 6 (March 1978): 77–83.
32 Susan P. Douglas and C. Samuel Craig, "Collaborative and Iterative Translation: An Alternative Approach to Back Translation," *Journal of International Marketing* 15 (No. 1, 2007): 30–43.
33 "Rising," *PROMO*, April 2001, 53ff.
34 Hans Baumgartner and Jan-Benedict E.M. Steenkamp, "Response Styles in Marketing Research: A Cross-national Investigation," *Journal of Marketing Research* 38 (May 2001): 143–56.
35 Graham Hooley *et al.*, "Market Orientation in the Service Sector of the Transition Economies of Central Europe," *European Journal of Marketing* 37 (No. 1, 2003): 86–106.
36 Jungbok Ha, Kiran Karande, and Anusorn Singhapakdi, "Importers' Relationships with Exporters: Does Culture Matter?", *International Marketing Review* 21 (Nos 4/5, 2004): 447–61.
37 Susan P. Douglas and C. Samuel Craig, "On Improving the Conceptual Foundations of International Marketing Research," *Journal of International Marketing* 14 (No. 1, 2006): 1–22.
38 Kjell Toften and Svein Ottar Olsen, "The Relationships Among Quality, Cost, Value, and Use of Export Market Information: An Empirical Study," *Journal of International Marketing* 12 (No. 2, 2004): 104–31.
39 Leonidas C. Leonidou and Marios Theodosiou, "The Export Marketing Information System: An Integration of the Extant Knowledge," *Journal of World Business* 39 (February 2004): 12–36.
40 Craig Conway, President and CEO, Peoplesoft, Keynote address, Digital Economy Conference, December 2001.
41 "Worldwide-friendly Sites Draws Returns," *Marketing News*, September 2, 2002, 24.
42 "Quick Studies," *Business Week*, November 18, 2002, 48–9.
43 Chris O'Leary, Sally Rao, and Chad Perry, "Improving Customer Relationship Management Through Database/Internet Marketing: A Theory-building Action Research Project," *European Journal of Marketing* 38 (Nos 3/4, 2004): 338–54.

Chapter 9

# Foreign market entry strategies

A merchant, it has been said very properly, is not necessarily the citizen of any particular country. It is in great measure indifferent to him from what places he carries on his trade; and a very stifling disgust will make him move his capital, and together with the industry which it supports, from one country to another.

Adam Smith

## Chapter outline

## Marketing strategy

### Raging Bull

Chaleo Yoovidhya, the founder of T.C. Pharmaceutical Co. in Thailand, developed several decades ago a formula for Krating Daeng, an energy drink. The brand is a huge success in Thailand, predominantly among blue-collar workers (e.g., truckers, laborers).

Then came Dietrich Mateschitz, an Austrian salesman of a cosmetics company that was represented in Thailand by the Yoovidhya family. The salesman was intrigued by Krating Daeng and obtained a license to make it in Austria. Krating Daeng became Red Bull, a literal translation. Yoovidhya and Mateschitz formed Red Bull GmbH, each taking a 49 percent stake. Yoovidhya's son got the other 2 percent. Red Bull was marketed in Austria in 1987 before charging into Hungary, its first foreign market, in 1992.

Energy drinks, heavy on caffeine and sugar (seven teaspoons in a can), are particularly popular among young Americans. The number of young drinkers more than doubled in three years to some 7.6 million teens. Red Bull aggressively gives a sample of its product at sporting events and on campuses. In the U.S.A., the company's marketing teams use dance halls, disc jockeys, alternative sports venues, and cab drivers to promote the brand. They may drive Red Bull cars (with a large Red Bull can mounted on the back) to hand out samples. Red Bull is the sponsor of some 500 extreme athletes. Its fleet of Flying Bulls show planes can be seen at air shows all over the world.

Red Bull's sleek blue-and-silver cans have become a standard package for the product category. Many other competitors imitate the shape and colors of the can. Over 500 new energy drinks were introduced worldwide in 2006.

Unlike the way it is marketed in its motherland (Thailand), Red Bull is promoted aggressively as a trendy product associated with extreme sports. In the U.S.A., the product is highly popular with high-school and college students. At about $2 for an 8-ounce can, Red Bull is pricey, but the price does not deter students from drinking it.

Red Bull has become a global success. With a sales volume of more than one billion cans a year in 83 countries, Red Bull commands 70 percent of the world's energy drink market – in spite of a slew of imitators that compete by offering lower prices or greater quantity per can. The worldwide success is enough to propel Yoovidhya to the top of Thailand in terms of wealth. In the process, he has joined the world's billionaires as ranked by *Forbes* magazine.

*Sources*: "Red Bull Tycoon Joins Elite Club," *Bangkok Post*, March 1, 2003; "Energy Drinks Hook a Generation," *San José Mercury News*, November 13, 2006; and "Hansen Natural Charging at Red Bull with a Brawny Energy Brew," *Business Week*, June 6, 2005, 74–7.

## Purpose of chapter

Red Bull has demonstrated a practical way to enter foreign markets. Likewise, Heineken has not entered all markets with a one-track mind and a single-entry method. Even a large multinational corporation, with all its power, still has to adapt its operating methods and formulate multiple entry strategies. The dynamic nature of many overseas markets makes it impossible for a single method to work effectively in all markets.

This chapter is devoted to a coverage of the various market entry strategies. Some of these techniques – such as exporting, licensing, and management contracts – are indirect in the sense that they require no investment overseas. Other techniques, however, require varying degrees of foreign direct investment. These foreign direct investment methods range from joint-venture to complete overseas manufacturing facilities, with such strategies as assembly operations, turnkey operations, and acquisition falling somewhere in between. These strategies do not operate in sequence, and any one of them may be appropriate at any time. In addition, the use of one strategy in one market does not rule out the use of the other strategies elsewhere. The methods vary in terms of risk accepted and, to a certain extent, the degree of commitment to the foreign market.

Another purpose of this chapter is to discuss the advantages and disadvantages associated with each method of market penetration. Factors that have an impact on the appropriateness of entry methods are covered in order to provide guidelines for the selection of market entry strategies. The chapter ends with an examination of free trade zones, which can be used to complement most entry strategies.

## Foreign direct investment (FDI)

To enter a foreign market, a company needs to consider the risk–reward ratio. To minimize risk, the firm may try to enter the foreign market indirectly in the sense that it tries to minimize its foreign direct investment and physical presence abroad. Some of the indirect market entry strategies include exporting, licensing, and management contract. By trying to play it relatively safe, the reward potential is also reduced accordingly.

To maximize a profit potential while tolerating a higher degree of risk, a marketer may want to consider FDI. Economists usually advocate a free flow of capital across national borders because capital can then seek out the highest rate of return. Owners of capital can diversify their investment, while governments will be less able to pursue bad economic policies. In addition, a global integration of capital markets spreads best practices in corporate governance, accounting rules, and legal traditions.

However, some critics point out that free capital flows are driven by speculative and short-term considerations. Empirical evidence, however, shows that FDI flows are more stable than all other forms of capital (portfolio and other investment flows). In fact, FDI flows are a stabilizing factor even during a financial crisis. The stability is due to the fact that FDI focuses on positive longer term sentiment about a recipient country. In addition, physical investment in plant and equipment cannot be easily reversed.[1] Empirical evidence indicates that FDI benefits developing host countries.[2]

Figures 9.1 shows that the CEE-10 countries (EU members in Central and Eastern Europe) have attracted large FDI inflows, and Figure 9.2 shows the surging inflows of FDI to emerging market countries. One indisputable fact is that developed countries are both the largest recipients and sources of FDI. The phenomenon is dominated by the triad of the European Union, the U.S.A., and Japan. Over the past few decades, the share of the triad in total world inward FDI flows and stocks has been about 60 to 70 percent, with a shift in the direction of the EU and away from Japan. As a matter of fact, the EU commands almost half of global inward and outward flows and stocks. It is encouraging that developing countries have made a gain as recipients of FDI, as evidenced by their share in total world inflows rising from 20 percent in 1978 to 1980 to 35 percent in 2003 to 2005. Unfortunately for African countries, their share has fallen.[3]

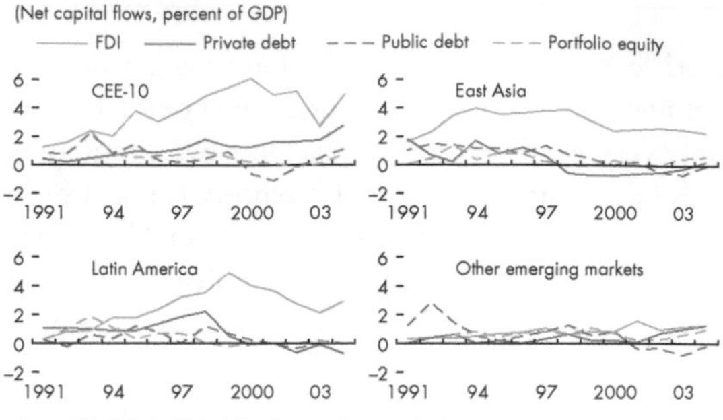
(Net capital flows, percent of GDP)
FDI
Private debt
Public debt
Portfolio equity
CEE-10
East Asia
Latin America
Other emerging markets
6
4
2
0
-2
1991
94
97
2000
03

Data: World Bank, Global Development Finance database.

**FIGURE 9.1** CEE-10 and FDI inflows

Source: *IMF Survey* (November 20, 2006, 334). © International Monetary Fund. Reprinted from *IMF Survey* (www.imf.org/imfsurvey) with the permission of the copyright holder.

Certain countries have managed to attract large amounts of FDI. The U.S.A. is the world's top recipient of FDI. In the case of Africa, to attract FDI, African countries have relied on their natural resources, locational advantages, and targeted policies. Above all, the countries that are successful in attracting FDI have certain traits: political and macroeconomic stability and structural reforms. "Strong, pro-democracy political leadership that has embraced policies to overcome social and political strife and a firm commitment to economic reform are key factors linked with sizable FDI inflows."[4] Therefore, even those countries that lack natural resources or location advantages can still attract foreign investors by adopting sound economic policies within an open political environment. Figure 9.3 shows that Cyprus has been successful in attracting a number of multinational corporations to locate their operations there.

Countries may be classified in terms of their FDI potential and performance. According to the United Nations Conference on Trade and Development, there are four groups: (1) front-runners (e.g., Australia, Bahamas) that have high FDI potential/high FDI performance, (2) above potential

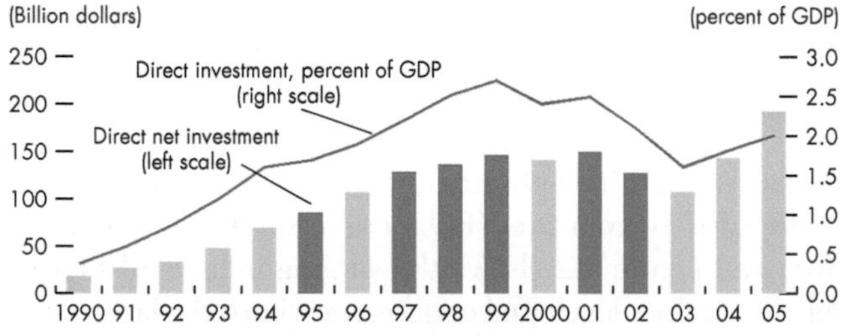
(Billion dollars)
(percent of GDP)
Direct investment, percent of GDP
(right scale)
Direct net investment
(left scale)
250
200
150
100
50
0
3.0
2.5
2.0
1.5
1.0
0.5
0.0
1990 91 92 93 94 95 96 97 98 99 2000 01 02 03 04 05

Note: Includes countries in the Emerging Markets Bond Index, India, and Czech Republic. Darker bars indicate the years of financial crisis: 1995–Mexico; 1997–Korea and Thailand; 1998–Brazil, Indonesia, Philippines, Russia, and Ukraine; 1999– Ecuador; 2001–Argentina and Turkey; 2002–Uruguay.

**FIGURE 9.2** Emerging markets and FDI inflows

Source: "Why FDI may not be as Stable as Governments Think," *IMF Survey* (January 29, 2007, 26). © International Monetary Fund. Reprinted from *IMF Survey* (www.imf.org/imfsurvey) with the permission of the copyright holder.

Cyprus supports global business
Strategically located with convenient regional and international air links.
Excellent telecommunications - direct dialling to over 200 countries.
Thirty-two double tax treaties covering 40 countries.
Highly qualified bilingual staff and very competitive operating costs.
A pleasant environment including one of the lowest crime rates in Europe.
CYPRUS
Europe's Business Island
If you want to know more about Cyprus contact CENTRAL BANK OF CYPRUS, International Division
P.O.Box 25529 • CY-1395 Nicosia • Cyprus • Tel: + 357 22 714225 (8.00 a.m. - 2.00 p.m. Cyprus time) • Fax: + 357 22 378164 • E-mail: idoe@centralbank.gov.cy • Web: http://www.centralbank.gov.cy

**FIGURE 9.3** Cyprus and FDI

(e.g., Albania, Angola) due to low FDI potential/high FDI performance, (3) below potential (e.g., Algeria, Argentina) due to high FDI potential/low FDI performance, and (4) underachievers (e.g., Bangladesh, Benin) that have low FDI potential/low FDI performance.[5] Based on the Inward FDI Performance Index, the top five countries are Azerbaijan, Brunei Darussalam, Hong Kong, Estonia, and Singapore.

Russia, one of the so-called BRIC (Brazil, Russia, India, and China) economies, has grown significantly as a market. Not surprisingly, Russia attracted a record $16.7 billion in FDI in 2005. Consumer-related sectors did very well. Coca-Cola Co. spent $600 million to acquire Russian fruit-juice market Multon, while Dutch brewer Heineken spent $750 million in acquisitions. Nestlé has so far invested $500 million, and its $120 million instant-coffee factory was its first international greenfield investment for two decades.[6]

Corruption has a negative impact on FDI. From the ethics standpoint, foreign investors generally avoid corruption because it is morally wrong. From the economic standpoint, investors prefer not to have to manage such costly risks.[7] A recent study, however, found that host-country corruption was not viewed as a significant market barrier. Instead, the negative effect of corruption was in the form of a discount on local takeover synergies. A deterioration in the corruption index by 1 point on a 10-point scale resulted in a reduction of 21 percent of local targets' premiums.[8]

## Exporting

Exporting is a strategy in which a company, without any marketing or production organization overseas, exports a product from its home base. Often, the exported product is fundamentally the same as the one marketed in the home market.

The main advantage of an exporting strategy is the ease in implementing the strategy. Risks are minimal because the company simply exports its excess production capacity when it receives orders from abroad. As a result, its international marketing effort is casual at best. This is very likely the most common overseas entry approach for small firms. Many companies employ this entry strategy when they first become involved with international business and may continue to use it on a more or less permanent basis.

The problem with using an exporting strategy is that it is not always an optimal strategy. A desire to keep international activities simple, together with a lack of product modification, make a company's marketing strategy inflexible and unresponsive.

The exporting strategy functions poorly when the company's home-country currency is strong. In the 1970s, the Swiss franc was so strong that Swiss companies found it exceedingly difficult to export and sell products in the U.S. market. Swiss companies had to resort to investing abroad in order to reduce the effects of the strong franc. During the first term of the Reagan administration, the U.S. dollar had also gained an extremely strong position. U.S. firms not only found it extremely difficult to export U.S. products but they also had to contend with a flood of inexpensive imports that became even more inexpensive as the dollar became stronger. A currency can remain strong over a stretch of several years, creating prolonged difficulties for the country's exports. Continuing the long-term trend, the Japanese yen surged 20 percent against the U.S. dollar in early 1995 and greatly harmed Japanese exporters.

Austria represents a small but open economy that requires international exchange. Based on a study of the effects of determinants on export performance, the most promising predictors of export performance are firm size, management's motives to internationalize, and use of the differentiation strategy.[9]

One study of Portuguese small and medium-sized exporters found a crucial role of past performance on their commitment to exporting.[10] Another study of small and medium-sized exporters found that decision-makers' cosmopolitanism influenced export initiation. These decision-makers often learned of foreign opportunities through their existing social ties – rather than through formal scanning and market research. The findings were consistent across different industrial settings.[11] In addition, a study of export behavior found a negative relationship between the psychic distance index and firms' actual selection of export markets.[12]

One study measured the export-entrepreneurial orientation construct so as to derive a high versus low export-entrepreneurial taxonomy. While Nigerian firms in the study perceive domestic environmental problems, high export-entrepreneurial firms appear to be better able to adapt and subsequently exhibit a higher tendency to initiate exporting. In addition, high export-entrepreneurial firms are more proactive and innovative in developing exporting while being less averse to exporting risks.[13]

It should be noted that research in international exchange tends to focus on the perspective of exporters. A more complete understanding requires an inclusion of the perspective of importers in the dyad. Based on a study of 36 exporter–importer dyads operating in four countries, the best-performing dyads exhibited a maintenance of close relationships by people on either side.[14]

## Licensing

When a company finds exporting ineffective but is hesitant to have direct investment abroad, licensing can be a reasonable compromise. Licensing is an agreement that permits a foreign company to use industrial property (i.e., patents, trademarks, and copyrights), technical know-how and skills (e.g., feasibility studies, manuals, technical advice), architectural and engineering designs, or any combination of these in a foreign market. Essentially, a licensor allows a foreign company to manufacture a product for sale in the licensee's country and sometimes in other specified markets.

Examples of licensing abound. Some 50 percent of the drugs sold in Japan are made under license from European and U.S. companies. *Playboy* used to take licensed materials from France's *Lui* for its *Oui* magazine, which was distributed in the U.S. market. *Playboy*'s more common role, however, is that of a licensor, resulting in nine *Playboy* foreign editions. *Penthouse* magazine, likewise, has Japanese and Brazilian versions under license in addition to those in Spain, Australia, and Italy. German-speaking countries account for *Penthouse*'s largest overseas edition. As of 2006, Starbucks has more than 13,000 stores worldwide and is opening seven new stores each day. Out of the total number, more than 5,000 are licensed locations. Retail store licensing accounts for 45 percent of the company's specialty revenue of $1.2 billion.[15]

Licensing is not only restricted to tangible products. A service can be licensed as well. Chicago Mercantile Exchange's attempt to internationalize the futures market led it to obtain licensing rights to the Nikkei stock index. The exchange then sublicensed the Nikkei index to the SIMEX for trade in Singapore in 1986.

In spite of a general belief that FDI is generally more profitable and thus the preferred scheme, licensing offers several advantages. It allows a company to spread out its research and development and investment costs, while enabling it to receive incremental income with only negligible expenses.

In addition, granting a license protects the company's patent and/or trademark against cancellation for nonuse. This protection is especially critical for a firm that, after investing in production and marketing facilities in a foreign country, decides to leave the market either temporarily or permanently. The situation is especially common in Central and South America, where high inflation and devaluation drastically push up operating costs.

There are other reasons why licensing should be used. Trade barriers may be one such reason. A manufacturer should consider licensing when capital is scarce, when import restrictions discourage direct entry, and when a country is sensitive to foreign ownership. The method is very flexible because it allows a quick and easy way to enter the market. Licensing also works well when transportation cost is high, especially relative to product value. Although Japan banned all direct investment and restricted commercial loans in South Africa, Japan's success there was due to licensing agreements with local distributors.

A company can avoid substantial risks and other difficulties with licensing. Most French designers, for example, use licensing to avoid having to invest in a business. In another example, Disney gets all of its royalties virtually risk-free from the $500 million Tokyo Disneyland theme park owned by Keisei Electric Railway and Mitsui. The licensing and royalty fees as arranged are very attractive: Disney receives 10 percent of the gate revenue and 5 percent of sales of all food and merchandise. Moreover, Disney, with its policy of using low-paid young adults as park employees, does not have to deal with the Japanese policy of lifetime employment.

An owner of a valuable brand name can greatly benefit from brand licensing. In addition to receiving royalties from sales of merchandise bearing its name or image, the trademark owner receives an intangible benefit of free advertising which reinforces the brand's image. Another benefit is that the brand is extended into new product categories in which the trademark owner has no expertise. Coca-Cola, for example, has licensed its brand name to more than 3000 products which are marketed by 200 licensees in 30 countries.

Recognizing the value of the licensing approach as well as the contributions of licensees in European countries, McDonald's has made a strategic adjustment. In Europe, the share of restaurants that are directly owned by McDonald's will decline from the current 30 percent to 20 or 25 percent. Compared to directly owned restaurants there, franchise outlets achieve better profit margins. However, outside of Europe and the U.S.A., the company plans to rely on its own know-how. McDonald's wants to grow in Russia and other regions with its directly owned restaurants since the business there has only recently been established.[16]

Nevertheless, licensing has its negative aspects. With reduced risk generally comes reduced profit. In fact, licensing may be the least profitable of all entry strategies.

It is necessary to consider the long-term perspective. By granting a license to a foreign firm, a manufacturer may be nurturing a competitor in the future – someone who is gaining technological and product knowledge. At some point, the licensee may refuse to renew the licensing contract. To complicate the matter, it is anything but easy to prevent the licensee from using the process learned and acquired while working under license. Texas Instruments had to sue several Japanese manufacturers to force them to continue paying royalties on its patents on memory chips.

Another problem often develops when the licensee performs poorly. To attempt to terminate the contract may be easier said than done. Once licensing is in place, the agreements can also prevent the licensor from entering that market directly. Japanese laws give a licensee virtual control over the licensed product, and such laws present a monumental obstacle for an investor wishing to regain the rights to manufacture and sell the investor's own product.

Inconsistent product quality across countries caused by licensees' lax quality control can injure the reputation of a product on a worldwide basis. This possibility explains why McDonald's goes to extremes in supervising operations, thus ensuring product quality and consistency. McDonald's was successful in court in preventing a franchisee from operating the franchises in France because the franchisee's quality was substandard. Anheuser-Busch, likewise, requires all licensees to meet the company's standards. The licensees must agree to import such ingredients as yeast from the U.S.A.

Even when exact product formulations are followed, licensing can still sometimes damage a product's image – that is, psychologically. Many imported products enjoy a certain degree of prestige or mystique that can rapidly disappear when the product is made locally under license. The Miller brewery became aware of this perception problem when it started brewing Lowenbrau, a German brand, in Texas.

In some cases, a manufacturer has no choice at all about licensing. Many developing countries force patent holders to license their products to other manufacturers or distributors for a royalty fee that may or may not be fair. Canada, owing to consumer activism, is the only industrialized nation requiring compulsory licensing for drugs.

Licensing, in spite of certain limitations, is a sound strategy that can be quite effective under certain circumstances. Licensing terms must be carefully negotiated and explicitly treated (see Figure 9.4). In general, a license contract should include these basic elements: product and territorial coverage, length of contract, quality control, grantback and cross-licensing, royalty rate and structure, choice of currency, and choice of law.

When licenses are to be granted to European firms, a firm must consider the anti-trust rules of the EU, specifically Article 85 of the Rome Treaty. This article prohibits those licensing terms (with some exemptions) that are likely to adversely affect trade between EU countries. Such arrangements as price fixing, territorial restrictions, and tie-in agreements are void.

A prudent licensor does not "assign" a trademark to a licensee. It is far better to specify the conditions under which the mark can or cannot be used by the licensee. From the licensee's standpoint, the licensor's trademark is valuable in marketing the licensed product only if the product is popular. Otherwise, the licensee would be better served by creating a new trademark to protect the marketing position in the event that the basic license is not renewed.

Licensing should be considered a two-way street because a license also allows the original licensor to gain access to the licensee's technology and product. This is important because the licensee may be able to build on the information supplied by the licensor. Unlike American firms, European licensors are very interested in grantbacks and will even lower the royalty rate in return for product improvements and potentially profitable new products. Thus, an intelligent practice is always to stipulate in a contract that licenses for new patents or products covered by the return grant are to be made available at reasonable royalties.

Finally, the licensor should try not to undermine a product by overlicensing it. For example, Pierre Cardin diluted the value of his name by allowing some 800 products to use the name under license. Subsequently, he created Maxim's as the second brand for restaurants, hotels, and food items. Similarly, fashion legend Yves Saint Laurent put his name (YSL) on numerous products ranging from baseball caps to plastic shoes. A luxury brand can lose its cachet when it has too much exposure. Gucci Group paid $1 billion for YSL's ready-to-wear and perfume businesses and quickly moved to restore the brand's image. Production, marketing, and distribution were overhauled. Even though YSL's licensing agreements contributed 65 percent of YSL's revenues, Gucci Group decided to walk away from revenues for the sake of the brand's luxury image. In three months, 11 franchised stores

Your licenses and royalties are like children.
They need to be valued, invested in, and protected.
Licenses and royalties comprise an important part of your bottom line. However, licensees half a world away aren't as worried about your bottom line as you are. At Ernst & Young, our global reach and auditing abilities enable us to advise whether your partners are abiding by your agreements. We can even set up internal systems that would enable you to self-monitor your arrangements. This way, your licenses can grow up to be the big, strong profit makers you always wanted them to be.
newrules
neweconomy
ey.com/thoughtcenter
ERNST & YOUNG
FROM THOUGHT TO FINISH.™

**FIGURE 9.4** Licensing strategy

were bought back, and a ready-to-wear factory in Tours was sold. Overall, Gucci terminated 152 of 167 licenses to stop the brand's slide in quality and reputation. Some critics believed that Gucci paid too much for YSL by underestimating how far the brand has fallen.[17]

Neither extreme of overlicensing nor underlicensing is desirable. Underlicensing results in potential profit being lost, whereas overlicensing leads to a weakened market through overexposure. Overlicensing can increase income in the short run, but it may in the long run mean killing the goose that laid the golden egg. Some of the risks associated with licensing are suboptimal choice, opportunism, quality, production, payment, contract enforcement, and marketing control. The methods to manage such risks include planning, licensee selection, compensation choices, ongoing relationship, contract specification, and organization of the licensing function.[18]

## Management contract

In some cases, government pressure and restrictions force a foreign company either to sell its domestic operations or to relinquish control. In other cases, the company may prefer not to have any FDI. Under such circumstances, the company may have to formulate another way to generate the forfeited revenue. One way to generate revenue is to sign a management contract with the government or the new owner in order to manage the business for the new owner. The new owner may lack technical and managerial expertise and may need the former owner to manage the investment until local employees are trained to manage the facility.

Management contracts may be used as a sound strategy for entering a market with a minimum investment and minimum political risks. Club Med, a leader in international resort vacations, is frequently wooed by developing countries with attractive financing options because these countries want tourism. Club Med's strategy involves having either minority ownership or none at all, even though the firm manages all the resorts. Its rationale is that, with management contracts, Club Med is unlikely to be asked to leave a country where it has a resort.

Management contract is a common strategy in the hotel business. Accor SA, a French hotel giant, for example, has purchased a large stake in Zenith Hotels International.[19] Zenith itself manages nine hotels in China and one hotel in Thailand without owning them, and most of its hotels do not carry the Zenith name. Accor's acquisition is an attempt to catch up in China with Bass PLC, the parent of Holiday Inn. It hopes to use Zenith's connections and experience to land more management contracts. Accor's Sofitel brand also has a hotel in China. In the U.S.A., the Motel 6 chain is also operated by Accor.

## Joint venture

The joint venture is another alternative a firm may consider as a way of entering an overseas market. A joint venture is simply a partnership at corporate level, and it can be domestic or international. For the discussion here, an international joint venture is one in which the partners are from more than one country.

Similar to a partnership formed by two or more individuals, a joint venture is an enterprise formed for a specific business purpose by two or more investors sharing ownership and control. Time Warner Entertainment and Taiwan Pan Asia Investment Company, for instance, have formed a joint venture in Taiwan called Tai Hua International Enterprise Co. Ltd. for the purpose of providing products and services to Taiwan's emerging cable TV industry. The U.S.-based McDonald's owns 50 percent of McDonald's Holdings in Japan.

One recent joint venture involves Advanced Micro Devices (AMD) and Fujitsu to replace a previous joint venture (Fujitsu–AMD Semiconductor Ltd.). The previous joint venture allowed the partners jointly to develop flash memory chips. The arrangement was for them to have separate sales forces and geographic territories while competing against each other in selling these jointly developed chips in Europe. Unlike the previous 50–50 joint venture, AMD owns 60 percent of the new company (called FASL LLC), while Fujitsu owns the rest. The three manufacturing plants in Japan, owned by the former joint venture, are folded into the new venture. With the new joint venture, both partners combine all sales, research, engineering, and marketing.[20]

Joint ventures, like licensing, involve certain risks as well as certain advantages over other forms of entry into a foreign market. In most cases, company resources, circumstances, and the reasons for wanting to do business overseas will determine if a joint venture is the most reasonable way to enter the overseas market. According to one study, firms tend to use joint ventures when they enter markets that are characterized by high legal restrictions or high levels of investment risks.[21]

Marketers consider joint ventures to be dynamic because of the possibility of a parent firm's change in mission or power (see Legal Dimension 9.1). There are two separate overseas investment processes that describe how joint ventures tend to evolve. The first is the "natural," nonpolitical investment process. In this case, a technology-supplying firm gains a foothold in an unfamiliar market by acquiring a partner that can contribute local knowledge and marketing skills. Technology tends to provide dominance to the technology-supplying firm. As the technology partner becomes more familiar with the market, it buys up more or all equity in the venture or leaves the venture entirely. A contributor of technology, however, is not likely to reduce its share in a joint venture while remaining active in it. The second investment process occurs when the local firm's "political" leverage, through government persuasion, halts or reverses the "natural" economic process. The foreign, technology-supplying partner remains engaged in the venture without strengthening its ownership position, the consequence being a gradual takeover by the local parties.[22]

There are several reasons why joint ventures enjoy certain advantages and should be used. One benefit is that a joint venture substantially reduces the amount of resources (money and personnel) that each partner must contribute.

Frequently, the joint-venture strategy is the only way, other than through licensing, that a firm can enter a foreign market. This is especially true when wholly owned activities are prohibited in a country. Centrally planned economies, in particular, usually limit foreign firms' entry to some sort of cooperative arrangement. China has made it quite clear that only those automakers with long-term commitments will be allowed to assemble foreign models with local partners. Foreign manufacturers must agree to have less than 50 percent control of the joint ventures.

Sometimes *social* rather than legal circumstances require a joint venture to be formed. When Pillsbury planned to market its products in Japan, it considered a number of options, ranging from exporting and licensing to the outright purchase of a Japanese company. Although foreign ownership laws had been relaxed, Pillsbury decided to follow traditional business custom in Japan by seeking a good partner. It thus got together with Snow Brand to form Snow-Brand/Pillsbury.

Joint ventures often have social implications. The familial and tightly knit relationship between suppliers and middlemen is prevalent in many countries. In Japan, this relationship is known as *keiretsu*, which means that family-like business groups are linked by cross-ownership of equity. Such

## Legal Dimension 9.1

**From Russia – without love**

Russia has the world's largest reserves of natural gas, and the country is No. 6 in oil. In 2003 BP PLC put $8 billion into TNK–BP, a 50–50 joint venture between BP and three Russian billionaires. As noted by the CEO in 2007, the Russian joint venture TNK–BP Ltd. "has been a very profitable investment." BP's share in TNK–BP amounts to one-fifth of BP's global reserves, a quarter of its production, and almost one-tenth of its global profits. Unfortunately, the investment environment and political climate have drastically changed. President Vladimir Putin has made clear his desire for Russian control of energy resources and control over large energy companies. The desire appears to be achieved at the expense of Western investors.

Russia has threatened to cancel TNK–BP's license for Kovykta because BP and its partners did not meet production targets. Putin questioned how the Russian shareholders in Kovykta managed to acquire their stakes in the 1990s. Interestingly, Russian regulators indicated that license issues could be resolved if Gazprom, the state-controlled gas monopoly, could enter into the project. Kovykta may hold nearly as much natural gas as Canada. Facing pressure from the Kremlin, BP has agreed to sell its majority stake. It would cede its holdings in a $20 billion Russian natural-gas project to state-controlled gas monopoly OAO Gazprom. TNK–BP would sell its 62.7 percent stake in the Kovykta field for almost $1 billion.

Earlier, Russian regulators threatened to shut down the Sakhalin-2 energy project due to alleged environmental violations. As a result, Royal Dutch Shell PLC found it necessary to sell control of the project to Gazprom.

*Source*: "BP Set to Leave Russia Gas Project," *Wall Street Journal*, June 22, 2007.

customs and business relationships make it difficult for a new supplier to gain entry. Even in the event that the new supplier is able to secure some orders, the orders may be terminated as soon as a member of the family is able to supply the product in question. A joint venture thus provides an opportunity for the foreign supplier to secure business orders through the back door.

A joint venture can also simultaneously work to satisfy social, economic, and political circumstances since these concerns are highly related. In any kind of international business undertaking political risks always exist, and a joint venture can reduce such risks while it increases market opportunities. In this sense, a joint venture can make a difference between securely entering a foreign market or not entering at all. Many American firms seek Saudi partners to establish joint ventures so that they can deal effectively with Saudi Arabia's political demands.

Joint ventures are not without their shortcomings and limitations. First, if the partners to the joint venture have not established clear-cut decision-making policy and must consult with each other on all decisions, the *decision-making process* may delay a necessary action when speed is essential. Partners' commitment to a joint venture is a function of the perceived benefits of the relationship. Conflict, on the other hand, reduces efficiency and the perceived benefits.

When two individuals or organizations work together, there are bound to be *conflicts* due to cultural problems, divergent goals, disagreements over production and marketing strategies, and weak contributions by one or the other partner. Although the goals may be compatible at the outset, goals and objectives may diverge over time, even when joint ventures are successful. Dow–Badische was set up in the U.S.A. with BASF providing the technology to make chemical raw materials and fibers and Dow supplying the marketing expertise. A split eventually occurred despite good profits when BASF wanted to expand the fiber business – Dow felt that the venture was moving away from Dow's mainstream chemical business. BASF ultimately bought out Dow and made the business its wholly owned subsidiary.

Another potential problem is the matter of *control*. By definition, a joint venture must deal with double management. If a partner has less than 50 percent ownership, that partner must in effect allow the majority partner to make decisions. If the board of directors has a 50–50 split, it is difficult for the board to make a decision quickly or at all. Dow's experience with its Korea Pacific Chemical joint venture illustrates this point. When prices plunged, the joint venture lost $60 million. To stem the loss, Dow wanted to improve efficiency but was opposed by its Korean partner. The government-appointed directors boycotted board meetings and a decision could not be reached. Both sides eventually ended up bringing lawsuits against each other.

There are four types of partitioning of management control: split management control, shared management, multinational-enterprise-partner-dominant management, and local-partner-dominant management. In the case of international joint ventures in Korea, the split control approach is superior to the others. As a result, multinational corporations and their local partners should split control by matching particular activities with the firm-specific advantages.[23]

There are several factors that may determine whether a company wants to take equity ownership in international joint ventures. These source country factors are exchange rate, cost of borrowing, export capability, and management orientation. Based on a study of 8078 international joint ventures in China, parent firms are more likely to take equity ownership when they are from a source country with a strong currency, low cost of borrowing, strong export capability, and high uncertainty avoidance.[24]

It is interesting to note that, while cultural differences indeed affect international joint-venture performance, culture distance stems more from differences in organizational culture than from differences in national cultures. A survey of Indian executives and their partners from other countries confirmed this relationship.[25]

With regard to performance, based on a study of 1335 Japanese joint ventures in 73 countries (excluding Japan), there is no significant relationship between the number of joint-venture partners and the performance of the venture.[26] According to another study involving a cross-sectional sample of more than 700 joint ventures, three sponsor categories may be identified: (1) partners from developed countries, (2) partners from newly industrialized countries, and (3) partners from developing countries. These categories result in U.S. firms' differential market performance.[27] In addition, partners' cooperation strongly affects performance in equity joint ventures, especially when market uncertainty is present.[28]

The "softer" (behavioral) side of international joint ventures needs to be considered. There are five stages of formation (need determination, partner search, partner selection, negotiations, and operations), four dimensions of trust (personal, competence, contractual, and goodwill), and three dimensions of commitment (intentions-based, contractual, and affective). The knowledge of these stages and dimensions can improve chances of success.[29] In addition, tie strength, trust, and shared values and systems play a role in the transfer of tacit knowledge, especially for mature international joint ventures.[30]

## Manufacturing

The manufacturing process may be employed as a strategy involving all or some manufacturing in a foreign country. The success of Ford Motor Co. in Russia has to do with the company's major commitment to the market. In 1999, Ford spent $150 million on the first foreign-owned automobile factory. The plant opened in 2002. Production has been climbing as Russian consumers step up purchases of automobiles. Local manufacturing has made it possible for Ford to keep prices down. Ford is able to sell its Focus sedans for about $3000 less than similarly equipped imports which have to deal with a 25 percent duty.[31]

Central Europe has gained attention as a manufacturing base for companies that want to enter the EU. The former Soviet bloc countries that are now the new members of the EU offer wages that are just a fraction of those in Western Europe, and they are eager to attract FDI so as to create jobs. Taiwan's Foxconn Technology Co. and Chinese electronics manufacturer Sichuan Changhong have received 10-year tax holidays in the Czech Republic. Another benefit is that manufacturing in the EU lets foreign manufacturers avoid the 14 percent tariff imposed on television sets made in China.[32]

One kind of manufacturing procedure, known as **sourcing**, involves manufacturing operations in a host country, not so much to sell there but for the purpose of exporting from that company's home country to other countries. This chapter is concerned more with another manufacturing objective: the goal of a manufacturing strategy may be to set up a production base inside a target market country as a means of invading it. There are several variations on this method, ranging from complete manufacturing to contract manufacturing (with a local manufacturer) and partial manufacturing.

From the perspective of the host countries, it is obvious as to why they want to attract foreign capital. Although job creation is the main reason, there are several other benefits for the host country as well. Foreign direct investment, unlike other forms of capital inflows, almost always brings additional resources that are very desirable to developing economies. These resources include technology, management expertise, and access to export markets.

There are several reasons why a company chooses to invest in manufacturing facilities abroad. One reason may involve gaining access either to raw materials or to take advantage of resources for its manufacturing operations. As such, this process is known as *backward vertical integration*. Another reason may be to take advantage of lower labor costs or other abundant factors of production (e.g., labor, energy, and other inputs). Hoover was able to cut its high British manufacturing costs by shifting some of its production to France. The strategy may further reduce another kind of cost – transportation. British publishing firms have begun to do more printing abroad because they can save 25 to 40 percent in production and shipping costs. Figure 9.5 shows how the Galician Institute for Economic Promotion has attracted more than 10,000 companies to do business in Galicia, Spain.

Manufacturing in a host country can make the company's product more price-competitive because the company can avoid or minimize high import taxes, as well as other trade barriers. Honda, with 68 percent of its car sales coming from exports and 43 percent from the U.S. market, has a good reason to be sensitive to trade barriers. In order to avoid future problems of this nature, it set up plants in Ohio. Likewise, Honda has committed itself to the market in China and will even work with its partner to create a new brand just for this market.[33]

A manufacturer interested in manufacturing abroad should consider a number of significant factors. The important incentives include: freedom of intercompany payments and dividend remittances, import duty concessions, tax holidays, and guarantees against expropriation.

the best
PSA Peugeot Citroën
car industry
Pescanova
frozen foods
Inditex
textiles & clothing
Zeltia
biotechnology
and 10000 other companies
...are doing business in GALICIA (Spain)
Come and join them in the region with the greatest facilities
and the best investment profitability rate in Europe.
NEW YORK
GALICIA
DÜSSELDORF
TOKYO
For further information:
HQ: Santiago de Compostela • Ph: +34 981 541 143 • promocion@igape.es
Offices:
Düsseldorf • Ph: 0211 935 0141 • IGAPE-Dusseldorf-U.Schneider@t-online.de
New York • Ph: 212 832 3942 • igape@idt.net
Tokyo • Ph: 03 3584 1861 • igapejap@gol.com
www.igape.es
XUNTA DE GALICIA
Galician Government Ministry of Economy and Finance
IGAPE
GALICIAN INSTITUTE FOR ECONOMIC PROMOTION

**FIGURE 9.5** Doing business in Spain

From the marketing standpoint, *product image* deserves attention. Although Winston cigarettes are made in Venezuela with the same tobaccos and formula as the Winston cigarettes in the U.S.A., Venezuelans still prefer the more expensive U.S.-made Winston. Philip Morris and R.J. Reynolds faced this same problem in Russia when setting up manufacturing plants there. Unilever had a similar problem when it began manufacturing locally in Nepal where people prefer Indian-made products.

*Competition* is an important factor, since to a great extent competition determines potential profit. Another factor is the resources of various countries, which should be compared to determine each country's comparative advantage. The comparison should also include production considerations, including production facilities, raw materials, equipment, real estate, water, power, and transport. Human resources, an integral part of the production factor, must be available at reasonable cost.

Manufacturers should pay attention to absolute as well as relative changes in *labor costs*. A particular country is more attractive as a plant's location if the wages there increase more slowly than those in other countries. The increase in labor costs in Germany led GM's Opel to switch its production facilities to Japan and led Rollei to move its production to Singapore. Several Japanese firms have been attracted by a low wage rate in Mexico, a rate even lower than the hourly pay in Singapore and South Korea. A manufacturer must keep in mind, however, that labor costs are determined not only by compensation but also by productivity and exchange rates. Mexico's labor costs, already extremely low, become even lower if the peso is weak, but this advantage is offset somewhat because Mexican workers are relatively unskilled and thus produce more defective products.

The *type of product* made is another factor that determines whether foreign manufacturing is an economical and effective venture. A manufacturer must weigh the economies of exporting a standardized product against the flexibility of having a local manufacturing plant that is capable of tailoring the product to local preferences.

*Taxation* is another important consideration. Countries commonly offer tax advantages, among other incentives, to lure foreign investment. Puerto Rico does well on this score. In addition, there are no exchange problems since the currency is the U.S. dollar.

Just as important as other factors is the *investment climate* for foreign capital. The investment climate is determined by geographic and climatic conditions, market size, and growth potential, as well as by the political atmosphere. As mentioned earlier, political, economic, and social motives are highly related, and it is hardly surprising that countries, states, and cities compete fiercely to attract foreign investment and manufacturing plants.

Multinational corporations have been investing more and more overseas, with Asia and Latin America as their prime targets. It should be pointed out that the importance of cheap, unskilled labor in attracting manufacturing investment has been diminishing. Because of technology development in products and processes, there is a greater need for human skill in product manufacturing. Therefore, developing countries that can successfully influence plant location decisions will be those that have more highly skilled labor at relatively low wages.

## Assembly operations

An assembly operation is a variation on a manufacturing strategy. According to the U.S. Customs Service, "Assembly means the fitting or joining together of fabricated components." The methods used to join or fit together solid components may be welding, soldering, riveting, gluing, laminating, and sewing.

In this strategy, parts or components are produced in various countries in order to gain each country's comparative advantage (see Figure 9.6). Capital-intensive parts may be produced in advanced nations, and labor-intensive assemblies may be produced in a less developed country, where labor is abundant and labor costs are low. This strategy is common among manufacturers of consumer electronics. When a product becomes mature and faces intense price competition, it may be necessary to shift all of the labor-intensive operations to less developed countries.

An assembly operation also allows a company to be price-competitive against cheap imports, and this is a defense strategy employed by U.S. apparel makers against such imports. As far as pattern design and fabric cutting are concerned, a U.S. firm can compete by using automated machines, but sewing is another matter altogether, since sewing is labor-intensive and the least-automated aspect of making the product. To solve this problem, precut fabrics can be shipped to a low-wage country for sewing before bringing them back for finishing and packaging. Warnaco and Interco save on aggregate labor costs by cutting fabrics in the U.S.A. and shipping them to plants in Costa Rica and Honduras to be sewn. The duties collected on finished products brought back are low.

Assembly operations also allow a company's product to enter many markets without being subject to tariffs and quotas. The extent of freedom and flexibility, however, is limited by local product-content laws. South American countries usually require that more than 50 to 95 percent of components used in products be produced domestically. Note that as the percentage of required local content increases, the company's flexibility declines and the price advantage erodes. This is so because domestic products can be sheltered behind tariff walls, and higher prices must be expected for products with a low percentage of local content.

In general, a host country objects to the establishment of a screwdriver assembly that merely assembles imported parts. If a product's local content is less than half of all the components used, the product may be viewed as imported, subjected to tariffs and quota restrictions. The Japanese, even with joint ventures and assembly operations in Europe, keep local content in foreign production facilities to a minimum while maximizing the use of low-cost Japanese components. British Leyland's Triumph Acclaim is one such example. Made in the United Kingdom under license from Honda, Acclaim contained over 55 percent of Japanese parts. Italy considered Acclaim to be a Japanese, not a European car. Since the EU's rule of thumb seemed to be at least 45 percent local content, Italy asked the European Commission to decide what percentage of local content a product must have to be considered "made in Europe." An assembly manufacturing operator must therefore carefully evaluate the tradeoff between low-cost production and the process of circumventing trade barriers.

## Turnkey operations

A turnkey operation is an agreement by the seller to supply a buyer with a facility fully equipped and ready to be operated by the buyer's personnel, who will be trained by the seller. The term is sometimes used in fast-food franchising when a franchisor agrees to select a store site, build the store, equip it, train the franchisee and employees, and sometimes arrange for the financing. In international marketing, the term is usually associated with giant projects that are sold to governments or government-run companies. Large-scale plants requiring technology and large-scale construction processes unavailable in local markets commonly use this strategy. Such large-scale projects include building steel mills; cement, fertilizer, and chemical plants; and those related to such advanced technologies as telecommunications.

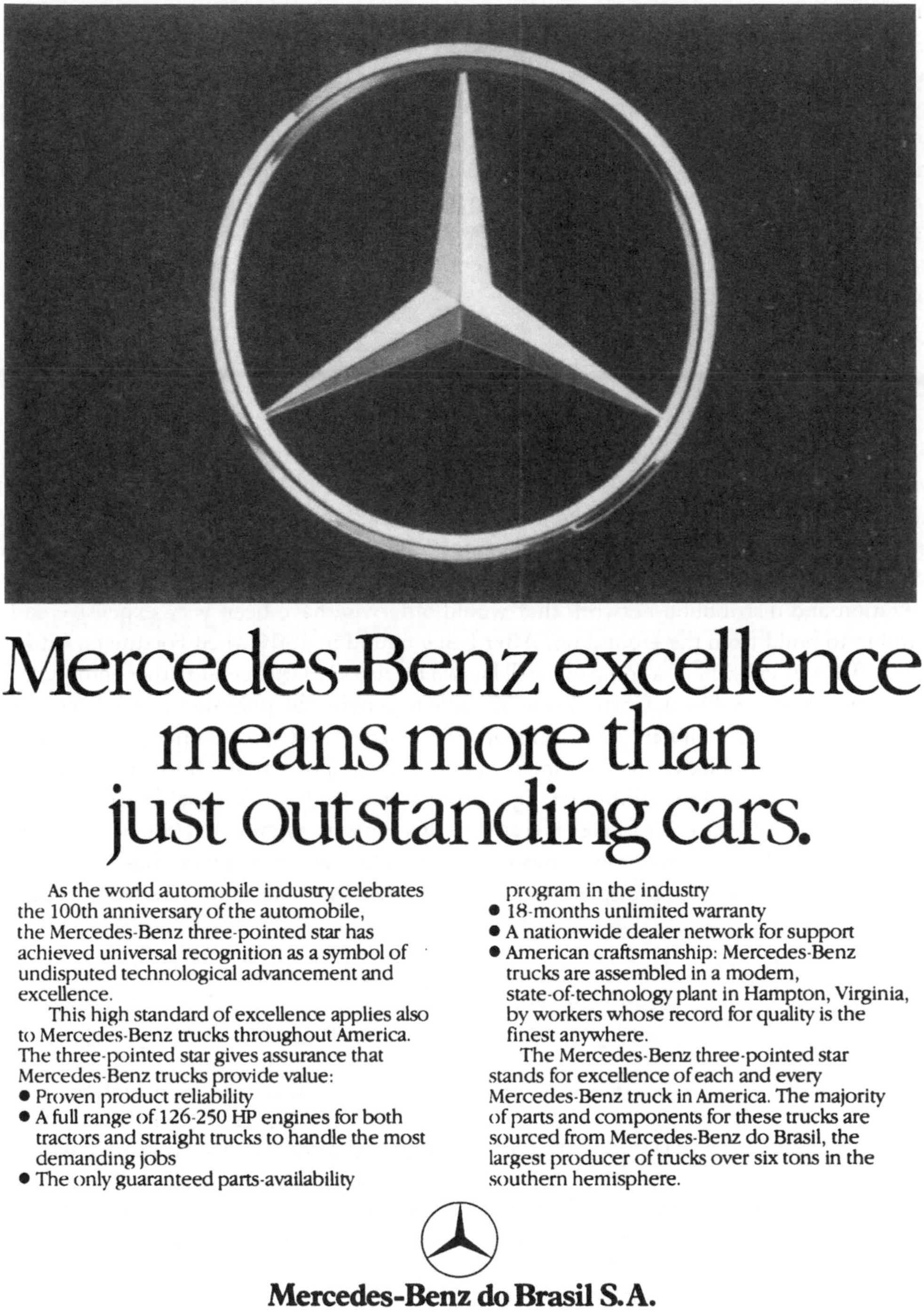
Mercedes-Benz excellence means more than just outstanding cars.
As the world automobile industry celebrates the 100th anniversary of the automobile, the Mercedes-Benz three-pointed star has achieved universal recognition as a symbol of undisputed technological advancement and excellence.
This high standard of excellence applies also to Mercedes-Benz trucks throughout America. The three-pointed star gives assurance that Mercedes-Benz trucks provide value:
• Proven product reliability
• A full range of 126-250 HP engines for both tractors and straight trucks to handle the most demanding jobs
• The only guaranteed parts-availability program in the industry
• 18-months unlimited warranty
• A nationwide dealer network for support
• American craftsmanship: Mercedes-Benz trucks are assembled in a modern, state-of-technology plant in Hampton, Virginia, by workers whose record for quality is the finest anywhere.
The Mercedes-Benz three-pointed star stands for excellence of each and every Mercedes-Benz truck in America. The majority of parts and components for these trucks are sourced from Mercedes-Benz do Brasil, the largest producer of trucks over six tons in the southern hemisphere.
Mercedes-Benz do Brasil S.A.

**FIGURE 9.6** Assembly operations

*Source*: Reprinted with permission of Mercedes-Benz do Brasil S.A.

Owing to the magnitude of a giant turnkey project, the winner of the contract may expect to reap huge rewards. Thus, it is important that the turnkey construction package offered to a buyer is an attractive one. Such a package involves more than just offering the latest technology, since there are many other factors important to less developed countries in deciding on a particular turnkey project. Financing is critical, and this is one area in which U.S. firms are lacking. European and Japanese firms are much more prepared to secure attractive financing from their governments for buyers. Another factor for consideration involves an agreement to build a local plant. All equipment must be installed and tested to make certain that it functions as intended. Local personnel must be trained to run the operation, and after-sale services should be contracted for and made available for the future maintenance of the plant.

## Acquisition

When a manufacturer wants to enter a foreign market rapidly and yet retain maximum control, direct investment through acquisition should be considered (see Cultural Dimension 9.1 and Ethical Dimension 9.1). The reasons for wanting to acquire a foreign company include product/geographical diversification, acquisition of expertise (technology, marketing, and management), and rapid entry. For example, Renault acquired a controlling interest in American Motors in order to gain the sales organization and distribution network that would otherwise have been very expensive and time-consuming to build from the ground up. After being outbid in 1994 when Forstmann Little & Co. bought Ziff-Davis Publishing, a company well known for its *PC Magazine* and other computer-related publications, Japan's Softbank Corp. was finally able to acquire the publisher a year later, albeit at a much higher price ($2.1 billion). The deal made the Japanese software company the world's largest computer magazine publisher and the largest operator of computer trade shows including Comdex.

Acquisition is viewed in a different light from other kinds of foreign direct investment. A government generally welcomes foreign investment that starts up a new enterprise (called a **greenfield** enterprise), since that investment increases employment and enlarges the tax base. An acquisition, however, fails to do this since it displaces and replaces domestic ownership. Therefore, acquisition is

### Cultural Dimension 9.1

**How to make a successful acquisition**

Jack Welch, the highly successful and former CEO of General Electric, lists the "six sins" of mergers and acquisitions. First, any "merger of equals" sounds good in theory but is a mess in practice. Second, the cultural fit of the two partners is as important as (if not more so than) a strategic fit. Third, run away from a "reverse hostage" situation when an acquirer makes so many concessions to the point that the acquired company will be in charge. Fourth, "be not afraid" as boldness is necessary and sensible for integration. Fifth, avoid the "conqueror syndrome" by installing own people everywhere in the new territory. Sixth and finally, "don't pay too much."

*Source*: Jack Welch and Suzy Welch, "The Six Sins of M&A," *Business Week*, October 23, 2006, 148.

very likely to be perceived as exploitation or a blow to national pride – on this basis, it stands a good chance of being turned down. There was a heated debate before the United Kingdom allowed Sikorsky, a U.S. firm, to acquire Westland, a failing British manufacturer of military helicopters. That episode caused the Thatcher government to halt its negotiation with Ford concerning the acquisition of British Leyland's Austin-Rover passenger-car division. A greenfield project, while embraced by the host country, implies gradual market entry.

## Ethical Dimension 9.1

### In the name of free trade: dying for profits

It is an undeniable fact that cigarette smoking kills 4.9 million people every year. Once young people start smoking, many will be hooked for life. If cigarettes are a brand new product that is introduced to the market for the very first time, it is doubtful whether any governments could allow this harmful product to be marketed. A case can be made that cigarettes should be classified as an illegal drug.

Health officials all over the world have been prodding their governments to discourage smoking as well as the marketing of cigarettes. After all, health costs are enormous. While the U.S.A. has forced tobacco firms to curtail their marketing activities in the U.S. market, it seems to have taken the opposite approach abroad. While the U.S. cigarette market is now a mature or even declining one, such overseas markets as China and Russia are very attractive. The Chinese and Russian markets are big, and people there are not as concerned about the health issues. There is no question that cigarettes are a highly profitable industry and that American tobacco firms have dominated markets worldwide. But should the U.S.A. push to open up markets abroad for American cigarettes by using free trade as an excuse? The Bush administration has even tried to interfere with international controls on tobacco by opposing the Framework Convention on Tobacco Control.

The World Health Organization has spent three years working out an agreement with 171 countries to control the spread of smoking-related diseases. The treaty bans tobacco advertising, except where such a ban would be in conflict with national laws. The treaty additionally imposes a substantial tax on tobacco products and mandates warning labels on cigarette packages. Strangely, the U.S.A., citing free speech, seems to be more concerned with the welfare of the tobacco industry, which happened to give $6.4 million to the 2002 campaign chests of Republican candidates. But then the Bush administration has rejected a global warming agreement, an international criminal court, and a treaty on women's rights.

Japan Tobacco Inc. acquired Britain's Gallaher Group PLC in 2006 for $14.7 billion. Gallaher's brands include Benson & Hedges and Silk Cut. Because of health concerns in the U.S.A., coupled with falling tobacco sales in Japan, Japan Tobacco is seeking profits in fast-growing economies that do not have strict smoking-related regulations. Gallaher's largest factory in Moscow produces 65 billion cigarettes. The combined entity will have almost 35 percent of the hugely profitable Russian market. The market share in neighboring Kazakhstan will be 50 percent.

*Sources*: "Deadly Export," *San José Mercury News*, May 21, 2002; "Tobacco Treaty Changes Sought," *San José Mercury News*, April 30, 2003; "U.S. Feeds the World's Tobacco Habit," *San José Mercury News*, May 4, 2003; and "Japan Tobacco Makes Big Bet," *Wall Street Journal*, December 18, 2006.

When host states and investors bargain over the terms of investment in sensitive sectors of the economy, there are political and economic tensions. Private ownership is positively related to greenfield investment (vs. divestiture) and joint venture (vs. wholly owned) projects.[34]

Although greenfield is a favored investment from the perspective of a host country, it is necessary to assess both the short-term and long-term benefits of this type of investment. A merger or acquisition merely involves ownership change, while greenfield FDI adds productive capital and employment – at least over the short term. However, after the initial period, it is difficult to assess the impact on host countries based on entry mode.[35]

A special case of acquisition is the **brownfield** entry mode. This mode occurs when an investor's transferred resources dominate over those provided by an acquired firm. In addition, this hybrid mode of entry requires the investor to extensively restructure the acquired company so as to assure fit between the two organizations. This is not uncommon in emerging markets, and the extensive restructuring may yield a new operation that resembles a greenfield investment. As such, integration costs can be high. Still, brownfield is a worthwhile strategy to consider when neither pure acquisition nor greenfield is feasible.[36]

Due to the sensitive nature of acquisition, there are more legal hurdles to surmount. In Germany, the Federal Cartel Office may prohibit or require divestiture of those mergers and acquisitions that could strengthen or create market domination. As in the case of Nestlé's acquisitions of U.S. companies in quick succession, it paid $10.3 billion in cash for Ralston Purina Co. (a pet-food powerhouse), over $2.6 billion in stock for a controlling stake in Dreyer's Grand Ice Cream Inc. (the largest U.S. maker of ice cream), and another $2.6 billion for Chef America Inc. Nestlé had to spend almost a year convincing American regulators to let it acquire Dreyer's Grand Ice Cream. The U.S. Federal Trade Commission blocked the proposed deal because the takeover would eliminate brand and price competition for such premium brands as Häagen Dazs and Godiva. Nestlé, Dreyers, and Unilever control 98 percent of superpremium ice cream sales in the U.S.A.

There does not appear to be any sign that mergers and acquisitions are abating. Vivendi paid $2.09 billion to Bertelsmann in 2006 to acquire the BMG Music Publishing Group which has the world's largest collection of music catalogs and songs.[37] Barclays decided to acquire ABN Amro in 2007 for 67 billion euros.[38]

Several of Ford Motor Co.'s premium brands are a result of acquisitions (see Figure 9.7), and they include Volvo (1999), Jaguar (1989), and Aston Martin (1987). A 2000 acquisition was a payment of nearly $3 billion to BMW Group for the British-born Land Rover line of sport-utility vehicles. BMW acquired Rover Group Ltd. in 1995 and lost $1.25 billion on this investment over five years. To cut the loss, BMW sold Rover Group's Rover and MG brands to a British investment group and Land Rover to Ford.

The value of a currency may either reduce or increase the costs of an acquisition. A buyer whose home currency is getting weaker will see its costs go up but will benefit if its currency becomes stronger. As in the case of Hoechst, a German chemical giant, it bid $7.2 billion for the U.S.-based Marion Merrell Dow Inc. and was able to save at least $250 million because the value of the dollar plunged in the meantime.

International mergers and acquisitions are complex, expensive, and risky. The problems are numerous: finding a suitable company, determining a fair price, acquisition debt, merging two management teams, language and cultural differences, employee resentment, geographic distance, and so on. Acquirers must thus exercise due diligence. Sometimes, it may be better to walk away from a deal. The reasons for exiting from a deal include: high price, no agreement on governance

Now available in regular,
high-test and field corn.
85
ETHANOL
We know we don't control the price of gas, but we can innovate to reduce the need. That's why we're building cars that can go 500 miles on a single tank and producing 250,000 E-85 ethanol vehicles this year. We even have 12 vehicles that get 30 mpg or more.* At Ford, innovation is the guiding compass of everything we do.
Bill Ford, Chairman and CEO
Ford Motor Company
Ford
LINCOLN
MERCURY
mazda
VOLVO
JAGUAR
LAND-ROVER
ASTON MARTIN
DRIVING AMERICAN INNOVATION
*Based on EPA estimated hwy mpg.
ford.com/innovation

**FIGURE 9.7** Ford's acquisitions and brands

issues, no synergies, poor quality of management, environmental issues, ethical reasons, no strategic fit, detection of significant unrecorded/undisclosed liability, potential problem with anti-trust laws, and uncertainty about legal/tax aspects.[39]

Quite often, the future synergies due to vertical integration are elusive. Unicord PLC, a large fish processor located in Thailand, paid $280 million to acquire Bumble Bee Seafood Inc., a San Diego tuna canner. The acquisition was a failure, and the founder of Unicord committed suicide in 1995 as lenders sought payment. Japan's Bridgestone Corp. paid $2.6 billion to acquire money-losing Firestone Tire & Rubber Co. and lost $1 billion in the first five years after the acquisition while enduring a bitter and lengthy strike. Overall, foreign acquirers pay almost twice as much as domestic buyers would. The U.S. market in particular, due to its market size, tends to force foreign acquirers to pay a premium price.

Major differences in national culture hurt foreign acquisition performance if the acquirer tightly integrates the acquired unit, but performance is enhanced if there is a limited degree of post-acquisition integration.[40] The parties should also consider a performance-contingent payout structure to mitigate risk of adverse selection. There is evidence that firms lacking acquisition experience rely on contingent payouts when purchasing targets in high-technology and service industries. There is a tendency to avoid contingent payouts in host countries which have problems with investor protection and legal enforceability.[41] In any case, pre-acquisition experience of both target and a multinational enterprise is important.[42]

Country differences in intellectual property rights protection can affect the choice of market entry. When protection is not secure, companies choose R&D joint ventures over contractual partnerships.[43]

According to a study by *Business Week* and Mercer Management Consulting Inc. of 150 deals worth at least $500 million, mergers and acquisitions do not benefit stockholders. When judged by stock performance in relation to Standard & Poor's industry indexes, about half of the 150 deals harmed shareholder wealth, while another one-third hardly contributed anything. Yet, in spite of the high failure rate for cross-border acquisitions, more and more international deals can be expected. A follow-up study showed that transatlantic mergers had a better chance to succeed – far better than the usual success ratio of American domestic or intra-European deals. One contributing factor is that such deals tended to expand geographic reach, reducing the need to cut costs by disruptively merging overlapping operations. In addition, because of the hassles of having to pass the scrutiny of anti-trust regulators on both sides of the ocean, companies choose to pursue only the most promising prospects.[44]

## Strategic alliances

As discussed, to gain access to new markets and technologies while achieving economies of scale, international marketers have a number of organization forms to choose from: licensing, partially owned or wholly owned subsidiaries, joint ventures, and acquisitions. A relatively new organizational form of market entry and competitive cooperation is **strategic alliance**. This form of corporate cooperation has been receiving a great deal of attention as large multinational firms still find it necessary to find strategic partners to penetrate a market.

There is no clear and precise definition of strategic alliance. There is no one way to form a strategic alliance. An alliance may be in the areas of production, distribution, marketing, and research and development. America Online is a good example of strategic alliances. In 2000, America Online and Bertelsmann AG formed a global alliance to expand the distribution of Bertelsmann's media content and electronic commerce properties over America Online's interactive brands worldwide. As an example of R&D alliances, Sony and Philips ally to compete with another alliance led by Toshiba in developing DVDs.

Strategic alliances may be the result of mergers, acquisitions, joint ventures, and licensing agreements. Joint ventures are naturally strategic alliances, but not all strategic alliances are joint ventures. Unlike joint ventures which require two or more partners to create a separate entity, a strategic alliance does not necessarily require a new legal entity. As such, it may not require partners to make arrangements to share equity. Instead of being an equity-based investment, a strategic alliance may be more of a contractual arrangement whereby two or more partners agree to cooperate with each other and utilize each partner's resources and expertise to penetrate a particular market.

Airlines are a good example of the international nature of strategic alliances. Almost all major airlines have joined one of the three strategic groups: Star, SkyTeam, and Oneworld. The SkyTeam group consists of Delta, Air France, Aeromexico, Alitalia, Czech Airlines, and Korean Air. Oneworld has American, British Airways, Aer Lingus, Cathay Pacific, Finnair, Iberia, Japan Airlines, LanChile, and Qantas. The Star alliance, the largest group, comprises United, Air Canada, Air New Zealand, ANA, Austrian, British Midland, Lauda, Lufthansa, Mexicana, Scandinavian, Singapore, Thai, Tyrolean, and Varig. Turkish Airlines was accepted in 2006 as the 21st member. While the alliances vary in size and degree of integration, most of them have code sharing by offering seats on a partner's flights. In addition, passengers earn frequent-flier points on their home carrier when flying with the alliance members. These members also provide reciprocal access to their airport lounges.

Companies enter into alliance relationships for a variety of reasons. Those in the emerging Latin American economies are similar to their counterparts in many other nations in terms of their motivations. In general, through alliances with foreign partners, they seek resource acquisition, competitive posturing, and risk/cost reduction.[45] While companies have paid attention to the hard side of alliance management (e.g., financial issues and other operational issues), the soft side also requires attention. The soft side has to do with the management of relationship capital in an alliance. Relationship capital focuses on the socio-psychological aspects of the alliance, and the two important areas of relationship capital are mutual trust and commitment.[46]

## Analysis of entry strategies

To enter a foreign market, a manufacturer has a number of strategic options, each with its own strengths and weaknesses. Many companies employ multiple strategies. IBM has employed strategies ranging from licensing, joint ventures, and strategic alliances on the one hand to local manufacturing and subsidiaries on the other hand. Likewise, McDonald's uses joint ventures in the Far East while licensing its name without putting up equity capital in the Mid-East. Walt Disney Co. has a 39 percent stake in Euro Disney while collecting management and royalty fees which amount to $70 million a year.

One would be naive to believe that a single entry strategy is suitable for all products or in all countries. For example, a significant change in the investment climate can make a particular strategy ineffective even though it worked well in the past. There are a number of characteristics that determine the appropriateness of entry strategies, and many variables affect which strategy is chosen. These characteristics include political risks, regulations, type of country, type of product, and other competitive and market characteristics.

Viacom Inc. appears to take culture into account in deciding on entry strategies. In the case of its MTV channel, the company generally does not have partners, but in the case of its Nickelodeon channel, the firm has made an effort to have local partners. It is difficult to tell Europeans that they should have the same cultural underpinnings inherent in American children's programming. Although children may watch programming from other countries, they are more inclined to watch their own programs.

Markets are far from being homogeneous, and the type of country chosen dictates the entry strategy to be used. In free-enterprise economies, an MNC can choose any entry strategy it deems appropriate. In controlled economies, the options are limited. Until recently, the most frequent trade entry activity in controlled economies was exporting, followed by licensing for Eastern Europe.

Market entry strategies are also influenced by *product type*. A product that must be customized or that requires some services before and after the sale cannot easily be exported to another country. In fact, a service or a product whose value is largely determined by an accompanied service cannot be practically distributed outside of the producing country. Any portion of the product that is service-oriented must be created at the place of consumption. As a result, service-intensive products require particular modes of market entry. The options include management contract to sell service to a foreign customer, licensing so that another local company (franchisee) can be trained to provide that service, and local manufacturing by establishing a permanent branch or subsidiary there.

A product that is basically a *commodity* may require local production in order to reduce labor and shipping costs. For a *value-added or differentiated product*, a firm can depend on the exporting mode because of the higher profit margin. Furthermore, local manufacturing may destroy the product's mystique and thus diminish a previously existing market.

There are two schools of thought that explain how multinational corporations select ownership structures for subsidiaries. The first has to do with what the firm wants, and MNCs want structures that minimize the transaction costs of doing business abroad (e.g., whole ownership). Factors affecting what the firm wants include the capabilities of the firm, its strategic needs, and the transaction costs of different ways of transferring capabilities. The second school of thought, related to what the firm can get, explains that what it wants may differ from what it can get (e.g., joint venture). In this case, ownership structures are determined by negotiations, whose outcomes depend on the relative bargaining power of the firm and that of the host government.

In practice, American manufacturers prefer joint ventures in the Far East because of legal and cultural barriers. Regarding how American manufacturers want to enter the European Union market, the preferred methods of entry are: joint venture, sales representative, branch/subsidiary, and distribution facility.

A company's entry choice of joint ventures versus wholly owned subsidiaries may be influenced by its competitive capabilities as well as market barriers. In the case of Japanese investors entering the U.S. market, they choose joint ventures when facing high market barriers. But they prefer to establish wholly owned subsidiaries when they possess competitive capabilities. These ownership decisions are influenced more by marketing variables than by technological factors. One caveat: the results vary across industries (low technology vs. high technology) and products (consumer products vs. industrial products).[47] The costs of organizing a business in transition economies influence entry mode choice. Host-country institutions have an impact because underdeveloped institutions drive up costs of establishing wholly owned ventures.[48]

Institutional isomorphism seems to exist as later entrants often use the entry mode patterns established by earlier entrants. In addition, this behavior exists within a firm as companies exhibit consistency in their entry mode choices across time.[49]

In the case of China, a company's timing of entry is associated with non-equity modes, competitors' behavior, and lower levels of country risk. Firms cannot delay their entry when the competitors are moving in. In addition, a firm's entry is accelerated if a non-equity mode of entry is chosen. Favorable risk conditions (locational features), likewise, accelerate entry timing. In addition, corporate size facilitates early entry. A firm of good size is able to muster resources, extend support among the related products sectors, and capitalize on economies of scale. This is consistent with the resource-based arguments that early entrants differ from late entrants in terms of resources and capabilities.[50]

One study focuses on conflicting results which show that cultural distance is associated with wholly owned modes in some studies and with joint ventures in other studies. The evidence shows that, for Western firms investing in Central and Eastern Europe, investment risk moderates the relationship between cultural distance and entry mode selection. Firms entering culturally distant markets that are low in investment risk prefer cooperative modes of entry. However, if such culturally distant markets pose high investment risk, wholly owned modes of entry are preferred.[51] Conversely, although cultural distance is routinely used as an independent variable that supposedly influences performance and entry mode choice, it is conceivable that the relationship may be reversed. A case can be made that cultural distance is a dependent variable because entry mode and performance may affect the perceived distance.[52]

With regard to Spanish FDI in Latin America, cultural affinity is the most important factor in the selection of the destination.[53] A review of 26 studies reveals that the nationality of companies affects entry mode decisions. The effect, however, varies due to some cultural and economic factors.[54] The effect of cultural distance is not straightforward. While it is negatively related with international diversification for high-technology industries, the relationship is positive for other industries. For U.S.-based multinationals, there is a strong negative association between cultural distance and entry mode choice.[55] Logically, multinationals need to conform to the institutional environment of the host country. Therefore, FDI should be utilized when there is minimal institutional distance between the home-country and host-country environments.[56]

It may make sense to differentiate between hard- and soft-service firms. Hard-service suppliers can learn from the experience of manufacturing companies going abroad. Soft services, however, are unique because of the importance of interaction between soft-service suppliers and their clients. Based on a study of 140 Swedish service firms, soft-service firms are likely to prefer a high control entry mode to a low control entry mode.[57]

## Free trade zones (FTZs)

When entering a market, a company should go beyond an investigation of market entry modes. Another question that should be asked is whether a free trade zone (FTZ) is involved and needs consideration. The decisions concerning market entry and FTZs are somewhat independent. An FTZ can be used regardless of whether the entry strategy is exporting or local manufacturing.

An **FTZ** is a secured domestic area in international commerce, considered to be legally outside a country's customs territory. It is an area designated by a government for the duty-free entry of goods. It is also a location where imports can be handled with few regulations, and little or no customs duties and excise taxes are collected. As such, goods enter the area without paying any duty. The duty would be paid only when goods enter customs territory of the country where an FTZ is located.

Variations among FTZs include freeports, tariff-free trade zones, airport duty-free arcades, export-processing zones, and other foreign grade zones. FTZs are usually established in countries for the convenience of foreign traders. The zones may be run by the host government or by private entities. FTZs vary in size from a few acres to several square miles. They may be located at airports, in harbor areas, or within the interior of a country (e.g., Salt Lake City). In addition to the FTZs (general-purpose zones), there are also subzones throughout the U.S.A. Subzones are special-purpose facilities for companies unable to operate effectively at public zone sites.

One popular misconception about FTZs is that they are used basically for warehousing. Although goods can be stored for an unlimited length of time in an FTZ, any gain from doing so is small when compared to the alternative of a bonded warehouse, which allows temporary storage without duty. Actually, the future of FTZs lies in manufacturing (product manipulation), not storing.

FTZs offer several important benefits, both for the country and for companies using them. One benefit is job retention and creation. When better facilities and grants are provided to attract MNCs, FTZs can generate foreign investment and jobs. For example, the Buffalo, New York, FTZ was able to attract a Canadian automobile assembly operation and a Japanese camera importer to establish operations there. China has set up special economic zones (SEZs) for manufacturing, banking, exporting and importing, and foreign investment. Figure 9.8 mentions Macedonia's incentives as well as its free economic zones.

Some countries, for political reasons, are not able to open up their economies completely. Instead they have set up **export-processing zones**, a special type of FTZ, in order to attract foreign capital for manufacturing for export.

The benefits of FTZ use are numerous. Some of these benefits are country-specific in the sense that some countries offer superior facilities for lower costs (e.g., utilities and telecommunications). Other benefits are zone-specific in that certain zones may be better than others within the same country in terms of tax and transportation facilities. Finally, there are zone-related benefits that constitute general advantages in using an FTZ. Some of the zone-related benefits are: lower theft rate, lower insurance costs, delay of tax payment, and reduction of inventory in transit.

FTZs provide a means to facilitate imports. Imported merchandise may be sent into FTZs without formal customs entry and duty payment until some later date. Both foreign and domestic goods can be moved into FTZs and remain there for storage, assembling, manufacturing, packaging, and other processing operations. Goods that were improperly marked or cannot meet standards for clearance may be remarked and salvaged. Moreover, goods may be cleaned, mixed, and used in the manufacturing of other products. One Swiss cosmetics company imports in bulk and employs U.S. labor to repackage its goods for retailing. In fact, importers can even display and exhibit merchandise and take orders in FTZs without securing a bond. For retailers, benefits derived by using FTZs include the sorting, labeling, and storing of imports.

FTZs not only facilitate imports but can also facilitate export and re-export, though the gain from this practice is small when compared to the alternatives of duty drawback and temporary import bond. Still, domestic goods can be taken into an FTZ and are then returned free of quotas and duty, even when they have been combined with other articles while inside the zone. Sears uses the New Orleans FTZ to inspect foreign cameras it subsequently ships to Latin America. Seiko Time corporation of America opened a 200,000-square-foot facility in the New Jersey FTZ to store and ship watches to Canada and Latin America. One European medical supply firm that makes kidney dialysis machines use German raw materials and American labor in a U.S. FTZ for assembly purposes, and then exports 30 percent of the finished product to Scandinavia.

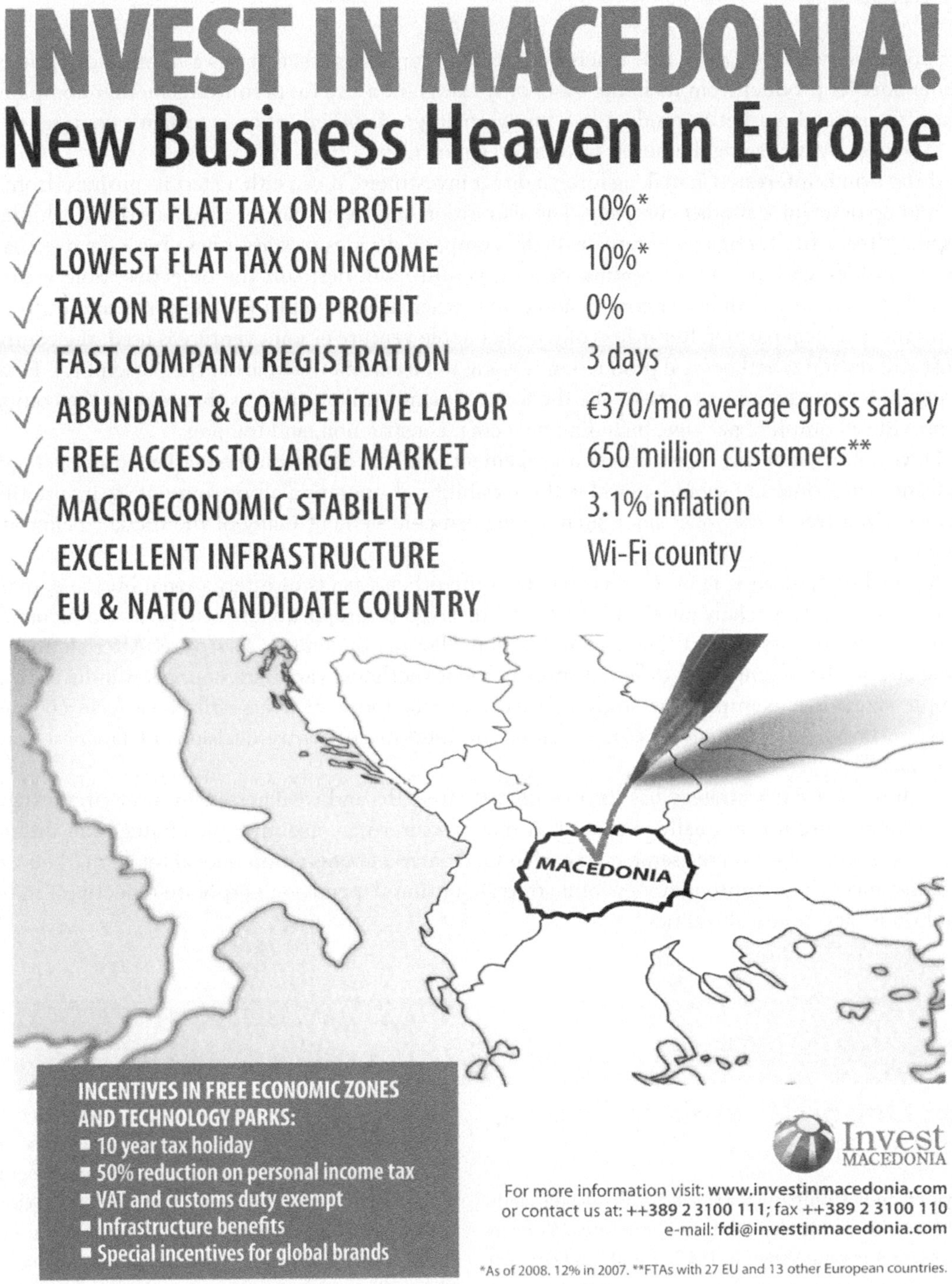
INVEST IN MACEDONIA!
New Business Heaven in Europe
LOWEST FLAT TAX ON PROFIT 10%*
LOWEST FLAT TAX ON INCOME 10%*
TAX ON REINVESTED PROFIT 0%
FAST COMPANY REGISTRATION 3 days
ABUNDANT & COMPETITIVE LABOR €370/mo average gross salary
FREE ACCESS TO LARGE MARKET 650 million customers**
MACROECONOMIC STABILITY 3.1% inflation
EXCELLENT INFRASTRUCTURE Wi-Fi country
EU & NATO CANDIDATE COUNTRY
MACEDONIA
INCENTIVES IN FREE ECONOMIC ZONES AND TECHNOLOGY PARKS:
10 year tax holiday
50% reduction on personal income tax
VAT and customs duty exempt
Infrastructure benefits
Special incentives for global brands
Invest MACEDONIA
For more information visit: www.investinmacedonia.com
or contact us at: ++389 2 3100 111; fax ++389 2 3100 110
e-mail: fdi@investinmacedonia.com
*As of 2008. 12% in 2007. **FTAs with 27 EU and 13 other European countries.

**FIGURE 9.8** Macedonia's incentives and free economic zones

## Conclusion

If a company wants to avoid FDI when marketing in foreign markets it has a number of options. It can export its product from its home base, or it can grant a license permitting another company to manufacture and market its product in a foreign market. Another option is to sign a contract to sell its expertise by managing the business for a foreign owner.

If the firm is interested in making foreign direct investment, it can either start its business from the ground up or acquire another company. The acquisition, however, may receive a less than enthusiastic response from the foreign government. If the company decides to start a new business overseas, it must consider whether a sole venture or joint venture will best suit the objective. Sole ventures provide a company with better control and profit, whereas joint ventures reduce risk and utilize the strengths of a local partner. Regardless of whether a sole venture or joint venture is used, the company must still decide whether local production is going to be complete or partial (i.e., assembly). Finally, foreign sales to governments often take the form of giant turnkey projects that require the company to provide a complete package, including financing, construction, and training.

Once a particular market is chosen, management needs to decide on the market entry strategy. In addition, the company should consider the feasibility of operating all or some of its international business in a free trade zone, since such a zone can complement many of the market penetration options.

A word of caution is in order. Compared to the other aspects of international business, market entry strategies (especially joint ventures) have received disproportionate attention. Unfortunately, contradictory results abound. These contradictions should not come as a surprise. After all, many of these studies have employed different measurement methods, variables, countries, industries, and sample sizes. For example, one study focused on entry forms of five small Norwegian computer software firms,[58] while another study focused on 4000 market entry decisions of Japanese multinationals.[59]

Each market entry strategy has its own unique strengths and weaknesses. In most circumstances the strategies are not mutually exclusive. A manufacturer may use multiple strategies in different markets as well as within the same market. No single market penetration is ideal for all markets or all circumstances. The appropriateness of a strategic option depends on corporate objectives, market conditions, and political realities.

## CASE 9.1 TAYLOR CANDY COMPANY AND THE CARIBBEAN MARKET

### Jun Onishi, Hirosaki University, Japan

Taylor Candy Company is a small, family-owned candy company located in the southern Florida area. When it was originally established in 1957, it sold candy only in that area. Over the years, its candy bars have grown in popularity and are now distributed throughout the southeastern U.S.A.

Its most popular product is the Coco-Loco bar, which has a toasted coconut outside with a crisp peanut crunch inside. Because coconuts are not grown in the U.S.A., this candy bar is marketed as an "exotic, island treat." The wrapper shows palm trees and a thatch-roofed beach bungalow, emphasizing this image. The advertisements for the product feature someone relaxing on a tropical beach, eating the candy bar. Market research shows that most of the consumers of this candy bar are working and in the lower-middle class, making lower-than-average to average incomes. Consumers interviewed said that the candy bar's flavor is the main reason why they purchased it, but they also indicated that they were influenced by the tropical image. Some consumers said that, since they could not afford to vacation on a tropical island, eating the candy bar made them feel as if they were on an island. A large percentage of consumers also indicated that they were influenced by the company's aggressive anti-littering and pro-recycling stance.

At this point in time, attempts to distribute the candy bar in the U.S.A. outside of the southeastern region have not been successful due primarily to competition from other, longer established companies with a similar line-up of candy. Several years ago, the company looked into the possibility of distributing its candy in the Caribbean area, but several factors discouraged the company from distributing the product there. These factors included the high cost of transportation, poor transportation and distribution infrastructure within the islands, corrupt governments, and uncertain demand.

Recently, Tom Taylor, Director of Marketing, was vacationing in the Bahamas and discovered that a small general store near a popular tourist resort was selling one of his candy bars. Tom asked the owner of the store about where he got the candy bars. The owner told him that he had a friend who flew between Miami and the Bahamas on business several times a year and who always brought a big box of the candy bars as a favor. In exchange, the owner, who knows many local officials, helped the businessman with his local deals. He said that the store always sold out of the candy bar within a few days, mainly to tourists, but also to the middle- and upper-class locals.

Taylor decided that the fact that the store always sold out of the Coco-Loco bar within a few days indicated a high potential demand. However, he wanted to be sure that this demand was not strictly local. So he did some research to find out what kind of demand there might be for candy bars in the Caribbean. He found that very few U.S. candy companies exported to the Caribbean, which indicated that there was not a high demand. However, additional research indicated that Caribbean people were fond of sweets. Chocolate, which originated in Central America, was very popular in the Caribbean and was used in many desserts. He found a website with recipes which showed that many Caribbean cakes, pastries, and pies were made using fruits, rum, chocolate, spices, and lots of sugar.

Based on this information, Taylor decided that there might be demand for Taylor Candy Company candy bars. He decided to gather updated information on other factors that had previously led the company to decide against trying to distribute to the Caribbean. He discovered that transportation costs between Florida and the islands had decreased considerably over the past few years. He also learned that the local transportation and distribution infrastructures had improved on the largest and most populated islands.

He also researched several websites to obtain current information on the political situation in the region. He discovered that there was still little true democracy and that a great deal of corruption still existed, but that, in general, things had become more politically stable with a higher degree of political and economic freedom. While he did not think that it would be a good idea to try to do business in a country that was extremely corrupt or unstable, he thought that there could be some Caribbean countries which would have an acceptable political and social environment.

Taylor decided that the idea of exporting to the Caribbean was worth exploring; so he discussed it with the President of the company. They decided that they should consider several additional factors.

First, they thought it would be important to identify the islands that would be the best target markets in terms of being able to support sufficient demand. They reasoned that the best islands would be those with either high numbers of tourists or those with large local populations and relatively high average incomes. They decided that a country would have to have either a population of at least 100,000 people, an average income of at least US$5000, or a total national tourism income of at least US$100 million per year to support significant sales. Any country meeting at least one of these requirements would also have to be politically stable.

The second item considered was whether they could price the candy bars for the local market and make a profit on those islands where they were not going to depend on sales from tourists. They knew that even the islands with the highest average local incomes would have average incomes far lower than incomes in the U.S.A. The shop in the Bahamas where he had found the candy bars selling at a very low price was due to the merchant being a friend of the owner who gave him the candy bars free in exchange for favors.

Third, they knew that, to make a worthwhile profit, they would have to ship the candy bars in sufficiently large quantities every couple of months. Thus, there would have to be a local distributor who could handle those quantities of candy stock and keep the product fresh for approximately two months. They also knew that the climate in the Caribbean was hot and humid, and that it would be necessary to keep the stock in a climate-controlled warehouse and distribute it to each store in small amounts.

The fourth factor that was considered was whether there were any cultural factors that might affect sales. They of course knew the story about Chevrolet's failure to market the Nova in Latin America because "nova" means "no go" in Spanish and the story about Coca-Cola's name in China sounding like "bite the wax tadpole." Would it be possible that the name "Coco-Loco" would have some meaning in a local language that would be strange or offensive to someone in that market? Could consumers be suspicious of the ingredients within the product because of the name? Taylor felt more confident by comparison with English-speaking countries where the company's products were sold.

They were also concerned about general attitudes within the population toward the U.S.A. and American products. Would there be any anti-American sentiment which could discourage people from buying their candy bars? Could they be perceived as a luxury item even though they were priced to be affordable? In 1997, a lawsuit was initiated against Coco-Loco by an Indian businessman who claimed that the trade name 'Coco-Loco' was registered as the product name of his company. After a lengthy trial, Taylor Candy Company won this suit since the court held that the registration was valid only in India, but this incident created a negative image of the company among Indians.

Because of their close location to the U.S.A., there are ambivalent feelings among Caribbean people toward American products. A stable political environment is also an important criterion for Taylor Candy Company. A disruptive political incident by Cambodians in 2003 against Thailand reminded Taylor of the importance of having political stability.

The sixth item that was given consideration was the environmental issue. In the U.S.A., Taylor Candy Company pursues a strict policy of environmental protection. The production process is set up to minimize energy usage and waste generation. The company also tries to promote anti-littering and recycling of candy bar wrappers in their advertisements. They know that this is an important concern with many of their customers in the U.S.A., and the company wants to maintain its reputation as a pro-environmental company. The company felt so strongly about this issue that it decided to market in the Caribbean only if consumers there would be receptive to its anti-littering and pro-recycling promotional messages. Taylor Candy Company goes so far as to include notices on candy bar wrappers asking people to recycle the wrappers.

Finally, the company considered the possibility of a decrease in tourism travel by Americans due to the terrorist attacks on the World Trade Center and the Pentagon on September 11, 2001. They knew that a very large percentage of tourism revenue in the Caribbean came from the U.SA. If tourism to the Caribbean area significantly decreased, they felt that this would have a negative effect on sales to tourists.

Taylor collected additional information on population, average income, and average annual tourism expenditures for several Caribbean countries (see Table 9.1). The company then reviewed the information he had previously collected on the politics and culture of each of the above countries. All of the Caribbean countries have predominantly black populations, with varying percentages of white (mainly Spanish, French, or British ancestry), East Indian, and mixed-race minorities.

Some of Taylor's observations about the various countries included the following: Haiti is nominally a democracy, but there is a long history of political and social violence that is still continuing. An organization that rates the level of political freedom of various countries, on a scale of 1 (completely free) to 15 (no freedom), gave Haiti a 9.

Antigua is a member of the British Commonwealth and is also nominally a democracy. However, one

**TABLE 9.1** Country statistics

| Country | Population | Purchasing power parity (U.S.$) | Tourism expenditure (million U.S.$) |
|---|---|---|---|
| Haiti | 7,000,000 | 1800 | 58 |
| Dominican Republic | 8,600,000 | 5700 | 1755 |
| Jamaica | 2,700,000 | 3700 | 1100 |
| Trinidad and Tobago | 1,200,000 | 9500 | 105 |
| Guyana | 700,000 | 4800 | 38 |
| Suriname | 435,000 | 3400 | 17 |
| Bahamas | 298,000 | 15,000 | 1450 |
| Belize | 257,000 | 3200 | 84 |
| Grenada | 89,000 | 4400 | 60 |
| Antigua | 67,000 | 8200 | 257 |

political party has control of the media and a monopoly on patronage, making it effectively a one-party state. Antigua was given a freedom score of 7.

The Dominican Republic is also a nominal democracy, but there have been numerous charges of election fraud. The government is very conservative and has strong links to the military.

The Dominican Republic and Suriname also have a history of military governments, but recently have had elections. Both of these countries were given a freedom score of 6.

Jamaica is considered a working democracy, with a freedom score of 5, but there is much social violence in the country. Jamaica also has a small East Indian minority within its population.

Guyana has multiple parties with elections that appear to be fair. However, the current government, led by a Marxist prime minister, has been in power for a long period of time. It was given a freedom score of 4. It also has a small East Indian minority.

The Bahamas is a multi-party democracy and was given a freedom score of 3. However, since the opposition party does not generally win elections there is very little change in government. The government is considered by some to be very corrupt. It has a small East Indian minority.

Trinidad, Belize, and Grenada are among the most successful democracies in the Caribbean, with respective freedom scores of 3, 2, and 3. Trinidad has a large East Indian population. A recent coup attempt in that country by dissatisfied Muslims was successfully put down. Belize has had successful elections in which the government has changed hands without violence. Grenada has strong ties to the U.S.A.

In researching cultural factors that influence acceptance of the candy bar, Taylor found that the word "loco" means "crazy" in Spanish and that "coco" might suggest "cocaine".

Taylor also read an article about the effect of the terrorist attacks on tourism in the Caribbean area. The article stated that tourism had been adversely affected. One of the effects of the attacks was that many cruise lines were selling cabins at drastically reduced prices, well below the price at which Caribbean hotels could compete. However, cruise lines still account for only 7 percent of tourism revenue in the Caribbean. He wondered that, if so many of the Caribbean countries were so heavily dependent on the tourism industry for economic prosperity and if tourism travel suddenly declined, some countries might not be suitable target markets for Taylor Candy Company to export its products to those countries.

## Questions

1 Briefly explain these market entry strategies: exporting, licensing, joint venture, manufacturing, assembly operations, management contract, turnkey operations, and acquisition.
2 What is cross-licensing or grantback?
3 What are the factors that should be considered in choosing a country for direct investment?
4 What is an FTZ? What are its benefits?

# Discussion assignments and minicases

1 Since exporting is a relatively risk-free market entry strategy, is there a need for a company to consider other market entry strategies?
2 Can a service be licensed for market entry purposes?
3 In spite of the advantages of free trade zones, most companies have failed to utilize them effectively. What are the reasons? Can anything be done to stimulate interest?
4 One of the most celebrated joint ventures is NUMMI (New United Motor Manufacturing, Inc.), a joint venture between General Motors and Toyota. It seems surprising that the two largest competitors would even think of joining forces. GM is the number one manufacturer in the U.S.A. as well as in the world. Toyota, on the other hand, is number one in Japan and number two worldwide. NUMMI is a 50–50 joint venture with the board of directors split equally between the two companies. Initially, the venture was to manufacture the Toyota-designed subcompact, and the name chosen for the car was Nova. At present, the plant manufactures Toyota Tacoma, Toyota Corolla, and Toyota Voltz.

   What are the benefits each partner may expect to derive from the NUMMI joint venture? Do you foresee any problems?
5 Each year, foreign companies generate some $10 billion in capital and 300,000 new jobs for the U.S. economy. As may be expected, U.S. politicians, states, and local governments have aggressively competed for foreign direct investment. Discuss the business of attracting foreign corporations from the viewpoints of both the companies and states. What are the matters of concern to companies which they will take into consideration when making their location decisions? What are the incentives which states can offer to lure businesses to locate in a particular state?

## Notes

1 "Why FDI May Not Be As Stable As Governments Think," *IMF Survey*, January 29, 2007, 26–7.
2 Prakash Loungani and Assaf Razin, "How Beneficial Is Foreign Direct Investment for Developing Countries?" *Finance & Development*, June 2001, 6–9.
3 United Nations Conference on Trade and Development, *World Investment Report* 2006.
4 "FDI in Africa: Why Do Select Countries Do Better?" *IMF Survey*, March 25, 2001, 91–2.
5 *World Investment Report 2006: FDI from Developing and Transition Economies*, UNCTAD, 2006, 17.
6 "Shoppers Gone Wild," *Business Week*, February 20, 2006, 46–7.

7 Mohsin Habib and Leon Zurawicki, "Corruption and Foreign Direct Investment," *Journal of International Business Studies* 33 (Second Quarter 2002): 291–307.

8 Utz Weitzel and Sjors Berns, "Cross-border Takeovers, Corruption, and Related Aspects of Governance," *Journal of International Business Studies* 37 (November 2006): 786–806.

9 Artur Baldauf, David W. Cravens, and Udo Wagner, "Examining Determinants of Export Performance in Small Open Economies," *Journal of World Business* 35 (No. 1, 2000): 61–75.

10 Luis Filipe Lages and David B. Montgomery, "Export Performance As an Antecedent of Export Commitment and Marketing Strategy Adaptation: Evidence from Small and Medium-sized Exporters," *European Journal of Marketing* 38 (Nos 9/10, 2004): 1186–214.

11 Paul Ellis and Anthony Pecotich, "Social Factors Influencing Export Initiation in Small and Medium-Sized Enterprises," *Journal of Marketing Research* 38 (February 2001): 119–30.

12 Paul A. Brewer, "Operationalizing Psychic Distance: A Revised Approach," *Journal of International Marketing* 15 (No. 1, 2007): 44–66.

13 Kevin I.N. Ibeh and Stephen Young, "Exporting as an Entrepreneurial Act – An Empirical Study of Nigerian Firms," *European Journal of Marketing* 35 (No. 5, 2001): 566–86.

14 Ashley Lye and R.T. Hamilton, "Search and Performance in International Exchange," *European Journal of Marketing* 34 (No. 1, 2000): 176–89.

15 "Starbucks to Grow 'a Latte,'" *San José Mercury News*, October 29, 2006.

16 "McDonald's in €800m Push to Lift Profile Across Europe," *Financial Times*, August 21, 2007.

17 "Saint Laurent's Newest Look," *Business Week*, July 31, 2000, 82, 84; and "Making Over YSL Is No Stroll Down the Catwalk," *Business Week*, January 28, 2002, 54.

18 Sandra Mottner and James P. Johnson, "Motivations and Risks in International Licensing: A Review and Implications for Licensing to Transitional and Emerging Economies," *Journal of World Business* 35 (No. 2, 2000): 171–88.

19 "Accor Buys Zenith Stake to Life China Exposure," *The Asian Wall Street Journal*, January 4, 2001.

20 "AMD to Form New Venture with Fujitsu," *San José Mercury News*, March 31, 2003; and "Fujitsu, AMD Expand Venture," *San José Mercury News*, April 1, 2003.

21 Keith D. Brouthers, "Institutional, Cultural and Transaction Cost Influences on Entry Mode Choice and Performance," *Journal of International Business Studies* 33 (Second Quarter 2002): 203–21.

22 Linda Longfellow Blodgett, "Partner Contributions as Predictors of Equity Share in International Joint Ventures," *Journal of International Business Studies* 22 (No. 1, 1991): 63–78.

23 Chang-Bum Choi and Paul W. Beamish, "Split Management Control and International Joint Venture Performance," *Journal of International Business Studies* 35 (May 2004): 201–15.

24 Yigang Pan, "Equity Ownership in International Joint Ventures: The Impact of Source Country Factors," *Journal of International Business Studies* 33 (Second Quarter 2002): 375–84.

25 Vijay Pothukuchi *et al.*, "National and Organizational Culture Differences and International Joint Venture Performance," *Journal of International Business Studies* 33 (Second Quarter 2002): 243–65.

26 Paul W. Beamish and Ariff Kachra, "Number of Partners and JV Performance," *Journal of World Business* 39 (May 2004): 107–20.

27 Hemant Merchant, "The Structure–Performance Relationship in International Joint Ventures: A Comparative Analysis," *Journal of World Business* 40 (February 2005): 41–56.

28 Yadong Luo and Seung Ho Park, "Multiparty Cooperation and Performance in International Equity Joint Ventures," *Journal of International Business Studies* 35 (March 2004): 142–60.

29 Chris Styles and Lisa Hersch, "Executive Insights: Relationship Formation in International Joint Ventures: Insights from Australian–Malaysian International Joint Ventures," *Journal of International Marketing* 13 (No. 3, 2005): 105–34.

30 Charles Dhanaraj *et al.*, "Managing Tacit and Explicit Knowledge Transfer in IJVs: The Role of Relational Embeddedness and the Impact on Performance," *Journal of International Business Studies* 35 (September 2004): 428–42.

31 "They've Driven a Ford Lately," *Business Week*, February 26, 2007, 52.

32 "Made in China – Er, Veliko Turnovo," *Business Week*, January 8, 2007, 43.
33 "Honda Will Create Brand for China's Auto Market," *Wall Street Journal*, July 19, 2007.
34 Jonathan P. Doh, Hildy Teegen, and Ram Mudambi, "Balancing Private and State Ownership in Emerging Markets' Telecommunications Infrastructure: Country, Industry, and Firm Influences," *Journal of International Business Studies* 35 (May 2004): 233–50.
35 *World Investment Report 2006*, 17.
36 Klaus E. Meyer and Saul Estrin, "Brownfield Entry in Emerging Markets," *Journal of International Business Studies* 32 (Third Quarter 2001): 575–84.
37 "Vivendi Plans to Pay $2.09 Billion to Buy BMG," *San José Mercury News*, September 7, 2006.
38 "Barclays to Acquire Dutch Bank ABN Amro," *San José Mercury News*, April 24, 2007.
39 Philippe Very and David M. Schweiger, "The Acquisition Process as a Learning Process: Evidence from a Study of Critical Problems and Solutions in Domestic and Cross-Border Deals," *Journal of World Business* 36 (No. 1, 2001): 11–31.
40 Arjen H. L. Slangen, "National Cultural Distance and Initial Foreign Acquisition Performance: The Moderating Effect of Integration," *Journal of World Business* 41 (June 2006): 161–70.
41 Jeffrey J. Reuer, Oded Shenkar, and Roberto Ragozzino, "Mitigating Risk in International Mergers and Acquisitions: The Role of Contingent Payouts," *Journal of International Business Studies* 35 (January 2004): 19–32.
42 Klaus Uhlenbruck, "Developing Acquired Foreign Subsidiaries: The Experience of MNEs in Transition Economies," *Journal of International Business Studies* 35 (March 2004): 109–23.
43 Jeffrey J. Reuer, Oded Shenkar, and Roberto Ragozzino, "Mitigating Risk in International Mergers and Acquisitions: The Role of Contingent Payouts," *Journal of International Business Studies* 35 (January 2004): 19–32.
44 "Mergers: Will They Ever Learn?", *Business Week*, October 30, 1995, 178; and "Is the European Grass Greener?", *Business Week*, January 29, 2001, 28.
45 Masaaki Kotabe *et al.*, "Strategic Alliances in Emerging Latin America: A View from Brazilian, Chilean, and Mexican Companies," *Journal of World Business* 35 (No. 2, 2000): 114–32.
46 John B. Cullen, Jean L. Johnson, and Tomoaki Sakano, "Success Through Commitment and Trust: The Soft Side of Strategic Alliance Management," *Journal of World Business* 35 (Fall 2000): 223–40.
47 Shih-Fen S. Chen and Jean-François Hennart, "Japanese Investors' Choice of Joint Ventures versus Wholly-owned Subsidiaries in the U.S.: The Role of Market Barriers and Firm Capabilities," *Journal of International Business Studies* 33 (First Quarter 2002): 1–18.
48 Klaus E. Meyer, "Institutions, Transaction Costs, and Entry Mode Choice in Eastern Europe," *Journal of International Business Studies* 32 (Second Quarter 2001): 357–67.
49 Jane W. Lu, "Intra- and Inter-organizational Imitative Behavior: Institutional Influences on Japanese Firms' Entry Mode Choice," *Journal of International Business Studies* 1 (First Quarter 2002): 19–37.
50 Vibha Gaba, Yigang Pan, and Gerardo R. Ungson, "Timing of Entry in International Market: An Empirical Study of U.S. Fortune 500 Firms in China," *Journal of International Business Studies* 33 (First Quarter 2002): 39–55.
51 Keith D. Brouthers and Lance Eliot Brouthers, "Explaining the National Cultural Distance Paradox," *Journal of International Business Studies* 32 (First Quarter 2001): 177–89.
52 Oded Shenkar, "Cultural Distance Revisited: Towards a More Rigorous Conceptualization and Measurement of Cultural Differences," *Journal of International Business Studies* 32 (Third Quarter 2001): 519–35.
53 José I. Galan and Javier Gonzalez-Benito, "Distinctive Determinant Factors of Spanish Foreign Direct Investments in Latin America," *Journal of World Business* 41 (June 2006): 171–89.
54 Ulrike Mayrhofer, "International Market Entry: Does the Home Country Affect Entry-mode Decisions?", *Journal of International Marketing* 12 (No. 4, 2004): 71–96.
55 Laszlo Tihanyi, David A. Griffith, and Craig J. Russell, "The Effect of Cultural Distance on Entry Mode Choice, International Diversification, and MNE Performance: A Meta-analysis," *Journal of International Business Studies* 36 (May 2005): 270–83.

56 Len J. Trevino and Franklin G. Mixon Jr., "Strategic Factors Affecting Foreign Direct Investment Decisions by Multinational Enterprises in Latin America," *Journal of World Business* 39 (August 2004): 233–43.

57 Anders Blomstermo, D. Deo Sharma, and James Sallis, "Choice of Foreign Market Entry Mode in Service Firms," *International Marketing Review* 23 (No. 2, 2006): 211–29.

58 Oystein Moen, Morten Gavlen, and Iver Endresen, "Internationalization of Small, Computer Software Firms: Entry Forms and Market Selection," *European Journal of Marketing* 38 (Nos 9/10, 2004): 1236–51.

59 Christine M. Chan, Shige Makino, and Takehiko Isobe, "Interdependent Behavior in Foreign Direct Investment: The Multi-level Effects of Prior Entry and Prior Exit on Foreign Market Entry," *Journal of International Business Studies* 37 (September 2006): 642–65.

Part 4

# International marketing decisions

Chapter 10

# Product strategies

## Basic decisions and product planning

Benchmark brands should be studied, but solutions can seem a lot more accessible when you can see how someone fell and picked themselves up.

Jez Frampton, CEO, Interbrand

## Chapter outline

- Marketing strategy: East is East and West is West
- What is a product?
- New product development
- Market segmentation
- Product adoption
- Theory of international product life cycle
    - Stages and characteristics
    - Validity of the IPLC
    - Marketing strategies
- Product standardization vs. product adaptation
    - Arguments for standardization
    - Arguments for adaptation
- A move toward world product: international or national product?
- Marketing of services
    - Importance of services
    - Types of services
    - The economic and legal environment
    - Are services different?

- ❑ Marketing mix and adaptation
- ❑ Market entry strategies

- ■ Conclusion
- ■ Case 10.1 McDonaldization

## Marketing strategy

**East is East and West is West**

In spite of the global economy, product design must still take local cultures into consideration. Lenovo's Opti Desktop PC was designed with the Chinese consumer culture in mind. When submitted for consideration for a design award, the unusual design initially put off the judges. They were later won over once they realized that research showed that Chinese tech-centric gamers did not want a sleek U.S. design but that they preferred something of their own. Lenovo's design research was dubbed "Search for the Soul" of the Chinese customer. In order to identify the design elements which had meaning and value, Lenovo immersed itself in Chinese music, history, and objects of desire (e.g., mobile phones). It observed how families lived, worked, and played. The research was able to identify five "technology tribes": Social Butterflies, Relationship Builders, Upward Maximizers, Deep Immersers, and Conspicuous Collectors. Each tribe revealed different needs. The Opti has shapes and colors for Chinese Deep Immersers who escape by immersing themselves in games online. The design won a gold award in 2006.

Dell's EC 280 system is available only in China. Designed by Dell's engineers in Shanghai, the system has two configurations. Based on the amount of storage, the prices range from $223 to $515. EC 280 offers a low price, low power consumption, and compact size (about one-eighth the size of a traditional desktop PC).

Electrolux, a Swedish appliance maker, relaunched a mini-dishwasher in Italy and targeted households with one or two people. Full-size dishwashers force people to wait for a full load and are thus run only once or twice a week. Infrequent use makes it more difficult to clean dishes, and favorite coffee mugs or plates are not available for use every day. Engineers made home visits and acquired insights for product design. By watching how consumers loaded their dishwashers, the baskets and racks were repositioned for the U.S. market.

*Sources*: "Annual Design Awards 2006," *Business Week*, July 10, 2006, 77; "Dell Unveils Computer to Be Sold Only in China," *San José Mercury News*, March 26, 2007; and "Electrolux Redesigns Itself," *IN*, November 2006, 13–15.

## Purpose of chapter

Just because a product is successful in one country, there is no guarantee that it will be successful in other markets. A marketer must always determine local needs and tastes and take them into account. Some products have universal appeal, and little or no change is necessary when these products are placed in various markets. But for every so-called universal product, there are many others, as mentioned above, that have a narrower appeal. For products in this category, modification is necessary in order to achieve acceptance in the marketplace. The cases of Lenovo, Dell, and Electrolux show why products have to be adapted for the target market.

It is generally easier to modify a product than to modify consumer preference. That is, a marketer should change the product to fit the needs of the consumer rather than try to adjust consumers' needs to fit product characteristics. An awareness of application of this marketing concept in an international setting would provide definite advantages to an international merchant. Although the principle has been universally accepted in domestic marketing, it has often been ignored in international marketing.

The purpose of this chapter is to study *product* in an international context. The discussion focuses on the meaning of product and the necessities of market segmentation and product positioning. Other topics include product development and services. There is also a critical look at the controversial issue of product standardization versus product adaptation, as well as the theory of international product life cycle and that theory's marketing applications.

## What is a product?

A product is often considered in a narrow sense as something tangible that can be described in terms of physical attributes, such as shape, dimension, components, form, color, and so on. This is a misconception that has been extended to international marketing as well, because many people believe that only tangible products can be exported. A student of marketing, however, should realize that this definition of product is misleading since many products are intangible (e.g., services). Actually, intangible products are a significant part of the American export market. For example, American movies are distributed worldwide, as are engineering services and business-consulting services. In the financial market, Japanese and European banks have been internationally active in providing financial assistance, often at handsome profits. Even when tangible products are involved, insurance services and shipping are needed to move the products into their markets.

In many situations, both tangible and intangible products must be combined to create a single, total product. Perhaps the best way to define a product is to describe it as *a bundle of utilities or satisfaction*. Purchasers of Porsche cars certainly expect to acquire more than just the cars themselves. As was asked in one of Porsche's print advertisements (see Figure 10.1), "Do I want a car, or do I want a Porsche?"

For automobiles and many products, warranty terms and equipment are a part of the bundle of utilities, and can be adjusted as appropriate (i.e., superior versus inferior warranty terms). In hot and humid countries, there is no reason for a heater to be part of the automobile's product bundle. In the U.S.A., it is customary for automatic transmission to be bundled with other standard automobile equipment.

One marketing implication that may be drawn is that a multinational marketer must look at a product as a total, complete offering. Consider the case of designer handbags. The average price of fashionable designer bags is about $1500. Hermes has a waiting list for a crocodile version of its Birkin bag which costs $148,000. Women love handbags because handbags are an easy way to update a wardrobe and because handbags communicate a person's style and success. Manufacturers and retailers are more than happy with the fat profit margins. After all, customers do not seem to mind paying an outrageous sum for status goods.[1]

Contact us at 1-800-PORSCHE or porscheusa.com. ©2007 Porsche Cars North America, Inc.
Porsche recommends seat belt usage and observance of all traffic laws at all times. Specifications for comparison only. Cayenne Turbo shown includes optional equipment at additional cost.
Eventually it all boils down to:
Do I want a car, or do I want a Porsche?
The decision couldn't be more clear-cut. Legendary Porsche handling. A potent, new, 500-hp engine that uses less fuel. And all tightly wrapped in a newly refined, more muscular stance. Now do you want a Cayenne, or did you just want a car? Porsche Cayenne Turbo. There is no substitute.
The new Cayenne. Available in March.
PORSCHE

**FIGURE 10.1** A differentiated product: when a car is not just a car

Porsche, Cayenne and the Porsche Crest are registered trademarks, and Cayman and the distinctive shapes of the Porsche automobiles are trademarks of Dr. Ing.h.c.F. Porsche AG. Used with permission of Dr. Ing.h.c.F. Porsche AG and Porsche Cars North America, Inc. © Porsche Cars North America, Inc. Photographer: Stephan Romer.

Ethical Dimension 10.1

**A night to remember**

It was a night to remember – if you can afford to pay $25,000 for a 10-course gourmet dinner. In early 2007, Lebua Hotel in Bangkok offered a dinner titled "Epicurean Masters of the World." Each course was created by a world-renowned chef. There were six three-star Michelin chefs – four from France, one from Germany, and one from Italy. Guests indulged themselves by eating Beluga caviar, Perigord truffles (about $350), Kobe beef, and Brittany lobster. Each dish was accompanied by a rare and vintage wine. The guests who attended this culinary extravaganza came from the U.S.A., Europe, the Middle East, and Asia. Some arrived in their private jets. In spite of the fine foods, there was only so much of a fine thing that one could consume. After a while, it was somewhat too much of a good thing.

*Source*: "Bangkok's Gorging Gourmets," *San José Mercury News*, February 11, 2007.

Since a product can be bundled, it can also be unbundled. One problem with a bundled product is the increased cost associated with the extra benefits. With the increased cost, a higher price is inevitable. Thus a proper marketing strategy, in some cases, is to unbundle a product instead so as to get rid of the frills and attract price-sensitive consumers. As an example, Serfin is a mid-tiered bank in Mexico, and is owned by Spain's Banco Santander Central Hispano. Serfin has launched Serfin Light, a new credit card that offers no points or air miles. Instead, its key feature is an interest rate of 24 percent rather than the 40 percent charged by the main competitors. The word Light is appropriate because Mexico is the world's largest consumer per capita of soft drinks, and Diet Coke is sold as Coke Light. The "light" concept has a significant meaning in Mexico. The success of Serfin Light prompted Banorte, the largest bank in northern Mexico, to change its slogan to "better than a light card, a strong card."[2]

## New product development

There are six distinct steps in new product development. The *first step* is the *generation of new product ideas*. Such ideas may come from any number of sources (e.g., salesperson, employees, competitors, governments, marketing research firms, customers). As in the case of Japan, already one out of five Japanese is aged 65 or older, and the trend has adversely affected baby food. Searching for new sources of revenue, Japanese food companies were intrigued to learn that the same characteristics that make baby food appealing to babies (soft, small morsels, low salt, easy preparation) also attracted old people. Thus food manufacturers have come up with ready-to-eat treats: soft-boiled fish, bite-sized shrimp meatballs, chop suey with tofu, and dozens of others. These "Fun Meals" or "Food for Ages 0–100" only hints at the target demographic group without embarrassing older consumers.[3]

The *second step* involves the *screening of ideas*. Ideas must be acknowledged and reviewed to determine their feasibility. To determine suitability, a new product concept may simply be presented to potential users, or an advertisement based on the product may be drawn and shown to focus groups to elicit candid reactions. As a rule, corporations usually have predetermined goals that a new product

Cultural Dimension 10.1

**Japan's most influential invention: *ramen***

*Ramen* is the Japanese word for *lo mein* (Chinese boiled noodles). Momofuku Ando first introduced his instant chicken *ramen* in 1958 which had flavoring already infused in the noodles. At the time, at a price of 10 cents a packet, the product cost six times the price of a bowl of fresh *ramen*. Ando persevered and ultimately succeeded even though it took nearly half a century for the world to come around. China consumes 17.8 billion packets, while the figures for Indonesia, Japan, South Korea, and the U.S.A. respectively are: 9.9 billion, 5.35 billion, 3.64 billion, and 3 billion.

Ando's Nissin Food Products has perfected a process to preserve cooked noodles. Fresh *ramen* is steamed, molded into blocks, dried, cooled, and packaged. He improved the flavor by packaging powdered soup mix separately from the brick of wavy noodles.

When asked to name Japan's most influential invention of the twentieth century, people ranked *ramen* first, ahead of Sony Walkman, Toyota cars, and Nintendo video games. No longer limited to mild variations, *ramen* now comes in a variety of hot and spicy flavors.

The global noodle king produces more than four billion packs and cups a year, controls 40 percent of the Japanese market, and 10 percent of the world market. Nissin operates 25 plants in eight countries and uses shrimp from India and cabbage from China. To conquer the world, Nissin has adapted its products to the peculiarities of foreign markets. Shorter noodles are offered to accommodate forks rather than chopsticks.

*Sources*: "The Universal Appeal of Ramen," *San José Mercury News*, February 26, 2003; and Chicken Ramen Maker Used His Noodle," *San José Mercury News*, February 12, 2001.

must meet. Kao Corporation, a major Japanese manufacturer of consumer goods, is guided by the following five principles of product development: (1) a new product should be truly useful to society, not only now but also in the future, (2) it should make use of Kao's own creative technology or skill, (3) it should be superior to the new products of competitors, from the standpoint of both cost and performance, (4) it should be able to stand exhaustive product tests at all stages before it is commercialized, and (5) it should be capable of delivering its own message at every level of distribution.[4]

The *third step* is *business analysis*, which is necessary to estimate product features, cost, demand, and profit. Xerox has small so-called product synthesis teams to test and weed out unsuitable ideas. Several competing teams of designers produce a prototype, and the winning model that meets preset goals then goes to the "product development" team.

The *fourth step* is *product development*, which involves lab and technical tests as well as manufacturing pilot models in small quantities. At this stage, the product is likely to be handmade or produced by existing machinery rather than by any new specialized equipment. Ideally, engineers should receive direct feedback from customers and dealers. When Nokia showed a mock-up of a silver-colored, 10-millimeter-thick phone to focus groups in London, Mumbai, Moscow, Bangkok, Shanghai, and Boston, it received a positive response for this 6500 classic. However, some users, especially women, felt that the silver color was "a little bit too cold" and that it made the phone feel sober. The design team switched to black metal on portions of the phone but accented it with a silver border around the screen. As for the U.S.A., which uses different cellphone standards, Nokia does not offer the 6500 classic. Nokia has a team at its U.S. research facility to design phones specifically for American consumers. U.S. consumers prefer clamshell-shaped and slider phones to candy-bar-shaped phones which are popular outside the U.S.A.[5]

The *fifth step* involves *test marketing* to determine potential marketing problems and the optimal marketing mix. PepsiCo International chose Thailand as the first test market for its innovative twin-cola concept. To launch the two flavors, Pepsi used Thai pop diva Tata Young to represent Pepsi Fire, while Vanness Wu of the Taiwanese boy band F4 represented the coolness of Pepsi Ice.[6]

Finally, assuming that things go well, the company is ready for *full-scale commercialization* by actually going through with full-scale production and marketing.

It should be pointed out that not all of these six steps in new product development will be applicable to all products and countries. Test marketing, for example, may be irrelevant in countries where most major media are more national than local. If the television medium has a nationwide coverage, it is not practical to limit a marketing campaign to one city or province for test marketing purposes.

Many new products are tested and marketed each year. In Japan, because consumers constantly demand fresh, new products, some 700 to 800 drinks are launched annually. To keep pace, Coca-Cola has built a product development center which allows it to cut launch time for new drinks from 90 days to a month, enabling it to release 50 new beverages a year.

Unfortunately, it is easier for a new product to fail than to succeed. Naturally, so many things can go wrong. Therefore, it is just as critical for a company to know when to retreat as when to launch a product. Coca-Cola's Ambasa Whitewater, a lactic-based drink, was removed from the market after 18 months when sales started to decline.

## Market segmentation

Market segmentation is a concept to which marketers and academics like to pay a great deal of attention. All conceivable possibilities for segmenting the U.S. market have been thoroughly studied. For example, Visa has designed its consumer credit products and non-credit products for diverse market segments. Some of its products are: Visa Classic, Visa Gold, Visa Platinum, Visa Signature, Visa Infinite, Visa check card, and Visa Buxx.

Yet on the international scale, American marketers are prone to treat market segmentation as an unknown and unfamiliar concept, and they apparently leave their knowledge about market segmentation at home when they go abroad. More often than not, there is hardly any serious or conscious attempt by American businessmen to segment a foreign market. This phenomenon probably derives from an assumption that, by going abroad, geographic segmentation has been implemented. But geographic segmentation, an obvious choice, is often overemphasized and is usually inappropriate. Marketers fail to realize that the purpose of segmentation is to satisfy consumer needs more precisely – not to segment the market just for the sake of the segmentation. In India, for example, Japanese car manufacturers are successful in cultivating the "minicar" segment. Suzuki Motor Corp.'s Zen Estilo is a big success.

Another mistake marketers make in foreign countries is attempting to capture the total market at once. The resulting disappointment in market performance demonstrates that two major problems have been overlooked. First, consumers in a foreign country are unlikely to be homogeneous. Usually, marketers must distinguish urban consumers from rural consumers. Even in largely homogeneous Japan, American Express found it necessary to segment Japanese consumers. It introduced the luxury gold yen card for the affluent segment and the green card for the middle-income segment.

Second, a "total market" strategy places the company in head-to-head competition with strong, local competitors. The success of Japanese products in the U.S.A. and in many other countries can be explained in part by the explicit and conscientious attempts by the Japanese to segment the market. Japanese firms usually pick their targets carefully, avoiding head-to-head competition with major U.S. manufacturers in mature industries. Starting at the low end of the product spectrum, a Japanese firm establishes a reputation for product excellence, and eventually gets customers to trade up over time. The strategy has worked exceedingly well in the automobile and consumer electronics industries. Japanese computer makers have used the same marketing strategy in breaking into the U.S. computer market. Japanese firms market commodity products such as personal computers, disc drives, printers, and other peripherals before attempting to trade up with their customers to the larger systems, which have the highest profit margins. This strategy makes a great deal of strategic sense because the marketer does not arouse the U.S. giants early in the game. U.S. toolmakers' strategic mistake was their emphasis on large machines for major users, while leaving room at the low end for entry to foreign competitors with product lines at the $150,000 price level.

The most important reason behind the utilization of market segmentation is market *homogeneity/heterogeneity*. According to one study of industrial service buyers in the U.S.A. and Japan, based on the purchasing process, there are three unique market segments: (1) "networkers" who are heavy referral users, (2) "opportunists" who both directly and indirectly purchase services, and (3) "independents" who are heavy direct buyers of certain types of services. These segments have both American and Japanese companies.[7]

Based on the national boundary, homogeneity can be *vertical* (i.e., homogeneous within the same country) or *horizontal* (i.e., homogeneous across countries). Therefore, two countries exhibiting the lack of vertical homogeneity within their borders may still be homogeneous horizontally when a particular segment of one country is similar to an equivalent segment of another country.

Nevertheless, market segmentation is not always necessary or desirable. This is especially true either when consumer needs within a country are largely homogeneous or a mass market exists.

## Product adoption

In breaking into a foreign market, marketers should consider factors that influence product adoption. As explained by diffusion theory, at least six factors have a bearing on the adoption process: relative advantage, compatibility, trialability/divisibility, observability, complexity, and price. These factors are all perceptual and thus subjective in nature.

For a product to gain acceptance, it must demonstrate its *relative advantage* over existing alternatives. Products emphasizing cleanliness and sanitation may be unimportant in places where people are poor and struggle to get by one day at a time. Wool coats are not needed in a hot country, and products reducing static cling (e.g., Cling Free) are useless in a humid country. A sunscreen film attached to auto windshields to block out sunlight may be a necessity in countries with a tropical climate, but it has no such advantage in cold countries. Dishwashing machines do not market well in countries where manual labor is readily available and inexpensive.

A product must also be *compatible* with local customs and habits. A freezer would not find a ready market in Asia, where people prefer fresh food. In Asia and such European countries as France and Italy, people like to sweep and mop floors daily, and thus there is no market for carpet or vacuum cleaners. Dryers are unnecessary in countries where people prefer to hang their clothes outside for sunshine freshness. Kellogg's had difficulties selling Pop Tarts in Europe because many homes have no toaster. Unlike American women, many Asian and European women do not shave their legs, and thus have no need for razors for that purpose. The Japanese, not liking to have their lifestyles altered by technology, have skillfully applied technology to their traditional lifestyle. The electrical *kotatsu* (foot warmer) is a traditional form of heater in Japan. New *kotatsu* are equipped with a temperature sensor and microcomputer to keep the interior temperature at a comfortable level.

A new product should also be compatible with consumers' other belongings. If a new product requires a replacement of those other items that are still usable, product adoption becomes a costly proposition.

A new product has an advantage if it is capable of being *divided* and *tested* in small trial quantities to determine its suitability and benefits. This is a product's *trialability/divisibility* factor. Disposable diapers and blue jeans lend themselves to trialability rather well. But when a product is large, bulky, and expensive, consumers are much more apprehensive about making a purchase. Thus, washers, dryers, refrigerators, and automobiles are products that do not lend themselves well to trialability/divisibility. This factor explains one reason why foreign consumers do not easily purchase American automobiles, knowing that a mistake could ruin them financially. Many foreign consumers therefore prefer to purchase more familiar products, such as Japanese automobiles, that are less expensive and easier to service and whose parts are easier to replace.

*Observation* of a product in public tends to encourage social acceptance and reinforcement, resulting in the product being adopted more rapidly and with less resistance. If a product is used privately, other consumers cannot see it, and there is no prestige generated by its possession. Blue jeans, quartz watches, and automobiles are used publicly and are highly observable products. Japanese men flip their ties so that labels show. Refrigerators, on the other hand, are privately consumed products, though owners of refrigerators in the Middle East and Asia may attempt to enhance observability (and thus prestige) by placing the refrigerator in the living room where guests can easily see it. In any case, a distinctive and easily recognized logo is very useful.

*Complexity* of a product or difficulty in understanding a product's qualities tends to slow its market acceptance. Perhaps this factor explains why ground coffee has had a difficult time in making headway to replace instant coffee in many countries. Likewise, 3M tried unsuccessfully in foreign markets to replace positive-acting printing plates with presensitized negative subtractive printing plates, which are very popular in the U.S.A. It failed to convert foreign printers because the sales and technical service costs of changing printers' beliefs were far too expensive. Computers are also complex but have been gradually gaining more and more acceptance, perhaps in large part because manufacturers have made the machines simpler to operate. Ready-made software can also alleviate the necessity of learning computer languages, a time-consuming process.

The first four variables are positively related to the adoption process. Like complexity, *price* is negatively related to product adoption. Americans may look at rice cooking as a mundane chore. For many Japanese though, cooking rice is a serious business. Toshiba Corp. sold the world's first automatic electric rice cooker in 1955, forever freeing housewives from using heavy pots on wood-fire stoves. Toshiba's latest device is an $830 "vacuum pressure cooker." The machine can withstand 264 pounds of pressure, and is coated with silver and powdered diamonds to distribute heat evenly.

This cooker can boil water at a higher temperature and thus makes fatter, shinier, and sweeter grains of rice. Every grain of rice will have the same texture. Ultra high-end rice cookers are made only for the Japanese market. Outside of Japan, there are very few people who are willing to pay that much for the better taste of plain white rice.[8]

Undoubtedly, culture can exert influence on product adoption. Based on a study of the impact of national culture on the cross-national diffusion of innovations in 13 European countries, cross-national product diffusion is linked to the four cultural dimensions of individualism, masculinity, power distance, and long-term orientation.[9] Similarly, power distance and uncertainty avoidance influence ICT adoption.[10] According to the results of another study, innovativeness is associated with small power distance, weak uncertainty avoidance, and masculinity. Consumers from a large power distance, strong uncertainty avoidance, and/or feminine cultures are persuaded through normative influences (rather than interpersonal communications) to adopt new products.[11]

## Theory of international product life cycle

The international product life cycle theory (IPLC), developed and verified by economists to explain trade in a context of comparative advantage, describes the diffusion process of an innovation across national boundaries. The life cycle begins when a developed country, having a new product to satisfy consumer needs, wants to exploit its technological breakthrough by selling abroad. Other advanced nations soon start up their own production facilities, and before long less developed countries do the same. Efficiency/comparative advantage shifts from developed countries to developing nations. Finally, advanced nations, no longer cost-effective, import products from their former customers. The moral of this process could be that an advanced nation becomes a victim of its own creation.

IPLC theory has the potential to be a valuable framework for marketing planning on a multinational basis. In this section, the IPLC is examined from the marketing perspective, and marketing implications for both innovators and initiators are discussed.[12]

### *Stages and characteristics*

There are five distinct stages (Stage 0 through Stage 4) in the IPLC. Table 10.1 shows the major characteristics of the IPLC stages, with the U.S.A. as the developer of innovation in question. Figure 10.2 shows three life-cycle curves for the same innovation: one for the initiating country (i.e., the U.S.A. in this instance), one for other advanced nations, and one for LDCs (less developed countries). For each curve, net export results when the curve is above the horizontal line; if under the horizontal line, net import results for that particular country. As the innovation moves through time, directions of all three curves change. Time is relative, because the time needed for a cycle to be completed varies from one type of product to another. In addition, the time interval varies from one stage to the next.

#### *Stage 0 – Local innovation*

Stage 0, depicted as time 0 on the left of the vertical importing/exporting axis, represents a regular and highly familiar product life cycle in operation within its original market. Innovations are most likely to occur in highly developed countries because consumers in such countries are affluent and

**TABLE 10.1** IPLC stages and characteristics (for the initiating country)

| *Stage* | *Import/export* | *Target market* | *Competitors* | *Production costs* |
|---|---|---|---|---|
| (0) Local innovation | None | U.S.A. | Few: local firms | Initially high |
| (1) Overseas innovation | Increasing export | U.S.A. and advanced nations | Few: local firms | Decline due to economies of scale |
| (2) Maturity | Stable export | Advanced nations and LDCs | Advanced nations | Stable |
| (3) Worldwide imitation | Declining export | LDCs | Advanced nations | Increase due to lower economies of scale |
| (4) Reversal | Increasing import | U.S.A. | Advanced nations and LDCs | Increase due to comparative disadvantage |

*Source*: Sak Onkvisit and John J. Shaw, "An Examination of the International Product Life Cycle and Its Application within Marketing," *Columbia Journal of World Business* 18 (fall 1983, 74).

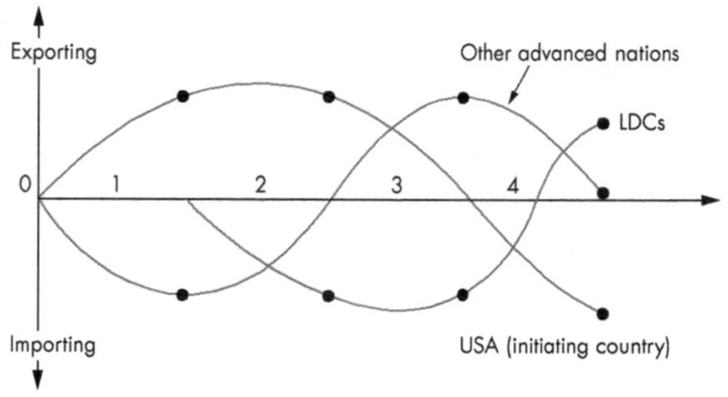
Exporting
Other advanced nations
LDCs
0
1
2
3
4
Importing
USA (initiating country)

**FIGURE 10.2** IPLC curves

*Source*: Sak Onkvisit and John J. Shaw, "An Examination of the International Product Life Cycle and Its Application within Marketing," *Columbia Journal of World Busines* 18 (fall 1983: 74).

have relatively unlimited wants. From the supply side, firms in advanced nations have both the technological know-how and abundant capital to develop new products.

Many of the products found in the world's markets were originally created in the U.S.A. before being introduced and refined in other countries. In most instances, regardless of whether a product is intended for later export or not, an innovation is initially designed with an eye to capture the U.S. market, the largest consumer nation.

### *Stage 2 – Overseas innovation*

As soon as the new product is well developed, its original market well cultivated, and local demands adequately supplied, the innovating firm will look to overseas markets in order to expand its sales and profit. Thus, this stage is known as a "pioneering" or "international introduction" stage. The technological gap is first noticed in other advanced nations due to their similar needs and high income levels. Not surprisingly, English-speaking countries such as the United Kingdom, Canada, and Australia account for about half of the sales of U.S. innovations when first introduced to overseas countries with similar cultures. Their economic conditions are often perceived by exporters as posing less risk and thus they are approached first before proceeding to less familiar territories.

Competition at this stage usually comes from U.S. firms, since firms in other countries may not have much knowledge about the innovation. Production cost tends to be decreasing at this stage because by this time the innovating firm will normally have improved the production process. Supported by overseas sales, aggregate production costs tend to decline further due to increased economies of scale. A low introductory price overseas is usually not necessary because of the technological breakthrough; a low price is not desirable because of the heavy and costly marketing effort needed in order to educate consumers in other countries about the new product. In any case, as the product penetrates the market during this stage, there will be more exports from the U.S.A. and, correspondingly, an increase in imports by other developed countries.

### *Stage 2 – Maturity*

Growing demand in advanced nations provides an impetus for firms there to commit themselves to starting local production, often with the help of their governments' protective measures to preserve infant industries. Thus, these firms can survive and thrive in spite of relative inefficiency.

Development of competition does not mean that the initiating country's export level will immediately suffer. The innovating firm's sales and export volumes are kept stable because LDCs are now beginning to generate a need for the product. Introduction of the product in LDCs helps offset any reduction in export sales to advanced countries.

### *Stage 3 – Worldwide imitation*

This stage means tough times for the innovating nation due to its continuous decline in exports. There is no more new demand anywhere to cultivate. The decline will inevitably affect the U.S. innovating firm's economies of scale, and its production costs thus begin to rise again. Consequently, firms in other advanced nations use their lower prices (coupled with product differentiation techniques) to gain more consumer acceptance abroad at the expense of the U.S. firm. As the product becomes more and more widely disseminated, imitation picks up at a faster pace. Toward the end of this stage, U.S.

export dwindles to almost nothing, and any U.S. production still remaining is basically for local consumption. The U.S. automobile industry is a good example of this phenomenon. There are about 30 different companies selling cars in the U.S.A., with several more on the rise. Of these, only two (General Motors and Ford) are U.S. firms, with the rest being from Western Europe, Japan, South Korea, and others.

### *Stage 4 – Reversal*

Not only must all good things end, but misfortune frequently accompanies the end of a favorable situation. The major functional characteristics of this stage are *product standardization and comparative disadvantage*. This innovating country's comparative advantage has disappeared, and what is left is comparative disadvantage. This disadvantage is brought about because the product is no longer capital-intensive or technology-intensive but instead has become labor-intensive – a strong advantage possessed by LDCs. Thus, LDCs – the last imitators – establish sufficient productive facilities to satisfy their own domestic needs as well as to produce for the biggest market in the world, the U.S.A. U.S. firms are now undersold in their own country. The U.S.A. hardly produces color TV sets. Consumers' price sensitivity exacerbates this problem for the initiating country.

## Validity of the IPLC

Several products have conformed to the characteristics described by the IPLC. The production of semiconductors started in the U.S.A. before diffusing to the United Kingdom, France, Germany, and Japan. Production facilities are now set up in Hong Kong and Taiwan, as well as in other Asian countries. Similarly, at one time, the U.S.A. used to be an exporter of typewriters, adding machines, and cash registers. However, with the passage of time, these simple machines (e.g., manual typewriters) are now being imported, while U.S. firms export only the sophisticated, electronic versions of such machines. Other products that have gone through a complete international life cycle are synthetic fibers, petrochemicals, leather goods, rubber products, and paper. A deficit has also occurred at the same time for communications equipment, following the trend set by semiconductors in 1982.

RCA researchers first demonstrated the liquid crystal display (LCD) in the U.S.A. in 1968. It was Japan, however, that pioneered high-volume production. Japan's dominance lasted only a few years before South Korea took the lead. Korean manufacturers not only increased production efficiency but also learned how to advance the manufacturing technology to the next phase. Leadership for some categories of LCDs has shifted to manufacturers in Taiwan.[13]

The IPLC is probably more applicable for products related through an emerging technology. These newly emerging products are likely to provide functional utility rather than aesthetic values. Furthermore, these products likely satisfy basic needs that are universally common in most parts of the world. Washers, for example, are much more likely to fit this theory than are dryers. Dishwashing machines are not useful in countries where labor is plentiful and cheap, and the diffusion of this kind of innovation as described in the IPLC is not likely to occur.

## Marketing strategies

For those advanced economies' industries at the worldwide imitation stage (e.g., automobiles) or the maturity stage (e.g., computers), things are likely to get worse rather than better. The prospect, though bleak, can be favorably influenced. What is critical is for firms in the advanced economies to understand the implications of the IPLC so that they can adjust marketing strategies accordingly.

## *Product policy*

The IPLC emphasizes the importance of cost advantage. It would be very difficult for firms in advanced economies to match labor costs in low-wage nations such as China. Still, the innovating firm must keep its product cost competitive. One way is to cut labor costs through automation and robotics. IBM converted its Lexington (Kentucky) plant into one of the most automated plants in the world. Japanese manufacturers of electronics products are counting on automation to help them meet the challenge of South Korea.

Another way to reduce production costs is to eliminate unnecessary options, since such options increase inefficiency and complexity. This strategy may be critical for simple products or those at the low end of the price scale. In such cases, it is desirable to offer a standardized product with a standard package of features or options included.

To keep costs rising at a minimum, an initiating firm may use local manufacturing in other countries as an entry strategy. The company can not only minimize transportation costs and entry barriers but can also indirectly slow down potential local competition from starting up manufacturing facilities. Another benefit is that those countries can eventually become a springboard for the company to market its product throughout that geographic region. In fact, sourcing should allow the innovator to hold labor costs down at home and abroad and hold on to the original market as well.

Manufacturers should examine the traditional vertical structure in which they make all or most components and parts themselves because in many instances outsourcing may prove to be more cost-effective. **Outsourcing** is the practice of buying parts or whole products from other manufacturers while allowing a buyer to maintain its own brand name. For example, Ford Festiva is made by Kia Motors, Mitsubishi Precis by Hyundai, Pontiac Lemans by Daewoo, and GM Sprint by Suzuki.

A modification of outsourcing involves producing various components or having them produced under contract in different countries. That way, a firm takes advantage of the most abundant factor of production in each country before assembling components into final products for worldwide distribution.

Solectron and Flextronics are examples of contract manufacturers that do manufacturing for many well-known brands. Solectron, a contract electronics maker, makes components and finished products for electronics companies, and its customers include Cisco Systems, HP, and Ericsson. Flextronics, based in Singapore and San José, is a $12 billion global electronics manufacturing services company. In 2007, its offer to acquire Solectron was cleared by the European Union.

Once in the maturity stage, the innovator's comparative advantage is gone, and the firm should switch from producing simple versions to producing sophisticated models or new technologies in order to remove itself from cut-throat competition. Japanese VCR makers used to make 99 percent of the machines sold in the U.S.A. and 75 percent of all machines sold worldwide, but they still cannot compete with low-wage Korean newcomers strictly on price, because labor content in VCRs is substantial. To retain their market share, the Japanese rely on new technology, such as 8-mm camcorders.

For a relatively high-tech product, an innovator may find it advantageous to get its product system to become the industry's standard, even if it means lending a helping hand to competitors through the licensing of product knowledge. Otherwise, there is always a danger that competitors will persevere in inventing an incompatible and superior system. A discussion of product adoption earlier should make it clear that several competing and incompatible systems serve only to confuse potential adopters who must acquire more information and who are uncertain as to which system will survive over the long term.

The worst scenario for an innovating firm is when another system supplants the innovators' product altogether to become the industry's standard. Sony's strategic blunder in guarding its Betamax video system is a good case to study. Matsushita and Victor Co. took the world leadership position away from Sony by being more liberal in licensing its VHS (Video Home System) to competitors. Philips and Grundig did not introduce their Video 2000 system until VHS was just about to become the industry's standard in Europe and the world. By that time, despite price cutting, it was too late for Video 2000 to attract other manufacturers and consumers. The problem was so bad that Philips' own North American subsidiary refused to buy its parent's system. Ironically, Sony itself had to start making VHS-format machines in 1988. By 2002, Sony ended its bitter experience by discontinuing the Betamax machines.

A more recent case of competing technologies and strategic alliances involves the digital videodisc (DVD) which can also store audio and computer data and software. Toshiba's system competed with the Multimedia Compact Disc system offered by Sony and Philips. In addition, Toshiba aggressively courted movie makers (e.g., Warner Bros., MCA, and MGM/UA) while offering "open" licensing to other electronics companies. As a result, such manufacturing giants as Matsushita, Thomson, and Pioneer chose to ally with Toshiba. In the end, Sony and Philips had to come to a compromise by adopting a single format that was closer to Toshiba's system than theirs.

Matsushita and Sony recently faced off again as both tried to make their products the industry standard so as to control the market of related digital consumer products. The battle involved flash memory cards which are used to record data on digital cameras, music players, and next-generation mobile phones and computers. Matsushita, playing catch-up, has the support of nearly 90 manufacturers worldwide, while Sony has 58. In addition, Matsushita's DVD audio player is not compatible with Sony's SACD (Super Audio CD), and its first recordable DVD player uses DVD-RAM that is not compatible with the DVD-RW format led by Pioneer and supported by Sony. A bigger battle involving high-definition DVDs is also being fought. Sony's Blu-Ray format appears to have an edge.

## *Pricing policy*

Initially, an innovating firm can afford to behave as a monopolist, charging a premium price for its innovation. But this price must be adjusted downward in the second and third stages of the IPLC to discourage potential newcomers and to maintain market share. Anticipating a Korean challenge, Japanese VCR makers cut their prices in the U.S.A. by 25 percent and were able to slow down retailers' and consumers' acceptance of Korean brands. IBM, in comparison, was slow in reducing prices for its PC models. The error in judgment was the result of a belief that the IBM PC was too complex for Asian imitators. This proved to be a costly error because the basic PC hardly changed for several years. Before long, the product became nothing but an easily copied, standardized commodity suitable for intensive distribution – the kind that Asian companies thrive on. Commodity pricing now dominates the market. In the end, IBM decided to get out of this cut-throat business by selling its PC operations to Lenovo.

In the final stage of the IPLC, it is not practical for the innovating firm to maintain a low price due to competitors' cost advantage, but the firm's above-the-market price is feasible only if it is accompanied by top-quality or sophisticated products. A high standard of excellence should partially insulate the firm's product from direct price competition. U.S. car manufacturers failed in this area – high prices are not matched by consumer perception of superior quality.

### *Promotion policy*

Promotion and pricing in the IPLC are highly related. The innovating firm's initial competitive edge is its unique product, which allows it to command a premium price. To maintain this price in the face of subsequent challenges from imitators, uniqueness can only be retained in the form of superior quality, style, or services.

The innovating marketer must plan for a nonprice promotional policy at the outset of a product diffusion. Timken is able to compete effectively against the Japanese by offering more services and meeting customers' needs at all times. For instance, it offers technological support by sending engineers to help customers design bearings in gearboxes.

One implication that may be drawn is that a new product should be promoted as a premium product with a high-quality image. By starting out with a high-quality reputation, the innovating company can trade down later with a simpler version of the product while still holding on to the high-priced, most profitable segment of the market. One thing the company must never do is to allow its product to become a commodity item with prices as the only buying motive, since such a product can be easily duplicated by other firms. Aprica has been very successful in creating a status symbol for its stroller by using top artists and designers to create a product for mothers who are more concerned with style than with price. The stroller is promoted as "anatomically correct" for babies to avoid hip dislocation, and the company uses the snob appeal and comfort to distinguish its brand from those of Taiwanese and Korean imitators. Therefore, product differentiation, not price, is most important for insulating a company from the crowded, low-profit market segment. A product can be so standardized that it can be easily duplicated, but image is a very different proposition.

A more recent example is a treatment for impotence. Viagra was the first to hit the market, generating an incredible amount of discussion worldwide. It is important for Viagra to create brand awareness and preference. Within a few short years, a number of rivals entered the market with improved products. Bayer and GSK, using vardenafil, markets Levitra that works regardless of the cause of a patient's impotence – depression, heart disease, high blood pressure, diabetes. Eli Lilly's Cialis claims to work for up to 36 hours or seven times as long as Viagra, thus having an advantage in terms of picking the right moment.

### *Place (distribution) policy*

A strong dealer network can provide the U.S. innovating firm with a good defensive strategy. Because of its near-monopoly situation at the beginning, the firm is in a good position to be able to select only the most qualified agents/distributors, and the distribution network should be expanded further as the product becomes more diffused. Caterpillar's network of loyal dealers caused difficulty for Komatsu to line up its own dealers in the U.S.A. In an ironic case, GM's old policy of limiting its dealers from carrying several GM brands inadvertently encouraged those dealers to start carrying imports. A firm must also watch closely for the development of any new alternative channel that may threaten the existing channel.

When it is too late or futile to keep an enemy out, the enemy should be invited in. U.S. firms – manufacturers as well as agents/distributors – can survive by becoming agents for their former competitors. The tactic involves providing a distribution network and marketing expertise at a profit to competitors who in all likelihood would welcome an easier entry into the marketplace. American car manufacturers and their dealers seem to have accepted the reality of the marketplace and have become partners with their Japanese and foreign competitors, as evidenced by General Motors' joint ventures with Toyota, Suzuki, and Isuzu (to produce Nova, Sprint, and Spectrum respectively), American Motors' with France's Renault (before the subsequent sale to Chrysler), Chrysler's with Mitsubishi and Maserati, and Ford's with Mazda and the Korean Kia Motors. In 2007, DaimlerChrysler announced that it would ally with Chery Automotive in China to build small cars there. These small cars would then be sold in the U.S.A. as well as around the world.[14]

Once a product is in the final stage of its life cycle, the innovating firm should strive to become a specialist, not a generalist, by concentrating its efforts in carefully selected market segments where it can distinguish itself from foreign competitors. To achieve distinction, U.S. firms should either add product features or offer more services. For the alert firm, there are early warning signals that may be used to determine whether the time has come to adopt this strategy. One signal is that the product becomes so standardized that it can be manufactured in many LDCs. Another warning signal is a decline in U.S. exports owing to the loss or narrowing of the U.S. technological lead. By that time, certain forms of market segmentation and product differentiation are highly recommended. As in the case of consumer electronics, such great American brands as Marantz and Scott were once synonymous with good sound and top quality but have since been bought up or driven out of business by Japanese and European manufacturers. American firms still dominate the segment of high-end stereo equipment where top systems may cost up to $100,000. American firms are successful because of the precision required and because production runs are short and items are usually done by hand.

## Product standardization vs. product adaptation

Product standardization means that a product originally designed for a local market is exported to other countries with virtually no change, except perhaps for the translation of words and other cosmetic changes. Revlon, for example, used to ship successful products abroad without changes in product formulation, packing (without any translation, in some cases), and advertising. There are advantages and disadvantages to both standardization and individualization.

### *Arguments for standardization*

The strength of standardization in the production and distribution of products and services is in its **simplicity** and **cost**. It is an easy process for executives to understand and implement, and it is also cost-effective. If cost is the only factor being considered, then standardization is clearly a logical choice because economies of scale can operate to reduce production costs. Yet minimizing production costs does not necessarily mean that profit increases will follow. Simplicity is not always beneficial, and costs are often confused with profits. Cost reductions do not automatically lead to profit improvements, and in fact the reverse may apply. By trying to control production costs through standardization, the product involved may become unsuitable for alternative markets. The result may be that demand abroad will decline, which leads to profit reduction. In some situations, cost control can be achieved but at the expense of overall profit. It is therefore prudent to remember that cost should not be overemphasized. The main marketing goal is to maximize profit, and production cost reductions should be considered as a secondary objective. The two objectives are not always convergent.

When appropriate, standardization is a good approach. For example, when a **consistent company** or **product image** is needed, product uniformity is required. The worldwide success of McDonald's is based on consistent product quality and service. Hamburger meat, buns, and fruit pies must meet strict specifications. This obsession with product quality necessitates the costly export of french fries from Canada to European franchises because the required kind of potato is not grown in Europe. In 1982, a Paris licensee was barred through a court order from using McDonald's trademarks and other trade processes because the licensee's 12 Paris eateries did not meet the required specifications.

Some products by their very nature are not or cannot be easily modified. **Musical recordings** and **works of art** are examples of products that are difficult to differentiate, as are books and motion pictures. When this is the case, the product must rise and fall according to its own merit. Whether such products will be successful in diverse markets is not easy to predict. Films that do well in the U.S.A. may do poorly in Japan. On the other hand, movies that were not box-office hits in the U.S.A. have turned out to be moneymakers in France (e.g., most of Jerry Lewis' films). But in the case of Ricky Martin, his worldwide fame has to do in part with his France '98 World Cup theme song ("The Cup of Life") – in Spanish, English, and French.

With regard to high-technology products, both users and manufacturers may find it desirable to reduce confusion and promote compatibility by introducing **industry specifications** that make standardization possible.

A condition that may support the production and distribution of standardized products exists when certain products can be associated with particular **cultural universals**; that is, when consumers from different countries share similar need characteristics and therefore want essentially identical products (see Cultural Dimension 10.2). Watches are used to keep time around the world and thus can be standardized. The diamond is another example. Levi Strauss' attempt to penetrate the European market with lighter weight jeans failed because European consumers wanted the standard heavy-duty American type.

Industrial managers and managers of consumer goods may view certain marketing-related factors differently, thus implying that product standardization or customization depends in part on the type of product. While market conditions tend to support localization, Western companies tend to favor standardization. But there is some logic behind the practice. Most Central and Eastern European countries are too small to pay off for customization. In addition, within a decade, these markets may converge to Western Europe market structures and rules.[15]

There is evidence that exporters have a status quo bias. Because of this bias, there is a tendency for managers to under-adapt their host-market strategies.[16] In the field of ICT (information and communication technology), globalizing internationals (companies that globalize their operations after the domestic period) lean toward standardized product strategy alternatives.[17]

## Cultural Dimension 10.2

### Ice cream is cool

While Cold Stone Creamery sells its mix-and-match ice cream to the masses in shopping malls in the U.S.A., it wants a different image in Japan: ice cream for the ultra-cool. The company targets young urbanites who will make its frozen desserts fashionable. It aims to attract "influencers." These people are edgy high school students as well as fashion-conscious "office ladies" who are young, single, female professionals. On average, a high school girl will send about 200 cell-phone text messages every day, and this kind of word-of-mouth advertising can make or break a brand.

Talking about fashion, Cold Stone grabs retail space near Louis Vuitton and Versace stores, and it even sponsors fashion shows. One fashion show for young women, Tokyo Girls Collection, has attracted media attention, which enhances its fashion-forward image.

Although cotton candy and cake batter are unfamiliar in Japan, Cold Stone holds on to its American ingredients so that it can stand out. Just like their U.S. counterparts while preparing customers' orders, the company's Japanese employees sing songs such as "Hi Ho, Hi Ho! It's Off to Work We Go!" in Japanese.

*Source*: "Cold Stone Aims to Be Hip in Japan," *Wall Street Journal*, December 14, 2006.

## *Arguments for adaptation*

There is nothing wrong with standardized products if consumers prefer those products. In many situations, domestic consumers may desire a particular design of a product produced for the American market. But when the product design is placed in foreign markets, foreign buyers are forced either to purchase that product from the manufacturer or not purchase anything at all. This manner of conducting business overseas is known as the "big-car" and "left-hand-drive" syndromes. Both describe U.S. firms' reluctance and/or unwillingness to modify their products to suit their customers' needs.

According to the **big-car syndrome**, U.S. marketers assume that products designed for Americans are superior and will be preferred by foreign consumers. U.S. car manufacturers believe (or used to believe) that the American desire for big cars means that only big cars should be exported to overseas markets.

The **left-hand-drive syndrome** is a corollary to the big-car syndrome. Americans drive on the right side of the road, with the steering wheels on the left side of the automobile. But many Asian and European countries have traffic laws requiring drivers to drive on the left side of the road, and cars with the steering wheel on the left present a serious safety hazard. Yet exported U.S. cars are the same left-hand-drive models as are sold in the U.S.A. for the right-hand traffic patterns (see Figure 10.3). According to the excuse used by U.S. car manufacturers, a small sales volume abroad does not justify converting exported cars to right-hand steering. And as explained by GM's president, "there's a certain status in having a left-hand steer in Japan." This is one good reason why American automobile sales abroad have been disappointing. A half-hearted effort can only result in a half-hearted performance. American exporters have failed time and time again to realize that when in Rome one should do as the Romans do. Japanese car manufacturers have not shown the same kind of indifference to market needs; Japanese firms have always adapted their automobiles to American driving customs.

What's right with this picture?
You won't see very many Accord Coupes that look like this one. There is no question about that. Unless, of course, you happen to work at Honda's factory located in Marysville, Ohio. Or live in Japan.
Carefully built and assembled at one of the automotive industry's most advanced manufacturing facilities, the Accord Coupe is made only in America. But that's not the only place it's sold.
Thousands of new Accord Coupes are exported to Japan each and every year. Where they are prized for their engineering, craftsmanship and value. Just as they are here.
But the other reason the Japanese are fond of this car is because it comes with right-hand drive. Which is fitting since they drive on the opposite side of the road in Japan.
Mind you, producing both right-hand and left-hand drive cars from the same assembly line takes a lot of extra effort. The fact that Honda is the only U.S. carmaker to do so speaks for itself.
It's this kind of innovation and true commitment to people's needs which makes Honda, well, Honda.
Because even though we sell more Accord Coupes in America, it's just as important to satisfy our customers in other parts of the world.
After all, when you look at the big picture, that's what it's all about.
HONDA

**FIGURE 10.3** Honda: built-in product adaptation

*Source*: Reproduced courtesy of American Honda Motor Co., Inc.

Those American firms that have understood the need for product modification have done well even in Japan. Du Pont has customized its manufacturing and marketing for the Japanese market, and its design units work with Japanese customers to design parts to their specifications. Yamazaki-Nabisco's Ritz crackers sold in Japan are less salty than the Ritz crackers sold in America.

Firms must choose the time when a product is to be modified to better suit its market. According to the Conference Board, important factors for product modification mentioned by more than 70 percent of firms surveyed are long-term profitability, long-term market potential, product–market fit, short-term profitability, cost of altering or adapting (e.g., retooling), desire for consistency (e.g., maintaining a world image), and short-term market potential. These factors apply to consumer nondurable and durable products as well as to industrial products.

Product adaptation is necessary under several conditions. Some are mandatory, whereas others are optional. In addition, firm characteristics and environmental characteristics have a significant impact on a firm's overall performance and marketing mix strategy.[18]

## *Mandatory product modification*

The mandatory factors affecting product modifications include the following: government's mandatory standards (i.e., country's regulations), electrical current standards, measurement standards, and product standards and systems.

The most important factor that makes modification mandatory is **government regulation**. To gain entry into a foreign market, certain requirements must be satisfied. Regulations are usually specified and explained when a potential customer requests a price quotation on a product to be imported. Avon shampoos had to be reformulated to remove the formaldehyde preservative, which is a violation of regulations in several Asian countries. Food products are usually heavily regulated. Added vitamins in margarine, forbidden in Italy, are compulsory in the United Kingdom and Holland. In the case of processed cheese, the incorporation of a mold inhibitor may be fully allowed, allowed up to the permissible level, or forbidden altogether.

Frequently, products must be modified to compensate for differences in **electrical current standards**. In many countries, there may even be variations in electrical standards within the country. The different electrical standards (phase, frequency, and voltage) abroad can easily harm products designed for use in the U.S.A., and such improper use can be a serious safety hazard for users as well. Stereo receivers and TV sets manufactured for the U.S. 110- to 120-volt mode will be severely damaged if used in markets where the voltages are twice as high. Therefore, products must be adapted to higher voltages. When there is no voltage problem, a product's operating efficiency may be impaired if the product is operated in the wrong electrical frequency. Alarm clocks, tape-recorders, and turntables designed for the U.S. 60 Hz (60 cycles per minute) system will run more slowly in countries where the frequency is 50 Hz. To solve this problem, marketers may have to substitute a special motor or arrange for a different drive ratio to achieve the desirable operating RPM or service level.

Like electrical standards, **measurement systems** can also vary from country to country. Although the U.S.A. has adopted the old English (imperial) system of measurement (feet, pounds), most countries employ the metric system, and product quantity should or must be expressed in metric units. Starting in 2010, the EU countries will no longer accept nonmetric products for sale. Many countries even go so far as to prohibit the sale of measuring devices with both metric and imperial markings. One New England company was ordered to stop selling its laboratory glassware in France because the markings were not exclusively metric (see Legal Dimensions 10.1 and 10.2)

Legal Dimension 10.1

**The metric**

The metric system is the international standard of measurement and most countries require, or will soon require, metric units for measurements. Many non-metric U.S. products are not readily exportable to certain markets. More importantly, customers in other nations have lifelong experience with the metric system and expect products made to metric measures. They are neither familiar nor comfortable with U.S. pints, ounces, inches, and pounds.

The International System of Units, universally abbreviated to SI, is the modern metric system of measurement. The General Conference on Weights and Measures (CGPM) established the SI in 1960 and is the international authority that ensures SI dissemination and modification to reflect the latest advances in science and technology. The CGPM is an intergovernmental treaty organization which boasts 49 member states, including the U.S.A. and all the major industrialized countries, and remains the basis of all international agreements on units of measurement.

Every industrialized nation in the world, except the U.S.A., prefers the metric system for weights and measures. Thus, the trading partners of the U.S.A. require at least dual labeling (U.S. units and metric units), if not metric-only measurement units on product labels.

The European Union (EU) Metric Directive mandates that all products sold in the EU must specify and label in metric measurements only. The European Commission recommended a 10-year deferral of the implementation of the metric-only directive, allowing companies to use dual labeling through 2009. After the EU Directive takes effect, U.S. exporters can no longer label or print inches, pounds, or any other non-metric measurement on shipments (i.e., labels, packaging, advertising, catalogs, technical manuals and instructions). Legal units of measurement are referred to as SI units (Système International).

South Korea's revised Korean Metrology Law mandates that measurements be expressed only in SI units. Strict punishment for non-compliance may include fines and a prison term. The Japanese Measurement Law requires that all imported products and shipping documents show SI units. Chile requires that all labels must contain, in Spanish, size and weight converted to the metric system. In Brazil, product labels should have a Portuguese translation and use metric units or show a metric equivalent. Countries in Africa have similar metric requirements. All items entering Nigeria must be labeled in metric terms exclusively; products with dual or multi-markings will be confiscated or refused entry.

Source: David Averne and Jim McCracken, "The Metric System: The International System for Measurement and Commerce," *Export America*, January 2002, 14–15.

In 1982, in order to save $2 million, the U.S. Congress abolished the U.S. Metric Board as well as a voluntary program for conversion to the metric system. That decision was shortsighted. Metric demands adversely affect U.S. firms' competitiveness because many American firms do not offer metric products. A Middle East firm, for example, was unable to find an American producer that sold pipe with metric threads for oil machinery. A European firm had to rewire all imported electrical appliances because the U.S. standard wire diameters did not meet national standards. It is difficult to find a U.S. firm that cuts lumber to metric dimensions. Fortunately, the new trade act now requires the U.S. government and industry to use metric units in documentation of exports and imports as

## Legal Dimension 10.2

### Give them an inch, and they will take a kilometer

The European Union directive, passed in the mid-1980s, gave Great Britain more time to go metric. The time came on January 1, 2000. All shops are now required to operate in metric measurements. In spite of the agreement, the metric requirement has created uproar. British politicians and consumers are angry. Tesco PLC, Britain's largest supermarket chain, interviewed 1000 customers and learned that more than half felt that metric measurements were confusing. According to Tony Bennett of the UK Independence Party, "We gave away shillings and pence in 1971, then we had to switch from gallons to litres in 1995. Gradually we've been forced to give up Fahrenheit for Celsius, and now it's pounds for kilos." A fishmonger, upset with having to measure fish in kilograms, states: "If it's good enough for [British Prime Minister] Tony Blair to have his new baby weighed in pounds and ounces, then it's good enough to sell fish in." Likewise, a butcher declares: "It's disgusting how a person can go into an Englishman's shop and make him into a criminal for selling in pounds and ounces." Of course, the EU officials are not amused either.

For whatever reason, the European Commission announced in 2007 that it would no longer force England to use the metric system. Merchants are now free to describe their products in non-metric terms without facing fines or criminal punishment. According to Commission Vice-President Gunter Verheugen, the decision "honours the culture and tradition of Great Britain and Ireland." Yet he went on to make a seemingly contradictory statement: "I hope that the U.S.A. will also accept metric-only labelled goods on its territory."

*Sources*: "Weighty Matter: Tradition Hangs in the Balance of English Kilo War," *Asian Wall Street Journal*, July 24, 2000; and "Brussels Admits an Inch is as Good as a Kilometer," MarketWatch.com, September 11, 2007.

prescribed by the International Convention on the Harmonized Commodity Description and Coding System. The Harmonized System is designed to standardize commodity classification for all major trading nations. The International System Units (Système International d' Unites [SI]) is the official measurement system of the Harmonized System.

Very few countries still cling to the obsolete nonmetric systems. Among them are the U.S.A., Burma, Brunei, and Liberia. Robert Heller of the Federal Reserve Board of Governors made the following comment:

> Only Yemen and India have as low an export-to-GDP ratio as the United States. Would it come as a surprise to you to know that the U.S. and Yemen share something else in common? They are the only two countries in the world that have not yet gone metric! If an American manufacturer has to retool first in order to sell his wares abroad, his incentive to do so is considerably reduced, and it makes his first step into export markets all that much more expensive.[19]

Some products must be modified because of different **operating systems** adopted by various countries. Television systems provide a good example (see Exhibit 10.1). There are three different TV

Exhibit 10.1

**World television standards**

**NTSC**

| | | | |
|---|---|---|---|
| Antigua | Costa Rica | Japan | Samoa |
| Bahamas | Cuba | South Korea | Surinam |
| Barbados | Dominican Republic | Mexico | Taiwan |
| Belize | Ecuador | Netherlands Antilles | Trinidad |
| Bermuda | El Salvador | Nicaragua | Tobago |
| Bolivia | Greenland | Panama | U.S.A. |
| Burma | Guam | Peru | Venezuela |
| Canada | Guatemala | Philippines | Virgin Islands |
| Chile | Honduras | Puerto Rico | |
| Colombia | Jamaica | Saipan | |

**PAL**

| | | | |
|---|---|---|---|
| Afghanistan (Kabul) | Gibraltar | Netherlands | Sudan |
| Algeria | Hong Kong | New Guinea | Swaziland |
| Argentina | Iceland | New Zealand | Sweden |
| Australia | Indonesia | Nigeria | Switzerland |
| Austria | Ireland | Norway | Tanzania |
| Bangladesh | Italy | Oman | Thailand |
| Belgium | Jordan | Paraguay | Turkey |
| Brazil | Kenya | Portugal | United Arab Emirates |
| Brunei | North Korea | Qatar | United Kingdom |
| China | Kuwait | Saudi Arabia | Uruguay |
| Cyprus | Liberia | Sierra Leone | Yemen |
| Denmark | Luxembourg | Singapore | Yugoslavia |
| Finland | Malaysia | South Africa | Zambia |
| Germany | Malta | Spain | Zimbabwe |
| Ghana | Monaco | Sri Lanka | |

**SECAM**

| | | | |
|---|---|---|---|
| Albania | Guadeloupe | Martinique | Senegal |
| Benin | French Guyana | Mauritius | Syria |
| Bulgaria | Haiti | Mongolia | Tahiti |
| Congo | Hungary | Morocco | Togo |
| Czechoslovakia | Iran | New Caledonia | Tunisia |
| Djibouti | Iraq | Niger | Vietnam |
| Egypt | Ivory Coast | Poland | Zaire |
| France | Lebanon | Reunion | |
| Gabon | Libya | Romania | |
| Greece | Madagascar | Russia | |

operating systems used in different parts of the world: the American NTSC (National Television Systems Committee), the French SECAM (Système Electronique Pour Couleur Avec Memoire), and the German PAL (Phone Alternating Lines). In 1941, the U.S.A. became the first country to set the national standards for TV broadcasting, adopting 525 scanning lines per frame. Most other nations later decided to require 625 lines for a sharper image. In most cases, a TV set designed for one broadcast system cannot receive signals broadcast through a different operating system. When differences in product-operating systems exist, a company unwilling to change its products must limit the number of countries it can enter, unless proper modification is undertaken for other market requirements.

## *Optional product modification*

The conditions dictating product modification mentioned so far are mandatory in the sense that without adaptation a product either cannot enter a market or is unable to perform its function there. Such mandatory standards make the adaptation decision easy: a marketer must either comply or remain out of the market. Italy's Piaggio withdrew its Vespa scooters from the U.S. market in 1983, choosing not to meet U.S. pollution control standards for its few exports. One study found that firms exporting to the most developed markets are more likely than firms exporting to the most competitive environments to adapt marketing strategy.[20]

A more complex and difficult decision is optional modification, which is based on the international marketer's discretion in taking action. Nescafé in Switzerland, for instance, tastes quite different from the same brand sold just a short distance across the French border. Yum has tailored its menu to local tastes. In China, its menu includes Dragon Twister which is a sandwich stuffed with chicken strips, Peking duck sauce, cucumbers, and scallions. It also serves rice porridge and bamboo shoots. Its Chinese mascot is a child-friendly character called Chicky.[21] In India, McDonald's does not serve hamburgers. One of its popular burgers there is made of alu tikki, which uses a potato-based spicy dumpling as its patty.[22]

One condition that may make optional modification attractive is related to **physical distribution**, and this involves the facilitation of product transportation at the lowest cost. Since freight charges are assessed on either a weight or a volume basis, the carrier may charge on the basis of whichever is more profitable. The marketer may be able to reduce delivery costs if the products are assembled and then shipped. Many countries also have narrow roads, doorways, stairways, or elevators that can cause transit problems when products are large or are shipped assembled. Therefore, a slight product modification may greatly facilitate product movement.

Another determinant for optional adaptation involves **local use conditions**, including **climatic conditions**. The hot/cold, humid/dry conditions may affect product durability or performance. Avon modified its Candid moist lipstick line for a hot, humid climate. Certain changes may be required in gasoline formulations. If the heat is intense, gasoline requires a higher flashpoint to avoid vapor locks and engine stalling. In Brazil, automobiles are designed to run on low-quality gas, to withstand the country's rough dusty roads, and to weather its sizzling temperatures. As a result, these automobiles are attractive to customers in developing countries, especially when the automobiles are also durable and simple to maintain. American automobiles can experience difficulties in these markets, where people tend to overload their cars and trucks and do not perform regular maintenance, not to mention the unavailability of lead-free gasoline.

Another local use condition that can necessitate product change is **space constraint**. Sears' refrigerators were redesigned to be smaller in dimensions without sacrificing the original capacity so that they could fit into the compact Japanese home. Philips, similarly, had to reduce the size of its coffee-maker. In contrast, U.S. mills, for many years, resisted cutting plywood according to Japanese specifications, even though they were told repeatedly that the standard Japanese plywood dimensions were 3 by 6 ft – not the U.S. standard of 4 by 8 ft. In a related case, Japanese-style homes have exposed wood beams, but U.S. forest-products firms traditionally allow 2-by-4 studs to be dirty or slightly warped, since in the U.S.A. these studs will almost always be covered over with wallboard. The firms have refused to understand that wood grain and quality are important to the Japanese because an exposed beam is part of the decor. Furniture is not easily exported because it has two inherent problems: size/weight and the different ways furniture is designed and used in other cultures. Some foreign manufacturers are still able to be successful in Japan, especially those who are willing to reduce the size of some products and make necessary modification so as to appeal to Japanese consumers.[23]

IKEA was initially unsuccessful in penetrating the Japanese market due to its failure to consider the space constraints of typical Japanese residences. There is now better market acceptance after IKEA redesigned its products to fit Japanese homes.

Consumer demographics as related to **physical appearance** can also affect how products are used and how suitable those products are (see Cultural Dimension 10.3). Habitat Mothercare PLC discovered that its British products were not consistent with American customs and sizes. Its comforters (duvets) were not long enough to fit American beds, and its tumblers could not hold enough ice. Philips downsized its shavers to fit the smaller Japanese hand. One U.S. brassière company did well initially in Germany but failed to get repeat purchases. The problem was that German women have a tendency not to try on merchandise in the store and thus did not find out until later that the product was ill-fitting because of measurement variations between American and German brassières. Furthermore, German customers usually do not return a product for refund or adjustment.

Even a doll may have to be modified to better resemble the physical appearance of local people. The Barbie doll, though available in Japan for decades, became popular only after Mattel allowed Takara (which holds the production and marketing agreement) to reconstruct the product. Of 60 countries, Japan is the only market where the product is modified. Barbie's Western-style features are modified in several ways: her blue eyes become brown, her vividly blonde hair is darkened, and her bosom size is reduced.

Local use conditions include **user's habits**. Since the Japanese prefer to work with pencils – a big difference from the typed business correspondence common in the U.S.A. – copiers require special characteristics that allow the copying of light pencil lines. Software companies such as Microsoft, Oracle, and SAP have teams that are in charge of localization of their software products. For non-English-language countries, the words on the screen have to be first translated. For many countries, the program may also have to be adapted to the national operating system. Cadillac's China-designed version of its SLS sedan is four inches longer than the U.S. model. Chinese owners, like many other Asian counterparts, want a roomy back seat because they have chauffeurs.[24]

Finally, other **environmental characteristics** related to use conditions should be examined. Examples are endless. Detergents should be reformulated to fit local water conditions. IBM had to come up with a completely new design so that its machine could include Japanese word-processing capability. Kodak made some changes in its graphic arts products for Japanese professionals, most of whom have no darkrooms and have to work in different light environments.

**Price** may often influence a product's success or failure in the marketplace. This factor becomes even more critical abroad because U.S. products tend to be expensive, but foreign consumers'

## Cultural Dimension 10.3

### Not so hairy

Norelco's target customers are men between the ages of 35 and 54 who want a premium razor. The company interviewed 5000 American, European, and Chinese men. According to the research, Chinese men have less hair. Furthermore, Asian hair is stronger but slower growing because it is rounder in shape and thicker in diameter than Caucasian hair. As a result, Chinese shavers may not need Norelco's high technology with three rotating blades. Instead, Norelco plans to launch a double-headed razor.

Appealing to 1.1 billion Muslims, LG Electronics has introduced a mobile phone that includes an electronic compass. Muslims pray five times a day facing Mecca. The phone, equipped with location-tracking software, is able to point toward Mecca.

Japanese owners, like other Asians, wash their cars a lot. While washing, they get more intimate with areas of the car not seen by others. That is one reason why NUMMI has to remove three burrs – tiny metal bumps – from the tailpipe of its Voltz vehicles during the assembly process. One was inside the tailpipe, while another was outside it. The third was about where the tailpipe was welded to the main exhaust system. When Japanese customers clean their cars, they will want to clean inside of the pipe where some exhaust residue has accumulated so that they get a nice shiny appearance. American buyers do not notice these burrs in the exhaust pipes that bother their Japanese counterparts.

KFC's name in Chinese is *kendeji* (kun-duh-jee) or Kentucky. Blending local cuisine with its American-style fowl fare, KFC offers Beijing duck. This new item is Chicken Roll of Old Beijing, rolled in a thin pancake with scallions, cucumber slivers and traditional sauce – typical accounterments of Beijing-style roast duck. The product contains fried chicken instead of duck meat. Certainly, to maintain global success, KFC cannot afford to cling to American tastes without giving any due consideration to the diversified cultures and customs of local consumers in other countries.

*Sources*: "LG Reaches Out to Muslim Callers," *San José Mercury News*, 9 September 2003; "Fremont Plant to Produce Autos for Japan Sale," *San José Mercury News*, 18 May 2002; and "KFC's New Secret Recipe in China Draws on Traditional Beijing Duck," *San José Mercury News*, 15 February 2003; and "Case Study: Philips' Norelco," *IN*, June 2007, 18–19.

incomes tend to be at lower levels than Americans' incomes. Frequently, the higher quality of American products cannot overcome the price disadvantage found in foreign markets. To solve this problem, American companies can reduce the contents of the product or remove any nonessential parts or do both. Foreign consumers are generally not convenience-oriented, and an elaborate product can be simplified by removing any "frills" that may unnecessarily drive up the price. This approach is used by General Motors in manufacturing and selling the so-called Basic Transportation Vehicle in less industrialized nations. India is an important market for Siemens. With some $1 billion in sales, Siemens comfortably leads General Electric Co. and other competitors. Its Medical Solutions Division sells X-ray scanners without some nonessential features to make them more affordable in India.[25]

The non-profit One Laptop Per Child project is a good example of taking a drastically different approach to create a product for low-income consumers. The goal of the project is to improve education by equipping each child with a computer. This bright-colored, hand-cranked, wireless-enabled portable computer has unique design elements. It uses the free Linux operating system, flash memory instead of a hard drive and a microprocessor that requires minimal power. The project attracted the attention of Intel which used its financial muscle to grab the potential market. Fortunately, a truce was called, and the two sides agreed in 2007 to cooperate.[26]

One reason why international marketers often voluntarily modify their products in individual markets is their desire to maximize profit by **limiting product movement across national borders**. The rationale for this desire to discourage gray marketing is that some countries have price controls and other laws that restrict profits and prices. When other nearby countries have no such laws, marketers are encouraged to move products into those nearby countries where a higher price can be charged. A problem can arise in which local firms in countries where product prices are high are bypassed by marketers who buy directly from firms handling such products in countries where prices are low. In many cases, due to anti-trust laws, international marketers who wish to maintain certain market prices cannot ban this kind of product movement by threatening to cut off supply from those firms re-exporting products to high-priced countries. Johnson & Johnson, for example, was fined $300,000 by the EU for explicitly preventing British wholesalers and pharmacists from re-exporting Gravindex pregnancy tests to Germany, where the kits cost almost twice as much.

In spite of authorities' efforts to prevent companies from keeping lower priced goods out of higher priced countries, marketers may do so anyway so long as they do not get caught. Some manufacturers try to hinder these practices by deliberately varying packaging, package coding, product characteristics, coloring, and even brand names in order to spot violators or to confuse consumers in markets where products have moved across borders.

Perhaps the most arbitrary yet most important reason for product change abroad is **historical preference**, or **local customs and culture**. Product size, color, speed, grade, and source may have to be redesigned in order to accommodate local preference. Kodak altered its film to cater to a Japanese idea of attractive skin tones. Kraft's Philadelphia Cream Cheese tastes different in the U.S.A., Great Britain, Germany, and Canada. In Asia, Foremost sells chocolate and strawberry milk instead of low-fat and skim milk. Asians and Europeans by tradition prefer to shop on a daily basis, and thus they desire smaller refrigerators in order to reduce cost and electrical consumption.

When products clash with a culture, the likely loser is the product, not the culture. Strong religious beliefs make countries of the Middle East insist on halalled chickens. In soup-conscious Brazil, Russia, and China, Campbell soups did not take hold because homemakers there have strong cultural traditions of a homemaker's role, and serving Campbell soup to their families would be a soup served not of their own making. As a result, these homemakers prefer dehydrated products manufactured by Knorr and Maggi, used as a soup starter to which homemakers can add their own flair and ingredients. Campbell soups are usually purchased to be put aside for an emergency, such as if the family arrives home late.[27]

Product changes are not necessarily related to functional attributes such as durability, quality, operation method, maintenance, and other engineering aspects. Frequently, aesthetic or secondary qualities must also be taken into account. There are instances in which minor, cosmetic changes have significantly increased sales. Therefore, functional and aesthetic changes should both be considered in regard to how they affect the total, complete product.

One company that incorporates multiple features of product modification in appealing to local tastes is Pillsbury. In marketing its Totino's line of pizzas in Japan, Pillsbury found it wise to make several mandatory and optional changes in its product. Japanese food standards ban many preservatives and dyes, and thus necessitate an extensive redesign of a product. Totino's pizzas are basically a "belly stuffer" in the U.S.A., a confirmation of many foreigners' perceptions that Americans have pedestrian tastes in food. But the Japanese "eat" with their eyes, too – all foods have an aesthetic dimension. They perceive American foods as being too sweet, too large, and too spicy, making it necessary to alter the ingredients to suit the Japanese palate. Furthermore, the pizza size had to be reduced from the U.S. 12-ounce size to the Japanese 6.5-ounce size to fit into smaller Japanese ovens. In effect, Totino's frozen pizza and package were completely redesigned for the Japanese market, and Pillsbury's success confirms that its efforts were worthwhile.

In conclusion, marketers should not waste time resisting product modification. As one study has demonstrated, the performance of Korean exporters of electronics is enhanced by adaptation of products to foreign customers' tastes, adjustment of export prices to foreign market conditions, direct marketing, and trade promotions toward overseas distributors. Expenditure on overseas advertising seems to have no impact on export performance.[28]

The reluctance to change a product may be the result of an insensitivity to cultural differences in foreign markets. Whatever the reason for this reluctance, there is no question that it is counter-productive in international marketing. Product adaptation should rarely become an important issue to the marketer. A good marketer compares the incremental profits against the incremental costs associated with product adaptation. If the incremental profit is greater than the associated incremental cost, then the product should be adjusted – without question. In making this comparison, marketers should primarily use only future earnings and costs.

## A move toward world product: international or national product?

Product standardization and modification may give the impression that a marketer must choose between these two processes and that one approach is better than the other. In many instances, a compromise between the two is more practical and far superior than in selecting either procedure exclusively. Black and Decker has stopped customizing products for every country in favor of a few global products that can be sold everywhere. Such U.S. publishers as Prentice-Hall and Harper have also adopted the "world book" concept, which makes it possible for an English-language world book to have world copyrights. Publishers change, if necessary, only the title page, cover, and jacket.

World product and standardized product may sometimes be confused with each other. A **world product** is a product designed for the international market. In comparison, a **standardized product** is a product developed for one national market and then exported with no change to international markets. A German subsidiary of ITT makes a world product by producing a "world chassis" for its TV sets. This world chassis allows assemblage of TV sets for all three color TV systems of the world (i.e., NTSC, SECAM, and PAL) without changing all the circuitry on the various modules.

A move toward a world product by a company is a logical and healthy step. If a company has to adapt its product for each market, this can be a very expensive proposition, but without the necessary adaptation, a product might not sell at all. Committing to the design of a world product can provide the solution to these two major concerns faced by most firms dealing in the international marketplace. GE, for example, produces a numerical control system suitable in both metric and imperial measures. In addition, it has designed machines to operate under the wide differences in voltage among the different European countries. GE refrigerators are built in such a way that they can be used regardless of whether the frequency is 50 Hz or 60 Hz. This emerging trend toward world products is also attractive for items with an international appeal or for those items purchased by international travelers. Electrical shavers made by Norelco have a universal-voltage feature.

### Ethical Dimension 10.2

**A global product: universally deadly**

In 2004, Playboy published its lists of "50 Products That Changed the World." The AK was surpassed by only the Apple Macintosh, the birth control pill, and the Sony Betamax.

During the Vietnam War, American troops fought with the automatic M-16 rifle. To prevent jamming, M-16 requires careful cleaning. The Vietnamese relied on a Soviet weapon.

Mikhail Kalashnikov, as a young tank commander in 1941, witnessed the devastating power of the Nazi invaders' Schmeisser submachine-guns. Vowing to create a weapon to defend the motherland, he invented The Avtomat Kalashnikova 1947. The AK 47 boasted 600-rounds-per-minute bursts of firepower. Unveiled by the Soviet Army during the 1956 Hungarian uprising, it played a major role in the deaths of 50,000 civilians. The Kalashnikov assault rifle proved to be effective in Vietnam as it was immune from heat, cold, sand, and mud.

The first large-scale production of this low-tech weapon of mass destruction began in 1947. The Soviets neither asserted patent claims nor charged licensing fees, and the weapon was freely produced in numerous countries. Since then, more than 100 million AKs have been manufactured, and they have found their way into conflicts in just about all parts of the world. In El Salvador, Guatemala, Honduras, and Colombia, small conflicts became large wars. Although trained by Americans, Iraqi soldiers asked to be equipped with the indestructible AK.

*Source*: Larry Kahaner, *The Reliable Killer* (Hoboken, NJ: John Wiley & Sons, 2007).

One might question whether a world product would be more expensive than a national or local product, since the world product may need multipurpose parts. Actually, the world product should result in greater savings for two reasons. First, costly downtime in production is not needed to adjust or convert equipment to produce different national versions. Second, a world product greatly simplifies inventory control because only one universal part, not many individual parts, has to be stocked.

A world product may also be able to lower certain production costs by anticipating necessary local adaptation and thus being adaptation-ready. As an example, the Japanese government requires 32 changes on most U.S.-built cars, and the changes include: replacing headlamps that, because of left-hand drive, dip in the wrong direction; changing "sharp-edged" door handles; replacing outside rearview mirrors, and filling the space between the body and the rear bumper to prevent catching the sleeves of kimono-clad women. Honda is able to sell its U.S.-made cars in Japan at relatively low prices because it produces the car ready for sale in Japan (see Figure 10.3, p. 350). Because cars manufactured by GM, Ford, and Chrysler are built for the American market, they must undergo expensive alterations to meet Japanese regulations. The American car manufacturers have taken some steps to remedy the problem.

It must be pointed out that a world product has some inherent problems as well. As illustrated by Ford Escort, the car was designed in Europe as Ford's world car. The company's American executives, however, proceeded to thoroughly redesign it for the U.S. market. Similarly, design choices are often a source of conflict between Toyota's Japanese headquarters and its U.S. subsidiary. Even interior color schemes, while minor, are also a cause of dispute.[29] Therefore, corporate commitment is a necessity. There must be mechanisms to take care of the conflicting views of executives working in the different countries.

The Ford 2000 project, relying on centralization, uses vehicle centers to better utilize common parts and engineering ideas. However, due to differences in gasoline prices, consumer income, and tastes, the same vehicle does not have the same appeal in many parts of the world. While Americans are crazy about Ford's trucks and sport-utility vehicles, Europeans like smaller, more fuel-efficient passenger cars. While Europeans prefer flashier interiors, their American counterparts want wider seats while toning down the interiors.

As a product of compromise, a world product may have to be bland enough to partially please everyone while not really pleasing anyone. That is, it must satisfy the lowest common denominator of taste in different markets. Ford's Mondeo has done well in Europe, but American consumers have found the back seat of the American versions (Ford Contour and Mercury Mystique) to be too tight. Likewise, GM's 1997 front-drive minivan is just right for Europeans but a little too small for Americans. As far as the automobile industry is concerned, a world car has another problem; it has to meet the world's toughest environmental and safety rules, thus increasing costs.

The trend toward an international or world product and away from a national product will continue as MNCs become more aware of the significance of world marketing. The willingness of several companies to consider designing a universal product for the world market is indeed a good indicator that this trend will continue. Consider the case of Vaillant.[30] This German boiler company is Europe's biggest maker of central-heating boilers. The boiler market does not accommodate the pan-European plans well. Because of a huge variation in customer tastes and building standards, a company has to offer hundreds of different models. As a result, local suppliers largely dominate individual countries' boiler markets, and the industry's cross-border selling is much less developed than that found in most other industries. As noted by Vaillant's manager, products such as toilet cisterns and refrigerators have far less product divergence across the continent. Still, Vaillant's strategy is to focus on a few common components while producing hundreds of different types of boiler. While boilers must still be developed to meet individual countries' specifications, they will share as many common features (e.g., burners and controls) as is logical. Therefore, the costs of customization can be minimized without minimizing customer choice.

International marketers pursuing a global strategy will need to consider how to standardize the existing product offerings and marketing activities while making unique adjustment in a local market. According to one study investigating 16 supposedly global product attributes across three product categories in France and Malaysia, two attributes (product quality and appearance) are universal and may thus be standardized. The relevance of the other 14 attributes though is based on international market contingencies.[31]

Theoretically, the concepts of mass customization and global product may be compatible. After all, both strategies embody standardization and adaptation. They share the same goal of efficiency and effectiveness.

## Marketing of services

Services, broadly defined, encompass all economic activities – other than agriculture, manufacturing, and mining. The service section has a great variety of industries that include: banking and insurance, travel and tourism, entertainment, wholesale and retail trade, legal and other business services, telecommunications, healthcare, education and training, publishing, transportation, energy, and environmental services, as well as architecture, construction, and engineering services.

The impact of service can also be indirect. As countries become more developed economically, they also become more service-oriented. Firms in mature Western markets seem to gain a competitive advantage with a strong service orientation. Likewise, the evidence, while quite limited, shows that a private, more service-oriented Slovenian bank outperformed a large, older, state-supported bank.[32]

## *Importance of services*

Internationally, the "invisible" trade is responsible for one-fifth of the value of world exports. The share of commercial services in world trade has been rising. Due to information technology, communication costs will further decline. As a result, trade in services is very likely to continue to expand rapidly. In Hong Kong, the services sector has traditionally dominated the economy, accounting for 85 percent of GDP (mostly financial services and trade and tourism).[33]

The U.S.A. is the world's leading producer and exporter of services. The service sector is the largest component of the U.S. economy. It accounts for 79 percent of the private sector output and 83 percent of the private non-farm employment (93 million people).[34] The top U.S. services exports are: tourism, transportation (see Figure 10.4), financial, education and training, business, telecommunications, equipment (installation, maintenance, and repair), entertainment, information, and healthcare. The major markets for American services exports, in order, are: the European Union, Japan, and Canada.

Education and tourism in particular are significant earners for the U.S.A. Some 583,000 foreign students attend U.S. colleges and universities, and one-third or more of science and engineering degrees are awarded to foreigners.[35] Likewise, travel and tourism exports are unique because buyers must travel to the United States to buy and consume the products. The top three reasons why international visitors travel to the U.S.A. are: vacation, visiting friends and relatives, and business meetings.

## *Types of services*

There are two major categories of services: consumer and business services. Business services that are exported consist of numerous and varied types, including advertising, construction and engineering, insurance, legal services, data processing, and banking. Among the consulting and technical services are personnel training and supervision, management of facilities, and economic and business research.

Services such as haircuting are often cited as a classic example of non-tradables. However, technological advancement has made it possible for many services to be embodied in goods that are traded internationally (e.g., software on CD and films on DVD). Technology has also greatly benefited information-intensive services (e.g., research and development, accounting, legal services) as well as knowledge-based services (e.g., professional and technical services, banking, insurance, education). The Indian software industry has been able to capture about 12 percent of the international market for customized software. Figure 10.5 shows the international nature of management education.

Imagine an international airline that gave your money back if it didn't arrive on time.
Now imagine if that airline only took packages.
UPS INTRODUCES THE WORLDWIDE EXPRESS ON-TIME GUARANTEE. We promise to deliver your package on time to hundreds of cities around the world or we'll deliver it for free. Kind of makes you wish we also took people, doesn't it? For guarantee details, call 1-800-PICK-UPS. The package delivery company more companies count on.
UPS

**FIGURE 10.4** Marketing of services: transportation

#1 in Europe
and #2 worldwide*
IMD
Real World. Real Learning
www.imd.ch
ARE YOU READY FOR
THE NEXT BIG STEP?
PED
Program for Executive Development
Program starting dates:
January 8, 2003
March 17, 2003
July 28, 2003
October 6, 2003
Your next big career move will offer a challenge, with opportunity. A tough economy, increasing competition, new people. Now is the time to prepare for increased management responsibility.
That's the purpose of IMD's Program for Executive Development (PED). It prepares you for a move into general management positions by giving you a comprehensive understanding of the company and the business environment. It's a unique program that can extend into an Executive MBA.
Sign up now for the session starting January 8, 2003. Visit our website today for a full course description: www.imd.ch/ped
For more information about all IMD degree and Executive Education programs visit us at www.imd.ch
IMD
Chemin de Bellerive 23, PO Box 915
CH-1001 Lausanne, Switzerland
Tel: +41 21 618 03 42
Fax: +41 21 618 07 15
E-mail: info@imd.ch
* Financial Times Executive Education 2002 survey ranks IMD #1 in Europe in executive education overall and #2 worldwide in custom programs.


**FIGURE 10.5** Marketing of services: management education

## The economic and legal environment

Like merchandise trade, exports of services are influenced by changes in relative economic conditions and exchange rates. As shown by the travel industry, when the dollar was strong in the early 1980s, the increased buying power of the dollar made foreign travel for Americans a bargain. When the dollar weakened, however, foreign travelers vacationed in the U.S.A.

The primary competition for American service firms comes from Western Europe, with new challenges being mounted by Latin American and East Asian companies. Countries such as India view service as an infant industry that must be nurtured and protected. Not surprisingly, service exports/imports are subject to many non-tariff trade barriers (e.g., local labor and content of service requirements, ownership restrictions, foreign exchange controls, employment bans, quotas, local standards, and discriminatory taxation policies). International marketers may even face outright bans on investing in certain businesses altogether. For example, foreign life insurers are not allowed to set up shop in South Korea.

The National Committee for International Trade in Education publishes a report on barriers to trade in education services. The report states that American providers face numerous barriers when delivering their services abroad. The barriers highlighted include: national legislation and policy that inhibit foreign education providers from obtaining national licenses; qualifications authorities that have difficulty recognizing foreign educational credentials; telecommunications laws that restrict the use of national satellites and receiving dishes; foreign currency controls that limit direct investment by foreign education providers, place minimum capital investment requirements on foreign-owned firms and assess prohibitively high taxes on all revenue made by foreign entities; limitations on foreign ownership; and disregard for international agreements concerning intellectual property rights.[36]

Although service providers must abide by local laws, they may still want to try to change unfavorable laws or oppose proposed regulations that can adversely affect business activities. Since the move for fixed exchange rates will threaten the existence of the Chicago Mercantile Exchange's currency contracts, the CME established the American Coalition for Flexible Exchange Rates to present the alternative point of view to that of the advocates of fixed rates.

One good sign is that services are being liberalized. One successful aspect of the Uruguay Round is the adoption of the General Agreement on Trade in Services (GATS). This agreement has extended multilateral rules (e.g., most-favored-nation status, national treatment, removal of quantitative restrictions) to services. Unfortunately, services are one of the areas of heated discussion, and the controversy is one reason why the WTO's Doha round has not been concluded in spite of years of negotiations.

## Are services different?

Virtually all marketing textbooks proclaim that services are different products, requiring adjustment to marketing approaches. Services have several unique characteristics: they are intangible, person-oriented, and perishable. Based on a conceptual model differentiating between the technical (physical good quality) and functional (service quality and servicescape) elements of the service encounter, differences were found between fast-food and grocery customers. In addition, the effects of the technical and functional service elements on behavioral intentions varied across eight countries.[37] In terms of advertising, a review of the international services advertising literature found that advertising strategies for goods could not be automatically transferred to services.[38]

It is premature to conclude that products and services are different and that they require different marketing strategies. Certainly, there are studies which show that products and services have different characteristics and that they may be perceived or received differently. In addition, there are studies which show that perceptions of services (as well as perceptions of products) differ from country to country. Still, it may not be wise to lump all services together and to treat them as a homogeneous group. Likewise, it does not make sense to lump together products from the many industries just because they happen to have one common element (i.e., tangibility). The characteristics of particular services are quite different from those of the other service counterparts, while having more in common with certain products. A great deal more research is necessary to determine whether products and services should be marketed in different ways. The particular circumstances must also be identified.

## Marketing mix and adaptation

Whether products and services are different, virtually all marketing concepts and strategies used to market tangible products are relevant to the marketing of services.

Like a product, a company's service should be broadly defined. American Express, for instance, does not look at itself as being in the credit-card business. Instead, the company is in the communications and information-processing business, and its computer center in Phoenix processes a quarter of a million credit-card transactions each day from all over the world.

Should services be internationally standardized? Based on a study of business-to-business repair service quality for mission-critical equipment, perceptions in both the U.S.A. and Europe are remarkably similar.[39] This homogeneity implies standardization possibilities. In contrast, another study found that the U.S.A. was systematically and significantly different from India and the Philippines with regard to perception of service quality dimensions. A study of financial service firms in Australia and the U.S.A. found that some of the new service-development practices were common to all countries but that some other practices had to be adjusted to account for national variations.[40] These studies should alert researchers and practitioners to investigate whether it is necessary to distinguish developed countries from developing economies (as well as to determine country differences that may exist within each group).

According to a study of public relations firms with regard to professional service employee standardization preferences, greater standardization is preferred by employees from higher power distance, high uncertainty avoidance, and high-context cultures. Employees from high individualism cultures, in contrast, prefer less standardization. In addition, standardization preference is positively associated with work interdependence but negatively associated with local embeddedness.[41]

Services require adaptation from time to time for foreign markets. Even movies distributed abroad, more often than not, must be packaged differently. At the very least, movies distributed internationally require subtitles or overdubbing. Most Japanese were perplexed by Disney's policies of serving no alcohol and prohibiting bringing in food from outside the park. Disney, however, has made a few changes. It has added a Japanese restaurant to serve older patrons. There was no Nautilus submarine. In addition, to protect against rain and snow, more areas are covered.

Walt Disney Co. has got together with Yash Raj Films to make Disney-branded animated films, with the voices of Bollywood stars. Its animated films will be released in at least three languages: Hindi, Tamil, and Telugu. It plans to make live-action movies specifically for the southern part of India, which has different tastes in movies and is an important market. The move is not surprising. After all, India's population under 14 years old is larger than the U.S. population. To win in high-growth foreign markets (particularly India, China, Russia, Latin America, and South Korea), Disney has decided to discard its traditional obsession with going it alone and with force-feeding its American products. It will now join local experts to make culturally customized movies.[42]

Service providers usually have more flexibility in providing services than products because it is more difficult for consumers to ascertain and compare the quality of services among suppliers. Their prices must still be competitive, especially when the services offered are standardized (see Table 10.2).

**TABLE 10.2** Prices of services

| *City* | *U.S.$* | *Index New York = 100* |
|---|---|---|
| Amsterdam | 500 | 83.3 |
| Athens | 420 | 70.0 |
| Auckland | 420 | 70.0 |
| Bangkok | 270 | 45.0 |
| Barcelona | 500 | 83.3 |
| Beijing | 230 | 38.3 |
| Berlin | 440 | 73.3 |
| Bogotá | 310 | 51.7 |
| Bratislava | 230 | 38.3 |
| Brussels | 500 | 83.3 |
| Bucharest | 230 | 38.3 |
| Budapest | 300 | 50.0 |
| Buenos Aires | 220 | 36.7 |
| Caracas | 290 | 48.3 |
| Chicago | 520 | 86.7 |
| Copenhagen | 640 | 106.7 |
| Delhi | 200 | 33.3 |
| Dubai | 470 | 78.3 |
| Dublin | 550 | 9.17 |
| Frankfurt | 500 | 83.3 |
| Geneva | 570 | 95.0 |
| Helsinki | 600 | 100.0 |
| Hong Kong | 420 | 70.0 |
| Istanbul | 440 | 73.3 |
| Jakarta | 210 | 35.0 |
| Johannesburg | 350 | 58.3 |
| Kiev | 290 | 48.3 |
| Kuala Lumpur | 140 | 23.3 |
| Lima | 300 | 50.0 |
| Lisbon | 400 | 66.7 |
| Ljubljana | 350 | 58.3 |
| London | 640 | 106.7 |
| Los Angeles | 510 | 85.0 |

**TABLE 10.2** *continued*

| *City* | *U.S.$* | *Index New York = 100* |
|---|---|---|
| Luxembourg | 500 | 83.3 |
| Lyon | 540 | 90.0 |
| Madrid | 490 | 81.7 |
| Manama | 430 | 71.7 |
| Manila | 250 | 41.7 |
| Mexico City | 390 | 65.0 |
| Miami | 480 | 80.0 |
| Milan | 500 | 83.3 |
| Montreal | 500 | 83.3 |
| Moscow | 420 | 70.0 |
| Mumbai | 170 | 28.3 |
| Munich | 520 | 86.7 |
| Nairobi | 210 | 35.0 |
| New York | 600 | 100.0 |
| Nicosia | 400 | 66.7 |
| Oslo | 740 | 123.3 |
| Paris | 590 | 98.3 |
| Prague | 240 | 40.0 |
| Riga | 260 | 43.3 |
| Rio de Janeiro | 370 | 61.7 |
| Rome | 460 | 76.7 |
| Santiago de Chile | 360 | 60.0 |
| Sao Paulo | 380 | 63.3 |
| Seoul | 440 | 73.3 |
| Shanghai | 240 | 40.0 |
| Singapore | 420 | 70.0 |
| Sofia | 200 | 33.3 |
| Stockholm | 600 | 100.0 |
| Sydney | 450 | 75.5 |
| Taipei | 340 | 56.7 |
| Tallinn | 310 | 51.7 |
| Tel Aviv | 330 | 55.0 |
| Tokyo | 690 | 115.0 |
| Toronto | 530 | 88.3 |
| Vienna | 530 | 88.3 |
| Vilnius | 280 | 46.7 |
| Warsaw | 360 | 60.0 |
| Zurich | 620 | 103.3 |

*Note*: Methodology weighted basket of 27 services.

*Source*: Prices and Earnings (Zurich: UBS AG, 2006, 24)

## *Market entry strategies*

Regarding market entry strategies, a service firm's unique characteristics may have some impact on entry-mode choice. In general, service firms prefer full-control modes. A study of 174 entry decisions of service companies found that some variables routinely used in the studies of the manufacturing sector were not significant (or exhibited different results) in different groups of service activities.[43]

In practice, service firms can use virtually all market entry strategies where appropriate. In the financial services industry, American firms have entered into partnership and joint venture agreements with European and Japanese firms. Wells Fargo and Nikko Securities have formed a joint venture to operate a global investment management firm. Merrill Lynch and Société Génerale have discussed a partnership to develop a French asset-backed securities market.

In the case of Toronto-based Four Seasons Hotels Inc., it was relatively unknown in Asia even though it manages Inn on the Park in Europe and The Pierre and The Ritz-Carlton in North America. To quickly become a dominant high-end hotelier worldwide, Four Seasons paid $122 million for a 25 percent stake in the Hong Kong-based Regent International Hotels Ltd. (which is owned by Japan's EIE International Corp.). As part of the deal, Four Seasons also gained the rights to manage the luxury chain, thus managing 43 hotels in 17 countries. This acquisition strategy coupled with the management contract strategy has made it possible for Four Seasons to gain an exposure in Asia that otherwise would have taken years to develop on its own. In the end, the Regent brand has been replaced with Four Seasons.

## Conclusion

A product provides a bundle of satisfaction that the consumer derives from the product itself, along with its promotion, distribution, and price. For a product or service to be successful in any market, whether at home or overseas, it must therefore primarily satisfy consumer needs. In order to satisfy these needs more precisely, marketers should employ market segmentation, product positioning, and other marketing techniques. In the past, American marketers have been slow to realize that they must adapt their marketing practices when selling abroad. American marketers have overlooked the particular preferences and needs of customers overseas and have not adapted exported products, brands, and packages to meet those needs. For companies that have committed themselves seriously to their international market needs, performance can be very encouraging. Texas Instruments and Du Pont, for example, have done remarkably well in Japan, a market misunderstood by many, by assigning their best marketing personnel in that market. Du Pont, recognizing the importance of this market, maintains 13 laboratories in Japan to work closely with customers in order to tailor products to meet customers' needs.

As explained by Theodosiou and Leonidou,

> based on an integrative analysis of 36 studies centering around strategy standardization/adaptation, its antecedents, and performance outcomes, this stream of research was found to be characterized by non-significant, contradictory, and, to some extent, confusing findings attributable to inappropriate conceptualizations, inadequate research designs, and weak analytical techniques.[44]

Although product modification for local markets is a necessity in many cases, it does not mean that all products must be changed. A standardized product designed for one market may fit many other markets as well. But this situation is relatively rare, and the standardized product that is suitable in many markets should be considered as a fortunate random occurrence. A world product, on the other hand, should be created with the world market in mind in order to maximize consumer satisfaction and simplify the production process in the long run. If a world product is not possible due to environmental diversity or other circumstances, a marketing manager should re-examine product characteristics and consumer needs. If there is a possibility that there is a convergence on the characteristics and needs, then it may be possible to standardize the product. When the characteristics and need variables do not converge, then it becomes a matter of changing the product to fit consumer needs, as long as the associated costs are not prohibitive. The time has clearly come for the export marketer to think less nationally and more internationally. It may in fact be as fundamental as determining that, if the product can satisfy a need at a reasonable price, the product will sell itself in its international market.

## Questions

1 By marketing in a foreign country, must a firm automatically utilize geographic segmentation or other segmentation bases?
2 Explain (in the international context) how these product attributes affect product adoption: relative advantage, compatibility, trialability/divisibility, observability, complexity, and price.
3 Describe briefly the IPLC theory and its marketing implications.
4 Describe the factors that make it feasible to offer a standardized product.
5 Offer your arguments for product adaptation.
6 Explain the "big-car" syndrome and "left-hand-drive" syndrome.
7 Why do foreign governments erect barriers to U.S. exports of services?

## Discussion assignments and minicases

1 Provide examples of products for each of these IPLC stages: (0) local innovation, (1) overseas innovation, (2) maturity, (3) worldwide imitation, and (4) reversal.
2 Given the implications of the IPLC theory, how should U.S. innovating firms adjust their marketing strategies?
3 Why are U.S. manufacturers unwilling to modify their products for overseas customers?
4 Is it practical to offer a world product? (Note: this term should be differentiated from a standardized product.)
5 Can standard marketing techniques (e.g., market segmentation) be used to market services locally and internationally?

6 Fresh Choice, Inc. operates some 50 casual restaurants in the U.S.A., mainly in California. The company's goal is to create a distinctive dining experience that combines the selection, quality, and ambiance of full-service, casual restaurants with the convenience and low-price appeal of traditional buffet restaurants. In essence, the company offers the soups-and-salads concept which should appeal to health-conscious diners who are focused on the nutritional content of their meals.

Fresh Choice restaurants feature high-quality, freshly made specialty and traditional salads, hot pastas, soups, bakery goods, and desserts, offered in a self-service format. Each restaurant includes a salad bar offering specialty tossed and prepared salads with an extensive choice of salad ingredients and dressings. All specialty tossed salads and specialty prepared salads are clearly marked, and low-fat and fat-free items are prominently identified. Throughout the day, several employees maintain the salad bar and replenish individual salads and ingredients from the opposite side of the salad bar, minimizing interference with customers. Separate exhibition-style cooking areas offer fresh soups, gourmet pizzas, hot pastas, baked potatoes, hot muffins, country-herbed biscuits, fresh-baked breads and other bakery goods, and fresh fruits and desserts.

You have been charged with the responsibility of opening and operating restaurants outside of the U.S.A. based on the same concept. Evaluate Fresh Choice's restaurant concept. Do you think that this product concept can be successfully introduced into your chosen country without any modification? What are the factors that may facilitate or impede the acceptance of the soups-and-salads concept among foreign (local) consumers? In the case that the existing concept is not totally appropriate, what are the modifications that you will make? Explain your rationale.

## CASE 10.1 MCDONALDIZATION

McDonald's Corp. is often used as an example of Americanism (and globalization) owing to its strict quality control and worldwide success. McDonald's has some 30,000 outlets in 121 countries to serve about 46 million customers every day, totaling more than $41 billion in annual sales.

The company has highly detailed specifications and rules that must be strictly followed. In England, its high standard for coffee aroused the ire of a British coffee supplier, and the company built its own plant when it could not obtain quality hamburger buns. McDonald's provides assistance to Thai farmers for cultivation of Idaho russet potatoes. When suitable supplies are unavailable in Europe, the company does not hesitate to import french fries from Canada and pies from Oklahoma.

As reported by *Advertising Age*, the *Wall Street Journal*, and *Direct Marketing*, the company, however, permits some degree of flexibility and creativity on the part of its franchisees. In Southeast Asia, it serves durian-flavored milk shakes made from a tasty tropical fruit whose aroma is acceptable to Asians but is considered foul by Westerners. Coconut, mango, and tropical mint shakes may be found in Hong Kong.

Menu changes are also necessary in Europe. McDonald's sells near beer, which does not require a liquor license in Switzerland, and chicken on the Continent (to head off Kentucky Fried Chicken). McDonald's on the Champs Élysées offers a choice of vin blanc or vin rouge, and the coffee comes in a tiny cup with about half a dozen spoonfuls of very strong black coffee. In England, tea is available and will have milk in it unless black tea is ordered.

McDonald's Australian outlets formerly offered mutton pot pie; outlets in the Philippines, where noodle houses are popular, offer McSpaghetti. Likewise, in Mexico, McDonald's offers the McPollo chicken sandwich and jalapeno sauce as a hamburger condiment. Because eating the Midwest-American beef is like eating soft pebbles to the Japanese, McDonald's hamburger in Japan has different texture and spices. In many countries, consumers consider fast food to be primarily a snack rather than a regular meal.

Furthermore, the company's operating philosophy has to be altered as well. In order to attract foreign partners who are well qualified and well financed, McDonald's grants territorial franchises instead of the usual practice of granting franchises store by store.

In spite of its strong American image and sandwiches, McDonald's has done quite a bit of localization. Consider the following non-U.S. products: Taiwan (rice dishes with curry beef, ginger beef and spicy tomato chicken), India (vegetarian sandwich with eggless tomato mayonnaise), New Zealand (hamburger with a fried egg and slice of pickled beet), Turkey (spicy meat patty with a yogurt and tomato sauce), the Philippines (pasta in a red sauce), Egypt (deep-fried patties of ground beans and spices), India (aloo tikka), Japan (teriyaki burgers), Amman (flatbread McArabia), Israel (kosher McNuggets), and France (cheese and ham between two thin slices of toasted bread).

McDonald's Restaurants Taiwan is almost entirely run by Taiwanese. It added rice dishes in late 2002, following the trend in Hong Kong, the Philippines, Indonesia, and Thailand. McDonald's controls 70 percent of Taiwan's fast-food market and hopes that rice dishes will add to the market share by enticing adults to eat with their children in its outlets. Still the management is mindful of the fact that the success in Taiwan is due to the core business (i.e., the traditional McDonald's business).

McThai Co. Ltd. adds a Thai feeling to McDonald's. About 15 percent of menu items are locally oriented products to suit local tastes. The menu includes *khao man somtan* (coconut milk rice with spicy papaya salad) and desserts such as sago and coconut pie. In addition, the managing director plans to introduce the concept of *eatingtainment* that combines entertainment and eating. Activities such as karaoke hours and contests have been planned.

In Europe, a local flavor is evident. The McDonald's outlets in England are the first in the world to sell fresh fruit (grapes and sliced apples), fruit juice with "no extra sugar," and a 266-calorie pasta salad with less than 5 percent fat. France is perhaps even more critical to McDonald's, and the company opens a new outlet every six days. Surprisingly, a typical French customer spends $9 per visit, more than twice as much as the U.S. average of $4. For McDonald's which is a model of efficiency, McDonald's France appears to ignore the model. It refits restaurants with chic interiors and extras (e.g., music videos) to encourage customers to linger over their meals. Instead of streamlining its menus to speed up service like its U.S. counterparts, the French outlets add items. A hot ham-and-cheese sandwich (Croque McDO) is especially popular. In terms of architecture, McDonald's France has adapted the restaurant designs to blend with local architecture. Some outlets in the Alps have wood-and-stone interiors reminiscent of a chalet. While the updated styling found in half of the more than 900 French outlets adds 20 percent more to the standard designs, sales at these outlets have also gone up by as much as 20 percent.

Conceivably, the French approach may not work in the U.S.A. because fast-food customers simply want quick service and cheap, tasty foods. The McCafé concept from Australia was imported but failed in the U.S.A. McDonald's did not do well either with pizza.

Historically, McDonald's idea is to sell the same food in the same restaurant environment to consumers everywhere. The strategy has played an important role in making the company become the world's largest fast-food chain. McDonald's has planned to invest up to €800 million in 2007 in its European business. Europe would receive as much investment as its U.S. counterpart even though the number of European outlets is only half of the number in the U.S.A. As explained by McDonald's, "we are an American brand, but we have to become more European. We have to become more locally relevant than we have been in the past."

## Points to consider

Some managers of McDonald's, buoyed up by the success in Asia and Moscow, want to "McDonaldize" the world. Discuss the implications of this statement. Should McDonald's try to standardize its product mix? What aspects of McDonald's are universal and thus can be exported to other countries? Should the company introduce in the U.S.A. the products that are successful in Europe and Asia?

## Notes


1 "Handbags Now a Status Sale," *San José Mercury News*, February 25, 2007.
2 "Credit Due for Tranparency," *Financial Times*, May 28, 2002.
3 "Eat Your Baby Food, Gramps," *Business Week*, March 3, 2003, 14.
4 Masashi Kuga, "Kao's Marketing Strategy and Marketing Intelligence System," *Journal of Advertising Research* 30 (April/May 1990): 20–5.
5 "Nokia Tries to Answer the Call of Design Again," *Wall Street Journal*, June 4, 2007.
6 "Pepsi Pitching Fire and Ice to Win Back Young Consumers," *Bangkok Post*, December 2, 2004.
7 Martin S. Roth, R. Bruce Money, and Thomas J. Madden, "Purchasing Processes and Characteristics of Industrial Service Buyers in the U.S. and Japan," *Journal of World Business* 39 (May 2004): 183–98.
8 "Making Perfect Rice the Japanese Way Can Cost Big Bucks," *Wall Street Journal*, June 4, 2007.
9 Sean Dwyer, Hani Mesak, and Maxwell Hsu, "An Exploratory Examination of the Influence of National Culture on Cross-National Product Diffusion," *Journal of International Marketing* 13 (No. 2, 2005): 1–28.
10 Abdul Azeez Erumban and Simon B. de Jong, "Cross-country Differences in ICT Adoption: A Consequence of Culture?", *Journal of World Business* 41 (December 2006): 302–14.
11 Sangeeta Singh, "Cultural Differences in, and Influences on, Consumers' Propensity to Adopt Innovations," *International Marketing Review* 23 (No. 2, 2006): 173–91.
12 This section is based largely on Sak Onkvisit and John J. Shaw, "An Examination of the International Product Life Cycle and Its Application within Marketing," *Columbia Journal of World Business* 18 (Fall 1983): 73–9.
13 Stephanie Ann Lenway and Thomas P. Murtha, "Book Review," *Journal of International Business Studies* 35 (November 2004): 560–3.
14 "Chery Assembly Deal Makes Chrysler a Model in Exporting from China," *Wall Street Journal*, July 5, 2007.
15 Arnold Schuh, "Global Standardization as a Success Formula for Marketing in Central Eastern Europe?", *Journal of World Business* 35 (No. 2, 2000): 133–47.
16 Douglas Dow, "Adaptation and Performance in Foreign Markets: Evidence of Systematic Under-adaptation," *Journal of International Business Studies* 37 (March 2006): 212–26.
17 Peter Gabrielsson *et al.*, "Globalizing Internationals: Product Strategies of ICT Manufacturers," *International Marketing Review* 23 (No. 6, 2006): 650–71.
18 Aron O'Cass and Craig Julian, "Examining Firm and Environmental Influences on Export Marketing Mix Strategy and Export Performance of Australian Exporters," *European Journal of Marketing* 37 (No. 3, 2003): 366–84.
19 "How to Compete," *San José Mercury News*, February 18, 1990.
20 Luis Filipe Lages and David B. Montgomery, "Export Performance As an Antecedent of Export Commitment and Marketing Strategy Adaptation: Evidence from Small and Medium-sized Exporters," *European Journal of Marketing* 38 (Nos 9/10, 2004): 1186–214.
21 "A Finger-Lickin' Good Time in China," *Business Week*, October 30, 2006, 50.
22 "Globalising, Indian-style," *DNA India*, December 29, 2006.

23 "U.S. Consumer Goods," *Export America*, August 2001, 18–23.
24 "Cadillac Floors It in China," *Business Week*, June 4, 2007, 52.
25 "The Sweet Smell of Demand," *Business Week*, January 29, 2007, 46.
26 "$100 Laptops Feature Enhanced Security Measures," *San José Mercury News*, October 7, 2006.
27 "Can M'm, M'm Good Translate?", *Wall Street Journal*, July 9, 2007.
28 Chol Lee and David A. Griffith, "The Marketing Strategy–Performance Relationships in an Export-Driven Developing Economy: A Korean Illustration," *International Marketing Review* 21 (No. 3, 2004): 321–34.
29 "The Americanization of Toyota," *Business Week*, April 15, 2002, 52–4.
30 "Fired Up to Introduce New Ideas," *Financial Times*, December 10, 2002.
31 G. Tomas M. Hult, Bruce D. Keillor, and Roscoe Hightower, "Valued Product Attributes in an Emerging Market: A Comparison between French and Malaysian Consumers," *Journal of World Business* 35 (No. 2, 2000): 206–19.
32 Monty L. Lynn, Richard S. Lytle, and Samo Bobek, "Service Orientation in Transitional Markets: Does It Matter?", *European Journal of Marketing* 34 (No. 3, 2000): 279–98.
33 "Hong Kong SAR Projected to See Significant Effects from China's WTO Accession," *IMF Survey*, June 19, 2000, 207–8.
34 Josephine Ludolph, "Services: Exporting's Hidden Giant," *Export America*, May 2001, 14–16.
35 "How the War on Terror Is Damaging the Brain Pool," *Business Week*, May 19, 2003, 72–3.
36 Jennifer R. Moll, Susan Gates, and Lesley Quigley, "International Education and Training Services: A Global Market of Opportunity for U.S. Providers," *Export America*, May 2001, 19–21.
37 Bruce D. Keillor, G. Tomas M. Hult, and Destan Kandemir, "A Study of the Service Encounter in Eight Countries," *Journal of International Marketing* 12 (No. 1, 2004): 9–35.
38 Maria Royne Stafford, "International Services Advertising," *Journal of Advertising* 34 (spring 2005): 65–86.
39 Mark Peterson, Gary Gregory, and James M. Munch, "Comparing U.S. and European Perspectives on B2B Repair Service Quality for Mission-critical Equipment," *International Marketing Review* 22 (No. 3, 2005): 353–68.
40 Ian Alam, "Service Innovation Strategy and Process: A Cross-national Comparative Analysis," *International Marketing Review* 23 (No. 3, 2006): 234–54.
41 William Newburry and Nevena Yakova, "Standardization Preferences: A Function of National Culture, Work Interdependence and Local Embeddedness," *Journal of International Business Studies* 37 (January 2006): 44–60.
42 "Disney Rewrites Script to Win Fans in India," *Wall Street Journal*, June 11, 2007.
43 Esther Sanchez-Peinado, José Pla-Barber, and Louis Hebert, "Strategic Variables That Influence Entry Mode Choice in Service Firms," *Journal of International Marketing* 15 (No. 1, 2007): 67–91.
44 Marios Theodosiou and Leonidas C. Leonidou, "Standardization Versus Adaptation of International Marketing Strategy: An Integrative Assessment of the Empirical Research," *International Business Review* 12 (April 2003): 141–71.

Chapter 11

# Product strategies

## Branding and packaging decisions

The protection of trademarks is the law's recognition of the psychological function of symbols.
Justice Felix Frankfurter, U.S. Supreme Court

### Chapter outline

- Marketing strategy: global brands and mega brands
- Branding decisions
- Branding levels and alternatives
  - Branding vs. no brand
  - Private brand vs. manufacturer's brand
  - Single brand vs. multiple brands
  - Local brands vs. worldwide brand
- Brand consolidation
- Brand origin and selection
- Brand characteristics
- Brand protection
- Packaging: functions and criteria
- Mandatory package modification
- Optional package modification
- Conclusion
- Case 11.1 Planet Ralph: the global marketing strategy of Polo Ralph Lauren

## Marketing strategy

### Global brands and mega brands

In the 1990s, Samsung Electronics Co. was simply another manufacturer of lower end consumer electronics with such brands as Wieseview, Tantus, and Yepp which did not mean much to consumers. Wanting to move up the value chain, Samsung needed a stronger brand identity. Discarding the weak brands, Samsung put all resources behind the Samsung brand and used quality, design, and innovation to build a more upscale image. In 2001, Samsung brought out mobile phones and digital TVs that showcased the company's technical expertise. It wanted the brand to be "in users' presence 24/7." It helps that consumers are attached to their cell phones and TVs. Most consumers carry their handsets with them everywhere, and their TV is the center of the family room. Samsung's products all make the same reassuring tone when they are turned on. Over five years, Samsung's brand value has jumped 186 percent and has surpassed the brand value of arch rival Sony. Now LG Electronics Inc., another Korean brand, is taking the same path.

In 1998, Hyundai was considering pulling out of the U.S. market where it had acquired a poor reputation from a decade of quality problems. Realizing that a car manufacturer without a U.S. presence cannot be a global brand, the company chose to stick it out. Plant managers were told to be obsessed with quality and to stop production lines if defects were found. It aggressively offers a 100,000-mile/10-year warranty. The extended warranty costs the company hundreds of millions of dollars a year in extra provision costs. Hyundai's perseverance has paid off. Its sales volume rose from 100,000 units in 1998 to more than 455,000 units in 2005. In addition, the quality scores from J.D. Power & Associates show Hyundai to be the top-rated non-luxury brand, even ahead of Toyota. Based on the quality survey of new car owners, Hyundai trails only Porsche and Lexus.

ACNielsen's Global Mega Brand Franchises report uses a number of criteria to identify mega brands. A mega brand must be available in at least 15 out of the 50 countries that account for 95 percent of global economic output. It must be marketed under the same name in at least three different product categories in three or more regions. Based on these criteria, the mega brands are dominated by the highly extendable personal care and cosmetics manufacturers and by food and drinks manufacturers. The queen of mega brands is Nivea, a brand owned by the German consumer products group Beiersdorf. This skin-care brand is a huge success, and has been extended to at least 19 product categories (shampoos, aftershave, wrinkle lotion, and bath foam) in every part of the world. In contrast, Coke as a brand does not have much of this power of extendability.

Table 11.1 shows the world's top 10 brands in terms of brand value.

*Sources*: "Global Brands," *Business Week*, August 1, 2005, 86–94; "The 100 Top Brands," *Business Week*, 7 August 2006, 60; "The 100 Top Brands," *Business Week*, August 6, 2007, 59; and "Nivea, Nestlé (AAC) Extend Bounds in Global Mega Brand Survey," *Bangkok Post*, April 3, 2003.

**TABLE 11.1** Top brands

| *Rank* | *Brand* | *Brand value ($millions)* |
|---|---|---|
| 1 | Coca-Cola | 65,324 |
| 2 | Microsoft | 58,709 |
| 3 | IBM | 57,091 |
| 4 | GE | 51,569 |
| 5 | Nokia | 33,696 |
| 6 | Toyota | 32,070 |
| 7 | Intel | 30,954 |
| 8 | McDonald's | 29,398 |
| 9 | Disney | 29,210 |
| 10 | Mercedes-Benz | 23,568 |

*Source*: "The 100 Top Brands," *Business Week* (August 6, 2007, 59).

## Purpose of chapter

The purpose of this chapter is to acknowledge the strategic significance of branding and packaging and to examine some of the problems commonly faced by MNCs. Among the subjects discussed are brandless products, private brands, manufacturers' brands, multiple brands, local brands, worldwide brands, brand consolidation, brand protection, and brand characteristics. The strengths and weaknesses of each branding alternative are evaluated. The chapter also examines both mandatory and optional packaging adaptation. The emphasis of the chapter is on the managerial implications of both branding and packaging.

## Branding decisions

To understand the role of trademark in strategic planning, one must know what a trademark is from a legal standpoint. According to the U.S. Lanham Trade-Mark Act of 1947, trademark "includes any word, name, symbol, or device or any combination thereof adopted and used by a manufacturer or merchant to identify these goods and distinguish them from those manufactured or sold by others." If a trademark is registered for a service, it is known as a service mark (e.g., Berlitz).

According to the WTO's Article 15 of Annex 1C (Agreement on Trade-related Aspects of Intellectual Property Rights),

> any sign, or any combination of signs, capable of distinguishing the goods or services of one undertaking from those of other undertakings, shall be capable of constituting a trademark.

> Such signs, in particular words including personal names, letters, numerals, figurative elements and combinations of colours as well as any combination of such signs, shall be eligible for registration as trademarks. Where signs are not inherently capable of distinguishing the relevant goods or services, Members may make registrability depend on distinctiveness acquired through use. Members may require, as a condition of registration, that signs be visually perceptible.

A trademark can be something other than a name. Bibendum, the roly-poly corporate symbol, is Michelin's trademark in France, and it is known as Bi-bi-deng in China. It should be noted that the Michelin Man, a 100-plus-year-old mascot, seems to have recently lost some weight while becoming more muscular. Nipper, the familiar fox terrier sitting next to a phonograph along with the phrase "His Master's Voice," is RCA's official symbol. Other easily recognized logos include Ralph Lauren's polo player and Goodyear's wingfoot. Figure 11.1 shows the logos of General Foods' well-known brands. Figure 11.2, in contrast, shows the trademarks of multinational firms that have direct investment in Cyprus.

A trademark can be more than a name or logo. Harley Davidson tried unsuccessfully to register the sound of its heavy motorcycles as a trademark. H.J. Heinz Company had better luck in registering a color in England. While words and logos account for a vast majority of trademarks registered in England and while it is unusual to a food company to be granted a trademark on a color alone, the Trademarks Registry granted legal protection to Heinz Baked Beans' distinctive use of turquoise. The Trademarks Registry has determined that Heinz Baked Beans' turquoise has "achieved distinctiveness through use." As the number one brand of baked beans in the United Kingdom for generations, the product is an important part of the British culture, and almost everyone recognizes the turquoise can.[1]

A logo, when inappropriate, ineffective, or dated, should be modified. Audi, which wanted to further differentiate itself from its parent Volkswagen, replaced its corporate logo in 1995 with a new one featuring the four silver rings with the Audi name written underneath in red. In 2007, Citi, the largest U.S. bank, launched a new branding campaign. The word "group" was dropped from the corporate name; so was the red umbrella. Going forward, the company will use only the "Citi" name topped with a red arc for all marketing activities.

In many countries, branding may be nothing more than the simple process of putting a manufacturer's name, signature, or picture on a product or on its package. Many U.S. firms did precisely this in the old days, as illustrated by King Gillette's own portrait being used as a trademark for his Gillette razor-blades.

The basic purposes of branding are the same everywhere in the world. In general, the functions of a brand are to: (1) create identification and brand awareness, (2) guarantee a certain level of quality, quantity, and satisfaction, and (3) help with promotion. All of these purposes have the same ultimate goal: to induce repeat sales. The Spalding name, for example, has a great deal of marketing clout in Japan. In fact, a group of investors bought the company in 1982 because they felt that Spalding was the best-known name in sports in the free world and that the name was underused.

For American consumers, brands are important. Overseas consumers are just as brand-conscious – if not more so – because of their social aspirations and the social meanings that brand names can offer. Eastern European consumers recognize many Western brand names, including some that are unavailable in their countries. Among the most powerful brand names are Sony, Adidas, Ford, Toyota, Volvo, BMW, and Mercedes. When International Semi-Tech Microelectronics Inc. acquired troubled SSMC Inc., the most important asset was probably the Singer trademark.

Brands are promises.
GENERAL FOODS
So is this.
Our new corporate mark is a promise to our consumers. It symbolizes our dedication to providing superior consumer satisfaction — through quality food and beverage products that reflect the world's changing times, tastes, lifestyles and needs.
This promise motivates every aspect of our business, from product development to production, from packaging to distribution. It is the moving force of General Foods, the basis of our success to date — and the foundation for future growth.
GENERAL FOODS
SUPERIOR CONSUMER SATISFACTION

**FIGURE 11.1** General Foods' registered trademarks and logos

*Source*: Reprinted with permission of General Foods Corporation.

The choice of connoisseurs
BARCLAYS
HSBC Republic
La vache qui rit
Moody's Interbank Credit Service Ltd
GENERALI INTERNATIONAL
REUTERS
gsk GlaxoSmithKline
SC Johnson A FAMILY COMPANY
CREDIT SUISSE FIRST BOSTON
SIEMENS
KARDEX
Amdocs
CAPITAL Intelligence
AgrEvo
NCR
MSD
Royal Skandia
Raychem
Roche
SG
BNP PARIBAS BNPI
AFP
Organon
LONDON FORFAITING
Bull
JCB
CYPRUS
EUROPE
ASIA
AFRICA
At the hub of 3 continents
MATURE CHOICE
QUALITY CHOICE
▪ Strategically located with convenient regional and international air links.
▪ Excellent telecommunications - direct dialling to over 200 countries.
▪ Numerous and attractive tax incentives including 32 double tax treaties.
▪ Highly qualified bilingual staff and very competitive operating costs.
▪ A pleasant environment including one of the lowest crime rates in Europe.
CYPRUS
Europe's Business Island
If you want to know more about Cyprus contact CENTRAL BANK OF CYPRUS, International Division
P.O.Box 25529 • CY-1395 Nicosia • Cyprus • Tel: + 357 22 714225 (8.00 a.m. - 2.00 p.m. Cyprus time) • Fax: + 357 22 378164 • E-mail: idoe@centralbank.gov.cy • Web: http://www.centralbank.gov.cy


**FIGURE 11.2** Cyprus: trademarks and FDI

When a company is for sale, the remainder of the purchase price after deducting the fair value of the physical assets is called goodwill, "going concern value," or an intangible asset. In the case of service businesses, nearly all of the purchase price that companies generate tends to be goodwill. The brand has brand equity when there is value that is attached to that brand. Perhaps, Coca-Cola's most valuable asset is its brand equity which is worth $39 billion.

Taking into consideration the importance of branding as a marketing tool, one would expect that corporate headquarters would normally have a major role in brand planning for overseas markets. As a component of an MNC's marketing mix, branding is the area in which standardization appears to be relatively high. Westinghouse, for example, requires its Westinghouse do Brasil affiliate to use the common logo, resulting in all the MNC's Brazilian companies using the familiar circled W symbol in their promotion programs. Thus, brand centralization is a common practice. In 2003, a startup founded by two Taiwanese-American entrepreneurs licensed the brand and distinctive W logo from CBS Corp. subsidiary Westinghouse Electric Corp. Today, Westinghouse Digital ranks No. 5 in liquid-crystal-display TVs in North America, with 7.7 percent of the market.[2]

International marketing managers should consider cultural and socioeconomic conditions of foreign countries in making global brand image strategy decisions. If the markets are similar, a firm may be able to use the standardization strategy by extending its brand image theme to the other markets. However, when markets differ in cultural uncertainty avoidance, individualism, and national socioeconomics, managers tend to employ the image customization strategy.

Other than merely using the same brands worldwide, MNCs are also interested in creating a global identity via some degree of standardization of a corporate visual identity system (CVIS) in their multinational operations. As in the case of British companies operating in Malaysia, they have increasingly adopted a standardized CVIS, stimulated in part by global restructuring, merger, or acquisition.[3] Their reasons include aiding the sale of products and services, creating an attractive environment for hiring employees, and increasing the company's stature and presence.

## Branding levels and alternatives

There are four levels of branding decisions: (1) branding versus no brand, (2) private brand versus manufacturer's brand, (3) single brand versus multiple brands, and (4) local brands versus worldwide brand.

Figure 11.3 shows an outline of the decision-making process when branding is considered. Figure 11.4 provides a branding model for decision-making. Exhibit 11.1 lists the advantages of each branding alternative.

### *Branding vs. no brand*

To brand or not to brand, that is the question. Most products are branded, but that does not mean that all products should be. Branding is not a cost-free proposition due to the added costs associated with marking, labeling, packaging, and legal procedures. These costs are especially relevant in the case of commodities (e.g., salt, cement, diamonds, produce, beef, and other agricultural and chemical products). **Commodities** are "unbranded or undifferentiated products which are sold by grade, not by brands." As such, there is no uniqueness, other than grade differential, that can be used to distinguish the offerings of one supplier from those of another. Branding is then probably undesirable

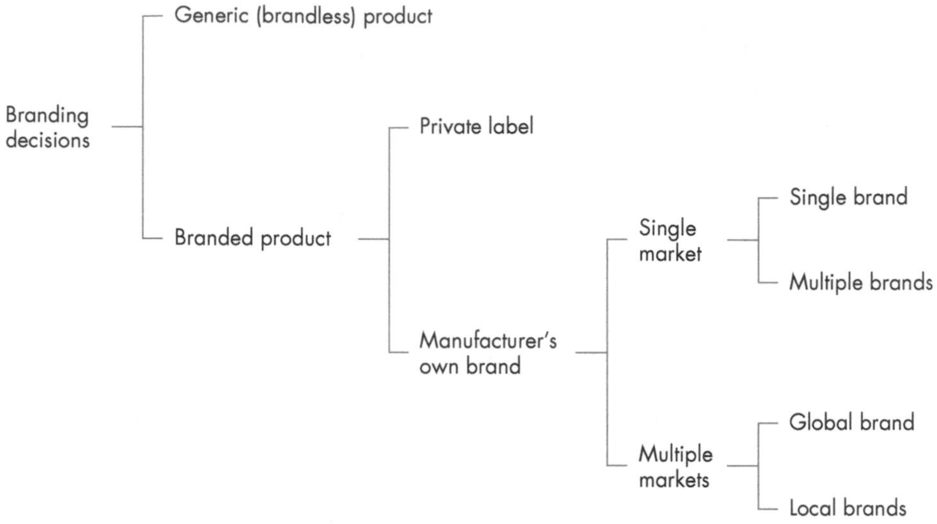
Branding decisions
Generic (brandless) product
Branded product
Private label
Manufacturer's own brand
Single market
Multiple markets
Single brand
Multiple brands
Global brand
Local brands

**FIGURE 11.3** Branding decisions

because brand promotion is ineffective in a practical sense and adds unnecessary expensesto operations costs. The value of a diamond, for example, is determined by the so-called four Cs – cut, color, clarity, and carat weight – and not by brand. This is why De Beers promotes the primary demand for diamonds in general rather than the selective demand for specific brands of diamonds.

On the positive scale, a brandless product allows for flexibility in quality and quantity control, resulting in lower production costs along with lower marketing and legal costs.

The basic problem with a commodity or unbranded product is that its demand is strictly a function of price. The brandless product is thus vulnerable to any price swing or price cutting. Farmers can well attest to this vulnerability because prices of farm products have been greatly affected by competition from overseas producers. Yet, there are ways to remove a company from this kind of cutthroat competition.

Branding, when feasible, transforms a commodity into a product (e.g., Chiquita bananas, Dole pineapples, Sunkist oranges, Morton Salt, Holly Farms fryers, and Perdue fryers). A **product** is a "value-added commodity," and this bundle of added values includes the brand itself as well as other product attributes, regardless of whether such attributes are physical or psychological and whether they are real or imaginary. 3M Company developed brand identity and packaging for its Scotch videotapes for the specific purpose of preventing them from becoming just another commodity item in the worldwide, price-sensitive market.

Branding makes premium pricing possible due to better identification, awareness, promotion, differentiation, consumer confidence, brand loyalty, and repeat sales (see Cultural Dimension 11.1). According to one Supreme Court decision (No. 649, May 4, 1942, Mishawaka Rubber and Woolen Manufacturing Co. v. S. S. Kresge, 53 USPQ 323), "The owner of a mark exploits this human propensity by making every effort to impregnate the atmosphere of the market with the drawing power of a congenial symbol. . . . Once established, the trademark owner has something of value."

Chesbrough's taxonomy of business types may be relevant to how a product can acquire value. There are six business models that are progressive in managing innovation. Type 1 companies sell

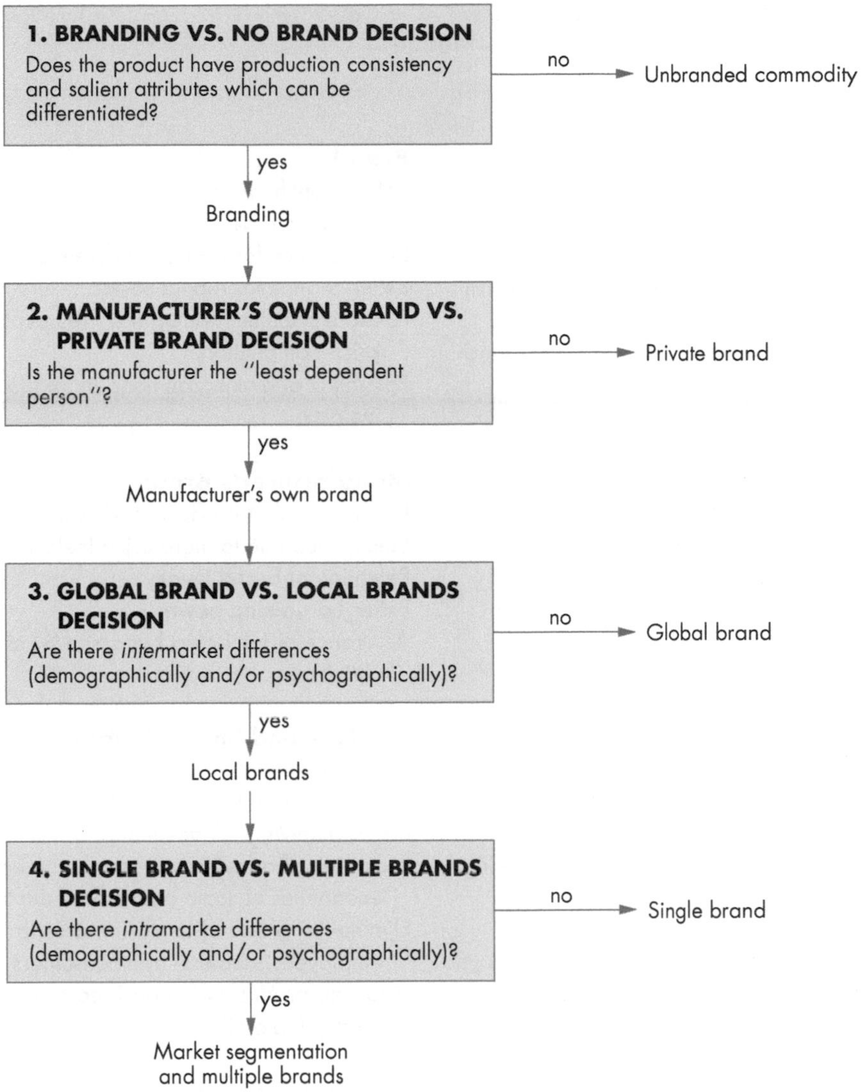

1. BRANDING VS. NO BRAND DECISION
Does the product have production consistency and salient attributes which can be differentiated?
no
Unbranded commodity
yes
Branding
2. MANUFACTURER'S OWN BRAND VS. PRIVATE BRAND DECISION
Is the manufacturer the "least dependent person"?
no
Private brand
yes
Manufacturer's own brand
3. GLOBAL BRAND VS. LOCAL BRANDS DECISION
Are there intermarket differences (demographically and/or psychographically)?
no
Global brand
yes
Local brands
4. SINGLE BRAND VS. MULTIPLE BRANDS DECISION
Are there intramarket differences (demographically and/or psychographically)?
no
Single brand
yes
Market segmentation and multiple brands


**FIGURE 11.4** A branding model for decision-making

Source: Sak Onkvisit and John J. Shaw, "The International Dimension of Branding: Strategic Considerations and Decisions," *International Marketing Review* 6 (2) (1989: 29).

commodities and compete on price and availability. As such, they are the most primitive. Type 2 companies, while using product differentiation, are reactive and manage innovation on an ad hoc basis. For Type 3 companies, innovation is planned instead of happening at random. In the case of Type 4 companies, they open themselves up to external technologies and incorporate these ideas into their internal operations. Type 5 companies have advanced to integrate suppliers and customers into their creative process. Finally, Type 6 companies are able to innovate their own business model through spin-offs and joint ventures, and new ideas flow freely in and out.[4]

Exhibit 11.1

**Advantages of each branding alternative (from manufacturer's viewpoint)**

**No Brand**
- Lower production cost
- Lower marketing cost
- Lower legal cost
- More flexibility in quality and quantity control (i.e., possibility of less rigidity in control)
- Good for commodities (undifferentiated items)

**Brand**
- Better identification
- Better awareness
- Better chance for product differentiation
- Better chance for repeat sales
- Possible premium pricing (i.e., removal from price competition)
- Possibility of making demand more price inelastic

**Private Brand**
- Ease in gaining dealers' acceptance
- Possibility of larger market share
- No promotional hassles and expenses
- Good for small manufacturer with unknown brand and identity

**Manufacturer's Brand**
- Better control of products and features
- Better price due to more price inelasticity
- Retention of brand loyalty
- Better bargaining power
- Assurance of not being bypassed by channel members

**Multiple Brands (in single market)**
- Utilization of market segmentation technique
- Creation of excitement among employees
- Creation of competitive spirits
- Avoidance of negative connotation of existing brand
- Gain of more retail shelf space
- Retention of customers who are not brand loyal
- Allowance of trading up or down without hurting existing brand

**Single Brand (in single market)**
- Better marketing impact
- Permitting more focused marketing
- Brand receiving full attention
- Reduction of advertising costs due to better economies of scale and lack of duplication
- Elimination of brand confusion among employees, dealers, and consumers
- Good for product with good reputation and quality (halo effect)

**Local Brands**
- Legal necessity (e.g., name already used by someone else in local market)
- Elimination of difficulty in pronunciation
- Allowance for more meaningful names (i.e., more local identification)
- Elimination of negative connotations
- Avoidance of taxation on international brand
- Quick market penetration by acquiring local brand
- Allowance of variations of quantity and quality across markets

**Worldwide Brand**
- Better marketing impact and focus
- Reduction of advertising costs
- Elimination of brand confusion
- Good for culture-free product
- Good for prestigious brand
- Easy identification/recognition for international travelers
- Good for well-known designer

## Cultural Dimension 11.1

**Teachers as rock stars**

"Cram schools" are a staple in Asia. They help students to excel in any particular subject of study and to prepare them for universities' highly competitive admission exams. Parents in Japan, Thailand, and the like are willing to pay for their children to attend these schools to complement what they learn in their regular schools. Nowhere are these schools more important than in South Korea. Among the 28,000 cram schools, Megastudy is the biggest. Popular teachers are treated like rock stars. Cramming is a $15-billion-a-year industry. The famous schools are able to charge a monthly fee of $1,000, even though Korea's average annual income is $16,000. Korean parents are willing to shell out large sums of money to give their children an edge. After all, a degree from a leading university will open the door to a good job and high-powered connections, not to mention attracting the right spouse.

*Source*: "Where a Teacher Can Make Millions," *Business Week*, December 11, 2006, 46.

Although branding provides the manufacturer with some insulation from price competition, a firm must still find out whether it is worthwhile to brand the product. In general, the following prerequisites should be met:

1 Quality and quantity consistency, not necessarily the best quality or the greatest quantity.
2 The possibility of product differentiation.
3 The degree of importance consumers place on the product attribute to be differentiated.

### *Private brand vs. manufacturer's brand*

Branding to promote sales and move products necessitates a further branding decision: whether the manufacturer should use its own brand or a distributor's brand on its product. Distributors in the world of international business include trading companies, importers, and retailers, among others; their brands are called private brands. Many portable TV sets made in Japan for the U.S. market are under private labels. In rare instances, Japanese marketers put their brands on products made by U.S. companies, as evidenced by Matsushita's purchases of major appliances from White and D&M for sale in the U.S.A. The Oleg Cassini trademark is put on shirts actually made by Daewoo.

Even though it may seem logical for a distributor to carry the manufacturer's well-known brand, many distributors often insist on their own private brands for several reasons. First, a distributor may be able to create a unique product by bundling or unbundling product attributes and then adjusting the price to reflect the proper value.

Carrefour, a French retail giant, sells some 3,000 in-house products at prices about 15 percent lower than national brands. J. Sainsbury PLC, a British retailer, has a private brand that is able to corner 30 percent of the detergent market, moving it ahead of Unilever's Persil and just behind Procter & Gamble's Ariel which is the market leader. It is believed that private-label products now account for one-third of supermarket sales in the United Kingdom and a quarter in France.

Second, a private brand is a defensive strategy which guarantees that a distributor is not bypassed by its supplier. For example, Ponder and Best, after losing the Rolleiflex and Olympus distributorships, came up with its own brand of photographic products, Vivitar.

Third, distributors can convert fixed production costs into variable costs by buying products made by others. Sperry's products are made by more than 200 manufacturers (e.g., Sperry's personal computer is manufactured by Mitsubishi). Through this practice, Sperry is able to save cash and research and development expenses. Of course, it is important for a distributor with a private brand to have a reliable supplier.

Fourth, and perhaps the most important reason for a distributor's insistence on a private brand, is brand loyalty, bargaining power, and price. In spite of the lower prices paid by the distributor and ultimately by its customers, the distributor is still able to command a higher gross margin than what a manufacturer's brand usually offers. The lower price may also be attributed to the distributor's refusal to pay for the manufacturer's full costs. A distributor may want to pay for the manufacturer's variable costs but not all of the fixed costs. Or a distributor may want to pay for production costs only but not the manufacturer's promotional expenditures, because a distributor gets no benefit from the goodwill of a manufacturer's advertised brand. If a firm has any problem with the supplier (manufacturer), it has the flexibility of switching to another supplier to manufacture the identical product, thus maintaining brand loyalty and bargaining power without any adverse effect on sales. RCA, for example, switched from Matsushita to Hitachi for its portable units of video-cassette recorders.

There are a number of reasons why the strategy of private branding is not necessarily bad for the manufacturer. First, the ease in gaining market entry and dealers' acceptance may allow a larger market share overall while contributing to offset fixed costs. Toronto-based Cott Corp., once an obscure regional bottling company, has emerged as a leading private-label player by being involved with dozens of store brand sodas. It sells more than one billion servings of soft drinks to Wal-Mart Stores Inc. under the label of Sam's American Choice. Cott bottles Sainsbury Classic Cola for J. Sainsbury PLC which is a top food retailer in Britain. In the U.S.A., Safeway Inc. is one of Cott's largest customers. Safeway feels that it can give consumers value while earning better margins than on national brands.

Second, there are no promotional headaches and expenses associated with private branding, thus making the strategy suitable for a manufacturer with an unknown brand. Suzuki cars are sold in the U.S.A. under the GM Sprint brand name. Ricoh's fax machines are sold under AT&T's well-known name. Brother has had virtually no name recognition because it has marketed its many products under the private labels of U.S. major retail chains; to secure recognition, it has begun to mount a major campaign.

Third, a manufacturer may judge that the sales of its own product are going to suffer to a greater or lesser degree from various private brands. In that case, the manufacturer might as well be cannibalized by one of those private brands made by the manufacturer.

There are also reasons why private branding is not good for the manufacturer. By using a private brand, the manufacturer's product becomes a commodity, at least to the distributor. To remain in business and retain sales to the distributor, the manufacturer must compete on the basis of price, because the distributor can always switch suppliers. Cott Corp., for example, lost its contract to brew its President's Choice beer for Loblaw Cos., Canada's top supermarket, when John Labatt Ltd paid Loblaw $28 million for the contract.

By not having its own identity, the manufacturer can easily be bypassed. Furthermore, it loses control over how its product should be promoted – this fact may become critical if the distributor does not do a good job in pushing the product. For example, Mitsubishi, which manufactures Dodge Colt and Plymouth champ for Chrysler, felt that its products did not receive Chrysler's proper attention. As a result, Mitsubishi began to create its own dealer network and brand identity (e.g., Mitsubishi Mirage). Ricoh used to sell copiers in the U.S.A. only under such private brands as Savin and Nashua, whose sales lagged. After switching to its own brand name in 1981, Ricoh's sales increased tenfold to take second place in unit sales behind only Canon.

The manufacturer's dilemma is best illustrated by Heinz's experience in the United Kingdom, where consumer recognition for its brand is stronger than in any other country in the world. Whereas Campbell Soup and Nestlé's Crosse & Blackwell make some products under private labels to accommodate giant supermarkets' insistence, Heinz produces products only under its own brand because, as the largest supplier of canned foods there, it has the most to lose. To preserve its long-term market leadership at the expense of short-term earnings, Heinz has held down prices, stepped up new product introductions, launched big capital-spending programs, and increased advertising. Heinz does make private-label merchandise in the U.S.A., where private brands account for 10 percent of its U.S. sales. Its logic is that the slow growth of U.S. private labeling does not pose a serious threat as it does in the United Kingdom.

Clearly, the manufacturer has two basic alternatives: (1) its brand or (2) a private brand. Its choice depends in part on its bargaining power. If the distributor is prominent and the manufacturer itself is unknown and anxious to penetrate a market, then the latter may have to use the former's brand on the product. But if the manufacturer has superior strength, it can afford to put its own brand on the product and can insist that the distributor accept that brand as part of the product.

The hypothesis of the "least dependent person" can be quite applicable in determining the power of the manufacturer and that of its dealer. The stronger party is the one with resources and alternatives, and that party can demand more because it needs the other party less. The weaker party needs the other partner more due to a lack of resources and/or alternatives, and thus the weaker party must give in to the "least dependent" party. In most cases, the interests of both parties are interdependent, and neither party may have absolute power. For instance, Kunnan, a maker of high-quality tennis rackets, lost some of its well-known customers when they began doing their own manufacturing. When those companies later discovered that they could not produce as well in terms of cost and quality, they came back to Kunnan for the private-brand manufacturing.

Private branding and manufacturer's branding is not necessarily an either/or proposition: a compromise can often be reached to ensure mutual coexistence. If desired, both options can be employed together. Michelin, for instance, is world renowned for its own brand, and most people do not realize that Michelin also makes tires for Sears and Venture. Sanyo, another major international brand, is relatively unknown in the U.S.A. because it has relied heavily on private-label sales to Sears and other large companies. To rectify this identity problem, Sanyo has been pushing its own name simultaneously.

Manufacturers cannot treat private brands as simply generic competitors. After all, retailers that carry the private labels are both customers and competitors at the same time.[5] The popularity of private brands varies from country to country. In England, the key factors that have contributed to the evolution of retail brands within British grocery retailing are changing the basis and use of retail power in the distribution channel, centralization of management activities, and appreciation of what constitutes retail image. British grocery retailers have successfully managed these factors. As a result, their retail brands are regarded by consumers as being as good as, if not better than, the established manufactured brands.[6]

Perceived risk is relevant in differentiating between store brands and national brands. The two categories differ in terms of perceived quality, familiarity, and confidence in a product's extrinsic attributes to assess its quality.[7] Consumers make a switch to store brands during bad economic times at a faster pace than when they switch back to national brands during economic recovery. Even when bad economic times end, some consumers continue buying private brands. These findings imply the vulnerability of national brands.[8]

The discussion thus far has focused primarily on the practice of distributors or middlemen having their own private brands manufactured by other companies. A new trend in the high-technology arena is for manufacturers with top brands to have their products manufactured by someone else.

High-technology firms have been relying more on contract manufacturers and original design manufacturers (ODMs). Quanta Computer Inc. is a contract manufacturer that does all the manufacturing and logistics.[9] This Taiwan company makes Apple's Titanium G4 PowerBook. It also takes care of just about everything in less than 48 hours for HP's notebook unit, from hardware to software and from testing the final product to shipping it to customers. Compaq Computer did not design or make its iPaq Pocket PC. This handheld device and its system of interchangeable accessory sleeves are actually the products of HTC, an ODM in Taiwan. Samsung, LG Electronics, and Acer are ODMs that make products for others as well as their own brands. Samsung's Q10 notebook looks almost indistinguishable from Dell Latitude X200 and Gateway 200. In the end, customers cannot rely on tangibles to tell these brands apart and must rely on such intangibles as warranty and technical support.

The branding and manufacturing strategy just mentioned illustrates the potential benefits and problems of private branding. By putting their brands on the computers made by outside suppliers, the brand owners are able to take care of the gap in their product lines quickly and economically while solving their inventory problems. However, this new strategy will make product differentiation more difficult. Well-informed consumers may not see a good reason to pay extra for these brands.

## Single brand vs. multiple brands

When a single brand is marketed by the manufacturer, the brand is assured of receiving full attention for maximum impact. However, a company may choose to market several brands within a single market based on the assumption that the market is heterogeneous and thus must be segmented. Consequently, a specific brand is designed for a specific market segment. In the case of Intel, it spent several hundred million dollars to promote Centrino, a new brand for wireless computing. Samsonite Corp. manufactures and distributes luggage and travel-related products by using such brand names as Samsonite, American Tourister, Lacoste, and Timberland.[10] Figure 11.5 shows Anheuser-Busch's various brands for the U.S. market.

The watch industry provides a good illustration for the practice of using multiple brands in a single market for different market segments. Bulova is a well-known brand, as are the Accutron and Caravelle brands. Citizen, in its attempt to capture the new youth and multiple-watch owners' market, traded down to include a new brand called Vega. Likewise, Hattori Seiko is well known for its Seiko brand, which is sold at the upper-medium price range in better stores; to appeal to a more affluent segment, the firm traded up with the Lassale name. Seiko's strategy is to deliberately divorce the Seiko and Lassale names, once used together in the public mind, with the gold-plated Lassale line and the karat-gold Jean Lassale line. Lassale watches have Seiko movements but are made only in the U.S.A. and Western Europe in order to curb parallel trading, and they are distributed only through

HERE'S TO YOU, AMERICA.
MICHELOB
MICHELOB Light
MICHELOB
Budweiser
BUD LIGHT
BUSCH
Natural Light
LA
"Somebody still cares about quality."
ANHEUSER-BUSCH, INC.
ST. LOUIS, MO.

**FIGURE 11.5** Anheuser-Busch's multiple brands for a single market

*Source*: Reprinted with permission of Anheuser-Busch, Inc.

jewelers and department stores. The company also trades down, with Pulsar, Lorus, and Alba for Asia. Swatch Group Ltd. has more than 50 percent of the Swiss watch industry. Swatch owns a number of well-known brands that include Omega, Longines, Tissot, and Calvin Klein. It recently spent $75 million to acquire the French watchmaker Breguet.

Multiple brands are suitable when a company wants to trade either up or down because both moves have a tendency to hurt the firm's main business. If a company has a reputation for quality, trading down without creating a new brand will harm the prestige of the existing brand. By the same rationale, if a company is known for its low-priced, mass-produced products, trading up without creating a new brand is hampered by the image of the existing products. Casio is perceived as a manufacturer of low-priced watches and calculators, and the name adversely affects its attempt to trade up to personal computers and electronic musical instruments. To overcome this kind of problem, Honda uses the Acura name for its sporty cars so that Acura's image is not affected by the more pedestrian Honda image.

China has a long way to go before it can become synonymous with quality in the eyes of Western consumers. Not surprisingly, Chinese companies have downplayed the origin of their products. In the case of TCL Corp., a TV and cell phone maker, it acquired the bankrupt German TV manufacturer Schneider in 2002. Although the TCL name has done well in Asia, the company believes that it needs a better known brand to succeed in Europe. Toward this end, Schneider, a century-old brand, should do better.[11]

## Local brands vs. worldwide brand

When the manufacturer decides to put its own brand name on the product, the problem does not end there if the manufacturer is an international marketer. The possibility of having to modify the trademark cannot be dismissed. The international marketer must then consider whether to use just one brand name worldwide or different brands for different markets or countries. To market brands worldwide and to market worldwide brands are not the same thing.

A single, worldwide brand is also known as an *international*, *universal*, or *global* brand. A Eurobrand is a slight modification of this approach, as it is a single product for a single market (i.e., the European Union and the other Western European countries), with an emphasis on the search for intermarket similarities rather than differences.

For a brand to be global or worldwide, it must, by definition, have a commonly understood set of characteristics and benefits in all of the countries where it is marketed. Coca-Cola is a global brand in the sense that it has been successful in maintaining similar perceptions across countries and cultures. However, most other brands do not enjoy this kind of consistency, thus making it debatable whether a global brand is a practical solution.

A worldwide brand has several advantages. First, it tends to be associated with status and prestige. Second, it achieves maximum market impact overall while reducing advertising costs because only one brand is pushed. Bata Ltd, a Canadian shoe marketer and retailer in 92 countries, found out from its research that consumers generally thought Bata to be a local concern, no matter the country surveyed. The company thus decided to become an official sponsor of World Cup soccer in order to enhance Bata's international stature. For Bata and others, it is easier to achieve worldwide exposure for one brand than it is for multiple local brands. Too many brands create confusion and fragmentation.

Third, a worldwide brand provides a convenient identification, and international travelers can easily recognize the product. There would be no sense in creating multiple brands for such international products as *Time* magazine, American Express credit-card, Diner's Club credit-card, Shell gasoline, and so on.

Finally, a worldwide brand is an appropriate approach when a product has a good reputation or is known for quality. In such a case, a company would be wise to extend the brand name to other products in the product line. This strategy has been used extensively by General Electric Co. In another case, 3M Company perceived commonalities in a consumer demographics and market development worldwide; in response, it devised a "convergence marketing" strategy to develop global identity for its Scottish brand of electronic recording products, whose design prominently displays the Scottish name and a globe-like logo.

Global consumer culture positioning (GCCP) is a positioning tool which suggests one pathway through which a brand can be perceived by consumers as "global." GCCP is a construct which associates a brand with a widely understood and recognized set of symbols that constitute an emerging global consumer culture. A significant number of advertisements employ GCCP (instead of positioning the brand as a member of a local or specific foreign consumer culture).[12]

As noted by *Business Week* in 2005, most companies with the biggest increase in brand value operate as single brands everywhere. A single worldwide identity offers efficiency, consistency, and impact.[13]

The use of multiple brands, also known as the *local* or *individual* approach, is probably much more common than many people realize. Discover Financial Services, while using the Discover name in the U.S.A., issues a consumer credit-card in England under the Morgan Stanley Dean Witter. In the case of Unilever, its fabric softener is sold in ten European countries under seven names. Due to decentralization, the multinational firm allows country managers to choose names, packages, and formulas that will appeal to local tastes. More recently, the company, while keeping local brand names, has been gradually standardizing packaging and product formulas.

There are several reasons for using local brands. First, developing countries resent international brands because the brands' goodwill is created by an advertising budget that is much greater than research and development costs, resulting in no benefit derived from research and development for local economies. In addition, local consumers are forced to pay higher prices for advertising and goodwill, benefiting MNCs but hindering the development of local competitive capacity. Such resentment may explain why India's ministries, responding to domestic soft drink producers' pressure, rejected Pepsi's 35 percent Pepsi-owned joint venture. Some governments have considered taxing international brands or limiting the use of such brands, as in the case of South Korea, which has considered placing restrictions on foreign trademarks intended for domestic consumption.

Second, when the manufacturer is unable to ensure uniform product quality across countries or when it wants to vary its quality level for different countries, it should consider local brands. Shanghai Automotive Industry Corp. is a joint-venture partner of both General Motors Corp. and Volkswagen AG, and it has rolled out cars under its own brand. Honda Motor Co. will start selling cars with its Chinese partner (Guangzhou Automobile Group Co.) under a new brand in 2010, becoming the first foreign car manufacturer to develop an original brand in China. The first few models will be derived from existing Honda cars and will likely be priced below $10,000, targeting the low end of the market. The new brand will allow it to penetrate China's growing market for low-cost cars without diluting its image. Toyota, in contrast, has no plans to establish a new brand in China.[14]

Third, when an existing brand is difficult to pronounce, a new brand may be desirable. Sometimes, consumers avoid buying a certain brand when it is difficult pronounce because they want to avoid the embarrassment of a wrong pronunciation.

Fourth, a local brand is more easily understood and more meaningful for local consumers. By considering foreign tastes and preferences, a company achieves a better marketing impact. Post-it note pads made by 3M are marketed as Yellow Butterflies in France. Grey, an international advertising agency, worked with Playtex to create appropriate names for Playtex's brassières in different languages. The result was Wow in England and Traumbugel (dream wire) in Germany. Translation can also make a brand more meaningful. This approach is sometimes mistaken for a single-brand approach when in fact a new brand is created. Close-Up (toothpaste) was translated as Klai-Chid (literally meaning "very close") in Thailand; the translation retained the meaning and the logo of the brand as well as the package design.

Fifth, a local brand can avoid a negative connotation. Pepsi introduced a non-cola under the Patio name in America but under the Mirinda name elsewhere due to the unpleasant connotation of *patio* in Spanish.

Sixth, some MNCs acquire local brands for quick market penetration in order to save time, not to mention money, which would otherwise be needed to build the recognition for a new, unknown brand in local markets. Renault would have been foolish to abandon the AMC (American Motors) name after a costly acquisition. Thus, Renault 9, for example, became AMC Alliance in the U.S.A. Chrysler subsequently bought AMC from Renault, one reason being AMC's coveted Jeep trademark.

Seventh, multiple brands may have to be used, not by design but by necessity, due to legal complications. One problem is the restrictions placed on the use of certain words. Diet Coke in countries that restrict the use of the word *diet* becomes Coke Light. Anti-trust problems can also dictate this strategy. Gillette, after acquiring Braun A.G., a German firm, had to sign a consent decree not to use the name in the U.S. market until 1985. The decree forced Braun to create the Eltron brand, which had little success.

Eighth, and perhaps the most compelling reason for creating new local brands, is because local firms may have already used the names that multinational firms have been using elsewhere. In such a case, to buy the right to use the name from a local business can prove expensive. Unilever markets Sure antiperspirant in the United Kingdom but had to market test the product under the Trust name in the U.S.A., where Sure is Procter & Gamble's deodorant trademark.

In an interesting case, Anheuser-Busch bought the American rights to the Budweiser name and recipe from the brewer of Budweis in Czechoslovakia; Budejovicky Budvar Narodni Podnik, the Czech brewer, holds the rights in Europe. Operating from the town of Ceske Budejovice, known as Budweis before the First World War, this brewer claims exclusive rights to the Budweiser name in the United Kingdom, France, and several European countries. Courts have ruled that both companies have the right to sell in the United Kingdom, but Anheuser-Busch has to use the Busch name in France and the corporate name in other parts of Europe.

Budejovicky Budvar NP, owned by the Czech government, has argued that the Budweiser name has been associated with beer made in the Ceske Budejovice area since about 1265. Anheuser Busch, on the other hand, has pointed out that it began using the name in 1876 but that Budejovicky Budvar was not founded until 1895. Anheuser Busch applied for several EU-wide trademarks in 1996, and most of them were granted over Budvar's objections. In 2007, a European Union court rejected Budvar's appeals.[15]

Ninth, a local brand may have to be introduced due to price control. This problem is especially acute in countries with inflationary pressures. Price control is also one reason for the growth of the so-called gray marketers, as the phenomenon contributes to price variations among countries for the same product. Thus, instead of buying a locally produced product or one from an authorized distributor/importer, a local retailer can buy exactly the same brand from wholesalers in countries where prices are significantly lower. A manufacturer will have a hard time prohibiting importation of gray market goods, especially in EU countries where products are supposed to be able to move freely. Parallel trading can be minimized by having different national brands rather than just a worldwide brand.

As mentioned earlier, brand standardization is a common strategy. Companies tend to brand globally but advertise locally. Interestingly, although the McDonald's logo is one of the most recognizable trademarks in the world, McDonald's has changed its advertising logo just for Quebec, perhaps the only market in the world receiving this special treatment. The most well-known logo in Quebec is J'M. This is a play on "j'aime" which means "I love" in French.

The strategy of using a worldwide brand is thus not superior (or inferior) to using multiple local brands. Each strategy has its merits and serves its own useful functions. This is where managerial judgment comes in. Unilever, for example, considers consumer responses to a particular brand mix. It uses an international brand for such products as detergents and personal products because common factors among countries outweigh any differences. Food products, however, are another story. Food markets are much more complex due to variations in needs and responses to different products. The southern half of Europe mainly uses oil for cooking rather than margarine, white fats, or butter. The French more than the Dutch consider butter to be an appropriate cooking medium. German homemakers, when compared to British homemakers, are more interested in health and diet products. Soup is a lightweight precursor to the main dish in Great Britain but can almost be a meal by itself in Germany. Under such circumstances of preferential variations, the potential for local brands is greatly enhanced.

It is interesting to note that local brands may sometimes be viewed as foreign brands. As in the case of pizza, which is a foreign product category in India, consumers experience local brands as foreign brands. It is thus reasonable to believe that hamburgers, a staple item in the U.S.A., will also be viewed as a foreign product in Asia and Latin America. Fried chicken, on the other hand, is probably more common (i.e., not foreign) among the various cultures.[16]

Any domestic market is unlikely to be homogeneous, and there is room for both international and local brands. There is empirical evidence to show that consumers buying imported brand clothing have lifestyle and shopping orientations that differ from those who prefer domestic brand clothing.[17]

While it is often assumed that an international brand is more prestigious than a local brand, this assumption must be carefully assessed. After all, local brands have their own strengths and are perceived in a favorable manner with regard to several aspects. Local brands tend to generate more awareness, trust, value, and image of reliability and being "down to earth."[18] Compared to global brands, local brands are not necessarily inferior. Foreign brands' market shares are driven by their superior core advantages. Conversely, the market shares of domestic brands are significantly affected by their local advantages.[19]

When creating local brand names in the multilingual international market, companies have three translation methods to consider: phonetic (i.e., by sound), semantic (i.e., by meaning), and phonosemantic (i.e., by sound plus meaning). The effectiveness of translation depends on the emphasis of the original English name and the translation method previously used for brand names within the same category. When the phonetic naming method is used, brand name evaluations are more favorable for names that emphasize an English word than for those names that emphasize a Chinese word.[20]

## Brand consolidation

Frequently, it is either by accident or lack of coordination that multiple local brands result. Despite the advantages offered by the multiple brand strategy, it may be desirable to consolidate multiple brands under one brand when the number of labels reaches the point of being cumbersome or confusing. National BankAmericard used to issue cards around the world under 22 names before consolidating them all under the Visa umbrella. Unilever markets a vast array of beauty, home-care, and food products under numerous names. Some of its well-known brands include: ice cream (Breyer's, Good Humor), soap (Dove, Caress, Lever 2000, Lifebuoy), hair care (Suave, ThermaSilk), oral care (Close-Up, Pepsodent, Aim), fragrances (Calvin Klein, Elizabeth Arden, Elizabeth Taylor), and personal care (Vaseline, Q-Tips, Pond's). However, this portfolio of 1600 brands, although well recognized, has proven to be unmanageable. So Unilever has decided to focus mainly on some 400 brands while eliminating up to 75 percent of its products.

Another way of consolidating the brand franchise is simply to drop weak brands. Assuag-SSIH weeded out all but its most prominent watch brands. Its Eterna brand, for example, was never marketed in the U.S.A., and that brand was eventually sold to another company.

Brand consolidation on a global scale is a strategy that has been hotly debated. As in the case of Scott Paper Co., the company felt that the Scott name, just like Coca-Cola, should command respect all over the world. In addition, global branding would allow Scott to use common advertising messages internationally while saving costs. So the company has been phasing out local brand names in its 80 national markets. Even Andrex, a top-selling toilet tissue in England, may suffer the same fate, thus diluting or destroying the goodwill that has been earned.

When a marketer wants to change brands or consolidate them under one brand in order to unify all marketing efforts, the process on an international scale is complex and extremely costly. Although a unified brand across frontiers provides cost savings by eliminating duplication of design and artwork, production, distribution, communications, and other related issues, such a change is fraught with pitfalls and, if not well planned and executed, can cause more problems than it solves. Nestlé used a gradual, evolutionary process in preparing its European brands for 1992. Its package–design unification involved having the Nestlé name appear along with that of the local brand. The Nestlé name was gradually enlarged over a period of four or five years until it replaced the local brand names entirely.

Another kind of problem presents when a brand is well known but the corporate name is not, complicating communication for the company. In this situation, it is probably easier to change the corporate name to fit the better known brand, a strategy used by Sony, Aprica, Olympus, and Amoco.

Nissan's name change, in comparison, was risky because it followed an opposite route. Nissan's half-hearted entry into the U.S. market led to the use of the Datsun name to avoid embarrassment just in case the effort failed. But the company was also unhappy that the proud corporate name was not as widely recognized as its Datsun brand, which enjoyed an 85 percent recognition rate in the U.S.A. (compared to 10–15 percent for Nissan). The company decided to institute a worldwide brand by phasing out Datsun and phasing in Nissan. Some critics questioned the move because the change cost Nissan $150 million. Furthermore, years of goodwill gained from the Datsun name would be lost. To minimize this problem, both Nissan and Datsun names appeared together at first. Its initial TV commercials and print advertisements emphasized that Datsun was a product of Nissan.

It is debatable whether the corporate name and the product's brand name should even be the same. When the name is the same, a brand that performs poorly or gains notoriety through bad publicity hurts the corporate image as well, as the images of the corporation and the product are so intertwined. Firestone is a prime example of how a brand could damage the same corporate name due to the accidents caused by its tires. The strategy is even riskier for fashion products because fashion comes and goes. Using the same name, however, is a relatively safe strategy and should work well if a firm has good quality control and the reputation of its non-fashion products has withstood the test of time.

Brand consolidation is never an easy process, especially when well-known brands have to be replaced. Because of BP's acquisition of Amoco, BP Amoco has rebranded Amoco gas stations to erase the Amoco name from all 9,000 stations in the U.S.A. The decades-old Amoco torch has been replaced by a new, lower case BP logo and an 18-point green-and-yellow sun. The remodeling of all 19,000 BP stations worldwide could cost up to $4.5 billion over four years. The 1,725 recently acquired Arco stations are keeping the Arco name.

It will be interesting to see how Philips fares with its attempt to unify all products under one brand name. For many years, Philips marketed its products in the U.S.A. under many names, including Norelco for its electric shavers. The company plans to phase out the Norelco name. Initially, the Philips logo appears above the Norelco logo on the packaging.[21] It is debatable whether a company should get rid of the brand name that is a leader in the world's largest market.

Figures 11.6 and 11.7 show how Agere Systems and Wyeth promote their new corporate names. In the case of Unilever, it has had to deal with complications related to its effort to replace its Jif brand with the Cif brand.

## Brand origin and selection

Brand names can come from a variety of sources, such as from a firm's founders (e.g., François Michelin, Albert G. Spalding, Pierre Cardin, and Yves St. Laurent), places (e.g., Budweiser), letters and numbers (e.g., IBM), and coined words (e.g., Ikea based on a combination of the initials of the Swedish-born founder, Ingvar Kamprad, with those of the farm, Elmtaryd, and the village, Agunnaryd, where he grew up).

Sometimes, it is easier simply to purchase an existing brand from another company. Hong Kong's Universal International bought Matchbox, a British toy car manufacturer. W. Haking enterprises, another Hong Kong company, acquired the Ansco name from GAF, and most Americans do not realize that the brand of Haking's low-priced cameras is actually a Hong Kong brand. North American Philips (NAP) bought the Schick shaver trade name. Underscoring the value of this name, Remington even filed a complaint alleging that the Schick name enabled NAP to avoid spending $25 million needed to launch a new shaver to supplement the Norelco line.

Brand selection is far from being an exact science, as illustrated by the origins of many successful brands. Gabrielle Chanel liked the scent of the fifth sampled bottle in 1921. Feeling that 5 was a pretty number, she named the perfume Chanel No. 5. Denmark's Lego Group, well known for its interlocking plastic bricks, is the world's fifth-largest toy maker with annual sales of about $1 billion. The founder, Ole Kirk Kristiansen, named his company Lego which is a combination of the Danish words *leg godt*, meaning "play well."

More recently, brand selection has shifted away from being an art and is becoming more of a science. There are several companies that specialize in creating brand and corporate names, and they use computer programs that can run prefixes, suffixes, and other word combinations.

Still, it must be pointed out that marketers often do not have the luxury of picking and choosing names that they like. Nor is it always feasible to conduct market research to investigate the

agere
world leader new name
OR,
WHY ALL OUR
LAB COATS
ARE OUT GETTING
NEW LOGOS.
www.agere.com
Once we were Lucent's Microelectronics Group. Today we're Agere Systems. A company that has put generations of innovations to work. A world leader in optical components and communications chips. An organization with the focus, expertise and global resources to lead the way in communications technology. Agere Systems. Same smart people. New lab coats.
agere systems
How communications happens.™
© 2001 Agere Systems Inc. Agere, the Agere Systems logo and How communications happens are trademarks of Agere Systems Inc.

**FIGURE 11.6** Agere Systems: a corporate name change

*The future of medicine has a new name.*

**Wyeth**

Announcing the new name of American Home Products Corporation.

As it has grown over its 76-year history, American Home Products has become one of the world's most advanced pharmaceutical companies, with a rich portfolio of innovative medicines.

We've built a research powerhouse unique in its ability to discover and develop novel treatments across three platforms: pharmaceuticals, vaccines and biotechnology. Equally important, we link these efforts to maximize our potential to find solutions to health care problems around the world.

To better reflect our focus and mission, we have selected Wyeth – a name that expresses our pharmaceutical heritage – as our Company's new corporate name. Our symbol on the New York Stock Exchange changes to WYE.

In addition to prescription medicines, Wyeth will continue to bring you leading non-prescription brands as well as innovative products in the field of animal health.

With a proud past and an exciting pipeline to the future, we at Wyeth renew our commitment to a single mission: Leading the way to a healthier world.

WYE
LISTED
NYSE

*Pharmaceuticals. Vaccines. Biotechnology. All add up to* **Wyeth®**

©2002 Wyeth

www.wyeth.com

**FIGURE 11.7** Wyeth: a corporate name change

appropriateness of a name. In Brazil, Philip Morris chose the Galaxy name without conducting market research because it happened to be one of the company's registered names. NUMMI's use of the Nova trademark for cars produced jointly with Toyota and General Motors was due in part to GM's ownership of the Nova brand name.

## Brand characteristics

A good brand name should possess certain characteristics, and such characteristics are thoroughly discussed in most advertising and marketing textbooks. In essence, a brand name should be short, distinctive, easy to pronounce, and able to suggest product benefits without negative connotations. In the international arena, these qualities are also relevant (Cultural Dimension 11.2).

In selecting a brand name, a marketer should first find out whether a brand name has any negative connotation in the target market. One company in the business of brand name selection felt that Probe was an inappropriate name for Ford's car, having an unpleasant gynecological reference. One reason why Japan's Daihatsu Motor Co. Ltd. did not succeed in the U.S.A. may have to do with its name. According to research, many American consumers thought that the company was Korean, and it was a negative association.

### Cultural Dimension 11.2

**Branding: Russian style**

In Russia, it is desirable for a corporate or brand name to: (1) match the product, (2) show the product's advantages, and (3) be easy to remember. The following tactics are common.

- ✓ Imitating a leader (or just a successful name). Nescafé – Ruscafé, "Forest balsam" – "Cedar balsam".
- ✓ Disclosing benefits to a customer in an obvious fashion. "Quick-o-soup" (a soup that is quick to prepare); "Nestarin" (a remedy able to make you ageless); "Negrystin" (takes one's sadness away); "Fornouse" (medical treatment).
- ✓ The use of associative neologisms. "Savory" (ketchup); "Vkoosnoteevo" (dairy products: *vkoosno* means delicious).
- ✓ The use of neologisms that include product category. "Froogurt" (yogurt); "Chickland" (frozen chicken).
- ✓ Stressing advantages or special features of a product with the help of "speaking" last names. "Bochkarev" (*bochka* means barrel); "Solodov" (*solod* means malt); "Bystrov" (*bystro* means quickly). "Bystrov" is a brand name of porridge. "Bochkarev" and "Solodov" are brand names of beers.
- ✓ The use of superlatives in names. "Extra"; "Super"; "Mega."
- ✓ Parts of the names that rhyme with each other. "Hoobba-Boobba"; "Hully-Gully."
- ✓ Unexpected emotional names. "Merry milkman" (dairy products).
- ✓ The use of the word "Euro" as a European quality guarantee. "EuroSet" (electronics); "EuroDom" (*dom* means house).
- ✓ An appendix of the word "Russian" to appeal to customers' patriotism. "Russian product"; "Russian standard" (vodka).

*Source*: A. Purtov, "Naming in Russia: The Right Selection of a Company's Name or a Trademark," *Promotional Technologies* (No. 8, 2003): 12–14.

An international brand name should reflect the desired product image. Toward this end, consumer perception should be taken into account. For instance, worldwide consumers usually perceive French perfumes to be superior, and French-sounding names for this kind of product may prove beneficial. Likewise, good watches are perceived to be made in Switzerland, toiletries in the U.S.A., machinery and beers in Germany, and so on. If appropriate, brands should reflect such images. Russian-sounding names may be used to position a vodka brand positively. Smirnoff originated in the Soviet Union but has been made in the U.S.A. for decades – a fact not known by many Americans.

Marketers may want to consider *foreign branding* which is a strategy of pronouncing or spelling a brand name in a foreign language. Foreign branding, by triggering cultural stereotypes, may influence product perceptions and attitudes.

One way of creating a desired image is to have a brand name that is unique or distinctive. Exxon has this quality. Aprica, a status-symbol stroller, is also unique in several respects. In choosing the name, Kenzo Kassai, the company's owner, wanted something cute like "apple" for his folding stroller. During a trip to Italy, he found *apri* – an appropriate name for something that opens and closes. As "stroller" in Japanese is translated as "baby car," the *ca* syllable (for "car") is a natural ending. In effect, Aprica is a blend of English, Italian, and Japanese, meaning "open to the sun."

A unique name often renders itself to graphic design possibilities, another desirable feature of a trademark. Exxon was chosen due to its distinctiveness, usefulness in work markets, and graphic design possibilities. After rejecting Hot-Line and Sound-About for not being appealing, Sony selected Walkman because of the distinctive logotype with two legs sticking out from the bottom of the letter *A* in *walk*.

An international product should have an international brand name, and this name should be chosen with the international market in mind. When possible, the name should suggest significant benefits. Although Emery Air Freight ships everything large and small anywhere in the world, its name gave no indication of this advantage. To overcome a secretary's fear of shipping a letter to foreign countries with a carrier specializing in freight, the corporate name was changed to Emery Worldwide. Not wanting the trademark to be closely identified with the U.S.A., U.S. Rubber adopted Uniroyal to reflect its diverse businesses around the world. The former French-born chairman of Revlon viewed Amoresse as unsuitable for a fragrance for the international audience; consequently, the name was changed to Jontue.

One way of making a brand name more international is by paying special attention to pronunciation. Many languages do not have all the alphabet characters and the English language is no exception. The Spanish alphabet does not include the letter w, and the Italian language has no j, k, w, or y. Exhibit 11.2 examines the vowels and consonants that prose pronunciation problems to the Chinese.

Stenographers can easily see why many American words are misunderstood overseas because shorthand notations are based on how a word is pronounced and not on the way it is spelled. In general, any prefix, suffix, or word containing such letters as ph, gh, ch, and sh invites difficulty. Phoenix sewing machines provide a good example – it is inconceivable to many foreign consumers how the brand can be pronounced fe-nix and not pe-nix or fo-nix. It is difficult to understand why the o and not the e is silent in this case. In addition, if the o is silent, why should it be in there in the first place? By the same token, people in many countries do not make any distinction, as far as pronunciation is concerned, for the following pairs: v and w; z and s; c and z; and ch and sh. A similar lack of distinction often exists with the trio of j, g, and y. The letter c in English words can be confusing because it can be pronounced like an s, as in the words audience and fragrance, or like a k,

### Exhibit 11.2

**"A brief guide to pronunciation of Romanized Chinese"**

There are four Romanized Chinese consonants which cause pronunciation problems. Here is a guide to pronouncing them accurately:

- *c* equals the *ts* of *tsar* or i*ts*; thus "cai" (finance) sounds like "tsai"
- *q* equals the *ch* of *Ch*ina or *ch*ile; thus *Qin* (a Dynasty) sounds like *chin*
- *x* equals the *sh* of *sh*ine or *sh*eet; thus xi (west) sounds like *shee*
- *zh* equals the *j* of *J*im or *j*ig; thus Zhang (a surname) sounds like Jang

Chinese vowels are broader and longer than American vowels; otherwise they are very close in pronunciation, except for the Chinese *e* as in the names Hebei and Henan. The Chinese *e* is somewhat like the *o* of *other*.

Unless otherwise indicated, two Chinese vowels placed next to one another are pronounced as one sound, i.e. as a dipthong. The sister state of Illinois, Liaoning, is a two syllable word – *lyao-ning*.

Chinese surnames come first. The given names are not hyphenated in modern Chinese. Thus Huang Zhirong (the Chinese consul general) should be addressed as Mr. Huang.

Sometimes, Chinese, especially those from Beijing, have a tendency to add an *r* sound at the end of certain words. Don't be confused by it. It is analogous to a Harvard *r*.

*Source*: U.S. Department of Commerce.

as in the words cat and cost. The letter y also poses some problems because it can sound like a at one time and i at another. Consider the hair product Brylcream. Foreign consumers may think that the e is silent and that the y should sound like a long i. A simple test could have easily revealed any pronunciation difficulties. Figure 11.8 shows how Hoechst tried to overcome the pronunciation difficulty while producing a promotional message at the same time.

Finally, the legal aspect of branding definitely cannot be overlooked (see Ethical Dimension 11.1 and Legal Dimension 11.1). A name that is similar to other firms' trademarks should be avoided. Toyota's Lexus was sued in 1988 by Lexis which is Mead Data Central Inc.'s information retrieval service. Lexus was originally prevented from using the name nationally in the U.S.A. until winning a decision from an appeals court. Likewise, Altima Systems Inc., a California computer business, wanted to stop Nissan also using the name before finally reaching a confidential agreement in 1992. Directed Electronics Inc., another California automobile security company, is the owner of the name Viper for its line of automobile security alarm systems. A legal challenge followed when Chrysler started using the name for its Dodge car. Both sides reached an out-of-court settlement in 1992, agreeing to coexist.

## Brand protection

The job of branding cannot be considered done just because a name has been chosen. The brand must also be protected. The first protective step is to obtain trademark registration (see Legal Dimension 11.2 and Ethical Dimension 11.2). Because of the cost involved, it may be neither practical nor desirable to register the name in all countries, especially in places where demand seems weak. It is

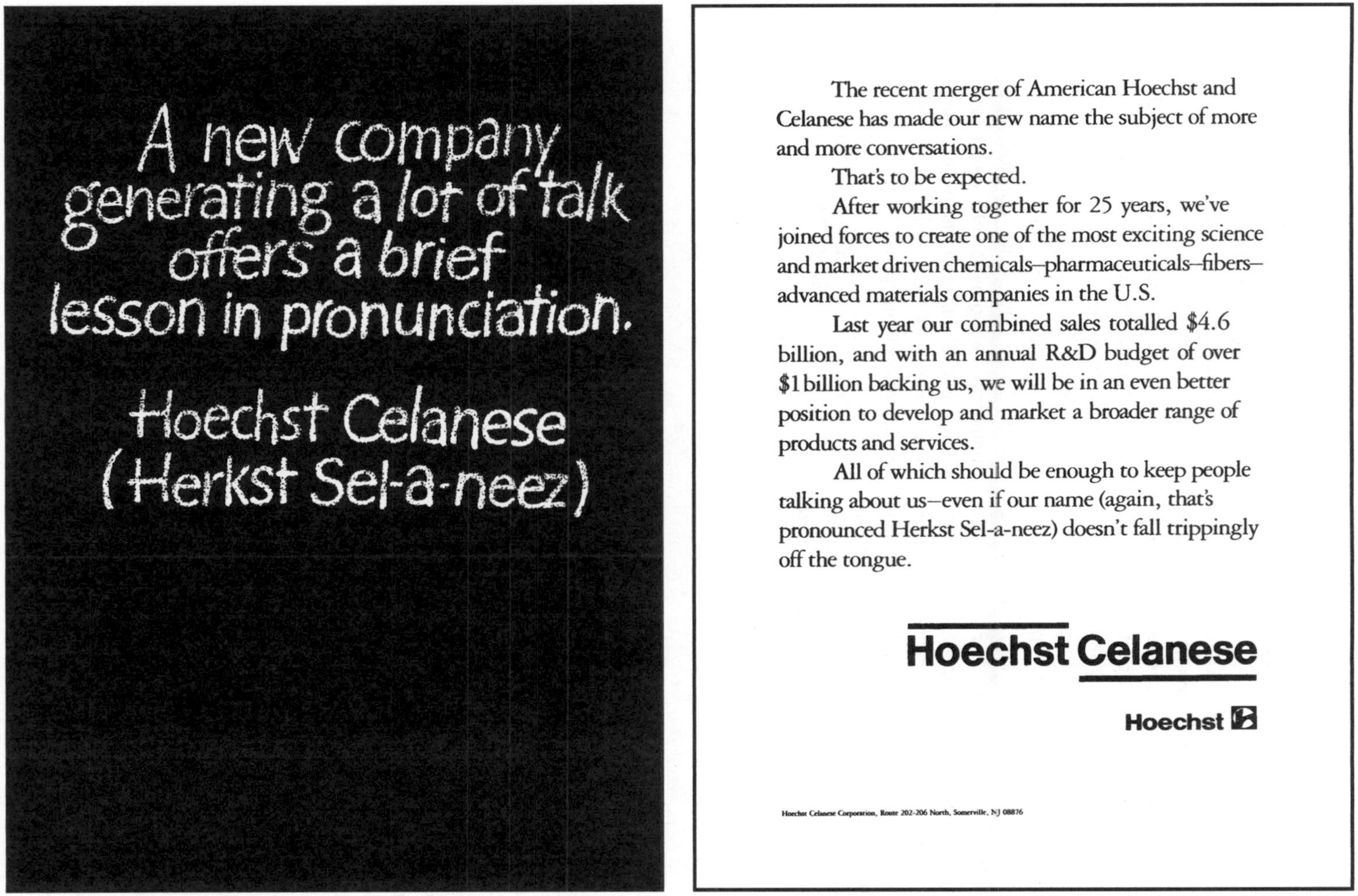
A new company generating a lot of talk offers a brief lesson in pronunciation.
Hoechst Celanese (Herkst Sel-a-neez)
The recent merger of American Hoechst and Celanese has made our new name the subject of more and more conversations.
That's to be expected.
After working together for 25 years, we've joined forces to create one of the most exciting science and market driven chemicals–pharmaceuticals–fibers–advanced materials companies in the U.S.
Last year our combined sales totalled $4.6 billion, and with an annual R&D budget of over $1 billion backing us, we will be in an even better position to develop and market a broader range of products and services.
All of which should be enough to keep people talking about us—even if our name (again, that's pronounced Herkst Sel-a-neez) doesn't fall trippingly off the tongue.
Hoechst Celanese
Hoechst
Hoechst Celanese Corporation, Route 202-206 North, Somerville, NJ 08876

**FIGURE 11.8** Hoechst: overcoming a pronunciation difficulty

*Source*: Reprinted with permission of Hoechst Celanese Corporation.

## Ethical Dimension 11.1

### Putin's legacy: Putinka vodka

Many or most Russians admire Russian President Vladimir Putin. That admiration has been used to the advantage of Vinexim. The company markets Putinka vodka which exploits an affectionate diminutive form of the President's surname for the brand. Putinka has emerged from nowhere in 2003 to become the second most popular vodka brand in Russia, with a market share of 4.2 percent. While the connection to President Putin is intentional, this relationship is neither sanctioned nor licensed. Because Putinka is not an exact copy of the President's surname, the company has managed to avoid restrictions on trademarking proper names without permission. In addition, the brand name sounds similar to a Russian fishing term. The brand uses heavy advertising. Its use of billboards circumvents a ban on outdoor liquor advertisements by using the Putinka name (without mentioning vodka) to promote essay contests or telephone hotlines to suggest ideas for toasts.

Putin is certainly not happy about the exploitation of his name for commercial purposes. Unlike what he can do to his political foes, there is nothing much that Putin can do about his commercial antagonists. No one knows how Putinka vodka will perform once Putin leaves office. Could it be that Putinka may have a more lasting impact than Putin?

Source: "Will Russia's Putinka Outlast the President?", *Wall Street Journal*, May 29, 2007.

## Legal Dimension 11.1

### The end of the long and winding road

Apple Corps Ltd. started out as Apple Records in the mid-1960s. The company was formed by the Beatles to distribute their music, and the trademark was registered in nearly all countries where the Beatles' music was sold.

Steve Jobs and Steve Wozniak formed Apple Computer in 1977. The founders chose the Apple name because they wanted their company to be listed ahead of rival Atari Corp. in the telephone book. Apple Computer's logo is a multi-colored apple with a bite taken out of it. Apple Records, on the other hand, has a logo which is a shot of the exterior of a green apple and the inside of an apple sliced in half.

Apple Corps asserted its right to the trademark and wanted to collect royalties on Apple Computer's computer sales. The lengthy negotiations led to an agreement in 1981. Apple Computer agreed to pay an undisclosed sum for the right to use the Apple name on apparel, personal computers, and related equipment "that didn't synthesize or reproduce music."

The legal problem resurfaced in 1984 When the Macintosh computer was introduced in 1984 because the Mac had a semiconductor chip that made it possible for the machine to record and synthesize sound. In 1988, Apple Corps claimed that the Macs were musical instruments and demanded royalties from Apple Computer.

Apple Computer counter-attacked by filing legal actions in many countries to have Apple Corps' trademark cancelled or declared invalid based on the time that has elapsed since the breakup of the Beatles. Apple Corps, however, was able to obtain an injunction from the British Court to stop Apple Computer from challenging the validity of Apple Corps' trademark country by country. According to Apple Corps' argument, the 1981 settlement required the computer firm to respect the validity of the Beatles' trademark in other countries and to recognize British law as the ultimate authority on the matter. Apple Corps wanted tens of millions of dollars in royalties, interest, and legal fees. While continuing its legal fight, Apple Computer wrote off $38 million in 1991 as a reserve for a lawsuit against it by Apple Corps. Later, the two companies signed an agreement which specified the rights each would have to use the Apple trademark.

Subsequently, Apple Computer got into the music business in a big way with its iTunes Music Store and iPod music player, and Apple Corps was back to sue for another trademark infringement. Apple Computer issued a written statement: "Unfortunately, Apple and Apple Corps now have differing interpretations of this agreement and will need to ask a court to resolve this dispute."

For almost 30 years, Apple Corps and Apple Computer battled over the rights to the Apple name and symbol. Apple Corps sued Apple Computer for the third time in 2003, alleging that the launch of iTunes violated the 1991 agreement. After all, Apple Computer agreed earlier not to enter the music business. A British court ruled in favor of Apple Computer in 2006, and Apple Corps appealed. The two sides reached an agreement in early 2007, giving ownership of the name Apple, the Apple logos, and all related trademarks to Apple Computer. Some of the trademarks are licensed back to Apple Corps.

*Sources*: "You Say It's Your Trademark," *San José Mercury News*, October 27, 1990; "Apple Against Apple," *San José Mercury News*, February 23, 1989; "Let it Be? Not on Your Life," "*Business Week*, August 5, 1991, 31; "The Long and Winding Trademark Dispute," *San José Mercury News*, September 13, 2003; and "Apple, Beatles Give Peace a Chance," *San José Mercury News*, February 6, 2007.

## Legal Dimension 11.2

### Trademark registration

Practically anyone can file for and own a registered trademark for just about every good or service imaginable. A registered trademark provides public notice as to the origin and source of a product or service and establishes a property interest.

**Costs**. Costs for filing a single class trademark application vary, but usually range from $800 to $2000 for a smooth filing with few obstacles to publication and registration. To minimize your costs, keep in mind the range of products or services you wish to use the trademark with and a good idea of what you want the trademark to look like. In addition, if there is a design element to your mark, record the image on a transferable medium, such as a disk.

Most important to cutting costs is to have some idea of whether you are the only user of the proposed trademark. In fact, the most common but easily avoidable legal obstacle is when someone else has previously filed for, or holds, a registration to the same mark as yours for the same or similar goods or services. To aid your attorney, you can easily conduct what is called a "common law" search by checking the U.S.

Patent and Trademark Office (USPTO) online trademark database (www.uspro.gov), surfing the Internet, and checking phone books, trade journals, and other product listings, such as the *Thomas Register*.

**Filing process**. The trademark application process begins by filing with the appropriate government authority. The process is called ''prosecuting a trademark" and entails communication between the trademark authority and your representatives. Following the filing, the application is reviewed by an examiner. Once the examiner finds that the application has no defects, or all defects have been properly addressed, the application is passed for publication. It is rare for a trademark application to have no defects. If detects are found, the examiner issues an official report or "action to the attorney of record' detailing the defects and statutory deadline for response. In many countries, an examiner is obligated by law to issue at least two actions before making a rejection final. When the corrective actions are not sufficient and the rejection by the examiner is made final, only an appeal will enable the mark to be reviewed again.

However, once all defects are resolved the application is passed for publication, which can take several months. Depending on the country, the mark is published in the official trademark reporter or allow a time period for the public to submit comments. If comments concerning your mark are received, they will be considered before the mark can continue. If the mark passes publication unscathed, it will move on to registration.

Once registered, the mark can be safely marked as registered by using the registration symbol or the ®, as a superscript to your mark. This demarcation gives notice to the world that you are rightfully using the word, phrase or design as a lawful trademark for the goods or services to which it is attached.

**Maintenance of trademark**. Continued maintenance of your trademark registration is an important responsibility of trademark ownership. Careful attention should be paid to deadlines for such filings, as the dates differ from jurisdiction to jurisdiction. Many businesses not only maintain the registration of their trademarks in use, but also actively protect their marks from improper use by other entities. These trademark owners do so by hiring law firms or "trademark watch" firms to ensure that no one except authorized users is using their trademarks in conjunction with certain goods and services.

*Source*: Jaylene M. Sarracino, "Small Business Primer to Filing for Trademarks in a Foreign Country," *Export America*, March 2001, 16–17.

inexcusable, however, not to do so in major markets. Even Queen Elizabeth II has registered her two private homes (Sandringham in Norfolk and Balmoral Castle in Scotland) as trademarks so that she can sell her own merchandise under the brand names of Sandringham and Balmoral. The names have been registered with the British Trade Marks Registry and represent the first time that the Queen has exploited the names of her houses for commercial purposes.

There are international arrangements that simplify the registration process. The **Paris Convention (International Convention for the Protection of Industrial Property)** is the most significant multilateral agreement on trademark rights because it establishes reciprocity, which allows a foreign trademark owner to obtain the same protection in other convention-member countries as in the owner's home country. Although preventing discrimination against non-nationals, the degree of protection varies with individual national laws. In the case of the **Madrid Convention**, nationals of the participating countries can have simultaneous trademark filing among all member countries. The **Trademark**

## Ethical Dimension 11.2

### The birthplace of coffee

Ethiopia claims to have pioneered the coffee trade more than 500 years ago. Starbucks Corp. trumpets Ethiopia as the birthplace of coffee. While Ethiopian growers receive 75 cents a pound for their coffee, Starbucks is able to fetch as much as $13 for half a pound of the processed product. About 25 percent of the beans are lost in roasting, and there are costs related to transportation, storage, and insurance.

Ethiopia has attempted to trademark Sidamo, Harar, and Yirgacheffe, the names of the country's most famous coffee regions. The idea is to develop stronger brands for its most valuable export so as to earn higher prices. Canada, Japan, and the European Union have granted trademarks for some of Ethiopia's regional names. While the U.S. Patent and Trademark Office has awarded a trademark for Yirgacheffe, it blocked the application for Sidamo because of Starbucks's application to trademark the name "Shirkina Sun-dried Sidamo." The National Coffee Association, a U.S. trade group, opposed Ethiopia's trademark applications, arguing that Sidamo and Harar are generic names. The trademark office concurred. Later, Starbucks withdrew its application for Shirkina Sun-dried Sidamo and has renamed the product Ethiopia Sun-dried Shirkina.

Ethiopia offered Starbucks a royalty-free trademark licensing agreement. Starbucks refused, claiming that the agreement was legally doubtful and that the company had to bear too much responsibility to defend Ethiopia's trademarks. The refusal eroded goodwill that Starbucks earned from its coffee-buying practices. In 2006, Starbucks bought 6 percent of its coffee from "fair trade" certified co-ops and 53 percent from sellers who adhered to guidelines that promoted economic sustainability for growers. According to the company, its guidelines are more comprehensive than the fair-trade standards.

Ethiopian officials and the local media felt that Starbucks was engaging in "coffee colonialism." Critics believe that Starbucks did not support Ethiopia's trademark approach because the company was concerned that the other supplying countries might do the same, thus increasing its coffee costs. Starbucks buys only 2 percent of its coffee from Ethiopia and obtains the rest mainly from Latin American countries. Starbucks, on the other hand, argued that Ethiopia, instead of seeking trademarks, should seek "geographic certifications," a different legal method used by Guatemala, Colombia, and other coffee-growing regions to build their reputations.

In 2007, after months of refusal, Starbucks announced a deal to license and market coffees named after several of Ethiopia's coffee-growing regions. The agreement does not call for the company to pay a licensing fee for the use of the regional names on the company's packages.

*Sources*: "Starbucks, Ethiopia Agree on Licensing," *Wall Street Journal*, June 21, 2007.

**Registration Treaty (TRT)** allows a company to file for trademark protection with the International Bureau of the World Intellectual Property Organization (WIPO) without being required, as in the case of the Madrid Agreement, to have a prior home registration. Other treaties include the **Central American Arrangement** and the **African Intellectual Property Organization (OAPI)**. The **Arrangement of Nice [France] Concerning the International Classification of Goods and Services to Which Trade Marks Apply** is the most widely used trademark classification system. Adopted by the U.S.A. and some 60 countries, the system has 34 product and seven service categories.

The U.S.A. has two registers. The **Principal Register** provides federal protection, a benefit not provided for by the Supplemental Register. A trademark owner who is unable to place a mark on the Principal Register may be able to do so later when the mark has acquired distinctiveness over the years. The **Supplemental Register** is still useful for U.S. marketers who must obtain registration in the home country before becoming eligible to do the same in host countries.

The courts have developed a hierarchy of registration eligibility. Moving from highly protectable to unprotectable, these categories are: fanciful (Kodak), arbitrary (Camel), suggestive (Eveready), descriptive (Ivory), and generic (aspirin). In general, for a trademark to be eligible for registration, it must be "distinctive" or, if not, must be "capable of being distinctive."

A **fanciful mark** is a term that is coined solely for the purpose of identifying a particular product. An **arbitrary mark** is an ordinary word that is used on a product in a totally nondescriptive way. A **suggestive mark** subtly indicates something about a product, and consumers thus must use their imagination to understand that the mark represents a product's characteristic. A **descriptive mark**, in contrast, immediately conveys, without requiring use of imagination, a product's characteristic, quality, or feature. Interestingly, pharmaceutical companies are quite good at creating fanciful marks. Based on the total cost of direct-to-consumer advertising, the top ten are: Nexium, Vioxx, Celebrex, Viagra, Allegra, Advair Diskus, Zocor, Paxil, Zoloft, and Zyrtec.

Although a valid brand name can suggest or imply a product's benefits, it cannot merely describe the fact or the product. A suggestive mark is registrable, but a descriptive name is not legally acceptable unless it has acquired distinctiveness through long-continued exclusive use. Even if the descriptive mark may somehow have been registered, the mark can still be cancelled for lack of distinctiveness. Of course, it is not always easy to distinguish a suggestive mark from a descriptive mark. Weedless, as a lawn-care product, may be either suggestive or descriptive.

A **generic mark** merely identifies the product rather than the maker of that product. As such, it receives no protection and cannot function as a trademark. Labatt, a Canadian brewer, attempted to win U.S. trademark protection for the name "ice beer" by claiming that it invented the manufacturing process. Anheuser-Busch Cos. sued and was awarded $5 million in punitive damages when a St. Louis jury ruled that ice beer was not a trademark.

The policy of the U.S. government is to contest applications for generic trademarks abroad (e.g., Wash-and-Wear or such foreign variants as Lava y Listo). If allowed to be registered, such trademarks could create significant problems in international trade. A U.S. exporter, for example, will find it impossible to use common product names in advertising abroad without the risk of being sued for trademark infringement, or the exporter may find that the goods are refused entry into a foreign country altogether.

Most countries do not require the display of a trademark in a specific language or the translation of the trademark. Still, to be registered, a foreign trademark may have to be written in a local language in such a way as to give the equivalent pronunciation. China requires a trademark to be displayed in Chinese characters. Coca-Cola, depending on a group of Chinese characters used, may have the right sound but the wrong interpretations. The original registered characters (Koo-kah- koo-lah), when translated, mean either "a wax-fattened mare" or "bite the wax tadpole." The company then switched slightly to the new characters to read Kah-koo-kah-lah, which translate to "may the happy mouth rejoice."

Unlike patents, trademark registrations may be renewed indefinitely. To keep registrations in force, trademark owners are required to pay an annual tax or maintenance fee in most countries (though not in the U.S.A.). The technical requirements must also be observed. Some countries (e.g.,

Australia) allow the fees to be paid by a foreign trademark owner residing abroad or by the owner's representative/agent in a third country. In other countries (e.g., Brazil), the fees can be paid by only a local or domestically domiciled representative/agent.

Politics may make the registration and maintenance of a trademark difficult. Most U.S. companies have lost their trademarks in Vietnam due to invalidation of those trademark registrations which were obtained in South Vietnam before 1975 and which were not re-registered in the Socialist Republic of Vietnam by 1982. While McDonald's registered its trademark in South Africa in 1968, the company did not open a restaurant there due to international economic sanctions. According to South African law, a foreign company could lose its right for not using the trademark for five years. As a result, when McDonald's finally entered the market in 1995, a local court ruled that the company did not have an exclusive right to its various trademarks. As a matter of fact, Dax Properties, which opened its own MacDonald's hamburger outlet there selling such things as Little Mac, even tried to bar the real McDonald's from using the name. Under international pressure, South Africa passed a new law in 1995 to conform to international law and to offer protection to world-recognized names.

Registration by itself does not offer automatic or complete protection. Other legal requirements must be met in order to maintain copyright. **Use** is a universal requirement. In China, publication, advertising, and exhibiting of a product with the trademark all constitute use. To establish use in most countries, a manufacturer must sell or make that product in the intended market.

The legal procedure to acquire and maintain a trademark varies from country to country. Whereas some countries recognize registration but not prior use, other countries do exactly the opposite. In most countries, a company can register a mark subject to cancellation if that mark is not used or continued to be used within a reasonable period of time. The failure to register, even with actual prior use, may force the company to forfeit its rights to another person who registers the same mark later but before anybody else. The first user can be held to ransom this way.

The WTO states: "Members may make registrability depend on use. However, actual use of a trademark shall not be a condition for filing an application for registration. An application shall not be refused solely on the ground that intended use has not taken place before the expiry of a period of three years from the date of application." Furthermore, "If use is required to maintain a registration, the registration may be cancelled only after an uninterrupted period of at least three years of non-use."

Going back as far as the 1870s, trademark rights in the U.S.A. were based on the "no trade, no trademark" premise. Until recently, the U.S. Patent and Trademark Office was practically alone in the world in requiring a potential mark owner to put the trademark into interstate or foreign commercial use first before it could even be registered. The U.S. Trademark Act of 1946 (the Lanham Act) has been updated, and several changes have been made. One change involves intent-to-use trademark applications; the change permits companies to file an application based on projected future use. Now a declaration of a bona fide intent to use the mark in commerce is sufficient. A trademark registration is subsequently issued when the applicant files a statement showing evidence of actual use of the mark in commerce. To demonstrate use of the mark, specimens in the form of containers, labels, tags, or displays associated with the goods must be filed. There is no penalty for reserving names that are never actually used. The second change is the constructive-use provision. For goods or services specified in the Principal Registration, an applicant receives a nationwide priority effect as though the applicant had used the mark throughout the nation as of the filing date. The definition of "use of the mark" has been changed to require that use be in the ordinary course of trade, and token use is prohibited. To reserve a mark, the intent-to-use application becomes the sole avenue. Finally, the term of federal registration has been reduced from 20 to 10 years to clear out trademarks that are no longer used.

Although a single use of a mark may be adequate to register that mark, a company must exploit the mark commercially in good faith to prevent its loss.[22] The rationale is to prevent a company from abusing the law to its advantage when the owner has no intention of using the trademark other than to bar potential competitors with genuine interests from utilizing a competitive tool. An example is Snob perfume, a name owned in France by Le Galion, a French company, and in the U.S.A. by Jean Patou, an American company. Le Galion was able to challenge Patou's rights successfully because Patou (1) sold only 89 bottles of Snob perfume in 21 years, (2) never supported the product with promotion, and (3) made only $100 in gross profit. Thus, Patou was suspected of registering the name just to bar a potential competitor from entering the market.

The quickest way to lose a trademark is by not using it. A failure to use a registered trademark for three years terminates all rights in China. In the case of South Korea, nonuse after a period of one year is grounds for cancellation of registrations. In Central and South America, due to inflation, currency devaluations, and political uncertainty, a manufacturer may find it difficult to maintain operations there. However, the company risks losing its trademark if it stops the business activities. It is thus wise to consider some temporary licensing agreements with local firms until the situation improves. By doing so, brand awareness and trademark ownership are sustained. This is exactly what some international firms did while being forced to retreat from South Africa at the height of the anti-apartheid movement.

Another caveat is to make sure that the brand does not become so generic that it is identified with the product itself. A loss of trademark can occur if the name becomes part of the language; that is, when members of the consuming public use the brand name to denote the product or its common function rather than the producer of the product. Yo-Yo (a foreign trademark), Roquefort cheese, and Champagne are proprietary names in France but generic names in the U.S.A. The reverse is true of Ping-Pong, a U.S. registered trademark that is a generic name in China for table tennis. In Japan there is no word for vulcanized rubber, and the Goodyear name is used to identify this product. Cyanamid has had to fight to keep Formica from denoting all plastic laminate or laminated wood. Bayer's loss of the Aspirin trademark in the U.S.A. was due partly to the anti-German sentiment during World War II and partly to its failure to create a generic word for the product, whose chemical name is acetylsalicylic acid. Bayer would have been on more solid legal ground if it had established a generic term for household use (e.g., headache tablet or pain relief tablet).

To avoid this problem of a brand name becoming a generic name, a firm must never use the brand name in a generic sense (i.e., using it as a verb or adjective to denote the product). Promotional materials should reflect the proper usage, and the public should be informed accordingly. Willy Motors always emphasizes that Jeep is a trademark and uses an advertisement to inform consumers not to use Jeep as an adjective (e.g., jeeplike, jeepy, or jeep-type), a verb (e.g., jeep around or go jeeping), a plural (e.g., jeeps), or a generic without the capital J. In the Philippines, however, Jeep has become a generic name, and people there use privately owned small buses known as jeepnies for transportation. Jeep is now a registered trademark of DaimlerChrysler.

It is not legally sound to combine trademarks. It may seem remote that Honda will have trouble with its Honda Accord and Honda Civic marks, but the fact remains that the second mark (Accord, Civic) is in jeopardy through inference that it is the product's generic name. The public may thus assume that manufacturers other than Honda also make Accord and Civic cars.

Tabasco provides a good illustration of the various legal issues that have been discussed. Unlike Worcestershire Sauce and Soy Sauce, Tabasco is a properly registered trademark. It is the name of a river and a state of southern Mexico. One may question how a geographic name could ever have been accepted for registration, as the name is not distinctive. The answer is that the name was capable of being distinctive and did become distinctive because it has been used continuously and exclusively by the manufacturer for a long time. Thus, the name has become associated with this particular company. Furthermore, Tabasco is the official botanical name of red hot peppers, but those peppers were actually named for the sauce (i.e., product) and not the other way around. Tabasco is aware that consumers might use the brand to denote the product (i.e., hot sauce) rather than the maker of the product. It has thus hired two legal firms to police the world for any misappropriation of the trademark. Its vigorous enforcement enabled it to defeat F.F. Trappey Sons' legal bid for the right to use the word.

To hold the legal rights to a registered trademark is one thing, but to prevent others from illegally using it through counterfeiting is another matter altogether (see Legal Dimension 11.3). In fact, counterfeiters, though acknowledging the illegality of the activity, may see nothing morally wrong with the activity. In China, the basic cultural values relevant to counterfeiting are neutral – it is not a violation to copy someone's ideas. Great artists' works, for example, are copied as a sign of respect.

To prevent the importation into the U.S.A. of counterfeits and, to a lesser extent, gray market goods, a trademark owner whose mark is accepted for the Principal Register can register a mark with the U.S. Customs Service for the purpose of preventing entry of goods bearing an infringing mark. The Customs Service distinguishes colorable imitation from counterfeit trademark. A **colorable imitation** is a mark so similar as to be confused with a registered mark, whereas a **counterfeit trademark** is basically indistinguishable from a registered trademark. Colorable imitations are treated more leniently in that they can still gain entry so long as the objectionable mark is removed. However, in the case of counterfeits, the Customs Reform and Simplification Act of 1978 allows the seizure as well as forfeiture to the government of any articles bearing a counterfeit trademark.

## Legal Dimension 11.3

### Hijacking a brand

MAG Engineering & Manufacturing, a manufacturer of locks and security equipment, was surprised when shipments from several suppliers in the southern Chinese province of Guangdon were held up in 2004 by local customs officials. An investigation revealed a problem – a big problem. Taixing Lock Industry Manufacturing, one of MAG's suppliers, had registered MAG's trademark in China as its own. It then told customs officials that other suppliers were not authorized to produce and ship MAG products. After spending almost $40,000 in legal fees, MAG has still not completely resolved the problem. Chinese law emphasizes first registration, unlike the U.S.A. which respects first use. In the meantime, the company has spent another $15,000 to file nearly 350 separate trademark applications. It is a good idea to include a clause in a contract that prohibits suppliers or other contractees from violating a trademark in question.

## Packaging: functions and criteria

Similar to the brand name, packaging is another integral part of a product. Packaging serves two primary purposes: functional and promotional. First and foremost, a package must be functional in the sense that it is capable of protecting the product at minimum cost.

If a product is not manufactured locally and has to be exported to another country, extra protection is needed to compensate for the time and distance involved. A country's adverse environment should also be taken into account. When moisture is a problem, a company may have to wrap pills in foil or put food in tin boxes or vacuum-sealed cans. However, the type of package chosen must be economical. In Mexico, where most consumers cannot afford to buy detergents in large packages, detergent suppliers found it necessary to use plastic bags for small packages because cardboard would be too expensive for that purpose.

For most packaging applications, marketers should keep in mind that foreign consumers are more concerned with the functional aspect of a package than they are with convenience. As such, there is usually no reason to offer the great variety of package sizes or styles demanded by Americans. Plastic and throw-away bottles are regarded as being wasteful, especially in LDCs, where the labor cost for handling returnables is modest. Non-American consumers prefer a package to have secondary functions. A tin box or a glass bottle may be used after the product content is gone to store something else. Empty glass containers can be sold by consumers to recoup a part of the purchase price.

From the marketing standpoint, the promotional function of packaging is just as critical as the functional aspect. To satisfy the Japanese preference for beautiful packaging, Avon upgraded its inexpensive plastic packaging to crystalline glass. Similarly, BSR packs its product into two cartons, one for shipping and one for point-of-purchase display, because Japanese buyers want a carton to be in top condition. The successful campaign for Bailey's Irish Cream in the U.S.A. included a fancy gold foil box package that promotes this whiskey-based drink's upscale image. In any case, packaging does not have to be dull. Novel shapes and designs can be used to stimulate interest and create excitement.

## Mandatory package modification

A package change may be either mandatory or at the discretion of the marketer. A mandatory change is usually necessitated by government regulations. Sometimes, it is for safety and other reasons. Sometimes, packaging regulations are designed more for protection against imports than for consumer protection.

Several countries require bilinguality (e.g., French and English in Canada and French and Flemish in Belgium). This requirement may force the manufacturer to increase package size or shorten messages and product name, as a bilingual package must have twice the space for copy communications. In some cases, modification is dictated by mechanical or technical difficulties, such as the unavailability of certain typographic fonts or good advertising typographers.

In many cases, packaging and labeling are highly related. Packages may be required to describe contents, quantity, manufacturer's name and address, and so on in letters of designated sizes. Any pictorial illustration that is used should not be misleading. In Singapore, certain foods must be labeled to conform to defined standards. When terms are used that imply added vitamins or minerals (e.g., enriched, fortified, vitaminized), packages must show the quantities of vitamins or minerals added per metric unit. In addition, if the product is hazardous in any way, marketers should adopt the United Nations' recommendations for the labeling and packaging of hazardous materials.

Exporters of textile products must conform to countries' varying regulations. Spain has specific and extensive requirements concerning fiber content, labeling, and packaging. In addition to its flammability requirements, Sweden's labeling regulations include size, material, care, and origin. Venezuela requires all packaged goods to be labeled in metric units while specifically prohibiting dual labeling to show both metric and nonmetric units. Germany wants the description of fiber content to be in German, but labeling for Denmark must be in Danish or a related language. In the case of France, care labeling (if used) must meet an International Standardization Organization (ISO) directive.

As discussed in Chapter 10, countries' different measurement systems may necessitate some form of product modification, and this applies to packaging as well. Products, toiletries included, cannot be sold in Australia in ounces. The Australian regulations require products to be sold in metric numbers, in increments of 25 mm. In Germany, liquid products must be bottled or packaged in standard metric sizes. Interesting, the U.S.A., a nonmetric nation, has the same requirement for liquor products.

The European Union's Directive on packaging and packaging waste, taking effect in 1994, harmonized the national measures on the management of packaging waste among the member states while ensuring that restrictions on packaging do not create trade barriers. Setting targets for both recovery and recycling of waste, the Directive requires the member states to ensure that 50 to 65 percent of all waste is recovered for waste stream and that 25 to 45 percent is recycled.

## Optional package modification

Optional package modification, although not absolutely necessary, may have to be undertaken for marketing impact or for facilitating marketing activities. Through accidents and history, users in many countries have grown accustomed to particular types of packages. Mayonnaise, cheese, and mustard come in tubes in Europe, but mustard is sold in jars in the U.S.A. Orange bottles are popular in the Netherlands. While non-Dutch beer drinkers all over the world readily recognize a green Heineken bottle, the domestic Heineken beer comes in a brown bottle. Alfred H. Heineken designed the famous green bottle and logo with red star and the black banner bearing the brand name.

The package of Red Bull, the world's number one brand of energy drinks, can be easily recognized around the world. The tall, slender can is decorated with the brand's logo and blue color. This design has become a standard scheme for this product category, with newcomers trying to imitate the design. However, in Thailand where Red Bull originated, the brand comes in a short, square, glass bottle.

In selecting or modifying a package, a marketer should consider local conditions related to purchasing habits. Products conventionally sold in packs in the U.S.A. are not necessarily sold that way elsewhere and may require further bulk breaking. This phenomenon is due in part to lower income levels overseas and in part the result of a lack of unit pricing, which makes it difficult for buyers to see any savings derived from the purchase of a bigger package. Foreign consumers may desire to buy one bottle of beer or soft drink at a time instead of buying a six-pack or eight-pack. Likewise, one cigarette, not the whole pack, may be bought in a purchase transaction.

For Unilever, the $50 billion Anglo-Dutch consumer goods multinational has mastered the art of selling products in tiny packages costing a few cents each. Its Indian subsidiary, Hindustan Lever Ltd., began selling single-use sachets of Sunsilk shampoo for 2 cents to 4 cents. These mini-packages now account for half of Hindustan Lever's $2.4 billion in sales in India. Unilever's Rexona brand deodorant sticks sell for 16 cents and over and are very popular in India, the Philippines, Bolivia, and Peru. A nickel-size Vaseline package and a tube containing enough Close-Up toothpaste for 20 brushings sell for about 8 cents each. In Nigeria, Unilever sells 3-inch-square packets of margarine that do not need refrigeration.[23]

In addition to conditions of use, other cultural factors should be taken into consideration because such factors often determine and influence consumer preference. Although the UHT (ultra-high temperature) process for packaging milk and juices in unrefrigerated cartons has long been popular in Europe and Asia, it took some time for American consumers who were accustomed to fresh products to start accepting aseptic packaging.

Symbols and colors of packages may have to be changed to be consistent with cultural norms. If packages are offensive, they must be made more acceptable if the product is to be marketed successfully. For example, the controversial Jovan packages, with their sexual connotations, can prove to be too suggestive in some countries. In Japan, because manufacturers of condoms have female customers in mind, packaging tends to be cute.

Sometimes, it is difficult to tell whether package modification is mandatory or optional. Take the case of Germany's "green dot" packaging laws. Since the early 1990s, Germany has required manufacturers, distributors, and retailers to take back sales packaging (used packaging materials) either directly from the consumer's domicile or from designated local collection points. Those manufacturers who participate in the "green dot" program are exempted from this requirement. The green dot is the symbol which has been adopted by the Duales System Deutschland GmbH (DSD – Dual System of Germany), a corporation established in 1990, with over 400 participating companies (shareholders). The DSD collects a fee from the participating manufacturers for the right to display the green dot symbol on the products. The revenue is used to finance local packaging waste-collection and recycling programs. The green dot tells consumers that such packaging may not be returned to the retailer but should be consigned to specially dedicated collection containers or be taken to the local recycling center. The symbol also indicates that the packaging will be recycled or reused rather than dumped or incinerated. While goods not displaying the green dot are not illegal, they are unlikely to be accepted by the market – retailers, wholesalers, and importers. The DSD estimates that over 10 billion units currently being marketed in Germany carry the green dot.

Most other European Union countries have initiated similar green dot programs. Japan's Packaging Recycling Law requires manufacturers to pay costs associated with collection, sorting, transportation, and recycling of all paper and plastic containers and packaging. Importers are held responsible for paying the recycling costs of imported products.

One helpful sign that should reduce packaging confusion is the European Union's standardization attempt. Changes in the EU's food-packaging requirements should allow foreign food manufacturers and packaging agents to follow one unified EU regulation. Although size requirements differ by product, the EU has harmonized the sizes of sealed packages and containers. This uniformity assists consumers in comparing prices for the same quantity, thus abolishing the need for unit pricing. EU packaging regulations also help to promote conservation by decreasing the amount of paper used in packaging.

Because there is no EU-wide general product-labeling directive, manufacturers have to label their products differently for each country, thus increasing expenses. There is also a question about language requirements. The EU suggests that most products should have at least two EU official languages so as to increase the marketability of the products. In terms of what is to be placed on the product label, EU officials recommend the following: (1) the name of the product, (2) the name of the manufacturer or distributor within the marketing country, (3) any care conditions, (4) special storage conditions, (5) country of origin, especially where labels might mislead, (6) metric requirements, and (7) list of chemicals/ingredients included.

## Conclusion

A product is a bundle of utilities, and the brand and package are part of this bundle. There is nothing unusual about consumers' reliance on brand names as a guide to product quality. As shown by the perfume industry, the mystique of a brand name may be so strong as to overshadow the product's physical attributes. When practiced and well executed, branding allows a commodity to be transformed into a product. In doing so with the aid of product differentiation, brand loyalty is created, and the product can command a premium price.

Branding decisions involve more than merely deciding whether a product should be branded or not. Branding entails other managerial decisions. A manufacturer must decide whether to use its own brand or that of its dealer on its product. A marketer must also determine whether to use a single brand for maximum impact or multiple brands to satisfy the different segments and markets more precisely. Regardless of the number of brands used, each brand name must be selected carefully with the international market in mind. Once selected, the brand name must be protected through registration, and other measures should be taken to prevent any infringement of that name.

Like the brand name, which may have to be varied from one country to another, packaging should be changed when needed. Mandatory modification of packaging should not be considered a problem because the marketer has no choice in the matter – if a marketer wants to market a product, the marketer must conform to the country's stated packaging requirements. Unilever, for instance, has to conform to the French requirement of selling cube-shaped packs, not rectangular packs, of margarine. Its descriptions for mayonnaise and salad dressing also have to vary from country to country.

Optional or discretionary packaging modification, in contrast, is a more controllable variable within a marketer's marketing mix. Usually, discretionary packaging is more related to product promotion, and it can take on the same importance as mandatory packaging. Soft-drink containers are a good example of how packaging requirements must be observed. In many countries, bottles are manufactured in metric sizes due to government requirements, and the containers must be made of glass because consumers abroad regard plastic throw-away bottles as being wasteful. Therefore, both mandatory and optional packaging changes should be considered at the same time.

## CASE 11.1 PLANET RALPH: THE GLOBAL MARKETING STRATEGY OF POLO RALPH LAUREN

**Helen M. Caldwell and Deidre Bird, Providence College**

Polo Ralph Lauren (PRL) is considered to be one of the most successful premium lifestyle brand companies in the world with 2006 sales exceeding $5.3 billion. The fortieth anniversary of the company has been covered in glowing terms across the world. *Time* magazine's May 8, 2006 issue of the "100 Most Influential People" included Ralph Lauren and described him as the "Dream Weaver." *Harper's Bazaar* March 2006 issue profiled him as "Fashion's Number One" and proclaimed him the bestselling designer in the world and outlined his successful rise from the Bronx kid Ralph Lifschitz to the world-famous Ralph Lauren.

## The Polo Ralph Lauren concept

PRL is a family-controlled company in that its Chairman and CEO is designer and founder Ralph Lauren. However, it is publicly quoted on the New York Stock Exchange. The company derives its revenues from three sources: retail, wholesale, and licensing.

The retail segment operates over 279 full-price and outlet stores, including the magnificent flagship stores in Manhattan, London, Paris, Milan, Tokyo, and now Moscow. There is also an extensive website, Polo.com, which is growing rapidly and now has 800,000 customers worldwide. It also provides an opportunity to showcase the broad range of products and reinforce the luxury lifestyle message to consumers outside of the retail reach. According to the Luxury Institute's 2006 Luxury Website Effectiveness Index (LWEI) for fashion designers, Polo Ralph Lauren has the top-rated website. The LWEI incorporates four components of a luxury website's effectiveness: usefulness of content, ease of navigation, overall look and feel, and trust with personal information. Retail now accounts for 42 percent of total revenues.

The wholesale segment consists of two units: Polo Brands and Collection Brands, with each unit selling its own discrete brands to department and specialty stores, and to PRL-owned and licensed stores.

The licensing segment accounts for almost 10 percent of total sales, generating revenues from royalties through licensing alliances whereby the licensee is granted the right to use the company's trademarks in connection with the manufacture and sale of certain products in specific geographical areas. As part of its global strategy, PRL purchased its Japanese licensee of men's, women's, and jeans apparel and accessories. "We will look to reinforce the brand's image and elevate the distribution in Japan to better align with our business globally," Polo Ralph Lauren President Roger Farah said at a press conference. "Japan is a key luxury market," he added.

In early 2007, Polo Ralph Lauren Corporation started a new group named Global Brand Concepts (GBC), which will develop new lifestyle brands for specialty and department stores. The first such endeavor is J.C. Penney Company, Inc. (NYSE: JCP) which has announced its plans to launch American Living, a new lifestyle brand created exclusively for the J.C. Penney customer by Polo Ralph Lauren's (NYSE: RL) Global Brand Concepts. The launch will be the largest in J.C. Penney's history and will include a full range of merchandise for women, men, and children, as well as intimate apparel, accessories, and home furnishings. American Living will be available in J.C. Penney's stores, catalog and industry-leading website jcp.com, beginning in spring 2008.

The Company's brand names, which include "Polo by Ralph Lauren," "Ralph Lauren Purple Label," "Ralph Lauren," "Black Label," "Blue Label," "Lauren by Ralph Lauren," "Polo Jeans Co.," "RRL," "RLX," "Rugby," "RL Children's Wear," "Chaps," and "Club Monaco" among others, constitute one of the world's most widely recognized families of consumer brands.

## The Polo Ralph Lauren strategy

PRL intends to grow by brand extension and by globalization. In its brand extensions, the company aims to expand by "creating luxury lifestyle brands that inspire people to live their dreams." Planet Ralph is a place where all the women are beautiful, the men are handsome, the children are adorable, and even the pup is well bred. The houses are elegant in an old-world manner, replete with family crests and antiques. Of course this leads to opportunities for selling everything from clothes and accessories for men, women and children, an array of fragrances, home furnishings, and even paint.

This lifestyle marketing and brand extension strategy requires a large advertising budget with highly controlled images and messages communicating the qualities of the brand. The company uses a combination of multi-page magazine ads along with full-page ads in key newspapers and some television commercials.

PRL is now the Official Outfitter of Wimbledon, and Boris Becker is its brand ambassador. Boris will wear Ralph Lauren throughout the duration of the tournament in his role as a Wimbledon commentator and brand ambassador. This connection with the prestigious tennis tournament and internationally renowned player will add further to the Ralph Lauren cachet, especially in the British market.

## The PRL global strategy

In 2006, 70 percent of PRL revenues were from the U.S.A., followed by 14 percent from Europe and 9 percent from Japan. Based on a belief that there are numerous growth opportunities outside the U.S.A., the company has opened splendid flagship stores in London, Paris, Milan, Tokyo, and most recently in Moscow. Europe and Asia are considered to be key markets for international growth. These retail emporiums are in the most elite shopping neighborhoods and offer the best merchandise in the most elaborate setting imaginable.

In March 2006, Lauren opened his brand's largest store ever in Tokyo's upscale district of Omotesando – an area that he sees to have potential to become a new global fashion center. The Tokyo store features one-of-a-kind antiques and vintage pieces, as well as many more exclusive limited-edition Ralph Lauren designs, punctuating this unique fusion of great American spirit with Japanese sophistication. With frequent visits, customers will be introduced to the ever-changing world of Ralph Lauren.

The most recent additions are two opulent stores in Moscow, both in partnership with Russia's Mercury distribution group.

> There the Muscovites will find the world of Ralph Lauren – an Old World of molded ceilings, wrought iron chandeliers, a gentlemanly glass and mahogany elevator and floors dedicated to menswear (including made-to-measure) and to both glamour and sporty ease for women. Significantly, the main floor offers a new universe of extreme luxury accessories, from sunglasses framed in translucent tortoise-shell to alligator bags, named for Lauren's wife Ricky, and with a gilded identity plaque inside worthy of a czar.

## The world market for luxury brands

The primary customers for luxury goods tend to be women aged 25 to 50 in the upper-income brackets, where the household income exceeds $100,000. However, in what is referred to as the "democratization of luxury," people in all income brackets want to participate in the luxury market, even if that means buying a $4 chai latte at Starbucks, or a $60 Coach scarf. Ralph Lauren recognized this himself when he described the desire for luxury as aspirational.

Approximately 35 companies share 60 percent of the luxury goods market. The six top competitors, one of which is PRL, have annual revenues exceeding $1 billion. The top three luxury brand conglomerates are Louis Vuitton Monet Hennessey (LVMH), Richemont, and Gucci.

Luxury sales worldwide exceeded $150 billion in 2006, with only 30 percent coming from the U.S.A. The largest luxury market is Japan which accounts for about 40 percent of the world's total sales. There is a saying in Japan that aptly describes the country's attitudes toward buying luxury brands: "Your coat is your home." Japanese consumers often communicate their status through their bags, shoes, watches, jewelry, clothes, and other visible luxury brand goods. A phenomenon referred to as "parasite singles," namely well-educated young women who work in secretarial or administrative assistant jobs and live at home with their parents, leads to their having money to spend on luxury goods. These women are the largest consumer segment for luxury brands in Japan. If PRL can succeed at attracting this market, it will certainly prove lucrative.

## Points to consider

As Lauren ponders the corporation's future, the following questions will need to be addressed:

1 Can an American brand built on the quintessential "American Dream" succeed globally?
2 Will the PRL form of lifestyle marketing succeed globally?
3 Which brands would represent the best global opportunities for PRL?
4 Which countries would represent the best opportunities for additional retail expansion? Would India be a viable option?

*Sources*: Polo Ralph Lauren Annual Report, 2006; "Ralph Lauren: To Russia With Love," *Women's Wear Daily*, May 16, 2007; Anne D"Innocenzio, "Luxury Goods Go Over the Top," *Forbes.com*, June 14, 2007; "Every Cloud Has a Silver Lining," *The Economist*, March 21, 2002; Radha Chadha and Paul Husband, *The Cult of the Luxury Brand in Asia* (London: Nicholas Brealey International, 2006); "Top Fashion Brand Web Sites Ranked by Their Overall Effectiveness," *Women's Wear Daily*, November 30, 2006; and PRL Press Release, "Polo Ralph Lauren Announce Signing of Boris Becker as Official Brand Ambassador for Wimbledon 2007"; and Suzy Menkes, "Ralph Lauren Returns to his Russian Roots," *International Herald Tribune*, May 14, 2007,

## Questions

1 What are the requirements that must be met so that a commodity can effectively be transformed into a branded product?
2 Explain the "least dependent person" hypothesis and its branding implications.
3 When is it appropriate to use multiple brands in (a) the same market and (b) several markets/countries?
4 What are the characteristics of a good international brand name?
5 Explain these legal requirements related to branding: (a) registration, (b) registration eligibility, (c) use, (d) renewal, and (e) generic trademark.
6 Distinguish colorable imitation from counterfeit trademark.
7 Cite the factors that may force a company to modify its packing for overseas markets. Discuss both mandatory and optional modification.

# Discussion assignments and minicases

1 Should U.S. farmers brand their exported commodities (e.g., soybean, corn, beef)?
2 Some retailers (e.g., Sears) and manufacturers (e.g., General Motors) place their trademarks on products actually made by foreign suppliers. Discuss the rationale for these actions by these firms.
3 Discuss how certain English letters, prefixes, suffixes, syllables, or words create pronunciation difficulties for those whose native language is not English.
4 Is Hyundai a good name to use for an international brand? On what do you base your evaluation?
5 Go to the soft-drink section of a supermarket. How many different types of soft-drink packages are there (e.g., in terms of size, form)? Should any of them be modified for overseas markets?

6 Majorca is a place well known for its pearls. One Spanish firm, Majorica SA, has used Majorica, an ancient name for Majorca, since 1954 as its trade name as well as a brand name to describe its pearls. Majorica was alarmed to learn that R. H. Macy, a major U.S. department store chain, was selling Majorca-labeled pearls that were made by Hobe Cie. Ltd., a competitor of Majorica SA. Contacts with Macy produced no fruitful results in resolving the difficulty. Macy felt that it had a right to use the name in question because Majorca was the name of an island and because the pearls in questions were indeed made there.

Subsequently, Majorica filed a lawsuit in a federal court, asking for a judgment to stop Macy using the name. Majorica SA cited trademark infringement as the reason for seeking relief. It argued that Macy's action caused confusion among consumers as well as erosion of goodwill. Is Majorica a valid brand name or just a generic trademark? Does the fact that it is the name of a place (i.e., island) affect the registration eligibility and legal protection of Majorica SA? Was Macy's action legally defensible? Assuming that you are a federal court judge, do you think that Macy's use of the name could cause consumer confusion? Do you think that Macy's labeling constituted trademark infringement? Can the branding/labeling be somehow modified to prevent consumer confusion?

## Notes

1 *H.J. Heinz Company 2000*, Second Quarter, 9.
2 "Flat Panels, Thin Margins," *Business Week*, February 26, 2007, 50–1.
3 T.C. Melewar, John Saunders, and John M.T. Balmer, "Cause, Effect and Benefits of a Standardised Corporate Visual Identity System of UK Companies Operating in Malaysia," *European Journal of Marketing* 35 (No. 3, 2001): 414–27.
4 Henry Chesbrough, *Open Business Models: How to Thrive in the New Innovation Landscape* (Boston, MA: Harvard Business School Press, 2006).
5 Peter C. Verhoef, Edwin J. Nijssen, and Laurens M. Sloot, "Strategic Reactions of National Brand Manufacturers Towards Private Labels: An Empirical Study in the Netherlands," *European Journal of Marketing* 36 (No. 11, 2002): 1309–26.
6 Steve Burt, "The Strategic Role of Retail Brands in British Grocery Retailing," *European Journal of Marketing* 34 (No. 8, 2000): 875–90.
7 Celina Gonzalez Mieres, Ana Maria Diaz Martin, and Juan Antonio Trespalacios Gutierrez, "Antecedents of the Difference in Perceived Risk Between Store Brands and National Brands," *European Journal of Marketing* 40 (Nos 1/2, 2006): 61–82.
8 Lien Lamey *et al.*, "How Business Cycles Contribute to Private-Label Success: Evidence from the United States and Europe," *Journal of Marketing* 71 (January 2007): 1–15.
9 "Quanta's Quantum Leap," *Business Week*, 5 November 2001, 79–81; and "Don't Be Fooled by the Name on the Box," *Business Week*, June 17, 2002, 18.
10 "Samsonite Agrees on Sale to CVC," *Wall Street Journal*, July 6, 2007.
11 "Breaking Into the Name Game," *Business Week*, 7 April 2003, 54.
12 Dana L. Alden, Jan-Benedict E.M. Steenkamp, and Rajeev Batra, "Brand Positioning Through Advertising in Asia, North America, and Europe: The Role of Global Consumer Culture," *Journal of Marketing* 63 (January 1999): 75–87.
13 "Global Brands," *Business Week*, August 1, 2005, 86–94.
14 "Honda Will Create Brand for China's Auto Market," *Wall Street Journal*, July 19, 2007.

15 "EU Court Upholds Anheuser Trademarks," *Wall Street Journal*, June 13, 2007.
16 Giana M. Eckhardt, "Local Branding in a Foreign Product Category in an Emerging Market," *Journal of International Marketing* 13 (No. 4, 2005): 57–79.
17 Cheng-Lu Wang, Noel Y.M. Siu, and Alice S.Y. Hui, "Consumer Decision-making Styles on Domestic and Imported Brand Clothing," *European Journal of Marketing* 38 (Nos 1/2, 2004): 239–52.
18 Isabelle Schuiling and Jean-Noel Kapferer, "Real Differences Between Local and International Brands: Strategic Implications for International Marketers," *Journal of International Marketing* 12 (No. 4, 2004): 97–112.
19 Gerald Yong Gao *et al.*, "Market Share Performance of Foreign and Domestic Brands in China," *Journal of International Marketing* 14 (No. 2, 2006): 32–51.
20 Shi Zhang and Bernd H. Schmitt, "Creating Local Brands in Multilingual International Markets," *Journal of Marketing Research* 38 (August 2001): 313–25.
21 "Case Study: Philips' Norelco," *IN*, June 2007, 18–19.
22 Sidney A. Diamond, *Trademark Problems and How to Avoid Them*, rev. edn (Chicago, IL: Crain Books, 1981), 20–2.
23 "Ideas for a Changing World," *Business Week*, August 26, 2002, 112–14.

Chapter 12

# Channels of distribution

In a market system, all aspects of economic activity are interdependent, and the whole cannot function properly if any major element is not in its place.

Michel Camdessus, Managing Director, International Monetary Fund

## Chapter outline

- Marketing strategy: blood diamonds and De Beers (Part 1)
- Direct and indirect selling channels
- Types of intermediaries: direct channel
  - Foreign distributor
  - Foreign retailer
  - State-controlled trading company
  - End user
- Types of intermediaries: indirect channel
  - Export broker
  - Manufacturer's export agent or sales representative
  - Export management company (EMC)
  - Cooperative exporter
  - Purchasing/buying agent
  - Country-controlled buying agent
  - Resident buyer
  - Export merchant
  - Export drop shipper
  - Export distributor
  - Trading company
- Channel development

- Channel adaptation
- Channel decisions
- Determinants of channel types
  - Legal regulations
  - Product image
  - Product characteristics
  - Middlemen's loyalty and conflict
  - Local customs
  - Power and coercion
  - Control
- Distribution in Japan
- Selection of channel members
- Representation agreement and termination
- Black market
- Gray market
  - Causes
  - Legal dimension
  - Ethical dimension
  - Product quality
  - Manufacturers' marketing strategies
- Distribution of services
- Conclusion
- Case 12.1 Managing channel conflict in the global IT industry
- Case 12.2 Schwarzkopf, Inc. distribution network

## Marketing strategy

**Blood diamonds and De Beers (Part 1)**

One needs money to wage war, and diamonds are just as good as any kind of money. Diamonds are precious, portable, and anonymous. Most of Sierra Leone's diamonds are smuggled into Liberia for sale. It is practically impossible to identify the origins of diamonds. As a result, diamonds are a currency of choice for thugs and rebels in Africa. At one time, diamonds from the African war zones accounted for 10 to 15 percent of the world supply.

In Angola, diamonds helped Unita, an Angolan rebel group, to launch a civil war in 1990s. Such blood diamonds resulted in half a million Angolans being killed and four million Angolans being displaced. The Revolutionary United Front, a rebel unit that barters diamonds for weapons, is unbelievably brutal. Its soldiers chopped off the limbs of innocent people to instill fear. Unita's cruelty led the U.S.A. to impose a diamond embargo in 1998 on the group. While the United Nations Children's Fund has declared that Angola is the worst place on Earth to be a child, it took the United Nations six years before imposing the embargo.

Unita does not act alone. It has many accomplices to help it to use diamonds to finance its ruthless operations. Corrupt governments, pitiless rebels, and porous borders in Angola, Congo, and Sierra Leone have allowed diamonds to become agents of slave labor, dismemberment, murder, mass exodus, and economic collapse. Many diamond dealers in Antwerp do not care to know where the stones are from, and the world's largest diamond bourse in Antwerp has "extremely lax regulations." At the same time, Liberia, Uganda, Rwanda, and Zimbabwe have passed off smuggled diamonds as their own by supplying false but official certificates of origin. Diamonds, in spite of their image of romance, have played a major role in the cross-border conflict that ravaged Liberia and Sierra Leone for more than a decade.

Fortunately, governments and the diamond industry have reached a global accord that stops trade in diamonds from the conflict zones. For rough diamonds to be exported, they must be certified that they are not from the territory held by the rebels. Any private exporters or importers who break the rules will lose their trading licenses. Countries that break the rules will be barred from selling diamonds, and they may face international sanctions. UN sanctions blocking the export of blood diamonds were finally lifted, and Liberia shipped its first consignment of diamonds worth $222,000 in 2007.

To maintain its control on the supply of diamonds, De Beers bought Unita's diamonds. In its defense, De Beers claimed that it did not deal directly with the rebels and that it stopped all deals after the 1998 embargo. The company's own annual reports nonetheless showed that the cartel's deals had brought large amounts of money to the rebels. As the world was flooded with diamonds, De Beers found it difficult to maintain expensive inventory and prices, and its image was also taking a heavy beating. The company managed to solve both problems at the same time by not buying diamonds from Angola any longer, except from a government-controlled mine. It has also warned Antwerp traders that they could be cut off for failure to follow industry rules against money laundering. Police there have raided offices and seized papers and gems as evidence of money laundering and tax evasion. Antwerp is the world's top diamond center, and 80 percent of the world's uncut diamonds pass through the city.

*Sources*: "Africa's Gems: Warfare's Best Friend," *New York Times*, April 6, 2000; "New Rules Set for Diamond Trading," *San José Mercury News*, November 6, 2002; "'Blood Diamond' Ban Over, Liberia Ships Gems," *San José Mercury News*, September 10, 2007; and "Are the Diamonds Forever?", *Business Week*, June 4, 2007, 50.

## Purpose of chapter

All products need competent distribution. Unfortunately, the distribution of blood diamonds is relatively competent. In any case, any products, no matter how good they are, are unlikely to gain market acceptance without being made available at the time and place that are convenient to the final users.

The purpose of this chapter is to discuss the various channels of distribution that are responsible for moving products from manufacturers to consumers. Both international and domestic channels are examined. The chapter describes the varieties of intermediaries (i.e., agents, wholesalers, and retailers) involved in moving products between countries as well as within countries. The tasks and functions of the various intermediaries will be examined. It should be kept in mind that certain types of intermediaries do not exist in some countries and that the pattern of use as well as the importance of each type of intermediary varies widely from country to country.

A manufacturer is required to make several decisions that will affect its channel strategy, including the length, width, and number of distribution channels used. This chapter examines the various factors that influence these decisions. For an operation to be a success, a good relationship among channel members is vital. There is no one single distribution method always ideal in all markets. Thus, the chapter examines channel adaptation.

## Direct and indirect selling channels

A manufacturer can sell directly to end users abroad, but this type of channel is generally not suitable or desirable for most consumer goods. In foreign markets, it is far more common for a product to go through several parties before reaching the final consumer. Figures 12.1 and 12.2 show how two major Japanese companies (Sony and Kikkoman), by acting as middlemen, offer their distribution expertise to help American firms market their products in Japan.

Companies use two principal channels of distribution when marketing abroad: (1) direct selling and (2) direct selling. **Indirect selling**, also known as the *local* or *domestic* channel, is employed when a manufacturer in the United Kingdom, for example, markets its product through another British firm that acts as the manufacturer's *sales intermediary* (or middleman). As such, the sales intermediary is just another local or domestic channel for the manufacturer because there are no dealings abroad with a foreign firm. By exporting through an independent local middleman, the manufacturer has no need to set up an international department. The middleman, acting as the manufacturer's external export organization, usually assumes the responsibility for moving the product overseas. The intermediary may be a **domestic agent** if it does not take title to the goods, or it may be **domestic merchant** if it does take title to the goods.

There are several advantages to be gained by employing an indirect domestic channel. For example, the channel is simple and inexpensive. The manufacturer incurs no start-up costs for the channel and is released from the responsibility of physically moving the goods overseas. Because the intermediary very likely represents several clients who can help share distribution costs, the costs of moving the goods are further reduced.

An indirect channel does, however, have limitations. The manufacturer has been relieved of any immediate marketing costs but, in effect, has given up control over the marketing of its product to another firm. This situation may adversely affect the product's success in the future. If the chosen intermediary is not aggressive, the manufacturer may become vulnerable, especially in the case where competitors are careful about their distribution practices. Moreover, the indirect channel may not necessarily be permanent. Being in the business of handling products for profit, the intermediary can easily discontinue handling a manufacturer's product if there is no profit or if a competitive product offers a better profit potential.

Export intermediaries' performance is a function of their possession of valuable, unique, and hard-to-imitate resources. Such resources reduce their client's transaction and agency costs.[1] A related study, focusing on 20,000 French firms, found that export intermediary firms tend to export products

SONY
PLAZA
WANTS
MORE
U.S. PRODUCTS TO SELL IN JAPAN
"International trade requires efforts in importing as well as in exporting. There's an excellent market for American products in Japan. Our economy is strong. Japanese customers want diversity and are attracted by American brands. Sony has the sales force and knowledge of the Japanese market to help American firms find ready acceptance among Japanese consumers. This kind of trade will be beneficial both to Japan and to the American firms coming into the market."
——A. MORITA SONY Chairman
With this philosophy, Sony Plaza Co., Ltd. was established by Sony Corporation, a Company known for it's own fine exports. Sony Plaza has made famous such names as Fieldcrest, Royal Copenhagen, Paddington Bear, Famous Amos, Goody, etc. in the Japanese market.
And you? Sony Plaza wants to import yours.
If you're interested please talk to us.
In the U.S. please write to: Ms. Michele Classe, Sony Corp of America, America Export to Japan Div., 9 West 57th Street, New York, N.Y. 10019.
In Japan: Mr. Y. Maki, Sony Plaza Co., Ltd., Sony Bldg. 5-3-1 Ginza, Chuo-ku, Tokyo. 104, Japan.
SONY plaza

**FIGURE 12.1** Sony's distribution expertise

*Source*: Reprinted with permission of Sony Corporation of America.

A Nose for Taste
Tastes as American as Del Monte tomato ketchup. As English as Lea and Perrins Worcestershire sauce. And as French as a Grand Vin Bordeaux.
The favored flavors of the West have been brought to Japan by Kikkoman Corporation.
Three centuries' experience, early market globalization, and consumer involvement give Kikkoman a keen sense for successful cross-cultural marketing ventures.
Further testimony to leadership and innovation are Kikkoman's far-ranging biotechnology and food development activities.
So the next time you think of Kikkoman, think again. We're a whole lot more than soy sauce.
KIKKOMAN
Kikkoman Corporation
1-25, Kanda Nishiki-cho, Chiyoda-ku, Tokyo 101, Japan
Production facilities: Japan, USA and Singapore; Subsidiaries: Hawaii, Canada, West Germany, Hong Kong and Australia.

**FIGURE 12.2** Kikkoman's distribution expertise

*Source*: Reprinted courtesy of Kikkoman Corporation.

with a high commodity content rather than products with a low commodity content, thus confirming the role of product complexity.[2]

**Direct selling** is employed when a manufacturer develops an *overseas* channel. This channel requires that the manufacturer deal directly with a foreign party without going through an intermediary in the home country. The manufacturer must set up the overseas channel to take care of the business activities between the countries. Being responsible for shipping the product to foreign markets itself, the manufacturer exports through its own internal export department or organization.

One advantage gained in using the direct-selling channel is active market exploitation, since the manufacturer is more directly committed to its foreign markets. Another advantage is greater control. The channel improves communication because approval does not have to be given to a middleman before a transaction is completed. Therefore, the channel allows the company's policy to be followed more uniformly.

Direct selling is not without its problems. It is a difficult channel to manage if the manufacturer is unfamiliar with the foreign market. Moreover, the channel is time-consuming and expensive. Without a large volume of business, the manufacturer may find it too costly to maintain the channel. Hiram Walker, a Canadian distiller, used to have its own marketing operation in New York City to distribute such brands as Ballantine Scotch, Kahlua, and CC Rye. Poor earnings finally forced the company to phase out its costly U.S. selling organization along with its New York City marketing operation.

In the case of multinational corporations with foreign subsidiaries, cooperation can enhance performance of products across markets. Cooperative marketing operations between the headquarters and its foreign subsidiaries enhance performance of products in subsidiaries' markets. National culture in foreign markets moderates the effect of trust on relational behaviors. As a firm attempts to standardize its marketing programs, subsidiaries' acquiescence becomes increasingly important.[3]

## Types of intermediaries: direct channel

There are several types of intermediaries associated with both the direct and indirect channels. Figure 12.3 compares the two channels and lists the various types of domestic and foreign intermediaries.

### *Foreign distributor*

A foreign distributor is a foreign firm that has exclusive rights to carry out distribution for a manufacturer in a foreign country or specific area. Fore example, when Don Wood returned to Detroit,

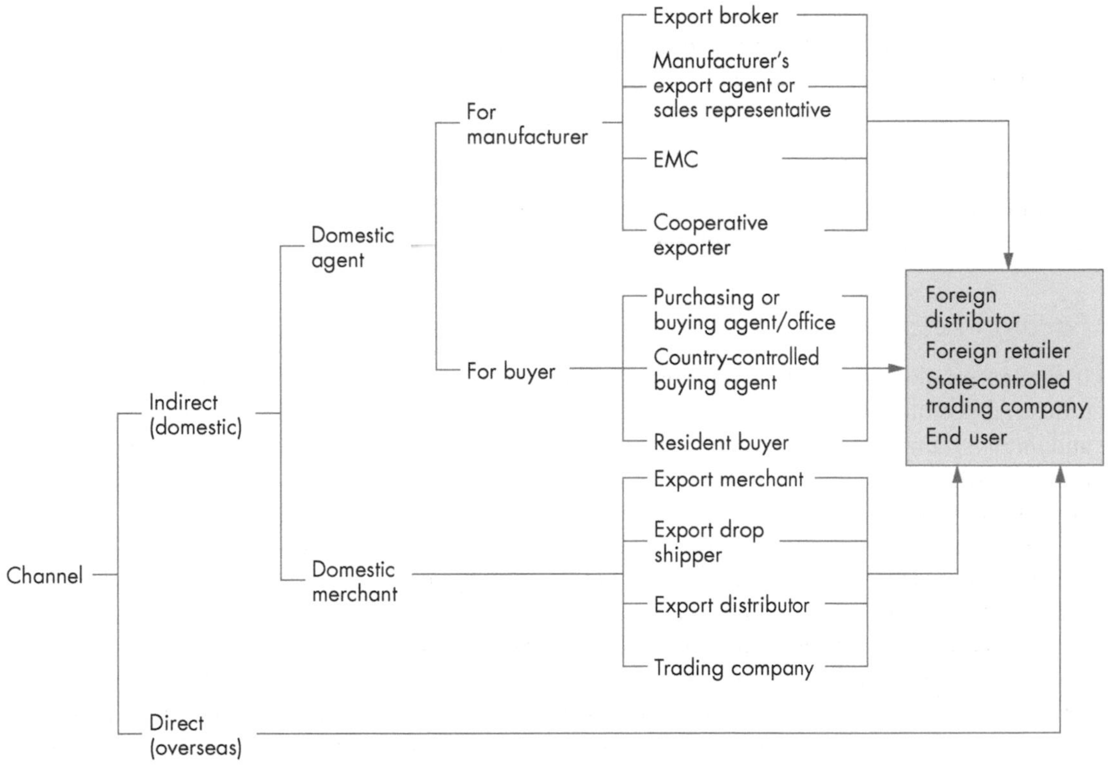
Channel
Indirect (domestic)
Direct (overseas)
Domestic agent
Domestic merchant
For manufacturer
For buyer
Export broker
Manufacturer's export agent or sales representative
EMC
Cooperative exporter
Purchasing or buying agent/office
Country-controlled buying agent
Resident buyer
Export merchant
Export drop shipper
Export distributor
Trading company
Foreign distributor
Foreign retailer
State-controlled trading company
End user

**FIGURE 12.3** International channels of distribution

he still remembered the MG sports car he drove in England during World War II. His letter asking MG's chairman to sell and ship one car to him brought the response that MG's policy was to sell only through authorized distributors. But MG was willing to appoint Wood its Midwest distributor if he would order two cars instead. Wood agreed to do so and went on to become a successful distributor.

Orders must be channeled through the distributor, even when the distributor chooses to appoint a subagent or subdistributor. The distributor purchases merchandise from the manufacturer at a discount and then resells or distributes the merchandise to retailers and sometimes final consumers. In this regard, the distributor's function in many countries may be a combination of wholesaler and retailer, but in most cases the distributor is usually considered as an importer or foreign wholesaler. The length of association between the manufacturer and its foreign distributor is established by a contract that is renewable provided the continued arrangement is satisfactory to both.

In some situations, the foreign distributor is merely a subsidiary of the manufacturer. Seiko U.S.A., for example, is a distributor for its Japanese parent (Hattori Seiko), which manufactures Seiko watches. More frequently, however, a foreign distributor is an independent merchant. Charles of the Ritz Group has been the U.S. distributor for Opium, a very popular perfume made in France. A distributor may sometimes take on the name of the brand distributed, even though the distributor is an independent operator and not owned by the manufacturer. Brother International Corp. is an independent U.S. distributor of Brother Industries, Ltd, a Japanese firm. Longines-Wittnauer Watch Co. distributes the Swiss-made Longines watch in the U.S. market. This distributorship is actually a subsidiary of the Westinghouse Electric Corp.

There are a number of benefits in using a foreign distributor. Unlike agents, the distributor is a *merchant* who buys and maintains merchandise in its own name. This arrangement simplifies the credit and payment activities for the manufacturer. To carry out the distribution function, the foreign distributor is often required to warehouse adequate products, parts, and accessories and to have facilities and personnel immediately available to service buyers and users. However, the manufacturer must be careful in selecting a foreign distributor or it may end up with a distributor who is deficient in marketing and servicing the product.

## Foreign retailer

If foreign retailers are used, the product in question must be a consumer product rather than an industrial product. There are several means by which a manufacturer may contact foreign retailers and interest them in carrying a product, ranging from a personal visit by the manufacturer's representative to mailings of catalogs, brochures, and other literature to prospective retailers. The use of personal selling or a visit, although expensive due to travel costs and commissions for the manufacturer's representative, provides for a more effective sales presentation as well as for better screening of retailers for the distribution purpose. The use of direct mail, although less expensive, may not sufficiently catch the retailers' attention.

For such big-ticket items as automobiles or for high-volume products, it may be worthwhile for a manufacturer to sell to retailers without going through a foreign distributor. In fact, most large retailers prefer to deal directly with a manufacturer. In Europe, for example, a number of retail food chains are becoming larger and more powerful, and they prefer to be in direct contact with foreign manufacturers in order to obtain price concessions.

In the case of Guess Inc., it has shortened its distribution channel by assuming the role of a retailer as well. The company operates both wholesale and retail businesses. Its licensing network has nearly

800 stores in 57 countries. It has bought out foreign distributors by buying back licensing agreements in order to capture more of the retail markup for itself. In Europe, fancy specialty stores carry the Guess brand and have an average price of $168. In South Korea, Guess bought back a 17-year-old license. By opening its own stores, Guess can feature more of its own merchandise such as watches, shoes, handbags, and fragrances as well as its other labels (e.g., Marciano, a higher end clothing line for women). The company plans to open 30 stores for its new G by Guess concept (which tops the jeans prices at $65 a pair).[4]

### State-controlled trading company

For some products, particularly utility and telecommunication equipment, a manufacturer must contact and sell to state-controlled companies. In addition, many countries, especially those in Eastern Europe, have state-controlled trading companies, which are companies that have a complete monopoly in the buying and selling of goods. Hungary has about 100 state trading organizations for a variety of products, ranging from poultry to telecommunication equipment and for both imported and exported products.

Being government sanctioned and controlled for trading in certain goods, buyers for state-controlled trading companies are very definitely influenced by their governments' trade policies and politics. Most opportunities for manufacturers are limited to raw materials, agricultural machinery, manufacturing equipment, and technical instruments rather than consumer or household goods. Reasons for this limitation include shortage of foreign exchange, an emphasis on self-sufficiency, and the central planning systems of the communist and socialist countries.

### End user

Sometimes, a manufacturer is able to sell directly to foreign end-users with no intermediary involved in the process. This direct channel is a logical and natural choice for costly industrial products. For most consumer products, the approach is only practical for some products and in some countries. A significant problem with consumer purchases can result from duty and clearance problems. A consumer may place an order without understanding his or her country's import regulations. When the merchandise arrives, the consumer may not be able to claim it. As a result, the product may be seized or returned on a freight-collect basis. Continued occurrence of this problem could become expensive for the manufacturer.

To solicit orders, a manufacturer may use publications to attract consumers. Many U.S. magazines receive overseas distribution, and the advertisements inside are read by foreign consumers. Other U.S. magazines including *Time*, *Newsweek*, and *Business Week* facilitate the ordering process because they publish international editions. Of course, an advertiser can also place its advertisements directly with foreign publishers. This is the process many countries follow in order to promote the local tourism industry. The 7-Eleven outlets in Japan also facilitate the manufacturer–end user-channel by allowing consumers to come in to inspect the merchandise shipped to them before making a payment.

## Types of intermediaries: indirect channel

For the majority of products, a manufacturer may find it impractical to sell directly to the various foreign parties (i.e., foreign distributors, foreign retailers, state-controlled trading companies, and end-users). Other intermediaries, more often than not, have to come between these foreign buyers and the manufacturer. This section examines the roles of those middlemen located in the manufacturer's country.

With an indirect channel, a manufacturer does not have to correspond with foreign parties in foreign countries. Instead, the manufacturer deals with one or more domestic middlemen, who in turn move and/or sell the product to foreign middlemen or final users. Although there are many kinds of local sales intermediaries, all can be grouped under two broad categories: (1) domestic agents and (2) domestic merchants. The basic difference between the two is *ownership* (*title*) rather than just the physical *possession* of the merchandise. **Domestic agents** never take title to the goods, regardless of whether the agents take possession of the goods or not. **Domestic merchants**, on the other hand, own the merchandise, regardless of whether the merchants take possession or not. An agent represents the manufacturer, whereas a merchant (e.g., distributor) represents the manufacturer's product. The merchant has no power to contract on behalf of the manufacturer, but the agent can bind the manufacturer in authorized matters to contracts made on the manufacturer's behalf.

Agents can be further classified according to the principal whom they represent. Some agent intermediaries represent the buyer; others represent the interest of the manufacturer. Those who work for the manufacturer include export brokers, manufacturers' export agents or sales representatives, export management companies, and cooperative exporters. Agents who look after the interests of the buyer include purchasing (buying) agents/offices and country-controlled buying agents.

## Export broker

The function of an export broker is to bring a buyer and a seller together for a fee. The broker may be assigned some or all foreign markets in seeking a potential buyer. It negotiates the best terms for the seller (i.e., manufacturer) but cannot conclude the transaction without the principal's approval of the arrangement. As representative of the manufacturer, the export broker may operate under its own name or that of the manufacturer. For any action performed, the broker receives a fee or commission. An export broker does not take possession or title to the goods. In effect, it has no financial responsibility other than sometimes making an arrangement for credit. An export broker is less frequently involved in the export (shipping) of goods than in the import (receiving) of goods.

The export broker is useful due to its extensive knowledge of the market supply, demand, and foreign customers. This knowledge enables the broker to negotiate the most favorable terms for the principal. The broker is also a valuable associate for highly specialized goods and seasonal products that do not require constant distribution. An export broker may be thus used on a one-time basis by small manufacturers with limited financial resources who are selling in broad markets.

## Manufacturer's export agent or sales representative

Because of the title of this intermediary, one might easily mistake an export agent or sales representative for a manufacturer's employee when, in fact, this is an independent businessperson who usually retains his or her own identity by not using the manufacturer's name. Having more freedom than the manufacturer's own salesperson, a sales representative can select when, where, and how to work within the assigned territory. Working methods include presenting product literature and samples to potential buyers. An export agent pays his or her own expenses and may represent manufacturers of related and noncompeting products. The person may operate on either an exclusive or nonexclusive basis.

Like a broker, the manufacturer's export agent works for commission. Unlike the broker, the relationship with the manufacturer is continuous and more permanent. The contract is for a definite period of time, and the contract is renewable by mutual agreement. The manufacturer, however, retains some control because the contract defines the territory, terms of sale, method of compensation, and so on.

The manufacturer's export agent may present some problems to the manufacturer because an agent does not offer all services. Such services as advertising, credit assistance, repair, and installation may be excluded. An export agent may take possession but not title to the goods and thus assumes no risk – the risk of loss remains with the manufacturer. Finally, the manufacturer relinquishes control over marketing activities, and this can hurt a manufacturer whose volume is too small to receive the agent's strong support. The experience of Arthur C. Bell, a British firm, is a case in point. James B. Beam, its previous agent in the U.S.A., neglected Bell because its salespeople had too many other products to handle. Bell switched to Monsieur Henri as its new agent. However, this hardly improved the situation because Henri also preferred to concentrate on larger accounts. As a result, Bell was left out of Christmas catalogs or dropped by many retailers. Bell thus contemplated acquiring a U.S. importer to exercise stronger control over its own marketing destiny.

Under certain circumstances, it may not be justifiable for a small manufacturer to set up its own sales force and distribution network. Such circumstances include the following:

1 When the manufacturer has a geographically widespread market – the usual case in international marketing.
2 When some overseas markets are too thin.
3 When the manufacturer's product is new and the demand is uncertain.
4 When the manufacturer is inexperienced in international marketing.
5 When the manufacturer wants to simplify business activities.

A manufacturer can avoid fixed costs associated with having its own sales and distribution organization when it employs an agent, since the commission is paid only when sales are made. A manufacturer's export agent has extensive knowledge of specific foreign markets and has more incentive to work than the manufacturer's own salesperson. In addition, the agent carries several product lines, and the result is that the expense of doing business is shared by other manufacturers. This arrangement allows the manufacturer to concentrate time, capital, and expertise on the production of goods rather on having to deal with the marketing aspect. Of course, if the product is successful, the manufacturer can always set up its own sales force.

## Export management company (EMC)

An export management company manages, under contract, the entire export program of a manufacturer. An EMC is also known as a **combination export manager (CEM)** because it may function as an export department for several allied but noncompeting manufacturers. In this regard, those export brokers and manufacturer's export agents who represent a combination of clients can also be called EMCs. When compared with export brokers and manufacturer's export agents, the EMC has greater freedom and considerable authority. The EMC provides extensive services, ranging from promotion to shipping arrangements and documentation. Moreover, the EMC handles all, not just a portion, of its principal's products. In short, the EMC is responsible for all of the manufacturer's international activities.

Foreign buyers usually prefer to deal directly with the manufacturer rather than through a third party. Therefore, an EMC usually solicits business in the name of the manufacturer and may even use the manufacturer's letterhead. Identifying itself as the manufacturer's export department or international division, the EMC signs correspondence and documents in the name of the manufacturer. This may be an advantageous arrangement for small and medium-sized firms that lack expertise and adequate human and financial resources to obtain exports. This arrangement may be a good way for a firm to develop foreign markets while creating its own identity abroad. The EMC, on the other hand, faces a dilemma because of a double risk: it can easily be dropped by its clients either for doing a poor job or for making the manufacturer's products too successful.

American EMCs are typically small, and a majority of them have six employees or fewer. It is normal for an EMC to have only one or a few managers or market specialists. An EMC typically requires at least a one-year contract to handle a manufacturer's products. More often, it is a three-year contract. This is understandable because it takes at least six to twelve months to produce significant results.

EMCs are compensated in several ways. Frequently, compensation is in the form of a commission, salary, or retainer plus commission. Depending on the product, the commission may be as high as 20 percent, with the 6 percent to 10 percent range being the most prevalent. Some EMCs may require a manufacturer to pay a one-time project fee, and such start-up costs may range from a few hundred dollars to tens of thousands of dollars. Meridian Group, a Los Angeles EMC, has stated that it can help handle sales, distribution, credit, shipping, and everything else. Typically, an export manager charges a fee of between 10 percent and 15 percent of a shipment's wholesale value.

Many EMCs are also traders (i.e., export merchants). As both agents and merchants, they sometimes act as agents and rely on the commission arrangement. When acting as merchants, they engage in the buy-and-resell arrangement. In such cases, they buy merchandise outright and thus take title to the goods. They are compensated by receiving discounts on goods purchased for resale overseas, and such discounts may be greater than what other middlemen receive for the domestic market. They may receive promotion allowances as well. As in the case of Overseas Operations, Inc., it markets builders' hardware, housing accessories, door closures and locks, and computer software and accessories. As an exclusive representative of a number of American manufacturers, the company buys products when orders are received and makes its profit on the markup.

There are several reasons why a firm might use an EMC. It has international marketing expertise and distribution contacts overseas. For the many services provided, an EMC's costs are relatively low due to the efficiencies of scale; that is, costs can be spread over the products of several clients. In addition, the EMC provides shipping efficiency because it can consolidate several manufacturers' products in one shipment. The orders are consolidated at the port and shipped on one ocean bill of lading to the same foreign buyer. By consolidating shipments of products from several principals, a company obtains better freight rates. In addition, many EMCs provide financial services. By guaranteeing payments and collecting from overseas buyers, a manufacturer is assured of immediate payment. By providing all of these services, the EMC allows the manufacturer to concentrate on internal efforts and its domestic market.

Using EMCs, like using other types of intermediaries, does have its disadvantages. First, an EMC prefers new clients whose products complement the EMC's existing product lines. The EMC is very likely not interested in unknown products or new technologies that require too much time and effort in opening new markets overseas. A problem for a small manufacturer may be the extent of support it receives. If a firm seeks to do business with a large EMC, the EMC is not likely to give the small client adequate attention. If a small EMC is used, the EMC may be too small to give attention to all the products of its clients. In general, most EMCs do put in serious effort and are willing and able to provide sufficient services for new clients.

## Cooperative exporter

A cooperative exporter is a manufacturer with its own export organization that is retained by other manufacturers to sell in some or all foreign markets. Except for the fact that this intermediary is also a manufacturer, the cooperative exporter functions like any other export agent. The usual arrangement is to operate as an export distributor for other suppliers, sometimes acting as a commission representative or broker. Because the cooperative exporter arranges shipping, it takes possession of goods but not title.

The cooperative exporter's motive in representing other manufacturers primarily involves its own financial interest. Having fixed costs for the marketing of its own products, the cooperative exporter desires to share its expenses and expertise with others who want to sell in the same markets abroad. Because of these activities, a cooperative exporter is often referred to as a *mother hen*, a *piggyback exporter*, or an *export vendor*. Examples of cooperative exporters include such well-known companies as GE, Singer, and BorgWarner. By representing several clients, the cooperative exporter is regarded as a form of EMC.

The relationship between the cooperative exporter and its principal is a long-term one. The arrangement provides an easy, low-risk way for the principal to start marketing overseas, and the relationship should ordinarily continue so long as unrelated or noncompetitive products are involved. A problem may arise if the principal decides to market a new product that competes directly with the cooperative exporter's own product or those of the exporter's other clients.

## Purchasing/buying agent

An export agent represents a seller or manufacturer; a purchasing/buying agent represents a foreign buyer. By residing and conducting business in the exporter's country, the purchasing agent is in a favorable position to seek a product that matches the foreign principal's preferences and requirements. Operating on the overseas customer's behalf, the purchasing agent acts in the interest of the buyer by seeking the best possible price. Therefore, the purchasing agent's client pays a fee or commission for the services rendered. The purchasing agent is also known by such names as commission agent, buyer for export, export commission house, and export-buying agent. This agent may also become an export-confirming house when confirming payment and paying the seller after receiving invoice and title documents for the client.

The buying agent is valuable for manufacturers because it seeks those firms out and offers them its services. However, since the agent operates on an order basis, the relationship with either seller or buyer is not continuous. This arrangement thus does not offer a steady volume of business for the manufacturer and neither does it offer any reduction in financial risk. In any case, the transaction between the manufacturer and the buying agent (or the agent's customer) may be completed as a domestic transaction in the sense that the agent will take care of all shipping arrangements. Otherwise, the manufacturer will have to make its own arrangements.

## Country-controlled buying agent

A variation on the purchasing agent is a country-controlled buying agent. This kind of agent performs exactly the same function as the purchasing/buying agent, the only distinction being that a country-controlled buying agent is actually a foreign government's agency or quasi-governmental firm. The country-controlled buying agent is empowered to locate and purchase goods for its country. This agent may have a permanent office location in countries that are major suppliers, or the country's representative may make formal visits to supplier countries when the purchasing need arises.

## Resident buyer

Another variation of the purchasing agent is the resident buyer. As implied by the name, the resident buyer is an independent agent that is usually located near highly centralized production industries. Although functioning much like a regular purchasing agent,, the resident buyer is different because it is retained by the principal on a continuous basis to maintain a search for new products that may be suitable. The long-term relationship makes it possible for the resident buyer to be compensated with a retainer and a commission for business transacted.

The resident buyer provides many useful services for a manufacturer. It can offer a favorable opportunity for a supplier to maintain a steady and continuous business relationship so long as the supplier remains competitive in terms of price, service, style, and quality.

For a foreign buyer, the resident buyer offers several useful services, one of which is the purchasing function. The resident buyer uses its judgment to make decisions for its overseas client, which does not have the time to send someone to visit production sites or firms, or which cannot wait to examine samples. Another service provided by the resident buyer is the follow-up function. The resident buyer can ensure that delivery is made as promised. A late delivery can make the purchase meaningless, especially in the case of seasonable or fashion products. If the foreign client decides to visit manufacturing plants or offices, the resident buyer can assist by making hotel reservations, announcing the visit to suppliers, arranging vendor appointments, and so on.

## Export merchant

The intermediaries covered thus far have certain factors in common: they take neither risks nor title, preferring to receive fees for their services. Unlike these middlemen, domestic merchants are independent businesses that are in business to make a profit rather than to receive a fee. There are several types of domestic merchants. Because they all take title, they are distinguished by other features, such as physical possession of goods and services rendered.

One kind of domestic merchant is the export merchant. An export merchant seeks out needs in foreign markets and makes purchases from manufacturers in its own country to fill those needs. Usually the merchant handles staple goods, undifferentiated products, or those in which brands are unimportant. After having the merchandise packed and marked to specifications, the export merchant resells the goods in its own name through contacts in foreign markets. In completing these arrangements, the merchant assumes all risks associated with ownership.

The export merchant's compensation is a function of how product is priced. The markup is affected by the profit motive as well as by market conditions. In any case, the export merchant hopes that the price at which the product is sold will exceed all costs and expenses in order to provide a profit. An export merchant may sometimes seek extra income by importing goods to complement its export activities. The merchant may or may not offer a steady business relationship for its supplier.

## Export drop shipper

An export drop shipper, also known as a *desk jobber* or *cable merchant*, is a special kind of export merchant. As all these names imply, the mode of operation requires the drop shipper to request a manufacture to "drop ship" a product directly to the overseas customer. It is neither practical nor desirable for the shipper to physically handle or possess the product. Based on this operational method, the shipper's ownership of the goods may only last for a few hours.

Upon the receipt of an order from overseas, the export drop shipper in turn places an order with a manufacturer, requesting the manufacturer to deliver the product directly to the foreign buyer. The manufacturer collects payment from the drop shipper, who in turn is paid by the foreign buyer.

Use of a drop shipper is common in the international marketing of bulky products of low unit value (e.g., coal, lumber, construction materials). The high freight volume relative to the low unit value makes it prohibitively expensive to handle such products physically several times. Minimizing physical handling reduces the cost accordingly.

One may question why a manufacturer does not simply deal directly with a foreign buyer, bypassing the drop shipper and saving money in the process – the shipping instructions would reveal the name and address of the foreign buyer. The answer is that the manufacturer can reduce the risk while simplifying the transactional tasks. It is a great deal easier for the manufacturer to call the export drop shipper in the manufacturer's own country instead of trying to sell to and collect from the buyer in a far-away destination.

There are also good reasons why the foreign buyer may not be able to or want to bypass the export drop shipper. The buyer may not have adequate product knowledge or supply knowledge, and the buyer's order may be too small to entice the manufacturer to deal directly. The drop shipper is thus valuable because this kind of merchant is highly specialized in knowing the sources of supply and markets. The drop shipper also has information and advice about the needed product and can arrange all details for obtaining it.

## Export distributor

Whereas export merchants and drop shippers purchase from a manufacturer whenever they receive orders from overseas, an export distributor deals with the manufacturer on a continuous basis. This distributor is authorized and granted an exclusive right to represent the manufacturer and to sell in some or all foreign markets. It pays for goods in its domestic transaction with the manufacturer and handles all financial risks in the foreign trade.

An export distributor differs from a foreign distributor simply in location. The foreign distributor is located in a particular foreign country and is authorized to distribute and sell the product there. The export distributor, in comparison, is located in the manufacturer's country and is authorized to sell in one or more markets abroad. Consider Mamiya, a Japanese manufacturer. J. Osawa is Mamiya's worldwide distributor (i.e., export distributor). Bell and Howell: Mamiya is in turn J. Osawa's exclusive U.S. distributor (i.e., foreign distributor).

The export distributor operates in its own name or in that of the manufacturer. It handles all shipping details, thus relieving the manufacturer of having to pay attention to overseas activities. In other words, the sale made to the export distributor is just like another domestic transaction for the manufacturer. Because the export distributor, as a rule, represents several manufacturing firms, it is sometimes regarded as a form of EMC.

The export distributor usually sells the manufacturer's product abroad at the manufacturer's list price and receives an agreed percentage of the list price as remuneration. That is, the export distributor is either paid commission or is allowed a discount for its purchase. The manufacturer may bill a foreign buyer directly or may allow the distributor to bill the buyer to obtain the desired margin.

## Trading company

Those that want to sell and those that want to buy often have no knowledge of each other or no knowledge of how to contact each other. Trading companies thus fill this void. In international marketing activities for many countries, this type of intermediary may be the most dominant form in volume of business and in influence. Many trading companies are large and have branches wherever they do business. They operate in developing countries, developed countries, and their own home markets. Half of Taiwan's exports are controlled by trading companies. In Japan, general trading houses are known as *sogo shosha*, and the largest traders include such well-known MNCs as Mitsubishi, Mitsui, and C. Itoh. The nine largest trading firms handle approximately half of Japan's imports and exports. Even large Japanese domestic companies buy through trading companies.

A trading company performs many functions: the term describes many intermediaries that are neither brokers nor import merchants. A trading company may buy and sell as a merchant. It may handle goods on consignment, or it may act as a commission house for some buyers. By representing several clients, it resembles an EMC, except for the fact that it (1) has more diverse product lines (2) offers more services, (3) is larger and better financed, (4) takes title (ownership) to merchandise, (5) is not exclusively restricted to engaging in export trade, and (6) goes beyond the role of an intermediary (which provides only export facilitation services) by engaging directly in production, physical distribution channel development, financing, and resource development.

As the name implies, the trading company trades on its own account for profit. By frequently taking title to the goods it handles, its risks of doing business greatly increase. A trading company does not merely represent manufacturers and/or buyers, thus reducing risks, because increased risks are usually accompanied by increased rewards. In the case of WSJ International, which is a trader as well as a representative, profit margins gained on trading are about four times greater than margins on representative sales. It is thus not surprising that trading accounts for half of the company's revenues.

Manufacturers and buyers use trading companies for good reasons. The trading company gathers market information; does market planning and finds buyers; packages and warehouses merchandise; arranges and prepares documents for transportation, insurance, and customs; provides financing for suppliers and/or buyers; accepts business risks; and serves foreign customers after sales. It is, in short, a valuable entity in overcoming cultural and institutional barriers. Nanodata, for example, concluded that it was too expensive to reach unfamiliar and distant market areas. The company hired TKB Technology Trading Corporation, a trading company, to identify suitable European markets for Nanodata's computer and to develop a distribution channel by choosing agents, distributors, or direct subsidiaries. TKB offered entry without expensive staff buildup until Nanodata was ready to do so on its own.

Like other intermediaries, however, the trading company must always face the possibility of being bypassed by its clients, and it thus must offer something of value to its customers. This holds true even for Mitsubishi, the world's largest trader with more than $164 billion in sales. Without its own production, this company could be squeezed out by Japanese clients that would set up their own marketing departments. Mitsubishi's solution in keeping old customers and getting new ones is to give buyers and sellers an incentive to do business with it. It has formed joint ventures with American and Japanese partners with an aim to acquire ownership influence with both its suppliers and customers. Furthermore, this firm cannot be easily replaced due to its long experience, expertise, and established networks.

### *Japanese trading companies*

Because of the spectacular success of the huge Japanese trading companies, many companies – especially those in the U.S.A. – would like to emulate or duplicate them. Japanese trading companies perform a number of marketing functions: market identification and analysis, sales forecasts, buying goods from manufacturers, selling goods to customers, and bearing financial risks (see Figure 12.4).

Japanese trading companies have several distinct characteristics. They are supported by domestic Japanese business. They are partners with groups of banks and other financial intermediaries, allowing them to have easy, convenient, and almost permanent access to enormous amounts of capital and financing.

Traditionally, Japanese manufacturers prefer to separate manufacturing from marketing, leaving the marketing function to trading firms. A new breed of Japanese manufacturers, however, prefers to have more marketing control and has been shifting away from this pattern of specialization by pursuing forward integration. Responding to this adverse trend, the *sogo shosha* is emphasizing its core competence: information gathering. It has transformed itself into an information-based organization.

### *Export trading companies*

In the U.S.A., the Export Trading Company (ETC) Act was passed in 1982. Title III of the 1982 Act allows domestic competitors to obtain binding anti-trust pre-clearance for specified export activities. By granting prior anti-trust immunity, the anti-trust threat was removed, creating a favorable environment for the formation of joint export ventures.

The firms that have recently formed ETCs are from various backgrounds. Some are manufacturers with subsidiaries that have ready access to the parents' products. GE Trading Company, for example, has access to GE's 300,000 products. Retailers such as Sears and Kmart have a great deal of bargaining power because of their enormous purchases, and this leverage serves them well in marketing U.S. exports through foreign retail chains. Other organizations forming ETCs are banks, which seem natural for this purpose. Because banks can own up to 100 percent of an ETC's stock, these ETCs are guaranteed to have adequate financial resources. In some cases, banks and other business firms may want to form a joint venture, as in the case of First Chicago and Sears World Trade, Inc.

One problem with ETCs is that the ETC Act is designed to promote only U.S. exports. Thus ETCs' import activities must adopt a secondary position, undertaken only when they are needed to promote exports. Consequently, ETCs may lack an efficient infrastructure for developing two-way trade. In this regard, ETCs differ greatly from Japanese trading companies, which achieve their efficiencies through domestic, foreign, and third-country trading activities. American ETCs may thus lack a comprehensive international perspective.

WE EXPORTED

# $3.3 Billion

TO JAPAN LAST YEAR FROM AMERICA

Marubeni has built some big markets for the U.S.A. in Japan, in close tie with its subsidiary Marubeni America. And not by chance. Success like this takes more than sales skills: it requires deep insight into the realities that create the Japanese marketplaces, and investment to help shape them. We're the kind of "hands on" trading companies that are geared to meet these challenges squarely.

Consider our record with American high-tech products. Marubeni's had tremendous success marketing sophisticated computers and semiconductor manufacturing equipment from the U.S.A. in Japan. The reason: we've built a complete subsidiary, Marubeni HYTECH, and staffed it with specialists and engineers who know these products inside out. Far beyond sales, our people provide a brand of on-call support and service to customers that's much better than what other importers can do. We even feed back user comments to makers, for product improvement.

Right now, HYTECH is handling sales and support of electronic-industry design systems from such U.S. companies as ECAD, Zycad, Viewlogic and others. Sales of these systems to Japan's IC manufacturers are growing rapidly.

Of course we handle a great many more "Made in U.S.A." goods, too: we export America's agricultural produce and consumer products, we license its services and sell its high-fashion clothing, and we introduce partners for the venture businesses that build the future. Marubeni America Corp. is today, in fact, one of the leaders in increasing U.S. exports, as its $3.3 billion in sales to Japan and $2.2 billion elsewhere attest.

We build world trade in other ways as well. By providing customized financing, investment, leasing, supply of natural resources—even turnkey plant or infrastructure project management.

Take advantage of our skills. Marubeni's 192 offices worldwide are on-line channels of business opportunity, linked by 24-hour satellite telecommunications. Our 13 offices in America are waiting and willing to talk over the business potentials in Japan, or anywhere, any time you'd like.

Always with and for you.

**Marubeni**

C.P.O. Box 595, Tokyo 100-91, Japan

**Marubeni America Corporation Head Office:**
42nd Fl., Pan American Bldg., 200 Park Avenue, New York, N.Y. 10166 Tel. 212-599-3700

**Los Angeles** Tel. 213-972-2700 **San Francisco** Tel. 415-954-0100 **Chicago** Tel. 312-222-6211 **Houston** Tel. 713-654-4000 **Seattle** Tel. 206-624-5850 **Portland** Tel. 503-224-3760 **Dallas** Tel. 214-880-9001 **Detroit** Tel. 313-353-7060 **Boston** Tel. 617-273-4940 **St. Louis** Tel. 314-291-1127 **Washington D.C.** Tel. 202-331-1161 **Nashville** Tel. 615-885-2530

**FIGURE 12.4** Japanese trading company

*Source*: Reprinted with permission of Marubeni America Corporation

## Channel development

The suitability of a particular channel depends greatly upon the country in which it is used. A particular type of intermediary that works well in one country may not work well elsewhere or may lose effectiveness over time. This does not necessarily mean that each country requires a unique channel. However, a company may find that a country classification system is useful, a system that may be used to determine how the distribution strategy should be set up from one group of countries to another.

Litvak and Banting suggest the use of a country temperature gradient to classify countries.[5] Their classification system is based on these environmental characteristics: (1) political stability, (2) market opportunity, (3) economic development and performance, (4) cultural unity, (5) legal barriers/ restrictions, (6) physiographic barriers, and (7) geocultural distance. Based on these characteristics, countries may be classified as hot, moderate, or cold. A hot country is one that scores high on the first four characteristics and low on the last three. A cold country is exactly the opposite, and a moderate one is medium on all seven characteristics.

The U.S.A. generally falls in line with the characteristics of a hot country. So does Canada, even though its cultural unity is moderate (rather than high) and its physiographic barriers are moderate (rather than low). Germany, likewise, is a hot country in spite of some slight interference in the sense that its legal barriers and geocultural distance are moderate rather than low. Brazil, in contrast, largely conforms to a cold country's characteristics.

It is a judgment call whether so many characteristics are necessary for the purpose of classifying countries. The level of economic development could be used as the sole indicator, but such a classification would be misleading because hot countries are not the same as industrialized countries. Still, one must question whether the refinement and improvement in the classification process justifies the extra effort necessary to wade through all relevant characteristics, especially since the level of economic development correlates well with these characteristics. For practicality, a short cut appears to be desirable.

Classification is a means to an end, and the purpose of the country temperature gradient is to determine which intermediary should be used in a given country. The temperature gradient also indicates which kind of intermediary is likely to be functioning in a country. In a cold country, competitive pressures on institutional change are not dynamic. Legal restrictions, for example, can prevent or slow down new distribution innovations. Consider Egypt as an example. Only those born of Egyptian fathers or Egyptian legal entities can represent foreign principals. Being "comfortably cold," middlemen see few threats to their existence. In China, all tobacco must be sold through the China National Tobacco Co. monopoly.

For a hot country, environmental forces may be so hot that new institutional structures arise. Middlemen who fail to adjust will be bypassed and go out of existence. The survival of a channel member is thus a function of the ability to adapt to changing environmental conditions because the channel member cannot hide behind local regulations for protection. For example, in the United Kingdom, either the principal or the intermediary can terminate an agency relationship provided there is a reasonable notice.

The country temperature gradient has implications for all channel members. A foreign manufacturer can exercise maximum control over the evolutionary process in the distribution channel. The firm can initially rely on middlemen/distributors. If sales increase, the manufacturer can bypass the intermediary by setting up a sales branch or subsidiary. This is the trend being followed by foreign liquor suppliers in the U.S. market. These suppliers now very much control their own destiny by being responsible for their own distribution. E. Remy Martin & Co. took its cognac away from Glenmore Distillers and became its own U.S. distributor through its Premier Wine Merchants. Distillers Co., a Scottish firm, did likewise by buying Somerset Importers from Esmark. Pernod Ricard and Monet-Hennessy adopted the same strategy by buying Austin Nichols and Schieffelin, respectively.

A local manufacturer should be alert to any new channel since the new channel may pose a threat to this existing channel. When possible, the manufacturer must pre-empt the competition from utilizing it. Xerox was successful and secure with its direct sales force channel – so secure that, when Japanese competition entered the market, Xerox was totally unprepared. The Japanese invaded the U.S. market quickly and cheaply by using independent office equipment dealers, a channel that had been ignored by Xerox. The Japanese firms had their own direct sales force in large metropolitan areas, but they also supplied their machines to such U.S. firms as IBM, Monroe, and Pitney Bowes, thus exploiting these U.S. firms' extensive sales and distribution networks. Xerox was forced to experiment with such alternative channels as retail stores, direct mail, and part-time representatives.

Wholesalers, especially those involved in high-margin, low-volume operations, are particularly vulnerable to the threat posed by modern institutions. Wholesalers can easily be bypassed if they are successful in promoting their principals' products. Superscope, for example, lost the Sony franchise. On the other hand, if wholesalers do the job poorly, they are also likely to be eliminated or their authority and responsibility reduced. Mitsubishi was so unhappy with Chrysler's performance that the Japanese company developed its own independent dealer network in order to catch up with Toyota and Nissan.

Innovations tend to take place in a hot country before spreading to other hot countries and finally developing countries. Retailing innovations that conform to this description include self-service stores, discount houses, and supermarkets, all of which initially developed in the U.S.A. Hypermarche, on the other hand, is a mass-merchandising method developed in Europe. This retail store is an enormous self-service combination of food and general merchandise, generally displayed in shipping containers. A single set of checkout counters is used. This innovation has had only limited success when introduced in the U.S.A.

The success of an innovation is affected not only by the country temperature gradient but also by several other factors. A certain minimum level of economic development is required to support any form of outlet beyond simple retailing methods. General stores, a dying breed in the U.S.A., are still very common in many countries. Firms' aggressive behavior will also be a determinant of the success of a new retailing method. Other cultural, legal, and competitive factors play an important role too. In developing countries where there is plenty of low-cost labor and where people are accustomed to being waited on, self-service stores, discount houses, and supermarkets are slow in gaining widespread acceptance. In developed countries, by comparison, various factors work in the favor of large modern discount stores/supermarkets, including high population density, urbanization, literacy, and labor costs. In addition, the high income level and relatively even income distribution make refrigerators and automobiles affordable and accommodate infrequent shopping trips and large purchases.

Due in part to globalization, a country's temperature gradient can change over time. India's characteristics have shifted in the direction of a "hot" country. For decades, Indian consumers have mainly relied on *kirana* stores (small neighborhood shops) and produce markets. There are 12 million mom-and-pop stores. Now a retail revolution is taking place. Reliance Industries Ltd and other Indian conglomerates as well as foreign investors are expected to spend more than $25 billion over five years to change the shopping scene.[6] This retail market is expected to more than double to $637 billion by 2015.

## Channel adaptation

Because the standardized approach to international marketing strategy may not apply to distribution strategy in foreign markets, it is imperative that international marketers understand the distribution structures and patterns in those markets. Toward this end, comparative marketing analysis should be conducted. Distribution is likely to be highly adapted to the different conditions in Africa, Latin America, and Asia. These regions' government regulations as well as local customs act as a barrier to distribution standardization.

Some channel adaptation is frequently a necessity. Suspicion and privacy can limit the effectiveness of door-to-door selling or other direct-selling methods. Avon has had to develop other distribution methods in Japan and Thailand. Discount retailing may not be effective in countries where there are many middlemen handling small volumes of merchandise. A traditional distribution channel may seem inefficient, but it may maximize the use of inexpensive labor, leaving no idle resources.

A manufacturer must keep in mind that, because of adaptation, a particular type of retailer may not operate in exactly the same manner in all countries. Whereas a U.S. supermarket emphasized low gross margin, its foreign counterpart may have a relatively high gross margin, emphasizing specialty goods and imported goods to a high degree. Furthermore, that foreign counterpart often operates a ready-to-eat food section. Interestingly, American supermarkets, especially those that have converted into superstores, have begun to do the same.

A particular distribution concept proven useful in one country may have to be further refined in another. Although 7-Eleven pioneered the convenience food store concept in Japan, the Japanese operation has evolved into being more sophisticated than its original counterpart in the U.S.A. 7-Eleven Japan offers its customers steaming fish cakes, canned tea, and rice balls, while accepting payment for utility bills and accepting orders from the Tiffany's catalog. To provide the most popular and latest products, about two-thirds of a typical store's 3000 items will change in a year.

It will be interesting to see how Tesco, a retail giant in the UK, fares in the U.S. market. Tesco's strategy is to start with 300 stores in California, Arizona, and Nevada. These Fresh & Easy stores are positioned as neighborhood stores and compete with quick service restaurants, convenience stores, and supermarkets. Most of them are located in underserved urban neighborhoods, and they target women between the ages of 35 and 54. While the format for Fresh & Easy is based on Tesco's Express convenience stores in the UK, Fresh & Easy is tailored for American shoppers who shop more frequently and in more types of stores than their British counterparts. Tesco's flagship grocery format, with private-label goods accounting for about 40 percent of total merchandise, is deemed inappropriate for the U.S. market. In addition, a convenience store relying on only private label will not compete head-on with U.S. supermarkets.[7]

## Channel decisions

As in any domestic market, the international market requires a marketer to make at least three channel decisions: length, width, and number of channels of distribution. **Channel length** is concerned with the number of times a product changes hands among intermediaries before it reaches the final consumer. The channel is considered long when a manufacturer is required to move its product through several middlemen. The channel is short when the product has to change hands only once or twice. If the manufacturer elects to sell directly to final consumers, the channel is direct.

While Dell Inc. used direct sales on the Internet to surge to number one, it later slipped to second place because HP chose to shift the balance of power toward the retail channel. Dell finally has to adjust its distribution model by starting to ship its computers to Wal-Mart Stores Inc. Acer feels that effective use of the "channel" marketing model has served it well. The approach is to pair Acer with local distributors so as to target small and medium-sized businesses, educational institutions, and home use.[8]

**Channel width** is related to the number of middlemen at a particular point or step in the distribution channel. Channel width is a function of the number of wholesalers and the different kinds that are used, as well as a function of the number and type of retailers used. As more intermediaries or more types are used at a certain point in the channel, the channel becomes wider and more **intensive**. If only a few qualified intermediaries are needed to provide proper product support at a particular level or at a specific location, the channel is **selective**. The product, though perhaps not available everywhere, is still carried by at least a few qualified middlemen within the same area. Finally, the distribution becomes **exclusive** if only one intermediary of one type is used in that particular area.

The watch industry and its distribution strategies provides a good illustration of an industry with various channel widths. Timex, as a low-priced, mass-market product, is intensively distributed in the sense that any intermediary, no matter what kind, is allowed to carry the brand. Seiko is more selective. Seiko, as an upper-medium-priced brand, is sold through jewelry stores and catalog showrooms and is less likely to be found in discount or drug stores. Patek Philippe, in order to promote an image of elegance and exclusivity, limits its U.S. outlets to 100 meticulously selected fine jewelry stores. Figure 12.5 shows that Patek Philippe chooses a channel that enhances an image. A 5970 model, priced for its complex movements, can fetch $103,200.[9]

Channel width is relative. Both Seiko and Omega employ selective distribution, though Omega is much more selective. Omega's tighter policy of selective, limited distribution results in the brand being available only in top jewelry, specialty, and department stores. Because of the relative nature of channel width, it is inappropriate to compare width at the retail level with wholesale width. Because there are many more retailers than wholesalers, the issue of channel width applies only to a particular distribution level rather than through distribution levels. The degree of selectivity depends on the relative, not the absolute, number of intermediaries at a particular distribution level. As a product moves closer to end-users, the distribution channel tends to become broader. At a point closer to the manufacturer, the channel is not as broad. For example, at the distributor level, Brother International is the exclusive U.S. distributor for Japan's Brother Industries.

A wider channel offers greater availability for a product, but it may also dilute the product's image. As in the case of Coach, it has done well in the luxury goods segment. But as it expands its product varieties while opening new stores, the luxury image may suffer from overexposure.[10]

Another decision that concerns the manufacturer is the **number of distribution channels** to be used. In some circumstances, the manufacturer may employ many channels to move its product to consumers. For example, it may use a long channel and a direct channel simultaneously. The use of dual distribution is common if the manufacturer has different brands intended for different kinds of consumers. Another reason for using multiple channels may involve the manufacturer setting up its

A PATEK PHILIPPE DOESN'T JUST TELL YOU THE TIME.
It seems to us that there are certain unique qualities that can be found among the men and women who, over the centuries, have chosen to wear Patek Philippe watches.
Intelligence, for one thing. A delight in logic, for another. An appreciation of beauty. And perhaps most important, as great a respect for *internal* integrity as for *external* appearance.
Of course, we have the advantage of knowing the names of many of the great historical and contemporary figures who have been clients of Patek Philippe.
But we believe that even if you were to judge the watch solely on its own merits, without reference to some of its notable owners, you would come to the same conclusions about their characters as we have.
Here are some of the things that might guide your opinions. For esthetics, as well as function, every working part, down to the tiniest screw or the finest wheel, is microscopically rounded off and polished by hand, to a tolerance of no more than one-hundredth of a millimeter–a virtually frictionless state.
Cutting and pivoting the wheels and pinions alone involve 100 different operations, each one done by hand. And the pinions are lapped and polished on both sides.
In the Patek Philippe mechanical watch as well as the Patek Philippe quartz watch, many internal parts are plated with gold, again for function *and* appearance.
Our *horlogers complets*, complete watchmakers, mount the tiniest parts of a Patek Philippe by hand during the eight to nine month span that it takes to create each individual watch.
And once it is totally assembled, it is taken apart for further refinements.
During manufacture, each movement undergoes a total of 600 or more hours of testing, including testing for its response to cold, heat, humidity, and for wear, in five different positions. Actually, almost half the time of our watchmakers is spent on examination and re-examination of parts and final polishing.
Our quartz watch has only one-third fewer mechanical parts than our mechanical watch, and takes eight months to complete. Almost as long as our mechanical watch.
And the tiny 2.5mm Patek Philippe quartz movement comes from our own electronics factory, where we have been honing our skills in this twentieth century science of electronic timekeeping since 1952.
Ultimately, there is as much difference between a Patek Philippe quartz watch and other quartz watches as there is between a Patek Philippe mechanical watch and other mechanical watches.
For 144 years, our single-minded dedication to perfection has been the context for our company's existence–ever since the French watchmaker, Adrien Philippe, joined forces with the exiled Polish nobleman, Count Antoine de Patek–to create the world's finest watches.
Now that you know a little about the details of our meticulous timepieces, what do you think the ownership of a Patek Philippe, mechanical or quartz, might tell you about yourself?
Something very reassuring, perhaps?
*The Patek Philippe pictured is self-winding, mechanical, with date. For a new and comprehensive presentation of Patek Philippe timepieces, please send $5–or for a brochure of current styles write–to Patek Philippe, 10 Rockefeller Plaza, Suite 629-B, NY, NY 10020.*
PATEK PHILIPPE
IT TELLS YOU SOMETHING ABOUT YOURSELF.

**FIGURE 12.5** Patek Philippe's channel of distribution

*Source*: Reprinted with permission of Henri Stern Watch Agency, Inc.

own direct sales force in a foreign market where the manufacturer cannot remove the original channel (e.g., agents) for strategic or legal reasons. Although Seiko, Lassale, and Jean Lassale are all made by the same Japanese firm, dual channels are used for these brands. Seiko and Lassale are sold through distributors in the U.S.A., whereas Jean Lassale is sold by the manufacturer directly to retailers (jewelers).

## Determinants of channel types

There is no single across-the-board solution for all manufacturers' channel decisions; yet there are certain guidelines that can assist a manufacturer in making a good decision. Factors that must be taken into account include legal regulations, product image, product characteristics, intermediary's loyalty and conflict, local customs, power and coercion, and control.

### *Legal regulations*

A country may have specific laws that rule out the use of particular channels or middlemen. France, for example, prohibits the use of door-to-door selling. Saudi Arabia requires every foreign company with work there to have a local sponsor who receives about 5 percent of any contract. Not surprisingly, many Saudis, acting as agents, have become millionaires almost overnight.

The overseas distribution channel often has to be longer than desired. Because of government regulations, a foreign company may find it necessary to go through a local agent/distributor. In China, foreign firms cannot wholly own retail outlets, and they cannot engage in wholesaling activities. In addition, only 14 foreign retail ventures have direct import authority, forcing those without direct import authority to add another layer of middlemen. Foreign retailers are required to operate through joint ventures, and they can own a maximum of 65 percent of such joint ventures. It is an Asian tradition, however, to circumvent ownership restrictions by having silent partners who have nothing to do with daily operations. Carrefour SA, for example, essentially wholly owned its three north-eastern supermarkets – until the government cracked down on the practice. As a result, Carrefour was forced to transfer 35 percent of the ownership to two domestic trading firms.

Similarly, Bharti Enterprises has formed an alliance with Wal-Mart to open hundreds of stores. The strategic alliance is due in part to restrictions on foreign companies which are not allowed to operate multi-product retail chains in India. Wal-Mart has insisted that it cannot and will not own stores. Instead, it will focus on the back-end supply chain management. The front end will be fully owned and operated by Bharti which has access to Wal-Mart's proprietary know-how in logistics and retail chain management.[11]

Channel width may be affected by the law as well. In general, exclusive representation may be viewed as a restraint of trade, especially if the product has a dominant market position. In Germany, the Federal Cartel Office may intervene with exclusive dealing and distribution requirements. Due to the EU's single market program, geographic barriers between national markets have blurred, making it possible for consumers outside national sales territories to gain greater access to products and services. Therefore, EU anti-trust authorities have increased their scrutiny of "national" and exclusive sales agreements. The Treaty of Rome prohibits distribution arrangements that affect trade or restrict competition (i.e., restrictions on territory, non-competition clauses, and grants of exclusivity). As a matter of fact, in the case of automobiles, the Commission has determined that exclusive distribution limits trade between the member countries, and manufacturers thus have less incentive to price cars on a competitive basis. It has directed the manufacturers to allow the distributors to sell to other dealers and consumers throughout the EU.

## *Product image*

The product image desired by a manufacturer can dictate the manner in which the product is distributed (see Cultural Dimension 12.1). A product with a low-price image requires intensive distribution. On the other hand, it is not necessary or even desirable for a prestigious product to have wide distribution. Clinique's products are sold in only 64 department stores in Japan. Waterford Glass has always carefully nurtured its posh image by limiting its distribution to top-flight department and specialty stores. At one time, it did not take on any retail accounts for a period of a year. Its effort to create an air of exclusivity has worked so well that Waterford Glass commands a quarter of the U.S. market, easily making it the bestselling fine crystal.

### Cultural Dimension 12.1

#### Exposure but not overexposure

To better compete with discount stores, department stores pushed Polo Ralph Lauren, Calvin Klein, Guess, and the other established brands to lower the prices of their jeans. As a result, the average prices fell from $68 to $29. In 2002, Guess had an $11 million loss. Instead of continuing to lower prices and further dilute the image of its brand, Guess? Inc. made its Euro-trendy look more upscale and shifted its denim sources from the U.S.A. to the finer weaves of Italy and Japan. The jeans are stitched and washed in smaller batches. The company opened more Guess stores, and the number has climbed from 118 in 2001 to 706 in 2006. At these stores, the average price of women's jeans is $103, twice as much as what it was a few years ago. There is no resistance from customers, who understand that the higher price is for quality.

Guess has 375 stores outside of the U.S.A. The brand is sold in Europe in fancy specialty stores where the average price of jeans is $168. To keep more of the retail markup, the company has bought back licensing agreements from foreign distributors. Having its own stores allows Guess to feature more Guess products such as watches, shoes, handbags, and fragrances.

In the U.S.A., Samsonite's quality image has taken a hit, as its luggage was even found in Wal-Mart. In Europe and Asia, Samsonite is a premier brand. About 60 percent of the company's sales come from outside the U.S.A. Samsonite is now trying to spruce up its image. It has added leather shoes (available for years in Italy), wallets, and stationery.

Burberry knew that it had a problem when its lower-end products such as stadium hats and scarves became popular, actually too popular, with British soccer fans. These products sold for less than $50, and their popularity undermined the brand's image. To reduce its overexposure, the company discarded those low-end items and launched the Icons luxury collection. The brand has recovered smartly, as evidenced by a 40 percent increase in the stock price.

Sources: "How Guess Got Its Groove Back," *Business Week*, December 18, 2006, 126; "Sleek. Stylish. Samsonite?" *Business Week*, February 26, 2007, 106; and "Best Global Brands," *Business Week*, August 6, 2007, 56–8.

Although intensive distribution may increase sales in the short run, it is potentially harmful to the product's image in the long run. This is a problem faced by Aprica as it moves its strollers beyond department and specialty stores into mass-market outlets such as J.C. Penney and Sears. Tiffany & Co. lost many upper-class customers when it broadened its clientele base. Cartier, trying to restore its esteem, has pared down its retail distribution network, which had proliferated unwisely, by 50 percent in the U.S.A. and 25 percent worldwide.

## Product characteristics

The type of product determines how the product should be distributed. For low-priced, high-turnover convenience products, the requirement is for an intensive distribution network. The intensive distribution of ice cream is an example. Walls' (formerly Foremost's) success in Thailand may be attributed in part to its intensive distribution and channel adaptation. Walls has tailored its distribution activities to the local Thai scene by sending its products (ice cream, milk, and other dairy products) into the market in every conceivable manner. Such traditional channels as wholesalers and such new channels as company-owned retail outlets (modern soda fountains) and pushcarts are also used. Pushcarts are supplied by the company and manned by independent retailers (i.e., sidewalk salesmen) who keep a 20 percent margin. However, traditional channels employing wholesalers, small stores, restaurants, hotels, and schools still account for a majority of sales.

For high-unit-value, low-turnover specialty goods, a manufacturer can shorten and narrow its distribution channel. Consumers are likely to do some comparison shopping and will more or less actively seek information about all brands under consideration. In such cases, limited product exposure is not an impediment to market success.

One should always remember that products are dynamic, and the specialty goods of today may be nothing more than the shopping or even convenience goods of tomorrow. Consider computers, which were once an expensive specialty product that required a direct and exclusive channel. Since the early 1980s, computers have become more of a shopping good, necessitating a longer and more intensive channel. Now computers are sold like TV sets in discount stores.

## Middlemen's loyalty and conflict

One ingredient for an effective channel is satisfied channel members. As the channel widens and as the number of channels increases, more direct competition among channel members is inevitable. Some members will perceive large competing members and self-service members as being unfair. Some members will blame the manufacturer for being motivated by greed when setting up a more intensive network. In effect, intensive distribution reduces channel members' cooperation and loyalty as well as increasing channel conflict. Michelin has been accused of undercutting its own dealers in the U.S. market by not only expanding its dealer network by 50 percent but also adding a direct channel to take national accounts away from dealers. Both actions increased price competition and reduced dealers' loyalty. Apple's problems in Japan were due in part to its addition of new channels even though it already had a major distributor.

One survey measured cooperative decisions involving export managers from the U.S.A. and Peru, during a sequence of three simulated interactions with business partners. During the initial stage of the relationship, decisions made by Peruvian export managers reflected less trust than did those of their American counterparts. During the second stage, Peruvian exporters responded differently to a low level of cheating. Results are generally consistent with cultural differences in attitudes toward in-group vs. out-group members. However, the influence of cultural differences gradually erodes in favor of personal characteristics and relationship-specific history. Therefore, cultural differences between business partners decline in importance as they get to know each other.[12]

## *Local customs*

Local business practices, whether outmoded or not, can interfere with efficiency and productivity and may force a manufacturer to employ a channel of distribution that is longer and wider than desired. Because of Japan's multi-tiered distribution system, which relies on numerous layers of middlemen, companies often find it necessary to form a joint venture with a Japanese firm, such as Pillsbury with Snow Brand, Xerox with Fuji, and KFC with Mitsubishi. Japan's many-layered distribution system is not entirely unique in that part of the world, since the custom in many Far Eastern countries is to have multiple intermediary markups on imported goods. Yet the rule of thumb in Hong Kong is that there should be no more than two layers between a U.S. exporter of finished goods and Hong Kong consumers, usually consisting of an importer, agent retailer, or distributor.

Domestic customs can explain why a particular channel is in existence. Yet customs may change or may be overcome, especially if consumer tastes change. For example, there are some 82,000 British pubs, 50,000 of which are owned by brewing companies; the problem they face is the trend toward beer consumption at home. The pubs have had to adjust by turning themselves into "gastro pubs" – offering stylish up-market food. Some have emulated trendy American bars, selling more wine, and food such as hamburgers.

It is difficult for new firms to enter Russia. The market has a great deal of structural and institutional impediments. The impediments include: horizontal dominance (significant seller and

### Ethical Dimension 12.1

**Organs for sale**

China has attracted a great deal of unwanted attention. Reports have been circulated regarding the growing business of organ transplants. Voluntary organ donations are not common in China since Confucian heritage requires the body to be kept intact out of respect for parents and ancestors. Yet wealthy Chinese and foreign patients are able to secure kidneys, livers, and corneas – so long as they pay hundreds of thousands of dollars for them. Brokers are more than happy to offer their services to arrange transplants. There is a suspicion of prisoners being executed for their organs.

After years of denial, China has admitted that many organs used in transplants are indeed taken from executed prisoners. China, however, claims that permission was granted by executed prisoners. Critics, on the other hand, doubt that death-row prisoners are truly free to give consent or withhold it. Instead, they may have been coerced to become donors. In July 2006, China outlawed all sales of organs.

*Sources*: "Mystery Shrouds Organ Transplants," *San José Mercury News*, May 7, 2007; and "China Admits Executions Feed Organ Transplants," *San José Mercury News*, November 18, 2006.

buyer contraction in regional markets), a high degree of vertical integration and exclusive buyer–seller relationships in certain industrial sectors, geographic segmentation, interregional barriers to trade and investment, and policies that make entry difficult for new firms. The anti-competitive market structure, coupled with the existing dominant firms' anti-competitive conduct, does not leave enough structural economic space for new entrants.[13]

## Power and coercion

The "least dependent person" hypothesis, mentioned earlier in Chapter 11, states that the one party with resources and alternatives can demand more because it needs the other party less. As such, the least-dependent member of the channel has more power and may be able to force other channel members to accept its plan. This hypothesis explains why it has been difficult for Japanese and Korean semiconductor manufacturers to recruit U.S. distributors to reach customers who are too small to buy directly from computer-chip manufacturers. The major U.S. semiconductor manufacturers have long adopted a tacit policy of not allowing their distributors to sell Japanese competitors' products. Avnet Inc., the largest distributor in the U.S.A., had to stop buying chips from Japan's NEC Corp.. Samsung Semiconductor was initially happy when Arrow Electronics Inc., the nation's second-largest distributor of semiconductors, agreed to sell its products. Arrow abruptly terminated the agreement a few weeks later, citing changing business conditions. What happened was that Intel Corp. and Texas Instruments reduced the amount of business conducted with Arrow. It is thus not surprising that only one of the electronics industry's top ten distributors distributes Japanese or Korean chips.

Conceivably, dealers in a developing country do not retaliate against a manufacturer's use of coercive influence strategies. When dealers are highly dependent on manufacturers, they have higher tolerance than dealers in other channel contexts.

One must be careful in applying Western models overseas because their impact may differ in developing countries. The applicability of those models may vary from country to country as well. How distributors perceive influence can affect control and conflict in the relationship. Consequently, influence, as practiced in Western channels, may not be effective in relationships with Asian or Latin American firms. Existing Western literature on channel behavior suggests that a channel member's power stems from the other's dependence. However, in the case of department stores and their suppliers in China, the data show that some dimensions of dependence do not have an impact on channel members' perception of power.[14]

One study investigated how resource- and market-based assets influenced power in international relationships. Based on a sample of distributors from Canada, Chile, Great Britain, and the Philippines, a distributor's power is influenced by asset specificity, predictability, and market knowledge gap. Investment in assets specific to the relationship that cannot be easily obtained by an American manufacturer provides an overseas distributor with power over its U.S. manufacturer.[15]

In the case of fashion retailers, they have several significant concerns about international relationships. They have to cope with strategy non-compliance, perceptual disagreements, and disputes related to decision-making responsibility.[16] International retail franchisors exert control over their franchise networks by employing the following methods: franchise contract, support mechanisms, franchise partner selection, franchise relationship, and use of master/area franchising.[17]

### Control

If it has a choice, a manufacturer that wishes to have better control over its product distribution may want to both shorten and narrow its distribution channel. The EU integration and competitive pressures may encourage manufacturers to get closer to final customers by setting up sales subsidiaries instead of relying on distributors or agents. Absolut vodka, a product of Vin and Sprit (a company in Sweden), is distributed in the U.S.A. by Future Brands. The product is distributed in Europe by Maxxium. To maintain a measure of control, Vin and Spirit bought 49 percent of a joint venture with Future Brands, and it became a partner in Maxxium.

Channel members must be evaluated so that trust can be established. According to one study, it is somewhat surprising that Mainland Chinese sellers and Hong Kong Chinese intermediaries do not have close ties. Because these sellers constrain their use of social information, the intermediaries have to resort to commercial information transfers so as to evaluate the sellers' trustworthiness. Likewise, the Hong Kong intermediaries have to rely on commercial information interactions because their Western buyers do not prefer social information interactions either.[18]

In conclusion, there are a number of factors that affect channel decisions. Some of these factors are interrelated. Empirically, it has been shown that overseas distribution channel choice is affected by culture and other product constraints.

## Distribution in Japan

One good way to understand how a foreign distribution system might differ from that of the Western world is to examine Japan's distribution system. Japan's many-layered distribution system appears to be counterproductive. In modern societies where production is revered, Japan's distribution system seems ancient and inefficient. Employing 8.6 million people, the system consists of multiple layers of overstaffed intermediaries – overstaffed in part due to nepotism. The distribution network has more wholesalers and retailers per capita than any of the advanced industrial nations.

At the wholesale level, Japanese wholesalers perform the warehousing and financing functions in great detail. Because retailers are small and inadequately financed, the retailers shift warehousing and financing responsibilities to their suppliers by placing frequent but small orders. Wholesalers are expected to extend lengthy credit and accept the risk of selling on consignment. Wholesalers are also expected to stock an extensive assortment of goods and to provide rapid delivery. Supplier reliability and wholesaler ability to deliver with a short lead time outweigh any concern about price advantage.

Another distinctive feature of the Japanese wholesaling business is the close and frequent interaction among wholesalers. It is common business practice for wholesalers there to resell products to other wholesalers. Distribution channels in Japan are characterized by multiple layers of wholesalers and many small retailers. Japanese wholesalers have close, personal relationships with other wholesalers, manufacturers, importers, and retailers. Because of these intimate relationships which serve as an informal barrier, foreign firms have difficulties in reaching directly end-users or retailers. Even though the population of Japan is about half that of the U.S.A. and Japan is smaller in geographic size than the state of California, the number of retail outlets in Japan is nearly the same as that in the U.S.A. Overall, the Japanese system of distribution is both complex and inefficient.

The Japanese distribution system exists to serve social as much as economic purposes, and the social or societal goal sometimes overshadows economic logic. Channel members are not altogether different from family members, with all levels and members being tightly interlocked by tradition and emotion. It is a traumatic and sometimes tragic decision if channel members have to be dropped, and such members may be unable to bear the social consequence of losing face.

The familial relationship of firms makes doing business easier, and it is customary for members of the same family unit to prefer sourcing from one another to sourcing on the outside. This tightly knit vendor–customer family relationship is perceived by some foreign firms as a trade barrier, but it is more likely that these foreign manufacturers have failed to understand the system. However, it is not as much a case of the Japanese versus foreign suppliers but rather of an insider against an outsider. Any newcomer, Japanese or foreign, will have a difficult time penetrating the family unit's close organizational ties. The key to succeeding within this network is to work long and hard to become part of the family.

Compared to corporate groups in Germany, Spain, France, and Korea, the well-diversified industrial groups of Japan called *keiretsu* are similar but larger. There are six major *keiretsu* in Japan: Mitsui, Mitsubishi, Sumitomo, Fuyo, Sanwa, and Dai-Ichi. The *keiretsu* system has three major characteristics: (1) cross-ownership of equity (which allows the costs of a negative industry-specific shock to be shared by all other member firms from other industries), (2) close ties to the group's "main bank" (which provides the majority of the firm's debt financing), and (3) product market ties with the other firms in the group (which limit competition by discriminating against outside buyers/sellers).

Legal barriers pose a problem for distribution efficiency. Foreign car manufacturers have to contend with the high cost of opening dealerships in Japan. Japanese regulations prohibit local automobile dealers from sharing facilities with importers even though these dealers may sell products that have nothing to do with automobiles. In the U.S.A., Japanese exporters have no difficulty in lining up American dealers to share their outlets.

For almost 30 years, Japan's controversial Large Scale Retail Store Law protected small and medium-sized retailers by restricting a larger store's size, hours, and operating days. Large retailers, the ones most likely to carry imported goods, were thus unable to modernize the distribution system. One has to be careful about what one may wish for, however. Because of the pressure from the U.S.A. to open up its economy to more efficient international competitors, Japan finally abolished the law in 2000. Unfortunately, Japan has replaced it with the Large Scale Retail Store Location Act that has even more restrictions. Store developers must build enough parking spaces so that, even on the busiest shopping days, no shopper will ever have to wait for a parking space. This requirement is easier said than done. After all, in Japan, land is expensive, and lot sizes are narrow, not to mention a burdensome task of land transfer. On top of all these obstacles, it is exceedingly difficult for any developer to do enough to reduce traffic so as to win building approval.

In spite of the apparent rigidity which exists in Japan, it must be pointed out that Japan, as a "hot" country, is ripe for changes. Japanese retailing, once highly weak and fragmented, has been evolving rapidly. Small retail firms have declined in number by 20 percent, and the total number of retail establishments has decreased as well. These developments clearly show a consolidation of the Japanese retail sector.

Due to structural change in Japan, foreign manufacturers may want to experiment with alternative distribution channels. It is possible to circumvent the Japanese distribution system. Instead of cracking Japan's multi-tiered distribution system, foreign marketers may want to employ certain alternative distribution channels. One channel is to use direct marketing (telemarketing, mail order, and door-to-door selling). Amway Japan Ltd. has been spectacularly successful by adopting the parent's highly effective direct-sales technique. The company rewards Japanese distributors for performance and gives them such titles as Diamond Direct distributors.

Another alternative channel is to establish a retail store. This is what Toys 'Я' Us has done. Costco has followed suit. Costco operates more than 390 outlets worldwide to sell merchandise in big packages under a membership system. It will take time for Japanese consumers to get used to this type of distribution. Many Japanese are accustomed to go on foot to shop daily at local stores. In addition, Japanese homes are small and have only limited storage space. In the end, though, the convenience of driving to big stores and stocking up at lower prices may change their attitudes.[19]

Carrefour has withdrawn from Japan, and Wal-Mart has problems there. As explained by the CEO of Tesco PLC,

> We did not go in a big way. We could see it was complex. We lived in Japanese homes and spent three years researching Japan. We did not bring our format in. Carrefour brought in the French hypermarket. We bought a small business in the convenience sector, which we thought suited shopping in Japan. People shop every day. Small is beautiful in Japan. Western concepts of large, big, extra value don't work.[20]

## Selection of channel members

Because the success of a product depends so much on the efforts of channel members, a manufacturer must carefully screen all potential members. Most Hong Kong trading companies handle such a wide range of products that they may have inadequate time to devote to any additional product. To make matters worse, some agents in Hong Kong are known to take on a new product line for the sole purpose of denying it to other agents, knowing full well that they are not capable of being of much assistance to the new client.

Manufacturers and their intermediaries should determine whether their marketing plans are compatible. It is unwise to assume that a common European (or Asian) business mentality exists across European (or Asian) countries.

Since it is difficult for a manufacturer to learn about distant potential dealers short of a personal and lengthy visit, there is a need to depend on other sources of information. Countries with export promotion programs usually have local offices in their major foreign markets that can provide information about how exporters may contact importers in such markets. Figure 12.6 illustrates how Hong Kong tried to attract U.S. importers.

One good source of information in the U.S.A. is the International Trade Administration, which has available trade lists by industry and country. The U.S. Department of Commerce's *Agent/Distributor Service (ADS)* is designed for firms seeking to identify potential foreign agents or distributors interested in a business relationship. It is a customized overseas search for interested and qualified foreign representatives on behalf of a U.S. client. U.S. commercial officers abroad conduct the search and prepare a report identifying up to six foreign prospects that have personally examined the U.S. firm's product literature and have expressed an interest in representing it.

How the Hong Kong Trade Development Council helps you trade with Hong Kong
SUPPOSE YOU WANTED TO IMPORT SOLAR POWERED PENCIL SHARPENERS?
Or cotton knitwear? Or space-age toys? Or integrated circuit boards? In fact, if you're thinking of importing virtually anything into the United States, you owe it to your company to talk to the Hong Kong Trade Development Council.
Talk to the HKTDC first
A major part of our job worldwide is to put importers like you in touch with suitable manufacturers and exporters in Hong Kong. Our computerised trade enquiry service contains over 22,000 companies currently exporting quality Hong Kong products to the world.
The HKTDC in the United States.
Here in the U.S., there are four HKTDC offices waiting to help answer any questions you may have regarding suppliers, products, quotas, shipping, or anything else. Plus you can see Hong Kong products at most of the big trade fairs in U.S. each year.
To begin, simply visit your HKTDC office and we can tell you who's manufacturing what, where and when. From toys to garments to construction materials.
Talk to us...free
We've been saving the best news for last. Our services in the U.S. offices are absolutely free. So why not visit us soon? You've got absolutely nothing to lose, and everything to gain.
Hong Kong Trade Development Council
Promoting Hong Kong trade worldwide
548 Fifth Avenue, 6/F., New York, N.Y. 10036, U.S.A.
Telephone: (212) 730-0777 Telex: 710 581 6302 HKTDC NYK

**FIGURE 12.6** A trade inquiry service

*Source*: Reprinted with permission of Hong Kong Trade Development Council.

## Representation agreement and termination

Firms often assume that, in the absence of provisions to the contrary, clauses appointing foreign distributors or agents are nonexclusive. Actually, the opposite is often the case. Indonesia prohibits a supplier from appointing more than one distributor or representative in the same territory. Colombia presumes that a sales agent's appointment is exclusive unless the agreement specifically states that the appointment is a nonexclusive one.

It may not be easy to terminate a representation agreement. Based on the assumption that an agent or distributor often invests considerable effort and money to develop the local market for the principal, many countries have enacted **agency termination laws** to protect the interests of agents and distributors. Such laws have a tendency to penalize unilaterally foreign principals that have terminated the agency relationships. These laws often forbid a manufacturer from terminating its relationships with even incompetent channel members without a lengthy notice in advance or without an expensive settlement. For example, without just cause, Bolivia may not allow a principal's product to enter the country. In Abu Dhabi, an agent with a compensation claim pending can legally prevent the importation of the former principal's products.

Despite some variations, contract termination laws of various countries have several common characteristics. First, these laws are constructed in such a way that they provide the agent with considerable leverage. The principal can terminate or refuse to extend an agency agreement without being penalized economically only upon a showing of just cause. For example, the reasons and situations under which the agreement may be validly terminated in Chile are: (1) expiration of the contract term, (2) agent's resignation, (3) death, (4) bankruptcy or insolvency of either party, (5) legal incompetence of either party, (6) marriage of a woman agent, and (7) termination of the functions of the principal, if the agency was based on the exercise of such functions.

Second, the principal is obliged to compensate the agent when the relationship is terminated without just cause. If a fixed-term contract has run for more than one year, Mexico sets the compensation at the value of six months' remuneration plus 20 days' remuneration for every year of service after the first year. In Austria, the damage payment may amount to between one year's and 15 years' average commission. Puerto Rico's required compensation in the event of unjust termination can be excessive, since it includes (1) actual value of expenses incurred by the agent in setting up and running the business, (2) value of the agent's inventories and stock, (3) loss of the agent's profits, and (4) value of the agent's goodwill. The agent may also claim an amount equal to the agent's profit experience for the previous five years or five times the average annual profit.

Third, the compensation and other rights granted to the agent may in some countries not be waived. Sweden, for instance, does not allow the agent to waive the termination notice requirements.

Fourth, the agency contract may not allow the parties to elect another country's law to govern the contract. Bolivia voids choice-of-law clauses since Bolivian law is the sole applicable law.

Fifth, the agent may be considered as an employee of the principal and is thus entitled to the protection of local labor laws concerning dismissal and compensation. The compensation may take the form of a pension.

Sixth, the principal may be required to give notice prior to termination, and the agent may have the right to contest the termination decisions. Sweden stipulates that the notice term be three months when an indefinite-term agreement has been in effect for at least one year. In Switzerland, the law requires a two-month minimum period for termination notice after the first year, and the termination can be effective only at the end of each calendar quarter.

To minimize risk and problems, the principal should carefully structure the representation agreement. In general, certain contract terms must be included. The written contract should identify the parties and their rights and obligations. A time period during which the agreement will be in effect should be stated. When legally permissible, the contract should specify the jurisdiction to handle legal disputes. Arbitration clauses specifying the arbitration body should be included. To avoid ambiguity, it is highly advisable to have an English version that is expressly allowed to prevail.

In Italy, most distribution agreements involve repeated sales of stock to distributors because there is no compensation upon expiration of the contract unless otherwise stipulated. It is more favorable for a manufacturer to avoid an agency relationship which will entitle an agent to certain guarantees. When an agency relationship is established, the manufacturer must make a contribution to an agent's insurance fund (ENASARCO) in order to provide sickness, termination, and pension benefits. Upon termination, the agent receives compensation for the termination itself from the ENASARCO fund. In addition, the agent will also receive compensation for the clientele already provided to the principal, and the compensation is based on the annual value of clientele served by the agent.[21]

MNCs should avoid **evergreen contracts**, which allow agreements to remain in effect or to be automatically renewed until terminated by one of the parties.[22] Such a contract may substantially increase the potential compensation obligations of the exporter under foreign laws on termination of distributors' and sales representatives' contracts. Exporters should therefore have specific expiration dates in their foreign distributorship and sales representative agreements. Many countries regard the third or fourth renewal of even one- or two-year agreements as evidence of an evergreen contract. When renewing agreements, it is thus a good practice for the exporter to change the language of prior texts sufficiently in order to avoid creating the appearance of an evergreen contract. Another useful method of reducing or avoiding compensation payments is to include "just cause" termination provisions. The agreement should have the legally permissible grounds (just causes) for terminating distributors' and sales representatives' contracts in the foreign country in question.

## Black market

Economic activities in search of profit will always take place regardless of what the laws say. Naturally, virtually all countries, regardless of their religious, political, and legal orientations, must contend with the black market. For millennia, smuggling has been a way of life in land-locked Afghanistan. Smuggling is facilitated by the Afghan Trade Transit Agreement (ATTA), signed in 1950, that allows goods to pass from the port of Karachi through Pakistan and over the Afghan border duty-free. Almost all goods bound for Afghanistan make a "U-Turn" and end up back in Pakistan. As an example, a buyer in Afghanistan may import air-conditioners through the Karachi port and move them across the Afghan border 620 miles away. After the trucks unload the appliances on the Afghan side, they go back to Pakistan and wait for the very same appliances to re-enter Pakistan illegally, carried by donkeys, camels, or on tribesmen's backs. Such goods sell for a great deal less in Pakistan than legally imported items. Incidentally, a trucking industry largely controlled by Afghan refugees is used for the transportation of these products. According to the World Bank, this illegal trade amounted to $2.5 billion in 1997.[23]

While the legality of a gray market is uncertain, a black market is most certainly illegal. While a black market usually conjures up an image of small-time crooks and mafia-type organizations, several large multinationals have been accused of smuggling or abetting it. JTI-Macdonald, a Canadian tobacco manufacturer, and its four U.S.-based affiliates were charged with fraud and evasion of hundreds of millions of dollars in duties and taxes. These companies were accused of supplying Canada's black market. The scheme involved exporting their Canadian-brand cigarettes, manufactured in Canada and Puerto Rico, to the U.S.A., "knowing that these products were being smuggled back into Canada and onto the commercial market."[24] According to internal documents obtained by anti-smoking groups, some cigarette companies engage in smuggling their own brands into countries. The tactic is employed for the purpose of using cheap illegal products to increase sales. The average value of the illegal tobacco trade is believed to be 8 percent of global cigarette sales. In Brazil, the rate may reach 30 percent.[25]

## Gray market

A gray market exists when a manufacturer ends up with an unintended channel of distribution that performs activities similar to the planned channel; hence the term **parallel distribution**. Gray market

### Legal Dimension 12.1

**American Coke vs. Japanese Coke**

Japan is Coca-Cola's most lucrative market, making the company $1 billion in profits before taxes. About 50 percent of Coca-Cola's products in Japan are sold through vending machines, resulting in a profit of $1.26 per case – compared with 94 cents in Germany and only 28 cents in the U.S.A. Some entrepreneurs want to share that profit. As a result, consumers in Japan can buy either Japan-made Coke or Coke that comes from the U.S.A. The price of American Coke is roughly 40 percent lower, in spite of the shipping costs. Coca-Cola certainly does not like it and has gone after two small exporters – Omni Pacific and Dependable Vending. Coke's lawsuits state that sale of its products outside the specified regions raises quality-control issues, infringes its trademark rights, and violates bottlers' contracts.

The exporters have fought back and filed a countersuit contending that Coca-Cola itself has provided some Japanese bottlers with the discounted American-made Coke so as to undercut the exporters. Coca-Cola is accused of unfairly trying to control prices worldwide by using such methods as threats of legal action, requiring bottlers not to do business with suspected transshippers, and issuing blacklists of certain companies that distributors cannot sell to. These methods violate foreign fair-trade laws and American anti-trust statutes. Ironically, Dependable Vending gets its goods from Coca-Cola Enterprises, the biggest bottler, which eagerly sells to anyone in order to meet its targets.

Coca-Cola also went after Mushi Pardhan, a Tanzanian immigrant in Canada. Pardhan bought Coke products wholesale in Canada and shipped the "gray goods" to Hong Kong and Japan for a 14 percent profit margin. He bought a case for $4.25 (plus transport cost) and resold it for more than $6. The sales reached $4.8 million on a weekly basis. Coca-Cola, suing for trademark infringement, shut Pardhan down in 1995. A federal judge subsequently ruled that Pardhan bought and sold the products legally, and the Canadian Supreme Court refused to accept Coca-Cola's appeal.

*Sources*: "Coke Flips Its Top over Japan Sales," *San José Mercury News*, January 26, 2000; and "Distributor Dilemmas," *PROMO*, August 2000, 20.

goods move through this extra channel, internationally as well as domestically. In an international context, a gray market product is one imported by an unauthorized party. Products notably affected by this method of operation include watches, cameras, automobiles, perfumes, and electronic goods. The problem is particularly acute for Seiko, because one out of every four Seiko watches imported into the U.S. market is unauthorized.

A gray marketer may acquire goods in two principal ways. One method is to place an order directly with a manufacturer by going through an intermediary, in order to conceal identity and purpose. Another method is to buy the merchandise for immediate shipment on the open market overseas. Asian countries in general and Hong Kong in particular are favorite targets because the wholesale prices there are usually much lower than elsewhere. The importance of the gray market even prompts some countries to specialize in handling such goods for the third country, primarily the U.S.A. Germany stimulates the practice by rebating all import duties and local VAT for re-exports. Paris' Roissy Airport is popular with international brokers because of its duty-free warehouse space for transshipments, which are not taxed either. The airport also allows quick delivery because goods simply move through it without any intermediate delivery.

The existence of the gray market has stimulated a great deal of debate. Complaints are made, and responses to the charges offered. At least four questions must be asked. First, why does the gray market exist? Second, are gray market goods illegal? Third, do gray marketers perform any useful functions? Fourth, are gray market goods inferior?

## Causes

Gray marketing of a product within a market often takes place because of the channel structure and margins. A manufacturer which wants to eliminate the potentially profitable gray marketing activity should restructure its pricing and discount policies. Parallel importation of trademarked products occurs for several reasons: (1) gray marketers can easily locate sources of supply because many trademarked products are available in markets throughout the world, (2) price differences among these sources of supply are great enough, and (3) the legal and other barriers to moving goods are low.

Although there are several causes, price differential is the only true reason for the gray market to exist. There is no justification for the existence of the gray market unless prices in at least two domestic markets differ to the extent that, even with extra transportation costs, reasonable profits can be made. This is a good example of economic forces at work. Gray market goods can be purchased, imported, and resold by an unauthorized distributor at prices lower than those charged by manufacturer-authorized importers/distributors. As a result, identical items can carry two different retail prices.

## Legal dimension

At one time, the question of whether gray market goods are illegal or not could not be answered with a great degree of certainty. Unlike the black market, which is clearly illegal, the gray market, as its name implies, is neither black nor white – legality is in doubt. For the U.S. market, all U.S.-registered trademark owners are protected under the Tariff Act of 1930 and Section 42 of the Lanham Act. The law *protects an independent American trademark owner* who invests money in promoting a brand to the extent that the owner becomes identified with that brand in the U.S.A. The protection is granted to protect the mark owner from unfair competition by those seeking to sell the same goods without authorization. If the owner of a U.S. trademark bought distribution rights from an "unrelated" foreign manufacturer, that owner is thus able to obtain an exclusion order from the Customs Service to forbid entry of goods bearing his brand name. Thus, only *independent American firms* are entitled to seek this protection. An exclusion order is not granted to foreign companies, and this includes those using their own U.S. subsidiaries to import their goods into the U.S.A. As a result, Canon and Minolta were unable to register their trademarks with U.S. Customs for the purpose of banning entry of gray market goods.

At present, the law seems to be more on the side of parallel distributors (see Legal Dimension 12.2). The U.S. Court of Appeals ruled that a trademark owner receives no injury to its reputation because there is no confusion about the product's origin and that a manufacturer is capable of labeling and advertising to inform the public of the lack of warranty of gray market merchandise. Courts in other countries often adopt the same position. Japanese judges repeatedly rule for gray market importers. The British Fair Trading Act allows wholesalers to sell to any retailers, who in turn can buy from any wholesalers. The Ninth U.S. Circuit Court of Appeals held that "this country's trademark law does not offer [the manufacturer] a vehicle for establishing a discriminatory pricing scheme simply through the expedient of setting up an American subsidiary with nominal title to its mark."

The U.S. Supreme Court's rulings on two separate cases, though somewhat contradictory, appear to endorse gray marketing. Sharp electronics Corp. stopped selling calculators to Business Electronics Corp., a Houston discount retailer, after receiving a complaint from a full-price retailer. The Supreme Court rules that such a cut-off is not an automatic violation of federal anti-trust law because Sharp did not explicitly set prices. The High Court, arguing that higher prices lead to better service which

## Legal Dimension 12.2

### Black market

The European Union filed lawsuits against Philip Morris and R.J. Reynolds, accusing them of organizing and running a multibillion-dollar international cigarette smuggling operation. The federal civil racketeering lawsuits alleged a conspiracy that evaded billions of dollars in customs payments, duties, fees, and taxes from the EU. To facilitate smuggling, these tobacco giants knowingly mislabeled or did not label their cigarettes, and they arranged practically untraceable payments for smuggled cigarettes that included money re-routed to Swiss bank accounts. In the case of R.J. Reynolds, the smuggling trail started in its Miami office. Winstons were sold there to Copaco, a Panama company. Cigarettes were shipped from North Carolina to Panama and then to the Netherlands. Shippers in the Netherlands next attached documents to show that the cigarettes were sent to the Canary Islands or Eastern Europe. Actually, the shipment was trucked to be sold in Spain.

The European Union later filed another lawsuit in New York against R.J. Reynolds to seek compensation for money laundering. According to the EU's estimates, it lost several billion dollars in taxes every year due to smuggling of cigarettes from Eastern Europe and the Middle East into the EU. American companies supposedly and intentionally oversupplied Eastern European countries and elsewhere so that the surplus could be smuggled into the EU.

*Sources*: "Two Tobacco Giants Accused of Smuggling in Europe," *San José Mercury News*, November 7, 2000; and "EU Files New Suit Against R.J. Reynolds," *San José Mercury News*, November 1, 2002.

benefits consumers, held that manufacturers can cut off "free riders" who take unfair advantage of the greater service provided by full-price firms. In a five-to-four vote in another case, however, the Supreme Court legitimized the gray market. The Tariff Act of 1930 allows imports to be blocked only when requested by a U.S. firm that was authorized by an unaffiliated foreign trademark owner to distribute its products. Foreign goods can be imported when the foreign and domestic trademark holders are "subject to common ownership and control."

At one time, certain exclusive sales territories were supported by non-tariff barriers between member states of the European Union. However, the EU's elimination of non-tariff barriers and border controls has made it possible for parallel imports to move freely across the EU, resulting in price competition. Under the EU concept of parallel imports, suppliers and distributors of products in one member state cannot use exclusive sales arrangements to conspire to block parallel imports of identical products from dealers in other member states. Such actions are a violation of EU anti-trust laws.

The only industry-specific exception to the EU's normal competition principles is the automobile industry. The rules governing new car sales, known as "block exemption," restrict car dealers' competition. Even then, the rules still require manufacturers to sell their cars to any EU citizens regardless of where they live. Volkswagen was found to have prevented Germans and Austrians from buying Volkswagen and Audi cars in Italy where the prices were cheaper. The European Commission fined Volkswagen a massive amount of 102 million euros. The amount was later reduced to 90 million euros because the EU's Court of First Instance ruled that the European Commission did not prove that Volkswagen cancelled some dealer franchises so as to punish them for facilitating cross-border sales. In the end, the European Court of Justice, the EU's High Court, upheld the ruling in 2003.

### Ethical dimension

To manufacturers and authorized dealers, parallel distributors are nothing but freeloaders or parasites who take advantage of the legitimate owners' investment and goodwill. Manufacturers also feel that these discounters deceive buyers by implying that gray market goods are of the same quality and warranties as items sold through authorized channels.

Gray marketers naturally see the situation differently. They feel that manufacturers try to have it both ways – tolerating gray marketing when they need to get rid of surplus merchandise and condemning gray marketers when that need subsides. Gray marketers also accuse manufacturers of not wanting to be price competitive and view manufacturers' distribution restrictions as a smokescreen for absolute price control. Parallel distributors claim to align themselves more with consumers by providing an alternative and legal means of distribution, a means capable of delivering the same goods to consumers at a lower but fair price under the free enterprise system. Some parallel distributors have even sued Mercedes-Benz for restraint of trade, which is a violation of the Sherman and Clayton Acts. As pointed out by them, trademarks are designed to counter fraud rather than limit distribution.

### Product quality

With regard to the charge that gray market goods are inferior, manufacturers and authorized dealers refuse to service such goods by pointing out that gray market goods are not for U.S. consumption.

Therefore, such goods are adulterated, second-rate, or discontinued articles, and consumers may be misled into believing that they receive identical products with U.S. warranties. One study found that price–quality inference and risk averseness negatively affected consumer attitude toward gray-market goods.[26]

Gray marketers, however, do not buy this argument. According to them, there is really no proof that the products they handle are inferior. It is inconceivable that a manufacturer would stop a production line just to make another product version for the non-U.S. market. As such, gray market goods are genuine products subject to the same stringent product controls. Concerning the inferior warranty and the manufacturer's refusal to service gray market goods under warranty terms, parallel distributors show no concern because they have their own warranty service centers that can provide the same, if not better, service. Their service offers are often closer to the market being served. Gray marketers also point out that they would not survive in the long run if they did not provide service and quality assurance.

## *Manufacturers' marketing strategies*

The arguments used by both sides are legitimate and have merits. Only one thing is certain: authorized distributors are adversely affected by parallel distribution. They lose market share as well as control over price. They may have to service goods sold by parallel competitors, and loss of goodwill follows when consumers are unable to get proper repair.

Manufacturers and authorized distributors definitely see the need to discourage gray marketing. There are several strategies for this purpose, and each strategy has both merits and problems. Although tracking down offenders costs money, disenfranchisement of offenders is a stock response. This move sends loud signals of commitment to distributors who abide by the terms of the franchise agreement. A one-price-for-all policy can eliminate an important source of arbitrage, but it ignores transaction costs and forecloses valid price discrimination opportunities among classes of customers who are buying very different benefits in the same product. Another strategy is to add distributors (perhaps former gray market distributors) to the network, but this approach may create disputes among current distributors.

There are both reactive and proactive strategies that may be employed (See Tables 12.1 and 12.2).[27] Reactive strategies to combat gray market activity are strategic confrontation, participation, price cutting, supply interference, promotion of gray market product limitations, collaboration, and acquisition. Proactive strategies are product/service differentiation and availability, strategic pricing, dealer development, marketing information systems, long-term image reinforcement, establishing legal precedence, and lobbying.

Certain strategies warrant further attention. When wanting to track the trail of gray market goods, manufacturers can use serial numbers on products and warranty cards to identify those who are involved in unauthorized distribution. There are two problems related to this strategy. First, using special model numbers or identifying special model numbers or identifying marks on products increases inventory costs and affects the manufacturer's flexibility in re-routing products quickly and cheaply to markets with a sudden surge in demand. Second, even when unauthorized dealers are identified, there is a question of whether anything can be done to rectify the situation. When Canon stopped shipments to the Netherlands, Dutch dealers simply imported Canon cameras from Germany instead. Furthermore, any overt and concerted action against gray market dealers may be construed as an illegal restraint of domestic and international commerce.

**TABLE 12.1** Reactive strategies to combat gray market activity

| *Type of strategy* | *Implemented by* | *Cost of implementation* | *Difficulty of implementation* | *Does it curtail gray market activity at source?* | *Does it provide immediate relief to authorized dealers?* | *Long-term effectiveness* | *Legal risks to manufacturers or dealers* | *Company examples* |
|---|---|---|---|---|---|---|---|---|
| Strategic confrontation | Dealer with manufacturer support | Moderate | Requires planning | No | Relief in the medium | Effective | Low risk | Creative merchandizing by Caterpillar and car dealers |
| Participation | Dealer | Low | Not difficult | No | Immediate relief | Potentially damaging reputation of manufacturer | Low risk | Dealers wishing to remain anonymous |
| Price cutting | Jointly by manufacturer and dealer | Costly | Not difficult | No, if price cutting is temporary | Immediate relief | Effective | Moderate to high risk | Dealers and manufacturers remain anonymous |
| Supply interference | Either party can engage | Moderate at the wholesale level, high at the retail level | Moderately difficult | No | Immediate relief or slightly delayed | Somewhat effective if at wholesale level; not effective at retail level | Moderate risk at wholesale level; low risk at retail level | IBM, Hewlett-Packard, Lotus Corp., Swatch Watch U.S.A., Charles of the Ritz Group Ltd., Leitz, Inc., NEC Electronics |

| | | | | | | | | |
|---|---|---|---|---|---|---|---|---|
| Promotion of gray market product limitations | Jointly, with manufacturer leadership | Moderate | Not difficult | No | Slightly delayed | Somewhat effective | Low risk | Komatsu, Seiko, Rolex, Mercedes-Benz, IBM |
| Collaboration | Dealer | Low | Requires careful negotiations | No | Immediate relief | Somewhat effective | Very high risk | Dealers wishing to remain anonymous |
| Acquisition | Dealer | Very costly | Difficult | No | Immediate relief | Effective if other gray market brokers don't creep up | Moderate to high risk | No publicized cases |

*Note*: Company strategies include, but are not limited to, those mentioned here.
*Source*: S. Tamer Cavusgil and Ed Sikora, "How Multinationals Can Counter Gray Market Imports," *Columbia Journal of World Business* 23 (winter 1988, 78).

**TABLE 12.2** Proactive strategies to combat gray market activity

| *Type of strategy* | *Implemented by* | *Cost of implementation* | *Difficulty of implementation* | *Does it curtail gray market activity at source?* | *Does it provide immediate relief to authorized dealers?* | *Long-term effectiveness* | *Legal risks to manufacturers or dealers* | *Company examples* |
|---|---|---|---|---|---|---|---|---|
| Product service differentiation and availability | Jointly, with manufacturer leadership | Moderate to high | Not difficult | Yes | No; impact felt in medium to long term | Very effective | Very low risk | General Motors Ford, Porsche, Kodak |
| Strategic pricing | Manufacturer | Moderate to high | Complex; impact on overall profitability needs monitoring | Yes | Slightly delayed | Very effective | Low risk | Porsche |
| Dealer development | Jointly, with manufacturer leadership | Moderate to high | Not difficult; requires dealer participation | No | No; impact felt in long term | Very effective | No risk | Caterpillar, Canon |

| | | | | | | | | |
|---|---|---|---|---|---|---|---|---|
| Marketing information system | Jointly, with manufacturer leadership | Moderate to high | Not difficult; requires dealer participation | No | No; impact felt after implementation | Effective | No risk | IBM, Caterpillar Yamaha, Hitachi, Komatsu, Lotus Development, insurance companies |
| Long-term image reinforcement | Jointly | Moderate | Not difficult | No | No; impact felt in long term | Effective | No risk | Most manufacturers with strong dealer networks |
| Establishing legal precedence | Manufacturer | High | Difficult | Yes, if fruitful | No | Uncertain | Low risk | COPIAT, Coleco, Charles of the Ritz Group, Ltd. |
| Lobbying | Jointly | Moderate | Difficult | Yes, if fruitful | No | Uncertain | Low risk | COPIAT, Duracell, Porsche |

*Note*: Company strategies include, but are not limited to, those mentioned here.

*Source*: S. Tamer Cavusgil and Ed Sikora, "How Multinationals Can Counter Gray Market Imports," *Columbia Journal of World Business* 23 (winter 1988, 82).

Another strategy involves educating consumers. Minolta ran advertisements to inform consumers that gray market cameras have inferior warranty. This strategy is risky because the message implies that something is wrong with the manufacturer's own products.

The most effective way to eliminate the gray market is to eliminate the cause – price discrepancy between markets. Price matching can put gray retailers out of business overnight. But this method requires the manufacturer to reduce prices in the most profitable markets. Another problem with this strategy is that it adversely affects the product's prestige image and brand value. Certain brands are successful due to their snob and exclusivity appeal, and they are promoted as luxury articles that must be expensive. In the case of automobiles, price cutting would disrupt both insurance rates and resale values, creating a peculiar situation by making new cars less expensive than used ones.

To resolve some of the problems pointed out above, the strategy of product differentiation should be used. Porsche makes its cars for the U.S. market more powerful and better equipped in order to reflect the higher price. The assumption here is that the differences in features are noticeable and justify the price differential. Multiple brands can also be employed for the same product, with each brand assigned to a certain market. Like other strategies, however, the use of multiple brands affects the economies of scale and increases the production, inventory, and marketing costs.

One study uses the gray market activity as an independent variable and strategic export performance and economic export performance as the dependent variables. Gray marketing does not greatly harm exporters' economic performance because it also generates sales of its own. However, gray marketing interferes with exporters' efforts to achieve their strategic goals. Contrary to traditional thinking, foreign currency and inflation rate fluctuations do not appear to spur gray marketing. Likewise, it is often assumed that a company's exposure to overseas markets should give it internal skills to create an organizational environment that is capable of combating gray marketing. However, according to the empirical evidence, a company's international experience and the number of its markets have insignificant relationships with unauthorized imports. On the other hand, the low level of gray marketing is associated with distribution control, integrated channels, centralization, and product standardization.[28]

Some companies rely on severe enforcement to deter gray marketing. Based on the results of one study, however, enforcement severity per se has no impact. Deterrence occurs when the multiple facts of enforcement are combined. The certainty and enforcement speed may deter violations.[29]

## Distribution of services

Services, just like products, also need distribution. As such, service providers need to design their distribution channels. The various determinants and decisions previously discussed should apply to the marketing of services as well.

In general, services can be exported through four distinct modes: cross-border, consumption abroad, commercial presence, and movement of personnel.[30] The first mode is *cross-border*. This mode occurs when neither the producer nor the consumer physically moves. Instead, the services are provided through a common channel such as the Internet. Education and training (i.e., distance learning) and professional services such as accounting are typical cross-border supply services.

*Consumption abroad* is the second mode. This takes place when the consumer/buyer is in the supplier's country. Tourism is a good example of this mode of delivery.

*Commercial presence*, as the third mode, occurs when the supplier establishes a local office in the country where the service is to be provided. Typical services that employ this mode include financial and consulting services.

Finally, *movement of personnel* consists of staff from the service company moving to the country where the service export is provided. Temporary ventures, such as engineering or construction projects, are examples of this type of service delivery. Employees from the firm travel to and provide contracted services for the duration of the project.

Let us consider the case of the education and training sector (see Figure 12.7). The sector includes services defined at the level of post-secondary education, and it includes education services ranging from diploma and certificate through doctoral and post-doctoral degrees. Regarding distribution, the four modes of supply mentioned above certainly apply to the exporting of post-secondary education and training. A U.S. institution may deliver online courses to foreign students based in their home countries. A more familiar form is for foreign students to travel to an American or European university for consumption abroad. Several European and American universities have now established a commercial presence by opening a branch campus/training facility in a foreign country through which they offer their courses and programs. Last but not least, Western institutions and corporations have also relied on movement of personnel in the sense that their faculty and trainers are sent abroad to deliver a course to consumers in another country.

## Conclusion

A product, no matter how desirable, must be made accessible to buyers. A manufacturer may attempt to use a direct distribution channel by selling directly to end-users abroad. The feasibility of this channel depends on the type of product involved. Generally, the sales opportunity created by direct selling is quite limited. Intermediaries are usually needed to move the product efficiently from the manufacturer to the foreign user.

This chapter has discussed the roles of domestic and overseas middlemen. The manufacturer has the option of selling or assigning sales responsibility to intermediaries in its own country and letting them decide about reselling the product elsewhere. Another option for the manufacturer involves bypassing intermediaries and dealing directly with foreign buyers, assuming that the manufacturer has enough expertise, market familiarity, resources, and commitment. With myriad intermediaries available, it is impossible to prescribe a single distribution method ideal for all products and markets.

A number of factors – such as product type, regulations, customs, power, control, and intermediary loyalty – must be taken into account in designing and developing an international channel of distribution. These factors determine how long, how wide, and how many channels are appropriate. Ordinarily, those intermediaries that fail to add some value to the product as it moves through them are likely to be bypassed or dropped from the channel. But the manufacturer cannot afford to dictate terms, because an intermediary will carry a manufacturer's product only if the manufacturer minimizes channel conflict as well as providing some value to these sales intermediaries in return.

A WORLD-CLASS MBA
WITHOUT INTERRUPTING
YOUR CAREER
Top-ranked Duke University's Fuqua School of Business delivers an MBA degree that prepares students for global success through a world-class combination:
FORMAT - Three distinct programs tailored to different stages of careers and personal lives allow students to maintain career momentum and apply their knowledge immediately.
FACULTY - Ranked No.1 by Business Week in intellectual capital for quality of scholarship.
PEERS - Collaboration with high-caliber professionals from around the world.
THE DUKE MBA - WEEKEND EXECUTIVE
This established and highly respected program meets alternate weekends on the Durham, NC campus. Gain strategic vision while participating on diverse teams with managers averaging 11+ years of work experience.
THE DUKE MBA - GLOBAL EXECUTIVE
This pioneering program, designed for executives with an average of 14 years' experience and global responsibilities, combines traditional teaching with Internet-enabled distance learning. Residencies in Asia, South America, Europe and the U.S. enhance understanding of global business.
THE DUKE MBA - CROSS CONTINENT
This unique 20-month program is geared toward high-potential professionals with 3 to 9 years of experience. Maximizes flexibility by combining week-long residencies in either Durham, NC or Frankfurt, Germany with Internet-enabled distance learning from anywhere in the world.
FOR A WORLD-CLASS EDUCATION SUITED TO YOUR NEEDS, JOIN US AT THE FUQUA SCHOOL OF BUSINESS.
Telephone: 919.660.7804 USA
Telephone: 49.69.9726990 EUROPE
www.fuqua.duke.edu
We Educate Thoughtful Business Leaders Worldwide
DUKE'S EXECUTIVE MBA RANKED #2 BY U.S. NEWS & WORLD REPORT
DUKE
THE FUQUA SCHOOL OF BUSINESS
Duke University
The Fuqua School of Business

**FIGURE 12.7** Distribution of education

# CASE 12.1 MANAGING CHANNEL CONFLICT IN THE GLOBAL IT INDUSTRY

**Carol Reade, San José State University**

With continued reduction of trade barriers and liberalization of markets, global corporations are making inroads into new markets and using local distribution channels. Competency and trustworthiness are well-known considerations for the selection of channel members. What is less well known is the extent to which the relationship between channel members may impact upon business success. This case, based on the author's consulting work, illustrates the challenge of managing channel conflict in a South Asian operation of a large, international manufacturer of computer hardware. All names are pseudonyms.

## The conflict

Fabulous Computers International manufactures computer hardware. Its marketing campaign focuses not only on quality computers, but increasingly on quality customized solutions and quality after-sales service. Paradise Computers (Paradise) is a subsidiary of Fabulous Computers International. Paradise distributes Fabulous computers through a network of local vendors which provide customized software and hardware systems solutions. The vendors operate on a quota system. Each vendor is rewarded for making the sales quota, and receives a bonus for every sale made beyond quota.

Recently, Paradise received two complaints against its oldest and largest vendor, Vendor A. Vendor A, which was the first in the country to sell Fabulous computers, has an established reputation for selling Fabulous products and achieves high sales volume. Vendor A has a highly motivated and aggressive sales force which is good at identifying new clients. One of the complaints against Vendor A came from a new client, Starbrite, which has a rapidly expanding garment business. Starbrite claims that Vendor A did not have the expertise to install the agreed-upon customized software solution. As a result Starbrite's system continually crashed for two months, causing loss of business.

The second complaint against Vendor A came from Vendor Z. Vendor Z, which has been associated with Paradise for less than a year, has an excellent reputation for the design and installation of sophisticated systems. It is new to selling computer platforms. Vendor Z has complained that Vendor A continually poaches potential clients, either by accepting thinner margins on the same product or by talking the client into less costly, lower capacity products which are not in the customer's best interest over the long term. Starbrite was one such potential client.

## The management challenge

The Paradise management is very concerned about these complaints. Vendor A has been Paradise's most loyal and valuable vendor in terms of sales volume. The complaint from Starbrite reveals that Vendor A has limited expertise with designing sophisticated solutions. Starbrite had talked extensively with Vendor Z about its systems needs, and incorporated Vendor Z's recommendations into its tender specifications. Vendor A responded to the tender notice proposing a lower capacity, lower cost solution. Although Vendor A assured Starbrite that the lower capacity system would be fine, it proved to be inadequate. Vendor A's strength is in selling and installing solutions for cost-conscious clients with simple business models.

The market has become more competitive with a flood of competing brands. At the same time, client needs are becoming more sophisticated. While the Fabulous brand continues to be strong, Paradise's competitive edge rests increasingly on customized systems solutions and after-sales service.

In keeping with this trend, Paradise has taken on vendors like Vendor Z, which has a team of software engineers with expertise in the design, installation, and trouble-shooting of sophisticated systems. These vendors are not yet as loyal to Fabulous products as the older vendors, and may shift to selling other brands if they feel they are blocked from selling Fabulous products. Vendor Z has expressed an intention to pull out of the arrangement with Paradise if Vendor A continues to poach its potential clients. The Paradise management feels that losing Vendor Z would be a blow to its competitive strategy. Moreover, management are concerned that if they do not find ways to manage this conflict among their business partners, they may lose their competitive advantage in the market.

Put yourself in the shoes of the Paradise management. How would you manage the conflict between Vendor A and Vendor Z?

## *Points to consider*

1 What are the concerns and interests of Fabulous Computers International, Paradise Computers, Vendor A and Vendor Z?
2 What is the root cause of the channel conflict?
3 Develop options that could reduce conflict between the channel members.
4 If the channel conflict remains unresolved, what effect might it have on Paradise and on Fabulous products?

# CASE 12.2 SCHWARZKOPF, INC. DISTRIBUTION NETWORK

**Daniel M. Evans, San José State University and Heinz Bieler, Schwarzkopf Professional**

Schwarzkopf is one of the leading hair care companies in the world. The "Professional Product" lines office is based in Hamburg, Germany. Professional Products are sold solely to beauty salons and beauty schools worldwide (see Figure 12.8).

An enterprising merchant named Hans Schwarzkopf established a chemist's shop on a bustling street in Berlin, Germany. He produced medicinals, perfumes, and beauty care products favored by the men and women of his day. In 1898, he compounded the world's first formula for shampooing hair. The news spread rapidly of the new Schwarzkopf powder shampoo, and the House of Schwarzkopf grew and became known throughout Europe as a maker of distinctive hair and beauty products.

Today, Schwarzkopf offers, worldwide, everything needed for beautiful hair, such as hair color, shampoos, conditioners, permanent waves, and styling products.

In 1978, Schwarzkopf was introduced in the U.S.A. for the first time. Schwarzkopf decided to follow tried and true European distribution methods. In Europe, especially in Germany, it is customary to offer products through direct sales to the clientele; in this case, the beauty salons. Schwarzkopf has its own sales force which visits all the salons in Germany. Considering the size of Germany, the direct sales system works well. Furthermore, since the salon owners and workers are themselves products of the extensive German occupational training system, the direct sales force does not need to engage in fundamental training in the use of the hair care products.

Schwarzkopf established one warehouse in Los Angeles, and hired a few "educators" to call on prospective buyers. Schwarzkopf became an instant success in the Los Angeles area, but it proved difficult to service prospective customers in the rest of the U.S.A. Schwarzkopf tried until 1993 to service customers directly as in Germany, but realized that the German distribution methods were not adequate for the U.S. market. Furthermore, sales personnel reported frustration at the inability of salons to use the Professional Products properly.

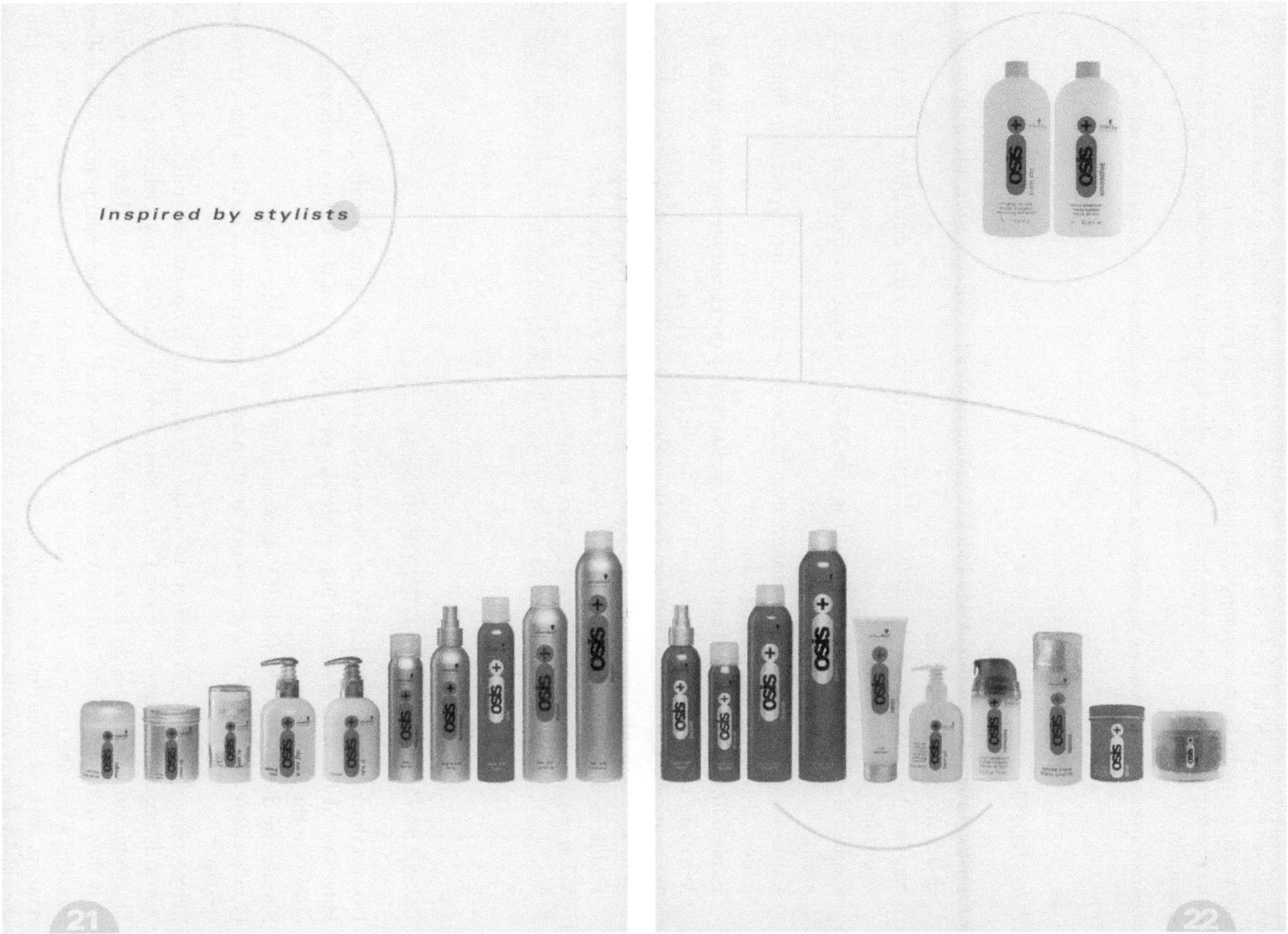
Inspired by stylists
21
22

FIGURE 12.8 Schwarzkopf's product line

### Points to consider

1 Why do you think it was difficult for Schwarzkopf to achieve satisfactory distribution throughout the U.S.A.?
2 In what other way did German assumptions about the U.S. market prove inadequate?
3 If you were responsible for Schwarzkopf in the U.S.A., what changes in the distribution system would you recommend?

## Questions

1 Distinguish between direct and indirect selling channels. What are the advantages and disadvantages of these channels?
2 Explain these types of direct-channel intermediaries: foreign distributor and state-controlled trading company.
3 Explain these types of indirect-channel agents: EMC, cooperative exporter, and purchasing agent.
4 Explain these types of indirect-channel merchants: export merchant, export drop shipper, export distributor, and trading company.
5 Explain hot, moderate, and cold countries as classified by the country temperature gradient. What are the channel implications of this classification system?
6 What are the factors that affect the length, width, and number of marketing channels?
7 Why is it difficult – financially and legally – to terminate the relationship with overseas middlemen? What should be done to prevent or minimize such difficulties?
8 What are gray market products? Are they legal?

## Discussion assignments and minicases

1 Do you think that the U.S. ETCs can compete effectively with Japanese trading companies?
2 How should Japan be classified: hot, moderate, or cold? Do you think this classification may change in the future?
3 Should the distribution channels of Volkswagen and Porsche be the same?
4 Honda created a separate dealer network for its Acura brand. Is there a need for this expensive strategy?
5 Sony Corp. of America, in an effort to include retailing in its operations, runs its own licensed stores in Japan and Europe. In the U.S.A., Sony has opened the Sony Gallery of Consumer Electronics in Chicago. Inside the store, "boom boxes" and camcorders are displayed on pedestals as if they were art objects, and the Walkman is displayed on trendy mannequins. The gallery includes a life-size mock-up of an apartment with a built-in Sony home theater system. Some retailers are concerned that Sony might turn out to be both their supplier and competitor. How should Sony deal with this concern?

6 Do gray marketers serve useful marketing functions – for consumers and manufacturers?
7 U.S. Customs regulations require watches to have a small inked stamp on the movement. Seiko thus charged that the gray market Seiko watches imported into the U.S.A. were unfit because the opening for marking harmed dust- and water-resistant seals and contaminated the watch movement.
   - Do you feel that gray marketers' marking to comply with customs regulations is harmful to the product?
   - Because Seiko is a popular brand and gray market Seiko watches are carried by a number of discounters and catalog showrooms, what should Seiko do to alleviate the problem of unauthorized imports?

## Notes


1 Mike W. Peng and Anne S. York, "Behind Intermediary Performance in Export Trade: Transactions, Agents and Resources," *Journal of International Business Studies* 32 (Second Quarter 2001): 327–46.
2 Harald Trabold, "Export Intermediation: An Empirical Test of Peng and Ilinitch," *Journal of International Business Studies* 33 (Second Quarter 2002): 327–44.
3 Kelly Hewett and William O. Bearden, "Dependence, Trust, and Relational Behavior on the Part of Foreign Subsidiary Marketing Operations: Implications for Managing Global Marketing Operations," *Journal of Marketing* 65 (October 2001): 51–66.
4 "How Guess Got Its Groove Back," *Business Week*, 18 December 2006, 126; and "Guess Inc.'s Torrid Global Growth Raises Eyebrows," *Wall Street Journal*, June 19, 2007.
5 Isaiah A. Litvak and Peter M. Banting, "A Conceptual Framework for International Business Arrangements," in *Marketing and the New Science of Planning*, ed. Robert L. King (Chicago: American Marketing Association, 1968), 460–7.
6 "Widening Aisles For Indian Shoppers," *Business Week*, April 30, 2007, 44.
7 "The British Invasion," *PROMO*, March 2007, 20.
8 "Taiwan's Acer Gains Ground on Chinese Rival Lenovo," *San José Mercury News*, April 2, 2007.
9 "The Wrist Watchers," *Business Week*, August 6, 2007, 80–1.
10 "The Best Performers," *Business Week*, March 26, 2007, 75.
11 "Wal-Mart Joins with India Firm to Open Stores," *San José Mercury News*, November 28, 2006; and "Retail's Coming Face-off," *Business Today*, December 31, 2006, 90.
12 R. Scott Marshall and David M Boush, "Dynamic Decision-making: A Cross-cultural Comparison of U.S. and Peruvian Export Managers," *Journal of International Business Studies* 32 (Fourth Quarter 2001): 873–93.
13 Harry G. Broadman, "Competition and Business Entry in Russia," *Finance & Development*, June 2001, 22–5.
14 Guijun Zhuang and Nan Zhou, "The Relationship Between Power and Dependence in Marketing Channels," *European Journal of Marketing* 38 (Nos 5/6, 2004): 675–93.
15 David A. Griffith and Michael G. Harvey, "A Resource Perspective of Global Dynamic Capabilities," *Journal of International Business Studies* 32 (Third Quarter 2001): 597–606.
16 Christopher M. Moore, Grete Birtwistle, and Steve Burt, "Channel Power, Conflict and Conflict Resolution in International Fashion Retailing," *European Journal of Marketing* 38 (No. 7, 2004): 749–69.
17 Anne Marie Doherty and Nicholas Alexander, "Power and Control in International Retail Franchising," *European Journal of Marketing* 40 (Nos 11/12, 2006): 1292–1316.
18 Michael Trimarchi and Peter W. Liesch, "Business Communication in Interactions Between Mainland Chinese and Western Firms Through Hong Kong Chinese Intermediaries," *European Journal of Marketing* 40 (Nos 11/12, 2006): 1210–35.

19 "Warehouse Giant Costco Growing in Crowded Japan," *San José Mercury News*, September 22, 2002.

20 "Tesco Studies Hard for U.S. Debut," *Wall Street Journal*, June 28, 2007.

21 Vincenzo Sinisi and Thomas M. Federman, "Commercial Aspects of Italian Law," *Business America*, October 5, 1992, 12–14.

22 John T. Masterson, Jr., "Drafting International Distributorship and Sales Representative Agreements," *Business America*, November 21, 1988, 8–9.

23 "Dark Days for a Black Market," *Business Week*, October 15, 2001, 60–1.

24 "Canadian Maker Charged with Fraud," *San José Mercury News*, March 1, 2003.

25 "Smuggled Tobacco Costing Countries Billions in Lost Revenue," *The Nation*, 22 March 2007.

26 Jen-Hung Huang, Bruce C. Y. Lee, and Shu Hsun Ho, "Consumer Attitude Toward Gray Market Goods," *International Marketing Review* 21 (No. 6, 2004): 598–614.

27 S. Tamer Cavusgil and Ed Sikora, "How Multinationals Can Counter Gray Market Imports," *Columbia Journal of World Business* 23 (winter 1988): 75–85.

28 Matthew B. Myers, "Incidents of Gray Market Activity Among U.S. Exporters: Occurrences, Characteristics, and Consequences," *Journal of International Business Studies* 30 (First Quarter 1999): 105–26.

29 Kersi D. Antia et al., "How Does Enforcement Deter Gray Market Incidence?", *Journal of Marketing* 70 (January 2006): 92–106.

30 Tony Michalski, "Going Global With Services Exports: A Guide to Available Support," *Export America* (May 2001): 17–19.

Chapter 13

# Physical distribution and documentation

Imagine a world without lawyers, accountants, and insurance agents.

Murray L. Weidenbaum, former Chairman, Council of Economic Advisers

## Chapter outline

- Marketing strategy: Booming economies and headaches
- Modes of transportation
  - Land
  - Air
  - Water
- Cargo or transportation insurance
- Packing
  - Weight
  - Breakage
  - Moisture and temperature
  - Pilferage and theft
- Containers
- Freight forwarder and customs broker
- Contract logistics
- Documentation
  - Shipping documents
  - Collection documents
- Conclusion
- Case 13.1 Who can best introduce the "City Adventurer" into Saudi Arabia?

## Marketing strategy

### Booming economies and headaches

The economies of India and Russia are booming, and multinational corporations want to be part of the action. Doing business in India and Russia, however, is not easy. In particular, the aspect of physical distribution poses a daunting challenge.

In 2006, Nokia Corp. lost thousands of its cellular phones that were soaked by rain because the local airport did not have room to warehouse the crates of handsets that were shipped from its Chennai factory. Because the ports are very slow, Cisco Systems has to resort to flying parts in.

Maruti Suzuki has learned that it can take up to ten days to truck its cars 900 miles from its factory in Gurgaon to the port in Mumbai. The Japanese car manufacturer has to cope with delays at the three state borders, where drivers are stalled as officials check their papers. In addition, big rigs are barred from India's congested cities during the day. Once the cars are at the port, the problem is still not over. Because there is not enough dock space for cargo carriers to load and unload, the vehicles may have to wait weeks for the next outbound ship.

The Russian market, with 11 time zones, is geographically dispersed. There are vast climatic and geographical variations. To make matters worse, the country's infrastructure – both air and road – is poor. There are shortages of trucks from Kotka, and the capacity in St. Petersburg's port is limited.

Warehousing is concentrated in Moscow and Moscow Oblast, which account for half of the nation's warehousing supply and demand. In the Moscow region alone, there is a deficit of quality warehousing space of between one and two million square meters. New warehouse locations are being added. However, because more than half of warehouse facilities are concentrated around Moscow, the rest of the country's large industrially developed territories is relatively "naked."

The booming economy has brought transportation systems to the brink of crisis. Because Russia's distribution structure is not well developed, retailers need to use different gateways and transport modes to import and deliver goods. It is thus essential to use a logistics provider that has representation in different gateways in Russia.

Less than a decade ago, Western firms believed that it was too risky to transport goods to Russia. They instead sold goods in Europe, and specialized importers and distributors within Russia then transported the goods. The restored political and legal stability has now made it feasible for Western companies to control their own supply chains. Toward this end, they want a single partner that can offer the same kind of service transport and logistics services found in the U.S.A. and Europe.

The express and logistics industry is an $8-billion business. Russia needs more than 1,000 logistics specialists a year. At present, the talent pool can meet only 10 percent of the demand.

*Sources*: "The Trouble with India," *Business Week*, March 19, 2007, 49–58; Tarek Liddawi, "Optimizing Supply Chains in the Retail Sector," *AmCham News* 13 (October–November 2006): 6; Mark Jordan, "Challenges for the Express & Logistics Industry in Russia," *AmCham News* 13 (October–November 2006): 8; and Alex Geller, "Warehousing and Logistics," *AmCham News* 13 (October–November 2006): 10.

## Purpose of chapter

Distribution is a necessary as well as a costly activity. According to one executive at Procter & Gamble, the average time required to move a typical product from "farm to shelf" is four to five months. Although it takes only about 17 minutes to actually produce a product, the rest of the time is spent in logistical activities – storage, handling, transportation, packing, and so on.

In the developed economies, the distribution sector typically accounts for one-third of the gross domestic product (GDP). Furthermore, international logistics costs can account for 25 to 35 percent of the sales value of a product, a significant difference from the 8 to 10 percent for domestic shipment.

Examples are endless that could demonstrate some of the difficulties in physically moving products overseas. Firms can become easily frustrated by the physical distribution problems overseas. Port congestion coupled with the lack of efficient materials handling equipment can cause long delays. Even inland movements can be a problem because some road networks cannot accommodate long containers and rail gauges vary across countries. China, for example, intentionally uses different rail gauges for security reasons (i.e., to prevent quick troop movement in the case of a foreign invasion). Not only must a company make arrangements for transportation, but it must also pay attention to how the product is packed for shipping. The process requires a great deal of paperwork throughout.

Paperwork is a global problem. It impedes trade, chokes flow of trade, costs jobs, and loses government revenue. To move goods across borders worldwide, nine billion documents are required each year. According to the United Nations Conference on Trade and Development, an average customs transaction involves 27 parties, 40 documents, 200 data elements (30 of them are repeated at least 30 times), and the retyping of 70 percent of all data at least once. Of course, in many countries, the import–export paperwork is worse.[1]

This chapter examines the various issues related to the process of moving a product from one country to another, beginning by comparing and contrasting the major transportation modes. The discussion then focuses on insurance and packing for export. Next, the chapter examines two kinds of intermediaries that, in the area of physical distribution, are virtually indispensable – freight forwarders and customhouse brokers. Finally, a significant portion of the chapter is devoted to a discussion of documentation, including both shipping and collection documents.

## Modes of transportation

The availability of transportation is one important factor affecting a company's site selection, as noted in Figure 13.1. To move a product both between countries and within a country, there are three fundamental modes of transportation: air, water (ocean and inland), and land (rail and truck). Ocean and air shipments are appropriate for transportation between countries, especially when the distance is considerable and the boundaries are not joined. Inland water, rail, and highway are more suitable for inland and domestic transportation. When countries are connected by land (e.g., North America), it is possible to use rail and highway to move merchandise from locations, such as from the U.S.A. to Canada. In Europe, rail (train) is an important mode of transport due to the contiguity of land areas and the availability of a modern and efficient train system.

The appropriate transportation mode depends on (1) market location, (2) speed, and (3) cost. A firm must first consider **market location**. Contiguous markets may be served by rail or truck, and such

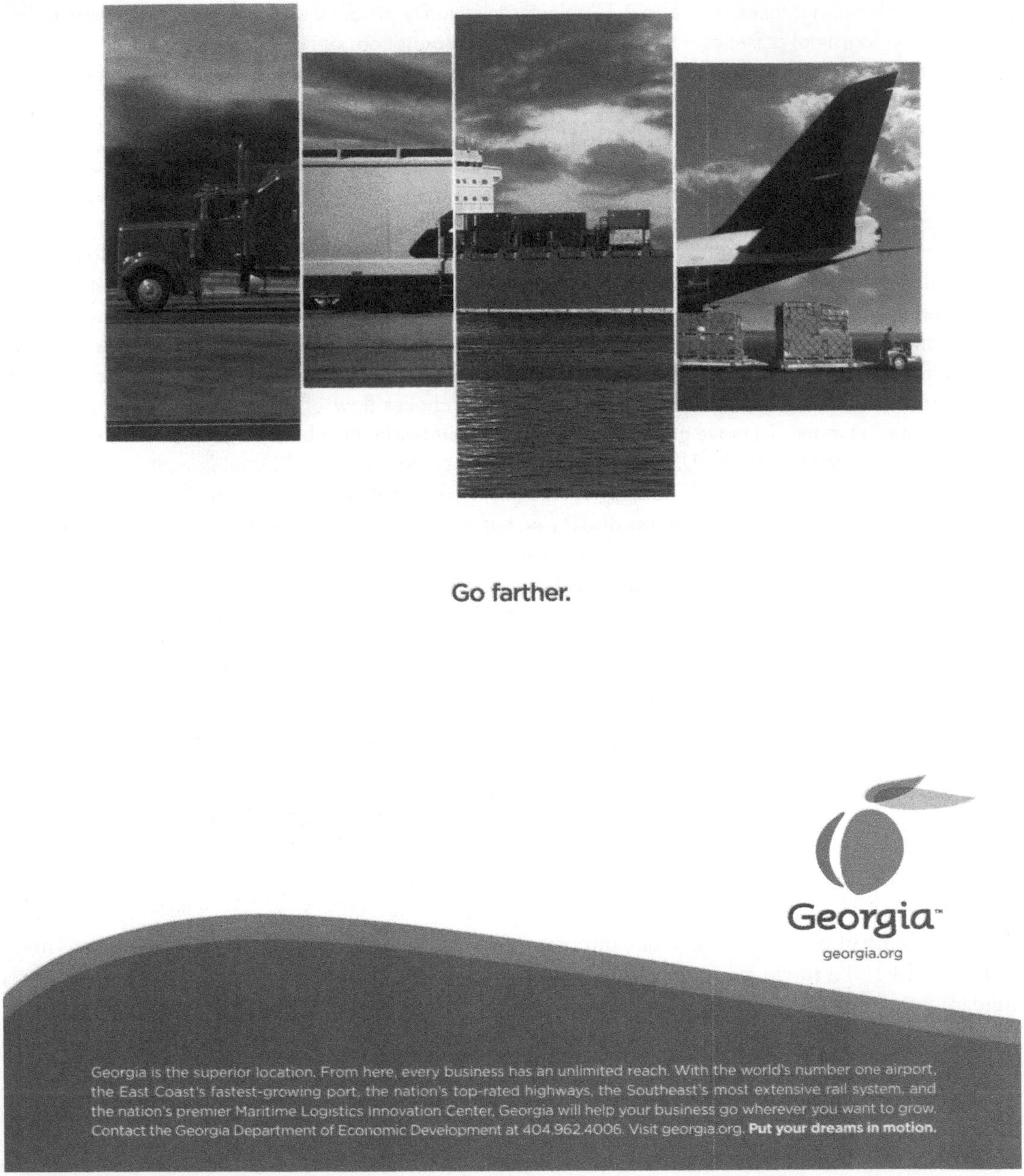
Go farther.
Georgia™
georgia.org
Georgia is the superior location. From here, every business has an unlimited reach. With the world's number one airport, the East Coast's fastest-growing port, the nation's top-rated highways, the Southeast's most extensive rail system, and the nation's premier Maritime Logistics Innovation Center, Georgia will help your business go wherever you want to grow. Contact the Georgia Department of Economic Development at 404.962.4006. Visit georgia.org. Put your dreams in motion.

**FIGURE 13.1** Transportation and site selection

*Source*: Reprinted by permission of Georgia Department of Economic Development.

is the case when goods are shipped from the U.S.A. to Canada or Mexico. To move goods between continents, ocean or air transportation is needed.

**Speed** is another consideration. When speed is essential, air transport is without question the preferred mode of distribution. Air transport is also necessary when the need is urgent or when delivery must be quickly completed as promised. For perishable items, a direct flight is preferable because a shorter period in transport reduces both spoilage and theft.

Finally, **cost** must be considered as well. Cost is directly related to speed – a quick delivery costs more. But there is a trade-off between the two in terms of other kinds of savings. Packing costs for air freight are less than for ocean freight because for air freight the merchandise does not have to be in transit for a long period of time, and the hazards are relatively fewer. For similar reasons, the air mode reduces the inventory in float (i.e., in the movement process). Thus, there is less investment cost because the overall inventory is minimized and inventory is turned over faster.

A firm must understand that there is no ideal transportation mode. Each mode has its own special kinds of hazards.[2] Hazards related to the ocean/water mode include wave impact, navigation exposures, water damage, and the various vessel motions (rolling, pitching, heaving, surging, swaying, and yawing). Hazards related to the air mode include ground handling and changes in atmospheric pressure and temperature. Hazards related to the rail and highway modes include acceleration/deceleration (braking), coupling impact, swaying on curves, and shock and vibration.

Figure 13.2 describes the services of Yellow Freight System, an international carrier.

## *Land*

Land transportation is an integral part of any shipment, whether locally or internationally. Some type of land transportation is necessary in moving goods to and from an airport or seaport. The land transportation mode involves rail and truck. When goods in a large quantity must be moved over a long distance inland, rail can prove to be quite economical. Europe and Japan have modern train systems that are capable of moving merchandise efficiently.

On the other hand, trucks are capable of going to more places. In addition, trucks may be needed to take cargo to and from a railway station. When countries have joint boundaries, moving cargo by truck or train is often a practical solution. As a matter of fact, the U.S. trucking industry is quite concerned about a NAFTA agreement which allows Mexican drivers to drive their trucks into the U.S.A. It is debatable whether the real issue is a safety concern or a trade barrier.

Less developed countries generally rely on road transport. In sub-Saharan Africa, road transport is the dominant form of transport.[3] This form of transport accounts for 80 to 90 percent of the region's passenger and freight movements. Unfortunately, the nearly two million kilometers of roads in Africa have been greatly damaged due to years of neglect. In any case, road transport may be the only access to most rural communities – a situation common in Africa as well as other developing economies.

## *Air*

Of all the various transportation modes, air accounts for only about 1 percent of total international freight movement; yet it is the fastest-growing mode and is becoming less confined to expensive products. Air transport has the highest absolute rate, but exporters have discovered that there are many advantages associated with this mode. First, air transport speeds up delivery, minimizes the time the goods are in transit, and achieves great flexibility in delivery schedules. Second, it delivers

CLEAR BORDERS IN A SINGLE BOUND.
If your business knows no boundaries look to the carrier with the best coverage. In Mexico, Canada and the Caribbean, for example, we offer extensive networks of our own local professionals and strategically situated terminals to help move your freight smartly through customs. And we've launched YFM Direct™ with one of Europe's largest carriers to give you date-certain transatlantic door-to-door service to and from Europe. So if you're shipping international, ship with Yellow...the seamless, single-source, transborder machine.
Times have changed, and we're moving further, faster.
ASK FOR AN INTERNATIONAL SPECIALIST AT 1-800-531-1649.
BECAUSE IT'S NOT BUSINESS AS USUAL.®
YELLOW

**FIGURE 13.2** International carrier

perishables in prime condition (see Cultural Dimension 13.1). Harris Ranch uses a 747 jumbo jet to fly live cattle from the U.S.A. to Japan. A premium price commanded by high-quality beef in Japan makes it possible to use air freight.

Third, it can respond rapidly to unpredictable and urgent demand. For instance, quick replacement of broken machinery, equipment, or a component part can be made by air. Fourth, it reduces to a minimum damage, packing, and insurance costs. Finally, it can help control expensive inventory and other hidden costs, including warehousing, time in transit, inventory carrying costs, inventory losses, and the paperwork necessary to file claims for lost or damaged goods. These costs will increase as the time in transit increases. Furthermore, opportunity costs (e.g., lost sales and customer dissatisfaction) also adversely affect profit, especially in the long term. All of these costs can be minimized with air transport.

Traditionally, the appropriateness of air freight was determined solely by a **value-to-weight equation**, which dictated that air cargo should be confined to high-value products. One reason for that determination was that transport cost is a small proportion of such products' value. Another reason was that the amount of capital tied up with these products while in transit is high and should be released as soon as possible.

Shippers have begun to shift their attention to the **freight rates–density effect**, which determines true costs rather than absolute costs of each transportation mode.[4] Air freight rates are usually quoted per unit of weight, and sea freight rates are usually quoted per unit of weight and volume (which ever yields more revenue for the steamship). For example, assume the freight rates are $350/ton by air and $60/ton and/or cubic ft by sea. At first, it would appear that surface (sea) transportation is a great deal cheaper. However, for a product that is 1 ton and 7 cubic ft, the cost of sea freight ($420) is actually higher than that of air freight ($350). Therefore, sea freight is cheap when goods are very dense (i.e., low volume per unit of weight). But as density declines (i.e., the increase in bulk in relation to constant weight), the charge for sea freight rises rapidly. Consequently, air freight is quite

## Cultural Dimension 13.1

### Tuna and air travel

The year was 1971, and Akira Okazaki was working in Japan Airlines' cargo division. While the planes heading to North America were full, they returned home empty. Okazaki, looking for cargo to air freight to Japan, contacted a member of staff in Toronto to ask about the tuna catch off Prince Edward Island in Canada. The reply mentioned that the tuna were plentiful. After a great deal of experimentation to keep the fish fresh, the tuna were exportable. As a result, the tuna trade center in the Tsukji wholesale seafood market in Tokyo leapt forward.

Sushi started as a fast-food snack in Japan and its colonies in Asia. It was virtually unknown outside of Japan. Things began to change in the 1950s, thanks to the development of shipping containers. By the 1970s, thanks to the adaptation of containers to Boeing jetliners, coupled with sophisticated packing and improvements in cooling technology, tuna became a major export out of North America as well as one of the most profitable sectors of the world's cargo business.

*Source*: Sasha Issenberg, *The Sushi Economy: Globalization and the Making of a Modern Delicacy* (New York: Gotham Books, 2007).

competitive for such low-density goods as ladies' shoes, men's shoes, computers, color TV sets, refrigerators, and towels.

The dominant form of the international transportation of merchandise has always been ocean transport. Its main advantage is its low rate, though the savings achieved for many products are not necessarily greater than other transport modes on an overall basis. This helps explain why, when all the hidden costs related to ocean transportation are considered, air transportation is growing at a very rapid rate (see Figure 13.3).

Half a century ago, virtually all overseas trade went by ship. The use of air freight for high-value, time-sensitive products has jumped since then. The air mode has made it possible to outsource high-technology products (e.g., computers). A reduction in transit time by one day can reduce a product's price by 0.8 percent. Based on over $800 billion of manufactured imports per year, an extra day can add $7 billion to the costs. Because an ocean shipment, on average, takes 20 days, a shift from a 20-day ocean shipment to a one-day air shipment can lower the price of a product by about 15 percent.[5]

## Water

Bulk shipping is important in international trade because it is one of the most practical and efficient means of transporting petroleum, industrial raw materials, and agricultural commodities over long distances. About 51 percent of the global bulk fleet consists of oil-tankers, while dry bulk carriers account for 43 percent. The remainder of the fleet is made up of combination carriers which are capable of carrying either wet (crude oil and refined petroleum products) or dry (coal, iron ore, and gain) bulk cargoes. The bulk shipping industry, being highly fragmented, has no one organization which holds more than 2 percent of the total world fleet.[6]

Quotations for ocean shipping may be obtained from a shipping company or a freight forwarder. Steamship rates are commonly quoted on weight and measurement. Goods are both weighed and measured, and the ship will use the method that yields a higher freight charge. Less-than-container shipments carry a higher rate than full-container shipments

There are three basic types of shipping company: (1) conference lines, (2) independent lines, and (3) tramp vessels. An ocean freight **conference line** is an association of ocean carriers that have joined together to establish common rules with regard to freight rates and shipping conditions. Consequently, the operators in the group charge identical rates. The steamship conference has also adopted a dual rate system, giving preferential treatment to contract exporters. A contract exporter agrees to ship all or a large portion of its cargo on a regular basis on vessels of conference member lines – in exchange for a lower rate than charged for a noncontract shipper. Nevertheless, the contract exporter is allowed to use another vessel, after obtaining the conference's permission, when no conference service is available within a reasonable period of time.

An **independent line**, as the name implies, is a line that operates and quotes freight rates individually and independently without the use of a dual-rate contract. Independent lines accept bookings from all shippers. When they compete with conference lines for noncontract shippers, they may lower their rates. In general, independent lines do not offer any special advantage for a contract shipper because they do not have significant price advantage. Furthermore, their services are more limited and not as readily available.

Finally, a **tramp vessel** is a ship not operating on a regular route or schedule. That is, tramp steamers do not have the established schedules of the other two types of carriers. Tramp vessels operate on a charter basis whenever and wherever they can get cargo. They operate mainly in carrying bulk cargoes.

Our international passengers start clearing customs before our planes even land.
United Parcel Service
ups
While we're flying your packages overseas, detailed shipment information is flying ahead on UPSnet,™ our global data network.
That gives UPS customs brokers in destination countries a sizable head start: from 2 to 36 hours. And that gives us extra time to sort out potential clearance problems before the packages even arrive.
As a result, UPS international shipments are well on their way while other delivery companies are still getting their paperwork in order.
What's more, this technology doesn't just make us faster and more reliable. It makes us more efficient. So we can deliver to over 180 countries and territories, usually for a lot less than other companies charge.
So next time you have an international shipment to send, just send it UPS.
After all, many companies can fly your packages overseas.
It's what we're doing while they're flying that makes all the difference in the world.
UPS®
We run the tightest ship in the shipping business.®
© 1991 United Parcel Service of America, Inc.

**FIGURE 13.3** Air freight and customs

In some circumstances, a shipper may not have an option on the vessel to be used. Because of certain laws enacted to protect a country's interests, mandatory use of a particular vessel is not uncommon. Brazil's shipping restrictions require goods imported for use by public or public-supported enterprises to be transported aboard vessels with a Brazilian flag. All exported Japanese automobiles must be shipped on Japanese-owned ships, and the same restriction applies to all tobacco leaf imported to Japan.

The U.S.A., while accusing other nations of erecting trade barriers, has the Federal Cargo Preference Act, which supports and favors U.S. shipowners and maritime workers over foreign-flag vessels. Shipping between American coastal ports, including the movement of Alaskan oil, is legally reserved primarily to U.S. flag vessels owned by American citizens, crewed by U.S. seafarers, and built in the U.S.A. without construction subsidies and operated without operating differential subsidies. Such vessels also receive preference in carrying U.S. military and U.S. government-sponsored shipments throughout the world.

In general, the rates charged by U.S. conference lines are higher than the rates charged by lines of other nations. Foreign operators are able to charge lower rates because of the subsidies and support received from their governments. Soviet ships at one time were able to quote rates as much as two-thirds lower than U.S. conference lines' published prices. Subsequently, conference lines (e.g., Seatrain) decided to give illegal rebates to major customers in order to win back cargo shipments lost to the Soviets.

Ships need ports, and efficient ports attract ocean shippers. It is somewhat surprising that U.S. ports are not efficient. Shippers and importers have been complaining about aging warehouses, limited hours of operation, and space shortage, all of which delay getting the cargo off the ships and on to trucks and trains. Ships may have to wait a week for unloading, while truckers can do nothing but wait for the cargo.[7]

In contrast, automated houses such as those in Hong Kong allow efficient flow of goods. A port's efficiency is measured by speed. Ocean shippers are preoccupied with moving containers of goods through a port in the shortest amount of time possible. The world's top two container ports are Hong Kong and Singapore. They lead all other ports in terms of TEUs (20-foot equivalent unit containers) that can be processed. These two ports' authorities have won their competitive advantage by building new automated rail and warehouse facilities and switching to 24-hour operations. Shangai, Rotterdam, and others are trying to attain such an advantage by building new deep-water facilities. At present, the world's top three ports based on container traffic are: Singapore (23,200 thousand TEUs), Hong Kong (22,480), and Shanghai (18,080). Long Beach (14,194), ranking No. 5, is the top U.S. port, while New York (4,792) comes in at No. 16. Tokyo (3,594) is No. 21.

Globally, most large shipping companies transporting containers are moving away from the traditional cargo delivery system's use of only one mode of transportation. They have adopted an integrated approach – a *multi-modal* cargo transport approach.

Development of the multi-modal cargo transport market in Russia has been impeded by the fragmentation of the expediting segment, the sector's weak professional development of employees, customs clearance, inadequate number of customs posts at borders, and lack of modern technologies at the customs posts. To compound the problems, Russia's aviation fleet is not equipped for the extensive use of container transport because passenger carriers have narrow fuselages. Cargo planes carrying pallets and oversized loads do not use standards and sizes corresponding to international norms. Extensive use of container cargoes in the aviation fleet is thus difficult, and there is no equipment at Russian airports for on-the-ground service of air shipments. Things are changing for the better though at airports in Moscow, Novosibirsk, and Krasnoyarsk. Shippers have witnessed the commissioning of foreign-made wide-bodied cargo planes, use of pallets and standard-sized containers, and mechanized on-the-ground service equipment. These are the preconditions for a multi-modal cargo transport system.[8]

## Cargo or transportation insurance

Inland carriers generally bear the responsibility for any damage to goods while in their possession. The same thing cannot be said for ocean carriers. Their reluctance to accept responsibility is due to the numerous unavoidable perils found at sea. Such perils include severe weather, seawater, stranding, fire, collision, and sinking. As a result, ocean carriers refuse to accept any liability for loss or damage unless a shipper can prove that it was purposefully negligent – a difficult task indeed. To protect against loss or damage and to avoid disputes with overseas buyers, exporters should obtain marine insurance.

**Marine cargo insurance** is an insurance that covers loss or damage at sea, though in practice it also applies to shipments by mail, air, and ship (see Figure 13.4). It is similar to domestic cargo insurance but provides much broader coverage. The purpose of this insurance is to insure export shipments against loss or damage in transit. The insurance may be arranged by either a buyer or a seller, depending on the terms of sale.

There are two basic forms of marine insurance: (1) special (one-time) coverage and (2) open (blanket) coverage. A **special policy** is a one-time policy that insures a single specific shipment. One-time insurance is relatively expensive because the risk cannot be spread over a number of shipments. Nevertheless, it is a practical insurance solution if a seller's export business is infrequent.

An **open policy** is an insurance contract issued to a firm in order to cover all its shipments as described in the policy within named geographic regions. The policy is open in the sense that it is continuous by automatically providing coverage on all cargo moving at the seller's risk. The policy is also open in the sense that the values of the individual shipments cannot be known in advance. Under this policy, no reports of individual shipments are required, although the insured must declare all shipments to the underwriter. The underwriter agrees to insure all shipments at the agreed rates within the terms and conditions of the policy. Open marine cargo policies are written only for a specified time period. A single premium is charged for this time period, based on the insured's estimated total value of goods to be shipped under the policy during the term of the contract. The contract has no predetermined termination date, though it may be cancelled by either party. A firm can also insure profit through a Valuation Clause in the cargo policy, which insures exports and contains a fixed basis of valuation. The following is an example of a typical valuation clause in a marine policy: "Valued at amount of invoice, plus 10 percent."

## Packing

Packaging may be viewed as consisting of two distinct types: industrial (exterior) and consumer (interior). Consumer packaging is designed for the purpose of influencing sales. The aim of industrial packaging is to prepare and protect merchandise for shipment and storage, and this type of packaging accounts for 7 cents of each retail dollar as well as 30 percent of total packaging costs.[9] Packing is

ONE THIRD IS COVERED BY LAND, TWO THIRDS BY WATER, AND ALL OF IT BY CIGNA.
The world's a big place. 27,459,880 square miles to be exact.
And if you're an international business buying insurance country by country, it can seem even bigger.
Dealing with other customs, policies and peculiarities can be more than just complicated. It can leave you unsure of your coverage. If not completely uncovered.
Thus the need for comprehensive global coverage. The kind of coverage that the CIGNA companies can provide.
As a truly global organization, CIGNA companies offer a wide range of property and casualty insurance all around the world. On both land and water. With local operations in nearly 80 countries, led by experienced representatives who know local customs inside and out.
Our global coverage can also help eliminate overlapping policies and gaps in protection.
What's more, we have a network of loss control specialists to help you prevent accidents.
As well as a worldwide claims-handling system that can process claims quickly should any accidents occur.
And with over 48,000 employees worldwide and almost 200 years of global experience, few companies can match our strength.
To learn more about our worldwide property and casualty coverages, write CIGNA Companies, Dept. R8, 1600 Arch Street, Philadelphia, PA 19103.
And find out just how small the world can be.
CIGNA

**FIGURE 13.4** Insurance

*Source*: Reprinted courtesy of CIGNA Companies.

even more critical for overseas shipment than for domestic shipment due to the longer transit time and a greater number of hazards. Consumer packaging is covered extensively in Chapter 11; this section concentrates instead on industrial packaging.

There are four common packing problems, some of which are in direct conflict with one another: (1) weight, (2) breakage, (3) moisture and temperature, and (4) pilferage and theft.

## *Weight*

Overpacking not only directly increases packing costs but also increases the weight and size of cargo. Any undue increase in weight or size only serves to raise freight charges. Moreover, import fees or customs duties may also rise when import duties are based on gross weight. Thus, overprotection of the cargo can cost more than it is worth.

## *Breakage*

Although overpacking is undesirable, so is underpacking because the latter allows a product to be susceptible to breakage damage. The breakage problem is present in every step of ocean transport. In addition to normal domestic handling, ocean cargo is loaded aboard a vessel by use of a line (with several items together in a net), conveyor, chute, or other methods, all of which put added stress and strain on the package. Once the cargo is on the vessel, other cargo may be stacked on top of it, or packages may come in violent contact during the course of the voyage. To complicate matters, handling facilities at an overseas port may be unsophisticated. The cargo may be dropped, dragged, pushed, and rolled during unloading, moving in and out of customs, or in transit to the final destination. In China, primitive methods (i.e., carts, sampans, junks, and so on) are used to move a great deal of cargo. Therefore, packaging must be sufficient to accommodate rough manual handling.

To guard against breakage, it may be desirable to use such package-testing equipment as vibration, drop, compression, incline-image, and revolving drum. The cargo must not exceed the rated capacity of the box or crate. Attempts should be made to ensure that internal blocking and bracing will distribute the cargo's weight evenly. Cushioning may be needed to absorb the impact. Cautionary markings, in words and symbols, are necessary to reduce mishandling because of misunderstanding.

One universal packing rule is "Pack for the toughest leg of the journey." To accommodate this rule, cargo should be unitized or palletized whenever possible. **Palletizing** is the assembly of one or more packages on a pallet base and the securing of the load to the pallet. **Unitizing** is the assembly of one or more items into a compact load, secured together and provided with skids and cleats for ease of handling. These two packing methods force cargo handlers to use mechanical handling equipment to move cargo.

Shipments by air do not usually require the heavy packaging that ocean shipments require. Standard domestic packing should prove sufficient in most cases. When in doubt, however, a company should consult the carrier or a marine insurance company for the best packing strategy. Where a firm is not equipped to do its own packing, there are professional firms that package exports.

## *Moisture and temperature*

Certain products can easily be damaged by moisture and temperature. Such products are subject to condensation even in the hold of a ship furnished with air-conditioning or dehumidifying equipment.

Another problem is that the cargo may be unloaded in the rain. Many foreign ports do not have covered storage facilities, and the cargo may have to be left out in the open and subjected to heat, rain, cold, and other adverse elements. In Morocco, bulk cargo and large items are stored in the open. Mozambique does the same with hazardous, bulk, and heavy items. Cargo thus needs extra strong packing, containerization, or unitization in order to have some measure of protection under these conditions.

One very effective means of eliminating moisture is **shrink wrapping**, which involves sealing merchandise in a plastic film. Waterproofing can also be provided by using waterproof inner linings or moisture-absorbing agents and by coating finished metal parts with a preservative or rust inhibitor. Desiccants (moisture-absorbing materials), moisture-barrier or vapor-barrier paper, or plastic wraps, sheets, and shrouds will also protect cargo from water leakage or condensation damage. Cargo can be kept away from water on the ground if placed on skids, pallets, or dunnage while having drain holes for crates.

There are several steps to ensure the proper way of packing to minimize moisture and breakage problems.[10] These steps are as follows:

1. Place water-barrier material on interior of sides and roof.
2. Use vertical sheathing.
3. Block, brace, and tie down heavy items.
4. Use new, clear, dry lumber and provide adequate diagonals.
5. Unitize multiple similar items.
6. Use waterproof tape to seal fiberboard boxes.
7. Palletize shipping bags.
8. Use proper gauge, type, and number of straps.

## Pilferage and theft

Cargo should be adequately protected against theft. Studies have fixed such losses in all transportation modes in a range from $1 billion to in excess of $5 billion.[11] In the U.S.A. alone, the annual value of cargo stolen in transit exceeds $2.5 billion. Annual loss through theft is well over £100 million in Great Britain, with employees' criminal activity being the main contributing factor.[12] Pilferage levels are consistently high in Bangladesh and substantial in India. There are a few techniques that may be used as deterrents. One method of discouraging theft is to use shrink wrapping, seals, or strapping. Gummed sealing tapes with patterns, when used, will quickly reveal any sign of tampering. In addition, only well-constructed packing in good condition should be used.

According to the RF Federal Customs Service and the International Road Transportation Union, non-delivery of shipments to their final destinations is a major security problem in Russia. Non-delivery occurs either due to cargo theft or shippers' use of dubious import schemes resulting in the seizure of products at borders.[13]

Another area of concern is marking. The main purpose of marking is to identify shipments so that the carrier can forward the shipment to the designated consignee. Markings thus should not be used to advertise the contents, especially when they are valuable or highly desirable in nature. A firm is also wise to avoid mentioning the contents, trade names, consignees' names, or shippers' names on the package because these markings reveal the nature of the contents. Because markings are still a necessity, they should be permanent, though so-called blind marks should be used. To avoid handlers becoming familiar with the markings, blind marks should be changed periodically. Bright color coding helps in spotting the pieces.

Packing alone should not be expected to eliminate theft. Packing should be used in conjunction with other precautionary measures. One of the most effective means of reducing exposure to theft, pilferage, and hijacking is to insist on prompt pickup and delivery. Another good idea is to avoid shipping the cargo if it will arrive at its destination on a weekend or holiday. One Chicago importer of jewelry found on Monday, when he went to pick up his merchandise at the O'Hare Airport, that the cargo had already been claimed by someone else over the weekend.

Cargo theft is a significant concern everywhere, especially in developing countries. In Mexico, since the mid-1990s, truck hijackings have become an epidemic. Criminals prefer medicines, clothing, food, and consumer electronics because these items can be quickly sold. Because of the rising claims and losses, insurance companies have drastically increased the premiums on cargo insurance while requiring higher deductibles. As a result, some companies (e.g., Nestlé) no longer insure cargo, choosing to cover losses themselves. For protection, they have beefed up security. Trucks may travel in convoys, or they are accompanied by armed escorts. Global positioning systems are used to track trucks.[14]

## Containers

An increasingly popular method of shipment is **containerization**. The growth in the use of containers has been explosive. About 90 percent of the world's cargo now travels via containers. The shipping container has been instrumental in spurring world trade. In the early 1960s, moving goods from one country to another was often prohibitively expensive. Nowadays, thanks to the creation of containers, freight costs are largely negligible.[15]

A container is a large box made of durable material such as steel, aluminum, plywood, and glass reinforced plastic. A container varies in size, material, and construction. Its dimensions are typically 8 ft high and 8 ft wide, with lengths usually varying in multiples of 10 ft up to a maximum of 40 ft. A container can accommodate most cargo but is most suitable for packages of standard size and shape. Some containers are no more than truck bodies that have been lifted off their wheels and placed on a vessel at the port of export. These containers are then transferred to another set of wheels at the port of import for inland movement. This type of container can be put on a ship, or can become a barcar when placed on a railway flatcar, or can be made into a trailer when provided with a chassis. Containers are ordinarily obtained from either carriers or private parties.

Containers can take care of most of the four main packing problems. Because of a container's construction, a product does not have to have heavy packing. The container by itself provides good protection for the product against breakage, moisture, and temperature. Because breaking into a container is difficult, this method of shipment discourages pilferage and theft as well. In addition, containers have substantially reduced the average transit time of ocean-shipped goods.

It is important to select the right container because containers come in varying sizes and types. Two basic types of container may be identified: (1) *dry cargo containers* and (2) *special purpose containers*. Some of the various types of dry cargo containers are end loading, fully closed; side loading, fully enclosed; and open top, ventilated, insulated. Special purpose containers come in different types for refrigerated, liquid bulk, dry bulk, flat rack, auto, livestock, and sea shed.

Exporters may have to plan for the return of secondary packaging or the container or both. Argentina's inefficient exports force those who do business with Argentina to ship most containers back empty.[16] One U.S. car manufacturer, after experimenting with containers, resumed shipping parts in wooden crates instead. Japanese firms have partially solved the Argentina problem by using collapsible racking and shipping systems so that items can be more densely packaged for return shipment.

## Freight forwarder and customs broker

There are two intermediaries whose services are quite essential in moving cargo for their principals, across counties as well as within countries: freight forwarders and customhouse brokers. Their various roles in the distribution process are shown in Figure 13.5. A freight forwarder generally works for exporters, whereas the customs broker generally works for importers. Because their functions are similar, freight forwarders sometimes act as customs brokers and vice versa.

A freight forwarder is a person responsible for the forwarding of freight locally as well as internationally. He or she is an independent businessperson who handles shipments for compensation. The kind of freight forwarder of concern here is the foreign or international freight forwarder who moves goods destined for overseas destinations.

A foreign freight forwarder is an exporter's agent (shipping agent) who performs virtually all aspects of physical distribution necessary to move cargo to overseas destinations in the most efficient and economic manner. To comply with export documentation and shipping requirements, the freight forwarder can take care of cargo from "dock to door." The services, when needed, include "the correct filing of export documentation, all arrangements with carriers, packing, crating and storage needs."[17] The freight forwarder can represent shippers in both air and ocean freight shipments because the procedures and documents required are very similar.

The freight forwarder's major contribution to the exporter is his or her ability to provide traffic and documentation responsibilities for international freight movements. This middleman handles the voluminous paperwork required in international trade, and is highly specialized in (1) traffic operations (methods of shipping), (2) government export regulations, (3) overseas import regulations, and (4) documents connected with foreign trade and customs clearance. In brief, the freight forwarder arranges all necessary details for the proper shipping, insuring, and documenting of overseas shipments.

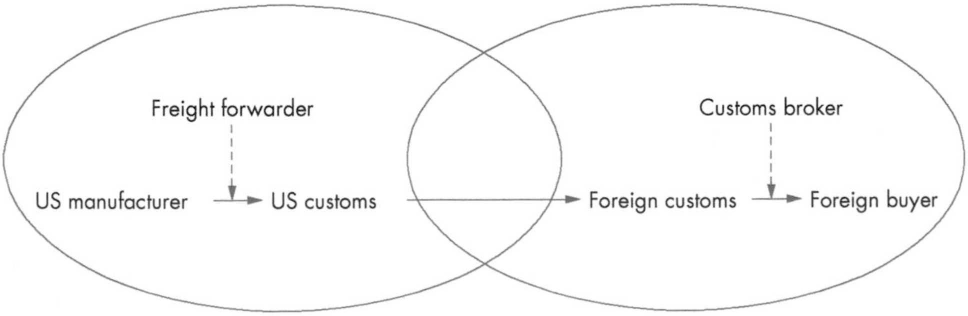
Freight forwarder
Customs broker
US manufacturer
US customs
Foreign customs
Foreign buyer

**FIGURE 13.5** Intermediaries that facilitate physical distribution

The freight forwarder can assist an exporter from the very beginning in getting a shipment ready for overseas. Once the exporter receives an inquiry, it can turn to the freight forwarder for assistance in preparing its quotation. The freight forwarder can advise the exporter on freight costs, port charges, consular fees, cost of special documentation, insurance costs, and the forwarder's handling fees, as well as recommend the degree of packing needed or arrange to have the merchandise packed or containerized.

The freight forwarder also prepares ocean bills of lading and any special consular documents, and reviews letters of credit, packing lists, and so on to ensure that all procedures are in order. After the shipment is made, the freight forwarder forwards all documents to the customer's paying bank with instructions to credit the exporter's account.

The freight forwarder can assist the exporter in other areas. This person can reserve space aboard an ocean vessel. He or she may consolidate small shipments into full container loads and, by doing so, can receive a lower rate from the carrier and pass on the savings to the shipper. The freight forwarder can arrange to clear goods through customs and have the goods delivered to the pier in time for loading. This middleman then handles the goods from exit port to destination. If desired, the freight forwarder can further move goods inland in a foreign country through various affiliates. According to one study, freight forwarders feel that the United Kingdom is the easiest and China the most difficult with regard to arranging international freight operations.[18]

The freight forwarder receives a fee from exporters. The service cost is a legitimate export cost and should be figured into the contract price charged to buyers. In addition, this person may receive brokerage fees and/or rebates from shipping companies for booked space. In such cases, the freight forwarder's commission is paid by the shipping lines. Because freight forwarders control most of the smaller shipments and because the less-than-container (LTC) traffic accounts for 17 to 18 percent of the business, carriers woo freight forwarders with extra rebates.

The counterpart of the freight forwarder for an exporter is the customs broker for an importer. As an individual or firm licensed to enter and clear goods through customs, a customs broker is a person or firm employed by an importer to take over the responsibility of clearing the importer's shipments through customs on a fee basis. A licensed customs broker named in a Customs Power of Attorney can effect entry. This broker is bonded, and the broker's bond provides the required coverage to carry on the responsibilities of the job. A customs broker may also act as a freight forwarder once the shipment is cleared. In the U.S.A., a customs broker must be licensed by the Treasury Department in order to perform these services.

The customs broker is indispensable in the receipt of goods from overseas. The services are valuable because the requirements for customs clearance are complicated. To effect entry, a person must have evidence of the right to make entry (carrier's certificate), in addition to the commercial invoice, packing, and surety. Moreover, the person must fill out forms with regard to dutiable status and must also have the goods examined under conditions that safeguard the goods before they are released. Overall, entry is a two-step process – getting goods released and providing information for duty assessment and statistical purposes. The customs broker is in the best position to provide for these requirements.

## Contract logistics

In many or perhaps most cases, marketers may find that it is much more practical to leave the physical distribution activities to specialists. Dell Computer Corp., for example, sells computers in 115 countries. It has arranged for Roadway Services Inc. to handle Dell's worldwide shipping. Earlier, Dell had to deal with dozens of carriers and found that it would have to hire 1,000 to 2,000 additional workers to meet the projected growth. Roadway, as a single-source provider, subcontracts and manages all customer shipments – both inbound and outbound.

For years, it might take a month for Ford Motor Co. to get its cars to its dealers' lots. It was not unusual for Ford to lose track of trainloads of cars. To overhaul its inefficient distribution network, Ford formed a joint venture with United Parcel Services Inc. UPS employs a tracking system like the one it uses to keep track of some 14 million packages daily. As a result, delivery time has been reduced to ten days, saving Ford millions of dollars in working capital each year.

UPS wants to serve as a traffic manager for companies. It has expertise to schedule planes, trains, and ships, and it can manage warehouses and distribution centers. While contract logistics offers high revenue growth, profit growth is probably not high. UPS's delivery business yields margins of about 15 percent. Contract logistics is a lower margin business, and it may be as low as 2 percent for work such as freight forwarding, management of warehouses, or order fulfillment.[19]

## Documentation

It is not an exaggeration to say that "paper moves cargo." To move cargo, documentation is a necessity. American firms used to complain about the cost of documentation and shipping in the EU. Documentation alone added 3 to 5 percent of the total cost of goods sold (see Legal Dimension 13.1).

Africa has many problems related to physical distribution. On the one hand, companies and consumers have to put up with bad roads, inefficient ports, and unreliable or even nonexistent electricity supply. All of these factors contribute to longer transit time. On the other hand, the bigger problems causing goods to be held up are the paperwork, inspections, and customs procedures.[20]

International direct marketers need to ensure that their delivery methods are convenient for their customers. As in the case of WearGuard Work Clothes, a U.S. company, it has four options to fulfill orders for Canadian customers: U.S. Postal Service parcel post, courier companies, bulk shipment,

### Legal Dimension 13.1

**Less is more**

At one time, New Zealand Customs officials inspected every shipment as well as interacting with every person at the border. Certainly, these practices are time-consuming and inefficient. So the country has begun to use risk-management strategies that allow officials to focus on a truly suspicious activity while permitting legitimate goods and persons to quickly cross the border. Prior to customs reforms, for example, boat builders had to pay a duty on imported boat parts and later apply for a refund after the exportation of a completed craft. The process necessitated a great deal of paperwork flowing back and forth. The reforms have made it possible for boat makers to merely register the parts with the Customs Service without having to tie up capital for months – not to mention less paperwork. New Zealand now collects relevant taxes and duties with a minimum of intervention.

*Source*: Mike Moore, "Tariff Reductions Aren't Enough," *Asian Wall Street Journal*, June 19, 2001.

and local fulfillment. In the end, it chose TNT Mailfast to bring WearGuard's parcels into Canada, clear them at customs, and give them to Canada Post for local delivery. This method allows Canadian customers to receive the merchandise without having to pay duties or additional fees. The company also has a Canadian address so that Canadian customers can conveniently mail packages in case of customer returns.[21]

Product transportation in the European Union has become easier and more efficient. As of 1993, border controls were removed. Border stops are limited to checking on legal matters such as illegal immigration and drug trafficking. Since 1995, some EU states have allowed people to move freely within the EU without having to show their passports.

To facilitate cargo movement, nations have been working toward automated customs – paperless international customs procedures. The Customs Cooperation Council, representing more than 130 nations, has approved a plan by which customs administrations around the world can work toward electronic data interchange. The main standards body for international electronic message is a United Nations-backed group called Edifact (Electronic Data Interchange for Administration, Commerce, and Transport). While Japanese companies do business with one another electronically, they use their own standards which force outsiders wanting to establish computerized links to engage in expensive programming and translation efforts. Edifact, however, works everywhere. Japan has finally agreed to join with Singapore to create a regional Edifact board. By sending standardized digital messages at computer speeds, importers can bypass piles of bureaucratic paperwork. Use of paperless trading technology should significantly improve the speed and efficiency of data and global trade. Unfortunately, only about 10,000 out of two million customs declarations in Russia are processed electronically.[22]

Exporters may want to consider purchasing an export-automation software. Some of the export software incorporates the electronic data interchange (EDI) technology, making it possible for exporters to send computer-generated forms electronically rather than mailing the documents to freight forwarders, customers, banks, and government agencies.

To fill out the required documents, a company must insert the proper identification number for its product. All products must be "shoehorned" into some kind of category. If a product is constructed out of several materials, it may be classified by the material that gives it its essential character. On January 1, 1989, the Harmonized Tariff System (HTS) went into effect. This system, designed to replace previous systems for classifying exports, contains logically structured nomenclature. There are 21 sections and 99 chapters to arrange commodities according to general economic activity. The sections and chapters are arranged according to levels of processing, with primary commodities classified first, followed by the technically more complex products.

The HTS assigns a number to each product which is traded internationally to ensure that customs officers and statisticians around the world are referring to the same thing when they classify a particular product. Almost all countries now use the HTS. The HTS number refers to a six-digit product-specific code. To meet each country's statistical and tariff requirements, the remaining digits are country-specific. Certain countries also use either alphabetical subdivisions after the six digits or combined alphanumerical systems, making the entire number 10 digits. This is what the U.S.A. does with its Schedule B system when describing U.S. imports.[23] As an example, the HS code for "widgets" is 12.34.56.78.90, the breakdowns are 12 (chapter), 12.34 (heading), 12.34.56 (subheading), 12.34.56.78 (tariff item), and 12.34.56.78.90 (HS Classification Number). When researching tariff rates for any region, it is important to first have a Harmonized System Number (HS) that corresponds to the product in question in order to obtain the exact rate.

Because of terrorist actions, security has assumed much greater prominence. The focus has shifted from drug smuggling to smuggling of biological, chemical, and nuclear weapons. In the aftermath of September 11, 2001 attacks on the U.S.A., a more secure shipping network is a necessity. Some security measures that can be employed are: greater security at a plant or loading dock, greater security during transport, submitting information on cargo in advance, and using electronic seals for container shipments.[24]

Documentation now plays a significant role in combating terrorism. The 24-hour rule requires a filing of detailed cargo information a full day before containers are loaded aboard U.S.-bound vessels. In the past, it was hardly unusual for a container to be loaded at the last minute. Once on board, the cargo could still be sold, necessitating a change in destination. Freight forwarders could simply forward cargo information just five days before the cargo reached a U.S. port. The cargo descriptions could be vague (e.g., "freight-any-kind" or "general freight." These descriptions are no longer accepted. U.S. Customs now requires shippers and freight forwarders to electronically submit a cargo manifest (a complete description of the cargo) to the National Targeting Center. Any suspicious or incomplete lists receive "no-load" messages. There are plans to require air, rail, and truck companies (just like their ocean counterparts) to list cargo manifests well in advance of arrival at airports, rail yards, and truck depots. Before the September 11 events, only 2 percent of cargo containers were inspected. The percentage has gone up to only 3 or 4 percent due to the sheer number of containers at U.S. ports.[25]

The summer of 2006 was another nightmare for delivery trucks on Russia's borders with Latvia, Estonia, and Finland. There were 30-kilometer- long lines of carriers waiting to clear Russian customs. A one-week delay to clear customs adds $1,000 to the transportation costs. Russian facilities at cross-points with EU countries do not have adequate space, equipment, and manpower to cope with the flow of imports that has gone up 457 percent since 1996. To make matters much worse, Russian customs officers excessively review documents and try to inspect all incoming goods. When facing unclear regulations, customs officers are afraid to make decisions that might cost them penalties or even their jobs in case their decisions are later overturned. To protect themselves, customs brokers may require additional documents to verify the declared value of goods even though they are not required by customs. They do so because the customs code requires them to provide security guarantees of 50 million rubles. They also use this extortionate practice to extract extra fees from clients. An importer facing this problem has to wait for extra documents, and a three-day delivery may turn out to take 17 days for the goods to arrive at the destination. The delay is also expensive in another way since storage fees of up to $3,000 a week add to the burden.[26]

There are many kinds of documents, and they can be grouped under two broad categories: (1) shipping documents and (2) collection documents. Shipping documents are prepared to move shipments through customs, allowing the cargo to be loaded, shipped, and unloaded. Collection documents, in contrast, are submitted to a customer or the customer's bank for payment.

## Shipping documents

There are several kinds of shipping documents. Such documents include the export license and shipper's export declaration forms, among others.

### Export license

An export license is a permit allowing merchandise to be exported, and virtually all countries require some form of export permit. In the case of the U.S.A., an export license is needed on all exports, except for shipments going to Canada and U.S. territories and possessions. The U.S.A. has two broad categories of export license: general and validated. The difference between the two has to do with whether a particular license requires prior, written approval from the U.S. Department of Commerce. The type of license required depends on the sophistication of the product, the destination country, the end-use, and the end-user.

## General license

A general license is a license for which no application is required and for which no document or written authorization is granted. It is a general authorization permitting the export of certain commodities and technical data without the necessity of applying for a license document. A general license allows the export through the Export Administration Regulations of all goods published in an authorization list and covers the export of nonstrategic goods (commodities not under restriction or control). Products that meet specific conditions can be shipped by merely inserting a correct General License symbol on the export control document known as a Shipper's Export Declaration.

## Validated export license

If an exporter does not qualify for a general license, the exporter may apply for a validated export license which, in effect, is a formal authorization document. The U.S.A. requires this kind of licensing for reasons of national security (strategic significance), short supply, or foreign policy. National security controls were necessary to prevent the export of strategic commodities and technical data to communist countries. Foreign policy controls, such as the restrictions placed on exports to South Africa and Namibia, are instituted by such licensing to promote U.S. foreign policy. In the case of short-supply controls, the licenses are granted with an eye to preventing the depletion of scarce materials (e.g., Western red cedar and petroleum).

Many of the products shipped under individual validated licenses (IVLs) and special licenses need pre-export paperwork (e.g., a foreign consignee/purchaser statement or a government-issued import certificate) to obtain the necessary license. IVLs authorize individual sales of a certain product to a certain customer in a certain country. Special licenses (e.g., project and distribution licenses) authorize the sale of a range of products to many customers if exporters can show that they have implemented a strict control process.

For control purposes, the U.S.A. regulates computer exports by creating four tiers of countries. The Tier 1 countries are the closest allies. Tier 2, the largest group, has most of the rest of the world. Countries in Tier 3 are those that U.S.A. is wary of, and they include China, Israel, and Russia. The Tier 4 countries are American enemies and rogue states (Cuba, Iran, Iraq, Libya, North Korea, Sudan, and Syria), and computer exports to them are prohibited.[27]

Foreign and U.S. firms that illegally export U.S. products risk losing their export privileges. Exhibit 13.1 describes how business firms can watch out for illegal export schemes.

The U.S. State Department processed 66,000 export authorization requests recently for items and services under arms controls. In spite of the export control, many U.S. companies have been found to violate export laws. Hughes Electronics and Boeing Satellite Systems, the two top U.S. aerospace companies, paid a record $32 million in fines in 2003 for unlawfully transferring rocket and satellite data to China in 1990s. The technology used to launch civilian rockets and satellites is similar to the technology for launching missiles. The companies "express regret for not having obtained licenses that

Exhibit 13.1

**Possible indicators of illegal export schemes**

The following are some possible indicators that an illegal diversion might be planned by an export customer:

- The customer or purchasing agent is reluctant to offer information about the end use of a product.
- The product's capabilities do not fit the buyer's line of business: for example, an order for several sophisticated computers for a small bakery.
- The product ordered is incompatible with the technical level of the country to which the product is being shipped. Semiconductor manufacturing equipment would be of little use in a country without an electronics industry.
- The customer is willing to pay cash for a very expensive item when the terms of the sale call for financing.
- The customer has little or no business background.
- The customer is unfamiliar with the product's performance characteristics but still wants the product.
- Routine installation, training, or maintenance services are declined by the customer.
- Delivery dates are vague, or deliveries are planned for out-of-the-way destinations.
- A freight forwarding firm is listed as the product's final destination.
- Packaging is inconsistent with the stated method of shipment or destination.
- When questioned, the buyer is evasive and especially unclear about whether the purchased product is for domestic use, export, or re-export.

*Source*: U.S. Department of Commerce.

should have been obtained" and "acknowledge the nature and seriousness of the offenses charged by the Department of State, including the harm such offenses could cause to the security and foreign policy interests of the United States."[28] To settle similar cases, Lockheed Martin and Loral Space and Communications paid fines of $13 million and $20 million. While regulations can be complex, it is difficult to see how these large companies, with all their resources and export knowledge, have failed to understand the export regulations of the U.S.A. In the case of ITT Corp., some of its managers even viewed internal compliance officials "as obstacles to getting business done." ITT, in its effort to reduce costs, outsourced production of components for advanced night vision equipment for the U.S. military. The company gave technical drawings and specifications for the components to a Singapore firm, which gave some of the work to companies in China and Britain. Having to admit guilt to two counts of violations of the 1976 Arms Export Control Act, ITT paid $100 million in penalties.[29]

## *Shipper's export declaration (SED) form*

In the majority of cases, exporters need to declare their shipments. American exporters, for example, are required to file SEDs for virtually all shipments, including hand-carried merchandise, and they must be deposited with an exporting carrier regardless of the type of export license. Exemptions apply to shipments to certain countries when the value is $2500 or less and when the shipment is not moving under a validated export license.

The SED is a multipurpose document. One of its purposes is to serve as an export control document. It declares the proper authorization for export by making reference to some type of export license. Another purpose of the SED is to compile basic statistical information on export shipments. These data are compiled and published to show the types of commodities exported and the countries that imported them.

### Hazardous certificate

To export hazardous cargo, an exporter must use a shipper's certification or declaration of dangerous cargo. This document, required for all hazardous shipments, is used to describe the contents by providing the details and qualities of the items being shipped, their proper classification, required labels, and so on. This declaration must always be completed by the shipper (preferably on the shipper's letterhead) and signed by the shipper. There is no prescribed form for ocean shipments of hazardous materials at the present time. For all hazardous shipments moving via air freight, a shipper's declaration of dangerous cargo (air cargo) must be submitted to the airline.

### Packing list

A packing list is a document that lists the type and number of pieces, the contents, weight, and measurement of each, as well as the marks and numbers. Its purpose is to facilitate customs clearance, keep track of inventory of goods, and assist in tracing lost goods. For insurance purposes, the packing list may be used in determining the contents of a lost piece. Furthermore, it is also useful in estimating shipping cost prior to export.

### Shipper's letter of instructions

The shipper's letter of instructions is a form provided to the freight forwarder from the shipper giving all pertinent information and instruction regarding the shipment and how it is to be handled. When signed by the shipper, it also authorizes the forwarder to issue and sign documents on behalf of the shipper.

### Dock receipt

A dock receipt is proof of delivery for goods received at the dock or warehouse of the steamship line. This document is required for shipments sailing from ports on the U.S. East and Gulf coasts. Six copies of the dock receipt must be lodged at the receiving warehouse before freight can be accepted.

## Collection documents

Before a seller can request payment, the seller must provide the buyer with a number of documents showing that the terms agreed upon have been fulfilled. The buyer requires such documents to protect itself and to satisfy its government's requirements.

### Commercial invoice

To collect payment, an invoice is needed. There are two kinds of invoices: (1) *pro forma* and (2) *commercial*. A pro forma invoice is an invoice provided by a supplier prior to the shipment of merchandise. The purpose of this invoice is to inform the buyer of the kinds and quantities of goods to be sent, their value, and import specifications (weight, size, and so on). The buyer may also need the pro forma invoice in order to be able to apply for an import license and/or a letter of credit.

A commercial invoice is a document that provides an itemized list of goods shipped and other charges. As a record of the business transaction between two parties, it provides a complete description of merchandise, quantity, price, and shipping and payment terms. It is desirable that this invoice contains a breakdown of charges such as those related to inland transportation, loading, insurance, freight, handling, and certification. Because the invoice is required to clear goods through customs, all necessary information required by the buyer's government must be included.

The requirements of the exporter's country must be satisfied as well. The U.S.A. prohibits certain goods from being diverted to countries such as North Korea and Cuba. Therefore, the invoice may have to be prepared so that it includes an anti-diversion clause or destination control statement. According to section 387.6 of the Export Administration Regulations,

> No person may export, dispose of, divert, direct, mail or otherwise ship, transship, or re-export commodities or technical data to any person or destination or for any use in violation of or contrary to the terms, provisions, or conditions of any export control document, any prior representation, any form of notification of prohibition against such action, or any provision of the Export Administration Act or any regulation, order, or license issued under the Act.

### *Foreign customs invoice*

A customs invoice is a special format invoice required by customs officials in some countries in lieu of the commercial invoice, as those officials may not recognize the commercial invoice for customs purposes. A foreign customs invoice is shown in Figure 13.6. This type of invoice generally contains the same information as the commercial invoice and may also contain certifications with regard to value and origin of the shipment.

### *Consular invoice*

In addition to the regular commercial invoice, several countries, notably those in Latin America, require legalized or visaed documents that often include a special kind of invoice known as a consular invoice. A consular invoice is a detailed comment prepared by a seller in the importing country's language on an official form supplied by the importer's government. Its purpose is to monitor merchandise and capital flows. Exhibit 13.2 lists those countries that require such documents.

A consular invoice must have an official stamp, seal, or signature affixed to it. This is the responsibility of the consulate general, who is a representative of the government of the importing country. The resident consul is supposed to verify the contents of the invoice (e.g., value, quantity, and nature of shipment) and to certify its authenticity and correctness. Usually, there is a fee for this service; Bolivia's consular fees for the notarization of invoices are 1 percent of the FOB value.

It is significant to keep in mind that the consulate is not obligated to facilitate imports by approving the submitted documents quickly. Because the consul may take his or her time in returning the visaed documents, an exporter should allow reasonable time for the processing of a consular invoice. It can be a frustrating experience to rush the consulate for the documents while the shipment is waiting.

**COMMERCIAL INVOICE FOR THE CARIBBEAN COMMON MARKET**

| SELLER (Name, Full Address, Country) | INVOICE DATE AND NO. | CUSTOMER'S ORDER NO. |
|---|---|---|
| ABC COMPANY<br>84609 SOUTH LANE<br>DETROIT, MICHIGAN 00000<br>U.S.A. | DATE: 10/1/87<br>NO: A495Z | PR8097 |
| | OTHER REFERENCES | |
| CONSIGNEE (Name, Full Address, Country)<br>ANTIGUA WHITE SANDS MOTEL<br>P.O. BOX 655<br>ST. JOHNS, ANTIGUA | BUYER (If Other Than Consignee) | |
| | PRESENTING BANK<br>XYZ BANK, ST. JOHNS | |
| | COUNTRY OF ORIGIN OF GOODS<br>UNITED STATES OF AMERICA | |
| PORT OF LADING<br>MIAMI | TERMS AND CONDITIONS OF DELIVERY AND PAYMENT<br>C AND F ST. JOHNS, ANTIGUA<br>SIGHT DRAFT, DOCUMENTS AGAINST PAYMENT | |
| COUNTRY OF FINAL DESTINATION: ANTIGUA<br>SHIP/AIR/ETC.: CARICOM V.109 | | |
| OTHER TRANSPORT INFORMATION<br>B/L NO. 185 | CURRENCY OF SALE<br>U.S. DOLLARS | |

| MARK AND NUMBERS | DESCRIPTION OF GOODS | GROSS WEIGHT(Kg.) | CUBIC METRES |
|---|---|---|---|
| A W S M<br>ANTIGUA<br>1/2 | RESTAURANT SUPPLIES | 130 Kgs | 1.354m3 |

| NO. AND KIND OF PACKAGES | SPECIFICATION OF COMMODITIES (IN CODE AND/OR IN FULL) | NET WEIGHT (Kg.) | QUANTITY | UNIT PRICE | AMOUNT |
|---|---|---|---|---|---|
| 2 CRATES | KITCHEN KNIFE A203 | 108 Kgs | 50 DOZ | 19.00/DZ | 950.00 |
| | | PACKING | | | 25.00 |
| | | FREIGHT | INLAND | | 35.00 |
| | | | OCEAN | | 120.00 |
| | | OTHER COSTS (Specify) | FORWARDING FEE | | 50.00 |
| | | INSURANCE | N/A | | |
| | | TOTAL INVOICE AMOUNT | C&F ST. JOHNS | | US$ 1,180.00 |

IT IS HEREBY CERTIFIED THAT THIS INVOICE SHOWS THE ACTUAL PRICE OF THE GOODS DESCRIBED, THAT NO OTHER INVOICE HAS BEEN OR WILL BE ISSUED AND THAT ALL PARTICULARS ARE TRUE AND CORRECT.

J. Doe

J. DOE, Clerk — 10/9/87 — DETROIT

SIGNATURE AND STATUS OF AUTHORIZED PERSON — DATE — PLACE

**FIGURE 13.6** Foreign customs invoice

*Source*: Reprinted with permission of Radix Group International, Inc.

Exhibit 13.2

**Countries that require a consular invoice**

**Near and Middle East**
Saudi Arabia
Kuwait
Lebanon
Oman
Jordan
Bahrain
Syria
Yemen
Iraq
Iran
United Arab Emirates

**South America**
Colombia (by request)
Argentina
Uruguay
Paraguay

**Central America**
Panama
Nicaragua
Honduras
Guatemala

**Far East**
Philippines (by request)

**Europe and Asia**
Greece (by request)
Spain (by request)
Turkey

**Africa**
Libya

**Caribbean**
Dominican Republic

*Source*: Reprinted with permission of Radix Group International, Inc.

Because a consular invoice is a legal document, any errors noted later require special consideration. An exporter cannot simply make corrections on a consular invoice that has been certified. Such corrections are considered forgery, and the criminal penalty can be quite severe.

Although a consular invoice usually contains the same information as a commercial invoice, the actual information required by the consulate depends on where the shipping is to be made. The best way to find out what is specifically required is to speak directly with the consulate or consult one of the reference manuals available, such as *Dun and Bradstreet* or the *International Trade Reporter* of the Bureau of National Affairs (BNA).

## Certificate of origin

A certificate of origin is a document prepared by the exporter and is used to identify or declare that the merchandise originated in a certain country. It assures the buyer or importer of the country of manufacture. This document is necessary for tariff and control purposes. Some countries may require statements of origin to establish possible preferential rates of import duties under the Most Favored Nation arrangements. This certificate also prevents the inadvertent importation of goods from prohibited or unfriendly countries. The forms can vary, ranging from a shipper's own letterhead certificate to a countersigning by the Chamber of Commerce (see Figure 13.7). In some cases, such

# CERTIFICATE OF ORIGIN

**2. EXPORTER** *(Principal or seller-licensee and address including ZIP Code)*

SHIPPER OF AMERICA
1234 NORTH STREET
CHICAGO, ILLINOIS
U.S.A.

ZIP CODE: 60000

**5. DOCUMENT NUMBER**

**5A. B/L OR AWB NUMBER**

**6. EXPORT REFERENCES**

9246

**3. CONSIGNED TO**

IMPORTER OF SAUDI ARABIA
P.O. BOX 740
JEDDAH, SAUDI ARABIA

**7. FORWARDING AGENT** *(Name and address - references)*

RADIX GROUP INTERNATIONAL
P.O. BOX 66213
CHICAGO, ILLINOIS 60666 FMC 232

**8. POINT (STATE) OF ORIGIN OR FTZ NUMBER**

IL

**4. NOTIFY PARTY/INTERMEDIATE CONSIGNEE** *(Name and address)*

GULF BROKERS LTD.
P.O. BOX 2009
JEDDAH, SAUDI ARABIA

**9. DOMESTIC ROUTING/EXPORT INSTRUCTIONS**

**12. PRE-CARRIAGE BY**

**13. PLACE OF RECEIPT BY PRE-CARRIER**

**14. EXPORTING CARRIER**

A VESSEL

**15. PORT OF LOADING/EXPORT**

NEW YORK

**10. LOADING PIER/TERMINAL**

**16. FOREIGN PORT OF UNLOADING** *(Vessel and air only)*

JEDDAH

**17. PLACE OF DELIVERY BY ON-CARRIER**

**11. TYPE OF MOVE**

**11.a CONTAINERIZED** *(Vessel only)* ☐ YES ☒ NO

| MARKS AND NUMBERS (18) | NUMBER OF PACKAGES (19) | DESCRIPTION OF COMMODITIES *in Schedule B detail* (20) | GROSS WEIGHT *(Pounds)* (21) | MEASUREMENT (22) |
|---|---|---|---|---|
| I.S.A.<br>JEDDAH<br>MADE IN U.S.A.<br>NO. 1/4 | 4 | BOXES: POWER TOOLS<br><br>MANUFACTURER:<br>SHIPPER OF AMERICA<br>1234 NORTH STREET<br>CHICAGO, ILLINOIS 60000<br>U.S.A. | 843# | 97' |

The undersigned......JANE DOE.................(Owner or Agent), does hereby declare for the above named shipper, the goods as described above were shipped on the above date and consigned as indicated and are products of the United States of America Dated at.....CHICAGO, IL....................... on the..10th..day of....OCTOBER.............................19.87.

Sworn to before me this ..10th.. day of ..OCTOBER.................. 19.87.

Debra Uvelli

.....NOTARY PUBLIC.........

"OFFICIAL SEAL"
DEBRA UVELLI
Notary Public, State of Illinois
My Commission Expires 6/11/91

Jane Doe
SIGNATURE OF OWNER OR AGENT

The.....ANY TOWN ASSOCIATION OF COMMERCE AND INDUSTRY......................., a recognized Chamber of Commerce under the laws of the State of .......ILLINOIS...................., has examined the manufacturer's invoice or shipper's affidavit concerning the origin of the merchandise, and, according to the best of its knowledge and belief, finds that the products named originated in the United States of North America.

Secretary .........M. H. JONES.............................

**FIGURE 13.7** A certificate of origin

*Source*: Reprinted with permission of Radix Group International, Inc.

forms must be visaed by an importing country's resident consul. For international use, this document is generally notarized and chamberized.

### Inspection certificate

An inspection certificate is a document certifying that the merchandise was in good condition immediately prior to shipment. Many foreign buyers protect themselves by requiring a shipper's affidavit or an independent inspection firm to certify quality and quantity and conformity of goods in relation to the order, as well as to ensure that the goods contracted for have actually been shipped. This certificate is normally prepared by an independent firm other than the exporter, attesting to the quality or quantity of goods being shipped.

### Special purpose documents

As in the case of an inspection certificate, an importer may request other special documents, such as a certificate of weight/measurement and certificate of analysis in order to protect the importer's interests. A certificate of weight/measurement is issued by an independent party attesting to the weight or measurement of the merchandise to be shipped. A certificate of analysis contains an expert's report on the findings or grading of the substance or composition of the product shipped. The document assures the buyer that the goods are those that an exporter contracted for shipment.

### Insurance certificate

A certificate of insurance is a negotiable document issued to provide coverage for a specific shipment. It briefly describes the transaction and its coverage. Usually, an insurance certificate is issued as an open-coverage policy to protect any and all shipments and transportation as long as a certificate is filed for each shipment. Generally, the policy will cover most losses sustained during transit. Not restricted only to ocean shipments is a marine insurance policy, which covers all modes of transportation.

### Air waybill

An air waybill is basically a bill of lading issued by air carriers for air shipments. This transport instrument is not a negotiable document. As a result, a carrier will release goods to a designated consignee without the waybill.

### Bill of lading

A bill of lading is a document issued to record shipment transportation (see Figure 13.8). Usually prepared by a shipper on the shipper's carrier's forms, this document serves three useful functions. First, as a *document of title*, it is a certificate of ownership that allows a holder or consignee to claim the merchandise described. Second, as a *receipt of goods*, it is issued by the carrier to the shipper for goods entrusted to the carrier's care for transportation. A bill of lading is thus proof of the carrier's possession of the freight. Third, as a *contract of carriage*, the bill of lading defines the contract terms between the shipper and his carrier. The conditions under which the goods are to be carried and the carrier's responsibility for the delivery are specified.

UNION STAR LINE

**SAMPLE BILL OF LADING**

| | |
|---|---|
| SHIPPER/EXPORTER<br>SHIPPER OF AMERICA INC.<br>1234 NORTH STREET<br>CHICAGO, ILLINOIS 60000<br>U.S.A. | DOCUMENT NO.<br><br>EXPORT REFERENCES<br>9876 |
| CONSIGNEE<br>OVERSEAS IMPORTS LTD.<br>5678 JOHN AVENUE<br>D-2000 HAMBURG, WEST GERMANY | FORWARDING AGENT — REFERENCES<br>RADIX GROUP INTERNATIONAL<br>P.O. BOX 66213<br>CHICAGO, IL 60666 FMC 232<br><br>POINT AND COUNTRY OF ORIGIN<br>IL |
| NOTIFY PARTY<br>SAME | DOMESTIC ROUTING/EXPORT INSTRUCTIONS |

| | | |
|---|---|---|
| PRECARRIAGE BY | PLACE OF RECEIPT<br>CHICAGO | |
| VESSEL<br>DAS BOOT V.01 | PORT OF LOADING<br>MONTREAL | ONWARD INLAND ROUTING |
| PORT OF DISCHARGE<br>HAMBURG | PLACE OF DELIVERY | |

PARTICULARS FURNISHED BY SHIPPER

| MARKS AND NUMBERS | NO. OF PKGS. | DESCRIPTION OF PACKAGES AND GOODS | GROSS WEIGHT | MEASUREMENT |
|---|---|---|---|---|
| OVERSEAS IMPORT<br>9876<br>MADE IN U.S.A.<br>NOS. 1/5 | 5 | SKIDS S.T.C. 10 CARTONS: BOOKS<br><br>FREIGHT COLLECT | 2000#<br><br>LADEN ON BOARD<br>OCT 10 1987 jws. | 100' |

These commodities licensed by U.S. for ultimate destination WEST GERMANY.
Diversion contrary to U.S. law prohibited.

FREIGHT CHARGES PAYABLE AT DESTINATION

| | PREPAID | COLLECT |
|---|---|---|
| | | |

Received from the aforenamed shipper, the goods as described above by the shipper in apparent external good order and condition unless otherwise indicated herein or hereon to be transported in accordance with all of the terms printed, written, typed or stamped in or on this B/L of two (2) pages to which the merchant agrees by accepting this B/L any local privileges or customs notwithstanding

In witness whereof, three (3) original BS/L have been signed, and if one (1) is accomplished by delivery of the Goods, issuance of a delivery order or by some other means, the others shall be void if required by the carrier, one (1) original B/L must be surrendered, duly endorsed in exchange for the goods or a delivery order

Dated at Port of Loading UNION STAR LINE

10 (MO) 10 (DAY) 1987 (YEAR) By J.W. Smith — J.W. SMITH FOR THE MASTER

B L No 911999-01

FIGURE 13.8 A bill of lading

*Source*: Reprinted with permission of Radix Group International, Inc.

Bills of lading can be issued for inland (overland), ocean, or air transport. An inland bill of lading is issued by railroad or truck lines. It authorizes the movement of goods from the shipper's warehouse to the port or point of export. An ocean bill of lading, in contrast, applies to goods shipped by water and is issued by steamship lines. When the document is issued by an air carrier, it becomes an air waybill. In the case of a so-called **through bill of lading**, shipment is provided for two or more transportation modes for delivery to a final destination. Another type of bill of lading is the NVOCC, which is issued by a "nonvessel operator common carrier" which consolidates freight into a container for shipping by regular liner vessels.

According to the International Chamber of Commerce, the bill of lading is acceptable only when it is marked **clean** and **on board**. The bill of lading is clean when the carrier sees no evidence of damage to the packing or condition of the cargo. The cargo thus must be received in good order and condition without exception or irregularity. A bill of lading is **foul** when there is indication of damage to the goods received. For an on-board bill of lading to be issued, the cargo must be loaded aboard the named vessel on the specified date of loading. In comparison, even though a received-for-shipment bill of lading also mentions a particular vessel, this document only implies that the goods have been received by the steamship company. In such a case, because the goods are not yet loaded on board a particular vessel, it is possible that the goods may end up on another vessel instead.

In addition to being classified as clean or foul and by types of transportation carriers, a bill of lading can be straight or negotiable. A **straight** bill of lading, under international law, is non-negotiable. It is consigned directly to a consignee rather than to order. As such, it allows delivery only to the consignee or party named on the bill. The carrier must be certain that the party receiving the goods is actually the named party. To obtain possession of the shipment, the foreign buyer simply shows proof of identity.

A shipper's **order** or **negotiable** bill of lading is a negotiable instrument that is consigned to order. When endorsed, it allows transfer of title to the holder of documents, and delivery can be made to a named party or anyone designated.

Both the straight and order bills of lading serve as collection documents. The buyer must pay for the goods, post bond, or meet other specified conditions before obtaining the bill of lading to claim the goods. The shipper endorses the bill and presents it to the bank for collection as evidence of satisfying the conditions stated in the letter of credit.

## Conclusion

Moving cargo to an overseas destination is a much more complex task than transportation of freight locally. Other than the usual package designed to protect and/or promote a product while on display, packing (shipping package) is necessary if the merchandise is to be properly protected during shipment. Because of a greater number of hazards, the length of time during which the cargo is in transit, and a carrier's limited liability, the shipper should obtain marine insurance. In addition, the shipper should take necessary packing precautions to minimize any chance of damage. Containerization is one of several transportation modes that can achieve this goal.

Cargo cannot move without proper documentation. There are a great number of documents that must be filed to satisfy an exporter's government requirements and an importer's legal requirements. To compound this problem, the document requirements of the various countries are far from being uniform. The shipper, however, does not have any options – the shipper simply must submit all required documents if a cargo is to be moved and if the shipper is going to collect payment from the buyer. There are specialists in cargo movement who can facilitate the process for a fee. Freight forwarders and customhouse brokers work for the shipper and the importer, respectively. They are capable of taking over all aspects of physical distribution and documentation. When the shipper wants to be relieved of these responsibilities, these intermediaries can help.

## Questions

1 What are some of the hazards associated with the air, water, and land modes of transportation?
2 Explain how the freight rates–density effect can affect the choice of transportation.
3 Distinguish among conference lines, independent lines, and tramp vessels.
4 Distinguish between special coverage and blanket coverage.
5 When is an export license needed?
6 Explain these documents: SED, dock receipt, invoice (commercial, foreign customs, and consular), certificate of origin, inspection certificate, air waybill, and bill of lading.
7 Distinguish among these types of bill of lading: clean, foul, straight, and negotiable.

## Discussion assignments and minicases

1 Is there an ideal mode of transportation based on market location, speed, cost, and hazard criteria?
2 What products are suitable for air shipping?
3 Explain how containerization can solve the four packing problems of weight, breakage, moisture, and temperature, and pilferage and theft.
4 What are the functions of a freight forwarder and a customhouse broker? Is it worthwhile to use these agents?

## CASE 13.1 WHO CAN BEST INTRODUCE THE "CITY ADVENTURER" INTO SAUDI ARABIA?

### Jun Onishi, Hirosaki University, Japan

Jack Hamilton, an American, is the overseas sales manager of the Swiss-made watch "Rogart." He is concerned about a decrease in sales. Overseas sales of Rogart enjoyed double-digit sales growth until the past year, when its major competitors, Omega and IWC, introduced new watch models whose prices were 20 percent lower than comparable Rogart models.

In the watch industry, Rogart is regarded as an expensive watch and competes with Omega, IWC, and even Rolex. The company was established in Geneva, Switzerland, in 1870. Its earliest products were clocks, but eventually its skill in developing small-size movements allowed it to shift into manufacturing wristwatches. In 1970, its bicentennial model "Bon Vivant" received the first prize at the International Watch Trade Fair in Munich, which resulted in Rogart being recognized as a world-famous wristwatch manufacturer. George Shneider, CEO of Rogart, provides the following sentiment of what a Rogert watch is:

> A wristwatch like Rogart is not only a timepiece. People buy our watch because they want to buy the atmosphere of elegance and beauty. They want to wear our watch because they want to be treated differently. Therefore, we must offer showrooms and service centers that help our customers feel different from those of other watchmakers. Our distributors should be first-class service-minded people. They also should be connoisseurs who can fully appreciate the masterpieces of Rogart.

In 2001, Rogart introduced a new type of wristwatch, the so-called "City Adventurer." The perceptual image intended for this watch was to allow the wearer to feel a sense of adventure while still in the city. The target market for this watch was people in their early to mid-thirties who liked to identify with nature. This model was offered with a stainless steel wristband with a gold dial, and the dial face had Arabic numbers with a marine blue background.

Although "City Adventurer" falls into the premium watch category, the price is 30 percent lower than other Rogart models. Since the concept of "City Adventurer" is still the same as the traditional concept of Rogart (as described in the quote from Shneider), this model has sold very well in Europe and the U.S.A. Hamilton thinks that there are two reasons for these strong sales. Because there was a slight economic recession in these two regions, consumers were attracted to lower priced timepieces. His other reason is that, because the watch reminds consumers of the outdoors, they have a preference for purchasing this watch. However, for the current year, he anticipates that sales within these markets could also decrease. The latest models introduced by competitors are also pro-ecology, and their prices are lower. He surmises that he has to find substitute markets where he could cover the sales decline.

One possible market where Hamilton is considering introducing the "City Adventurer" is the Middle East, and in particular Saudi Arabia. Rogart has had a very good reputation in the Middle East. Since the new model, "City Adventurer," has not yet been introduced in this market, consumers there still perceive Rogart to be an expensive premium watch. In order to sell this model, Rogart will have to change people's perceptions. Hamilton must convince them that this is a premium watch even though it is priced lower than those of other Rogarts. Rogart has exclusive dealer contracts with distributors in Kuwait, UAE, Qatar, Bahrain, and Oman. However, it does not have an exclusive dealer under contract in Saudi Arabia. He feels that it will be advantageous to introduce the new "City Adventurer" model into Saudi Arabia before expanding its sales into Rogart's other Middle Eastern markets. He is aware that Saudi consumers have traveled to neighboring Bahrain in order to purchase Rogart watches. He believes that Saudi Arabia will make a very attractive market location because sales in neighboring Bahrain amount to nearly the same as those in Egypt, even though the population of Bahrain is less than one million, compared to that of Egypt which is over 70 million.

In determining the feasibility of Saudi Arabia as a potential market, Hamilton tried to take everything that he knew about Saudi Arabia into consideration. First he reviewed the geographic, demographic, political, and economic situation. He knows that Saudi Arabia is a large country, just over one-fifth the size of the U.S.A. The population of Saudi Arabia is about 22 million. Some of its larger cities include Riyadh (3.6 million), Jeddah (2.7 million), Damman (675,000), Taif (634,000), and Al Khobar (185,000). Jeddah is the chief commercial city, accounting for about 60 percent of all commerce in Saudi Arabia.

Saudi Arabia borders on six other Arab countries (Iraq, Jordan, Kuwait, Oman, Qatar, and Yemen) and has about 2,640 miles of coastline on the Persian Gulf and Red Sea. Much of the country is harsh and dry, with temperatures ranging between 20° and 45° C (68–113° F). However, some areas are extremely humid. For example, humidity in Jeddah often approaches 100 percent.

Saudi Arabia has a hereditary monarchy that is governed according to a fundamentalist interpretation of the Sharia, or Islamic law. The current king is Fahd bin Abd al-Aziz Al Saud, who acts as both head of state and head of government (Prime Minister). The crown prince acts as First Deputy Prime Minister. There is no written constitution or elected legislature. The Al Saud family exerts strict control over the government. Although based on Islamic law, several secular codes have been introduced and commercial disputes are handled by special committees.

Political parties, labor unions, and professional associations are banned. Informal political activity is centered around the male members of the royal family, with the king seeking a consensus on important policy matters among the senior princes. The king also consults senior religious scholars (called the ulama) and leaders of main tribal families. The Western-educated professional and technocratic elite have restricted influence through alliances with various Saudi princes.

Saudi Arabia is a founding member of the United Nations (UN), the League of Arab States, the Organization of the Islamic Conference, and the Gulf Cooperation Council (GCC). Its main foreign policy concerns are security, Arab nationalism, and Islam. It is a member of the Organization of the Petroleum Exporting Countries (OPEC). Historically, Saudi Arabia has maintained close ties with the U.S.A., despite differences over Israel.

As most people know, the country's chief source of wealth is petroleum. With its extensive coastline on the Red Sea and Persian Gulf, Saudi Arabia also exercises strong control over shipping in that area. In 2000, Saudi per capita GNI was about U.S.$7,000, compared to $34,000 for the U.S.A. Saudi per capita income has dropped sharply over the past 20 years as the population has doubled while GDP has fallen. However, there are still many wealthy Saudis.

Prior to the economic recession in Saudi Arabia, 70 percent of the watches sold in Saudi Arabia were sold to foreigners working on large construction projects. However, since the recession and the decrease in construction, sales to foreign residents have decreased, and, at this time, about 60 percent of watch purchases are made by Saudi citizens. Because of the pro-ecology image of the "City Adventurer," Hamilton feels that foreigners will still be the primary customers. To successfully launch "City Adventurer," advertising in English newspapers will be important. However, he believes that Rogart should continue to use both Arabic and English newspapers to promote its corporate identity to foreign consumers.

Hamilton also considers everything that he knows about Saudi culture and business practice. Recently he read a book, *Culture and Organizations, Software of the Mind*, written by Dutch Sociologist Geert Hofstede. According to Hofstede, there are four dimensions that are commonly observed in each culture but to different degrees: power distance, uncertainty avoidance, individualism, and masculinity. Based on his research, Saudis, in general, are high in power distance but are mid-level (neither very high nor very low) in individualism, masculinity, and uncertainty avoidance. On the other hand, Hamilton is from the U.S.A., which is described as low in power distance and uncertainty avoidance and high in individualism and masculinity. Other books explain that Hofstede's "masculinity" dimension has to do with task/achievement orientation. Hamilton prefers this terminology because he thinks that the term "masculinity" suggests some kind of gender issue, which

**TABLE 13.1** Cultural dimensions

| *Dimension* | *Saudi Arabia* | *U.S.A.* |
|---|---|---|
| Power distance | High | Low |
| Uncertainty avoidance | Middle | Low |
| Individualism | Middle | High |
| Task/achievement orientation | Middle | High |

could create misunderstanding about the real nature of this dimension.

Hamilton also knows from experience that Arab retailers can be very competitive with each other; so distributors should always be careful to treat all retailers fairly. For example, if a special price is offered to one retailer, it should also be offered to all the others. He also knows that Saudi businessmen tend to maintain close relationships and share information with their competitors. Therefore, he feels that it is important not to share company secrets with distributors or retailers.

The fact that relationships are very important to Saudi businessmen creates a problem for Hamilton. Each time he goes to Saudi Arabia, he has to spend at least two hours with each of his business contacts, drinking tea and chatting, before he can do any business. He is also frustrated by Saudi business hours, which run from about 8 a.m. to noon, then, after a five-hour break, resume at about 5 p.m. and run to 9 p.m. The "rest" days in Saudi Arabia are a half day on Thursdays and Fridays, as opposed to Saturdays and Sundays in European countries. Some European businessmen whom he met in Saudi Arabia complained that often important business decisions were delayed because of these holiday differences.

Hamilton knows that trust is also very important in Saudi business dealings. Retail stores must demonstrate that they trust their customers and that they can be trusted in return. Therefore, offering Saudis a warranty on premium watches will not be an effective sales strategy, as retailers are expected to offer free repairs on such expensive merchandise. However, offering international warranties (one year) to foreign purchasers who may leave Saudi Arabia would be an effective strategy.

One aspect of Saudi culture that will be relevant is the issue of gender. Almost 80 percent of Saudi purchasers of luxury watches are men, and about 20 percent are women. Hamilton suspects that this is related to the fact that Saudi women are required to wear a veil and be accompanied by their husband or a male relative when they are in public or in the presence of anyone who is not a relative. The requirement that women be accompanied by a husband or male relative restricts the times that they can go shopping, and the requirement that they wear a veil makes it difficult to examine merchandise such as watches. Although having female sales clerks for female customers may be a good solution, Saudi law forbids women from working. Thus, most retail shops have difficulty promoting watches to female customers. Some shops offer rooms where a woman and her husband or relative can examine merchandise in private, allowing the woman to remove her veil.

Another item that Hamilton takes into consideration is Saudi commercial law. When foreign companies enter into business relationships with Saudi companies, they must follow strict Saudi rules. One of these rules is that a foreign company which terminates a business relationship with a Saudi company must pay that company a large amount in compensation.

Hamilton is particularly concerned about the commercial law issue because of an incident that happened to one of Rogart's competitors, Alpha Watches. Alpha wanted to cover the market across Saudi Arabia, including Damman, Al Khobar, Riyadh, Jeddah, and Taif. To do this, Alpha hired two distributors, Arabian Trading Co. and Ahmed Corp., which had complementary markets. Arabian Trading Co. specializes in commodities and some brand items. It owns a chain of retail stores with locations in the two largest cities, Riyadh and Jeddah. Ahmed Corp. specializes in watches. It has retail outlets only in Al Khobar. The plan was that each distributor would sell to retailers in different markets.

But Alpha's plan backfired. The two distributors entered into a price war, trying to sell to the same retailers. This caused prices to drop, which Alpha had not anticipated. The price dropped so much that retailers began to re-export the watches to other countries (e.g., Bahrain, Jordan, Kuwait, Oman), where the price was higher. Alpha wanted to terminate its relationship with Ahmed Corp. in order to restore the retail price, but it did not want to pay the high compensation required by Saudi law. So Alpha decided to minimize export to Saudi Arabia, but its contracts with both distributors specified a five-year minimum trading period.

In addition to considering Saudi culture and business practices, Hamilton has to consider logistical and other related issues. Rogart will use air freight to ship merchandise to Saudi cities. Rogart has its own distribution center in Kuwait, and it has established a network to distribute merchandise from there to other distributors in the Middle East. However, "City Adventurer" is a new product. Although it is very popular in Europe, where production cannot meet current demand, Rogart does not yet know what the level of demand will be in the Middle East. Therefore, Hamilton believes that it will be better to ship watches directly from Switzerland to his Saudi distributor instead of passing stock through the Kuwait distribution center.

The major Arabian cities where airports are located are Jeddah, Riyadh, and Dhaharan (near Al Khobar). Transportation between cities is by truck. Often during the winter the transportation between Riyadh and Al Khobar or Jeddah is disrupted by sandstorms. For shipment, Rogart has used European Insurance Company and Pan European Airlines for more than 20 years. Rogart has an annual contract with European Insurance Company which covers all products exported from Switzerland, and Rogart has also received special air freight charges from Pan European Airlines which are 15 percent less expensive than rates offered by other airlines. Whenever Rogart exports products from Switzerland, Rogart has used these two companies. Hamilton will likely take this into account when he negotiates prices of products with Saudi distributors.

Another important factor in shipping watches to the Middle East is the product's fragility, and warehouses where the watches will be stored should control for dust, temperature, and humidity. Warehouses in Jeddah meet international standards for these conditions, but those in Riyadh and Al Khobar do not and are thus not suitable for storing watches. Where the watches are to be stored is a serious concern, because dust is one of the major factors leading to watch repair. Rogart's experience in watch repair in Kuwait, Bahrain, and Oman indicates that almost 5 percent of products sold are returned for repair within the warranty period because dust has got into the watch mechanism. Some of the products are returned to Rogart soon after the product is sold, indicating that dust had entered the watches during warehousing.

Finally, Hamilton realizes that it will be a problem for his Saudi distributor if retail shops continue to import Rogart watches from Bahrain. One solution is to raise the price of watches to the Bahraini distributors, so that those watches will be priced higher and will not be able to compete in Saudi Arabia with the Saudi distributors' watches. However, that will increase the retail price of the watches in Bahrain, making them less competitive than those of other watchmakers. Another possibility is to use service to differentiate between the Saudi and Bahraini distributors. If his Saudi distributor offers a free yearly cleaning service for watches purchased from them, it may prevent retailers from buying watches from Bahraini distributors.

Because of the above considerations, Hamilton is very cautious about signing a contract with any distributor and has decided to carefully study the background of each potential distributor. He has received inquiry letters from three companies interested in distributing Rogart watches in Saudi Arabia. Each company has submitted its estimated sales turnover of Rogart watches using its sales channels.

Ashraf Co., Ltd, owned by a Lebanese merchant, is a wholesaler and retailer of expensive branded items. It handles products of Chanel, Louis Vuitton, Cross, Canon, Sony, Christian Dior, Mont Blanc, Panasonic, and Omega. Its two sales outlets are tastefully decorated and create a very luxurious atmosphere. For distribution, it has a strong sales network in the eastern Saudi cities of Damman, Al Khobar, and Riyadh. Although it is the sole distributor of Omega watches, its repair and service facility cannot handle complicated or delicate repairs. Since it has well-trained technicians at its branch in Kuwait, the Saudi repair and service facility usually requires Omega watches to be sent to the Kuwait branch for repair. As a distributor, estimated sales turnover of Rogart is lower than that of other distributors.

Detami Trading, owned by a Saudi billionaire, is an agent for Japanese and European cars and premium watches. The owner has a strong personal relationship with many wealthy Saudis, and transfers orders from these people and receives commissions from manufacturers. Detami Trading has showrooms with good repair services in Jeddah, Riyadh, and Damman. As an agent, it does not carry products in inventory. Customers usually have to wait a week or two before they receive products. However, it has a strong nationwide direct relationship with customers.

The final company, Dolphin Corporation, is a Saudi-owned chain of specialty stores of marine products. Its main products are motor boats, scuba diving gear, and diving watches. It has specialty stores in Damman and Jeddah. The Damman store has a small share of the local watch market, while the Jeddah store enjoys a major share of the local watch market. Dolphin Corporation's products are very popular among adventurers, not only of Saudi nationality but also expatriates. It also handles Breitening, which is famous as a pilot's watch. It has offered an excellent repair service for this watch. Its specialty shops are tastefully decorated and encourage people to engage in outdoor sports.

Ashraf Co. and Dolphin Corp. have their own warehouses near their offices in the major cities of Saudi Arabia. Detami does not have warehouses but plans to ship watches by air freight courier (e.g., FedEx) directly to each customer. This will increase the price by 10 percent compared to the other two distributors, but inventory and storage costs will be reduced.

Ashraf Co. has a good relationship with the major Arabic newspapers and regularly advertises in Arabic newspapers, such as *Itidal* and *Jazirah*. Mohammed Abu-issa, who is President of Ahraf Co., has told Hamilton that it is not necessary to place advertisements in local English newspapers, since the number of local expatriates has been decreasing steadily. Detami, as an agent, indicates that it likes Rogart to place advertisements in international newspapers and magazines (such as in-flight magazines) that are available in Saudi Arabia. Dolphin Corp. traditionally has a good relationship with local expatriates, since most of the staff speak English very well. The company's after-sales service is also well known by expatriates. Ahmed Abdullah, who is Managing Director of Dolphin Corp., has told Hamilton that it will not be too difficult to promote the product to locals, since Dolphin is a Saudi company. He likes to start advertising in the Jeddah area, to see how the market responds to Rogart watches.

*Sources*: Library of Congress (U.S.A.) website, www.loc.gov; and Central Intelligence Agency (U.S.A.) website, www.cia.gov.

## Points to consider

If you were a market consultant to Jack Hamilton, what would your recommendations be to him? As you respond to the following questions, be certain to provide reasons and justification for your recommendations.

1 Identify the important characteristics for doing business in Saudi Arabia. Do not copy from the case but summarize using your own words.
2 Hamilton realizes that the U.S.A. and Saudi Arabia are different. Identify possible cultural conflicts that may be encountered based on Hofstede's cultural dimensions. Use the format below to analyze the cultural dimensions.

| *Hofstede dimension* | *Comparison* | *Possible source of conflict* |
|---|---|---|
| Power distance | Saudi Arabia is higher than U.S.A. | Hamilton's frankness will be treated as arrogance |

3 If Rogart introduces "City Adventurer" which will be priced 30 percent lower than other models, it may be difficult for Rogart to introduce other, more expensive, models in the future. Provide some advice to Rogart about how it can introduce other, more expensive watch models to the Saudi Arabia market in the future.
4 In your view of the distributors being considered, identify the best company to sell "City Adventurer" in the Saudi Arabian market and provide your rationale for making this choice.

## Notes


1 Mike Moore, "Tariff Reductions Aren't Enough," *Asian Wall Street Journal*, June 19, 2001.
2 *Ports of the World: A Guide to Cargo Loss Control*, 13th edn (CIGNA), 46–7.
3 Rupert Pennant-Rea and Ian G. Heggie, "Commercializing Africa's Roads," *Finance & Development*, December 1995, 30ff.
4 David Ross, "Air Freighting," in *Handbook of Physical Distribution Management*, 3rd edn, ed. John Gattorna (Aldershot: Gower, 1983), 223–37.
5 "Security as a Trade Barrier," *Business Week*, December 31, 2001, 36.
6 Overseas Shipholding Group, Inc. 1993 Annual Report, 13–14.
7 "The Quiet Revolution in Transportation: The Rise of Efficiency," *Wall Street Journal*, April 24, 2007.
8 Anna Krasnova, "Development of Multi-modal Cargo Transport in Russia," *AmCham News* 13 (October–November 2006): 12.
9 Charles A. Taff, *Management of Physical Distribution and Transportation*, 7th edn (Homewood, IL: Irwin, 1984), 261.
10 *Ports of the World*, 51.
11 *Ports of the World*, 52.
12 John Wilson, "Security in Distribution," in *Handbook of Physical Distribution Management*, 3rd edn, ed. by John Gattorna (Aldershot: Gower, 1983), 365–96.
13 Yoanna A. Gouchtchina and Michael H. Lane, "A Chain Without Links," *AmCham News* 13 (October–November 2006): 18.
14 "Sounding the Alarm in Mexico," *Business Week*, June 26, 2000, 74.
15 Marc Levinson, *The Box: How the Shipping Container Made the World Smaller and the World Economy Bigger* (Princeton, NJ: Princeton University Press, 2006).
16 John F. Magee, William C. Copacino, and Donald B. Rosenfield, *Modern Logistics Management* (New York: Wiley, 1985), 196.
17 Patterson Brown, "Freight Forwarders, Customs Brokers and Incoterms: Making Exporting Easier," *Export America*, November 2001.
18 Paul R. Murphy, James M. Daley, and Douglas R. Dalenberg, "Doing Business in Global Markets: Perspectives of International Freight Forwarders," *Journal of Global Marketing* 6 (No. 4, 1993): 53–68.
19 "Big Brown's New Bag," *Business Week*, July 19, 2004, 54–6.
20 Michael Klein, "Taking Care of Business," *Finance & Development*, December 2006, 30–3.
21 "WearGuard Does It Right in Canadian Launch," *DM News*, April 18, 1994, 22, 43.
22 Konstantin Antipov and Art Franczek, "Delays at Customs Cause Logistics Headaches," *AmCham News* 13 (October–November 2006): 14.
23 Jim Robb, "Ask the TIC," *Export America*, 14–15.
24 "U.S. Customs Lays Stress on Secure Cargo," *Bangkok Post*, November 30, 2001.
25 "Anti-terrorism Cargo Rules Please Nobody," *San José Mercury News*, February 19, 2003.
26 Antipov and Franczek, "Delays at Customs."
27 "Export Controls," *San José Mercury News*, February 2, 2000.
28 "Hughes, Boeing to Pay Fines," *San José Mercury News*, March 6, 2003.
29 "U.S. to Probe Outsourcing After ITT Case," *Wall Street Journal*, March 28, 2007.

Chapter 14

# Promotion strategies

## Personal selling, publicity, and sales promotion

Everyone lives by selling something.
Robert Louis Stevenson

## Chapter outline

- Marketing strategy: book worms
- Promotion and communication
- Promotion mix
- Personal selling
  - Personal selling vs. advertising
  - Varying quality and style of personal selling
  - Intercultural negotiation
  - Motivation
  - Telemarketing
  - Expatriate personnel
- Publicity
  - The nature of publicity
  - The management of publicity
  - Negative publicity
- Sales promotion
  - The nature of sales promotion
  - Restrictions
- Overseas product exhibitions
- Conclusion

- Case 14.1 Selling in the EU
- Case 14.2 A new system installment of Sanki Denki (Thailand)

## Marketing strategy

**Book worms**

Book clubs serve older customers in the U.S.A. They used to prosper in the U.S.A. and Western Europe, but the business has slowed down significantly. In Eastern Europe and Central Europe, it is a different story. Family Leisure, a unit of Bertelsmann, sold 12 million books in Ukraine and enjoyed a 55 percent sales growth in 2006. The company is Ukraine's largest bookseller, commanding 12 percent of the market. Family Leisure Club has some 2 million members, and almost half of them are under 30 years old.

Bertelsmann's units include the Book-of-the-Month Club and Literary Guild in the U.S.A., and the global profit margins average 4 percent. Ukraine easily surpasses that figure as its profit margins are triple the average.

The countries that were once members of the Soviet bloc have well-educated populations, and their citizens enjoy reading. Because good bookstores are few, Bertelsmann has become the biggest book publisher in the Czech Republic, and it has been highly successful in Poland, Russia, and the other countries in the region.

Ukraine, a country of 47 million people, has only about 300 bookstores. Bertelsmann's strategy is to sign up hot young Ukrainian authors and to serve as their exclusive distributor. Because the average income is less than $8000 a year, the company keeps prices low. A typical title sells for under $5. Family Leisure Club ships books to post offices, where customers go to pick up their books. While Internet access is still out of reach of most people, these citizens happen to be world leaders in sending mobile phone text messages to place orders. Family Leisure's goal is "not to be a book club, but an integrated bookseller."

*Source*: "Where the Book Business Is Humming," *Business Week*, May 14, 2007, 50.

## Purpose of chapter

The Bertelsmann example in the marketing illustration above provides clear evidence that a product must be promoted and that advertising is not the only means. A well-rounded marketing plan must include a proper promotion mix. This mix should not rely solely on advertising – personal selling, publicity, and sales promotion should also be included. This chapter examines the communication process in general as well as those promotional components other than advertising that are part of the process. Attention is given to the role of personal selling, internationally and locally. The pros and cons of employing local nationals for selling are also discussed.

One section is devoted to the treatment of publicity, examining the principles related to a sound publicity campaign, with an emphasis on how to deal with negative publicity. A further section investigates the use of sales promotion and the influence of local regulations on the various sales promotion techniques.

## Promotion and communication

The purpose of promotion is both to communicate with buyers and to influence them. Effective promotion requires an understanding of the process of persuasion and how this process is affected by environmental factors. The potential buyer must not only receive the desired information but should also be able to comprehend that information. Furthermore, the information must be sufficiently potent to motivate the buyer to react positively.

To communicate effectively with someone means that certain facts and information are shared in common with that person. **Communication** is basically a five-stage process consisting of source, encoding, information, decoding, and destination (see Figure 14.1). Encoding is a step that transforms the idea or information into a form that can be transmitted (e.g., written or spoken words). For a receiver to understand the coded information, that person must be able to decode these words.

The source can encode and the receiver can decode only through the experience each has had. The two large circles in Figure 14.1 represent the **fields of experience** of each party. If the two circles have a large common area, communication is relatively easy because both individuals have similar psychological and social attributes. Communication is more difficult if the overlapping area is smaller. Such is often the case with international communication. If the circles do not meet, communication is likely impossible; that is, the sender and the receiver have nothing in common, and they therefore have an extremely difficult time understanding each other. Moreover, "**noise**" (interference) can easily affect any one of the five stages, making the effect on the communication difficult to predict. Thus, the sender must be receiver-oriented. The message must consist of information that the receiver can relate to, and the information must be encoded with relevant images and words common to the receiver's experience and language.

It is not sufficient just for the receiver to be informed by the message; the receiver must also be persuaded to accept the information and to act as suggested. A promotional message thus must be designed in such a way that the purchaser reacts favorably. Effective motivation requires that the principles of mass persuasion be followed.[1]

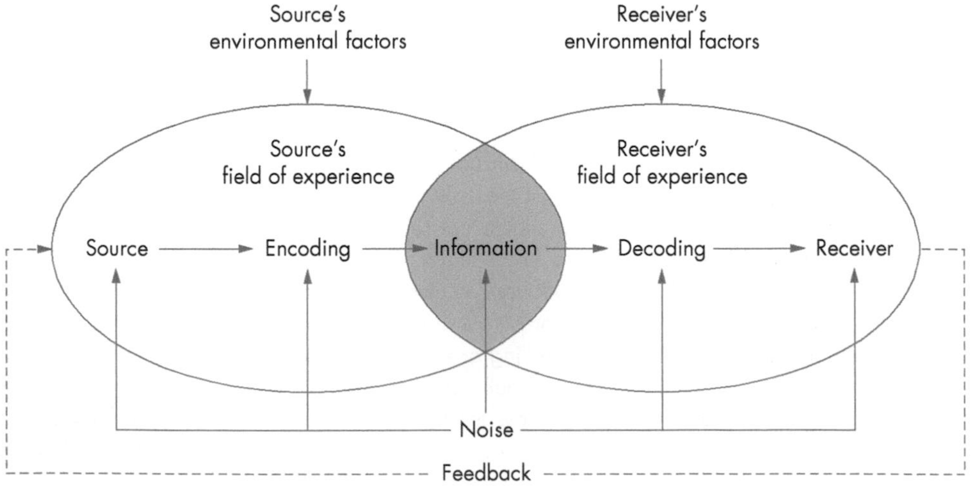
Source's
environmental factors
Receiver's
environmental factors
Source's
field of experience
Receiver's
field of experience
Source
Encoding
Information
Decoding
Receiver
Noise
Feedback

**FIGURE 14.1** The process of communication

The first principle is that the message must reach a person's sense organs. This may sound simplistic, yet frequently the message sent is not received by the intended audience. To ensure reception, the message must gain the attention of the receiver. If the right media are not available or if the wrong message channel is used, the message may never reach the intended receiver. Furthermore, if the cue is not appealing, the receiver may never open his or her senses to the message due to a lack of interest. Note that what is interesting in one culture may not be so in another. A message that refers to historical events in a home country (e.g., July 4) may have little meaning in a host country.

The second principle requires that the message should not contradict a person's cultural norms. It is possible, though not probable, that a message which is not consistent with the receiver's beliefs may sometimes be potent enough to make the buyer re-evaluate traditional beliefs. In most cases such a message is likely to be rejected, discarded, or distorted. The effective promotional message is thus one that is accepted as part of the receiver's attitude and belief structure.

The third principle requires that the sender create a message which arouses the receiver's need and suggests a particular action that will enable the receiver to achieve a desired goal. If the suggested action results in several goals being realized simultaneously, the potency of the message correspondingly increases. An advertiser thus should identify relevant needs and motives. Motives can differ greatly among countries, even when the same product is involved. Consider the automobile. American car buyers usually replace their automobiles every few years, and styling is important to them. A typical British car owner, however, views the purchase as a lifetime commitment. For the Briton, the motive of functions in terms of durability outweighs the emotional appeal of styling.

The last principle suggests that the message must gain control of the receiver's behavior at the right place and time. The message should offer a well-defined path to reach the goal. If the purchaser is placed in a situation requiring action, the chances are increased that the buyer will take the suggested action. For example, Tokyo Toyopet, a division of Toyota, has done remarkably well by adhering to this principle. Its Toyota salesperson contacts a potential new car buyer just after the latter's car has completed its "shaken," a mandatory inspection in Japan for a three-year-old automobile. The timing is effective because this is when the car owner is most likely to think about trading in the old vehicle for a new one.

Infiniti's communication campaign to introduce the brand seems to largely contradict the principles of mass persuasion. Although novel, the promotion campaign was severely criticized for failing to directly communicate the features and benefits of the Infiniti brand. The introductory TV spots and magazine advertisements did not show the product (i.e., car). Instead, they showed pictures of rocks, trees, hay, and so on. The TV spots included "Distant Leaves," "Misty Tree," "Delicate Branches," "Flock of Geese," and "Summer Storm." Infiniti dealers were also upset.

## Promotion mix

To communicate with and influence customers, several promotional tools are available. Advertising is usually the most visible component of promotion, but it is not its only component. The promotion mix also consists of three other distinct but interrelated activities: personal selling, publicity, and sales promotion.

The four promotional components are not mutually exclusive, and it can be difficult at times to determine which one of the four activities a particular promotional tool may be. Consider the common trade fair. Promotion for a trade fair may be viewed as advertising because a fair sponsor, as well as participating companies, generally uses direct mail and newspapers to advertise the event. Since the media receive both advertising orders and news releases, they may be willing to provide free publicity for the fair as well. Furthermore, staffing at a display booth is necessary, and there will be plenty of opportunity for a company's representative to use personal selling to make sales. Finally, it is not uncommon for fair participants to offer free gifts and special prices during the display, and these techniques are classified as sales promotion tools. This chapter concentrates on personal selling, publicity, and sales promotion.

## Personal selling

According to the American Marketing Association, personal selling is an "oral presentation in a conversation with one or more prospective purchasers for the purpose of making sales." Personal selling, also commonly known as salesmanship, is used at every distribution level. The cost of personal selling is high. One extreme case is German software maker SAP, the world's leader in applications packages for client-server networks. In the U.S.A., SAP America has removed the $140,000 annual limit on sales commissions, making it possible for a salesperson to earn as much as $2 million a year – more than what the company's top German executives make.[2]

In spite of the high cost, personal selling should be emphasized when certain conditions are met. Industrial buying or large-volume purchases, characterized by a large amount of money being involved, justify personal attention. Personal selling has also proven to be effective when the market is concentrated or when a salesperson must develop a measure of confidence in the customer for the

### Cultural Dimension 14.1

**"Stocking Fellas"**

Marks & Spencer PLC is a mid-priced retailer that sells a quarter of all lingerie in England. In the month before Christmas, male shoppers triple in number. Lingerie is highly popular as Christmas gifts for women, but it is also one of the most returned items after Christmas. For male buyers, lingerie is a tricky proposition. If the chosen item is too big, he may be accused of thinking of his partner as being fat. If the item is too small, his partner will wonder why he bought an item fit for a child.

The company's research found that only one-third of women were happy with the underwear that they got from their partners. This is not surprising, given the fact that only one-third of all men know the size or favorite color of their wife or girlfriend.

To solve the problem, the retailer employs "Stocking Fellas" or salesmen who help male customers shopping for lingerie. Men are advised to peek at their partners' underwear drawers. They are also urged to consider shades like silver or brown instead of rushing to red items. Because not all salesmen are suitable as Fellas, the company chooses those who are talkative and who work in departments that require precise sizing (e.g., men's suits). The Fellas are trained by veteran lingerie saleswomen.

*Source*: "For a Delicate Sale, A Retailer Deploys 'Stocking Fellas,'" *Wall Street Journal*, December 21, 2006.

purchase. The effectiveness of personal selling is also a function of product type. In general, personal selling works well with high-unit-value and infrequently purchased products. Such products usually require a demonstration, are custom-made or fitted to an individual's need, or involve trade-ins (see Cultural Dimension 14.1).

In the Far East, Asian businesspeople do not like to discuss business deals with a foreigner who does not come highly recommended by some mutual acquaintance. Personal contact is important to selling in South Korea, not only because of the value placed on personal relationships but also because such contact serves to bring the end-user in touch with new processes and equipment. Because Japanese suppliers often visit their Korean customers, U.S. suppliers need to visit Korea to augment the efforts of the local representative. At the same time, it is advisable to hold demonstrations, seminars, and exhibitions of their products in Korea.

Note that not all salespersons are directly involved in selling. So-called missionary salespersons, for example, have the task of educating potential buyers about product benefits and promotional campaigns in order to create the goodwill that may result in subsequent sales. When Foremost first introduced milk and ice cream products to the Thai market in 1956, the company sent sales representatives (missionary salespersons) to educate people by giving talks on sanitation and nutrition in schools and by providing free samples to students.

## *Personal selling vs. advertising*

Personal selling is similar to advertising in the sense that both aim to create sales and both must be understandable, interesting, believable, and persuasive. However, advertising differs from personal selling in several aspects. Advertising relies on a non-personal means of contact and sales presentation. When compared to advertising, personal selling commands a much larger share of aggregate promotional dollars and accounts for several times more in terms of the number of personnel. This relationship exists in all countries. In fact, the abundant labor supply in developing countries makes it easy and inexpensive to employ sales personnel. Shoplifting problems also encourage the use of personal selling, making self-selection and self-service relatively rare.

The differences between advertising and personal selling can also be contrasted in terms of the communication process.[3] Advertising is a one-way communication process that has relatively more "noise," whereas personal selling is a two-way communication process with immediate feedback and relatively less "noise." Controlling the message is more difficult in personal selling than in advertising because salespersons may react in unforeseen situations in such a way that may differ from the company's policy. Yet advertising is usually less persuasive because advertisements are prepared in advance by those who have minimal contact with customers and because the message must be kept simple to appeal to a large number of people. Personal selling, on the other hand, is more flexible, personal, and powerful. A salesperson can adapt the message to fit the client at the time of presentation, and stimuli can be presented to appeal to all five senses.

## *Varying quality and style of personal selling*

The quality of personal selling varies widely from product to product, from employer to employer, and from one target group to another. In general, salespersons selling for manufacturers are better trained and more qualified than those working for wholesalers and retailers. In terms of the target market, salespersons who sell to industrial users are more likely to be "order-getters" and are generally aggressive, well trained, and well informed. Industrial salespeople, receiving high compensation, must be capable of mixing easily with top management. Those selling to wholesalers, retailers, and consumers have a more routine selling job, and these salespersons are "order-takers" and generally less aggressive in securing new business. Expensive products require a higher quality of personal selling than low-unit-value, high-turnover products.

Personal selling is not viewed as a prestigious occupation in most countries. It is often taught in trade schools or vocational schools rather than in colleges, and thus the quality of personal selling outside the U.S.A. is far from exemplary. In Brazil, for example, salespeople are not very well trained by U.S. standards.

Selling styles differ significantly. In Japan, employers are agreeable to the practice of having salespersons call on their employees at the workplace. Japanese salespersons sell cars door-to-door. Subaru went one step further. With its image as a vehicle for outdoor types, Subaru equipped its door-to-door salesperson with Sportsman's Guide catalogs. Sportsman's Guide, a U.S. firm selling a proprietary line of sporting goods and accessories, was optimistic about this unique distribution channel.

In the U.S.A., salespersons entertain clients at either breakfast or lunch. Overseas, it is much more common to meet for entertainment after business hours and to have sales discussions over dinner or in a nightclub. The after-hours business contacts are much more important overseas than they are in the U.S.A. Clients expect attention to be given to social functions in addition to business functions, including golf, drinking, dining, and so on. Potential customers expect to be extensively wined and dined. A salesperson commonly takes customers to bars and nightclubs for social contacts with members of the opposite sex. Under such circumstances, salespersons must be prepared to be far more than order-takers.

The personal selling tactic may have to be modified in some markets. Avon is able to use door-to-door selling in the U.S.A. and Latin America, but it found that the practice is anathema in some cultures. Asians, for example, are wary of strangers; as a result, Avon's sales representatives only call at the homes of friends and relatives. Neighborhood parties sponsored by Avon are a modified promotional technique that seems to work well in Asia, and the technique has been tested in Germany as well. In France, the prohibition of door-to-door selling has compelled Avon to shift to direct-mail sales.

Personal selling must receive proper support in terms of training and information. It is difficult for salespersons to be effective without advertising support. Advertising creates awareness and helps make customers more receptive. Tokyo Toyopet's advertising, for instance, does not take the form of direct-action advertising. Rather, it tells customers to be patient and to wait for one of the company's salesmen to call. Such advertisements are not product-oriented since the intent is to sell a company image. These advertisements are employed not to attract customers to the showroom but to aid in the salesmen's door-to-door sales activities.

## Intercultural negotiation

Successful negotiations require some understanding of each party's culture and may also require adoption of a negotiation strategy that is consistent with the other party's cultural system. One strategy is to rely on stereotyping. It is possible, for example, to use stereotyped preconceptions to identify the personality traits of negotiators from different ethnic groups or countries. Although stereotyping allows an easy label, it is also risky because generalization may lead one to believe that members of the group must share the same traits. These prejudices, if believed, may affect business negotiations and their outcomes.

International marketers are interested in the effects of cultural adaptation on intercultural communication. Studies should be conducted to identify conditions that make it desirable for businesspeople to adapt their behavior in response to the culture of the other party.

## Motivation

Like other employees, salespeople need to be motivated. In many countries, Western firms find it difficult to retain and motivate salespeople. The concept of individual recognition of sales representatives is at odds with Japan's team approach to business and its aversion to a compensation system that pays for performance. According to a study of the impact of sales management control in Greece, India, and Malaysia, incentive pay has no effect on salesperson performance.[4]

Based on the results of one study, compensation method and control system are important determinants of ethical behavior of salespeople. Age, but not education, also plays a role. While a salesperson's ethical behavior does not lead to higher performance, it results in a lower level of role conflict and a higher level of job satisfaction.[5]

In Saudi Arabia, where selling is considered an undesirable occupation, qualified local sales representatives are hard to find due to a labor shortage. Because of India's various languages and social caste system, it is difficult for sales representatives to sell outside their own social level. In Brazil, the determination of sales force compensation and product pricing is affected by rampant inflation and national labor laws. It is thus a problem to pay someone less than the amount paid the previous year.

Amway (Japan) Ltd, the subsidiary of privately held Amway Corp., is the corporation's top overseas affiliate as well as the ninth most profitable foreign company in Japan. Amway is able to bypass local retailers and wholesalers who often demand enormous markups. Amway conducts all its direct selling in homes through some 500,000 distributors (salespeople). Amway's cult-like corporate culture appeals to the Japanese who prefer to identify strongly with their employers. As in the U.S.A., Amway motivates salespeople by offering 30 percent commissions, bonuses, and trips abroad, and its pyramidal structure generously rewards distributors who bring new salespeople into their group (see Figure 14.2). Distributors are attracted by the unusual brand of fraternal capitalism as much as by potential earnings.

Avon's joint venture with the Guangzhou Cosmetics Factory is the first foreign as well as Chinese company authorized to sell directly to Chinese consumers. Avon's concern about Chinese women's ability to understand the concept of direct sales quickly disappeared when local representatives told Avon to double the prices and sold one month's allocation of cosmetics in five days. Most representatives like the self-esteem, independence, and extra income (commissions).

## Telemarketing

Personal selling does not always require a face-to-face conversation. For instance, personal selling may be done over the telephone. Although telephone selling has been in existence for a considerable period of time, the growth of the direct marketing field has pushed this method of selling to the forefront. This marketing practice, now known as **telemarketing**, has become very popular among sellers – but not necessarily with consumers, who feel they are being inundated with such calls. Because of the effective lobbying of telemarketing firms, U.S. lawmakers have been reluctant to pass

# Building a worldwide business... from Michigan.

*Amway's world headquarters in Ada, Michigan, putting the final touches on the metal globe sculpture situated among 60 national flags representing Amway's worldwide presence.*

Amway Corporation is proud to be one of the many worldwide operations that got its start in Michigan. In 35 years, Amway has grown from a neighborhood business to a world leader in the direct sales of diverse, high-quality consumer products. Independent Amway distributors are the heart of this company... but Michigan will always be our home.

Amway®

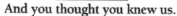

**And you thought you knew us.**

*If you'd like more information on Amway and its international operations, call 1-800-544-7167.*
*Amway Corporation, 7575 Fulton St. East, Ada, Michigan 49355-0001*

**FIGURE 14.2** Amway and direct marketing

*Source*: Reprinted with permission of Amway Corporation.

laws restricting the use of telemarketing. As part of the lobbying effort, the firms pointed out that legislators' own fund-raising efforts would be impeded by the proposed restrictions. However, the U.S. and state governments finally implemented the do-not-call lists in 2003.

In overseas markets, telemarketing is not as far developed as it is in the U.S.A. The limited availability of telephones for private households is one problem. The privacy laws are another obstacle. **Cold calling** (unsolicited sales calls) is receiving close scrutiny in the name of consumer protection and respect for privacy. A statutory cooling-off period may apply to sales closings over the telephone. Germany is even more restrictive. It prohibits cold calls on the grounds of privacy invasion, and this ban even applies to an insurance salesperson's announcement of a visit.

## *Expatriate personnel*

One controversial subject for which there is no definite solution is the nationality of the personnel to be used in a market abroad. Some marketers argue for the use in a foreign market of expatriate salespersons and managers, or those from the home country. Others take the opposite point of view by contending that the best policy is to use local nationals or those who were born in the host country.

Expatriate personnel are favorably viewed because they are already familiar with their company's product, technology, history, and policies. Thus the only kind of preparation they would need is knowledge of the foreign market. Yet this may be the greatest obstacle for the expatriate salesperson. Whereas some may enjoy the challenge and adjustment, other expatriate personnel find it difficult to cope with a new and unfamiliar business environment. The failure to understand a foreign culture and its customs without question will hinder the effectiveness of an expatriate sales force. British managers, for instance, have difficulty in running retail stores in the highly competitive U.S. market, which is characterized by longer shopping hours and sizing differences.

Not only must an expatriate cope with new business conditions, but the expatriate's family must also share in the burden of making social adjustments. Life can be difficult both physically and psychologically for those who are unable to make the necessary adjustments for an assignment that requires a lengthy relocation overseas. The expatriate may have second thoughts about accepting such an assignment, fearing that the distance from headquarters may eliminate chances for promotion or that the company may want to keep him or her abroad. Moreover, an overseas assignment may not be easy for American salespersons and their spouses because they may become frustrated with shopping and schooling, and the limited entertainment opportunities. Some may be driven by boredom and frustration and may initiate an affair or begin to drink excessively. It is thus crucial that the personnel for overseas assignments be selected carefully. In fact, their families should also be interviewed to determine the suitability of their temperament for an overseas assignment. Firms should seek a spouse's opinion.

Successful expatriates possess certain qualities that include cultural adaptability, patience, flexibility, and tolerance for others' beliefs. One study of network ties focuses on three characteristics of international managers – nationality, cultural distance, and expatriate status. Based on a network analysis of cross-subsidiary interactions among 457 managers in a multinational corporation, managers form strong, expressive ties with peers with a smaller cultural distance and from the same status group, but in the case of instrumental ties, they are stronger when peers differ in these background characteristics.[6]

According to the cultural similarity hypothesis, differences between the home and host cultures for a sojourner affect one's adaptation to the host culture. The personal fit hypothesis on the other hand states that a person's successful cultural adaptation depends on his or her idiosyncratic response to the cultural environment. The findings of one study show that successful adaptation is related to a person's ability to fit into the host culture, rather than the cultural similarity.[7] Another study focusing on 194 expatriate managers and 505 subordinates working in the multinational hotel industry has found support for a model of expatriate adjustment that describes the relationships between organization antecedents (i.e., reasons for assignment), a more comprehensive set of adjustment behaviors, self-reported performance, and subordinate-rated managerial effectiveness.[8]

Expatriates are likely to perform more effectively overseas if they are satisfied with their jobs. A company should design new job assignments based on past skills and experiences while opening up opportunities for future growth and development. In addition, international mentoring (and the use of multiple mentors) should be useful in assisting expatriates to adjust and develop during the predeparture, expatriation, and repatriation stages of international assignments.[9]

An expatriate's commitment to the local operation and the parent company is determined in part by one's satisfaction with the host culture. This satisfaction is in turn determined by one's consumer experiences. Market alienation, having a negative effect on satisfaction, can be reduced by participation in the host marketplace. While cultural knowledge is not directly related to one's satisfaction with the host culture, it has an indirect impact through its association with participation in the host marketplace.[10] Based on a sample of Japanese multinational companies, those companies with control ability over international subsidiaries are those with expatriate personnel possessing adequate cultural knowledge of the host country.[11]

Despite the problems associated with the use of expatriate personnel, local workers or the host country's own nationals may present another set of unique problems. Rather than having a multinational perspective, they may be more closely identified with their home country. They may also not possess an understanding of the headquarters' business cultures and objectives. Furthermore, they may be geographically immobile in the sense that they may prefer staying in their own country rather than accepting a new position with more responsibilities abroad. Empirically, however, one study found no support for the widespread belief that expatriate personnel are more loyal to the company than host-country nationals.[12]

In all fairness, some disadvantages of using locals very likely apply to expatriates as well. More important is that these criticisms point to the problem of ethnocentrism. Companies that are truly multinational realize that good foreign personnel, though somewhat different in their thinking and approach, can be valuable and effective employees. Foreign personnel may also be able to provide knowledge and information that can be very valuable to American companies. Hewlett Packard is one example of an American multinational company that owes its success to the use of foreign personnel. Its European operations are run autonomously by Europeans. Local pools of technical expertise are tapped to develop products for worldwide distribution. New management ideas, such as flexible working hours and a program to introduce the company to schoolchildren, were first developed in Germany before being adopted in the U.S.A.

There are several advantages to be gained by an MNC in using foreign-born native personnel working in their own country. One advantage is that the company can avoid political, sensitive, or embarrassing situations. Since the government and the local community undoubtedly prefer that their own nationals be hired instead of outsiders, the MNC can avoid charges of exploitation while gaining goodwill at the same time. Visa's European organization has been staffed and directed by Europeans in an effort to dilute its image as an American company.

Another advantage to be gained is that the company can compete quite strongly for high-quality local personnel. An MNC can offer above-market pay, which may likely be still lower than the pay scale in the MNC's home market. This situation applies to Japan as well. The stigma associated with the Japanese working for foreign companies has recently been crumbling. In the past, the Japanese were reluctant to work for U.S. companies because they felt that it would be difficult to be promoted. They were also apprehensive about the role of politics within the organization. However, younger Japanese are now more internationally oriented and are eager to join U.S. companies, since these workers resent the Japanese system of seniority, dedication, and loyalty.

When the host country's people are locally employed, expatriate relocation and travel expenses can be avoided. The costs of keeping expatriates overseas can be exorbitant. Cost-of-living adjustments may equal 80 percent of basic salaries. In addition, a modest house in a Tokyo suburb may cost $11,000 a month. It is not unusual for GM to have to spend $750,000 to $1 million on a manager and his or her family during a three-year stay overseas.[13]

The use of local personnel allows a company to proceed with its business more quickly, since the adjustment period is eliminated. Language barriers and cultural difficulties are minimized. For example, it is difficult for an American salesperson to entertain his or her foreign clients without an understanding of the local culture. Without a knowledge of the local language, even simple or casual interaction such as telling a joke is a struggle. In Japan, a majority of business is conducted verbally in face-to-face interaction, whereas in the U.S.A. much greater emphasis is placed on correspondence and report preparation. Realizing that the American business culture is different, Ricoh uses American personnel to run its U.S. operations. Furthermore, Ricoh recognizes that local nationals, being identified as part of the local scene, can be both efficient and effective, since they have business and government contacts.

One study examined a decision whether to appoint an expatriate as the managing director of 844 Japanese manufacturing affiliates in Asia. A parent's strategic dependence on an affiliate was found to increase the likelihood of appointing an expatriate for the purpose of control and coordination. Organizational experience in the host country (both by the affiliate and the firm) increased the propensity to use localization through appointments of local nationals.[14] Another study investigated expatriate localization programs in 67 multinational companies with operations in the Peoples' Republic of China. It found that the success of the localization of management (i.e., replacing expatriates with locals) could be enhanced by planning aspects of the localization program and efforts to improve selection.[15]

When personnel in key positions and at headquarters are examined, usually most American companies employ only Americans. In a way, this is understandable due to the vast supply of local talent available to fill such positions, but some American MNCs are now realizing that a well trained American may not be well-trained to work on a worldwide basis. American Standard has instilled a stronger global orientation into its corporate decision-making process by using foreign managers to run many of its important U.S. operations. Such heterogeneity provides a company with linguistic capabilities, exporting know-how, skills in negotiating with foreign governments, and international flavor that many U.S. managers lack.

Women tend not to get international assignments. The reasons often offered range from the reluctance of women or their companies, to prejudice against women in foreign countries. One study found that women and their supervisors had different views on women's interst in pursuing international assignments as well as different expectations concerning the prejudice. Therefore, women and their supervisors should openly discuss the issues.[16] Interestingly, at least in the case of India,

Indian host-country nationals have a preference for female expatriates from the U.S.A. as co-workers.[17]

From the viewpoint of employees, based on an analysis of 4605 individual evaluations of the 60 companies in the Reputation Quotient Annual 2000 study, firms' foreignness (measured by whether companies have foreign headquarters) makes the companies less attractive as employers. On the other hand, a company's degree of internationalization is an attractive factor. Gender, race, respondent age, and education level also interact with the foreignness variables in predicting company attractiveness.[18]

While it is understandable as to why attention must be given to expatriate personnel, it is just as important to pay attention to **inpatriate managers**. A program or process should be designed to overcome the stigmatization and stereotyping of inpatriate managers located in the home-country organization. A negative stereotype could threaten both the performance of the inpatriate managers as well as the performance of the corporation that is attempting to globalize its operations.[19]

## Publicity

### *The nature of publicity*

Publicity is the nonpersonal stimulation of demand that is not paid for by a sponsor which has released news to the media. Advertising and publicity are similar in the sense that both require media for a nonpersonal presentation of the promotional message. One difference between the two is that, with publicity, a company has less control over how the message will be used by the media. Another difference is that publicity is presumed to be free in the sense that the media are not paid for the presentation of the message to the public. In practice, a publicity campaign is not cost-free because someone must be assigned to generate the publicity, and there are several direct and indirect costs. Still, the cost for publicity is minimal when compared to the benefit.

Publicity offers several advantages. In addition to the low cost, the material presented is not recognized as paid advertising per se because it occurs in an editorial setting which makes it appear to have been generated by the approval of the editorial staff. The material thus has more credibility, and consumers tend to accept it as news information rather than as advertising. This perception is particularly useful in countries where it is difficult to buy commercial time or advertising space.

Publicity should be used when a company advertises heavily, since advertising increases the likelihood that the media that have been used will reciprocate by using the company's news releases. Publicity is also effective when the editorial content can influence purchase, a point proven by Perrier. Publicity was the important part of Perrier's marketing program, because the company determined that it needed third-party endorsement by editors in news and lifestyle publications and broadcast media. Perrier therefore invited 60 editors and TV personnel to the mineral spring in France.

There are several methods that may be used to gain publicity. Such methods include the following: contribution of prizes; sponsorship of civic activities; release of news about the company's product, plant, and personnel; and announcements of the company's promotional campaign, especially with regard to such sales-promotion techniques as games and contests. Nike was able to overtake Adidas in the U.S.A. with effective publicity and sales promotion campaigns. In addition to asking athletes to help design shoes, Nike signed professional athletes to exclusive promotional contracts involving cash, free shoes, and promotion appearances. Shoes were given to top college teams, and the company gained additional exposure when these teams appeared on TV. Moreover, it sponsored running clinics, sporting events, and women's pro tennis events.

## The management of publicity

Publicity is often viewed as a promotional component that is not possible to manage. News releases to the media may not be utilized by the media. If they are, they may not be utilized in the manner intended. In reality, the problem is not so much that publicity cannot be managed but that publicity is usually managed in a haphazard way.

Proper management is required for all publicity campaigns. Every campaign must first have a well-defined objective. Without a precise objective it is difficult to coordinate activities, and conflicting messages or items of little news value might be released. Confusion usually follows.

Similar to the other three activities of promotion, the effectiveness of publicity must be measured. The effectiveness of publicity is not determined by the number of news releases or publication space and air time generated. Similar to advertising, personal selling, and sales promotion, the effectiveness of publicity should be measured by sales inquiries and changes in the attitude or response pattern of the public.

A person responsible for a publicity campaign should keep the needs of the media in mind. Any request for information should be handled promptly because any requested information is likely to be used. In most countries, magazines have small editorial budgets and are understaffed. A publicity placement is more likely to be accepted if it is submitted in the form that is ready to be used. For example, photos and materials that are camera-ready relieve the publication of budget and time constraints.

## Negative publicity

Some publicity received can be far from being favorable (see Ethical Dimension 14.1). Ajinomoto, a brand of monosodium glutamate, has been able throughout the company's history to dispel false rumors. A rumor was spread in the 1910s that Ajinomoto came from snakes. Another rumor, circulating in Islamic countries, was that Ajinomoto was processed from pig bones.

No company wants negative publicity. Without the proper handling of publicity, a situation may deteriorate. The adverse publicity generated by its powdered infant formula became a publicity nightmare for Nestlé. The company's idea of marketing a breast-milk substitute in developing countries to save babies from disease, malnutrition, and death backfired very badly. Church groups and consumer groups accused the company of promoting the product to those who could least afford it or who were unable to use it properly. The poor handling of the animosity that developed engaged the company in a long and costly conflict.

Ford and Firestone generated a great deal of negative publicity related to Ford Explorer and Firestone tires.[20] The Ford SUVs and Firestone tires were connected to more than 1,400 accidents and other mishaps, and almost 100 people died as a result. Ford blamed the accidents on the Firestone tires and offered replacement tires to its customers, resulting in a recall of some 6.5 million tires. Firestone, on the other hand, put the blame in part on Ford's user instructions to underinflate these tires. Neither side appeared to handle the crisis well, and the termination of the cooperation did not help the matter.

Much has been learned from the Tylenol case, in which Johnson & Johnson was able to deal effectively with the contamination that occurred in its capsules. Marketers should carefully review how the company was able to turn the negative publicity around and how it was able to regain sympathy and trust. Based on these experiences, there are several "do's" and "don'ts" that should be kept in mind.

## Ethical Dimension 14.1

**Expensive water**

According to the 2006 Human Development Report, produced by the United Nations, the water crisis and poor sanitation kill 1.8 million children each year and cause health problems to almost 50 percent of all people in developing countries. The irony is that people living in urban slums pay five to ten times more for a liter of water than people living in high-income areas. People in the poorest parts of Accra and Manila pay more than those living in London, New York, and Paris.

Water is often taken for granted by people in developed economies. Unfortunately, more than 1.2 billion people do not have access to safe drinking-water. About 40 percent of the world's population (or 2.6 billion people) lack proper sanitation. As a consequence, water-borne diseases result in about 2 million deaths each year.

Coca-Cola Co. and Pepsi, as major users of water, have been severely criticized. Water, after all, is the largest ingredient in most of Coca-Cola's more than 400 beverage brands. Coca-Cola and its bottlers consume more than 73 billion gallons of water annually.

The public relations nightmare is particularly acute in India. According to the Centre for Science & Environment, soft drinks there were found to contain pesticides. The amount of pesticides found in Pepsi was 36 times higher than the European Economic Commission standards for water. In 2004 amid a drought, Coca-Cola was ordered by government officials to shut down a bottling plant. Local communities claimed that the plant was draining groundwater. The company said that a government study concluded that it was not using excessive amounts of water.

To eliminate the water controversy, Coca-Cola has about 70 clean-water projects in 40 countries. These are community water partnerships with groups that include CARE and the U.S. Agency for International Development. In Kenya, the company provides water supplies, treatment and storage systems, sanitation and hygiene education in schools and communities. In India, it has invested in 270 rainwater-harvesting structures, with more being planned. This is a strategy to show the company as a local benefactor and global diplomat. The effort should help local economies while broadening the company's consumer base.

*Sources*: "Paying a High Price for Polluted Water," *Finance & Development*, December 2006, 3; "Why Coke Aims to Slake Global Thirst for Safe Water," *Water Street Journal*, March 15, 2007; and "Pepsi: Repairing a Poisoned Reputation in India," *Business Week*, June 11, 2007, 46–54.

To begin with, it is not wise to criticize the media for reporting unfavorable news. The criticism serves to alienate the media by inflaming the issue and prolonging the attention being given to it. It is also not wise to ignore adverse publicity. This behavior may give the impression of arrogance, and it wastes critical time that could be used to solve the problem if the problem is serious. A company should also avoid the "no comment" response because it conveys the impression of uncooperativeness and it implies guilt. If a full disclosure is not possible for security reasons, the company's spokesperson should say so and ask for understanding from the media.

When preparing to respond to inquiries about a newsworthy event, it is critical to review the facts, prepare news reports, and perhaps seek professional assistance. Personnel should be immediately organized to handle inquiries from consumers and reporters. Even when the problem is still unclear, contingency plans should be devised so that personnel can be put into action quickly. In fact, there should be a contingency crisis management plan that forces executives to think in advance about how to deal with unforeseen crises.

Those companies facing the greatest levels of industrial and environmental risk are more likely than others to have crisis communication plans. Such companies include those in the extractive industries and food and drug manufacturers. It is thus surprising that, given the nature of the business, Union Carbide failed to anticipate potential problems that could have occurred. As a result, the company was severely criticized for its handling of the devastating Bhopal (India) gas leak. Many inquiries in the early stages went unanswered, and at times the company appeared evasive when it did issue a response.

In dealing with the media, candor, preparedness, speed, and cooperation are all essential. If a company's guilt is undeniable, it is better to admit it at the outset so that attention can be shifted to the steps being taken to resolve the situation. Although a team effort is likely taking place, it is highly desirable that a top executive acts as the company's sole spokesperson so that inconsistencies can be minimized. The executive should be prepared to communicate quickly and professionally. He or she must possess accurate information and be ready to answer all questions. Since the media are eager to receive information, they can and should be accommodated, as well as exploited. The company can call news conferences that allow it to relay the information to the public through the media at no cost. At such conferences, the spokesperson can outline the steps being taken to protect the public interest. In effect, this tactic provides the company with free advertising and positive publicity.

If the product has serious potential ramifications, corporate image advertising may be used to reinforce the trustworthiness of the company and the product. Marketing research can be valuable in tracking the public mood so that appropriate communication strategies may be adopted. Figure 14.3 shows how South Africa attempted to use advertising to deal with its country's negative image and bad publicity.

The company should also be decisive. Its decision should be based on the public good rather than cost as an overriding motive. If product recall is warranted because a situation is potentially dangerous to the public, the recall should proceed immediately. A company should avoid vacillation or hedging. Procter & Gamble poorly handled a problem of contaminated cake mixes in California by making contradictory announcements about the product's recall. A decisive response does not mean, however, that product recall is always the preferred strategy. Gerber Foods took legal action against those states that wanted its baby food taken off the shelves because of broken glass found in some jars. The company's rationale was that the incident was an isolated one not related to its normal manufacturing process and that any recall would unduly alarm the public. Its position was subsequently supported by the results of an investigation.

## Sales promotion

### *The nature of sales promotion*

Sales promotion consists of those promotional activities other than advertising, personal selling, and publicity. As such, any promotional activities that do not fall under the other three activities of the promotion mix are considered sales promotion. Qantas, for example, offers its passengers Connection Cards that may be used to purchase London Fog coats wholesale. The trade often uses the term indiscriminately. Businesspersons may use the term "promotion" when they actually mean "sales promotion." In this book, *promotion* is a broad term that encompasses sales promotion as well as the other three promotional activities.

South Africa
Houses for sale: $16 000 and less
Imagine buying a four-roomed, State-built house for as little as $880. Or a five-roomed house for between $2 331 and $16 000. It's happening right now – in South Africa.
SHARING A BETTER QUALITY OF LIFE
South Africa is involved in a remarkable process of providing fair opportunities for all its population groups. The South African Government is committed to ensure that each of South Africa's many nationalities have the ability and resources to realize their social, economic and political aspirations.
Housing is a leading example of South Africa's development process. And as an integrated part of its drive towards home ownership for everyone, the South African Government has given the go-ahead for the sale of 500 000 State-financed homes at discounts of up to 40 % of their market value.
MEETING THE HOUSING CHALLENGE
South Africa's urban Black population is expected to rise from 9 million currently to around 20 million by the turn of the century. It is estimated that an additional 4.9 million housing units will have to be provided to accommodate this phenomenal urbanisation.
The housing challenge is being met by both the Government and the private sector. Government initiatives are directed mainly towards providing the machinery and support for self-help building projects, while private enterprise provides loans, subsidies and guarantees.
THE FUTURE – BETTER PROSPECTS FOR ALL
A recent survey indicated that 82 % of all employers were prepared to provide their Black staff with assistance to buy their own homes.
The facts on housing present only part of the picture. Many aspects of South African life have changed – and are changing at an ever-increasing rate. The future is exciting because we have the people, the dedication and a buoyant economy to enable us to keep on providing opportunities and improving the quality of life of all our people.
Because South Africa is a microcosm of so many of the world's sensitivities, it is often a contentious subject. If you are faced with a decision regarding South Africa, make sure you have all the facts.
For more information, simply complete the coupon below.
To: The Minister (Information), The South African Embassy, 3051 Massachusetts Avenue, Washington D.C., 20008 N.W.
Please send me more information on socio-economic and political developments in South Africa.
Name
Address
Code
We're looking forward to the future.

**FIGURE 14.3** Management of negative publicity

*Source*: Reprinted with permission of the South African Consulate General, Washington, DC.

## Cultural Dimension 14.2

**Generous return**

Acer Inc. ranks No. 4 among the branded personal computer makers, behind Hewlett-Packard, Dell, and Lenovo. In 2006, it made a profit of $338 million from sales of $11.1 billion. It is a strong competitor in Asia and Europe. Gianfranco Lanci, president of the company, shuttles weekly between his home in Milan and his corporate duty in Taiwan.

In the 1990s, Acer attempted to compete in the U.S. market. The U.S.A. is the world's largest market but also a highly competitive place. Acer misjudged the market and its peculiarity. For one thing, Acer failed to realize that American consumers expected and would take full advantage of retailers' generous return policies. It was an expensive venture and experience for Acer. During the 10-year period, Acer suffered a loss of a couple of billion dollars, ten times greater than what was expected. The company was forced to withdraw from the U.S. market but is now making a new attempt to conquer the market.

Taiwan and China have maintained their uneasy economic cooperation. Beijing has stated its intention to attack Taiwan if Taiwan formally declares its independence. Politics aside, both parties have greatly benefited from their economic ties. Taiwanese companies have invested more than $100 billion in China since the early 1990s. Acer is one of the many companies that outsource manufacturing there.

Acer does not want to pursue market share by marketing cut-rate products that sacrifice function and computing power. Even in developing countries with limited spending power, the company's "research shows that people with smaller incomes don't want inferior products."

*Sources*: "Acer Chairman Takes Global Approach," *San José Mercury News*, November 26, 2006; "A Racer Called Acer," *Business Week*, January 29, 2007, 48; and "Taiwan's Acer Gains Ground on Chinese Rival Lenovo," *San José Mercury News*, April 2, 2007.

The techniques of sales promotion are varied and numerous. The most common ones used are coupons, sweepstakes, games, contest, price-offs, demonstrations, premiums, samples, money refund offers, and trading stamps. According to a study of consumer evaluations of sales promotion, immediate price reduction exerts the greatest amount of influence on brand choice.[21]

A combination of these techniques may be used and sometimes are used in the same campaign. When Kelloggs expanded its business abroad, it had to enlighten consumers in South and Central America, the Middle East, and Asia about dry cereal and cold breakfasts. To instill this new eating habit, Kelloggs used samples and demonstrations in conjunction with a heavy advertising campaign.

Sales promotion is temporary in nature. Not being self-sustaining, its function is to supplement advertising, personal selling, and publicity. To launch Budweiser beer in Great Britain, Anheuser-Busch employed the "American" theme. Its TV commercials on July 4 and Thanksgiving day were spots filmed in California with American actors. To supplement its advertising effort, the company used a variety of sales promotion techniques. It made posters, bunting, flags, pennants, T-shirts, and sweatshirts available to pubs and discos for promotional parties. Bud ashtrays, bar towels, coasters, football pennants, and similar items were offered for sale. Moreover, American disc jockeys were brought in to program American music nights.

Sales promotion is not restricted to the stimulation of demand at the consumer level. It may be used to gain middlemen's support as well. Moreover, the use of sales promotion is not limited to consumer products. It may be used with industrial selling too. Misawa Homes promoted its House 55 by sending samples to U.S. Homes and Germany's Okal. Pfizer, like other drug firms, attracts drug wholesalers by sponsoring trips and other events. Gifts are given to doctors, and doctors' wives are taken on shopping tours.

Sales promotion is effective when a product is first introduced to a market. It also works well with existing products that are highly competitive and standardized, especially when they are of low unit value and have high turnover. Under such conditions, sales promotion is needed to gain that "extra" competitive advantage.

The effectiveness of sales promotion can be tempered by psychological barriers, and this fact is applicable to middlemen as well as consumers. Some foreign retailers are reluctant to accept manufacturers' coupons because they fear that they will not be reimbursed. Consumers, on the other hand, may view rebates, mail-in coupons, and money-back guarantees with suspicion, thinking that something must be wrong with the product.

International marketers need to confirm the validity of a statement concerning the effectiveness of a sales-promotion technique. Sometimes, casual observation and hearsay have a way of making a particular claim become a statement of fact without the support of empirical evidence.

## Restrictions

Although sales promotion is generally received enthusiastically in developing countries, the activity is still largely underutilized, which may be due more to legal barriers than to psychological barriers. European countries have a larger number of restrictions than the U.S.A. in this area. The legal requirements are so diverse that the European Association of Advertising Agencies (EAAA) decided that the standardization of promotion regulations was very unlikely in the near future.

Since it would be impossible to know the specific laws of each and every country, marketers should consult local lawyers and authorities before launching a promotional campaign. For example, Belgium requires a government tax stamp on window signs. The purpose of this section is to show how certain sales promotional tools might be affected by local regulations (see Legal Dimension 14.1).

### *Premiums and gifts*

Most European countries have a limit on the value of the premium given. Colgate was sued by a local blade manufacturer in Greece for giving away razor-blades with shaving cream. Austria considers premiums to be a form of discriminatory treatment toward buyers. In France, it is illegal to offer premiums that are conditional on the purchase of another product. In Finland, premiums are allowed so long as the word *free* is not used with them. A gift is usually subject to the same restriction as a premium. Compared to the U.S.A. and the United Kingdom, which are very lenient, Belgium, Germany, and Scandinavia have strict laws concerning promotion owing to their desire to protect consumers from being distracted from the true value of a given product or service. Argentina, Austria, Norway, and Venezuela virtually ban the use of merchandise premiums. Other countries, being less restrictive, do not permit the value of the premiums to exceed more than a certain percentage (e.g., 10 percent in Japan) of the value of the product that must be purchased to receive the premium.

## Legal Dimension 14.1

### Sales promotion techniques and legal restrictions

Germany's national safety standards for consumer products are higher than those of the United Kingdom. While the U.S.A., the United Kingdom, Poland, and Spain have by and large minimal regulations on promotional bonuses, this is not the case in Germany, Belgium, and the Scandinavian countries. In the latter group, retail sales that are combined with free mail-ins, cash off purchases, free draws (sweepstakes), free gifts with purchase, and so on are either forbidden or strictly regulated.

In Sweden, the authorities ordered TV4 to stop its broadcast of a Swedish version of a popular quiz show, "Who Wants to Be a Millionaire." The government's Lottery Inspection Agency concluded that the program was not a real contest but more of a lottery. The TV station director begged to differ. He denied that contestants relied on guess work rather than knowledge.

Austria has a discount law prohibiting cash reductions that give preferential treatment to different groups of customers. Discounts in Scandinavia are also restricted. In France, it is illegal to sell a product for less than its cost. In Germany, marketers must notify authorities in advance if they plan to have a sale. Unlike in the U.S.A., where there are all kinds of sales for all occasions (e.g., manager's sale, assistant manager's sale, buyer's sale), a sale in Germany is limited to such events as going out of business, giving up a particular product line, end of January (winter), end of July (summer), and a twenty-fifth anniversary. Both Austria and Germany are similar in the sense that special sales may be made only under certain circumstances or during specified periods of time (seasonal sales). Moreover, discounts for payment on delivery may not exceed 3 percent, and any quantity discounts must be within the applicable industry's usual numerical range.

### *Samples*

In Russia, tobacco firms freely distribute samples. The "Lucky Strike girls," for example, move around in Moscow bars to offer patrons a smoke and a light. Due to public criticism, Philip Morris has stopped the sampling practice in the U.S.A. In addition, the U.S.A. does not allow alcoholic beer to be offered as a free sample, and this law also holds for taste tests. Germany restricts door-to-door free samples that limit population coverage as well as the size of the sample pack.

### *Sweepstakes, games, and contests*

For a sweepstake to be legal in France, an entry form must be separate from an order form. Germany permits sweepstakes so long as they do not create psychological pressure on customers. In addition, they cannot be misleading, and they must not offer a prize of substantial value.

Lotteries tend to be illegal in many countries (e.g., France, England, the U.S.A.). A lottery has three elements – chance, consideration, and price. For a sweepstake, game, or contest not to become an illegal lottery, a company must ensure that at least one of these three elements is missing.

## Overseas product exhibitions

One type of sales promotion that can be highly effective is the exhibition of a product overseas. This type of promotion may be very important because regular advertising and sales letters and brochures may not be adequate. For certain products, quality can be judged only by physical examination, and product exhibition can facilitate this process.

One very effective way to exhibit products abroad is to use trade fairs. Unlike trade shows in the U.S.A. where the social or party atmosphere is prevalent, European trade fairs are an important part of the marketing mix that must be prepared with great care. These shows can account for one-third of a European firm's marketing budget. The State of Colorado helped Alpine Map Co. to pay for a booth at an international sporting goods show in Munich. The company has been going back there ever since, and now foreign sales account for 40 percent of its total sales. As a matter of fact, the company is probably better known in Europe than at home.

There are two main types of trade shows: *horizontal* and *vertical*. At one end of the spectrum are broad, well-established, annual affairs (horizontal trade shows). The Hamburg Fair, for instance, exhibits almost everything in both consumer and industrial goods. At the other end of the spectrum are specialized types for products in specialized industries (vertical trade shows). Electronica, held annually in Munich, is a vertical trade show.

There are more than 800 international trade fairs each year. Trade fairs allow thousands of firms from many countries to set up "temporary stores or offices" right in the marketplace to display their products. A strong feature of a trade fair is that prospectors are in a buying mood. Another advantage is that buyers are seeking out sellers at a central location. Obviously, a trade show presents a much easier contact situation for a salesperson because there is no travel to many diverse locations to call on potential buyers.

A new phenomenon is the "**virtual exhibition**." This concept stems from an excess of demand over supply of traditional or physical exhibitions. Based on a sample of European and Middle Eastern senior managers who organize Middle East exhibitions, the virtual exhibition can be a useful medium to support international marketing activities.[22]

An exhibitor should investigate whether it is worthwhile to use a carnet for products that will be shipped or taken to the exhibition. A **carnet** is an international customs document that facilitates the temporary duty-free importation of product samples in lieu of the usual customs documents required to bring merchandise into several major trading countries (see Figures 14.4 and 14.5). That is, a carnet is a series of vouchers listing the goods and countries involved where the product will be exhibited. For a fee based on the value of the goods to be covered, a carnet may be purchased in advanced in the U.S.A. by American firms. Foreign firms can turn to their local carnet associations, which are members of the International Bureau of the Paris-based International Chamber of Commerce. By issuing carnets, these associations in effect guarantee the payment of duties that may become due on goods temporarily imported and not re-exported. A carnet holder is required to post security equal to 40 percent of the value of the goods to cover duties and taxes in cases where goods were not re-exported and duties were not paid.

Because different national customs regulations can act as trade barriers, the World Customs Organization adopted the "Customs Convention on the ATA Carnet for the Temporary Admission of Goods" in 1961. The initials ATA are from the French and English words "Admission Temporaire/ Temporary Admission." A carnet offers a number of benefits: no temporary import bonds, no registration of goods when departing a country, unlimited reuse for all products listed on a carnet for

INTERNATIONAL GUARANTEE CHAIN ................ INTERNATIONAL GUARANTEE CHAIN
*CHAINE DE GARANTIE INTERNATIONALE* — *CHAINE DE GARANTIE INTERNATIONALE*

B.I.C.C.

**GENERAL LIST** / ***LISTE GENERALE***
**(May be used for Continuation Sheets / *Feuille Supplementaire*)**

x Patricia Cohen x
Signature of Holder / *Signature du titulaire*

Signature of authorized official and stamp of the issuing Association /
*Signature du delegué et timbre de l'association émettrice*

Sample

VOUCHER No. ............ CONTINUATION SHEET No. 0 ............ Carnet No. 00-XXXXX
*VOLET DE No.* — *FEUILLE SUPPLEMENTAIRE No.* — *Carnet A.T.A. No.*

| Item No./ *No. d'ordre* | Trade description of goods and marks and numbers, if any/ *Désignation commerciale des marchandises et, le cas échéant, marques et numéros* | Number of Pieces/ *Nombre de Pièces* | Weight or Volume/ *Poids ou Volume* | *Value/ *Valeur* | **Country of origin/ *Pays d'origine* | For Customs Use/ *Réservé à la douane* |
|---|---|---|---|---|---|---|
| 1 | 2 | 3 | 4 | 5 | 6 | 7 |
| | TOTAL CARRIED OVER / *REPORT* | | | | | |
| 1 | P917 18KT CYNNABAR AND PLATINUM BRACELET | 1 | 46DWT | $472 | USA | |
| 2 | B251-22 18KT DIAMOND AND SABI BACELET | 1 | 22DWT | $930 | USA | |
| 3 | Z003 18 KT FACETED CUFFLINKS | 2 | 19DWT | $157 | USA | |
| 4 | BQ88CYN 18KT CYNNABAR AND PLATINUM BUCKLE AND TIP ON 1-1/4" BELT | 1 | 55DWT | $456 | USA | |
| 5 | G994RKT 18KT DIAMOND AND PEARL EARRINGS 8 DIA = 2.28CT 2 SOUTH SEA PEARLS | 2 | 17DWT | $7425 | USA | |
| 6 | Aubergine Satin Pants Sytle #D953321 | 1 | 1.5 lb | $100 | EC | |
| 7 | Beige Brocade Dress Style #BOT22 | 1 | 2 lb | $75 | DE | |
| 8 | Purple Sequin Long Dress Style #PT21 | 1 | 2 lb | $200 | IT | |
| 9 | 1998 Sony TCD Headphones, model TCD[illegible], serial J712349985 | 1 | 1 lb | $225 | JP | |
| 10 | Sony PVM 8041GT Monitor, Serial #2519587 | 1 | 8 lb | $840 | JP | |
| 11 | Wireless Microphone System, Lectrosonics #1038 | 1 | 1 lb | $1600 | US | |
| 12 | Fujinon Camera Lens, #060184 | 1 | 2 lb | $5000 | JP | |
| | NO CHANGES, OR ADDITIONS, ABOVE OR BELOW THIS LINE. | | | | | |
| | General List includes 0 *(number)* "Continuation Sheets". | | | | | |
| | TOTAL or CARRIED OVER / *TOTAL ou A REPORTER* | 14 | 60 lbs | $17,480.- | | |

Sample

*Commercial value in country of issue and in the currency, unless stated differently. / *Valeur commerciale dans le pays d'émission et dans sa monnaie sauf indication contraire.*
**Show country of origin if different from country of issue of theCarnet, using ISO country codes. / *Indiquer le pays d'origine s'il est différent du pays d'émission du Carnet en utilisant le code international des pays ISO.*

**FIGURE 14.4** Carnet

# ATA Carnet Application

**A. Holder Information:**

1. Carnet Holder (Corporation or Individual):
Street Address (No P.O. Box):
City: State: Zip: Phone: Fax:
2. IRS/SS No.: E-mail:
3. Parent Company: IRS No. of Parent Company:
4. Person Duly Authorized & Title:
5. Authorized Representatives (individuals or agents) who will be shipping or hand-carrying the merchandise on the Carnet:

**B. Carnet Preparation/Country Information:**

6. Goods to be exported as: (mark more than one if applicable)
☐ Professional Equipment (PE)
☐ Commercial Samples (CS)
☐ Exhibitions and Fairs (EF)

7. Approximate Date of Departure from U.S.: (enter date as "MM/DD/YY")

8. Type the NUMBER of visits in the space provided beside each country you expect to visit:

| | | | |
|---|---|---|---|
| __ Andorra (AD) | __ Germany (DE) | __ Macedonia (MK) | __ South Africa (ZA) |
| __ Algeria (DZ) | __ Gibraltar (GI) | __ Malaysia (MY) | __ Spain (ES) |
| __ Australia (AU) | __ Greece (GR) | __ Malta (MT) | __ Sri Lanka (LK) |
| __ Austria (AT) | __ Hong Kong (HK) | __ Mauritius (MU) | __ Sweden (SE) |
| __ Belgium (BE) | __ Hungary (HU) | __ Morocco (MA)[2] | __ Switzerland (CH) |
| __ Bulgaria (BE) | __ Iceland (IS) | __ Netherlands (NL) | __ Taiwan (TW) - Call First |
| __ Canada (CA)[1] | __ India (IN)[2] | __ New Zealand (NZ) | __ Thailand (TH) |
| __ China (CN)[2] – Call First | __ Ireland (IE) | __ Norway (NO) | __ Tunisia (TN)[4] |
| __ Croatia (HR) | __ Israel (IL)[3] | __ Poland (PL) | __ Turkey (TR) |
| __ Cyprus (CY) | __ Italy (IT) | __ Portugal (PT) | __ United Kingdom (GB) |
| __ Czech Republic (CZ) | __ Ivory Coast (CI) | __ Romania (RO) | __ Other: |
| __ Denmark (DK) | __ Japan (JP) | __ Senegal (SN) | |
| __ Estonia (EE) | __ Korea (KR)[3] | __ Singapore (SG) | |
| __ Finland (FI) | __ Lebanon (LB)[4] | __ Slovakia (SK) | |
| __ France (FR) | __ Luxembourg (LU) | __ Slovenia (SI) | |

[1] certain PE items are admitted [2] only EF items for certain events [3] 100% security required [4] CS items are not admitted

9. Number of times your merchandise will be leaving and re-entering the U.S.:__________
10. Number of countries transiting(s): ____ List Countries to be transited: ____________________

**C. Delivery Instructions:**

11. Courier Service (Include completed airway bill with your account number OR to use our courier service, include $20.00 for Shipping & Handling)
12. Messenger Pick-up
13. Regular Mail

**D. Processing Fees:**

14. Basic Processing Fee: Ship to:
15. Expedited Service:
16. Additional Certificate Sets Fee: ($5 each add'l set after 8)
17. Continuation Sheet Fee: ($0 first sheet, $5 each add'l)
18. Shipper's Export Declaration Fee: ($5 each)
19. Refundable Claim Deposit:
(for government agencies only; waiver must be download and submitted)
20. Shipping and Handling:
21. Country Surcharge:
Total:

Continue to next page for Security and Obligation.

FIGURE 14.5 Carnet application

one year, and coverage of most business-related items. The system is recognized by 58 countries and 27 territories worldwide.

In the U.S.A., the U.S. Council for International Business (USCIB), appointed by the U.S. Treasury Department, is the sole issuer and guarantor of carnets. All carnet applicants submit a security deposit in the form of cash or a bond. The deposit is collateral and will be drawn upon to reimburse the USCIB if it incurs a liability or loss in connection with the carnet. When the original carnet is returned, assuming no anticipation of claims, the cash deposits will be returned in full, and the bonds terminated. The value of shipment and type of application (paper or electronic) determine the carnet fees.

For countries that do not accept carnets, a company has two other alternatives. It can either apply for a **Temporary Importation Under Bond (TIB)**, a document sold by a customs broker at the time of entry; or it can rely on the duty drawback for temporary imports. This process requires an importer to register the goods at the time of entry into a foreign country and deposit the applicable duties and taxes. Later, at the time of departure, the foreign customs authority inspects and collects the appropriate paperwork for the product in question. A full refund follows.[23]

Overseas exhibits are a costly form of promotion. There are costs related to the design and construction of a booth. There are also the transportation costs of the booth and products for display. Labor is required for setting up and later dismantling the booth. In addition to the rental costs of space and furniture, other costs include staffing and transportation, and accommodation of representatives.

There a few suggestions that exhibitors at trade fairs should keep in mind. Space cost is only a small portion of the total cost. Thus it is better to rent adequate space, since overcrowding discourages potential clients from visiting the exhibit. Exhibit contents should be kept simple, and only the most important items displayed. To avoid having to set up the booth late and dismantle it early, a company may want to locate its booth away from the freight entrance area. Mailing lists of prospects should be obtained, and letters sent to them before the opening day. It is also important to have a qualified representative at the booth who can make sales decisions. This representative should arrive early and leave late. Early arrival also gives the representative time to become acclimatized. Plenty of business cards and brochures should be kept on hand. Finally, the local traffic patterns should be taken into account. Unlike in the U.S.A. where people are used to turning right and walking on the right-hand side, many countries drive on the left side of the street and people thus walk on the left side of an aisle. An exhibitor may gain an advantage if it locates the exhibit on the left side of an aisle, since the visitors will traffic on that side.

An exhibitor should notice and respect cultural differences in dress formality and the exchange of business cards. Trade shows overseas are serious affairs, and only businesspeople and buyers (not the general public) are admitted. Because most buyers want time to think about products, some serious follow-up after the show should be carried out. It may be worthwhile to spend a few extra days making calls on the most promising prospects. Later, the exhibitor should send letters with additional material or have a local representative call the visitors who stopped at the booth.

A trade show is not the only means of exhibiting products overseas. Companies can also rent space in trade centers to display merchandise on a more permanent basis. Vienna (Austria) and Taipei (Taiwan) are examples of two such trade centers located in different parts of the world .

Because of the high cost of overseas exhibition, exporters should consult with their governments concerning their assistance and the other related promotional activities. It is not unusual for governments to sponsor official participation in certain major international exhibitions. In the case of the U.S.A., the Department of Commerce additionally organizes a *trade mission* from time to time. It may, for example, send a boat full of merchandise to an overseas port. Based on the belief that foreign sales of U.S. consumer products are best developed through *in-store promotion*, its sponsored events are designed to promote sales of consumer merchandise directly to consumers in major department stores and mail order houses from Finland to Hong Kong.

## Conclusion

A product, no matter how superior, should not be expected to sell itself. It must be promoted so that prospectors can learn about the benefits provided by the product. The State of Pennsylvania, for example, had only one overseas office before 1980 but now has several to promote its exports. The State of Ohio has determined that, for each $1 spent to promote its exports, it derives $260 in export sales.

A product may be promoted in several ways – advertising, personal selling, publicity, and sales promotion. Although advertising is the most prominent technique, the other three methods are no less important. For promotion to be most effective, however, all four of the promotional techniques should be used and coordinated. Two chapters are devoted to a discussion of the various aspects of promotion. This chapter has concentrated on the treatment of personal selling, publicity, and sales promotion. The next chapter is primarily concerned with international advertising.

Personal selling usually commands the largest proportion of promotional expenditures. It is used internationally as well as locally at every distribution level and for all kinds of products. When expatriate sales personnel are to be employed, these personnel and their families should be screened for suitability before being given overseas assignments. For a variety of good reasons, qualified local nationals should be used whenever possible. If MNCs do not hire these qualified individuals, local progressive competitors are likely to employ them.

With limited media time and space available in many countries, it is necessary to develop some rapport with media people in order to try to gain free publicity. Finally, the efforts in advertising, personal selling, and publicity activities should be supplemented and supported by sales promotion.

## CASE 14.1 SELLING IN THE EU

### Antonis C. Simintiras, University of Wales

It was a pleasant, warm Sunday afternoon when Michael had to rethink his selling strategies for his region. Michael was born in England and after studying for four years at a major UK university he joined a leading British pharmaceutical company. Following a successful career in sales within the UK, he was promoted to sales representative for Southeast Europe. Based in Thessaloniki, Greece, he was made responsible for selling the entire range of products for the company's division to pharmacists, doctors, and hospitals. Michael went through a rigorous and intensive training program for three months and learned a lot about cultural differences between the British and Southern Europeans. Although he was responsible for covering three countries in the Balkan region (Greece,

Bulgaria, and Yugoslavia), Michael had recently come to the conclusion that his selling strategies in Greece were somewhat inappropriate.

After six months of hard work, Michael was happy with the progress he had made. He had managed to open several accounts with hospitals in all three countries and had built up a network of pharmacists and doctors, many of whom had either bought or agreed to buy his company's products. Recently, however, he had noticed a change in the attitude of some of his most important customers, especially in Greece, which was the first, in terms of priority, market for development. Until a few months previously, almost all of his customers had shown a strong interest in his products and were happy to place orders. During the past two months however, Michael had noticed that the level of interest and willingness to buy had deteriorated, to the extent that some of his customers were delaying reordering, despite the fact that their safety stocks were not allowing them such a relaxed attitude toward stock replenishment. Constant feedback from customers indicated that there was nothing wrong with either the products or his selling approach. Both his customers and their patients were very pleased with the products and a lot of positive publicity in the relevant press had been generated throughout the region since Michael went there.

Sitting in his rocking-chair and overlooking the Aegean Sea from his balcony, Michael was trying to figure out what might have gone wrong. He thought he was consistent with his selling approach. He made professional presentations, used a problem-solving approach, followed up his sales, and made sure that products were delivered on time. The service level that he offered was exceptional, and above all, his strong interest in helping his customers by providing suggestions for growing their business was the best he could do to win the minds and hearts of all of his customers. His selling experience in the UK had helped him immensely with the above approach. He scrutinized his behavior but did not find any shortcomings or reasons for the apparent customer loyalty problem that he saw as forthcoming.

He played back mentally many of his encounters with his customers and was convinced that he always delivered a personalized and value-added solution to all of them. He could not recall any instance of not keeping his promises or not making an effort to see and discuss things from his customers' point of view. Being the only interface between the customers and the company in that region, his name had become synonymous with the firm and this was something that his customers seemed to value. He believed that this approach was the most appropriate for establishing strong and lasting relationships with his customers that, in turn, could prove to be a significant barrier for competitors entering the market.

Michael remembered his training times and the interesting lectures about cultural differences between North and South. He shook his head in an affirmative way as if he wanted to say categorically that this was absolutely true. Then he recalled that profits came from repeat customers, and customer retention could produce a disproportional return on investment. He could afford no more time thinking! He had to take some sort of action. He realized that the solution (if there was one) to this problem was hidden somewhere in the cultural make-up of the customers with whom he was dealing. He decided to telephone one of his customers (a Greek whom he had met in England during his university years) and invite him over to his house for dinner. This was the first time that Michael decided to socialize with a customer. His customer accepted the invitation and the following is an extract from their conversation after they had finished their dinner and Michael's problem had been discussed.

*Customer*: Michael, I do not think that you fully understand our culture.

*Michael*: I do not claim I do, but what do I miss or do wrong?

*Customer*: I think there is nothing that you do wrong. The issue perhaps is "what you do not do right."

*Michael*: What is it that I am not doing right then?

*Customer*: A salesperson interested in developing long-term relationships with his customers has to do certain things. Other than being professional in his dealings with the customers, a salesperson is expected to interact frequently with doctors, pharmacists, and hospital officials in a social context in order to build trust. Frequent social interaction (i.e., in a non-stressful environment) indicates commitment over and above to what is required by the protocol, enhances the feelings of trust, contributes to satisfaction of the customer, and facilitates conditions for building attitudinal loyalty. This is something that we used to call "relationship selling" in England, as far as I remember.

*Michael*: I think I understand what you are trying to tell me. Much of the relationship-building activity takes place in social as opposed to work environments. Very much like the meeting we have here. I have got it, and I am ever so grateful to you for your help.

*Customer*: You are, as I remember you from the university years, "a fast learner"!

## Points to consider

1 What is relationship selling and how does its application vary among different cultures?
2 Are business relationships that are enhanced by social interactions better for global selling?
3 Would you agree that commitment and trust are qualities that can be sold in a similar way to products and services? If so, is "relationship selling" a selling from a relationship-building point of view, or is it simply a traditional selling activity?

# CASE 14.2 A NEW SYSTEM INSTALLMENT OF SANKI DENKI (THAILAND)

## Jun Onishi, Hirosaki University, Japan

Sanki Denki Corporation is one of the largest manufacturers of household electrical appliances in Japan. In the mid-1980s, the steep rise in the Japanese yen against the U.S. dollar, supplemented by the Plaza Agreement of seven advanced countries, forced Sanki Denki's management to locate some of its manufacturing facilities outside of Japan in order to absorb the increase in the export price of products by reducing production costs. After careful analysis of several countries, Sanki Denki decided to establish several overseas production plants in Southeast Asia.

In 1987, Sanki Denki (Thailand) was established at the province of Chonburi as the company's third overseas plant under an export tax-free concession granted by the BOI (Board of Investment). During the first five years, Sanki Denki's primary markets were Europe and the U.S.A. However, the economic boom in Thailand, which began in the late 1980s, changed the marketing strategy of the company from doing business in export markets to concentrating on domestic markets. In 1995, the company's gross sales amounted to 20 billion baht, and 87 percent of the total sales were generated by the domestic market.

The economic sluggishness initiated by Thailand's devaluation of the baht against foreign currencies in July 1997 spread throughout Asia "in the blink of an eye" and affected the sales of consumer product manufacturers in many Asian countries. In particular, domestic market-oriented companies began downsizing unless they were in the fortunate position of being able to offer lower product prices. Sanki Denki (Thailand) was also caught up in the re-evaluations and decided to reduce production costs by installing a JIT (just-in-time) inventory system. Tamura, manager of human resources of Sanki Denki (Japan), was given the responsibility of installing the newly developed JIT inventory system at Sanki Denki (Thailand). This system has had great success in reducing costs in other factories across Asia. As soon as Tamura was transferred to Sanki Denki (Thailand) as managing director, he started to install the new JIT system not only in sales offices but also in the company's factories. Since Tamura had never worked in a factory, he promoted Somkiat, a very capable assistant production manager, to production manager.

After Somkiat had completed his Master's degree in the U.S.A. and returned home, he worked for Mitsubishi Electric (Thailand) for five years. He was in charge of production efficiency, including quality control, cost reduction, and logistics. During these five years, he was sent to Japan for job training on three occasions. He also learned some Japanese during these training conferences. He had worked for Sanki Denki (Thailand) since he was recruited as assistant manager of the Chonburi factory in 1999. He had worked for the "Kaizen" system at the factory. Tamura thought that Somkiat would be an ideal person for installing the new JIT system, since this system required frequent communication with workers and with Tamura. Tamura's confidence in Somkiat was confirmed when Tamura interviewed Somkiat who expressed, with full confidence, that he would be a very capable and excellent production manager. Tamura had interviewed many Japanese employees when he was in the personnel department at the head office, and he consistently noticed that Japanese employees talked modestly and understated the capabilities they possessed. A typical case involved a female applicant. When asked about her English proficiency, she replied hesitantly that she could not speak English very well. Later, however, he heard that her English-language level was excellent. Tamura came to give more credit to Japanese interviewees who, in his estimation, seemed to be very modest in acknowledging their capabilities. He came to believe, however, that he had overestimated Somkiat's abilities after working with him on the JIT project. He felt that Somkiat was different from the typical Japanese employee applicant because he had been influenced by Western culture when he was a student in the U.S.A. Tamura realized that there may be a tendency in Western culture for an interviewee to exaggerate his or her abilities and thus mislead an interviewer such as Tamura.

Tamura believed that the installation of the JIT system could be completed within six months which was a shorter projection period than that expressed by head office. However, after six months, he realized that the installation of the JIT system was behind schedule. One day, when Tamura returned from lunch, he received a telephone call from Suzuki, director in charge of operations in Southeast Asia. The following exchange transpired:

*Suzuki*: Tamura, I got your report this morning. What does it mean that you cannot complete this project by the end of October? This project is not a difficult one. You only have to install our new JIT system at our Thai operation. We have done it in Indonesia and Singapore within a six-month period. It is already September. Although you have spent almost seven months, it has not yet been completed. Now, you say that you cannot finish by the end of October?

*Tamura*: Well, Mr. Director, I apologize for the delay, but the situation here is different from those of the other two countries. I have successfully installed the new JIT system in the sales offices. But there is strong resistance against this system in the factory. Factory workers are afraid of lay-offs, since the new JIT system will increase the efficiency of work, which may reduce the amount of manpower needed for production. According to Somkiat, our new factory manager, the system cannot be installed until he receives a consensus from the workers. Not receiving a consensus will create a disturbance in the factory.

*Suzuki*: What does a disturbance mean? Somkiat is a factory manager. To persuade factory workers to accept the new system is his job, isn't it? And to direct him to do this is your job. Do it and complete the project by the end of November!

After a long, painful conversation with the director in the Tokyo head office, who blamed Tamura for the delay of the new JIT system installation in its Thailand factory, Tamura decided to push factory workers more to accept the new JIT system.

Tamura complained that his American-educated production manager, Somkiat, was not cooperating with him in implementing the new JIT system which he was trying to set up company-wide. In an interview, Tamura stated the following:

*Tamura*: Most of the sales office staff members seem to understand the new system, and, even though what they have used so far is not cost-effective, they are at least trying to follow through. But my production people seem to be going nowhere with it. I've met with my production manager Somkiat and his staff several times to discuss the new JIT system and to make certain that they understand it. The staff people say nothing, and Somkiat just smiles and assures me that they do understand. Yet, when I ask him for the objective statements for his department, he continually puts me off with one lame excuse or another. When I call him on it, he just smiles and tells me that the statements are forthcoming – he needs a little more time. It's infuriating. I've got a deadline to meet, and he knows it. I'm going to have the head office on my back if I don't show them some results very soon. Short of going down to the production department and bulldozing the system through myself, I don't know what to do. I thought Somkiat would be perfect for this job when I first met him and promoted him to production manager. But now I'm beginning to wonder.

A follow-up interview with Somkiat to get his side of the story revealed that he did understand the necessity of installing the new JIT system and strongly supported it. As he explained:

*Somkiat*: I know that, if we cannot reduce the cost of production, we will not be able to survive in the market. It means that we will have to downsize our factory or, worse yet, possibly close down the factory. But what I can't seem to get Mr. Tamura to understand is that you can't just push something like that through here overnight. It's totally outside my people's experience, and they are afraid that they will be laid off since the new JIT system also reduces the number of workers.

Mr. Tamura arranged an orientation of the new JIT system for all company personnel shortly after the new policy was announced. I thought the orientation provided a good overview of the system's philosophy, but it did not really explain exactly how the system would be applied here or how, specifically, it would benefit the employees. Opportunities were given for people to ask questions, but no one did because, I guess, no one knew enough about the system to know what to ask, and because Tamura was there, no one wanted him to think "lay-off" if it was not in his mind. Tamura seems to have two very different faces which confused our employees very much. In general he is very nice. He greets his workers in the morning and purchases souvenirs from Thailand to give to the staff whenever he goes back to Japan. He always attends weddings or funerals of the employees if he is asked. I am, however, surprised that his behavior is completely changed when he finds a mistake. He does not care even if there are other staff members there. He criticizes the employee with a loud voice and uses impolite words. I think this kind of criticism makes employees dislike him, and he is now rather isolated from the Thai employees. No one asks him to attend funeral or wedding ceremonies any more. I know that the sales office staff have already started working on setting up department and individual objectives based on the new JIT system, but from what I have heard, people are not happy about it. It seems that they think that the new JIT system is just a poorly disguised attempt to try to gain more control over them and to try to force them to do more work for the same amount of pay. I have heard that several employees are already looking for jobs elsewhere. Tamura doesn't have a clue.

I have met with the same resistance among my people, especially my supervisors. Shortly after that orientation, rumors started spreading around the plant that the new system was going to be used to get rid of people and other such things. Productivity and quality dropped while absences have gone up. I realized pretty fast that, if I could not convince the supervisors to support the installation of the JIT system, it would never be successfully implemented. So, I have spent a lot of time talking informally with them about it to try to find out what the problems are. I have been taking small groups of supervisors out for dinner after work, and, after talking about topics of general interest, we gradually move into work-related issues and to the new JIT system. More than half of them are now clear on what the system is, how it works, and how it will benefit them, and I am sure that, with their help, I can win the other half over within a month. Once that happens, I'll have a committed supervisory staff who will be able to help me communicate the same message to the workers, and then we'll be able to implement the system smoothly and successfully.

I have tried to explain all this to Mr. Tamura several times but, like so many Japanese managers I have known, he discussed it with Japanese colleagues or consulted the main office. For the first six months, he gave me the authority to handle this matter. However, once he noticed that he would not be able to meet the deadline set by the main office, he became autocratic and austere. As I told you already, he has essentially blamed me and even criticized me in front of a few of my employees. He has never tried to explain this situation to the main office. He is not making my job easier, and if he does not change his attitude, I might be looking elsewhere for a job myself. He has been here almost a year and, during this period, his attitude toward Thais has changed very much. He had tried to study the Thai language for six months, but he has given up. He also avoids speaking the Thai he knows. He eats lunch alone and is not aware of his staff's feeling or of the confusion which exists about the new system. But, because I'm the only one who's actually tried to confront him with the problem, he thinks I'm the trouble-maker. I have stopped trying to explain things to him, and I've stopped arguing with him as this has become a waste of time and ends up making him and myself look bad in front of the workers.

After three months, Tamura was sent back to the Tokyo head office because of his failure to install the JIT system at the Thai factory. Sanki's products have lost price competitiveness, and market share has dropped by 10 percent. Suzuki decided to shift the production site away from Thailand and to China where Sanki Denki could install the JIT system successfully. In April 2001, after 15 years of operation, Sanki Denki terminated all 400 factory employees. Somkiat accepted a position as an assistant manager of a factory with a German company. At that factory, he is in charge of ISO and has been very successful in that work. Tamura was transferred to the procurement department at Sanki Denki and is in charge of managing the spare parts inventory. In reflecting on his time with Sanki Denki (Thailand), he still cannot figure out what went wrong.

*Tamura*: I tried to help as much as I could. I tried to educate the Thai staff to be ready to work with the JIT system. Sometimes, I had to be hard on the employees, and I thought this to be a kind of "whip of love." After a few months Thai employees did improve their efficiency very much. Though I did not admire them publicly, I was satisfied with their improvement. Is there anything that I did wrong?

## Questions

1 Explain how personal selling overseas may differ from how it is used in the U.S.A.
2 What are the requirements of a good publicity program?
3 What is a carnet?
4 Explain why standard sales promotion tools (e.g., premiums, coupons) may not be applicable or effective abroad.

# Discussion assignments and minicases

1 Compare domestic communication with international communication. Explain why "noise" is more likely to occur in the case of the international communication process at all five stages (source, encoding, information, decoding, and receiver).
2 Why is telemarketing not as widely used outside of the U.S.A.?
3 Should expatriate personnel be used? What are some of the difficulties that they may encounter overseas? What may be done to minimize these problems?

## Notes


1 Wilbur Schramm (ed.), "How Communication Works," in *The Process and Effects of Mass Communication* (Urbana, IL: University of Illinois Press, 1961), 3–26.

2 "America's Latest Software Success Story Is German," *Business Week*, August 8, 1994, 46.

3 Harold C. Cash and W.J.E. Crissy, "Comparison of Advertising and Selling," The *Psychology of Selling*, Vol. 12 (Personnel Development Associates, 1965).

4 Nigel F. Piercy, George S. Low, and David W. Cravens, "Examining the Effectiveness of Sales Management Control Practices in Developing Countries," *Journal of World Business* 39 (August 2004): 255–67.

5 Sergio Roman and José Luis Munuera, "Determinants and Consequences of Ethical Behaviour: An Empirical Study of Salespeople," *European Journal of Marketing* 39 (Nos 5/6, 2005): 473–95.

6 Ivan M. Manev and William B. Stevenson, "Nationality, Cultural Distance, and Expatriate Status: Effects on the Managerial Network in a Multinational Enterprise," *Journal of International Business Studies* 32 (Second Quarter 2001): 285–303.

7 Sunkyu Jun and James W. Gentry, "An Exploratory Investigation of the Relative Importance of Cultural Similarity and Personal Fit in the Selection and Performance of Expatriates," *Journal of World Business* 40 (February 2005): 1–8.

8 Jeffrey P. Shay and Sally A. Baack, "Expatriate Assignment, Adjustment and Effectiveness: An Empirical Examination of the Big Picture," *Journal of International Business Studies* 35 (May 2004): 216–32.

9 John M. Mezias and Terri A. Scandura, "A Needs-driven Approach to Expatriate Adjustment and Career Development: A Multiple Mentoring Perspective," *Journal of International Business Studies* 36 (September 2005): 519–38.

10 Sunkyu Jun, James W. Gentry, and Yong J. Hyun, "Cultural Adaptation of Business Expatriates in the Host Marketplace," *Journal of International Business Studies* 32 (Second Quarter 2001): 369–77.

11 Yongsun Paik and Junghoon Derick Sohn, "Expatriate Managers and MNC's Ability to Control International Subsidiaries: The Case of Japanese MNCs," *Journal of World Business* 39 (February 2004): 61–71.

12 Moshe Banai and William D. Reisel, "Expatriate Managers' Loyalty to the MNC: Myth or Reality? An Exploratory Study," *Journal of International Business Studies* 25 (No. 2, 1994): 233–48.

13 "The Fast Track Leads Overseas," *Business Week*, November 1, 1993, 64ff.

14 Rene A. Belderbos and Marielle G. Heijtjes, "The Determinants of Expatriate Staffing by Japanese Multinationals in Asia: Control, Learning and Vertical Business Groups," *Journal of International Business Studies* 36 (May 2005): 341–54.

15 Gerald E. Fryxell, John Butler, and Amanda Choi, "Successful Localization Programs in China: An Important Element in Strategy Implementation," *Journal of World Business* 39 (August 2004): 268–82.

16 Linda K. Stroh, Arup Varma, and Stacey J. Valy-Durbin, "Why Are Women Left at Home: Are They Unwilling to Go on International Assignments?" *Journal of World Business* 30 (fall 2000): 241–55.

17 Arup Varma, Soo Min Toh, and Pawan Budhwar, "A New Perspective on the Female Expatriate Experience: The Role of Host Country National Categorization," *Journal of World Business* 41 (June 2006): 112–20.

18 William Newburry, Naomi A. Gardberg, and Liuba Y. Belkin, "Organizational Attractiveness Is in the Eye of the Beholder: The Interaction of Demographic Characteristics with Foreignness," *Journal of International Business Studies* 37 (September 2006): 666–86.

19 Michael Harvey *et al.*, "Reducing Inpatriate Managers' 'Liability of Foreignness' by Addressing Stigmatization and Stereotype Threats," *Journal of World Business* 40 (August 2005): 267–80.

20 "A Crisis of Confidence," *Business Week*, 18 September 2000, 40–2; "Jac Nasser's Biggest Test," *Fortune*, 18 September 2000, 123ff.; and "Ford vs. Firestone: A Corporate Whodunit," *Business Week*, June 11, 2001, 46–7.

21 Begona Alvarez Alvarez and Rodolfo Vazquez Casielles, "Consumer Evaluations of Sales Promotion: The Effect on Brand Choice," *European Journal of Marketing* 39 (Nos 1/2, 2005): 54–70.

22 Liz Lee-Kelley, David Gilbert, and Nada F. Al-Shehabi, "Virtual Exhibitions: An Exploratory Study of Middle East Exhibitors' Dispositions," *International Marketing Review* 21 (No. 6, 2004): 634–44.

23 "Ask the TIC: Temporary Imports, ATA Carnet," *Export America*, March 2001, 14–15.

Chapter 15

# Promotion strategies

## Advertising

A brand is not meaningful for the brand itself. The brand becomes meaningful when you have a sustainable, profitable, long-term business.

J.T. Wang, Chairman, Acer Inc.

### Chapter outline

- Marketing strategy: soft and not-so-soft drinks
- The role of advertising
- Patterns of advertising expenditures
- Advertising and regulations
- Advertising media
  - Television
  - Radio
  - Newspapers
  - Magazines
  - Direct mail
  - Outdoor
  - Internet
  - Screen (cinema)
  - Directories
  - Rural media
  - Stadium
  - Other media
  - Media mix
- Standardized international advertising
  - Three schools of thought

## Marketing strategy

**Soft and not-so-soft drinks**

Coca-Cola Co. acquired the Thums Up brand in India in 1993. Thums Up is a sweeter local cola that once commanded more than 60 percent of carbonated beverage sales. Due to Coca-Cola's neglect, Thums Up's market share plunged to just 15 percent by 1998. Finally, the chief of operations in India managed to obtain approval from Coca-Cola to push local brands as much as Coca-Cola. Advertising and distribution have been strengthened. Within a year, Thums Up made it back to become the No. 2 soda in India.

In the case of Coke itself, the operations chief introduced a new advertising campaign that equates Coke with *thanda*, the Hindi word for "cold." He also uses Bollywood movie star Amir Khan as Coke's celebrity spokesman. The advertising campaign has been a huge success.

In India, beer advertisements are banned. To build a brand on a national scale, brewers have to be creative. As in the case of SABMiller, it sells a mineral water called Royal Challenge. The brand name for the water is not an accident. Royal Challenge is also the brand name for one of SABMiller's lagers. TV commercials for the water are indistinguishable from traditional beer advertisements, including the label on the bottle. The water commercials, however, show actors drinking a clear liquid rather than amber-colored beers.

*Sources*: "Finally, Coke Gets It Right," *Business Week*, February 10, 2003, 47; and "The Great Indian Beer Rush," *Business Week*, April 23, 2007, 50.

## Purpose of chapter

The water and beer examples in the marketing illustration above emphasize the need to communicate with buyers and to endow a product with a distinct image. A product must not only be physically superior but also psychologically desirable. Frequently, a product's psychological attributes are even more important than its physical characteristics. To convince consumers that a product is psychologically superior, a company uses advertising. A product has to be differentiated from competitive brands, and the differences can be either real or imagined.

The marketing of products overseas underscores the necessity for the adaptation of communication. To advertise internationally, a firm cannot simply repeat the same message indiscriminately in all markets. A message that elicits a favorable response in one country can easily fail to communicate with an audience in another country. To complicate matters, there are constraints on advertising that preclude the use of certain kinds of media in certain countries.

The purpose of this chapter is to examine the advertising practices in various countries. The variations in advertising practices are discussed, as well as particular problems associated with the utilization of advertising media abroad. Finally, the chapter closely analyzes the most controversial subject in international advertising – standardized advertising. Some practical guidelines are offered that may be useful in resolving the controversy.

## The role of advertising

Developing and socialist/communist countries, emphasizing production and distribution efficiency, usually attack advertising as a wasteful practice whose primary purpose is to create unnecessary wants. Yet advertising serves a very useful purpose – consumers everywhere, irrespective of their countries' political systems and level of economic development, need useful product information.

Since the 1950s, China has prohibited foreigners from advertising there because advertising was considered politically inappropriate. In the 1980s, however, China changed its policy in order that the Chinese population could be informed of available products, just as in a modern industrial society. Virtually all media are now available for advertising. TV advertising is quite a bargain, since a 60-second spot for the nationally broadcast China Central Television I network costs only $5000. Chinese viewers generally enjoy watching the commercials shown.

A correlation has been shown to exist between advertising expenditures and a country's GDP and level of economic development. As a country becomes more industrialized, the level of advertising expenditure tends to increase as well. The U.S.A. is highest in per capita advertising. Regarding the Commonwealth of Independent States (CIS), foreign companies are responsible for about half of the advertising done there. Advertising expenditures in the CIS are quite tiny and represent only the amount of a small advertising account in the U.S.A.

Many of the largest advertisers in the U.S.A. also advertise heavily overseas. Procter & Gamble and General Motors, for example, are among the largest advertising spenders in France and Canada. Local firms in markets outside the U.S.A. often view this kind of expenditure as an unfair trade practice. They fear that American firms could easily overwhelm local firms in terms of advertising dollars.

## Patterns of advertising expenditures

Advertising expenditures vary widely from industry to industry. Mars allocates 5 percent of the company's total sales to advertising. Manufacturers of dolls and stuffed toys maintain an advertising-to-sales ratio of more than 15 percent.

The relationship between advertising expenditure and sales generated has been well documented. Certain variables determine the size of the advertising budget as well as the size of the overall marketing budget. According to the well-publicized ADVISOR models, the size of an advertising budget is a function of: sales (+), number of users and other participants (+), customer concentration (–), fraction of sales made to order (–), stage in life cycle (–), and product plans (+). The size of a marketing budget is a function of: prospect–customer attitude differences (–), proportion of direct sales (+), and product complexity (–). It should be pointed out that the importance of particular predictor variables is not uniform across countries.

It is important to note variations in the various kinds of marketing expenses – when expressed as a percentage of sales – across countries and product categories. The variations in the marketing expense ratios indicate that executives should be careful when they approach advertising budget decisions in other cultures.

## Advertising and regulations

Advertising can be affected in several ways by local regulations. The availability of media (or the lack of it) is one example. When and how much media time and space are made available, if at all, is determined by local authorities. Belgium prohibits the use of electricity for advertising purposes between midnight and 8 a.m. German laws regulate TV advertising content and limit advertising on the national TV channels to 20 minutes a day, forcing advertisers to switch from state-run TV to private channels. Greece and South Korea ban the erection of new signs. Furthermore, nationalism may intrude in the form of a ban on the use of foreign languages and materials in advertising.

The advertising industry may have a local self-regulatory organization which monitors the style and content of promotional activities. In Australia, similar to the U.S.A., the most important reason to reject an advertisement is a breach of taste. Unlike their American counterparts, Australian managers appear to be more ready to defer to the judgment of their more numerous and active trade associations.[1]

The legitimacy of comparative advertising has not been fully settled in many countries. Some products are banned altogether from certain media or from advertising in certain countries. A number of countries have complete bans on cigarette advertising. Interpreting the law creatively, R.J. Reynolds attempted to circumvent Norway's ban on cigarette advertising by advertising "Camel boots" instead. The advertisement used the same model, trademark, and the lettering in the word *Camel* as those used in Camel's cigarette advertisements. After a protest, the advertisement was eventually withdrawn. Advertisements in France are limited to a picture of a cigarette package with no "seductive imagery." To overcome this restriction, cigarette makers create products such as Marlboro cigarette lighters and Pall Mall matches that are purposefully made to resemble cigarette packages because there is no restriction on how such products can be advertised. In Sudan, Philip Morris advertised by having the Marlboro cowboy hold a Marlboro lighter.

## Advertising media

**International advertising** is the practice of advertising in foreign or international media when the advertising campaign is planned, directly or indirectly, by an advertiser from another country. To advertise overseas, a company must determine the availability (or unavailability) of advertising media. Media may not be readily available in all countries or in certain areas within countries. Furthermore, the techniques used in media overseas can be vastly different from those employed in the U.S.A.

## Television

For Americans, television is taken for granted because it is available everywhere and in color. Outside of the U.S.A., even in other advanced nations, it is a different story altogether. This difference may explain why U.S. advertisers spend $20 billion each year on TV commercials, four times the amount European advertisers spend.

In most countries, television is not available on a nationwide basis due to the lack of TV stations, relay stations, and cable TV. Color television, for the poor, may be a rarity. Nevertheless, the viewing habits of people of lower income should not be underestimated due to the "group viewing" factor. For example, a TV set in a village hall can attract a large number of viewers, resulting in a great deal of interaction among the villagers in terms of conversation about the advertised products.

In many countries, TV stations are state controlled and government operated due to military requirements. As such, the stations are managed with the public welfare rather than a commercial objective in mind. The programming and advertising are thus closely controlled. The programs shown may vary widely and are usually dubbed in the local languages. European governments particularly abhor the U.S. private-broadcast model with its degenerate mass programming. More recently, however, European restrictions have been reduced on featuring films with frequent interruptions from advertisements. The reduction is due in part to an attempt by European countries such as France to end the government monopoly on media and to privatize the broadcast business by making available private broadcasting franchises.

Commercial TV time is usually extremely difficult to buy overseas (see Legal Dimension 15.1). This is true even in Europe and Japan, where television is widespread. The usual practice in Tokyo is to use TV advertising to bombard the market, but the challenge for the marketer is to get air time. There are several reasons why television advertising time is severely limited. Many countries only have a few TV channels which may not schedule daytime television or late-night programs. With less broadcast time comes less advertising time. Some countries do not allow program sponsorship other than spot announcements. Belgium, Denmark, Norway, and Sweden ban advertising on television altogether. Some governments permit advertising only during certain hours of operation. In Germany, advertising on television is permitted only between 6.15 and 8 p.m. (except Sundays and holidays) for a total advertising time available of 20 minutes. That same number of commercial minutes also applies to Switzerland. The problem of getting a fraction of the available television time was so severe for Unilever that the firm had to make adjustments in media strategy by relying more on other media. In most countries, the situation is such that an advertiser is fortunate to get air time at all.

There are at least two tactics an advertiser can employ to overcome the problem of lack of broadcast time for advertising. One is to use shorter commercials. Although disputed in the U.S.A., 15-second spots have become the norm in a number of countries. Spots shorter than 30 seconds are an overwhelming majority in France, Japan (79 percent), and Spain. As a matter of fact, the Japanese even have eight-second spots that function almost like billboards on TV.

Another tactic is to purchase TV time well in advance. With a waiting list of 100 companies, TV advertising time in the Netherlands must be booked with a year's notice. Those advertisers able to get air time still face other advertising hurdles. For example, commercial interruptions can be long and frequent, creating a severe problem of clutter.

Advertisers sometimes use TV stations in one country to reach consumers in another country. Canada is a prime example. More than 75 percent of Canadians are clustered within 100 miles of the U.S. border, and 95 percent are within 200 miles. Thus, nearly all Canadians are within the broadcast range of U.S. stations. U.S. advertisers often U.S. TV stations to communicate with Canadian

## Legal Dimension 15.1

### South Korea's advertising law

Unlike expensive TV shows in the U.S.A., South Korea utilizes the just-in-time and very cheap production process for its TV dramas. Some of these shows have been exported to other countries around the world. The most notable series is *Dae Jang Geum* ("Jewel in the Castle") which tells a story about a cook who became a doctor in the royal household of a Korean dynasty. *Jumong*, an 81-part epic, proved to be another spectacular success, and its final episode challenged the 58 percent share, a record set by *Dae Jang Geum*. President Roh Moo Hyun was highly criticized for allowing his state-of-the-nation address to cut into one episode of the series.

Korean shows' low production budgets are necessitated by an unusual advertising law. All TV commercials must be priced about the same regardless of whether the TV shows are a hit. The country's three commercial networks thus need to limit expenses and to spread out their production money for shows that may be hits or misses. The length of a series has to be decided before production, without any allowance to extend a hit show.

*Source*: "South Korean TV Creates Low-budget Ratings Warrior," *Wall Street Journal*, March 7, 2007.

consumers. In fact, Canadian advertisers themselves make it a practice of using U.S. stations at the border (e.g., Detroit, Spokane, and Buffalo) to air commercials aimed primarily at the Canadian market. Reasons for this practice are that American TV stations have higher program ratings than Canadian stations, and that the Canadian audience in total spends some 26 billion hours a week viewing U.S. shows – the equivalent of 78 percent of the total hours spent watching Canadian English-language TV programs.

New technology may allow advertisers to solve some of the problems related to TV time and government regulation (e.g., a ban on the advertising of certain products or to certain groups). Cable TV is available in Western Europe. Commercial programs, for example, can be beamed from the United Kingdom to cable networks in Norway, Finland, and Switzerland. Retransmitting the signal, however, is still illegal in Norway.

Satellite TV may present another solution and is gaining wider acceptance. McDonald's and Mars have begun to funnel some advertising dollars to the Sky Channel satellite network. Cable TV and satellite TV are often international media in the sense that they reach multiple countries outside the country where the broadcast originates. Turner Broadcasting's Cable News Network has a global reach of more than 60 million households in more than 200 countries and territories. MTV's 33 channels across the world have access to almost 375 million households. MTV, VH1, and Nickelodeon altogether reach 1 billion people in 18 languages in 164 countries.[2]

The two cable or satellite channels that are truly international are CNN and British Broadcasting Corp. BBC World, as the largest channel in the BBC network, is viewed by almost 65 million people in 200 countries every week. Recently, BBC World has stopped broadcasting TV programs tailored for Indian audiences. Shows like Question Time India and Mastermind India have been dropped. According to BBC World, "Our target viewer is an international traveler or someone interested in international events." Unlike CNN, which has joined hands with TV18 (a local partner in India) to launch CNN-IBN, "BBC World is an English channel and will continue to remain so."[3] Interestingly, BBC World is virtually unavailable in the U.S.A. where the BBC instead offers the BBC America channel.

Because of CNN's U.S.-centric approach during the Iraq War in 2003, the BBC was able to attract new audiences all over the world with its authoritative coverage of the war. Its balanced coverage frustrated those from the right as well as those from the left. Those on the right called the BBC the Baghdad Broadcasting Corp., while those on the left dubbed it the Blair–Bush Corp. For those in the middle, BBC stood for better, balanced coverage.[4] France has TV5 that broadcasts internationally, but this French-language channel primarily offers movies and general programming. France is in the process of creating a government-supported all-news channel to present its point of view that may counter those of CNN and the BBC.[5]

Regionally, Channel V is an Asian alternative to MTV. Channel V is 87.5 percent owned by Star Group, News Corp.'s wholly owned subsidiary. Both Channel V and Star Group have their headquarters in Hong Kong. In order to localize its operations, Channel V has moved the production of its Channel V International from Hong Kong to Malaysia. Its other six channels have local production teams that focus on China, Taiwan, Korea, India, Thailand, and Australia.[6]

One advertising problem with this new technology has been that, when an advertisement is aired, consumers in all countries are exposed to an identical message. However, improved technology has now made it possible for advertisers to beam particular advertising versions to different countries.

## Radio

Radio is no longer king of the media in the U.S.A., but it retains its status in many countries as the only truly national medium. In Mexico, for example, radio provides coverage for 83 percent of the country. It is popular for several reasons. A radio set is inexpensive and affordable – even among poor people. It is virtually a free medium for listeners: the programs are free and the costs of operating and maintaining a radio set are almost negligible. Furthermore, illiteracy poses no problem for this advertising medium. As a communication medium, radio is entertaining, up-to-date, and portable. The medium penetrates from the highest to the lowest socioeconomic levels, with FM stations being preferred by high-income and better educated listeners. Not surprisingly, radio commands the largest proportion of advertising expenditures in a great number of markets.

In order for radio stations in the U.S.A. to survive and counter the threat of television, they have adopted the "magazine" format by specializing in a particular type of programming. Advertisers must not assume that stations have adopted this same approach abroad. In many countries, radio stations have not become specialized in a particular program format and see no need to be selective in order to attract the listening audience. Radio stations commonly vary their programming format throughout the day, sometimes as often as every half hour. An audience shift should thus be expected, and a consequence of this practice is that it may not be easy to reach the target market effectively.

Unlike U.S. stations, which do their own programming and hire their own announcers or disc jockeys, overseas stations are quite liberal in selling air time to outside operators. This is true in spite of the fact that for security reasons most overseas stations are owned, controlled, and operated by the government. Once the air time has been sold, the program format is determined by the sponsor or independent disc jockey. Thus, listeners' loyalty is not so much to the station but to the disc jockey who may roam from one station to another throughout the day.

## Newspapers

In virtually all urban areas of the world, the population has access to daily newspapers. In fact, the problem for the advertiser is not one of having too few newspapers but rather one of having too many

In the U.S.A., large cities can rarely support more than two dailies. In other countries, a city may have numerous newspapers dividing the readership market. Lebanon, with a population of 1.5 million, has some 200 daily and weekly newspapers, with the average circulation per paper of only 3500.

Newspapers in communist countries are controlled by the government and are thus used for propaganda purposes. China's newspapers, for example, tend to carry news items that the government deems to express some moral and social value.

Believing that sensational news attracts readership, most non-U.S. newspapers in the free world are set up in a sensational news format. It is a rule rather than the exception for these newspapers to concentrate on murders, robberies, scandals, and rapes. Even the United Kingdom, where citizens are known for their reserved manner, is not exempt from this practice. World news and nonscandalous political news often take a back seat to the more sensational news. As a result, non-U.S. newspapers look more like such weekly U.S. tabloids as the *National Enquirer* and *Star*. A newspaper that concentrates on news of substance and quality (i.e., unsensational news) must pay for this in terms of low readership.

Many countries have English-language newspapers in addition to the local-language newspapers. The English-language newspapers are patterned more like the traditional American paper, with an emphasis on world, government, and business news. This vehicle would be appropriate for an advertiser to reach government and business leaders, educated readers, upper-class people, and those with affluence and influence. The aim of the *Asian Wall Street Journal* is to supply economic information in English to influential businesspersons, politicians, top government officials, and intellectuals. It was not designed to be a newspaper for mass readers.

Many countries have nationally distributed newspapers, as shown in Figure 15.1. However, it is difficult to find a true national newspaper because almost every newspaper tries to be somewhat local in nature. Even in the U.S.A., before *USA Today*, the closest thing to a national newspaper was perhaps the *New York Times*, with the *Washington Post* in second place. Clearly, it is even more difficult to have an international newspaper. Those papers distributed internationally include the *International Herald Tribune* and such financial newspapers as the *Wall Street Journal* (with the *Asian Wall Street Journal* for Asian countries), and the United Kingdom's *Financial Times*. As might be expected, these newspapers are not available everywhere, and the circulation is low. The *Financial Times*, a century-old daily covering British business, international business, and economic and political news, has a worldwide circulation of about 230,000, with only 6000 sold in the U.S.A. and Canada. Still, the *Financial Times* offers U.S. advertisers access to upscale readers in Europe and other parts of the world.

American advertisers are accustomed to having separate editorial sections in American newspapers and are often frustrated by foreign papers. A 20-page newspaper may still have sections for sports, entertainment, fashion, business, and science, but each section may be only one page. Thus, it becomes difficult for an advertiser to match the product to the proper section or environment (e.g., tire and automotive products in the sports section) in a local newspaper.

Furthermore, with so many newspapers dividing a small market, it is expensive to reach the entire market. There are some 380 and 800 newspapers in Turkey and Brazil, respectively. With advertisements in just one paper, the reach would be quite inadequate. Advertising in several papers, on the other hand, is also impractical. It is fortunate for advertisers that people often read or subscribe to two or more dailies and often share newspapers. Despite a small circulation, readership may still be high. Usually, the pass-along rate in foreign markets is much higher than that in the U.S.A., but reliable estimates of the circulation of overseas newspapers are difficult to obtain. The figure provided

THE NIKKEI WEEKLY
Expansion in Japan defies critics
World Business, the NIKKEI View
Japanese businessmen know where you get your business information. But do you know where they get theirs?
While top business people follow the Nikkei Average, Japan's leading stock index, Nikkei is much, much more. It's the multi-media network that most Japanese businessmen consult every day.
Above all, Nikkei is The Nihon Keizai Shimbun—the world's largest business daily—with more than 3 million subscribers.
Nikkei is also specialized papers, and Japan's top English-language business newspaper, The Nikkei Weekly.
Nikkei is database, too, including Nikkei Telecom, a real-time 24-hour service in English and Japanese.
All this plus books and periodicals, new media and broadcasting, events and more.
Nikkei. It's the information network Japanese businessmen live by.
NIKKEI®
Nihon Keizai Shimbun, Inc., 1-9-5 Otemachi, Chiyoda-ku, Tokyo 100-66, Japan Tel: (03) 3270-0251
Nihon Keizai Shimbun America, Inc. New York Office: Suite 1802, 1221 Avenue of the Americas, New York, NY 10020 U.S.A. Tel: (212) 512-3600 or 1-800-322-1657
Los Angeles Office: 725 South Figueroa Street, Suite 1515, Los Angeles, CA 90017 U.S.A. Tel: (213) 955-7470
Nihon Keizai Shimbun Europe Ltd. London Office: Bush House, North West Wing, Aldwych London, WC2B 4PJ, U.K. Tel: (071) 379-4994
Frankfurt Office: Kettenhofweg 22, 6000 Frankfurt/M 1, Germany Tel: (069) 720214
For further information on Nikkei, just fill out this coupon and mail.
Planning & Development Dept., Projects Development Bureau, Nihon Keizai Shimbun, Inc., 1-9-5 Otemachi, Chiyoda-ku, Tokyo 100-66, Japan
Your Name
Company
Position
Address
City
State
Zip Code
BW-7/91

**FIGURE 15.1** Japan's top English-language business newspaper

by the newspaper publisher may be highly inflated, and there is no meaningful way, at least for advertisers, to measure or audit the circulation figures.

In the U.S.A., newspapers have been enduring a steady decline in readership for a decade or two. London, with ten national dailies, is still newspaper-centric. Still, the traditional newspapers in England are facing the similar and familiar problems of the loss of younger audiences and new competitors such as free newspapers and websites. The *Financial Times* lost a total of almost $80 million in 2003 and 2004. To retain readers, the *Guardian* has adopted an unusual approach. It has launched three websites that contain "user-generated content" because readers want to gather and chat. The company has not yet figured out how to make money from this new avenue. Its main goal though is to keep its readers from fleeing.[7]

## Magazines

Nowhere in the world are there so many and varied types of consumer magazines as there are in the U.S.A. Because U.S. magazines segment the reading market in every conceivable manner, there are magazines for the masses as well as for the few and selected. This makes it possible for advertisers to direct their campaigns to obtain **reach** (the total number of unduplicated individuals exposed to a particular media vehicle at least once during a specified time period) or **frequency** (the intensity or the number of times within a specified period that a prospect is exposed to the message), or both. Foreign magazines are generally not highly developed in terms of a particular audience. They do not segment their readers as narrowly as U.S. magazines do, and they do not have the same degree of accurate information about reader characteristics. In Brazil there are very few magazines, and people read all three or four of them. This results in **duplication** which can be a waste of promotional effort unless frequency is the objective.

Marketers of international products have the option of using international magazines that have regional editions (e.g., *Time, Business Week, Newsweek*, and *Life*). In the case of *Reader's Digest* and several other popular magazines, local-language editions are distributed. Allen-Edmonds, a shoe company, was able to increase its foreign sales by advertising its shoes in the international editions of such magazines. For technical and industrial products, magazines can be quite effective. Technical business publications tend to be international in their coverage. These publications range from individual industries (e.g., construction, beverages, textiles) to worldwide industrial magazines covering many industries. A trade magazine about China, for example, is a suitable vehicle for all types of industrial products of interest to the Chinese government. In Europe, the number of business publications is seven times as high as that in the U.S.A. There are more than 1000 technical and trade journals in Scandinavia. Canada, in contrast, usually has only one trade magazine for each market segment, making it easier to cover the entire Canadian market.

Local (i.e., national) business magazines are an effective vehicle to reach well-defined target audiences. *Nikkei Business* is one such magazine in Japan (see Figure 15.2). Not surprisingly, one study of TV, newspapers, and magazines has confirmed that, as far as reaching China's upscale and status-seeking consumers, "magazines have the highest targetability among the three most popular mass media."[8]

Unlike the U.S. market, which has an organization such as the ABC (Audit Bureau of Circulations) to audit the circulation figures for most magazines, the circulation figures of overseas magazines are somewhat unreliable. Furthermore, overseas magazines tend to depend more on news-stand sales than on subscription sales, making it difficult to calculate consistent volume or to predict the size of

JAPAN'S BUSINESS LEADERS ALL LOOK ALIKE.
It's easy to spot business leaders in Japan. There's a Japanese business leader lurking behind every copy of NIKKEI BUSINESS.
NIKKEI BUSINESS is exclusively for Japan's corporate crème de la crème – a very choice body of 200,000 subscribers selected by NIKKEI BUSINESS' own publishers: Nikkei-McGraw-Hill.
To our readers, we're a valued cover-to-cover information source for international business, with a wealth of informed articles written exclusively by an in-house staff of experts.
To our advertisers, we're unparalleled advertising effectiveness. 100% on-target. With no spillover. And no wastage.
So get behind NIKKEI BUSINESS and put NIKKEI BUSINESS behind you. And follow Japan's leaders right to the top.
Subscriptions: 202,677 (as of Aug. 5, 1985 issue)
Net paid circulation is regularly audited and certified by Japan ABC.
186,830 (1984)
For further information write to Yoshihiko Shimada, Advertising Manager, 1-14-6 Uchikanda, Chiyoda-ku, Tokyo 101, Japan Tel. (03)233-8031 Telex: J29902 NKMCGRAW
日経ビジネス
NIKKEI BUSINESS
Nikkei-McGraw-Hill, Inc., Publishers of Nikkei Business
North American Sales Network: New York Tel. (212) 997-2806, Chicago Tel. (312) 751-3716, Los Angeles Tel. (213) 480-5221, Houston Tel. (713) 462-0757, Toronto Tel. (416) 259-9631

**FIGURE 15.2** A national business magazine

*Source*: Reprinted with permission of Nikkei-McGraw-Hill, Inc.

readership in advance. Because many magazines are unaudited, either by choice or through lack of an audit bureau, it is not sensible to exclude unadited publications from the media schedule. Even when publications are audited, the information given may not be adequate. The English ABC provides minimum information, whereas the German IVW audit is very thorough.

## Direct mail

Confusion usually arises when such terms as direct mail, direct advertising, direct marketing, and mail order are discussed. It is important to understand that direct marketing is a broad term that encompasses the other related terms. According to the Direct Marketing Association (DMA), **direct marketing** is "the total of activities by which products and services are offered to market segments in one or more media for informational purposes or to solicit a direct response from a present or prospective customer or contributor by mail, telephone, or personal visit." This is a more than $1-billion business in the U.S.A. As a system, direct marketing has two distinct components: (1) promotion and (2) ordering/delivery (see Figure 15.3).

Direct marketers can promote their products through all advertising media. They can solicit orders by making announcements on television or in magazines (usually with coupons or order forms). Television home shopping is a form of direct marketing. Some cable TV channels (e.g., the Home Shopping Network in the U.S.A. and the Canadian Home Shopping Network) are designed specifically for this purpose.

Frequently, marketers rely on **direct advertising** in media created for that purpose. These media consist of direct mailings and all forms of print advertisements distributed directly to prospects through a variety of methods (i.e., advertising materials distributed door to door, on the street, or inside the store or those placed inside shopping bags and on auto windshields). **Direct mail** is thus only one kind of direct advertising medium, which is in turn a part of general advertising media or the promotional methods of direct marketing. Of course, the use of direct mail is not limited to just direct marketing.

With regard to ordering, buyers can place orders by telephone (often with a toll-free number), through a personal visit, or by mail. An order that is sent in by mail and fulfilled by mail delivery is

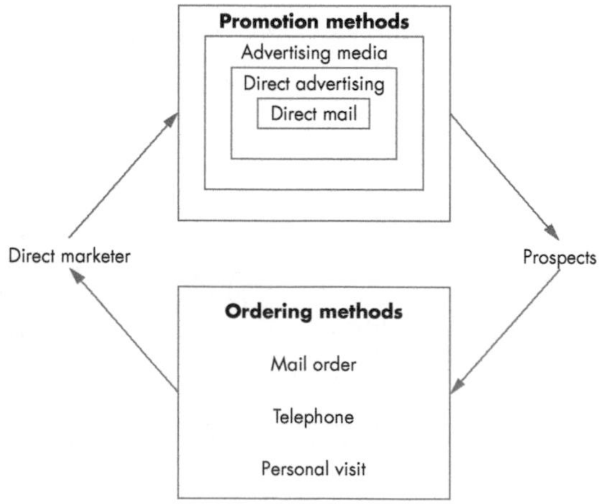
Promotion methods
Advertising media
Direct advertising
Direct mail
Direct marketer
Prospects
Ordering methods
Mail order
Telephone
Personal visit

**FIGURE 15.3** Direct marketing

called a mail order. Thus, **mail order** is not a medium; rather it is just one of several means that may be used to place and handle orders. An ordering method is one of the two components of the direct-marketing system.

For this discussion, direct mail and direct marketing are considered together. There are several reasons for doing so. Direct mail generally accounts for a major portion of direct-marketing advertising expenditures. In addition, many reports on direct-marketing campaigns do not provide a detailed breakdown of the advertising dollar accounted for by media other than direct mail.

Direct mail is largely undeveloped in many countries. This is especially true where labor is cheap and abundant and where it is just as easy to use a salesperson to make sales calls. Furthermore, for countries with high illiteracy, this medium is not suitable for promoting consumer products.

Without doubt, the U.S.A. is the most developed market for the advertising medium of direct mail. Foreign marketers as well as American marketers have a wide selection of buyer lists that permit them to contact the intended target audience with minimum waste.

U.S. practices in using direct mail require some modification when taken abroad. There is difficulty in making a direct transposition of a U.S. mailing piece without change into a European mailing kit due to various weight rules and other unique regulations. Population direct-mail lists are another serious problem since foreign list owners do not trust renters and brokers. List generation and management is still primitive abroad. American list owners enhance their lists with such information as buyer's frequency, recency, and dollar value, but direct marketers used to those practices can become frustrated with list brokers in Europe (except in Germany) because basic selection criteria are not even provided. In addition, privacy laws are more restrictive abroad than in the U.S.A. For example, Germany allows only two unique selection criteria per order when renting a list.

## Outdoor

Outdoor advertising includes posters, billboards, painted bulletins, roadside and store signs, and electric spectaculars (large illuminated electric signs with special lighting and animated effects). Given the great impact and impressiveness of size and color, outdoor advertising serves well as reminder promotion for well-known products.

Outdoor advertising is frequently used overseas due to the low cost of labor in painting and erecting such displays. In addition, this is considered a free medium, because an advertiser can simplify place its posters on any available wall, bus-stop shelter, tree, or fence without paying for it. The practice also encourages one advertiser to replace other advertisers' posters with one of its own.

Unlike most media, outdoor advertising is one medium in which the U.S.A. seems to lag behind other countries in terms of per capita advertising expenditures and sophistication. This is an advanced and dominant medium in Europe and Canada. Outdoor advertising is also very important in countries without commercial TV (e.g., Belgium). In Saudi Arabia, outdoor and transit posters account for more than a quarter of all media spending, approximately ten times the U.S. percentage.

Outdoor advertising does not have to be uninteresting. One advertiser changes its outdoor illustration and message frequently – with the model removing an item of clothing each time the poster board was changed. Another advertiser made it appear that the billboard was gradually being eaten away by termites.

New technologies have added such design options as backlighting, projection, Day-Glo paints, three-dimensionals, extensions, reflective disks, bows, and cutouts. Fiber optics may eventually replace neon because fiber optics are much more energy efficient and weigh less than neon glass tubing. Some advertisers have turned to video billboards that can show a 20-second commercial repeatedly.

When using outdoor advertising, certain rules need to be followed. Illustrations should be large, and words kept to a minimum. A rule of thumb is to say "what must be said" and not "what can be said." Simple, contrasting colors should be used: white on black or red seems to work well. The right typeface is critical; certain typefaces are difficult to read. Having all letters in capitals can be equally difficult and should be avoided.

### *Internet*

One recent medium that has gained worldwide attention is the Internet. Unlike other media, the Internet is global in nature, creating both worldwide opportunities and problems. It is unknown whether the law governing an Internet promotion should be the law of the upload site or that of the download site. Although all the other media allow marketers to a certain extent to restrict delivery of their messages, the Internet is an all-or-nothing proposition. Thus, it is easy to violate many domestic laws. In addition, given its international nature, the Internet requires global planning, and the cultural dimension must be considered. A successful website is one that has been carefully planned, taking into account the various languages and cultures.

One significant development is that new software has allowed a multinational marketer to make users' locations dictate a particular website to which users will be exposed. For example, those in Western Europe trying to access the Coca-Cola website may end up with a European site rather than the one seen by their American counterparts. In addition, due to technological improvements coupled with marketing goals, the Internet has become a more selective medium. Yahoo has created regional portals. Many international marketers such as Coca-Cola have added local websites in local languages.

The Coca-Cola Company has stated that, in spite of the core brand being well recognized all over the world, it is still "very much a local operation, meeting the demands of local tastes and cultures in nearly 200 countries." Visitors to its website are encouraged to select the country of interest. At one time, Atlanta dictated everything, and the local divisions were not allowed to set up their own websites and instead had to show only the corporate home page. Coca-Cola's Belgian website now reflects the more international approach, and the trilingual (Dutch, French, and English) site draws more than three million hits per month.[9]

While Internet usage is a worldwide phenomenon, it does not mean that a marketer should standardize its Internet strategies on a worldwide basis. A study of advanced Internet users from 20 countries reveals differences in beliefs, attitudes, perceptions, and Internet buying behavior based on user experience and home country or region. Such differences remain even after controlling for social, cultural, and macroeconomic variables.[10]

In the case that an international marketer wants to offer only one website (unlike Coca-Cola's strategy), its website must be designed to accommodate global users. While graphics are appealing, they slow things down, especially when users in most countries have slower connections. Thus by limiting graphics and other high-bandwidth features, the site is faster and universally appealing. By adopting a global perspective for the website, a company can enhance its international opportunities. Global functionality and language concerns should be addressed.[11]

While shopping and Internet use are global behavior, shopping habits and the determinants of the Internet sites' attractiveness may be culture-bound. To determine the critical characteristics of a website, one study investigated the shopping habits of 299 respondents from 12 countries. In general, site quality, trust, and positive affect toward it are related to both purchase intentions and site visitors' loyalty. Because the impact of these factors varies across regions and product categories, a website should probably be tailored to each region as well as to each product category.[12]

It is not a simple task to build a multilingual e-commerce site.[13] Other than the language that must be overhauled, a site must be able to handle different currencies, characters, and measurements. Some languages have words that must be read from right to left. Certain U.S. Net icons such as shopping carts are alien in some countries. Therefore, a global website has to be culturally sensitive.

One study of 206 websites created by U.S. firms for the UK, France, Germany, and Spain has examined the four basic functions of website content (transaction, communication, relationship, and interactivity). The research has yielded some useful results. While maintaining a minimum level of uniformity for logo, color, and layout, American firms have tailored the specific content to each market. Website standardization is influenced by image reinforcement, direct sales functions, and availability of choice. Furthermore, durable goods firms are more likely than non-durables to standardize their websites.[14]

A study of international website usage has found that cultural adaptation is an important factor in technology acceptance.[15] Local country websites depict a particular country's cultural values. While companies adapt their foreign websites to the target country's cultural values, the adaptation is not yet extensive at the present time.[16] Furthermore, a culturally unique web style, rather than a "transnational" web style, is emerging.[17] A content analysis of American, British, Japanese, and Korean corporate websites also indicates that Western websites are likely to emphasize consumer–message and consumer–marketer activity. Eastern websites, in contrast, tend to stress consumer–consumer interactivity.[18]

A study of 30 websites of the world's largest consumer packaged goods companies involved consumers from 23 countries on three continents with regard to how they perceived value derived from visiting a website. Consumers from countries with a weak rule of law pay attention to privacy/security protection. Those from countries that emphasize national identity focus more on cultural congruity between the website and themselves. In their perceived value judgments, consumers who are from more individualist countries give more weight than those from collectivistic countries to pleasure, privacy/security protection, and customization.[19]

## *Screen (cinema)*

In virtually all countries, the cinema is a favorite activity for social gatherings. People are avid moviegoers due to the limited television broadcasting and because of people's natural desire to go out to a place of social gathering. Cinemas (or theaters, as they are called in many parts of the world) are classified as first class or second class and sometimes even third class, depending on how soon new films are shown there. Theaters usually operate on a reserved-seat basis, with advance reserve bookings being highly encouraged.

Similar to outdoor advertising, the cinema is a very popular advertising medium outside of the U.S.A. Cinemas sell commercial time to agencies or advertisers. The usual practice is for a theater to begin its program with a showing of slides of advertised products, and this slide show is followed by commercials. The theater may then proceed to show newsreels and documentaries that may contain paid news items such as a store opening. Then, just before the showing of the main feature, there are short promotional films or teaser trailers of future attractions. An intermission can present another opportunity for advertising.

Cinema advertising has several advantages. It has the impact of outdoor advertising without the drawback of being stationary. It has sight and sound like television but with better quality. Furthermore, cinema advertising has a truly captive audience. A disadvantage is that some moviegoers may resent having to watch commercials, but such resentment is likely a minor problem, since moviegoers are usually in a positive and receptive mood. The more serious problem is that patrons, knowing that there will be some commercials shown first, take their time in showing up and may be wandering into and about the theater until the main feature begins.

## Directories

Directories are books that provide listings of people, professions, and institutions. The yellow page telephone directories, with a listing of various types of companies, are a prime example. Directories may be sold or given away free of charge. Because the telephone is not widely available in many areas and the information is not accurate, this medium has been underutilized outside of the U.S.A. In some countries, governments and private entities publish trade directories of local exporters and their advertisements.

The popularity of cellular or mobile phones presents another unique problem. In Japan, the number of mobile phones has now exceeded the number of fixed telephones. Given the fact that cellular phone owners may switch the telephone services from one company to another, their telephone numbers are somewhat temporary. In addition, there is no compilation of cellular phone numbers so as to publish a directory.

## Rural media

In marketing to developing countries, marketers must understand the use of rural media. Mobile units, for example, may be sent to areas lacking access to mass media. Such vehicles can play recorded music and advertising messages over amplifiers or loudspeakers attached to the vehicles' rooftops. A marketer can also attract an audience by arranging for some type of festival advertising held at a temple or school. A free outdoor movie can be shown during the festival while advertising is broadcast through loudspeakers to the captive audience. In a way, such rural media are not that different from the traveling "medicine" shows of the American past.

## Stadiums

Stadium advertising is also appropriate, especially in soccer stadiums, because soccer (i.e., "football") is the most popular and passionate sport in the world. Signs can be displayed on stadium walls, and the advertising rules for outdoor advertising should be applied. The objective of this advertising is not so much to communicate with those in a basketball or football stadium but rather to communicate with TV viewers. For nonstop games such as soccer and hockey, a broadcaster can show the entire game while including logos or brief advertising messages on the edges of the screen – at the top, bottom, side, or all around, with the game being shown in the middle part of the screen.

Cigarette marketers are major sponsors of sports and cultural events (e.g., billiards, horse-racing, rugby, and symphony orchestras) in a number of countries because these events receive extensive TV coverage. In effect, the prominent display of names and logos allows companies to associate their brands with glamour, health, vitality, and success.

### Other media

There are several other advertising media that are traditional and common in developing countries and elsewhere. Some of these media are **advertising specialties**, a variety of inexpensive items (e.g., pens, calendars, letter openers) carrying the advertiser's name, address, and a short sales message. In spite of the cost, such items are relatively durable. Because of their attractive appearance and low production cost, Ajinomoto's calendar-type products are an effective display in Japan and other Asian countries. A charming, attractive young girl (Miss Ajinomoto) serves as an "eye-catcher" to help advertise products. Ajinomoto provides three-ounce bottles to restaurants as toothpick holders or seasoning containers. In addition to using the traveling cinema, a popular form of entertainment, Ajinomoto also uses the traveling cooking school, which combines the expertise of a cook and a nutritionist to provide instruction and education to many institutions such as schools.

Marketers have never ceased to search for a new advertising medium. One novel medium is fortune cookies. Enjoy China Holdings has used restaurants and bars in Shanghai to distribute its messages (websites). For example, the message stating "You will soon find your true love" has the website for personal advertisements. The irony is that fortune cookies did not actually originate in China. In any case, 99 percent of people read the messages contained in the fortune cookies that they have got.[20]

### Media mix

There is no one single advertising medium that is suitable for all countries and products. The media mix has to vary from one target market to another.

The basic principles of media selection apply in all markets. In general, an advertising medium should be selective and cost-effective in reaching a large number of the intended audience. It should deliver the kind of reach, frequency, and impact desired, assuming that there are no particular legal restrictions.

Tokyo Toyopet provides a good illustration of how advertising media are selected to promote cars – in this case, Toyota cars. Newspapers and magazines, due to their national circulation in Japan, are unsuitable because this division of Toyota only concentrates on the Tokyo market. TV time is not readily available and much too expensive. As a result, radio advertising is the clear-cut choice.

## Standardized international advertising

Standardized international advertising is the practice of advertising the same product in the same way everywhere in the world. The controversy of the standardization of global advertising centers on the appropriateness of the variation (or lack of it) within advertising content from country to country. The technique has generated a heated and lively debate for four decades and has been both praised and condemned – passionately.

Doing research is difficult in this area due to the ambiguous *definition* of standardization itself. Strictly speaking, a standardized advertisement is an advertisement that is used internationally with virtually no change in its theme, copy, or illustration (other than translation). More recently, a new breed of advocates of standardization has claimed that an advertisement with changes to its copy or illustration (e.g., a foreign model used in an overseas version) is still a standardized advertisement so long as the same theme is maintained. This new and broadened definition can cloud the issue even more with the added element of subjectivity. Because standardization is a matter of degree rather than an all-or-nothing phenomenon, a more precise definition of standardized advertising, conceptually and operationally, would go a long way toward solving the confusion created by contradictory claims.

Dewar's advertising is a good example of how difficult it is to state with certainty whether a certain advertisement is a standardized advertisement or not. After 20 years, the highly regarded U.S. "Profiles" campaign for Dewar's Scotch whisky was tailored to markets around the world. The format is the same in every country. It provides biographical information, hobbies, and philosophies to portray the successful lifestyle of an entrepreneurial "life-achiever" who also happens to be a typical and famous Dewar's drinker (see Figure 15.4). Previously, Dewar's overseas advertising used translations of American advertisements, but research revealed that the use of local personalities would communicate a stronger message. The localized profile advertisements used in Spain featured profiles of a Spanish author and a 29-year-old Spanish flight instructor and former hang-gliding champion. The Australian campaign gave Dewar's profiles of a 33-year-old Melbourne entrepreneur, a jewelry designer, and a photojournalist. In Thailand, the advertisement featured a Bangkok architect. These campaigns were handled by the local Leo Burnett offices.[21] Because of the inclusion of both the standardization and localization elements, it is very difficult to determine whether these campaigns are more standardized than localized (or vice versa) – without a precise definition of the concept of standardization.

The issue of advertising standardization, without doubt, has far-reaching implications. If it is a valid strategy, international business managers should definitely take advantage of the accompanying benefits of decision simplification, cost reduction, and efficiency. On the other hand, if the premise of this approach is false, the indiscriminate application of standardized advertising in the marketplace will cause more harm than good since it can result in consumers misinterpreting the intended message. Consequently, the important function of advertising to facilitate a consumer's search process can be seriously impaired.

## Three schools of thought

There are three schools of thought on the issue of standardized advertising: (1) standardization, (2) individualization, and (3) compromise.[22] The **standardization** school, also known as the *universal, internationalized, common,* or *uniform* approach, questions the traditional belief in the heterogeneity of the market and the importance of the localized approach. This school of thought assumes that better and faster communication has forged a convergence of art, literature, media availability, tastes, thoughts, religious beliefs, culture, living conditions, language, and, therefore, advertising. Even when people are different, their basic physiological and psychological needs are still presumed to remain the same. Therefore, success in advertising depends on motivation patterns rather than on geography. British Airways' image advertising featuring movie stars, which was designed by Saatchi and Saatchi in the 1970s to trumpet the newly sleek British Airways, has been cited as an example of a successful standardized campaign.

The opposite view of the standardization school is the **localization** school, also known as the *nonstandardization, specificity, individualization, adaptation,* or *customization* approach. This conventional school of thought holds that advertisers should take particular note of the differences among countries (e.g., culture, taste, media, discretionary income). These differences make it necessary to develop specific advertising programs to achieve impact in the local markets. A good illustration of

DEWAR'S PROFILE:
MARK SALZMAN
HOME: Los Angeles, California.
AGE: 29.
PROFESSION: Author, actor, martial artist. "I know everyone in L.A. says that, but really, I am."
HOBBY: Going to the zoo. "It's the one place I won't be asked about China–except by, maybe, the pandas."
LAST BOOK READ: *Discos and Democracy: China in the Throes of Reform*, Orville Schell.
LATEST ACCOMPLISHMENT: Writing the script and starring in the movie "Iron and Silk," based on his book about his experiences as an English teacher in China.
WHY I DO WHAT I DO: "What else do you do with a degree from Yale in Chinese Language and Literature?"
QUOTE:
PROFILE: Animated, ebullient and prone to colorful exaggeration.
HIS SCOTCH: Dewar's® "White Label®," straight up. "After years of drinking nothing but rice wine, it was a pleasure to return to a place where my Scotch was always on the menu."

**FIGURE 15.4** A standardized advertisement?

*Source*: Reprinted with permission of Schenley Industries, Inc.

the importance of localization is the Shiseido case. The Japanese corporation, the world's third largest cosmetic company, did poorly in its first attempt to penetrate the U.S. market because its advertisements featured only Japanese models.

Between these two extreme schools is the **compromise** school of thought. While recognizing local differences and cautioning against a wholesale or automatic use of standardization, this middle-of-the-road school holds that it may be possible, and in certain cases even desirable, to use U.S. marketing techniques everywhere under certain conditions.

## Feasibility and desirability

For an international advertising manager, the decision is affected by his or her perception of whether it is "feasible" and "desirable" to implement standardization. In some cases, it may be feasible but not desirable to use a standardized advertisement; in other cases, it may be desirable but not feasible to do so. The applicability of advertising standardization is a function of these two conditions.

The *feasibility* issue has to do with whether environmental restrictions or difficulties may prohibit the use of a standardized campaign. Three common problems are *literacy* (for print advertisements), *local regulations*, and *media and agency availability*.

Because illiteracy adversely affects the comprehension of advertising copy, the text portion of an advertisement must frequently be minimized or replaced with pictures. Visual aspects influence perceived similarity of advertising.[23] Nevertheless, not all types of pictures are universal in their meanings, and some may not be an effective means of communicating with nonliterate market segments. Therefore, although pictures are more universal than words, international marketers should still research their markets before attempting to communicate with them through pictures.

Indonesia is a big market, trailing only China, the U.S.A., Russia, and Japan. Compared to almost 24 percent of American men, two-thirds of adult males in Indonesia smoke. While governments all over the world have been placing more restrictions on cigarette advertising, Indonesia is quite tolerant. Cigarette brand names are basically free to appear in advertisements. Tobacco companies are among the largest buyers of TV advertising time. Cigarette-branded banners are in public parks, and billboards show young, glamorous models. PT Gudang Garam, Indonesia's largest cigarette producer, uses "The real man's taste" as its slogan. Sampoerna, a unit of Philip Morris International, tries to stand out by using satirical ads that poke fun at aspects of Indonesian society. Still there are some advertising restrictions. Tobacco advertisements cannot show cigarettes or the act of smoking. TV spots for cigarettes also cannot be aired before a set time in the evening.[24]

Germany's emphasis on fair competition results in the prohibition of slander against competitors. As a result, the advertiser must be wary of using comparatives (e.g., better, superior) and superlatives (e.g., best, most durable). In China, Duracell battery commercials were taken off the air because the drumming bunny's endurance claim violated the rules that prohibit superlative claims and comparative advertising. Likewise, Budweiser's "King of Beers" slogan was found to be unacceptable.

A multinational advertiser wishing to use a standardized advertising campaign needs to rely on an advertising agency with a worldwide network to coordinate the campaign across nations. Unfortunately, almost no agencies, regardless of size, are in a position to control local agencies overseas.

It should be noted that the use of a single agency to handle worldwide advertising, while resembling the standardization approach, does not necessarily mean that the approach is purely standardization. While Colgate-Palmolive believes that there is no need to reinvent a winning formula, the directive of IBM's Personal Systems Group is "do it once, replicate, and localize."

## Ethical Dimension 15.1

### Malaysia: "downgrading local faces"

About a decade ago, Malaysia's "Made in Malaysia" campaign was introduced. The government requires that all advertisements for the local market use Malaysian talent. The TV commercials are to be filmed and edited locally. The guidelines have not been strictly enforced.

Now the government wants to reduce the number of Eurasian faces in advertisements. According to the Information Minister, "many advertisements on TV now, especially on private TV, feature more faces which are not Malaysians. This, to me, is downgrading local faces." His logic is that, instead of the usual white-mixed faces, there should be more opportunities for talents and models who look more like Malays, Chinese, or Indians. For those TV commercials featuring pan-Asian talents, they should be for the international market instead of being shown in Malaysia.

The Information Ministry's proposed guidelines have caused outrage. In particular, Malaysian models of mixed heritage feel that they are being discriminated against in the multicultural country.

*Source*: "KL's Crackdown on Eurasian Faces Triggers Furore," *Bangkok Post*, February 8, 2007.

A study of ethical perceptions provides another relevant perspective. Relative to the U.S.A., hiring personnel from other advertising agencies was viewed more negatively in Korea. Also in Korea, clients' expectations of favors as well as social obligations arising from gifts received may require a different response.[25]

Degree of feasibility varies from country to country, facilitating the implementation of standardization in some countries while creating problems in others. A study of 66 New Zealand firms operating in two or more EU countries has come to the conclusion that the marketing environment is not likely to be similar across all EU countries. However, some country pairs (e.g., UK–France, UK–Germany, UK–Ireland, Germany–France, Germany–Italy, and Germany–Sweden) may offer some degree of similarity that permits standardization.[26] A study of European tour operators within the Nordic region shows that it is a challenge for these firms to practice the philosophy of "think regional, act local" or "cooperative centralization." While they manage marketing regionally, certain activities have to be adapted due to situation-specific factors such as product and industry characteristics.[27]

It should be noted that an environment may change, permitting either more or less opportunity for standardization in the future. Therefore, feasibility is dependent on the situation and does not offer solid support for either of the two extreme schools of thought.

Three major criteria exist to judge the degree of *desirability* of a standardized advertisement. One of these is the amount of *cost savings* that might be achieved. Thus, standardization is desirable only when the saving derived in the production cost of this type of advertisement is significant. One structural model explores the factors that encourage standardized advertising. The results obtained from Japanese and U.S. subsidiaries in the EU show that standardized advertising can enhance a company's financial and strategic performance if the external environment and internal resources are conducive to standardization.[28]

Another criterion of desirability is *consumer homogeneity*, a major assumption of the uniform approach. One model developed to address the issue of standardization/localization considers three factors. These factors are homogeneity of customer response to the marketing mix, transferability of competitive advantage, and degree of economic freedom.[29]

If consumers were indeed homogeneous across countries, the debate would be resolved, since consumers could then be motivated in exactly the same way. Are consumers homogeneous (see Cultural Dimension 15.1)? The proponents of each school of thought have offered real-life examples that are subjective and highly judgmental. Consumers would be better served if the collection of empirical data were based on research designs that eliminate the effect of confounding factors.

The results of the literature review of management responses, consumer characteristics, and consumer responses indicate that there is no theoretical or empirical evidence to support the standardization perspective in its current form.[30] As an example, a sample of Dutch respondents exhibited a somewhat negative attitude toward the use of the English language in TV commercials. The use of a foreign language (English, in this case) made it more likely for a commercial to be misunderstood.[31] Language thus poses a challenge. In an experiment involving advertisements using image and utilitarian appeals, Americans (presumed to be from a "masculine" culture) liked the utilitarian advertisement better and felt that it was more believable. In contrast, participants from Taiwan (primarily an "androgynous" culture) responded equally well to both types of appeal.[32]

The third criterion of desirability has to do with the degree of *cooperation of an MNC's foreign subsidiaries and national managers*. Because of subsidiaries' involvement, it is a good idea to investigate the standardization decision-making process by studying two organizational factors (decision powers of subsidiaries and familiarity with foreign markets at headquarters) and two cultural factors (similarity in market position and country environmental conditions). MNCs are more likely to centralize control and adopt standardization when they understand similarities in market position, when they are familiar with foreign contexts, and when they develop shared values and beliefs among subsidiary managers and headquarters managers. Otherwise, standardized decisions are likely to be challenged by local subsidiaries.[33] Similarly, another study confirmed that a global company's ability

### Cultural Dimension 15.1

**Language of luxury**

While wealth may be a universal desire, it also has its own local languages. First of all, rich people are different from poor people. Second, wealth has a hierarchy, and the super-rich are different from those who are merely rich. Third, the manner in which wealth is displayed differs from one geographic region to another.

Americans and Asians like cars, jets, and yachts. In Asia, conspicuous consumption is the norm. Europeans (in part due to their longer traditions) and Latin Americans prefer to spend big on art. Wealthy Latin Americans, due to personal safety issues, are not big on jewelry. In contrast, the rich in the Middle East like "heavy luxury" and spend the largest percentage of their wealth on status jewelry and watches. The preference may be due in part to their nomadic traditions and the fact that jewelry is quite portable.

The super-wealthy have one thing in common. Regardless of country, they spend more and differently than those who are "only" rich. As wealth increases, there is a tendency to spend more on art, travel, and wine and less on jewelry.

*Source*: "All Luxury Is Local," *Wall Street Journal*, June 29, 2007.

to foster successful relationships in terms of marketing operations between headquarters and its foreign subsidiaries can enhance product performance across markets. As a firm tries to standardize its marketing programs, the subsidiaries' acquiescence becomes increasingly important.[34]

## Research and empirical evidence

At present, the research focus has shifted toward a more limited level of *horizontal homogeneity*. Instead of showing that multiple countries are basically equivalent (when it is now quite clear that they are not), several researchers have moved away from the country as a unit of analysis. Instead, they focus on examining whether a subset of one national market is similar to the subset of another national market.

At present, the available empirical data deal with the effectiveness of standardization only in an indirect manner. The available data are primarily concerned with showing how national markets differ in some ways without showing whether such differences actually affect the effectiveness of international standardization. Most of the recent studies have shifted the emphasis to *national advertising practices*. The evidence is rather overwhelming that certain advertising methods (e.g., use of symbols, comparative advertising) may be the norm in some countries but the exception in others. The researchers are virtually unanimous in cautioning against the automatic use of standardization. According to them, since consumers are used to a certain advertising method which is predominant in their country, these consumers may not be receptive to other advertising tactics.

With regard to TV commercials in Hong Kong and South Korea, femininity plays an important role in explaining the differences. Korea, supposedly a country of high uncertainty avoidance, displays more values of low uncertainty avoidance in its commercials.[35]

One group of researchers has focused on *corporate responses* by investigating whether multinational firms prefer to standardize or localize their campaigns. Overall, companies are more likely to employ localization rather than standardization, and advertising in particular is the component of the marketing mix that is most adapted. However, a recent interview with 150 Norwegian exporters, focusing on standardization and cooperative climate, found that companies with high local market knowledge had better performance. While the researcher believed that this relationship partially supported the standardization approach, it should be noted that standardization usually focuses on the home country while ignoring the preference of the host countries. As also noted by the author, standardization programs should not be initiated without a thorough understanding of local market conditions.[36]

In spite of the expected convergence of EU markets that should be amenable to standardization, both Japanese and American managers still recognize obstacles to the utilization of advertising standardization. In terms of motivation, both groups value cost savings. However, American managers also place more emphasis on a uniform brand image, while Japanese managers are interested in the higher level of control that can be derived from standardization. In any case, the overall level of advertising standardization is somewhat moderate.[37]

Examinations of advertisement content have repeatedly found that, in practice, the content or message of advertisements varies significantly from one market to another. In the case of children's TV commercials from China and the U.S.A., a content analysis found that Chinese commercials reflect China's traditional cultural values and its social and economic development level. Still there appears to be a shift in China from the elderly to the young, reflecting the country's one-child policy. There is also some evidence of Western values creeping in.[38] Another study compared the U.S. and

Chinese advertising appeals in terms of cultural values. The youth/modernity appeal, supposedly reflecting Westernization, is equally and prominently displayed in both sets of commercials. However, Chinese commercials emphasize the following cultural values more frequently: (1) the soft-sell appeal in seven product categories, (2) the veneration elderly/tradition appeal in six product categories, (3) the oneness with nature appeal in two product categories, and (4) the group consensus and status appeals each in one product category. In contrast, U.S. advertisements more frequently use the hard-sell appeal, the time-oriented and individual/independence appeals, and the product merit.[39]

Japanese advertisements are also distinct. A content analysis of how teenage girls and "girlish" images were portrayed in eight issues of *Seventeen* magazine (four being in the U.S. edition and four in the Japanese version) found culture-based differences. There is a higher frequency of verbal and visual girlish images in the Japanese issues.[40] An analysis of women's magazine advertisements in Germany and Japan focused on ad format, usage of models, male and female role portrayal, and value appeals. While there are some similarities, there are also distinct cross-national differences in the way that marketers adapt their strategies. The non-traditional approaches in targeting women are more culturally specific than the traditional approaches. Male role portrayal is an important element of the non-traditional approaches in women's magazines.[41] Similarly, a study of TV commercials from Japan, Russia, Sweden, and the U.S.A. in terms of the masculine–feminine continuum found that feminine countries show a higher degree of utilization of relationships for male and female characters. Since not all cultures share the same values, advertising standardization appears to be strategically unwise.[42]

One content analysis examined advertisements from the U.S.A., Egypt, Lebanon, and the United Arab Emirates. In Arabic magazine advertisements, people are depicted less frequently. When these advertisements show women, the women wear long dresses. The American advertisements, in contrast, provide more information content, price information, and comparative advertising.[43] Yet another content analysis found that standardization could be a flexible policy that could be adapted to accommodate different market circumstances.[44]

One content analysis investigates the seven local editions of *Cosmopolitan*, a relatively global magazine. Compared to domestic product advertisements, multinational product advertisements are more likely to use standardized strategies. In addition, product category plays a role as beauty products (cosmetics, fashion) are more likely than other products (e.g., cars, food, household goods) to be attracted to standardization.[45] Another content analysis of over 400 magazine advertisements distinguishes cultures in terms of Hofstede's cultural dimensions. The results suggest that, with regard to services, it is possible for advertisers to standardize the type of advertising appeal and specific service quality dimension. It is considerably more common to use rational appeals rather than emotional appeals to reach Korean consumers, and such cues as reliability and assurance should be employed.[46]

It should be pointed out that even the meanings of the visual aspect of an advertisement may vary from one culture to another. According to one quasi-experimental study of the effectiveness of standardized visual images, a high-context audience is more likely than a low-context audience to overread into the meaning of the visual. The audience's perceived social identity also has an impact.[47]

While Hollywood movies are an international medium, the acceptance of these movies as well as products placed in them may vary from one country to another. Unlike commercials that can be adapted for a particular country, product placement is not so adaptable because a movie shows a product being placed in the same way all over the world. Consumers in the U.S.A., France, and Austria exhibited varying responses with regard to acceptability and purchase behavior. As an example,

Americans were more likely to accept and purchase the products shown in the movies. There was also some degree of convergence however. For example, women were less positive than men, and this less positive attitude was persistent across all three countries. In any case, one implication is that it is a good idea to identify specific segments in terms of country, product, and individual differences.[48]

In practice, the degree of standardization depends in part on corporate policy and strategic planning. At the same time, it also depends on the importance of a particular overseas market and the insistence of the head of that subsidiary. It must be pointed out though that while some advertisers practice standardization, it is unknown whether this is an effective approach.

After having seen or experienced difficulties in implementing the standardization concept, most international advertisers today have had second thoughts about standardization and have moved toward some degree of localization. Parker Pen Co. launched an ambitious "one world, one voice" program in 1984 to sell writing instruments all over the world. The campaign was a big disappointment, and the company has once again tailored advertisements to local markets. As Procter & Gamble's international chief has pointed out, although "technology" (e.g., gel toothpaste) is global, other aspects such as taste, coloring, packaging, and advertising of the technology are usually local.

In conclusion, an overwhelming number of studies do not show evidence that supports standardization. Instead, most studies have found consumer, market, and media differences. However, the empirical evidence that contradicts the use of standardization is indirect in nature. This is not surprising, since it is very difficult to design a study that truly proves the validity (or lack of it) of advertising standardization. It is possible though to design a more rigorous study that will address the issue in terms of cause and effect.[49]

As for future research, Taylor has proposed a number of questions to be pursued (see Exhibit 15.1).[50] Exhibit 15.2 provides some items that may be used for measurement purposes.[51]

### Exhibit 15.1

**Advertising standardization: some research questions**

1 What factors are correlated with firms' use of standardized advertising? Under what circumstances is standardization of (1) strategy, (2) execution, and (3) language appropriate?
2 Is standardized advertising more effective than localized advertising in terms of traditional measures such as attitude toward the ad and attitude toward the brand? Does global advertising help lead to improved ROI, and other measures of financial performance? Does it contribute to improved strategic performance?
3 Does standardized advertising help to build a uniform brand image? How valuable is a uniform brand image to a company and does it contribute to brand equity? If a uniform brand image helps build brand equity, what are the mechanisms by which this happens?
4 To what extent are global advertisers able to reach cross-market segments? How do they identify segments and how do they reach them? Can cross-market segmentation be effective on a large scale?

*Source*: Abridged from Charles R. Taylor, "Moving International Advertising Research Forward: A New Research Agenda," *Journal of Advertising* 34 (spring 2005): 7–16.

Exhibit 15.2

**Advertising standardization: measurement of constructs**

Perception of advertising infrastructure (alpha = .65)

- Similar advertising media are available in these markets.
- Advertising regulation is similar across these markets.
- Media costs are similar across these markets.

Use of standardized advertising strategies (alpha = .77)

- We use the same general strategy for our ads in all of the countries where we advertise.
- The main ideas or themes are similar across the European markets in which we advertise.
- We use a similar budgeting process in the European markets in which we advertise.
- We use similar media strategies across the markets in which we advertise.

*Source*: Abridged from Charles R. Taylor and Shintaro Okazaki, "Who Standardizes Advertising More Frequently, and Why Do They Do So? A Comparison of U.S. and Japanese Subsidiaries' Advertising Practices in the European Union," *Journal of International Marketing* 14 (No. 1, 2006): 98–111.

## A decision-making framework

All forms of advertising standardization should not be ignored by the marketer. This technique may be appropriate on a modest scale, though definitely not on a worldwide basis. A limited homogeneity does exist in many cultures around the world. Thus it is a good idea to find out when and where this limited scale of homogeneity exists so that some level of standardization may be considered.

For decision-making purposes, market segmentation can provide a practical framework for standardizing advertising, as shown in Figure 15.5. If the world is treated as one whole market, a standardized advertisement may then be used. But if the world is divided into several segments (i.e., regions or countries), each segment probably requires its own custom-made marketing mix (i.e., a localized advertisement).

A market should be segmented when five requirements are met: identification, accessibility, differential response, segment size, and cost/profit. Each country (or region) should be considered as a distinct segment if the following conditions are met:

1 The marketer can identify the country's unique demographic characteristics.
2 The responses to a unique marketing mix of customers in the country will be appreciably different from those of other countries.
3 The country is accessible through available selective advertising media with minimum promotion waste.
4 The country's population size is large enough to justify the specially designed marketing campaign.
5 Incremental cost as a result of the segmentation is less than incremental profit.

When all of these segmentation criteria are met, market segmentation is applicable but advertising standardization is not. There is no question that the U.S.A. is a market segment of its own because of its unique characteristics and responses, media availability, market size, and great profit potential. As such, Asian and European marketers as a rule design advertisements specifically for the U.S. market. In contrast, these marketers are more likely to introduce in, say, Asian countries (except Japan) the advertisements they have already used in their own countries. This action may be due to their belief that these other markets are either similar or not economically significant enough to justify nonstandardized advertising.

In a number of cases, it may not be strategically sound to localize an advertisement for a particular market. Some countries are just too small to warrant that kind of special attention and the associated cost. It is almost impossible to justify why an international firm should design an advertisement specifically for Tuvalu. Tuvalu, whose economy relies on fishing and coconuts, has a population of

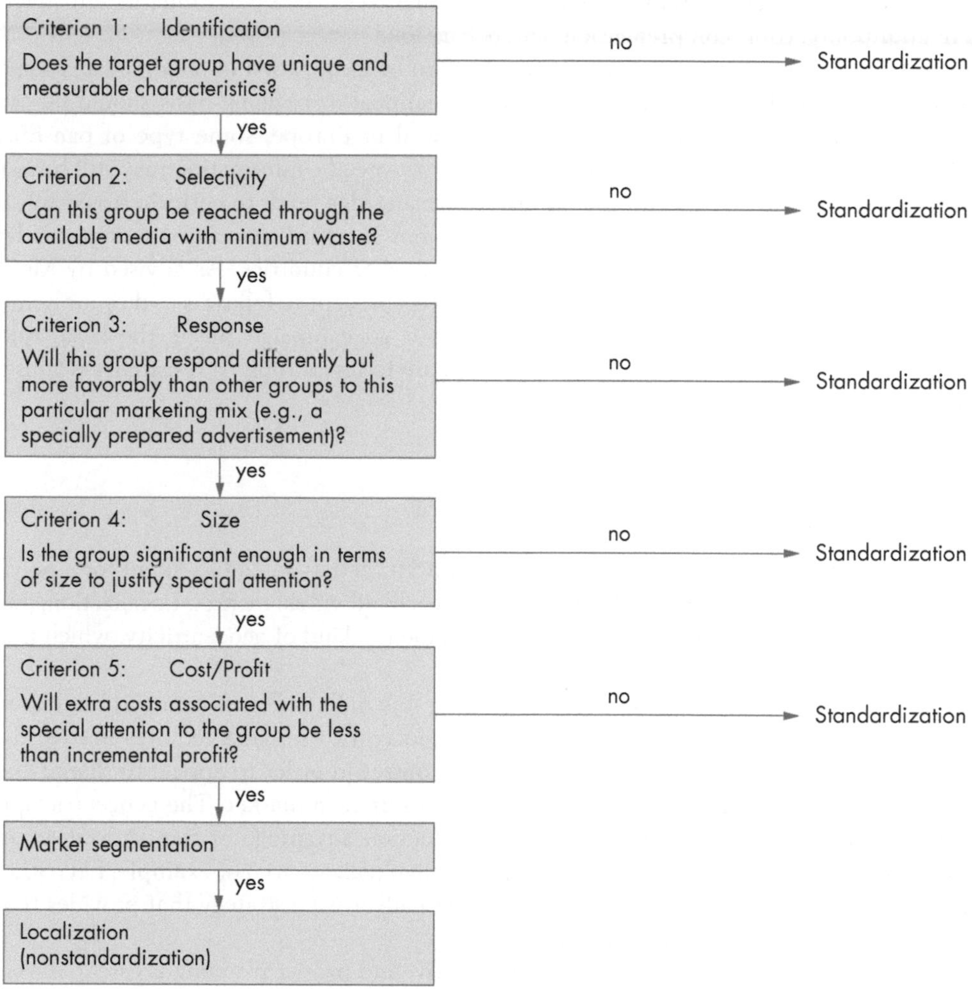
Criterion 1: Identification
Does the target group have unique and measurable characteristics?
no
Standardization
yes
Criterion 2: Selectivity
Can this group be reached through the available media with minimum waste?
no
Standardization
yes
Criterion 3: Response
Will this group respond differently but more favorably than other groups to this particular marketing mix (e.g., a specially prepared advertisement)?
no
Standardization
yes
Criterion 4: Size
Is the group significant enough in terms of size to justify special attention?
no
Standardization
yes
Criterion 5: Cost/Profit
Will extra costs associated with the special attention to the group be less than incremental profit?
no
Standardization
yes
Market segmentation
yes
Localization (nonstandardization)

**FIGURE 15.5** A decision-making framework for advertising standardization

*Source*: Sak Onkvisit and John J. Shaw, "Standard International Advertising: A Review and Critical Evaluation of the Theoretical and Empirical Evidence," *Columbia Journal of World Business* 22 (fall 1987: 53).

only 10,000. Even on a bigger scale, it may be easier to justify why, in many instances, standardization should be employed when marketing in the CIS countries. In spite of their new-found independence, they are still similar in many ways. Perhaps, more importantly, their market sizes may not be adequate: Armenia (3.8 million citizens), Azerbaijan (8.1 million), Georgia (5.4 million), Kazakhstan (14.9 million), Kyrgyzstan (4.7 million), Tajikistan (6.2 million), Turkmenistan (5.4 million), and Uzbekistan (25 million).

Marketers should understand that standardization is not a universal tool that can be automatically used without proper consideration. It makes no sense to forge worldwide uniformity and conformity for management's convenience if consumers seek diversity and individuality. Standardization and advertising are not synonymous. Advertising is supposed to (1) inform and (2) persuade customers (3) effectively. Standardization may fail to perform any (or all) of these three objectives. Thus, it is critical to pretest each advertisement in an international context to determine its effectiveness in terms of attention-getting, comprehension, and persuasion.

It is probably a mistake to use either standardization or localization on a wholesale basis. Some degree of standardization or localization on an international or regional basis should be carefully considered. While a U.S. campaign may not work well in Europe, some type of pan-European advertising may be possible, but even then, some country-specific information may still be required. It is important to realize that a well-thought-out advertising idea tends to perform reasonably well in multiple markets without a great deal of adjustment, but any flaws associated with a standardized advertisement will multiply in tandem with the number of countries. As advised by McCollum Spielman, Worldwide's Chief Executive Officer, "the best precept to follow is to do your homework. When entering another country, make sure that your ad campaign meets the basic rules and preconditions of its targeted culture. Test it! And be sure to test through a researcher who is part of that culture."[52]

## Global advertising: true geocentricity

Criticisms of myopic standardization should not be interpreted as an endorsement for a polycentric approach which requires custom-made campaigns for each individual market. Localization, practiced for its own sake, can be just as myopic. What is desirable is a kind of geocentricity, which is not the same thing as standardization.

Standardization is basically a campaign designed for one market (home country) but exported to other markets regardless of justification. In contrast, a geocentric campaign requires an advertisement to be designed for the worldwide audience from the outset in order to appeal to shared common denominators while allowing for some modification to suit each market. The geocentric approach combines the best of both worlds (i.e., the cost-reduction advantage of standardization and the advantages of local relevance and effective appeal of individualization). For example, Levi Strauss has switched from all localized advertisements to a pattern advertising strategy that provides the broad outlines, but not the details, of the campaign.

Devising a global advertisement is anything but easy, and proper planning is essential. As in the case of Coca-Cola, it has launched a campaign called "The Coke Side of Life" as its new global marketing platform. The localized version in Thailand features Thai artists, and the slogan used there is: "Choose Coke – the good side of life." Apparently, the original slogan cannot be literally translated if the proper meaning is to be retained.[53]

With proper planning, it is possible to create an advertisement which can maintain the main theme internationally while allowing necessary adaptation. A global advertisement should be adaptation ready in the sense that necessary and desirable adaptation is planned at the time of conception rather than after the fact. Coca-Cola Co.'s "General Assembly" campaign is a good example. The campaign shows 1000 children singing the praises of Coke. Because each McCann office had permission to edit the film to include close-ups of a youngster from its market, at least 21 different versions of the spot existed.

The success of IBM's Subtitles campaign has demonstrated that it is possible to integrate global and local action if the markets are similar and if the product/brand is perceived similarly in those markets. Previously, the company allowed each of its core 13 semi-autonomous business entities to develop its own independent business strategy. Seeing greatness in the sum of the parts, IBM's chairman reintegrated these units into a cohesive whole in 1993. One advertising agency was appointed in 1994 to have the prime responsibility for executing IBM's communication programs with a single voice worldwide.

The Subtitles campaign achieved global imagery through the use of the same footage in each country while employing local subtitles to translate the foreign language of the commercial. Local subtitling permits each country to retain its home cultural accent. The message of the campaign was that IBM could deliver simple yet powerful solutions to manage information anywhere and at any time for individuals and companies of all sizes. The company wanted to communicate that it was vigorous and innovative while maintaining the latent strengths of global scope, leadership, and reliability. Naturally, the international implementation encountered some local difficulties ranging from limited access to television commercials to the common practice of dubbing for foreign language films and commercials.

The campaign was run in 47 countries, and it was pretested and/or tracked in over 20 markets worldwide. Although individual markets showed some response variation, the responses to the campaign were considerably consistent. Among those who were aware of the campaign, their responses showed that the company's key attribute dimensions improved significantly while measures of negative attribute dimensions declined. In comparison, the other brands tracked did not show a positive movement. Thus, the Subtitles campaign has proved to be one of IBM's longest and most successful runs of the company's image campaign in recent history.[54]

In designing a global advertisement, a marketer should take certain attributes into account.[55] The characteristics of a global advertisement are: (1) it should be visual, (2) it must have some universal appeal, (3) it must be adaptation-ready, (4) it combines both standardization and localization, (5) it assumes both homogeneity and heterogeneity, (6) it combines efficiency with effectiveness, and (7) it is simultaneously global and local. These characteristics are essential in meeting the needs of the marketer as well as the needs of worldwide consumers.

## Conclusion

In developing countries, advertising is often viewed as something wasteful. In socialist/communist countries, it may be seen as incompatible with political objectives. It is undeniable that certain advertising practices are misleading, deceptive, and wasteful. Just as undeniable, however, is that advertising serves a useful function by providing customers with relevant information for intelligent decision-making. Although the U.S. style of advertising is not necessarily suitable for all other countries, it does make a significant contribution to the high standards of living in the U.S.A.

U.S. advertisers need to realize and understand that foreign media are not always readily available. Many of the media, especially the broadcast media, are government operated and controlled for security reasons. Broadcast media are considered sensitive instruments because the equipment may be used for espionage or for supporting a coup attempt. It is a common practice for revolutionaries staging a coup to seek control of radio and TV stations for psychological warfare.

Even when foreign media are available, American advertisers must appreciate their different style and approach. Such media as outdoor, cinema, and rural advertising are used extensively outside the U.S.A. Moreover, advertisers in many parts of the world rely more on a repetitive effect than on sophistication within a message. Direct-action advertising and the hard-sell approach may have to give way to an indirect-action approach, emphasizing the reputation and image of a company or brand name even though this usually does not result in immediate sales.

Because of the variations found in advertising regulations, media availability, media approaches, and consumer characteristics, there is a high degree of risk in employing standardized advertising on a worldwide basis. Studies have shown time and time again that the world market is basically heterogeneous. Although a global advertisement may have the advantage of lower cost, cost reduction should not always be the overriding motive. Advertisers need to be less ethnocentric and to show more consideration and regard for foreign consumers. All advertisements, standardized or not, should be tested for suitability for the intended audience before being utilized in the marketplace.

## CASE 15.1 INTERNATIONAL ADVERTISING: STANDARDIZED, LOCALIZED, OR GLOBAL?

Indonesia is the world's fifth largest cigarette market, trailing only China, the U.S.A., Russia, and Japan in volume. About 24 percent of adult American males smoke, as do two-thirds of adult Indonesian males. Advertising restrictions are few. The main restriction is that advertisements cannot show the act of smoking. There is no restriction on the use of a brand name in advertisements or at public events, and there is no minimum age for smokers.

Altria Group Inc.'s Philip Morris International acquired a controlling stake in PT Hanjaya Mandala Sampoerna in 2005 for $5.2 billion, the largest investment amount by a foreign investor. While Marlboro has 50 percent of the segment of traditional cigarettes, this particular segment is small. In Indonesia, *kretek* (sweet clove) cigarettes command 90 percent of the market. Planning to use its premium brand to gain more market share, Philip Morris plans to launch a clove-flavored cigarette under the Marlboro name.

Nokia Corp.'s global campaign carries the slogan "1001 reasons to have a Nokia imaging phone." Unlike past campaigns that employed different images and messages in different countries, the idea is to use one message in all countries. The rationale is that consumers should receive a uniform message wherever they travel, while the company could gain from the benefits of standardization. Nokia believes that it is now more practical to advertise its products on a global basis because most parts of the world have finally used the same technology, making it possible for Nokia to offer new products around the world at the same time. Until recently, a unified advertisement was not feasible because the company had to launch different products in different regions at different times. To provide local flavor, Nokia uses local actors (e.g., in Africa, Asia, Europe, and the U.S.A.). Local settings (e.g., a marketplace in Italy or a bazaar in the Middle East) are chosen and modified to showcase a Nokia phone in a certain region.

Peninsula Hotels operates seven deluxe hotels (three in the U.S.A. and four in Asia). The company is known for the exacting image of its luxury hotels. Until recently, Peninsula allowed its advertising to be generated locally by each hotel. Now the company wants a stronger and uniform brand identity. It has designed a global campaign that targets a niche audience. In particular, it focuses on high-spending Americans who make up the largest group of customers at any location of the hotel chain, but it will also try to attract British customers. The print advertisements appear in magazines as well as the *Economist* and the *International Herald Tribune*.

The campaign, called Portraits of Peninsula, is based on portraits by Annie Leibovitz, who is known for her celebrity portraits. She made news in 2007, unintentionally and globally, when she was commissioned to do the portraits of Queen Elizabeth. The BBC reported that the Queen was upset when Leibovitz suggested that she be "less dressy."

For Peninsula Hotels, Leibovitz's work provides a series of black-and-white photographs of the hotel's personnel and guests. One photo shows a vintage Rolls Royce being polished by a Hong Kong fleet manager. Another shows a white-gloved page walking six dogs on Fifth Avenue in New York. There is a group photo of maids, chefs, and housekeepers (together with their children dressed in tiny page uniforms).

## Points to consider

1 The Marlboro cowboy is a legend (see Figure 15.6). The image is so strong that it is not necessary for the copy of a Marlboro advertisement to say much. It is the image of the cowboy that carries virtually all the message. How should Marlboro advertise its brand in Indonesia? In addition, choose another country and explain whether Marlboro can use its standardized campaign or whether it will need to adopt a localized campaign, taking into consideration the legal requirements.
2 Evaluate Nokia's "1001 reasons" campaign. How should it be classified: standardized, localized, or global? Offer evidence to support the theoretical basis that you use for your critical evaluation.
3 Evaluate Peninsula's Portraits campaign. How should it be classified: standardized, localized, or global? Offer evidence to support the theoretical basis you use for your critical evaluation.
4 Offer suggestions with regard to how the Nokia and Peninsula campaigns may be improved so as to achieve a global appeal.

*Sources*: "Altria Seeks Indonesian Smokers," *Wall Street Journal*, July 2, 2007; "Nokia Bets One Global Message Will Ring True in Many Markets," *Wall Street Journal*, September 24, 2004; and "Peninsula Hotels Launches Global Ad Campaign," *Wall Street Journal*, October 6, 2004.

## Questions

1 Cite some foreign regulations that restrict the use of either advertising in general or certain advertising practices in particular, and offer the rationale of these regulations.
2 Why is it difficult in most countries to buy (a) TV time and (b) newspaper space?
3 Outside of the U.S.A., why is radio probably the closest thing to a national medium of communication?
4 Although the U.S.A. is well known for the creation of many new media, what are some media that are more popular overseas than in the U.S.A.?

Marlboro
Marlboro
Marlboro
LIGHTS
Famous Marlboro Red and Marlboro Lights—
either way you get a lot to like.
Lights: 10 mg "tar," 0.7 mg nicotine—
Kings: 16 mg "tar," 1.0 mg nicotine
av. per cigarette, FTC Report Feb '85
SURGEON GENERAL'S WARNING: Smoking
Causes Lung Cancer, Heart Disease,
Emphysema, And May Complicate Pregnancy.

**FIGURE 15.6** The Marlboro Man

*Source*: Reprinted by permission of Philip Morris U.S.A.

5 Offer the arguments for each of the three schools of thought: standardization, individualization, and compromise.
6 Is there any empirical evidence supporting standardized advertising (or its homogeneity assumption)?
7 Are standardization and market segmentation compatible strategies?

## Discussion assignments and minicases

1 Does advertising serve any useful purpose in developing countries and socialist/communist countries?
2 Explain how the programming approach of the U.S. television industry may differ from those used in other countries.
3 Do you think there is a market for a world or international newspaper?
4 Many American consumers consider direct mail to be the same as junk mail, a term that is offensive to the direct marketing industry. At present, this medium is largely underdeveloped outside of the U.S.A. What is your assessment of the future of direct mail overseas?
5 As an advertising manager, do you plan to use a standardized advertisement?
6 Harman Kardon audio and video products are aimed at the high-end segment of the market. The company has decided to advertise its products with the same graphic throughout the world. By producing basically one advertisement in six languages (English, Dutch, French, German, Italian, and Japanese), the company expected to save at least $200,000. The Zagoren Group was assigned the duty of coordinating the cooperative effort. The U.S. full-page version appearing in *Audio* and *Stereo Review* showed a Harman Kardon amplifier on a grand piano with a black background and "The Components of High Performance" as the headline. For this advertisement to be used overseas, must there be any changes necessitated by production and other requirements?

## Notes

1 Herbert Jack Rotfeld, Colin Jevons, and Irene Powell, "Australian Media Vehicles' Standards for Acceptable Advertising," *Journal of Advertising* 33 (winter 2004): 65–73.
2 "MTV's World," *Business Week*, February 18, 2002, 81–4.
3 "Beeb Changes Tack in India," *Business Today*, December 31, 2006, 42.
4 "Suddenly, the BBC Is a World-beater," *Business Week*, April 28, 2003, 98.
5 "France Plans an All-news Broadcast," *San José Mercury News*, May 13, 2003.
6 "Channel V Plans Move to Malaysia," *Bangkok Post*, June 11, 2002.
7 "London's New Media Lessons," *Business Week*, December 4, 2006, 26.
8 Kineta Hung, Flora Fang Gu, and David K. Tse, "Improving Media Decisions in China," *Journal of Advertising* 34 (spring 2005): 49–63.
9 "For Coke, Local Is It," *Business Week*, July 3, 2000, 122.
10 Patrick D. Lynch and John C. Beck, "Profiles of Internet Buyers in 20 Countries: Evidence for Region-specific Strategies," *Journal of International Business Studies* 32 (Fourth Quarter 2001): 725–48.

11 "Worldwide-friendly Sites Draws Returns," *Marketing News*, September 2, 2002, 24.

12 Patrick D. Lynch, Robert J. Kent, and Srini S. Srinivasan, "The Global Internet Shopper: Evidence from Shopping Tasks in Twelve Countries," *Journal of Advertising Research* 41 (May–June 2001): 15–23.

13 R. Crockett, "Surfing in Tongues," *Business Week E.Biz*, December 11, 2000, EB 18.

14 Shintaro Okazaki, "Search the Web for Global Brands: How American Brands Standardise Their Web Sites in Europe," *European Journal of Marketing* 39 (Nos 1/2, 2005): 87–109.

15 Nitish Singh *et al.*, "Understanding International Web Site Usage," *International Marketing Review* 23 (No. 1, 2006): 83–97.

16 Nitish Singh, Vikas Kumar, and Daniel Baack, "Adaptation of Cultural Content: Evidence from B2C E-commerce Firms," *European Journal of Marketing* 39 (Nos 1/2, 2005): 71–86.

17 Nitish Singh, Hongxin Zhao, and Xiaorui Hu, "Analyzing the Cultural Content of Web Sites: A Cross-national Comparison of China, India, Japan, and U.S.," *International Marketing Review* 22 (No. 2, 2005): 129–46.

18 Chang-Hoan Cho and Hongsik John Cheon, "Cross-cultural Comparisons of Interactivity on Corporate Web Sites," *Journal of Advertising* 34 (summer 2005): 99–115.

19 Jan-Benedict E.M. Steenkamp and Inge Geyskens, "How Country Characteristics Affect the Perceived Value of Web Sites," *Journal of Marketing* 70 (July 2006): 136–50.

20 "Seeking a Fortune in Shanghai," *Business Week*, November 13, 2006, 10.

21 "Dewar's Profiles Travel Well," *Advertising Age*, August 14, 1989, 28.

22 For a comprehensive review of the theoretical issues and empirical evidence, see Sak Onkvisit and John J. Shaw, "Standardized International Advertising: A Review and Critical Evaluation of the Theoretical and Empirical Evidence," *Columbia Journal of World Business* 22 (fall 1987): 43–55.

23 Klaus Backhaus, Katrin Muhlfeld, and Jenny Van Doorn, "Consumer Perspectives on Standardization in International Advertising: A Student Sample," *Journal of Advertising Research* 41 (September–October 2001): 53–61.

24 "Indonesian Tobacco Ads Pack in Humor," *Wall Street Journal*, March 8, 2007.

25 Young Sook Moon and George R. Franke, "Cultural Influences on Agency Practitioners' Ethical Perception: A Comparison of Korea and the U.S.," *Journal of Advertising* 29 (spring 2000): 51–64.

26 Henry F.L. Chung, "An Investigation of Crossmarket Standardisation Strategies," *European Journal of Marketing* 39 (Nos 11/12, 2005): 1345–71.

27 Angela Roper, "Marketing Standardisation: Tour Operators in the Nordic Region," *European Journal of Marketing* 39 (Nos 5/6, 2005): 514–27.

28 Shintaro Okazaki, Charles R. Taylor, and Shaoming Zou, "Advertising Standardization's Positive Impact on the Bottom Line," *Journal of Advertising* 35 (fall 2006): 17–33.

29 Nanda K. Viswanathan and Peter R. Dickson, "The Fundamentals of Standardizing Global Marketing Strategy," *International Marketing Review* 24 (No. 1, 2007): 46–63.

30 Onkvisit and Shaw, "Standardized International Advertising."

31 Marinel Gerritsen *et al.*, "English in Dutch Commercials: Not Understood and Not Appreciated," *Journal of Advertising Research* 40 (July–August 2000): 17–31.

32 Chingching Chang, "Cultural Masculinity/Femininity Influences on Advertising Appeals," *Journal of Advertising Research* (September 2006): 315–23.

33 Michel Laroche *et al.*, "A Model of Advertising Standardization in Multinational Corporations," *Journal of International Business Studies* 32 (Second Quarter 2001): 249–66.

34 Kelly Hewett and William O. Bearden, "Dependence, Trust, and Relational Behavior on the Part of Foreign Subsidiary Marketing Operations: Implications for Managing Global Marketing Operations," *Journal of Marketing* 65 (October 2001): 51–66.

35 Young Sook Moon and Kara Chan, "Advertising Appeals and Cultural Values in Television Commercials: A Comparison of Hong Kong and Korea," *International Marketing Review* 22 (No. 1, 2005): 48–66.

36 Carl Arthur Solberg, "The Perennial Issue of Adaptation or Standardization of International Marketing Communication: Organizational Contingencies and Performance," *Journal of International Marketing* 10 (September 2002): 1–21.

37 Charles R. Taylor and Shintaro Okazaki, "Who Standardizes Advertising More Frequently, and Why Do They Do So? A Comparison of U.S. and Japanese Subsidiaries' Advertising Practices in the European Union," *Journal of International Marketing* 14 (No. 1, 2006): 98–120.

38 Mindy F. Ji and James U. McNeal, "How Chinese Children's Commercials Differ from Those of the United States: A Content Analysis," *Journal of Advertising* 30 (fall 2001): 79–92.

39 Carolyn A. Lin, "Cultural Values Reflected in Chinese and American Television Advertising," *Journal of Advertising* 30 (winter 2001): 83–94.

40 Michael L. Maynard and Charles R. Taylor, "Girlish Images Across Cultures: Analyzing Japanese versus U.S. Seventeen Magazine Ads," *Journal of Advertising* 28 (spring 1999): 39–64.

41 Katharina M. Dallmann, "Targeting Women in German and Japanese Magazine Advertising: A Difference-in-differences Approach," *European Journal of Marketing* 35 (No. 11, 2001): 1320–41.

42 Laura M. Milner and James M. Collins, "Sex-role Portrayals and the Gender of Nations," *Journal of Advertising* 29 (spring 2000): 67–73.

43 Fahad S. Al-Olayan and Kiran Karande, "A Content Analysis of Magazine Advertisements from the United States and the Arab World," *Journal of Advertising* 29 (fall 2000): 69–82.

44 Greg Harris and Suleiman Attour, "The International Advertising Practices of Multinational Companies: A Content Analysis Study," *European Journal of Marketing* 37 (No. 1, 2003): 154–68.

45 Michelle R. Nelson and Hye-Jin Paek, "A Content Analysis of Advertising in a Global Magazine Across Seven Countries: Implications for Global Advertising Strategies," *International Marketing Review* 24 (No. 1, 2007): 64–86.

46 Hae-Kyong Bang *et al.*, "A Comparison of Service Quality Dimensions Conveyed in Advertisements for Service Providers in the U.S.A. and Korea: A Content Analysis," *International Marketing Review* 22 (No. 3, 2005): 309–26.

47 Michael Callow and Leon G. Schiffman, "Sociocultural Meanings in Visually Standardized Print Ads," *European Journal of Marketing* 38 (Nos 9/10, 2004): 1113–28.

48 Stephen J. Gould, Pola B. Gupta, and Sonja Grabner-Krauter, "Product Placements in Movies: A Cross-cultural Analysis of Austrian, French and American Consumers' Attitudes Toward This Emerging, International Promotional Medium," *Journal of Advertising* 29 (winter 2000): 41–58.

49 Sak Onkvisit and John J. Shaw, "Standardized International Advertising: Some Research Issues and Implications," *Journal of Advertising Research* 39 (November/December 1999): 19–24.

50 Charles R. Taylor, "Moving International Advertising Research Forward: A New Research Agenda," *Journal of Advertising* 34 (spring 2005): 7–16.

51 Charles R. Taylor and Shintaro Okazaki, "Who Standardizes Advertising More Frequently, and Why Do They Do So? A Comparison of U.S. and Japanese Subsidiaries' Advertising Practices in the European Union," *Journal of International Marketing* 14 (No. 1, 2006): 98–111.

52 Harold McCollum Spielman, "Local Partnerships: The Strategic Asset in Multicultural Research," *Journal of Advertising Research* 35 (January/February 1995): RC8-15.

53 "New Local Campaign for Coke," *The Nation*, January 5, 2007.

54 Wayne R. McCullough, "Global Advertising Which Acts Locally: The IBM Subtitle Campaign," *Journal of Advertising Research* 36 (May/June 1996): 11–15.

55 Sak Onkvisit and John J. Shaw, "Marketing/Advertising Concepts and Principles in the International Context: Universal or Unique?", in *New Directions in International Advertising Research, Advances in International Marketing*, Vol. 12, ed. Charles R. Taylor (Amsterdam: JAI, 2002), 85–99.

Chapter 16

# Pricing strategies

## Basic decisions

Overseas operations should be told never to forget three no's. Never get involved in legal issues, never allow the formation of labor unions, and never fail to collect accounts receivable.

Takashi Kiuchi, general manager of planning and administration, International Operations Group, Mitsubishi Electric Corporation

### Chapter outline

- Marketing illustration: the price is right
- The role of price
- Price standardization
- Pricing decisions
    - Supply and demand
    - Cost
    - Elasticity and cross-elasticity of demand
    - Exchange rate
    - Market share
    - Tariffs and distribution costs
    - Culture
- Alternative pricing strategies
- Dumping
    - Types of dumping
    - Legal aspects of dumping
    - How to dump (legally and illegally)
- Price distortion
- Price fixing

## Marketing strategy

**The price is right**

Ryanair Holdings PLC is a successful model for how to operate a low-cost airline. Customers can forget about receiving any perks. Checking in luggage can cost $9.50. Getting a bottle of water in flight costs $3.40. Priority boarding and assigned seating cost extra. Employees do not fare better. Flight crew members pay for their uniforms, and staff members at the headquarters at Dublin Airport have to supply their own pens.

Curiously, while there is a charge for every little thing, the seat is free or nearly free. About 25 percent of the seats are given away for free. Ryanair is able to do so because the planes and website resemble retail stores. The website offers insurance, hotels, car rentals, and online bingo. Flight attendants sell perfume, digital cameras, and scratch-card games. The planes are basically giant billboards for Vodafone Group, Jaguar, and Hertz. When the seatback trays are up, advertisements will stare each passenger in the eye.

With more than 90 percent of the tickets being sold online, administration costs and travel agent commissions are reduced. Since window shades require time to be reset by flight crew between flights, Ryanair removes them. Likewise, there are no seatback pockets for any clutter. The seats do not recline, and there is no in-flight entertainment.

The company's founder and CEO is no stranger to controversy or "cheap publicity stunts." He labeled European Union commissioners "communist morons" and the British Airport Authority "overcharging rapists."

In spite of its average fare of $53, Ryanair's net margins are 18 percent or more than double the 7 percent of Southwest which has an average fare of $92.

Wizz Air is a leading low-cost airline company that specializes in flying Eastern and Central Europeans to and from Western Europe. A one-way fare starts at less than 20 euros. Wizz Air is not interested in business travelers because their number is too small. Leisure traffic is seasonal, and vacationers usually choose a new destination each year, making it complicated for the company's network planning. While the Poles, Hungarians, and others do not pay much to go to and from their home countries, they offer a reliable traffic market.

*Sources*: "Wal-Mart with Wings," *Business Week*, November 27, 2006, 44–5; and "Growth Market for Airlines: Cheap Travel for Immigrants," *Wall Street Journal*, March 7, 2007.

## Purpose of chapter

The air travel business is a complicated one in terms of pricing. There are millions and millions of fares. Just like other businesses, airlines need to offer attractive prices while being able to make a reasonable return.

While price is important, it is not a wise strategy to sell on price as a continuing policy. A product's price must reflect its proper value in the eye of the consumer. To demonstrate the complexity of pricing decisions, in the case of Japanese firms, the need to adjust their prices is derived from an attempt to neutralize any threat from newcomers. For the Korean manufacturers, the strategy of offering lower prices is to penetrate the advanced economies and to compensate for the unknown quality of their goods. The low prices, however, still allow the Korean manufacturers to make sufficient profit margins because of their lower labor costs. In both cases, the pricing strategies are somewhat constrained by host-country regulations, such as the anti-dumping laws.

This chapter examines pricing decision in an international context. The chapter begins with a discussion of the role of price in general. It proceeds to cover the various factors that can affect price, with special attention given to certain variables that are unique to the international market (e.g., foreign exchange rate, dumping, and price control). Methods for dealing with a foreign country's hyperinflation and transfer prices will also receive some attention.

## The role of price

Price is an integral part of a product – a product cannot exist without a price. It is difficult to think or talk about a product without considering its price. Price is important because it affects demand, and an inverse relationship between the two usually prevails. Price also affects the wider economy because inflation is caused by rapid price increases. Yet among the marketing decision variables, price has received the least attention. "The export-pricing literature is characterized by a distinct lack of sound theoretical and empirical works."[1]

Price, however, is no more important than the other three Ps. One should not forget that price should never be isolated from the other parts of the marketing mix. Price should never be treated as an isolated factor.

Price is often misunderstood, especially by many executives. Consumers do not object to price. What they object to is the lack of relationship between the perceived value of the product and the price being charged. They want a fair price, and a fair price can be either high or low, so long as it reflects the perceived value of the product in question. Too high a price causes consumers to resist making a purchase because the value is not there.

Price can be absolutely high from a cost standpoint yet relatively low from a demand standpoint in relation to its value and other features. Therefore, price must be lower than the perceived value or exactly reflect the perceived value. For example, a markdown may be needed for damaged or obsolete goods. But a "high" price may appear to be quite reasonable when extra value is added to a product. Consumers around the world do not mind a high price if they indeed "get what they pay for." However, this is too often not the case.

## Price standardization

One area of pricing that has received some attention is the issue of pricing standardization. Conceivably, American firms that do not rely greatly on foreign sales and do business primarily with industrialized countries may attempt to standardize their prices internationally. In contrast, those companies that are more committed to international business localize their prices and are more successful overseas.

Whether price should be uniform worldwide is a subject of much debate. One school of thought holds that, from the management's viewpoint, there is no reason for an export price to differ from the home price. In addition, economists believe that arbitrage will eliminate any price differential between markets. This is especially the case with the European Union due to the free movement of goods, the elimination of customs barriers, and the harmonization of VAT rates. In addition, the free movement of people will enable them to easily observe prices of the same products in neighboring countries. As a result, internationally recognized consumer goods with wide European distribution are likely to have a more uniform pricing system.

Based on the responses of managing directors of electronics exporters in South Korea, their companies' performance is influenced in part by the adjustment of export prices to foreign market conditions.[2] As explained by Solberg, Stottinger, and Yaprak,

> globalization of markets did not necessarily lead to standardized prices; price differentiation across markets was still well practiced. Market idiosyncrasies, such as different levels of country risk market size, and strategic importance of the market to the firm, typically justified adapted prices in local markets. This held true even in cases in which markets were intertwined (i.e., Scandinavian countries) but had different sets of local conditions. Moreover, companies were actively exploiting these differences. For example, even global price leaders that had the power to implement uniform prices deliberately used differentiated prices when necessary.[3]

A multinational corporation needs to coordinate prices across its multiple markets – without violating national laws. A study of South Korean, Taiwanese, Hong Kong, and Singaporean firms operating in Europe found that they had closer relationships with their parent firms and that they had greater autonomy in strategy and pricing decisions.[4] In the case of Nintendo, it was fined $147 million by the European Commission for price collusion with seven European distributors. The company organized a cartel that operated from 1991 to 1998, and it allowed companies to keep prices for its games and game consoles artificially high in certain countries. These distributors agreed to refuse to sell to buyers from the other European countries, resulting in extraordinarily large differences in prices among countries.

## Pricing decisions

Pricing is one area of marketing that has been largely overlooked. Of all the four Ps of marketing, pricing is probably the one that receives the least attention, especially in an international context.

One problem with an investigation of pricing decisions is that theories are few and vague. Most of the theories that do exist reduce the large number of pricing variables to a discussion of demand and supply. Because the few theories are inadequate, many pricing decisions are based on intuition, trial and error, or routine procedures (e.g., cost-plus or imitative pricing).

When pricing a product, a company must consider a number of factors. Such factors as cost and supply are always relevant – domestically and internationally. Other factors such as exchange rate, tariffs, and culture are more applicable in the case of international marketing.

## Supply and demand

The law of supply and demand is a sound starting point in explaining companies' price behavior. A common practice is to reduce the large number of pricing factors to two basic variables: demand and supply. In an efficient, market-oriented economy, demand is affected by competitive activity, and consumers are able to make informed decisions. Price, as a measure of product benefit, acts as the equilibrator of supply and demand. On the supply side, suppliers compete for consumers' limited funds by constantly cutting costs and enhancing product value. On the demand side, any increase in demand is followed by a higher price, and the higher price should in turn moderate demand. The higher price, however, usually induces manufacturers to increase the supply, and more supply should lead to a reduction in price which will then stimulate demand once again.

The demand–supply model of pricing seems to work best with commodities under a monopoly situation. OPEC, an oil cartel, once controlled the supply of oil so tightly that the cartel was able to push oil prices up sharply. The demand remained high for a period of time because consumers were unable to adjust their driving habits immediately. In the long run, however, high prices curbed excessive demand, and oil prices tumbled during the mid-1980s. The law of supply and demand, in this circumstance, operated in the predicted manner. The moral could be that even a monopolist cannot continue increasing prices without eventually reducing demand. Unfortunately, consumers have also adjusted their behavior when prices improve by embracing SUVs and fuel-inefficient vehicles, thus allowing OPEC's control on supply to boost price to an all-time high in 2008.

However, this pricing model based strictly on demand and supply is oversimplified. The straightforward relationship between supply and price can be affected by several factors. Numerous products have been so differentiated that supply alone as a factor is essentially irrelevant. If a product has a distinct, prestigious image, price may become secondary in importance to image. For such a product, supply can be reduced and price increased without curtailing demand. Waterford Glass became the bestselling fine crystal in the U.S.A. by carefully nurturing its "posh image" as well as by controlling the supply. Waterford held down volume while maintaining premium prices. According to the company, there is no advantage in owning a product that anyone can buy.

Because demand-and-supply analysis can only broadly explain companies' price behavior, it is necessary to consider other relevant factors that affect demand or supply, or both, and that ultimately influence pricing decisions.

## Cost

In pricing a product, it is inevitable that cost must be taken into account. British Airways at one time blindly matched the competition's prices without carefully considering its cost structure. By instituting carefully considered restrictions on discount seats, the company was able to increase its yield significantly.

The essential question is not whether cost is considered but rather what kind of cost is considered and to what extent. The typical costs associated with international marketing include: market research; credit checks; business travel; international postage, cable, and telephone rates; translation costs; commissions, training charges, and other costs involving foreign representatives; consultants and freight forwarders; product modification; and special packaging.

For one school of thought, the thinking is that export price should be lower than home price because the home market actually gains in its overhead expenses by spreading these costs over an expanded production volume. Furthermore, a low price may be necessary, at least at the beginning, to penetrate a foreign market.

The second school of thought, however, argues that the **cost-plus method** (i.e., **full cost**) should be used in pricing a product for the overseas market. All costs – including domestic marketing costs (e.g., sales and advertising expenses, marketing research costs) and fixed costs (e.g., research, development, and engineering) – must be paid for by all other countries. As such, the company begins with a domestic price and then adds to its various overseas costs (e.g., freight, packing, insurance, customs duties). This pricing practice, with its high degree of centralization, is also ethnocentric. In effect, with an allowance for transportation costs and tariffs, the same price prevails everywhere in the world. Although the method is simple and straightforward, it is far from being ideal, because it is easy for the price to end up being too high.

Traditionally, Mercedes-Benz used the cost-plus method when pricing its cars, making engineers insensitive to costs. The company found that its costs were 30 percent above Lexus. Now the company has shifted toward setting prices according to the competition. Engineers and plant managers are required to meet the market-driven target price.

A number of international marketers use **marginal-cost pricing**, which is more polycentric and decentralized. This pricing method is oriented more toward incremental costs. An implicit assumption is that some of the product costs, such as administration costs and advertising at home, are irrelevant overseas. In addition, it is likely that research and development costs and engineering costs have already been accounted for in the home market and thus should not be factored in again by extending them to other countries. The actual production costs plus foreign marketing costs are therefore used as the floor price below which prices cannot be set without incurring a loss. Japanese companies often rely on this type of pricing strategy to penetrate foreign markets, as well as to maintain market share. For the Japanese, breaking even is regarded as a success. The Japanese are thus willing to sacrifice profit in order to keep their factories going.

The incremental cost method has the advantage of being sensitive to local conditions. Subsidiary or affiliate companies are allowed to set their own prices. A potential shortcoming in using this method is that, because research and development costs and the costs of running the headquarters' operation must be borne solely by the home-country market, full cost may not be adequately taken into account by overseas subsidiaries.

In the long run, it is dangerous to be price competitive without being cost competitive. Grundig, for example, tried to gain market share in the VCR market by lowering its higher priced product model, only to realize that it was losing $40 for every unit sold. There is, however, a possible solution for firms with high costs resulting from high tariffs, transportation costs, and high manufacturing costs at home. They have a choice of either producing their products in the overseas market or granting licenses to local producing firms there.

If a company is unable to control costs or to price its product sufficiently high to cover costs, sooner or later the company will be forced to leave the market.

## *Elasticity and cross-elasticity of demand*

Because of the elasticity and cross-elasticity of demand, a company does not usually have the option of changing or holding its price steady, independent of action taken by its competitors. Ford, thinking that its number one position in England was insurmountable, moved unilaterally to end price wars by eliminating discounts and incentives. This action proved to be a strategic error because competitors

## Ethical Dimension 16.1

**Unethical consumers?**

Could consumers in wealthy countries be the culprits as far as low pay and harsh work conditions in China are concerned? Could it be that these consumers are addicted to low prices, thus forcing Wal-Mart, Nike, and so on to go to China for cheap labor? After all, other low-wage nations have higher costs due in part to the fact that they enforce labor laws more effectively. In addition, these countries simply cannot match China in terms of efficient workforce, infrastructure, component supply base, and massive manufacturing capacity.

Many Chinese workers, on the other hand, may have aggravated their own work conditions by wanting to work as many hours as possible while being willing to forgo overtime pay.

American and European multinationals are sensitive to the issue of sweat labor. Some have joined together to improve work conditions. The Fair Labor Association is a coalition of U.S. retailers and name brands. It strives to relieve audit overload at factories by advocating a single set of standards instead of companies relying on their varying corporate codes of conduct. Along the same line, The Fair Factories Clearinghouse represents a joint effort of L.L. Bean, Reebok, Timberland, and others. Social-compliance information on thousands of factories is pooled. If a plant is certified by a reputable agency, the results can be accepted by other buyers.

*Source*: "How to Make Factories Play Fair," *Business Week*, November 27, 2006, 58.

did not follow suit, and Ford's dominant market share dropped from 32 percent to 27 percent. Always remember that it takes only one company to start or continue a price war.

To be competitive does not mean that a company's price must be at or below the market. A superior or unique product can command a higher price. U.S. beef, generally from grain-fed cattle, sells better in Japan than does low-priced Australian and New Zealand beef because cattle in those countries are raised on grass and yield leaner meat. A product with a desirable image can also hold its price above the market. This has always been Sony's strategy, and Sony has stayed away from price wars that might damage its image. But Sony has on occasion been forced to lower prices when, as a result of competitors' price cuts, the price gap between it and other competitors has widened too far.

A company can insulate itself against cut-throat pricing to a certain extent by cultivating a unique and desirable image. A prestigious image allows a firm to act more or less as a monopolist and to gain additional pricing freedom. Cartier takes full advantage of its reputation. A watch made by its subcontractor for $125, for example, was sold by Cartier for almost five times that amount. More than two-thirds of BMW owners are repeat buyers. Because of their brand loyalty, BMW is able to price its cars 10 to 30 percent above the competitors' comparable models.[5] D. Porthault is a maker of ultra-upscale linens. As one of France's most prestigious luxury brands, Porthault wants to manufacture only in France. After all, consumers do not object to paying a high price for quality and the "Made in France" label.[6]

For most consumer goods, a country's per capita income is a good indicator of a market's ability to pay which may indirectly determine a product's elasticity of demand. However, some chic products have a strong demand, and low per capita income is not a deterrent. As in the case of Levi's 501 jeans, the product's worldwide success indicates that a high price can succeed in countries with low per capita income. As a matter of fact, it is possible that, for such products, a higher price may even propel the rise in demand.

## Exchange rate

One pricing problem involves the currency to be used for billing purposes. As a rule, a seller should negotiate to bill in a strong currency, and a buyer should try to gain acceptance in a weak currency. European firms can also minimize exchange risk by using euros in place of an individual currency for quotation and billing.

The exchange rate is one factor that generally has no impact in domestic marketing but is quite critical in international marketing. Since March 1985, a severe drop in the dollar value against other major currencies caused the earnings of U.S. MNCs to jump because their overseas profits when repatriated brought extra dollars after exchange. In contrast, the devalued dollar brought nothing but displeasure to Japanese exporters. Because of the upward spiral of the yen, Komatsu was forced to raise its prices three times in 1985 and 1986. Komatsu's loss of price advantage forced the company to open a plant in the U.S.A. in 1986. Other companies such as Nissan, Honda, and Toyota also had to increase their prices several times. The largest price increase was in a market virtually controlled by the Japanese (e.g., expensive consumer electronics such as CD players and fancy VCRs). Their ability to increase price was, however, more limited at the low end of the market, where the Koreans were right on their heels.

Domestic manufacturers cannot expect to gain competitive advantage solely because of the drop in their home currency. Since its peak in 1985, the foreign exchange value of the U.S. dollar had dropped more than 50 percent by 1987. In 1994, the U.S. dollar lost more than 10 percent in value against the Japanese yen. In the first three months of 1995, the dollar dropped about 20 percent more in rapid succession to hit one new all-time low after another against the Japanese yen. Japanese car manufacturers had to increase their U.S. prices repeatedly in the 1990s. According to Nissan Motor Co., for each single yen increase against the German mark, Nissan's revenue and net income were reduced by four billion yen. For each one-yen increase against the dollar, the company lost six billion yen annually in sales and profits.

The significant decline of the U.S. dollar should have dramatically reduced – but did not – the deficit in U.S. international trade. Instead, the deficit in U.S. merchandise trade rose. Explanations ranged from the J-curve to the dollar's strengths against the currencies of Canada and many newly industrialized countries.

Even though dollar prices of imports to the U.S.A. indeed increased substantially, a depreciating dollar by itself cannot close the trade gap. A falling dollar, although making imports more expensive, has little meaning if prices for domestic substitutes increase to allow imports to maintain a price advantage. The potential price effects on trade resulting from an exchange-rate change require taking into account the domestic price developments for competing goods. One must examine how importers, exporters, and domestic producers price their products in terms of the falling dollar.

The real issue is the relationship between import prices and prices for domestically produced competitive goods. These exchange rate/price relationships are basic in measuring the impact of an exchange-rate change on countries' actual trade balances. In 2008, the U.S. dollar kept falling against the other major currencies, repeatedly hitting an all-time low against the euro. Over a period of three years, the Korean won went up 25 percent against the dollar.[7] In general, Japanese, Korean, and European manufacturers, wanting to maintain market share, do not like to pass on the full cost of appreciation to the U.S. market. But American manufacturers and exporters appear to be unable to resist the urge to fully benefit from the sinking dollar. As a result, U.S. import prices do not go up as much and as fast as U.S. export prices. By thinking about the short-term profit instead of growing market share, U.S. firms will have a hard time increasing market share when the dollar recovers.[8]

## *Market share*

A high market share provides pricing flexibility because the company has the advantage of being above the market if it so chooses. The company may also choose to lower its price because of the better economies of scale derived from lower production and marketing costs. Market share is even more critical for late entrants because market share acts as an entry barrier. That is, without market share, a company cannot achieve the high volume necessary to improve its efficiency.

The first hard drive originated in San José in 1956. In the mid-1980s, there were 77 manufacturers worldwide. Only six significant manufacturers remain in this brutal industry. The 2006 worldwide market share for hard-disk drives is: Seagate (34.9%), Western Digital (20.5%), Hitachi (17.3%), Samsung (10.4%), Toshiba (8.5%), Fujitsu (7.5%), Excelstore (0.7%), and Cornice (0.1%).[9] As for personal computers, servers, and printers, HP has done quite well. For personal computers, the market share is: HP (18%), Dell (17%), Lenovo (7%), Acer (6%), Toshiba (5%), and others (47%). With regard to servers, the market share is IBM (32%), HP (27%), Sun (11%), Dell (10%), Fujitsu/Fujitsu Siemens (5%), and others (15%). In the case of printers, the market share is: HP (44%), Epson (11%), Canon (10%), Xerox (7%), Lexmark (6%), and others (22%).

Market share can be bought with a very low price at the expense of profit. Compaq shocked the Japanese market in 1992 by selling desktop PCs for less than half the price of Japanese manufacturers. Other U.S. firms soon joined in and grabbed one-third of the market. Fujitsu, Japan's biggest computer company, then started dumping in its home market and lost $300 on each $2,000 machine that it sold, amounting to more than $1 million each day.Various hypotheses explain the differences in pricing behavior between U.S. and Japanese firms, ranging from the dollar's dominant international role and the substantial market power of U.S. goods to the large size of the U.S. domestic market, which permits insensitivity to exchange-rate fluctuations. Another explanation is a model based on differences in planning horizons and hysteresis.[10]

**Hysteresis** is a type of market inertia which indicates that the relationship between two or more variables critically depends on past history. Hysteresis may occur when a firm has increasing returns to scale or when consumers are loyal to particular brands, making it very difficult for new entrants to sell their products at the same level of profit as established firms. In a hysteretic environment, when there is a differentiated shock (i.e., something that temporarily changes costs for some but not other producers), those firms facing higher costs must either raise prices to maintain profits in the short term and risk losing market share in the long run, or raise prices less sharply to keep market share in the long run and maximize long-run profits. Japanese price behavior may thus be a rational strategy for long-term profit maximization rather than a predatory, singled-minded obsession with market share.

Because U.S. manufacturers usually do not practice price discrimination between domestic and foreign customers, a change in the value of the dollar appears to be reflected entirely in the foreign currency price of U.S. exports (i.e., complete pass-through of the exchange rate change). Japanese manufacturers, on the other hand, have a tendency to maintain stable yen prices domestically while keeping their export prices fairly stable by absorbing a significant part of yen fluctuation in the form of flexible profit margins. This pricing behavior, reflecting incomplete pass-through, generates "dumping" when the yen appreciates and lower prices domestically than abroad when the yen depreciates.

## Tariffs and distribution costs

As a rule, when dumping and subsidies are not involved, a product sold in a host country should cost more than an identical item sold in a manufacturer's home market. This is the case because the overseas price must be increased to cover tariffs and extra distribution costs. In Japan, both tariffs and quotas combine to restrain imports and force the prices of imported goods upward. In addition, the long distribution channel (i.e., many middlemen) common in many countries around the world is responsible for price escalation, often without any corresponding increase in distribution efficiency. Foreigners in Japan may be shocked to find that an order of plain toast (without coffee) can cost a few dollars.

## Culture

U.S. manufacturers should keep in mind that neither the one-price policy nor the suggested list price will be effective in a number of countries. In the U.S.A., a common practice is for retailers to charge all buyers the same price under similar buying conditions. In most other countries, a flexible or negotiated price is common practice, and buyers and sellers often spend hours haggling about price. Thus, price haggling is an art, and the buyer with the superior negotiating skills may be expected to do better on price than those unfamiliar with the practice.

One very common pricing practice in the U.S.A. is odd-number pricing. One study investigated the effectiveness of 9-ending prices. While "9-ending prices" are popular in the U.S.A., they are not

### Cultural Dimension 16.1

**Lucky numbers**

In China, numerology is a stock trading strategy. Part superstition and part self-fulfilling prophecy, there is a traditional belief that numbers are related to good fortune. The homonyms of numbers hold deep meaning. Numbers have special meaning for phonetic reasons. Numbers spoken in the languages of both Mandarin and Cantonese have homonyms that imply luck of both kinds.

The pronunciation of number 8 (*ba* in both Mandarin and Cantonese) sounds similar to words for "wealth" or "fortune." Not surprisingly, the kickoff time for Beijing Olympic Games is 8 p.m. on 8.8.2008.

For investment purposes, it is an auspicious sign when an 8 is a digit in a share price or when it is part of a particular stock's six-number identity code. The numeral 4, however, is pronounced "*si*," and it is the same pronunciation for the word "death," which is the last thing any investors want.

According to Mandarin pronunciation, the meanings for these numbers are as follows: 1 (together, want), 2 (love, easy), 3 (earn, live), 4 (death), 5 (me, not), 6 (smooth), 7 (together), 8 (fortune, wealth), and 9 (long time).

*Source*: "Chinese Investors Crunching Numbers Are Glad to see 8s," *Wall Street Journal*, May 24, 2007.

well received in a Central European country (Poland).[11] Because people in China are used to beginning negotiation with a high price, they are surprised by eBay's auction system that allows bids to go up.[12]

## Alternative pricing strategies

Pricing involves more than simply marking up or down, and a price that can change in terms of an increase or decrease is not the only answer to moving a product. There are several other alternatives available for making price changes that should be considered. These strategies include the timing of the price change, number of price changes, time interval to which price change applies, number of items to change, use of discount and credit, and bundling and unbundling. U.S. car manufacturers have become rather ingenious in employing these strategies. They change the price by small amounts a number of times over the year. By increasing price significantly at the end of the current model year and then doing it again for the new model year one month later, the company can claim that the price increase for the new model is small because the calculation of the increase is based on the last price of the current year's model. Not surprisingly, GM saves the heftiest price increase for the end of the year in order to facilitate high sticker prices on the new models that are shortly introduced.

The effect of price can be masked and greatly moderated by *financing* or *credit terms*. Airbus, a European consortium jointly owned by four companies from France, Germany, the United Kingdom, and Spain, assembles and markets airplanes as an alternative for carriers that prefer not to buy American. In its eagerness to penetrate the U.S. market, the consortium provided export financing that subsidized Eastern Air Lines by more than $100 million. For Boeing, the consortium engaged in predatory export financing just to get sales.

*Discounts* (cash, quantity, functional, and so on) may be used to adjust prices indirectly. Major buyers are in a position to command a larger discount if it can be granted legally. Although a quantity discount may provide an incentive for dealers to work harder, it often discriminates against smaller middlemen. Ricoh, concluding that it was not a sound practice to compete on price, decided to ignore tiered pricing that rewarded dealers with large orders. Ricoh uses only flat-rate prices, and small dealers pay the same price as large dealers.

Another method used to moderate the price effect is to *bundle* or *unbundle* the product. The price reflects the bundling or unbundling of the product. Bundling adds value and increases prices a little or not at all for added value. This is the strategy used by Japanese car manufacturers, who increase the base price of their cars just enough to cover actual costs. The Japanese also sell cars in the U.S.A. with more standard equipment and fewer options. The strategy makes sense because their vehicles must be shipped from overseas factories, and any custom orders would only serve to delay production and shipment. Moreover, the price charged covers a "bundle" of standard equipment and represents good value for buyers.

Detroit takes the opposite route. U.S. car manufacturers keep prices low by offering a base price for a bare-bones product. Any other equipment is optional and at an added cost. U.S. car manufacturers thus offer a car with several hundred options. By letting a buyer choose any equipment combination at extra cost for each option, a fully equipped U.S. car can become quite expensive, as Detroit charges and seeks to make a profit from each additional item in the option combination.

Ford has begun to experiment with the bundling approach by making available three levels of trim (bundling), each containing many items as standard equipment. The approach provides several benefits. It simplifies the production-and-assembly system while cutting costs and speeding up delivery time. Without having to stock a large and confusing number of options, better inventory control is achieved. With fewer combinations available, quality control should also be improved. The method also provides a clearer market image for the brand.

It cannot be said that a bundling strategy is always superior or inferior to an unbundling strategy. Bundling offers a buyer more product for less money while simplifying production and marketing activities. The overall bundle, of course, is not likely to match the buyer's need completely. On the other hand, a product can be unbundled so that the buyer does not have to pay for any unwanted extras. In effect, the price can be made more affordable by unbundling the product.

When a company faces escalating export prices due to the addition of transportation charges, customs duties, extra packing costs, and so on, it should consider strategies to moderate the impact of price escalation.

Foreigners usually regard U.S. and German goods as being of good quality and performance but also as being too expensive. Because they are price conscious, exporters should consider means to keep prices reasonable. They may want to adapt their products by taking out those features that are nice but not critical. Larger shipments will lower freight costs, or they may want to consider local manufacturing so as to eliminate expensive freight altogether. On the other hand, exporters should realize that affordable prices will result in repeat business. Furthermore, an initial order for a piece of equipment will lead to demand for spare parts and components and auxiliary equipment. Finally, they should stress that the superior quality of their products ultimately results in lower production costs.

## Dumping

Dumping, a form of price discrimination, is the practice of charging different prices for the same product in similar markets. As a result, imported goods are sold at prices so low as to be detrimental to local producers of the same kind of merchandise. Boeing and McDonnell Douglas, for example, accused Airbus of receiving $9 billion in subsidies from the government consortium, enabling the company to price each airplane at some $15–20 million less than the true cost. Dumping also applies to services. Japanese banks in California were accused of dumping money in the U.S. market by pricing their loans at an interest rate lower than that charged by U.S. banks.

### *Types of dumping*

There are several types of dumping: sporadic, predatory, persistent, and reverse. **Sporadic dumping** occurs when a manufacturer with unsold inventories wants to get rid of distressed and excess merchandise. To preserve its competitive position at home, the manufacturer must avoid starting a price war that could harm its home market. One way to find a solution involves destroying excess supplies, as in the example of Asian farmers dumping small chickens in the sea or burning them. Another way to solve the problem is to cut losses by selling for any price that can be realized. The excess supply is dumped abroad in a market where the product is normally not sold.

**Predatory dumping** is more permanent than sporadic dumping. This strategy involves selling at a loss to gain access to a market and perhaps to drive out competition. Once the competition is gone or the market established, the company uses its monopoly position to increase price. Some critics

## Legal Dimension 16.1

### Fish and chips

In 2003, the U.S. Department of Commerce made a final determination in two cases. It ruled that South Korea's Hynix Semiconductor had received unfair subsidies for its DRAMS from 2001 to mid-2002. If the U.S. International Trade Commission decides that these imports harm or threaten American industries, the U.S.A. could impose countervailing duties of 44.71 percent against Hynix.

In another case, the final determination was that Vietnam was dumping its products on the U.S. catfish market. If confirmed by the U.S. International Trade Commission, anti-dumping tariffs of up to 64 percent could be imposed. Vietnam strongly denied the dumping charges and accused the U.S.A. of protectionism. It claimed that its low-priced exports were due to the ability of Vietnamese producers to breed whiskered fish far more cheaply than American farmers. The U.S.A. countered by saying that, due to Vietnam's "non-market economy," its supposedly low labor costs could not be measured properly against those of a free market. In addition, U.S. farmers were successful in persuading the U.S. Congress to force Vietnam to change the name of its catfish to the Vietnamese terms "tra" and "basa."

*Sources*: "U.S. May Slap Big Tariffs on Two Imports," *Bangkok Post*, June 19, 2003; and "Vietnam Fears Tariffs on Shrimp," *San José Mercury News*, July 26, 2003.

question the allegation that predatory dumping is harmful by pointing out that if price is subsequently raised by the firm that does the dumping, former competitors can rejoin the market when it becomes more profitable again.

Hitachi was accused of employing predatory pricing for its EPROM (electrically programmable read-only memory) chips. A memo prepared by the company urged U.S. distributors to "quote 10 percent below competition (until) the bidding stops, when Hitachi wins." The Justice Department, after a year-long investigation, dropped the probe because it found that there was insufficient evidence to prosecute.

Zenith has long accused Japanese television manufacturers of using predatory dumping. It charged in its anti-trust suit that major Japanese manufacturers, through false billing and secret rebates, conspired to set low, predatory prices on TV sets in the U.S. market with the purpose of driving U.S. firms out of business in order to gain a monopoly. Both the Japanese and U.S. governments defended the Japanese firms' cooperation on the grounds of "sovereign compulsion." In other words, the defendants' cooperation was the result of compliance with Japanese government's export policy. After 16 years of legal maneuvering, the U.S. Supreme Court dismissed the conspiracy theory but ordered a trial concerning the dumping charge.

**Persistent dumping** is the most permanent type of dumping, requiring consistent selling at lower prices in one market than in others. This practice may be the result of a firm's recognition that markets are different in terms of overhead costs and demand characteristics. For example, a firm may assume that demand abroad is more elastic than it is at home. Based on this perception, the firm may decide to use incremental or marginal-cost pricing abroad while using full-cost pricing to cover fixed costs at home. This practice benefits foreign consumers, but it works to the disadvantage of local consumers. Japan, for example, is able to keep prices high at home, especially for consumer electronics, because it has no foreign competition there, but it is more than willing to lower prices in the U.S. market in order to gain or maintain market share. Japanese consumers, as a result, suffer by paying higher prices for Japanese products that are priced much lower in other markets.

The three kinds of dumping discussed above have one characteristic in common: each involves charging lower prices abroad than at home. It is possible, however, to have the opposite tactic – **reverse dumping**. In such a case, the overseas demand must be less elastic and the market will tolerate a higher price. Any dumping will thus be done in the manufacturer's home market by selling locally at a lower price.

## Legal aspects of dumping

Whether or not dumping is illegal depends on whether the practice is tolerated in a particular country. Switzerland has no specific anti-dumping laws. Most countries, however, have dumping laws that set a minimum price or a floor on prices that can be charged in the market.

Illegal dumping occurs when the price charged drops below a specified level. What is the unfair or illegal price level? And what kind of evidence is needed to substantiate a charge of dumping? The case of Melex golf carts from Poland illustrates the difficulty in determining a fair price. The success of Melex in the U.S.A. led to an accusation of dumping. The U.S. Treasury Department was unable to ascertain whether Melex's U.S. price was lower than prices at home in Poland because Poland has no golf-courses and no demand for such a product. The cost of production was unsuitable for determining its fair price. Poland, as a socialist economy, does not allow market forces to fully dictate the costs of factors of production. For this reason, the 1974 Trade Act does not allow production costs in a communist/socialist country to be used for comparison purposes.

To determine fair costs, the Treasury began to use a small Canadian manufacturer's costs as reference prices, only to see the Canadian firm stop making golf carts. In addition, Poland protested that the Canadian firm's production costs were too high and were unsuitable for comparison. The Treasury's next step was to rely on reference prices of a comparable product from free-market countries. Mexico and Spain were chosen because they were considered to be similar to Poland in terms of their level of economic development. Even though Mexico and Spain do not produce golf carts, they were used anyway to determine what their production costs would be if they produced such a product. After extensive review and discussion, the ruling was that the "constructed" value did not differ appreciably from Melex's actual price.

The 1980 ruling did not end the matter. The American producers still wanted Melex to pay the dumping charges for the years 1979 to 1980, and the Commerce Department's 1992 review imposed a duty of $599,053.51 plus interest. Melex has continued to fight the case which has outlasted five U.S. administrations, Poland's martial law, and the Soviet Union empire.[13]

One item of evidence of dumping occurs when a product is sold at less than fair value. The Commerce Department, for example, made a final determination that imports of certain small business telephone systems and sub-assemblies from Japan and Taiwan were being sold in America at less than fair value. Subsequently, the U.S. International Trade Commission made final determinations and found injury to industries in the U.S.A. from such imports. The Commission's injury finding led to anti-dumping duties being placed on imported products to offset their price advantage.

Another example of dumping evidence is a product sold at a price below its home-market price or production cost. The U.S.A. relies on the official U.S. trigger price, which is designed to curb dumping by giving an early signal of an unacceptable import price. In the case of steel, the trigger price sets a minimum price on imported steel that is pegged to the cost of producing steel in Japan. According to the General Accounting Office, some 40 percent of all imports at one time were priced below the trigger price.

To provide relief, the Antidumping Act requires the U.S. Department of Commerce to impose duties equal to the dumping margin. The anti-dumping duty is based on the amount by which the foreign market value or constructed value exceeds the purchase price or an exporter's sale price.

Petitioning or threatening to petition can create harassment effects by forcing foreign firms to restrain sales. Due to investigations and the threat of duties, importers frequently reduce shipments, increase prices, or do both.

It is understandable why domestic firms want anti-dumping policies. However, whether such policies benefit the economy is another issue altogether. As concluded by an economist of the International Monetary Fund, "antidumping, as currently practiced, is anticompetitive, threatens to further distort trade patterns, and undercuts the benefits of multilateral liberalization efforts."[14] Indeed, the U.S. International Trade Commission's study ("The Economic Effects of Antidumping and Countervailing Duty Orders and Suspension Agreements") has come to the conclusion that the overall effect of anti-dumping duties is negative.

The U.S.A. deems dumping to be illegal if: (1) the Department of Commerce makes a final determination that dumping has taken place, and (2) the International Trade Commission rules that such imports harm or threaten the U.S. industries. In the case of dynamic random access microchips (DRAMs), most American producers ceased production under pressure of low-price imports, primarily those from South Korea. Micron Technologies, the only significant remaining producer, suspected Taiwanese and Korean manufacturers of unfair trade practices. In the end, the U.S. International Trade Commission ruled that the U.S. computer-chip industry was not harmed or threatened with injury by Taiwan imports that were sold for less than fair value, thus ending Micron's complaint. However, with regard to Korea, the Import Administration ruled that Korean manufacturers sold DRAMs in the U.S.A. at prices below their cost of production, and duties were imposed at the border.

Dumping is a controversial practice. Just as controversial are the anti-dumping laws, especially those of the U.S.A. The 1916 Antidumping Act of the United States infuriated the trading partners. As may be expected, these partners asked the WTO to intervene. The WTO ruled that the ancient U.S. law violated international trade rules. The U.S.A. appealed, arguing that the law was not about dumping but about anti-trust. The WTO appeals panel confirmed the lower court ruling, explaining that the penalties were too severe and that the standards for applying them were too weak.

Economists generally argue that the widely used anti-dumping measures have been abused for protectionist purposes. Over 1800 anti-dumping investigations have been initiated since 1995. While industrial countries have traditionally been the main users of such measures, developing countries have been more active in recent years; between 1994 and 2001, they initiated almost two-thirds of all investigations. Most anti-dumping actions have been concentrated in a small number of sectors, especially steel, chemicals, textiles, and consumer electronics, often at the low-tech end of product range.[15] For the U.S.A., import-sensitive companies (especially steelmakers) are responsible for filing nearly half of all dumping petitions.[16]

## How to dump (legally and illegally)

Dumping is a widespread practice. Exporters and their importers insist on its use when necessary, and will find ways to cancel the practice. One can learn from the Mitsui case. Mitsui was responsible for generating the largest dumping case and pleaded guilty to all 21 counts involving kickbacks and the falsifying of documents to customs officials in order to sell steel below trigger prices. Mitsui attempted to conceal its dumping activities through several means. It hid the origin of the Japanese steel products by disguising them as U.S. made (e.g., wire rope imported to Houston). It submitted false documents to conceal the true merchandise value and backdated invoices to avoid trigger prices. Furthermore, it gave its U.S customers a rebate equal to the difference between the nominal exchange rate and the actual exchange rate, and the calculations were made after product entry. These illegal rebates totaled $1.3 million between 1978 and 1981. Another deceptive method involved the use of damage claims. Mitsui honored false claims that goods were damaged during shipment and granted credits of $22,676 for damaged Korean wire nails without investigating or reporting these losses to its insurance company. In spite of these ingenious methods, Mitsui was exposed, and paid heavy fines for dumping and fraud.

Without doubt, dumping is a risky practice that can cause a great deal of embarrassment, in addition to the payment of large financial penalties. Thus, a preferable strategy is to use other means to legally overcome dumping laws. One method that can help avoid charges of dumping is to differentiate the exported item from the item being sold in the home market. By deliberately making the home product and its overseas version incomparable, there is no home-market price that can be used as a basis for price comparison. This may be one reason why Japanese car manufacturers market their automobiles under new or different names in the U.S.A. Another method used to circumvent dumping laws is to provide financing terms that can have the same effect as price reduction.

The dumping problem can also be overcome if the production of a product, rather than its importation, is carried out in the host country. This option has become necessary for Japanese manufacturers, who have no desire to lower prices in Japan because they do not have to contend with foreign competitors. The high prices at home, however, work to the disadvantage of Japanese manufacturers because it is easy to prove that they are engaged in dumping in the U.S. market. For Japanese DVD manufacturers, there is a dilemma: they cannot make their U.S. prices too low without violating dumping laws and yet the prices charged cannot be so high as to encourage Korean firms to move in and take market share away. One solution may be to manufacture the sets in the U.S.A. To minimize the higher costs prevailing in the U.S.A., Japanese firms could import as many components and parts from Japan as practical. As in the case of Japanese forklift makers, they were accused of dumping by the Hyster-Yale unit of NACCO Industries Inc. When the International Trade Commission ruled in Hyster's favor and when the U.S. government imposed import duties of up to 51.3 percent on Japanese models, the Japanese firms quickly set up U.S. assembly plants and were able to avoid paying the duties. By doing so, they held their U.S. market share at about 50 percent.

## Price distortion

Dumping laws are not the only cause of price variations. The power of the market force in setting prices can be moderated by a government's price policy. Few governments allow the market to set prices completely on its own accord. When a government is actively involved in buying and selling local and foreign goods, price deviations usually and readily follow. Because of the political influence of the agricultural sector in Japan, Japanese rice farmers are able to price their rice at several times more than U.S. prices, resulting in Japanese consumers paying double or triple the world price.

On most occasions, a government sets the price artificially high in order to discourage the domestic consumption of imported products. Generally, however, government policy is to keep prices artificially low in the case of necessities that are essentially for public welfare. A government's licensing policy and patent enforcement can affect market prices indirectly as well.

Inflation is often the primary cause of price controls. Inflation affects public welfare and encourages workers to demand higher wages. In addition, inflation increases the pressure of currency devaluation which will affect prices of virtually all products and services.

When a situation of price distortion exists, a company must devise a strategy to deal with it. In 1985, Argentina was experiencing an inflation rate of 1000 percent. Merchants knew that price controls were inevitable, and they increased prices rapidly and drastically in order to circumvent the restrictions when price controls were implemented. Another method of dealing with price controls involves the creation of a "new" product that is not subject to old or existing prices. A new brand name or a new package may or may not be adequate for this purpose.

Companies themselves are sometimes responsible for price distortion. The European Union has initiated an investigation to determine whether major film companies may have deliberately introduced mechanical differences in their products so as to enforce price differences across markets. The investigation centers on whether Disney and six other major film companies may have made their DVDs incompatible in different regions so as to prevent a disc bought in one country (e.g., the U.S.A.) from being played in Europe or elsewhere.[17]

Gruma is the world's top tortilla maker, and it derives more than two-thirds of its $3 billion-plus in sales from Mexico, its home market. Because of the skyrocketing prices, the Mexican government has imposed price controls on finished tortillas as well as the flour used to make them. While these price controls hurt Gruma's profit, the company is helped by its global expansion. It has been a supplier for Taco Bell Corp. for more than 20 years, and it makes tortillas and chips in 80 factories around the world, including one in Shanghai making tens of millions of tortillas a year for KFC in China. As commented by the Gruma's CEO, "We're able to think globally but respect tastes and preferences of each country where we operate."[18]

Price distortion can also happen because of counterfeiting. In China, an illegal copy of a DVD may be bought for less than a dollar. While Warner Bros sold a DVD for about $3 there, a relatively low price for a movie that was shown in the U.S.A. a few months earlier, the price was still too high. So the company has adopted a new pricing policy. The new price is now less than $2, and buyers get a genuine item that has higher quality, accurate subtitles, and other extras.[19]

## Price fixing

For a long time, Europe has tolerated or encouraged corporate cooperation. Some governments have supported price fixing to protect small shops. Germany does not permit retailers to reduce more than 3 percent off manufacturers' suggested prices, and books cannot be discounted. Cartels were legal in the Netherlands until 1996. The beer industry does not seem to have vigorous competition. Major brewers enjoy huge market shares in their home markets. Interbrew, the owner of brands Stella Artois and Abbaye de Leffe, makes almost 60 percent of beer consumed in Belgium. Heineken's market share in the Netherlands is about the same. These brewers own a large number of bars and often use exclusive deals that last up to 10 years, shutting out new entrants. Because of almost nonexistent price competition, critics believe that the brewers have a long history of collusion. Breweries naturally deny any price fixing or market conspiracy. A new EU law has taken effect which prohibits brewers dominant in their home markets from owning restaurants or cafés.[20]

The EU has begun to aggressively pursue anti-trust cases. European car manufacturers have long kept domestic prices 30 percent higher or more than they are abroad. When Volkswagen tried in 1998 to prevent German dealers from importing cheaper cars from Italy, the European Commission fined it more than $100 million. In addition, 15 shippers, including Britain's P&O Nedlloyd, Denmark's Maersk Line, and the U.S.'s Sea-Land Service, were fined a record $314 million. Furthermore, eight steel producers were fined $95 million for conspiring to fix prices of seamless-steel tubes.[21]

The European Commission assessed a fine of 750.7 million euros against a number of companies for operating a multinational cartel of electric-power switchgear makers. For 19 years, the cartel implemented an elaborate scheme. It fixed prices, allocated projects to each other, shared markets, and exchanged commercially important and confidential information. These manufacturers coordinated their bids, and European tenders were allocated according to the cartel rules based on global cartel quotas. Japanese companies agreed not to sell in Europe, and European companies agreed not to enter Japan. Germany's Siemens AG, France's Alstom SA, and Areva SA played leadership roles and thus had their fines increased by 50 percent. Siemens was given a fine of 419 million euros. Among the Japanese firms, Mitsubishi Electric Corp was fined 118 million euros.[22]

Many former communist and socialist countries have now moved in the direction of market-oriented prices. Since the start of the reforms in 1992, Russia has lifted price controls on more than 90 percent of wholesale and retail goods and has privatized most state-owned enterprises to varying degrees.[23]

Table 16.1 shows how prices in general differ greatly from country to country. Table 16.2, in contrast, shows prices of automobiles in particular. Table 16.3 shows the work time required to buy staple items (bread and rice) as well as a somewhat more discretionary item (Big Mac).

## Inflation

Once the price is set, it must still be adjusted periodically because of the impact of inflation. During 1985, the runaway inflation in Argentina made it easy to see that prices had to be adjusted upward on a sharp and continuous basis. Supermarkets there adjusted prices twice each day, and restaurants marked their prices in pencil to make easy daily changes. Argentine consumers rushed out to purchase goods as soon as they were paid, as a one-day delay could cost them dearly in terms of higher prices.

An inflationary environment creates numerous problems. A firm's price may be constrained by government price controls. In addition, it is difficult to guarantee prices over an extended period of time. Catalog houses, for example, face a dilemma because they can neither maintain the prices printed in their catalogs nor print new catalogs frequently. Any installment payment plan adds to the complexity.

Domestically and internationally, marketers must take time lag in getting payments into account. A country's inefficient banking system may be a cause of the delay. For example, Gosbank was once the central bank for all the states within the Soviet Union. The bank's dissolution drastically reduced the efficiency of the interstate banking system. Exporters and importers had to wait two or three months to clear payment orders, and the risk was too great at the time when inflation was high.

When a marketer operates within a highly inflationary environment, it must think like its customers in order to protect itself. There are several strategies that may be devised for this purpose.

**TABLE 16.1** Prices around the globe

| *City*[1] | *Excl. rent New York = 100* | *Incl. rent New York = 100* |
|---|---|---|
| Oslo | 121.5 | 94.6 |
| London | 110.6 | 105.5 |
| Copenhagen | 109.2 | 86.3 |
| Zurich | 107.4 | 87.3 |
| Tokyo | 106.8 | 93.4 |
| Geneva | 102.9 | 85.8 |
| New York | 100.0 | 100.0 |
| Dublin | 98.3 | 84.3 |
| Stockholm | 98.1 | 75.8 |
| Helsinki | 97.0 | 77.3 |
| Paris | 95.6 | 78.1 |
| Vienna | 95.0 | 74.0 |
| Luxembourg | 93.3 | 76.6 |
| Chicago | 92.2 | 82.2 |
| Los Angeles | 91.6 | 80.6 |
| Toronto | 88.5 | 71.4 |
| Brussels | 88.4 | 68.5 |
| Munich | 88.4 | 71.2 |
| Amsterdam | 87.7 | 73.0 |
| Montreal | 87.5 | 71.2 |
| Lyon | 87.2 | 66.0 |
| Miami | 87.0 | 70.5 |
| Frankfurt | 86.9 | 69.3 |
| Seoul | 85.8 | 73.9 |
| Milan | 83.1 | 68.5 |
| Berlin | 82.3 | 64.6 |
| Hong Kong | 82.1 | 73.0 |
| Barcelona | 81.5 | 65.6 |
| Rome | 81.3 | 67.6 |
| Sydney | 80.4 | 69.0 |
| Madrid | 80.0 | 66.2 |
| Singapore | 76.6 | 62.9 |
| Istanbul | 76.3 | 61.6 |
| Nicosia | 74.7 | 66.2 |
| Auckland | 74.4 | 60.6 |
| Dubai | 74.0 | 66.1 |
| Athens | 73.0 | 57.4 |
| Lisbon | 72.3 | 62.1 |
| Tel Aviv | 69.2 | 55.2 |

**TABLE 16.1** *continued*

| *City*[1] | *Excl. rent New York = 100* | *Incl. rent New York = 100* |
|---|---|---|
| Taipei | 68.9 | 57.2 |
| Moscow | 65.6 | 56.8 |
| Sao Paulo | 65.1 | 53.6 |
| Rio de Janeiro | 64.8 | 55.1 |
| Ljubljana | 64.4 | 48.7 |
| Manama | 64.0 | 54.8 |
| Warsaw | 63.7 | 49.5 |
| Caracas | 63.4 | 52.8 |
| Santiago de Chile | 63.1 | 54.3 |
| Tallinn | 62.0 | 48.6 |
| Mexico City | 60.7 | 49.2 |
| Johannesburg | 59.7 | 47.2 |
| Budapest | 58.6 | 46.7 |
| Bogotá | 56.9 | 42.3 |
| Bangkok | 55.3 | 41.0 |
| Prague | 53.8 | 42.6 |
| Riga | 52.7 | 40.2 |
| Jakarta | 51.8 | 44.4 |
| Bucharest | 51.6 | 43.3 |
| Bratislava | 50.4 | 39.6 |
| Shanghai | 50.3 | 39.3 |
| Sofia | 50.1 | 40.0 |
| Beijing | 49.6 | 39.6 |
| Vilnius | 49.4 | 37.7 |
| Lima | 49.1 | 35.9 |
| Nairobi | 48.4 | 39.7 |
| Kiev | 47.8 | 40.6 |
| Manila | 46.7 | 35.2 |
| Delhi | 42.8 | 34.6 |
| Buenos Aires | 41.9 | 32.1 |
| Mumbai | 38.5 | 41.5 |
| Kuala Lumpur | 36.8 | 28.2 |

*Notes*

**Methodology**: the cost of a weighted shopping basket geared to Western European consumer habits containing 122 goods and services.

1 Listed according to value of index (price level without rent).

*Source*: *Prices and Earnings* (Zurich: UBS AG, 2006, 8).

**TABLE 16.2** Car prices and maintenance costs

| *City* | *Mid-price car* | *Price*[1] *U.S.$* | *Tax*[2] *U.S.$* | *Fuel*[3] *U.S.$* |
|---|---|---|---|---|
| Amsterdam | VW Golf Comfortline 2.0 FSI | 31,843 | 362 | 1.72 |
| Athens | VW Passat 2.0 2005 | 33,538 | 449 | 1.16 |
| Auckland | Toyota Corolla GL 1.8 | 19,651 | 131 | 1.02 |
| Bangkok | Toyota Corolla 1.8 | 22,460 | 46 | 0.69 |
| Barcelona | Seat Ibiza | 25,407 | 82 | 1.27 |
| Beijing | Hyundai Elantra | 16,164 | 20 | 0.55 |
| Berlin | VW Golf Comfort | 25,154 | 136 | 1.61 |
| Bogotá | Renault Megane | 20,484 | 241 | 1.13 |
| Bratislava | Skoda Oktavia | 21,634 | 97 | 1.26 |
| Brussels | Renault Megane Sedan 2.0 | 24,611 | 406 | 1.61 |
| Bucharest | Skoda Octavia Classic 1.9 TDI | 19,114 | 20 | 1.24 |
| Budapest | Opel Astra 1.8 Ecotec | 18,098 | 92 | 1.26 |
| Buenos Aires | Peugeot 206 | 13,925 | n.a. | 0.64 |
| Caracas | Chevrolet Aveo 1.6 | 15,614 | 31 | 0.50 |
| Chicago | 2005 Honda Accord | 23,300 | 78 | 0.77 |
| Copenhagen | Toyota Corolla 1.6 | 40,098 | 404 | 1.66 |
| Delhi | Mitsubishi Lancer 2.0 | 17,918 | n.a | 1.12 |
| Dubai | Mitsubishi Lancer 2006, 1.3GL | 10,491 | 127 | 0.41 |
| Dublin | Peugeot 307 1.6 HDI | 30,432 | 499 | 1.38 |
| Frankfurt | Golf Sportline | 30,818 | 163 | 1.53 |
| Geneva | VW Golf 2.31 V5 | 28,341 | 193 | 1.31 |
| Helsinki | Toyota Corolla 1.6VVT | 26,565 | 154 | 1.59 |
| Hong Kong | Honda Civic | 20,621 | 747 | 1.90 |
| Istanbul | Peugeot 307 | 21,348 | 365 | 1.97 |
| Jakarta | Toyota Altis G 1.8 2006 | 30,596 | 209 | 0.53 |
| Johannesburg | VW Golf | 21,210 | 20 | 0.89 |
| Kiev | Skoda Fabia | 18,190 | 10 | 0.83 |
| Kuala Lumpur | Proton | 15,083 | 32 | 0.46 |
| Lima | Toyota Corolla | 14,276 | 201 | 1.12 |
| Lisbon | VW Golf 1.9TDI | 36,663 | 150 | 1.51 |
| Ljubljana | Skoda Octavia | 19,513 | 126 | 1.18 |
| London | Ford Focus 1.8 Zetec | 19,609 | 307 | 1.61 |
| Los Angeles | Honda Civic Sedan | 16,000 | 98 | 0.82 |
| Luxembourg | VW Golf GT 2000 TDI | 29,768 | 25 | 1.31 |
| Lyon | Renault Megane 21 | 25,395 | 162 | 1.54 |
| Madrid | Renault Megane | 20,992 | n.a | 1.31 |
| Manama | Toyota Corolla | 15,822 | 53 | 0.27 |
| Manila | Nissan Sentra GX 1.3 | 11,983 | 34 | 0.75 |
| Mexico City | Sentra Nissan | 12,697 | 299 | 0.68 |

**TABLE 16.2** *continued*

| *City* | *Mid-price car* | *Price*[1] *U.S.$* | *Tax*[2] *U.S.$* | *Fuel*[3] *U.S.$* |
|---|---|---|---|---|
| Miami | Honda Civic | 23,000 | n.a. | n.a. |
| Milan | Grande Punto Sedan 1.4 | 18,820 | 212 | 1.57 |
| Montreal | Toyota Corrola LE 1.81 | 14,470 | 221 | 0.94 |
| Moscow | Toyota Avensis 2.0 | 29,888 | 11 | 0.64 |
| Mumbai | Maruti Suzuki Esteem | 11,241 | n.a. | 1.09 |
| Munich | VW Golf 5 1.9 TDI | 26,059 | 113 | 1.56 |
| Nairobi | Peugeot 406 2l | n.a. | n.a. | 1.03 |
| New York | Ford Focus ZX4-S | 13,745 | 85 | 0.83 |
| Nicosia | Opel Vectra 1800cc | 33,584 | 94 | 1.13 |
| Oslo | Volvo V50 2006 | 39,148 | 433 | 1.73 |
| Paris | Peugeot 307 1.4 | 21,535 | 290 | 1.60 |
| Prague | Skoda Octavia 1.8 | 21,107 | 378 | 1.26 |
| Riga | Toyota Avensis 1.8 | 26,249 | 42 | 1.03 |
| Rio de Janeiro | VW Golf 1.8 | 22,785 | 548 | 1.24 |
| Rome | Fiat Punto 1.9 MJT | 22,439 | 325 | 1.60 |
| Santiago de Chile | Peugeot 206 | 11,416 | 210 | 1.06 |
| Sao Paulo | Ford Fiesta Sedan 1.6 | 14,566 | 549 | 1.32 |
| Seoul | Samsung AM5 | 23,034 | 124 | 0.89 |
| Shanghai | Fiat Siena | 9,947 | 249 | 0.57 |
| Singapore | Toyota Camry 2000cc | 49,318 | 1233 | 1.12 |
| Sofia | Opel Astra Classic | 15,481 | 36 | 1.09 |
| Stockholm | Volvo S 40 | 26,576 | 211 | 1.46 |
| Sydney | Toyota Corolla Ascent Sedan | 14,754 | 187 | 0.89 |
| Taipei | Toyota Altis 1.8E 2006 | 25,064 | 348 | 0.81 |
| Tallinn | Toyota Corolla 1.61 | 20,050 | n.a. | 1.10 |
| Tel Aviv | n.a | n.a | n.a | n.a. |
| Tokyo | Honda Accord 20A | 19,819 | 338 | 1.23 |
| Toronto | Ford Focus ZX3 SE | 19,993 | 64 | 0.89 |
| Vienna | VW Golf 1.9 TDI | 25,449 | 526 | 1.30 |
| Vilnius | VW Passat Comforline | 27,501 | 24 | 1.12 |
| Warsaw | Ford Focus II 1,6 | 17,241 | 408 | 1.22 |
| Zurich | VW Golf 1.6 L | 22,240 | 255 | 1.22 |

*Notes*

1 Purchase price (including sales taxes) of a popular mid-range car (five-door, standard equipment).

2 Annual vehicle tax and/or annual registration fee.

3 Gas price per liter at the time of the survey (February to the end of April 2006).

n.a. = not available.

*Source*: *Prices and Earnings* (Zurich: UBS AG, 2006, 21).

**TABLE 16.3** Work time required to buy . . .

| *City* | *1 Big Mac in minutes* | *1kg of bread in minutes* | *1kg of rice in minutes* |
|---|---|---|---|
| Amsterdam | 19 | 10 | 9 |
| Athens | 26 | 10 | 20 |
| Auckland | 14 | 13 | 5 |
| Bangkok | 67 | 49 | 22 |
| Barcelona | 21 | 16 | 10 |
| Beijing | 44 | 42 | 29 |
| Berlin | 17 | 10 | 17 |
| Bogotá | 97 | 59 | 25 |
| Bratislava | 55 | 21 | 20 |
| Brussels | 20 | 12 | 12 |
| Bucharest | 69 | 31 | 25 |
| Budapest | 48 | 14 | 24 |
| Buenos Aires | 56 | 18 | 24 |
| Caracas | 85 | 76 | 13 |
| Chicago | 12 | 18 | 10 |
| Copenhagen | 18 | 12 | 6 |
| Delhi | 59 | 22 | 36 |
| Dubai | 25 | 11 | 12 |
| Dublin | 15 | 7 | 9 |
| Frankfurt | 16 | 9 | 17 |
| Geneva | 16 | 10 | 7 |
| Helsinki | 19 | 17 | 9 |
| Hong Kong | 17 | 26 | 11 |
| Istanbul | 48 | 14 | 36 |
| Jakarta | 86 | 47 | 36 |
| Johannesburg | 30 | 12 | 11 |
| Kiev | 55 | 19 | 21 |
| Kuala Lumpur | 33 | 21 | 9 |
| Lima | 86 | 37 | 19 |
| Lisbon | 32 | 20 | 10 |
| Ljubljana | 35 | 37 | 30 |
| London | 16 | 5 | 5 |
| Los Angeles | 11 | 18 | 10 |
| Luxembourg | 17 | 14 | 12 |
| Lyon | 24 | 15 | 15 |
| Madrid | 19 | 15 | 8 |
| Manama | 24 | 28 | 22 |
| Manila | 81 | 64 | 29 |
| Mexico City | 82 | 53 | 22 |
| Miami | 12 | 20 | 11 |

**TABLE 16.3** *continued*

| *City* | *1 Big Mac in minutes* | *1kg of bread in minutes* | *1kg of rice in minutes* |
|---|---|---|---|
| Milan | 20 | 17 | 15 |
| Montreal | 17 | 17 | 9 |
| Moscow | 25 | 12 | 12 |
| Mumbai | 70 | 14 | 32 |
| Munich | 17 | 11 | 15 |
| Nairobi | 91 | 32 | 33 |
| New York | 13 | 16 | 8 |
| Nicosia | 19 | 9 | 8 |
| Oslo | 18 | 14 | 6 |
| Paris | 21 | 16 | 13 |
| Prague | 39 | 14 | 14 |
| Riga | 28 | 24 | 23 |
| Rio de Janeiro | 53 | 40 | 19 |
| Rome | 25 | 23 | 19 |
| Santiago de Chile | 56 | 32 | 21 |
| Sao Paulo | 38 | 30 | 11 |
| Seoul | 29 | 28 | 13 |
| Shanghai | 38 | 35 | 23 |
| Singapore | 22 | 26 | 10 |
| Sofia | 69 | 19 | 31 |
| Stockholm | 21 | 18 | 15 |
| Sydney | 14 | 15 | 5 |
| Taipei | 20 | 18 | 11 |
| Tallinn | 39 | 24 | 21 |
| Tel Aviv | n.a. | n.a. | n.a. |
| Tokyo | 10 | 16 | 12 |
| Toronto | 14 | 10 | 6 |
| Vienna | 16 | 13 | 10 |
| Vilnius | 43 | 18 | 24 |
| Warsaw | 43 | 17 | 18 |
| Zurich | 15 | 10 | 5 |

*Notes*

**Methodology**: price of the product divided by the weighted net hourly wage in 14 professions.

n.a. = not available.

*Source*: *Prices and Earnings* (Zurich: UBS AG, 2006, 11).

First, merchants must collect their accounts receivable quickly. To protect itself, American Express requires its Argentine cardholders to pay their charge account purchases even before the bills are sent. Second, a product may be modified by reducing the quantity or eliminating extra frills so that an affordable price can be achieved. Third, sometimes it may be better not to make a sale. Some Argentine retailers and distributors felt that they would come out ahead by closing their stores for a month instead of making sales because their inventories would greatly appreciate in value over the interval. Fourth, the marketer can insulate itself against the declining value of a depreciating local currency by posting its prices in terms of an appreciating hard currency.

Another means of protection is through the accounting system. A company has the option of valuing its inventory and costs of goods sold based on either the **FIFO** (first in, first out) or **LIFO** (last in, first out) basis. During a period of stable prices, it may not matter much which method is used, but in a country experiencing high inflation, it may turn out to be a matter of survival for a marginal company as to which accounting inventory valuation method is used.

The FIFO method will understate the cost of goods sold during a period of high inflation, and this will result in excessive paper profits that are subject to the payment of higher taxes and dividends. The problem is made more difficult because there is less cash available for the replenishment of inventory, which when purchased is acquired at much higher prices. Thus, a firm is wise to adopt the LIFO system, which will improve the amount of cash flow. By assuming that the last item bought at a higher price will be the first item to be sold, the cost of goods sold is overstated, resulting in less profit being generated. Subsequently, less tax and dividends will be paid, and there are more funds remaining for the purchase of new inventory. Anderson Clayton, for example, uses the LIFO method to reduce its tax liability in Mexico. The improvement in cash flow reduces the need to borrow funds in that uncertain monetary environment.

After World War I, several European economies experienced hyperinflation. Unbelievably, Germany recorded an astronomical 3.25 million percent in a single month in 1923. So modern hyperinflation is quite mild by comparison. The recent episodes of modern hyperinflation include Argentina (with a peak 12-month inflation rate of 20,266 percent in 1990), Bolivia (23,447 percent in 1985), Brazil (6821 percent in 1990), Peru (12,378 percent in 1990), and Ukraine (10,155 percent in 1993).[24] The most notorious case recently is Zimbabwe (100,000 percent).

It should be noted that there is a relationship between inflation and regulations.[25] For the EU members to join the monetary union, one of the criteria is that they must achieve an inflation rate of no more than 1.5 percent above the average of the three EU member countries with the most stable prices. The purpose of this requirement is to bring a country in line with low-inflation countries before introducing the euro.

## Transfer pricing

A common practice is for an MNC's many subsidiaries to trade among themselves or with the parent firm. For example, almost one-third of all U.S. exports go to U.S. subsidiaries and business affiliates overseas. According to the United Nations World Investment Report, intrafirm trading of goods and services among multinational corporations has soared, amounting to about one-third of total world trade.

Initially, it may seem that any price charged should be acceptable because the sales are among subsidiaries. If the selling price is relatively low, the profit is made by the buying unit. If the price is relatively high, the profit is made by the selling subsidiary. In the final analysis, the same amount of profit is still made by the parent firm whichever is the case. This situation, however, is complicated by taxation. The transfer prices used, therefore, must be carefully considered (see Figure 16.1). To comply with the complicated tax laws, the 500 biggest U.S. companies spend more than $1 billion a year, with half of the cost attributed to international tax rules.[26]

There are four basic methods used to determine transfer prices. The first method involves transfers at **direct manufacturing costs**. The problem with this method is that when a buying subsidiary acquires merchandise at a very low price it has no incentive to hold down expenses or to maximize profits. The selling unit is also likely to be unhappy for not showing profit, feeling that it is subsidizing an affiliate of the firm's operations.

The second technique involves a transfer at **direct manufacturing cost plus a predetermined markup** to cover additional expenses. Profit is produced and added at every stage. The disadvantage with this method is that the price generated may be too high because market conditions are given secondary consideration to the markups taken.

The third course of action involves the use of a **market-based transfer price**. The price, though competitive, may end up being too low for the selling subsidiary because production cost may not be considered.

The fourth and final process employs an **arm's length price** as a basis for determining transfer price. This price would be the price that unaffiliated traders would agree on for a particular transaction. The problem with using this method occurs when the product has no external buyers or is sold at different prices in different markets.

Cost-plus and market-based pricing were the most popular methods used both in more developed countries and less developed countries. The findings show that size and legal considerations (e.g., compliance with tax and custom regulations, anti-dumping and anti-trust legislation, and financial reporting rules of host countries) are influential in the use of market-based transfer pricing. However, the extent of economic development in host countries and economic restrictions (e.g., exchange controls, price controls, restrictions on imports, and political and social conditions) are either unimportant or secondary determinants of a market-based transfer pricing strategy. U.S. Treasury Regulation 1.482 prescribes the following transfer pricing methods: the uncontrolled price method, the resale method, the cost-plus method, and some other appropriate method when none of the methods described above is applicable.

Ordinarily, the parent firm should attempt to maximize its income in low-tax countries and minimize profit in high-tax markets. To minimize the income of a buying subsidiary in a high-tax country, use of the arm's length price is appropriate. In fact, any permissible costs should be added so that the price charged will be so high that it leaves the buyer with only a small profit subject to tax.

On the other hand, if the buying subsidiary is located in a low-tax country, its income should be maximized. This can be achieved by using a transfer price based on only direct production costs. In this case, the buyer will acquire the product for resale or use at a very low price. Its high profit is, however, subject only to low tax rates in this market. Although Cartier's corporate home is in low-tax Luxembourg, it wisely prices its watches so that most of the markup is collected by its lower taxed Swiss subsidiary.

Section 482 of the U.S. Internal Revenue Code requires arm's length dealing between related parties. An arm's length price or charge is defined as the amount or price that would be charged or would have been charged for the same product or service if independent transactions with unrelated

Where else can you find so many foreign tax specialists under one roof?
In whatever country you do business, you can benefit from the objective advice of Ernst & Young's foreign tax specialists. From M&A to transfer pricing, from business realignment to exploring the capital markets, our specialists do more than just advise on the tax implications of doing international business—they deliver integrated solutions that help you realize your goals. Visit our international tax website today. It will make a world of difference.
newrules
neweconomy™
ey.com/internationaltax
ERNST & YOUNG
FROM THOUGHT TO FINISH.™

**FIGURE 16.1** Tax laws and transfer pricing

parties under similar conditions were carried out. This requirement applies to (1) loans; (2) both goods and services (e.g., performance of marketing, managerial, technical, or other services for an affiliated party); and (3) possession, use, occupancy, loan, and assignment of tangible and intangible property.

If the IRS finds that adjustments are needed to correctly reflect a company's income, it is empowered to distribute, allocate, or apportion gross income, deductions, credits, or allowances among related organizations regardless of whether they are organized in the U.S.A. The purpose of the Internal Revenue code is to prevent a low intercompany transfer price that shifts income away from the U.S.A. At the same time, the application of the code is intended to be certain that the transfer price of a sale from a foreign company to a related U.S. company is not so high as to result in a small income being realized in the U.S.A. The U.S. Customs Service, however, has a different perspective – it keeps an eye out for low transfer prices, which in turn reduce customs duties and which may result in dumping.

The IRS employs several methods to determine an arm's length price. When available, comparable uncontrolled sales must be used. When such sales do not exist, the resale price method is the next alternative to be used. When the first two methods are not applicable, it is permissible to use the cost-plus method. Any other appropriate pricing method may be used only when it is reasonable and when the first three methods are not relevant.

In general, U.S. firms with foreign subsidiaries can minimize their U.S. taxes by overpaying the foreign subsidiaries for goods and services received or undercharging them for goods and services rendered. In the case of DHL Corp., the world's largest international air express network which links more than 80,000 cities in more than 200 countries, it was ordered by the IRS to pay $194 million in back income taxes and $75 million in penalties. The IRS determined that DHL and its subsidiaries shifted taxable income to a Hong Kong subsidiary. The IRS has also determined that, between 1966 and 1988, the various Hyatt companies underreported income by $100 million because they paid too little for the Hyatt brand and other services provided by the U.S. parent. A 1999 ruling has determined that the $10,000 one-time fee that Hyatt International paid for each hotel bearing the Hyatt name was much too low.[27]

According to President Clinton, the U.S.A. could bring in $45 billion in four years by taking care of the transfer pricing problem. The new U.S. regulations allow companies to have greater flexibility, judgment, and subjectivity in determining what they charge foreign operations for certain services. At first, it seems that the new regulations may encourage firms to be even more aggressive in their transfer pricing schemes to maximize profits. The IRS, however, feels that firms will have to be more careful because the "best method rule" requires them to identify the best way to determine the prices that they charge their other operations.

When possible and applicable, a U.S. company should try to maximize foreign tax credits since they can be used to reduce U.S. income tax. Moreover, it should consider locating a tax haven to shelter and maximize its income by using the tax haven to collect royalties, fees, dividends, and so on.

The OECD has published guidelines on transfer pricing. Most countries use the OECD guidelines to determine an arm's length price. Since 1990, the U.S. government has imposed penalties on companies that deviated from the OECD standard. One study assessed the impact of the penalty on the stock market valuation of Japanese multinationals with U.S. subsidiaries in the 1990s. It found that the U.S. transfer pricing penalty led to a loss of $56.1 billion in the cumulative market value of these firms.[28]

## Conclusion

To set a price, the concerns of all affected parties must be addressed. A manufacturer needs to make a profit. So do resellers, who demand an adequate margin for their services. Moreover, competitors' reactions in terms of their price responses must be anticipated. Finally, it is necessary to take into account both consumers and the value they place on the product.

Several factors must be taken into consideration in setting price, including cost, elasticity of demand, supply, product image (prestige), turnover, market share/volume, product life cycle, and the number of products involved. The optimum mix of these ingredients varies by product, market, and corporate objectives.

Price setting in the international context is further complicated by such factors as foreign exchange rates, relative labor costs, and relative inflation rates in various countries. Other important considerations are export packing costs and charges, transportation costs, tariffs, tax laws, and profit remittance restrictions.

## CASE 16.1 BLOOD DIAMONDS (PART II)

De Beers maintains its power by using a system that sells exclusively to 125 "sightholders" (diamond merchants from the world's leading diamond-cutting centers). These sightholders gather ten times a year in London to buy stones from De Beers' exclusive sales unit, the Central Selling Organization. They are a crucial link in the supply chain of brokers, cutters, and wholesalers that produce engagement rings and other jewelry of the world's fragmented $56 billion diamond retail trade. Sightholders do not have to buy what De Beers offers, but they will not be invited back for another "sight."

De Beers has two major problems. On the one hand, human rights groups accuse it of buying illicit (blood or conflict) diamonds from African rebels and rulers who use the proceeds to finance their wars. On the other hand, the company's usual strategy of hoarding diamonds is becoming more and more expensive. For a very long time, De Beers has accumulated raw gems so as to monitor the supply made available to the world as well as to control the world diamond prices. However, the strategy has become an expensive proposition because there are so many diamond producers, making it difficult for the company to keep absorbing the ever-increasing supply on its own.

De Beers has found a way to kill two birds with one stone. It uses the social problem (the controversy over blood diamonds) to address its commercial problems. The company has suspended all buying of diamonds outside of its own proprietary stones and its contractual purchases. It has announced plans to certify all diamonds sold to sightholders as non-conflict stones. It has told 125 sightholders that they will lose access to De Beers stones if they deal in blood diamonds.

The plan is to use its refusal to handle conflict diamonds to reinvent De Beers as a socially responsible crusader. To improve its image, De Beers has positioned itself as a "supplier of choice." While still wanting to maintain its global leadership for uncut diamonds worth $7 billion to $8 billion a year, it aims to become a branded, high-value diamond trader.

De Beers, also known as the syndicate, has another motive. It wants the world in general and the U.S. government in particular to forgive and forget its monopoly or cartel status. It is hopeful that the new image will help to convince American anti-trust regulators that it is no longer a monopolist that fixes prices of industrial diamonds. With the anti-trust problems being unresolved, De Beers cannot set up operations in the U.S.A. which is the world's largest retail market for polished stones. Half of the world's retail sales take place in American jewelry stores. As part of its rebranding campaign, the Central Selling Organization has become the Diamond Trading Co.

Diamonds have traditionally been graded and valued based on the four Cs – cut, color, clarity, and carat. Is it possible to make "country of origin" the fifth C in grading system? Canada is doing just that by touting its diamonds as politically correct.

Skeptics dismiss the idea as a gimmick. Some players, however, are counting on it, claiming that the fifth C is not just any country of origin but Canada. Boasting Canada's reputation as a peaceful, socially progressive country, and stressing that Canadian diamonds are mined under ethical, environmentally friendly conditions, these organizations are striving to distinguish Canadian diamonds from blood diamonds. If country of origin has always played a part in defining the quality of a product (e.g., Swiss watches, Italian leather, French wines), it is conceivable that it may work for Canadian diamonds.

Sirius Diamonds Inc. laser-engraves a polar bear on its Canadian stones. Henry Birks & Sons Inc. engraves its Canadian diamonds with a maple leaf and serial number. The government of the Northwest Territories provides a certificate for each diamond that is mined, cut, and polished there. Each certificate has a serial number that is engraved by laser on the diamond. However, some retailers complain that wholesalers are charging as much as 20 percent more for Canadian diamonds.

### Points to consider

1 Evaluate De Beers' pricing practice.
2 Evaluate De Beers' attempt to promote a new image.
3 Will consumers care where a diamond comes from?

*Sources*: "Why De Beers Washed Its Hands of Blood Diamonds," *San José Mercury News*, August 27, 2000; and "Political Correctness by the Carat," *Wall Street Journal*, April 20, 2003.

## Questions

1 Explain how exchange rate and inflation affect the way you price your product.
2 What is dumping? When does it become illegal? What can a seller do to circumvent antidumping regulations?
3 What methods may be used to compute a transfer price (for transactions between affiliated companies)?

## Discussion assignments and minicases

1 How should U.S. farmers price their products?
2 To protect itself, how should a marketer price its product in a country with high inflation?
3 Price haggling is an art. Discuss how one can haggle effectively.
4 Explain why U.S. car manufacturers prefer to use the "unbundling" approach in pricing their cars while their foreign competitors tend to use the "bundling" pricing approach.

## Notes


1 Matthew B. Myers, S. Tamer Cavusgil, and Adamantios Diamantopoulos, "Antecedents and Actions of Export Pricing Strategy: A Conceptual Framework and Research Propositions," *European Journal of Marketing* 36 (No. 1, 2002): 159–88.
2 Chol Lee and David A. Griffith, "The Marketing Strategy–Performance Relationships in an Export-driven Developing Economy: A Korean Illustration," *International Marketing Review* 21 (No. 3, 2004): 321–34.
3 Carl Arthur Solberg, Barbara Stottinger, and Attila Yaprak, "A Taxonomy of the Pricing Practices of Exporting Firms: Evidence from Austria, Norway, and the United States," *Journal of International Marketing* 14 (No. 1, 2006): 23–48.
4 Ivy S.N. Chen and Veronica Wong, "Successful Strategies of Newly Industrialised East Asian Firms in Europe," *European Journal of Marketing* 37 (No. 1, 2003): 275–97.
5 "BMW: Speeding Into a Tight Turn," *Business Week*, November 5, 2001, 54–5.
6 "Snuggling into the Voile Sheets," *Business Week*, December 4, 2006, 110–12.
7 "Hyundai Still Gets No Respect," *Business Week*, May 21, 2007, 68–70.
8 "A Cash-grab U.S. Exporters May Regret," *Business Week*, January 29, 2007, 28.
9 "Survival of the Biggest," *San José Mercury News*, April 15, 2007.
10 Jack L. Hervey, "Dollar Drop Helps Those Who Help Themselves," *Chicago Fed Letter*, March 1988.
11 Rajneesh Suri, Rolph E. Anderson, and Vassili Kotlov, "The Use of 9-ending Prices: Contrasting the U.S.A. with Poland," *European Journal of Marketing* 38 (No. 1/2, 2004): 56–72.
12 "EBay's China Lesson: Go Local," *San José Mercury News*, December 24, 2006.
13 "Legal Charges Keep Electric Golf Cart Going – to Court," *Wall Street Journal*, May 24, 1995.
14 Michael Leidy, "Antidumping: Unfair Trade or Unfair Remedy?" *Finance & Development*, March 1995, 27–9.
15 Hans Peter Lankes, "Market Access for Developing Countries," *Finance & Development*, September 2002, 8–13.
16 "A U.S. Trade Ploy That Is Starting to Boomerang," *Business Week*, July 29, 2002, 64–5.
17 "EU Launches DVD Price Probe," *The Nation*, June 13, 2001.
18 "Wrapping the Globe in Tortillas," *Business Week*, February 26, 2007, 54.
19 "Take That, You Pirates," *Business Week*, October 9, 2006, 57.
20 "Invasion of the Cartel Cops," *Business Week*, May 8, 2000, 130.
21 "Cartel Cops."
22 "Japan Firms Fined by EU," *Wall Street Journal*, January 25, 2007.
23 Harry G. Broadman, "Competition and Business Entry in Russia," *Finance & Development*, June 2001, 22–5.
24 Carmen M. Reinhart and Miguel A. Savastano, "The Realities of Modern Hyperinflation," *Finance & Development*, June 2003, 20–1.
25 "The Maastricht Inflation Criterion: Lessons to Learn," *IMF Survey*, October 16, 2006, 305.
26 "Taxing Multinationals: The Donnybrook Ahead," *Business Week*, September 9, 2002, 86–7.
27 "The Corporate Tax Game," *Business Week*, March 31, 2003, 81–2.
28 Lorraine Eden, Luis F. Juarez Valdez, and Dan Li, "Talk Softly but Carry a Big Stick: Transfer Pricing Penalties and the Market Valuation of Japanese Multinationals in the United States," *Journal of International Business Studies* 36 (2005): 398–414.

Chapter 17

# Pricing strategies

## Countertrade and terms of sale/payment

Money often costs too much.
Ralph Waldo Emerson

## Chapter outline

## Marketing strategy

**Noncash trade**

Malaysia's 15 billion ringgit ($3.95 billion) plan aims to expand and electrify 635 kilometers of railway that runs down the spine of Peninsular Malaysia. Most of the project will be financed by barter trade. The country will use palm oil to pay Indian and Chinese state-owned railway companies for more than 10 billion ringgit in construction contracts. Funds from palm oil sales are put in a special account and will be paid out to Indian and Chinese contractors as progress payments on the railway job. In the 1990s, Malaysia also used palm oil to buy Russian-built combat planes. Just like Malaysia, many Asian and Eastern and Central European countries have done countertrade deals. Thailand, for example, has exchanged 200,000 tons of 15 percent broken rice for such Indonesian goods as aircraft, freight train carriages, and ammonia. Indonesia, being cash-strapped, set up a countertrade agreement with Russia in 2003. In order to obtain four Sukhoi Su-30 fighter jets, four helicopters, and spare parts, Indonesia agreed to trade palm oil, tea, coffee and 15 other commodities. The deal was worth $150 million to $175 million.

*Sources*: "Indonesia Reportedly to Deal Goods for Arms," *San José Mercury News*, April 11, 2003.

## Purpose of chapter

The trade practices of Asian countries (e.g., Malaysia, Indonesia) and Eastern/Central European countries illustrate the fact that money is not the only means of payment. Due to the fact that many Eastern European countries and less developed nations often lack hard currency, they resort to alternative pricing mechanisms. International marketers may thus be forced to enter into some kind of countertrade scheme so as to do business with those countries. Although countertrade may be complex and time consuming, it is manageable. A section of this chapter is devoted to the examination of countertrade as an alternative method of trading. The various types of countertrade are discussed.

Another section of this chapter deals with pricing terms used in international quotations. To be competitive, it is the job of a responsible exporter to provide a quotation that is complete and meaningful. It is important for both the buyer and the seller to specify and know the point of delivery where risk shifts from one party to another. A poorly prepared quotation results in confusion and possibly a loss of sale.

Finally, the chapter ends with a review of payment methods. The different payment methods involve a certain degree of financing and risk. It is thus critical to specify the timing and means of payment that are satisfactory to both parties. A misunderstanding regarding delivery terms may cause an exporter to become responsible for unintended shipping costs. To make the matter worse, by unknowingly failing to meet contractual obligations, the exporter may not be able to collect payment. While certain safeguards are necessary, they should not be so cumbersome or costly as to deter business.

## Countertrade

**Countertrade**, one of the oldest forms of trade, is a government mandate to pay for goods and services with something other than cash. It is a practice which requires a seller, as a condition of sale, to commit contractually to reciprocate and undertake certain business initiatives that compensate and benefit the buyer. In short, a goods-for-goods deal is countertrade.

Unlike *monetary trade*, suppliers are required to take customers' products for their use or for resale. In most cases there are multiple deals that are separate yet related, and a contract links these separable transactions. Countertrade may involve several products, and such products may move at different points in time while involving several countries. Monetary payments may or may not be part of the deal.

There are three primary reasons for countertrade: (1) countertrade provides a trade financing alternative to those countries that have international debt and liquidity problems, (2) countertrade relationships may provide developing countries and MNCs with access to new markets, and (3) countertrade fits well conceptually with the resurgence of bilateral trade agreements between governments.[1] The advantages of countertrade cluster around three subjects: market access, foreign exchange, and pricing. Table 17.1 lists potential motives for countertrade.

Countertrade offers several advantages. It moves inventory for both a buyer and a seller. The seller gains other benefits, too. Besides the tax advantage, the seller is able to sell the product at full price and can convert the inventory to an account receivable. The cash-tight buyer that lacks hard currency is able to use any cash received for other operating purposes.

**TABLE 17.1** Potential motives for countertrade

| | *Types of countertrade* | | | | |
|---|---|---|---|---|---|
| | *BT*[1] | *CA/ST*[2] | *CP*[3] | *BB*[4] | *OF*[5] |
| Avoids using foreign exchange | Yes | Yes | No | Rarely | No |
| Avoids repayment of external debt | Yes | Yes | No | No | No |
| Hides price discounts | Yes | Yes | No | No | No |
| Shifts risk | Yes | Yes | Yes | Yes | Sometimes |
| Substitute for foreign direct investment | No | No | Yes | Yes | Yes |
| Political factors dominant | No | Yes | No | No | Yes |

*Notes*
1 BT Barter
2 CA/ST Clearing arrangement/switch trading
3 CP Counterpurchase
4 BB Buyback
5 OF Offset.

*Source:* Jean-François Hennart, "Some Empirical Dimensions of Countertrade," *Journal of International Business Studies* 21 (2) (1990, 248).

Countertrade constitutes an estimated 5 to 30 percent of total world trade. Countertrade greatly proliferated in the 1980s. Perhaps the single most important contributing factor is LDCs' decreasing ability to finance their import needs through bank loans.

Regarding Russia, its officials have estimated that 90 percent or more of the transactions having to do with "critical imports" involve reciprocal trade exchanges. Countertrade in Russia may proliferate because, with the Russian banking system in disarray, it is difficult to arrange traditional export financing (e.g., letter of credit). Non-cash forms of payment may account for as much as two-thirds of all transactions in Russia. There are thousands of intermediaries acting as barter specialists. One deal involves a governor paying for a $17 million airplane by trading gas paid to his government in lieu of energy royalties, giving a middleman commission of 10 percent. Velta Co., once one of the Soviet Union's biggest bicycle makers, stays in business by swapping its bicycles for raw materials and electric power. The company's 4000 employees have to accept one bicycle a month in lieu of a paycheck.[2]

Russia is a virtual economy dominated by barter, mutual nonpayment, and money surrogates, such as promissory notes (veksel), and tax authorities have been forced to collect in-kind tax payments. Countertrade is a consequence of failures in corporate governance. In this regard, countertrade is both a means of avoiding payment of private or public debts in cash and a way of concealing the real state of affairs – not only from the tax authorities but also from minority shareholders and employees. Noncash settlements make it possible for owner-managers to degrade assets and divert cash flows in a less transparent way.[3]

Countertrade is pervasive in Russia for a number of reasons. Direct subsidies to enterprises were cut, and demand for many industrial products fell after price and trade liberalization. The ensuing credit crunch could not be solved by banks because bank lending to enterprises is very limited. As a result, the enterprises ran up arrears to suppliers and finally used offsets to settle these arrears. The state itself also fostered the non-cash economy by allowing tax offsets. The federal and local governments accepted goods in lieu of tax payments, and state utilities also accepted most of their receipts in kind.[4]

Non-cash transactions, by substituting for trade and bank credit, help firms to survive in a credit-constrained environment. In the case of time-lagged nonmonetary deals, an enterprise essentially enjoys a credit from its partner because a payment does not have to be made until later. Even in the case of a spot barter, a seller is forced to accept either goods now or money later, being mindful of the fact that "later" may turn out to be "never." This artificial demand allows goods to be produced by the old-style, inefficient enterprises that should have gone out of business.[5]

Because of the nontransparent nature of countertrade, there are implicit subsidies from the state in the form of tax offsets which amount to tax discounts. Because barter prices are arbitrary, tax evasion is facilitated. In addition, by allowing inefficient enterprises to remain, countertrade acts as an entry barrier for new firms. There is a vicious cycle: barter makes it harder to screen firms and monitor their performance. As their access to bank credit is further reduced, they have to barter even more.

## Types of countertrade

There are several types of countertrade, including barter, counterpurchase, compensation trade, switch trading, offsets, and clearing agreements. Figure 17.1 provides a classification of countertrade.

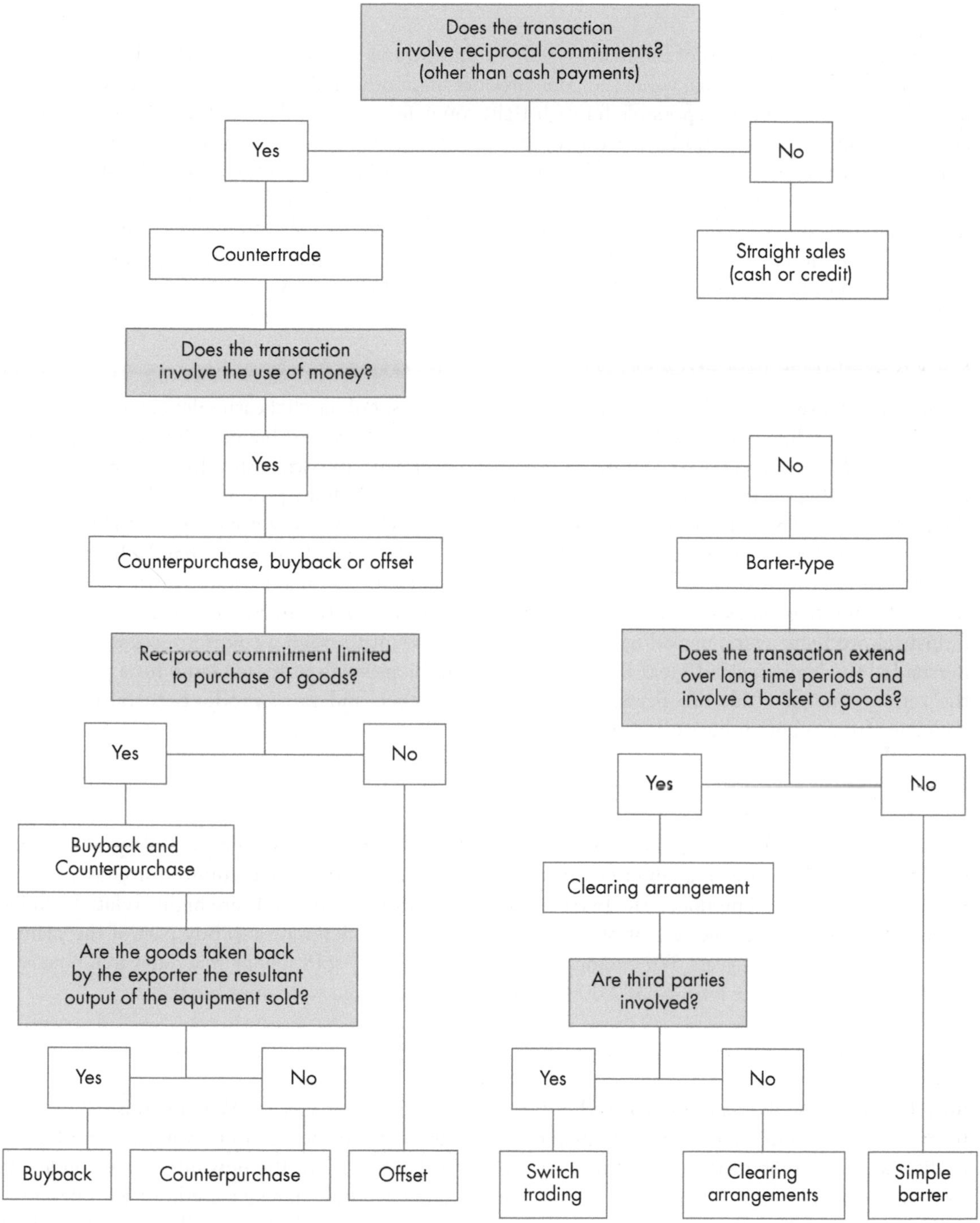
Does the transaction involve reciprocal commitments? (other than cash payments)
Yes
No
Countertrade
Straight sales (cash or credit)
Does the transaction involve the use of money?
Yes
No
Counterpurchase, buyback or offset
Barter-type
Reciprocal commitment limited to purchase of goods?
Does the transaction extend over long time periods and involve a basket of goods?
Yes
No
Yes
No
Buyback and Counterpurchase
Clearing arrangement
Are the goods taken back by the exporter the resultant output of the equipment sold?
Are third parties involved?
Yes
No
Yes
No
Buyback
Counterpurchase
Offset
Switch trading
Clearing arrangements
Simple barter

**FIGURE 17.1** Classification of forms of countertrade

*Source*: Jean-François Hennart, "Some Empirical Dimensions of Countertade", *Journal of International Business Studies* 20 (245).

### Barter

**Barter**, possibly the simplest of the many types of countertrade, is a one-time direct and simultaneous exchange of products of equal value (i.e., one product for another). By removing money as a medium of exchange, barter makes it possible for cash-tight countries to buy and sell. Although price must be considered in any countertrade, price is only implicit at best in the case of barter. For example, Chinese coal was exchanged for the construction of a seaport by the Dutch, and Polish coal was exchanged for concerts given by a Swedish band in Poland. In these cases, the agreement dealt with how many tons of coal were to be given by China and Poland rather than the actual monetary value of the construction project or concerts. It is estimated that about half of the U.S. corporations engage in some form of barter, primarily within the local markets of the U.S.A.

### Counterpurchase (parallel barter)

**Counterpurchase** occurs when there are two contracts or a set of parallel cash sales agreements, each paid in cash. Unlike barter, which is a single transaction with an exchange price only implied, a counterpurchase involves two separate transactions – each with its own cash value. A supplier sells a facility or product at a set price and orders unrelated or nonresultant products to offset the cost to the initial buyer. Thus, the buyer pays with hard currency, whereas the supplier agrees to buy certain products within a specified period. Therefore, money does not need to change hands. In effect, the practice allows the original buyer to earn back the currency. GE won a contract worth $300 million to build aircraft engines for Sweden's JAS fighters for cash only after agreeing to buy Swedish industrial products over a period of time in the same amount through a counterpurchase deal. Iraq persuaded the New Zealand Meat Board to sell $200 million-worth of frozen lamb for a purchase of the same value of crude oil. Brazil exports vehicles, steel, and farm products to oil-producing countries from whom it buys oil in return.

### Compensation trade (buyback)

A **compensation trade** requires a company to provide machinery, factories, or technology and to buy products made from this machinery over an agreed-upon period. Unlike counterpurchase, which involves two unrelated products, the two contracts in a compensation trade are highly related. Under a separate agreement to the sale of plant or equipment, a supplier agrees to buy part of the plant's output for a number of years. For example, a Japanese company sold sewing machines to China and received payment in the form of 300,000 pairs of pajamas. Russia welcomes buyback.

### Switch trading

**Switch trading** involves a triangular rather than bilateral trade agreement. When goods, all or part, from the buying country are not easily usable or saleable, it may be necessary to bring in a third party to dispose of the merchandise. The third party pays hard currency for the unwanted merchandise at a considerable discount. A hypothetical example could involve Italy having a credit of $4 million for Austria's hams, which Italy cannot use. A third-party company may decide to sell Italy some desired merchandise worth $3 million for a claim on the Austrian hams. The price differential or margin is accepted as being necessary to cover the costs of doing business this way. The company can then sell the acquired hams to Switzerland for Swiss francs, which are freely convertible to dollars.

### Offset

In an **offset**, a foreign supplier is required to manufacture/assemble the product locally and/or purchase local components as an exchange for the right to sell its products locally. In effect, the supplier has to manufacture at a location that may not be optimal from an economic standpoint. Offsets are often found in purchases of aircraft and military equipment. One study found that more than half of the companies countertrading with the Middle East were in the defense industry and that the most common type of countertrade was offset.[6] These companies felt that countertrade was a required element in order to enter these markets.

In China, foreign car manufacturers are not permitted to produce cars there unless they have a local partner. China wants to gain manufacturing skills and has been pressuring global car manufacturers to share knowledge. To accelerate the pace of technology transfer, the government has pushed state-controlled car companies to go beyond making foreign-brand cars. Honda and its local partner have decided to create a new brand exclusively for the Chinese market.[7]

### Clearing agreement

A **clearing agreement** is a clearing account barter with no currency transaction required. With a line of credit being established in the central banks of the two countries, the trade in this case is continuous, and the exchange of products between two governments is designed to achieve an agreed-upon value or volume of trade tabulated or calculated in nonconvertible "clearing account units." For example, the former Soviet Union's rationing of hard currency limited imports and payment of copiers. Rank Xerox decided to circumvent the problem by making copiers in India for sale to the Soviets under the country's "clearing" agreement with India. The contract set forth goods, ratio of exchange, and time length for completion. Any imbalances after the end of the year were settled by credit into the next year, acceptance of unwanted goods, payment of penalty, or hard currency payment. Although nonconvertible in theory, clearing units in practice may be sold at a discount to trading specialists who use them to buy saleable products.

## Problems and opportunities

Although countertrade is a common and growing practice, it has been criticized on several fronts. First, countertrade is considered by some as a form of protectionism that poses a new threat to world trade. Such countries as Sweden, Australia, Spain, Brazil, Indonesia, and much of Eastern Europe demand reciprocity in order to impose a discipline on their balance of payments. In other words, imports must be offset by exports. Indonesia links government import requirements in contracts worth more than Rp. 500 million to the export of Indonesia products, other than oil and natural gas, in an equivalent amount to the foreign-exchange value of the contract.

Second, countertrade is alleged to be nothing but "covert dumping." To compensate any supplying partners for the nuisance of taking another product as payment, a countertrading country frequently trades its products away at a discount. If the countertrading country discounts directly by selling its goods itself in another market instead of through a foreign firm, dumping would clearly occur. However, according to an International Trade Commission study, the practice does not seem to be harmful to the U.S.A. Countertrade activity actually results in U.S. exports always greatly exceeding the value of imports. Thus, it would appear that many products which U.S. firms agree to take from their customers for overseas marketing are not dumped back in the U.S. market.

Third, countertrade is alleged to increase overhead costs and ultimately the price of a product. Countertrade involves time, personnel, and expenses in selling a customer's product – often at a discount. If another middleman is used to dispose of the product, a commission must also be paid. Because of these expenses, a selling company has to raise the price of the original order to compensate for such expenses as well as for the risk of taking another product in return as payment. The fact that the goods are saleable – either for other goods or, in the end, for cash somewhere else – means that additional and probably unnecessary costs must be incurred. As explained by Fitzgerald, "Countertrade requirements, like any trade restrictions, increase the cost of doing business. These costs cannot be passed into the international market but must be borne within the country imposing the requirements."[8] It is believed that barter transactions are responsible for reducing Russia's revenues by 500 billion rubles.[9]

Related to this charge of increasing costs is the problem of marketing unwanted merchandise that may remain unsold. A company may have to take on the added job of marketing its customer's goods if it does not want to lose business to rivals who are willing to do so. McDonnell Douglas was able to secure a contract to sell 250 planes to former Yugoslavia only after agreeing to market such Yugoslav goods as hams and other foods, textiles, leather goods, wine, beer, mineral water, and tours. The company had a difficult time selling the $5-million-worth of hams and finally did so to its own employees and suppliers. With regard to the Yugoslavian tours, the best the company could do was to offer the trips as incentives to employees.

Financing, essential in virtually all types of conventional transactions, becomes more complicated in the case of countertrade. This is especially true when the sale of one product is contingent on the purchase of an unrelated product in return. Understandably, banks may hesitate to provide credit for such a deal because of their concern that the exporter may not be able to profitably dispose of the product given to the exporter as payment.

When a company is unable or does not want to be concerned with disposing of the product taken from its customer, it can turn to companies that act as intermediaries. The intermediaries may agree to dispose of the merchandise for a commission or they may agree to buy the goods outright. The Mediators is one such middleman organization that operates a $500-million-a-year business globally.

An examination of countertrade literature found that an overwhelming number of the published articles were theoretical rather than empirical.[10] There are a few empirical studies, however, that have shed some light on the practice of countertrade. According to one model, developing countries which impose countertrade have the following characteristics: declining foreign exchange reserves, commodity terms of trade, balance of trade, and increasing debt service ratios. There is some evidence that these variables can help exporters identify those countries which are likely to be countertraders.[11]

The results of one study dispel some widely held views about countertrade. First, the relationship between a country's credit rating and its propensity to countertrade is not as strong as commonly believed. Second, buyback and counterpurchase are substitutes to foreign direct investment. Third, there is a surprisingly large volume of countertrade between developing countries themselves. Fourth, each countertrade type seems to have its own separate motivation (see Table 17.1). Barter allows exchange without the use of money and explicit prices. Barter is therefore useful in order to bypass: (1) exchange controls, (2) public or private price controls, and (3) a creditor's monitoring of imports.[12]

Those firms that tend to benefit from countertrade are the following: (1) large firms that have extensive trade operations from large, complex products; (2) vertically integrated firms that can accommodate countertrade takebacks; and (3) firms that trade with countries which have inappropriate exchange rates, rationed foreign exchange, import restrictions, and importers inexperienced in assessing technology or in export marketing. In contrast, firms whose characteristics are the opposite of those just enumerated are likely to encounter significant barriers to countertrade operations and to receive few benefits.[13]

In general, the U.S. government is opposed to government-mandated countertrade. However, recognizing that countertrade is a fact of life, the U.S. government has maintained a hands-off policy toward countertrade arrangements which do not have government intervention or which American exporters choose to pursue. It does not oppose participation by American firms in countertrade transactions when they do not have a negative impact on national security, but the U.S. policy prohibits federal agencies from promoting countertrade in their business and official contacts.[14]

Interestingly, the U.S. government itself has published a guide on countertrade practices so that U.S. firms can take advantage of marketing opportunities in the former Soviet Union.[15] The irony is that the Russian government, seeking hard currency earnings, now appears to prefer cash transactions and has begun to discourage countertrade transactions of marketable commodities. However, those Russian products that do not have a ready market will probably still require some form of countertrade.

Likewise, Ukraine's economic improvement is due to its first-generation institution reforms that took place in 1999 and 2000. The reforms focusing on the energy sector are responsible for the reduction in barter payments and arrears. The reforms should result in a more efficient allocation of resources, while promoting a working financial system.[16]

There is no question that countertrade is a cumbersome process. Yet a firm is unwise not to consider it. Much like other trade practices, countertrade presents both problems and opportunities. More often than not, problems of countertrade are more psychological than real obstacles. Problems can be overcome. One need only remember that in the final analysis all goods can be converted into cash.

## Price quotaton

A quotation describes a specific product, states the price for that product as well as a specified delivery location, sets the time of shipment, and specifies payment terms. When a company receives an inquiry from abroad, the quotation must be very detailed in terms of weight, volume, and so on because of the customer's unfamiliarity with foreign products, places, and terms (see Cultural Dimension 17.1 and Legal Dimension 17.1). Since the time of shipment is critical, the prepared quotation should specify whether the time mentioned is from the factory or the port of export and whether it includes the estimated inland transit time. Furthermore, price quotations should state explicitly that they are subject to change without notice. It is a good idea to specify the precise period during which a specific price or offer remains valid.

Because it is often requested by a buyer, a **pro forma invoice** may have to be prepared and supplied with or instead of the quotation. Even when it is not requested, it is still good business practice to include it with any international quotation. This type of invoice is not for payment purposes; it is essentially a quotation in an invoice format. The buyer uses it to apply for an import license or when arranging for funds. A pro forma invoice should be conspicuously marked "pro forma invoice," and it should include a statement certifying that the pro forma invoice is true and correct as well as a statement describing the country of origin of the products.

Cultural Dimension 17.1

**Quotation**

A quotation describes the product, its price, time of shipment, and terms of sale, and terms of payment. A good quotation should include the following:

1 buyer's name and address
2 buyer's reference number and date of inquiry
3 brief description of requested products
4 price of each item
5 gross and net shipping weight
6 total cubic volume and dimensions packed for export
7 trade discount
8 delivery point
9 terms of sale
10 terms of payment
11 insurance and shipping costs
12 validity period for quotation
13 total charges to be paid by customer
14 estimated shipping date to factory or U.S. port
15 estimated date of shipment arrival.

*Source*: "Price, Quotations, and Terms of Sale Are Key to Successful Exporting," *Business America*, October 4, 1993, 12–15.

Legal Dimension 17.1

**Lawful and wholesome returns**

Capital managed according to *sharia* (Islamic law) is a $750 billion market. However, due to the Islamic prohibition against earning interest, companies could not sell bonds. Now investment bankers have found ways to get bonds to co-exist with Islamic law. Bankers from Merrill Lynch in London and Beirut-based Bemo Securitisation managed to sell $166 million of debt-like certificates for East Cameron Gas, a Houston natural gas producer. These certificates are *sharia*-compliant because of how they are structured. Islamic investors receive a fixed rate of return (11.25 percent per annum) and are considered to be owners of the underlying assets. An official sharia adviser declares that the instrument "will yield returns, Allah willing, that are lawful and wholesome."

*Source*: "Returns Muslims Can Live With," *Business Week*, July 17, 2006, 9.

## Terms of sale

### *Trade terms*

The quotation must include terms of sale. In the U.S.A., it is customary to ship FOB factory, freight collect, or COD. Such terms, however, are inappropriate for international business, and other terms such as EXW, FAS, FOB, CFR, CIF, DEQ, and DDP should be used instead.

All companies should use **Incoterms** which are a set of international rules that are used to interpret the most common terms in foreign trade. Developed under the auspices of the International Chamber of Commerce, Incoterms are recognized by the United Nations Commission on International Trade Law as a global standard. By defining the responsibilities of buyers and sellers for delivery of goods under sales contracts, the use of Incoterms reduces uncertainties by eliminating varying interpretations of foreign trade terms. Because there are several versions of Incoterms, the seller should clearly refer to Incoterms 2000 whenever the terms are used (e.g., FOB London Incoterms 2000).[17]

Incoterms have four basic categories. The *E terms* are used when the seller will make goods available to the buyer on the seller's own premises. *F terms* are used when the seller will be required to deliver goods to a carrier appointed by the buyer. *C terms* are used when the seller will be required to contract for carriage, but will not assume risk of loss or damage to goods, or of additional costs that may occur after shipment and dispatch. Finally, *D terms* require the seller to bear all costs and risks needed to bring goods to the place of destination. In general, Incoterms base the interpretations on the party who is best equipped to handle the task. For example, loading and unloading obligations have been shifted to the seller under the Free Carrier Seller's Place term because this shipment is being unloaded at the seller's place and because the seller will have personnel and equipment available to load.

Table 17.2 describes the point of delivery and risk shift for these different terms of sale. These terms are discussed below.

## *Ex works (EXW) or ex – named point of origin*

*Ex* means *from*, and the price quoted is calculated from the point of origin. There are several variations of this term, and they include *ex factory, ex warehouse, ex mill, ex plantation,* and *ex mine*. Under these terms, the seller makes goods available to the buyer at a specific time and place, usually at the seller's place of business or warehouse. The buyer takes delivery at the seller's premises and bears all risks and expenses from that point on.

## *FAS – named port of shipment*

FAS stands for *free alongside ship*. Under this term, the price includes delivery of goods alongside the vessel or other mode of transportation, and the seller pays all charges up to that point. This term does

**TABLE 17.2** Point of delivery and where risk shifts from seller to buyer

| | EXW | FAS | FOB | CFR | CIF | DEQ | DDP |
|---|---|---|---|---|---|---|---|
| Supplier's warehouse | X | | | | | | |
| Export dock | | X | | | | | |
| On board vessel | | | X | X | X | | |
| Import dock | | | | | | X | |
| Buyer's warehouse | | | | | | | X |
| Main transit insurance risk on | Buyer | Buyer | Buyer | Buyer | Seller | Seller | Seller |

not include the cost of loading. It is customary to use the port of export as the point of origin for this transaction. The seller's legal responsibility ends once it has obtained a clear wharfage receipt. A significant change should be noted. Under Incoterms 2000, the seller is required to clear the goods for export. Previous Incoterms versions required the buyer to arrange for export clearance.

### FOB – named point

FOB stands for *free on board*. Like the other terms within the quotation, the point where the price is applicable must be mentioned. There are a number of classes, and the point in question may be any one of these: the named inland carrier at the named inland point of departure, the named inland carrier at the named point of exportation, the named port of shipment, and the named inland point in the country of importation.

Nevertheless, the point used for quotation is usually the port of export. In such a case, the price includes local delivery and loading. The seller's responsibility does not end until goods have actually been placed aboard the ship and a bill of lading issued. The buyer arranges for overseas transportation and bears all costs and risks from the time the goods are placed on board (i.e., passes the ship's rail).

### CFR – to named point of destination

CFR stands for *Cost and Freight*. Usually, this term will name the overseas port of import as the point in question. The price generally includes the cost of transportation to the named point of debarkation. The buyer, in turn, is expected to pay for insurance. Like FOB, the risk of loss or damage to the goods is transferred from the seller to the buyer when the goods pass the ship's rail.

### CIF – to named point of destination

CIF stands for *cost, insurance, and freight*. Again, the point used for quotation can be any location, but the International Chamber of Commerce recommends that this point should be the destination. The CIF price includes the cost of goods, insurance, and all transportation charges to the point of debarkation (destination). The delivery costs are thus extended beyond the country of export. Although the price covers more items or activities than FOB, the seller's obligations still end at the same stage (i.e., when goods are aboard or loaded). The seller pays for insurance, and the seller's insurance company assumes responsibility once the goods are loaded. Firms exporting to the EU should note that duties are imposed on the CIF value of the shipment.

### Delivered ex quay (DEQ) – named port of destination

The seller is required to deliver the goods to the quay at the predefined port of destination and clear them for importation. The seller must also take on all risks and costs including duties, taxes, and any other charges. To avoid confusion, the term should mention either "duty paid" or "duty unpaid."

### DDP – delivered duty paid

An example of this kind of quotation is "duty paid landed U.S." With the payment of this price, the seller undertakes the delivery of goods to the place named in the country of import, most likely the buyer's warehouse, with all costs and duties paid. The seller obtains an import license if required and arranges for an overseas customhouse broker to clear the merchandise through customs and to act as a freight forwarder by forwarding the goods locally to the final destination.

The terms of sale mentioned above also have some variations. For example, **CPT** (carriage paid to) and **CIP** (carriage and insurance paid to) – to a named place of destination – are used in place of CFR and CIF respectively for shipment by modes other than water.[18] In the case of **FCA** (free carrier) to a named place, the term replaces "FOB named inland port" and may be used for multimodal transport, container stations, and any mode of transport (including air).

## Quotation guidelines

Although the potential buyer will probably specify the terms to be used, the seller should make certain that the quotation or price is meaningful when specific terms are not requested. It is unwise for a company in a suburb of Chicago to quote a price as "FOB Evanston, not export packed." The buyer may have no way of knowing that Evanston is a suburb of Chicago. Even if the buyer does know where Evanston is, that firm would have difficulty determining how much the local transportation or freight charges would be to move the goods from Evanston to the Chicago port. Moreover, the buyer would surely be interested in knowing what the packing costs for export are, since the merchandise would have to be packed for export. Without a meaningful quote, it is difficult to receive serous consideration from a potential buyer.

Whenever possible, the exporter should quote CIF. Better yet, the quote should include a breakdown for the C(ost), I(nsurance), and F(reight). The buyer is then aware of all the relevant costs needed to get the product to the port in its country, and the buyer can decide whether it should arrange for the insurance and/or freight. If the seller needs assistance, a freight forwarder would be helpful in determining the CIF price.

Although the CIF price yields the greatest amount of information for the buyer, terms other than CIF may prove more appropriate under certain circumstances. If the exporter needs to conserve cash, the exporter should not quote CIF or any terms beyond it (e.g., delivered duty paid). If currency convertibility is a problem, FOB terms may be more desirable for both parties. That is, the buyer pays freight in its own currency or arranges to use a ship from its own country. In Russia, cost of goods and cost of delivery of goods to shelves are by far a retailer's two largest expense items. A Russian retailer may want to purchase goods on FOB or EXW terms so that the company can have better control over the cost of transportation from the production country. It may try to minimize expenditures through direct negotiation of ocean freight rates and outsourcing logistics.[19]

China often controls shipping arrangements for imports and exports in order to preserve foreign exchange and retain the insurance business. The country's foreign trade corporations (FTCs), responsible for most foreign trade, prefer selling on CIF terms while buying FOB in order to underwrite all freight charges and insurance themselves. One potential problem encountered in this case is that ships arranged for the Chinese FTCs have been known to arrive considerably late, incurring high interest and warehousing costs for American firms. Moreover, delays at Chinese ports are another problem, and can hold up the payment even more.

## Methods of financing and means of payment

There are several payment methods. It should be noted that how buyers handle payments can vary from one part of the world to another. In Asia, the typical payment terms of 60 to 90 days are common and considerably longer than those in the U.S.A. Credit-cards and checks are pretty much a U.S. phenomenon. In Europe and elsewhere, credit-cards are mainly used by the affluent. For online purchases beyond the U.S. border, account-to-account (A2A) payments seriously challenge credit- and debit-cards. A2A payments make it possible for consumers to move money between their own accounts, send cash to a friend or relative, or pay a merchant or utility. Not requiring a plastic card, paper checks, or cash handling, the transfer of funds takes place via a direct electronic link between a user's bank and a recipient's bank. A2A transfers are not only easy to use, but also enable merchants to receive a payment more quickly without having to wait for a check in the mail. "There are cultural differences between the U.S. and other countries that extend to the way consumers pay for a purchase. Not only are there still a lot of cash-oriented societies, but a lot of countries don't have the same approach to card acquiring and processing as the U.S."

Some methods provide financing to buyers, whereas other methods assure sellers of prompt payment.[20] Table 17.3 compares these payment methods. Figure 17.2 shows payment terms risk/cost tradeoff.

### *Consignment*

When consignment is used, goods are shipped but ownership is retained by the seller. This means that the product is furnished on a deferred-payment basis, and when the product is sold, the seller is reimbursed by the consignee. In effect, the seller is providing full financing for the consignee. The problem with consignment sales is that a high degree of risk prevails. First of all, it is costly to arrange for the return of merchandise that is unsold. In addition, because of the distance involved, the seller has difficulty keeping track of inventory and its condition. Certain safeguards are thus necessary. For example, the contract should specify the party responsible for property insurance in the event that there is damage to the merchandise while in the possession of the consignee. Because of these problems and difficulties, the method is not widely used by American exporters. Consignment, however, can be a satisfactory arrangement when the sale involves an affiliated firm or the seller's own sales representative or dealer.

Risk to exporter
Least risk
Highest risk
Cash in advance
Confirmed irrevocable letter of credit
Irrevocable letter of credit
Bank collection sight draft
Bank collection time draft
Open account
Cost to buyer
Highest cost
Least cost

**FIGURE 17.2** Export payment terms risk/cost trade-off

*Source*: Business America (February 1995, 6).

**TABLE 17.3** Methods of payment

American firms involved in international trade face a unique set of problems. Ultimately, the goal of any exporter is to make a sale and be paid. In return, the importer wants to receive the agreed upon goods. Factors such as distance, time, language, culture, and country regulations must be taken into consideration by the prospective parties if their needs are to be satisfied. The importer or exporter should ask himself some of the following questions before selecting the most appropriate method of payment.

- How reliable is the exporter?
- How long has the exporter been shipping?
- Is the exporter's product subject to inspection?
- How creditworthy is the importer?
- Has the importer demonstrated the ability to pay promptly?
- Can the importer count on getting the goods on time?
- What credit terms are offered by the competition?
- What are the political and economic conditions within the importer's and exporter's countries?
- What is the value of the goods?
- Is this a one-time shipment or does the possibility exist for additional orders?
- Is the product standardized or specialized, and is it resaleable?

After carefully evaluating the previous questions the importer or exporter is now prepared to select the proper payment method.

| *Method* | *Payment* | *Goods available to buyer* | *Risk to exporter* | *Risk to importer* |
|---|---|---|---|---|
| Cash in advance | Before shipment | After payment | None | Relies on exporter to ship goods as ordered |
| Letter of credit | When goods shipped and documents comply, with L/C* | After payment | Little or none depending on L/C* | Relies on exporter to ship goods described in documents |
| Sight draft, documents against payment | On presentation of draft to buyer | After payment | Buyer can refuse goods | Same as L/C* unless he can inspect goods before payment |
| Time draft, documents against acceptance | On maturity of draft | Before payment | Relies on buyer to pay draft | Same as above |
| Open account | As agreed | Before payment | Relies completely on buyer to pay his account | None |

*Note*
* L/C denotes letter of credit.

*Source: International Workbook* (Chicago: Unibanc Trust, 1985, 1). Reprinted with permission of Unibanc Trust.

## Open account

With an open account, goods are shipped without documents calling for payment, other than the invoice. The buyer can pick up goods without having to make payment first. The advantage with the open account is simplicity and assistance to the buyer, who does not have to pay credit charges to banks. The seller in return expects that the invoice will be paid at the agreed time. A major weakness of this method is that there is no safeguard against default, since a tangible payment instrument does not exist. The lack of payment instrument also makes it difficult to sell the account receivable. To compound the problem, the buyer often delays payment until the merchandise is received – a standard practice in many countries.

Because of the inherent risks of an open account, precautions should be taken. The seller must determine the integrity of the buyer by relying on prior experience, or through a credit investigation. Toward this end, there are several organizations that can provide some assistance in terms of credit information. First, there are commercial credit agencies such as the International Dun & Bradstreet's American Foreign Credit Underwriters Corp. Second, such organizations as chambers of commerce and trade associations can be contacted. In addition, commercial banks and their overseas branches or correspondent banks usually have some useful credit information. Finally, government sources can also be valuable. World Traders Data Reports, for example, has a great deal of information on foreign firms. In any case, a prudent credit decision should take into account an importing country's political risk and economic conditions.

Before granting credit, an exporter needs to assess a buyer's creditworthiness. Credit bureaus overseas should be consulted. In addition, **credit scoring** is another useful technique. Credit scoring is a process that converts customer credit and financial information into a numerical format that is then combined to create a score. The scores will represent the levels of risk. There is a general consensus that international business involves many risks that include customer creditworthiness, and country (eco and political), bank (transactional and portfolio), transitional market, currency, legal (contract), regulatory, and systematic failure. However, credit executives do not agree on whether it is possible to construct an automated scoring model that is robust enough to address all the risks simultaneously without requiring a judgmental factor.

**Credit insurance** is another useful tool to mitigate risks. This is standard practice in European business-to-business transactions. The advantages are protection against buyer insolvency, greater borrowing power, and greater sales. However, the insurance, while covering a buyer's inability to pay, does not cover the buyer's unwillingness to pay. As such, disputes related to a buyer's dissatisfaction with the goods are not covered. Some sellers are hesitant to pay the cost of insurance, typically between 0.1 and 0.4 percent of sales for domestic accounts and between 0.25 to 1 percent of covered sales for export accounts. They do not realize that their own bad debt reserves are actually a form of credit insurance.[21]

## Cash in advance

The seller may want to demand cash in advance when:

1 The buyer is financially weak or an unknown credit risk.
2 The economic/political conditions in the buyer's country are unstable.
3 The seller is not interested in assuming credit risk, as in the case of consignment and open account sales.

Ethical Dimension 17.1

## Nigerian scams

Nigerian scam artists have made headlines in the U.S.A. The *Wall Street Journal*, for example, has published lengthy articles describing how they have defrauded American firms and citizens. Crooks have gone high-tech. Instead of mailing or faxing their scam letters, they now rely on e-mail. In one year alone, Americans fell for the scam and lost $100 million after giving out their account numbers. If unreported losses can be accounted for, the total should be much higher. The Nigerian scams have been successful to the point that they are Nigeria's No. 3 or 4 export.

The most prevalent method involves money transfer schemes. Claiming to try to defraud the Nigerian government, the scam artists typically propose to transfer millions of U.S. dollars to an overseas bank account owned by a foreign firm which is promised a percentage of the transferred funds as "commission." The funds are alleged to be overpayments from previous government contracts. The crooks then request information about the company's bank, as well as blank, signed company letterhead and pro forma invoices. The firm owning the account is told it will receive a percentage of the transferred funds as "commission." The American firm may also be solicited for a "transaction fee" to enable the supposed transfer of funds. Invariably, American firms, instead of receiving any money for their assistance, would find that the Nigerian fraud artists have used the letterhead and bank information to withdraw money from their U.S. accounts.

The following is an example of a scam letter.

NIGERIA NATIONAL PETROLEUM CORPORATION (NNPC)
PLOT 19
FALOMO ROAD
IKOYI-LAGOS
NIGERIA

ATTN: Managing Director/CEO

I am Dr Buba Ahmed, director of procurement and contracts with Nigeria National Petroleum Corporation (NNPC). I have decided with my director general in office to contact you quickly on this business of transferring the sum of US$30,000,000.00 (thirty million United States dollars only) into a foreign bank account.The need is very urgent. I got your contact from Nigerian chambers of commerce and it is with business trust that made me to contact you in this matter. I write to solicit for the transfer of this money into your account. This money was generated from an over-invoiced contract sum in my corporation (NNPC). We have generally agreed that 20 percent of this said fund is for you as compensation for using your bank account in transferring this money. Ten percent should be for all expenses made for this business,while 70 percent is for us. Please note that we will arrange to meet you immediately after successful conclusion of this transfer. The 70 percent share of ours will be used for investment overseas.Your assistance and cooperation is highly needed. I assure you that this business is 100 percent risk free and as such you should not entertain any fear in dealing with us.

Should this interest you, we will require your banking information as mentioned below: 1. YOUR BANK NAME AND ADDRESS 2. YOUR ACCOUNT NUMBER WITH THE BANK 3. NAME TO BE USED AS BENEFICIARY 4. YOUR BANK TELEPHONE AND FAX NUMBER. Contact me on the above e-mail address and we hope to conclude this business within 14 working days. Please while writing to me don't forget to include your personal telephone and fax numbers, for easy and quicker communication. I anticipate your urgent positive reply.

Best Regards,

Dr Buba Ahmed

*Sources*: "Doing Business in Nigeria: Distinguishing Between the Profitable and the Questionable," *Business America*, December 1997, 30–2; "Nigerian Financial Scam Generating Reader Responses," *San José Mercury News*, April 17, 2003; "The List: Gotcha!", *Business Week*, July 16, 2001, 10; and "Ask the TIC," *Export America*, July 2001, 16–17.

Because of the immediate uses of money and the maximum protection, sellers naturally prefer cash in advance. The problem, of course, is that the buyer is not eager to tie up its money, especially if the buyer has some doubts about whether it will receive the goods as ordered. By insisting on cash in advance, the seller shifts the risk completely to the buyer, but the seller may end up losing the sale through this insistence.

## *Bill of exchange (draft)*

A means of financing international transactions is through a bill of exchange or draft, which is a request for payment (see Figure 17.3). The request is an unconditional order in writing from one person (drawer) requiring the person to whom it is addressed (drawee) to pay the payee or bearer on demand or at a fixed or determinable time. The drawer, usually the exporter, is the maker or originator of the draft requesting payment. The drawee, usually the buyer, is the party responsible for honoring or paying the draft. The payee may be the exporter, the exporter's bank, the bearer, or any specified person. In short, a draft is a request for payment. It is a negotiable instrument that contains an order to pay a payee. As noted by John Stuart Mill many years ago, the purpose is to save expense and minimize the risk of transporting precious metals from place to place as payment of imports. The bill of exchange simply allows banks to make adjustments by debiting or crediting accounts maintained in buyer or seller names with other banks.

The transaction process occurs in this way. The drawee accepts the draft by signing an acceptance on the face of the instrument. If the buyer does not accept (sign) the bill, the buyer is not given the attached documents to obtain goods from the steamship company, since the shipment is made on the negotiable order bill of lading. In practice, banks are responsible for payment collection. The original order bill of lading is endorsed by the shipper and sent to the buyer's bank along with the bill of exchange, invoices, and other required documents (e.g., consular invoice, insurance certificate,

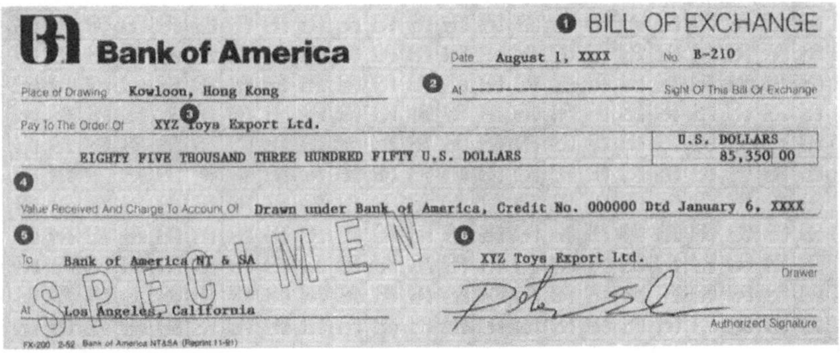

Bank of America

① BILL OF EXCHANGE

Date August 1, XXXX No. B-210

Place of Drawing Kowloon, Hong Kong ② At ------------ Sight Of This Bill Of Exchange

Pay To The Order Of ③ XYZ Toys Export Ltd.

EIGHTY FIVE THOUSAND THREE HUNDRED FIFTY U.S. DOLLARS U.S. DOLLARS 85,350 00

④ Value Received And Charge To Account Of Drawn under Bank of America, Credit No. 000000 Dtd January 6, XXXX

⑤ To Bank of America NT & SA ⑥ XYZ Toys Export Ltd. Drawer

At Los Angeles, California Authorized Signature

SPECIMEN

FX-200 2-52 Bank of America NT&SA (Reprint 11-91)

BILL OF EXCHANGE
1. A bill of exchange or draft is an instrument, much like an ordinary check in appearance, which is used as a formal demand for payment in a business transaction.
2. This bill of exchange is a sight draft and is drawn in accordance with both the application for the commercial latter of credit on page 12 and the irrevocable documentary letter of credit on page 16.
3. XYZ Toys Export Ltd., the beneficiary, is the payee, or recipient of funds.
4. As established by the irrevocable letter of credit on page 16, all drafts must be marked with Bank of America's credit number for identification purposes.
5. Bank of America, Los Angeles, is the drawee, or bank to which this bill of exchange is presented for payment.
6. The drawer is the party who signs an order directing the drawee, Bank of America, Los Angeles, to pay a specified sum of money to the payee. In this situation, XYZ Toys Export Ltd. is both the drawer and the payee.

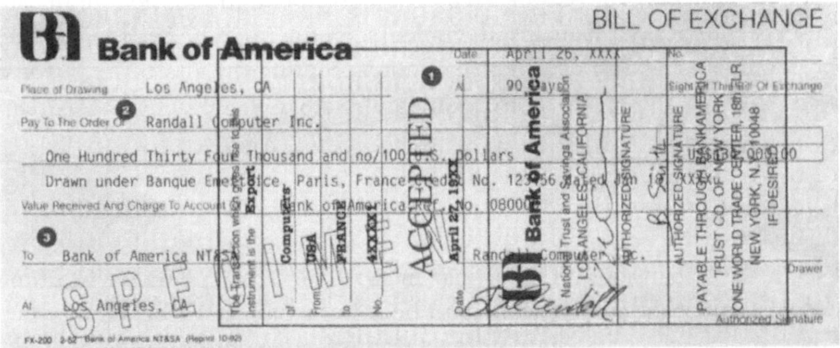

Bank of America

BILL OF EXCHANGE

Date April 26, XXXX No.

Place of Drawing Los Angeles, CA ① At 90 Days Sight Of This Bill Of Exchange

Pay To The Order Of ② Randall Computer Inc.

One Hundred Thirty Four Thousand and no/100 U.S. Dollars U.S. $134,000.00

Drawn under Banque Emettrice, Paris, France Credit No. 123456 dated Jan 16, XXXX

Value Received And Charge To Account Of Bank of America Ref. No. 08000

③ To Bank of America NT&SA Randall Computer Inc. Drawer

At Los Angeles, CA Authorized Signature

ACCEPTED April 27, 19XX

The Transaction which gives rise to this instrument is the Export of Computers from USA to FRANCE No. 4XXXXX

Bank of America National Trust and Savings Association LOS ANGELES, CALIFORNIA

AUTHORIZED SIGNATURE

PAYABLE THROUGH BANKAMERICA TRUST CO. OF NEW YORK ONE WORLD TRADE CENTER, 18th FLR NEW YORK, N.Y. 10048 IF DESIRED

SPECIMEN

FX-200 2-52 Bank of America NT&SA (Reprint 10-92)

BILL OF EXCHANGE—BANKERS' ACCEPTANCE
1. This "usance" bill of exchange or time draft is Randall Computer Inc.'s demand for payment at 90 days sight, under Banque Emmettrice Internationale's irrevocable usance letter of credit. Randall Computer Inc. would endorse the draft on the reverse side at the time they present it to Bank of America, Los Angeles with their documents.
2. Bank of America, Los Angeles, is the drawee and accepts the draft on April 27, XXXX. The draft will mature on July 26, XXXX, 90 days from the acceptance date. Randall Computer can either retain the acceptance until maturity or discount the draft through Bank of America, Los Angeles, and receive an amount less than its full face value.
3. On the maturity date of the acceptance, July 26, XXXX, Bank of America, Los Angeles, will pay Randall Computer Inc., or the presenter of the draft if it was discounted and sold in the secondary market, and charge the account of Banque Emettrice Internationale. Unless the acceptance was discounted, Randall Computer Inc. will receive payment for the goods sold to Produits Electroniques S.A. 90 days after sight, in accordance with their agreement.

**FIGURE 17.3** A bill of exchange

*Source*: *Trade Banking Services* (Bank of America Corporation, 1994, 24–5). Reprinted with permission of Bank of America.

inspection certificate). Once notified by the bank, the buyer pays the amount on the draft and is given the bill of lading, which allows the buyer to obtain the shipment.

There are two principal types of bill of exchange: sight and time. A **sight draft**, as the name implies, is drawn at sight, meaning that it is paid when it is first seen by the drawee. A sight draft is commonly used for either credit reasons or for the purpose of title retention. A **time (usance or date) draft** is drawn for the purpose of financing the sale or temporary storage of specified goods for a specified number of days after sight (e.g., 30, 60, 90 days, or longer). It specifies payment of a stated amount at maturity. As such, it offers less security than a sight draft since the sight draft demands payment prior to the release of shipping documents. The time draft, on the other hand, allows the buyer to acquire shipping documents to obtain merchandise when accepting the draft, even though the buyer can actually defer payment.

At first sight, it may seem that a time draft is not really different from an open account, since the goods may be obtained or picked up by the buyer before making payment. There is one crucial difference, however. In the case of the time draft, there is a negotiable instrument evidencing the obligation. Since this document can be sold to factors and discounted immediately, the seller can obtain cash before maturity. In the U.S.A., factors are financial institutions that buy accounts receivable from manufacturers.

There are other variations of this kind of draft. If bills of lading, invoices, and so on accompany the draft, this is known as **documents against payment (D/P)**. If financial documents are omitted to avoid stamp tax charges against such documents or if bills of lading come from countries where drafts are not used, this type of collection is known as **cash against documents**. Frequently, the draft terms may read "90 days sight D/A" or **documents against acceptance**. Upon accepting this draft, the buyer is permitted to obtain the documents and the merchandise, while not being obliged to make payment until the draft matures.

## *Bankers' acceptance*

A bankers' acceptance assists in the expansion of credit financing. A bankers' acceptance is a time draft whose maturity is usually less than six months. The draft becomes a bankers' acceptance when the bank accepts it; that is, the bank on which the draft is drawn stamps and endorses it as "accepted." Drafts drawn on and accepted by nonbank entities are called **trade acceptances**. U.S. dollar bankers' acceptances are negotiable instruments and may be used in conjunction with letters of credit.[22]

An acceptance becomes the accepting bank's obligation, and once accepted it becomes a negotiable instrument that may be bought or sold in the market like a certificate of deposit (CD) or commercial paper. Daily newspapers usually list the daily prices of bankers' acceptances in the financial section. The acceptance commission is the reason why a bank lends its name, integrity, and credit rating to the instrument. The discount charge is computed at the current prime bankers' acceptance rate from date of purchase to maturity. The bank has primary responsibility for payment to the acceptance holder at maturity, but the draft originator still has secondary liability in case the accepting bank does not honor the claim.

## *Letter of credit*

An alternative to the sight draft is a sight letter of credit (L/C). As a legal instrument, it is a written undertaking by a bank through prior agreement with its client to honor a withdrawal by a third party for goods and services rendered (see Figure 17.4). The document, issued by the bank at the buyer's request in favor of the seller, is the bank's promise to pay an agreed amount of money on its receipt of certain documents within the specified time period. Usually, the required documents are the same as those used with the sight draft. In effect, the bank is being asked to substitute its credit for that of the buyer's. The bank agrees to allow one party to the transaction (the seller, creditor, or exporter) to collect payment from that party's correspondent bank or branch abroad. Drafts presented for payment under the L/C are thus drawn on the bank. The importer can repay the bank by either making an appropriate deposit in cash or borrowing all or part of the money from the bank. The drawee (buyer) is usually responsible for the collection charges by banks at home and overseas. Figure 17.5 examines the process involved in a letter of credit.

Several banks may be involved in the process. The *issuing bank*, as a rule, issues letters of credit for its current customers only, even if collateral is offered by someone else. In contrast, the *advising bank* is the bank that notifies the exporter that an L/C has been issued. The issuing bank forwards the L/C to the advising bank (its foreign correspondent), which is usually selected for its proximity to the beneficiary. In the case of a *confirming bank* the same services are performed as the advising bank but the confirming bank also becomes liable for payment.

There are several types of letters of credit, including revocable, irrevocable, confirmed, unconfirmed, standby, back-to-back, and transferable.

## Revocable letter of credit (L/C)

With a revocable L/C, the issuing bank has the right to revoke its commitment to honor the draft drawn on it. Without prior warning or notification to the seller, the bank can cancel or modify its obligation at any time before payment – even after shipment has already been made. Since the bank's commitment is not legally binding, the protection to the seller is minimal. Exporters generally do not want to accept a revocable L/C.

## Irrevocable letter of credit

This type of L/C is greatly preferred to the revocable letter of credit. In this case, once the L/C is accepted by the seller, it cannot be amended in any way or cancelled by the buyer or the buyer's bank without all parties' approval. It is possible, however, for the buyer who receives proper documents but unsuitable goods because of fraud to obtain an injunction preventing the banker from paying the fraudster. When Worlds of Wonder, a U.S. toy company, filed for bankruptcy protection, four Hong Kong creditors/suppliers were able to use irrevocable letters of credit to collect $16.5 million from an undisclosed bank. Another Hong Kong manufacturer, Applied Electronics, could not recover any of its debt since it held no outstanding letters of credit.

## Confirmed letter of credit

For the exporter, it is highly desirable for the L/C to be confirmed through a bank in the exporter's country because the exporter then receives an additional guarantee of payment from a second bank (i.e., the confirming bank). The advising bank sends a cover letter along with the original L/C to the exporter, stating that the L/C has been confirmed. A U.S. exporter is in a much better position if there is a U.S. bank that accepts the responsibilty of paying the letter of credit in case of refusal to

CABLE ADDRESS:
Conill Bank Telex 02-5233

TELEPHONE (312) 828-6340

CONTINENTAL BANK
CONTINENTAL ILLINOIS NATIONAL BANK AND TRUST COMPANY OF CHICAGO
231 SOUTH LA SALLE STREET, CHICAGO, ILLINOIS 60693

ORIGINAL

APRIL 2, 19--

CREDIT NUMBER 6000000
DOCUMENTARY CREDIT IRREVOCABLE

| ADVISING BANK | APPLICANT |
|---|---|
| UNDERWRITERS BANK OVERSEAS, LTD.<br>AMERICAN INTERNATIONAL TOWERS<br>HONG KONG, HONG KONG | CHICAGO IMPORTERS CO., LTD.<br>CHICAGO, ILLINOIS<br>U.S.A. |
| **BENEFICIARY** | **AMOUNT** |
| CHUNG LEE ELECTRIC INDUSTRIAL MFG. LTD.<br>CHAI WAN, HONG KONG | US $74,750.00<br>Seventy Four Thousand Seven Hundred Fifty And 00/100 US Dollars |
| | **EXPIRY** |
| | 07/08/19-- IN HONG KONG<br>JULY 08, 19-- |

DEAR SIR(S),

We hereby establish in your favor our Irrevocable Letter of Credit No. 6000000 which is available for negotiation of your drafts at SIGHT, drawn on us, and bearing the clause "DRAWN UNDER CONTINENTAL ILLINOIS NATIONAL BANK AND TRUST COMPANY OF CHICAGO, CHICAGO, ILLINOIS, CREDIT NO. 6000000" and accompanied by:

-Commercial invoice in triplicate.
-Special customs invoice in triplicate.
-Packing list in duplicate.
-Certificate of origin Form "A" in duplicate.
-Full set of at least 3 originals of clean on board Bills of Lading consigned to Chicago Importers Co., Ltd. C/O Freight Forwarder Inc., Elk Grove Village, IL 60007, marked freight collect, notify Chicago Importers, 200 West Jackson, Chicago, IL 60646.

-Covering shipment of: MOTOR AS PER PURCHASE ORDER #15875", to be shipped from F.O.B. vessel Hong Kong port to Los Angeles, California.

-The insurance is covered by the buyer.
-The documents must be presented for negotiation within 7 days after shipment.
-Partial shipments permitted. Transshipments prohibited.

-The first negotiating bank to send one original of each documents directly by airmail to: Chicago Importers Co., Ltd., Chicago, IL and the remaining documents with a certificate that this has been done must accompany the draft.

We hereby engage with drawers and/or bonafide holders that drafts drawn and negotiated in conformity with the terms of this Letter of Credit will be duly honored on presentation and that drafts accepted within the terms of this Letter of Credit will be duly honored at maturity. The amount of each draft must be endorsed on the reverse of this Letter of Credit by the negotiating bank.

CONTINENTAL ILLINOIS NATIONAL BANK AND TRUST COMPANY OF CHICAGO

L. Taylor — FOR CASHIER          A. Smith — FOR CASHIER

NO. 093090 Except so far as otherwise expressly stated, this documentary credit is subject to the "Uniform Customs and Practice for Documentary Credits" (1974 revision) International Chamber of Commerce (Publication No. 290)

**FIGURE 17.4** Import commercial letter of credit

*Source*: Reprinted with permission of Continental Illinois National Bank and Trust Company of Chicago.

**Sight letters of credit**

***The letter of credit process is more complex than other payment methods previously discussed. The principal steps that occur in a letter of credit process are outlined in Exhibit 1.***

***Exhibit 1***

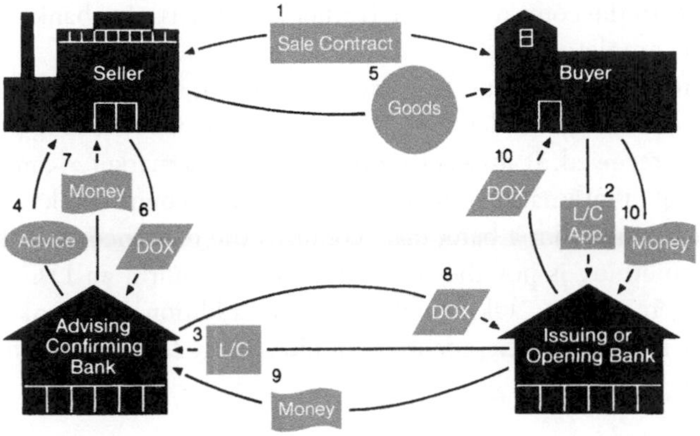
1
Sale Contract
Seller
Buyer
5
Goods
7
Money
4
6
Advice
DOX
10
DOX
2
L/C App.
10
Money
8
DOX
Advising Confirming Bank
3
L/C
Issuing or Opening Bank
9
Money

*Note: Money denotes money and/or acceptance.*

***Sight Letter of Credit Process***

1. A sales contract is entered into between the seller and buyer. This contract specifies: terms of payment, contract price, goods to be shipped, etc.
2. The buyer (applicant, importer, accountee) requests from his bank (issuing or opening bank) a letter of credit by completing an application. The account officer must then approve the request since this is an extension of credit to the buyer.
3. The issuing bank will transmit the letter of credit to another bank (the advising bank) usually located in the seller's country. The advising bank may confirm the credit, whereby payment is guaranteed to the seller if all terms and conditions are met.
4. The advising or confirming bank informs the seller (beneficiary, exporter) that the letter of credit has been issued.
5. After reviewing the letter of credit, the seller is now in a position to meet the terms and conditions in the letter of credit and ship the merchandise.
6. The seller submits documents to the negotiating bank which is normally the advising and/or confirming bank.
7. The advising or confirming bank will examine the documents against the terms of the letter of credit. If the seller has met the terms of the letter of credit, the paying bank will remit payment. (If discrepancies exist, please refer to the section on Handling Discrepancies.)
8. The advising bank forwards the documents to the issuing bank where they will also be checked.
9. If documents meet the requirements under the letter of credit (or discrepancies have been waived), the issuing bank pays the advising bank.
10. The issuing bank charges the buyer's account and forwards the documents to the buyer so that goods can be released from customs.

**FIGURE 17.5** Process involved in a sight letter of credit

*Source*: *International Workbook* (Chicago, MA: Unibanck Trust, 1985, 3). Reprinted with permission of Unibank Trust.

do so by the buyer and/or the buyer's bank (i.e., issuing bank in a foreign country). In the early 1980s, the political crisis in Iran, for example, made it impossible for many American sellers to enforce the payment terms specified in unconfirmed letters of credit. Naturally, a confirmed L/C is more desirable when payment is guaranteed by two banks instead of one, especially if there is some doubt about the issuing foreign bank's ability to pay. Moreover, since the confirming bank is located in the same country as the exporter, the exporter is able to receive payment more readily by presenting documents to the confirming bank (rather than the issuing bank abroad) to show that all obligations have been completed.

Honesty is a virtue that cannot be taken for granted in international trade. A seller may, for example, ship unordered or inferior goods while collecting payment. A buyer may refuse to pay for goods received. It must be emphasized that a marketer can never be too cautious or careful when dealing in international trade. In the case of a confirmed letter of credit, the seller should not accept a statement from a bank that "confirms the existence of an L/C" because to confirm the existence of something is not the same thing as to confirm an L/C. A confirmed L/C requires the bank's engagement (i.e., taking obligation). In addition, the bank that confirms the L/C must be financially sound, and the exporter should specify that "the confirming bank must be acceptable to the seller."

### *Unconfirmed letter of credit*

When the L/C is not confirmed by a bank in the seller's country, the certainty is less and payment slower. An unconfirmed letter of credit may still be acceptable so long as the foreign bank that issues it is financially strong. In fact, some multinational banks are so well known that they prohibit letters of credit issued by them to be confirmed because confirmation would tarnish their prestige. However, letters of credit can still be confirmed confidentially.

It is possible to combine the several types of L/C. A letter of credit can be revocable and confirmed, irrevocable and unconfirmed, and so on. For maximum security and earliest payment, the seller should ask for an irrevocable and confirmed L/C. Japan's MITI, for example, requires irrevocable letters of credit before it will issue insurance coverage for exporters to Brazil.

### *Standby letter of credit (bid or performance L/C)*

Unlike the purpose of a commercial L/C, which is trade-related, the purpose of a standby L/C (special purpose or bid or performance L/C) is to guarantee a seller's obligation under a contract or agreement. It is used for such purposes as a performance bond, bid bond, surety bond, and loan agreement (see Figure 17.6). In this case, it is the buyer that requires the seller to open an L/C naming the buyer as a beneficiary, instead of the other way around. The reason for this arrangement is that the subsequent failure of the seller to fulfill the agreement can be quite damaging to the buyer, since a period of time has elapsed and the buyer has to seek a new supplier all over again. Because of the possibility of a loss of profit as a result of a delay or failure of the seller, the buyer needs to be assured that the seller is indeed capable of delivering goods or completing the project as promised. A standby L/C is thus a bank's guarantee to the beneficiary that a specific sum of money will be received by the beneficiary under certain conditions. If the beneficiary is the buyer, the firm can draw under the standby L/C only when the applicant (seller) fails to meet its obligations. On the other hand, the beneficiary can also be the exporter, which can ask for full or partial payment as the project progresses. Thus, the

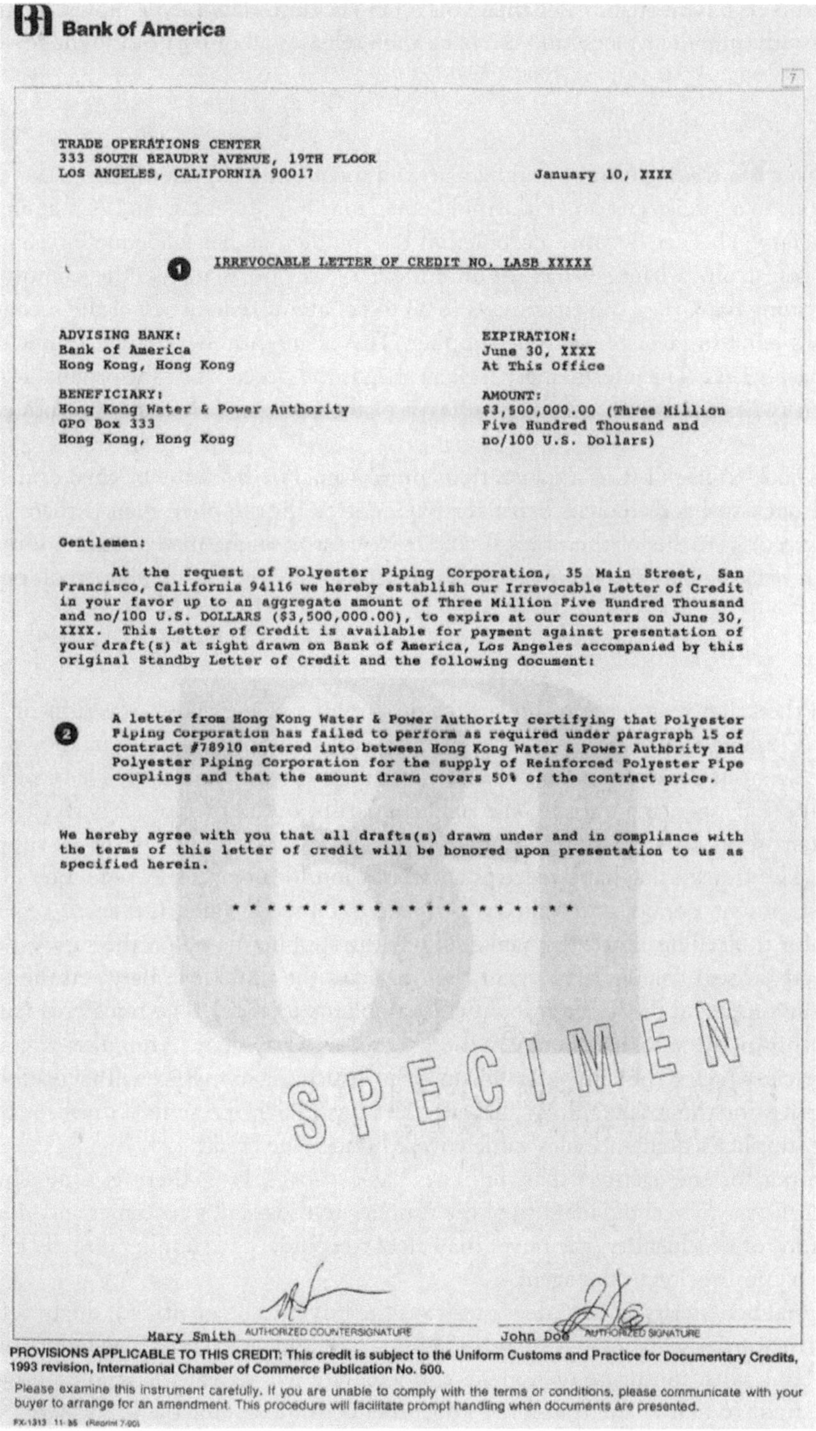

Bank of America

7

TRADE OPERATIONS CENTER
333 SOUTH BEAUDRY AVENUE, 19TH FLOOR
LOS ANGELES, CALIFORNIA 90017

January 10, XXXX

1 IRREVOCABLE LETTER OF CREDIT NO. LASB XXXXX

ADVISING BANK:
Bank of America
Hong Kong, Hong Kong

EXPIRATION:
June 30, XXXX
At This Office

BENEFICIARY:
Hong Kong Water & Power Authority
GPO Box 333
Hong Kong, Hong Kong

AMOUNT:
$3,500,000.00 (Three Million Five Hundred Thousand and no/100 U.S. Dollars)

Gentlemen:

At the request of Polyester Piping Corporation, 35 Main Street, San Francisco, California 94116 we hereby establish our Irrevocable Letter of Credit in your favor up to an aggregate amount of Three Million Five Hundred Thousand and no/100 U.S. DOLLARS ($3,500,000.00), to expire at our counters on June 30, XXXX. This Letter of Credit is available for payment against presentation of your draft(s) at sight drawn on Bank of America, Los Angeles accompanied by this original Standby Letter of Credit and the following document:

2 A letter from Hong Kong Water & Power Authority certifying that Polyester Piping Corporation has failed to perform as required under paragraph 15 of contract #78910 entered into between Hong Kong Water & Power Authority and Polyester Piping Corporation for the supply of Reinforced Polyester Pipe couplings and that the amount drawn covers 50% of the contract price.

We hereby agree with you that all drafts(s) drawn under and in compliance with the terms of this letter of credit will be honored upon presentation to us as specified herein.

* * * * * * * * * * * * * * * * * * * *

SPECIMEN

Mary Smith AUTHORIZED COUNTERSIGNATURE

John Doe AUTHORIZED SIGNATURE

**PROVISIONS APPLICABLE TO THIS CREDIT: This credit is subject to the Uniform Customs and Practice for Documentary Credits, 1993 revision, International Chamber of Commerce Publication No. 500.**

Please examine this instrument carefully. If you are unable to comply with the terms or conditions, please communicate with your buyer to arrange for an amendment. This procedure will facilitate prompt handling when documents are presented.

FX-1313 11-95 (Reprint 7-90)

**FIGURE 17.6** Standby letter of credit

*Source*: *Trade Banking Services* (Bank of America Corporation), 30–1. Reprinted with permission of the Bank of America.

seller is assured of payment for sales made on open account. The buyer draws by presenting the seller's draft with unpaid invoices, and the bank then releases all or part of the money to the seller.

### *Back-to-back letter of credit*

When the seller is a trading firm or middleman who must pay a supplier before asking the supplier to deliver goods to a foreign customer, the middleman may have to obtain an L/C naming the supplier as the beneficiary. This can become a problem if the middleman has inadequate resources to obtain a loan or a L/C from a bank. What the intermediary can do is to use the commitment of the customer's issuing bank (i.e., the customer's L/C) to collateralize issuance of the second L/C by the intermediary's bank in favor of, say, the supplier. This is an entirely separate transaction from the original or master L/C. The intermediary (seller) assigns the proceeds of the original L/C to its bank, which in turn issues the bank's own L/C in favor of the supplier for an amount not exceeding the original L/C.

Because a back-to-back L/C is a transaction entirely separate from the original or master L/C, the bank issuing back-to-back credit is liable for payment to the supplier even if there is a failure to complete the requirements of the original credit. Not surprisingly, many banks are reluctant to be involved with back-to-back transactions, preferring to handle the transferable credit option instead.

### *Transferable letter of credit*

Again, when the seller is an agent or broker for the supplier of the goods, it is difficult for the agent to have an L/C issued to the supplier if the agent's credit standing is weak or unknown. To solve the problem, the agent or broker may request a transferable L/C from the buyer. This type of L/C allows the beneficiary (i.e., agent) to transfer *once* rights in part or in full to another party. The agent as the first beneficiary requests the issuing or advising bank to transfer the L/C to its supplier (second beneficiary). The transferring bank receives a commission for doing so. A reduction in the amount, unit price, shipment period, and validity period are allowed. Since the agent receives a fee or commission for the selling effort, the bank will pay the supplier based on the supplier's invoices for the transferred (lesser) amount. The agent then receives the difference between the full price (the agent's own invoice) and the lesser amount (the supplier's invoice). The transferee (supplier), after making the shipment, submits documentation to receive payment. After this is completed, the original beneficiary (agent) obtains a commission by substituting its invoice with any other documents evidencing price for the total value of the sale. The beneficiary presents a draft for the difference between the supplier's draft and sales value covered under the credit.

The dilemma for the agent is that, unlike a back-to-back L/C, there is a possibility that the transferable L/C may reveal the identity of the supplier to the agent's customer and vice versa. Once the buyer learns of this identity, the buyer may elect to contact the supplier directly in the future to avoid paying a commission to the agent.

If the original beneficiary (agent) does not want the buyer to be identified, the beneficiary's name or a neutral (forwarder's) name may be substituted for the buyer's name. The failure of the agent to provide the bank with substitute documents immediately will defeat the whole purpose, since the bank has the right to deliver the transferee's documents to the issuing bank.

## *Advantages and disadvantages of letters of credit*

The L/C offers several advantages. First, it offers security while minimizing risk. The bank's acceptance of the payment obligation is a better credit instrument than a bill of exchange that has been accepted by the buyer. An L/C creates a better relationship with the buyer since all terms are specified and both parties are protected. In addition, the exporter can receive payment before maturity by discounting the L/C. An L/C can be discounted at a lower rate because it offers greater security than a bill of exchange. The discount charge is usually computed at the current prime bankers' acceptance rate from date of purchase to maturity.

For the buyer, the L/C also offers several benefits even though the buyer may have to bear the burden of financing. First, the buyer can buy now and pay later. Second, the L/C offers the assurance of prompt delivery. There is also an expired date for credit, and no payment is made until the goods are placed in the possession of a transport carrier for shipment. In addition, the seller must complete the terms specified in the L/C before payment is released. Third, the buyer may receive a better price since the seller does not have to adopt unnecessary safeguards or to sell the L/C at deep discount. The buyer, as a result, may even qualify for the seller's cash discount.

It is imperative that the seller carefully examine the L/C terms to make certain that he or she understands them and can meet the requirements. The seller must examine such items as the description of the merchandise, trade terms, price, delivery date, required documents, the party responsible for insurance, departure and entry points, and so on. The seller must also determine whether the L/C received is confirmed and irrevocable if requested as such. The seller should not accept an L/C requiring that the inspection certificate be signed by a particular individual because if that individual, due to death or other reasons, cannot sign the certificate, the exporter is unable to fulfill all the requirements and cannot collect payment. A precautionary measure may be to insist that the certificate be issued by a particular inspection company rather than a specific person associated with the company.

In spite of the many advantages, the L/C does have disadvantages as well. The instrument lacks flexibility, is cumbersome, and is the most complex method of obtaining payment. Any changes in the terms require an amendment to the L/C. Although suitable for a routine transaction, the L/C does not work well when the transaction is unusual and requires flexibility. It can also be expensive for the buyer if the government requires a prior deposit before establishing the L/C. For example, Lebanon requires banks to have their customers make a 15 percent deposit on documentary letters of credit on goods to be sold in Lebanon.

Another reason why the L/C can be a burden to the buyer is that it entails credit exposure. As such, the buyer's credit must be approved in advance by the buyer's bank. This is understandable because the L/C is issued on an unsecured basis, and the buyer-applicant only pays when the issuing bank is called upon to make payment. Without a satisfactory credit standing, the bank may require cash or other collateral for its own protection. In fact, a cash deposit may not even be acceptable if the importer has financial difficulties or an unknown credit reputation, since prior creditors may later lay claim to that amount of money in the event of the importer's bankruptcy. As a result, the bank will treat a request for an L/C as a request for a loan or line of credit. As such, the practice will tie up a portion of the buyer's available line of credit. Furthermore, L/C fees may range from 1 to 3 percent or perhaps even higher of the L/C amount.[23] These fees, of course, add to the importer's costs.[24]

It must be pointed out that an L/C is not a foolproof document. Guria, a private company based in the Republic of Georgia, was persuaded by an American businessman to relax the terms under which he could collect on an L/C for his handling of the purchase of 2,900 metric tons of sugar on behalf of Guria. The businessman then withdrew $768,500, but the sugar was never delivered. In another case, National Westminster Bank PLC paid out $1.8 million on an L/C to an Italian businessman who forged documents to show the bank that 5,000 metric tons of sugar were on the way to a buyer in Saudi Arabia. The Saudis found out that the shipment never took place, and the Czechoslovakian bank that issued the L/C refused to pay the British bank.[25] Certainly, the existence of an L/C is not a substitution for proper business investigation.

The most significant portion of the cost for an L/C is confirmation. The confirmation cost, being variable, may range from about 1 percent for a low-risk country to 6 percent or more for a high-risk country (e.g., Russia). The instrument, because of its relative greater degree of safety, has a much lower incidence of losses, reschedulings, or restructurings than the other normal term international loans. For almost two decades, there appear to be no losses on the confirmed letters of credit, except for the Dominican Republic, Nigeria, and Iraq – countries that after all failed to meet the minimum country risk standards at the time.[26]

## Conclusion

The exporter must make an effort to quote a meaningful price by using proper international trade terms. When there is doubt about how to prepare a quotation, freight forwarders should be consulted. These specialists can provide valuable information with regard to documentation (e.g., invoice, bill of lading) and the costs relevant to the movement of goods. Special financial documents such as letters of credit, however, require a bank's assistance. International banks have international departments that can facilitate payment and advise clients regarding the pitfalls in preparing and accepting documents.

Even when an exporting firm is assured of payment, it still needs to consider the source of payment and determine whether it is legitimate. The company should adopt money-laundering prevention rules. It is important to know one's client and to exercise due diligence so as to avoid undue scrutiny from law enforcement agencies.

## CASE 17.1 COUNTERTRADE: COUNTERPRODUCTIVE?

In modern times barter and its numerous derivations, which have conceptually been gathered together under the rubric "countertrade," have gained renewed stature in international trade. This has occurred despite the fact that international money and credit markets have attained unparalleled levels of sophistication.

Where readily acceptable forms of money exchange and viable credit facilities are available, markets shun cumbersome and inefficient barter-type transactions. However, international liquidity problems and government restrictions on the operation of markets have prompted many less developed countries (LDCs) and nonmarket economies (NMEs), as well as industrial countries, to promote "creative" trade transactions that circumvent the normal exchange medium of modern markets.

The shortcomings of countertrade include the following:

1. Countertrade has a high inherent transaction cost.
2. Countertrade limits competitive markets.
3. Countertrade contributes to market distortions that lead to inappropriate economic planning.

## Inefficiency in transactions costs

The underlying weakness of countertrade as a mechanism of trade and exchange is its inefficiency. The indivisibility of goods made barter inefficient, for example, and forced those involved with such trade to seek a better way. Barter gave way to goods/services-for-money exchange, which permitted transactions to incorporate divisibility as well as time shifting.The opportunity for more convenient (i.e., efficient), multiparty trade became a reality.

A major factor in the expansion of world trade during the last half of the twentieth century has been the emergence of a few widely accepted currencies, especially the U.S. dollar, as settlement currencies for international transactions. The development of international credit markets to support trade depended on the fact that transactions could be entered into without undue concern by the parties involved as to the delivery of the specific quantity and quality of goods and the timeliness of payment. A key characteristic of this type of market is that the channels of communication and exchange are well defined and relatively simple.

As a consequence of this clarity and simplicity, such markets are efficient. Specifically, the direct and indirect costs involved in the process of exchange account for a relatively small proportion of the total cost of the transaction.

Such efficiency is not present in the conditional transactions that make up countertrade. The inefficiency cost must be borne by one or more of the parties involved.

Many countertrade transactions are entered into because the importing country is unable to obtain financing in the international markets and is short of hard-currency reserves. The lack of access, or limited access, to the credit markets may be due to restrictions on the country, placed as a condition for specific new lending by the International Monetary Fund (IMF) or foreign commercial banks. In this environment countertrade is sometimes viewed by an LDC government as a means of engaging in trade without the cost of entering the international finance markets.

Whereas it is correct that countertrade may mean that the international financial markets may not have to be tapped, it is not correct to assume that there are no financing costs associated with a countertrade transaction. In fact, due to the complexity associated with carrying out a countertrade transaction, the cost is higher than if the LDC had access to those credit markets. Moreover, countertrade may end up subverting the capital and austerity restrictions that in some cases are a part of an IMF/LDC lending agreement.

In countertrade the costs of financing are shifted. They become implicit rather than explicit. The seller may absorb this cost in the form of accepting the obligation to buy or use or resell goods it otherwise would not accept (thus reducing its return on the transaction). Alternatively, the seller may build the transaction's finance costs into the price the buyer must pay. The finance costs are there, albeit hidden.

## Limiting competition

There is another implicit cost when countertrade is required by the LDC or nonmarket economy (NME) buyer as a condition of the transaction. Countertrade limits the potential number of sellers in the market. Not every seller firm is willing or able to engage in countertrade; thus, an LDC or NME buyer that insists on countertrade as part of a trade package limits its potential for obtaining a competitive product, service, or price.The fact is that engaging in countertrade costs the LDC or NME economy more in terms of real resources than a straight commercial transaction.

## Market distortions and false signals

Developing countries may not have well-developed international marketing facilities. As a result they often find it difficult to break into international markets with goods and services that are nontraditional for their economy.

In other cases an LDC or NME may choose to develop a new domestic industry by buying the technology and plant from abroad. Domestic demand may not be adequate for an efficient plant size. In response, they may opt for a larger, more efficient (but possibly from a world supply view, redundant) plant with the expectation of placing the marginal production on the international market.

Under such conditions counterpurchase or buyback agreements may be sought by the LDC or NME to finance the importation of plant and equipment for a new industry (as in a buyback agreement) or general imports (as in a counterpurchase agreement).The LDC or NME may also be seeking a more knowledgeable partner to handle the international marketing of goods for which it does not have the expertise.

The difficulty with this approach is that countertrade may be used to get goods on to the international market that would not "make it" under the usual conditions and will not be competitive once the buyback agreement expires.

Further, the industrial country firm that accepted the countertraded goods may dump them, which would be disruptive to international markets. The result may be that the LDC or NME producer may falsely interpret the signals and overestimate the real market demand for the dumped goods as being stronger than a longer term, unsubsidized, market can bear.

Moreover, the secondary consequences of countertrade transactions are not benign. The inefficiencies of countertrade – the false price signals that result in the building of redundant plant and equipment – tend to promote the establishment of bureaucracies within governments and private firms that have "bought into" countertrade. In turn, these bureaucracies have a vested interest in maintaining the economic distortions that undergird the growth in countertrade.

## Summing up

Countertrade is a significant factor in modern international trade. In its different forms it is used as a marketing tool, as a competitive tool, as a tool to restrict trade alternatives, and as a tool to tie the trade of one country to another country. Countertrade in a modern world economy with highly developed goods, capital, and financial markets appears on its face to be an incongruous development. Countertrade is a costly, inefficient, and disruptive anomaly. Yet observers of international trade suggest that the volume of countertrade is growing.

Countertrade takes place in a world of imperfection where the political and economic policies of government and industry distort the relationships between and within the goods, capital, and financial markets.

### *Points to consider*

1 Discuss the pros and cons of countertrade as a form of trade.
2 As a manufacturing firm located in a developed country, you are interested in taking advantage of the Eastern European markets' movement toward market-oriented economies. However, your potential customers lack hard currency and have asked you to consider countertrade. Are you willing to engage in countertrade? Why or why not?

*Source*: Abbreviated and adapted from Jack L. Hervey, "Countertrade – Counterproductive?", *Economic Perspectives* (January/February 1989): 17–24.

## Questions

1 Explain these terms of countertrade: *barter, counterpurchase, buyback, offsets, clearing agreement,* and *switch trading.*
2 Explain these terms of sale: *EXW/DEQ, FAS, FOB, CFR, CIF,* and *DDP.*

3 Explain: (a) bill of exchange and (b) bankers' acceptance.
4 Explain these types of letter of credit: *revocable*, *irrevocable*, *confirmed*, *unconfirmed*, *back-to-back*, and *transferable*.

## Discussion assignments and minicases

1 Given that countertrade is a fact of life which is not going to go away, is there any valid argument from a *theoretical* standpoint for this method of doing business?
2 Assume you are a manufacturer being asked to submit a quotation to a potential buyer. How are you going to prepare your quotation in (a) terms of sale and (b) terms of payment?

## Notes


1 Jack L. Hervey, "Countertrade – Counterproductive?", *Economic Perspectives*, January/February 1989, 17–24.
2 "Russia: What Happens When Markets Fail," *Business Week*, April 26, 1999, 50–2.
3 Raj Desai and Itzhak Goldberg, "Stakeholders, Governance, and the Russian Enterprise Dilemma," *Finance & Development*, June 2000, 14–18.
4 "Noncash Transactions Increase in Russia after Transition to Market Economy," *IMF Survey*, November 20, 2000, 381–2.
5 "Noncash Transactions."
6 John A. Angelidis and Nabil A. Ibrahim, "Countertrading with the Middle East: An Empirical Investigation of Challenges and Opportunities," *Journal of Global Marketing* 8 (No. 2, 1994): 97–114.
7 "Honda Will Create Brand for China's Auto Market," *Wall Street Journal*, July 19, 2007.
8 Bruce Fitzgerald, "Countertrade Reconsidered," *Finance & Development*, June 1987, 46–49.
9 Ann Ring, "Countertrade Business Opportunities in Russia," *Business America*, January 11, 1993, 15–16.
10 Sam C. Okoroafo, "An Integration of Countertrade Research and Practice," *Journal of Global Marketing* 6 (No. 4, 1993): 113–27.
11 Sam C. Okoroafo, "A Managerial Approach to Predicting Countertrade Demands by Developing Countries," *Journal of Global Marketing* 6 (Nos 1/2, 1992): 171–83.
12 Jean-François Hennart, "Some Empirical Dimensions of Countertrade," *Journal of International Business Studies* 21 (No. 2, 1990): 243–70.
13 Donald J. Lecraw, "The Management of Countertrade: Factors Influencing Success," *Journal of International Business Studies* 20 (spring 1989): 41–59.
14 Pompiliu Verzariu, "Trends and Developments in International Countertrade," *Business America*, November 2, 1992, 2–6.
15 *A Guide on Countertrade Practices in the Newly Independent States of the Former Soviet Union* (Washington, DC: U.S. Department of Commerce, 1995).
16 "Institutional Improvement in Ukraine Could Lead to Growth Boom," *IMF Survey*, October 16, 2006, 301.
17 "Incoterms 2000," *Export America*, 11–12. See also the website of the International Chamber of Commerce for Incoterms 2000; and www.look4logistics.com.
18 "Price, Quotations, and Terms of Sale Are Key to Successful Exporting," *Business America*, October 4, 1993, 12–15.

19 Tarek Liddawi, "Optimizing Supply Chains in the Retail Sector," *AmCham News* 13 (October–November 2006): 6.
20 Banks with international departments have publications that explain the various types of collection methods and documents. For example, see *Trade Banking Services* (BankAmerica Corporation, 1994).
21 "What's This Credit Worth?", *Collections and Credit Risk*, November 2000, 43ff.
22 *Trade Banking Services*, 5.
23 D. Grant McKinnon, "Export Sales – The Importance of Setting Competitive Payment Terms," *Business America*, February 1995, 6–7.
24 For an in-depth discussion, see John F. Dolan, *The Law of Letters of Credit: Commercial and Standby Credits* (2nd edn) (Boston, MA: Warren Gorham Lamont, 1991).
25 "Deals Too Sweet to Be True," *Business Week*, July 10, 1995, 122.
26 "Export Payment Terms Adjust the Risk to Exporters and the Cost to Importers," *Business America*, 26–8.

# Part 5

# Financial decisions

Chapter 18

# Financial strategies

## Financing and currencies

Owe your banker a thousand pounds, and you are at his mercy. Owe him a million, and the position is reversed.

John Maynard Keynes

## Chapter outline

- Marketing strategy: the Big Mac Index
- Trade finance
- Nonfinancial institutions
  - Self-financing and debt financing
  - Equity financing
- Financial institutions
- Government agencies
- International financial institutions/development banks
- International Monetary Fund (IMF)
- Money
- Foreign exchange
- Foreign exchange market
- Foreign exchange rate
  - Currency equilibrium
  - Effect of devaluation
- Exchange rate systems
  - Gold Standard
  - Par value (adjustable peg)
  - Crawling peg (sliding or gliding parity)

- Wide band
- Floating (flexible) system

- Official classification of exchange rate regimes
- Evaluation of floating rates
- Financial implications and strategies
  - Early warning systems
  - Hedging
  - Leading and lagging
  - Invoicing
  - Pass-through costs
  - Other strategies
- Conclusion
- Case 18.1 Ups and downs: a foreign exchange simulation game

## Marketing strategy

### The Big Mac Index

*The Economist* charts the cost of a Big Mac at McDonald's restaurants in 120 countries. The Big Mac Index is a measure of what it costs to buy a Big Mac in various parts of the world. Some people use the Big Mac Index as a convenient substitute for the purchasing–power–parity theory, which states that, although short-term factors may once in a while unduly affect exchange rates, purchasing power should be the same all over the world. If a Big Mac costs $3.43 in New York City, but costs $2.29 (or 33 percent less) in Tokyo, then the interpretation is that the Japanese yen is 33 percent undervalued compared to the U.S. dollar.

The Big Mac Index is a surprisingly accurate comparative of international currency. It found in 1994, for example, that the Japanese yen was overvalued by more than 60 percent. While it is true that short-term factors (e.g., politics, trade deficits, and interest rates) can greatly affect currency valuations, economic fundamentals tend to assert themselves over the long term. Therefore, in the case of Japan, according to the purchasing–power–parity theory, it is just a matter of time before the dollar would rise and the yen would fall.

The Big Mac Index's greatest triumph has to do with the euro. When the euro was launched in January 1999, virtually all economists predicted the euro's rise against the dollar. The Big Mac Index instead suggested that the euro started off significantly overvalued. One of the best-known hedge funds, Soros Fund Management, considered but disregarded the sell signal given by the Big Mac Index. When the euro tumbled, Soros was not happy.

In 2002, while the U.S. dollar was riding high, the Big Mac Index determined that the dollar was more overvalued than at any time in the measure's 16-year history. Not long after, the dollar began its decline, and the weakness persisted throughout 2003.

One problem with the Big Mac Index is that it is unable to predict when the change in currency value will take place. In 1995, in spite of the acknowledgment that the dollar was greatly undervalued against the yen, the dollar kept sinking and hitting new record lows. However, there was some evidence of the validity of the index. In March 1995, McDonald's Co. Japan

Ltd., the largest restaurant chain in Japan, announced that it would cut the prices on its hamburgers by about 30 percent. The price cut was attributed to the rising value of the yen against the dollar and lower operating expenses since McDonald's imports many of its supplies. In April 1995, McDonald's cut its price again in Tokyo by 38 percent from \$2.53 to the unheard price of \$1.56 in Japan.

In mid-2007, a Big Mac cost 11 yuan in China (or only \$1.45 at the exchange rate at the time), meaning that the Chinese yuan was undervalued by 58 percent. At the other end, Iceland, Norway, and Switzerland had the most overvalued currencies. While the euro was 22 percent above its fair value, the Swiss franc was 53 percent overvalued. At the time, the Japanese yen was found to be 33 percent undervalued. Soon after that, the yen rallied sharply against the U.S. dollar.

Based on the price of \$3.43 for a Big Mac in the U.S.A., the prices in selected countries (and undervaluation or overvaluation against the dollar) are: Brazil (\$3.61, +6%), China (\$1.45, –58%), Denmark (\$5.08, +49%), Egypt (\$1.68, –51%), Hong Kong (\$1.54, –55%), Japan (\$2.29, –33%), New Zealand (\$5.89, +73%), Russia (\$2.03, –41%), Switzerland (\$5.20, +53%), and Thailand (\$1.80, –47%).

*Sources*: George Anders, "What Price Lunch?", *Wall Street Journal*, September 23, 1988; "Shorting the Yen," *Worth*, September 1994, 61; "Big Mac Currencies," *The Economist*, April 21, 2001, 74; "Hamburger Helper," *CBSMarketWatch.com*, April 29, 2003; "The Big Mac Index: Sizzling," *The Economist*, July 7, 2007, 74.

## Purpose of chapter

The Big Mac Index serves as an introduction to the value of money as well as the impact of foreign exchange. Even a highly regarded professional trader could be wrong about the direction of a certain currency. All currency traders, international bankers, exporters, and multinational corporations realize that volatility exists in the international financial markets. For example, foreign exchange fluctuations probably cost Lufthansa AG 200 million marks in 1995. For each one-yen increase against the dollar, Nissan will lose six billion yen annually in sales and profits. Therefore, for firms with international activities, foreign exchange risk is inevitable and must be managed to keep it at a minimum.

The purpose of this chapter is to discuss the critical role that financing and financial strategies play in securing overseas projects. Financing is important to the operations of both importers and exporters. Importers seek financing for the purchase of merchandise. Exporters likewise need financing for the manufacturing of their products and the maintenance of their inventories. Furthermore, overseas buyers attempt to shift the financing function to their suppliers. If an exporter agrees to extend credit, the exporter must in turn obtain financing for this purpose. Financing is not a problem only for small firms. In fact, in the case of international multimillion-dollar projects, sellers' financing is usually expected, and financing terms often separate winners from losers.

This chapter will place greater emphasis on the various issues relating to international finance. First, it examines the meaning of money as a medium of exchange. It then examines the role of foreign exchange in international trade while discussing the functions of foreign exchange markets. Next, it focuses on the effect of currency devaluation and appreciation. There is also an evaluation of the various systems of foreign exchange and their implications. Finally, some practical guidelines are offered about hedging options used to reduce foreign exchange risk.

## Trade finance

**Trade finance** arises from the export of goods and services, when the buyer and seller negotiate the amount, time, and terms of payment. The financing needs of the seller and buyer are almost always not compatible, and they may even sometimes be in conflict. Naturally, the buyer desires a competitive price and a payment arrangement that does not tie up one's credit line, whereas the seller wants a financing arrangement that offers quick payment and protection against default. The method of trade finance attempts to accommodate these differences. Trade finance can be supplied by parties in the private sector (e.g., the buyer's cash in advance payment) or by parties in the public sector (e.g., a bank's financing of the sale).

There are both local and international sources of financing that are available to public and private buyers, including the various private and nonprofit financial institutions. Any business, no matter how large or small, domestic or international, always requires some kind of financing for its operations. Because international financing must deal with financial and economic conditions in more than one country, this activity involves more uncertainty and complexity than domestic financing. The greater complexity of international financing, however, is accompanied by a greater number of financing options. In addition to the standard channels, there are also other sources available almost exclusively for international business. These sources include: (1) nonfinancial institutions, (2) private financial institutions, (3) international agencies, and (4) the International Monetary Fund (IMF).

## Nonfinancial institutions

### *Self-financing and debt financing*

There are several nonfinancial institutions that can provide financing. First, there is self-financing because a business can use its own *capital* or can withhold *dividends* so that profits may be plowed back into the organization for further business expansion (see Legal Dimension 18.1). Second, retailers and manufacturers alike may be able to seek *trade credit* and financial assistance from certain middlemen, such as export merchants and trading companies. Third, when joint ventures are formed, *foreign partners* can also lend a helping hand. Fourth, subsidiaries of MNCs may borrow from *affiliated firms* as well as from the *employee retirement fund*.

In addition, the business may decide to raise equity capital by selling stocks, or it may depend on debt financing by selling *commercial paper* or *bonds*. Bond buyers or holders are the firm's creditors rather than its owners. One study found that a company's increased foreign involvement raised bondholder value while decreasing shareholder value.[1]

U.S. firms can sell bonds in either the U.S.A. or foreign countries, with Eurobonds as a prime example. Treasurers of U.S. firms must decide whether their bonds to be sold abroad are to be denominated in dollar or foreign currencies. In any case, it should be noted that debt financing requires the services of investment banks. Virtually every multinational bank or multinational brokerage house has a division that acts as an investment bank.

Another source of financing is **venture capital**. Venture capitalists invest funds in a firm in exchange for a share of ownership. Although known for their investments in high-technology firms, venture capitalists have diversified their portfolios. There are about 600 venture capital firms in the U.S.A. Private investors, however, fund most ventures. Venture Capital Network in Durham, New

## Legal Dimension 18.1

### Tax havens

Companies will go anywhere in their pursuit of profits (or avoidance of taxes). They are not bashful in exploiting low tax rates abroad. The idea is to maximize income in low-tax countries while shifting expenses to high-tax nations. Perhaps, the most aggressive scheme is to incorporate in a tax haven. While this tactic usually creates uproar in the home country, these companies feel that it does not pay to be nationalistic.

As in the case of Tyco International Ltd., it followed the moves of Cooper Industries, Ingersoll-Rand Co., and others. By moving to Bermuda, it has managed to cut its effective tax rate from 36 percent to 23 percent. The company is now saving $600 million a year. Tyco has since set up 150 subsidiaries in Barbados, the Cayman Islands, and Jersey.

Tourism accounts for 40 percent of the $4.5 billion economy of the Bahamas. Financial services, accounting for almost 20 percent of economic activity, are an increasingly important factor. More than 400 banks and trust companies and 600 mutual funds have offices there. These entities manage nearly $600 billion in assets.

Nassau, the tiny capital of the Bahamas, has liberal trust laws and no income tax to go with its balmy weather. There are no taxes on corporate profits, retail sales, capital gains, or income from inheritances. Another attraction is that Nassau promises inviolable secrecy because only signatories on an account can access bank records.

In 2000, OECD accused 35 jurisdictions of engaging in "harmful tax practices." These jurisdictions included the Bahamas, Barbados, the U.S. Virgin Islands, and 12 other Caribbean regimes. The Bahamas fought back by stating that the OECD's action was a retribution against the smaller countries' competitive tax regimes.

It is an irony that the U.S. tax laws are so complicated and inefficient to the point that the U.S. Treasury may be better off by simply exempting overseas income from taxes. This will encourage American companies to bring their profits home, and the U.S.A. may end up collecting $7 billion more. The nation's 500 biggest companies are forced to spend more than $1 billion a year in their effort to comply with tax laws. Half of these costs are probably linked to international tax rules.

*Sources*: "Taxing Multinationals: The Donnybrook Ahead," *Business Week*, September 9, 2002, 86–7; "The Corporate Tax Game," *Business Week*, March 31, 2003, 79–83; and "Taxing Times for Tax Havens," *Business Week*, October 30, 2000, 96ff.

Hampshire, is a nonprofit service affiliated with the University of New Hampshire. Attempting to match entrepreneurs with investors, the Network charges investors $200 a year and those seeking capital $500 annually for registration. While most European venture capital firms focus on their own national markets, Mangrove Capital Partners target the whole of Europe. One of its notable successes is Skype Technologies, which was rejected by 20 venture capital groups for its plan to offer free telephone calls over the Internet.[2]

Interestingly, one study found that the venture capital industry in East Asia exhibited different behavior from that in the West, even though East Asian venture capitalists were trained in Western venture capital firms.[3] Apparently, the regulatory environment and culture of East Asia can play a role in shaping the industry.

## *Equity financing*

Instead of relying on debt financing, companies may raise equity capital by selling stocks. One study examined the relationship between market valuation and geographic scope of U.S. MNCs' foreign operations. According to the evidence, based on the importance of the location of MNC operations, MNCs with presence in developing economies have significantly higher market values than MNCs that operate only in advanced economies. In addition, the market value impact of intangible assets increases with the degree of an MNC's expansion into developing locations only.[4]

Naturally, companies list their stocks in their own national stock markets. For multinational corporations however, they want to additionally offer their stocks in multiple countries. While many firms limit the listing of their securities to their domestic exchanges, the growing internationalization of capital markets suggests that more and more firms perceive that the benefits of listing their stocks on foreign exchanges outweigh the related costs. As in the case of News Corp., Australian-turned-American citizen Rupert Murdoch has moved the company and the stock listing to the U.S.A. so as to broaden the shareholder base while gaining better access to the capital markets. Indeed, the restrictions which some major U.S. institutions face in owning foreign stocks would be lifted, and News Corp.'s likely addition to the Standard & Poor's 500-stock index will attract more investors. The company gets about 75 percent of its revenues, profits, and cash flow from the U.S.A.[5]

Chinese companies have taken an unusual approach so that their stocks can be publicly traded in the U.S.A. A Chinese company may appear to be acquired by a U.S. shell company which has nothing, but because the U.S. company is publicly traded, the Chinese board will then take over the U.S. company and change its name before issuing new stock to raise capital. This kind of reverse merger allowed Sinovac Biotech Ltd., a maker of vaccines in Beijing, to raise $12 million in the U.S.A.[6]

Emerging stock markets vary greatly in terms of the number of firms listed, the number of new listings per year, market capitalization, and so on. Naturally, such markets carry significant risk, but emerging stock markets are likely to play an increasingly important role in financing companies' growth.

The Milken Institute's Capital Studies group has developed an index to compare the quality of the financial infrastructures that support entrepreneurial activity. The index consists of seven components: (1) the efficiency of savings–loan intermediaries; (2) the breadth and liquidity of equity markets; (3) the efficiency and size of bond markets; (4) the development of alternative sources of finance from venture capital to credit cards; (5) the environment for foreign investment, both direct and indirect; (6) the macroeconomic environment (measuring price stability and low interest and tax rates), and (7) the institutional environment (measuring the enforceability of property and contract rights, the efficiency of bankruptcy procedures, and freedom from corruption). The last two components carry disproportionate weight. Based on the 2006 index, the top countries are: (1) Hong Kong, (2) Singapore, (3) the United Kingdom, (4) Canada, (5) the U.S.A., (6) Australia, (7) Switzerland, (8) the Netherlands, (9) Ireland, and (10) Sweden.[7]

# Financial institutions

International companies have several options in financial institutions that have the capability of dealing in international finance (see Figure 18.1). The most common alternative is banks (and nonbank banks), both domestic and overseas. In addition to the well-known giant banks that operate

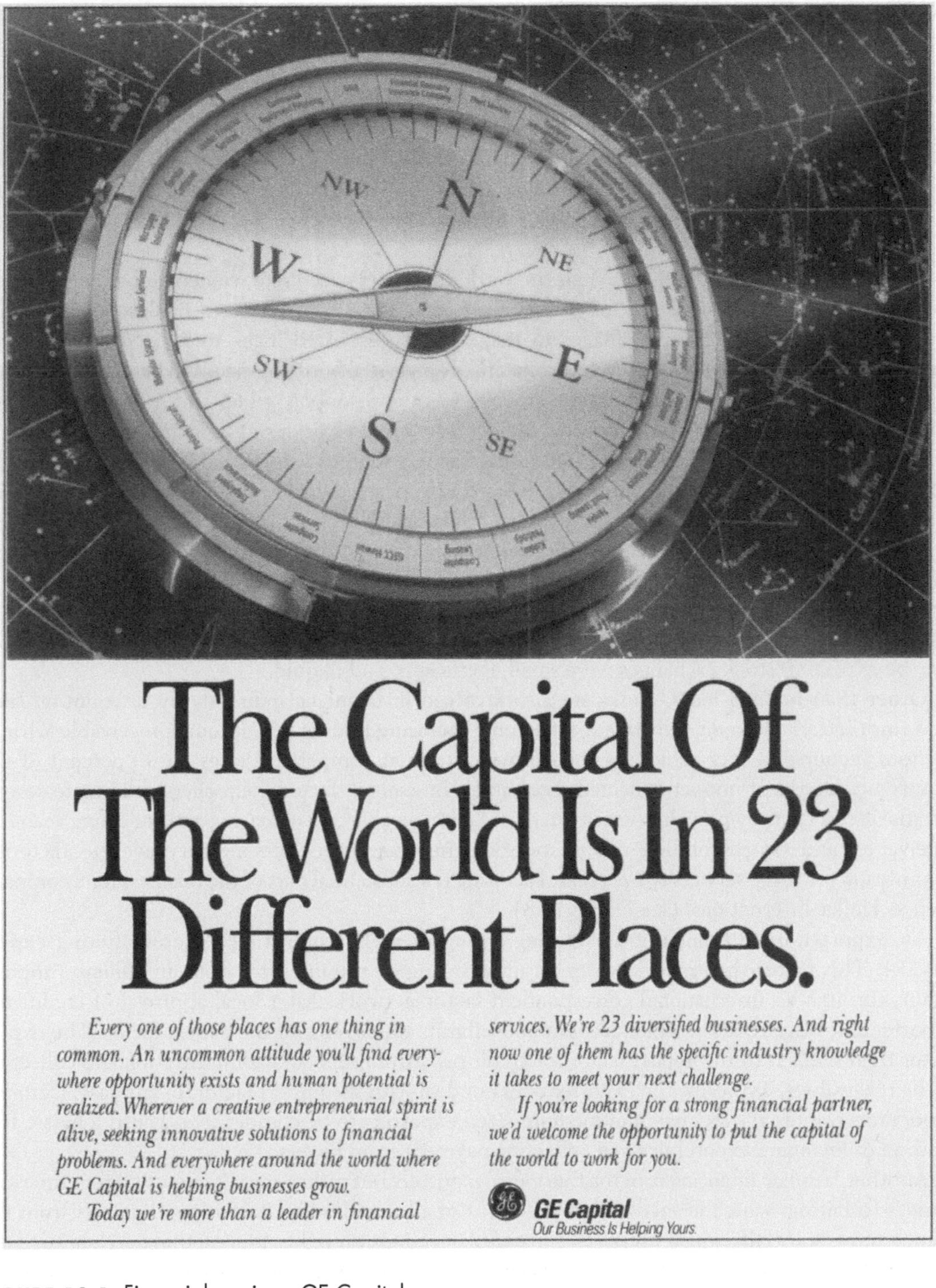
NW
N
NE
W
E
SW
S
SE
The Capital Of The World Is In 23 Different Places.
Every one of those places has one thing in common. An uncommon attitude you'll find everywhere opportunity exists and human potential is realized. Wherever a creative entrepreneurial spirit is alive, seeking innovative solutions to financial problems. And everywhere around the world where GE Capital is helping businesses grow.
Today we're more than a leader in financial services. We're 23 diversified businesses. And right now one of them has the specific industry knowledge it takes to meet your next challenge.
If you're looking for a strong financial partner, we'd welcome the opportunity to put the capital of the world to work for you.
GE Capital
Our Business Is Helping Yours.

**FIGURE 18.1** Financial services: GE Capital

globally, there are many medium-sized banks that have international banking departments. The multinational banks can make arrangements to satisfy all kinds of financing needs.

Although markets play a dominant role in Anglo-Saxon countries such as the U.S.A. and England, continental Europe and Japan are dominated by banks. Due to national culture, countries having higher uncertainty avoidance are more likely to have a bank-based system.[8] In Asia, there is still too much dependence on bank financing.[9] While banks in most regions lend 60 percent or more of their resources to the private sector, banks in Africa lend only about 30 percent. African banks do not lend much because of perceived lending risk. They have been accused of "a lack of banking nerve."[10]

The concept of **microcredit**, based on the work of Nobel Peace Prize winner Muhammad Yunus, has attracted a great deal of attention worldwide (see Figure 18.2). Grameen Bank sends thousands of people to urban slums and villages to make small unsecured loans to poor people. Female borrowers can obtain $100 or so without collateral. A potential borrower needs to band together with four other people from the community. The five work as a support group and must approve each other's proposals. The idea is to empower the poorest women by offering collateral-free credit.[11]

Because of various regulatory and traditional barriers to entry, stocks have historically played a relatively minor role in corporate financing in many European countries. In the case of German equity markets, for example, until recently, the largest banks that had a monopoly on brokerage effectively controlled access to the stock exchange. Small firms, being kept from issuing equity, remained captive loan clients. In addition, the integration of banking and commerce in Germany has contributed to large German firms' traditional reliance more on bank credit and bonds than on equity to finance growth. German firms use their equity holdings to exert ownership control over industrial firms. As may be expected, stock exchanges were small, inefficient, and illiquid.

Other than making loans, banks are also involved in financing indirectly by discounting (i.e., factoring) letters of credit and time drafts. Some **factoring houses** buy accounts receivable with or without recourse at face value and then provide loans at competitive rates on 90 percent of the factors' acquired but not-yet-collected receivables. In general, factors help clients eliminate several internal credit costs by providing credit guarantee of receivables, by managing and collecting accounts receivable, and by performing related bookkeeping functions. The industry average factoring commission for these services is 1 percent. Factoring is a substantial part of the business for a company such as Heller International (see Figure 18.3).

An exporter usually initiates a factoring arrangement by contacting a factor offering export services. This factor then requests a credit undertaking on the importer from an affiliate (import) factor, through an international correspondent factor network. After local approval of credit, the exporter ships the goods on open account and submits the invoice to the export factor. The export factor then sends it to the import factor for credit risk assumption and administration and collection of the receivables. Typically, the exporter does not deal with the import factor. In any case, factoring export receivables allows small and medium-sized exporters to be competitive, as it is a hassle-free method of financing export sales and collecting payment from buyers.

Another familiar financing tool for European exporters but rather an unknown tool for American firms is forfaiting, which finances about 2 percent of all world trade. **Forfaiting** originates from the French term "a forfait" which means to surrender or relinquish rights to something. When used, an exporter surrenders possession of export receivables by selling them at a discount. The cost depends on country risk. For sales to Japan and France, the discount rate may be 6.75 percent, and terms may reach five years, whereas sales to Pakistan may boost the discount rate to 7.75 percent with a

The loan she'll pay back. Her dignity she'll keep.
Rosaria is poor, but she doesn't need charity. She just wants a little credit. With a loan as small as $100, she can grow her tiny business, feed her family, and send her kids to school. Today, ACCION microloans are helping more than one million women and men work their way out of poverty. But to reach millions more, we need your support.
To help others like Rosaria succeed, please call us now or visit www.accion.org to donate online.
ACCIÓN
ACCION INTERNATIONAL
56 Roland Street, Suite 300
Boston, Massachusetts 02129
Phone: 617.625.7080
www.accion.org

**FIGURE 18.2** Microloans

*Source*: ACCION International.

For a total perspective
to serve your financial world best...
Heller is the one.
The one that zeros in on creative solutions that answer all your needs. Get the Heller point of view for any or all of your financing needs, which include:
Asset-Based financing expertise to assist you in major acquisitions or mergers, meeting working capital needs or other types of financing. Professionals with the deal structuring expertise, funding capacity and service capabilities to serve your industry and market.
Factoring to provide specialized credit and collection expertise and working capital funds in marketing your products throughout the U.S. and around the world.
Equipment financing programs to facilitate the sale of equipment from the manufacturer to the end user. An integrated multi-service offering which satisfies financing requirements for each step in your distribution process.
Commercial Real Estate financing to support you in every phase of your project's development—from site development to permanent financing.
Heller wants to be involved in your financial planning process. As part of Heller International, there are 72 offices worldwide, staffed with professionals dedicated to a high level of performance. We've recently changed our name to Heller Financial emphasizing our commitment to set standards of excellence no one in the industry can match. We welcome you to test our commitment.
For more information and a copy of our 1984 Annual Review call: 1-800-458-4924. (In Illinois, call: 1-800-621-2429. In Canada, call: 1-416-482-4012.)
Heller Financial
Asset-Based Financing • Factoring • Equipment Financing • Real Estate Financing
105 West Adams Street, Chicago, Illinois 60603.
Heller Financial, Inc. is an operating subsidiary of Heller International Corporation.
© Heller Financial, Inc. 1985

**FIGURE 18.3** Factoring: Heller Financial

*Source*: Reprinted with permission of Heller Financial.

one-year term limit. Generally, an exporter consults with a forfaiter before incorporating the discount rate into the final selling price.

Export factoring and forfaiting are similar, since both involve selling export receivables to a third party at a discount. There are a few differences, however, between the two parties. First, factors like a large percentage of an exporter's business, but forfait houses do not mind working on a one-shot basis. Second, while factors specialize in short-term receivables (up to 180 days), forfaiters tend to work with medium-term receivables. Finally, forfaiters are more willing to deal with high-risk countries. To protect themselves, forfait houses require a guarantee from a reputable commercial bank in the importer's country. The guarantee is in the form of an **aval** (bank guarantee). An endorsement with the words "PER AVAL" or "GUARANTEED PER AVAL" is stamped directly on to the notes or bills by the guarantor bank.[12]

Banks may provide **equipment leasing** as another alternative form of financing. The most attractive benefit of leasing is its low cost while allowing an exporter to conserve capital and improve cash flow. Leasing may involve 100 percent financing with no down payment (see Figure 18.4). It may be used in conjunction with conventional lending sources.

In the United Kingdom, companies have a number of financial institutions to contact for loans. These institutions include foreign banks, British clearing banks, merchant banks (factor houses), finance houses, investment trust companies, pension funds and insurance companies, leasing firms, and development capital and other specialist venture capital organizations. In Germany, companies may be able to obtain short-term loans for German and foreign banks, usually by overdraft.

Figures 18.5 and 18.6 show two international banks with a strong presence in the world's financial markets.

## Government agencies

It is not unusual for governments to provide **concessionary financing**. Such public loans, as a rule, carry lower than market interest rates, and their terms are more favorable than those of private financial institutions. Governments' role in financing can also be indirect but significant. Japan, for example, uses qualification for public loans as an inducement for private banks to co-finance. The qualification carries this significance by implying that any investment would be in the national interest and that the firm in question is financially sound.

To win a project in a developing nation, an exporting country may provide **tied aid** which is concessionary financing terms conditional upon the purchase of the equipment and services from the donor country. Trade-motivated tied aid may thus persuade a buyer to lean in the direction of the donor – not necessarily on the merit of product quality and true price. Ellicott Machine Corp. International, a small U.S. company, lost market share in Indonesia where the Indonesian government has been the company's largest single customer for dredging equipment for over 100 years. The market share loss was due to European competitors' use of tied aid soft loans.

European governments have been offering **mixed** or **blended credit**. This type of financing package combines an official, conventional loan with either outright grants or foreign aid grants at below-market rates, in effect reducing the actual interest rate based on the condition that donor countries' products are bought. France, the heaviest user of this technique, won Malaysia's contract for a $200-million turnkey power plant by disguising its 30-year loan at a 4.5 percent rate as an aid grant, which made up almost half of the financing package. Mixed credit is particularly important in the sale of

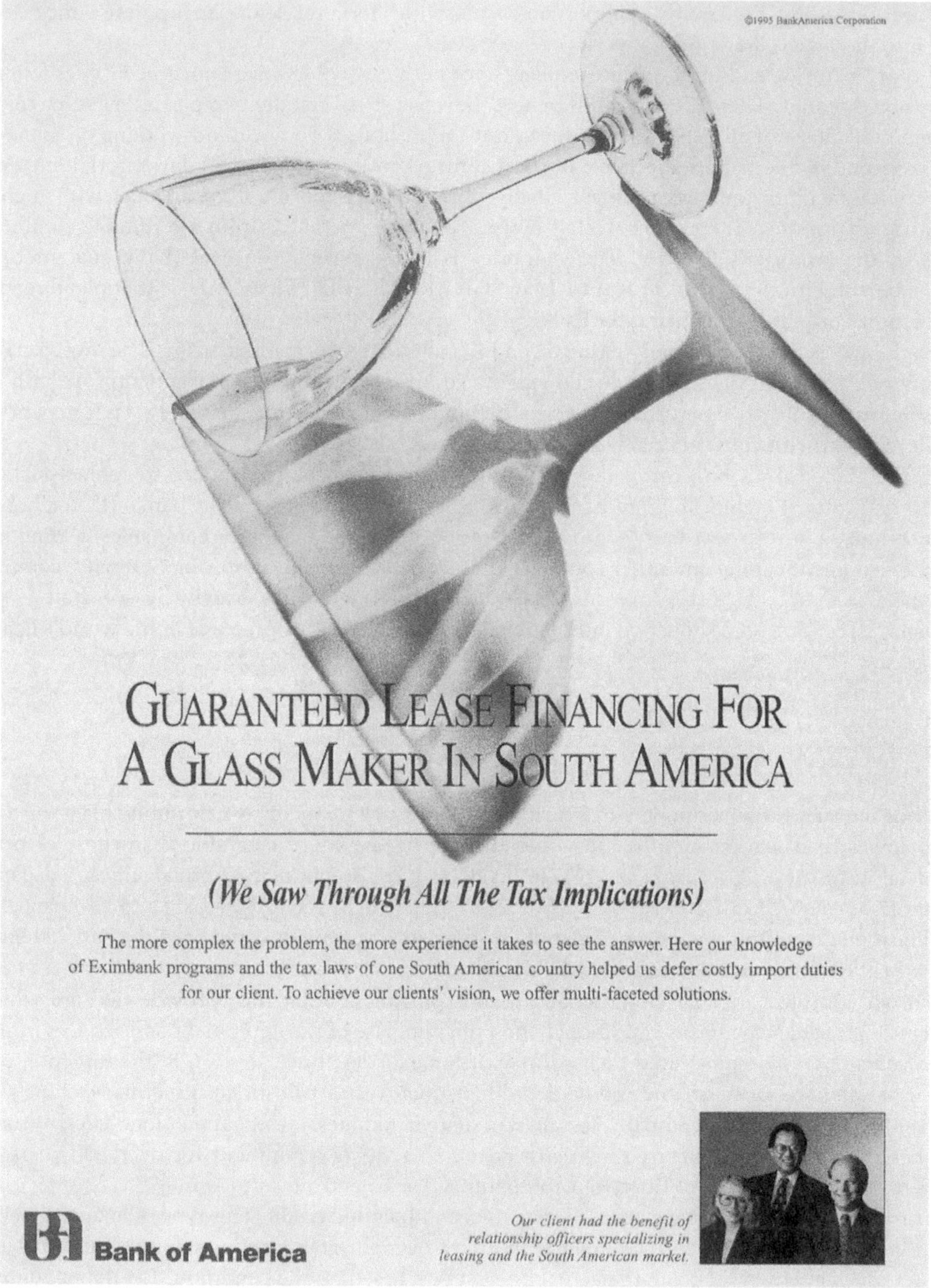
©1995 BankAmerica Corporation
GUARANTEED LEASE FINANCING FOR
A GLASS MAKER IN SOUTH AMERICA
(We Saw Through All The Tax Implications)
The more complex the problem, the more experience it takes to see the answer. Here our knowledge of Eximbank programs and the tax laws of one South American country helped us defer costly import duties for our client. To achieve our clients' vision, we offer multi-faceted solutions.
Bank of America
Our client had the benefit of relationship officers specializing in leasing and the South American market.

**FIGURE 18.4** Lease financing: Bank of America

*Source*: Reprinted with permission of Bank of America.

SANWA BANK INTRODUCES
*GLOCAL BANKING.*
THERE IS NO ALTERNATIVE.
In the world of financial services, most banks are following one of two courses.
Global banking. And local banking.
But global banking often loses sight of local conditions, local needs.
While local banking lacks the reach and the perspective to serve your needs around the world.
Which is why the introduction of *glocal banking* – from Sanwa Bank – is important news.
Sanwa provides a full range of financial services tailored to meet *local* needs in every city where Sanwa does business.
And, beyond that, access to the Sanwa *global* network; a formidable resource only a bank that ranks among the four largest in the world* could provide.
Local needs. Global strength.
For corporate finance. For public projects. To meet your every financial need. From rapid fund access to swift financing to M&A services to credit analysis. And etc., etc., etc.
So see Sanwa.
And see what a difference *glocal banking* can make.
Sanwa Bank
*Capital strength. Capital ideas.*
*FORTUNE, August 22, 1994
The Sanwa Bank U.S.A. & Canada Network
U.S.A.-
Branches: New York:212-339-6300 Chicago:312-368-3000 San Francisco:415-597-5200 Los Angeles:213-896-7407
Agencies: Atlanta:404-586-6880 Dallas:214-744-5555
Loan Production Office: Boston:617-654-2930
Rep. Offices: Houston:713-654-9970 Cleveland:216-736-3380
Subsidiaries: Sanwa Bank California:213-896-7000 Sanwa Business Credit Corporation:312-782-8080 Sanwa Leasing Corporation: 810-637-4100
Sanwa General Equipment Leasing:410-821-7200 Sanwa Securities (U.S.A.) Co., L.P.:212-527-2500
Sanwa Futures L.L.C.:312-341-6530 Sanwa Financial Products Co., L.P.:212-407-3500 Sanwa Bank Trust Company of New York:212-361-2111
Canada
Rep. Offices: Toronto:416-366-2583
Subsidiaries: Sanwa Bank Canada
Toronto Head Office:
416-366-2583
Sanwa McCarthy Securities Limited
Toronto Head Office:
416-862-9160

**FIGURE 18.5** An international bank and financial services: Sanwa Bank

*Source*: Reprinted with permission of Sanwa Bank.

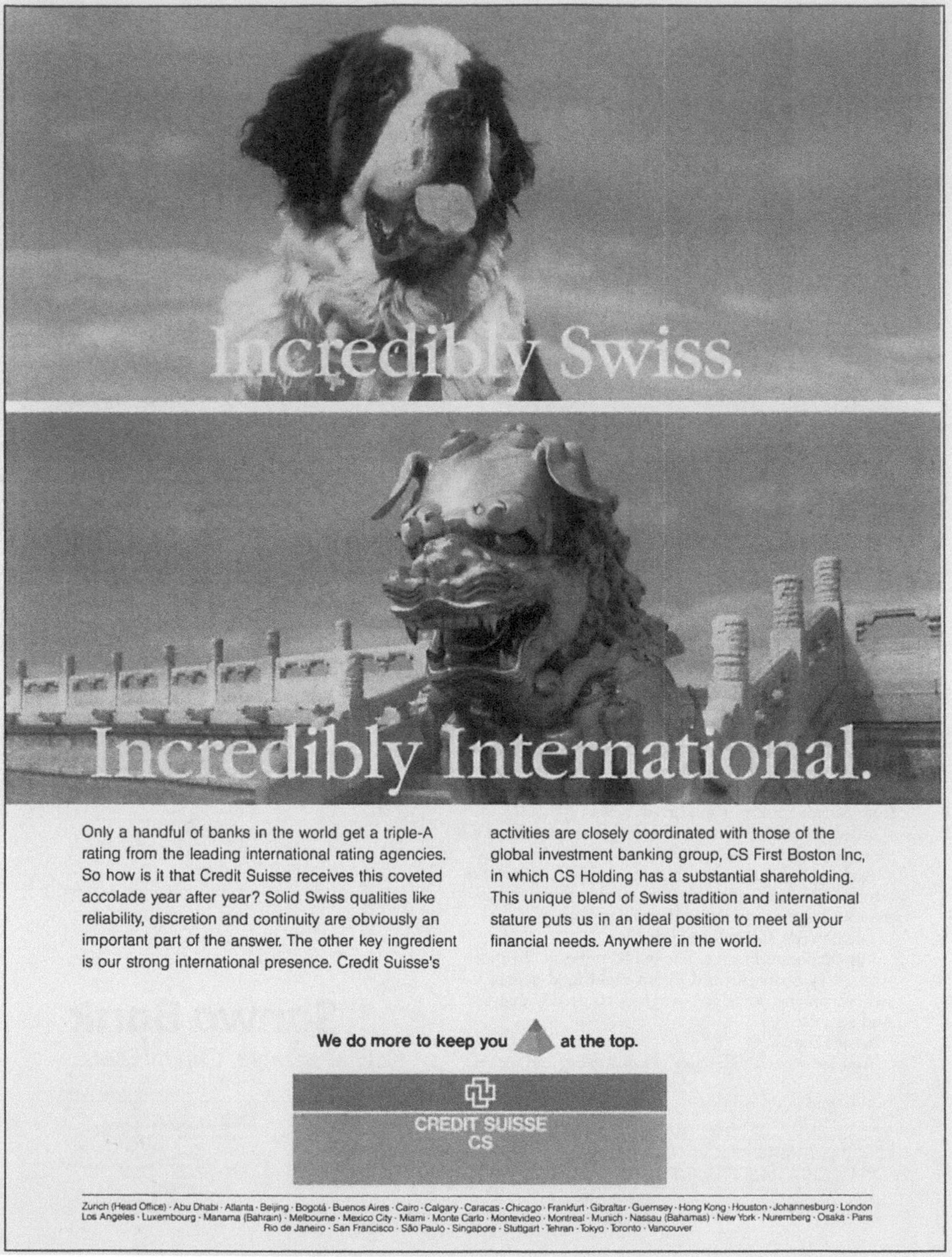
Incredibly Swiss.
Incredibly International.
Only a handful of banks in the world get a triple-A rating from the leading international rating agencies. So how is it that Credit Suisse receives this coveted accolade year after year? Solid Swiss qualities like reliability, discretion and continuity are obviously an important part of the answer. The other key ingredient is our strong international presence. Credit Suisse's activities are closely coordinated with those of the global investment banking group, CS First Boston Inc, in which CS Holding has a substantial shareholding. This unique blend of Swiss tradition and international stature puts us in an ideal position to meet all your financial needs. Anywhere in the world.
We do more to keep you at the top.
CREDIT SUISSE
CS
Zurich (Head Office) · Abu Dhabi · Atlanta · Beijing · Bogotá · Buenos Aires · Cairo · Calgary · Caracas · Chicago · Frankfurt · Gibraltar · Guernsey · Hong Kong · Houston · Johannesburg · London
Los Angeles · Luxembourg · Manama (Bahrain) · Melbourne · Mexico City · Miami · Monte Carlo · Montevideo · Montreal · Munich · Nassau (Bahamas) · New York · Nuremberg · Osaka · Paris
Rio de Janeiro · San Francisco · São Paulo · Singapore · Stuttgart · Tehran · Tokyo · Toronto · Vancouver

**FIGURE 18.6** An international bank and financial services: Credit Suisse

high-technology capital goods, and the indiscriminate use of this technique in foreign aid/export financing packages has fostered a built-in expectation of it on the part of buyers.

## International financial institutions/development banks

One major source of financing is international nonprofit agencies. There are several regional development banks, such as the Asian Development Bank, the African Development Bank and Fund, and the Caribbean Development Bank. The primary purpose of these agencies is to finance productive development projects or to promote economic development in a particular region. The Inter-American Development Bank, for example, has as its principal purpose the acceleration of economic development of its Latin American member countries. The European Bank for Reconstruction and Development (EBRD), located in London, is funded by 39 countries and two European Union organizations. The U.S.A., with a 10 percent share, is the largest single shareholder. The bank targets 60 percent of its loans for the private sector in Central and Eastern Europe. The five multilateral development banks (World Bank, Inter-American Development Bank, Asian Development Bank, African Development Bank, and the European Bank for Reconstruction and Development) have annual commitments topping $45 billion. They are active in all major economic sectors and offer good long-term export opportunities for equipment suppliers, contractors, and consultants. Therefore, they are an important financing source.

In general, both public and private entities are eligible to borrow money from such agencies so long as private funds are not available at reasonable rates and terms. Although the interest rate can vary from agency to agency, these loan rates are attractive and very much in demand.

Of all the international financial organizations, the most familiar is the World Bank, formally known as the International Bank for Reconstruction and Development (IBRD). The World Bank Group consists of five associated institutions. They are: (1) IBRD, (2) IDA, (3) IFC, (4) MIGA, and (5) ICSID. Each institution has a distinct role in the mission to fight poverty and improve living standards.

## International Monetary Fund (IMF)

During the Great Depression of the 1930s, many countries resorted to competitive currency devaluation and trade restrictions to maintain domestic income, resulting in lower trade and employment for everyone. Concern over these "beggar-thy-neighbor" policies led to a July 1–22, 1944 conference at Bretton Woods, New Hampshire, attended by delegates from 44 countries. The IMF was born there on December 27, 1945, to institute an open and stable monetary system. Through consultation, collaboration, and financing members with balance-of-payments problems, the IMF facilitates the growth of international trade, raises levels of income and employment, and develops the productive resources of all members.

The IMF is a cooperative apolitical intergovernmental monetary and financial institution. It began financial operations on March 1, 1947. The IMF has 185 countries as members. Montenegro joined as the institution's 185th member in 2007.

As a "pluralist" international monetary organization, its multiple activities encompass financing, regulatory, and promotional purposes. It acts as a source of balance-of-payments assistance-cum-adjustment to members, as a source and creator of international liquidity, as a reserve depository and intermediary for members, as a trustee, and as a catalyst. The use of the IMF's resources is based on balance-of-payments need, on equal and on discriminatory treatment of members, and on due regard for members' domestic, social, and political systems and policies.

Guided by its charter (Articles of Agreement), the IMF has six prescribed objectives:

1 To promote international cooperation among members on international monetary issues.
2 To facilitate the balanced growth of international trade and to contribute to high levels of employment, real incentive, and productive capacity.
3 To promote exchange stability and orderly exchange arrangements while avoiding competitive currency devaluation.
4 To foster a multilateral system of payments and transfers while eliminating exchange restrictions.
5 To make financial resources available to members.
6 To seek reduction of payment imbalances.

Membership in the IMF is open to any nation that controls its own foreign relations and is willing and able to fulfill the obligations of membership. Each member has a quota based on its subscription contribution to the fund. This quota determines the member's voting power and access to the IMF's financial resources.

## Money

Money is so simple that most users take it for granted. Actually, it is one of the great innovations in history.[13] Being so simple, useful, and common, money facilitates the exchange of goods and services. In the U.S.A., numerous currencies circulated during the late 1700s and throughout most of the 1800s. It took nearly 140 years after becoming one nation for the U.S.A. to have a successful central bank in 1914.[14]

A **hard currency** is hard because of the solid trust that people have in the currency and not because of its gold backing. Businesspeople must have faith that the country issuing the currency will fulfill its obligations. For money to function as a store of value, there must exist something of value to store. Even though Russia has gold and oil, people still have doubts about the ruble as a store of value.

An Act of Parliament does not make a currency hard or international. Currencies become internationalized only because they meet the needs of official institutions and private parties more effectively than other financial assets can. According to the Federal Reserve Board, nearly two-thirds of the $300 billion of U.S. currency in circulation are outside of the U.S.A. Ex-communist economies and South America's inflation-wracked countries demand U.S. dollars in their attempt to seek economic stability. Panama and Liberia have long used the U.S. dollar as their official currencies. Honduras, Hong Kong, and several Asian countries have pegged their money to the dollar. While it is true that the U.S. dollar now comprises only half of official foreign exchange reserves, the dollar is still the world's most instantly and easily recognized international currency. Due to historical reasons, the former Soviet economies were hesitant to accept the German mark. Japan, on the other hand, is reluctant to allow the yen to become an international transaction currency.

An international currency fulfills three basic functions in the global monetary system: it serves as a medium of exchange, a unit of account, and a store of value. As a *medium of exchange*, private parties

## Cultural Dimension 18.1

### Paper money

With credit cards, debit cards, online banking, and so on, paper and metal currency should be obsolete, but that is not the case in the U.S.A. where the currency per capita (held by the public) exceeds $620 billion, basically $2200 for every man, woman, and child. Per capita holdings of currency in Europe are lower but still significant, exceeding $1000 in most countries, with Germans and Austrians having over $1800 per person. Japan, however, leads them all with more than $4000 for every living person.

One advantage of cash over electronic money is that it promises anonymity to the holder. For criminals and money launderers, cash is a currency of choice. As a matter of fact, the euro, because of its 400 euro notes, should be more popular than the U.S. dollar whose largest notes are $100 bills. But if cash facilitates illegal activities and tax evasion, should governments then not try to outlaw paper money?

The cost of the production of a bill is 4 cents, while it costs 20 cents to mint a coin. However, a bill's life is 18 months, but a coin can last for more than 30 years. Switching from a dollar bill to a dollar coin could save the U.S. government $500 million a year.

However, the first three rounds of dollar coins ended in a knock-out for the challengers. The U.S. public simply shunned the Eisenhower (1971–78), Susan B. Anthony (1979–81), and Sacagawea (2000) coins. By not withdrawing $1 bills, the U.S. government did not help the matter. Yet it introduced another new dollar coin in 2007. Chances are that the new coin will go nowhere either.

Canada and several European countries have eliminated the smaller currencies. The euro's smallest bill is a 5-euro note, similar to Britain's £5 note. The other currencies' smallest bills are 1000 yen, 10 Swiss francs, $5 Canadian, $5 Australian note, and 20 Mexican peso notes.

South Korea is not doing much better than the U.S.A. The highest denomination bank note is for 10,000 won (or about U.S.$10 or so). Certainly, it would be hard work to try to smuggle Korean notes. However, Seoul plans to issue notes of 50,000 won and 100,000 won within a few years.

*Sources*: Kenneth S. Rogoff, "The Surprising Popularity of Paper Currency," *Finance & Development*, March 2002, 56–7; "Treasury Never Gives Up Trying to Sell Us on Dollar Coins," *San José Mercury News*, February 25, 2007; "Presidential Dollar Coins Ready to Serve," *San José Mercury News*, November 20, 2006; and "Seoul Has Plan to Thin Wallets, Lighten Purses," *Wall Street Journal*, May 3, 2007.

use an international currency in foreign trade and international capital transactions, whereas official agents use it for balance-of-payments financing and to intervene in foreign exchange markets. As a *unit of account*, private parties use an international currency for invoicing merchandise trade and for denominating financial transactions, whereas official agents use it to define exchange rate parities. As a *store of value*, international currencies are held by private agents as financial assets (e.g., in the form of bonds held by nonresidents), and by official agents (such as central banks) as reserve assets. Table 18.1 shows the various countries' inflation rates.

The economic and political policies of Zimbabwe's President Robert Mugabe are misguided and ill-conceived. It should thus surprise no one, except Mugabe, that Zimbabwe's economy has shrunk about 30 percent since 1999. One farmer told the BBC that his farm used to have a rental income of $2000 a year but that what he now received would buy him only one-third of an egg. Ordinary

Legal Dimension 18.2

**Money: the ultimate counterfeit**

During the American Revolution, the British counterfeited U.S. currency in large amounts and rendered the currency worthless. During the U.S. Civil War, it was estimated that one-third to one-half of the currency in circulation was counterfeit.

During World War II, the Nazis forced about 140 Jewish prisoners to forge the British currency. These prisoners were chosen because of their artistic skills. By 1945, 12 percent of all pound-sterling bills were fake. So many fake pounds were in existence in Europe and the Middle East that the pound sterling lost 75 percent of its value on the black market. Altogether, nearly £133 million were forged. In current value, those bills would amount to about $6 billion. Unfortunately for Germany and fortunately for the United Kingdom, most of the bills did not reach England. Germany did not have planes to drop them. Otherwise, the pound would have been undermined, and it would have crippled the British economy.

*Sources*: "Actionline," *San José Mercury News*, December 21, 2006; and "How a Counterfeiting Ring Saved Adolf Burger at Nazi Camps," *Wall Street Journal Asia*, January 25, 2007.

citizens have to put up with oppression and starvation. Sadly, the leaders of the other African countries as well as Malaysia have kept silent. As a matter of fact, they even gave Mugabe a warm welcome at international conferences.

Yet one may be surprised to hear that the biggest stock market rally during the first half of 2007 took place in Zimbabwe. Astonishingly, the Zimbabwe Industrials Index rocketed about 4000 percent. There is a rational explanation. The rise in stocks has nothing to do with economic or corporate performance. Instead, it has all to do with Zimbabwe's surging inflation. At an annual rate of 7500 percent, the country had the world's highest inflation rate. While the official exchange rate was 250 Zimbabwe dollars to one U.S. dollar, the reality is that Zimbabwe had to give up more than 50,000 Zimbabwe dollars to fetch one U.S. dollar. Desperate to preserve their capital, Zimbabwe residents have been switching from a declining asset (Zimbabwe dollar) to an appreciating one (stocks).[15] In 2008, Zimbabwe's inflation rate reached 100,000 percent.

Looking on the bright side, Zimbabwe's inflation pales when compared to Germany's inflation rate which topped 1 million percent after World War II. The reality though is very grim. In September 2007, Zimbabwe devalued its currency by more than 99 percent.

For a currency to be used internationally, two sets of factors are essential. First, there must be confidence in the value of the currency and in the political stability of the issuing country. Second, a country should possess financial markets that are substantially free of controls. These markets should be broad (i.e., contain a large assortment of financial instruments) and deep (i.e., have well-developed secondary markets). The country should also possess financial institutions that are sophisticated and competitive in overseas financial centers.

**TABLE 18.1** Inflation (CPI) 2003 to 2006

| *City (countries)* | *2003* | *2004* | *2005* |
|---|---|---|---|
| Amsterdam (Netherlands) | 2.2 | 1.4 | 1.5 |
| Athens (Greece) | 3.5 | 3.0 | 3.5 |
| Auckland (New Zealand) | 1.8 | 2.3 | 3.0 |
| Bangkok (Thailand) | 1.8 | 2.8 | 4.5 |
| Barcelona (Spain) | 3.1 | 3.1 | 3.4 |
| Beijing (China) | 1.2 | 3.9 | 1.8 |
| Berlin (Germany) | 1.0 | 1.8 | 1.9 |
| Bogotá (Colombia) | 7.1 | 5.9 | 5.0 |
| Bratislava (Slovakia) | 8.5 | 7.5 | 2.8 |
| Brussels (Belgium) | 1.5 | 1.9 | 2.5 |
| Bucharest (Romania) | 15.3 | 11.9 | 9.0 |
| Budapest (Hungary) | 4.7 | 6.7 | 3.5 |
| Buenos Aires (Argentina) | 13.4 | 4.4 | 9.6 |
| Caracas (Venezuela) | 31.1 | 21.7 | 15.9 |
| Chicago (United States) | 2.3 | 2.7 | 3.4 |
| Copenhagen (Denmark) | 2.1 | 1.2 | 1.8 |
| Delhi (New Delhi, India) | 3.8 | 3.8 | 4.2 |
| Dubai (United Arab Emirates) | 3.1 | 4.6 | 6.0 |
| Dublin (Ireland) | 4.0 | 2.3 | 2.2 |
| Frankfurt (Germany) | 1.0 | 1.8 | 1.9 |
| Geneva (Switzerland) | 0.6 | 0.8 | 1.2 |
| Helsinki (Finland) | 1.3 | 0.1 | 0.9 |
| Hong Kong (China) | –2.6 | –0.4 | 1.1 |
| Istanbul (Turkey) | 25.2 | 8.6 | 8.2 |
| Jakarta (Indonesia) | 6.8 | 6.1 | 10.5 |
| Johannesburg (South Africa) | 5.8 | 1.4 | 3.4 |
| Kiev (Ukraine) | 5.2 | 9.0 | 13.5 |
| Kuala Lumpur (Malaysia) | 1.1 | 1.4 | 3.0 |
| Lima (Peru) | 2.3 | 3.7 | 1.6 |
| Lisbon (Portugal) | 3.3 | 2.5 | 2.1 |
| Ljubljana (Slovenia) | 5.6 | 3.6 | 2.5 |
| London (Great Britain) | 1.4 | 1.3 | 2.1 |
| Los Angeles (United States) | 2.3 | 2.7 | 3.4 |
| Luxembourg (Luxembourg) | 2.0 | 2.2 | 2.5 |
| Lyon (France) | 2.2 | 2.3 | 1.9 |
| Madrid (Spain) | 3.1 | 3.1 | 3.4 |
| Manama (Bahrain) | 1.7 | 2.3 | 2.6 |
| Manila (Philippines) | 3.5 | 6.0 | 7.6 |
| Mexico City (Mexico) | 4.5 | 4.7 | 4.0 |
| Miami (United States) | 2.3 | 2.7 | 3.4 |

**TABLE 18.1** *continued*

| *City (countries)* | *2003* | *2004* | *2005* |
|---|---|---|---|
| Milan (Italy) | 2.8 | 2.3 | 2.3 |
| Montreal (Canada) | 2.7 | 1.8 | 2.2 |
| Moscow (Russia) | 13.7 | 10.9 | 12.6 |
| Mumbai (Bombay, India) | 3.8 | 3.8 | 4.2 |
| Munich (Germany) | 1.0 | 1.8 | 1.9 |
| Nairobi (Kenya) | 9.8 | 11.6 | 10.3 |
| New York (United States) | 2.3 | 2.7 | 3.4 |
| Nicosia (Cyprus) | 4.1 | 2.3 | 2.6 |
| Oslo (Noway) | 2.5 | 0.4 | 1.6 |
| Paris (France) | 2.2 | 2.3 | 1.9 |
| Prague (Czech Republic) | 0.1 | 2.8 | 1.8 |
| Riga (Latvia) | 2.9 | 6.3 | 6.7 |
| Rio de Janeiro (Brazil) | 14.8 | 6.6 | 6.9 |
| Rome (Italy) | 2.8 | 2.3 | 2.3 |
| Santiago de Chile (Chile) | 2.8 | 1.1 | 3.1 |
| Sao Paulo (Brazil) | 14.8 | 6.6 | 6.9 |
| Seoul (South Korea) | 3.6 | 3.6 | 2.7 |
| Shanghai (China) | 1.2 | 3.9 | 1.8 |
| Singapore (Singapore) | 0.5 | 1.7 | 0.5 |
| Sofia (Bulgaria) | 2.3 | 6.1 | 5.0 |
| Stockholm (Sweden) | 2.3 | 1.1 | 0.8 |
| Sydney (Australia) | 2.8 | 2.3 | 2.7 |
| Taipei (Taiwan) | –0.3 | 1.6 | 2.3 |
| Tallinn (Estonia) | 1.3 | 3.0 | 4.1 |
| Tel Aviv (Israel) | 0.7 | –0.4 | 1.3 |
| Tokyo (Japan) | –0.3 | 0.0 | –0.3 |
| Toronto (Canada) | 2.7 | 1.8 | 2.2 |
| Vienna (Austria) | 1.3 | 2.0 | 2.1 |
| Vilnius (Lithuania) | –1.2 | 1.2 | 2.6 |
| Warsaw (Poland) | 0.8 | 3.5 | 2.1 |
| Zurich (Switzerland) | 0.6 | 0.8 | 1.2 |

*Note:*

1 Modification of the consumer price index (CPI) January 2003–January 2006.

*Source*: *Prices and Earnings* (Zurich: UBS AG, 2006, 49).

## Foreign exchange

Foreign exchange transactions involve the purchase or sale of one national currency against another. The easiest way to understand this type of transaction is to view money as just another product that customers are willing to buy and sell. Like other products, money can be branded, and the U.S. dollar, Swiss franc, Japanese yen, and so on are simply some of the brand names for a money "product." Some of these brand names carry more prestige and are more desirable than others, similar to the brand names of consumer products.

People often wonder why it is necessary to have so many different currencies. Obviously, it would be preferable to have just one worldwide currency that could be used anywhere on Earth, similar to the U.S. dollar being used and accepted in all 50 states. However, a global currency is currently impossible because of two uncontrollable factors – national sovereignty and inflation.

Under normal circumstances, it is very rare for a country to adopt another country's currency as its own. One exception is Liechtenstein, which signed a customs treaty with Switzerland in 1923, making the Swiss franc its official currency. Moreover, Liechtenstein's customs affairs are administered by Switzerland.

Many Americans, knowing that the dollar is widely accepted, do not understand why the U.S. dollar cannot become a global currency and why other nations resist replacing their national currencies with the U.S. dollar. This resistance may perhaps be better understood if one imagines the tables being turned. Would the American public be willing to abandon the dollar and replace it with a new global currency? The fact that the U.S.A. is so unwilling to embrace the metric system in spite of its demonstrated superiority underscores this point clearly. Because of *national pride*, no nation wants to give up its identity and sovereignty, and this includes its national currency. National pride may also explain Great Britain's reluctance to allow the pound to join the European Monetary System (EMS), especially since the British believe that the pound has a more important role in the international financial world. Great Britain withdrew the pound from the EMS in 1992 and has so far refused to switch to the euro.

A less emotional but often uncontrollable issue is *inflation*, which reduces the value of money (i.e., purchasing power). Since it is impossible for all nations to have an identical inflation rate, the effect of inflation on the value of various currencies is uneven. In Argentina, the inflation rate was greater than 400 percent in 1984, and it accelerated to more than 800 percent later, forcing the government to adopt the austral as its new currency in 1985. Inflation in the U.S.A. at the same time was running in the single digits. In China during the 1940s, the currency had so little value that the Chinese had to cart their money around in wheelbarrows. After World War I, the value of the German mark stood at 4 trillion marks to a dollar.

These examples should make clear that it is impractical for any single currency to be used on a worldwide basis while maintaining constant value in all countries.

## Foreign exchange market

Firms needing to make payment for foreign business transactions never seem to have enough currency on hand, and it is cumbersome for them to seek out those with adequate amounts to sell. There is thus a need for a foreign exchange market for all individuals and institutions in order that they may contact one another for this purpose. The foreign exchange market as it exists has no central trading

### Cultural Dimension 18.2

**Currency quotient**

Match the country with the currency.

**Elementary level**

| | | | |
|---|---|---|---|
| 1 | France | A | dollar |
| 2 | Hong Kong | B | euro |
| 3 | Japan | C | dollar |
| 4 | United Kingdom | D | pound |
| 5 | U.S.A. | E | yen |

**Intermediate level**

| | | | |
|---|---|---|---|
| 1 | Australia | A | dollar |
| 2 | Mexico | B | won |
| 3 | Russia | C | peso |
| 4 | South Africa | D | rand |
| 5 | South Korea | E | ruble |

**Advanced level**

| | | | |
|---|---|---|---|
| 1 | Bangladesh | A | tugrik |
| 2 | Burma | B | pataca |
| 3 | Cambodia | C | riel |
| 4 | Macau | D | kyat |
| 5 | Mongolia | E | taka |
| 6 | Latvia | F | koruna |
| 7 | Slovakia | G | lat |

floor where buyers and sellers meet. Most trades are completed by banks and foreign exchange dealers using telephones, cables, and mail. As a worldwide market, the foreign exchange market operates 24 hours a day.

The foreign exchange market facilitates financial transactions in three different ways. First, it provides *credit* or *financing* for firms engaged in international business. This may be achieved through a variety of means, such as letter of credit, time draft, forward contract, and so on. Second, it performs a *clearing* function similar to a domestic bank's clearing process for checking-account customers. Clearing is a process by which a financial transaction between two parties involving intermediation between banks is "settled." In the case of international clearing, the funds are transferred on paper from a commercial customer to its local bank, from there to a New York bank, and finally to a foreign bank abroad. The process allows payments to be made for foreign goods without a physical transfer or movement of money across countries.

Third, the market furnishes facilities for *hedging* so that businesses can cover or reduce their foreign exchange risks. **Hedging** is an activity that is used as a temporary substitute purchase or sale for the actual currency. This temporary transaction allows users to protect the price they secure from fluctuations because it establishes equal and opposite positions in the market.

The rationale for hedging lies in the exchange rate fluctuation, which can move significantly and erratically, even within a short time. For example, due to inflation and instability, the Russian ruble lost 27 percent of its value against the U.S. dollar in a single day in 1994. The panic started when the central bank stopped supporting the declining ruble. The ruble tumbled from 3081 to the dollar to 3926, and it was a record fall. In just about three months, the ruble lost half its value. Consumers, to hedge against price increases, bought as much merchandise as they could afford, while merchants sharply marked up prices.

Figure 18.7 provides a good illustration of the high degree of volatility in the foreign exchange market. Since it is common for a customer to take some time in accepting the quoted price, placing an order, and making payments, financial loss caused by exchange rate movement can easily occur. Without a hedge, an American exporter selling to an Italian customer will suffer financially when the

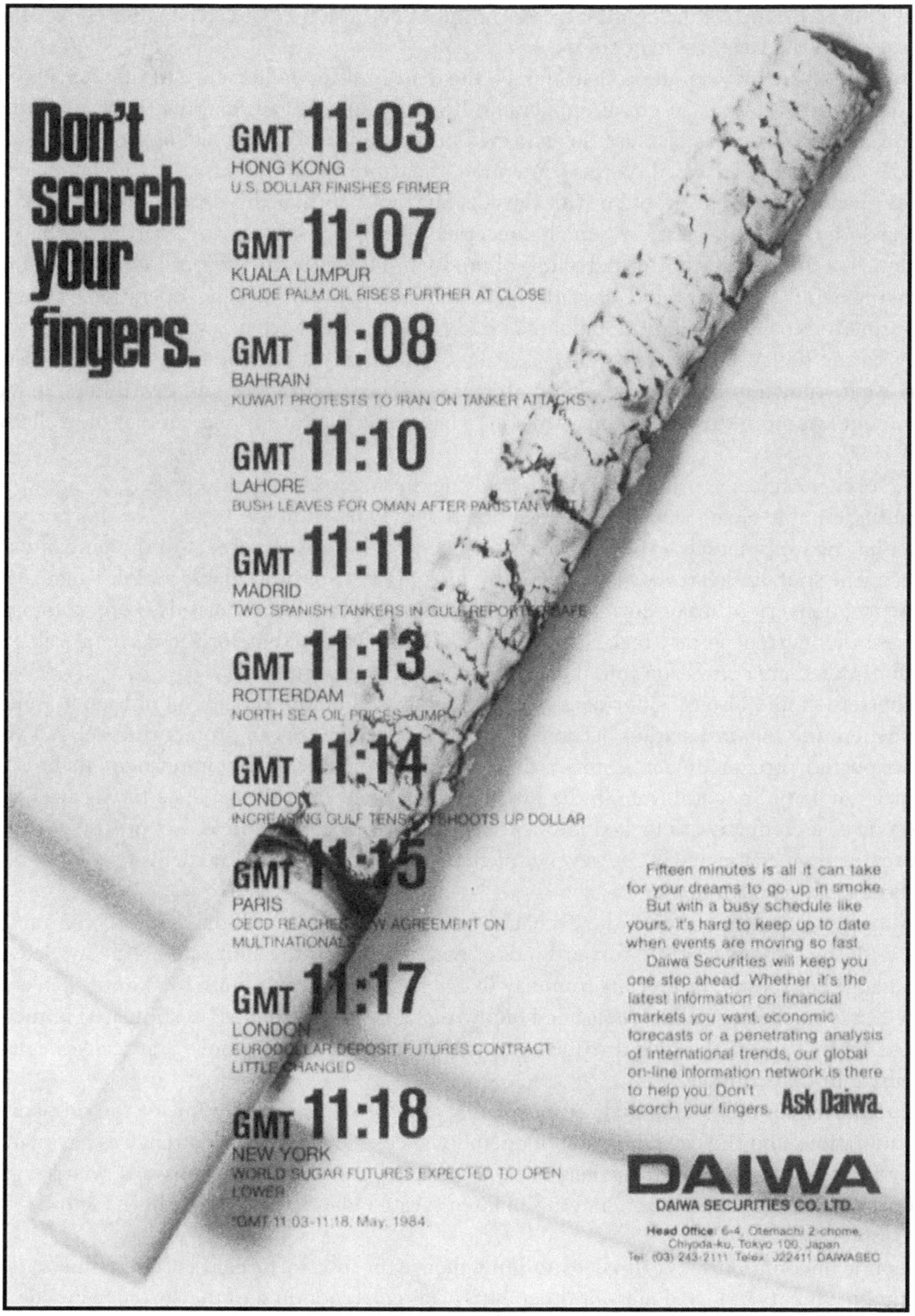
Don't scorch your fingers.
GMT 11:03
HONG KONG
U.S. DOLLAR FINISHES FIRMER
GMT 11:07
KUALA LUMPUR
CRUDE PALM OIL RISES FURTHER AT CLOSE
GMT 11:08
BAHRAIN
KUWAIT PROTESTS TO IRAN ON TANKER
GMT 11:10
LAHORE
BUSH LEAVES FOR OMAN AFTER
GMT 11:11
MADRID
TWO SPANISH TANKERS IN
GMT 11:13
ROTTERDAM
NORTH SEA OIL
GMT 11:14
LONDON
GULF SHOOTS UP DOLLAR
GMT
PARIS
OECD AGREEMENT ON
MULTINATIONAL
GMT 11:17
LONDON
DEPOSIT FUTURES CONTRACT
GMT 11:18
NEW YORK
SUGAR FUTURES EXPECTED TO OPEN
GMT 11:03-11:18, May, 1984.
Fifteen minutes is all it can take for your dreams to go up in smoke.
But with a busy schedule like yours, it's hard to keep up to date when events are moving so fast.
Daiwa Securities will keep you one step ahead. Whether it's the latest information on financial markets you want, economic forecasts or a penetrating analysis of international trends, our global on-line information network is there to help you. Don't scorch your fingers.
Ask Daiwa.
DAIWA
DAIWA SECURITIES CO. LTD.
Head Office: 6-4, Otemachi 2-chome, Chiyoda-ku, Tokyo 100, Japan
Tel: (03) 243-2111 Telex: J22411 DAIWASEC

**FIGURE 18.7** Volatility of the foreign exchange rate

*Source*: Reprinted with permission of Daiwa Securities Company Limited.

euro declines in value (or the dollar increases in value) because the euros paid, after conversion, will yield fewer dollars than first expected.

Some observers may conclude that, though the danger of the falling euro to the U.S. exporter is real and serious, there is an equal opportunity for the euro to gain in value instead. Under this scenario, the exporter can increase the expected profit – once from the sale of the goods and again from the exchange gain. Based on this contention, the exporter would miss the windfall profit if the exporter had hedged. The problem with this idea, however, is that the exporter is in reality a mere amateur so far as the speculation game is concerned. He or she may be an expert in and have great knowledge of the manufacturing and selling of products. However, the exporter is not in the business of making windfall profits and should concentrate on familiar trading operations rather than attempting to be a gambler in the unfamiliar and risky game of currency speculation. This warning applies to the Italian importer as well, especially when payment is to be made in dollars instead of euros. As demonstrated by Shell Sekiyu, a Japanese-Dutch oil refiner and distributor, its finance department lost more than $1 billion by making a bad bet in the futures market that the dollar would rise in 1993.

The foreign exchange market provides a hedging mechanism needed to protect corporate profits against undesirable changes in the exchange rate that may occur in the future. For this purpose, the market has two submarkets – spot and forward. The two differ with respect to the time of currency delivery. The **spot market** is a *cash* market where foreign exchange is available for immediate delivery. In practice, delivery of major currencies occurs within one or two business days of the transaction, whereas other currencies may take slightly longer. A U.S. firm holding foreign currency can go to its bank for immediate conversion into dollars based on the spot rate for that day.

Exporters should also consider doing some hedging well before the arrival of foreign funds, and this is where the **forward market** becomes significant. Companies can protect themselves by selling their expected foreign exchange forward. A forward contract is a commitment to buy or sell currencies at some specified time in the future at a specified rate. By signing a forward contract of, say, 45 days, a company has locked into a certain rate of exchange and knows precisely how many dollars, after conversion, it will get – even though payment, conversion, and delivery will not be made until later (i.e., 45 days after).

It should be understood that the exchange rate specified in the 45-day forward contract is not necessarily the same rate as the forward rate of the next day or the spot rate of 45 days later. Both rates change constantly, fluctuating from day to day and even from minute to minute. The only rate that will stay unchanged is the one agreed on by the bank and the hedger as stipulated in the signed forward contract, even though subsequent forward and spot rates may move drastically the day after the signing of that contract.

An exporter should realize that, in most cases, the spot rate is irrelevant for the preparation of price quotations and the determination of operational costs since foreign currency as payment is not received until a later date. Since there is no immediate conversion, the forward rate is the more appropriate one. The expectation in terms of interest rate inflation has already been factored into the agreed-upon forward rate.

It is not uncommon for companies to limit their exposure to foreign currency fluctuations by requiring payments in U.S. dollars or other currencies corresponding to the currency in which costs are incurred. They may use forward exchange contracts to hedge foreign currency transactions. These contracts allow the companies to exchange, say, U.S. dollars for foreign currencies at maturity at rates agreed to at the inception of the contracts.

For Texas Instruments, its functional currency for financial reporting is the U.S. dollar. To minimize the adverse earnings impact from exchange rate fluctuations affecting its non-U.S. dollar net balance sheet exposures, the company uses forward currency exchange contracts. At year-end 2006, for example, it had forward contracts of $85 million to sell euros, $82 million to sell British pounds, and $48 million to sell Japanese yen. Based on such hedging activities, a hypothetical 10 percent plus or minor fluctuation in non-U.S. currency exchange rates should keep a pre-tax currency exchange gain or loss at less than $1 million.[16]

## Foreign exchange rate

The foreign exchange rate is simply a *price* – the price of one national currency as expressed by the value of another. This exchange price, once established, allows currencies to be exchanged one for another. The exchange rate, however, is more than just the price of a currency. It affects the cost of imported goods and exported goods; the country's rate of inflation; and a firm's profit, output, and employment.

Similar to the price of any other product, the price of a currency is determined by the demand and supply of that currency. When the currency is in demand, its price increases, but if a currency's supply increases without any corresponding increase in demand, its value declines.

With excess imports comes an excess supply of money because a large volume of money must be generated to pay for all the imports. With excess money in circulation, the business community, as well as the general population, begins having doubts about its value, making the currency appear overvalued. In contrast, excess export results in too much demand for the exporting nation's currency, since foreign buyers require large amounts to pay for goods. The currency then becomes expensive due to its scarcity, and its real value increases.

The demand for a currency is determined by several factors. Some of these include the following:

1 Domestic and foreign prices of goods and services.
2 Trading opportunities within a country.
3 International capital movement as affected by the country's stability, inflation, money supply, and interest, as well as by speculators' perceptions and anticipations of such conditions.
4 The country's export and import performance.

During the first term of the Reagan administration, the demand for dollars was extraordinarily strong due to cheap land, huge markets, economic growth, low inflation, and a relatively high interest rate in the U.S. market. The perception that the U.S.A. was the most stable country was further bolstered by investors' confidence in former President Reagan. These favorable factors, operating in conjunction, were more than enough to push the dollar sky-high despite the huge trade deficits of the U.S.A. at the time.

Inflation discourages lending but encourages borrowing, because a loan when due can be repaid with less expensive money. A country with high inflation tends to have a weak currency, which is usually accompanied by high interest rates. The higher interest costs do not necessarily make it an undesirable place to take out loans.

## Currency equilibrium

A nation's currency is in equilibrium when its rate creates no net change in the country's reserve of international means of payment. The equilibrium rate operates to keep the nation's balance of payments in proper perspective over an interval of time by making imports equal to exports. When in equilibrium, the foreign exchange rate is stable, perhaps fluctuating slightly before returning to its parity position.

Despite most nations' desire to maintain currency equilibrium, currency has a tendency to get out of balance. The equilibrium is affected by the intensity of such fundamental problems as inflation and excess import. Both inflation and excess import are negatively related to the subsequent price of the currency. In theory, neither persistent trade surpluses nor deficits are desirable. Persistent trade surpluses are unwelcome because they make the surplus nation's currency too cheap and imported products too expensive, resulting in a loss of local consumers' buying power.

More serious than the surplus problem is that of persistent trade deficits. When this occurs, an adjustment of the disequilibrium is necessary to restore the equality of demand and supply. The adjustment may be achieved through several techniques. For instance, the disequilibrium within limits can be temporarily financed while waiting for the disequilibrium to reverse itself. Persistent deficits cannot be financed for long periods because the country would soon exhaust its reserves and credits in the effort to pay for imports. The country may opt to choose to control its money supply in order to correct the situation. Trade deficits eventually cause a country to take steps to tighten its money supply. By buying up excess supplies of money, the government makes money less available for imports, and the economy ultimately slows down.

There are other methods that can help in restoring equilibrium by shifting demand away from foreign goods. Trade restrictions such as tariffs and foreign exchange controls achieve this purpose by making imports more expensive. If all else fails, the government may resort to changing its exchange rate in order to alter the price relationship of goods traded between two countries. The new rate would reflect a new equilibrium, which would be reinforced by an increase in the cost of imported goods.

## Effect of devaluation

Devaluation is a reduction in the price of one currency in terms of other currencies. As in the case of Russia before its economic crisis in August 1999, it gave up 6.7 rubles for each dollar. Then the crisis hit, and the exchange rate jumped to about 23 rubles per dollar by the end of the year. Turkey did not fare any better. In early 2001, the country's currency lost 28 percent of its value in a single day. Turkey was forced to allow its currency to float freely to prevent capital flight and stabilize its stock market.[17]

To the layperson, devaluation carries negative connotations, but countries that wish to stimulate exports normally want to devalue their own currency. To understand the effect of devaluation, one might consider two possible exchange rates: assume that the Japanese yen is going to be devalued from 110 yen to the dollar to 120 yen to the dollar. A question one might then ask is whether the new rate (i.e., 120 yen) is better than the old rate as far as Japanese exporters are concerned. The answer is a definite yes. One dollar now receives 10 more yen, meaning that a dollar spent in U.S. currency will purchase 120 yen worth of Japanese goods rather than 110 yen worth. In effect, it becomes attractive for others to buy from Japan because they essentially get 10 extra yen worth of merchandise for free. This effect helps to explain why Komatsu had a $20,000 price advantage at one time over Caterpillar on a $100,000 tractor. The explanation for the differential is that the dollar was too expensive in relation to the yen.

Another question one might ask is what effect devaluation will have on Japanese importers. This time, the effect is unfavorable because Japanese importers are required to spend 10 more yen to get the same amount of goods for each dollar as before. The yen devaluation has therefore made imported goods more expensive for Japanese importers and consumers.

Likewise, if the U.S.A. elects to pursue the goal of full employment, the 110 yen rate is preferred because this rate makes it easier for Japan to import more American goods without having to spend a relatively larger amount of yen. This increase in demand in Japan is accompanied by a rise in employment in the U.S.A.

However, if the U.S. goal is to maximize consumer welfare, the 120 yen rate is better because American consumers can get more of the relatively inexpensive imported products without having to spend relatively more dollars for them. Yet this positive effect is countered by a negative one – the demand for imported goods reduces the demand for domestic products, and unemployment increases in the U.S.A.

How well does devaluation really work? Although devaluation is supposed to expand exports and reduce imports, in practice the actual impact is often not as great as one might expect, especially in the short term. There are several reasons for this. Initially, the trade balance may worsen instead of improve. The country in difficulty often has a low marginal propensity to save, and buying habits and long-term contracts make it difficult in the short run to alter the physical trade volume.

Devaluation, instead of correcting the problem, can aggravate inflation – the very thing it is intended to control. Workers, seeing imported goods more expensive than before, often demand wage increases to compensate for their loss of buying power. To compound the problem, domestic industries usually take advantage of the situation by boosting their own domestic prices. This is the route frequently taken by the U.S. steel and automobile industries whenever import prices are driven up by devaluation or other restrictive measures. Therefore, devaluation cannot work in the long run because if these effects continue to cycle and recycle, a collapse of the economy is the result. Devaluation, in order to be effective, must be accompanied by a program to urge local firms to exert self-restraint and to encourage people to consume less and save more. In February 1989, the Sandinista government of Nicaragua devalued its currency (cordoba) and raised prices for petroleum products for the third time that year. The devaluation was designed to contain hyperinflation that had reached 20,000 percent in 1988.

One must also keep in mind that a substantial time lag occurs between the change in currency value and its impact on the physical flow of trade. The lag occurs because suppliers and buyers need time to adjust their habits and decisions before they start getting used to the new exchange rates. Furthermore, although devaluation makes imports more expensive, consumers may fail to curtail their purchases of those imports. This phenomenon is known as the **J curve** because it takes quite a while for the economy to round the turn of the J. One should then expect a modest swelling of the trade deficit to occur after devaluation, before a sharp recovery can follow if the right steps have been taken. In general, economists believe that it takes some 18 months before an increase in import prices can have a significant impact on the volume of trade adjustment.

If the economy is successful in expanding exports and reducing imports as intended, devaluation should increase the national income, which in turn will stimulate the volume of imports once again. Thus, the initial effect of devaluation can be reversed in the long run. Moreover, any deliberate devaluation carried on will result in a beggar-my-neighbor policy, which will export domestic unemployment to other countries. The deliberate practice of devaluation can easily provoke other trading partners to retaliate by lowering their own money value. Because of these consequences, the net gain from devaluation in the longer term is not going to be as large as its initial gain.

## Exchange rate systems

There should be no doubt that an exchange rate can be quite volatile and that anyone who is unfortunate enough to make an incorrect decision about the rate's direction will pay for it dearly. Anyone having any doubts about the validity of this statement need only consider Argentina. In 1981, the Argentine peso plunged to only one-seventh of the value of what it had been at the beginning of the same year.

The concern over such a severe reduction in value has led economists and government officials into a heated and continuing debate over the best exchange rate system. All existing systems have strengths as well as weaknesses, and there is probably no such thing as a perfect exchange rate system. The major exchange rate systems may be ranked in terms of increasing flexibility: fixed rate (Gold Standard and adjustable peg), semifixed (wide band and crawling peg), and flexible or floating rate.

### *Gold Standard*

The Gold Standard was the start of modern exchange rate systems. Gold was first developed as the standard of international exchange in the United Kingdom in the late 1700s, and many other nations had followed suit by the mid-1800s. In the case of the U.S.A., the U.S. Coinage Act placed the dollar on the Gold Standard in 1873.

Each country was required to link its currency value to gold by legally defining a *par value* based on a specified quantity of gold for its standard monetary unit. Thus, exchange rates had fixed par values as determined by the gold content of the national monetary links. A modification of this system occurred at a later date, and it became known as the Gold Exchange Standard. Created in 1922, the modified system allowed countries to use both gold and the U.S. dollar for international settlement because the U.S.A. stood ready to redeem dollars in gold on demand.

In 1930, a dollar was defined as containing 23.22 grains of fine gold (with 480 grains in a troy ounce), whereas a British pound had 113 grains. In 1971, the gold content of the dollar was redefined from 0.888671 grams of gold to 0.73666 grams. The price of gold, being $20.67 per fine troy ounce in 1879, was later changed to $35 in 1933. The increase in gold price in effect devalued the dollar. Because each national currency had to be backed by gold, each country's money supply, in turn, was determined by its gold holdings.

Because of this common denominator (i.e., gold), all currencies' values were rigidly fixed. Although the values were fixed by law, that does not mean that these exchange rates could not fluctuate to some small degree in accordance with the demand and supply of a currency. The fluctuation had to be within the limits set by the costs of interest, transport, insurance, and handling of gold from one country to another.

The Gold Standard functioned to maintain equilibrium through the so-called *price–specie–flow mechanism* (or, more appropriately, the *specie–flow–price mechanism*) with *specie* meaning gold. The mechanism was intended to restore the equilibrium automatically. When a country's currency inflated too fast, the currency lost competitiveness in the world market. The deteriorating trade balance resulting from imports being greater than exports led to a decline in the confidence of the currency. As the exchange rate approached the gold export point, gold was withdrawn from reserves and shipped abroad to pay for imports. With less gold at home, the country was forced to reduce its money supply, a reduction accompanied by a slow-down in economic activity, high interest rates, recession, reduced national income, and increased unemployment. The onset of hard times would pressure inflation to be reduced. As domestic prices declined, demand for domestic products increased, and demand for imports declined. Price deflation thus made domestic products attractive both at home and abroad. The country's balance of payments improved, and gold started to flow into the country once again. The price–specie–flow mechanism also restored order in the case of trade surpluses by working in the opposite manner.

There are several reasons that the gold standard could not function well over the long term. Because gold is a scarce commodity, gold volume could not grow fast enough to allow adequate amounts of money to be created (printed) to finance the growth of world trade. The problem was further aggravated by gold being taken out of reserve for art and industrial consumption, not to mention the desire of many people to own gold. The banning of gold hoarding and public exporting of gold bullion by President Franklin Roosevelt was not sufficient to remedy the problem.

Another problem of the system was the unrealistic expectation that countries would subordinate their national economies to the dictates of gold as well as to external and monetary conditions. In other words, a country with high inflation and/or trade deficit was required to reduce its money supply and consumption, resulting in recession and unemployment. This was a strict discipline that many nations could not force upon themselves or their population. Instead of having sufficient courage to use unemployment to discourage imports, importing countries simply insisted on intervention through tariffs and devaluations instead. Nations insisted on their rights to intervene and devalue domestic currencies in order to meet nationwide employment objectives. Due to the rigidity of the system, it was only a matter of time before major countries decided to abandon the Gold Standard, starting with the United Kingdom in 1931 in the midst of a worldwide recession. With a 12 percent unemployment rate at the time, the United Kingdom chose to leave the Gold Standard rather than exacerbate the unemployment problem. Monetary chaos followed in many countries.

## Par value (adjustable peg)

The need to restructure the international monetary system after World War II was the incentive for the delegates of 44 countries to meet at Bretton Woods, New Hampshire, in 1994. The result of the meeting was the creation of the World Bank to finance development projects and the International Monetary Fund to promote monetary stability while facilitating world trade expansion. The IMF system, also known as the par value, adjustable, or Bretton Woods system, was created to overcome the problems associated with the Gold Standard. The inadequacy of gold as an international currency was overcome by turning to the U.S. dollar. As the other international currency, the dollar provides added reserves for stability as well as liquidity for gold and currencies.

The IMF required a fixed exchange ratio or par value. The agreement fixed the world's paper currencies in relation to the U.S. dollar, which was fully convertible into gold. Regarding the dollar as the acceptable store of value, countries were willing to receive it in settlement for international balances. Based on policies designed to avoid disruptive fluctuations and rate rigidity, members had to establish a par value for their currency, either directly in terms of gold or indirectly by relating the par value to the gold content of the U.S. dollar (within a margin of 1 percent on either side of parity). The IMF prohibits any unauthorized use of multiple exchange rates.

A correction of the par of exchange was possible in the case of a fundamental disequilibrium. The IMF was required to concur with a change from the initial par value through a cumulative amount of up to 10 percent. Any change in par value beyond this amount required the IMF's approval. However, there was difficulty in determining (1) when a fundamental disequilibrium existed, (2) whether the currency was overvalued or undervalued, and (3) the extent of the overvaluation or undervaluation.

To discourage speculation, the change in par value was kept infrequent, resulting in a late adjustment. In addition, during a crisis, there was no time for mutual consultations as called for by the IMF's Articles of Agreement. In fact, mere rumors of pending consultations would probably be more than enough to encourage intense speculation. For instance, if the dollar sank in value to its lower limit but was not allowed to go further, no one would want to buy it at that point because its value was being kept artificially high. Its high price did not reflect its actual lower value. Speculators, knowing that devaluation had to follow soon and that the dollar had nowhere to go but down once devaluation took effect, would sell dollars first before buying them back at a new lower rate or price. With only sellers and no buyers, the resulting panic could force the financial markets to close.

One more problem with the par value system was the burden it placed on the dollar. The constant requirements for more and more dollars to finance the ever-expanding trade volume made foreign central banks and private holders nervous, weakening their confidence in the dollar and heightening speculation. After starting strong, the dollar ended up being weak and unwanted, just as predicted by Gresham's law: bad money drives out good money.

An analogy may be used to explain this problem. A man of wealth and reputation is able to obtain credit to buy anything he desires, but as he begins to overextend himself or as he prints his own money, the confidence of creditors in him and his money would severely erode. This analogy may serve to explain why Japan does not want its yen to become a reserve currency.

The consequent lack of confidence in the U.S. dollar drove creditors to turn to gold once again as an alternative. As the gold price rose, a gold pool was created in 1961 to stabilize its market price. When the pool sold gold to bring its price down, it had a negative impact on the dollar because 59 percent of the pool was a contribution of the U.S.A. As the U.S. gold reserve shrank from $24 billion to $12 billion in 1970, the gold price remained stubbornly high, and confidence in the dollar further eroded. The pool was finally dissolved, and a two-tier gold price came into being. That is, central banks agreed to continue to buy and sell gold at the official price of $35 an ounce, but the free market price was allowed to seek its own level.

To many people, the adjustable peg lacks the certainty of the gold system as well as the flexibility of the floating system. In spite of the periodic growth in world trade, low inflation, and low interest rates under the IMF system, the problems created for the dollar were so great that President Richard Nixon finally severed the link between the dollar and gold in August 1971, thus ending the Bretton Woods international monetary system. Citizens of the U.S.A. were once again allowed to own or trade gold on December 31, 1974, and the dollar was permitted to float to seek its own value.

## Crawling peg (sliding or gliding parity)

A cross between a fixed rate system and a fully flexible system are the semi-fixed systems such as the crawling peg and the wide band. They differ from fixed rates because of their greater flexibility in terms of the exchange rate movement, but they are not a floating system either because there is still a limit with regard to how far the exchange rate can move.

Because the infrequent adjustment of the IMF's par value system necessitated a large devaluation at a later date, the crawling peg rate was developed. The idea is to adjust the rate slowly by small amounts at any point in time on a continuous basis to correct for any overvaluation and undervaluation. The continuous but small adjustment mechanism (e.g., as little as 0.5 percent a month or 6 percent for the whole year) was designed to discourage speculation by setting an upper limit that speculators could gain from devaluation in one year.

The crawling peg system requires countries to have ample reserves for the prolonged process of adjustment. In addition, the minor adjustments may not correct the currency's overvaluation or undervaluation. Mexico has devalued the peso at a controlled rate that proved too small to reflect the peso's proper value. In the first part of 1985, the peso lost more than 85 percent of its value against the dollar on the free market. In contrast to the official rate of 24 pesos to the dollar, the free market exchange houses charged 325 pesos, and the rates at the border were even higher. Considering that only a few years earlier the exchange rate was less than 100 pesos to the dollar, it may at first seem that the extent of the devaluation was dramatic. However, it was not enough. In mid-1986, the peso plunged a great deal more, resulting in each U.S. dollar fetching more than 700 pesos. Near the end of 1987, the peso lost as much as 59 percent in value in just a few days and ended the year at the rate of 2,200 pesos to a U.S. dollar. Such large devaluations are exactly what speculators wait for.

In late 1994, *Business Week* magazine mentioned that Mexico's use of crawling peg to systematically devaluing the peso had worked well in controlling inflation while boosting exports; yet only a month later, the peso was in full crisis. The collapse of the Mexican peso at the end of 1994 as well as the economic crisis which ensued in 1995 was a result of Mexico's attempt to keep the value of the peso artificially high, but when the government ran out of reserves to support the currency, the peso collapsed and savagely hurt Mexican citizens.

## Wide band

The purpose of the wide band is to compensate for the rigidity of the fixed rate systems. Similar to and yet different from the adjustable peg system, the wide band allows the currency value to fluctuate, say, 5 percent on each side of the par. Not primarily dedicated to exchange rate changes, this system uses the more flexible movement to warn speculators of the more adverse consequences when their guess about the direction of the exchange rate proves to be wrong.

To pursue the elusive goal of exchange rate stability, the European Monetary System (EMS) incorporated certain features in order to force member countries to make adjustments to correct their divergent economic conditions. As a miniature Bretton Woods system, the EMS employed the so-called grid parity system to link the members' currencies so tightly that they almost became a single currency. The EMS had a fixed exchange rate among members, and the participating currencies could fluctuate by up to 2.25 percent on either side of their bilateral "central rates" against other members, with the exception of the volatile lira's 6 percent fluctuation on either side.

The EMS created a currency bloc known as the European currency unit (ECU) in the 1980s to provide a substitute as well as a complement to the U.S. dollar. The ECU was a composite of several national currencies. The weights for each currency were based on the relative GNP of each country and each country's share in intra-European trade. The weights were examined every five years or if the relative value of any currency changed by 25 percent.

Under the wide band scheme, a country pursuing more inflationary policies will find the prices of its international goods going up, necessitating a depreciation program to correct the country's balance of payments in order to slow growth and curb inflation, while eventually risking recession. The country's exchange rate would then sink toward the floor under its par value. Once the fixed limit is reached (i.e., after hitting either the floor or the ceiling), the country is back to the rigidity of the fixed rate all over gain. Moreover, if a wide band is desirable due to the increase in flexibility, a country may be better off with no limit for movement at all.

## Floating (flexible) system

Under the fixed systems, excessive demand for gold developed and the U.S.A. was forced to suspend the sale of gold in 1968, except to official parties. However, taking this action did not help, and by the late 1960s the dollar came under increasing pressure due to the prolonged and steep deterioration of the balance of payments. A crisis of confidence developed and foreigners' reluctance to hold dollars resulted in a change in the dollar's historic value. On August 15, 1971, the U.S.A. suspended the convertibility of the dollar into gold and other reserve assets altogether, and it floated the dollar to force a change in the parity as well as a review of the IMF. The subsequent Smithsonian Agreement resulted in a revaluation of other currencies and the devaluation of the dollar by 10.35 percent. In February 1973, following a great deal of speculation against the dollar, the crisis was renewed, and a second 10 percent devaluation followed. The crisis forced the official foreign exchange markets to close in Europe and Japan for about two and a half weeks. When these markets reopened, all major currencies were allowed to float.

After an initial period of remarkable stability, the dollar sank rapidly for seven weeks due to balance-of-payments deficits, Watergate revelations, renewed inflation in the U.S.A., and a tightening of money abroad. Had the fixed systems been in effect, a traditional crisis would have resulted. Foreign exchange markets would have been closed, and large-scale adjustment of parities would have been necessary. With the dollar free to float, however, the beneficial effect was that speculative pressures were reflected in a sharp drop in the exchange value of the dollar without a closing of the market. The resultant devaluation, in turn, helped the U.S.A. to improve its trade performance.

In October 1978, another crisis came along for the U.S. dollar. Concerns over inflation in the U.S.A. prompted a panic selling of the dollar, and the stock market plunged. In spite of the risk of recession, the Carter administration was forced to take drastic measures. Among the measures taken were an increase in the Federal Reserve's discount rate, gold sale, and dollar buying. Initially, the magnitude of the action took the market by surprise. Gold prices dropped, and the bond market, stock market, and dollar all rose significantly. Yet by the end of the month, the strong anti-inflation policies themselves weakened confidence in the government, and chaos ensued. Additional panic selling drove the dollar to record lows. Once again, by allowing the dollar to float, the traditional adverse consequences of market closings and official devaluation were averted.

Under a flexible or floating system, market force, based on demand and supply, determines a currency's value. A surplus in a country results in an appreciation of its currency, immediate higher prices, mass reserve, and opportunity costs. In addition, too much money on reserve leads to a loss of investment opportunities. On the other hand, a country's deficit will lower its currency value, making it easier to export more later.

In the absence of government intervention, the float is said to be *clean*. It becomes *dirty* (i.e., managed) when there is a central bank intervention to influence exchange rates, which is a common action, especially by those with inflation and trade problems. A country experiencing inflation must reduce public spending and the money supply to cool its economy. However, because of the delayed impact of devaluation on trade improvement, such restrictive measures need time to achieve their intended purpose before inflationary pressures work themselves back into the economy through higher import prices. Therefore, the country must continuously monitor and defend its currency over the time that the changes are taking effect.

Interventions are unlikely to change a market trend. Central banks' combined resources are just not adequate to reverse a fundamental trend in the foreign exchange market. The foreign exchange reserves held by central banks total only $1 trillion, about the average daily volume of currency trading. On June 24, 1994, the Federal Reserve Board and 16 other central banks spent more than $3 billion to support the U.S. dollar. Market forces, determined to send the dollar the other way, fought back. By the end of the day, the dollar was even worse off than it had been before the intervention, proving an old rule in currency intervention (i.e., "Do not try to row upstream").

## Official classification of exchange rate regimes

The IMF has identified eight types of exchange rate regimes.[18] These regimes may be divided into three broad groups: floating, intermediate, and hard peg.

**Floating exchange rate regimes** include independently floating regimes (in which the exchange rate is market determined, with intervention only to moderate exchange rate fluctuations) and managed floating regimes with no predetermined path for the exchange rate.

**Intermediate exchange rate regimes** include soft pegs (conventional pegs to a single currency or a basket of currencies, horizontal bands, and crawling pegs with and without bands) and tightly managed floating regimes (under which the authorities attempt to keep the exchange rate stable without any commitment to a predetermined path).

**Hard peg regimes** include currency boards and exchange rate regimes with no separate legal tender (such as formal dollarization and currency unions like the CFA franc zone and the euro area).

It must be noted that a country's official classification of its exchange rate regimes may be more fiction than fact. The declared regime often differs from actual country practices. A study of 153 countries dating back to 1946 found that, in the 1950s, 1960s, and early 1970s, 45 percent of the countries that officially claimed a pegged exchange rate actually had some variant of a float. In the 1980s and 1990s, a new type of misclassification emerged: 53 percent of the official "managed floats" turned out to be de facto pegs or crawling pegs. These misclassifications may have led to a false conclusion that a freely floating exchange rate might be an unwise choice for policy-makers. The countries with official floating exchange rates experienced an average annual inflation rate of 174 percent while achieving a meager annual per capita growth rate of 0.5 percent. However, after weeding out countries with de facto pegs or "freely falling" episodes (cases whether the 12-month inflation rate was 40 percent or more), countries with true floats actually had annual inflation rates below 10 percent and an annual per capita growth of 2.3 percent.[19]

In practice, exchange rate regimes vary along a continuum. There is also evidence that countries have moved away from intermediate exchange rate regimes toward floating and, to a lesser extent, hard pegs.[20] For countries that have integrated themselves closely with global capital markets, they need to choose between the two extremes – either a floating currency or a hard peg. Some economies (e.g., Hong Kong and Argentina) have hardened their pegs by introducing currency boards. A monetary union provides even harder pegs.[21]

Article IV of the IMF's Articles of Agreement basically allows member countries to choose their own exchange rate regime. They can either float or peg their currencies. They can do so as long as they collaborate with the IMF to promote a stable system of exchange rates and so long as they do not manipulate exchange rates to gain an unfair competitive advantage over other countries.[22]

Figure 18.8 shows the slow appreciation of the Chinese currency. China has been a target of criticism for not allowing its currency to appreciate freely. On the other hand, one may argue that China simply wants a stable exchange rate. It does not appear to manipulate its exchange rate to gain an unfair trade advantage. After all, by keeping the value of its currency stable (i.e., relatively low), China ends up paying more for imports (especially oil).

## Evaluation of floating rates

Given that a perfect system does not exist, how does one go about evaluating existing systems? A system is acceptable when, given a certain rate of inflation in a country, the value of that country's currency is reduced in the international exchange markets by the same extent, while the value of the currency in a country with no inflation holds steady or moves up accordingly. The system being used should not allow countries to manipulate their rates to gain an unfair advantage over rival trading partners. In essence, a good system promotes stability, certainty, and inflation control.

The fixed rate and floating rate systems have diverse natures and characteristics. Therefore, both of the systems cannot meet the same goals of certainty, stability, and inflation control. Advocates of the fixed rate plan believe that the certainty and rigidity of exchange rates can promote economic efficiency, public confidence, and inflation control. In recent years, several U.S. public officials have

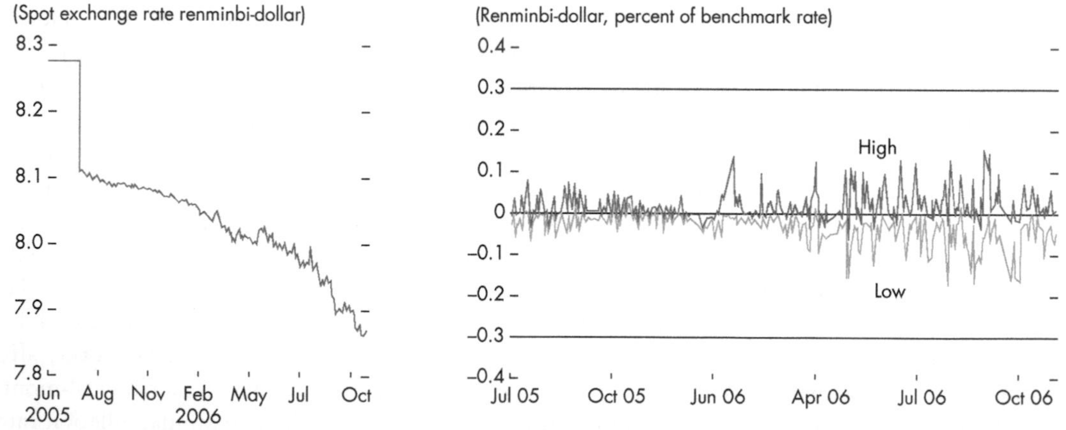
(Spot exchange rate renminbi-dollar)
8.3
8.2
8.1
8.0
7.9
7.8
Jun 2005
Aug
Nov
Feb 2006
May
Jul
Oct
(Renminbi-dollar, percent of benchmark rate)
0.4
0.3
0.2
0.1
0
−0.1
−0.2
−0.3
−0.4
High
Low
Jul 05
Oct 05
Jun 06
Apr 06
Jul 06
Oct 06

Data: National Bureau of Statistics of China and IMF staff estimates.

**FIGURE 18.8** The quiet renminbi

*Source*: *IMF Survey* (December 11, 2006, 351). Credit: © International Monetary Fund. Reprinted from *IMF Survey* (www.imf.org/imfsurvey) with the permission of the copyright holder.

been encouraging the return to some kind of Gold Standard. If this system could indeed work as intended, there would probably be no need to have more than one world currency.

Experience has shown that fixed rates do not work well for a prolonged period. For fixed rates to work, the gold price must remain fixed to control inflation – a difficult if not impossible requirement. In addition, making fiat money convertible into gold cannot guarantee the willingness to achieve long-term stability in the purchasing power of money. Furthermore, while gold prices and general prices tend to move together over long periods of time, short-term movements of gold prices have been much more erratic than movements in general prices. Other commodity indices provide better early warnings of fluctuations in inflation than gold. Therefore, there are better alternatives than a Gold Standard on which to base monetary policy.

Other problems associated with fixed rates include massive capital flows during a crisis and the closing of financial markets. According to Morgan Guaranty, between 1976 and 1985, citizens of Mexico and Venezuela sent $53 billion and $30 billion, respectively, out of their countries. It is also unrealistic to believe that the U.S.A. wants its money supply to be backed by gold and to be at the mercy of major gold producers such as South Africa.

Critics of floating exchange rates contend that the system causes uncertainty, which discourages trade while promoting speculation. In fact, world exports climbed steadily for eight years after the float was put in place, and it is apparent that the system does not interfere with world exports.

The claim that uncertainty encourages investors to speculate and destabilize exchange rates is probably invalid. The fixed rate system is more likely to encourage speculation by giving speculators a one-way, no-lose bet to make money, as the exchange rate can only move in one direction once the upper limit is reached. Whatever the fault of the floating rates, the fixed rate regime is subject to the same fault, probably to a greater magnitude.

Because of a lack of the inherent discipline imposed by fixed rates, floating currencies are said to encourage inflation. In reality, the flexible rate system makes the consequences of inflationary policies more readily apparent to the general public, labor, and employers in the form of a declining foreign value of the currency and an upward trend in domestic prices. This public awareness makes it easier to implement proper policies to correct the situation without reacting in a crisis atmosphere as otherwise might occur. These countries are then able to pursue the mixture of unemployment and price objectives that they prefer and that are consistent with international equilibrium.

The floating system should be accepted with reservations. One problem occurs because of a high degree of short-term volatility and the large medium-term swings in exchange rates. In addition, floating rates do not work well during recessions or through a faltering economic recovery. The float may exacerbate inflationary problems by quickly feeding higher import costs into local wages and prices. When Mexico devalued its peso in 1976, labor unions won a 23 percent wage increase, which only served to force the government to make a second devaluation just two months later. The plunging value of the peso in late 1994 and 1995, on the other hand, created a great deal of unemployment and hardship in Mexico.

A decade of floating exchange rates has shown that developing countries have realized more benefits than problems. Floating rates do not necessarily result in a currency's free fall, and they do not imply higher inflation or lower output. Of the 12 countries surveyed for the period 1985 to 1992, inflation declined in six countries following floating and accelerated in only one (Nigeria). Regarding output, of the 11 countries surveyed, six experienced faster GDP growth; only Brazil and Paraguay showed decline in growth after floating.

The financial crises experienced by many emerging market economies appeared to have one thing in common. These economies maintained soft pegs by pegging their exchange rates in value to either a particular currency or a basket of currencies. As in the case of the Asian economic crisis, the five Asian economies (Thailand, Indonesia, Malaysia, the Philippines, and Korea) were actively managing their exchange rates, partly to promote their competitiveness.

To maintain soft pegs, the authorities were committed to defend it but would allow rate changes under a significant attack. However, the increased integration of their national capital markets and the international capital markets makes it just about impossible to sustain soft pegs over extended periods.[23] The international capital markets simply will not allow domestic policy mistakes to go unnoticed and unpunished.

In spite of some limitations, the floating system was able to carry the world through a number of economic crises quite smoothly. The floating system has proven itself through several periods of raging inflation, deep recession, and massive money movements. Many observers continue to find fault with it, but other systems have just as much, if not more, of the same flaws. At present, there does not appear to be a superior alternative that can be used.

## Financial implications and strategies

One study found evidence of a larger magnitude of foreign exchange exposure for multinational firms with greater foreign operations.[24] In practice, size is irrelevant because any prudent firm must manage foreign exchange risks. It is extremely difficult to predict the movement of a currency. As an example, the U.S. dollar depreciated approximately 10 percent against the German mark and the Japanese yen during the first half of 1994 even though the Federal Reserve Board pushed up the federal funds rate while the Bundesbank lowered its rates and while the Japanese prime minister resigned. During the first few months of 1995, the dollar dropped about 20 percent more against the Japanese yen before beginning a surge of 25 percent. The euro was introduced at $1.18 to the dollar on January 1, 1999, floated to below 83 cents in October 2000, and floated back to $1.18. In four years, it was down 31 percent and back up 44 percent, with no obvious economic fundamentals to explain the gyrations.

Between the start of 2005 and mid-2007, the South Korean won rose 10 percent against the U.S. dollar, increasing more than any other Asian currencies. The country's export-oriented companies did not cheer the strength of their currency. A shipbuilder receiving a $100 million dollar order for a ship to be delivered in 2010 needs to protect itself. It may hedge by agreeing to pay a bank that amount in dollars in 2010 if the bank will give the shipbuilder the equivalent value of won in return in 2010 (based on the exchange rate at the present time). The bank will immediately acquire the required won and will keep it in an account designated for the shipbuilder. When the bank acquires the won at the present time so that it will be available a few years from now, the acquisition adds to the demand for the won and thus strengthens the won even more. As the won strengthens, Korean exporters need to further hedge their transactions, and the vicious cycle continues.

Because of the rising won, a Korean company's dollar sales and euro sales result in fewer won after conversion. Just like other exporters who got hurt, Hyundai Motor's net profit dropped 35 percent in 2006. To make matters worse, while the won was appreciating, the Japanese yen was dropping against the U.S. dollar and the euro. As a result, Hyundai and other Korean exporters were simply not in a position to raise prices.[25]

## Ethical Dimension 18.1

### The man who could move markets: a loose cannon vs. a moron

George Soros is perhaps the world's most powerful and successful investor. To communicate his views, he uses articles in newspapers, statements to wire services, and letters to the editor. His actions and words have rocked the world financial markets and angered the countries' central banks. He played a major role in derailing the European currency system. When central banks were on the opposing side of Soros' trades, they often lost.

Soros went against the British pound in 1992 and won. In 1993, he made an announcement on German TV that he was selling the German mark while buying U.S. dollars. According to his letter to *The Times of London*, the Bundesbank had kept interest rates high for too long and had to reduce short-term rates sharply. The mark did indeed decline, while the U.S. dollar climbed. His opinions, being so respected, have become self-fulfilling in several instances.

He shorted the Thai baht in early 1997, forcing the economies of Thailand and several other countries to collapse. So when it was time for Soros to attend Thailand in 2001 to promote his new book, the Thai people certainly did not forget. Some promised to throw eggs and excrement at him. Others wanted to file criminal charges against Soros for his role in starting the Asian economic crisis. Thailand's senior police officers warned that they could not guarantee his safety. Logic prevailed, and Soros cancelled his trip.

In defense of Soros, the collapse of the Asian currencies and economies could not have happened without the systems' flawed fundamentals. It was the Bank of Thailand that chose to gamble tens of billions of dollars to defend its indefensible exchange rate system. It was the Thai government leaders who funneled billions of baht into various pockets and who spent lavishly on mega-projects without addressing social, educational, and health needs. Soros certainly did not urge the Thai banks to lend recklessly to those who speculated on real estate or stocks.

Occasionally, even George Soros could be wrong. In 1994, he believed that Japan would lower interest rates and that the Japanese yen would fall in value against the U.S. dollar. However, trade talks between Japan and the U.S.A. broke down. When markets reopened, traders concluded that the U.S.A. would try to push up the yen in order to narrow the U.S. trade deficit. The yen surged by nearly 5 percent. As a result, the $12 billion of assets held by Soros' Quantum Group lost nearly 5 percent. He suffered a loss of $600 million in a single day on February 14, 1994.

There is no love lost between the billionaire hedge fund financier George Soros and Malaysian Prime Minister Mahathir Mohammed. Mahathir declared that all currency trading should be illegal. He was certainly upset with Soros, calling him "a moron" who had set Malaysia back 20 years. Soros countered by saying that Mahathir was "a loose cannon" who was "a menace to his own country." Explained Soros: "Markets cannot be left to correct their own mistakes because they are liable to overreact and to behave in an indiscriminate fashion."

*Sources*: "Asia Official, Financier Face Off over Free Trade," *San José Mercury News*, September 22, 1997; "The Man Who Moves Markets," *Business Week*, August 23, 1993, 50ff.; "A $600 Million Valentine's Day Massacre," *San José Mercury News*, February 26, 1994; and "Editorial: Soros Alone Cannot Be Blamed for Crisis," *Bangkok Post*, February 1, 2001.

## Early warning systems

While exchange rate movements are predictable at longer horizons based on the countries' varying interest rates, business firms have to find certain practical ways to deal with short-term volatility. It may be worthwhile to consider some early warning systems.

While some models have as many as 20 indicators, the IMF researchers have developed a simple five-variable macroeconomic model for an after-the-event analysis. The indicators are: degree of real exchange rate overvaluation, size of current account deficit as a share of GDP, growth rate of exports, growth rate of reserves, and ratio of short-term external debt to reserves. The model worked reasonably well, producing results with relatively high warning signals for Korea, Thailand, Indonesia, and Malaysia, but not for the Philippines.[26]

Investment banks have been developing their own in-house models to predict currency crises. One such economic model is Deutsche Bank's Alarm Clock (DBAC). While these models are certainly not perfect, they seem to be far superior to some of the alternative indicators often used by the markets and analysts. Even though there were many false alarms, the models were able to anticipate potentially dangerous pressures at work in foreign exchange markets.[27] In addition, they are objective and mechanical, thus minimizing analysts' biases.

## Hedging

"Hedges protect yards from dogs and businesses from financial exposure."[28] There are a number of hedging methods, and they include forward contracts, swaps, or options. One method involves the interbank market, which offers both spot and forward transactions. An importer or buyer can purchase foreign currency immediately on the **spot** (or *cash*) **market** for future use. When the foreign exchange is not needed until sometime in the future, the seller (or buyer) can turn to the **forward market**, usually entering into a forward contract with a bank agreeing on the purchase and sale of currencies at a certain price at some future time. Smaller companies often have trouble obtaining forward contracts from their banks for two reasons. First, they are not well known. Second, their transaction sizes are too small to attract banks' interest.

Dell Computer's idea of managing its exposures to foreign currency exchange rate fluctuations is to minimize the impact of adverse fluctuations on earnings and cash flows associated with foreign currency exchange rate changes. Its strategy is to utilize foreign currency option contracts and forward contracts to hedge its exposure on transactions in more than 20 currencies. The principal currencies hedged are the euro, British pound, Japanese yen, and Canadian dollar. The company estimates that, based on its foreign currency cash flow hedge instruments outstanding at one time, it has a maximum potential one-day loss of about $43 million. Because of its hedging activities, foreign currency fluctuations did not have a material impact on the results of its operations and financial position during the fiscal years of 2004, 2005, and 2006.[29]

Although Intel Corporation transacts a substantial majority of its business activities in U.S. dollars, it still has certain operating costs in other currencies. To reduce currency risks, the company uses currency forward contracts and currency options. Its balance sheet and forecast transaction risk management programs, based on historical trends in currency exchange rates, should keep any adverse impact on income before taxes to less than $30 million a year in the cases that it experiences adverse changes in exchange rates of 20 percent for all currencies.[30]

Regardless of corporate size, any company can use the **futures market** for hedging. The main difference between forward and futures contracts is the "standardized" sizes and delivery dates of futures transactions. The standardization feature provides market liquidity, making it easy to enter and exit the market at any time, but this same feature excludes the likelihood of meeting individual needs exactly.

The most dominant futures market for foreign currencies is the International Monetary Market (IMM) division of Chicago Mercantile Exchange (CME) in Chicago (see Figure 18.9). These global commodities demand 24-hour attention. To meet this need, the LIFFE (London International Financial Futures Exchange) and the SIMEX (Singapore International Monetary Exchange), both patterned after the IMM, make 24-hour trading a reality. SIMEX is examined in Figure 18.10.

**Currency options**, once illegal in the U.S.A., provide another hedging alternative. The most important characteristic of options is an option buyer's ability to limit the loss, if the buyer's guess is wrong, to the premium paid. A buyer of a currency option acquires the right either to buy or sell a fixed amount of foreign currency at a set price within a specified time period, and the buyer can exercise this right when it is profitable to do so.

Both *futures* and *options on futures* reduce risk significantly. However, there are two key advantages of options on futures over futures. First, because a trader is able to take positions smaller than standard futures contracts, options on futures allow small businesses to hedge more effectively. Second, compared to futures, options on futures provide greater flexibility by allowing hedgers to cap their exposure.

Although banks have been and are still the first choice of corporations seeking to manage foreign exchange risk, exchanges have devised new ways to attract firms or to get banks to work through exchanges. Coca-Cola Co. hedges its foreign earnings by buying options. GAF Corp., a New Jersey specialty chemicals and building materials conglomerate with $1 billion in sales, works with either a bank or an exchange, depending on the dollar volume. It uses exchanges for most of its options transactions when they fall in the range of $5 million to $25 million because exchanges are more competitive in transactions of that size. When the amounts exceed $25 million, GAF uses banks instead.[31]

Table 18.2 provides a comparison of a variety of hedging methods. One study found that it is not common practice to adopt innovative foreign exchange risk management products. As a matter of fact, the simple, first-generation product (i.e., forward contracts) is still more popular among American corporations than the second-generation (e.g., swaps, futures contracts, and options) and third-generation products (e.g., cylinder options, synthetic homemade forwards/options, foreign currency warrants).

There have been many new financial products introduced within the past few years. One popular vehicle is the **ETFs** (exchange traded funds) which allows stock indices and currencies to be traded as if they were stocks. As a result, investors can easily buy and sell ETFs during trading hours instead of having to rely on the less flexible mutual funds that focus on the same underlying markets. A new development is the **ETNs** (exchange traded notes) that allow investors to hedge their assets denominated in U.S. dollars. Barclays Bank has listed three currency ETNs on the New York Stock Exchange. These ETNs provide exposure to the movement of the euro, Japanese yen, and British pound against the U.S. dollar. With ETFs, investors buy a portion of a portfolio. With ETNs, investors get the index return plus any accrued interest. In the case of Barclays Bank's ETNs, the bank's products capture currency moves plus the yield of the underlying market, but investors have to assume credit risk related to Barclays being able to meet its obligations when they want to sell their shares.[32]

Hedging, just like buying insurance, can be expensive. It costs about $26 million to hedge $500 million worth of earnings. A forward contract costs half a percentage point per year of the revenue

Risk control for businesses that bruise easily.
When you ship $1.2 billion worth of bananas worldwide, a small flip in currency exchange rates could make a big difference in profits.
Chiquita, like many smart international companies, gets a good grip on those risks with currency options at the Chicago Mercantile Exchange. Hedging Deutschemarks, Pound Sterling and Yen, Chiquita has successfully guarded against financial bruising for years. And because 80% of all the exchange-traded currency worldwide was traded on the CME's International Monetary Market, they've found it easy to slip in and out of currency options quickly.
"The IMM is where all information that impacts foreign exchange prices comes together," says David Groelinger, Chiquita VP and Treasurer. "That's where the most efficient pricing takes place."
Even more efficient when Globex™ becomes available next summer. The new electronic system will operate after regular trading-hours, making it possible to trade around the world, around the clock.
If you're like the top bananas at Chiquita, and don't want your international earnings frittered away, the CME's currency futures and options should hold great appeal for you.
CHICAGO MERCANTILE EXCHANGE®
The Exchange of Ideas
1-800-331-3332 (US) 01-920-0722 (Europe) 03-595-2251 (Pacific)

**FIGURE 18.9** Chicago Mercantile Exchange

*Source*: Reprinted courtesy of Chicago Mercantile Exchange.

SIMEX
The Exchange with foresight
SIMEX, the Singapore International Monetary Exchange, is an innovator in the financial futures market. As Asia's first international financial futures exchange, SIMEX has grown rapidly by developing new ways to meet the changing needs of participants around the world.
SIMEX was the first to introduce an unprecedented mutual-offset system with the Chicago Mercantile Exchange (CME); this allows investors to establish a position on one exchange and transfer it to or liquidate it on the other. Equally important, SIMEX has similar rules and trading systems as the CME's for safeguarding its market participants.
In response to the need for a way to hedge Japanese equities, SIMEX launched trading in Nikkei Stock Average Futures, the first exchange to offer a futures contract on what is now the largest stock market in the world. This offers more efficient and economical participation in the Japanese stock market together with greater flexibility.
It is innovations such as these and the efficient, well-regulated trading that keep SIMEX in the vanguard of futures trading.
Futures contracts currently traded on SIMEX include Eurodollars, Nikkei Stock Average, Deutschmark, Japanese Yen, British Pound, US Treasury Bond and Gold.
It's not surprising, therefore, that participants from all over the world have discovered the benefits of using SIMEX and have recognised its foresight in futures trading.
The Singapore International Monetary Exchange Limited
1 Maritime Square, #09-39 World Trade Centre, Singapore 0409. Tel: (65) 278 6363. Telex: RS 3800. Cable: SINMEX. Fax: 2730241
Call us today to discuss how SIMEX can play a part in your financial plans.

**FIGURE 18.10** SIMEX

*Source*: Reprinted with permission of the Singapore International Monetary Exchange Limited.

**TABLE 18.2** How foreign exchange products compare

| *Product* | *Who arranges* | *Credit line required* | *Margin required* | *Front-end premium* | *When valuation occurs* | *Extent of limitation of risk* | *Type of taxation* | *Minimum size* | *Ease of offset* | *Need for in-house supervision* |
|---|---|---|---|---|---|---|---|---|---|---|
| Borrow the foreign currency | Bank | Yes | No | No | Periodic | Both directions (upside and downside) | Ordinary | Effectively none[1] | Easy | Yes |
| Foreign exchange forward | Bank | Yes | No | No | Maturity | Both directions | Capital gains | Effectively none[1] | Difficult | No |
| Swap | Bank | Yes | No | No | Periodic (settlement) | Both directions | Ordinary | Effectively none[1] | Difficult | No |
| Over-the-counter (OTC) option | Bank | No | No | Yes | Maturity | One direction | (Review) | Effectively none[1] | Easy | No |
| Hybrid: Buy one OTC option, sell another | Bank | Yes | No | No | Maturity | Within a range only, then unlimited | (Review) | Effectively none[1] | Easy | No |

| | | | | | | | | | | |
|---|---|---|---|---|---|---|---|---|---|---|
| Hybrid: Collar | Bank | Yes | No | No | Maturity | Risk, within a range then limited both directions | Capital gains | Effectively none[1] | Difficult or easy | No |
| *Exchange options:* | | | | | | | | | | |
| on physicals | Exchange | No | No | Yes | Maturity | One direction | (Review) | Fixed by exchange | Easy | Possibly |
| on futures | Exchange | No | No | Yes | Maturity | One direction | Capital gains | Fixed by exchange | Easy | Possibly |
| Futures | Exchange | No | Yes | No | Daily | Both directions | Capital gains | Fixed by exchange | Easy | Yes |

*Note*:

1 Although less than $1 million is rare.

*Source*: Joe Stein, "Forex Products Treasures Like," *Futures* (December 1988, 35). Reprinted from *Futures* magazine, 219 Parkade, P.O. Box 6, Cedar Falls, Iowa 50613, U.S.A.

being hedged.[33] This explains why Eastman Kodak Co. has decided to abandon hedging, believing that the ups and downs of currencies would simply even out in the long run.

Multinationals, due to the nature of their operations, may be able to employ a natural hedge. The technique involves matching revenues and costs in the same currency. One variation of the technique is to manufacture and buy supplies locally. By using locally earned revenues to pay for the production of local goods, a company can minimize the earnings that must be translated or repatriated. Another variation of the method is to look at the net exposure. Coca-Cola manages most of its foreign currency exposures on a consolidated basis by using natural offsets to determine the net exposure. In addition, the weakness in one currency is often offset by the strengths in others over time.

It should be noted that a firm's ability to construct operational hedges has an impact on its exchange rate risk exposure. Those multinationals with greater breadth are less exposed to currency risk. In contrast, those with more highly concentrated networks (greater depth) are more exposed.[34]

## *Leading and lagging*

In order to deal with the complexity of international trade, two strategies should be considered: leading and lagging. For an MNC with a network of subsidiaries, several techniques may be used to reduce foreign exchange. Subsidiaries with strong currencies could delay or lag the remittances of dividends, royalties, and fees. Those in weak currency countries could try to lead, or pay promptly, their liabilities. It is important to recognize, however, that these strategies involve speculation, since no one really knows the timing and extent of the movement of a currency.

## *Invoicing*

The currency to be used for the purpose of invoicing should be considered carefully. Toyota Motor Corp. operates two factories in England. Because the United Kingdom has so far refused to give up the pound sterling for the euro, Toyota faces a risk of losing money when it converts its euro revenues into pounds to pay for British-made components. To solve the problem, Toyota has told its local suppliers to set prices in euros for any new business. Ideally, Toyota wants to eventually pay bills in Europe in euros as it expands operations in the region.[35]

When the buyer is in a soft currency but the seller is in a hard currency, the invoice should use the seller's currency. But the buyer's currency (or that of another selected third country) should be used for invoicing when the buyer is in a hard currency but the seller is in a soft currency. When both the buyer and the seller are in soft currencies, they should consider a third currency as an alternative, but if both are in hard currencies, it may not matter much whether the buyer's currency or the seller's currency is employed. Note that these invoicing strategies apply also to an MNC's subsidiaries that trade with one another. Furthermore, when the volume justifies the cost, the MNC should coordinate invoicing activities by setting up a reinvoicing center.

Japan is the world's second-largest crude-oil importer after the U.S.A. Nippon Oil, Japan's largest refiner, buys about 120,000 barrels a day of crude from state-owned national Iranian Oil Co. It may start paying Iran in yen. Paying Iran in yen could be attractive for less export-oriented Japanese refiners, as it can reduce foreign exchange risks.[36] The Iranian government has asked India to pay in something other than U.S. dollars for natural gas. Iran is willing to bear currency conversion costs if India shifts payments out of U.S. dollars. All Iranian hard currency budget revenues must be calculated in euros – a move seen as both a response to political and financial pressure from the U.S.A.

and a reaction to the dollar's weakness. It is concerned about sanctions being imposed that may freeze dollar transfers.

Oil continues to be priced almost exclusively in U.S. dollars. There have been frequent predictions that oil producers will some day prefer a basket of currencies or an alternative, especially if the dollar weakens against other currencies over time. The U.S. currency remains by far the largest component of other countries' foreign exchange reserves. About two-thirds of all foreign exchange reserves are held in dollars, while a quarter of such reserves are in euros, with less than 4 percent in yen. Because of the market for dollar-denominated assets (e.g., U.S. Treasury debt), it is attractive for producers of oil and other commodities to hold dollars. For most Asian buyers it is more convenient to trade oil in dollars.

## Pass-through costs

Domestic firms should not expect to improve their performance solely on the basis of foreign competitors' misfortunes (i.e., appreciation of foreign competitors' currency). After all, foreign firms are still in a position to decide how much of the cost increase to pass on to buyers. Regarding the gap in percentage terms between the appreciation in the value of each country's currency measured in dollars and the price of its exports measured in dollars, Japan passed on far less of its currency-induced cost increases.

To preserve market share, Japanese, Korean, and European manufacturers generally do not pass along the full cost of appreciation to the U.S. market, but American manufacturers and exporters appear to be unable to resist the urge to fully benefit from the sinking dollar. As a result, U.S. import prices do not go up as much and as fast as U.S. export prices. By thinking about the short-term profit instead of growing market share, U.S. firms will have a hard time increasing market share when the dollar recovers.[37]

## Other strategies

Hedging techniques are not adequate in managing long-term exposure for foreign exchange risk. Other production and marketing strategies should be considered. Oki Electric Industry Co. Ltd. shifted production of high export-ratio products overseas. In the late 1980s, Komatsu was hit hard by the strong yen. To solve this problem, this Japanese firm established strategic alliances overseas to shift production abroad. Komatsu has a joint venture with Dresser Industries in the U.S.A. while being linked in Europe with Hanomag, which has 20 percent of the German wheel-loader and bulldozer market. In addition to its ties with Korea's Samsung Shipbuilding and Heavy Industries, Komatsu imports sheet metal parts from its Indonesian joint venture and has a long-standing agreement with Robbins, a U.S. firm, on underground machinery.

Ford Motor Co. made a bold move in Russia in 1999 by spending $150 million to become Russia's first foreign-owned automobile factory. Local production helps to keep prices low for Ford Focus sedans. Ford is able to sell the cars for $3000 less than imports which have a 25 percent duty.[38] During the second term of the Bush Administration, the U.S. dollar was weak, especially against the euro. Except for the Japanese yen, the dollar did not fare well against the Asian currencies either. Hyundai had to learn to cope with the rising won. Engineers were dispatched to the factories of the suppliers to assist in the development of less costly parts. In addition, Hyundai plans to make half of its vehicles abroad by 2010, up from the present 30 percent.[39]

Globalization offers protection from currency fluctuations. Renault, a French car manufacturer, believes that geographic diversification is a natural hedge. The assumption is that the many currencies will balance each other out. This assumption, however, may be occasionally debatable. Renault itself lost $108 million in one quarter in 1992 due partly to the sharp devaluations of the British and Italian currencies.

Japanese multinationals have demonstrated how they have been able to cope – painfully but successfully – with the strong yen. Japanese exporters have responded to the surging yen by sacrificing profit margins in order to hold the line on export prices in real terms. They have accelerated their direct investment in nearby Asia to capitalize on low-cost labor. At the same time, they have shifted production at home from commodity-type products to high-value quality products. In addition, geographic diversification has allowed Japanese firms to soften losses due to yen appreciations.

Finally, it should be pointed out that an exporter's overvalued currency may still have some unintended benefits. Japanese firms have been able to use their overvalued yen to buy raw materials from abroad at a lower cost, thus reducing their manufacturing costs. Furthermore, the adverse currency movement may allow a company to show market commitment while gaining market share.

## Conclusion

Any businessperson will surely appreciate the necessity of having adequate financing and cash flow. It is not uncommon for an importer to turn to its supplier for financial assistance. If the exporter insists on cash in advance or the equivalent (such as a letter of credit), the sale may be jeopardized.

To finance operations, a company, in addition to selling securities, can turn to middlemen and various financial institutions for loans. Over and above the U.S. market, there are other important capital markets, such as the Euromarket and the Asian Dollar Market, in which financial resources can be secured. For a financial arrangement of significant value, government assistance may be requested from a country's government-supported export–import bank, which has a variety of programs ranging from direct loans to participation arrangements with private lenders.

As for the government itself, borrowing can occur with the IMF to support its currency and to finance temporary trade deficits, or borrowing can be initiated with the World Bank and its affiliates (IDA and IFC) to finance development projects. Private enterprises can benefit indirectly from the funds made available by the World Bank and IDA, as they can contact the IFC directly.

This chapter, although somewhat technical in nature, has covered various financial circumstances related to international marketing. Borrowing money is one thing, but exchanging money is another matter altogether. There have been, there are, and there always will be dreadful accounts about how companies were caught short by the devaluation of a currency. For decades, authorities have debated the merits of the various competing currency exchange systems. Although no single system is able to eliminate completely the volatility of rate movements, there is at present no superior alternative to the system of managed floating rates.

Regardless of the exchange rate system used, rate changes are almost always a certainty, and thus some degree of risk is inevitable. Because MNCs have no determination with regard to the exchange systems – fixed or floating rates – they must attempt to reduce their foreign exchange exposure. To hedge, multinationals can consider any one of the following markets: spot, forward, futures, options, and brokers' services. Other alternatives may include using adjustable prices and billing in strong currencies.

Because of the varying rates of inflation among countries, the impact of inflation on the value of a currency cannot be overlooked. For companies with assets in a high-inflation country, the value of their assets may be substantially and adversely affected. Yet MNCs can benefit from inflation if they know how to borrow money wisely. With regard to the timing of payment, money managers should lead in soft currencies and lag in stronger currencies. For an MNC with subsidiaries in many countries, reinvoicing is a well-advised strategy.

In spite of an increasing number of techniques believed to minimize foreign exchange exposure, it is premature to expect that the methods discussed here are all the techniques that corporate managers can employ. With trends indicating movement toward further deregulation in an increasingly complex world of financial activities, it is just a matter of time before new strategies are created to manage exchange risks.

## CASE 18.1 UPS AND DOWNS: A FOREIGN EXCHANGE SIMULATION GAME

What goes up must come down. This applies to most currencies as well. The up and down movements greatly and eventually affect what consumers have to pay or are willing to pay for imported products.

For an international marketer, the effect of foreign exchange rate changes on operations and pricing is unavoidable. The marketer must estimate *how much* the value of a currency will go up or down and predict *when* the movement will occur. This, to say the least, is not an easy task, and it perplexes even the most experienced money manager. The marketer may be wrong about the direction of the move. Even if the guess is right, the timing may be off. The marketer may thus initiate a move too soon or too late. Without the right timing, the marketer may begin to question the decision concerning the direction.

Assuming that the marketer made the right decisions on the direction and timing, he or she still has to consider the *magnitude of change*. Or the marketer may think that the currency has moved enough and then begins to hedge or remove the hedge. In other words, there are short-term and long-term trends. They may move together or in the opposite direction. In effect, it is more than just making one basic decision. Every day (or even every minute) poses a new situation requiring a decision about whether the action is necessary.

Assume you are going to export your products to both Japan and Germany, and that the value of the merchandise is $100,000 for each country. You will receive payments in Japanese yen and euro respectively in three months. Your net profit margin is 5 percent. Consult the exchange rates for today by looking up the information in a daily newspaper. One convenient method is to consider the currency futures tables that may be found in the the *Wall Street Journal* and many daily newspapers. The *Wall Street Journal* and *New York Times* also provide options information (simply consider the nearby month as benchmark). It should be noted that the sizes of the currency contracts are the same for both futures and options.

### Points to consider

1 Since you will receive payments in three months, do you think there is any need to hedge your exposure?
2 Assuming that hedging is desirable, what is your hedging preference: cash, forward, futures, or options?
3 Do you want to hedge both the Japanese yen and euro?
4 When do you want to hedge? (Note: You can hedge any time within three months.)

5 Consider the exchange rates at the end of the three-month period and determine how the profit from the sale of your products is affected by the rate changes as determined by your decisions.

## Questions

1 Name some of the financing sources for exporters.
2 Is it possible to raise capital by issuing stocks in a foreign country?
3 What are the functions (or services) of a factor?
4 What is mixed or blended credit?
5 What are the goals and functions of the World Bank, IDA, and the IFC?
6 What are the role and functions of the IMF?
7 Explain how inflation and nationalism make it impossible for a single global currency to exist.
8 Why do companies involved in international trade have to hedge their foreign exchange exposure?
9 Distinguish between the spot market and the forward market.
10 Should an exporter use the spot rate or forward rate for quotation?
11 Is devaluation good for exports and imports? Why is the impact of devaluation usually not immediate?
12 Explain how these exchange rate systems function: (a) Gold Standard, (b) par value, (c) crawling peg, (d) wide band, and (e) floating.
13 How does a clean float differ from a dirty float?
14 How can an MNC hedge or cover its foreign exchange exposure?
15 How does the forward market differ from the futures and options markets?
16 How does inflation affect a country's currency value? Is it a good idea to borrow or obtain financing in a country with high inflation?
17 What are leading and lagging, and how should they be employed with regard to payment and collection?

## Discussion assignments and minicases

1 Given that foreign competitors through their governments' assistance are able to offer below-market interest rates or financing, how can U.S. firms fight back to remain competitive?
2 The Hawley Group has plans to widen its shareholder base: "In addition to common share lists in the U.K. and Bermuda, and its sponsored American Depository Receipt (ADR) facility in the U.S., Hawley has recently obtained share listings in both Australia and New Zealand, imminently expects listing on the international Division of Montreal Stock Exchange, and is holding active discussions in Frankfurt and Tokyo." Is there any need for Hawley to be listed in so many markets?

3 The worldwide demand of many financial products results in the mutual offset link by the Singapore International Monetary Exchange (SIMEX) to the Chicago Mercantile Exchange (CME), which allows a contract bought on one exchange to be sold on another. On the Chicago Mercantile Exchange (CME) floor, the most popular stock index traded is the S&P 500. The interest in overseas stocks explains why the CME holds exclusive rights outside Japan to create, market, and trade the Nikkei 225 Stock Average futures contract. The Nikkei Averages are a Japanese stock index based on stocks of all the major publicly held Japanese corporations. The averages are developed by NKS (Nihon Keizai Shimbun), which publishes the world's largest circulation daily business newspaper. The CME has sublicensed its rights for the Nikkei 225 to the SIMEX for trading in the Asian time zone because too few Japanese stocks are traded on U.S. security exchanges.

Some believe that, in future, that which is traded will be the averages based on stock prices of companies worldwide. One development in this direction is Morgan Stanley's granting the CME a license to trade futures based on the Morgan Stanley Capital International Europe, Australia, and Far East (EAFE) stock index. The EAFE index is a diversified portfolio on non-U.S. stocks that cover 38 industries and represents 63 percent of the total market value of these countries' stock exchanges. It is considered the performance benchmark of international market activity.

Do you think the day may come when U.S. stock indices (e.g., Dow-Jones Industrial Averages, S&P 500) may be overshadowed or even replaced by a world or global stock index that represents the movement of stock prices worldwide?

4 Should the world abolish all local currencies except the U.S. dollar, which would function as a global currency?

5 Should the world adopt a basket of the five or ten leading currencies (e.g., U.S. dollar, Japanese yen, Swiss franc) as a global currency for international trade?

6 Should European firms insist on the euro for all buying as well as selling transactions?

7 Japan has aggressively pursued the lower yen value. Is this strategy good for Japan?

8 Should the U.S.A. abandon the float in favor of the Gold Standard or some other type of fixed or semi-fixed system?

9 Both fixed and floating rates claim to promote exchange rate stability while controlling inflation. Is it possible for these two divergent systems to achieve the same goals?

10 How should an MNC reduce its foreign exchange risks?

11 Honda was the first of the Japanese firms to manufacture its cars in Ohio for the U.S. market. The success of its assembly plant in Marysville (Ohio) led to a second Ohio plant. Honda also began exporting its cars from the American plant to Japan. Mazda and Mitsubishi followed suit. Other Japanese companies that export or plan to export products or components made in the U.S.A. to Japan include Hitachi, Yamaha, Fujitsu, and Sony. Politically and financially, what are the benefits of (a) manufacturing cars in the U.S.A. for U.S. consumption and (b) exporting cars to Japan?

12 International travelers often wonder why it is necessary to have so many different currencies. Obviously, it would be preferable to have just one worldwide currency that could be used anywhere on Earth. After all, the 50 states of the U.S.A. use the U.S. dollar, and most members of the European Union use the euro. If the euro can replace the mark, franc, and others, it should also be theoretically possible to have a single world currency. If not, at the least, the big three currencies (the U.S. dollar, euro, and yen) should fix the exchange rates among themselves,

preferably at the rates of $1, 1 euro, and 100 yen. These currencies could form a common monetary policy that serves as the anchor for the world price level.

Nobel Prize economist Robert Mundell has been advocating a new world currency that merges the dollar, euro, and yen. All currencies will then be converted into this international money. The supply of this currency will be supervised by an international board, and monetary gains from its issue will be split along the IMF quotas. As suggested by Mundell, the name of the world currency should be the *dey* (dollar, euro, yen) or perhaps the *intor*.

Is it practical to create and introduce a world currency as envisioned? Assess the likelihood of success of this universal currency.

## Notes

1 John A. Doukas and Ozgur B. Kan, "Does Global Diversification Destroy Firm Value?", *Journal of International Business Studies* 37 (May 2006): 352–71.
2 "Searching for an Encore to Skype," *Business Week*, November 27, 2006, 46.
3 Garry Brouton, David Ahlstrom, and Kuang S. Yeh, "Understanding Venture Capital in East Asia: The Impact of Institutions on the Industry Today and Tomorrow," *Journal of World Business* 39 (February 2004): 72–88.
4 Christos Pantzalis, "Does Location Matter? An Empirical Analysis of Geographic Scope and MNC Market Valuation," *Journal of International Business Studies* 32 (First Quarter 2001): 133–55.
5 "Home, Sweet Delaware," *Business Week*, April 19, 2004, 46.
6 "Going Public Chinese Style," *Business Week*, March 5, 2007, 40.
7 "Capital Access: The Key to Productivity," *Wall Street Journal*, April 24, 2007.
8 Chuck C.Y. Kwok and Solomon Tadesse, "National Culture and Financial Systems," *Journal of International Business Studies* 37 (March 2006): 227–47.
9 "The Art of Reform," *Finance & Development*, June 2006, 20–3.
10 "African Banks Need More Lending Nerve, Says Author," *IMF Survey*, April 11, 2007, 93.
11 "Taking Tiny Loans to the Next Level," *Business Week*, November 27, 2006, 76–80; "Serving the Underserved," *Business Today*, December 31, 2006, 150–4; "Economist Earns Nobel's Top Honor," *San José Mercury News*, October 14, 2006; and "Micro-finance Can Become Global Model," *San José Mercury News*, December 11, 2006.
12 Mary Ann Ring, "Innovative Export Financing: Factoring and Forfaiting," *Business America*, January 11, 1993, 12–14; and Elnora Uzzelle, "Forfaiting Should Not Be Overlooked as an Innovative Means of Export Finance," *Business America*, February 1995, 20.
13 Robert D. Laurent, "Is There a Role for Gold in Monetary Policy?", *Economic Perspectives*, March/April 1994, 2–14.
14 Jack L. Hervey, "Europe at the Crossroads," *Chicago Fed Letter*, August 1993, 1–3.
15 "Don't Chase Big Stock Rally in Zimbabwe," *Wall Street Journal*, June 13, 2007.
16 Texas Instruments 2006 Annual Report, 55.
17 "Turkish Lira Plummets in Economic Crisis," *San José Mercury News*, February 22, 2001.
18 "A New Way of Looking at Exchange Rate Regimes," *IMF Survey*, November 4, 2002, 344–5.
19 "In Brief," *Finance & Development*, September 2002, 3.
20 "A New Way."
21 "Alan Blinder Draws Seven Key Lessons for International Finance from Tumultuous 1990s," *IMF Survey*, 20 November 2000, 383–4.
22 "IMF Strengthening Exchange Rate Advice to Member Countries," *IMF Survey*, June 18, 2007, 148–9.

23 "Have Asian Crisis Countries Reverted to Precrisis Exchange Rate Practices?", *IMF Survey*, 25 February 2002, 56–9.
24 Robert W. Faff and Andrew Marshall, "International Evidence on the Determinants of Foreign Exchange Rate Exposure of Multinational Corporations," *Journal of International Business Studies* 36 (September 2005): 539–58.
25 "Won's Rise Makes Waves," *Wall Street Journal*, June 11, 2007.
26 Andrew Berg and Catherine Pattillo, *The Challenge of Predicting Economic Crises, Economic Issues No. 22*, International Monetary Fund, 2000.
27 "Early Warning Systems: Fad or Reality?", *IMF Survey*, November 12, 2001, 347–48.
28 James T. Moser, "A Good Hedge Keeps Dogs Off the Yard," *Chicago Fed Letter*, November 1989.
29 Annual Report Pursuant to Section 13 or 15(d) of the Securities Exchange Act of 1934.
30 2006 Annual Report, 46. Intel Corporation.
31 Jon Stein, "Forex Products Treasurers Like," *Futures*, December 1988, 34–6.
32 "Move Over ETFs, As ETNs Hit the Scene," *Wall Street Journal*, May 15, 2007.
33 "Perils of the Hedge Highwire," *Business Week*, October 26, 1998, 74ff.; and "Business Won't Hedge the Euro Way," *Business Week*, December 4, 2000, 157.
34 Christos Pantzalis, Betty J. Simkins, and Paul A. Laux, "Operational Hedges and the Foreign Exchange Exposure of U.S. Multinational Corporations," *Journal of International Business Studies* 32 (Fourth Quarter 2001): 793–812.
35 "Toyota Tells U.K. Suppliers to Use Euros," *San José Mercury News*, August 11, 2000.
36 "Buyer May Shift to Yen for Iran Oil," *Wall Street Journal*, July 19, 2007.
37 "A Cash-grab U.S. Exporters May Regret," *Business Week*, January 29, 2007, 28.
38 "They've Driven a Ford Lately," *Business Week*, February 26, 2007, 52.
39 "Hyundai: Too Far, Too Fast?", *Business Week*, January 1, 2007, 39.

# Company and trademark index

# Country/city index

# Name index

# Subject index

# MARKETING RESEARCH

## AN APPLIED APPROACH

Visit the Marketing Research, Fourth Edition Companion Website at **www.pearsoned.co.uk/malhotra_euro** to find valuable **student** learning material including:

- Annotated links to relevant sites on the web
- Online glossary
- Flashcards to test your knowledge of key terms and definitions
- Foreword by the managing director of *Sports Marketing Surveys*, who has provided many of the case studies throughout the book.